D1452721

AN ENCYCLOPÆDIA OF PARLIAMENT

AN
ENCYCLOPÆDIA
OF
PARLIAMENT

NORMAN WILDING

and

PHILIP LAUNDY

COMPLETELY REVISED FOURTH EDITION

CASSELL · LONDON

CASSELL & COMPANY LTD
35 Red Lion Square · London WC1
and at
SYDNEY · AUCKLAND
TORONTO · JOHANNESBURG

First edition, February 1958
Second impression, May 1958
Second (revised) edition, 1961
Third (revised) edition, 1968
Fourth (revised) edition first published in Great Britain 1972

I.S.B.N. 0 304 93689 8

Set in 11 pt. Fournier type and printed in Great Britain
by T. and A. CONSTABLE LTD., Hopetoun Street,
Printers to the University of Edinburgh

571

TO CYNTHIA
AND TO THE MEMORY
OF MARIAN

PREFACE

WHEN the first edition of this work appeared in 1958 the Commonwealth consisted of ten fully independent members and numerous colonies and dependencies in various stages of constitutional development. To-day, thirteen years and four editions later, there are thirty-two full members and a small assortment of territories dependent in one way or another on an independent Commonwealth state, in most cases the United Kingdom. There have been some casualties along the road. South Africa withdrew from the Commonwealth in 1960; the West Indies Federation and the Federation of Rhodesia and Nyasaland both came to grief; and Southern Rhodesia, following the dissolution of the latter Federation, unilaterally declared its independence from Great Britain in 1965, an act which was regarded as illegal by the British Government and which has not been recognized by any other country either inside or outside the Commonwealth.

To-day, as in 1958, the parliamentary system remains the Commonwealth's principal common denominator, although it has been subjected to serious stresses and strains during the years which have elapsed. The most grievous has been the breakdown of parliamentary government and the accompanying civil war experienced in Nigeria. Pakistan has encountered difficulties in sustaining the parliamentary system, and other countries where it has undergone interruption include Ghana, Sierra Leone and Lesotho. In Ghana and Sierra Leone, happily, it has been successfully restored, but at the time of writing it remains in suspension in Lesotho. Difficulties have been experienced in Cyprus where the Turkish population has withdrawn from participation in the system of government.

Some countries, notably India and Ceylon, have achieved a remarkable success in maintaining parliamentary democracy in spite of prodigious social and economic problems. Most Commonwealth countries have successfully adapted the parliamentary system to their own conditions and requirements, and the transformation which it has undergone in countries such as Kenya, Tanzania, Uganda, Zambia and Malawi is an indication of its remarkable flexibility. The older countries of the Commonwealth and former British Empire, such as Canada, Australia, New Zealand, Jamaica, Trinidad and Tobago and Barbados have tended to preserve their fidelity to the original Westminster model.

Not only has the Commonwealth changed, but so have the procedures and practices of its Parliaments. The older Parliaments have modernized their rules and the younger ones have introduced innovations of their own, sometimes owing little or nothing to outside influences. In Great Britain, Canada, Australia and New Zealand the historic financial procedure, with its archaic requirements, has been swept away. Gone are the Committee of Supply and the Committee of Ways and Means. Gone is the requirement that a financial measure must originate in a Committee of

[vii]

the Whole House. The legislative process has been revised in many of its aspects, to such an extent, in fact, that it is to-day possible for a non-controversial Bill to pass through all its stages in the British House of Commons without once being considered on the floor of the House itself. The use of committees has greatly increased, not only to economize on time but also to involve members more closely in the processes of government. In those Parliaments where the volume of business is the heaviest, the problem of organizing the sessional programme and allocating time has engaged the continuing attention of overworked parliamentarians.

The impact of technology on Parliament has been felt in the interest shown in the broadcasting of parliamentary debates. Australia and New Zealand, where debates have been broadcast over sound radio for many years, gave the Commonwealth its lead in this area. Proposals for broadcasting parliamentary proceedings by sound and television have been under consideration in Great Britain, Canada, and elsewhere, together with the technical, political and legal implications involved.

Although this book covers the Parliaments of the Commonwealth, the emphasis in each edition has been upon the British practice, and so it is with this edition. The evolutionary nature of Parliament has been as evident in Great Britain, the Mother of Parliaments, as in the younger countries of the Commonwealth. Ancient ceremonies have been considerably modified. Peers have been permitted to disclaim their titles. Proposals for reforming the House of Lords have been critically examined. Long-standing practices involving parliamentary privilege have been questioned. Problems such as conflict of interest and the discussion of matters which are *sub judice* have been looked at afresh. New ministerial offices have been created while others have been rendered obsolete.

The various editions of the Encyclopædia have thus been published during a period of intensive change relating both to the constitutional development of the Commonwealth and the practices of its Parliaments. The current edition incorporates a great deal of new material and reflects the processes of a living institution which is in a continuous state of evolution.

Very little explanation is required with regard to the arrangement of material. The headings are arranged in one alphabetical sequence and in most instances are the obvious ones which will occur to the inquirer in connexion with the information he requires. It was decided, however, not to place under one heading a general historic survey of Parliament as such an article would necessarily have been of disproportionate length. Instead we have dealt with the parliamentary history of individual reigns from that of Elizabeth I to Victoria under the name of each Sovereign, the earlier history of Parliament being considered under the broad heading, 'Parliament'. This arrangement had the added advantage of enabling us to deal with the relations between the Crown and Parliament at different periods

of history under the heading of the Sovereign concerned. Read in consecutive chronological order these articles provide, within the limits of a
work of this nature, a reasonably detailed account of the origins and
development of Parliament.

Being strictly concerned with Parliament, this Encyclopædia does not
include biographical entries under the names of statesmen and politicians,
which are readily available in other works of reference. Where the
activities of such people concern parliamentary history they are dealt with
in the historical articles. Personal entries are confined to those individuals
who have in some way been directly concerned with the creation and
growth of the powers, privileges, and precedents of Parliament or who
have influenced its customs and procedure.

It would be impossible in the space of this preface to acknowledge our
indebtedness to the many authorities of which we have made use and the
many individuals who have advised us, supplied information and material,
and given us co-operation and support in the preparation of the various
editions of this book. Our parliamentary contacts and experience have
become greatly widened since the first edition was published and the
elimination of many of the imperfections of previous editions has been
due to our parliamentary colleagues and others throughout the Commonwealth who have drawn attention to inaccuracies and given us the benefit
of their criticisms and advice. Their kind co-operation has enabled us to
include information in the various editions of this Encyclopædia which
was not otherwise available in published form. We trust that they will
continue to place us further in their debt by drawing our attention to any
errors of commission or omission which they may discover, and for
which, of course, we alone are responsible.

To single out individuals for special mention may be invidious, but
perhaps we may be excused if we make an exception in the case of a
personal friend and former colleague, Mr. Erskine Grant-Dalton, who,
although no longer an officer of Parliament, was for many years one of
the Commonwealth's outstanding parliamentary practitioners.

Acknowledgments are due to the Erskine May Trustees for their permission to quote from successive editions of Erskine May's *Parliamentary
Practice*; to Mr. O. Hood Phillips for permission to quote from his
Constitutional Law of Great Britain and the Commonwealth, 1952, published
by Sweet & Maxwell; to Mr. Kenneth Mackenzie for allowing us to make
use of his excellent study for Penguin Books, *The English Parliament*;
to the editor of *Parliamentary Affairs* for permission to reprint an article
by Philip Laundy entitled 'Parliament and the Church' which first appeared in that publication; and to the Controller of H.M. Stationery
Office for permission to quote from various Government documents.

November 1970   N. W. W.
                                                  P. A. C. L.

A*   [ix]

A

ABJURATION ACT

An Act of 1701 specified that an oath of abjuration was to be 'tendered to every person entering any public office, to the effect that they renounced the title of the pretended Prince of Wales', i.e., the son of James II, to the English throne, and recognized the rights of the dynasty established under the Act of Settlement (q.v.). In 1858 one form of oath was substituted for the oaths of allegiance, supremacy and abjuration, and this Act was subsequently superseded by the Promissory Oaths Acts of 1868 and 1871.

See also OATHS.

ABSENCE, LEAVE OF

The formal granting of leave of absence to a Member of Parliament is a practice which has largely fallen into disuse. The attendance of members is not enforced in either House. Formerly members of the House of Commons who absented themselves without permission were directed to be punished, the penalty being forfeiture of wages. Although the penalty is no longer applicable the legislative declaration of the duty of a member remains on the Statute Book.

The formal granting of leave of absence by the House is not entirely obsolete, however, and since 1948 it has become customary to grant formal leave of absence to parliamentary delegations visiting other countries on behalf of the House. The usual purpose of such a delegation is to present a Mace or other gift from the House of Commons to the legislature of a new Commonwealth nation. The procedure of granting formal leave of absence may also be resorted to in the case of a member wishing to absent himself from a committee on which attendance is compulsory under Standing Orders.

Party organization has taken the place of compulsion in securing attendances, but some other Commonwealth Parliaments continue to enforce the attendance of members, who are required to obtain permission if they wish to absent themselves from a sitting of the House.

In the House of Lords, the Standing Order relating to leave of absence was considerably expanded in 1958. While it reaffirmed the right of the House to grant or refuse leave of absence, its main purpose was to relieve from the obligation implicit in a writ of summons those peers who by reason of age, health, disinclination or other commitments feel unable to attend the House of Lords. When the writs for a new Parliament are issued each peer receives a letter from the Lord Chancellor inquiring whether he desires leave of absence for the whole Parliament or for the coming session only or not at all. A peer who proposes to attend the House as often as he reasonably can is not expected to apply for leave of absence. Peers who do not reply within twenty-eight days are, after a further letter from the Lord Chancellor, deemed to have applied for leave of absence for the remainder of the Parliament. At the beginning of each subsequent session a letter similar to that sent at the beginning of the Parliament is sent to those peers whose leave of absence terminated with the previous session or who, not having been granted leave of absence, attended no sitting of the House during the previous session other than for the purpose of taking the oath of allegiance.

A peer who applies for leave of absence is never refused it. He is not, however, expected to attend the House, except for the purpose of taking the oath of allegiance, and should therefore regard himself as excluded from its service during the period of his leave of absence, unless he gives at least one month's notice to the Clerk of the Parliaments of his desire to attend.

It is interesting to record that in the House of Lords the practice is still observed of entering the name of each peer present each day in the Journal.

See also ATTENDANCE OF MEMBERS.

ACCESS TO SOVEREIGN

See PRIVILEGE; SOVEREIGN.

ACT OF ATTAINDER

An Act of Attainder (Conviction) was an Act of Parliament convicting a person of an offence and inflicting a punishment. This was not necessarily preceded by a trial, but if it was it was held before both Houses of Parliament and not before the Lords on the accusation of the Commons, as was the case in an impeachment (q.v.). The Act of Attainder procedure was commonly used from the 15th century until the reign of James I instead of impeachment, and Erskine May describes it as 'the highest form of parliamentary judicature'. It has not been employed since the early 18th century, and like impeachment is now obsolete. The latter had for its object the coercion of the King, and it would necessarily be in times of serious conflict between King and Parliament that it would be resorted to. Attainder was a sign that King and Parliament were in agreement, since the King must sign the Bill, although in theory attainder served the same purpose as impeachment—the parliamentary control of the King's minister.

[2]

ACT OF INDEMNITY

An Act of Indemnity, protecting persons against the consequences of any breach of law, can originate in either House and is proceeded with as an ordinary Bill, although the Bill is usually passed through all its stages at one sitting as being an urgent matter. A famous Bill of Indemnity was that passed by the Convention Parliament (q.v.) at the Restoration to exonerate, with certain exceptions, all those who had committed acts directed against the monarchy. Bills of Indemnity are now usually passed for the protection of Members of Parliament who are sitting illegally, and who would otherwise be committed to a fine of £500 for each day's attendance. A recent example of this was an Act passed in 1951 to indemnify the Rev. J. G. MacManaway, who was elected as member for Belfast West but disqualified from sitting under the House of Commons (Clergy Disqualification) Act of 1801. The passing of the House of Commons Disqualification Act in 1957 should almost eliminate the necessity for Indemnity Bills in that House, as prospective candidates can consult the list of disqualifying offices contained in the Act before offering themselves for election.

ACT OF PARLIAMENT

A Bill which has successfully passed through all its stages in both Houses and has received the Royal Assent (q.v.) becomes an Act of Parliament and thus a law of the land. An Act may be amended or repealed by another Act which in turn has undergone the same processes in the form of a Bill. A Bill is a draft statute which very often undergoes amendment during its committee stage (*see* BILL, PASSAGE OF); consequently the Act which eventually emerges sometimes differs from the Bill which was originally introduced into the House.

An Act of Parliament consists of the following parts:

i. *Citation and Short Titles.* The citation title is generally set out in the last section and is usually identical with the short title at the head of the Act. An Act of Parliament is always referred to by its short title (e.g., Education Act, 1944). Occasionally the short title and the citation title are not identical, as in the case of the Consolidated Fund (Appropriation) Act, which is always enacted as the Appropriation Act. An Act may also be cited by its regnal year and chapter number or, for Acts passed in 1963 and thereafter, by the year in which they were passed and the chapter number.

ii. *Long Title.* The long title sets out in general terms the purpose of the Act, and when the term 'title' is used without qualification it usually refers to the long title.

iii. *Preamble.* The preamble is not an essential part of an Act and is not often now incorporated in a Public Act. Its purpose is to state the reasons and intended effects of the legislation.

iv. *Enacting Formula.* The enacting formula is a short paragraph which precedes the sections of the Act. This formula, which was developed in the 15th century, now runs as follows: 'Be it enacted by the Queen's most Excellent Majesty, by and with the advice and consent of the Lords Spiritual and Temporal, and Commons, in this present Parliament assembled, and by the authority of the same, as follows:—.' The Parliaments of the other Commonwealth monarchies use a similar enacting formula in the drafting of their Acts, with the exception of the New Zealand Parliament which omits specific reference to the Sovereign. In Consolidated Fund and Finance Acts the usual formula is preceded by certain words which define the sole responsibility of the Commons for the grant of money.

v. *Sections.* The Act is divided into a series of numbered sections (known in the Bill form as 'clauses' (q.v.)), each with a descriptive note printed in the margin. Sections may be divided into subsections, subsections into paragraphs, and paragraphs into sub-paragraphs. Long and complicated Acts often have their sections grouped in parts distinguished by Roman numerals and titles in capitals, and these parts may again be broken up into small groups of sections with a group title in italics. A table of sections may be prefixed to an Act showing the numbered titles of the sections and also any grouping into parts. The order of the sections is usually so arranged that the leading principles of the Act are embodied in the opening section or sections. The formal sections, such as those devoted to definitions, are usually contained at the end of the Act. In the Acts of some other Commonwealth countries this practice is varied and the formal sections appear at the beginning.

vi. *Schedules.* At the end of many Acts of Parliament there are sets of schedules which contain matters of detail dependent on the provisions of the Act.

Unless otherwise provided in the Act itself, an Act of Parliament takes effect from the day it receives the Royal Assent. Under the Acts of Parliament (Commencement) Act, 1793, the Clerk of the Parliaments is required to endorse on every Act immediately after the title, the day, month, and year when it shall have been passed and received the Royal Assent. Formerly all Acts of Parliament of which the commencement was not specifically enacted were held in law to take effect from the first day of the session.

As soon as an Act has received the Royal Assent, a print of it in the form in which it was finally agreed to is prepared in the Public Bill Office of the House of Lords, and it is given a chapter number. Acts are numbered serially throughout each calendar year in the order in which they receive the Royal Assent. Prior to January 1963 they were numbered sessionally and by regnal year, but the passing of the Acts of Parliament Numbering and Citation Act, 1962, provided for the simpler method of chaptering now in use. Public General Acts form one series, Provisional Order Confirmation Acts and Local Acts form a second, and Personal Acts, if printed, form a third. After examination a proof copy of the Act is certified by the Clerk of Public Bills and sent to the Queen's Printer, and a request is sent to the Controller of the Stationery Office to issue instructions for its immediate publication. Two prints are prepared on a durable vellum. These are endorsed with the words by which the Royal Assent was signified and signed by the Clerk of the Parliaments, thus becoming the official copies of the Act. One is sent to the Public Record Office and the other is preserved in the House of Lords. In the case of Church Assembly Measures (q.v.) a third vellum copy is printed and sent to the Church Assembly. Paper prints of the Act are placed on sale to the public, and the original prints may be seen if desired and copies taken on payment of a fee.

(Further reading: Maxwell, *Interpretation of Statutes*, 1962.)

See also CITATION OF STATUTES; PRIVATE ACTS; PUBLIC GENERAL ACTS.

ACT OF SETTLEMENT

The statute of 1701 which provided for the Protestant succession and for the disqualification of any future successor not in communion with the Church of England.

The Act also provided (1) that the nation should not engage in any war for the defence of territories not belonging to the English Crown without the consent of Parliament; (2) that the Sovereign should not leave the kingdom without the consent of Parliament; (3) that matters cognizable in the Privy Council should be transacted there, and all resolutions signed by those of the Privy Council who had advised them, a provision which was designed to subordinate the Cabinet; (4) that no foreigner should be eligible to sit in the Privy Council or in either House of Parliament, or to hold office under or receive any grant from the Crown; (5) that no office holder or person receiving a pension from the Crown should be eligible to sit in the House of Commons; (6) that no pardon under the Great Seal of England be pleadable to an impeachment by the Commons in Parliament.

Of these provisions the first, fourth, and sixth remain upon the Statute Book, although the latter can have no practical effect to-day as the practice of impeachment has fallen into disuse. The second provision was repealed in 1716 and the third in 1705. The fifth, had it remained in force, would have excluded all ministers from the House of Commons. It was first revised in 1705, when it was provided that Members of Parliament appointed to ministerial offices must vacate their seats but could submit themselves for re-election. This condition remained in force until it was abolished by the Re-election of Ministers Act, 1919, as amended 1926.

ADDLED PARLIAMENT

The Parliament summoned by James I on 5 April 1614 in the hope of raising money. The Commons demanded the abolition of impositions (duties raised by the sole authority of the King), a demand which failed to receive the support of the Lords, and also the restoration of the ejected clergy to their livings. Neither the King nor the Commons were disposed to meet each other's demands, with the result that the Parliament was dissolved on 7 June 1614, having passed no Act and granted no supplies, thus receiving its nickname.

It was alleged that attempts had been made to influence the elections to this Parliament in order to secure the return of members in sympathy with the King, but the allegations were denounced by the King as utterly false.

(Further reading: Moir, *The Addled Parliament of 1614*, 1958.)
See also JAMES I AND PARLIAMENT.

ADDRESS

See CROWN AND PARLIAMENT.

ADDRESS, DEBATE ON THE

See DEBATE ON THE ADDRESS.

ADJOURNMENT OF THE DEBATE

A motion for the adjournment of the debate may be moved at any time, except while another member is speaking, by any member who has not already exhausted his right to speak. If such a motion is defeated or withdrawn no similar motion may be moved in the course of the same debate unless some other motion has intervened. The mover of a defeated motion to adjourn the debate loses his right to speak in the debate itself, and is not permitted to move a similar motion subsequently. Conversely, a member who has already spoken in the debate loses his right to move its adjournment, unless he makes the motion during the course of his speech. If the motion to adjourn the debate is carried, the motion which it supersedes lapses unless a day is named for the resumption of the debate. When the debate is resumed, the member who moved its adjournment is entitled to be called by the Speaker provided he rises immediately the question is again proposed.

A motion for the adjournment of the debate is a 'dilatory motion' (q.v.) and has been used for the purpose of preventing the House from reaching a decision on a question. The use of dilatory motions to obstruct business was common until the end of the 19th century; but the Standing Orders now empower the Speaker to refuse to accept them if he considers them to be an abuse of the rules of the House or to put the question upon them without allowing any debate. When debate is allowed it is strictly confined to the desirability or otherwise of the debate being adjourned.

Members wishing to prevent the House from reaching a decision on a question sometimes adopt the practice of alternating a motion for the adjournment of the debate with a motion for the adjournment of the House, thereby circumventing the rule which prohibits the moving of the same dilatory motion on two consecutive occasions in the course of the same debate. A motion for the adjournment of the debate cannot be moved while a motion for the adjournment of the House is under discussion.

Technically, a motion for the adjournment of the debate, if carried, merely postpones the taking of a decision on a question, but in practice, owing to the pressure of parliamentary time, the postponement of a decision on any question other than an item of government business is usually tantamount to defeating it.

ADJOURNMENT OF THE HOUSE

A temporary pause in parliamentary proceedings which, unlike a prorogation or dissolution of Parliament, has no effect on the course of parliamentary business. The House of Lords and the House of Commons may each adjourn at their own pleasure, and the adjournment of the one does not involve the adjournment of the other. The Crown cannot direct either House to adjourn. The Stuart Kings claimed this right, but it was never acknowledged. The Crown has, however, acquired the statutory power (by Acts of 1799 and 1870) to abridge an adjournment if it lasts longer than six days, in which case the resumption of the sittings may be ordered by proclamation not less than six days after the date of the proclamation.

The Lord Chancellor and the Speaker of the House of Commons are also empowered to recall their respective Houses during an adjournment if they believe an earlier meeting to be in the public interest. The Standing Orders of the House of Commons provide that the Speaker may recall the House on the representations of Her Majesty's ministers. The Lord Chancellor's power is conferred by sessional order of the House and the initiative in consulting with the Government rests with him.

In both Houses an adjournment is effected by the adoption of the motion, 'That this House do now adjourn'. In the case of the House of Commons there are circumstances in which an adjournment may take place without such a motion being carried, e.g., the Speaker may, in certain circumstances, be obliged to adjourn the House owing to the absence of a quorum (q.v.), and he is empowered to suspend a sitting in the event of grave disorder arising. Until 1888, when a fixed hour for the interruption of business was introduced, the House of Commons, like the House of Lords to-day, could adjourn only when a motion for

[7]

the adjournment had been carried, and the Speaker was sometimes left stranded in the Chair because members would hurry out of the Chamber before he could put the question. Although the Speaker is now protected from this predicament by the automatic adjournment, the House is still normally adjourned by motion, and the motion to adjourn the House provides frequent opportunities for debate. Subjects debated on adjournment motions have ranged from an alleged injustice suffered by a member's constituent to the conduct of the Second World War. The momentous debate which preceded the fall of Mr. Neville Chamberlain's Government took place on the motion, 'That this House do now adjourn'.

Motions for the adjournment of the House may be classified as substantive or dilatory. A substantive adjournment motion may be moved following the Question Period and before the Orders of the Day are entered upon or between Orders of the Day and can be moved only by a member of the Government. Any subject falling within the responsibilities of the Government may be discussed on a substantive adjournment motion provided it does not entail legislation, does not anticipate an Order of the Day or a Notice of Motion, and does not concern the conduct of the Sovereign or other holders of high office. A dilatory adjournment motion can be moved by any member during the course of a debate and has the effect of superseding the question before the House. Both forms of adjournment motion are considered below.

A substantive adjournment motion is used for various purposes and can take any one of the following forms:

The Daily Adjournment Motion. The motion, 'That this House do now adjourn' is made by a member of the Government at the conclusion of every sitting, either at the moment of the automatic interruption of business, or at the conclusion of exempted business (q.v.) or (should all business be concluded before the moment of interruption) at the premature conclusion of public business. When morning sittings were briefly introduced on Mondays and Wednesdays in 1967, the motion on these days was made at 12.30 p.m. prior to the luncheon adjournment. The motion may be debated for half an hour and is one of the recognized opportunities for private members to raise any matter they wish to discuss, subject to the limitations described above. These debates normally have nothing to do with the desirability or otherwise of adjourning. All manner of topics are raised during this daily half-hour and the adjournment motion is nothing more than a peg on which to hang them. Such is the competition among members for the right to raise a matter 'on the adjournment' that, following an arrangement made in 1955, the subjects for discussion on four days of the week are selected by ballot, while those for discussion on Thursdays are selected by the Speaker.

[8]

In making his selections the Speaker gives priority to individual or constituency grievances and to matters of immediate topical interest. Matters debated 'on the adjournment' frequently arise out of the answers to questions, and a member receiving what he deems to be an unsatisfactory reply to a question will often announce his intention of raising the matter again 'on the adjournment'.

Holiday Adjournment Motions. On the day that the House adjourns for one of its seasonal holidays it is customary to devote the whole day to a debate on the adjournment motion, the topics for discussion being selected by the Opposition or by private members. There are four such occasions in a normal session.

Adjournment Motions in Government Time. Adjournment motions are sometimes moved by the Government in order to debate a matter of its own choosing, usually in consultation with the Opposition. The procedure enables the House to consider a matter without coming to a decision upon it, and following the debate the motion is usually withdrawn by leave of the House. The adjournment motion may also be used by the Government to enable a minister to make a policy statement between two Orders of the Day or to enable an immediate debate to take place on a statement which has been made in the normal order of business. Since the introduction of the new financial procedure in December 1966 Supply debates have frequently taken place on a motion to adjourn the House, and it is anticipated that this will become a regular practice.

Extraordinary Adjournment Motions. There have been occasions when one or both Houses have adjourned in order to express respect or condolence when an eminent person has died. This procedure is normally followed upon the death of a distinguished member or ex-member, as in 1925 upon the death of the Earl of Oxford and Asquith, in 1945 on the death of Earl Lloyd George, in 1947 on the death of Earl Baldwin, and in 1965 on the death of Sir Winston Churchill. On 12 April 1945 the House of Commons set a precedent by adjourning as a mark of respect to the memory of Franklin D. Roosevelt, the first foreign head of State to whom such a tribute was paid. The precedent was followed on 25 November 1963 following the assassination of President Kennedy. Discussion on adjournment motions of this kind is restricted to the purpose for which the House is adjourning and the motion is invariably carried.

Emergency Adjournment Motions. The Standing Orders of the House of Commons make provision for emergency adjournment motions which any member is entitled to move and which are in the nature of emergency motions of censure upon the Government. The conditions relating to such motions while less rigid than they were prior to 1967 remain strict and the question cannot be put to the House unless the Speaker is satisfied that the matter raised complies with the conditions envisaged by the relevant Standing Order. Attempts to move such motions are frequently made but less frequently allowed. They are dealt with more fully under the heading EMERGENCY ADJOURNMENT MOTIONS.

A dilatory motion for the adjournment of the House may be moved at any time during a debate, except while another member is speaking, by any member who has not exhausted his right to speak to the question before the House. The use of this type of motion to obstruct the business of the House was common until the end of the 19th century, but the Standing Orders now empower the Speaker to refuse such a motion if he considers it to be an abuse of the rules of the House, or to put the question without allowing any debate upon it. When debate is allowed it must be confined to the desirability or otherwise of an adjournment and if the motion is defeated the House reverts to the question which was superseded by the adjournment motion. When a dilatory adjournment motion has been made and defeated, no similar motion may be moved again during the debate unless the question on some other motion has in the meantime been proposed from the Chair. This prohibition can be circumvented by alternating motions for the adjournment of the House with motions for the adjournment of the debate, and this practice is sometimes employed by members who wish to prevent the House from coming to a decision on the matter under consideration. Should a dilatory motion for the adjournment of the House be carried the motion which was before the House is dropped, notice of a fresh motion being required in order to revive the discussion.

ADMINISTRATION OF THE HOUSE OF COMMONS
See sub-heading under HOUSE OF COMMONS.

ADMIRALTY, FIRST LORD OF THE
See FIRST LORD OF THE ADMIRALTY.

ADMONITION
See PRIVILEGE, BREACH OF; REPRIMAND AND ADMONITION.

ADOPTIVE ACT
An Act of Parliament which does not come into operation unless and until it is adopted by a local authority or public body, e.g., the Public Libraries Acts, 1892–1919, now repealed. Such an Act applies only within the localities for which it has been adopted by the authorities concerned.

AFFIRMATION
Instead of taking the oath on taking his seat in the House of Commons a member, or in the House of Lords a peer, may make affirmation.

The form used in this case is: 'I . . . do solemnly, sincerely, and truly declare and affirm that I will be faithful and bear true allegiance to Her Majesty Queen Elizabeth, her heirs and successors, according to law.' The right to make affirmation is given by the Promissory Oaths Act, 1868. The Oaths Act, 1888, which gave a similar right to atheists, resulted from the objections to Bradlaugh (q.v.) making affirmation. The Quakers and Moravians Acts of 1833 and 1838 allowed persons of those persuasions to make a 'solemn affirmation or declaration instead of taking an oath'.

AGRICULTURE, FISHERIES AND FOOD, MINISTER OF

An Act of 1889 set up a Board of Agriculture consisting of the Lord President of the Council, the Secretaries of State, the First Lord of the Treasury, the Chancellor of the Exchequer, the Chancellor of the Duchy of Lancaster, and the Secretary of State for Scotland. The board was to promote the general welfare of agriculture and to publish information and statistics relating thereto. It also took over the work of a Privy Council Committee concerned with animal diseases, and the functions of the former Land Commissioners in relation to tithe commutation, copyholds, inclosures, allotments, and land drainage and improvement. Under an Act of 1903 the board took over the administration of fisheries from the Board of Trade, and became the Board of Agriculture and Fisheries, and in 1919 it became a Ministry. In 1944 the Minister established a National Agricultural Advisory Service for the purpose of giving free advice and instruction on agricultural matters, and he himself can be advised by several semi-independent boards, such as the Wheat Commission, the Agricultural Wages Board, and the Herring Industry Board. In October 1951, the policies of the Ministries of Food and of Agriculture were placed under the supervision and co-ordination of the Lord President of the Council, but in 1954 the two ministries were incorporated. The Minister is usually a member of the Cabinet, and his salary is £8,500 a year. He is assisted by two joint Parliamentary Secretaries with salaries of £3,750 each. All three, if they sit in the House of Commons, are entitled to draw an additional £1,250 of their parliamentary salaries.

A chronological list of holders of this office appears as Appendix 9.

AIRCRAFT PRODUCTION, MINISTER OF

Created in 1940, the post of Minister was first held by Lord Beaverbrook, followed by Lieut.-Col. Moore-Brabazon (afterwards Lord Brabazon), Col. The Rt. Hon. J. J. Llewellin (afterwards Lord Llewellin), Sir Stafford Cripps, A. E. Brown, and John Wilmot. The office was abolished early in 1946 following the general reorganization of Government which took place at the end of the War. The functions of the Minister were transferred to the Minister of Supply, the merging of the two Ministries having been forecast from the time the Labour Government took office, when they were put under one Minister, John Wilmot.

AIR FORCE ACT
See ARMY ACT.

AIR, SECRETARY OF STATE FOR

Originally a Minister of Cabinet rank with responsibility for the Royal Air Force and the Air Ministry, this office was abolished together with the Air Ministry, with the coming into force of the Defence (Transfer of Functions) Act, 1964. It was superseded by the office of Minister of Defence for the Royal Air Force, a Minister below Cabinet rank who was subordinate to the Secretary of State for Defence. This office was in turn abolished as the result of a ministerial reorganization in January 1967, direct responsibility for the Royal Air Force being vested in an Under-Secretary of State. (*See also* DEFENCE, SECRETARY OF STATE FOR.)

The Air Ministry and the office of Secretary of State for Air were originally constituted by the Air Force (Constitution) Act, 1917. The Air Navigation Acts, 1920–36, also assigned responsibility for civil aviation to the Air Ministry, but in 1945 it was taken over by the newly constituted Ministry of Civil Aviation and subsequently by the Ministry of Aviation (since abolished and incorporated with the Ministry of Technology). The Secretary of State for Air was the President of the Air Council, a body which has been replaced by the Air Force Board operating under the jurisdiction of the Defence Council. A chronological list of the holders of this office appears as Appendix 10.

ALBERTA LEGISLATIVE ASSEMBLY

Alberta formed part of the Canadian North-West Territories until 1905, when the Province was created. The Government is composed of the Lieutenant-Governor, the Executive Council, and the Legislative Assembly. The Legislative Assembly consists of 65 members (increased from 63 in 1967) elected for five years by popular vote, each electoral division returning one member. The Executive Council, or Cabinet, consists of 16 members of the legislature including the Premier, who presides. The Lieutenant-Governor is appointed by the Federal Government.

Since 1935 the Provincial Government of Alberta has been controlled by the Social Credit Party, which ranks as only a minor party at the federal level of Canadian politics. Shortly after it came to power in Alberta the Social Credit Government attempted to give legislative effect to its unorthodox monetary theories, thereby leading to one of the rare occasions on which the Federal Government has invoked its power to disallow provincial enactments. The Province sends 6 Senators and 19 members to the Canadian Parliament.

Alberta's magnificent Legislative Building of classic design was not completed when the first session of the Assembly was held there in 1911. It is of cruciform shape with a main rotunda, each wing being 130 feet long.

ALLOCATION OF TIME ORDERS
See GUILLOTINE.

ALLOTTED DAYS
See SUPPLY DAYS.

ALMON, JOHN (1737–1805)

The compiler of the Parliamentary Register, a monthly record of the proceedings of Parliament which was commenced in 1774. He subsequently compiled a summary of the debates from 1742 up to the beginning of the Parliamentary Register. Almon's Debates are one of the main sources from which Cobbett and Wright compiled the Parliamentary History (q.v.).

ALTERNATIVE VOTE

The alternative or preferential vote, not to be confused with proportional representation (q.v.), is an electoral system which provides for a single ballot in which the voter numbers the candidates in the order of his preference. In the event of no single candidate securing an overall majority of the total votes cast, the candidate at the bottom of the poll is eliminated and his votes are distributed among the remaining candidates according to the second preferences indicated on the ballot papers. If only three candidates are contesting a seat the second count will produce a result. If, however, there are four or more candidates in the poll and no candidate secures an overall majority even after the second count, a further candidate is eliminated and his votes are redistributed according to the second preferences (or third preferences where the second preference is given to the candidate already eliminated) expressed on the ballot papers, the process continuing until one candidate succeeds in securing an overall majority. This electoral system is widely used in Australia. It operates in respect of elections to the House of Representatives of the Commonwealth Parliament and the Legislative Assemblies of Victoria, New South Wales, South Australia, and Western Australia. In 1957 the alternative vote was adopted in Rhodesia, but it was abolished prior to the 1965 General Election.

The Borda system is a modified form of the alternative vote whereby a certain number of points is awarded for a first preference, a lesser number for a second preference, and so on. The winning candidate is then determined by the number of points he manages to accumulate. This system meets the objection of those who maintain that second and lesser preference votes should not have the same value as first preference votes.

The second ballot, a system which has been used in French elections, is an electoral method which bears a certain similarity to the alternative vote. Instead of requiring the expression of preferences on the ballot papers it provides for a second ballot in the event of the candidate at the top of the poll failing to secure an absolute majority. A restriction is normally placed on the number of ballots which can be taken but, like the alternative vote, it is based on the principle of eliminating the candidates at the bottom of the poll.

One of the terms of reference of the Speaker's Conference set up in 1965 in Great Britain was to examine methods of election, with particular reference to preferential voting.

(Further reading: Lakeman *Voting in Democracies*, 1955.)

AMENDMENT

A motion before the House may be agreed to or negatived as it stands, or it might be agreed to if it were altered in some way. This is done by moving an amendment (a subsidiary motion) which may be one of three classes. It may be designed to alter the motion by (1) leaving out certain words, (2) by adding or inserting certain words, or (3) by leaving out certain words and adding or inserting others. Amendments can be proposed at any stage of a debate, but the Speaker or Chairman is more likely to refuse an amendment, which they have power to do, if it is not written out and handed in before the debate commences.

In 1967 the words 'That the amendment be made' were adopted as the universal formula in which the question on an amendment is proposed, with one exception which is noted below. Previously an archaic and somewhat confusing formula was in use whenever an amendment involved the omission of certain words. In such a case the Speaker would say 'The original question was . . .' (stating the question at length), 'since which an amendment has been proposed to leave out the words . . .' (which were proposed to be omitted). He then put the question 'that the words proposed to be left out stand part of the question'. If that question were resolved in the affirmative it showed that the House preferred the original question to the amendment, and the question, as first proposed, was put by the Speaker. If, however, the question 'That the words stand part' were negatived, the question was put with the omission of those words, unless another amendment was then moved for the insertion or addition of other words. After the amendments had been disposed of the question itself remained to be put, as the rejection of an amendment did not constitute a final decision upon the original motion. This procedure has been retained only in the case of a 'six-months' amendment to the motion for the second reading of a Bill (*see* BILL, PASSAGE OF). The retention of this formula for such amendments enables the supporters of a Bill to continue to vote 'Aye'.

Amendments to amendments can be moved, but not if they propose to leave out all the words of the original amendment—if that is desired the first amendment must be negatived before the second can be offered. In the same way an amendment to the original question cannot propose to leave out all the words, and the initial word 'That' must, at least, be retained. In this case the rule that the debate must be restricted to the amendment is not adhered to, as the amendment and the motion are before the House as alternative propositions. Amendments must be moved after a question has been proposed by the Speaker and before it has been put, and must be intelligible and relevant to the question. The matter of relevance is modern practice—in 1831 an amendment was moved for the production of papers on the state of Poland to the question that the Speaker leave the Chair for the Committee on the Reform Bill.

See also BILL, PASSAGE OF; CONSEQUENTIAL AMENDMENT; REASONED AMENDMENT; SELECTION OF AMENDMENTS.

AMENDMENTS, CONSIDERATION OF
See BILL, PASSAGE OF.

AMENDMENTS, SELECTION OF
See SELECTION OF AMENDMENTS.

ANCILLARY MOTION
This kind of motion is dependent on an Order of the Day, e.g., that a Bill be read a second time, or that the House agrees with the report of a committee. Only the prescribed form of words may be used in moving an amendment to an ancillary motion, and if the object is to secure the rejection of a Bill, the formula is 'That the Bill be read a second time' (or whatever stage has been reached) 'upon this day six months'. Ancillary motions do not require notice, and the mover has no right of reply.

ANNE (1665–1714) AND PARLIAMENT
Queen Anne, the last monarch of the House of Stuart, ascended the throne on 8 March 1702, and was crowned on 23 April. Her reign was a distinguished one in many respects, but politically it was coloured by violent party strife and intense intrigue. Anne herself was a woman

of many virtues, but she was largely ruled in public affairs by her favourites, notable amongst whom were the Duchess of Marlborough and (after the Duchess's fall from favour) Abigail Masham. The greatest legislative achievement of the reign was the Act of Union with Scotland.

Prior to the reign of William III a Parliament automatically ceased to exist upon the death of the Sovereign, but an Act of that reign had provided for a continuation of Parliament for a period of six months after the demise of the Crown. Consequently, the last Parliament of William III was the first in history whose life extended into the following reign. In her first speech to Parliament on 11 March the Queen dwelt upon the proposed Union with Scotland and the prosecution of war against France and Spain, and declared 'that she knew her heart to be entirely English'. After her coronation she named as her successor the Princess Sophia of Hanover, in accordance with the Act of Settlement (q.v.). The members of both Houses were sworn as required by the Abjuration Act (q.v.), and Anne was voted the same revenue as that received by her predecessor, in return for which she announced her intention of applying £100,000 from the Civil List to the needs of the public service. War was declared on France and Spain, after which Parliament was prorogued on 25 May and dissolved on 2 July.

The first elections of the reign gave the Tories a majority in the House of Commons. The current trend of religious feeling tended towards High Church principles, an outlook which was reflected in the composition of Anne's first Parliament, which met on 20 October 1702. The Queen herself showed pronounced High Church sympathies in making her first ecclesiastical and government appointments, although Godolphin was appointed Lord Treasurer. She dismissed from his office of Lord Almoner the Bishop of Worcester, who had been accused of interfering unduly with the election of the successful Tory candidate for that county. Although church matters assumed some importance in this Parliament, the war necessarily claimed its first attention, and the necessary forces and supplies were voted. The Earl of Marlborough, who had already achieved brilliant military successes, was rewarded by the Queen with a dukedom and a pension of £5,000 a year during her own lifetime. It was her wish to settle this pension in perpetuity upon the title, but she was baulked in this desire by the opposition of the Commons.

The most contentious measure of the session was the Occasional Conformity Bill, which was designed to prevent Dissenters from complying with the provisions of the Test Act in order to qualify for certain offices. Although supported by the Queen, this obnoxious measure was rejected by the Lords no less than three times before it was eventually passed in 1711, only to be repealed in 1719. The

Prince Consort's Annuity Bill also gave rise to friction between the two Houses, as the Commons sent it up to the Lords with an additional clause exempting the Prince from the disability imposed upon foreigners by the Act of Settlement. This device of tacking a non-financial provision upon a Money Bill in order to overcome any anticipated opposition from the Lords had long been objected to in the upper House, where a Standing Order had been introduced condemning the procedure as unparliamentary and unconstitutional. The Commons had found in this method an effective means of getting their own way, for the Lords would have been compelled to reject a Bill in its entirety in order to get rid of the 'tack', and would thus have placed themselves in the embarrassing position of withholding supplies from the Crown. During the session of 1704 the two Houses were again brought into conflict over the Aylesbury election case. An elector who had brought an action against the Returning Officer who had rejected his vote obtained a verdict at the county assizes which was set aside by the Court of Queen's Bench on the ground that such a dispute could only be decided by the House of Commons. The matter was referred by writ of error to the House of Lords where the order of the Court of Queen's Bench was in turn set aside. At this the Commons became highly indignant, declared that the elector had been guilty of breach of privilege in bringing the action in the first place, and after further developments had taken place, committed him and others associated with him to prison. The prisoners moved for a writ of *habeas corpus* but the Court of Queen's Bench decided that it had no jurisdiction in the matter. This question was also brought before the Lords by writ of error, the Queen having rejected an address from the Commons praying that a writ of error should not be granted. Upon this the Lords agreed to a number of important resolutions directed against the Commons, amongst which the right of an imprisoned person to a writ of *habeas corpus* under any circumstances was upheld, and the right of either House to create any new privilege for itself was denied. The issue was never resolved conclusively as Parliament was shortly afterwards prorogued.

The year 1704 was notable for the inauguration of the fund known as Queen Anne's Bounty. It was created for the benefit of the poorer clergy and consisted of that part of the royal revenues arising from the First Fruits and Tenths which were originally paid to Rome. The income amounted to £17,000 a year, which Parliament supplemented with an annual grant of £100,000. Important ministerial changes which took place during this year brought Robert Harley, the Tory Speaker of the House of Commons, and Henry St. John, another Tory who had promoted the Occasional Conformity Bill, into the Government. Anne's first Parliament met on 29 October for its final session, and before its dissolution Marlborough won his great victory at Blenheim. The Duke received further rewards at the hands of the Queen and Parliament voted further substantial supplies for the prosecution of the war.

The elections of 1705 returned a Whig majority to the House of Commons and marked the beginning of a temporary Whig ascendancy. The leading Tories in the House of Lords incurred the extreme displeasure of the Queen by supporting a proposal that the heir presumptive to the throne should be invited to live in England. The suggestion was repugnant to Anne, as the Tory leaders well knew, and the remarks of Buckingham when speaking in support of it were such as to give grave personal offence to the Queen. Two measures affecting the succession were passed, however: an Act for the naturalization of the Princess Sophia and her issue (with a clause excluding anyone of the line who should embrace the Roman Catholic faith) and a Regency Act which provided for certain steps to be taken immediately on the death of the Queen. The trouble-making tactics of the Tories, which included a campaign designed to awaken alarm for the safety of the Church of England, embarrassed the Government so severely that the Queen was persuaded by her Whig ministers to remove their leaders from the Privy Council. Sunderland had been appointed Secretary of State in place of the Tory Hedges, and the promotions and peerages of the year 1706 were mainly in favour of the Whigs. Party strife was at this time very bitter but on the issue of the war there was fortunately unity. Marlborough's victory at Ramillies was received with great acclaim; supplies were quickly voted and a Bill was passed settling a pension of £5,000 a year from the Post Office revenue upon the Duke and his successors for ever.

The Act of Union with Scotland came into force on 1 May 1707, and the first Parliament of Great Britain met on 23 October. It pledged its support for the war and voted enormous supplies, but a ministerial crisis was soon to follow, resulting in the resignations of Harley and St. John. The latter was succeeded by the celebrated statesman Robert Walpole, then the most promising of the younger Whigs, and Somers was later brought into the Government as Lord President of the Council. With Godolphin still at the head of the Treasury the Whigs were now firmly installed in the Government.

On 20 October 1708 the Prince Consort died, and in the following January the two Houses prepared an address recommending a second marriage to the Queen. It was not well received by Anne, who, in her reply, pointed out that the Protestant succession was fully secured and concluded: 'The subject of this address is of such a nature that I am persuaded you do not expect a particular answer.'

The tide of events now began to turn against the Whigs, and their downfall was hastened by the impeachment of Dr. Sacheverell. This very High Church minister had preached a fanatical sermon in which

[18]

he had bitterly denounced the Whig ministry, and on the instigation of Godolphin and Sunderland he was brought to trial in Westminster Hall. He was found guilty and suspended for three years, but popular sympathy was on the side of Sacheverell and the Queen herself was favourably disposed towards him. The breach between the Queen and her Whig ministers widened shortly after this incident. She completely broke with her former favourite, the Duchess of Marlborough, and under pressure from the Tories she dismissed Godolphin and Sunderland from office. Harley was now called upon to form a ministry, and failing to secure any Whig support he formed a Government consisting entirely of Tories. On 21 September 1710 Parliament was dissolved, and a Tory majority was returned to the House of Commons at the ensuing elections. In the House of Lords also the Tory position was strengthened by the election of Tory peers to represent Scotland. The Property Qualification Act was introduced during the session of 1711, a measure by which ownership of land became an essential qualification for a Member of Parliament, and which remained in force until 1858. The same year saw the origin of the catastrophic South Sea scheme.

When Parliament met on 7 December 1711, the Queen announced the opening of peace negotiations. Harley had already taken the initiative in approaching the French some twelve months previously, and his popularity at home had been greatly strengthened by the attempt upon his life earlier in the year. But although there was considerable support in Parliament for the proposed articles of peace, bitter opposition came from Marlborough, Nottingham, Sunderland, and a majority of the peers, who carried an amendment against the Government by 62 votes to 54, and from a substantial minority in the House of Commons, where a similar amendment was defeated by 232 to 106. The Government was thus severely embarrassed, and realizing that drastic action alone could save them they resolved to strike at Marlborough. Accordingly they acted upon a report from a commission on public accounts which accused the Duke of receiving unauthorized payments. Marlborough protested that the payments complained of were no more than his rightful dues, but the Queen accepted the report of the commission and dismissed Marlborough from all his offices on the last day of the year. On the same day she created twelve new Tory peers to provide the Government with a majority in the upper House, one of them being the husband of her favourite, Abigail Masham.

The peace negotiations proceeded in the face of the spirited and undaunted opposition of Marlborough and his supporters, and on 31 March 1713 the Peace of Utrecht was concluded. Amongst other things the treaty provided for recognition of the Protestant succession in England, the expulsion of the Pretender from France, a permanent severance of the Crowns of France and Spain, and the acquisition by

Great Britain of Newfoundland, the Hudson's Bay Territory, and Gibraltar. Shortly after the conclusion of the peace dissension broke out within the Tory ministry on the question of the succession. Bolingbroke supported a Stuart restoration but Harley, now the Earl of Oxford, was pledged in favour of the House of Hanover. A breach between the two ministers developed, and the former, determined to overthrow the Lord Treasurer, promoted an extreme High Church measure which became known as the Schism Act, knowing that Harley could never be induced to accept it. The conflict resulted in the dismissal of Harley, and Bolingbroke would have appeared to have triumphed, but the Queen was suddenly stricken with her last illness and was persuaded before she died to appoint Shrewsbury, a staunch supporter of the Hanoverian dynasty, to the head of the Government.

Queen Anne died on 1 August 1714. A woman who had endured much private suffering, she had ever kept the welfare of her people close to her heart. Although by no means a born ruler her influence upon the age in which she lived may be justly described as a salutary one; and the achievements of her brief reign went far to merit the tribute implicit in the term Augustan Age.

ANNUNCIATORS

Electrically worked indicators which were formerly placed in rooms frequented by members in the House of Commons showing what the House was discussing, calls for and results of divisions, and the name of the member speaking. In August 1967 these annunciators, of which there were forty-four distributed throughout the building, each capable of showing words up to a total of twenty-six letters, were replaced by a system of closed-circuit television.

The House of Commons of Northern Ireland uses indicator boards in various parts of the building on which are listed the names of members. A light appears opposite the member speaking in the House, and counts, divisions and stages of business can also be indicated by lights on these boards. An economical system of television annunciators is described by E. Grant-Dalton in vol. 29 of *The Table*.

'ANOTHER PLACE'

In a bicameral legislature it is obvious that certain restrictions must be imposed upon comments made in one House upon the proceedings of the other, for an unguarded or a deliberately critical reference could well provoke something of a constitutional crisis. For this reason it has long been the rule in British Parliaments that a member of one House may make no reference at all to the proceedings of the other. For many years, however, members have found means of evading this rule by making veiled or indirect references to the other Chamber, with the result that it has become customary to refer to 'another place' when speaking of the other House. Nobody to-day objects to this practice and the rule against it is not rigidly enforced, but it is not permitted to refer to debates of the current session. Dispensations are granted in certain circumstances, for example, to ministers who find it necessary to refer to the debates of the other House in the course of an explanation and to Members when referring to official statements.

ANTICIPATION

It is recognized in all Parliaments as a general principle that a member must not discuss matters which are the subject of a forthcoming debate. However, there is no hard and fast rule on the subject of anticipation, and a wide discretionary power is reserved to the Speaker in this matter. Erskine May states that 'a matter must not be anticipated if it is contained in a more effective form of proceeding than the proceeding by which it is sought to be anticipated'. Thus, a motion may not anticipate a Bill or other order of the day because it is a less effective proceeding; similarly, an amendment or an adjournment motion may not anticipate a substantive motion.

At one time it was possible to prevent a debate taking place on a matter with the use of 'blocking' motions (q.v.), but this practice has to a great extent been eliminated by Standing Order No. 11 which provides:

In determining whether a discussion is out of order on the ground of anticipation, regard shall be had by Mr. Speaker to the probability of the matter anticipated being brought before the House within a reasonable time.

ANTIGUA PARLIAMENT

From 1871 to 1956 Antigua was a Presidency of the Leeward Islands Federation, an association which was abolished when the West Indies Federation was formed. Antigua became a member of the West Indies Federation, and in 1959 internal constitutional changes for Antigua were agreed upon by the Leeward and Windward Islands Constitutional Conference. The Legislative Council was reconstituted to consist of 10 elected members, 1 official member and 2 nominated unofficial members, and a Speaker was appointed to take the place of the Administrator who previously presided. With effect from 1 January 1960 the Executive Council was also reconstituted to comprise a Chief Minister, appointed from the unofficial members of the Legislative Council, 4 other unofficial members and 1 official member (the Law Officer).

In 1962 the West Indies Federation was dissolved as the result of Jamaica's decision to withdraw from it. When negotiations for an alternative form of federation for the smaller West Indian Colonies failed to produce agreement, new constitutional proposals were

[21]

published in 1965 (Cmnd. 2865) whereby six British territories of the Eastern Caribbean could, if they wished, enter into an associate status with Great Britain. Antigua was the first of these dependencies to initiate negotiations with Britain with a view to acquiring the new status.

Under the new arrangements Antigua has full control over internal affairs, Britain retaining responsibility for external affairs and defence which will be exercised in close consultation with Antigua. Certain powers in the field of external relationships are delegated to Antigua, including the right to apply for membership of certain international organizations, to conclude trade agreements, and to enter into certain other agreements.

The new Constitution provides for a Governor and a bicameral legislature consisting of a Senate and a House of Representatives. The Senate consists of 10 members appointed by the Governor, 7 on the advice of the Premier and 3 after consultation with the Premier. The House of Representatives consists of not less than 10 directly elected members and has a life of five years unless sooner dissolved. The Speaker need not be an elected member, in which case he becomes a member by virtue of his office. The Attorney-General may or may not be an elected member, and if non-elected he becomes a non-voting member of the House.

The Senate and the House both meet in the same Chamber and, therefore, do not sit simultaneously.

The association may be terminated voluntarily either by Great Britain or Antigua. If terminated by Antigua a Bill to end the association must be passed by the Antigua Parliament with a two-thirds majority and must also be approved by a two-thirds majority of the electorate at a referendum. No referendum is required, however, if Antigua should terminate the association for the purpose of entering into a union, federation or other constitutional association with an independent Commonwealth Caribbean country.

APPEAL COMMITTEE

A committee appointed by the House of Lords every session to consider matters relating to petitions for leave to appeal to the upper House in its judicial capacity. Normally it is attended only by the Lords of Appeal in Ordinary, although it is deemed to consist of all the peers present during the session. Three peers form a quorum.

APPELLATE COMMITTEE

A committee appointed every session by the House of Lords consisting of the Lords of Appeal (q.v.), to which are referred for hearing all appeals which come before the upper House. The delegation to it of the judicial work of the House, to which the committee reports its decisions, leaves the House of Lords free to proceed with its legislative and other business.

See also HOUSE OF LORDS.

APPLAUSE IN PARLIAMENT

'Hear, Hear' is the traditional parliamentary expression for the purpose of applauding a speech, approving a sentiment, or welcoming back after a successful mission or a long illness a prominent Member of Parliament. Its use is not limited to the confines of either House, however, as on certain public and royal occasions decorous cries of 'Hear, Hear' have been heard issuing from the stands occupied by Members of Parliament. The expression is an abbreviation of 'Hear him! Hear him!' which was in use at the beginning of the last century. In some Commonwealth Parliaments which have not adopted the benches of the British Parliament, applause is indicated by members rapping on their desks. No applause is permitted on the part of strangers seated in the galleries of a legislative chamber.

APPROPRIATION ACCOUNTS

See COMMITTEE OF PUBLIC ACCOUNTS.

APPROPRIATION ACT

The annual statute which gives legal force to the main Estimates (q.v.) after they have been agreed to in Parliament. The passing of the Act is generally the last financial business of the session. It is introduced in the House of Commons as the Consolidated Fund (Appropriation) Bill, and differs from other Consolidated Fund Bills in that it contains schedules, which to a great extent reproduce the main Estimates, specifying the purposes for which the money is to be used (hence Appropriation Act). Like Consolidated Fund Acts (q.v.) the Appropriation Act also authorizes the Treasury (q.v.) to borrow money in anticipation of revenue, the amount which may be borrowed being equal to the total sum of the money appropriated. The Act formerly authorized the service departments to make use of the power of 'virement' (q.v.), whereby money assigned to one vote could be transferred to meet the expenses of another vote, but the need has now fallen away following the introduction of a new procedure which provides for a Defence Vote on Account (*see* ESTIMATES).

The Appropriation Act is an Act to grant aids and supplies to the Crown, and its enacting formula expresses the predominance of the Commons in matters of finance, and runs as follows:

Most Gracious Sovereign, We, Your Majesty's most dutiful and loyal subjects, the Commons of the United Kingdom in Parliament assembled, towards making good the supply which we have cheerfully granted to Your Majesty in this Session of Parliament, have resolved to grant unto Your

Majesty the sum hereinafter mentioned; and do therefore most humbly beseech Your Majesty that it may be enacted, and be it enacted by the Queen's most Excellent Majesty, by and with the advice and consent of the Lords Spiritual and Temporal, and Commons, in the present Parliament assembled, and by the authority of the same, as follows:—

The formula is the same in the case of Consolidated Fund Acts.

The Consolidated Fund (Appropriation) Bill and all other Consolidated Fund Bills, having completed their passage through both Houses, remain in the custody of the House of Commons until they are presented for the Royal Assent (q.v.). When this ceremony takes place in the traditional manner they are carried to the Lords by the Clerk of the House of Commons, handed to the Clerk of the Parliaments by the Speaker, and receive the Royal Assent before all other Bills. The Royal Assent to all Bills for granting aids and supplies to the Crown is signified in the words, '*La Reyne remercie ses bons sujets, accepte leur benevolence, et ainsi le veult*'. With the passage of the Royal Assent Act 1967 the Royal Assent to Bills is now normally announced by the Lord Chancellor and the Speaker of the House of Commons in their respective Houses, and the procedure described above has probably undergone some modification as a result.

Consolidated Fund Bills provide opportunities for general debates on financial policy limited only by the various purposes for which the Bills seek to provide money. Since the introduction of the new financial procedure in December 1966 the Standing Orders have provided that the third reading of such Bills is not debatable. Like the Finance Bill they constitute 'Exempted Business' (q.v.) and proceedings upon them are not subject to interruption under the automatic adjournment or Ten o'clock Rule (q.v.).

See also ACT OF PARLIAMENT; FINANCE ACT.

APPROPRIATIONS-IN-AID

See ESTIMATES.

ARCHBISHOPS

See LORDS SPIRITUAL.

ARMY ACT

Until 1955 legislative provision for the Army was based on the Army Act of 1881. The Air Force Act which governed the junior service was in reality the Army Act as modified by the Air Force (Constitution) Act, 1917. Both these statutes were kept in force by a regular Army and Air Force (Annual) Act, which extended the application of the main legislation for a further period of twelve months and provided for such amendments as the current circumstances required. Provision for the Navy was, and still is, provided for by permanent statutes.

Until 1879 the whole code of military law was temporary, being re-enacted each session by a Mutiny Bill. In that year a permanent Act, the Army Discipline and Regulation Act, was passed, but in order to secure the right of Parliament to give or withhold its consent to a standing army, it also provided that the permanent Act is inoperative unless brought into force by an annual Act. The Army Act, 1881, was a consolidation of the Act of 1879 and the subsequent Acts amending it. It was the practice to introduce the Army and Air Force (Annual) Bill after the House had agreed to the resolutions voted in Committee of Supply determining the size of the armed forces for the coming year.

In 1952, during the debate on the Army and Air Force (Annual) Bill of that year, the inadequacy of the outdated legislation was discussed at length, and both sides of the House agreed that it was in need of revision. A Select Committee was therefore appointed 'to consider the Army Act and the Air Force Act, and to make recommendations for the amendment thereof; and to consider and report on the advisability of enacting the said Acts or parts thereof permanently'. The committee was given the usual power to send for persons, papers, and records, and was further empowered to communicate with the Departmental Drafting Committee appointed to assist them by the War Minister and the Air Minister. After detailed and extensive investigation, during the course of which a number of expert witnesses were examined, the committee reported in 1954, including with the report the proposed drafts of a new Army Bill and Air Force Bill.

The revised Bills were introduced into the House on 14 December 1954, and became Acts of Parliament in 1955. As recommended by the Select Committee both provide for the annual renewal of the Acts by Order in Council, but not beyond a period of five years from the date on which they come into operation unless Parliament otherwise determines. Parliament thus has the opportunity of reviewing the main legislation every five years should it so desire. Every such Order in Council must be laid before Parliament in draft and approved by resolution of each House.

ARMY AND AIR FORCE (ANNUAL) ACT
See ARMY ACT.

ARREST, FREEDOM FROM
See PRIVILEGE.

ASSENT, ROYAL
See ROYAL ASSENT.

[25]

ATTAINDER, ACT OF
See ACT OF ATTAINDER.

ATTENDANCE OF MEMBERS

The attendance of members is now controlled by the party Whips (q.v.), but before this pressure was brought to bear many efforts were made to compel early and full attendance at the House of Commons. Acts were passed in 1382 and 1515 enforcing attendance, and penalties for absence were sometimes imprisonment, but more frequently fines or the forfeiture of the member's 'wages'. During the first half of the 17th century several attempts were made to ensure punctuality by imposing fines on members arriving late, and one of these is described by D'Ewes. 'A motion made,' he says, 'as I came in, that such members as should not come up by eight, and be at prayers, should pay a shilling. Divers spake against it; but the greater number being for it, it passed.' Very little, however, as it would seem, to the benefit of Mr. Speaker, seeing that next morning he did not make his appearance till a quarter to nine. 'The House by this time,' D'Ewes remarks, 'was very full at prayers, by reason of the order made yesterday. Sir H. Mildmay, after prayers, stood up and said he was glad to see this good effect of yesterday's order, and said to the Speaker that he did hope that here-after he would come in time; which made the Speaker throw down twelvepence upon the table. Others as they came in did each pay his shilling to the Serjeant. I spake to the orders of the House: That the order made yesterday was to fine "after" prayers, and therefore you (I spake to the Speaker) cannot be subject to pay; and for coming a little after eight, that was no great difference. Although I spake truly, the Speaker, having cast down his shilling, would not take it up again.'

The infliction of fines seems to have ceased towards the close of the 17th century in England, but provision for the imposition of fines exists in some of the Parliaments of the Commonwealth. In Canada, for example, a Member who absents himself without permission for more than twenty-one days is liable to a fine of $120 for each day's unexcused absence. This rule is largely inoperative, however, as no attendance records are kept apart from a statutory declaration made by the member himself. It is interesting to note the contrasting practice in the Senate where a roll-call takes place every sitting day.

In most Commonwealth Parliaments the penalty for absenteeism is forfeiture of membership. In Australia the attendance of members is governed by the Constitution which provides that a member's place becomes vacated if he fails to attend for two consecutive months without the leave of the House. The attendance of members is also recorded in the Votes and Proceedings. In Singapore, similarly, a member absenting himself for two consecutive months without leave is liable to lose his seat. In Ceylon a member's seat is vacated if he fails to attend for three consecutive months, while in Barbados a member forfeits his seat if he is absent without leave for more than forty days. In New Zealand a member is held to be in contempt of Parliament if he is absent without leave for more than seven consecutive sitting days.

The question of attendance of Members of the House of Lords is dealt with in a Report by a Select Committee on the Powers of the House (of Lords) in Relation to the Attendance of its Members which was published as a House of Lords Paper in 1956.

See also ABSENCE, LEAVE OF; CALLING THE HOUSE.

ATTORNEY-GENERAL
See LAW OFFICERS OF THE CROWN.

AUDITOR GENERAL
See COMPTROLLER AND AUDITOR GENERAL.

AUSTRALIAN PARLIAMENT

Although the first Federal Parliament of the Commonwealth of Australia met in 1901, agreement as to the site of the federal capital was not reached until 1909, and the first Parliament was not held there until eighteen years later. Until then the Federal Parliament met in Melbourne. The total area of the Australian Capital Territory, originally part of New South Wales, is 910 square miles, of which about 20 square miles was reserved for the federal capital, Canberra. The Australian Parliament's powers are limited and enumerated, the State Parliaments retaining the residuary power of government over their respective territories, but a federal law prevails where it is inconsistent with a state law. However, the Governor-General of Australia cannot disallow state laws as the Governor-General of Canada can disallow, in certain circumstances, laws made by the provincial Parliaments. The Federal Parliament's main concerns are external affairs, foreign and inter-State trade and commerce, taxation, postal services, defence, currency and coinage, banking, aliens and naturalization, social services, railways, and customs and excise. It has an upper House, the Senate, and a lower House, the House of Representatives, and since the 1949 elections the membership of both has been nearly doubled. There are now 60 Senators (36 from 1901 to 1949), 10 from each State, while the number of members of the House of Representatives to be elected in the six States is determined on a population formula contained in the Constitution. The maximum life of a Parliament is three years, and elections for the House of Representatives are held following the dissolution of each Parliament. Senators, however, are elected for six years, each State voting as a single electorate, half of them retiring every three years. Until 1949 the lower House consisted of 74 members, but its present strength is 124 comprising 46 from New South Wales, 33 from Victoria, 18 from Queensland, 11 from South Australia, 9 from Western Australia, 5 from Tasmania and 2 representing the Northern Territory and the Australian Capital Territory, territories which are administered by the Federal Government. The 2 members last mentioned, who now have full voting rights, formerly fell into a rather curious category. Prior to 1968 in the case of the former and 1967 in the case of the latter, their rights were restricted and they were permitted to vote only on Bills relating solely to their own territories and on motions for the disallowance of ordinances relating to their own territories, although they could take part in all debates. They did not count towards a quorum and were ineligible to be chosen as Speaker or Chairman. The Northern Territory was represented in this manner from 1923, the Australian Capital Territory from 1950.

Qualifications for the Commonwealth franchise are possessed by any British subject over twenty-one, including aborigines, who has lived in Australia for six months continuously, and is not otherwise disqualified. For those who thus qualify (except aborigines), voting is compulsory. The system of voting for the House of Representatives is preferential (*see* ALTERNATIVE VOTE), and for the Senate, since the passing of the Commonwealth Electoral Act of 1948, proportional representation (q.v.).

The Australian system of government makes provision for the referendum (q.v.). Any proposal to amend the Constitution must be submitted to the electors and can be enacted only if approved by a majority of the States as well as by a majority of the electors. Bills seeking to amend the Constitution must be passed by an absolute majority in each House.

Australian parliamentary procedure is based on that of Great Britain and, in spite of important variations in practice, the fundamental principles are common to both systems. For example, the financial initiative is reserved to the lower House, and the Senate may neither originate nor amend a Money Bill. The House of Representatives does not, however, enjoy the power conferred on the House of Commons under the Parliament Acts (q.v.), and Bills must be passed by both Houses before they can be presented for the Royal Assent. In the event of disagreement between the two Houses, provision is made for conferences of Managers appointed by each House, and also for joint sittings. In the event of a deadlock both Houses may be dissolved by the Governor-General under Section 57 of the Constitution. A double dissolution has been proclaimed twice since the inception of the Commonwealth of Australia—in 1914 and in 1951. In considering the powers of the Australian Senate it is important to bear in mind that, unlike the House of Lords and the Canadian Senate, it is a directly elected Chamber.

The procedure of the House of Representatives underwent extensive revision in 1963, the most radical changes concerning financial procedure. Following the report of the Standing Orders Committee, the House of Representatives decided to dispense with 'the obsolete system of preliminary consideration of financial proposals' inherited from the British Parliament. It was felt that the retention of a system which was established during the 17th century as the result of a constitutional struggle between Crown and Parliament was no longer consistent with modern parliamentary needs. Accordingly, the Committees of Supply and Ways and Means and all other financial committees on whose resolutions Money Bills were previously based have been abolished. Under the new procedures Money Bills are introduced in exactly the same way as non-financial Bills, no preliminary resolutions being required. The Budget debate takes place on the second reading of an Appropriation Bill, and amendments of the widest scope relating to public affairs may be moved and debated at this stage. When the second reading is passed the details of estimated expenditure, included in a schedule to the Bill, are debated at the committee stage, these debates corresponding with those which previously took place in Committee of Supply. Taxation proposals are also now initiated by way of a Bill, the committee stage being the occasion for the debate which formerly took place in Committee of Ways and Means. The Governor-General's message recommending an appropriation or taxation is announced by the Speaker at the time of the introduction of the Bill.

It is of interest to note that in 1967 the British House of Commons also abolished the Committees of Supply and Ways and Means (*see* PROCEDURE, FINANCIAL). However, the requirement that financial legislation should be based on a preliminary financial resolution has been retained, and the Australian procedure thus continues to differ from the British in very important respects.

Differences between the Australian and British Parliaments also exist in matters of tradition and custom. For example, the Speaker of the House of Representatives does not necessarily hold himself aloof from the party political conflict. Although he discharges his duties with impartiality when in occupation of the Chair, the office has not attained that total detachment from political partisanship which characterizes its counterpart in Great Britain. As a result the Speaker's seat is invariably contested at a General Election and, if the Speaker's party is defeated at the polls, he himself can expect to be replaced by the nominee of the majority when the new Parliament meets. The principle of continuity of the Speakership has never been conceded in Australia, although at least one Speaker attempted to assert his independence by abstaining from voting during a crucial division in committee. His action, however, brought about the fall of the

Government and its subsequent electoral defeat. His party never forgave him and he never again held any office. When the Labour party has held office in Australia the Speaker has usually discarded his wig and robe of office in deference to the party's distaste for such insignia.

Among further Australian variations from British parliamentary procedure and practice the following may be noted:

1. The committee stage of a Bill may be dispensed with and the third reading moved forthwith provided no member objects.
2. The committee stage of a Bill, when debated, is always taken in a Committee of the Whole House, there being no counterpart to the Standing Committee system of the House of Commons.
3. Fairly rigid time limits are provided both for speeches and debates. For example, in speaking on the Address in Reply to the Throne Speech a member is limited to 25 minutes; on the second reading of a Bill 30 minutes; in committee 20 minutes; on an adjournment motion 10 minutes; and on the election of the Speaker 5 minutes. A debate on a definite matter of urgent public importance is limited to 2 hours and each speech to 10 minutes. A debate on a motion for the allotment of time may last not more than 20 minutes, each member being limited to 5 minutes. Certain exemptions from these limitations are provided for in order to accommodate ministers, Opposition spokesmen and the movers of motions.
4. Rulings from the Chair may be challenged from the floor of the House and summarily voted on.
5. No provision exists for the automatic adjournment of the House except in the event of the absence of a quorum.
6. Questions may be put to ministers *without* notice. Such questions are asked daily at the commencement of business.
7. If the closure is moved, the Speaker or Chairman, as the case may be, is obliged to put the question to the House.
8. Since 1 April 1965 a member has not been prohibited from reading his speech.
9. The election of the Speaker is conducted by secret ballot.
10. Provision is made for 'grievance' debates on every alternate Thursday. Debate takes place on a question proposed by the Speaker, 'That grievances be noted', any member being permitted to speak or move an amendment.
11. Divisions are taken in the Chamber with members sitting in their places.
12. Private Bills have no place in Australian parliamentary procedure.
13. Public Bills introduced by private members are very rare.
14. For ease of consultation the Prime Minister and the Leader of

the Opposition sit opposite one another at either side of the Table of the House.

The Australian Cabinet system is directly derived from that of Great Britain and is presided over by the Prime Minister. Originally the Cabinet consisted of all ministers of Cabinet rank but, in January 1955, the British practice was adopted whereby only selected ministers form the Cabinet, the others remaining outside the supreme policy-making body. Approximately one half of the ministers are normally members of the Cabinet. At the beginning of 1970 Mr. Gorton's Government comprised 12 ministers in the Cabinet and 14 outside it. When the Liberal Party is in power the formation of the ministry is largely a matter for the Prime Minister, as in Great Britain. However, the power of the party caucus is particularly strong in Australia, and when the Labour Party was last in office the then Prime Minister yielded the right of selecting his colleagues to the caucus which chose them by ballot. In addition to the Cabinet there is an Executive Council which is a purely formal constitutional agency, giving legal force to certain Cabinet decisions and appointments. It is presided over by the Governor-General, and all ministers are *ex-officio* members.

The broadcasting of debates is controlled by a Joint Committee of 3 Senators, including the President, and 6 members of the lower House, including the Speaker. The committee allocates the time given to each House and makes the final decision as to which debates will be broadcast. Both sides of the House receive equal coverage and the debates are broadcast live from the Floor of the House.

Parliament House is a rectangular building covering about $3\frac{1}{2}$ acres. The centre portion is the King's Hall, from which the Senate and the House of Representatives lie right and left respectively. This arrangement follows Westminster, where the House of Lords and the House of Commons occupy the same position in relation to the Central Hall. All the usual amenities are provided for members, including a post office and a barber's shop. A Joint Select Committee was appointed in August 1965 to inquire into the accommodation and service needs of a new and permanent Parliament House. The Committee reported on 8 April 1970 (Parliamentary Paper No. 32 of 1970) and a detailed account of the Committee's recommendations was published in an article written by the President of the Australian Senate, Sir Alister McMullin, and published in *The Parliamentarian* for October 1970.

AVIATION, MINISTER OF

This office was created after the General Election of 1959, and Mr. Duncan Sandys was appointed as the first Minister with a seat in the Cabinet. He was succeeded in 1960 by Mr. Peter Thorneycroft. This Minister took over responsibility for all matters concerned with civil aviation from the Minister of Transport and Civil Aviation (who reverted to his former title of Minister of Transport) and responsibility for the development and production of civil and military aircraft, guided missiles, and atomic weapons, and all research connected therewith, from the Minister of Supply, now a defunct office.

Under a ministerial reorganization in 1967 the Ministry of Aviation was abolished and incorporated with the Ministry of Technology. The then Minister of Aviation, Mr. John Stonehouse, became a Minister of State within the Ministry of Technology, responsible for aviation affairs. In 1970 the Ministry of Technology and the Board of Trade were merged into a single Department of Trade and Industry under a Minister styled the Secretary of State for Trade and Industry and President of the Board of Trade.

AVIATION SUPPLY, MINISTER OF

This Minister's Department was set up temporarily under a major reorganization of the machinery of central government which took place in 1970. He is responsible for aerospace research and the development and procurement of aircraft and similar equipment for defence purposes, functions formerly exercised by the Minister of Technology (q.v.). When the Ministry of Technology was absorbed by the new Department of Trade and Industry, these particular functions were not taken over.

It is intended that the functions of the Minister of Aviation Supply will be transferred to the Secretary of State for Defence by 1 April 1972.

AYRTON LIGHT

The lantern above Big Ben (q.v.) which takes its name from a First Commissioner of Works, Mr. Acton Smee Ayrton, and which has shone since 1885 to denote that the House of Commons is sitting.

B

BACK-BENCHER

The term applied to the 'private member' who does not hold any ministerial office. He occupies a back bench, the front benches being reserved on the Government side for ministers and parliamentary secretaries, and on the other side for the leading members of the Opposition.

BADGE MESSENGER

House of Commons messengers are thus called because of their silver-gilt badges of office which are suspended from a chain round the neck. These badges consist of the royal arms beneath which is hung a figure of Mercury, and some of them date from 1755. The Rhodesian Parliament adopted a similar badge for its Chief Messenger in 1928. A visitor who wishes to see a Member of Parliament at the House fills in his name and business on a green card, and these cards are taken round the building by a badge messenger, to whom no doors are barred, until the member is found.

BAD PARLIAMENT

The Parliament dominated by John of Gaunt which met in January 1377, and so called in contradistinction to the 'Good Parliament' (q.v.), which met in the previous year. Reforms instituted by the Good Parliament were annulled by the following Bad Parliament, which also reinstated Edward III's mistress, Alice Perrers, who had been partly responsible for the disgrace and imprisonment of the Speaker, Sir Peter de la Mare.

BAHAMAS PARLIAMENT

Discovered by Columbus in 1492, the Bahamas were already regarded as British less than a hundred years later. They were included in Royal Grants to Sir Robert Heath, the Attorney-General, in 1629, to the 'Eleutherian Adventurers'—a company formed in London to colonize the islands—in 1647, and again in 1670 when Charles II vested the Bahamas in 6 Lords Proprietors. Their Charter provided for an elected House of Assembly, and the Constitution was finally settled in 1729, when the Crown assumed direct control of the Colony. The bicameral legislatures of the Bahamas, Barbados and Bermuda were until recently the only surviving examples in the Colonies of the old representative system which existed before Crown Colony government was introduced.

The Bahamas achieved internal self-government with Cabinet responsibility in January 1964, and a new Constitution further enhancing the constitutional status of the islands came into force in 1969. Under the new Constitution the Bahamas are known as 'The Commonwealth of the Bahama Islands'. Parliament consists of the Queen represented by the Governor, the Senate and the House of Assembly. The Senate consists of 16 members, 9 of whom are appointed by the Governor on the advice of the Prime Minister, 4 on the advice of the Leader of the Opposition and 3 by the Governor, following consultation with the Prime Minister and any other persons he may wish to consult. Under the 1964 Constitution the Senate had consisted of 15 members of whom 8 were nominated by the Governor, 5 on the advice of the Premier and 2 on the advice of the Leader of the Opposition. The former Legislative Council which the Senate replaces had been created by Letters Patent in 1841 and had originally consisted of 9 members nominated for life by the Crown. The House of Assembly consists as before of 38 members, its size having been increased in 1967 from 33. The life of a Parliament is five years unless sooner dissolved, the life of the Senate being concurrent with that of the House. The delaying power of the Senate over Bills has been reduced from 15 to 9 months.

Universal suffrage for adult males was introduced in 1959 and the vote was extended to women in 1962.

The 1964 Constitution had introduced a ministerial system, providing for a Premier and a Cabinet. Under the 1969 Constitution, the Premier was restyled the Prime Minister. The Governor retains his ultimate responsibility for external affairs, the police force, defence and internal security, but in recognition of the desire of Bahama ministers to be more closely associated with these important areas of government the 1969 Constitution provides for a Security Council consisting of the Governor and the Prime Minister among others which would discuss questions of policy relating to the reserved areas. It is provided in addition that immediate responsibility for the police and internal security should be entrusted to a minister designated on the advice of the Prime Minister.

BALLOT

See PRIVATE MEMBERS' BILLS; PRIVATE MEMBERS' TIME.

BALLOT ACT, 1872

This Act was passed to make elections free from corrupt influences by substituting a secret ballot for open voting. As passed it was of temporary duration, but was extended by the Expiring Laws Continuance Acts and made permanent by the Representation of the People

Act, 1918. The Act also included detailed rules for the holding of parliamentary and municipal elections, the duties of Returning Officers and penalties for election offences. This Act also removed the distinction between county and borough members as 'Knights of the Shire', 'Citizens of the City', or 'Burgesses of the Borough', all representatives being grouped as 'Members of the House of Commons'. South Australia first introduced the secret ballot in 1856.

BARBADOS PARLIAMENT

As early as twelve years after its settlement by the British in 1627 Barbados had its elected House of Burgesses to advise the Governor and his Councillors on the administration of the island. This House soon became a body possessing the right to initiate legislation, and Barbados thereafter enjoyed a large measure of self-government. It was so far independent by the time of the struggle between King and Parliament that it decided to remain neutral during the Civil War. Although Cromwell subdued the island he was anxious to avoid any decline in its main product—sugar—and in 1652 his Parliament agreed 'that no taxes, customs, imports, loans or excise shall be laid, nor levy made on any inhabitants of this island without their consent in a General Assembly'. Charles II placed a brake on the rapid constitutional development of Barbados by assuming proprietorship and exacting a tax of $4\frac{1}{2}$ per cent on all its exports, and in 1663 the Governor dissolved the Assembly and legislated through ordinances made in Council. He was forced to issue new writs for an Assembly in 1665, and in 1710 it was finally ruled that the Assembly had sole right to the executive power in the matters of finance within the island. The growth of Boards or Committees of the Legislature which acted as government departments to spend the money voted by themselves caused the Colonial Office to create an Executive Council in 1876 to advise the Governor on the island's administration. The Assembly tried to retain its control of finance, but in 1881 an Executive Committee consisting of 4 members of the Assembly and 1 member of the Legislative Council was appointed to sit with the Governor and Executive Council to initiate legislation on all matters of supply and the general welfare of the island.

With the growth of party politics, Governor Bushe in 1946 was responsible for 4 members of the majority party being selected to form an Executive Committee, and this was the forerunner of the ministerial government inaugurated in 1954.

In 1958 the cabinet system was introduced and, in the same year, Barbados became a member of the short-lived West Indies Federation. Full internal self-government was achieved on 16 October 1961, while Barbados was still a member of the Federation, but in the following year the Federation was brought to an end after Jamaica and Trinidad withdrew. Following the dissolution of the West Indies Federation,

Barbados entered into discussions as to the possibility of a narrower federation with the Leeward and Windward Islands but, with the failure of these negotiations, the Barbados Government announced in 1965 its intention of seeking separate independence. Thus on 30 November 1966 Barbados became an independent member of the Commonwealth.

The Parliament of Barbados, which (together with the Parliaments of Bahamas and Bermuda) was a surviving example of the old colonial representative system, remains bicameral. In May 1964 the former Legislative Council was replaced by a Senate of 21 members who are nominated by the Governor-General, 12 on the advice of the Prime Minister, 2 on the advice of the Leader of the Opposition, and 7 to represent religious, economic and other interests. The House of Assembly consists of 24 members elected on a universal franchise, the voting age having been lowered from twenty-one to eighteen in 1963. The Senate may not introduce Money Bills, nor reject a Bill sent up from the House of Assembly in two successive sessions. The life of a Parliament is five years unless sooner dissolved.

Executive power is vested in the Governor-General who appoints the Prime Minister and acts in accordance with his advice, in conformity with normal constitutional practice. Barbados has its own Privy Council, which was established in 1961 and replaced the former Executive Council which included both the Governor and the Premier. The Constitution provides for the protection of fundamental rights and freedoms, and includes certain entrenched clauses which may be amended only with the approval of a two-thirds majority of both Houses of Parliament. A proposal that Barbados should enter into an association with any other state or territory of the Commonwealth will not, however, require a two-thirds majority.

Procedure varies slightly in the House of Assembly from that of the House of Commons—for instance the second and third readings of Bills can be taken on the same day and immediately after each other, and there is seldom any third reading debate. There is no fixed time for the adjournment, and no guillotine when the House is in committee.

Since 1874 both Houses have occupied a wing of the Public Buildings. The Assembly Chamber has thirteen stained-glass windows with portraits of the Sovereigns of England from James I, in whose reign Barbados was claimed, and other windows with names of past Speakers and Presidents of the Council. Members sit round a horse-shoe table with a division between Government and Opposition. The Mace was acquired in 1810.

BAREBONES PARLIAMENT

The Parliament of Nominees, also known as the Little Parliament, which was summoned by Cromwell on 4 July 1653, after his dismissal of the Long Parliament (q.v.). It consisted of 140 members, selected as being 'God-fearing men, who had given proofs of their fidelity, energy, and devoted zeal for the cause of God'. The Parliament received its strange nickname from one of its members, a staunch Puritan, who rejoiced in the name of Praise-God Barebone. The Parliament assumed the title of Parliament of the Commonwealth of England. The Speaker, Francis Rouse, was elected without ceremony and re-elected every month while the Parliament lasted.

The Barebones Parliament became the butt of much ridicule on account of its reforming zeal, in which it displayed little judgment. It eventually disagreed amongst itself over a scheme for the reorganization of the Church, and on arriving at a deadlock the minority, which included the Speaker, succeeded by a cunning artifice in causing the Parliament to resign its powers to the Lord General, Cromwell. On 12 December, the minority assembled early and resolved to terminate the Parliament and surrender its authority, and headed by the Speaker they proceeded to Whitehall where they signed an instrument of abdication.

(Further reading: Glass, *The Barbone Parliament*, 1899.)

See also CROMWELL AND PARLIAMENT.

BAR OF THE HOUSE

Members are not allowed to speak outside the Bar, which consists of two rods which can be drawn across the end of the benches to form the boundary of the House of Commons opposite the Speaker's Chair. Members may stand in the space between the Bar and the Door of the House, but if they cross the Bar they must take their seats. The House has authority to call persons indicted for breach of privilege to the Bar of the House, and either as culprits or suppliants many well-known historical figures have been seen there, accompanied by the Serjeant-at-Arms with the Mace. Until 1772 those who had incurred the displeasure of the Commons were made to kneel at the Bar, but after that they were allowed to stand. Perhaps the House was moved to take this action by a remark made by Baldwin, who was arrested for publishing the proceedings of the House in 1771 and appeared at the Bar. On rising from his knees, after being censured, he said, as he brushed the dust from his clothes, 'What a damned dirty House!' The Duke of Wellington was even given a seat when he came to receive the thanks of Parliament for his services in the Peninsular War. The Bar in the new Chamber of the House of Commons opened in 1950 was a gift from Jamaica.

Offenders who are called before the House of Lords also stand at the Bar of the House, likewise the Speaker and Members of the House of Commons when they attend an Opening of Parliament or to hear the Royal Assent (q.v.) given to Bills. The Lords have not for many years required a prisoner to kneel at the Bar, but although the custom has declined it has never been formally renounced by them.

BARON

The ancient meaning, and even the derivation, of the word 'baron' is shrouded in obscurity. It may have meant a free man or a king's man, and it does not occur as a title of dignity in Saxon times. The Normans introduced it into England and changed the Anglo-Saxon thane into a baron, but it was some time before 'baron' implied a man of some particular distinction. The fact that 'baron' was not considered a title is shown by the British use of the word, whereby although it indicates a rank of the peerage, a baron is addressed as 'Lord X' and not 'Baron X'. Much controversy has arisen on the creation and continuance of baronies by tenure (the title being attached to the land or estates), but in the Berkeley case in 1811 the claim to such creation was finally disposed of. Since the 15th century the creation of a baron has generally been by letters patent, and not by the old writ of summons to the High Court of Parliament. The first instance of the present form of creation occurred in the reign of Richard II in 1387, when John Beauchamp de Holt was created Baron Kidderminster. A baron is styled 'Right Honourable' and addressed by the Sovereign as 'Right trusty and well-beloved cousin'. The mantles of barons are of crimson velvet edged with miniver, the cape furred with miniver pure, and powdered with two rows of ermine. The coronet is a plain circle of silver gilt, surmounted by six silver balls at equal distances. There are at present (1970) 720 barons and baronesses, including 181 life peers (q.v.).

BARRY, SIR CHARLES (1795–1860)

The architect who designed the Houses of Parliament at Westminster. The building was constructed after the great fire of 1834 had destroyed its predecessor and the formal opening took place in 1852. In 1941 the House of Commons Chamber was demolished by a bomb. The present Chamber, which was designed by Sir Giles Gilbert Scott, was opened in 1950.

BASUTOLAND

See LESOTHO PARLIAMENT.

BEAUCHESNE, ARTHUR (1876–1959)

Clerk of the Canadian House of Commons from 1925 to 1949, and author of *Rules and Forms: a Treatise on Parliamentary Procedure*.

BECHUANALAND PROTECTORATE

See BOTSWANA PARLIAMENT.

'BEHIND THE SPEAKER'S CHAIR'

Informal parliamentary discussions between the parties often take place off the Floor of the House (q.v.) in that part of the Chamber 'behind the Speaker's Chair'. The term is frequently used in connexion with such conversations. The understandings arrived at on these occasions often have an important bearing on the conduct of official business.

BELLAMY'S KITCHEN

The first attempt to provide any catering arrangements for M.P.s at Westminster was made by John Bellamy, the Deputy Housekeeper, in 1773. The House was then beginning to keep late hours, and as members found it inconvenient to leave the precincts of the House in search of refreshment, they persuaded Bellamy to provide them with food and drink, out of which he managed to make a very comfortable fortune. His famous Kitchen, described by Dickens in *Sketches by Boz*, continued under his son until the fire of 1834. When the new Houses of Parliament were built the catering was administered by a Kitchen Committee (q.v.) drawn from the Members of Parliament. The name 'Bellamy's' survives, however, in the New Zealand Parliament, where it is popularly applied to their refreshment department.

According to a story related by an old waiter of the House of Commons to Disraeli, soon after he entered Parliament, Pitt's last words before he died were, 'I think I could eat one of Bellamy's pork pies.' It is only right, however, to emphasize the apocryphal nature of this story!

'BELOW THE GANGWAY'

The gangway cuts across the House of Commons Chamber about half-way down. The position 'below the gangway' is generally occupied by minority groups not attached to the two main political parties or by dissenting groups within them. Sir Winston Churchill, during his years of political exile, was accustomed to occupy a seat 'below the gangway'.

BERMUDA PARLIAMENT

Bermuda was taken possession of by Admiral Sir George Somers in 1609, and the first settlers arrived in 1612. They were given legislative powers by a charter granted by James I in 1615, which stated that Bermudans 'were to be considered as free denizens, with full enjoyment of all liberties, franchises and immunities as though abiding and born in England'. Having begun as the property of the Virginia Company, and subsequently of the City of London Company, Bermuda came directly under the Crown in 1684, although it is not a

Crown Colony as its legislative powers were granted irrevocably and cannot be varied by Orders in Council.

The Parliament of Bermuda is the oldest British colonial legislature, the first General Assembly having been established in 1620. Prior to the adoption of its present Constitution, Bermuda was the only surviving example of the old colonial representative system where the upper House was entirely nominated and the representative character of the legislature lay in the lower House. Under the former Constitution, the Legislative Council consisted of 3 official and 8 nominated unofficial members, and the House of Assembly of 36 elected members. The Governor was assisted by an Executive Council of 3 official and 6 appointed unofficial members, the latter being nominated from the members of the House of Assembly. Government departments were controlled by statutory Executive Boards nominated by the Governor, their Chairmen being members of the House of Assembly. In 1966 the minimum voting age was reduced from 25 to 21 years. Women were enfranchised and became eligible for election to the House of Assembly in 1944. An additional vote formerly allotted to property owners was abolished in 1967.

The new Constitution was implemented by Order-in-Council under a British Act of Parliament in 1967, and the first General Election to be held under it took place in May 1968. It provides for a Governor appointed by the Crown which retains special responsibility for external affairs, defence, internal security and the police; a bicameral legislature; and an Executive Council appointed on the advice of the government leader. The size of the Legislative Council remains at 11, of whom 4 are appointed on the advice of the government leader, 2 on the advice of the opposition leader, and 5 by the Governor at his discretion. Its only power is one of delay. It cannot veto legislation, nor initiate or amend Money Bills. The House of Assembly consists of 40 members elected by two-member constituencies on the basis of universal adult franchise. The Executive Council consists of the government leader and not less than 6 other members of the legislature appointed on his advice, including one or two members of the Legislative Council. The Governor acts on its advice except on the matters reserved to the Crown. The government department boards lost their executive functions but now assist the members of the Executive Council in a consultative and administrative capacity.

The Constitution also provides for a Boundaries Commission consisting of 2 members appointed at the Governor's discretion, 2 on the advice of the government leader and 1 on the advice of the opposition leader. The members appointed directly by the Governor include the Chairman, who is required to be an eminent person from outside Bermuda with a knowledge of Bermudan affairs, and the other must be a person who holds or has held high judicial office in any part of the

Commonwealth. In drawing electoral boundaries no account may be taken of the racial distribution of the population.

BICAMERAL LEGISLATURE

A legislature consisting of two chambers, an upper and a lower. Both chambers can usually initiate legislation, but the more important and controversial measures are generally introduced in the lower chamber.

The advantages and disadvantages of the bicameral system have long been a subject of controversy, and it may therefore be useful to list the principal standard arguments for and against.

In Favour

A second chamber can relieve the pressure of work on the lower House which in these days of intense governmental activity easily tends to become overburdened.

It can act as a House of review and thus provide a brake on hasty or ill-considered legislation.

It can secure for the country the services of men and women who may be unable or unwilling to engage in the political campaign necessitated by a normal election.

It can check any tendency on the part of the lower House to abuse its power.

It can represent interests not otherwise represented in the lower House.

In a federal state it can safeguard the interests of the component states of the Federation.

Against

A second chamber, which usually tends to be conservative, is in a position to impede reform and obstruct progressive measures.

It makes for delay in the passage of legislation which could have serious consequences in a case where the national interest required that a measure should be passed into law as quickly as possible.

It is an additional burden on the public revenue which cannot be justified in view of the lack of public interest normally shown in the proceedings of a second chamber.

Given effective powers it can be obstructive; without effective powers it can only be held in contempt.

A seat in the upper House so often becomes a consolation prize for a political failure.

Any chamber other than one which is directly elected runs contrary to accepted democratic principles. So long as a single chamber is directly responsible to the electorate it has no opportunity to become despotic.

In Great Britain, Australia, and India, the upper House performs the further function of keeping a check on delegated legislation by appointing a scrutiny committee. John Stuart Mill had another reason for preferring bicameral legislatures. He wrote: 'A majority in a single assembly . . . easily becomes despotic and overweening, if released from the necessity of considering whether its acts will be concurred in by another constituted authority. The same reason which induced the Romans to have two consuls makes it desirable there should be two chambers: that neither of them may be exposed to the corrupting influence of undivided power, even for the space of a single year.' An upper chamber or Senate also provides for the representation of individual states in the case of a federal union, such as Australia, where each State sends 10 Senators to the Federal Parliament. In this case the representation is on a state and not a population basis. In the Indian Parliament the second chamber is actually called the Council of States.

Most of the older Commonwealth Parliaments have a second chamber although New Zealand has for the time being abandoned hers. In Australia, all the state legislatures with the exception of that of Queensland are bicameral. In Canada the Province of Quebec abolished its Legislative Council in 1967 so that all the provincial legislatures are now unicameral. The composition of the Quebec Legislative Council was comparable to that of the Canadian Senate, both chambers being survivals of the old colonial upper Chamber whose prototype was the House of Lords. The members of the Canadian Senate are appointed for life, although in 1965 a compulsory retirement age of 75 was introduced by way of a constitutional amendment. In India ten of the state legislatures are bicameral in addition to the central Parliament. Other bicameral Parliaments in the Commonwealth include those of Ceylon, Malaysia, Nigeria (prior to the military *coup* of 1966), Jamaica, Trinidad and Tobago, Bermuda, Bahamas, Barbados, Lesotho, Antigua, Grenada, British Honduras, Northern Ireland and the Isle of Man. The English Parliament assumed almost from the first a bicameral form, and except for eight years during the revolutionary period in the middle of the 17th century, has retained it ever since.

The Abbé Siéyès said: 'If a second chamber dissents from the first it is mischievous; if it agrees with it, it is superfluous.' In spite of this, however, the adoption of a second chamber has been considered advantageous by most of the world's legislatures, not because of any theoretical arguments that can be adduced in its favour but because its value has been recognized by long experience of the methods of parliamentary government.

Throughout the Commonwealth the principle of the predominance of the lower House in matters of finance is generally accepted (*see* PRIVILEGE, FINANCIAL).

[42]

(Further reading: Marriott, *Second chambers*, 1927; Roberts, *Functions of an English second chamber*, 1926.)

BIG BEN

The bell (13½ tons) which strikes the hours in the Clock Tower (q.v.) of the British Houses of Parliament, so called after Sir Benjamin Hall, First Commissioner of Works at the time it was hung. The name is now popularly applied to the clock itself, which was made by Messrs. Dent from the designs of Lord Grimthorpe, and began its long service on 31 May 1859. The four dials are 23 feet in diameter, the figures are 2 feet long, the minute hands are 14 feet long, and the hour hands 9 feet long. No other public clock has ever kept such accurate time as Big Ben. Twice a day since 1859 it has automatically telegraphed its performance to the Royal Observatory at Greenwich for checking, and for weeks it has remained correct to within one-tenth of a second. Apart from a few stoppages it has never deviated more than four seconds from Greenwich time. Big Ben was first broadcast at midnight on 31 December 1923, and now its voice is known and welcomed in the remotest parts of the world. Since 1885 a light has burnt at the top of the Clock Tower when the House of Commons is sitting, but, with all the other lights of London, this was extinguished during the last war. When Speaker Clifton Brown, afterwards Viscount Ruffside, pressed the switch on 24 April 1945 in the Commons Chamber to relight the lantern, he said: 'I pray that, with God's blessing, this light will shine henceforth not only as an outward and visible sign that the Parliament of a free people is assembled in free debate, but also that it may shine as a beacon of sure hope in a sadly torn and distracted world.' (*See* AYRTON LIGHT.)

(Further reading: Gillgrass, *Book of Big Ben*, 1946; Phillips, *Story of Big Ben*, 1959, H.M.S.O.)

BILL

See BILL, PASSAGE OF; BILL, RECOMMITTAL OF; MONEY BILLS; PRIVATE BILLS; PRIVATE MEMBERS' BILLS; PUBLIC BILLS.

BILL OF ATTAINDER

See ACT OF ATTAINDER.

BILL OF INDEMNITY

See ACT OF INDEMNITY.

BILL OF RIGHTS

A great and historic statute which was enacted in December 1689, its long title being, 'An Act declaring the Rights and Liberties of the

Subject and settling the Succession of the Crown'. Although an outstanding landmark in British constitutional history, the Bill of Rights introduced no new principle of law. It merely confirmed the existing rights of Parliament and the subject, which had been violated by James II, and was based upon the famous Declaration of Right which had been accepted, together with the Crown, by the Prince and Princess of Orange. The Bill of Rights thus embodies the conditions on which William and Mary succeeded to the Throne of England. It commences with a recital of the unconstitutional acts of James II, declares his actions to have been illegal, refers to his abdication and the subsequent summoning of the Convention Parliament (q.v.), and continues with the following declarations on the part of the Lords Spiritual and Temporal and Commons 'for the vindicating and asserting their ancient rights and liberties':

That the pretended power of suspending of laws or the execution of laws by regal authority without consent of Parliament is illegal;

That the pretended power of dispensing with laws or the execution of laws by regal authority, as it hath been assumed and exercised of late, is illegal;

That the commission for erecting the late Court of Commissioners for Ecclesiastical Causes, and all other commissions and courts of like nature, are illegal and pernicious;

That levying money for or to the use of the Crown by pretence of prerogative, without grant of Parliament, for longer time, or in other manner than the same is or shall be granted, is illegal;

That it is the right of the subjects to petition the king, and all commitments and prosecutions for such petitioning are illegal;

That the raising or keeping a standing army within the kingdom in time of peace, unless it be with consent of Parliament, is against law;

That the subjects which are Protestants may have arms for their defence suitable to their conditions and as allowed by law;

That election of members of Parliament ought to be free;

That the freedom of speech and debates or proceedings in Parliament ought not to be impeached or questioned in any court or place out of Parliament;

That excessive bail ought not to be required, nor excessive fines imposed, nor cruel and unusual punishments inflicted;

That jurors ought to be duly impanelled and returned, and jurors which pass upon men in trials for high treason ought to be freeholders;

That all grants and promises of fines and forfeitures of particular persons before conviction are illegal and void;

And that for redress of all grievances, and for the amending, strengthening and preserving of the laws, Parliaments ought to be held frequently.

The Bill of Rights goes on to confirm the succession of William and Mary to the throne and to provide for the succession on their decease.

In recent years there has been a tendency to incorporate within the Constitutions of the newly independent countries of the Commonwealth a Bill or Declaration of Rights reasserting certain fundamental human rights and freedoms. Their usual purpose is to provide constitutional guarantees to racial or religious groups which feel the need for some kind of insurance for their future security. India set the pattern in 1950 when a precise statement of fundamental rights was incorporated into her republican Constitution. In 1957 similar guarantees were built into the Constitution of the Federation of Malaya. In 1959 a list of fundamental rights was included in the Constitution of Nigeria in a form which has to some extent been used as a model for other countries. Since that time Bills or Declarations of Rights have been incorporated in the Constitutions of Sierra Leone, Uganda, Kenya, Malawi, Zambia, Rhodesia, the Gambia, Jamaica, Trinidad and Tobago, Malta, Guyana, Barbados, Botswana and Aden, although subsequent developments have altered the constitutional structure in some of these countries.

The Constitutions of the older Commonwealth countries contain no comparable provisions, but in 1960 the Parliament of Canada passed an Act for the Recognition and Protection of Human Rights and Fundamental Freedoms, the first part of which has come to be known as the Canadian Bill of Rights.

BILL, PASSAGE OF

A Bill is a statute in draft, and no Bill, public or private, whether it be introduced by the Government or a private member, can become law until it has received the approval of Parliament. Parliament must therefore have opportunities to consider all Bills both in general principle and detail, and every Bill must pass through a number of stages in both Houses. A Bill may be introduced in either the House of Commons or the House of Lords but the great majority are introduced in the lower House. Generally speaking, no Bill involving finance may be introduced in the House of Lords (but *see also* MONEY BILLS, final paragraph), and in practice only routine and non-controversial legislation is initiated in the upper House. The main function of the Lords in introducing legislation these days is to relieve the pressure of business on the generally overburdened Commons. Bills concerning the privileges of either House commence in the House to which they relate. Restitution Bills (q.v.) are always introduced in the House of Lords.

There are three ways in which a Public Bill may be introduced into the House of Commons: (1) upon an order of the House; (2) upon presentation by a minister or private member after notice has been given without previously obtaining leave from the House; and (3) upon being brought down from the House of Lords. (For procedure relating to Private Bills see under that heading.)

[45]

Under modern procedure the first method of introduction is mainly confined to financial Bills which, under the requirements of Standing Orders, are founded upon preliminary resolutions of the House and to Bills introduced under the ten minutes' rule (q.v.). At one time it was necessary to obtain the leave of the House before any Bill could be given a first reading, the motion for leave to introduce a Bill being a debatable stage.

The majority of Bills, whether presented by ministers or private members, are introduced by the second method, which was established in 1902 by the passing of a Standing Order permitting any member to present a Bill without an order of the House.

A Bill brought down from the House of Lords is not necessarily proceeded with unless a member signifies his intention of taking charge of it.

The first stage in the passage of a Bill after its introduction is the

First Reading. This is a purely formal stage and permits of no debate. The short title of the Bill is read by the Clerk of the House, the Bill is ordered to be printed, and a day is appointed by the member in charge of the Bill for the

Second Reading. This is the most important stage through which a Bill has to pass, as its entire principle is at issue. Matters of detail are not discussed at this stage, but the general application and desirability of the measure come under debate. The method of opposing the second reading of a Bill is to move an amendment to the question moved by the member in charge of the Bill: 'That the Bill be now read a second time', to make it read: 'That the Bill be read upon this day six (or three) months.' This is regarded as a courteous method of dismissing the Bill from further consideration, and a motion for the outright rejection of a Bill is not consistent with established practice. Members were not so polite in former times, when a motion that a Bill be 'rejected and torn' was not uncommon, and if carried entailed the literal tearing of the Bill. It is even recorded in the Journal of the House of Commons that a rejected Bill was kicked by members as they went out.

A member wishing to record a special reason for opposing the second reading of a Bill is permitted to move a reasoned amendment (q.v.).

The second reading debate normally takes place on the Floor of the House but, in October 1965, following a recommendation from the Select Committee on Procedure, provision was made for the reference of certain Government Bills to a Second Reading Committee (q.v.) for consideration in principle. Such a committee is not empowered to order that a Bill be read a second time but merely to recommend to the House whether or not a Bill should be given a second reading.

At the conclusion of the debate on the second reading a vote is taken on which there may or may not be a division (q.v.). If a Bill passes its second reading it moves on to the

Committee Stage. This is the stage at which a Bill is considered in close detail and is gone through clause by clause, line by line and, if necessary, word by word. For the committee stage a Bill is either referred to a Standing Committee (q.v.) or to a Committee of the Whole House. Before 1907 a Bill was always committed to a Committee of the Whole House unless a motion was carried committing it to a Standing or Select Committee, but since that year Bills after second reading have been automatically referred to one of the Standing Committees which are constituted every session. Exceptions to this practice are made in the case of Bills involving finance which are usually referred to a Committee of the Whole House, Bills for confirming provisional orders (q.v.) which are referred to the Committee of Selection (q.v.), and any Bill which on the affirmed motion of a member is referred to a Committee of the Whole House or a Select Committee. Bills committed to Standing Committees are distributed among the committees by the Speaker. Those relating exclusively to Scotland are considered by the Scottish Standing Committee.

The function of a Committee of the Whole House or a Standing Committee is to go through the text of a Bill in detail, and during the course of the debate amendments may be moved and voted upon. The selection of amendments for consideration is at the discretion of the Chairman.

The committee is bound by the decision of the House approving the Bill in principle at the second reading, and any amendment which does not accept the principle is out of order and cannot be considered. Amendments moved during the committee stage of a Bill are very often agreed to by the Government or the member in charge of the Bill if they tend to make the measure more acceptable. A Bill cannot be rejected during the committee stage as this power is reserved to the House. A committee can, however, negative a clause which is essential to the Bill and report the Bill to the House as amended, thus possibly achieving the same effect as rejection. In committee the rules of debate are relaxed and a member may speak more than once to the same question. The proceedings on a controversial clause of a Bill can thus be very long drawn out.

Report Stage. If a Bill has not been amended in committee this stage is purely formal and the third reading is proceeded with. In the case of an amended Bill the Bill as amended is considered by the House before the third reading takes place, and this stage amounts to a formal repetition of the committee stage with the Speaker in the Chair and the normal rules of debate applying. When a Bill is reported from a Committee of the Whole House the Chairman leaves the Chair, having put the question: 'That I do report the Bill without amendment (or as amended) to the House', and the Speaker resumes the Chair. The Chairman then reports to the Speaker in the following manner: 'I beg to report that the committee have gone through the Bill and directed me to report the same without amendment', or alternatively: '. . . and made amendments thereunto'. If a Committee of the Whole House is unable to complete its consideration of a Bill at one sitting the Chairman, on the motion of a member, puts the question: 'That I do report progress and ask leave to sit again.'

When a Bill is reported from a Standing Committee the formal proceedings described above are dispensed with. Since 1967 the report stage of a Bill which has been referred to a Second Reading Committee may be taken in a Standing Committee unless 20 or more members object.

A Bill may be recommitted to a Committee of the Whole House, a Standing Committee, or a Select Committee, and a motion for this purpose may be moved at the beginning or the end of the report stage or during the third reading.

Third Reading. Since December 1967 debate at this stage has been prohibited unless notice is given by not fewer than 6 members that a debate is required. When a debate does take place at this stage, the procedure is similar to that at second reading except that it is usually far more limited. A Bill is accepted or rejected at this stage by means of a vote which may or may not include a division, and if passed it has successfully secured its passage through the House of Commons. At one time there was a subsequent stage through which a Bill had to pass. Following the third reading it was customary for the motion, 'That the Bill do pass' to be formally proposed and carried, but this practice fell into disuse during the latter half of the 19th century.

The next step in the passage of a Bill is to refer it to the House of Lords. It then goes through the same stages in the upper House as those through which it has successfully passed in the lower House, the proceedings being mainly similar. After second reading the Bill is referred to a Committee of the Whole House, and amendments of substance may be moved during the third reading, whereas in the Commons verbal amendments only are permitted to be moved at this stage. If the Lords agree to the Bill without amendment it is not returned to the Commons unless it is a Bill involving finance. Instead, the Lords send a message to the Commons 'to acquaint them that the Lords have agreed to the said Bill without amendment'.

If the Lords have made amendments they return the Bill with the message: 'That the Lords have agreed to the same with amendments, to which their Lordships desire their concurrence.' The Lords are not empowered to amend Bills involving finance, over which the Commons exercise exclusive control. If the Lords amend a Bill there is yet a further stage through which it has to pass:

Consideration of Lords' Amendments. During this stage only the amendments and no other provisions of the Bill may be discussed.

The Clerk reads the amendments one by one, and a motion: 'That this House doth agree (or disagree) with the Lords in the said amendment' is considered in respect of each. The debate on the motion must be confined to the amendment under consideration. If the Lords' amendments are agreed to, the Commons send a message acquainting the Lords accordingly and the Bill is returned to await the Royal Assent (q.v.). If the Commons disagree with any of the Lords' amendments a Committee is appointed to draw up reasons for disagreement. The Committee retires to its deliberations immediately and reports at the same sitting. A message is then sent to the Lords communicating the reasons for disagreement, together with the Bill and any amendments which the Commons have made to the Lords' amendments. If, after consideration, the Lords insist on all or any of the amendments with which the Commons have disagreed, further proceedings are necessitated in the Commons to consider the Lords' reason for their insistence. This interchange of amendments can be carried still further, but in practice few Bills go beyond this stage. Every effort is made to reach agreement by compromise, and one House or other usually concedes its objections.

If the Commons amend a Bill which originated in the Lords the procedure described above is reversed.

Once a Bill has successfully passed through all its stages in both Houses it requires only the Royal Assent to make it an Act of Parliament (q.v.).

In the other Parliaments of the Commonwealth the procedure relating to the passage of Bills, like most other procedure, follows closely that of Westminster. Bills are taken through the same stages, although in the case of a unicameral legislature there is no upper House to which to refer any measure. In all bicameral Parliaments the principle seems to be firmly established that the upper House has no power to interfere with legislation involving finance. In Canada the first reading of a Bill is still preceded by a motion seeking leave to introduce it, but this stage is not debatable except in so far as it permits the minister or member in charge of the Bill to make a brief statement in explanation of its provisions. Nevertheless, a division can be expected on the motion if the Bill is a controversial one.

In December 1968 the Canadian House of Commons adopted the Westminster system in referring most Bills to Standing Committees for consideration in detail. In the Indian House of the People the Committee of the Whole House is not employed and Bills are referred to *ad hoc* Select Committees. In 1963 the Australian House of Representatives agreed that the committee stage of a Bill could be dispensed with altogether and the third reading taken immediately after the second reading in any case where no member objected.

See also PARLIAMENT ACTS, 1911 and 1949.

[49]

BILL, RECOMMITTAL OF

After a Bill has passed through its committee stage it may, if desired, be recommitted, either in whole or in part, to a Committee of the Whole House, a Standing Committee or a Select Committee (qq.v.). A motion for recommittal may be made at the beginning or end of the report stage or on the third reading. A Bill which has been considered by a Select Committee or a Joint Committee is afterwards recommitted to a Committee of the Whole House.

BISHOPS

See LORDS SPIRITUAL.

BLACK PARLIAMENT

A Scottish Parliament which met at Scone in 1320, so called because of the savage punishments it imposed on those concerned in the conspiracy of Sir William de Soulis. The Reformation Parliament (q.v.) of England was also called the Black Parliament by those who deplored its activities.

BLACK ROD

See GENTLEMAN USHER OF THE BLACK ROD; YEOMAN USHER OF THE BLACK ROD.

BLOCKADE, MINISTER OF

Created in 1916, he performed similar functions to those of the Minister of Economic Warfare in the Second World War. Lord Robert Cecil, who combined the office with that of Under-Secretary of State for Foreign Affairs, held it until it was abolished at the end of the First World War.

BLOCKING

The legitimate obstruction of a Bill or motion by invoking the Standing Orders relating to Opposed Business. Therein it is provided that after a certain hour each day a member is entitled to object to further proceedings on an opposed item of business. Another method of blocking a Bill or motion is to cause protracted debate to take place on the preceding Order of the Day.

BLOCKING MOTION

At one time it was out of order to anticipate any matter which stood upon the order paper, and a member could prevent a matter being debated merely by keeping on the order paper a motion which he never brought up. This use of 'blocking' motions is now largely prevented by the Standing Order relating to anticipation (q.v.).

BLUE BOOK

A popular name for an official report, statistical or other government publication which because of its bulk is provided with a blue cover of stouter quality than the inside pages. The term is said to have had its origin in the publication of Archbishop Laud's Diary, which he described as 'a thin book in folio in a blue coat'.

See also WHITE PAPER.

BOARD OF TRADE, PRESIDENT OF THE

See PRESIDENT OF THE BOARD OF TRADE.

BOROUGH FRANCHISE

See REPRESENTATION.

BOTSWANA PARLIAMENT

The Republic of Botswana, formerly the Bechuanaland Protectorate, became independent on 30 September 1966. The country's first legislature was established under the Constitution of 1961, which provided for a Legislative Council of 35 members, 21 of whom were elected. Under this Constitution the Executive Council consisted of 5 officials and 4 elected members (2 Africans and 2 Europeans). In 1965 the cabinet system was introduced and the Legislative Council was replaced by a Legislative Assembly. The Assembly consisted of 31 members elected by universal suffrage, 4 elected by the Assembly itself, and 2 *ex-officio* members, the Attorney-General and the Financial Secretary. The Cabinet comprised a Prime Minister, Deputy Prime Minister and not more than 5 other ministers, the Financial Secretary being *ex-officio* the Minister of Finance. Provision was also made for a House of Chiefs consisting of 12 members and having advisory powers.

Under the Constitution providing for independence the Bechuanaland Protectorate became the Republic of Botswana, the President being the chief executive as well as the Head of State. The Legislative Assembly became the National Assembly and one of its functions is the election of the President. The President must himself be a member of the National Assembly, although a non-member may be elected President provided he becomes a member within six months. The election of the President is held concurrently with the election of members to the National Assembly, and a dissolution of Parliament thus involves a presidential as well as a parliamentary election. A candidate for President must be nominated by not less than 1,000 registered voters and must receive the votes of a majority of the members of the National Assembly in order to be elected.

The composition of the National Assembly has not been greatly changed, and consists of 31 members elected by universal adult suffrage, 4 elected by the 31 elected members, and the Attorney-General, who, as a civil servant, is entitled to speak but not to vote. The House of Chiefs is retained in an enlarged form, and now consists of 8 tribal chiefs, 4 members elected by sub-chiefs in certain districts, and 3 additional members specially selected by the other 12. Bills passed by the National Assembly require the assent of the President, but the House of Chiefs has the right to consider Bills which affect tribal interests or which seek to alter the Constitution, and to make representations on such Bills.

The President presides over the Cabinet which also includes the Vice-President and 6 other ministers appointed by the President. The Cabinet is directly responsible to the National Assembly, and in the event of a vote of no confidence being passed in the National Assembly a dissolution of Parliament is automatic on the fourth day following the resolution if the President fails to resign or dissolve Parliament himself. The Vice-President is competent to exercise the powers of the President during the latter's absence or incapacity or following his death or resignation, except that he is not empowered to dissolve Parliament.

The Constitution, following similar recent precedents, incorporates a Bill of Rights designed to protect fundamental freedoms. While the Constitution may be amended by Parliament, its provisions are divided into three categories, 'ordinary', 'entrenched' and 'specially entrenched'. An amendment to an ordinary provision may be passed in the normal manner, subject to the publication of the amending Bill at least thirty days before its introduction in the National Assembly. A Bill to amend an entrenched provision must be passed twice by the Assembly, the second time, following a three-month interval, requiring a two-thirds majority of the members on its presentation. The requirement of thirty days prior to publication before the first introduction of the Bill also applies. Entrenched provisions include those relating to the office of President, the manner of his election, his tenure of office, the protection of fundamental rights and freedoms, the composition and functions of the House of Chiefs, the public service, the duties of the Attorney-General, and the establishment of the Consolidated Fund. A Bill to amend a specially entrenched provision of the Constitution is subject to the same procedure as a Bill to amend an entrenched provision, with the additional requirement that it must be submitted to the judgment of the electorate at a referendum and be approved by a majority of the persons voting. Specially entrenched provisions include those relating to Parliament (its powers, duration, dissolution, etc.), the judicial system, the electoral system and the franchise (including the non-political delimitation of constituencies and the appointment and duties of the Supervisor of Elections), and the procedure for the amendment of the Constitution itself.

BOUNDARY COMMISSIONS

The report of an all-party Speaker's Conference on Electoral Reform and Redistribution of Seats appeared in 1944 (Cmd. 6534) and resulted in the House of Commons (Redistribution of Seats) Act (now superseded by the 1949 and 1958 Acts of the same title). These Acts set up four Permanent Boundary Commissions for England, Scotland, Wales, and Northern Ireland to keep under review the representation in the House of Commons of the part of the U.K. with which they are concerned, and to submit reports to the Home Secretary as to the redistribution of seats not less than ten or more than fifteen years from the date of their last reports. The most recent report was submitted in 1969 and at the time of writing was still awaiting implementation. The Second Schedule of the 1949 Act sets out the rules to be observed by the Boundary Commissions.

See also CONSTITUENCY.

BOWING TO THE SPEAKER

The practice of bowing to the Speaker when passing in front of the Chair and entering or leaving the Chamber is now accepted as a mark of respect, but it may have arisen from the Commons' long association with St. Stephen's Chapel (*see* ST. STEPHEN'S HALL) where it had been customary to bow to the altar. However, this seems improbable in view of the fact that the first Parliament which met after the Chapel's deconsecration was so strongly Protestant. Some writers suggest that the genuflexion originated even earlier, when Parliament met in the Chapter House of Westminster Abbey where there was a statue of the Virgin Mary. It has also been suggested that the custom dates from the days before the separation of the two Houses when the monarch himself presided over Parliament. After the Houses separated the Commons continued the practice of bowing to the Chair as its occupant, the Speaker, was in those days regarded as the king's man.

BRADLAUGH, CHARLES (1833–1891)

The central figure in a struggle with the House of Commons, lasting six years, over the right of a new member to affirm instead of taking an oath on the Bible. Bradlaugh was elected for Northampton in 1880, and as he had no religious belief claimed the right to make affirmation. Although the objection to allowing this was merely technical, there was a strong feeling against him because of his heterodox opinions, and he was excluded from the House and unseated four times. He was re-elected every time, and on the fifth occasion, in 1886, a new Speaker (Peel) would not allow any objection being made when he took the oath in the ordinary form. In 1888 Bradlaugh succeeded in having his Oaths Bill passed, which authorized anyone objecting to be sworn to make an affirmation instead of taking an oath in all cases where an oath or affirmation was necessary. In 1933 a centenary volume entitled *Champion of Liberty: Charles Bradlaugh* was published which contained appreciations by many eminent writers and extracts from his own speeches covering many aspects of his life and work.

BRAND, SIR HENRY BOUVERIE WILLIAM, 1st Viscount Hampden and 23rd Baron Dacre (1814–1892)

Speaker of the House of Commons from 1872 to 1884, Brand's tenure of office is notable for a drastic innovation of procedure and for the creditable manner in which the Speaker fulfilled his arduous duties in the face of conditions of unprecedented difficulty and strain.

Brand was three times unanimously elected to the Chair. Prior to his first election, some doubts were expressed as to his fitness for the office of Speaker on the ground that he had been for many years the senior Liberal Whip. These doubts were soon dispelled by his demeanour in the Chair, and he retired as one of the most popular Speakers ever to preside over the House.

Brand's task was rendered difficult and harassing from the outset by the campaign of systematic obstruction evolved by Parnell and his supporters. After the General Election of 1880 had returned an increased number of Irish Nationalists, his position became even more unenviable. The obstructive tactics of the Irishmen reached a climax in January–February 1881, when the debate on the motion for leave to bring in the so-called Coercion Bill was protracted for over forty-one hours. The sitting began on 31 January and continued until 9 a.m. on 2 February, when the Speaker took his memorable decision to terminate the debate upon his own responsibility. 'The dignity, the credit and the authority of this House are seriously threatened,' declared Speaker Brand, 'and it is necessary that they should be vindicated.' This was the first time any check had been imposed upon the length of a debate. Brand's action was unprecedented but justified by sheer necessity. He was supported by the Prime Minister and the Leader of the Opposition, and the following day the powers of the Speaker were formally augmented by resolution. Thus the closure (q.v.) was first introduced into the rules of procedure, and the Speaker's powers of dealing with obstruction have subsequently been further strengthened.

BREACH OF PRIVILEGE

See PRIVILEGE, BREACH OF.

BRIBERY PARLIAMENT

The Parliament which was elected in 1841, so called because of the number of Bills for the disfranchisement of corrupt boroughs which were introduced and passed in the House of Commons but invariably rejected by the House of Lords.

BRITISH COLUMBIA LEGISLATIVE ASSEMBLY

The Colonies of Vancouver Island and British Columbia, whose legislatures dated from 1849 and 1858 respectively, were united in 1866 to form the Province of British Columbia. The new Province entered the Canadian Confederation in 1871, and has a local constitution similar to that of the other Provinces. It has a single-chamber legislature, the Legislative Assembly, which has 55 members elected for five years, the normal life of the legislature. Seven constituencies return 2 members, and all others return 1 member each. The franchise was extended to native Indians and Canadian-Chinese in 1947. The voting age is nineteen. Procedure in the Legislative Assembly differs in some details from the Westminster practice—for instance, there are no oral questions, adjournment motions are not debatable, preambles are allowed to motions, and only rarely are Bills, other than Private Bills, referred to a committee. When it is necessary for an amendment to be made to a Bill after the third reading, it is assumed that the Crown still retains its right of veto, and the Lieutenant-Governor sends a message recommending the amendment. The order for third reading is then discharged and the Bill recommitted. One feature of procedure, which is common to Canadian provincial legislatures, is that an appeal to the House is allowed from a ruling of the Speaker on questions of order. The Constitution Act 1960 limits the number of executive councillors to 17 of whom no more than 14 may receive a salary, the various ministerial offices being listed. The Premier is President of the Council, and the Lieutenant-Governor (who is appointed by the Federal Government) acts on the advice of the Premier in the appointment of ministers. The membership of the Legislative Assembly was increased from 52 in 1966 and from 48 in 1958. British Columbia sends 23 members to the Canadian House of Commons and 6 members to the Senate.

When the Legislative Assembly met early in 1950 in the imposing grey stone Parliament Buildings in Victoria, a hundred years of responsible government was marked by two events—the election of Mrs. Nancy Hodges as Speaker, the first woman in the history of the British Commonwealth to preside over a parliamentary assembly, and the swearing-in of the first full-blooded Indian to be elected to the legislature.

BRITISH CONSTITUTION

The Constitution, or fundamental principles by which the British nation is constituted and governed, is said to be 'unwritten' because it is not embodied in any enactment or formally related series of enactments. It includes some important milestones, from Magna Carta (q.v.) to the Statute of Westminster (q.v.), during the course of its historic evolution, but some of its most important features are no part of its formal and legal structure and have little sanction beyond tradition and precedent. British constitutional law forms a part of the general body of English law and is derived from the same sources, primarily statutes and judicial precedents and secondarily custom and books of authority. Its most important characteristic is the legislative supremacy of Parliament, which can legally pass any kind of law and cannot be overridden by the legislative power of any other body or person. As Dicey pointed out, the omnipotence or undisputed supremacy throughout the whole country of the central government and 'the Rule or Supremacy of Law' are the two main features from which all British constitutional development has proceeded. Although the British political system is monarchical it is a limited or 'constitutional' monarchy, and the governmental powers which are vested in the Sovereign are in practice exercised according to the laws, customs, and conventions of the Constitution, and they are exercised either by the Crown on the advice of its ministers or by the ministers in its name. The financial needs of the Crown long furnished the main lever by which Parliament increased its power, and from that interaction between the Crown and the people grew the system of government in and with Parliament, subject to the ever-increasing influence of public opinion and to periodic review by the nation as a whole. The Monarchy itself, divorced from arbitrary personal power, has become increasingly the symbol of the continuity of the British Constitution and the unity of the peoples of the British Commonwealth.

See also CROWN AND PARLIAMENT; PARLIAMENT; PRIVY COUNCIL; ROYAL PREROGATIVE; SOVEREIGN.

BRITISH GUIANA

See GUYANA PARLIAMENT.

BRITISH HONDURAS NATIONAL ASSEMBLY

The elected Legislative Assembly, which was opened in 1854, abolished itself in 1870 in favour of a nominated Legislative Council. It first met in 1871 and until 1892 had a majority of official members. The elective principle was re-introduced by the new Constitution of 1935, and the first General Election under this was held in 1936. The new Council still had 13 members, but of the 7 unofficials 5 were elected. In 1945 the membership was increased, and the unofficial element was given a majority of 6 in a Chamber of 14. At the same time a broadened franchise was adopted—previously women under thirty were not entitled to vote. A Commission of Inquiry was appointed in 1948 on the question of a more advanced Constitution and made its report in 1951. The following year the Council approved the proposals for reform, which were embodied in an ordinance passed in 1954, and the new Legislative Assembly met on 18 June of that year. It consisted of a Speaker appointed by the Governor, 3 official, 3 nominated, and 9 elected members. Universal adult suffrage was introduced in 1954. The Executive Council, the chief instrument of policy, had the Governor as Chairman and the 3 official and 6 other members of the Legislative Assembly (including 2 nominated members) elected by their fellow-members. From 1 January 1955 a modified form of semi-ministerial government was introduced.

Agreement on a new Constitution for British Honduras providing for a ministerial system and internal self-government was reached at a conference held in London in July 1963. The new Constitution came into force on 1 January 1964 but the inauguration of the new bicameral legislature, the National Assembly, was delayed until after the Election which took place on 28 February 1965.

The House of Representatives has 18 members elected by universal suffrage and the Senate has 8, 5 appointed on the advice of the Premier, 2 on the advice of the Leader of the Opposition and 1 appointed by the Governor after consultation with such persons as he thinks appropriate.

The Governor retains reserve powers in matters affecting defence, external affairs, internal security, the public service and finance, so long as British Honduras is in receipt of budgetary aid from the British Government. The Constitution provides for two consultative bodies concerned with security and external affairs, their functions being to advise the Governor and to familiarize ministers with matters for which they will ultimately be responsible.

BRITISH SOLOMON ISLANDS LEGISLATIVE COUNCIL

The Solomon Islands came under British protection at various dates between 1893 and 1899 and, until 1960, were administered by the High Commissioner for the Western Pacific, with the help of an Advisory Council.

On 18 October 1960, a new Constitution came into effect which provided for a Legislative Council and an Executive Council. The Legislative Council consisted of 11 official and 10 unofficial members, all nominated, but an Order in Council dated 25 September 1964 provided for the introduction of an elected element into the Council. It was provided that 8 of the 10 unofficial members would be elected to represent single-member constituencies, 7 being elected through electoral colleges and only one being directly elected. However, a new

Constitution which came into effect on 1 April 1967 provided for a Legislative Council consisting of 14 elected members, all directly elected, 3 *ex-officio* members (the Chief Secretary, the Attorney-General and the Financial Secretary) and up to 12 Public Service members, under the presidency of the High Commissioner. The Executive Council consists of the High Commissioner, the 3 *ex-officio* members of the Legislative Council and 5 other members of whom at least 4 must be elected members.

BRITISH VIRGIN ISLANDS LEGISLATIVE COUNCIL

In 1902 the Legislative Council was abolished, and the islands were governed by an Executive Council and the General Legislative Council of the Leeward Islands, to which federation they belonged. The Legislative Council was restored in 1950, and in 1954 it acquired an elected majority, which in 1966 consisted of the Administrator as President, 2 nominated official, 2 nominated unofficial, and 6 elected members.

The report of Dr. Mary Proudfoot, who was appointed Constitutional Commissioner for the islands, was published in August 1965 as Colonial Office pamphlet No. 361, and the constitutional changes agreed in October 1966 were based on her recommendations.

Under the new Constitution the Legislative Council consists of a Speaker, chosen from outside the Council, two *ex-officio* members (the Attorney-General and the Financial Secretary), one member nominated by the Administrator, and 7 members elected by single-member constituencies. The Constitution also provides for the introduction of the ministerial system, the Executive Council consisting of the 2 *ex-officio* members and 3 of the elected members, one of whom being appointed Chief Minister. The Administrator normally presides over the Executive Council and exercises control over finance, external affairs, defence, internal security, the public service and the judicial system, other powers being vested in the ministerial group. The Administrator's responsibility for finance was made subject to review within four years.

BROADCASTING IN PARLIAMENT

The broadcasting of Parliament over sound radio was first introduced in the British Commonwealth by New Zealand in 1936. At first it was done on a limited scale, but now practically the whole of the proceedings are broadcast, although whether transmission continues beyond 10.30 p.m. depends on the importance of the subject under discussion. The decision to broadcast parliamentary proceedings in New Zealand was a purely administrative one, and during the first years of the broadcasts they were entirely under ministerial control.

In 1962 the broadcasts and the day-to-day administration connected with them were taken over by the Broadcasting Corporation, and in the same year a Standing Order was introduced to provide for their regulation.

In 1946 Australia introduced the sound broadcasting of parliamentary debates in both Houses. The broadcasts are governed by statute and are under the control of a Joint Committee of both Houses consisting of 3 Senators, including the President of the Senate, and 6 members of the House of Representatives, including the Speaker. Matters such as the periods during which the broadcasts shall take place, the allocation of broadcasting time between the two Houses, re-broadcasting of debates and the extent to which comment should be permitted from the control booth are determined by the Committee in accordance with guide lines laid down by Parliament.

The Legislative Assembly of Saskatchewan was the first Canadian legislature to introduce the sound broadcasting of its proceedings. Coverage is mainly confined to the debate on the Address and the Budget debate, and the broadcasts take place on about 20 days of the session from 2.45 p.m. to 4.00 p.m. They are re-broadcast in the evenings.

No Commonwealth Parliament has yet permitted the televising of its proceedings on a regular basis, although the question of broadcasting parliamentary proceedings by sound and television has been under consideration by both houses of the British Parliament for some years. Mr. Amery, in his *Thoughts on the Constitution*, said that broadcasting would raise the standard of debate and increase public interest in the proceedings of Parliament, but there are several arguments against its adoption in England which call for consideration. For instance, there is the possible 'jockeying' for speech time; members would naturally seek the best listening-in period—usually early in the evening. Also members might tend to talk more about—and to—their constituencies, and while topics discussed in the New Zealand Parliament are more domestic and appeal to a wider audience, there are considerably fewer debates of really general interest in the British Parliament.

Canada was the first Commonwealth country to televise parliamentary proceedings. Television was installed at Ottawa on 14 October 1957 to cover part of the ceremony of the Opening of Parliament by the Queen. Senate, but not House of Commons, proceedings have been televised on two previous occasions. In the United Kingdom the ceremony of the Opening of Parliament was broadcast for the first time on 28 October 1958 over both the sound and television services of the B.B.C. In 1966, another year when the ceremony was broadcast, the House of Commons Chamber was shown on television for the first time as the cameras followed Black Rod arriving to summon the members to the Bar of the House of Lords to hear the Speech from the Throne.

In 1963 the Hansard Society published a pamphlet by Mr. Robin Day entitled 'The Case for Televising Parliament'. However, Mr. Colin Seymour-Ure, in an article for *Parliamentary Affairs* (vol. XVII, no. 2, spring 1964) entitled 'An Examination of the Proposal to Televise Parliament' points out the difficulties and dangers of introducing cameras into the Palace of Westminster.

Since 1964 the question of broadcasting parliamentary proceedings has been considered in its various aspects by a number of Select Committees of the House of Commons and the House of Lords. At the time of writing (1970) neither House has come to any final conclusions on the subject. On 15 June 1966 the House of Lords approved by a vote of 56 to 31 a resolution calling for the televising of its proceedings on an experimental basis and in February 1968 a closed-circuit experiment took place. On 24 November 1966 the House of Commons declined to follow the example of the Lords when it rejected by 131 votes to 130 a proposal that its proceedings be televised for an experimental period. However, in April and May of 1968 experiments in sound broadcasting were conducted in the House of Commons and in two of its Standing Committees. In 1969 the Joint Committee on the Publication of Proceedings in Parliament considered the broadcasting of debates from the point of view of its implications with respect to parliamentary privilege and the law of defamation. (*See* First Report of the Committee, 3 December 1969, H.L.26 and H.C.48.)

BRUNEI LEGISLATIVE COUNCIL

Brunei's first written Constitution was promulgated on 29 September 1959, providing for a Privy Council, an Executive Council and a Legislative Council. The Executive Council, under the presidency of the Sultan, and the Legislative Council, which was to include 16 elected members as well as 8 *ex-officio* and 9 appointed by the Sultan, were together designed to replace the former State Council. Until the holding of the first Elections in September 1962 the Legislative Council was wholly nominated. The Elections were won by the People's Party which was implicated in a revolution which broke out in the following December. As a result of the revolution the People's Party was banned and the Legislative Council was dissolved, to be re-established in July 1963 with nominated members replacing the former elected members.

On 26 August 1964 the Legislative Council approved new constitutional proposals which included the restoration of the elected element of the Council. It now consists of a Speaker, 6 *ex-officio* members, 5 official members and 10 elected members. The Executive Council is replaced by a Council of Ministers which sits under the presidency of the Sultan and includes the High Commissioner, the 6 *ex-officio* members and 4 elected members appointed as Assistant Ministers. A Chief Minister is appointed by the Sultan to whom he is responsible for the exercise of executive authority. The British Government retains the responsibility for external affairs and defence in Brunei and it is the responsibility of the High Commissioner to advise the Sultan on these matters.

Brunei declined to join the Federation of Malaysia in 1963.

BUDGET

'Budge', an anglicized form of the French *Bouge*, is an obsolete word meaning a small bag, and budget was derived from this. In a pamphlet of 1733 entitled 'The Budget Opened' Sir Robert Walpole, the Prime Minister and Chancellor of the Exchequer, is satirically pictured while explaining his financial measures as a quack doctor opening a bag filled with medicines and charms, and the expression 'budget' appears to have come into use about this time. It was originally applied only to the exposition annually given by the Chancellor at the opening of the financial year of the state of the country's finances and the measures rendered necessary thereby. It has, however, become customary, though less in England than elsewhere, to use the word as denoting the whole annual plan of finance (*see also* CHANCELLOR OF THE EXCHEQUER).

The following paragraphs describe the historic Budget procedure which was observed until the new procedure was implemented in 1967 in accordance with the recommendations of the Select Committee on Procedure of 1965–6.

The Budget is presented soon after the beginning of the financial year by the Chancellor of the Exchequer in Committee of Ways and Means, and in his speech he gives an account of the previous year's finances and his proposals for taxation for the coming year. The Finance Bill is founded on the resolutions of the Committee of Ways and Means passed after the Chancellor's opening statement. These resolutions, which form its usual basis, are the resolutions for the continuance, during the financial year, of the income tax, and the imposition or alteration of any duties necessary for the purpose of adjusting the revenue to the estimated expenditure. The secrecy with which changes in taxation have to be guarded, until the conclusion of the Chancellor's statement, makes debate on his proposals unprofitable until there has been time for his speech to be studied. The debate therefore on the first day is sometimes only formal. A general debate follows, in which considerable latitude is allowed—a survival from the times when the Commons claimed to discuss 'grievances before Supply'—and the committee must be able to consider the resolutions proposed by the Chancellor as forming, together with existing taxation, a complete scheme of revenue to be debated as a whole. (*See also* WAYS AND MEANS.)

In the interests of the revenue it is necessary that changes in taxation or the renewal of expiring taxes should have the force of law on the same day as they are proposed by the Chancellor. For many years before 1913 the Treasury (q.v.) had taken the Ways and Means resolutions as sufficient authority for continuing existing taxation and making such changes as would be imposed and made by the Finance Act (q.v.) when it was passed. The legality of this procedure was challenged by Gibson Bowles in 1912, and the High Court held that the deduction of income tax on the authority of a Ways and Means resolution was invalid. The difficulty was solved by passing the Provisional Collection of Taxes Act in 1913, by which a resolution comes into and continues in force as soon as it has been voted by the Committee of Ways and Means, provided that: (1) it is agreed to by the House within ten sitting days; (2) the Bill confirming it is read a second time within twenty sitting days after it has been agreed to by the House; (3) this Bill receives the Royal Assent within four months after the resolution has been voted; and (4) the resolution does not impose a new tax.

Under the new procedure, the Committee of Ways and Means is abolished, a change which required legislative action because of the provision of the Provisional Collection of Taxes Act. The Budget speech is now delivered and the Ways and Means resolutions are taken in the House. As soon as the Chancellor has delivered his Budget speech a resolution of a provisional nature is passed in place of the previous series of questions which were put on all the Budget motions save the last. The Budget debate now takes place on the first of the Budget resolutions and it is thus possible at the conclusion of the debate to reach considered decisions on each of the resolutions separately. The Provisional Collection of Taxes Act has been amended to apply to resolutions of the House in place of resolutions of the Committee of Ways and Means; to require that the provisional resolution of the House must be confirmed by the passage of the Budget resolutions within ten sitting days; and to provide that such resolutions shall cease to have statutory effect unless the Bill confirming them receives its second reading in the House of Commons within twenty-five sitting days and the Royal Assent by 5 August.

The Budget which aroused most opposition was that of Lloyd George in 1909, when he introduced the Land Tax. He then made the longest Budget speech in modern times—4 hours 51 minutes, less an interval of 30 minutes to relieve his voice. During the course of the ensuing debate, the closure was moved 106 times and 549 divisions were taken, which represent 90 hours in the Division Lobbies. The Lords threw this Budget out by 350 votes to 75, although there had been no precedent for such an action for many years. In the General Election which followed the consequent forced dissolution of Parliament, the question at issue was whether the Lords had the right to reject a Budget which the Commons had passed. The Parliament Act of 1911 destroyed the power of the Lords to veto legislation, and henceforth they could only delay measures sent up by the Commons.

Mr. Gladstone still holds the record for the longest Budget speech as he spoke for five hours when he introduced his first Budget in 1853, and Mr. Ward Hunt made the shortest speech in 1868.

While delivering his Budget speech the Chancellor of the Exchequer, in accordance with a custom of the House which is a departure from the normal practice, is permitted to regale himself with the liquid refreshment of his choice. Disraeli is said to have favoured brandy and water while Goschen preferred port. Some Chancellors have called for most unusual concoctions, and Gladstone is on record as having consumed sherry and beaten egg while presenting his Budget. In our own century Sir Stafford Cripps was far more orthodox in choosing plain water. Mr. Derick Heathcoat Amory preferred a more sustaining concoction of milk, honey, and rum, but Mr. Callaghan has been satisfied with tonic water.

(Further reading: Brittain, *The British budgetary system*, 1959.)

BURKE'S PEERAGE

Founded in 1826 by John Burke, this substantial work of reference has appeared regularly, and for many years annually, since its inception. In 1953 the 100th edition was published, the second edition to be issued after the war. Since then it has been published at intervals of three or four years.

Burke's Peerage is a complete genealogical and heraldic history of the peerage, baronetage, and knightage, in alphabetical arrangement. It also contains a considerable amount of related information, including tables of precedence, and special sections on the Royal Family and Royal Lineage. The companion work to the *Peerage, Burke's Landed Gentry*, was first published in 1837.

BUSINESS COMMITTEE

A Select Committee of the House of Commons appointed by Standing Order consisting of the Chairmen's Panel (q.v.) and 5 other members, 7 being the quorum. Its function is to allocate the time to be devoted in Committee of the Whole House and at the report stage to the various parts of a Bill on which debate has been limited by the application of the guillotine (q.v.) or by the previous consent of the House. It is important to note that the committee is not empowered to propose an overall allocation of time (except in certain circumstances

c*   [63]

under Standing Order 43A, but merely to allot the days or portions of days to be devoted to the various clauses or groups of clauses of a Bill to which a total time has already been allocated. The committee reports its recommendations to the House, which may accept or reject but not debate them. The 5 additional members are appointed specifically in respect of each Bill referred to the committee.

When an allocation of time order is passed by the House in relation to the proceedings of a Standing Committee (q.v.), a Business Sub-Committee of the Standing Committee is appointed by the Speaker with similar functions to those of the Business Committee. The sub-committee consists of the Chairman and 7 members of the Standing Committee, and reports directly to the Standing Committee.

BUSINESS OF THE HOUSE

The relative order of all the items of business in the House of Commons is not rigidly fixed, but in the extremely unlikely event of every possible item occurring at a single sitting the following list shows the probable order in which they would be taken. The list is based on that which appears in Erskine May's *Parliamentary Practice*, 17th ed., pages 339-40.

1. Prayers.
2. Business taken immediately after Prayers:
   (i) Reports of Queen's Answers to Addresses.
   (ii) Formal communications by the Speaker.
   (iii) Motions for new writs.
   (iv) Unopposed Private Business.
   (v) Presentation of public petitions.
   (vi) Motions for unopposed returns.

3. Questions:
   (i) Questions for oral answer.
   (ii) Private notice questions.

4. Business taken after questions:
   (i) Ministerial statements and statements by the Speaker.
   (ii) Introduction of new members.
   (iii) Adjournment motions on the ground of urgency.
   (iv) Motions for leave of absence (now practically obsolete).
   (v) Ceremonial speeches.
   (vi) Oral Notices of Motions and holding of ballot for private members' motions.
   (vii) Personal explanations.
   (viii) Motions to appoint 'Money' Committees.
   (ix) Consideration of Lords' Amendments (if not material) to a Public Bill or messages.
   (x) Raising a matter of privilege.

5. Business taken 'at the commencement of public business':
   (i) Presentation of Public Bills.
   (ii) 'Business' motions moved by the Government.
   (iii) Motions for leave to bring in Bills or nominate Select Committees under the 'Ten Minutes Rule'.

6. Privilege motions of which notice has been given.

7. Public Business: Orders of the Day and Notices of Motion.

8. Business which has been granted special precedence at 7 p.m.:
   (i) Proceedings on adjournment motions introduced earlier in the day on ground of urgency (*see* 4(iii) above).
   (ii) Opposed Private Business.

   Interruption of Business at 10 p.m.

9. Business motions moved by the Government for the purpose of exempting certain business from automatic interruption.

10. Business regularly taken after 10 p.m. (*see* EXEMPTED BUSINESS).

11. Half-hour debate on daily adjournment motion.

BUSINESS VOTE

A franchise enjoyed by virtue of the occupation of business premises. It was abolished by the Representation of the People Act, 1948. Prior to this Act, an elector who qualified for the business vote was entitled to exercise it in addition to his normal residential vote.

BY-ELECTIONS

See ELECTIONS.

C

CABINET

'The Cabinet,' writes Sir W. Ivor Jennings, 'is the core of the British constitutional system. It is the supreme directing authority. It integrates what would otherwise be a heterogeneous collection of authorities exercising a vast variety of functions. It provides unity to the British system of government.' Yet in spite of its essential nature it is a body without a legal existence. The Cabinet evolved from the Privy Council (q.v.) and eventually took its place as the executive organ of government, but its growth was a largely informal process. The word itself originally meant a small room or closet and thus came to signify a body of persons meeting together to deliberate in secret. As far back as Tudor times much of the work of the Privy Council was delegated to committees, either standing or *ad hoc*, in order to relieve the pressure of administrative work. The practice was continued under the Stuarts, and one of these committees, normally styled the Foreign Affairs Committee although it concerned itself with all matters of consequence, domestic as well as foreign, came to assume very great importance. It consisted of the King's most trusted and intimate counsellors and frequently took decisions of major importance before the Privy Council had even been consulted upon the matters under discussion. The Parliaments of the 17th century took strong exception to such committees, which were variously described as junctos, cabals, or cabinets. But in spite of its unpopularity the system not only survived but flourished until it became under Anne the accepted machinery of executive government. As the powers of 'the committee' (as it came to be called) increased, so the functions of the Privy Council came to be purely formal. The last serious attempt to restore the Privy Council to its former position was under the Act of Settlement (q.v.) in 1701. Until the accession of George I it had been customary for the Sovereign to preside over meetings of the committee, but from 1717 that monarch, being unable to speak English, ceased to attend and the business of government was transacted without royal participation. When attending upon the Sovereign the committee had been known as the Cabinet, and this was the name retained after the Sovereign's withdrawal from their meetings. In the absence of the King it was necessary for a minister to take over the presiding function and there thus emerged the office of Prime Minister (q.v.).

The Cabinet is thus a committee drawn from the ministers of the

[66]

Government, presided over by the Prime Minister, whose function is to frame the general policy of the Government and to co-ordinate its administrative activities. It accepts collective responsibility for all the activities of the Government, from which it follows that there must be no fundamental disagreement amongst its members. 'The major task of the Cabinet,' writes J. R. Mackintosh (*The British Cabinet*, 1962), 'is not to lead the party, to manage Parliament or to think out policy, but to co-ordinate administration, ensure that legislative proposals are acceptable to the departments concerned, to keep the senior ministers in touch with all the various lines of activity and to give the work of the government a measure of unity.' Every minister must abide by Cabinet decisions or resign, and an attack upon an individual minister is an attack on the Cabinet as a whole. Cabinet proceedings are of a strictly secret nature as it is obviously essential that all ministers should be able to speak with complete frankness. It would be foolish to pretend that argument and disagreement play no part in Cabinet meetings, but differences must be resolved by compromise in order to arrive at unanimous decisions. A minister refusing to accept a Cabinet decision would have no alternative but to resign from the Government, and if he found himself consistently in the minority at Cabinet meetings the same course would be forced upon him. There is one exception to the rule of secrecy. If a minister, finding himself unable to support the policy of the Government, takes the proper course of resigning he is permitted to make a personal explanation stating his reasons for his actions, but his statement must be limited to the circumstances leading up to his resignation.

A Cabinet is composed of the Prime Minister and such of his colleagues as he may select. There has long been a controversy over the comparative merits of a large and a small Cabinet. As the late Lord Morrison pointed out in his book *Government and Parliament*, a Cabinet may be one of three possible sizes: there is the Cabinet composed of substantially all the ministers of the Government, which was the general pre-war pattern; the very small Cabinet of the type which came into being during the two World Wars, sometimes limited to as few as 5 members; and finally the medium-sized Cabinet ranging from 16 to 23 members which follows the pattern set since the War, and which necessitates the omission of a number of departmental ministers. It seems to be generally agreed that the largest type tends to be too unwieldy to perform the function of a supreme policy-making body. Under the exceptional conditions imposed in wartime, the leading authorities seem to concur in the view that the central direction of a war is best entrusted to a small Cabinet capable of arriving at swift and firm policy decisions. Opinions are divided, however, on the desirability of a small Cabinet in peacetime. The small Cabinet has been advocated by L. S. Amery in his book *Thoughts on the*

[67]

Constitution, the main argument in its favour being that the function of the Cabinet could best be discharged by a small group of co-ordinating ministers free from departmental responsibilities, as the work of a minister in charge of a department is so heavy that he is unable to carry fully the additional burden of Cabinet membership, in consequence of which his contribution to Cabinet discussions must be inadequate, and that furthermore his outlook is liable to be coloured by his departmental interests. The case against the small Cabinet in peacetime was lucidly argued byLord Morrison. He pointed out that the Cabinet should be representative of all sections of the party in power, fully in touch with all shades of opinion, and able to give political leadership not only to the party itself but to the House of Commons and the country as a whole. It is unlikely that a small group of super-ministers could fulfil these requirements. Lord Morrison therefore advocated the medium-sized Cabinet, including a number of departmental ministers who can bring to the Cabinet 'that intimate experience of day-to-day affairs and work which is part of the valuable experience behind the contribution the departmental minister makes to Cabinet discussions'.

The delicate problem with which a Prime Minister is faced is, of course, the decision as to which ministers shall be included in the Cabinet and which shall be excluded. It is desirable to include two or three ministers without departmental responsibilities, such as the Lord President of the Council, the Lord Privy Seal, and perhaps the Chancellor of the Duchy of Lancaster, who are in a position to devote their time to the work of co-ordination and inter-departmental matters, and to undertake the chairmanship of Cabinet committees. It would obviously be unwise to exclude the leading departmental ministers such as the Foreign Secretary, Home Secretary, and Chancellor of the Exchequer, for apart from the vital importance of their offices, which are closely bound up with the framing of policy generally, they play major rôles in the co-ordination of Government activities. The Chancellor of the Exchequer, for instance, is by the very nature of his office responsible not only for the work of the Treasury but for co-ordinating financial and economic policy as a whole. To exclude the Secretary of State for Scotland and the Secretary of State for Wales would be open to serious objections, and could well be interpreted as an insult to the people of Scotland and Wales. Strong claims for inclusion can be put forward on behalf of other departmental ministers and of the Lord Chancellor on account of his legal eminence. In addition to departmental claims there are personal considerations involved. Some ministers are bound to be included in the Cabinet not by virtue of the offices they hold but because of their standing and influence in the party and in the country. To sum up in the words of Lord Morrison, 'the membership of the Cabinet should be of a character which will command the general respect of and exercise authority among its parliamentary supporters.'

In actual practice ministers not in the Cabinet are nevertheless summoned to Cabinet meetings when the affairs of their own departments come under discussion, and they also serve on Cabinet committees. Although there is an undoubted element of prestige attached to Cabinet membership, ministers not in the Cabinet are in no way subordinate to their Cabinet colleagues. They have the same rights and responsibilities, they receive the Cabinet agenda and conclusions and a large number of Cabinet papers (although not all), and they have the same discretion as Cabinet ministers in the raising of matters and the circulation of papers for Cabinet consideration. As members of Cabinet committees they are on an equal footing with their Cabinet colleagues. They are equally bound by Cabinet decisions and the principle of collective responsibility extends to them. In view of the growth of new departments in recent years a present-day Cabinet could number about 30 members if every minister was included, a size which would probably prove too unwieldy for the conduct of effective business. Although there is a tendency perceptible to exclude from the Cabinet the ministers in charge of the newer departments there is by no means a slavish adherence to this principle.

The nature of the Cabinet has undergone various changes since the days of the first Prime Minister, Sir Robert Walpole, whose 'inner cabinet' (a sort of cabinet within the Cabinet) consisted at first of the First Lord of the Treasury, the Lord Chancellor, the Lord President of the Council, and the 2 Secretaries of State. This small group, which was expanded to 8 members over the course of twenty-five years, came to supersede the Cabinet proper as the supreme responsible body. No appreciable increase in its composition becomes apparent until the 19th century when the creation of new and important offices imposed the necessity of swelling the total. Sir Robert Peel's Cabinet of 1841 consisted of 13 members. Disraeli's Cabinet of 1874 included only 12 members, but in order to keep its size so limited he was compelled to exclude such important office-holders as the President of the Board of Trade. Cabinets between the two World Wars averaged over 20 members. Since the Second World War the Cabinet has fluctuated in size between 16 and 23 members. Although the ministerial reorganization of January 1967 had the effect of reducing the Cabinet from 23 to 21 members, the general tendency up to that time had been for the size of the Cabinet to increase rather than decrease.

Until 1916 the business of the Cabinet was conducted in an informal and somewhat disorganized fashion. There was no Cabinet Secretariat in existence, no formal agenda prepared, no minutes kept, and no record taken of decisions. As a result it was not unusual for some doubt to exist amongst ministers as to what decisions had in fact been taken. Such was the emphasis upon the secrecy of Cabinet discussions that in those days ministers were known to object when their colleagues were seen making notes for their personal guidance. During the First World War it proved necessary to introduce some method into the organization of Cabinet business, and one of Lloyd George's first acts upon assuming office as Prime Minister was to establish a Cabinet Secretariat which was in fact the Secretariat of the Committee of Imperial Defence. To-day the Cabinet Secretariat is an indispensable office which serves both the Cabinet and its committees and performs many highly responsible functions, including the preparation of the agenda and the recording of conclusions. Lord Morrison referred to an interesting custom which is observed in Cabinet procedure when agreeing upon decisions. No actual vote is taken as this 'would not only be regarded as a breach of Cabinet decorum but would also be felt to symbolize and demonstrate, nakedly and unashamedly, a lack of Cabinet unity and solidarity which is always deprecated'. Usually the Prime Minister is able to state what appears to be the general view of the Cabinet and the decision is recorded accordingly. But sometimes it becomes necessary to 'collect the voices', when the view of each member is heard and the predominant view afterwards expressed by the Prime Minister, thus avoiding a formal vote.

In these days of heavy executive responsibility a considerable amount of work is delegated by the Cabinet to its committees. In the composition of these committees particular attention is given by the Prime Minister to the appointment of chairmen. They are normally chosen from among the ministers in the Cabinet, and wherever possible a minister without a department is selected for this work as he is in a better position to devote himself to the strenuous duties involved. The appointment of these committees is a confidential matter and the details concerning them, their composition, terms of reference, etc., are not revealed during the lifetime of a Government. There are sometimes exceptions to this rule as in the case of the Defence Committee which has the Prime Minister for its Chairman and is of such outstanding public importance that no secret is made of its existence. Not all Cabinet committees are of a permanent nature, some being appointed for special or temporary purposes.

In April 1969 Mr. Harold Wilson announced the establishment of a new Parliamentary Committee of the Cabinet comprising 6 senior ministers, later increased to 7, which would in effect constitute an inner Cabinet. In accordance with the usual practice the membership of this committee was not announced, although in view of its nature it was not difficult to speculate as to its probable composition.

The Machinery of Government Committee which reported in 1918 (Cd. 9230) defined the main functions of the Cabinet as (1) the final determination of the policy to be submitted to Parliament; (2) the supreme control of the national executive in accordance with the policy prescribed by Parliament; and (3) the continuous co-ordination and delimitation of the authorities of the several Departments of State. These statements aptly express the general and overall nature of the control which the Cabinet exercises over the administration. Matters of administrative detail are the concern of the departments and of the individual ministers responsible.

Cabinet government in the other countries of the Commonwealth bears a close relationship to the system which operates at home. The pre-eminence of the Prime Minister, the doctrine of collective responsibility, the principle of unanimity and the secrecy of Cabinet proceedings have all, broadly speaking, been embodied into the systems overseas. In the case of Ceylon the principal features of Cabinet government are actually specified in that country's Constitution. In Canada the composition of the Cabinet is heavily influenced by regional considerations and the desire of each Province to be adequately represented within it. In most Commonwealth countries the entire ministry is included in the Cabinet, but in January 1955 Australia adopted the British practice of including only selected ministers in the Cabinet. Since that time approximately half the ministers of Cabinet rank have been excluded from the inner circle of the Government. When the Labour Party is in office in Australia and New Zealand the party caucus is usually a powerful influence in the composition of the Cabinet.

(Further reading: Jennings, *Cabinet government*, 1959; Mackintosh, *The British Cabinet*, 1968; Wiseman, *The Cabinet in the Commonwealth*, 1958.)

CABINET COMMITTEES

The Cabinet is relieved of a large amount of work by the appointment of Cabinet committees, which enable some matters requiring more detailed consideration than it is possible for the Cabinet to give to be more thoroughly examined and explored. Some of these committees are Standing Committees, such as the Defence Committee, the Legislation Committee, which examines draft Bills and the general progress of the legislative programme during the session, the Future Legislation Committee, and the Lord President's Committee, which was a kind of sub-Cabinet or general purposes committee. The other Cabinet committees are temporary or special purpose committees, examples of such being the Housing Committee and the Committee on the National Health Service, which assisted the ministers concerned. It is considered undesirable during the lifetime of a Government to reveal the existence of Cabinet committees, their terms of reference, or the names of their Chairmen. There are exceptions—for example, no secret was made of the existence of the Defence Committee under the chairmanship of the Prime Minister, because it was the successor to the Committee of Imperial Defence and because of its exceptional public importance.

The composition of Cabinet committees varies—the more important ones consist of ministers both in and outside the Cabinet, with the Prime Minister as Chairman. The less important may consist of Parliamentary Secretaries and Civil Servants, with a Parliamentary Secretary as Chairman, but generally speaking the choice of Chairman is affected by the general set-up of the Government and the availability and suitability of ministers for the work. These committees and sub-committees are of course subordinate to the Cabinet, which in the case of temporary or special committees may authorize them to make decisions on its behalf and refer to the Cabinet if it is found necessary. As to the desirability of the Cabinet committee system, Lord Morrison said, 'It may be held that delegation of work to Cabinet committees impairs the doctrine of collective Cabinet responsibility. I hardly think so. Just as departmental Ministers must decide a host of things on their own responsibility, so also should Cabinet committees. They are, after all, composed of ministers and nearly always have a Cabinet Minister in the Chair. In any case they must keep in line with Cabinet policy, and the Prime Minister or the Cabinet can pull them up if they go wrong.'

In April 1969 Mr. Harold Wilson announced the establishment of a new Parliamentary Committee of the Cabinet comprising 6 senior ministers, later increased to 7, which would in effect constitute an inner Cabinet. In accordance with the usual practice the membership of this committee was not announced, although in view of its nature it was not difficult to speculate as to its probable composition.

CALLING THE HOUSE

The oldest method of increasing the attendance of Lords and Commons in Parliament, which at times has been irregular and often very poor, was by a 'Call of the House'. This was effected by reading the roll of members on a day of which due notice was given, and members not answering to their names and not sending an adequate excuse by a colleague were regarded as defaulters and punished. The earliest authenticated call of the House was on 16 February 1548/9, but there is no doubt that the practice goes back to medieval times. Usually a call was ordered when a large number of members had absented themselves from London, and at times the Speaker sent to the sheriffs letters directing them to summon all members who were staying in their counties to attend Parliament without fail on an appointed day. In the 19th century calls of the House became obsolete, and the last took place on 19 April 1836. Motions to have a call ordered were brought forward in the House of Commons on 10 July 1855 and 23 March 1882, but both were negatived.

The House of Lords has in the past ordered a call over when urgent business was deemed to require the attendance of its members, and this order was sometimes enforced by fines and imprisonment. When the bill for the degradation of Queen Caroline was before Parliament in 1820, the House of Lords was called over, and it was resolved, 'That no lord do absent himself on pain of incurring a fine of £100 for each day's absence, pending the three first days of such proceedings, and of £50 for each subsequent day's absence from the same; and in default of payment of being taken into custody'. The only excuses allowed were those of sickness, being abroad, old age (seventy and upwards), or the death of a near relative.

See also ATTENDANCE OF MEMBERS.

CAMPION, 1st BARON, formerly SIR GILBERT CAMPION (1882–1958)

Clerk of the House of Commons from 1937 to 1948, leading authority and author of books and other writings on Parliament and its procedure. He edited the 14th and 15th editions of Erskine May's *Parliamentary Practice*, and was editor consultant for the 16th edition. His most important individual work is his *Introduction to the Procedure of the House of Commons*, first published in 1929 (second edition 1947, third edition 1958).

Lord Campion was appointed Clerk of the Consultative Assembly of the Council of Europe in 1949. He was created a baron in 1950.

CANADIAN PARLIAMENT

On 1 July 1867 Canada became the first federal state in the British Empire, having been constituted by the British North America Act, an enactment of the British Parliament which was based on the recommendations of the Durham Report (q.v.). The Confederation originally consisted of four Provinces—Ontario, Quebec, Nova Scotia and New Brunswick—which were later joined by Manitoba (1870), British Columbia (1871), Prince Edward Island (1873), Saskatchewan and Alberta (1905) and Newfoundland (1949). Each Province has its own Legislature in addition to being represented in the Parliament of Canada. Apart from the ten Provinces there are two Territories, the Yukon Territory and the North-West Territory, which are directly administered by the federal Government. Ottawa, a city standing on the border between Ontario and Quebec, was designated the federal capital, and the first Parliament of the Confederation met there on 6 November 1867. The original Parliament building was destroyed by

[73]

fire in 1916, and the present building was completed in 1920 at a cost of £4,286,000.

The Canadian Parliament consists of the Governor-General, representing the Queen, and two Houses, the Senate and the House of Commons. The Senate consists of 102 members appointed for life by the Governor-General on the advice of the Cabinet, and may be regarded as a survival of the early colonial upper Chamber. However, an Act passed in 1965 now provides for the compulsory retirement of Senators on reaching the age of seventy-five, although this provision applies only to appointments made subsequent to the passing of the Act. A Senator must be at least thirty years of age, a resident of the Province for which he is appointed, and possessed of real property to the value of $4000. He may by writing resign his seat, and his place becomes vacant by reason of treason, felony, bankruptcy, or acquisition of foreign nationality, if he fails to attend Parliament for two consecutive sessions, or if he ceases to qualify in respect of property.

Provincial representation in the Senate is as follows: Ontario and Quebec, each 24; Nova Scotia and New Brunswick, each 10; Manitoba, British Columbia, Saskatchewan, Alberta and Newfoundland, each 6; Prince Edward Island, 4. The Senators from Quebec are appointed to represent 24 constituencies corresponding with the former electoral divisions of the old Province of Lower Canada. The other Senators have no designated constituencies but are appointed to represent their Provinces as a whole. The Canadian Senate, unlike that of Australia, was not designed to perform a strictly federal function, the Provinces being more concerned with representation in the Cabinet which is a truly federalized institution. Few Cabinet ministers are drawn from the Senate (in these days one minister is normally considered sufficient to represent the Cabinet in the Senate) and all important legislation is introduced in the House of Commons.

Under the British North America Act both Houses of Parliament are equal in their powers, and the Senate is therefore empowered, theoretically, to veto legislation initiated in the House of Commons and to amend Money Bills. This latter power was reasserted, in an academic way, as recently as 1957 in the Report of a Special Committee of the Senate on its Rights in Matters of Financial Legislation. In these days, however, the Senate is normally content to assume a passive rôle in the legislative process and would be very unlikely to invoke its powers to their fullest extent. Like the House of Lords, the Senate performs its most useful function as a House of review, and the investigatory work of its Standing and Special Committees is also of great value.

The Speaker of the Senate is appointed by the Governor-General and is himself a Senator. The rules and practice of the Senate are modelled to a great extent on those of the House of Lords—for example, Senators rising to speak address themselves not to the Chair but to the House itself. By a decision of the Judicial Committee of the Privy Council of 1929, women are eligible to sit in the Senate, and the first woman Senator was appointed in February 1930.

The House of Commons is directly elected by the people for five years, unless sooner dissolved, the representation of the Provinces being based on population. Originally consisting of 181 members, the membership of the House has been periodically increased over the years in accordance with population changes and the admission of new Provinces. The British North America Act, as amended in 1952, makes provision for the adjustment of provincial representation and the size of the total membership, while specifying that a Province shall always be entitled to a number of members in the House of Commons not less than the number of its Senators. The present membership (1970) stands at 264, of whom 88 represent Ontario, 74 Quebec, 23 British Columbia, 19 Alberta, 13 Manitoba, 13 Saskatchewan, 11 Nova Scotia, 10 New Brunswick, 7 Newfoundland and 4 Prince Edward Island. The Yukon and the North-West Territory are each represented by 1 member.

The Speaker of the House of Commons is elected by the House from among its own membership. In 1968 a Speaker without party affiliation was nominated for the first time with all-party support. It has been customary in the past to alternate an English-speaking Speaker with a French-speaking Speaker, both languages having official status at the federal level, although most Canadian Speakers have been fully or partially bilingual regardless of their racial origin. Language rights are also maintained by the appointment of a Deputy Speaker whose mother tongue is other than that of the Speaker, and when the Speaker of the House is of English origin the Speaker of the Senate is usually of French origin, and vice versa. Hansard reporters of both languages sit in the Chamber and the debates and other parliamentary publications are published in both languages.

The procedure and customs of the Canadian House of Commons are based on those of Westminster, although there are a number of significant differences to note. Of particular interest is the method of recording divisions. When it appears to the Speaker that all members intending to participate in a debate have done so he inquires: 'Is the House ready for the question?' Should no member rise he proceeds to put the question, and if a recorded division is required at least five members must rise when the Speaker gives his provisional verdict following the chorus of 'Yeas' and 'Nays'. On a division being called for the Speaker says, 'Call in the members,' upon which the division bells are rung. (A precedent also exists for the Speaker to call in the members on his own initiative.) No time limit is set for the ringing of the bells, and although ten minutes or so normally suffices, it is not unusual for the bells to ring for a considerably longer period, particularly when it is known that certain members beyond the precincts of the building are returning to record their votes. The division begins when the party Whips are satisfied that all the available members have arrived, at which point they enter the House together, bow to the Chair and take their seats. The Speaker then puts the question again and asks those who wish to vote in its favour to rise. Each member rises separately, and as he does so his name is called by the Second Clerk Assistant while the Clerk records the vote on a printed list. The members are taken in rows, the front benches rising first, the parties following each other in the order of their precedence in the House. As a matter of courtesy the Prime Minister, Leader of the Opposition, and leaders of minority parties are called first within their respective groups. When the votes in favour have been counted the Speaker calls on those who are opposed to the question to rise and a similar procedure ensues. The Clerk announces the result of the division to the Speaker who declares the motion or amendment carried or lost as the case may be. (This procedure applies only in the House. In Committee of the Whole House a vote is taken by means of a simple count.)

Another important area of procedure in which the Canadian House of Commons diverges from its counterpart at Westminster is the question period. Questions may be 'written' or 'oral', but while the Standing Orders have provided for written questions since 1867, the practice of asking oral questions, although of long standing, was not officially recognized by the rules until 1964. Written questions are listed on the Order Paper and may be answered in writing or orally in the House according to the discretion of the minister concerned, although if a written question is 'starred' he knows that the member asking it would prefer an oral reply. Some written questions remain upon the Order Paper for months as ministers do not consider themselves under any immediate pressure to reply to them. The highlight of the parliamentary day is the oral question period, and in its political content and the extent to which it engages public attention it corresponds to the question period at Westminster. Procedurally, however, it is very different. Oral questions may be asked 'on the Orders of the Day'—that is, before Government business at the commencement of each sitting—no notice being required. Any minister may be questioned on any day and little attempt is made to keep related questions together as at Westminster. Theoretically, oral questions must be concerned with matters of urgency, and the Speaker may disallow a question or direct that it be placed on the Order Paper. In practice, however, it is very difficult for the Speaker to enforce this rule, or indeed any of the rules relating to the abuse of questions. Most oral questions are asked on account of their political impact, and many of them are out of order in that they do not fall within the legitimate sphere of ministerial responsibility or are based on hearsay. The

Speaker is hampered by the fact that he has no advance notice of an oral question and that it is difficult to eradicate bad practices which are long established. No time limit was placed on the oral question period until 1965. In that year the House accepted a variable time limitation but in December 1968 a daily time limit of 40 minutes was established.

Prior to 1965 Canadian parliamentary procedure was in many respects cumbersome and outdated in spite of attempts to reform the rules through the appointment of a succession of Procedure Committees. A number of innovations were introduced on a provisional basis in 1965 but it was not until December 1968 that a permanent scheme of reform, providing for a radical revision of the Standing Orders, was implemented. The areas affected by the new rules included financial procedure, the legislative process, the committee structure of the House, emergency procedures and the powers of the Speaker. The Committees of Supply and Ways and Means were abolished and financial procedure was revised in accordance with principles which are also basic to the current British practice. The Estimates are automatically referred to Standing Committees for consideration in detail and a minimum of 25 days is allotted to the consideration of the business of Supply in the House. As in the British House of Commons these days are at the disposal of the Opposition and may be used for debating any matter coming within the jurisdiction of Parliament. The Supply days are divided between three periods ending respectively on 10 December, 26 March and 30 June. The main Estimates must be presented to the House before 1 March. Interim Supply to cover the months of April, May and June must be disposed of by 26 March, and the main Estimates must be disposed of by 30 June. Supply days may be used for the consideration of motions involving confidence in the Government not more than six times during a session, not more than two falling within each of the three periods.

With the abolition of the Committee of Ways and Means, the Budget is now introduced in the House itself and the Budget debate takes place on a resolution couched in very general terms and permitting a wide-ranging debate. The Ways and Means resolutions themselves are not separately debated, the opportunity for specific consideration of taxation proposals arising at the various stages of the Bills which seek to implement them. The preliminary resolution stage in Committee of the Whole House which was formerly required in respect of any Bill involving the expenditure of money is eliminated. Thus the ancient practice on which financial procedure was formerly based has been abolished as in the British House of Commons.

The legislative process was further amended by the automatic reference of all Bills, other than those based on Supply and Ways and Means resolutions, to Standing Committees for consideration in detail. In addition, the report stage has been revived for the consideration of amendments adopted in committee and to permit the introduction of subsequent amendments.

The Standing Committee structure, which had previously been established on a provisional basis, was confirmed, the terms of reference of most of the Standing Committees relating to the subject areas with which they deal. Matters are allocated to these committees in accordance with their subject content, each committee dealing equally with Bills, Estimates and *ad hoc* investigations. Thus each Standing Committee combines the functions of inquiry, legislation and financial scrutiny.

The procedure relating to Emergency Adjournment Motions was revised in such a way as to reduce the opportunities for its abuse. The Speaker's discretion in the interpretation of the rule was widened, notice of intention to ask for a debate under the Emergency Adjournment rule was made a requirement, and such a debate when granted no longer supersedes immediately the regular business of the House. Steps were also taken to ensure that a single dissenting voice should no longer be able to frustrate the otherwise unanimous will of the House when it is desired to waive the notice requirement for motions relating to the introduction and consideration of business or the hours and days of sitting.

Another important reform which was introduced in 1965 on a provisional basis and made permanent in December 1968 was the abolition of the rule which permitted a member to appeal against a Speaker's ruling from the floor of the House (a Chairman's ruling is now subject to an appeal to the Speaker). This rule was invariably used for political purposes without regard for precedent or good procedure. It was an ever-present threat to the Speaker's authority and there are several examples on the record of the Speaker being overruled by a majority vote in the House. Coupled with the abolition of appeals is the question of the continuity of the Speaker's office. This cause received an important boost in 1968 following the re-election of the Speaker in his constituency as an Independent with the endorsement of the two main parties and his subsequent re-election to the Chair with all-party support.

In July 1969 a further procedural change was implemented following a highly contentious debate providing for an allocation of time procedure in relation to Bills. This rule provides that in circumstances where time limitation on the passage of a Bill cannot be effected by all-party agreement, the Government shall have the right to initiate an allocation of time motion of its own which would be carried with the support of its majority in the House. Mention should also be made of the closure which was incorporated in the Standing Orders as far back as 1913. Although considerably less draconian in its operation than the closure rule at Westminster, it has seldom been invoked over the years because of the odium which it usually incurs for any government which resorts to it. The most notorious example of the use of closure occurred in 1956 during the Pipeline Debate. It was not called into operation again until 1964 when it was used to terminate the debate on the adoption of a national flag. The most recent example of its use was July 1969 when it was invoked to terminate the debate on the allocation of time procedure. Other devices designed to restrict debate for which the Standing Orders provide include time limits on speeches (from which the Prime Minister and the Leader of the Opposition are exempt), an 8-day limit to the debate on the address and a 6-day limit to the Budget debate.

The ceremonies observed in the Canadian Parliament are very similar to those of Westminster. The Speaker and the Clerks wear the traditional black uniform and gown but no wig, and they all wear tricorne hats when in procession. The Deputy Speaker, in contrast with his counterpart at Westminster, also wears the Speaker's uniform, without the gown, but neither the Speaker nor the Deputy Speaker wear knee-breeches and silver-buckled shoes. The Speaker wears a plain black gown on all occasions and is not equipped with a gold-embroidered ceremonial gown for special occasions. A practice peculiar to Canada is the employment of page boys who sit in the Chamber at the foot of the Speaker's Chair and act as messengers.

Although minority parties are usually represented in the Canadian Parliament, the federal political structure is based upon two major parties, the Liberals and the Progressive Conservatives, and power has always alternated between them. From 1935 to 1957 the Liberal Party was continuously in office. The Conservatives were returned to power by a very narrow margin in 1957, but in the following year they swept back into office with the largest parliamentary majority in Canadian history, winning 208 seats against the Liberals' 49. In 1962 the Conservatives managed to retain power as a minority Government, and in 1963 the balance was tipped precariously in favour of the Liberals. The Liberals were again returned as a minority Government in 1965 and with an overall majority in 1968. At the time of writing, two further parties are represented in the House of Commons, the New Democratic Party and Le Ralliement Créditiste. The former is a party based on moderate Socialist principles and in 1969 it won control of the Provincial Government of Manitoba. Its forerunner, the Co-operative Commonwealth Federation, controlled the Provincial Government of Saskatchewan from 1944 to 1964. During those years it was, as the government of Manitoba is now, the only Socialist Government in North America. The Ralliement Créditiste, a party which draws its support from the Province of Quebec, broke away in 1963 from the Social Credit movement of which it originally formed a part. Social Credit itself, a movement based on non-conventional monetary theories, has frequently been represented at Ottawa as a minority party but its effective strength lies in the provincial politics of Alberta and British Columbia in both of which Provinces it has controlled the Government for many years. Another French-Canadian party, the Union Nationale, was in power in Quebec, but it limits its activities to that Province and has never been represented at Ottawa.

Federal-provincial relations are governed by the British North America Act, and disputes between the Canadian and Provincial Governments as to their respective powers were originally settled by appeal to the Privy Council of the United Kingdom. In 1948 the Canadian Supreme Court became the final court of appeal, and in the following year the British Parliament passed an Act granting to the Canadian Parliament the right to amend the British North America Act in respect of federal matters. While the British Parliament in amending other sections of the Act does so only at the request of Canada, Canadians have long been dissatisfied with a machinery whereby the process of constitutional amendment is reserved to the Parliament of another country. The repatriation of the Constitution will depend, however, upon the acceptance of an agreed formula between the Canadian and Provincial Governments.

See also FRANCHISE; PEACE TOWER, OTTAWA; PRIVY COUNCIL.

CANDLES, MOTION FOR

In the House of Commons there was a time when an interruption to the business was caused by a member moving that candles be brought in, so by a Standing Order of 1717 it was ordered that the Serjeant-at-Arms should take care that candles be brought in at the appropriate time without any order being given. The old formula is still used when a member thinks the illumination in the Chamber is insufficient and he will rise and say, 'May candles be brought in, Mr. Speaker?'

Sir Geoffrey Shakespeare chose a very appropriate title for his autobiography when he called it *Let Candles Be Brought In*.

CASTING VOTE

In the House of Commons the Speaker has a casting vote when the voting in a division is equal, but the impartiality attached to his office obliges him when possible to vote in such a manner as not to make the decision of the House final. This principle was laid down by Mr. Speaker Addington in 1796. The Chairman also has a casting vote and uses it in the same way as the Speaker. In the House of Lords the Speaker and the Lord Chairman vote with the other peers. Under the ancient practice of the House, if the voting is equal the question is decided in the negative, but an amendment to the Standing Orders introduced in 1951 provided for certain exceptions to this rule. It is usual for the Speaker to give his reasons for casting his vote in a particular direction, and in 1673, during the Cavalier Parliament (q.v.), on a motion to adjourn the debate the voting was 105 to 105. The Speaker gave his casting vote for adjournment, remarking that 'he would have his reason for his judgment recorded, viz., because he was very hungry'.

'CATCHING THE SPEAKER'S EYE'

It often happens that several members who wish to speak in the House rise to their feet at the same time hoping to 'catch the Speaker's eye'. Up to 1625, when several members stood up, the House itself had decided whom they wanted to hear, but in that year the House resolved that 'if two rise up at once, the Speaker does determine. He that his eye saw first, has the precedence given'.

Thus, in theory, when more than one member rises to speak, the Speaker calls on the member first observed by him. In practice the Speaker uses his discretion in deciding whom to call, taking into account such factors as the wishes of the House and the right of all sections of opinion to a fair measure of expression. The competition among members to participate in debate is therefore not merely a matter of 'catching the Speaker's eye' although the expression has become an established phrase in parliamentary parlance.

CATERING, PARLIAMENTARY

See HOUSE OF COMMONS (SERVICES) COMMITTEE; KITCHEN COMMITTEE.

CATHOLICS IN PARLIAMENT

See ROMAN CATHOLICS IN PARLIAMENT.

CAUCUS

A private meeting or conference of the parliamentary members of a political party. The word is said to have originated in the United States and to have derived from a North American Indian word meaning 'to consult'. In the United States it usually means a meeting of the leaders of a political party previous to an election to select candidates for office, or to concert other measures for the furthering of party interests. The policy of deciding issues in caucus of the majority party before they have been submitted to Parliament has been prevalent in Australia and New Zealand. When decisions have been taken in caucus, from which a member cannot diverge, debate becomes a work of supererogation and the views of the Opposition mere tedious obstruction. As Sir Robert Menzies, the former Australian Prime Minister, remarked in 1945, 'Parliament might just as well not exist at present because legislation is first submitted to the caucus, and, if its approval is given, then the subsequent debate in Parliament becomes a mere formality.' Professor Crisp, in his *Australian National Government*, defends the practice. He writes (page 162): 'So long as caucus discussion and criticism are free and adequate they constitute another tempering agency in the democratic process, another barrier of healthy deliberation interposed between democratic government and the possible emergence of some form of plebiscitory dictatorship.' However, as Professor Bland points out, 'Surely it is Parliament and not caucus that is the forum of the nation—members in caucus hear only one set of political opinions. If Parliament is to be the nation's forum; if, as Professor Ernest Barker puts it, "law-making is the process of the good dialectic of public debate, in which thought clashes with thought until a reconciling compromise is found, which we can all accept because we can all see some little element of our thought, some little reflection of ourselves in the lineaments which that compromise presents", then this process of debate is utterly defeated by the caucus method, and parliamentary government has changed in character.'

In lighter vein, although he was alluding to the domestic politics of Oxford University, Lewis Carroll's contribution to the subject is worth repeating:

> 'We must combine, aye! hold a caucus meeting,
> Unless we want to get another beating.
> That they should "bottle" us is nothing new—
> But should they bottle us and *caucus* too?'

CAVALIER PARLIAMENT

The second Parliament of Charles II which first met on 8 May 1661, and has also been called the Pensionary Parliament and the Long Parliament of the Restoration. It sat for seventeen years until 30 December 1678, when it was prorogued for the last time and dissolved by proclamation on 24 January 1679.

When summoned, the House of Lords consisted of 142 peers and the House of Commons of 507 members. At the outset the Cavalier Parliament, as its name implies, was strongly Royalist in its sympathies and the newly restored monarchy faced little opposition from it. It pursued a repressive religious policy aimed against the Presbyterians and Nonconformists and its Royalist legislation reversed much of the work of the Long Parliament (q.v.). But over the years of its long life its attitude gradually changed. Misgovernment, the corruption and profligacy of the court, an unpopular foreign policy, and a general fear of the advance of popery combined to strengthen the ranks of the dissentients in both Houses and in the Commons an organized opposition developed which became known as the Country Party. The popular cause reasserted itself and a jealous and more characteristic regard for parliamentary rights and privileges took the place of sub-servience to the Crown. Amongst the gains of the Cavalier Parliament may be cited the strengthening of parliamentary control over finance, the assertion of the principle that a minister is responsible to Parliament for his actions, and the secure establishment of Protestantism.

This Parliament holds the record as the longest Parliament in British history, although this distinction has been accorded by some to the more famous Long Parliament by virtue of the fact that, although forcibly dismissed by Cromwell in 1653 and again by the army in 1659, it was never constitutionally dissolved until 1660, twenty years after it was originally summoned. However, as various other Parliaments intervened between the first dismissal of the Long Parliament and its subsequent recall, the record properly belongs to the Pensionary Parliament, which sat for seventeen consecutive years and derived its alternative nickname from its longevity.

See also CHARLES II AND PARLIAMENT.

CAVE, EDWARD (1691–1754)

The printer and publisher who first began the systematic reporting of parliamentary debates for popular consumption. In 1727 he was imprisoned and fined, together with his friend Robert Raikes, for supplying to the latter reports of parliamentary proceedings for publication in the *Gloucester Journal*. In 1731 he started the *Gentleman's Magazine* in which the reports of the debates of both Houses became a regular feature. The reports were based upon information smuggled out of the public galleries by Cave's friends, and occasionally Members of Parliament supplied Cave with copies of their own speeches. A writer named William Guthrie later constructed the reports from the information supplied to him, and he was followed in 1740 by the young Samuel Johnson (q.v.).

In 1738 Cave published a speech before it had been delivered and an important debate took place in the House of Commons on the subject of parliamentary reporting. Most speakers agreed in roundly con-demning the practice and the House passed a strongly worded resolu-tion to that effect. Cave did not cease to publish his reports, but he employed the subterfuge of disguising the locale and the names of the speakers. In 1747 Cave was in trouble with the House of Lords for publishing an account of Lord Lovat's trial, and he did not resume his reports until 1752, after which he seems to have carried on unmolested.

See also PRESS AND PARLIAMENT.

CAVENDISH, SIR HENRY (1732–1804)

The Member of the House of Commons for Lostwithiel in the Parliament of 1768 to 1774, who distinguished himself by reporting the debates of that Parliament. His record runs from 10 May 1768 to

13 June 1774, and consists of forty-eight small quarto volumes, which are lodged in the British Museum. An edited version in two volumes was published in 1841/2. He took his notes in Gurney's system of shorthand, and a portion of the existing manuscript remains in the shorthand form. He recorded many of the speeches of the most eminent parliamentarians of the day, and in particular those of Edmund Burke. It is due to Cavendish that any record at all exists of the proceedings of the so-called Unreported Parliament (q.v.).

CAYMAN ISLANDS LEGISLATIVE ASSEMBLY

Power to constitute a separate government for the Cayman Islands (previously administered as a dependency of Jamaica) was bestowed on the Crown by the Cayman Islands and Turks and Caicos Islands Act of 1958. An Executive Council and a Legislative Assembly with 12 elected members were established under a Constitution proclaimed in July 1959 but, as Jamaica still retained power to apply her laws to the islands, they received a new Constitution in 1962, when Jamaica became independent. This provided for an Administrator, and an Executive Council with 2 *ex-officio* members, 1 nominated from the nominated members of the Legislative Assembly and 2 elected by all members of the Assembly from among the elected members.

The Assembly has 2 or 3 *ex-officio*, 2 or 3 nominated and 12 elected members and is presided over by the Administrator or, in his absence, by a Deputy President elected by the Assembly and submitted to the Administrator for the Queen's Consent. The Administrator has power to enforce the passing of legislation if he considers it expedient.

CENSURE, VOTE OF

See VOTE OF CENSURE.

CENTRAL HALL and CENTRAL TOWER, PALACE OF WEST-MINSTER

The Central Hall is octagonal in shape, 75 feet high and 60 feet across. Four arched doorways at the north, south, east, and west of the Hall lead respectively to the Members' Lobby, House of Commons; the House of Lords; the Lower Waiting Hall, libraries, and dining-rooms; and St. Stephen's Hall (q.v.). Constituents visiting their Members of Parliament are normally directed to the Central Hall.

The Central Tower stands above the Central Hall and is 300 feet high and 75 feet across.

CEYLON PARLIAMENT

Ceylon became a self-governing Dominion in the British Common-wealth on 4 February 1948, following the passage by the United

Kingdom Parliament of the Government of Ceylon Act in 1947. Ceylon has a bicameral Parliament comprising a Senate and a House of Representatives. The Senate consists of 30 members, half elected by the lower House and half nominated by the Governor-General. It is a permanent body which remains unaffected by a dissolution of Parliament. Senators hold office for six years, one-third of them retiring every second year. Since the General Election of March 1960 the House of Representatives has consisted of 151 members elected by universal adult suffrage and 6 nominated by the Governor-General. Unless sooner dissolved, the House has a duration of five years.

Prior to the March 1960 election the House of Representatives consisted of 101 members, 95 of whom were elected. An unusual provision of Ceylon's Constitution empowers the Governor-General to nominate up to 6 additional persons as members of the House of Representatives if he is satisfied that any important interest in the island is inadequately represented or unrepresented.

The size of the House of Representatives was increased by the Ceylon Constitution (Amendment) Act, 1959, which also repealed legislation providing for the separate representation of Ceylonese citizens of Indian and Pakistani origin. In place of the 4 special seats which would have been allocated to this group in terms of the Ceylon Constitution (Special Provisions) Act, 1954, and the Indian and Pakistani (Parliamentary Representation) Act, 1954 (both now repealed), there has been substituted a machinery which provides for the creation of multi-member constituencies wherever the racial composition of a particular district renders concentrated representation desirable.

The Ceylon Parliamentary Elections (Amendment) Act, 1959, lowered the voting age to eighteen, but those under twenty-one were not enfranchised in time to participate in either of the two General Elections held in 1960.

In December 1959 the House of Representatives was dissolved following a political crisis which arose after the assassination of the Prime Minister, Mr. Bandaranaike. The election held in March 1960 failed to produce a stable majority for any single party, and the Government formed by Mr. Senanayake resigned in April after they had failed to win a vote of confidence. A second election held in July returned to power the party of the murdered Prime Minister, now under the leadership of his widow. Mrs. Bandaranaike became the world's first woman Prime Minister on 21 July 1960, when she was invited by the Governor-General to form a Government. She had not contested the election as a candidate, and was appointed to the Senate on 1 August, thus becoming the only Prime Minister in the Commonwealth to sit in an upper House. Her government was defeated in the General Election of 1965, but she was again returned to power in 1970.

The control of the Government is vested in a Cabinet which in 1970 consisted of 21 ministers, the Prime Minister being responsible also for defence, external affairs, planning and employment. Not fewer than 2 ministers, including the Minister of Justice, must be senators.

Although Ceylon now has only one official language—Sinhalese—Members of Parliament may deliver their speeches in Sinhalese, Tamil, or English. A speech is reproduced in Hansard in the language in which it was delivered.

One of the first acts of Mrs. Bandaranaike on regaining power in 1970 was to convene the House of Representatives as a Constituent Assembly with the responsibility for drafting a new Constitution for Ceylon. The new Constitution will establish Ceylon as a Republic 'pledged to realize the objectives of a socialist democracy' and will make provision for the protection of fundamental rights and freedoms. When the members of the House met for the first time as a Constituent Assembly on 19 July 1970, they assembled outside the precincts of Parliament in order to demonstrate the fact that they were not meeting in their normal legislative capacity. The Governor-General was absent from the meeting since his presence, as the representative of the Queen, would have been deemed inappropriate.

(Further reading for the colonial period: Namasivayam, *The legislatures of Ceylon*, 1951.)

CHAIRMAN OF COMMITTEES, HOUSE OF LORDS

A peer is appointed Chairman and first of the Deputy Speakers at the beginning of each session, or whenever the office becomes vacant. He takes the chair in all Committees of the Whole House, and he is also Chairman of all other committees of the House on Private Bills and other matters, unless the House directs otherwise. An important duty of the Lord Chairman is the supervision of Private Bills, and copies of these are supplied to him and his Counsel at each stage of the proceedings upon them. From the date of the institution of his office in 1800 this supervisory function was performed by the Lord Chairman alone, but as Private Business had increased in importance, the Commons decided in 1848 to entrust their Chairman of Ways and Means with a similar duty. In divisions the vote of the Lord Chairman, like that of the Speaker of the House of Lords, is taken in the House.

The Lord Chairman draws a salary of £4,875 a year.

CHAIRMAN OF WAYS AND MEANS

The member of the House of Commons who presides over a Committee of the Whole House (q.v.). When the House goes into committee the Speaker leaves the Chair and the Chairman of Ways and Means takes his place, not in the Speaker's Chair but at the Table of the House. At the same time the Mace is removed from the brackets on the Table and placed in those beneath the Table.

The Chairman presides in committee with the same impartiality as the Speaker in the House and his authority is final. There is no appeal from his rulings to the Speaker, he is empowered to accept the closure and to select amendments, and his conduct cannot be questioned except on a substantive motion. He is not empowered to inflict any serious form of punishment, but he can direct a member to withdraw. In committee he has a casting vote only, but when the Speaker is in the Chair his status is the same as that of any other member.

Unlike the Speaker, the Chairman is attended by no ceremonial and he wears neither wig and gown nor any other special form of costume. He and the Deputy Chairman are appointed for the duration of a Parliament by resolution of the House on a Government motion, the candidates normally being members of the governing party. Care is usually taken, however, to select candidates who are acceptable to the Opposition in order to secure a unanimous vote, and they seldom take an active part in political controversy. Their seats are nevertheless liable to be contested at General Elections, and they are unlikely to be reappointed by the next Parliament in the event of a change of Government.

Before 1841, the Chairman of Ways and Means, as his title implies, was Chairman of the Committee of Ways and Means only, but since that year he has acted as Chairman of all other Committees of the Whole House as well. Since 1910 he has been appointed at the beginning of each Parliament on a motion by the Leader of the House. Under the earlier practice the Leader of the House called upon a member to take the Chair after the House had resolved itself into a committee, and if another member was also nominated, the Speaker resumed the Chair and a vote was taken.

The Chairman of Ways and Means is also the Deputy Speaker (q.v.) and when acting in this capacity he occupies the Speaker's Chair. When presiding in committee he is addressed by name. Under the new financial procedure adopted in 1966 and 1967 he now presides as Deputy Speaker when Estimates and Ways and Means resolutions are considered in the House. On these occasions he has all the powers which he enjoyed when presiding over the Committees of Supply and Ways and Means, both of which are now abolished, including the power to accept the closure and to select amendments.

The Deputy Chairman was first appointed in 1902, and in the absence of the Chairman of Ways and Means he exercises the full powers of the latter, including his powers as Deputy Speaker. In the absence of both the Chairman and Deputy Chairman the Chair is taken by one of the members on the Chairmen's Panel (q.v.).

D

The Chairman of Ways and Means is also charged with special responsibilities in connexion with Private Business (*see* PRIVATE BILLS).

The Chairman and Deputy Chairman are paid salaries of £4,875 and £3,750 per annum respectively which are provided for in the Estimates and not, like the Speaker's salary, charged on the Consolidated Fund. They are entitled in addition to £1,250 of their parliamentary salaries.

CHAIRMEN'S LIAISON COMMITTEE

An informal committee consisting of the Chairmen of the Public Accounts Committee, Estimates Committee, Select Committee on Nationalised Industries, and the various Specialist Committees, the Chairmen's Liaison Committee was established in 1968 to consider applications from Select Committees wishing to travel overseas. The Committee has the task of scrutinizing each such application and determining whether or not it is justified. It also keeps a watchful eye on expenditure in connexion with the employment of outside specialists by committees. The Second Clerk Assistant acts as Clerk to the Committee.

CHAIRMEN'S PANEL

A panel consisting of the Chairman of Ways and Means, the Deputy Chairman and not less than 10 experienced Members of the House of Commons who are nominated by the Speaker at the commencement of each session to act as temporary Chairmen in Committees of the Whole House (q.v.) and as the regular Chairmen of Standing Committees (q.v.). The panel, of whom 3 form a quorum, settle points of procedure which are not covered by the rules of the House, and are empowered to report to the House from time to time any resolutions they may come to on matters of procedure relating to Standing Committees. A member of the panel acting as Chairman in Committee of the Whole House is not empowered to accept a motion for the closure (q.v.) or to select amendments.

CHAMBER

The majority of the Parliaments of the Commonwealth favour the type of debating chamber for which the House of Commons provides the model—one of rectangular shape with rows of benches facing each other along each of the longer sides. In some of the smaller Parliaments members enjoy the luxury of individual chairs and desks. The continental semicircular assembly, where members address the House from a rostrum, would be very much out of keeping with British parliamentary customs. In the course of a speech during a debate on the rebuilding of the House of Commons in 1943, Sir Winston Churchill said that the semi-circular Chamber 'appeals to political theorists, enables every individual or group to move round the centre, adopting various shades of pink according as the weather changes'. The British type of Chamber has undoubtedly encouraged the growth of two main parties instead of the numerous groups, many of them splinter factions, often found in foreign Parliaments. Having advocated the retention of the rectangular Chamber, Sir Winston went on to say that 'a Chamber formed on the lines of the House of Commons should not be big enough to contain all its members at once without overcrowding, and there should be no question of every member having a separate seat reserved for him. If the House is big enough to contain all its members, nine-tenths of its debates will be conducted in the depressing atmosphere of an almost empty or half-empty Chamber. The essence of good House of Commons speaking is the conversational style, the facility for quick, informal interruptions and interchanges. Harangues from a rostrum would be a bad substitute for the conversational style in which so much of our business is done. But the conversational style requires a fairly small space, and there should be on great occasions a sense of crowd and urgency.' The present House of Commons, with its large membership and restricted accommodation, fulfils all the requirements alluded to by Sir Winston. It is interesting to note that these debating traditions, so characteristically British, developed quite accidentally. When in 1547 King Edward VI allotted St. Stephen's Chapel to the Commons as their permanent debating Chamber it so happened that the chapel provided the very conditions calculated to encourage the type of discussion described by Sir Winston.

CHANCELLOR OF THE DUCHY OF LANCASTER

The Duchy of Lancaster estates and revenues are nominally controlled by the holder of this office, and he performs various duties such as appointing County Court Judges, which in other counties devolve upon the Lord Chancellor (q.v.) and the Home Secretary (q.v.). The Chancellor is appointed by letters patent and the delivery of the Seal of the Duchy. He has no heavy departmental duties and all but formal matters are dealt with by a small staff under the direction of the Vice-Chancellor. The Chancellor is thus available to perform a variety of temporary and pressing duties which are not assigned to any particular minister, such as membership of Government committees. Earl Winterton was given the office in 1938 with a seat in the Cabinet, to answer in the Commons (he was then an Irish peer and eligible to sit in the Commons) for the Air Ministry, whose head was then in the Lords. He has recorded that his official duties in connexion with the Duchy of Lancaster occupied him for about half an hour a week. In 1953 Lord Woolton combined the office of Chancellor with that of Minister of Materials. In 1957 Dr. Charles Hill was appointed to the office with the responsibility for the co-ordination of official information services at home and abroad. In 1970 Mr. Anthony Barber was appointed Chancellor of the Duchy with responsibility for leading the negotiations concerning Britain's entry into the European Common Market but on Mr. Iain Macleod's death succeeded him as Chancellor of the Exchequer, his place at the Duchy being taken by Mr. Geoffrey Rippon. The Chancellor of the Duchy of Lancaster is usually a member of the Cabinet, his salary being £8,500 a year, plus an additional £1,250 if he sits in the House of Commons.

The estates and jurisdiction of the Duchy and County Palatine of Lancaster have been attached to the Crown since 1399, but the Lancaster inheritance goes back to 1265.

A chronological list of Chancellors of the Duchy of Lancaster appears as Appendix 14.

CHANCELLOR OF THE EXCHEQUER

Britain's Finance Minister, who is in control of the imposition of taxes and the expenditure of national revenue. He is always one of the Commission of the Treasury (q.v.) and he is appointed Chancellor of the Exchequer and Under Treasurer by separate patents, and by the receipt of the Exchequer Seals. Originally Clerk to the Lord Chancellor, he came into existence during the reign of Henry II, when, the Great Seal being no longer used for Exchequer business, he was appointed to take charge of the Seal of the Exchequer and to keep a check on the Treasurer. He also had to discharge certain judicial functions in the Exchequer account—his more strictly financial duties then belonged to the Under Treasurer, which office he now includes with his own. The position of Chancellor of the Exchequer was not of great importance so long as the Treasury Board was in active working, but the meetings of the Board, consisting of the King (up to the accession of George III), the Lords of the Treasury, and the Chancellor of the Exchequer, became merely formal early in the 19th century and were discontinued in 1856. As the Treasury Board diminished, so the Chancellor of the Exchequer has risen in importance. While the duties of the old Exchequer were to the Crown, the duties of the Treasury and the Chancellor of the Exchequer are to the taxpayer. It is the Chancellor's business when he knows the amount of the public income, and the extent of the demands upon it, to adjust revenue to expenditure, to raise or remit taxation as the occasion may justify, and to discover how the largest amount of money may be raised by the cheapest methods and with the least effect on the economy and general prosperity of the country. The Chancellor steps into the limelight once a year when he presents his Budget (q.v.), which reviews the financial position of the country and contains his proposals for taxation during the ensuing year, for which he must obtain the assent of Parliament.

The work of the Chancellor is not only arduous but sometimes rather thankless, and its results are often not very favourably received—Gladstone called his office 'the most unpopular of the State', but went on to say that the only two Chancellors against whom he had never heard a word said were 'the two worst Chancellors of the Exchequer of the last forty years'. Anson says that 'the Chancellor and his staff may be regarded as living in perpetual vigilance against servants of the State, who want more pay than the Treasury thinks the country can afford—against departments of government, which want more money than the Chancellor is prepared to ask Parliament to grant—against the House of Commons, which contests the amount demanded, and the mode in which it is proposed to be raised—and against the taxpayer who wishes to have everything handsome about him, and does not like to pay for it'.

The complexities of fiscal and economic affairs have become such that the duties involved in controlling the whole range of public expenditure and supervising the general co-ordination of economic policy comprise far too great a burden for a single minister. Since the end of the Second World War various means have been devised for spreading the load, including the appointment of a second senior minister at the Treasury, the Chief Secretary to the Treasury (q.v.), who is sometimes given Cabinet rank, and the appointment of a Cabinet Minister with a separate though related sphere of jurisdiction, namely Economic Affairs. At the time of writing (November 1970) the Chancellor is assisted at the Treasury by the Chief Secretary, a Minister of State (q.v.), the Parliamentary Secretary to the Treasury, who is the Chief Government Whip, and the Financial Secretary to the Treasury. From 1964 to 1969 another senior Cabinet Minister, the Secretary of State for Economic Affairs, was generally reponsible for economic and industrial development, but this office was abolished in the government reorganization which took place in October, 1969. In broad terms the Chancellor's duties today embrace the control of national revenue and expenditure, long-range planning of public expenditure in relation to the growth of national resources, the development of international co-operation in economic and financial matters, investment and the problems of the nationalized industries, and the general co-ordination of economic policy in conjunction with other Ministers concerned with Economic Affairs.

There remains very little of the judicial power formerly possessed by the Chancellor. He sat with the Barons of the Exchequer when that Court sat as a Court of Equity, but this jurisdiction was taken away in 1841, and in 1873 the Judicative Act excluded the Chancellor from judicial powers in the High Court or Court of Appeal. But in the appointment of Sheriffs, which takes place at the High Court of Justice on 12 November each year, the Chancellor takes his old place as though in the old Exchequer of account among the judges and Great Officers of State. The salary of the Chancellor is £8,500, and like all other ministers in the House of Commons he draws £1,250 of his parliamentary salary. He has an official residence at 11 Downing Street.

A chronological list of Chancellors of the Exchequer appears as Appendix 16.

CHANDLER, RICHARD (d. 1744)

The compiler of an extensive collection of House of Commons debates which was published in 1742–4 under the title, *The History and Proceedings of the House of Commons from the Restoration to the present time, containing the most remarkable motions, speeches, resolves, reports, and conferences to be met with in that interval.* It ran to fourteen volumes. A companion work, entitled *The History and Proceedings of the House of Lords from the Restoration in 1660 to the Present Time,* was published in eight volumes by Ebenezer Timberland in 1742–3. This latter work is sometimes erroneously ascribed to Chandler. According to the *Dictionary of National Biography,* its publication was accompanied by an announcement from Timberland to the effect that the good reception which Chandler's work had enjoyed had induced him (Timberland) to publish the debates of the House of Lords during the same period.

The Debates of Chandler and Timberland form one of the sources from which Cobbett and Wright compiled the Parliamentary History (q.v.).

CHANNEL ISLANDS LEGISLATURES

The structure of the Channel Islands' government is based on that of feudal Normandy, of which Duchy they were once part, and their legislatures owe very little to Westminster. The islands in fact are not part of the United Kingdom, but occupy a political status in the Commonwealth somewhere between a fully self-governing member and a Crown Colony, and are quite independent in all matters of domestic policy. The Queen is still regarded in the Channel Islands as the Duchess of Normandy. The feudal atmosphere continued for many years, and until very recently only a privileged few were eligible for election to the legislatures. In Jersey and Guernsey these are called the Assembly of the States, and are presided over by their respective Bailiffs, who are appointed by the Crown. The two Lieutenant-Governors are the personal representatives of the Sovereign, and are the channel of communication between the U.K. Government and the island legislatures—there is a Standing Committee of the Privy Council which deals particularly with Channel Islands affairs. The Lieutenant Governors summon the States and have powers, subject to the U.K. Home Secretary and Secretary of State for Defence, in relation to the preservation of peace and defence. The right of the U.K. Parliament or the Queen in Council to legislate for the Channel Islands is denied by the Islanders, and although there can be no real doubt of the legislative competency of Parliament, the efficacy of legislation by prerogative Orders in Council is uncertain. In practice the consent of the States is obtained, and the statute or order is given legal effect by registration in the local Royal Court. As the result of the Report of the Committee of the Privy Council on Proposed Reforms in the Channel Islands (Cmd. 7074), which reforms were adopted in 1948, the States of Jersey now consists of the Bailiff as President, 12 Senators (elected for nine years, 4 retiring every third year), 12 Constables (triennial), and 28 Deputies (triennial). All these are elected on a universal adult suffrage. The Dean of Jersey, the Attorney-General, and the Solicitor-General also have seats, but no votes. Permanent legislation, but not certain temporary laws, requires the assent of the Queen in Council, and if the Lieutenant-Governor vetoes, or the Bailiff dissents from, proposed legislation it is suspended for the consideration of the Queen in Council. The Guernsey Legislative Assembly (the States of Deliberation), whose Constitution was amended at the same time, comprises the Bailiff as President, 12 Conseillers, 33 People's Deputies, 10 Douzaine (parish council) representatives, and 2 Alderney representatives. The Lieutenant-Governor and the law officers also have seats, and may speak but not vote. The Conseillers are elected by the States of Election, which consists of the Conseillers, the Jurats (magistrates who themselves are elected by the States of Election), the Rectors, the Crown officers, the People's Deputies, 34 Douzaine representatives, and, for the election of Conseillers only, 4 Alderney representatives. Most proposed laws are initiated by the various States Committees, the presidents of which are in fact ministers. There is a special provision for certain Acts of the U.K. to be registered and adopted when they are of mutual interest, such as the Copyright Act and the Civil Aviation Act.

Procedure in Jersey was laid down by the Code of 1771, and Bills (or *Projets de Loi*) are lodged *au Greffe* (the *Greffier* is the Clerk and the *Greffe* the Clerk's office) for fourteen days after presentation, during which time they are printed and circulated to members. The formal first reading follows, and the Bill is discussed in detail on second reading and any amendments proposed. If they are accepted, the Bill is lodged for a further fourteen days before the third reading, when it is passed or rejected as amended. When there are no amendments a Bill may pass its second and third readings on the same day. Bills which have become Acts of the States go to the Lieutenant-Governor for the Royal Assent and become law on registration by the Royal Court which, although administering justice, still retains this vestige of its former legislative powers. The States were originally an advisory body to the Royal Court, and in Guernsey all legislation is theoretically derived from it.

Although Alderney has its States—a President and 9 elected members—it has become since 1949 even more a subsidiary of Guernsey, to whose States it sends 2 representatives. The Sark Legislature is the Court of Chief Pleas, consisting of the Seneschal as President, 40 Tenants, and 12 Deputies elected by the remainder of the Islanders. Laws passed by the Guernsey States can be applied to Sark after ratification by the Chief Pleas.

CHAPLAIN TO THE SPEAKER
See SPEAKER'S CHAPLAIN.

CHARGES UPON THE PEOPLE
See WAYS AND MEANS.

CHARITY COMMISSIONERS

Until 1960, when the Charity Commission was reconstituted by the Charities Act passed in that year, one of the Charity Commissioners was a member of the House of Commons appointed in the same way as a minister by the government of the day. He was a member of the Board of Commissioners established under the Charitable Trusts Act, 1853, which had the responsibility of regulating the condition and management of charities in England and Wales. He was answerable to Parliament for the activities of the Charity Commissioners and, like a minister, he answered questions in the House on any matter which fell within their province. He was unpaid in order to avoid disqualification from membership of the House of Commons on the ground of holding an office of profit under the Crown.

In 1950 a committee was appointed under the chairmanship of Lord Nathan to investigate and make recommendations with regard to the law relating to charitable trusts. The committee reported in 1952, and in 1955 the Government published a white paper setting out its policy with regard to charitable trusts, accepting the general principles embodied in the recommendations of the Nathan Committee. A new Charities Act became law in 1960, providing *inter alia* for the reconstitution of the Charity Commission, none of whose members being Members of Parliament. The object of the Act is to preserve the independence of the Charity Commissioners while recognizing the need for adequate ministerial control over services which are supported by public funds. The Act makes the Home Secretary responsible for the appointment and removal of the Commissioners and answerable to Parliament for their work and for public expenditure incurred in support of charities. He receives an annual report from the Commissioners which is laid before Parliament, makes regulations in terms of the Act where necessary, and is responsible for Bills relating to individual charities which had previously been piloted through the House by the Parliamentary Charity Commissioner.

The last Member of Parliament to hold office as a Charity Commissioner was Sir Hugh Linstead.

CHARLES I (1600–1649) AND PARLIAMENT

Charles I succeeded to the throne on 27 March 1625, and was at variance with Parliament from the outset of his reign. Like his father, James I, he was a firm believer in absolute sovereignty and equally unsympathetic to the claims and aspirations of the Commons. It was inevitable, therefore, that the great constitutional conflict between Crown and Parliament should continue unabated throughout his reign, and develop into an issue upon which there could be no compromise. During the years Charles occupied the throne the struggle went far beyond the traditional dispute between the King asserting his prerogative and Parliament its privileges and resolved itself into the momentous issue of absolutism as opposed to popular government, or tyranny versus liberty. The fatal climax which brought the King to the scaffold was due as much to Charles's unfortunate character as to any other factor. Although a man of culture and personal virtue, his failings could only spell disaster to one on whom destiny had thrust the rôle of a King. He preferred intrigue to honest negotiation and regarded subterfuge as the natural solution to any problem. He would give any promise in order to gain his own ends and subsequently break it as lightly as he had made it. He lacked shrewdness, perception, and imagination. A dogmatic advocate of the Divine Right of Kings, he could not believe that an opposing view could be sincerely held. He constantly repeated his errors and could never learn from experience. Such a man on the Throne of England at such a time in the nation's history was inevitably ill-fated.

Charles's breach with Parliament originated before he had even ascended the throne. On 9 April 1624, he had made a solemn promise in the presence of the Commons to the effect that no concessions would be granted to British Catholics in the event of his marrying a Catholic. A few months later he violated this undertaking by agreeing to a secret clause in his marriage treaty with Henrietta Maria guaranteeing protection to Catholics at home, a guarantee he was later to repudiate in order to appease his first Parliament. Parliament thus had cause to mistrust the King from the very beginning.

Charles summoned his first Parliament on 18 June 1625. It was a Parliament grimly resolved to abolish the abuses of the prerogative and to use for the purpose its one effective weapon, the power to withhold Supply. Consequently, although the King made it clear that he required substantial grants in order to prosecute a war with Spain,

D*

[95]

the subsidies voted by the Commons were extremely meagre; moreover they took the bold step of granting to the King for only one year instead of for life the proceeds from the taxes known as tonnage and poundage, thus departing from the precedent of two centuries. The King was much taken aback, and when Parliament next met he was further incensed by the Commons, who proceeded to make known their distrust of his favourite counsellor, Buckingham, and demanded the replacement of this minister. The King replied by dissolving Parliament on 12 August.

Having failed to raise the money he required by other means, the King was forced to call his second Parliament on 6 February 1626. The Commons immediately asserted their right to question the conduct of Buckingham, but the King insisted that his executive government was not subject to parliamentary control and arrogantly informed the Commons that he would not tolerate their interference in the appointment of his ministers. He also claimed that the summoning and dissolving of Parliaments lay within his discretion and that they would remain or depart according to whether he liked or disliked their works. The reply of the Commons was to impeach the King's favourite. Furious at having his will disregarded, Charles impulsively ordered the arrest of Sir John Eliot and Sir Dudley Digges, two of the managers of the indictment, but was compelled to release them upon the Commons resolving 'not to do any more business until they are righted in their privileges'. At the same time Charles violated the privileges of the House of Lords, firstly by imprisoning the Earl of Arundel for an offence concerning the marriage of his son, and secondly by refusing a writ of summons to the Earl of Bristol, who had brought charges against Buckingham. In the face of the Lords' protests Charles was forced to yield to the upper House also, and to evade his difficulties and to save Buckingham he dissolved Parliament on 15 June. He refused a request by the Lords for a longer sitting, and on the Commons preparing a remonstrance in vindication of their proceedings he ordered the document to be burned.

Driven by his necessities, the King now resorted to illegal means to obtain money. He determined upon a forced loan, rich and poor alike being required to contribute to it. This tyrannical imposition was vigorously resisted, and amongst those who were imprisoned for refusing to subscribe were John Hampden and Sir Thomas Wentworth, who was later to become the Earl of Strafford and desert the popular cause for that of the King. A great constitutional issue was raised as a result of these arbitrary imprisonments when five gentlemen sought redress in the Court of King's Bench on the ground that their commitment was a violation of Magna Carta. Judgment was given for the Crown, but when the next Parliament was summoned the Commons were not to let the matter rest. Having failed to raise sufficient funds by his oppressive measures and the urgency of his situation being aggravated by a war with France, Charles called his third Parliament on 17 March 1628. The Commons immediately proceeded to pass resolutions complaining of their grievances, foremost amongst which were the matters of arbitrary imprisonment and taxation without the consent of Parliament. It was in this Parliament that Wentworth emerged as a leader and it was under his guidance that a Bill was brought in to secure the liberties of the subject. The King was unwilling to make any concessions on the matter of imprisonment, and on Wentworth's Bill being dropped the Commons drew up the famous Petition of Right (q.v.), which has been described as the greatest statutory vindication of the liberties of the subject since Magna Carta. It went further than Wentworth's Bill, for in addition to prohibiting unparliamentary taxation and imprisonment without warrant, it forbade the enforcement of martial law and the compulsory billeting of soldiers during peacetime. Sir Edward Coke proposed that the Lords should be asked to support the Commons, and the Petition of Right was agreed to by both Houses. Realizing the strength of the opposition ranged against him and being desperately in need of money, Charles, after a characteristic attempt at evasion, assented to this great statute, and the Commons voted him his subsidies.

Serious disputes remained outstanding between the King and Parliament, however. The matter of tonnage and poundage continued to be a contentious problem, for the King had been receiving the proceeds from these taxes without parliamentary sanction, and the Commons were determined to maintain parliamentary control over this grant. They proposed to continue the practice of granting tonnage and poundage for one year at a time, and on the King rejecting the proposal they reminded him that to receive the proceeds from any taxes without the consent of Parliament was contrary to the Petition of Right. The King protested that to take away the benefits derived from tonnage and poundage was to remove the Crown's chief source of income, and on 26 June he prorogued Parliament. Parliament met again on 20 January the following year under circumstances aggravated by a serious religious problem. There had arisen in opposition to the Puritans an Anglo-Catholic faction known as the Arminians, who were regarded by many as papists in disguise and consequently as traitors. They aimed to alter the established form of worship and introduce ceremonial into the churches, and with the active support of the King and under the leadership of William Laud, who eventually became Archbishop of Canterbury, their influence was steadily increasing. In 1628 the Commons, who were predominantly Puritan, had protested against Laud's influence, had called for the absolute suppression of Arminian teaching, and had adopted a resolution expressing their adherence to the articles of religion established under Elizabeth. Furthermore, Arminian

[97]

doctrine was repugnant to the Commons on political as well as religious grounds since it favoured the principle of absolute sovereignty. Completely disregarding their feelings in the matter, Charles created Laud Bishop of London. The circumstances under which Parliament reassembled in 1629 were thus far from favourable to the possibility of conciliation between the King and the Commons. The King's religious policy was obviously not calculated to induce the Commons to come to terms with him on the matter of tonnage and poundage, and these disputes came to a head on 2 March 1629, when an extraordinary incident took place in the House of Commons. The House having assembled, the Speaker, Sir John Finch, announced that it was the King's wish that the House should adjourn and proceeded to put the question to that effect. There were cries of 'No!' from the members and Sir John Eliot rose to speak. Finch informed the House that he had been commanded by the King to leave the Chair should anyone attempt to speak and he rose accordingly. Tumult followed, and several members rushed forward and forcibly held the Speaker down in the Chair, Holles declaring that he should sit there until it pleased them, the Commons, to adjourn. Eliot then spoke, asserted the right of the House to adjourn itself, and tendered a protestation which he demanded should be put to the vote. The Speaker, abject and in tears, refused to obey any but the King's commands. Meanwhile the King, who was growing impatient, sent for the Serjeant-at-Arms to bring away the Mace. The Commons permitted the Serjeant to depart but refused to relinquish the Mace, without which the House could not be constituted. The Gentleman Usher of the Black Rod was then heard knocking at the door, but the House refused to admit him. In the midst of the uproar, Holles proceeded to deliver Eliot's protestation from memory, which according to the Parliamentary History (q.v.) ran as follows:

Whosoever shall bring in innovation in religion, or by favour seek to extend or introduce popery or Arminianism, or other opinions disagreeing from the true and orthodox Church, shall be reputed a capital enemy to this kingdom and the commonwealth.

Whosoever shall counsel or advise the taking and levying of the subsidies of tonnage and poundage, not being granted by Parliament, or shall be an actor or an instrument therein, shall be likewise reputed an innovator in the government and a capital enemy to this kingdom and commonwealth.

If any merchant or other person whatsoever shall voluntarily yield or pay the said subsidies of tonnage and poundage not being granted by Parliament, he shall likewise be reputed a betrayer of the liberty of England and an enemy to the same.

Holles himself put the resolutions to the vote, the Speaker maintaining his refusal to fulfil his functions. They were carried by the House, which then voted its own adjournment.

On 10 March the King formally dissolved Parliament. He issued a declaration justifying his conduct in which he claimed that precedent entitled him to levy tonnage and poundage on his own authority, and alleged that the Commons had turned the matter into a pretext for their behaviour. He then turned his vengeance upon the leaders of the popular cause, and Eliot, Selden, Holles, Strode, and Valentine, amongst others, were committed to prison. Wentworth had by this time forsaken Parliament for the Crown and had become one of the King's ministers, Buckingham having been assassinated during the parliamentary recess. Various charges were framed against the prisoners, for even Charles felt it necessary to show some cause for their arrest so soon after consenting to the Petition of Right, but when brought to trial most of them pleaded parliamentary privilege and declined to return any other answer to the charges. The judges upheld the Crown and condemned them to imprisonment during the King's pleasure. Holles was released upon making submission, but Eliot remained in prison until his death in 1631, Selden was not released until 1633, and Strode and Valentine remained incarcerated until 1640. It was not until 1667 that these judgments were formally reversed by resolutions agreed to in both Houses of Parliament.

Having made known his absolute power in the calling and dissolving of Parliaments, Charles determined to govern without them, and for the next eleven years, the longest such period in English history, he did so. To raise money he again resorted to illegal methods. He enforced the payment of tonnage and poundage, introduced compulsory knighthoods, revived monopolies and the ancient forest laws, and exacted ship-money. Amongst those who resisted the latter tax was John Hampden, judgment being given against him but later reversed by the Long Parliament (q.v.). During this period also the people were further antagonized by the savage sentences inflicted by the Court of Star Chamber upon Puritans whose religious writings had given offence, and by the King's ecclesiastical policy generally as exemplified by the hated Laud, who in 1633 was promoted to the see of Canterbury. Their attempt to extend this policy to Scotland enflamed the resentment of the northern kingdom to an even greater extent. The final straw was an attempt to impose a new liturgy upon the churches of Scotland, an unwarrantable interference in the established form of worship which led, first, to the adoption of the National Covenant which pledged its signatories to resist this incursion to the death, and eventually, in 1639, to war. In the meantime Ireland was suffering under the oppressive administration of Strafford.

Although he was rigidly enforcing his exactions, lack of money remained the King's most pressing problem. He therefore decided to call a Parliament and seek the means to wage an effective war with Scotland. On 13 April 1640, Charles's fourth Parliament, the Short Parliament (q.v.), was opened. The Commons, however, were in sympathy with the Scots, and not only refused to grant Supply before their grievances were redressed but called for an end to the war with Scotland. On 5 May, to the exasperation of the Commons, Charles dissolved the Short Parliament and proceeded with the war, relying upon illegal exactions and some grants which Strafford had wrung from the Irish Parliament. These resources were soon exhausted and on 24 September Charles summoned together a Great Council of Peers at York to which he appealed for support. The Lords declined their assistance, and the King was left with no alternative but to call another Parliament.

Charles's fifth Parliament, that historic assembly which has become known as the Long Parliament, met on 3 November 1640. The King was disposed to be conciliatory, but he had gone too far and the Commons were beyond being pacified and were bent upon the removal of their grievances. A number of reforms were immediately introduced which the King was unable to resist. The Triennial Bill provided that the interval between Parliaments should never exceed three years; another Bill required the consent of Parliament to a dissolution, thus placing an effective, if unconstitutional, check upon the Royal Prerogative; the levying of ship-money and all other irregular means of raising money were declared illegal; the right of the Commons to impose taxation and appropriate supply was reasserted, and the payment of tonnage and poundage and all other duties was declared illegal without the consent of Parliament; the Star Chamber and other special courts with arbitrary powers were abolished. Concurrently with these measures, the Commons inquired into the conduct of Strafford in Ireland. He was first impeached, then, on the suggestion of Pym, proceeded against by way of a Bill of Attainder, the main charge against him alleging his intention to bring over an Irish army in order to crush the people of England. The Bill was passed in the Commons by 204 votes to 59, and was eventually agreed to in the Lords by the small majority of 26 votes against 19. The King had promised Strafford that Parliament should harm not a hair of his head but fearing that the mob which was demonstrating in Whitehall would imperil the life of the Queen, he reluctantly assented to the Bill and signed his minister's death-warrant. The impeachment of Laud quickly followed that of Strafford, and the Archbishop lay in prison until he was proceeded against in December 1644, and executed the following month.

The King was thus considerably divested of his arbitrary power, and a more reasonable man would probably have submitted to the restraints imposed upon him by the will of an almost unanimous people. Charles, however, his hatred of the parliamentary leaders enflamed by the execution of Strafford, accepted the limitations upon his authority with mental reservations and thought only of seeking a means of recovering his position. It was on the question of church administration that he recognized an opportunity of rallying adherents to his cause. An acute religious issue had developed within the Commons and parties had begun to form on either side. The Puritan majority favoured the total abolition of episcopacy, whilst the opposite group, although opposed to the doctrines of Laud, advocated moderate church reform and the retention of the bishops. The division between the two factions was not slow to widen and the minority formed themselves into a constitutional Royalist party. They were strongly supported in the House of Lords, where the reformers were headed by Bishop Williams, and Charles saw that his best hope of regaining his lost authority lay through an alliance with this movement. In the Commons a Bill to abolish episcopacy 'root and branch' passed its second reading but was dropped in committee. It was followed by a Bill to exclude the bishops from the House of Lords, which passed the Commons but was rejected by the upper House. In the meantime Charles went to Scotland hoping to gain the support of the Presbyterians whom he had so recently offended. His mission was attended with signal failure, and he became suspected of being involved in a plot, known as 'The Incident', to seize the Scottish opposition leaders. Shortly afterwards he was suspected of attempting to win over the Irish Catholics with a promise of freedom for their religion. The Irish, however, so recently the victims of Strafford's tyranny, saw their opportunity to shake off a hated foreign rule while Britain was torn by internal strife, and chose to rebel rather than trust the King. The rising was terrible in its magnitude and was only finally suppressed by Cromwell nine years later.

These events made the Commons more distrustful of the King than ever and gave rise to the Grand Remonstrance (q.v.). This document commenced with a recital of the King's misdeeds and the state of the nation, and continued with a statement of the reforms which had been effected by Parliament and those which were still required. It was vigorously opposed by the Royalist leaders in the Commons, but was eventually passed by the small majority of 159 votes against 148. Another division was taken on a motion that the remonstrance should be printed and was carried, having previously been defeated, by 135 votes to 83. The effect of the resolution was to turn the remonstrance into a direct appeal to the nation, a decision which hopelessly widened the breach between the King and Parliament and made Charles fearful of the lengths to which the Commons were prepared to go. It was rumoured that the leaders of the majority were preparing to impeach the Queen, whose intrigues on behalf of Catholics and whose influence over the King were well-known, and Charles decided to forestall his adversaries. He ordered the arrest of five of the most powerful leaders of the majority in the Commons, Pym, Hampden, Holles, Haselrig, and Strode, and one peer, Lord Mandeville, who had identified himself with their cause. They were charged on seven treasonable counts, including the subversion of the government and laws of England, incitement to riots, and even with the actual levying of war against the King. On 3 January the Attorney-General laid the charges before the Lords, who appointed a committee to inquire into the matter. In the Commons, meanwhile, Pym made it known that his study and chamber and those of Hampden and Holles had been sealed by command of the King, which the House declared to be a breach of both law and privilege. Whilst the Commons were thus deliberating, the King's Serjeant-at-Arms arrived with orders to arrest the five members. The House returned a deputation to the King stating that the demand concerned their privileges and an answer would be given as speedily as so important a matter would allow. The Speaker commanded the five members to remain in daily attendance and gave orders that the seals in their houses should be broken.

On the following day, 4 January 1642, Charles made a characteristically foolish and impulsive decision. He resolved to go in person to the House of Commons, attended by an armed escort, and seize the five members where they sat. News of the King's intention reached the Commons, however, and the five members were given leave to absent themselves. Arriving at Westminster Hall, Charles signed to his followers to remain in the hall and in the lobby, and entered the Commons Chamber alone, the first Sovereign ever to cross the Bar of the House of Commons, and the last. Tense silence greeted his entry as Speaker Lenthall stepped down from his Chair to meet the King. 'By your leave, Mr. Speaker, I must borrow your Chair a little,' were the King's first words. He then apologized for his visit, assured the Commons that he had no intention of violating their privileges, but reminded them that persons guilty of treason had no privileges. He then called on Pym and Holles by name, but receiving no reply he turned to the Speaker and asked him if any of the five members were present. Falling upon his knees, Lenthall delivered his historic reply: 'May it please Your Majesty, I have neither eyes to see, nor tongue to speak in this place, but as the House is pleased to direct me, whose servant I am here; and I humbly beg Your Majesty's pardon that I cannot give any other answer than this to what Your Majesty is pleased to demand of me.' For a moment the King was nonplussed, but maintaining his dignity he rejoined: 'Well, I see all the birds are flown. I do expect from you that you shall send them unto me as soon as they return hither. If not, I will seek them myself, for their treason is foul and such as you will thank me to discover.' The King left the Chamber pursued by cries of 'Privilege, privilege!'

4 January 1642 was a momentous day in the annals of parliamentary history. In forcing his way into the Commons Chamber, Charles

was unquestionably guilty of an outrageous breach of privilege, and through the mouth of their Speaker the Commons had successfully upheld their rights. Furthermore, in attempting to prosecute commoners before the Lords otherwise than on the impeachment of the House of Commons, the King's conduct was unparalleled in that it violated the traditional law which entitled every man to be tried by his peers. The Commons were not slow to make known their views on the matter. They are amply stated in the entry in the Journal for the following day, which also records the measures which were taken to guard against a recurrence of the outrage.

All hope of conciliation between the King and Parliament was now extinguished and the Civil War soon followed. Early in March, both Houses of Parliament concurred in a resolution that the state should begin defence preparations. The King issued a counter declaration, to which Parliament replied on 17 March with the resolution 'that when the Lords and Commons in Parliament, which is the Supreme Court of Judicature in the kingdom, declare what the law of the land is, to have this not only questioned and controverted, but contradicted, and a command given that it shall not be obeyed, is a high breach of privilege'. This was the point of the final rupture, although it was five months before hostilities actually broke out. In the meantime both sides manœuvred for military advantages and public support, and on 2 June Parliament issued its final demands embodied in the famous Nineteen Propositions (q.v.). There was no possibility of the King accepting them, and on 22 August he raised his standard at Nottingham and the Civil War began. On 14 June 1645, the Cavaliers were decisively beaten by Cromwell's forces at Naseby and a parliamentary victory was assured. Meanwhile the Solemn League and Covenant had been concluded, uniting England and Scotland in a common cause and in favour of the reformed religion. The King surrendered to the Scots, who delivered him to the English Parliament.

By this time dissension had developed within the Commons between the Presbyterians and the Congregationalists or Independents, and Charles hoped to turn their quarrel to his own advantage. The Presbyterians did not support the total abolition of the monarchy and in Cromwell and the Independents they recognized dangerous opponents. Although the Presbyterians held the majority in Parliament, the Independents controlled the army, and the former realized that if the power of Cromwell and his followers was to be reduced it would be necessary to disband the army. The army, however, seized the initiative and brought the King to London, where they assumed command. They proceeded to intimidate Parliament and establish military authority. Charles, pursuing his favourite policy of intrigue, negotiated with both parties independently, and undeterred by the discovery of the notorious Glamorgan Treaty he continued to correspond secretly with the Irish Catholics. Exasperated by his duplicity, Parliament and the army were induced to come to terms and they agreed on new proposals. The extreme republicans in Cromwell's party would not hear of any agreement with the King who, fearing for his safety, fled to the Isle of Wight. From here he offered fresh proposals to Parliament containing a number of concessions, but Parliament had lost patience. The Commons embodied their own proposals in four Bills which demanded the complete sovereignty of Parliament, including permanent control of the army. Charles rejected the Bills and, as far as Cromwell's party were concerned, lost his last chance.

On 3 January 1648, the House of Commons resolved to discontinue all negotiation with the King. The Scots were disturbed by the trend of events, however, and concluded a secret treaty with the King, a development which led to the second Civil War in which Cromwell marched north and decisively defeated the Scottish Presbyterians. During Cromwell's absence in the north, the English Presbyterians reopened negotiations with Charles which led to an alliance known as the Treaty of Newport. But the army, now in complete command of the situation, refused to consider any agreement. They were determined to bring the King to trial, but they realized that if the consent of the House of Commons was to be secured it would be necessary to exclude the Presbyterians from Parliament. This exclusion was accomplished on 6 December 1648, by the unconstitutional proceeding known as Pride's Purge (q.v.), when all members who favoured coming to terms with the King were forcibly prevented from entering the House. Henceforth the King was doomed. All former votes in favour of a treaty were annulled, and on 2 January 1649 a House of Commons unanimously hostile to the King resolved 'that by the fundamental laws of this kingdom, it is treason in the King of England, for the time being, to levy war against the Parliament and Kingdom of England'. Simultaneously they brought in a Bill constituting a High Court of Justice for the purpose of trying and judging Charles Stuart, King of England. Both resolution and Bill were rejected by the Lords, and on 4 January the House of Commons resolved 'that the Commons of England, in Parliament assembled, do declare that the people are, under God, the original of all just power. And do also declare, that the Commons of England, in Parliament assembled, being chosen by, and representing the people, have the supreme power in this nation. And do also declare, that whatsoever is enacted, or declared for law by the Commons, in Parliament assembled, hath the force of a law, and all the people of this nation are concluded thereby, although the consent and concurrence of King, or House of Peers, be not had thereunto'. A Bill constituting themselves a High Court of Justice was also passed.

The court as finally constituted consisted of 135 commissioners and John Bradshaw was appointed president of the tribunal. The trial commenced in Westminster Hall on 20 January. The King refused to recognize the court as a lawful authority and claimed the prerogative of Divine Right. The Commons for their part claimed that they sat in the name of the people of England. Thus in the final act of the drama the fundamental issue of sovereignty was argued with the same lack of compromise which had dogged the long struggle throughout, but this time the King was powerless. On 27 January the tribunal found him guilty of treason and sentenced him to death. On the 29th the warrant for his execution was signed by 59 of his accusers, and on the 30th the final tragedy was enacted.

There can be no question that Charles was tried and condemned illegally by a minority of the House of Commons representing his bitterest foes. The justice of the verdict and sentence is also questionable on the ground that the King could hardly have committed the offences with which he was charged without the approval and assistance of a large part of the nation. The King might also be defended on the ground that he held his opinions sincerely and acted in accordance with his firm convictions. There is no doubt that his execution profoundly shocked the majority of his subjects. But on the great constitutional issue involved there can be no doubt that Parliament was in the right. By its very nature and consequences the struggle was of vital concern not only to those who waged it but to generations then unborn, and its outcome established the sovereignty of Parliament for all time. The doctrine of Divine Right and the tyranny which it engendered were shattered for ever, and the popular will was asserted so conclusively that it could never again be effectively challenged.

CHARLES II (1630–1685) AND PARLIAMENT

The Convention Parliament (q.v.) which restored Charles Stuart to the throne met on 25 April 1660. The Lords assembled as of right and passed a resolution declaring that the government should consist of King, Lords and Commons in accordance with the ancient constitution of the realm. The Convention Parliament received from Charles the famous Declaration of Breda which embodied the proposals which had been put forward by General Monk. It conferred a free pardon upon all who had committed political offences since the Civil War save those whom Parliament should except, and guaranteed religious toleration and the holding of free Parliaments. Measures were taken for the immediate return and proclamation of the King, and Charles received a deputation of twelve peers and six commoners at The Hague, the spokesman for the Commons being Denzil Holles, one of the five members whom his father had attempted to impeach for treason in 1641. Charles landed in England on 25 May and entered London in triumph on the 29th. He recognized the Convention Parliament as a legally constituted authority and it proceeded to business requiring immediate attention. A Bill of Indemnity was introduced to exonerate, with certain exceptions, all those who had committed acts directed against the monarchy. It was a measure which provoked heated debates in both Houses, but a compromise was eventually agreed on, Vane and Lambert being amongst those who were excepted from the Bill. A number of regicides were condemned to death, and the bodies of Cromwell and others were exhumed and shamefully maltreated. The restitution of land next engaged the attention of Parliament and proved to be a question difficult of solution, causing dissatisfaction throughout the country. On the matter of revenue the Commons made no secret of their determination to maintain control of the purse-strings, but they voted the King an annual income of £1,200,000 to cover the ordinary expenses of government, together with an excise and tonnage and poundage, those taxes which had proved such a bone of contention between Charles I and his Parliaments, for life. This provision would have been reasonably generous had the sources of revenue been adequate to meet the amount granted, but as it was the King suffered financial embarrassment until his marriage to Catherine of Braganza in 1662 brought him certain monetary and other advantages.

Although the Convention Parliament restored the monarchy it by no means made itself the tool of the King. It introduced a number of popular reforms and set definite limits upon the King's prerogative. It also disbanded the army, although it left the King with the Guards regiments from which the present regular army ultimately developed. Parliament next turned its attention to the religious difficulties which existed, but Charles dissolved it before it could reach any decisions. Although he did not reveal his own views at this stage they were diametrically opposed to those of the Presbyterians who formed quite a strong group in the Convention Parliament, and Charles dissolved it in the hope of finding its successor more amenable to his wishes.

Charles's next Parliament, which has been variously called the Cavalier Parliament (q.v.), the Pensionary Parliament, and the Long Parliament of the Restoration, met on 8 May 1661, and sat through seventeen sessions until its final dissolution on 30 December 1678. It began as a subservient instrument of the King's will but by the time its long life was terminated it had reasserted the popular cause in the highest parliamentary tradition. The Cavaliers were predominant in the Commons, the Presbyterians having been returned in greatly reduced numbers. It immediately proceeded to take strongly Royalist measures and reversed much of the legislation of the Long Parliament. The person of the King was not only secured from hostile action but was even placed beyond criticism and the supreme military authority was vested in the Crown. The bishops were restored to the House of Lords and it was declared that no legislative power could exist in both or either House of Parliament without the King. Parliament also embarked on a programme of repressive legislation aimed against the Presbyterians and Nonconformists. Its first deed of the session was to pass a resolution compelling all its members to receive the Sacrament according to Anglican ritual, and a few days later the Solemn League and Covenant was ordered to be burned. The Corporation Act disqualified magistrates and civic officials from continuing in office unless they accepted the Anglican form of worship, and in subsequent sessions further such legislation was introduced, including the Act of Uniformity in 1662, under which many of the clergy were driven from the Church, and the Conventicle Act in 1664 which was designed to oppress the nonconforming clergy still further. The Act of Indemnity was honoured, however, although Sir Henry Vane, who had been excepted from the Act, was executed in spite of a promise that he should not suffer death.

Shortly after coming to the throne Charles began to seek for means to relieve his Roman Catholic subjects from their disabilities, for he was strongly sympathetic towards them although he insisted he was no papist himself. But on this question Parliament was staunchly opposed to him, and when in 1663 the King urged upon Parliament the acceptance of a Declaration of Indulgence in favour of the Catholic religion the proposals were rejected by both Houses. The Lord Chancellor, Clarendon, although an ardent upholder of the prerogative power, failed to support the King on this occasion, and the bishops in the House of Lords were unanimously opposed to any such concession. As a result of the stand he adopted on this matter Clarendon incurred the enmity of the Roman Catholics in the House of Lords, one of whom, the Earl of Bristol, attempted unsuccessfully to impeach him. Although he enjoyed the support of the Queen, strong forces, which were eventually to bring about his downfall, were working against this minister. His oppressive religious policy had already earned him the hatred of the Nonconformists, and his objection to the vices of a corrupt and immoral Court, as well as incurring the displeasure of the King, had made for him a powerful foe in the person of Lady Castlemaine, one of Charles's innumerable mistresses. His foreign policy, which was to lead to the costly and unpopular war with Holland, eventually led him into further difficulties until his position became untenable.

It was inevitable that a popular reaction should arise against the tyranny of the administration. Religious persecution had become intolerable, objectionable taxes pressed heavily upon the people, the Court was notorious for its profligacy, and the popular feeling opposed the Dutch war. To add to the burdens of the people at this time, London was ravaged first by the plague and afterwards by the Great

Fire. An opposition party gradually arose in the House of Commons and steadily gathered strength until it became a force to be reckoned with. In the session of 1665–6 a further great principle was established as a result of a proviso inserted in a Supply Bill—the right of the Commons to appropriate supplies to the purposes approved by them. They next asserted their right to examine the public accounts, and a Bill providing for the nomination of independent commissioners to inquire into public expenditure was carried in the lower House. It was violently opposed by Clarendon and did not finally become law until after his downfall, but when the commissioners eventually reported on their investigations they revealed flagrant abuses and misappropriation of public monies to the shame and discredit of the King and his government.

In 1667 the forces which had been steadily mounting against Clarendon brought about his downfall. He was dismissed from office by the King and the House of Commons proceeded to impeach him on a number of charges. He was accused amongst other things of raising a standing army for the purpose of establishing military government and circumventing Parliament, causing persons to be imprisoned beyond the confines of the kingdom in order to place them beyond the benefit of the law, engaging in corrupt transactions, and misleading and betraying the King in regard to his foreign alliances. Clarendon's courage failed him and he fled the country without attempting to answer the charges, with the result that a Bill for his banishment was carried by both Houses. The Commons reasserted through Clarendon's case their constitutional right of impeachment.

After the fall of Clarendon the country was largely governed by the Cabal administration, so called from the initial letters in the names of Clifford, Arlington, Buckingham, Ashley, and Lauderdale, who formed it. The Commons were by this time proving a thorn in the flesh of the King who, in order to ward off their frustration of his designs, resorted to continual prorogation of Parliament. He was anxious to avoid any diminution of his personal power and for this reason was desirous of maintaining a standing army. Parliament had called for the disbanding of the army on the termination of hostilities and the King, quite obviously, could not look to the Commons for the supplies necessary to keep an armed force in existence. He therefore needed to find a means of remaining independent of Parliament, and to this end he entered into a secret treaty with the King of France, promising to advance the Roman Catholic religion in Great Britain and to co-operate with the French in an attack on Holland in return for financial and military assistance. When particulars of this dishonourable agreement leaked out the opposition in the Commons consolidated its ranks and an organized party, the Country Party, came to be formed. It included in its ranks not only Presbyterians, Nonconformists, and Republicans, but Royalists who had become seriously disturbed at the trend of events, and others who, although adhering to the established Church of England, deplored the oppression of the Nonconformists. By 1673 a serious situation had developed. An unnecessary and unjust war had been declared against Holland under Charles's treaty with Louis XIV of France, and a Declaration of Indulgence, ostensibly favouring all non-Anglicans but in reality designed to benefit the Catholics alone, had been issued by proclamation and without parliamentary sanction. This declaration swept away all the penal laws and announced that the supreme power in ecclesiastical matters rested with the King. The Lord Keeper, Sir Orlando Bridgeman, at once resigned his office and was succeeded by Shaftesbury. Parliament met on 4 February, and although the Commons voted supplies for continuing the war with Holland the Declaration of Indulgence was rejected outright. The King thereupon complained to the House of Lords, where a heated debate took place. Shaftesbury, contrary to general expectation, opposed the Indulgence, and the dispute was eventually settled by the King withdrawing it. This incident was followed shortly afterwards by the passing of the Test Act which excluded all Catholics from holding office in the government. This measure effectively broke up the Cabal administration and disqualified the King's brother, the Duke of York, who was an acknowledged Catholic.

When Parliament met for its eleventh session on 20 October 1673, the opposition to the Dutch war and the French alliance, with which was associated the threat of an advance of popery, was seen to be formidable. Charles attempted to deal with his difficult situation in characteristic manner by proroguing Parliament, and during the recess he effected some drastic changes in his ministry. Shaftesbury was dismissed from office and replaced by Sir Heneage Finch, and the Earl of Danby became Lord Treasurer. But Charles's problems were renewed when Parliament assembled again on 7 January 1674. The Commons immediately declared against a continuance of the French alliance and called for further measures against the advance of Catholicism. Anxiety was expressed as to the security of the established Church in the event of the King's death, for he had no legitimate children and the succession would pass, in accordance with the Constitution, to the Duke of York. There had already developed an undercurrent of opinion favouring the exclusion of the Duke and his children from the succession and the declaration of the Prince of Orange, a grandson of Charles I, as the heir to the Throne of England. There was therefore good reason for desiring peace with Holland. A fear of hostile activity on the part of English Catholics was generally prevalent and both Houses of Parliament were united against what was regarded as the common menace. Before Parliament was prorogued again on 24 February, motions for the dismissal of the King's 'evil counsellors', Buckingham, Lauderdale, and Arlington, were introduced into the Commons, thus re-establishing the principle of the responsibility of ministers to Parliament, and a peace treaty was concluded with Holland which was to ensure good relations between the two nations thenceforward. This short session was thus notable for some important parliamentary achievements.

Parliament did not meet again until 13 April 1675. Although the Dutch war was over, the French influence remained strong and Charles was easily induced to prolong the parliamentary adjournment to suit the convenience of the King of France. He was nevertheless anxious to arrive at an agreement with Parliament if this should prove possible without upsetting his plans. The session was a singularly unproductive one, however, as a quarrel arose between the two Houses on a question of privilege and prevented the passage of any legislation. The same session was notable for a scene which took place in the House of Commons over the result of a division taken while the House was in committee, and which was settled by the Speaker solemnly taking the Chair and rebuking the House for its disorderly behaviour. The incident serves to illustrate the eminence and respect with which the Speaker has always been regarded, that by his merely taking the Chair he was able to quell an unruly House. Parliament was prorogued on 9 June and assembled again on 13 October. In his opening speech the King frankly admitted his extravagances and promised to observe greater thrift in the future; but Parliament was opposed to the King's French alliance and took great exception to the influence wielded by Louis XIV in the affairs of Great Britain, with the result that the Commons refused to grant supplies to pay for the late war. They agreed to vote money for the Navy, but with the proviso that the revenue derived from the receipt of customs should be applied to this purpose and to no other, the intention and the effect being to prevent the government waging any war which was not supported by Parliament. During this session the quarrel between the two Houses continued unabated, a fact of which Charles took advantage when he prorogued Parliament again on 22 November. Another long adjournment took place, for which Charles received a handsome bribe from the French King, and the Houses did not meet again until 15 February 1677. Long debates took place in the Commons on the King's foreign policy, and he was advised to renounce his treaty with France and join with Holland in the Grand Alliance. Charles's reaction was to prorogue Parliament yet again on 28 May, a violent scene ensuing when the Speaker announced the King's decision to the Commons. An interesting feature of this session was the passing of a resolution in the lower House to repeal the Act under which Members of Parliament received payment.

When Parliament met again on 15 January 1678, certain developments had changed the situation. The Prince of Orange had married

Mary, the elder daughter of the Duke of York, a match largely brought about by Danby, the Lord Treasurer, and a treaty had been concluded with Holland. This greatly pleased the Commons, who voted supplies in support of the new alliance, but the King had by no means decided to turn his back on France. He had decided it would be expedient to conciliate the opposition but was not prepared to go to the extent of abandoning his own position, which depended for its strength upon the friendship of Louis. The French King was studying the position very closely, and whilst concluding secret agreements with Charles, he simultaneously entered into negotiations with representatives of the popular faction in England, whose object it was to alienate Louis from Charles and thus frustrate the latter's bid for personal power. The intrigues of this period were highly complicated, for the allegiance of an individual to one side or another could be easily bought. The opposition leaders in England were eager for a dissolution of Parliament, believing they would be greatly strengthened by new elections, and such was the influence of the French King that it was to him they turned for the purpose of bringing this about.

Parliament was prorogued on 15 July, and several further adjournments followed before the Cavalier Parliament reassembled for its seventeenth and final session on 21 October. During the interim the country was seized with panic over the 'discovery' of the so-called Popish Plot which had been fabricated by Titus Oates, a charlatan with a deplorable record of conduct who had once taken holy orders. Such was the fear of popery which pervaded the country that the fantastic allegations of Oates and his confederates spread like wildfire and were believed, various circumstances lending credence to their stories. The sensation led directly to the most drastic measures being taken against the Catholics. Many were tried for their complicity in the imagined conspiracy and many innocent victims were judicially murdered. In Parliament a Bill for disabling papists from sitting in either House passed both Houses, although the Commons unexpectedly accepted a proviso inserted by the Lords excepting the Duke of York from its operation. In spite of this the feeling in the country was now stronger than ever in favour of excluding the Duke from the succession. To meet what they regarded as the emergency the Commons resolved to raise a military force which would come under their direct control, but the King rejected the resolution and further incensed the Commons against his brother whom they suspected of interceding with Charles on behalf of his fellow Catholics.

The King found himself faced by insurmountable difficulties which were now further aggravated by the impeachment of his minister Danby. Although an opponent of Catholicism and the French alliance, Danby had angered the Commons by his unconstitutional methods, which favoured the prerogative rather than the popular will, and in their present frame of mind some of their accusations tended to be unreasonable. Surrounded by these problems Charles decided to resolve them by dissolving Parliament, a step he was reluctant to take but which now offered itself as the only solution. On 30 December he prorogued Parliament until 24 January 1679, on which date he declared it to be dissolved.

The elections which followed went decisively against the King, and the Country Party was returned in great strength. When the result became clear, Charles resigned himself to the situation and took certain steps to conciliate the people's representatives. The Duke of York was sent out of the country to Brussels and the adoption of a strong policy against popery was announced; Danby was dismissed from office, and the disbandment of the army was commenced. Charles's third Parliament met for the first time on 6 March 1679, and a dispute immediately arose between the King and the Commons over the appointment of a Speaker. The Commons re-elected Sir Edward Seymour, who had presided over the previous Parliament, but the King rejected him. The Commons refused to accept Charles's nominee and the matter was eventually settled by compromise, Sir William Gregory being appointed to the Chair. The lower House then proceeded at once to the impeachment of Danby, the main charge against him being his complicity in the dishonourable bargains which had been concluded with France. It is true that he had acted under the express instructions of the King, but the Commons rejected this defence as conflicting with the entire principle of ministerial responsibility, a principle which Danby's trial went far towards establishing. The case also endorsed the precedent that impeachments and other proceedings interrupted by a dissolution are not necessarily annulled. The former Lord Treasurer was committed to the Tower where he remained for five years.

This Parliament is notable for the passing of the Habeas Corpus Act, one of the greatest pieces of legislation ever to reach the Statute Book. It secures the individual from arbitrary arrest and imprisonment without trial, and represents that guarantee and protection of personal liberty which characterizes any democratic society. Also during this year, 1679, the first Bill to exclude the Duke of York from the succession was introduced in the House of Commons, but its progress was arrested by the prorogation of Parliament. A dissolution followed on 12 July, Charles faintly hoping that fresh elections might improve his position. But once again they went against him, and the King adopted a policy of procrastination, as a result of which his fourth Parliament was not called together until 21 October 1680. It was during this period that the party names of 'Whig' and 'Tory' first came into use, the Whigs being the Country Party and the Tories the supporters of the Court who opposed the exclusion of the Duke of York. Repeated pressure was put upon the King to summon Parliament, and petitions to this effect were received at the Court in large numbers, emanating from corporations and persons of all classes. The supporters of the King endeavoured to stifle the popular demand by issuing addresses abhorring what they regarded as encroachments on the prerogative. The two factions thus acquired the names of Petitioners and Abhorrers.

When Parliament did eventually meet it showed itself as determined upon the destruction of popery as its predecessor. It also passed important resolutions in justification of the Petitioners, declaring, 'That it is and ever hath been, the undoubted right of the subjects of England to petition the King for the calling and sitting of Parliaments and redressing of grievances.' A second Exclusion Bill was introduced in the lower House, but was rejected in the Lords after a dramatic debate. But the Commons were not to be thus deterred and called upon the King for his assent to the measure in spite of the Lords' rejection. His Majesty refused, and in the face of further determined action by the Commons he first prorogued and later dissolved Parliament on 18 January 1681.

For the third time the elections produced an overwhelming majority in favour of the popular cause. Piqued by the City of London, which had strongly supported the Petitioners, the King decided to hold his next Parliament at Oxford as a mark of the disfavour with which he regarded the capital. He remained adamant in spite of a petition urging him to reverse his decision, and on 21 March 1681, he opened his fifth and last Parliament, the Oxford Parliament. The question of the succession was debated in both Houses, and various expedients were discussed. From the Lords came the suggestion that the Duke of Monmouth should be recognized as Charles's successor, whilst the Commons spent some time in discussing a compromise involving the separation of the Crown from the administration. Eventually it was decided to prepare and introduce another Exclusion Bill, but before the legislation could be proceeded with another quarrel broke out between the two Houses over the matter of an impeachment. On 28 March, before any further business could be undertaken, the King unexpectedly dissolved Parliament in a manner which amounted to a peremptory dismissal. On 8 April he published a declaration reproaching his last three Parliaments for their actions whilst proclaiming his love for the established Church and the institution of Parliament as such. In answer to the King's declaration a Member of the House of Commons, Sir William Jones, wrote a 'Just and modest vindication of the proceedings of the two last Parliaments of King Charles II'.

For the remaining years of his life Charles governed without Parliaments. He was duly rewarded by the King of France for getting rid of the people's representatives, and a campaign against the Whigs was initiated by the supporters of the Court. Shortly afterwards a conspiracy known as the Rye House Plot was uncovered involving a number of distinguished Whigs, of whom Lord Russell and Algernon

Sidney were most unjustly executed for their alleged complicity in the affair. Monmouth was also implicated but was later able to make his peace with the King. The Duke of York, who had returned from Brussels in 1679, was reinstated in the Privy Council, all attempts to exclude him from the succession having failed.

Charles II died suddenly on 6 February 1685. A man of loose principles and many grave faults, his virtues were hardly significant enough to redeem his deplorable conduct throughout his reign. He entirely lacked his father's saving graces, and if he emerges as less of a tyrant than the first Charles it should be borne in mind that the popular cause had registered many historic gains before he came to the throne and he inherited a severely limited prerogative. It is true that in its early days the Cavalier Parliament had tended to be subservient and reversed much of the work of the Long Parliament, but this had proved to be but a temporary reaction. On the whole Parliament had clung tenaciously to its rights and privileges, and in addition the Commons had asserted themselves, usually successfully, against the Lords. In spite of the many unsatisfactory features of the reign Parliament had continued its advance towards the ideal of popular government in the face of a false and unprincipled monarch.

CHARTISTS

A revolutionary working-class organization which was founded in 1838, and whose immediate object was parliamentary reform. Its programme was stated in the so-called 'People's Charter', which was drafted in the form of an Act of Parliament and set forth the famous 'Six Points', namely, adult male suffrage based on a residence qualification only, the abolition of property qualifications for the franchise, voting by ballot, the division of the country into equal electoral districts, the payment of Members of Parliament, and the holding of annual Parliaments. All but the last point have since been secured.

On 4 February 1839, a Convention or 'People's Parliament', representing the disfranchised working classes, was held in London, and resolved to present a petition to the House of Commons demanding the acceptance of its Charter and to call for strike action should the petition be rejected. The petition, to which over one and a quarter million signatures were attached, was rejected, but owing to lack of organization the Convention was unable to put its plans into effect. Shortly afterwards the moderate leadership of the movement was over-ridden by the inflammatory elements and violence and rioting broke out in a number of centres. Most of the ringleaders were arrested and imprisoned, but further agitation broke out upon their release, and nearly three and a half million signatures were collected for a second petition which was presented in 1842. Its rejection was followed by spasmodic strikes and rioting which achieved nothing, and thereafter the movement entered a period of decline. It underwent a temporary revival in 1848, stimulated by other revolutionary movements which flared up on the Continent during that year, but by 1853 it had virtually disappeared.

Chartism was born of the dissatisfaction of the working classes with the Reform Act of 1832, which conferred benefits upon the middle classes only. The great improvement in the lot of the working classes which began with the repeal of the Corn Laws in 1846 and the progressive reforms called for by Lord Shaftesbury contributed largely to the disintegration of the movement.

A history of Chartism was written by Mark Hovell and completed by Professor T. F. Tout (*The Chartist Movement*, 2nd ed., 1950).

CHIEF PLEAS

The Parliament of Sark, one of the Channel Islands. It consists of the Seigneur, the Seneschal, 40 Tenants, and 12 Deputies of the People. The Seneschal is the chief judicial officer of the island, and *ex-officio* President of the Chief Pleas. He is appointed for three years by the Seigneur, whose position is hereditary, with the approval of the Lieutenant-Governor of Guernsey. Sark is subject in certain respects to the authority of the Lieutenant-Governor and the States of Guernsey.

CHIEF SECRETARY TO THE TREASURY

First created in October 1961, this office was first held by Mr. Henry Brooke and coupled with that of Paymaster General (q.v.) until October 1964. The appointment resulted from the greatly increased duties of the Chancellor of the Exchequer (q.v.) and the functions of the Chief Secretary are concerned with the whole range of public expenditure, including scrutiny of departmental estimates and the framing of forward surveys. Although working under the general direction of the Chancellor, Mr. Brooke and his immediate successor in the office, Mr. John Boyd-Carpenter, both sat in the Cabinet.

The office was originally created under the Royal Prerogative, which meant that no salary was attached to it and, in order to receive a salary, it was necessary for the incumbent to hold an additional office which would entitle him to be paid. The Ministers of the Crown Act, 1964, gave it statutory authority and it is listed as an office in its own right in the second schedule to the Act. It now carries the status of a Minister of State (q.v.), and the salary attached to it lies within the discretion of the Prime Minister within the limit of £8,500—i.e., the salary of a Minister of Cabinet rank. The Chief Secretary, if a Member of the House of Commons, is entitled to an additional taxable allowance of £1,250.

CHILTERN HUNDREDS

Under parliamentary law a Member of the House of Commons may not directly resign his seat. A member wishing to vacate his seat has to follow a rather curious procedure known as 'applying for the Chiltern Hundreds'. The custom, according to Hatsell's *Precedents*, originated about 1750. No Member of Parliament may occupy an office of profit under the Crown, and by accepting such an office he automatically vacates his seat. The offices of steward or bailiff of Her Majesty's three Chiltern Hundreds of Stoke, Desborough, and Burnham and steward of the Manor of Northstead are nominally offices of profit, although in actual fact they have ceased to exist. They are the traditional appointments for which a member applies should he wish to retire from the House of Commons before a dissolution takes place. As Disraeli once remarked, 'The Parliamentary Constitution of England was born in the bosom of the Chiltern Hills; as to this day our parliamentary career is terminated among its Hundreds.' The practice is to issue the appointments alternately to enable two members to retire simultaneously if necessary. Each office is retained until the Chancellor of the Exchequer receives application from another member wishing to retire.

The effect of disqualification which these appointments impose upon a member who accepts them has been preserved by statute and until recently extended to two further obsolete offices: the stewardship of the Manors of East Hendred and Hempholme, which were last used for the purpose in 1840 and 1865 respectively.

In other Parliaments of the Commonwealth, a member is permitted to resign his seat directly.

CHURCH AND PARLIAMENT

The Church of England is one of the few Churches in the world to-day which is an established Church. This does not mean that it is a State Church, whose faith, rites, and doctrine are dictated by the state. On the contrary, Church and State in England each have a distinctly separate identity and have frequently disagreed. An established church is one whose laws are officially recognized by the state and which are incorporated with the laws of the land. The Church of England has never been established by any statute or decree. The first official reference to its establishment occurs in the canons of 1603 with the use of the words, 'the Church of England as by law established', but the Church was established long before this date. It was established before the Reformation settlement which merely gave formal recognition to a relationship which had long existed. In fact, establishment may be said to date from the time when the Anglo-Saxon kings were first converted to Christianity. In other words, there has never been a time during its existence when the Church of England was not established, except for a brief period under Cromwell.

[116]

Establishment provides the Church with certain guarantees and also places certain restrictions upon it. Certain ecclesiastical and academic appointments are reserved to clergy of the Church of England. The Sovereign must be in communion with the Church and her coronation is a religious ceremony in which she is consecrated as Head of State by the Archbishop of Canterbury, Primate of All England. The Lord Chancellor, as the traditional keeper of the Sovereign's conscience, must also be a member of the Church. No incumbent may be removed from office except after due trial and conviction according to law. The Church is guaranteed permanent representation in Parliament. It has never been without its representatives in the councils of the realm—indeed, throughout English history the Church has been the most permanent element in the representative system. The only thing which can be said with certainty about the composition of the ancient Witenagemot, Parliament's Anglo-Saxon ancestor, is that it always included bishops. After the Conquest, clergy and laity were combined in a single organ of government, the *Curia Regis* (q.v.), to deal with matters of Church and State alike.

When Edward I summoned the Model Parliament (q.v.) in 1295 he included in his summons the two archbishops and all the bishops, sixty-seven abbots, and for the first time representatives of the lower clergy as well. The latter were very reluctant to sit in Parliament with the laity, and when the Lords and Commons separated into two Houses in the fourteenth century they withdrew their attendance altogether. The House of Lords, in those days the more powerful of the two Houses, was dominated by the spiritual peers until the Reformation. With the expulsion of the abbots from the House of Lords by Henry VIII the lay peers found themselves in the majority for the first time, and simultaneously the Commons emerged as the more powerful of the two Houses. To-day, the spiritual peers are very much in the minority, but the two Archbishops, the Bishops of London, Winchester, and Durham, and twenty-one other bishops chosen according to their seniority and irrespective of their sees continue to sit in the House of Lords as of right. Under the House of Commons (Clergy Disqualification) Act, 1801, clergy of the Church of England and the Church of Ireland and ministers of the Church of Scotland are disqualified from membership of the House of Commons. The Act was passed in consequence of the case of John Horne Tooke when doubts were expressed as to the eligibility of ordained persons to sit in the lower House. Since the disestablishment of the Welsh Church in 1920 (the original Act was passed in 1914), clergy of the Church of Wales are no longer disqualified. Roman Catholic priests are disqualified under the Roman Catholic Relief Act, 1829, an Act which otherwise removed the most serious disabilities which were suffered by persons of the Roman Catholic faith. Nonconformist ministers are not disqualified. In spite of the fiction of the three estates of the realm which survives to-day notably in the enacting formula of an Act of Parliament, the clergy can no longer be regarded for practical purposes as a separate estate, particularly since the members of the House of Commons are elected by both clergy and laity voting together as a single electorate.

The Church thus enjoys the protection of the State and is accorded a measure of influence in the affairs of the State. In return, however, it surrenders a certain amount of autonomy. The Measures of the National Assembly of the Church of England are subject to parliamentary control and require the assent of the Queen in Parliament before they can become law. The Convocations of Canterbury and York may not meet without the authority of the Queen, nor may canons be drafted and passed into law without the assent of the Queen in Council. Appointments of archbishops, bishops and deans are made by the Sovereign on the advice of the Prime Minister (who need not himself be a member of the Church of England). The Judicial Committee of the Privy Council is the highest court of appeal in ecclesiastical cases, although its jurisdiction in respect of cases involving doctrine, ritual or ceremonial was removed by the Ecclesiastical Jurisdiction Measure, 1963. While disestablishment would free the Church from these restrictions it would also inevitably involve the Church in extreme difficulties, including the loss of property. In any case, only Parliament could pass the necessary legislation disestablishing the Church, and in view of the vast implications of such a step, and the fact that there exists no *status quo ante* to which the Church could revert, it is impossible to predict exactly what disestablishment would entail. Few of those who advocate reforms in the relationship between Church and State think in terms of disestablishment.

The Church has always played an important rôle in the conduct of state affairs. Originally its position was one of power, while to-day it is one of influence. From the earliest years of the English Church until the Reformation the highest offices in the state were often held by ecclesiastics. This was hardly surprising in an age when almost everybody else was illiterate. The practice of appointing churchmen to political offices continued well into modern times, the last to hold ministerial office being the Bishop of Bristol who was appointed Lord Privy Seal in 1711. Until the Reformation, in spite of disputes occasioned by papal interference, the spiritual jurisdiction of the Pope had never been called in question. By the time Henry VIII came to the throne the power of the papacy in England was at its height. It could influence Parliament through the majority of spiritual peers in the House of Lords; through the ecclesiastical courts which administered the canon law which in turn depended on the Pope, its power in the land had been greatly extended; the monasteries, with their great wealth, were under the direct control of Rome. Fierce resentment burned throughout the country against the manner in which the papacy abused its power and its frequent heavy exactions. The King was thus able to take advantage of the feeling prevalent in the country when he decided to strike at the authority of Rome. There can be no question that his success in bringing about the Reformation in England was due to the fact that he had the support of the country, and the measure of that support may be calculated from his boldness in denying the papal jurisdiction entirely. In the words of G. M. Trevelyan: 'The Reformation . . . was a lay revolution carried by the Crown and Parliament—more especially by Crown and Commons—against the will of the Church authorities.' The House of Lords is not on record as having offered any particularly strong resistance to the King and Commons. There is every reason to assume that the 16th century House of Lords, a traditionally conservative body then as now, regarded the revolutionary policy with considerable alarm and disfavour. Their passive attitude can no doubt be explained by the King's disconcerting habit of decapitating anybody who attempted to frustrate his will, and it is interesting to speculate on whether they might have shown fight in other circumstances as they did in later centuries over the Reform Bill and the Parliament Bill.

With the Reformation, power over the Church passed from the papacy to the Crown. In 1534 Parliament passed an Act styling the King Supreme Head of the Church of England. The King now appointed the bishops instead of the Pope; the King now summoned the Convocations which could pass canons only with his consent; money once paid to Rome now went to the Crown. Another Act of Parliament gave the King the right to issue edicts concerning both Church and State. He could take action directly concerning the Church, and even pronounce on heresy, without consulting the bishops. In short, the King took all possible steps to secure his position against the Pope by subordinating the Church to his own personal control. For a short time in Mary's reign the authority of the Pope was restored, and the world witnessed the spectacle of Mary's third Parliament humbly receiving absolution from Cardinal Pole. But with the accession of Elizabeth the Reformation was confirmed. Like her father before her, Elizabeth claimed personal supremacy over the Church, but she eschewed the title of Supreme Head and altered the style instead to Supreme Governor. The title remains to-day but the powers it confers, like all the prerogatives of a constitutional monarch, are exercised only on advice. Elizabeth I, again like her father, acted through Parliament, but was always ready to assert her prerogative if Parliament refused to be subservient. On various occasions throughout her reign she rebuked her Parliaments for meddling in ecclesiastical affairs without her approval. The rise of the Puritan movement during her reign brought about a gradual change in the relationship between

E   [119]

the Crown and the Church, and her closing years witnessed the beginnings of that alliance between them which was to be ranged against Parliament in the mighty constitutional struggle of the 17th century.

The first Parliament of Elizabeth's reign, which met in 1559, repealed the religious legislation of Mary's reign and repudiated once again the authority of the Pope. It passed an Act of Supremacy appointing the Sovereign the head of the Church and an Act of Uniformity enforcing the use of the Protestant prayer book. The Abbot of Westminster took his place in the House of Lords at the opening of this Parliament, the last occasion on which an abbot sat in Parliament. The second Parliament of the reign, meeting in 1563, enacted a penal statute requiring all priests to take the oath of supremacy on pain of severe penalties and imposing the same obligation on all future members of the House of Commons. The effect of this was to exclude all Roman Catholics from the lower House, but peers were exempted from this requirement, 'the Queen's Majesty being otherwise sufficiently assured of their faith and loyalty'. The Parliament of 1571 was the first in which the House of Commons included no avowed Roman Catholics. This Parliament, as a result of the famous papal bull of 1570 excommunicating Elizabeth and absolving her subjects from any allegiance towards her, passed many important measures to secure the Queen and the Church against papist conspiracies. It also enforced the Thirty-nine Articles of Religion by statute.

The anti-Roman fervour which was widespread throughout the country encouraged the rise of an extreme faction in the form of the Puritan movement. It stood for radical Church reforms and in the manner of most revolutionary movements in England it found its voice through the House of Commons. In 1571 a Puritan member attempted to introduce a Bill proposing to alter the prayer book. In 1581 another member moved a successful resolution calling for a fast. In 1587 an attempt was made to introduce a Bill which sought to abolish the canon law and proposed a revised form of prayer. All such activities were regarded by Elizabeth as an encroachment on her prerogative, and throughout her reign the Puritan members of the House of Commons were a source of constant irritation to her. In order to counter the growth of puritanism, the Court of High Commission was set up in 1583 for the trial of religious offences but it failed to impose the uniformity which was its object. During the eighth Parliament of the reign the government managed to secure the passage of a Bill through the House of Commons, at a time when attendance was slack, which extended the penalties imposed upon Roman Catholics to Protestant nonconformists. This measure and the general policy of the State towards them drove the Puritans more and more into open hostility against the Crown and the Church.

By the time James I ascended the throne of England the Church had come to look to the Crown as its protector. James was a staunch advocate of the authoritarian doctrine of the Divine Right of Kings (q.v.) and cherished an equal dislike of both Parliament and puritanism. The Church, now in firm alliance with the Crown, supported the King in his theories of government. The famous Hampton Court Conference failed in its aim of reconciling the Puritans to orthodox practices, and the Puritan clergy became determined to change the character of the Church from within. The House of Commons, now a strongly Puritan body, was resolved to resist any royal usurpation of its rights and privileges. Like Elizabeth I, James was for ever rebuking the Commons for meddling in affairs of religion, but he lacked the popularity and prestige of his illustrious predecessor, and the Commons were never slow to remind the King of their traditional liberties. King and Church thus combined against Parliament and the Puritans in a political as well as a religious struggle, the former representing absolutism, the latter constitutionalism. Only on one issue were the opposing factions in agreement, and that was on the need to suppress popery. The penal statutes of Elizabeth's reign were confirmed in the first session of James's first Parliament and their enforcement provoked the celebrated Gunpowder Plot (q.v.) which was timed for the opening of the second session in 1605. For a short time King and Commons were able to present a united front, caught up as they were in the general revulsion of feeling against popery which followed the revelation of the Plot. But except for the brief truce occasioned by this episode, James was at variance with all his Parliaments, and their differences were exacerbated by the attitude of the Anglican clergy in supporting the King's claim to absolute power.

Charles I succeeded to the throne in 1625 well schooled in the convictions of his father. The events of the previous reign had made it clear that a struggle had been embarked upon in which neither side was willing to compromise. The situation would have been a difficult one whatever monarch had come to the throne at this crucial period. With a man of Charles's unfortunate character at the head of Church and State the struggle could only become mortal. Through the alliance forged between the King and Archbishop Laud, another whose character could hardly have been more unsuited to the needs of the situation, the association between the Crown and the Church became such that the downfall of one could only spell the ruin of the other. While the popular cause in the House of Commons included such people as Eliot, Hampden, Selden, Pym, and Cromwell, it was obvious that the struggle could only end in disaster for one side or the other. Laud pursued a policy with the support of the King which made him detested throughout the country. It was based upon a rigid discipline within the Church and a ruthless intolerance of nonconformism. His weapons included a strict censorship of the Press and the Courts of

Star Chamber and High Commission which tried all kinds of religious offences and from whose decisions there was no appeal. The attempt to extend this policy to Scotland aroused the bitter resentment of the Presbyterians and eventually led to the Solemn League and Covenant uniting the Puritans and the Presbyterians in a common cause.

Finding, like his father before him, that none of his Parliaments was prepared to be compliant to his will, Charles attempted to govern without Parliament for eleven years, but in 1640 he was driven by his necessities to summon first the Short Parliament (q.v.) and towards the end of the year the historic Long Parliament (q.v.). Immediately it came into existence the Long Parliament became an irresistible force. All the nation's grievances were swept away before its reforming zeal. The Courts of Star Chamber and High Commission were abolished by statute and Archbishop Laud was impeached, to be finally condemned and executed in 1645. By this time the King was on the losing side and the power of Parliament was not to be challenged. But in its newly won supremacy serious differences developed within the House of Commons itself. The moderate faction became alarmed at the ruthless extremism of the Puritans. There were many who, while detesting the policies of Laud, remained loyal to the Crown, and the development of republican feeling among the Puritans gave rise to a constitutional Royalist party among the Commons. This faction advocated moderate Church reforms and were not prepared to go, as they saw it, too far. The famous 'Root and Branch' Bill, sponsored by Cromwell among others, aimed at the total abolition of episcopacy, but although it passed its second reading it was dropped in committee. A Bill to exclude the bishops from the House of Lords was passed by the Commons but rejected by the Lords. As the storm came nearer to bursting so the rift widened and when the Civil War began in August 1642 each man had decided by which standard he stood. The war, as every schoolboy knows, ended in victory for Cromwell and the Roundheads, but dissension broke out among the victors over the question of negotiating with the King. The Independents led by Cromwell were resolved to bring the King to trial but the Presbyterians did not wish to see the monarchy abolished. The Presbyterians were in the majority in the House of Commons but the Independents controlled the army, and the army had its own way. The Presbyterians were forcibly excluded from the House of Commons and the doom of the King was sealed.

The years of the Commonwealth (1649-60) were the only period of English history when the Church was severed from the State. Episcopacy was abolished by law and the liturgy was banned not only in churches but in private homes as well. Marriage became a civil ceremony and Christmas Day was observed as a day of fasting. The same harshness which Laud had employed against nonconformists was now employed by the Puritans against the Anglicans, and just as the Puritan movement had been strengthened by persecution, so did the national Church gain in its adversity. With the restoration of the monarchy came the re-establishment of the Church. The House of Lords, which had been abolished by Cromwell, assembled as of right, but the bishops did not take their seats until 1661 after an Act had been passed readmitting them to Parliament. The Anglican ritual was restored and the Solemn League and Covenant was ordered to be burned. Much repressive legislation was passed which had the effect of driving the nonconformists outside the Church of England. An Act of Uniformity made obligatory the use of a revised prayer book. The Corporation Act disqualified from holding office all magistrates and municipal officials who rejected the Anglican ritual. The Conventicle Act of 1664 imposed penalties for attending religious services other than those of the Church of England. In 1665 the Five Mile Act was passed against Puritan ministers, outlawing them from any towns in which they had preached unless they took an oath against promoting changes in Church or State. The persecution of Roman Catholics ceased during the early years of the Restoration, but fear and suspicion were aroused throughout the country by the government's policy towards nonconformists, the increasing number of Roman Catholics at Court, the fact that the King's brother who was the heir to the throne was an avowed Roman Catholic, and by a leakage of information concerning a secret agreement entered into between Charles II and Louis XIV of France in which Charles undertook to advance the cause of the Roman faith in England.

In 1673 a Declaration of Indulgence was issued which swept away all the penal laws and announced that the supreme power in ecclesiastical matters rested with the King. Although it appeared to relieve from their disabilities both Roman Catholics and nonconformists alike, it was in reality a subterfuge designed to benefit Roman Catholics only. This proclamation, issued as it was without the sanction of Parliament, produced an immediate sharp reaction. The Keeper of the Great Seal at once resigned and the Declaration was opposed in the House of Lords and rejected outright in the House of Commons. In the face of opposition on this scale the King was compelled to withdraw it. The fears of the country were now thoroughly aroused, and this incident was followed by the passing of the Test Act which excluded all Roman Catholics from holding office in the government. This measure disqualified the King's brother and a number of the King's ministers. The feeling against popery rose to fever pitch with the revelation in 1678 of the so-called 'Popish Plot' which had been dreamed up by the charlatan, Titus Oates. It resulted, among other things, in the enactment of the first law specifically to exclude Roman Catholics from sitting in either House of Parliament. The Commons unexpectedly accepted a Lords' amendment exempting the King's brother from its provisions.

James, the Duke of York, succeeded his brother as King in 1685, despite several attempts during the previous reign to pass legislation excluding him from the succession. It soon became clear that he was bent on restoring the Roman faith in England. Shortly after his accession he attended a public celebration of Mass and at his coronation the Anglican rites were curtailed. He violated the Test Act, revived the Court of High Commission, and in 1688 issued the Declaration of Indulgence which moved the seven bishops to draw up their famous petition for which they were committed to the Tower and tried on a charge of libel. The bishops at once became popular heroes and their acquittal was endorsed with the emphatic approval of the country. It was clear that such a King would have to go.

The Revolution of 1688, which established William and Mary on the throne, heralded the beginning of a new era for Church, State, and Parliament. One of the most vital changes occasioned by the settlement was the passing of the control of the Church from the Crown to Parliament. The effects of this great constitutional development did not immediately make themselves felt, as for many years to come Parliament was to be largely controlled by the executive. The Church also retained a considerable political influence as widespread fears could be easily aroused by the warning, 'The Church is in danger!' A Toleration Act was passed early in the new reign which removed some of the disabilities to which nonconformists had been subjected, a measure which, in the words of Macaulay, 'removed a vast mass of evil without shocking a vast mass of prejudice'. In 1701 the Act of Settlement was passed securing the Protestant succession and disqualifying from the occupancy of the throne any potential successor not in communion with the Church of England, regardless of hereditary claims. In the House of Lords the bishops were still able to exercise a crucial influence on vital issues. In 1733 Walpole's government was twice saved from an adverse vote in the upper House by the support of the bishops, and care was taken during the reigns of the first two Georges to ensure that the bishops were supporters of the Whigs. The bishops had, in fact, become dependent on the patronage of the ministry, and regular attendance in the House of Lords was expected of them. It was not long before the Church came to be regarded as a department of state and Parliament a combined spiritual and lay legislature. This misconception was encouraged to a great extent by the suspension of Convocation. After the Restoration Convocation had surrendered to Parliament its traditional right of taxing the clergy. Although this was a logical historical development it put an end to the regular summoning of Convocation, and in 1717, as the result of a dispute precipitated by

Bishop Hoadly, it was prorogued by the government and not summoned again until 1852.

Church affairs do not loom large in the political history of the 19th century, although nonconformism was identified to a great extent with liberalism and the Church tended towards conservatism. In 1831 only one spiritual peer, the Bishop of Norwich, voted in favour of the second Reform Bill. In the early years of the 19th century there was a certain amount of hostility to the presence of the bishops in the House of Lords. In 1826 a motion was introduced in the House of Commons that 'the attendance of the bishops in Parliament is prejudicial to the cause of religion'. In 1834 leave was sought in the House of Commons to introduce a Bill 'for relieving the bishops of their legislative and judicial duties in the House of Peers'. In 1835 it was moved that the presence of the bishops in Parliament 'tends to alienate the affections of the people from the Church'. These thrusts against the Lords Spiritual were all parried by sizeable majorities, and there have since been no further attempts to deprive the bishops of their seats in Parliament. In 1847, when the bishopric of Manchester was created, it was enacted that the number of bishops sitting in the House of Lords should not be increased in consequence. A similar provision has been made whenever other new bishoprics have come into being. Throughout the century many of the privileges of the Church were gradually whittled away by parliamentary action. The emancipation of Roman Catholics and the relief of dissenters through the repeal of the Test and Corporation Acts meant, among other things, that public appointments were no longer restricted to members of the Church of England. Legislation making provision for civil marriages and enabling the granting of divorces by secular courts brought the laws of the State into direct conflict with the laws of the Church. In the creation of state schools, the 1870 Education Act diminished the influence of the Church in a sphere in which it had always been especially active. The Church became as much subordinated to the power of Parliament as it had once been subordinated to the will of the Sovereign.

In the 20th century the business of government has become so extensive that there are few branches of the national life which it does not control. Since the Government is sustained by Parliament it follows that Parliament is the repository of all power, and this, for all practical purposes, means the House of Commons. Since the passing of the first Parliament Act in 1911 the House of Commons has been in a position to do anything it likes. This change in the character of Parliament has brought the Church face to face with considerable handicaps—not through any hostile action on the part of Parliament, but because the State has taken over so many former Church responsibilities and because Parliament is so overwhelmed with pressing business that it is seldom able to find time for Church affairs which require legislative action.

Until the passing of the Church of England Assembly (Powers) Act in 1919 many much-needed measures for Church reform were either held up through lack of parliamentary time or deliberately blocked by small groups of prejudiced obstructionists. Without its former political influence the Church was in no position to bring the necessary pressure to bear in order to promote Church legislation, neither was it able to resist measures which were calculated to hinder its work. It was evident that some means needed to be devised whereby a passage for Church legislation could be secured through Parliament. The means was found in the creation of the National Assembly of the Church of England.

Towards the end of the 19th century it had been recognized that a body consisting entirely of clergy could not adequately represent the Church of England, and the Convocations of Canterbury and York agreed to the constitution of a House of Laity in each province. Later the two Convocations and the two Houses of Laity met together to form a Representative Church Council. Early in 1919 a scheme was proposed to confer certain legislative powers on the Council and to re-name it the National Assembly of the Church of England. A Bill was accordingly drawn up and introduced in the House of Lords, which passed it without a division. The second reading in the House of Commons was moved by Sir E. Beauchamp who emphasized the pressing necessity for Church reforms and revealed that between 1880 and 1913, 217 Church Bills had come before Parliament of which 183 had never been heard of again. Mr. Broad moved an amendment calling for the disestablishment of the Church which was negatived by 304 votes to 16. The Bill eventually passed its third reading in the House of Commons without a division. A law passed by the Church Assembly is known as a Church Assembly Measure. It has the same authority as an Act of Parliament and similarly requires the Royal Assent. The Church Assembly consists of the House of Bishops, the House of Clergy and the House of Laity. The combined upper Houses and combined lower Houses of the Convocations constitute the first two, while the House of Laity is elected every five years by Church members who are registered on the parish electoral rolls, except for not more than 10 members who may be co-opted. The number of elected members of the House of Laity is determined by resolution of the Church Assembly in the year preceding that in which the election is to be held, in accordance with the procedure laid down in the Representation of the Laity Measure, 1956. Laymen usually comprise about one-half of the total composition of the Church Assembly which normally meets three times a year for four days at a time.

The Church Assembly is not concerned with faith or doctrine but only with administration. It debates a measure in very much the same way as Parliament debates a Bill. When a measure has passed through all its stages and has been approved by the majority of the Church

Assembly, it is referred to the Legislative Committee, composed of members of the Assembly, which decides when and how the measure will be presented to the Ecclesiastical Committee. The Ecclesiastical Committee consists of 15 members of the House of Lords nominated by the Lord Chancellor and 15 members of the House of Commons nominated by the Speaker. Its quorum is 12. Its function is to examine every measure and consider its implications. Its findings on the nature, effect, and expediency of the measure are embodied in a draft report which is sent to the Assembly's Legislative Committee. The Legislative Committee may recommend at this stage that in view of the findings of the Ecclesiastical Committee the measure should be amended or withdrawn. If it is decided to proceed with the measure the draft report of the Ecclesiastical Committee becomes a formal report, and both the report and the measure are laid before the two Houses of Parliament for their separate approval. Parliament cannot amend a measure but it can debate and reject it. A resolution must be passed in both Houses of Parliament before a measure can be presented for the Royal Assent.

The delegation of powers in ecclesiastical matters which the 1919 Act conferred on the Church Assembly has proved to be a progressive move bringing highly successful results. It has enabled the Church to implement a large number of very necessary reforms and has overcome the problem of finding parliamentary time. It has conferred the responsibility for legislating in Church matters upon people with suitable qualifications and experience. It has acknowledged the right of the clergy to a major voice in the framing of legislation on Church affairs while preserving the right of the laity to exert an equal influence. There is no doubt that Parliament would never have agreed to conferring the powers enjoyed by the Church Assembly on a body in which the laity were not generously represented. Between 1920 and 1969, 150 measures became law, and only four have been rejected by Parliament. Of the latter, one proposed the demolition of some ancient churches in the City of London and was strongly opposed by the City; another provided for the division of the diocese of Lichfield and was opposed by the diocese of Hereford; the remaining two, and the most significant, proposed the revision of the prayer book. This vital issue strained the relations between Church and Parliament, and the debates on the two measures concerned, which took place in 1927 and 1928, are of the utmost importance. The earlier measure was passed by the House of Lords but both were rejected by the House of Commons—a House whose voting strength included Roman Catholics, Jews, Presbyterians, Nonconformists, atheists, agnostics, Scotsmen, Welshmen, Irishmen, and even a Parsee, all of them entitled to pass judgment on a matter of vital concern to the Church of England alone. Here indeed was an expression, if one was needed, of the supremacy of Parliament over the Church!

E*

A position had arisen in which (to quote Mayfield) 'not even the English love of constitutional fictions could withstand ecclesiastical realities'. In 1952 a Commission of the Church Assembly on Church and State made various recommendations for changing the present state of affairs. The Commission considered disestablishment but recommended in preference a revision of the terms of the establishment. The recommendations concerned the appointment of bishops, the ecclesiastical courts, and, most important of all, the granting to the Church of some measure of independence from parliamentary control in the framing and revising of its forms of worship. No suggestion was made that Parliament should surrender its sovereignty over the Church or its ultimate authority to legislate on Church matters. The views of the Church Assembly have since been met to some extent with the passage of the Ecclesiastical Jurisdiction Measure, 1963, which reformed the system of ecclesiastical courts, and the Prayer Book (Alternative and Other Services) Measure, 1965, which permits certain variations in forms of service.

In 1966 the work of the Convocations and of the Church Assembly was further facilitated by the passage of the Church of England Convocations Act which provides that the duration of the Convocations shall coincide with the duration of the the House of Laity. Previously a dissolution of Parliament also involved a dissolution of the Convocations, thereby causing an unnecessary interruption of ecclesiastical business and the unwelcome expense to the Church of new elections of representative clergy. It is of interest to note that the Convocations can trace their origins back to an ecclesiastical synod held at Hertford in the year 673. When Parliaments began to be summoned regularly in the Middle Ages it became the custom to issue the writs of summons to the two Convocations simultaneously with the writs for the election of a new Parliament. After 1640, in which year certain canons made by the Convocations were declared invalid because Parliament was not sitting at the time, it became the established practice that the summoning and dissolution of Parliament and the Convocations should take place simultaneously. The change in the law (effected, it should be noted, by an Act of Parliament and not by a Church Assembly Measure) reflects a more realistic conception of the modern relationship between Church and State.

The report of 1952 recognized the benefits to the Church which are inherent in the establishment. To quote Mayfield again, '. . . to the English welfare state the Church of England brings a continuity of tradition older than that either of the Crown, or of Parliament. Throughout its history the Church has, by hook or by crook, remained in the lump that it may leaven it; and so it must continue, unless the State wills otherwise, for within the welfare state the pursuit of security can become both a rival faith and a great dilutant of the Christianity brought to England, and there maintained, by the Catholic and Apostolic teaching of the Church by law established'.

(Further reading: Garbett, *Church and state in England*, 1950; Mayfield, *The Church of England*, 1958.)

CHURCH ASSEMBLY MEASURES

In addition to Bills which have passed both Houses of Parliament, the Royal Assent is also given to Measures passed by the National Assembly of the Church of England. Measures must have been presented to the Queen for the Royal Assent in accordance with a resolution passed by both Houses of Parliament, and this cannot take place until a report by the Ecclesiastical Committee (q.v.) and the Measure concerned have been laid before them. Measures may relate to any matter concerning the Church of England and they have the same effect as an Act of Parliament. They are made under the authority of the Church of England Assembly (Powers) Act, 1919, and are published with the annual volumes of the Public General Acts (q.v.).

This legislative process is a novel system of devolution whereby the Church Assembly is able to present a Measure in its final form for the consideration of Parliament. Parliament cannot amend a Measure but, by declining to pass the necessary resolution, can reject it. Parliament thus retains control over Church legislation, and could, if it so wished, legislate for the Church without reference to the Church Assembly. For all practical purposes, however, the initiative in matters of Church legislation now rests with the Church Assembly.

Measures may not seek to alter the procedure for their consideration in Parliament or the composition and powers of the Ecclesiastical Committee.

See also CHURCH AND PARLIAMENT.

CHURCH COMMISSIONERS

Following the appointment in 1835 of two commissions 'to consider the state of the several dioceses of England and Wales', a permanent commission was appointed by the Ecclesiastical Commissioners Act, 1836. Its size was increased by the Ecclesiastical Commissioners Act, 1850, which provided for the appointment of three further commissioners to be known as Church Estates Commissioners, their function being to administer the estates of the Church in order to endow or augment benefices. It was specified that the First and Second Church Estates Commissioners must be lay members of the Church of England appointed by the Crown, the Third Church Estates Commissioner being appointed by the Archbishop of Canterbury from either laity or clergy. The First and Second Church Estates Commissioners may be Members of the House of Commons, and in practice the Second Church Estates Commissioner is always a member, being appointed by the government of the day in the same manner as a minister.

The Church Commissioners Measure, 1947, established the body corporate known as the Church Commissioners which was formed in 1948 from the union of Queen Anne's Bounty with the Ecclesiastical Commissioners. The three Church Estates Commissioners are now members of the Church Commissioners *ex-officio* but are appointed in the same manner as before. The other *ex-officio* members of the Church Commissioners are the two Archbishops, the diocesan Bishops of Canterbury and York, the Lord Chancellor, the Lord President of the Council, the First Lord of the Treasury (in practice the Prime Minister), the Chancellor of the Exchequer, the Home Secretary, the Speaker of the House of Commons, the Lord Chief Justice, the Master of the Rolls, the Attorney-General, the Solicitor-General, the Lord Mayors of London and York, and the Vice-Chancellors of the Universities of Oxford and Cambridge. There are thirty-five other Church Commissioners who are variously appointed.

The Second Church Estates Commissioner represents the Church Commissioners in the House of Commons and when necessary answers questions relating to matters within their jurisdiction. Under the Church Commissioners Measure, 1964, he is a member of the General Purposes Committee and is entitled to attend and speak at the meetings of every committee of Church Commissioners of which he is not a member.

CHURCH ESTATES COMMISSIONERS

See CHURCH COMMISSIONERS.

CHURCHILL ARCH

The stonework of the main doorway into the new Chamber of the House of Commons, bomb-chipped and smoke-blackened by German bombs when the Chamber was destroyed in 1941, has been re-erected and named the Churchill Arch as a memorial to Sir Winston's inspiring and redoubtable wartime leadership of Parliament and the British people.

CITATION OF STATUTES

Bills presented to Parliament must have a citation title, which usually appears in the last clause and is nearly always identical with the short title at the head of the Act. An exception is the Consolidated Fund (Appropriation) Act, which is always cited as the Appropriation Act. An Act may also be cited by its chapter number and calendar year. The Acts of Parliament Numbering and Citation Act, 1962, provided for the relatively simple method of numbering and citation now in use and, since 1 January 1963, Acts of Parliament have been numbered in a separate sequence for each calendar year—thus, the first Act to receive the Royal Assent in 1966 may be cited simply as

1966 c.l. Previously, Acts had been cited according to the session and regnal year in which they were passed: thus, the Income Tax Act of 1952 would have been cited as '15 & 16 Geo. 6 and 1 Eliz. 2, c.10', the 10th Act of the Parliamentary session which ran during the 15th and 16th years of the reign of George VI and the first year of the reign of Elizabeth II, reckoned from the dates of their accession. It is noteworthy that this cumbersome and confusing system of numbering and citation was in operation for seven centuries prior to the passing of the Act of 1962.

CIVIL AVIATION, MINISTER OF

Civil aviation was the responsibility of the Air Ministry until the Ministry of Civil Aviation Act, 1945, appointed a Minister to encourage the design, development, and production of civil aircraft, to promote air safety, and to organize research into air navigation. Under a consolidating statute of 1949 the Minister appointed the members of the Airways Corporations, and was responsible for the management of civil aerodromes and the compulsory purchase of land for their erection. When the Conservative Government took office in 1951 the Ministries of Transport and Civil Aviation were combined under one Minister, but with the creation of the Ministry of Aviation in 1959 all matters concerning civil aviation were separated from the Ministry of Transport. The Ministry of Aviation was abolished in 1967 and its functions absorbed by the Ministry of Technology.

The Ministers who held office between 1945 and 1951 were Lord Winster, Lord Nathan, Lord Pakenham, and Lord Ogmore.

CIVIL LIST

The provision made by Parliament for the expenses of the Royal Household. It includes the Sovereign's personal income and the allowances made to other members of the Royal Family. The Civil List is fixed by statute upon the accession of a Sovereign and charged directly upon the Consolidated Fund (q.v.). It is not subject to annual review by Parliament. The Civil List Act, 1952, provides that during the present reign and a period of six months afterwards the yearly sum of £475,000 shall be paid for the Queen's Civil List. In addition, an annual income of £40,000 is provided for H.R.H. the Duke of Edinburgh during his lifetime and provision is also made for Her Majesty's children. Other members of the Royal Family are provided for in previous Civil List Acts. The 1937 Act provided that Her Majesty the Queen, now Queen Mother, should receive during her life an annual income of £70,000 in the event of her surviving His Majesty the King. H.R.H. Princess Margaret was allowed an annual income of £6,000 under the same Act, and the 1952 Act provided that she should receive a further £9,000 in the event of her marriage.

The Civil List was originally intended to cover the ordinary expenses of government, and the practice of granting the Sovereign a regular annual income for this purpose was instituted at the Restoration. Charles II and James II both received £1,200,000 per annum to be disposed of as they thought fit, and extraordinary expenditure was met from annual grants of Supply (q.v.). The term 'Civil List' first appeared in 1697 when the House of Commons resolved 'that in a just sense and acknowledgement of what great things His Majesty has done for these kingdoms, a sum not exceeding the sum of £700,000 per annum be granted to His Majesty during his life for the support of the Civil List'. The first Civil List Act followed upon this resolution. Until 1715 the money for the Civil List was raised by assigning the proceeds of specific taxes to the purpose and it was customary to assign certain duties to the Sovereign for life. Owing to the haphazard nature of this arrangement effective supervision of public finance was impossible and the need for a common pool of revenue came to be realized. The first step in the direction of creating such a pool was taken in 1715 when an Aggregate Fund was established and an additional £120,000 for the Civil List was immediately charged upon it. In 1760 the hereditary revenues of the Crown were transferred to the Fund and the whole Civil List was charged upon it. In 1786 Pitt created the Consolidated Fund and all statutory expenditure (that is, all expenditure excluding annual grants of Supply) was charged upon it. By the middle of the 19th century the Consolidated Fund had become the great financial pool of the nation, receiving all revenue and bearing all charges.

Before the reign of George III Parliament never inquired into the disposition of the Civil List funds. Although Parliament provided the money it was regarded as belonging to the King who therefore was entitled to make use of it at his own discretion. In 1769 the King had accrued debts amounting to over half a million pounds and he asked Parliament to provide the funds to meet them. In consequence a proposal was made for the examination of Civil List expenditure but was turned down as being contrary to tradition and derogatory to the Crown, and the debts were paid. In 1777 the King was again in debt, but this time Parliament was less tolerant of the royal extravagances. The debt was again paid but not before accounts had been presented to Parliament. In 1780 Burke proposed his great plan of economic reform which, although rejected at the time, was to a great extent put into operation two years later. In 1782 Lord Rockingham insisted on the reform of the Civil List as one of the conditions of his forming a Government. It was still intended that the Civil List should cover the ordinary expenses of government, and it was divided for the purpose into eight classes including all civil pensions and salaries. These expenses were continually increasing, however, and it remained impossible to avoid deficits; it became necessary to meet more and more civil expenses from annual grants of Supply. Upon the accession of William IV in 1830 a decisive step was taken. Upon the recommendation of a Select Committee all expenditure not directly 'affecting the dignity and state of the Crown and the personal comfort of their Majesties' was removed from the Civil List. On the accession of Queen Victoria in 1837 the Civil List was further relieved of the royal pension list and reduced to the sum of £385,000. Thenceforward it became the personal income of the Sovereign and all expenses previously charged upon it were paid from the Consolidated Fund.

CLANDESTINE OUTLAWRIES BILL

See OUTLAWRIES BILL.

CLAUSES

The individual sections of a Bill which are numbered and become known as sections if the Bill becomes an Act of Parliament (q.v.). At the committee stage of a Bill each clause is considered separately, and if necessary in detail. New clauses and amendments to existing clauses may be considered at this stage, and the Chairman is empowered to select those which he feels the House would wish to consider. Any amendments made must be reported to the House at the report stage, when further amendments may be proposed.

CLERGY, DISQUALIFICATION OF

See DISQUALIFICATION FROM MEMBERSHIP OF PARLIAMENT.

CLERK OF THE CROWN

The Royal Proclamation dissolving a Parliament and fixing the date for the meeting of a new one also announces the making of an Order in Council directing the Lord Chancellor and the Governor of Northern Ireland to issue the necessary writs (q.v.). For a by-election the writ is issued on the authority of a warrant from the Speaker. The Crown Office, under the Clerk of the Crown in Chancery, and the Clerk of the Crown for Northern Ireland then prepare and send the writs summoning the peers and instructing the Returning Officers in the various House of Commons constituencies to hold elections and return the names of the members elected to the Crown Office, where they are recorded. Writs for an election in Northern Ireland are transmitted by the Clerk of the Crown there to the Clerk in England. After a General Election or a by-election the Clerk of the Crown receives all the ballot papers and other documents relating to the election and retains them for a year. In Scotland the ballot papers and marked electoral registers are kept by the sheriff clerk of the county in which the constituency is situated. The Lord Chancellor is head of the Crown

Office, and the Clerk of the Crown the head of the permanent staff. The office is one of great antiquity and dignity, the duties and emoluments of which were defined as far back as 1349. The Clerk of the Crown is appointed by sign manual warrant, and takes part in many important acts of the State, including the reading of the titles of Bills in the House of Lords when they receive the Royal Assent. It is in the Crown Office that the Great Seal (q.v.) is affixed.

CLERK OF THE HOUSE

The chief permanent officer of the House of Commons; his counterparts in the other Commonwealth Parliaments are similarly styled. The Clerk of the House of Commons is appointed by the Crown by letters patent in which he is described as 'Under-Clerk of the Parliaments, to attend upon the Commons'. His is a learned and highly specialized office, involving an expert knowledge of legislative procedure and a wide experience in parliamentary administration. He has the custody of all records and heads one of the five administrative departments of the House of Commons, the others being the Department of the Speaker, the Department of the Serjeant-at-Arms, the Department of the Library and the Administration Department. The Department of the Clerk of the House is responsible for the conduct of business and is divided into six offices—Public Bill Office, Journal Office, Committee Office, Private Bill Office, Table Office and the Overseas Office—each being responsible for different aspects of the work of the House.

The Clerk assists and advises the Speaker and members on matters of procedure. He is also the Accounting Officer for the House of Commons. He signs addresses, votes of thanks, and Orders of the House, endorses Bills sent or returned to the Lords, and reads whatever is required to be read in the House. He sits at the Table below the Speaker's Chair, and wears the traditional black uniform with wig and gown.

The Clerk of the House of Commons is mentioned in the earliest parliamentary records, and an excellent account of the history of the office is contained in Mackenzie's *The English Parliament*. The *Modus Tenendi Parliamentum*, an early account of the constitution of Parliament which was probably written in or about 1327, refers to a clerk specially assigned to the Commons, but the first appointment by letters patent of an 'Under-Clerk of the Parliaments' was that of Robert de Melton in 1363. Like the Clerk of the Parliaments (q.v.) the Under-Clerk was a chancery clerk, but his rewards were far more modest. His salary was a hundred shillings a year until 1529, when it was doubled, and he could hope for no more in recognition of his services than a living or a prebend, usually of St. Stephen's, Westminster.

The first known Commons Clerk to have kept any kind of record was Robert Ormeston, who held office from 1515 to 1545. The record which was to become the Journal of the House of Commons (q.v.) was originated by John Seymour, Commons Clerk from 1547 to 1567, and continued by his successor, Fulke Onslow, who held the appointment until 1602.

In the 17th century [writes Mackenzie] the House took an increasing interest in its forms and precedents, as the numerous resolutions recorded in the journals testify. In the stormy sessions of the Long Parliament, moreover, rule and order in proceeding acquired a new importance. The result was inevitably to raise the position of Clerk of the House of Commons from that of a merely mechanical recorder and preserver of records to that of an expert and adviser in procedure. Henry Elsyng, who was Clerk in the early years of the Long Parliament, was the first Clerk to appear in the role of guardian of procedure. He it was of whom it was said that for 'his abilities and prudence, more reverence was paid to his stool than to the Speaker's Chair'. . . . He was succeeded in 1649 by Henry Scobell, whose 'Memorials' is the main authority for 17th century procedure. In 1658 Scobell claimed to be Clerk of the 'Other House' which Cromwell substituted for the Lords and carried off the Commons Journals so that they could not be searched. In this awkward situation the Speaker remarked, 'The Clerk is gone, and you could not carry on business without one.'

John Hatsell, Clerk of the House of Commons from 1768 to 1797, made an elaborate collection of *Precedents of Proceedings in the House of Commons*, which is the best authority for 18th century procedure. Sir Thomas Erskine May was Clerk from 1871–86. His *Treatise on the Law, Privileges, Proceedings and Usage of Parliament* has been the authoritative statement of parliamentary rule and practice for the past hundred years.

The declaration made by the Clerk on taking office is as follows: 'I . . . do declare that I will be true and faithful and troth I will bear to our Sovereign Lady the Queen and to her Heirs and Successors. I will nothing know that shall be prejudicial to Her Highness, Her Crown Estate and Dignity Royal, but that I will resist it to my power and with all speed I will advertise Her Grace thereof, or at least some of her Counsel in such wise as the same may come Her knowledge. I will also well and truly serve her Highness in the Office of Under-Clerk of Her Parliaments to attend upon the Commons of this Realm making true entries Remembrances and Journals of the things done and passed in the same. I will keep secret all such matters as shall be treated in Her said Parliaments and not disclose the same before they shall be published but to such as it ought to be disclosed unto and generally I will well and truly do and execute all things belonging to me to be done appertaining to the said office of Under-Clerk of the Parliaments.'

The present salary of the Clerk of the House of Commons is £14,000 per annum. A chronological list of holders of the office appears as Appendix 6.

(Further reading: Marsden, *The officers of the Commons, 1363–1965*,

1966; Williams, *Clerical organization of the House of Commons, 1661–1850*, 1954.)

CLERK OF THE HOUSE OF LORDS
See CLERK OF THE PARLIAMENTS.

CLERK OF THE OVERSEAS OFFICE
A senior officer of the House of Commons, first appointed in 1952, as the Fourth Clerk-at-the-Table, who is charged with the special duty of conducting liaison between the House of Commons and the Clerks of overseas Parliaments. Co-operation between the Mother of Parliaments and her overseas progeny has always been encouraged. It is the practice for overseas Clerks to visit the House of Commons on periods of attachment to the various offices, and for officers from Westminster to visit overseas Parliaments to offer advice and assistance in such matters as the drafting of Standing Orders. The younger legislatures of the Commonwealth have thus been able to benefit from the accumulated experience of the oldest Parliament in the world.

This work, however, placed a heavy additional burden upon the existing staff of the Clerk's Department. It was therefore decided to appoint a Fourth Clerk-at-the-Table, redesignated the Clerk of the Overseas Office in 1967, who would couple his parliamentary duties with liaison work, for it was obvious that the official must be both free to travel and able to acquire the necessary experience at the Table of the House itself. The Clerk of the Overseas Office sits at the Table at all convenient times, and his special duties include travelling overseas when asked to assist legislatures in the Commonwealth (at the expense of the Parliament inviting him), arranging the attachment of Clerks from overseas, representing the Clerk of the House on committees dealing with seminars for overseas Speakers and legislators, and assisting in drafting or redrafting the Standing Orders of overseas legislatures.

CLERK OF THE PARLIAMENTS
The chief permanent officer of the House of Lords. He is appointed by the Crown by letters patent, and upon entering office he makes a declaration at the Table of the House of Lords 'to make true entries and records of the things done and passed' in the Parliaments and to 'keep secret all such matters as shall be treated therein and not to disclose the same before they shall be published but to such as it ought to be disclosed unto'. He controls four departments in the House of Lords: the Public Bill Office, the Private Bill and Committee Office, the Judicial Office, and the Accountant's Department. He is responsible for the preparation of the minutes of the proceedings of the House and he has the custody of all documents including the important collection of manuscript records stored in the Victoria Tower. He endorses all Bills sent

to the Commons and has the custody of those awaiting the Royal Assent with the exception of Money Bills. He is responsible for their subsequent promulgation as Acts of Parliament and for endorsing on every Act the date on which it received the Royal Assent. At the ceremony of the Royal Assent to Bills by the Lords Commissioners it is the Clerk of the Parliaments who pronounces the words by which the Royal Assent is signified. Like the Clerk of the House of Commons he is an authority on procedure and his advice is available to Members of the House of Lords. He exercises a general administrative control over the business of the House, and like his counterpart in the House of Commons he calls each item on the order paper as it is reached.

The office of Clerk of the Parliaments appears to date from the early Parliaments of the reign of Edward I, and according to Mackenzie it may be inferred from the frequent appearance of his name in the record of these Parliaments that a certain John of Kirby was the holder. Dasent names Sir Henry de Edenestowe as the first Clerk of the Parliaments to be appointed in 1330. In the reign of Edward III this official emerges more clearly, and one of his principal duties was to receive common petitions (as distinct from private petitions which were dealt with by the Receivers of Petitions), to bring them before the council, and also to read the replies to such petitions. In 1399 a salary of £40 per annum was attached to the office, and in 1510 the actual style of 'Clerk of the Parliaments' makes its first appearance. To-day the title would more aptly be 'Clerk of the House of Lords', but tradition has retained the original style. Similarly the Clerk of the House of Commons is to this day appointed as 'Under-Clerk of the Parliaments' although he can no longer be regarded as the former's assistant.

The appointment of the Clerk of the Parliaments is governed by the Clerk of the Parliaments Act, 1824. The salary attaching to the office is £14,000 per annum.

CLERKS ASSISTANT

The Clerk Assistant and the Second Clerk Assistant are the two officers of the department of the Clerk of the House (q.v.) next in seniority to the Clerk himself. They are appointed by the Crown on the recommendation of the Speaker, and when they sit at the Table of the House, they take their places on the left of the Clerk. Like the Clerk of the House they wear the traditional black uniform with wig and gown. Their duties at the Table are to keep the minutes of proceedings, to receive (and if necessary put in order) notices of motions, questions, and amendments, and to prepare the Notice Paper and the Order Book for future sittings. In Committee of the Whole House the Clerk Assistant officiates in place of the Clerk of the House whose chair is occupied by the Chairman of Ways and Means.

Important administrative duties devolve upon the Clerk Assistant, who has in effect become the Establishment Officer for the department of the Clerk of the House. He is the Chairman of the Staff Board, which consists of the Establishment Officers of all three departments of the House of Commons together with a representative of the Library. The Staff Board has various functions relating to staff including the consideration of pay claims and, when necessary, negotiation with trade unions.

The Second Clerk Assistant now has overall responsibility for committees and does not normally perform duties at the Table of the House any longer. The Clerk and Clerk Assistant are instead assisted at the Table by other officers of the Clerk's establishment.

There is also a Clerk Assistant in the House of Lords, next in seniority to the Clerk of the Parliaments.

The office of Clerk Assistant did not become permanent until 1640, the first holder of the appointment being John Rushworth (q.v.). Originally, the Clerk of the House had the right to nominate his subordinate officers and to receive payment from the nominees. The practice of selling these appointments was discontinued by Jeremiah Dyson, Clerk of the House from 1748 to 1762, who nominated Hatsell (q.v.) as his deputy without payment. The office of Clerk Assistant and that of Second Clerk Assistant (which was instituted in 1800) are now appointed by the Crown under statute, but the Clerk of the House retains the power of appointing the other officers of his department. The position of the Clerk of the House in his professional relationship with his fellow Clerks-at-the-Table is that of a *primus inter pares*.

The salaries of the Clerk Assistant and Second Clerk Assistant in the House of Commons are £9,000 in each case.

In Australia the Clerk Assistant was redesignated the Deputy Clerk in 1964, and the Second Clerk Assistant is now the Clerk Assistant.

CLERKS-AT-THE-TABLE

See CLERK OF THE HOUSE; CLERK OF THE PARLIAMENTS; CLERKS ASSISTANT; CLERK OF THE OVERSEAS OFFICE; READING CLERK.

CLERKS-AT-THE-TABLE IN COMMONWEALTH PARLIAMENTS, SOCIETY OF

See SOCIETY OF CLERKS-AT-THE-TABLE IN COMMONWEALTH PARLIAMENTS.

CLOCK TOWER, PALACE OF WESTMINSTER

Built on the site where an earlier clock tower stood for centuries. The old clock was granted to the vestry of St. Margaret's, Westminster, in 1698, but it was pulled down soon after under the directions of Sir Christopher Wren. It is not known what happened to the clock, but the bell, known as 'Great Tom of Westminster', was taken to St. Paul's Cathedral, recast in 1716 and now hangs in the Western Tower.

The present Clock Tower, which is a modified form of Barry's original design, is about 320 feet high to the top of the finial and 40 feet square. On the first floor is the room to which members are confined when 'committed to the Clock Tower'. Bradlaugh (q.v.) was the last member to be sent there in 1880.

See also BIG BEN.

CLOSURE

The procedure by which a debate may be terminated by a majority decision of the House, even though all members wishing to speak have not done so. Prior to 1881 there existed no means of limiting the length of a debate, and once a question had been proposed it could be debated as long as there were any members who wished to speak upon it. The closure was instituted as a result of the action taken by Speaker Brand on 2 February 1881, in terminating a debate on his own responsibility. After a sitting lasting $41\frac{1}{2}$ hours during which the Irish members had deliberately protracted the debate on the motion for leave to bring in the Protection of Person and Property Bill (the so-called Coercion Bill) for the unconcealed purpose of obstructing the business of Parliament, Speaker Brand took the initiative of putting the question on the motion although the Irish members still wished to continue the debate. 'The dignity, the credit and the authority of this House are seriously threatened,' he declared, 'and it is necessary that they should be vindicated.' He declined to call upon any more members to speak and proceeded to put the question. His action was supported by the Prime Minister and the Leader of the Opposition, and the following day the powers of the Speaker were formally augmented by resolution of the House. In 1882 the closure was embodied in a Standing Order and thus became a part of the permanent procedure of the House. Although originally introduced as an emergency measure in the face of a calculated assault upon the foundations of the parliamentary system, the closure has become a normal feature of procedure which is recognized as a method of expediting business. It has undoubtedly increased the efficiency of the parliamentary machine but has necessarily reduced the opportunities of the individual private member.

Under the present system, any member may move the closure by rising during a debate and moving, 'That the question be now put', and it lies within the discretion of the Speaker, or in Committee of the Whole House the Chairman of Ways and Means or Deputy Chairman, to allow or disallow the motion. It cannot be moved in the House with the Deputy Speaker in the Chair unless the Speaker's absence has been formally announced, except on Supply days or at the report stage of a Bill. If the motion appears to be an abuse of the rules of the House or an infringement of the rights of the minority it will not be accepted by the Chair. If it is accepted it must be put to the vote of the House immediately without amendment or debate. If it is negatived by the House the debate continues; if it is carried, the question which was before the House when the closure was moved must be put immediately and the debate ended. At least 100 members must vote with the majority for a closure motion in order for it to be carried. In a Standing Committee the Chairman is empowered to accept a closure motion, a quorum being required to vote in the majority in order to carry it. Formerly, at least 20 members were required to vote with the majority.

Although simple enough in outline, closure procedure is subject to certain variations according to the circumstances under which it is applied. The procedure described above is known as the 'simple closure'. The application of the closure to a debate on an amendment to the main question involves an extension of this procedure known as the 'contingent closure'. Once the closure motion has been accepted by the House and the question on the amendment has been put, a member may rise to claim that the main question be now put, and if in the opinion of the Chair the main question has been discussed sufficiently during the debate on the amendment, it will be put immediately. A further variation is the 'special closure' which can operate in respect of debates on specific clauses during the committee and report stages of Bills. It cannot be moved when an amendment is under consideration, but otherwise the motion can take various forms of which the following is a typical example: 'That the question "That the clause stand part of the Bill" be now put.' When such a closure motion has been carried and the motion consequential upon it has been put to the vote, any amendments standing to that part of the Bill affected by the motion fall away without discussion.

A closure motion is frequently made under the provisions of Standing Order No. 1 (3) which permits the closure to be moved at the moment for the interruption of business under the Ten o'clock Rule (q.v.). This entails certain complications which are fully discussed in Erskine May.

A development of the closure procedure, the 'closure by compartments' or 'guillotine', is dealt with under the heading GUILLOTINE.

CLOUGH, OWEN (1873–1964)

Founder of the Society of Clerks-at-the-Table in Commonwealth Parliaments (q.v.) and editor of the first twenty volumes of its Journal (1932–51). Clerk of the South African Senate from 1910 to 1929.

COALITION

A coalition is formed when political parties unite to secure a majority in Parliament over other groups, and also in times of war when a National Government takes over and political attachments give way to national necessity. In the latter case an electoral truce (q.v.) is declared. There were Coalition Governments in Britain from 1852 to 1855, from 1895 to 1905, from 1915 to 1922, and from 1931 to 1945. However, to quote Sir Ivor Jennings on peacetime coalitions, 'the exact point at which a coalition becomes a unified party government is not always clear. There is a tendency for coalitions to lose their party differences. It is not possible to fix the date on which the Peelites were absorbed into the Liberal Party, nor that at which the Liberal Unionists were merged into the Conservative Party'. But the situation of a Coalition Government in peacetime raises very different issues from those of a wartime coalition, as Mr. Amery pointed out. The former usually represents the effort of politicians to compromise principles in the hope of retaining power, while the latter emphasizes the national determination to unify its striking-power. A coalition and the temporary abandonment of party politics is now accepted as essential when the country is at war, but normally, as Disraeli remarked in the House of Commons in 1852, 'England does not love coalitions'.

COBBETT, WILLIAM (1762–1835)

An untiring advocate of parliamentary reform and the leading journalist concerned in the movement, Cobbett unsuccessfully contested Coventry (1820), Preston (1826), and Manchester (1832) before he eventually won a seat for Oldham in the reformed House of Commons.

In 1806, Cobbett began the compilation of the Parliamentary History (q.v.), an undertaking which was completed by J. Wright. Compiled from various sources, it runs to thirty-six volumes, the first twelve of which were edited by Cobbett, and it constitutes a great legislative history of the country from the Norman Conquest to the year 1803. In 1803, beginning where the Parliamentary History ceases, Cobbett began the Parliamentary Debates (q.v.) which he incorporated in his weekly *Political Register*. They were taken over in 1812 by Thomas Curson Hansard (q.v.).

COLLECTING THE VOICES

When the Speaker, or in committee the Chairman, puts the question at the end of the debate, he reads out the motion before the House and adds, 'As many as are of that opinion will say Aye.' Those members supporting the motion comply, after which the Speaker continues, 'As many as are of the contrary opinion will say No.' This procedure is known as collecting the voices, and may or may not be followed by a division.

COLLECTIVE RESPONSIBILITY

See CABINET.

COLONIAL LAWS VALIDITY ACT

A statute of 1865 which provides that any colonial law which is in any way repugnant to the provisions of any Act of the British Parliament extending to the Colony to which such law may relate (or to any order or regulation made in terms of such an Act) shall be void and inoperative to the extent of the repugnancy.

The Act, when originally passed, applied to all Her Majesty's realms and territories except the Channel Islands, the Isle of Man, and India, and continued to do so until the passing of the Statute of Westminster in 1931. In terms of the Statute of Westminster, the requirements of the Colonial Laws Validity Act no longer apply to the legislation of the fully self-governing members of the Commonwealth and the Provinces of Canada. They still apply to the legislation of the Australian States, and to that of all territories which have yet to emerge as full members of the Commonwealth.

Repugnancy to the Common Law of England does not constitute a ground for declaring a colonial law to be invalid.

COLONIAL LEGISLATURES

Colonies were annexed to the Crown either by means of settlement, or by conquest or cession. Where Colonies were settled it was usual to establish a system of representative government modelled on that of Great Britain. Colonies acquired by conquest or cession were allowed only such rights as the Crown saw fit to confer. It was in this latter class of Colony that the type of administration developed which became known as 'Crown Colony' government, the system under which the majority of British colonial dependencies came to be ruled, and under which they subsequently attained their independence.

The earlier form of colonial government was known as the old representative system, examples of which survived until recently in Barbados, the Bahamas and Bermuda. Under this system the colonial legislature was modelled on the British Parliament, comprising a Governor who took the place of the Sovereign, a permanently appointed upper House corresponding to the House of Lords, and an elected Lower House corresponding to the House of Commons. The general pattern for this system became established in 1689, although representative assemblies had been set up in Virginia and Bermuda as early as 1619 and 1620 respectively. The system was not a success for, while it conceded the principle of popular representation, there was no ministerial responsibility to Parliament. Executive authority was concentrated exclusively in the hands of the Governor, who was also empowered to veto legislation.

The character of the colonial Empire changed following the introduction of responsible government in Canada, a development which had been advocated by the Durham Report (q.v.). In Colonies without responsible government the old representative system began to give way to the new representative system, or 'Crown Colony' government. Under this system the legislature consists of a Governor and a Legislative Council which can include official, nominated unofficial and elected unofficial members. An Executive Council, consisting of official and unofficial members of the Legislative Council, sits under the chairmanship of the Governor and corresponds to a Cabinet, although its powers are much more limited. The Governor was responsible to the Secretary of State for the Colonies (q.v.) (an office which was abolished in 1966) and, as the representative of the Crown, the head of the executive and (sometimes) the President of the Legislative Council, he is the central institution of British colonial government. He is empowered to veto legislation, to enact laws independently of the legislature should he deem them to be essential to good government, and while bound to consult the Executive Council is not bound to accept its advice (although he would require very good reasons for not doing so). It follows that under a system of Crown Colony government the legislature is subordinate to the executive and the colonial government is subordinate to the imperial government.

A Colony's progress towards self-government is usually reflected in the increasing proportion of elected members in the Legislative and Executive Councils. A further symbol of advance towards self-government in recent years has been the appointment of a Speaker in the place of the Governor to preside over the Legislative Council. Once self-government is achieved the legislature becomes wholly elected and the cabinet system is introduced. The final stage in the constitutional evolution of a colony is the attainment of sovereign independence which normally follows shortly after the establishment of self-government.

Most of the newer members of the Commonwealth travelled the road to independence in the manner described above, and the colonial Empire has dwindled rapidly in recent years. The pace of colonial emancipation since the Second World War may be illustrated by the fact that in 1945 the Legislative Councils of Tanganyika (which has since united with Zanzibar to become Tanzania) and Nyasaland (now Malawi) were wholly nominated, while those of the Gold Coast (now Ghana), Nigeria, Sierra Leone, Kenya and Northern Rhodesia (now Zambia) included only a minority of elected members. To-day all these countries are fully independent members of the Commonwealth.

To quote from Wight's *British Colonial Constitutions*, 1947, 'The relation between the imperial government and the colonial government depends upon the relation within the colonial government between the executive and the legislature. And the relation between the executive and the legislature depends upon the relation between the legislature and the dependency as a whole. The executive can control the legislature so long as the legislature does not represent, or is not answerable to, an electorate. The imperial government can control the colonial government so long as the colonial government has not become the organ of a fully integrated and self-conscious colonial nation. The working out of these principles of subordination to the point at which they cease to apply, with the attainment of independent status, is inherent in the modern British tradition of colonial government.'

(Further reading: Wight, *Development of the legislative council*, 1946.)

COLONIES, SECRETARY OF STATE FOR THE

The first Colonial Secretary, the Earl of Hillsborough, was appointed in 1768, but his office was abolished in 1782. In 1801 the Secretary of State for War, Lord Hobart, afterwards the Earl of Buckingham, took over the Colonies, but with the advent of the Crimean War a Principal Secretary of State for War was appointed and the Secretary of State for War relinquished control of the Army and retained the Colonies.

On 1 August 1966 the Colonial Office became merged with the Commonwealth Relations Office, which was in turn integrated with the Foreign Office on 17 October 1968. The responsibilities of the Colonial Secretary diminished increasingly as Britain's former dependencies one by one obtained their independence. Enough colonial problems remained, however, to justify the continuance of the office until 1966, although from 1963–4, during the prime ministership of Sir Alec Douglas-Home, it was held jointly with the Secretaryship of State for Commonwealth Relations by a single minister. The Colonial Secretary was responsible to Parliament for the government of British Colonies, Protectorates and Trust Territories and was empowered under the Colonial Development and Welfare Acts to make provision for the development of the resources and the welfare of the peoples of these territories. He was responsible also for the promotion of constitutional progress in colonial territories and for finding means, where possible in consultation with the colonial administration and the people themselves, of leading them to independence. The Colonial Secretary was invariably in the Cabinet and was assisted at the time of the abolition of the office by two Parliamentary Under-Secretaries of State.

A chronological list of Colonial Secretaries appears as Appendix 11.

COMMAND PAPERS

Papers presented to Parliament by a minister technically by Command of Her Majesty. They are generally restricted to matters of Government policy likely to be the subject of debate or legislation,

Commonwealth and foreign affairs and treaties, and reports on the work of government departments. At first Command Papers were printed as appendixes to the House of Commons Journal, but in 1833 the system began of numbering them serially, at first with a plain number, afterwards with numbers preceded by letters indicative of 'Command'. So far there are five series:

In 1833 began No. [1], which ran to No. [4222] of 1868–9.
In 1870 began [C. 1], which ran to [C. 9550] of 1899.
In 1900 began [Cd. 1], which ran to [Cd. 9239] of 1918.
In 1919 began [Cmd. 1], which ran to [Cmd. 9889] of 1956.
In 1956 began [Cmnd. 1], which still runs.

COMMISSIONERS OF CROWN LANDS

The Minister of Agriculture, Fisheries and Food, the Secretary of State for Scotland (both *ex-officio* and unpaid), and a Permanent Commissioner, who is also the Secretary of the small department. The Commissioners are responsible for the collection and administration of the revenues from Crown land under the Crown Lands Acts, 1829–1943. They were incorporated by an Act of 1927, and in 1943 the Secretary of State for Scotland was added to the Commission. The revenues obtained from Crown lands in England and Wales, with the exception of the Duchies of Lancaster and Cornwall, have been surrendered to Parliament since 1760 in exchange for the Civil List (q.v.). The revenues from Crown lands in Scotland were transferred to the Commissioners in 1833. This department is subordinate to the Treasury, but its work is most closely connected with the Ministry of Agriculture.

COMMITTAL

See PRIVILEGE, BREACH OF.

COMMITTEE FOR PRIVILEGES

A Sessional Committee (q.v.) of the House of Lords whose functions are to consider claims for peerage and precedence and matters relating to the orders, customs and privileges of the House. Its membership consists of 'all the Lords who have been or shall be present this session': thus, any Lord who attends the committee is automatically a member of it, but it cannot function unless three Lords of Appeal (q.v.) are present. The committee may examine witnesses on oath, call for papers and hear counsel.

COMMITTEE FOR THE JOURNALS

A Sessional Committee (q.v.) of the House of Lords which is still regularly appointed even though it has not met for many years. It consists of all the Lords present during the Session, its quorum is 3, and its terms of reference are 'to peruse and perfect the Journals of this and former sessions of Parliament'.

COMMITTEE OFFICE

An office in the department of the Clerk of the House in the charge of the Second Clerk Assistant. It supplies the clerks for the majority of Select Committees (q.v.) and some Standing Committees (q.v.). In the House of Lords the Committee Office is combined with the Private Bill Office.

COMMITTEE OF GRIEVANCES

See PETITIONS.

COMMITTEE OF PRIVILEGES

A Sessional Committee (q.v.) of the House of Commons, consisting usually of 12 Members, 5 forming the quorum. The membership includes the Leader of the House, who is usually Chairman, the Leader of the Opposition and one of the Law Officers. Its function is to consider complaints alleging breach of privilege, and it meets only when a specific complaint is referred to it. When a case stands referred to the committee it is customary for the House to take no action in the matter until the committee has reported. The committee is empowered to send for persons, papers and records, and is thus able to examine witnesses, but it may not hear counsel or solicitors.

The Committee originated in the 17th century, but it was during the present century that it came to be regularly appointed at the commencement of each session. When a complaint alleging a breach of privilege is raised on the Floor of the House the Speaker is required to rule as to whether or not a *prima facie* case has been established. If he rules that a *prima facie* case has been made out, it becomes necessary for the member raising the complaint or the Leader of the House to move a resolution which either has the effect of disposing of the matter immediately or of referring it to the Committee of Privileges. In recent years, when such cases have arisen, the Leader of the House has frequently taken upon himself the responsibility of moving as a matter of course that the complaint be referred to the committee. However, it appears that the motion should more properly be made by the member raising the complaint, and a letter to *The Times*, of 25 February 1965, from Mr. L. A. Abraham pointed out that if the practice referred to persists it will become virtually impossible for the House to dispose of a matter of this kind out of hand. A motion to refer a complaint to the Committee of Privileges when the Speaker has ruled that a *prima facie* case has not been made out would nevertheless be in order, but it would not take precedence in the order of business.

The Select Committee on Parliamentary Privilege which reported in December 1967 recommended that the Committee of Privileges be renamed the Select Committee of House of Commons Rights.

See also PRIVILEGE, BREACH OF.

COMMITTEE OF PUBLIC ACCOUNTS

House of Commons Standing Order No. 79 provides: 'There shall be a select committee, to be designated the Committee of Public Accounts, for the examination of the accounts showing the appropriation of the sums granted by Parliament to meet the public expenditure, and of such other accounts laid before Parliament as the committee may think fit, to consist of not more than fifteen members, who shall be nominated at the commencement of every session, and of whom five shall be a quorum. The committee shall have power to send for persons, papers and records, and to report from time to time.'

The Public Accounts Committee is a very senior body with a highly important function to perform. Its members are drawn from all parts of the House in proportion to the representation of the parties in the House. Its Chairman is usually a leading Member of the Opposition, if possible one who has held office as Financial Secretary to the Treasury, and the holder of that office in the Government of the day is invariably an *ex-officio* member. The committee is assisted and advised by the Comptroller and Auditor General (q.v.) who sits with the committee in the capacity of a permanent witness, although in actual fact he takes a far more active part in the proceedings of the committee than this designation of his status would imply. He is in reality a part-member who works closely with the Chairman, sits with the body of the committee at its meetings, and, although not permitted to direct questions to witnesses himself, advises the Chairman as to the questions which should be asked. Two Treasury Officers of Accounts also attend the committee as permanent witnesses (although usually only one of them is required to be present); they represent their department and the committee benefits from their services as accounting experts.

The main function of the Public Accounts Committee and the purpose for which it was originally set up are to ensure that all public money is spent as Parliament intended. Two further functions which have been defined by a former Chairman of the committee, to ensure the exercise of due economy and to maintain high standards of public morality in all financial matters, are logical developments of the committee's activities and are, in a sense, self-imposed duties. The most important accounts to come before the committee are the Appropriation Accounts which detail the annual expenditure of the Army, Navy, Air Force, and Civil Service, and which correspond in form to the Estimates (q.v.). They are cash accounts and are accompanied by explanatory appendixes showing causes of discrepancies and other details, but they have been criticized as not revealing liabilities incurred but unpaid. They are generally regarded as adequate for the purpose, however, as they do not come before the committee until they have been examined by skilled auditors having access to any further information they may require. The accounts are considered by the committee in conjunction with the reports thereon of the Comptroller and Auditor General. The Accounting Officers of the various departments (who are usually the permanent heads of the departments) are summoned before the committee as witnesses and required to explain any difficulties or anomalies to which attention has been drawn. Any excess expenditure, which is automatically frowned upon although it may be justified in certain circumstances, must be fully accounted for, and invariably elicits a report from the committee. Any indications of extravagance or wastage are thoroughly investigated. It is not surprising that the committee is regarded with some dread by the permanent officials who are called upon to explain the financial activities of their departments. In such a vast administrative organization infringements of financial regulations are bound to occur, and although it is unlikely that the head of an offending department is directly at fault, he cannot avoid his overall responsibility. The committee itself can do nothing worse than submit an adverse report to the House, but such is the importance attached to its findings that the results of such a report could be far-reaching.

The committee usually commences its deliberations at the end of February when the first reports of the Comptroller and Auditor General become available, and continues to sit weekly, sometimes throughout the session. Its reports were considered in the Committee of Supply prior to its abolition in December 1966, and they are now considered in the House. In the session of 1960–1 it became customary to devote at least one Supply Day (q.v.) to debating them. (Following a statement by the Leader of the House in July 1960, three days were made available for debating the reports of the Public Accounts and Estimates Committees, two being Supply days and the third being provided in Government time.) To a great extent the committee's reports are for the benefit of the Treasury, and such is the committee's prestige that its recommendations almost carry the force of directives, although the Treasury has on occasion successfully resisted certain recommendations.

The Public Accounts Committee was originally set up in 1861 on a motion of Gladstone. Its establishment had been recommended by a previous committee, the Select Committee on Public Monies, which had also urged the presentation to Parliament of annually audited accounts for examination by the proposed committee.

The effectiveness of the Public Accounts Committee has frequently been criticized on the ground that it performs a *post-mortem* function. Perhaps the late Sidney Webb provided the right answer to this criticism when he said, 'The fact that post-mortem examination does nothing to keep the patient alive is no proof that the existence of a system of *post-mortem* examinations does not prevent murders.'

(Further reading: Chubb, *The control of public expenditure*, 1952; Einzig, *The control of the purse*, 1959.)

COMMITTEE OF SELECTION

A Sessional Committee (q.v.) appointed in each House by Standing Order.

HOUSE OF COMMONS. The Committee of Selection was first appointed in 1839, and since 1908 it has consisted of 11 members, 3 being the quorum. Its functions relate principally to Private Business, but it also performs important duties in the sphere of Public Business, notably the appointment of members to Standing Committees (q.v.). It appoints the Chairmen and members of Private Bill Committees and distributes Private Bills (q.v.) and Provisional Order Bills (q.v.) among the various committees concerned with them according to whether they are opposed or unopposed. It nominates 8 of the 10 members of the Standing Orders Committee (q.v.), the Commons members of Joint Committees on Private Bills, and the membership of other committees concerned with Private Business. It also participates in the nomination of members to serve on Hybrid Bill Committees.

HOUSE OF LORDS. In the House of Lords, the Committee of Selection consists of the Lord Chairman of Committees and such other Lords as are named by the House. It is concerned only with Private Business and matters related to Private Business, and within this sphere its functions largely correspond to those of the Commons Committee. It selects the 5 Lords who form the Committees on opposed Private Bills or Provisional Order Bills, and also nominates the Chairmen of such Committees, its appointments being subject to the formal approval of the House. Like the Commons Committee, it names the Bills to be considered by such committees at their first and subsequent meetings.

COMMITTEE OF SUPPLY

See COMMITTEE OF THE WHOLE HOUSE; ESTIMATES; PROCEDURE, FINANCIAL; SUPPLY.

COMMITTEE OF THE WHOLE HOUSE

A committee consisting of all the members of the House presided over by a Chairman instead of by the Speaker. Proceedings in Committee are conducted in a less formal manner and the rules of procedure are less rigid than when the Speaker is in the Chair—for example, a member may speak more than once to the same question. The House is entitled to refer to a Committee of the Whole House any matter which, in its opinion, may be better discussed in committee. However, following the implementation of the new financial procedure in 1966–7, there is now for all practical purposes only one type of Committee of the Whole House, namely a Committee of the Whole House on a Public Bill.

The effect of the new financial procedure is to abolish the Committee of Supply, the Committee of Ways and Means, and financial Committees of the Whole House in general. The traditional financial procedure of the House of Commons, which dated from the early 18th century, required that all financial legislation be based on resolutions passed in a Commitee of the Whole House. The new financial procedure has therefore introduced radical innovations, and for reasons of historic interest the operation of the three types of Committee of the Whole House which were concerned with finance is outlined below.

The requirement that all matters concerning the raising and granting of public money must be considered in Committee of the Whole House prior to the introduction of financial legislation was fundamental to the financial procedure of the House prior to December 1966. In considering the grant of aids and supplies for the public service, in other words the expenditure of public money, the House resolved itself into a Committee of Supply. The raising of money so voted, in other words taxation, was considered in Committee of Ways and Means. Both committees were automatically appointed at the beginning of every session immediately after the House had agreed to the address in answer to the Speech from the Throne. The function of the Committee of Supply was to consider and approve all estimates (q.v.) and reports from the Committee of Public Accounts and Estimates Committee (qq.v.). The Committee of Ways and Means had two functions. In the first place it gave preliminary authorization to the Budget proposals, and on its resolutions were founded Finance Bills and all Bills imposing taxation. Its second function was of a formal nature: namely, to authorize the issue from the Consolidated Fund (q.v.) of the sums of money required to make good the grants voted by the Committee of Supply. On these resolutions were founded the Consolidated Fund and Appropriation Acts.

A Committee of the Whole House on a financial resolution was appointed *ad hoc* and was concerned with a specific matter involving expenditure. A financial resolution required the Queen's Recommendation (q.v.) before it could be considered in committee, and it was customary for the Speaker to seek assurance that it had received the Queen's Recommendation, which could be signified only by a senior Minister, before he left the Chair. Following the passage of the resolution by the Committee of the Whole House, it then required the endorsement of the House itself. Under the new procedure a single financial resolution is made in the House itself and the Queen's Recommendation is signified in writing to the Clerk of the House and noted on the order paper.

The financial procedure of the House of Commons was reformed because the traditional procedure had in many respects become obsolete and unnecessary. In addition, it was also somewhat mystifying to those who were not familiar with the intricacies of parliamentary procedure. It is interesting to note that the Committee of Supply and the Committee of Ways and Means were abolished in the Australian House of Representatives in 1963.

The committee stages of Bills involving finance are still taken in a Committee of the Whole House. If it is desired to take the committee stage of a non-financial Bill in a Committee of the Whole House a motion to that effect must be moved immediately after second reading, otherwise it will automatically be referred to a Standing Committee (q.v.) (*see also* BILL, PASSAGE OF). The committee stage of a Bill is the stage at which it receives detailed, and if need be clause-by-clause, consideration.

Whenever the House of Commons goes into committee the Speaker leaves the Chair and the Mace is removed from the Table by the Serjeant-at-Arms and placed in the lower brackets. The Chairman of Ways and Means (q.v.) or the Deputy Chairman then presides, occupying not the Speaker's Chair but a chair at the Table. The occupant of the Chair enjoys the full authority of the Speaker, except that he is not empowered to inflict serious forms of punishment such as suspension from the service of the House or committal. Such powers are reserved to the House with the Speaker in the Chair, and if circumstances arise in committee to warrant such action it is for the Chairman to recall the Speaker and report the circumstances to the House. The Chairman is, however, empowered to direct a member to withdraw.

It was the customary practice when the House resolved itself into committee for a motion to be made 'That Mr. Speaker do now leave the Chair', but under present procedure the Speaker leaves the Chair automatically. Under the former Supply procedure, although the Speaker would normally leave the Chair without any question being put, arrangements were sometimes made to debate the motion 'That the Speaker do now leave the Chair'. The type of debate which was held is discussed under the heading 'GETTING THE SPEAKER OUT OF THE CHAIR'. The custom of the Speaker vacating the Chair when the House goes into committee is sometimes said to originate from the days when members had reason to doubt the loyalty of the Speaker, and preferred him to be absent when they wished to debate freely. This is a theory which is open to question, however.

F

In the House of Lords a Committee of the Whole House is appointed by an order: 'That the House be put into a committee', and the Chair is taken by the Lord Chairman of Committees.

A Committee of the Whole House is not permitted to adjourn a sitting or a debate, but a motion that the Chairman do report progress and ask leave to sit again may be moved in committee, and if carried has the effect of postponing debate on the matter under consideration. The motion, if carried, is reported by the Chairman to the Speaker when the latter resumes the Chair.

The earliest references to 'general committees' and 'grand committees' which comprised the total membership of the House are found during the reign of Elizabeth I. In subsequent reigns it became the general practice, when a committee was seized of a matter of great national importance, to admit any member who chose to attend. 'The statement made in many popular accounts that a Committee of the Whole House was first employed for the discussion of the Bill of Attainder against the Earl of Strafford (1641) is a pure legend.' (Redlich).

COMMITTEE OF WAYS AND MEANS

See BUDGET; COMMITTEE OF THE WHOLE HOUSE; PROCEDURE, FINANCIAL; WAYS AND MEANS.

COMMITTEE ON PUBLIC PETITIONS

A Sessional Committee (q.v.) of the House of Commons consisting of 15 members, 3 being the quorum, to which are referred all public petitions presented to the House with the exception of those affecting the privileges of the House or complaining of a personal grievance requiring immediate remedy. Its function is to classify and summarize the petitions referred to it in such a way as to convey to the House all requisite information respecting their contents. It is not empowered to verify the facts stated in a petition or to inquire into its substance. It may direct the printing in full or in part of any petition referred to it, in which case the petition or such parts of it as are printed would appear as an appendix to the committee's report.

The committee is not an overworked body as the public petition has largely been superseded by other methods of securing redress of grievances (*see* PETITIONS).

COMMITTEE ON UNOPPOSED BILLS

See PRIVATE BILLS.

COMMITTEE STAGE

See BILL, PASSAGE OF.

COMMON LAW

The Common Law may be regarded as being that part of the law of the land which is traditional and proceeding from the judgments of the Courts, as opposed to the part which is statutory and made in or under the authority of Parliament. The explanation of the adjective 'Common' is that in medieval times the law administered by the King's Superior Courts was the 'Common custom of the realm', as distinct from the particular customs with which local jurisdictions were concerned.

COMMONS AMENDMENTS, CONSIDERATION OF

See BILL, PASSAGE OF.

COMMONS, HOUSE OF

See HOUSE OF COMMONS.

COMMON WEALTH

Founded in July 1942 by Sir Richard Acland with a socialist policy founded on Christian morality and not Marxian 'scientific socialism', and advocating common ownership, social equality, colonial freedom, European federation, world unity, and a 'Second Front'. The party demanded an immediate ending of the Electoral Truce (q.v.) and declared its intention to fight by-elections where the previous member had not been Labour—or equally 'progressive'. In 1943 the National Executive of the Labour Party put Common Wealth on its list of proscribed organizations, membership of which was incompatible with membership of the Labour Party. In 1944 there were three Common Wealth members in the House of Commons, and although the party put up 23 candidates at the General Election of 1945 it only retained one of its seats. Sir Richard Acland was defeated, but was returned at a by-election in 1947 as a Labour member. Common Wealth has not contested an election since 1945.

COMMONWEALTH, 1658–1660

The Commonwealth was short-lived after the death of Oliver Cromwell. He had appointed his third son, Richard, as his successor, and according to the *Dictionary of National Biography* the new Protector was proclaimed some three hours after his father's death on 3 September 1658. Richard lacked the strength of his father and he was immediately caught up in the toils of dissension between the military and the civil power. To settle the difficulty and to obtain the money he required for meeting the expenses of the administration he summoned a Parliament, the only one of his brief career as head of the state. The new Parliament consisted of two Houses and the Commons were returned under the old method of election, the smaller boroughs again returning members. Richard Cromwell opened Parliament on 27 January 1659, and delivered 'beyond expectation, a very handsome speech' in which he paid tribute to his father and affirmed his resolve to govern through Parliament. But the republicans in the Commons lost no time in challenging the right of the new Protector to be recognized. They argued that he wielded too much power and that only Parliament was empowered to confer the office. The republicans were in the minority in Parliament, however, and Richard Cromwell's position was eventually confirmed by 223 votes to 134. Immediately afterwards the Commons also resolved to recognize the upper House. The army was antagonized by the proceedings of the Commons, and although the Protector's government controlled the majority in Parliament they feared the power of the military. To strengthen their own power the Commons passed resolutions diminishing that of the army, upon which the army demanded the dissolution of Parliament. Under pressure from the army leaders the Protector consented, and his one and only Parliament was dissolved by proclamation on 22 April.

Although once more in supreme control the army hesitated to raise taxes on its own authority and decided it was necessary to restore some form of civil power. At the instigation of General Lambert it was decided to recall the Long Parliament (q.v.) which was held never to have been legally dissolved. On 7 May the remnant of that once great assembly, or the Rump Parliament (q.v.) as it became known, returned to Westminster headed by Speaker Lenthall (q.v.). A temporary Committee of Public Safety was appointed, and the Commons passed resolutions abolishing the House of Lords and dispensing with a single person at the head of the state. Richard Cromwell was urged by his supporters to resist but he declined to do so, and is alleged to have said, 'I will not have a drop of blood spilt for the preservation of my greatness, which is a burden to me.' He resigned his claim to the Protectorship and Parliament undertook to discharge his debts.

On 14 May a new Council of State was elected consisting of 16 civilians and 15 army leaders. They included Haselrig, Vane, Ludlow, Fleetwood, Fairfax, Lambert, Bradshaw, St. John, and Whitelocke. An address was presented to Parliament on behalf of the army calling for certain assurances, including confirmation of the republican form of government, religious toleration for all but Catholics and Episcopalians, and a Constitution providing for a Parliament of two Houses as the legislative authority and a Council of State as the executive. The Commons accepted most of the clauses, but they ignored the request for a second Chamber and placed the army under parliamentary control, enacting that all commissions should be signed by the Speaker. It was inevitable that the old quarrel should flare up afresh. The army objected to the military authority being vested in the Commons, and under the influence of Lambert a petition was presented complaining of the army's grievances and making various demands which amounted to depriving Parliament of its control. The Commons rejected the petition, reaffirmed their claim to the military authority, and cancelled the commissions of those officers, including Lambert, who had offended them. They also took the extreme step of invalidating all measures which had been enacted since Oliver Cromwell forcibly dissolved the Long Parliament unless they received confirmation from the restored Rump. These proceedings provoked the army to action, and for the second time in its history the Long Parliament was forcibly expelled. On 13 October Lambert mustered his soldiers in and about the Palace of Westminster and prevented all members from entering the building.

The army was in supreme authority yet again, but all was far from well within the nation and there was much dissatisfaction over the trend of events. General Monk, who enters the pageant of history at this vital period, expressed concern at the situation in a letter from Edinburgh, and he also wrote to Speaker Lenthall affirming his adherence to parliamentary government. The army leaders who comprised the Committee of Safety attempted to negotiate with Monk, but the latter was determined on relieving the chaotic situation into which the country had fallen. Taxes remained uncollected and the army's administration was in dire financial need. Drastic remedies were imperative.

Although there was as yet nothing to indicate the likelihood of a restoration of the monarchy, events had already begun to move in this direction. Charles Stuart was eagerly watching developments from his exile on the Continent, but one can only conjecture whether or not Monk had already determined on his restoration as the solution to the country's problems.

On 26 December the Long Parliament was again recalled, but few of those who had sat in the previous Rump took the trouble to attend, and those members who had been excluded many years ago before the trial of Charles I and who attempted to regain admission were prevented from doing so. A new Council of State was elected and on 3 February 1660 General Monk came to London. He was welcomed and thanked by Parliament, but he demanded that a time should be fixed for a dissolution and writs issued for new elections. In view of the strong Royalist feeling in the country it was easy to appreciate the possible outcome of such a course. Moribund though it was, the Rump was nevertheless eager to cling to its precarious power. Parliament made an attempt to dissuade Monk from his purpose, but he remained adamant, and when writs were not issued within the time he had stipulated he made a move which Parliament had not anticipated by inviting the long-excluded members to return and take their seats. They immediately found themselves in an overwhelming majority. By this time the move towards a restoration of the monarchy had become a definite one. The restored members began to speak openly in favour of it and passed a number of measures designed to smooth its passage. On 16 March 1660 Parliament dissolved itself and the Commonwealth virtually came to a close. Monk opened secret negotiations with Charles, and a brief interregnum ensued before the Restoration was finally effected.

See also CHARLES II AND PARLIAMENT.

COMMONWEALTH AFFAIRS, SECRETARY OF STATE FOR

Until the Commonwealth and Foreign offices were merged on 17 October 1968, the Secretary of State for Commonwealth Affairs was a Cabinet minister in his own right, his office dating from July 1925. At that time a new secretaryship of State for Dominion Affairs was created to take over from the Colonial Secretary (q.v.) business connected with the self-governing Dominions, the self-governing Colony of Southern Rhodesia and the High Commission Territories of Basutoland, Bechuanaland and Swaziland. In July 1947 the Minister's title was changed to Secretary of State for Commonwealth Relations, and in August 1966 he became the Secretary of State for Commonwealth Affairs following the re-integration of the Colonial Office and Commonwealth Relations Office. The development of the Commonwealth Office from its establishment in 1925 to its integration with the Foreign Office in 1968 has reflected the growth of the Commonwealth from a small group of countries united under the British constitutional umbrella to a large association of widely scattered sovereign nations differing from each other in many fundamental respects.

The Commonwealth Secretary was responsible for the conduct of Great Britain's relations with the independent Commonwealth countries in much the same way as the Foreign Secretary was responsible for relations with foreign countries. Rhodesia's relationship with the United Kingdom was also conducted through the Commonwealth Office until normal communications were interrupted following the Rhodesian Government's unilateral declaration of independence in November 1965. The conduct of relations with all the sovereign countries of the world now comes under the responsibility of the Secretary of State for Foreign and Commonwealth Affairs (q.v.). A list of Commonwealth Secretaries appears as Appendix 12.

(Further reading: Walker, 'Commonwealth Secretary', in the *Journal of Commonwealth Political Studies*, vol. 1, no. 1.)

COMMONWEALTH OF NATIONS

An international association of states which has evolved from the former British Empire and which defies constitutional definition. The states which form the Commonwealth have little in common apart from the fact that they were once British Colonies, Protectorates or Trust Territories, and are now completely equal in status.

The evolution of the modern Commonwealth may be said to have started with the passage of the Statute of Westminster (q.v.) in 1931. Prior to this date the self-governing Dominions of the then British Empire—namely Canada, Australia, New Zealand, South Africa and the Irish Free State—were legally still Colonies. Their legislative competence was limited by the Colonial Laws Validity Act, 1865 (q.v.), and the United Kingdom Parliament was not debarred from legislating directly for them, although by convention this was never done except at their request or with their consent. The powers of the Dominions were also limited in respect to such matters as the waging of war, the making of treaties and the appointment of diplomatic representatives.

These disabilities were removed by the Statute of Westminster which gave effect to the declaration of the Imperial Conference of 1926 that Great Britain and the Dominions were 'autonomous Communities within the British Empire, equal in status, in no way subordinate one to another in any aspect of their domestic or external affairs, though united by a common allegiance to the Crown, and freely associated as members of the British Commonwealth of Nations'. This declaration implied that loyalty to the Crown was the common denominator of Commonwealth membership. It also implied the right to secede.

The right to secede received official confirmation in 1942 at the time of the Cripps Mission to India and was first acted upon in 1949 when the Irish Free State severed its links with the Crown and the Commonwealth, and the Republic of Burma elected to embark on its newly won independence outside the association. In the same year India, while announcing its intention to become a Republic, expressed the desire to retain Commonwealth membership, and a formula was agreed whereby India acknowledged the King as the head of the Commonwealth and the symbol of the association.

The Indian precedent was subsequently followed by other countries, although in the case of South Africa, a founder-member of the Commonwealth, the adoption of a republican form of government was followed by withdrawal from the association. The links binding the member-states inevitably became more tenuous, for with the admission of republics to the Commonwealth even the common denominator of allegiance to the Crown, previously regarded as a fundamental requirement, ceased to apply.

To-day the Commonwealth has abandoned all constitutional fictions and has no formal framework, apart from the Commonwealth Secretariat established in 1965. Its principal value is to serve as a forum for informal international co-operation and consultation, its main instrument for this purpose being the regularly convened Conference of Commonwealth Prime Ministers and Presidents. In addition, bodies such as the Commonwealth Parliamentary Association (q.v.) do much to further contacts between member-states. Certain sentimental ties perhaps remain within the Commonwealth, although some of its members probably have little regard for the historic basis of the association. The only conditions for admission to the Commonwealth appear to be the agreement of the other member-states, a willingness to recognize the Queen as head of the Commonwealth, and a constitutional status of sovereign independence. Only one member has been admitted from outside the family—namely Cyprus, which became independent outside the Commonwealth in 1960 but applied for re-admission as a full member in 1961. South Africa is the only former Commonwealth member to have withdrawn from the association as a result of pressure from other members, from which one may deduce that a country whose government is controlled by a racial minority is not acceptable to the Commonwealth as a whole. A democratic form of government is not, however, a *sine qua non* for Commonwealth membership as can be seen from developments which have taken place in some of the newer countries of the Commonwealth following the achievement of independence.

At the time of writing (1970) the Commonwealth consists of 12 monarchies acknowledging allegiance to the British Crown: United Kingdom, Canada, Australia, New Zealand, Ceylon, Jamaica, Trinidad and Tobago, Malta, Sierra Leone, Barbados, Mauritius, and Fiji; 15 Republics: India, Pakistan, Ghana, Nigeria, Cyprus, Tanzania, Uganda, Kenya, Zambia, Guyana, Singapore, Malawi, Botswana, Nauru, and The Gambia, and 5 independent monarchies: The Federation of Malaysia, Lesotho, Swaziland, Tonga, and Western Samoa. Ceylon is in the process of adopting a Republican Constitution and has already set up a constituent assembly for this purpose. Rhodesia, since its unilateral seizure of independence in November 1965, has been in an anomalous position, and in the eyes of the other member states is being governed by an illegal régime.

(Further reading: de Smith, *The New Commonwealth and its Constitutions*, 1964.)

COMMONWEALTH PARLIAMENTARY ASSOCIATION

An organization which has for its object the establishment of permanent machinery to facilitate the exchange of information, closer understanding and co-operation, and more frequent intercourse between members of the different Parliaments of the Commonwealth. It consists of main branches in the United Kingdom and each of the fully autonomous countries of the Commonwealth, state and provincial branches in states and provinces which, although united under a central or federal form of government, have also a local legislature; and auxiliary, affiliated and subsidiary branches, varying in status, in dependent states and territories having responsible or representative government. At present there are over sixty main, state and provincial branches and over thirty auxiliary, affiliated and subsidiary branches. In countries where parliamentary government has been suspended (e.g. Lesotho and Nigeria) certain branches are in abeyance. The Rhodesian branch was formally expelled from the Association following that country's unilateral declaration of independence in November 1965. The constitutions of the various branches of the Association have changed and are changing in accordance with the manner in which the Commonwealth itself has developed and is developing. In addition to the branches there are two associated groups, formed at the invitation of the General Council, in the United States of America and in the Republic of Ireland.

Full membership of the association is confined to sitting Members of Parliament throughout the Commonwealth, who are entitled to become members without election upon payment of the subscription. Ex-Members of Parliament may become affiliated members of the association. The association provides for visits and the holding of conferences and offers privileges to its members in the way of inter-branch hospitality, letters of introduction, travel facilities, and access to legislatures.

The association was formed in 1911 under the name of the Empire Parliamentary Association. The name was changed on the proposal of the Canadian branch at the first post-war Commonwealth Parliamentary Conference in 1948. At the same time it was resolved to establish a General Council of the Association as a means of regular contact between the branches, the representatives on the Council to be annually elected by the branches themselves. The Council meets annually at various places throughout the Commonwealth, issues an annual report, and elects its own Chairman and Vice-Chairman. It also appoints a Secretary-General who acts as liaison officer between the branches and whose office is a common information centre. Throughout the branches the Clerk of the House in each legislature concerned usually acts as the branch secretary.

The Commonwealth Parliamentary Association issues a regular publication entitled *The Parliamentarian* and also publishes other material on matters of parliamentary interest from time to time.

COMMUNICATIONS BETWEEN LORDS AND COMMONS

Frequent communications pass between the two Houses and a 'message' is used for sending Bills and amendments to Bills from one to the other, for requesting the attendance of witnesses, for the interchange of reports and other documents, and for communicating all matters of an ordinary description occurring in the course of parliamentary proceedings. Messages from the Commons were once conveyed by the Chairman or the member in charge of a Bill, accompanied by a number of other members, but in 1855 both Houses agreed to transmit messages by their Clerks. Until the middle of the last century 'conferences' between representatives of each House were held, the last being in 1860, but only written communications were delivered and there was no discussion. 'Free conferences' where debate was permitted fell into disuse even earlier, and only one, in 1836, has been held since 1740.

COMMUNIST PARTY IN PARLIAMENT

The British Communist Party was founded in 1920, and at the 1922 General Election two members of the party were elected, J. T. Walton Newbold and S. Saklatvala, a Parsee. The latter ran as an endorsed Labour Party candidate, having pledged himself to abide by the Labour Party Constitution. He was elected again for North Battersea in the 1924 election. The Parliamentary Labour Party rejected an application from Mr. Newbold after the election to receive the Labour Party Whip. William Gallacher, the next Communist to obtain a seat, was elected in 1935 for the Western Division of Fife, which seat he held until 1950. Another Communist member was P. Piratin, who was elected for the Mile End Division of Stepney in 1945 and held the seat until 1950. At the Communist Unity Conference of July 1920, a resolution was carried in favour of affiliation to the Labour Party, and soon after the Executive of the newly formed Communist Party of Great Britain made the first of its many applications for affiliation. The Labour Party executive replied that 'the basis of affiliation to the Labour Party is the acceptance of its constitution, principles and programme, with which the objects of the Communist Party do not appear to be in accord'. The Labour Party has continued to debar from affiliation 'political organizations . . . owing allegiance to any political organization situated abroad', and in 1923 voted that no member of the Communist Party should be eligible as a Labour Party candidate at parliamentary elections and that no Communist Party member should be allowed to join the Labour Party as an individual member.

The Communist Party has contested every General Election since the Second World War, but with a marked lack of success. The two seats held by the party in the 1945–50 Parliament were lost at the General Election of 1950, an election at which 100 Communist candidates stood, only 3 managing to save their deposits. Ten Communists stood in 1951, 17 in 1955, 18 in 1959, 36 in 1964, 57 in 1966, and 58 in 1970, all unsuccessfully. The party saved two of its deposits in 1955 and one in 1959, but forfeited all of them in 1951, 1964, 1966 and 1970.

However, although apparently doomed to failure at the polls, the party is now represented in the House of Lords by Lord Milford, the first and only Communist peer, who succeeded to his title in 1962. Lord Milford made his maiden speech on 4 July 1963 on the second reading of the Peerage Bill, in the course of which he declared that he could 'never support any measure which helps to perpetuate this Chamber'. In the course of the same debate, Earl Attlee remarked upon the curious anomaly which permits the voice of the Communist Party to be heard only in the House of Lords. Certainly, it is an outstanding example of the ironies which can result from the hereditary principle.

The Communist Party has members in the Parliaments of India and Ceylon. In the Indian elections of 1957 the party actually secured control of the state legislature of Kerala, but its tenure of office lasted only until July 1959. The Communist Government of Kerala was dismissed from office by the Government of India after rioting had taken place in the province, and it was defeated at the subsequent provincial election. However, in February 1967, the Communists and their allies again gained control of the state. For a short time a Communist held a seat in the Queensland Parliament, but this represents the party's only success in Australia.

COMPTROLLER AND AUDITOR GENERAL

The officer who is responsible for the auditing of all public accounts. His position is unique in that he is an Officer of Parliament yet, as head of the Exchequer and Audit Department, he controls a staff of Civil Servants. He is appointed by letters patent on the nomination of the Prime Minister (q.v.), his full title being 'Comptroller General of the Receipt and Issue of Her Majesty's Exchequer and Auditor General of Public Accounts'. His salary, like that of the Speaker (q.v.), is charged directly to the Consolidated Fund (q.v.) and not provided for in the Estimates (q.v.). His statutory duties are laid down in the Exchequer and Audit Department Acts, 1866 and 1921.

Although not himself a Civil Servant, the Comptroller and Auditor General has always held senior appointments in the Civil Service, usually in the Treasury (q.v.), for wide knowledge and experience of the administration of government departments are indispensable to his job. He need not necessarily be a trained auditor. His main duty is to conduct an examination of the Appropriation Accounts (i.e., the accounts of the various departments of government) and to satisfy himself that all moneys appropriated have been applied to the purposes intended and approved by Parliament. All other public accounts, including the Consolidated Fund accounts (i.e., accounts in respect of charges which are made directly on the Consolidated Fund and not provided for in the Estimates), are subjected to the same scrutiny. The immense amount of detailed work involved in this mighty task is carried out by the Exchequer and Audit Department, each division of the department being responsible for the accounts of a particular ministry or group of ministries.

The Comptroller and Auditor General submits an annual report to Parliament on his findings, which is referred to the Committee of Public Accounts (q.v.) for consideration. The Comptroller himself sits with the committee to offer any advice and assistance which may be required.

The appointment of Comptroller and Auditor General was created in 1866 by the first Exchequer and Audit Department Act. In terms of the Exchequer and Audit Department Act, 1957, his salary may be increased by resolution of the House of Commons. His present salary is £14,000, increased from £9,800 in 1970.

COMPULSORY VOTING

Australia is the only country in the British Commonwealth which imposes compulsory voting. It was first introduced in parliamentary elections in Queensland in 1915 and for the Australian Federal Parliament in 1924. All the other Australian States have since adopted compulsory voting, the last one to fall into line being South Australia, whose Act, passed in 1942, first came into operation at the 1944 election. Every elector who has not voted is sent a form after an election, on which must be stated the reason for failing to vote. If the Returning Officer decides that it is not true, valid, and sufficient, the elector becomes liable to a penalty of £2. Apart from the fact that compulsory voting reduces the cost of elections by removing any reason for candidates to convey electors to the polling-booths, its supporters have found very little to say in its favour. However, one Senator did state hopefully that it would compel people to take a keener interest in Parliament! Professor Crisp, the authority on politics and Parliament in Australia, says that the effects of compulsory voting cannot be assessed with precision or certainty, but that it has certainly not contributed to the serious political education of the electorate, and may even have discouraged it. He points out that it is arguable that as a voting population, which has only known a compulsory attendance at the polls, increases, there will be a growing number who regard voting as a burden and not a privilege of democracy. Professor Crisp says that there is no proof that compulsory voting has helped any particular party to power in Australia, and sums up this aspect of the question by quoting Sir Frederic Eggleston, a prominent Australian writer, politician, and diplomat, who concluded that 'compulsory voting assists a government which is moving with a live popularity: it punishes severely a government which is unpopular'.

CONCILIATION BILL

See SUFFRAGETTES.

CONCURRENT LIST

A list of subjects appended to a federal constitution in respect of which the federal legislature and the state or regional legislatures have power to make laws, federal law prevailing in case of conflict.

CONFEDERATION

A league or union of sovereign states where importance is attached to the independence of each of the constituent bodies, as opposed to a federation where stress is laid on the supremacy of the central government. However, the distinction between a confederation and a federation has become somewhat blurred, and even the most eminent constitutional writers have been known to use the terms as if they were synonymous.

CONFIDENCE, VOTE OF

See VOTE OF CONFIDENCE.

CONFLICT OF INTERESTS

The problems inherent in a situation where a Member of Parliament may find his public duty conflicting with his private interests have long been recognized by Parliament. There are various well-established practices governing the conduct of members in such circumstances. For example, they may not accept fees for professional services connected with proceedings in Parliament, neither may they vote on any matter in which they have a direct pecuniary interest. It is also customary for a member, if he has a personal interest in a subject under debate, to declare it, although the only such declaration actually required by the Standing Orders is in relation to opposed Private Bills.

While certain principles are clear, areas of uncertainty exist which call for a more precisely defined code of conduct, and it was to consider this matter that the House of Commons appointed a Select Committee on Members' Interests (Declaration) in 1969. Reporting on 4 December of that year the committee drew attention to certain activities in which modern Members of Parliament tended to engage and which had not come within the scope of the traditional practice of the House relating to conflict of interests. Such activities arose from the engagement of Members of Parliament as parliamentary consultants by public relations and similar organizations and the opportunities available to members of free travel and other benefits which could be used by pressure groups as a means of exerting influence. The committee rejected a suggestion that members should be required to register their private interests, but was favourably disposed towards a system which would require the public disclosure of the employment of Members of Parliament on

[163]

parliamentary matters, showing the object of the employment and the remuneration to be paid.

The committee recommended specifically that the House should adopt the two following resolutions, which would together comprise a code of conduct for members:

(1) That in any debate or proceedings of the House or its Committees or transactions or communications which a Member may have with other Members or with Ministers or servants of the Crown, he shall disclose any relevant pecuniary interest or benefit of whatever nature, whether direct or indirect, that he may have had, may have, or may be expecting to have.

(2) That it is contrary to the usage and derogatory to the dignity of this House that a Member should bring forward by speech or question, or advocate in this House or among his fellow Members any Bill, motion, matter or cause for a fee, payment, retainer or reward, direct or indirect, which he has received, is receiving or expects to receive.

The committee further recommended that the Committee of Privileges should review the code annually and that a serious breach of it should be held to be a contempt of the House.

CONSEQUENTIAL AMENDMENT

An amendment made to a clause in a Bill may affect other clauses where the same word or words occur, and amendments made to these other clauses in consequence are therefore called consequential amendments.

CONSERVATIVE PARLIAMENTARY PARTY

In the House of Commons this is composed of all members who take the Conservative Whip, thereby signifying their acceptance of the policy of the party as declared by the leader. Management rests with the Chief Whip, who is appointed by the leader of the party.

Unlike the Parliamentary Labour Party in the House of Commons, the leader of the Conservative Party is not appointed on a sessional basis, but once elected he remains the leader until he dies or resigns. He possesses powers much beyond those of the leader of the Labour Party, and the most striking fact about the Conservative Party is the pre-eminent rôle assigned to the leader under the constitution of the party. The Conservative Parliamentary Party has a committee known as the Nineteen Twenty-two Committee (q.v.) which all back-benchers are entitled to attend, and when in opposition a number of subject groups are formed which can examine the party's policy and actions and discuss the forthcoming business of the House.

CONSERVATIVE PARTY

The Conservatives are the successors of the old Tory Party, and as the Cavaliers had been called Tories—the word originally applied to Irish bandits—it is hoped by the opponents of the Conservatives who describe the party as Tories that some of the opprobrium once attached to the word still remains. The party did not acquire the description of Conservative until soon after the passing of the Reform Bill of 1832. The principles of Conservatism were defined by Disraeli in 1872—to maintain the institutions of the country, to uphold the Empire, and to ameliorate the condition of the people. Another Conservative M.P., Nigel Birch, wrote seventy-seven years later: 'Conservatism seeks to get out of every fresh development, each new line of thought, what is of value, but to prevent enthusiasm for the fashionable cure of the day leading to a state of unbalance which may do lasting damage to the country. The Tories took an active part in liberalizing our economy in the early part of the 19th century when it was encumbered by a tariff structure of great complexity, and still tied down by Tudor legislation, and took their stand against *laissez-faire* and for authority in the later years of the same century; and thus to-day they are seeking to preserve what was of lasting value in 19th-century Liberalism against the ever-increasing aggression of an authoritarian State.'

The Tories had triumphed in the restoration of the Stuarts to the throne, but with the coming of the Hanoverians the party's prestige declined and for nearly fifty years the Whigs were in power. The Jacobin tendencies in the party put it out of favour with the Court, but with the accession of George III it was restored to royal favour. The Coalition Governments with which the King hoped to break the Whig system of Cabinet government and increase his own power were, however, singularly unsuccessful. The experiment ended with the loss of the American colonies, and in 1783 the Tories began, under the leadership of William Pitt the Younger, a period of predominance which lasted until 1830. Pitt reorganized the financial system of the country, restored Cabinet government, remoulded the governments of Canada and India, and supported Wilberforce in his campaign against the slave trade. After the Napoleonic Wars the party was held together by Lord Liverpool as Prime Minister, although for some years before his retirement in 1827 it had become obvious that the Tory Party was divided into two main sections—the progressives who followed Canning and the reactionaries who looked to the Duke of Wellington. After Canning's death in 1827 the party split, and his disciples, who included Gladstone, drifted into Liberalism. From 1830 to 1874 the Tories were seldom in office and only once in power. Defeat caused the party to consider using a more suitable name, and the suggestion of J. W. Croker in 1833 of 'Conservative' was adopted since it implied that the party's essential characteristic was to maintain and preserve existing institutions. Sir Robert Peel started the work of reviving the party's fortunes by issuing a restatement of policy in the Tamworth Manifesto, and by setting up a central party organization in the hope of counteracting the bad impression left by the party's opposition to the Reform Bill in 1832. He was so successful that after achieving an Opposition 250 strong in the Parliament of 1835, he was returned with a comfortable majority in 1841. Everything seemed set fair for a generation of Tory rule when the party was again split in 1846 over the question of the abolition of the Corn Laws, which imposed a tax on imported wheat. Peel forced the abolition through in face of the bitter opposition of his party, led by Disraeli, and it was not until 1931 that the resulting agricultural depression which commenced towards the end of the century was relieved by any form of protection. Peel resigned after the break-up of the party, taking the 'Peelites' with him and leaving the rest of the party under the leadership of Lord Derby and Disraeli. During the following years Disraeli established his position and carried through the Electoral Reform Bill of 1867. In 1874 he was returned with the first clear Conservative majority since 1841, and until 1880, when they lost the election, the party was responsible for the passing of a number of Acts for the improvement of social conditions. After the death of Disraeli in 1881 the Conservatives were led for twenty-one years by Lord Salisbury, and as Lord Henry Bentinck said, 'The people gave its confidence (with a three years' break) from 1886 to 1900 with a remarkable constancy to the Tory Party, because the Party gave sufficient evidence of its honesty in the cause of the common weal.' By declaring for Home Rule for Ireland, Gladstone split the Liberal Party as Peel had split the Conservative Party over the Corn Laws, and the part played by the Peelites was taken by the Liberal Unionists led by Joseph Chamberlain, who formed an alliance with the Conservatives in their efforts to prevent the division of the United Kingdom which has lasted ever since. The name Unionist survives in the official name of the party, and is still used in Scotland and in Northern Ireland. During the later years of the 19th century the Liberals began to free themselves of Whig control and the Whig magnates began to turn to the Conservative Party. After the resignation of Lord Salisbury in 1902 the Conservatives became increasingly whiggish in their approach to political problems, and this, combined with the growth of 'big business' influence in Conservative counsels, had a disastrous effect on the party's fortunes. The so-called capitalistic tendencies in the party were emphasized by the Socialists to demonstrate that the Labour Party represented the workers and the Conservative Party the 'bosses', although the latter party had always been the champion of the small man. Even when it was soundly beaten in the election of 1906, working-class boroughs such as Hoxton and Stepney returned Conservative members to Parliament. This defeat in 1906 was caused by a division in the party over preferential tariffs within the British Commonwealth advocated by Joseph Chamberlain; then, after a brief revival of popularity, it allowed the Liberals to appeal to the electors on the cry of Peers *versus* People, with the result that two more General Elections were lost in succession. The outbreak of the First World War restored the prestige of the Conservatives, and it was remembered that they had always stood for effective armaments and a strong Navy. As the war progressed Conservative stock continued to rise, and in 1915 they entered a Coalition Government which they continued to support until 1922. The party, led by Baldwin, then broke with Lloyd George, mainly because of his unpredictable foreign policy, and apart from two short periods when the Labour Party was in office, the Conservatives, either alone or as the predominant partner in a coalition, were subsequently in power until the General Election of 1945. The National Government which was formed after the General Election of 1931 under Ramsay MacDonald included the Liberals and a few Labour members, but the Liberals split over the introduction of protective tariffs for agricultural products, and the Independent Liberals went into Opposition while the National Liberals supported the Government. In 1934 the Conservatives were subject to internal dissensions, on the subject of India, and later, when Neville Chamberlain became Prime Minister, over the attitude to be adopted towards Germany and Italy. On both occasions Sir Winston Churchill was in opposition to the official policy, and after he had become Prime Minister in 1940 his success during the Second World War redounded to his personal credit rather than to that of the party. After the War the Conservatives suffered such a severe defeat in the General Election of 1945 that they found it necessary to overhaul the party organization and programme. This resulted in almost equal support being given for the Conservative and Labour Parties at the 1950 General Election, and another election was held in 1951 which resulted in a Conservative Government under Sir Winston Churchill as Prime Minister with an overall majority of 17. The Conservative Party also won the General Election of 1955, under the leadership of Sir Anthony Eden, with a majority of 58. Eden's tenure of office was short-lived, however, his career being abruptly terminated by ill health and the effects of the Suez crisis in 1956. He was succeeded by Mr. Harold Macmillan at a time when the popularity of the party had suffered considerably as a result of the Suez débâcle, and under his leadership it made a spectacular recovery. In 1959 the Conservatives made electoral history by winning their third consecutive General Election with an increased majority of 100 over all their opponents and a House of Commons strength of 365.

During the Parliament of 1959–64 the fortunes of the party slumped to a very low ebb, a number of factors contributing to its decline. The stock of the Government was lowered by several serious policy failures, notably the abandonment of the Blue Streak missile following a vast expenditure on the project, the collapse of the negotiations for Britain's entry into the European Common Market, and the dissolution of the Federation of Rhodesia and Nyasaland. Economic problems continuously bedevilled the administration, and in 1962 Mr. Macmillan sought to restore public confidence in his Government by means of a drastic Cabinet reshuffle, involving the dismissal of the Chancellor of the Exchequer, the Lord Chancellor and the Minister of Defence among others. The main public reaction, however, was one of sympathy for the outgoing ministers. An even more damaging blow to the Government's prestige was dealt in 1963 when the country was rocked by a particularly sensational and sordid scandal involving a minister of Cabinet rank. The most serious aspect of the affair was that it suggested a deficient security system and a lack of control at the highest level of Government.

Later in the same year Mr. Macmillan retired from the leadership of the Conservative Party, and the manner in which his successor was chosen did little to enhance its blemished reputation. Traditionally the Conservatives had never elected a leader by straightforward ballot, but had allowed one to emerge through the somewhat obscure method of sounding opinion. In 1963 this procedure led to much bitter dissension and behind-the-scenes manœuvring, causing misgivings among supporters and opponents of the party alike. Sir Alec Douglas-Home eventually emerged as the leader and, on being invited to form a Government, he immediately disclaimed his peerages to enable himself to seek election to the House of Commons. A short period thus ensued during which the Prime Minister was without a seat in Parliament, giving rise to the taunt that the sovereign assembly of the nation was being made to wait upon the convenience of the Conservative Party. It is important to emphasize that no personal discredit was reflected on Sir Alec himself, who was later to take the initiative in promoting the reform of the Conservative Party's electoral procedure.

The continuing unpopularity of the party was reflected in its consistent losing of by-elections and the unparalleled success of the Labour Party in the Greater London Council elections of May 1964. A General Election held in October of the same year restored the Labour Party to power after 13 years in opposition with the narrow majority of 5 seats. Although this majority was shortly afterwards reduced to 4 through the loss of a by-election, the Labour Party went on to win the General Election of 1966 with the substantial majority of 97. Thereafter the fortunes of the Conservatives began to recover and during the ensuing four years they won numerous seats at by-elections and scored a success in the Greater London Council elections of 1967 even more spectacular than that won by the Labour Party three years previously. In June 1970, in spite of the Labour Party's apparent recovery of popularity as reflected by the public opinion polls, the Conservatives were again returned to power with an overall majority of 30.

In February 1965 the Conservative Party published the details of a new procedure for the election of a leader. The Conservative leader is now chosen by the Conservative Parliamentary Party (q.v.) and subsequently presented to a full meeting of the party at which extra-parliamentary members are represented. To be successful on the first ballot a candidate requires 15 per cent more of the votes cast than any other candidate, provision being made for a second and a third ballot if necessary. Sir Alec Douglas-Home relinquished the leadership in the following July, and Mr. Edward Heath was elected to succeed him, thus becoming the first Conservative leader to be chosen by a ballot of his colleagues.

PARTY ORGANIZATION. The National Union of Conservative and Unionist Associations is a federation to which are affiliated constituency and central associations throughout England, Wales, and Northern Ireland—there is a separate Scottish Unionist Association. Those eligible to attend the annual conference of the National Union include the members of the Central Council of the National Union and three additional representatives of each constituency association, together with accredited party agents. The Central Council itself meets twice a year and considers the report of the Executive Committee of the National Union. The Executive Committee in turn has a number of advisory committees such as the Advisory Committee on Policy, whose Chairman is appointed by the leader of the party. The Conservative Central Office co-ordinates the work of the party throughout the country and provides full-time professional party workers who operate the party organization's machinery under the ultimate direction of the leader, who is Prime Minister when the party is in office.

CONSIDERATION OF AMENDMENTS
See BILL, PASSAGE OF.

CONSIDERATION OF COMMONS' AMENDMENTS
See BILL, PASSAGE OF.

CONSIDERATION OF LORDS' AMENDMENTS
See BILL, PASSAGE OF.

CONSOLIDATED FUND
The great financial pool into which (with certain insignificant exceptions) all the nation's revenues are collected and from which all public expenditure issues. The bulk of the national income is provided

by taxation; other receipts include Post Office profits, revenue from Crown lands, and repayments on foreign loans. The Consolidated Fund is, in reality, an account kept by the Government at the Bank of England. On the authorization of Parliament sums of money are transferred from it into the account of the Paymaster-General (q.v.) (the Government's cashier) who in turn makes available to individual departments the amounts which have been stated and approved by Parliament in the Estimates (q.v.). In addition to the expenditure annually approved by Parliament certain expenses, known as Consolidated Fund Services, are charged to the Consolidated Fund under permanent legislation. These charges are considerable and include payments of interest on the National Debt and charges in respect of the Civil List (q.v.). The salaries of certain high officers, including the Speaker of the House of Commons, the Comptroller and Auditor General, the Parliamentary Commissioner for Administration (qq.v.), and the Judges of the High Court, are charged directly to the Consolidated Fund and not provided for in the Estimates, for the very good reason that the nature of their duties raises them above the controversy of the political arena, in tacit acknowledgment of which Parliament waives its right to review their salaries annually. The salary of the Leader of the Opposition is also charged directly to the Consolidated Fund, and is not therefore subject to annual review by a parliamentary majority controlled by his opponents.

The Consolidated Fund was established by Pitt in 1786. Prior to this date it was the practice to provide for each public service from the revenue yielded by taxes specifically assigned to the purpose. It was found impossible under this system to maintain an adequate supervision over the nation's finances as a whole, and although an Aggregate Fund had been instituted in 1715 for the concentration into a single pool of certain revenues designed to meet the Civil List expenditure, no real attempt at collective control was made until the creation of the Consolidated Fund. At first, however, only statutory expenditure, such as charges in respect of the National Debt and the Civil List, was defrayed from the Consolidated Fund; annual grants of Supply (q.v.) continued to be met from specially assigned sources of revenue. It soon came to be realized that it would make for greater efficiency if all public revenues were paid into the Consolidated Fund and all public payments issued therefrom, and with the passing of the Public Revenue and Consolidated Fund Charges Act, 1854, this practice became finally established.

See also PROCEDURE, FINANCIAL.

CONSOLIDATED FUND ACTS

The annual statutes which precede the Appropriation Act (q.v.), the main Act of the year for authorizing the grant of Supply (q.v.), and which give legal effect to the Supply voted prior to the passing of the main Estimates (q.v.). There are at least two such Acts passed each session, in addition to the Appropriation Act, and they are distinguished by means of numbers (e.g., Consolidated Fund (No. 2) Act). Under the new financial procedure of the House of Commons the first Consolidated Fund Bill is introduced in January and gives legislative authorization to the Civil Vote on Account and the Winter Supplementary Estimates. The second, which must be passed before the end of the financial year (31 March), gives legislative authorization to the Defence Vote on Account, together with any outstanding Supplementary Estimates for the current financial year and Excess Votes, if any, for the previous financial year (*see* ESTIMATES).

Consolidated Fund Acts differ from the Appropriation Act in that they merely authorize the Treasury to make a certain sum of money available to the public service, whereas the Appropriation Act specifies the purposes for which the money is to be used. Like the Appropriation Act, Consolidated Fund Acts also authorize the Treasury to borrow money by the issue of Treasury Bills, the amount which may be borrowed being equal to the total authorized expenditure. The enacting formula of a Consolidated Fund Act, and the procedure which is observed when, as a Bill, it receives the Royal Assent (q.v.), are the same as in the case of the Appropriation Act.

With the adoption of the new financial procedure in December 1966 the third reading stage of Consolidated Fund Bills is no longer debatable. The second reading stage has become the opportunity for enabling members to exercise their traditional right to debate 'grievances before supply'. The debate on the second reading stage of a Consolidated Fund Bill normally lasts all night and it is exclusively a backbencher's occasion. Private members are accorded priority in the debate and are permitted to raise any subject within the Government's responsibility. The heavy competition among members to participate in the debate is controlled by means of a ballot which decides the subjects which are to be raised. Under present procedure three such debates take place in a session including that on the main Consolidated Fund (Appropriation) Bill in July.

CONSOLIDATED FUND BILLS

See APPROPRIATION ACT; CONSOLIDATED FUND ACTS.

CONSOLIDATION BILL

A Bill introduced to consolidate a number of Acts of Parliament relating to the same subject, such as the Shops Bill of 1950 introduced to consolidate the Shops Acts from 1912 to 1938 and certain other enactments relating to shops. Before 1949, if corrections and minor alterations were necessary in a Consolidation Bill, it first had to be drafted, without alteration to the Acts composing it; an amending Act was then passed covering the desired corrections, and finally an Act consolidating the law as it existed after the amendments had been made. This procedure was simplified in 1949 by the passing of the Consolidation of Enactments (Procedure) Act, the first section of which says: 'If at any time it appears to the Lord Chancellor to be expedient that a Bill should be prepared for the purpose of consolidating the enactments relating to any subject, but that, in order to facilitate the consolidation of those enactments, corrections and minor improvements ought to be made in such enactments, he may cause to be laid before Parliament a memorandum proposing such corrections and minor improvements therein as he thinks to be expedient.' A Joint Committee consisting of 6 members from each House is appointed each session to consider Consolidation and Statute Law Revision Bills, and before reporting a Consolidation Bill this committee informs the Lord Chancellor and the Speaker what corrections and minor improvements mentioned in the Lord Chancellor's memorandum (or the Secretary of State's in the case of Scottish Bills) they are prepared to approve. When the Lord Chancellor and the Speaker have concurred, the emendations become law for the purposes of any further proceedings in Parliament relating to the Bill.

In the process of improving and clarifying the state of the law there are two necessary stages—the consolidation of the existing statute law and the reform and codification of the law as it ought to be. In an effort to reach the first stage a separate branch of the Parliamentary Counsel's Office was established in 1947 to deal with consolidation matters, and this tidying-up of the Statute Book is proceeding at a faster pace.

CONSTITUENCY

Since 1948 a constituency has been defined for statutory purposes as 'an area having separate representation in the House of Commons'. The previous statutory definition was 'any county, borough or combination of places, or university or combination of universities returning a member to serve in Parliament, and, where a county or borough is divided for the purpose of parliamentary elections, a division of the county or borough so divided'. Under the 1948 Act a constituency can be one of only two types, county or borough.

The *Oxford English Dictionary* defines the term as 'the body of voters who elect a representative member to a legislative or other public body'. It has apparently acquired its wider sense of an electoral district through common usage.

There are at present 630 constituencies in the United Kingdom, 511 of which are in England, 71 in Scotland, 36 in Wales, and 12 in Northern Ireland (*see also* REPRESENTATION). In 1944 permanent Boundary

Commissions were established for England, Wales, Scotland, and Northern Ireland, their function being to keep the constituency boundaries under review. They are required to submit periodic reports to the Home Secretary and the Secretary of State for Scotland not less than 10 or more than fifteen years from the date of their last reports, stating their recommendations, if any, for the redistribution of seats. The Speaker of the House of Commons is the *ex-officio* Chairman of the Boundary Commissions and judges are appointed Deputy Chairmen to each Commission.

In making their recommendations the Boundary Commissions are governed by the rules laid down in the Second Schedule to the House of Commons (Redistribution of Seats) Act, 1949, which consolidated the law on the subject. The number of constituencies for the whole of Great Britain must be not substantially greater or less than 613, and the number for Northern Ireland must remain at 12. Scotland must have not less than 71 seats and Wales not less than 35. Every constituency shall return a single member. The size of the electorate in each constituency must be as near as practicable to the electoral quota (q.v.), which is a figure obtained by dividing the total electorate of any of the three parts of Great Britain by the existing number of constituencies, and similarly for Northern Ireland. In determining constituency boundaries regard should be taken of existing local government boundaries, but where excessive disparities between electorates and the electoral quota would be created through strict adherence to this rule the Commissions are empowered to depart from it. Where geographical considerations render a departure advisable, the Commissions may depart from both or either of the rules relating to the electoral quota and local government boundaries.

When a Commission has decided upon its provisional recommendations they must be published in each constituency affected. One month is allowed during which representations may be made to the Commission, and local inquiries may be held. When the final reports of the Commissions are submitted to the Home Secretary and the Secretary of State for Scotland they must be laid before Parliament with a minimum of delay, together with draft Orders in Council embodying each recommendation which must be approved by the House of Commons before they can come into effect.

CONSTITUENT ASSEMBLY

A legislative body specifically charged with the task of framing or revising a Constitution. The name was first adopted by the National Assembly of France in 1789 after it had dropped the title of Third Estate. Constituent Assemblies were set up for both India and Pakistan when those countries became independent in 1947. Pakistan's Constituent Assembly also functioned as the federal legislature for a number of years. In 1970 the House of Representatives of Ceylon was convened as a Constituent Assembly for the purpose of drawing up a Republican constitution.

CONSTITUTION

A Constitution in its widest sense is the whole system of government of a country—the collection of rules which establish and regulate or govern the government, which rules are either part of the law of the land or are established by usage or convention. In its narrower sense a Constitution is a selection of these rules which have been embodied in one document. All the countries of the Commonwealth except the United Kingdom (and perhaps New Zealand), and indeed most of the nations of the world, have written Constitutions. The British Constitution is unwritten—in other words its rules have never been co-ordinated into one or even several documents. New Zealand's Constitution is based partly on the New Zealand Act, 1852, as amended from time to time, but otherwise it is 'unwritten' in the traditional British sense of the term. Dicey defines two types of Constitution—the flexible as 'one under which every law of every description can legally be changed with the same ease and in the same manner by one and the same body', and the rigid Constitution as 'one under which certain laws generally known as constitutional or fundamental laws cannot be changed in the same manner as ordinary laws'.

Unwritten Constitutions are necessarily flexible, but written Constitutions are not necessarily rigid, although most modern Constitutions are and cannot be altered or amended without some special legislative process. Australia, for example, cannot alter her Constitution without the amendment being passed by both Houses and agreed to by the people through the process of a referendum. Constitutions, as Thomas Jefferson once wrote, must not be deemed too sacred to be touched—laws and institutions must go hand in hand with the progress of the human mind.

CONSTITUTIONAL AND PARLIAMENTARY INFORMATION

The quarterly journal of the Association of Secretaries General of Parliaments. Its contents include summaries of the inquiries on parliamentary procedure conducted by the Association among the Parliaments of the world; information on changes in parliamentary procedure and new Standing Orders adopted by Parliaments; new constitutions and amendments to existing constitutions; and Acts of Parliament containing special features or innovations or which relate to the conduct of Parliament.

See also INTER-PARLIAMENTARY UNION.

CONSTITUTIONAL LAW

'The Constitutional Law of a State is the law relating to its Constitution. Where the Constitution is written, even though it may have to be supplemented by other materials, it is fairly easy to distinguish the Constitutional Law of a State from the rest of its legal system; but where, as in Britain, the Constitution is unwritten, it is largely a matter of convenience what topics one includes in Constitutional Law, and there is no strict scientific distinction between that and the rest of the law.

'It follows from what has been said that Constitutional Law deals, in general, with the distribution and exercise of the functions of government, and the relations of the government authorities to each other and to the individual in his character of a citizen or subject. More specifically, Constitutional Law embraces that part of a country's laws which relates to the following topics, amongst others: the mode of electing the head of the State, whether he be emperor, king, or president; his powers and prerogatives; the constitution of the legislative body: its powers and the privileges of its members; if there are two chambers their relations *inter se*; the status of Ministers and the position of the civil service which acts under them; the armed forces of the State and the liability of the citizen to be called on to serve in them; the relations of Church and State, if these are formally recognized; the relations between the central Government and local authorities to whom subordinate functions of government are delegated; the relations between the mother country and its colonies or dependencies; the treaty-making powers, and the rules which regulate intercourse with other States; the persons who constitute the body of citizens, the terms on which foreigners may be admitted to its territories and the privileges which they are permitted to enjoy; the mode in which taxation may be raised and the revenues of the State may be expended; the constitution of the Courts of justice and the tenure and immunities of the Judges; the right to demand trial by jury, and its limits; the limits of personal liberty, free speech, and the right of public meeting or association; the rights of the citizen to vote for elective bodies, central or local, and his liability to perform civic duties, such as serving on juries or aiding in the maintenance of order.'

HOOD PHILLIPS

CONTEMPTS

The distinction between a contempt and a breach of privilege lies in the fact that the latter is an offence against a specifically established privilege of Parliament, whereas the former is an offence based on precedents which are less easily defined. The distinction is explained in Halsbury's *Laws of England* (3rd ed., vol. 28, page 464) in the following terms:

The power of both Houses to punish for contempt is a general power similar to that possessed by the superior courts of law and is not restricted to the punishment of breaches of their acknowledged privileges. Any act or omission which obstructs or impedes any member or officer of the House in the discharge of his duty, or which has a tendency to produce such a result may be treated as a contempt even though there is no precedent of the offence. Certain offences which were formerly described as contempts are now commonly designated as breaches of privilege, although that term more properly applies only to an infringement of the collective or individual rights or immunities of one of the Houses of Parliament.

See also PRIVILEGE, BREACH OF.

CONVENTION PARLIAMENT

The term which is applied to those two Parliaments in English history which have restored the monarchy. The first was the Parliament of 1660 which restored Charles II to the throne, and the second was the Parliament of 1689 which offered the Crown to the Prince and Princess of Orange, afterwards William III and Mary, after the abdication of James II. These Parliaments first met without the formal summons of the Sovereign, and since under the British Constitution there can be no Parliament without a Sovereign, they were known initially not as Parliaments but as Conventions. In both cases the first act of the new reign was to convert the Convention to a Parliament.

COOK ISLANDS LEGISLATIVE ASSEMBLY

These islands were proclaimed a British Protectorate in 1888 and in 1901 were annexed and proclaimed part of New Zealand. Under the Cook Islands Amendment Act, 1957 (N.Z.), the Legislative Council with a majority of official members was replaced by a Legislative Assembly with an elected majority. However, laws governing the Islands could still be made by the New Zealand Parliament as well.

In July 1962 the Cook Islands declined the New Zealand Government's offer of full independence and adopted the alternative suggestion of full internal self-government. Proposals for the establishment of a ministerial system, providing for a cabinet of 5 ministers headed by a Chief Minister, were unanimously adopted by the Legislative Assembly, New Zealand remaining responsible for external affairs and defence only.

The Cook Islands Constitution Act, 1964, passed by the New Zealand General Assembly, provides that the Cook Islands, as a fully self-governing territory, shall be associated with New Zealand under the Queen and linked by a common citizenship. The old legislature was dissolved in February 1965 and a new Legislative Assembly of 22 members was elected by universal suffrage. The new Constitution came into full force on 4 August 1965, prior to which transitional arrangements were made for the substitution of the cabinet system for the former Executive Council. Five members headed by a Leader of Government Business were appointed to enable the members of the Legislative Assembly to gain more experience of the work of executive government. Since 4 August 1965 the Cabinet has consisted of a Premier and up to 5 other Ministers. The Resident Commissioner has become the High Commissioner representing both the Queen and the New Zealand Government. External affairs and defence, while remaining the responsibility of New Zealand, are matters which are subject to consultation between the Prime Minister of New Zealand and the Premier of the Cook Islands.

CO-OPERATIVE PARTY

In 1917 the Co-operative Congress meeting at Swansea decided to organize its own party, and out of 10 candidates at the General Election of 1918 one succeeded in winning a seat in the House of Commons and joined the Labour Party. Four Co-operative members were elected in 1922, in 1923 there were 6, and 5 were returned in 1924. In 1926 the Co-operative Congress and the Labour Party agreed to avoid contests between their respective candidates and to conduct joint electoral campaigns. From that time the Co-operative Party became a wing of the Labour Party, and 9 Co-operatives were returned at the General Election of 1929, their most prominent member, Mr. A. V. Alexander (afterwards Lord Alexander) becoming First Lord of the Admiralty. The Labour minority in the 1931–5 Parliament included 1 Co-operative member, but in 1935 9 candidates were successful out of 21. The party adopted a written constitution in 1938, and in 1941 the National Council of Labour was reconstituted to include equal representation of the Labour Party, the T.U.C., and the Co-operative Union. The Co-operative Party Conference in 1945, fearing political extinction, rejected a proposal that the party should affiliate nationally with the Labour Party, but endorsed negotiations for a new agreement with them, which was ratified by both parties in 1946. Affiliation between local Co-operative Society parties and constituency Labour parties was encouraged, and it was agreed that Co-operative candidates for Parliament would need to be selected by the constituency Labour party also, and would run under the designation 'Co-operative and Labour'. They would be expected, if returned, to join the Parliamentary Labour Party and abide by its standing orders. The membership of the House of Commons after the 1945 General Election included 23 Co-operatives out of 33 candidates, in 1950 18 out of 33, in 1951 and 1955 16 out of 38, in 1959 16 out of 31, in 1964 14 out of 27, in 1966 18 out of 24, and in 1970 16 out of 28. A new constitution covering both national organization and society parties was adopted in 1951, which altered the declaration made by members of the party to ensure that representatives of the retail societies on the National Committee should not be opponents of the Labour Party.

COUNCIL OF STATES

The name given to the upper House of the Indian Parliament (q.v.).

COUNT

See QUORUM.

COUNTY FRANCHISE

See REPRESENTATION.

COUPON ELECTION

When the dissolution of Parliament was announced at the conclusion of the First World War, the Labour Party decided to resume their independence and not to stand at the election as supporters of the existing Coalition Government. Lloyd George, ignoring the appeal of the Manchester Liberals that he should make his peace with Asquith and thus re-create a united Liberal Party, entered into a compact with Bonar Law. Under this arrangement all candidates who were classed as loyal to the coalition of Lloyd George Liberals and the Conservatives were to receive a certificate in the form of a letter of recommendation jointly signed by Lloyd George and Bonar Law. It was this certificate that was denounced by Asquith as a 'coupon' and which gave this designation to the election which was held in December 1918. This election was the first to be held following the passing of the Representation of the People Act of 1918 which gave the vote to women over thirty, abolished the property qualification for men, and extended the franchise to men in the services. The results of the election gave the supporters of the Coalition 533 seats, although they only polled 52 per cent of the total votes. Labour increased its representation to 59, and the Independent Liberals were reduced to 26. Asquith himself was defeated in East Fife, a seat he had held for thirty-two years.

COURT OF REFEREES

In the House of Commons the Court of Referees, established in 1864, consists of the Chairman and Deputy Chairman of Ways and Means, the Speaker's Counsel, and not less than seven members appointed by the Speaker. The Referees are concerned with determining the rights of petitioners to be heard against Private Bills when the promoters raise objections as to the petitioners' *locus standi*. The duty of the Referees, as defined by the Standing Orders relating to Private Business, is to decide 'upon all petitions against Private Bills (and Bills to confirm provisional orders), as to the rights of the petitioners to be heard upon such petitions, without prejudice, however, to the power of the committee to which the Bill is referred to decide upon any question as to such rights arising incidentally in the course of their proceedings'. The decisions of the Court of Referees constitute legal decisions against which there is no appeal.

COURT OF REQUESTS

A minor court of equity, closely connected with the Star Chamber, which flourished during the Tudor and early Stuart period. It was held in the Little Hall or White Hall of the Palace of Westminster, but it came to an end during the Long Parliament. The House of Lords moved into the Court of Requests building in 1801 and were still there at the time of the fire in 1834. After the fire it was used as a temporary House of Commons, the House of Lords moving to the Painted Chamber.

COURTYARDS OF THE PALACE OF WESTMINSTER

There are eleven open courtyards in the Palace of Westminster, five belonging to the House of Commons and six to the House of Lords. The former consist of Speaker's Court, Star Chamber Court, Cloister Court, Commons Court, and Commons Inner Court; the latter, Royal Court, Peers Court, Peers Inner Court, Chancellor's Court, State Officers' Court, and St. Stephen's Court. Speaker's Court at the north end of the palace is joined by a carriageway to Royal Court at the south end.

CROMWELL, OLIVER (1599–1658), AND PARLIAMENT

Oliver Cromwell first entered Parliament in 1628 for the borough of Huntingdon. In 1640 he was returned as a member for Cambridge in both the Short Parliament (q.v.) and the Long Parliament (q.v.). During the first session of the latter Parliament he served on eighteen committees and was one of the originators of the 'Root and Branch' Bill aimed at abolishing episcopacy. In the years 1641 and 1642 he was very active in urging and effecting defence preparations, and on the outbreak of the Civil War he entered the field and fought in the first engagement at Edgehill. The eventual defeat of the Royalists was due in great measure to Cromwell's masterly leadership in battle. In 1644 he was appointed a member of the committee of both kingdoms which resulted from the Solemn League and Covenant uniting England and Scotland against the King. A staunch Puritan, however, he was opposed to the influence of the Presbyterians, who soon recognized in him a dangerous opponent and were eager to curb his power. Cromwell and his supporters seized the initiative. Desirous of securing religious toleration within the army, they introduced the famous Self-denying Ordinance with the resolution 'that no member of either House of Parliament shall during the war enjoy, or execute any office or command, military or civil, and that an ordinance be brought in to that effect'. The ordinance passed the Commons on 19 December 1644, by 100 votes to 93, but was rejected by the Lords. A second Self-denying Ordinance was passed by the upper House on 3 April 1645, together with a scheme for remodelling the army. It is significant that Cromwell himself was exempted from the provisions of the Act and was allowed to continue as a lieutenant-general. After the surrender of the King, Cromwell's power as a political and religious leader greatly increased, and the struggle between the Presbyterians and the Independents—Cromwell's faction—flared up in earnest. The former were opposed to any form of toleration for Dissenters and were endeavouring to impose their system of worship upon the whole country. The Independents were strongly opposed to the Presbyterian system and upheld religious freedom, although Catholics and Episcopalians were excepted from their benevolence. In Parliament the Presbyterians were in the majority but the Independents were overwhelmingly strong in the army, and the former realized the necessity for disbanding the army if the power of Cromwell's party was to be weakened. On 8 March 1647, the Commons passed a resolution to the effect that no member should hold a command in the army, that no higher military rank than colonel should exist under the General-in-Chief, and that the army should accept the Covenant and conform to the church system established by Parliament. The army, however, forestalled the Presbyterians by taking possession of London and establishing military authority. The Commons were intimidated into reversing a vote of censure upon the army and the Presbyterians were divested of actual power inside Parliament, although outside their influence remained considerable.

Meanwhile the King, attempting to turn the quarrel to his own advantage, was negotiating with both parties independently. Cromwell himself was sincere in his desire to reach a settlement with Charles I, but the extreme republicans within his own party were violently opposed to any agreement. Angered by the King's intrigues and duplicity, the army and Parliament eventually came to terms and agreed on joint proposals which were submitted to Charles in the form of four Bills demanding, amongst other things, parliamentary control over the army and over all taxation and the resignation of all prerogative powers to Parliament. The King rejected the Bills and the moderates and extremists in Cromwell's party closed their ranks against him. On 3 January 1648, the House of Commons resolved to discontinue all negotiation with the King. The authority of the committee of the two kingdoms was renewed except in respect of Scotland and Independents replaced the excluded Presbyterians. The Scots, disturbed by the trend of events, concluded a secret treaty with the King. This development led to the second Civil War, and Cromwell took the field again, marched north and effectively crushed the Scots. During Cromwell's absence in the north the English Presbyterians concluded an alliance with the King which became known as the Treaty of Newport. But the army, refusing to countenance any agreement, determined to act. The army leaders were resolved on bringing the King to trial, but they realized that the agreement of the House of Commons could only be secured if the Presbyterians were excluded from Parliament. This exclusion was accomplished by the unconstitutional proceeding known as Pride's Purge (q.v.), by which all members to whom the army objected were prevented from entering the Chamber. Cromwell gave his tacit approval to the purge by taking his seat in the depleted House of Commons, which proceeded to annul all former votes for a personal treaty with the King and brought in an ordinance for bringing him to trial. There is no need to dwell here upon the trial and its tragic result.

On the death of the King the nation was faced with an unprecedented situation. Throughout the Civil War the ancient English Constitution had remained unchanged although its operation had been suspended. Now the state was without a monarch and without any legislation to provide for an alternative form of government, with the result that the remnant of the House of Commons wielded the sovereign power. It immediately took drastic measures. On 6 February 1649, it abolished the House of Lords with the resolution that 'the House of Peers in Parliament is useless, dangerous, and ought to be abolished'. On the 7th it abolished the monarchy, resolving 'that it hath been found by experience, and this House doth declare, that the office of a king in this nation, and to have the power thereof in any single person, is unnecessary, burdensome, and dangerous to the liberty, safety, and the public interest of the people of this nation, and therefore ought to be abolished, and that an Act to this effect be brought in'. On the 14th a Council of State was elected including Cromwell, Fairfax, Vane, Skippon, Haselrig, St. John, and Bulstrode Whitelocke, with Bradshaw as President. Its executive powers amounted to those of the King and Parliament combined. It was given control of the armed forces and was empowered to draw upon the public revenue, and its functions included the maintenance of peace at home and the restoration of order in Ireland, the suppression of royalism, the preservation of good relations with foreign powers, the protection of Englishmen abroad and the promotion of home trade. It took immediate measures against prominent Royalists and exiled the late King's two sons on pain of death. Cromwell then conducted campaigns against Ireland and Scotland, reducing the former to subjection, and completely defeating the Scots and the last manifestations of the Royalist cause at Worcester. The triumph of republicanism was complete, and Parliament agreed to an amnesty exonerating those who had supported the King provided they pledged their allegiance to the Commonwealth.

Domestic difficulties continued to multiply, however. Parliament and the army continued to be at loggerheads with one another, the latter being far from satisfied with the administration of the realm. The nation was without a head, which led to the growth of factions; religious conflict was as violent as ever; and the abuses of power amongst parliamentary leaders were flagrant and numerous. Parliament itself feared for its own existence. It shrank from holding new elections lest the results should be damaging to the Puritan cause. It was therefore proposed that all sitting members should retain their seats and be empowered to veto any new members elected to fill vacant seats if they deemed them unfit to serve. On the question of its own duration, Parliament resolved on 14 November 1651 that it should continue until 3 November 1654. Neither Cromwell nor the army approved the scheme. Cromwell maintained that the proposed new Parliament would merely be a continuation of the old, offering no security for religious liberty, and that the parliamentary leaders sought only to perpetuate their power. Eventually, driven by the widespread corruption which continued to flourish and by pressure from the army, Cromwell decided to act. It was typical of the man that once he had resolved upon the necessity for drastic action he used no half-measures. On 20 April 1653, Cromwell received news that Parliament was proceeding with its Bill to prolong its own life in spite of his objections. He left at once for the House of Commons, where he took his usual seat and remained silent until the question was put for the final division. At this point he rose and addressed the House. He began by praising the early works of the Long Parliament, but then he changed his tone and denounced it for its injustice and tyranny, its corruption and self-interest. His passion mounted and he turned upon the members individually, condemning each one for his personal vices without mentioning his name, but indicating by gesture the object of his wrath and scorn. Clapping his hat on his head to show his lack of respect for this Parliament, he paced up and down the Chamber, and stormed, 'You have sat too long here for any good you have been doing. Depart, I say, and let us have done with you. In the name of God, go!' Sir Peter Wentworth rose and reproached 'their servant whom they had so highly trusted and obliged', in response to which Cromwell cried, 'Come, come, I will put an end to your prating. You are no Parliament. I say you are no Parliament. It is not fit you should sit here any longer.' So saying he ordered in the detachment of soldiers which had accompanied him to the House and instructed them to clear the Chamber. The Speaker was forcibly plucked from the Chair, and as his eyes fell upon the Mace, Cromwell asked his famous question, 'What shall we do with this bauble?' adding, 'Here, take it away!' As the members departed he poured further invective upon them, and in justification of his action he cried out, 'It is you that have forced me to do this, for I have sought the Lord night and day that He would rather slay me than put me upon the doing of this work.' Then he snatched the offending Bill from the clerk at the table, pocketed it, and ordered the door to be locked. The same afternoon Cromwell informed the Council of State that its powers had ceased since Parliament was dissolved; but before they dispersed Bradshaw replied, 'Sir, we have heard what you did at the House this morning, and before many hours all England will hear it; but you are mistaken to think that the Parliament is dissolved; for no power under heaven can dissolve them but themselves: therefore take you notice of that.' Bradshaw was proved right in the end, for although no one in the country regretted the passing of the Long Parliament immediately after its expulsion, the constitutional ideal which that Parliament had represented was indestructible, and all Cromwell's attempts to provide reasonable alternatives were henceforth doomed to failure.

King, Lords, and Commons having been removed in turn, the country found itself without legislative or executive authority, and the only constituted authority remaining was Cromwell himself by virtue of his commission as Commander-in-Chief. He was thus an absolute dictator, but was nevertheless anxious to preserve constitutional forms and to resolve any doubts as to his motives. Accordingly, after declaring the cause of the dissolution of the Long Parliament, Cromwell and his officers called together a body of 140 nominees, which has been known variously as the Assembly of Nominees, the Little Parliament, and the Barebones Parliament (q.v.). The members were selected as being 'God-fearing men, who had given proofs of their fidelity, energy, and devoted zeal for the cause of God'. The Little Parliament met on 4 July 1653, and in his opening address Cromwell committed to it the supreme power and control of the nation. A Speaker was called to the Chair without ceremony and was re-elected each month while the Parliament lasted. It adopted the title of Parliament of the Commonwealth of England and was authorized to appoint another assembly before 3 November 1654, which should inherit its authority. For all its failings the Little Parliament was at least active and conscientious, and it embarked upon a programme of drastic reforms in which it exhibited more zeal than judgment. It abolished the Court of Chancery, revised the legal code, reformed judicial procedure, and established marriage as a civil ceremony. Simultaneously, it set about the reform of the Church, and far from reconciling the religious factions as Cromwell had hoped, further embittered relations between the sects. A proposal to abolish tithes, which would have deprived the clergy of their means of

G [183]

subsistence, was referred to a committee which drew up a scheme for church reform. The dissension over the scheme precipitated the downfall of the Little Parliament, for in the ensuing debate the first clause of the committee's report, which was regarded as vital to the scheme, was negatived, and the minority who had favoured it agreed upon a means of bringing the Parliament to an end. On 12 December they came early to the House and moved 'that the sitting of this Parliament any longer, as it is now constituted, will not be for the good of the Commonwealth, and that therefore it is requisite to deliver up to the Lord General Cromwell the powers which they had received from him'. A short debate took place on the motion which its opponents endeavoured to prolong until more of their supporters could be mustered, but the Speaker, who was with the minority in their conspiracy, terminated the debate by leaving the Chair without putting the question and, followed by a number of members, proceeded to Whitehall where they all signed an instrument of abdication surrendering their powers to Cromwell.

Once more Cromwell found himself in the position of a dictator, and this time Lambert and other military leaders persuaded him to accept the written constitution they had prepared, known as the Instrument of Government. Under this constitution authority was vested in a single person, styled the Lord Protector, and a Parliament. The Protector possessed the executive power and Parliament the legislative power, but both were subject to limitations. Bills passed by Parliament required the assent of the Protector, but he had no power to veto any legislation unless it conflicted with the constitution. In all administrative matters the Protector required the consent of a Council of State, which was to consist of not more than 21 persons appointed for life, a body described by Cromwell as 'the trustees of the Commonwealth in the intervals of Parliament'. The Protector, with the advice of the Council, was empowered to make ordinances until the first Parliament was called. Parliament was to be summoned every three years and could not be dissolved within the first five months of being called save by its own consent. Its control over finance was only partial, as it was not empowered to reduce the annual revenue required for the ordinary expenses of government. The Parliament was to consist of 400 members from England, 30 from Scotland, and 30 from Ireland. The representative system was revised and a number of small boroughs in England were disfranchised, their representatives being given to the counties or large towns previously unrepresented. County representation was increased, but the franchise was restricted to men owning £200 worth of property. The borough franchise remained unaltered. Roman Catholics and all those who had taken part in the Irish rebellion were permanently disfranchised, and those who had taken part in any war against Parliament since 1642 were ineligible to vote or to be elected for the first four Parliaments of the Protectorate. Power was thus divided in such a way as to render no one authority supreme. The constitution also embodied religious tolerance as one of its principles, with the usual proviso excluding Catholics and Episcopalians.

Cromwell was formally installed as Protector on 16 December 1653. He was dressed as a common citizen in a plain black coat to show that the period of military government was at an end. During the nine months which followed before the first Parliament of the Protectorate assembled, Cromwell proved his ability and sagacity as a ruler. He issued eighty-two ordinances aimed at laying the foundations of an enlightened society, and they included an Act reforming the Court of Chancery instead of abolishing it, and measures of legal and social reform. The first Parliament of the Protectorate met on 3 September 1654. To Cromwell's surprise and chagrin it immediately called in question the fundamental basis of the constitution. It objected to the Instrument of Government as representing the will of the army, and refused its unqualified acceptance of the principle of dividing authority between Parliament and a single person whose will would prevail in the event of conflict, particularly when that single person was the head of the army. They demanded that the office of Protector should be subject to parliamentary control. Cromwell, chastened by past experience, was reluctant to surrender too much control to Parliament, and on 12 September he addressed the assembly and stated his own views. He refused to agree to any alteration in the Instrument of Government, insisting that some basis of government was essential. On the 14th Parliament agreed to recognize the constitution in principle and a majority of the members signed a declaration of allegiance to the Lord Protector, but they refused to be bound by each of the forty-two articles of the Instrument of Government and thus reserved the right of Parliament to revise any part of it. During the next four months the various provisions of the Instrument of Government were debated at length and Parliament agreed to a number of resolutions having the effect of limiting the Protector's powers. They declared the office to be an elective and not an hereditary one, excepted the crimes of treason and murder from his special power of pardon, resolved that the Council of State should require the approval of Parliament, and demanded parliamentary control of the army. All these resolutions conflicted with the constitution, and Parliament's interminable discussions were holding up legislation necessary to the normal government of the country. The dissension was also encouraging renewed activity among the Royalists and a plot was afoot to overthrow Cromwell and the Commonwealth. In the face of these difficulties Cromwell decided to dissolve Parliament on the expiration of the five months guaranteed by the constitution, and he accordingly did so on 22 January 1655.

Because of the dangers which threatened the Commonwealth, Cromwell reverted to military government. He was loth to govern in an unconstitutional manner, but the time was one of crisis, and in the absence of any alternative means of raising revenue he levied taxes on his own authority. On 17 September 1655, faced with a war with Spain and conscious of the need for legislative sanction to endorse his actions, he summoned another Parliament. To avoid a repetition of the last Parliament, each member was subject to the approval of the Council of State, exercising a right held under the Instrument of Government. This resulted in the exclusion of about 100 members, some of whom were subsequently admitted to the House upon submitting a remonstrance. Cromwell opened the session with an impassioned appeal to the Parliament to support him and his government, and in response Parliament proceeded to pass some necessary measures, including the voting of a subsidy.

At the beginning of 1657, Parliament raised the question of reverting to a form of government more in accord with the ancient constitution with Cromwell as King. The matter was first formally discussed on 23 February, and Parliament drew up a scheme embodying their proposals known as the Humble Petition and Advice. The army was immediately opposed to the scheme, but Cromwell was more reserved in his judgment. He pointed out that as Protector he had no authority over parliamentary enactments whereas if he assumed the title of King he would exercise a right of veto. He therefore took time to consider the Humble Petition and Advice, whose eighteen articles amounted to a new constitution. It provided for a second chamber to be nominated by the Protector, gave the latter the right to appoint his successor, granted a fixed sum for the maintenance of the armed forces, and endorsed the principle of religious toleration with the usual proviso. The final article, which provoked bitter controversy, proposed 'that the Protector be requested to assume the name, style, title, dignity, and office of King of England, Scotland, and Ireland, and to exercise the same according to the laws of these nations.'

Eventually, after much personal consideration and deliberation with others, Cromwell rejected the title of King but accepted the proposed scheme in all its other articles. The new constitution was inaugurated with much pomp and ceremony on 26 June 1657, and henceforward Cromwell was King of England in all but name, his powers being much greater than they had been under the Instrument of Government. His difficulties were far from diminished, however, and in accepting the new constitution he alienated many of his republican supporters. Furthermore, one of the provisions of the Humble Petition and Advice opened the door to his opponents by prohibiting the exclusion of any candidates properly elected to Parliament.

In accordance with the second chamber provision of the constitution

Cromwell decided to re-create the House of Lords, and he summoned, in addition to the judges, 63 members, including existing and newly created peers. A fresh complication now arose, for the House of Commons, which now contained many ardent republicans, was reluctant to recognize the existence of an upper House. Cromwell was determined to govern according to the constitution and he informed the Commons of his intention in the most emphatic terms. But the crisis soon became acute. The Commons complained that they were being forced to recognize a body which had been abolished and declared that no authority had the right to overrule the Commons of England to whom sovereignty rightly belonged, and they proposed certain measures aimed at reducing the Protector's constitutional powers and restoring a unicameral Parliament. This decided Cromwell and he determined on a dissolution.

On 4 February 1658 Cromwell entered the chamber of the upper House and sent word to the Commons requiring their attendance. Addressing both Houses he told them that he had not sought his exalted position but had acted in accordance with the constitution thrust upon him by Parliament. The Protector continued, 'I would have been glad to have lived under my woodside, to have kept a flock of sheep, rather than undertaken such a government as this. But undertaking it by the Advice and Petition of you, I did look that you who had offered it unto me should make it good. I did tell you that I would not undertake it, unless there might be some other persons to interpose between me and the House of Commons, who then had the power, and prevent tumultuary and popular spirits: and it was granted I should name another House. I named it of men who shall meet you wheresoever you go, and shake hands with you, and tell you it is not titles, nor lords, nor parties that they value, but a Christian and an English interest. Men of your own rank and quality, who will not only be a balance unto you, but a new force added to you, while you love England and religion. Having proceeded upon these terms I thought I had been doing that which was my duty, and thought it would have satisfied you. But if everything must be too high or too low, you are not to be satisfied.' With mounting emotion Cromwell proceeded to reproach the Commons for their activities, and concluded, 'And if this be the end of your sitting, and this be your carriage, I think it high time that an end be put to your sitting. And I do dissolve this Parliament. And let God be judge between you and me.'

Thus ended Cromwell's parliamentary government, and until his death on 3 September 1658 he governed without Parliaments. A man of ability, honesty, and courage, fired by a deep religious fervour, the measure of Cromwell's success lay in his practical achievements. His government was well-ordered and enlightened and highly respected by foreign powers. His failure to establish himself as a constitutional ruler was due not to any personal failings in himself but to the irregular source of his power. He was too thoroughly English to question the necessity of the parliamentary system, but he failed to realize the impossibility of reconciling his own position with an institution deeply rooted in ancient law and custom.

The Commonwealth, having lost its strong man, did not long survive Cromwell. The Protector had appointed his third son, Richard, to succeed him, but the new Protector found himself little more than the tool of the army, and was neither slow nor reluctant to abdicate when circumstances forced this step upon him. The heightened dissension between Parliament and the army served only to emphasize the necessity for a return to the traditional form of government, and within two years of Cromwell's death the restoration of the monarchy had been established.

(For further reading see Trevor-Roper's essay, 'Cromwell and his Parliaments' contained in *Essays presented to Sir Lewis Namier*, 1956, edited by Pares & Taylor.)

See also COMMONWEALTH, 1658–1660.

CROSSING THE FLOOR

When a Member of Parliament changes his political allegiance he is said to have 'crossed the Floor'. The seating arrangement adopted in most of the Parliaments of the British Commonwealth, whereby the party in power and the Opposition sit facing each other, explains how the expression arose. As Sir Winston Churchill observed during the debate on the rebuilding of the House of Commons in 1943, 'The party system is much favoured by the oblong form of Chamber. It is easy for an individual to move through those insensible gradations from left to right' (referring to a semi-circular assembly) 'but the act of crossing the floor is one which requires serious consideration.' Added Sir Winston, 'I am well informed on this matter, for I have accomplished that difficult process not only once but twice.'

CROWN AND PARLIAMENT

Neither the House of Commons nor the House of Lords, whether acting separately or together, has any power to legislate without the assent of the Crown. It is now only for the purpose of reading the Speech from the Throne that the Queen is personally present in Parliament, the Royal Assent to Bills being given by a Commission appointed under the Great Seal. Although Charles II revived the practice of attending debates in the House of Lords it had already become unusual since the days of the *Curia Regis* (q.v.), but contact between the Crown and Parliament is maintained informally by ministers and formally by messages, both written and verbal, and by addresses. A written message under the Royal Sign Manual is usually delivered to both Houses, and generally acknowledged by an address similar in form to that presented in answer to the royal speech at the Opening of Parliament. The subject of a message usually relates to the Crown, its prerogatives, property, or financial provision for the Royal Family, otherwise to an important public event, such as a declaration of a state of emergency, which requires the attention of Parliament. A royal message is presented in the House of Commons at the Bar by a minister or member of the Royal Household and read by the Speaker. In the House of Lords the peer charged with the message announces it from his place, and it is read by the Lord Chancellor. Congratulatory and condolatory messages can also be sent by both Houses to members of the Royal Family. Verbal messages are delivered by a minister to the House of which he is a member, and are generally adapted to special forms of procedure, such as the 'Queen's Consent' and 'Queen's Recommendation' (qq.v.). Another form of verbal message is the signification of the Queen's pleasure in such formal and regularly occurring matters as prorogation, the opening of a new Parliament, and the election and royal approbation of the Speaker. Addresses to the Queen may be made jointly by both Houses, although this has not been done since 1842, and they are more often presented by each House singly. In the Commons the motion for an address is in the form 'That an humble address be presented to Her Majesty to . . .', and requires notice and admits of debate, amendment, and division. It may be presented by the Speaker and the whole House on great occasions such as the Silver Jubilee of George V, or the victorious conclusion of the last war, but is usually presented by a Privy Councillor or member of the Royal Household. In the House of Lords an address is usually ordered to be presented by the Lords with White Staves, i.e., the Lord Steward and the Lord Chamberlain. Her Majesty's reply to an address is reported to the House by the Speaker when it has been presented by the whole House, or by a member of the Royal Household (who is also an M.P.), who reads the answer at the Bar, when the address has been presented in the ordinary way. An address may deal with any matter regarding the government or welfare of the state.

From about 1783 in the reign of King George III, the Leader of the House of Commons sent daily reports to the Sovereign. This became a duty of the Leader of the House rather than the Prime Minister, presumably because the latter was more often than not a member of the House of Lords. The nature of this report and the question as to whether the Sovereign could take official cognisance of its contents was the subject of some controversy in the reign of King George V (*see* Nicolson's *Life of King George V*, page 429). In 1936 the practice of sending this report was discontinued on the instructions of King Edward VIII, the last such report being sent by Sir John Simon, then Leader of the House, on 1 August 1936.

For some time an additional report was made concurrently by the Vice-Chamberlain—an official of the Royal Household whose post is occupied by one of the Government Whips—describing incidents and the atmosphere in the House for the first part of the day.

On 6 November 1939, this report was also discontinued, except on special occasions, until after the end of the Second World War. It was recommenced at the request of King George VI on 17 October 1945, and has continued ever since. The report is in the form of a telegram sent to the Queen at about 7.45 p.m. each day.

See also PARLIAMENT; ROYAL PREROGATIVE; SOVEREIGN and individual sovereigns from Elizabeth I to Victoria.

CROWN OFFICE

See CLERK OF THE CROWN.

CRYPT CHAPEL, PALACE OF WESTMINSTER

Properly called the Chapel of St. Mary Undercroft, the Crypt Chapel lies beneath St. Stephen's Hall and was built between 1292 and 1327. It was severely damaged in the fire of 1834, but the original rich ornamentations in colour and gold were reproduced by E. M. Barry, son of Sir Charles Barry, the architect of the present Palace of Westminster. The Chapel has not been able to preserve its sacred character for all the six-hundred-odd years of its existence; it has been used at different times as a coal cellar, stable, and as the Speaker's dining-room. Marriages of M.P.s and the baptism of their children sometimes take place in the Crypt Chapel. Under the arrangements made for the control of the Palace of Westminster in April 1965, the Crypt Chapel is jointly controlled by the Lord Great Chamberlain, the Lord Chancellor and the Speaker of the House of Commons.

CURIA REGIS

The court of the Norman and Angevin Kings which conducted the business of central government in all its branches. It was partly descended from the Anglo-Saxon Witenagemot (q.v.) but it probably had more in common with its French counterpart, the *Curia Ducis*, the feudal council of the Dukes of Normandy. The King was the unquestioned and absolute ruler, but like any other feudal lord he sought the counsel of his vassals. Consultation between a lord and his tenants was deeply rooted in feudal custom, and the King must have been fully aware of the weight which would be attached to his decrees when consented to by the august assembly which constituted the *Curia Regis*. It included the King's barons or tenants-in-chief, officials of the Royal Household, the high officers of Church and State, and such other persons as the King chose to summon. The principal officers of State were the justiciar, the chancellor, the treasurer, the chamberlain, the constable, the marshall, and the King's justices.

The *Curia Regis* was a single organ of government exercising legislative, judicial, and executive functions. In the words of G. B. Adams, it was 'the mother of a numerous progeny', for from it there developed the Exchequer, the Courts of Common Law and Chancery, the House of Lords, the Privy Council—in fact most of the great institutions of government. In the reign of Henry I there is evidence of a large and a small assembly, the greater consisting of all the barons summoned for a special purpose, the smaller comprising the officials and such barons and bishops as were readily available, which remained in permanent session for the purpose of dealing with the regular business. But the latter was not in any sense a committee of the former. Both bodies were the *Curia Regis* with functions undistinguished from each other. It was only gradually and at the demand of practical convenience that the various organs of state began to separate. It is not possible to assign definite dates to these developments, but the Exchequer was the first department to acquire a separate identity in the 12th century. The Common Law Courts, the Court of Chancery, the House of Lords, and the Privy Council became separate institutions in the 13th and 14th centuries. The Privy Council is generally regarded as the continuation of the *Curia Regis* after the other branches of government had become dissociated from each other. The last full meeting of the *Curia Regis* as such took place as late as 1640.

(Further reading: Baldwin, *The King's Council*, 1913.)

CYPRUS PARLIAMENT

From 1882 to 1931 Cyprus was governed under constitutions which provided for an elected element in the Legislative Council, but as the result of serious disturbances in 1931 the Council was suspended and legislative power vested in the Governor, the Executive Council being retained to advise him. In 1946 and again in 1954 attempts were made by the British Government to initiate self-governing institutions, and from 1948 to 1954 the offer of a liberal Constitution remained open. In July 1956 Lord Radcliffe was appointed to consider the framework of a new Constitution, and his proposals (Cmnd. 42), which were accepted by the British Government, included the formation of a Legislative Assembly, with 30 elected and 6 unofficial nominated members, which would be responsible for all matters with the exception of defence, external affairs, and internal security. The Governor would have been empowered to legislate by ordinance in reserved matters—chiefly aspects of education, broadcasting, and matters of particular interest to the Turkish-Cypriot community. The Secretary of State for the Colonies announced in the House of Commons on 19 December 1956 that the new Constitution would be introduced as soon as the Government was satisfied that a situation existed in Cyprus in which genuine elections could be held, free from violence and intimidation. The Government's proposals proved unacceptable to the Cypriots, however, and the island continued in a state of unrest for two more years. As a result of discussions held in London and Zürich the dispute was settled on 19 February 1959. Great Britain, Greece, Turkey, and Cyprus agreed to the establishment of an independent Cypriot republic with a Greek-Cypriot President and a Turkish-Cypriot Vice-President, a Council of Ministers composed of 7 Greek-Cypriots and 3 Turkish-Cypriots, and a House of Representatives elected for five years by universal suffrage of each community separately in the proportion of seventy per cent for the Greek community and thirty per cent for the Turkish community. Elections were held in 1960 for 35 Greek-Cypriots and 15 Turkish-Cypriots, the numbers having been fixed by mutual agreement between the two communities. The Constitutional Law, with the exception of its basic articles, is subject to amendment by a majority comprising two-thirds of the Greek members and two-thirds of the Turkish members of the House of Representatives. The President and the Vice-President have the right (which may be exercised either separately or conjointly) to veto certain laws concerning foreign affairs and to return the Budget or any law or decision to the House of Representatives for reconsideration. In addition to the House of Representatives each community has its Communal Chamber with authority in religious, educational, and cultural matters and the right to impose certain taxes.

Early in 1961 the Cyprus Republic decided to apply for Commonwealth membership for an experimental period of five years, and her application was accepted by the Conference of Commonwealth Prime Ministers meeting in March of that year. It would appear, although the initial period of five years has elapsed, that Cyprus is still deemed to be, and still deems herself to be, a member of the Commonwealth.

Following the outbreak of fighting in December 1963, the Turkish-Cypriot members did not attend meetings of the House of Representatives, and on 22 July 1965 the Government published a draft electoral law having the effect of abolishing the separate representation of Greek and Turkish-Cypriots, and adopting a common voters' roll with no provision for guaranteed Turkish-Cypriot representation.

The Turkish members requested that they should be allowed to take part in the debate on this measure, but this was refused by the President of the House, unless the Turks resumed their seats permanently, agreed to the proposed change in the Constitution and recognized the present Cyprus Government.

These conditions were unacceptable and, as the Government had extended the term of office of the President (but not the Turkish Vice-

President) and the life of the existing Parliament for a period of up to twelve months, the Turkish-Cypriots responded by meeting and passing parallel resolutions with respect to the Vice-President and the Turkish members of the House of Representatives. The Turkish-Cypriot Communal Chamber similarly extended its term of office. Protests were made by the British and Turkish Governments on the 'unconstitutional' action of the Cyprus Government, which the latter rejected as being 'interference in the internal affairs of Cyprus'.

D

DEATH OF A MEMBER

In the House of Commons it is not usual to move a motion of condolence on the death of a member, but on 21 July 1937 Miss Thelma Cazalet (afterwards Mrs. D. Cazalet-Keir) asked Mr. Speaker Fitzroy if he would consider a request 'that some reference should be made in this House on the death of one of its Members . . . and whether you would consider making the appropriate statement yourself?' The Speaker said he would consider it, and on 28 July announced that he proposed to refer to the death of any member and to the loss sustained by the House as from the beginning of the next session (October 1937).

DEBATE, LIMITATION OF

See CLOSURE; GUILLOTINE; SUPPLY DAYS.

DEBATE ON THE ADDRESS

The Queen's Speech at the opening of each session of Parliament descends from the address made by the Chancellor in medieval times which explained to a Parliament the cause of its summons. Since the Cabinet system was established, the Speech from the Throne has been used to announce the programme of legislation for the session and to set forth the Government's policy. The address in reply is moved in both Houses and is limited to the expression of humble thanks for the Gracious Speech. The debate on the Speech occupies about two weeks and provides an opportunity for a general review of the Government's policy. Amendments to the motion are also moved which usually express regret for the omission of particular items from the legislative programme and any division which takes place is always on an amendment to the address, as it would be considered discourteous to oppose the address itself. It is considered an honour to be chosen by the Prime Minister to move and second the address in reply, and before the War civilian members wore court dress and service members uniform for the occasion. A member is expected to recognize the honour to his constituency as well, and to take the opportunity to praise its industries or its amenities. Canada, Australia, and New Zealand are other countries where a similar debate is held at the beginning of a new session on the address in reply to the speech of the Governor-General.

DEBATE, RULES OF

There are a number of basic rules and principles which govern all debate in the House of Commons, and which have been adopted in the main by the other Parliaments of the Commonwealth.

A member wishing to speak must rise in his place (unless he is prevented from doing so by some infirmity) and address the House from where he stands. This rule does not apply to ministers and members of the Opposition Front Bench who are permitted to address the House standing at the despatch boxes.

A member is allowed to wear a hat when seated but must always rise uncovered. Women members, however, are not bound by this rule. A further exception is made if a member desires to raise a point of order during a division (q.v.), in which case he addresses the Chair seated and covered.

A member may only speak when there is a question before the House, unless he is moving or seconding a motion or making a personal or a ministerial statement. He must address the House in English. He must not read a speech but is permitted to make use of notes. He may, however, read extracts from documents during the course of a speech, and there are certain other recognized exceptions to this rule. Ministers, for instance, may read the answers to questions, and when the Chancellor of the Exchequer delivers his Budget speech, or when a minister makes an important policy pronouncement or explains a highly technical Bill, considerable latitude is allowed.

A member may only speak when called upon to do so by the Speaker. According to Erskine May, 'When two or more members rise to speak, the Speaker calls on the member who, rising in his place, is first observed by him.' Hence the term 'catching the Speaker's eye'. In actual fact the choice lies within the discretion of the Speaker and his decision may not be challenged. Once in possession of the floor a member is entitled to be heard without interruption (except on a point of order), unless he is irrelevant, repetitive, or out of order, in which case he is liable to be checked by the Speaker. He may consent to yield to an interruption for the purpose of explanation or elucidation, but he is entitled to refuse to give way.

All speeches must be addressed to the Chair. It is out of order to address another member directly in the second person or to refer to him by name. If another member is referred to in the course of a speech it must be in the form of 'the Honourable Member for West Worthing' or 'the Honourable Member opposite' or some such suitable alternative. Privy Councillors are referred to as 'the Right Honourable Member'; ministers are usually referred to by the offices which they hold, although one often hears 'the Right Honourable gentleman' or 'my Right Honourable friend'. Commissioned officers of Her Majesty's forces are 'the Honourable (or Right Honourable) and gallant Member' and barristers are 'the Honourable (or Right Honourable) and learned Member'. A baronet is referred to as 'the Honourable Baronet' and a peer sitting in the House of Commons as 'the Noble Lord'. The purpose of these forms is to render criticism strictly impersonal, thus reducing the possibility of acrimonious debate and maintaining the dignity of the House.

Members must address the Chair from 'within the House'. The side galleries are technically within the House but not the cross benches below the Bar. Members often congregate at the Bar or behind the Speaker's Chair to listen to debates, but they would not themselves be permitted to speak from these positions.

Except in committee, no member is permitted to speak more than once to the same question except by leave of the House. This rule is relaxed in favour of the mover of a substantive motion (q.v.), who has the right of reply, and a member in charge of a Bill under consideration which has been amended by a Standing Committee. Leave to speak a second time is usually granted to a member wishing to clarify a misconception, a member wishing to answer a personal attack upon his conduct or character, or a minister wishing to sum up for the Government at the end of a debate.

No member may remain on his feet if the Speaker rises to intervene or to give a ruling.

Maiden speeches are always given priority and accorded special courtesy. A member making his maiden speech (q.v.) usually avoids controversial matters, and it is the custom for the member who follows him to congratulate him.

A member who has not concluded his speech at the moment of the automatic interruption of business, or who moves the adjournment of a debate, takes precedence on the resumption of that debate.

The following list of breaches of order while speaking is given by Erskine May:

(1) A member may not allude to a debate of the same session upon any question or Bill not then under discussion. This rule is not always strictly enforced, but exists to ensure that a matter cannot be reopened for discussion once a decision has been reached.

(2) A member may not speak against or reflect upon any determination of the House, unless he intends to conclude with a motion for rescinding it. This rule is always strictly enforced.

(3) A member may not allude to debates in the other House of Parliament. This rule is relaxed to permit reference to Government statements in the House of Lords, and it is also frequently evaded by referring to the upper House as 'another place'.

(4) A member may not utter treasonable or seditious words, or use the Queen's name irreverently or to influence debate.

(5) A member may not speak offensive or insulting words against the character or proceedings of either House.

(6) A member may not refer to matters pending a judicial decision. This rule is sometimes relaxed, and it is for the Speaker to intervene if he feels there is a danger of a debate prejudicing the conduct of judicial proceedings.

(7) A member may not, unless upon a substantive motion for that purpose, reflect upon the conduct of persons in authority. The persons covered by this rule are the Sovereign, the Heir to the Throne, Governors-General, the Lord Chancellor, the Speaker, the Chairman of Ways and Means members of either House of Parliament, and the Judges of the Superior Courts.

(8) A member may not make personal allusions to other Members of Parliament. The effect of this rule is to prohibit the making of derogatory references to the character, appearance, or private life of another member, or any suggestion that he is actuated by base motives.

(9) A member may not obstruct public business. The interpretation of this rule must obviously lie within the discretion of the Chair.

In addition to the rules listed above, it is out of order to anticipate a matter which has yet to be debated, and it is improper for a minister to cite documents which he is not prepared to 'lay on the Table' (i.e., make them available to other members).

Members who are not speaking are required to remain in their places unless they wish to leave the Chamber. They must enter and leave the Chamber in a decorous manner and are expected to bow towards the Chair upon entering and leaving. They should not cross the floor between the Chair and the speaker addressing the House. Reading, writing letters, and carrying on conversations are, strictly speaking, not allowed, but a certain latitude necessarily exists. A member may, for instance, wish to read something bearing upon the debate, and the need for a hurried consultation between a group of members might arise. Certain interjections such as 'Hear, hear', 'Order', 'Answer', and 'Divide' are permissible unless deliberately repeated for the purpose of obstructing a speaker. Clapping, hissing, and cries of 'Shame' are not in order. Needless to say, any language normally considered improper would never be overlooked if used by a member in the House.

In the House of Lords debate is usually conducted in a calmer and more sedate atmosphere, but similar rules and principles are required to be observed. A speaker, however, does not address the Chair; he addresses the House direct and commences his speech, 'My Lords'. He refers to another peer as 'the Noble Lord' or, according to his rank, as 'the Noble Earl', 'the Noble Viscount', etc.

DEBATES, LONGEST

The longest debate in the House of Commons on any one Bill was in 1893–4, when the stages of the Government of Ireland Bill took eighty-two days. The Budget resolutions and Finance Bill in 1909 took seventy-four days, of which ninety hours were spent on 554 divisions.

DEBATES, OFFICIAL REPORT OF

See HANSARD; PARLIAMENTARY DEBATES.

DEBRETT, JOHN (d. 1822)

In 1781, Debrett took over the publishing business of John Almon (q.v.), and from 1781 to 1822 he was the editor of the famous *Peerage* which still bears his name. It was first published as *The New Peerage; or Ancient and Present State of the Nobility of England*, and in 1802 was re-named *Debrett's Correct Peerage*. The companion work, *The Baronetage of England*, first appeared in 1808. Both are now published in consolidated form as *Debrett's Peerage, Baronetage, Knightage and Companionage*, and are also available separately. Debrett is a standard work of reference containing genealogical details of titled families, brief biographies of knights and companions, and illustrated with armorial bearings.

Debrett also compiled a record of parliamentary debates covering the years 1743 to 1774 and a *Register of Proceedings of both Houses from 1780 to 1803* which together comprise 63 volumes. Debrett's Debates were one of the sources from which Cobbett and Wright compiled the Parliamentary History (q.v.).

DECLARATION OF RIGHT

See BILL OF RIGHTS.

DEFENCE, SECRETARY OF STATE FOR

In terms of the Defence (Transfer of Functions) Act, 1964, the organization of defence is now centralized in a single ministry and under a single Minister known as the Secretary of State for Defence. The Admiralty, War Office and Air Ministry have ceased to exist as separate departments, and their former Ministers, the First Lord of the Admiralty and the Secretaries of State for War and Air, were replaced in the first instance by three new Ministers, subordinate to the Secretary of State for Defence and not of Cabinet rank, styled Minister of Defence for the Royal Navy, Minister of Defence for the Army and Minister of Defence for the Royal Air Force. In the Government formed by Mr. Harold Wilson in October 1964 a Deputy Secretary of State for Defence was appointed, his duties being coupled with those of the Minister of Defence for the Army, but in January 1967 a further ministerial reorganization took place. The posts of the three service Ministers were abolished and replaced by a Minister of Defence (Administration) and a Minister of Defence (Equipment) whose responsibilities covered all three services. In the Government formed by Mr. Edward Heath in June 1970 these two Ministers were replaced by a single Minister of State. In addition, three Parliamentary Under-Secretaries of State for Defence are directly responsible for the Royal Navy, Army and Royal Air Force respectively.

The Act makes provision for a Defence Council under the chairmanship of the Secretary of State for Defence, together with an Admiralty Board, Army Board and Air Force Board subordinate to the Council. Broad issues relating to defence remain subject to the supreme authority of the Prime Minister and the Cabinet as a whole, and are dealt with by a Cabinet Committee on Defence and Oversea Policy consisting of senior Cabinet ministers sitting under the chairmanship of the Prime Minister.

A Defence Minister was first appointed to the Cabinet in 1936 when Sir Thomas Inskip was designated Minister for the Co-ordination of Defence. The office fell into abeyance when Sir Winston Churchill assumed the title of Minister of Defence on becoming Prime Minister in 1940. When Lord Attlee became Prime Minister in 1945 he also assumed the title of Minister of Defence, but no department was formally constituted until the following year with the passing of the Ministry of Defence Act.

The salary of the Secretary of State for Defence is £8,500 a year and that of the Minister of State is £7,625. They receive an additional allowance of £1,250 if they are Members of the House of Commons.

Chronological lists of Defence Ministers and the former service Ministers appear with the appendixes.

The Estimates (q.v.) of the Ministry of Defence are published separately from the civil Estimates.

'DEFINITE MATTER OF URGENT PUBLIC IMPORTANCE'

See EMERGENCY ADJOURNMENT MOTIONS.

DELEGATED LEGISLATION

Laws (or rules and regulations with the effect of law) which Parliament by statute has sanctioned can be made by some authority other than itself. This delegation of powers is a comparatively modern practice, and prior to 1800 there are only about thirty specific instances. One of the earliest was a law of 1385 which provided that the Staple should be held at places and times and in such manner as should be ordained by the King's Council, with the authority of Parliament. The famous Statute of Proclamations of 1539 gave Henry VIII power to legislate by proclamation, but the intention here was not so much to delegate Parliament's powers but to define the King's. To this end the statute provided that the Common Law, statute law, and rights of property should not be affected by Royal Proclamations.

In the early 19th century the practice of delegating legislative powers was beginning to receive recognition, but even then Parliament was able to do most of the law-making that the country required. The Acts of that period are full of detail, and there were still only a few isolated instances where regulations were permitted to be made by some authority other than Parliament. With the advent of the Reform Bill of 1832 and the reforms in local government came a great increase in the volume of delegated legislation. According to Maitland, Parliament at this time began to legislate with remarkable vigour, to overhaul the whole law of the country, to lay down general rules and entrust their working to officials, ministers, and boards of commissioners. The First World War caused a further rapid rise in the tide of delegated legislation, but the powers conferred by the Defence of the Realm Acts of those years were small compared to those given by the Emergency Powers (Defence) Act of the Second World War. This Act empowered the Crown to make regulations by Order in Council 'for securing the public safety, the defence of the realm, the maintenance of public order and the efficient prosecution of any war in which His Majesty may be engaged, and for maintaining supplies and services essential to the life of the community'. To quote Professor Maitland again, 'We are becoming a much governed nation, governed by all manner of councils and boards and officers, central and local, high and low, exercising the powers which have been committed to them by modern statutes.' Indeed, there has been much public concern over the growth of bureaucracy in Britain, and the publication by Lord Hewart (who was then Lord Chief Justice) in 1929 of his book, *The New Despotism*, caused a considerable stir. Dr. Allen, in his *Law and Orders*, also stresses the dangers of delegating extensive legislative powers. However, apart from national emergencies when parliamentary processes are too slow in any case, Parliament has not sufficient time to deal with minute details of legislation, and while it continues to pour forth new laws, it must delegate the formulation of those details to the government department concerned.

In 1929 the Committee on Ministers' Powers (the Donoughmore Committee) was appointed to consider the whole question of the powers exercised by Ministers of the Crown, and their report was published in 1932. Although the committee considered that the system of delegated legislation was indispensable, it pointed out certain dangers inherent in it and made recommendations for further safeguards. Those existing at present include the examination of Statutory Instruments (the medium of delegated legislation) by a Sessional Committee in the House of Commons and by a similar committee in the House of Lords; the fact that certain orders require parliamentary approval before they can operate; the procedure by which other orders laid before Parliament can be annulled as a result of an adverse vote following a debate on a 'prayer'; and the fact that any order can be challenged in the courts and, if the court so decides, declared *ultra vires*. Parliament can also revoke delegated powers at any time. Further safeguards which were advocated by the Donoughmore Committee, including the appointment of a committee to scrutinize all Acts involving delegated legislation, have not yet been adopted. (The machinery of delegated legislation is dealt with under the heading STATUTORY INSTRUMENTS.)

A reference to practices observed in certain other Commonwealth countries in respect of delegated legislation might not be out of place under this heading.

In Australia the making of statutory regulations is governed by the Acts Interpretation Act of 1901, and the Senate Standing Committee, which was set up in 1932, is charged with the task of examining and reporting on subsidiary legislation. The yardstick which this committee adopts for the purposes of its scrutiny might well be adopted universally as a means of eliminating the evils inherent in any system of 'government by regulation'. In Australia statutory regulations must (1) be in accord with the statute under which they are made; (2) not trespass unduly on personal rights and liberties; (3) not make the rights and liberties of citizens depend upon administrative decisions, but only on judicial decisions; and (4) be concerned only with administrative detail and not amount to substantive legislation which is a matter for parliamentary enactment. Before considering a regulation the committee obtains from the Government department responsible for its issue a full explanation of its effects and the reasons for making it. Resolutions may be passed in either House disallowing a regulation.

New Zealand's Regulation Act of 1936 provides for the publication of subsidiary legislation in an official series of Statutory Regulations. The Attorney-General is required to examine all regulations before they are issued to determine whether or not they are desirable, and the Statutes Revision Committee may consider regulations to determine whether they trespass unduly on personal rights and liberties, or whether they appear to make some unusual or unexpected use of the powers conferred by the statute under which they are made. In addition, any regulation is subject to a motion in the House which, if carried, would have the effect of annulment.

Canada has never introduced any special procedures for debating subsidiary legislation, and the only opportunities which arise for objecting to it are during debates on the Address, Supply debates, and on continuing legislation. Even so, no provisions for annulment of regulations exist unless contained in the particular enabling Act.

Regulations which are not subject to annulment in this manner could only be repealed by passing a special Act of Parliament.

India's House of the People appointed a Committee on Subordinate Legislation in 1953 with functions similar to those of Australia's Senate Standing Committee. The power of the Government to make regulations and the extent of parliamentary control over them vary widely according to the provisions of the enabling Act. Some regulations must be laid before the House for a specified period and are subject to modification; others need to be approved by an affirmative resolution of Parliament; while the mere fact of publication in the Official Gazette is sufficient to bring certain of them into operation.

(Further reading: Kersell, *Parliamentary supervision of delegated legislative powers*, 1960; 'Upper chamber scrutiny of delegated legislation', published in *Public Law*, spring 1959.)

DELIBERATIVE VOTE

The normal vote cast by a member of a legislative chamber whenever a question is put, as distinct from a casting vote (q.v.) which can only be exercised by the occupant of the Chair in the event of the 'ayes' and the 'noes' being equal. The occupant of the Chair is not normally empowered to exercise a deliberative vote, the notable exceptions being the Lord Chancellor (q.v.) in the House of Lords and the President of the Australian Senate. In some Parliaments (e.g. the Rhodesian Parliament) the Speaker has neither a deliberative nor a casting vote. In countries where a special procedure for constitutional amendment is laid down requiring a two-thirds majority of the legislature, it has been known for the Speaker to depart from normal practice and cast a deliberative vote when the final division is taken. Precedents of this kind are to be found in South Africa and (before the adoption of the present Standing Orders) in Rhodesia.

DEMISE OF THE CROWN

Until 1867 the demise of the Crown affected the existence of Parliament, the reason being that the Sovereign summoned the estates of the realm, by writ, to confer with him, and on his death the invitation lapsed and Parliament was automatically dissolved. This inconvenience was met by a series of statutes, and an Act of 1695 provided that Parliaments should last for six months after the demise of the Crown, if not sooner dissolved by the new Sovereign. The Representation of the People Act, 1867, made the duration of a Parliament independent of the demise of the Crown. This is the only occasion upon which Parliament is required to meet without summons in the usual form, as by the Succession to the Crown Act, 1707, on the demise of the Crown Parliament has to meet immediately, whether it is already sitting or separated by adjournment or prorogation, and members then take the oath of allegiance to the new Sovereign. If the demise occurs subsequent to a dissolution but before the day appointed for the meeting of the new Parliament, the old one has to convene and sit for six months, unless sooner prorogued or dissolved by the new Sovereign (Meeting of Parliament Act, 1797). Most contingencies seem to have been provided for, but even now there is no provision for the remote possibility that a Sovereign might die after a dissolution and before the writs were issued.

DEPENDENT MOTION

See SUBSIDIARY MOTION.

DEPUTY CHAIRMAN

See CHAIRMAN OF WAYS AND MEANS.

DEPUTY PRIME MINISTER

Strictly speaking, the office of Deputy Prime Minister is unknown to the British Constitution, although this title was applied to Mr. Attlee when he held office in the Coalition Government during the Second World War and to Mr. Herbert Morrison during 1945 to 1950. More recently, Mr. R. A. Butler was designated Deputy Prime Minister by Mr. Harold Macmillan in 1962, although Mr. Butler had himself stated in the House of Commons in 1956 that 'the office of Deputy Prime Minister is not known to our Constitution'. The objection to the title is that it implies a line of succession and is thus an infringement of the Royal Prerogative. According to Sir John Wheeler-Bennett, King George VI objected on these grounds to the designation of Mr. Anthony Eden as Deputy Prime Minister in 1951. The new office of First Secretary of State (q.v.), first created in July 1962, appears to carry with it the status of Deputy Prime Minister, the latter title having lapsed with the resignation of Mr. Macmillan as Prime Minister in 1963.

DEPUTY SPEAKER

Before 1855 there existed no provision for a deputy to act as Speaker during an enforced absence. Consequently, if the Speaker fell sick the House was forced to adjourn for the duration of his indisposition, or, if the absence were likely to be prolonged, to elect a temporary Speaker who retired when the real Speaker recovered. In 1855, as the result of a Select Committee report, a Standing Order was introduced enabling the Chairman of Ways and Means (q.v.) to deputize for the Speaker whenever necessary, and in 1902 this provision was extended to the Deputy Chairman also. Either of these officers may take the Chair as Deputy Speaker whenever the House shall be informed by the Clerk of the unavoidable absence of the Speaker, or at the request of the

Speaker without any formal communication to the House. Under the new financial procedure, the implementation of which was begun in December 1966, the Deputy Speaker presides when the House debates the business of Supply and Ways and Means. On these occasions he is vested with the same powers he exercised when presiding as Chairman of Ways and Means over the now defunct Committees of Supply and Ways and Means. Until 1909, the consent of the House was still technically required before the Speaker could be relieved. The powers of the Deputy Speaker are confirmed and given statutory authority by the Deputy Speaker Act, 1855.

It is interesting to note that the extraordinary degree of health enjoyed by Speakers prior to 1855 was such that there were only twenty-nine absences during three centuries (1547–1853).

In Australia the title of Deputy Speaker was changed to Acting Speaker from 1 April 1965.

DESPATCH BOXES

In the House of Lords and House of Commons the two despatch boxes are placed on the Table of the House. That on the Government side contains two oath cards, an affirmation card, a Hebrew Old Testament, a Bible (Authorized Version), a Douay Bible (a translation of the Vulgate used by Roman Catholics), and two New Testaments. The despatch box on the Opposition side contains a New Testament and an oath card, so that the contents of both boxes are solely concerned with the swearing-in of members. The present despatch boxes in the House of Commons were a gift from New Zealand and are made of black bean wood. Their dimensions are 1 ft. 9 in. by 1 ft. 3 in. by 1 ft. 3 in. The old ones, which bore the impressions of Gladstone's signet ring received during moments of impassioned oratory, were lost when the Chamber was destroyed by bombs in 1941.

No account would seem to exist explaining the origin of the despatch boxes. The first authentic contemporary engraving of the House of Commons dated 1624 shows no despatch boxes, and on the evidence available it would be difficult to suggest the date when the despatch boxes became a permanent feature of the House. Before the advent of modern-style luggage the container in which a man normally carried his personal belongings was a box, and the likelihood is that Members of Parliament brought their papers and other accoutrements into the chamber with them in their boxes. Privy councillors sitting on the front benches probably stood their boxes, containing the papers they were likely to require during debate, on the Table of the House. Similarly the Clerk of the House probably kept his records and papers in a box which he kept upon the Table for convenience. Thus there was probably always one or more boxes deposited on the Table so that they became a recognized part of the furniture. If this is the explanation of their origin it is not difficult to appreciate how the despatch boxes became an established tradition of both Houses of Parliament. Ministers and leading opposition members are entitled to speak from the despatch boxes when addressing the House, and if a member neglects this privilege he is likely to be interrupted by cries of 'Box, box!'.

DEVOLUTION

In the constitutional sense, the passing of power and authority from one legislative body to another, e.g., Northern Ireland's independent powers with regard to her domestic affairs were conferred by devolution. The advantages of devolution are in theory that the labours of the central legislature are lightened, and the local region is given the chance of pursuing policies appropriate to the peculiarities of local conditions.

In 1919–20 a conference was held under the chairmanship of Speaker Lowther to consider a scheme of devolution which might be applied to England, Scotland, Ireland and Wales, but the problems encountered proved to be of great complexity and the conference failed to arrive at satisfactory solutions. It nevertheless produced a report (Cmd. 692) which was never debated in Parliament.

D'EWES, SIR SIMONDS (1602–1650)

The compiler of a work entitled *Journals of all the Parliaments during the Reign of Queen Elizabeth*, published in 1682. These journals constitute a valuable record of the proceedings of the Elizabethan Parliaments, and are one of the sources from which Cobbett and Wright compiled the Parliamentary History (q.v.). D'Ewes was also the author of a manuscript diary which is regarded as the best authority for the proceedings of the Long Parliament (q.v.) during its early years.

D'Ewes was knighted in 1626 and became Member of Parliament for the borough of Sudbury in 1640. The following year he was made a baronet, but the baronetcy became extinct in 1731. He was one of the members excluded from the House of Commons by Pride's Purge (q.v.) in 1648.

DILATORY MOTION

A motion which is intended to have a postponing or indefinitely delaying effect on a debate. If it is moved and carried 'That this House do now adjourn', or in committee 'That the Chairman do leave the Chair', the subject under discussion is shelved. If it is moved 'That the debate be now adjourned' or 'That the Chairman do report progress and ask leave to sit again', the debate is postponed. A dilatory motion is a superseding motion because if it is accepted by the Speaker he proposes the motion as a new question, which supersedes the original question and must be disposed of before the debate on the original question can be resumed. The adjournment can also be moved at the commencement of Public Business or between Orders of the Day by the Government and the motion then becomes almost a substantive one, especially if moved by a member with the object of affording an opportunity to criticize the Government. Dilatory motions cannot be amended, and lapse at the moment of interruption of business at the end of the day without question put. By virtue of a Standing Order the Speaker (or Chairman) has power to put the question forthwith on a dilatory motion, or he may decline to propose the question to the House if he considers the acceptance of the motion would be an abuse of the rules of the House.

DISORDER IN THE HOUSE

A member who flouts the authority of the Speaker, or otherwise seriously offends against the rules of conduct and good order during a debate, may be directed by the Speaker to withdraw from the House. If the member refuses, or the Speaker considers the offence sufficiently heinous, the Speaker may 'name' him (*see* 'NAMING' A MEMBER). In the case of general disorder in the House, the Speaker may suspend the sitting, although he very rarely has to resort to this method of restoring order.

In the House of Lords the Speaker is not invested with any disciplinary powers and the maintenance of order is the responsibility of the House itself. Any member has the right to call another member to order, to move that a member be no longer heard, or that the Standing Order relating to asperity of speech be read by the Clerk, the last occasion on which such a motion was moved being 2 May 1950.

DISQUALIFICATION FROM MEMBERSHIP OF PARLIAMENT

HOUSE OF LORDS

Aliens, other than naturalized aliens, bankrupts, and persons convicted of treason or felony are disqualified by statute from sitting and voting in the House of Lords. Peers under the age of twenty-one are disqualified in terms of a Standing Order dating from 1685. The disqualification on women was removed by the Life Peerages Act, 1958, under which women became eligible to sit in the House of Lords for the first time as life peers (q.v.). The disqualification on hereditary peeresses was removed by the Peerage Act, 1963.

A peer may also be disqualified by expulsion and, if imposed by sentence of the House acting in its judicial capacity, the disqualification could be permanent unless overruled by the Crown exercising the prerogative of pardon. A resolution by the Lords as a legislative body could not create a permanent disqualification.

[206]

HOUSE OF COMMONS

Disqualification from membership of the House of Commons is caused by some incapacity described by Anson as 'inherent, as in the case of an infant or lunatic, or acquired by profession or office, or incurred by bankruptcy, felony or corruption'. The disqualification of women was removed by the Parliament (Qualification of Women) Act, 1918, and the Representation of the People (Equal Franchise) Act, 1928, while the House of Commons Disqualification Act, 1957, greatly simplified the law relating to disqualification through the holding of certain offices. The main disqualifications still in force are as follows:

Peerage. Save as provided by the Peerage Act, 1963, which makes provision for the renunciation of a peerage, peers of England, Scotland, Great Britain and the United Kingdom are disqualified from membership of the House of Commons. The wives and sons of peers and Irish peers are not disqualified, but Irish peers are not eligible to sit in the House of Lords.

Clergy. Clergy of the Church of England and the Church of Ireland and Ministers of the Church of Scotland are disqualified by the House of Commons (Clergy Disqualification) Act, 1801. The passing of the Welsh Church Act, 1914, removed the disqualification on clergy of the Church of Wales, although the disestablishment of the Church of Ireland in 1869 did not remove it in respect of the clergy of that Church. Roman Catholic priests are disqualified under the Roman Catholic Relief Act, 1829. Nonconformist clergy are not disqualified.

Minors. The old Common Law disqualification which applied to persons under the age of twenty-one (although it was not always enforced) was made statutory by the Parliamentary Elections Act, 1695. In 1706 the Act of Union extended the disqualification to Scotland, while the Parliamentary Elections (Ireland) Act, 1823, makes similar provision in respect of Northern Ireland.

Aliens. The Common Law disqualification upon aliens received statutory confirmation under the Act of Settlement (q.v.). Under subsequent enactments, notably the Status of Aliens Act, 1914, and the British Nationality Act, 1948, the political incapacity of an alien is continued, but he can acquire political rights, including the removal of his disqualification from membership of Parliament, by naturalization.

Lunacy. Lunacy is also a disqualification under Common Law. Under the Mental Health Act, 1959, the Speaker has certain duties (formerly exercised under the Lunacy (Vacating of Seats) Act, 1886) in relation to the vacation of a member's seat by reason of his being of unsound mind. Having been notified in the manner provided by the Act of the detention of a member on the ground of mental illness, the Speaker makes arrangements for the examination of that member by two specialists in mental disorders. If the report of the specialists confirms the member's condition a further examination is arranged six months later, and if the member's condition is again confirmed his seat becomes vacant.

Bankruptcy. Bankruptcy is a statutory disqualification, the relevant statutes in respect of England and Wales being the Bankruptcy Acts, 1883–1914. An adjudged bankrupt is ineligible for election to the House of Commons, while in the case of a sitting member the disqualification comes into effect six months after the date of adjudication. Disqualification continues in force until removed by the annulment of the adjudication or by a grant of discharge accompanied by a certificate that the bankruptcy was not due to misconduct. The provisions of the law vary slightly in respect of Scotland and Northern Ireland.

Treason and Felony. The Forfeiture Act, 1870, as amended, provides for the disqualification of persons convicted of treason or felony and sentenced to death or to a term of imprisonment exceeding twelve months. It ceases when the offender has suffered the punishment to which he has been sentenced or has received a free pardon. In the case of persons convicted after election to Parliament, the Act does not specifically impose a disqualification from membership but only from sitting and voting. Thus, when such a case arose in 1954 the House carried a resolution for the expulsion of the member concerned before ordering the issue of a new writ.

Corrupt and Illegal Practices during Elections. Disqualification resulting from a conviction for corrupt or illegal practices at elections exists under Common Law and is amplified by the Corrupt and Illegal Practices Prevention Act, 1883, as amended by the Representation of the People Act, 1949. The nature of the disqualification varies with the nature of the offence—e.g., it can vary in length from five to ten years; it can be total or it can apply only to the constituency in which the offence was committed; and it can depend on whether the offence was committed by the candidate or his agent.

Offices of Profit under the Crown. The disqualification on the holders of certain offices of profit under the Crown is an historic one founded both in statute and Common Law. The House of Commons Disqualification Act, 1957, has, however, codified the law in relation to this matter. Broadly speaking, Civil Servants (whether established or not), members of the regular armed forces, members of police forces, judges and holders of certain other judicial offices, and members of certain commissions and tribunals are disqualified while they hold office. Certain office-holders, such as the sheriff of a county in England or Wales, are disqualified only for particular constituencies.

The principle of the exclusion of what subsequently became the Civil Service was established by the Succession to the Crown Act, 1707, which also excluded colonial Governors (now disqualified by the Act of 1957 in so far as they are members of the Overseas Civil

Service). Ministers of the Crown have always been largely exempted from the disqualification, although in terms of the Act of 1707 they were obliged on appointment to submit themselves for re-election until this requirement was modified in 1919 and finally abolished in 1926. The Act of 1957, since amended by the Ministers of the Crown Act, 1964, provided for a limitation on the number of Ministers of the Crown and junior ministers who may sit and vote in the House of Commons at any one time.

The Act of 1957 for the first time disqualified ambassadors, who had not previously been subject to any specific prohibition from membership of the House of Commons. The Act also removed the disqualification which previously applied to government contractors and the recipients of certain pensions from the Crown. Government contractors had been disqualified during the period of the contract under the House of Commons (Disqualification) Act, 1782, a disqualification extended to Ireland by a similarly entitled Act of 1801. Recipients of Civil Service and diplomatic pensions had never been disqualified, but certain other pensioners were disqualified under the Crown Pensions Disqualification Act, 1715. All three statutes were repealed by the Act of 1957.

Provision is made in the Act for the retention of the offices of steward of the Chiltern Hundreds (q.v.) and of the Manor of Northstead as offices incurring disqualification from membership of the House of Commons. Their existence remains a legal fiction but they are retained for the purpose of enabling a member to resign his seat.

See also OFFICE OF PROFIT UNDER THE CROWN.

DISQUALIFICATION OF VOTERS

See FRANCHISE.

DISSOLUTION OF PARLIAMENT

Parliament is dissolved by exercise of the Royal Prerogative (q.v.) and by means of a Royal Proclamation issued with the advice of the Privy Council. The Septennial Act of 1715 fixed the duration of Parliament at seven years. It was amended by the Parliament Act, 1911, which fixed the life of a Parliament at its present length of five years. The Parliaments sitting during the wars which began in 1914 and 1939 were prolonged beyond the statutory period, but in other cases Parliament has always been dissolved before the expiration of that period. If Parliament is sitting when dissolution is contemplated it is usually first prorogued and immediately afterwards dissolved. But if dissolution is decided on during the recess, as in 1900 and 1905, a considerable interval may elapse between prorogation and dissolution. Parliament was dissolved in person by Charles II in 1681 and by the Prince Regent in 1818, but since then it has been dissolved by proclamation, and the same proclamation which dissolves one Parliament calls another. The demise of the Crown (q.v.) does not automatically dissolve Parliament.

The prerogative of dissolution gives rise to many difficult and intricate questions and has produced a number of constitutional crises in the Commonwealth, notably those of Canada in 1926 and South Africa in 1939. These and other cases are considered in detail in Forsey's *The Royal Power of Dissolution of Parliament in the British Commonwealth*. The right of the Crown to dissolve Parliament is unquestionable, but William III, in 1701, was the last Sovereign to dissolve Parliament on his own responsibility. Since then, however, there have been cases of refusal by the Crown to grant dissolution in certain circumstances. In 1858 Lord Derby, when threatened with a vote of censure in the House, asked the Queen's leave to say that if the vote was carried Parliament would be dissolved, but she refused permission for this threat to be uttered.

The prerogative is now one which is exercised by the Sovereign on the advice and at the request of the Prime Minister, and for all practical purposes it can be assumed that a Prime Minister requesting a dissolution is by convention never refused. The request may be made for various reasons; a dissolution may be rightly demanded whenever there is reason to suppose that the House of Commons has ceased to represent the opinion of the majority of the country, or when a minister is defeated in the House on a measure which he believes will be acceptable to the country. A Government which is defeated in the House of Commons on an issue of confidence has no option in these days but to resign and submit to a test of its popularity at the polls. In any other circumstances the timing of a dissolution within the statutory five-year period which constitutes the maximum life of a Parliament is a matter for the Prime Minister to decide, and it is an accepted fact of political life that he will do his best to call an election at a time when he judges public opinion to be favourably disposed towards his Government.

DIURNAL OCCURRENCES OF PARLIAMENT

The first regular report of parliamentary debates, compiled in the form of a narrative. They were published by order of Parliament and were started in 1641, continuing until 1660.

DIVINE RIGHT OF KINGS

The doctrine which held that a King derived his authority direct from God and was therefore invested with an absolute power to override all other authorities. This principle of government formed the great political issue of the 17th century. Divine Right was claimed by Louis

XIV in France ('*L'état, c'est moi!*'), and by the Stuart Kings in England, where it became the primary factor in the struggle for supremacy between Parliament and the Sovereign. James I came to the throne with this concept of kingship as his guiding principle. Charles I, who through his background and upbringing had inherited his father's political convictions, continued to govern according to the same doctrine, and was very soon at variance with the House of Commons, which had emerged since the death of Elizabeth as a popular force, conscious of its growing power and effectiveness. Against the royal assertion of Divine Right, the Commons set their claim that a Sovereign's right to rule rests upon the consent of the governed. They further insisted that their hard-won privileges were a sacred right which no power, royal or otherwise, could alienate, whereas the King maintained that they were enjoyed by reason of his grace alone and were subject, like everything else, to the final and unchallengeable authority of his prerogative. In a dispute of such magnitude the unyielding attitude of both sides could lead only to conflict. The Civil War followed with its disastrous results for the monarchy, the King himself suffering the death of a traitor.

The monarchy was restored in 1660, the country having found itself unable to adapt itself to republican institutions, yet the concept of Divine Right had still not perished. The Anglican Church, which looked to the Crown for protection, was a staunch upholder of the doctrine, but with the accession to the throne of the Roman Catholic James II, the established Church found this same weapon being turned against itself. James was a typical Stuart, and his arbitrary principles of government soon led him into committing the same follies as his father, Charles I. For the second time in forty years England deposed its King, this time with less violence than on the former occasion. With the Revolution of 1688, which overthrew the Stuart dynasty and sent James II into exile, the doctrine of Divine Right suffered a mortal blow as a political creed of any consequence. Amongst English political theorists who have sought to justify this concept of government, Hobbes and Filmer are the most outstanding. (The standard work on this subject is *The Divine Right of Kings*, by J. N. Figgis (Cambridge University Press), 2nd ed., 1914.)

DIVISION LISTS

Lists of members voting in a division, the 'Ayes' and the 'Noes' (or in the House of Lords the 'Contents' and the 'Not Contents') being listed separately. Division lists for both Houses are printed in Hansard (q.v.), and with the daily Votes and Proceedings (q.v.).

Dasent records that the earliest instance known to him of the publication of a division list was when the names of the members who voted against Strafford's attainder in May 1641 were posted up outside

Westminster Hall and headed: 'These are the Straffordians, Betrayers of their Country.' The Parliamentary History (q.v.) records the more important divisions of the 18th century, although it was not until 1836 that the House of Commons officially published its own division lists, a reform which had been advocated by Edmund Burke in 1770.

DIVISION, POINT OF ORDER DURING A

In the House of Commons a member wishing to raise a point of order after a division has been called must address the Chair seated and covered. Women members are not required to be covered. This is the only occasion on which a member, other than a woman member, is permitted to address the Chair wearing a hat.

The custom is an ancient one which originated as a means of attracting the attention of the Speaker or Chairman while other members were moving into the division lobbies. For the particular benefit of members who are not provided with hats, a special hat is kept in the Chamber for the use of anyone wishing to raise a point of order during a division. Many varieties of headgear have been utilized on various occasions. A policeman's helmet has been known to serve the purpose, and obliging women members have loaned their hats on a number of occasions. At such times the hat is hurriedly passed from hand to hand until it reaches the member desiring to raise the point of order. Rulings from the Chair have established that a proper head covering is essential, and members who, in the urgency of the moment, have resorted to the use of handkerchiefs and order papers have been ruled out of order. In other Commonwealth Parliaments a member must remain seated when raising a point of order during a division, but a hat is not considered necessary. On 11 December 1947 the Speaker was asked whether a member could be covered in some other way than by a hat, order papers and handkerchiefs not being allowed. The Speaker said that some distinction needed to be made, because if a member stood up when other members were walking out to the Division Lobbies it did not indicate to the Speaker that that member was raising a point of order.

DIVISIONS

In both Houses of Parliament all questions are decided by a vote, a simple majority being required to affirm or negative a question. Sometimes a vote is carried to a division, which is a physical separation into two lobbies of those members wishing to vote for and those wishing to vote against a question. The procedure on divisions varies slightly in the two Houses, and the description which follows relates to the Commons, the points on which the Lords' procedure differs being noted below.

The present method of taking divisions in the House of Commons was established in 1836 after a select committee had recommended the building of division lobbies. The Speaker, or in Committee of the Whole House the Chairman of Ways and Means, states the question before the House at the conclusion of the debate upon it, and says, 'As many as are of that opinion say "Aye" ' and 'As many as are of the contrary opinion say "No" '. Judging by the strength of each separate chorus of 'Ayes' and 'Noes' he then says tentatively, 'I think the "Ayes" (or the "Noes") have it.' This opinion may be accepted by the House, in which case, after a pause, the Speaker or Chairman says definitely, 'The "Ayes" (or the "Noes") have it', and the question is decided. If, however, the opinion of the Chair is challenged by continuing cries of 'Aye' or 'No', as the case may be, the order, 'Clear the lobby', is given from the Chair, thus indicating that a division has been called. Immediately the exit doors of the Division Lobbies are locked, bells are rung throughout the building to acquaint members who are not in the Chamber that a division is in progress, and the policemen on duty call 'Division' through the corridors. After two minutes the Speaker or Chairman again puts the question, and it sometimes occurs that his opinion is accepted the second time and the division is called off. Usually, however, it is decided to continue with the division, although at this point the occupant of the Chair has a discretionary power which he can exercise if he considers that a division has been unnecessarily claimed. In adopting this procedure he calls upon the 'Ayes' and the 'Noes' to rise successively, and announces the result of the voting without further delay. This power is seldom used and exists only to counter irresponsible action. In proceeding with the division, the Chair appoints two tellers (usually Whips) from each side who take up their positions at the exits from the lobbies, an 'Aye' teller and a 'No' teller working together to check each other's counting. If two tellers are not forthcoming for one side no division can take place. The 'Ayes' and the 'Noes' are directed into their respective lobbies, which run parallel to and are entered from the Chamber, the 'Aye' lobby being to the right and the 'No' lobby to the left of the Chair. The exit doors are unlocked and the members, having given their names to the clerks stationed in the lobbies, file out and are counted by the tellers. Members who are prevented by infirmity from passing through the lobbies are counted in the House. After six minutes from the giving of the order, 'Clear the lobby', the order 'Lock the doors', is given, and the entrances to the lobbies are then locked and remain so until the result of the division is announced. When all the members taking part in the division have passed through the lobbies and the tellers have satisfied themselves that no one has been left uncounted, the respective figures are stated to a Clerk-at-the-Table, who enters them upon a division slip and hands it to the senior teller for the majority. The senior and junior tellers for the majority and the senior and junior tellers for the minority, in that order from right to left, then form up facing the Chair. They bow, advance a step forward together, and the senior teller for the majority reads out the figures. They bow once more and return to their seats, and the Speaker or Chairman then announces the result of the division himself.

Divisions consume an appreciable amount of parliamentary time; the average division lasts about ten minutes all told and when, as sometimes happens, a number of divisions take place during the course of a single sitting, the amount of time lost can be reckoned in hours. During the sitting of 20-21 March 1907, 43 divisions took place, the largest number ever to have occurred at one sitting.

The first division to be recorded in the Journal of the House of Commons took place on 23 March 1553/4. The largest division on record occurred on 11 August 1892, when the House voted by 350 to 310 in favour of Asquith's amendment to the address, expressing lack of confidence in the Government. The Budget of 1909 earned the distinction of surviving 549 divisions in the House of Commons, the largest number that any one issue has ever had to face. There have been a number of close divisions in which a majority of one has been recorded. On 22 March 1831 the second reading of the Reform Bill was carried by 302 votes to 301; on 4 June 1841 a vote of no confidence in the Government was carried by 312 votes to 311; and, more recently, on 27 July 1950, Sir Winston Churchill's motion that the House should go into secret session was rejected by 296 votes to 295.

Strangers are allowed to be present in the galleries during divisions but they are cleared from the Members' Lobby, a practice which survives from the days when persons liable to be affected by the result of a division had the habit of obstructing members on their way to vote.

The division lists record the names of the members taking part in a division and the manner of voting, and they constitute an official record which is reproduced in Hansard. A member's voting record is thus open to scrutiny.

Prior to 1906 the doors of the Chamber were locked after two minutes had elapsed from the calling of the division, and all members present were compelled to vote. Under the present practice the doors of the Chamber are left unlocked and members wishing to abstain from voting are not required to leave the Chamber. A member who was not present in the Chamber when the question was put is entitled to vote in a division.

The Select Committee on Procedure of 1966-7 in its third report recommended no radical change in the present method of holding divisions in the House of Commons and rejected, at least for the time being, the introduction of an electro-mechanical system of voting.

In the House of Lords, the 'Ayes' and 'Noes' in a division are known as the 'Contents' and the 'Not Contents'. Unlike the occupant of the Chair in the House of Commons, who has only a casting vote in the event of an equality of votes, the Lord Chancellor or Lord Chairman has a normal vote which is taken in the House and not in the Division Lobby. The tellers include themselves in the totals, whereas in the Commons they are excluded. The ancient practice in the event of an equality of votes was to award the decision to the 'Not Contents', but an amendment to the Standing Orders introduced in 1951 provided for certain exceptions to this rule. When a division is called the order is given to 'Clear the Bar'. The doors are locked after four minutes from the giving of the order, or after such shorter time as the tellers may agree upon, and after the question has been put the second time the Lords taking part in the division enter the two lobbies. If the division is on any stage of a Bill or on a question for approving or disapproving subordinate legislation at least 30 peers must vote, otherwise the Speaker declares the question not decided and the debate is adjourned to a subsequent sitting. Peers who wish to abstain from voting may go within the rails round the Throne, where they are not technically 'within the House'.

The procedure on divisions in other Commonwealth Parliaments is based on that of Westminster, and any minor variations are designed to suit local convenience and the size of the legislature. For instance, the lapse of time between the calling of the division and the locking of the doors is bound to vary; in some cases members wishing to abstain from voting must leave the Chamber; and in Parliaments where the members are not so numerous as in the House of Commons divisions sometimes take place in the Chamber itself, the members lining up on either side of the Speaker's Chair, and the tellers themselves cross the names from the division lists. The greatest variation from House of Commons procedure is probably to be found in the Canadian Parliament (q.v.).

See also FLASH VOTING; 'NODDING THROUGH'.

DOD'S *PARLIAMENTARY COMPANION*

A work of reference which is published annually and was established in 1832 by Charles Dod. It contains about 750 pages of information, including biographical details of peers and members of the House of Commons, a list of constituencies with details of the most recent General Election and subsequent by-elections, the composition of the Ministry, Royal Household, government and public offices, and the main details of British Parliaments overseas. It is bound in a dark blue cloth and its unusually small format makes it handy for the pocket.

DOMINICA PARLIAMENT

Formerly belonging to the Leeward Islands, Dominica was transferred to the Windward Islands group on 1 January 1940 and received a new Constitution on 29 September 1951. This provided for universal adult suffrage and a reformed Legislative Council with a majority of elected members—the Administrator as President, 2 *ex-officio*, 3 nominated, and 8 elected members. The Governor had reserved powers under the new Constitution and also the right to address the Council when he thought fit. The life of each Council was limited to a maximum of three years. The Administrator (as representative of the Governor of the Windward Islands) was assisted by an Executive Council consisting of 2 *ex-officio* members, 4 elected members of the Legislative Council chosen by that body, and a nominated member of the Legislative Council appointed by the Governor. The elected members were increased from 3 to 4 in March 1956, and the Executive Council became the principal instrument of policy with a majority of elected members, 3 of whom were appointed ministers.

In June 1959 constitutional changes for Dominica were agreed upon by the Leeward and Windward Islands Constitutional Conference. The Legislative Council was reconstituted to consist of 1 official member, 2 nominated unofficial members and 11 elected members, with an elected Speaker presiding instead of the Administrator. Further constitutional changes became effective on 1 January 1960 when a Chief Minister was appointed from among the elected members and the powers of the Governors of the Leeward Islands and the Windward Islands (whose posts were abolished) were transferred to the Administrators of the various islands comprising these groups.

In 1962 the West Indies Federation, of which Dominica had been a member, was dissolved, and when negotiations for an alternative form of federation for the smaller West Indian colonies failed to produce agreement, new constitutional proposals were published in 1965 (Cmnd. 2865) whereby six British territories of the Eastern Caribbean could, if they wished, enter into an associate status with Great Britain. Dominica decided to take advantage of these arrangements, and a new Constitution for the island was agreed at a conference held in April and May 1966 (Cmnd. 3021).

Under the West Indies Act, 1967, Dominica, together with certain other West Indian territories, has shed her colonial status and has entered into an associate status with Great Britain. Dominica's new Constitution provides for full internal self-government, control of external affairs and defence being reserved to Great Britain, who will discharge her responsibilities in these areas in close consultation with the Government of Dominica.

The Parliament of Dominica consists of the Queen and a House of

Assembly, the latter comprising 3 nominated members, 11 elected members and the Attorney-General sitting as an *ex-officio* member. Two of the nominated members are appointed by the Governor on the advice of the Premier and on the advice of the Leader of the Opposition. A nominated member is entitled to vote in the House except on a motion of no confidence in the Government or a Bill to amend the Constitution, and is removable by the Governor on the advice of the Premier or the Leader of the Opposition as the case may be. The elected members are elected by universal adult suffrage and the life of a Parliament is five years unless sooner dissolved. The Cabinet consists of the Premier and not more than 5 other ministers and is collectively responsible to Parliament.

The Constitution includes a number of basic clauses which relate to such matters as fundamental rights and freedoms, Parliament, the franchise and elections, citizenship, the judicial system, and other basic institutions of government. A Bill seeking to alter the Constitution requires the approval of not less than two-thirds of the elected members of the House of Assembly, and if it seeks to alter a basic clause it must in addition be submitted to the electorate at a referendum and approved by a majority of not less than two-thirds of the valid votes cast. The Constitution also provides for the termination of the association with Great Britain by either side, and if terminated by Dominica the process of constitutional amendment described above would be invoked. However, no referendum would be required in the event of Dominica terminating the association in order to enter into a federation, union or other association with an independent Commonwealth country in the Caribbean.

DOMINION STATUS

Dominion status was a concept which arose from the granting of self-government to the Colonies of the former British Empire. Lloyd George in the House of Commons in 1921 said it was difficult and dangerous to define it. It was something that had never been clarified by an Act of Parliament, and yet it worked perfectly. However, there were three characteristics of the ideal Dominion, enumerated by the Imperial Conference of 1926, which helped towards a definition of the term 'Dominion status'. First, a Dominion was a territorial community, other than Great Britain, which owed allegiance to the Queen in common with Great Britain; second, was equal in status with Great Britain and was in no way subordinate to her in any aspect of its domestic or external affairs; and third, was freely associated with Great Britain as a member of the British Commonwealth of Nations. The second was the vital characteristic, and it was to clarify the position in regard to this that, as a result of the Imperial Conference of 1930, the Statute of Westminster (q.v.) was passed by the Imperial

[217]

Parliament in 1931 and subsequently adopted by the other members of the British Commonwealth.

The term 'Dominion' is, however, now obsolete. The admission of a number of republics as full members of the Commonwealth (a precedent established by the acceptance of India as the first republican member in 1949) has undoubtedly hastened this process. These states, while they have ceased to recognize the Queen of England as their own Queen, recognize her as the Head of the Commonwealth. The monarchies of the Commonwealth continue to recognize the Queen of England as their own Head of State, although it is doubtful whether they still regard themselves as Dominions. The use of the term persists in Canada to some extent (for example, in the titles of certain Acts of Parliament) but it is not in general usage. The expression 'full member of the Commonwealth' is to-day normally used to describe a fully independent and self-governing member of the family, although the term 'Dominion status' has not yet been supplanted by 'Commonwealth status'. In 1947 the Secretary of State for Dominion Affairs was re-styled the Secretary of State for Commonwealth Relations. In 1966, following the integration of the Commonwealth Relations and Colonial Offices, the Minister's title became Secretary of State for Commonwealth Affairs. In 1968, the office was merged with that of Secretary of State for Foreign Affairs.

DRAFTSMEN

The lawyers responsible for the drafting of Bills. The office responsible for the drafting of Government Bills is that of the Parliamentary Counsel (q.v.) to the Treasury. Private members must arrange for the drafting of their own Bills, although they usually receive assistance from this office. Once it has been decided to introduce certain legislation, the Treasury instructs Parliamentary Counsel to draft a Bill on the lines stated. It is usually necessary for the Parliamentary Counsel to consult the minister or his delegate for more specific instructions. The first draft may be fairly rough in form, and very often several drafts have to be prepared before agreement is reached. In the case of a very complicated piece of legislation it is often necessary to prepare an Explanatory Memorandum (q.v.) and several months are sometimes required for the drafting of such a Bill. Draftsmen usually work in pairs, a senior and a junior draftsman working together. Only very small Bills are undertaken by the juniors without assistance. Even when the Bill has been introduced and is under the control of Parliament the draftsmen remain responsible for the language, and their responsibility extends to the drafting of any amendments which may be accepted by the House, and of consequential amendments.

Early legislation was drafted by judges, but by the end of the 18th century drafting was being undertaken by lawyers.

[218]

DRESS IN PARLIAMENT

The dress worn by parliamentary officials is indicative of Parliament's attachment to tradition and its reluctance to change its habits and customs. It drew the line at accepting trousers for its Speakers and Serjeants-at-Arms when they first became fashionable, and those officials continue to wear knee-breeches, the lace jabot or linen bands at the neck and the silver-buckled shoes of the 18th century. This costume has become known as Court dress, and normally the Speaker wears a cut-away jacket, breeches of black cloth, linen bands and a stiff wing-collar. Over this he has a black silk robe with a train and wears a full-bottomed wig and carries a black three-cornered hat. After his election, but before he receives the Royal Approbation from the Lord Chancellor, he wears Court dress with a bob wig but no gown. When he attends ceremonies where the Sovereign is present he appears in his State Robe of black satin damask trimmed with gold, over a black velvet Court suit. He then has a lace jabot at the neck, lace frills on the sleeves and white gloves. If the Court is in mourning he wears a black paramatta gown and lawn bands, white linen weepers and black buckles with his ceremonial dress, but instead of lace he would have a lawn frill and ruffles and black gloves instead of white.

The Clerks-at-the-Table wear the black dress coat and waistcoat with trousers instead of knee-breeches, a wing-collar with white evening bow-tie, a black silk gown, black patent leather shoes and a bob wig. The only change they make in case of mourning is to wear a black stuff instead of a silk gown. At the Opening of Parliament the Clerk of the House wears full Court dress with knee-breeches complete with lace jabot and lace at the cuffs. The lace is exchanged for lawn and the silk for a stuff gown if he attends an Opening of Parliament when the Court is in mourning.

The Serjeant-at-Arms wears Court dress with a plain, stiff linen collar, white gloves and a sword, and carries a cocked hat under his arm when attending the Speaker. At ceremonies where the Sovereign is present he wears lace at collar and cuffs and an SS collar (a chain worn round the neck, each link being fashioned like an S). For mourning he wears black buckles on shoes and breeches, black gloves and his sword (scabbard and sword sling are also black). For an Opening of Parliament in this case the lace is replaced by a broad-hemmed lawn frill and ruffles.

Decorations and medal ribbons are not worn with official dress in the British Parliament on normal sitting days, but on ceremonial occasions when the Sovereign is present, decorations are worn in miniature on the left breast of Court dress. Full-size war medals may also be worn. In the case of neck badges, the senior one is worn and others in miniature.

In many Commonwealth Parliaments, particularly the older ones, the costume worn by the officials follows the Westminster pattern with local variations. The Canadian Speaker dispenses with wig and knee-breeches but when in procession he wears a three-cornered hat. In Australia the Speaker wears a wig and gown except when there is a Labour Government, as this party does not favour any special insignia of office. The Indian Speaker wears no special costume but wig and gown are the standard dress for most Commonwealth Speakers. An interesting variation is to be found in Nova Scotia where the Speaker wears a top hat. The Rhodesian Speaker's costume resembles that of his British counterpart most closely. On State occasions he wears a gold embroidered gown which once belonged to Speaker Brand of the British Parliament.

It is impossible to deny that the standards of dress of the Members of Parliament themselves have declined since the formal costumes prescribed by the etiquette of earlier times have been abandoned. In the 17th century, knee-breeches, silk stockings and silver-buckled shoes were absolutely *de rigueur* for members. A hundred years later M.P.s always wore Court dress with bag wig and sword in the House, and only county members were entitled to wear spurs. At this time, too, Cabinet ministers were never seen in Parliament without the insignia of the various Orders to which they belonged. The 17th century costume survived in the Court dress which civilian movers of the Debate on the Address were required to wear until the last war.

The dress of Members of Parliament in general has become increasingly informal since the last century, when no member of either House would have appeared within the precincts of the Palace of Westminster wearing anything on his head but a high silk hat. In fact, as Harry Graham wrote in 1920: 'In both Houses the hat has long come to be regarded as a sacred symbol. It is with this article of clothing that the member daily secures his claim to a seat on the benches of the House of Commons; with a hat he occasionally expresses his enthusiasm or sympathy, on a hat does he sit at the close of a speech, with the certainty of raising a laugh; and without a hat he cannot speak upon a point of order when the House has been cleared for a division.' Although this latter restriction still holds, the aura attached to the hat has vanished, and if a member does wear one it is more often than not left in the cloakroom.

Obviously, Parliament cannot remain untouched by the general trend towards less formal dress, and it is interesting to note that any influence that Labour members may have been thought to have on the decline of sartorial elegance is discounted by Graham in his *Mother of Parliaments*. He writes: 'When the Labour Party began to take an important place in the popular assembly, it was thought that this democratic invasion would have an actively detrimental effect upon the dress of the House. Old-fashioned members shook their heads and prophesied an influx of hobnailed artisans clad in corduroys. These gloomy forebodings have not been realized. With very few exceptions the dress of Labour members is little calculated to offend the most sensitive eye, although it was certainly one of their number who first entered a startled House of Commons in a tweed stalking-cap; a form of head-dress which it is certainly difficult to forgive.'

DRUNKEN PARLIAMENT

The Scottish Parliament which met at Glasgow on 1 October 1662, so called because there was only one sober man present at the first day's sitting. This Parliament lasted only eight days, the first of which was taken up in constituting the House and choosing the Lords of the Articles. The Lords of the Articles then consumed nearly all the remaining time in preparing the Acts to be passed, which included several oppressive religious statutes. Parliament had its second and last meeting on the eighth day, when all the Acts were read, debated, voted, and passed.

DUKE

The highest title in the British peerage, and first introduced into it by Edward III, who created his son, the Black Prince, Duke of Cornwall, with remainder to his heirs, being the eldest sons of the Kings of England, by which charter the eldest son of the Sovereign becomes from birth or the accession of his parent, Duke of Cornwall. Otto the Great, Emperor of the Germans, is supposed to be the first to have constituted the title about A.D. 970, and it became hereditary in France and other parts of the Continent long before it was adopted in England. It is possible that one reason why it was not adopted in England earlier was because the Norman Kings were reluctant, as Dukes of Normandy themselves, to grant their subjects a title which resembled their own. In the reign of Queen Elizabeth I the whole ducal order became extinct or in abeyance, but it was revived by James I, who created his son Henry Duke of Cornwall. A duke is styled 'His Grace' and the 'Most Noble', and is officially addressed by the Sovereign as 'Our right trusty and right entirely beloved Cousin'. The mantle of a duke is the same as a baron's, but has four rows ot ermine on the cape. His coronet is a circle of gold, surmounted by eight strawberry leaves. There are now (1970) 24 dukes in addition to 4 Peers of the Blood Royal (the Prince of Wales and the Dukes ot Gloucester, Windsor and Kent) and a Royal Duke not of the Blood Royal (the Duke of Edinburgh).

DUMMY BILL

The document which is handed by a member to the Clerk of the House when introducing a Bill. It contains merely the title of the Bill and the names, which may not exceed twelve, of the members presenting and supporting it. Dummies are sometimes used to represent other documents which are presented to the House.

DURATION OF PARLIAMENT

Until 1694 the King could keep a Parliament in existence as long as he pleased, and Charles II retained for seventeen years the Parliament called at his accession. Events showed that a House of Commons, if it was kept in being for so long a time after its election, might cease to represent the people, and that if the House depended wholly on the Crown for the continuance of its existence it might be too ready to favour the policy of the Court. For this and other reasons, the Bill for Triennial Parliaments was passed in 1693 by both Houses, but William III withheld his consent until the Bill came before him in the following year, when it became law. By the end of the reign of Queen Anne, it was becoming apparent that with the unsettled state of the country a more stable House of Commons was desirable, and in 1715 the Septennial Act was passed which extended the life of a Parliament to a maximum of seven years. This period was again shortened by the Parliament Act of 1911, and now the British Parliament, if not sooner dissolved by the exercise of the Royal Prerogative, expires by the efflux of time at the end of five years.

Most other Commonwealth countries also fix the duration of their Parliaments at five years, although in Australia and New Zealand the life of a Parliament is only three years. An unusual practice obtains in Tasmania where, although the normal life of the lower House is five years, it may be reduced to three if the two political parties are returned in equal strength.

DURHAM REPORT

Following the insurrection of the French Canadians, the Legislative Assembly of Lower Canada was suspended in 1838 by a British Act, and provisions were made for the temporary government of the Province by a special council. The Earl of Durham was appointed High Commissioner in March 1838 and Governor-General of the British Provinces in North America, with the fullest powers to achieve a settlement of Canada's legislative problems. He was not supported in his actions by the British Government and resigned six months later. In 1839, after his return to England, Durham produced his famous 'Report on the Affairs of British North America', wherein he enunciated the principles of responsible government. The successful application of his ideas to Canada was followed later by their application to Australia, New Zealand, and South Africa, so that Lord Durham may truly be described as the principal founder of the British Commonwealth of Nations. The best edition of the Durham Report was published by the Clarendon Press in 1912 and edited by Sir C. P. Lucas, and a useful abridged version by Sir R. Coupland was issued by the same publishers in 1945.

E

EARL

The grade above a viscount in the English peerage. This is the only title which is derived from an English word—the Old English *eorl*. In Saxon times England was administered by several great earldoms, but as William the Conqueror considered them a threat to his authority they were split up among his followers. The great Palatine Earldoms of Chester and Shrewsbury and the Palatine of Durham, which was ruled by the Prince Bishop, were allowed to remain as a bulwark against the Welsh and the Scots. Under the Norman and later kings the earl became the ruler of a county, and the dignity in process of time became hereditary. The first known instance of such a creation was that of Geoffrey de Mandeville as Earl of Essex by King Stephen 'with inheritance of the title of heirs'. The Earldom of March, created in 1328, had no territorial connexion, and the precedent was set for the modern creations which are often attached merely to the family name of the nobleman concerned. The style of an earl is 'Right Honourable' and he is officially addressed by the Sovereign as 'Our right trusty and right well-beloved Cousin'. The mantle of an earl is the same as a baron's except that it has three rows of ermine on the cape. The coronet is a circle of silver gilt, surmounted by eight silver balls raised upon points, with gold strawberry leaves between the points. There are at present (1970) 162 earls and countesses.

EARLY DAY MOTION

A motion which is set down for no specific day and is thus described simply as a 'motion for an early day'. The purpose of such a motion is usually to give public expression to certain views, and it is often designed by its sponsors to stand on the order paper and attract as many signatories as possible in order to test the opinion of the House with regard to its subject matter.

EAST AFRICAN LEGISLATIVE ASSEMBLY

Before the end of the last war, inter-territorial collaboration between Kenya, Uganda, and Tanganyika had led to an organization which was in effect a form of central administration, but the Governors' Conference, on which this administration was based, had no juridical or constitutional foundations and no forum for public discussion and debate. This was remedied by the East Africa (High Commission) Order in Council, 1947, and a High Commission and a Central Legislative Assembly were established with effect from 1 January 1948. The three Governors formed the High Commission, which had the powers of a territorial administration in respect of the common services which the territories agreed it should administer. These High Commission services included railways and harbours, civil aviation, posts and telecommunications, customs and excise to ensure the operation of a common market, income tax (administrative and general provisions only), and various research organizations. The territorial Governments were, and still are, responsible for fixing tariff rates and income tax rates and allowances.

Following the report of the Raisman Commission (Cmnd.1279), which proposed a number of improvements in the working of the East Africa High Commission, Tanganyika, as the first of the three territories to achieve independence, took the initiative in proposing the necessary changes. By Independence Day (9 December 1961) an Agreement and Constitution had been signed replacing the High Commission by the East Africa Common Services Organization. Under the Organization, the East Africa Common Services Authority, consisting of the principal ministers of the three territories, replaced the High Commission of Governors as the body responsible for the policy of the Organization.

On 6 June 1967 the Presidents of the United Republic of Tanzania, Uganda and Kenya signed a treaty establishing the East African Community and Common Market. The agreement came into force on 1 December of the same year and the East Africa Common Services Organization was superseded by the new association. The Community has its headquarters in Arusha, Tanzania, and is under the immediate direction of the three East African Ministers, one nominated by each of the three countries. The Community includes five Councils, four Corporations and an East African Legislative Assembly which legislates on all matters relating to the Community. The five Councils are the Common Market Council, the Communications Council, the Economic Consultative and Planning Council, the Finance Council and the Research and Social Council. Each Council consists of the three East African Ministers plus one national Minister from each of the three countries in respect of the Communications and Finance Councils, and three in respect of the other Councils. The Corporations within the Community are the East African Railways Corporation, the East African Harbours Corporation, the East African Posts and Telecommunications Corporation and the East African Airways Corporation. Each has a Board of Directors and conducts its business on a commercial basis. The East African Legislative Assembly consists of a Chairman, the three East African Ministers, their Deputy Ministers, nine Members appointed by each of the three countries, the Secretary General and the Counsel to the Community.

The treaty provides for a transfer tax system for the protection of less developed industries, but otherwise trade between the three countries is virtually free. The collection of customs and excise is a common service which has been operating since 1949. The East African Development Bank was established on 1 July 1968.

ECCLESIASTICAL COMMISSIONERS

See CHURCH COMMISSIONERS.

ECCLESIASTICAL COMMITTEE

As laid down by the Church of England Assembly (Powers) Act, 1919, the Ecclesiastical Committee shall consist of 15 Members of the House of Lords, nominated by the Lord Chancellor, and 15 Members of the House of Commons, nominated by the Speaker. The quorum is 12. The function of the committee is to examine every Measure passed by the Church Assembly and to draft a report to Parliament on its nature, effect, and expediency. A Measure may relate to any matter concerning the Church of England and may extend to the amendment or repeal in whole or in part of any Act of Parliament. The report of the committee must be communicated in draft to the Legislative Committee of the Church Assembly, and if this committee so desires, the report and Measure are laid before both Houses of Parliament, and on a resolution being passed in each House the Measure is presented to Her Majesty the Queen for the Royal Assent in the same manner as an Act of Parliament. The Ecclesiastical Committee can meet even though Parliament is not sitting.

See also CHURCH AND PARLIAMENT; CHURCH ASSEMBLY MEASURES.

ECONOMIC AFFAIRS, SECRETARY OF STATE FOR

A Minister carrying this designation was first appointed to the Government formed by Mr. Harold Wilson in October 1964. Mr. George Brown became the first holder of the office, being simultaneously appointed First Secretary of State (q.v.). The Secretary of State for Economic Affairs was responsible for framing and supervising the plan for economic development and for the general co-ordination of action to implement the plan, and of all economic policy related to industrial expansion, allocation of physical resources, and regional implications of the expansion programme. He was also Chairman of the National Economic Development Council, a duty previously performed by the Chancellor of the Exchequer (q.v.). In August 1968 the Prime Minister took personal charge of the Department of Economic Affairs, and in October 1969 the department was abolished as a part of a major reorganization of the departments of government.

In September 1947, Sir Stafford Cripps had been appointed Minister of Economic Affairs with a seat in the Cabinet—a development which, together with the appointment of an Economic Secretary to the Treasury, had heralded a new conception of Treasury control over the national economy. However, Cripps became Chancellor of the Exchequer before the year was out, taking with him his responsibilities for the co-ordination of economic affairs, and no new Minister of Economic Affairs was appointed. In 1950 Mr. Hugh Gaitskell was appointed Minister of State for Economic Affairs outside the Cabinet, but this office lapsed temporarily when Gaitskell himself became Chancellor later the same year. It was revived when a Conservative Government came to power in 1951, but the office of Economic Secretary to the Treasury was allowed to lapse. Towards the end of 1952 the latter office was reinstated, replacing that of Minister of State for Economic Affairs. The appointment of Economic Secretary to the Treasury continued until 1964 when it was abolished in terms of the Ministers of the Crown Act of that year.

ECONOMIC WARFARE, MINISTER OF

The first Minister (R. H. Cross) was appointed at the beginning of the war in 1939, with similar responsibilities to those of the Minister of Blockade in the First World War—the prevention as far as possible of supplies of food and war materials reaching the enemy through neutral countries. Hugh Dalton followed Mr. Cross as Minister and then the Earl of Selborne, who held the office until it was abolished in 1945.

EDUCATION AND SCIENCE, SECRETARY OF STATE FOR

The governmental machinery with regard to education was restructured following the publication of two important reports towards the end of 1963—the Robbins Report on higher education (Cmnd. 2154) and the Newsom Report on the education of the thirteen to sixteen age group. The Government rejected the recommendation of the former report that a Minister of Arts and Science should be appointed with responsibility for all aspects of higher education, but instead the new office of Secretary of State for Education and Science was created, with full responsibility over the whole field of education and two Ministers of State to assist him (subsequently increased to three). Mr. Quintin Hogg became the first Secretary of State for Education and Science in April 1964 while concurrently holding office as Lord President of the Council. He was succeeded first by Mr. Michael Stewart and then by Mr. Anthony Crosland when the Labour Government came to power later in the year.

The Department controlled by the Secretary of State consists of two administrative units, one concerned with the schools system of

England and Wales, the other with civil science and (through the University Grants Commission) with the universities and other institutions of university status. Each unit is under the direct supervision of an Under-Secretary of State. The responsibilities of the Secretary of State for Scotland in respect of education in Scotland are not substantially changed by the reorganization.

The salary of the Secretary of State for Education and Science is £8,500 a year, with an additional taxable allowance of £1,250 if he is a Member of the House of Commons.

The new Secretaryship of State superseded the offices of Minister of Education, which dated from 1900, and Minister for Science, which was created in 1959.

Government involvement in education began in the first half of the 19th century when schools were all private and were mostly run by religious and other charitable bodies. In 1833 the Government began to make small grants towards the costs of education and, in 1839, an Education Committee of the Privy Council was appointed, provision being made by a statute of 1856 for its Vice-President to be a Member of Parliament. The Education Act of 1870 made education compulsory and gave local authorities the power to spend money on elementary education. The Board of Education Act of 1899 established a Board of Education in place of the Education Committee of the Privy Council. It consisted in theory of a President, the Lord President of the Council, the First Lord of the Treasury, the Chancellor of the Exchequer and the Secretaries of State, but in practice it never met, its responsibilities being vested in the President of the Board alone. The President of the Board of Education was a Minister of Cabinet rank. He controlled a Department and was assisted by a Parliamentary Secretary and a Consultative Committee. The Education Act of 1944 changed the name of the Department to the Ministry of Education and the President of the Board became the Minister of Education. The Act gave the Minister wider powers over local authorities, whose functions in respect of education it greatly extended, and defined the Minister's duty as being 'to promote the education of the people of England and Wales . . . and to secure the effective execution by local authorities, under his control and direction, of the national policy for providing a varied and comprehensive educational service in every area'.

A chronological list of Ministers concerned with education appears as Appendix 15.

EDWARD I (1239–1307)

Eldest son of Henry III, succeeded his father as King of England on 16 November 1272, the first King to begin his reign from the very moment of the death of his predecessor. His reign is of supreme importance in parliamentary history for it was at this period that

Parliament assumed the fundamental features which it has always retained. The Commons were represented in the Parliament of 1275 and by the end of the reign their presence in the national assemblies of the realm had become an established practice. The Model Parliament (q.v.) of 1295 is generally regarded as the first fully representative assembly to be summoned by an English King.

See also PARLIAMENT.

EDWARD II (1284–1327)

Fourth son of Edward I by his first wife, Eleanor of Castile, succeeded his father on 7 July 1307. A weak monarch, very much a tool in the hands of worthless favourites, Edward II was deposed by Parliament (q.v.) on 20 January 1327, and brutally murdered at Berkeley Castle later in the same year.

EDWARD III (1312–1377)

Eldest son of Edward II, succeeded to the Throne of England while still a child on the deposition of his father in January 1327, his coronation taking place on the 29th. His reign was one of great constitutional importance and of frequent Parliaments. The powers of Parliament developed substantially during these years, and to this period can be traced the division of the estates into two Houses and the establishment of a number of parliamentary practices.

See also PARLIAMENT.

EDWARD IV (1442–1483)

Son of Richard, Duke of York, and descendant of Edward III, seized the throne from Henry VI and was crowned on 28 June 1461.

EDWARD V (1470–1483)

Eldest son of Edward IV, succeeded to the throne on his father's death on 9 April 1483. His reign lasted only a matter of weeks and he was never crowned. He was murdered in the Tower together with his younger brother, probably in August, and supposedly at the instance of his uncle, the Duke of Gloucester, who assumed the crown as Richard III on 26 June.

EDWARD VI (1537–1553)

Son of Henry VIII and Jane Seymour, succeeded his father on the latter's death on 21 January 1547. During the first part of Edward's short reign the government of the country was in the hands of the Duke of Somerset, the Lord Protector. Somerset was overthrown in 1551 by the Duke of Northumberland, who, on the young King's death, made a vain attempt to secure the succession for Lady Jane Dudley, his daughter-in-law.

ELECTION PETITIONS

A person wishing to challenge the result of an election must do so by means of an election petition. If the constituency affected is in England or Wales the petition should be presented to the High Court in the Queen's Bench Division, if in Scotland to the Court of Session, and if in Northern Ireland to the High Court of Northern Ireland in the Queen's Bench Division. An election petition is tried by two judges sitting in open court without a jury and the case must normally be heard within the constituency concerned.

A petitioner must be an elector or a candidate in the election. A prescribed form must be observed in the drawing up of an election petition and the facts and grounds of the complaint must be fully stated.

The Election Petition Rules are contained in Statutory Instrument No. 543 of 1960.

See also ELECTIONS.

ELECTIONS

In the United Kingdom a dissolution of Parliament is always followed by a General Election. Parliament is dissolved when it has run its statutory course of five years' duration or, alternatively, before the expiry of this period should the Crown, on the advice of the Prime Minister, deem it advisable. The purpose of a General Election is to return representatives to sit in the lower House of Parliament. The political party securing the return of the largest number of representatives is entitled to form a Government. In order to fill a vacancy occurring during the lifetime of a Parliament, due to the death, retirement, or expulsion of a sitting member, a by-election is held in the area concerned. When Parliament is dissolved the Lord Chancellor is ordered by Royal Proclamation to issue writs for the holding of fresh elections throughout the country. The writs are issued from the office of the Clerk of the Crown in Chancery. In the case of a by-election the writ is issued on the warrant of the Speaker of the House of Commons to the Clerk of the Crown. Writs are issued as soon as practicable after the Royal Proclamation dissolving the old and summoning a new Parliament, or after the issue of the Speaker's warrant, as the case may be.

For the purposes of parliamentary elections the country is divided into a number of electoral divisions known as constituencies (q.v.). There are at present 630 constituencies in the United Kingdom, each returning a single member who is elected on a simple majority. A Registration Officer is appointed to every constituency, his duty being to compile the annual register of voters within his area. Provisional lists are displayed at post offices, public libraries, and other public offices from 28 November to 16 December each year. All claims and objections are decided by the Registration Officer, subject to appeal in the county court, and the register must be published in its final form not later than 15 February, coming into force on the 16th. (For details of persons entitled to vote and disqualified from voting *see under the heading* FRANCHISE.) Each constituency also has its own Returning Officer who is responsible for the conduct of an election. In England and Wales the Returning Officer is the sheriff of the county, the mayor of the borough, or the chairman of the urban district council. In Scotland he is the sheriff and in Northern Ireland the under-sheriff.

Electoral procedure is governed largely by the Representation of the People Act, 1949, which consolidated much previous legislation, and subsequent amending Acts. After the issue of the writs to the Returning Officers, notice of the election must be published in each constituency stating the place and times at which nomination papers must be delivered and the date of the poll. These notices must appear not later than four o'clock in the afternoon of the second day following that on which the writ was received. Each candidate must be nominated with his own consent by ten electors, including a proposer and seconder on a form specifically issued for the purpose. Most candidates are members of the main political parties contesting the election, but there are invariably a number of independent candidates throughout the country who offer themselves for election without any party backing. A candidate is not obliged to reside in the constituency he proposes to represent. Most qualified electors are also entitled to stand for Parliament. (Exceptions are dealt with under the heading DISQUALIFICATION FROM MEMBERSHIP OF PARLIAMENT.) Every candidate must deposit with the Returning Officer or cause to be deposited on his behalf the sum of £150 on or before nomination day. The deposit is returnable provided the candidate polls at least one-eighth of the total votes cast in the constituency for which he stands. The forfeiture condition is designed to discourage idle or frivolous contestants. A candidate may withdraw from the contest at any time before the final day for the submission of nominations. His notice of withdrawal must be signed by himself, attested by a witness, and delivered to the Returning Officer. Objections to nominations must be lodged at certain specified times, although not necessarily in writing, with the Returning Officer, who decides on their validity. Only a candidate, his proposer and seconder, and his election agent are entitled to lodge objections. When all objections have been dealt with, or when the time for receiving them has expired, the Returning Officer publishes the names of the candidates nominated together with their proposers and seconders. If only one candidate is nominated he is declared elected and no contest takes place.

In a General Election all polls must be held on the same day. Polling day is always the ninth clear day after nomination day, and polling takes place between the hours of 7 a.m. and 10 p.m., polling hours having been extended from 9 p.m. with effect from 1970. Each constituency is divided into a number of polling districts and the polling station for each district is in charge of a Presiding Officer. Since the passing of the Ballot Act in 1872 secret voting has been a legal requirement, and all Returning Officers, Presiding Officers, poll clerks, candidates and their agents are obliged to make a declaration undertaking to maintain the secrecy of the poll. Before voting commences the Presiding Officer shows the empty ballot boxes to those present at the polling station and then locks and seals them. Each voter entering the polling station must identify himself or herself to the Presiding Officer or poll clerk. If the name is on the register of voters the official calls out the voter's number and the other necessary details and marks the register accordingly. The ballot paper is stamped with the official mark, lack of which would render it invalid, the voter's number is entered upon the counterfoil, and the ballot paper is handed to the voter, who takes it to one of the screened booths provided. The names of the candidates are listed on the ballot paper in alphabetical order. Prior to 1970 no political affiliation was indicated on a ballot paper, but a candidate is now permitted to include a description of himself not exceeding six words in length. A central register of authorized political descriptions for use on nomination and ballot papers is now maintained and published twice a year. All that is required of the voter is to place a simple cross against the name of the candidate of his choice. Any writing or mark other than a cross by which the voter could be identified invalidates the vote. Having marked the paper the voter folds it in order to conceal his vote and places it in the ballot box in the presence of the Presiding Officer. If a ballot paper is spoilt by accident it must be returned to the Presiding Officer, who will issue the voter with a fresh paper provided he is satisfied that the spoiling was inadvertent. The spoilt paper is cancelled but not destroyed, and all such papers must be delivered to the Returning Officer after the close of the poll. A person who is illiterate or incapacitated in such a manner as to prevent him from marking a ballot paper may be assisted in voting by the Presiding Officer. A blind person may alternatively be assisted by a relative or friend.

Certain classes of persons are entitled to the special facilities accorded to absent voters and are permitted to record their votes by post or proxy. They include members of the armed forces and (if residing with their husbands overseas) their wives, Crown servants employed overseas and (if residing with them) their wives, and others who are prevented from voting personally by reason of physical incapacity or the nature of their occupations.

No votes may be received after the time for the close of the poll except from voters who were admitted to the polling station before that time. Before their removal from the polling station the ballot boxes are sealed, and the unused ballot papers, the counterfoils of used papers, the marked register of voters, and various other papers concerned in the poll are made up into separate packets in the presence of the candidates' agents and all delivered to the Returning Officer.

The votes must be counted as soon as practicable after the conclusion of the poll at a centre determined by the Returning Officer in each constituency. In addition to the Returning Officer and his counting staff, the candidates are entitled to be present at the count together with their wives or husbands and their agents. After an examination of the seals the ballot boxes are opened and the votes in each box are counted but not sorted. They are then mixed together and distributed amongst the counting staff who, working in pairs, sort the papers out according to the manner of voting. The candidates' agents are entitled to observe the counting. If any doubt should arise over the validity of a paper it is placed aside for the decision of the Returning Officer. A ballot paper may be rendered invalid for a variety of reasons including lack of the official mark, the presence of writing or other marks of identification, or doubt as to the voter's intention. If a close result is declared a candidate may ask for a recount, and it lies within the discretion of the Returning Officer to agree to or refuse the request. Subsequent recounts may also be requested. In the rare event of the two leading candidates polling an equal number of votes lots are drawn to determine the winner. The Returning Officer must publicly declare the result of the poll, and must return the writ, endorsed with the name of the successful candidate, to the Clerk of the Crown.

An election campaign must be conducted within the limits of certain statutory requirements. Under the Corrupt and Illegal Practices Prevention Act, 1883, every candidate must appoint an election agent, who is responsible for the conduct of the candidate's campaign according to the limitations imposed by law. A candidate may act as his own agent if he wishes but he may employ no more than one agent, although he is permitted to utilize the services of as many unpaid volunteers as he wishes for purposes such as canvassing. An election agent may be paid or unpaid and need not necessarily be an elector. No person is eligible to act as an election agent who has been convicted of corrupt or illegal practices within the last five years. An election agent must be appointed on or before nomination day and his name and address declared in writing to the Returning Officer. All expenses incurred during the course of a campaign must be paid through the election agent. Election expenses are strictly limited by statute and severe penalties are provided for any breach of the law in this respect, including the disqualification of a winning candidate if he is found to have exceeded the permitted maximum expenditure. This maximum consists of a basic £750 (increased from £450 with effect from 1970) throughout the constituencies of the United Kingdom plus an additional shilling for every six entries in the register of electors in a county constituency or for every eight entries in a borough constituency. None but the candidate or his agent may give orders for printing and advertising. All bills must bear the name of the printer and publisher and no payment is permitted for their exhibition. There is no restriction upon the number of meetings a candidate may hold, but they must be conducted with decorum and in such a manner as to cause no obstruction. Electioneering confers upon a candidate no immunity from the laws of libel and slander. A candidate is entitled to send post free to every voter in his constituency one election communication weighing not more than two ounces. Broadcasting is exempted from the calculation of election expenses. There is no limit to the fee which may be paid to an election agent as long as it is covered by the candidate's total permitted expenditure. The Representation of the People (Amendment) Act, 1957, made the law relating to election expenses uniform throughout the United Kingdom. Previously, certain differences existed in respect of Northern Ireland—e.g., the agent's fee could be additional to a candidate's other expenses. After an election an agent is required to render a return of all expenses.

During an election campaign the B.B.C. allows the main parties a certain amount of time on both its sound and television services for political broadcasts. The allocation of the time allotted is agreed upon between the leaders of the parties and is roughly in proportion to the respective strength of each party and the number of candidates which each has entered in the contest. It is usual for the two leading parties to have an equal allocation of time. Broadcasts run to twenty and thirty minutes for the major parties and to ten and twenty minutes for other parties with a reasonably substantial following. Any minor party with 50 or more candidates in the field is allotted one broadcast of ten minutes' duration.

Elections to-day are conducted with a fairness, honesty, and integrity which few would question. Every precaution which legislation can enforce is taken to keep an election free from corrupt practices such as bribery, personation, the intimidation of voters, and the exerting of undue influences. Such offences, together with others involving breaches of electoral law known as illegal practices, will render an election void if committed by, or with the knowledge and consent of, the candidate or his agent. They also render the offender liable to criminal prosecution and heavy penalties if convicted. The extreme rarity of such cases is a testament to the clean spirit of candidates and voters alike, and to the high standards of those responsible for the conduct of elections. The electoral system we enjoy to-day is of comparatively recent origin and coincident with the advent of parliamentary reform. Prior to the Reform Act of 1832 none of those safeguards existed which to-day ensure free and honest elections and popular representation.

The most outrageous corruption was openly practised and tolerated. Bribery, intimidation, and coercion, together with such devices as patronage, 'pocket' boroughs, and faggot voting all combined to produce a system as farcical as it was rotten. Yet in spite of its base foundations the House of Commons of the pre-reform era remained on the whole a creditable body, and although it could not claim to be honestly representative of the people its members were not unmindful of the popular liberties they were elected to uphold.

The following General Election records are of some interest. The highest poll ever recorded in a single constituency was that of 93·65 per cent at Darwen in 1929 when 38,470 electors voted out of a total of 41,077. Other high polls include those at Fermanagh and South Tyrone (Northern Ireland) in 1955 when 92·5 per cent of the electorate voted (60,797 out of a possible 65,685) and Clitheroe in 1950 when a 91·64 per cent poll was recorded (41,938 votes registered out of a possible 45,758). The largest personal majority on record was polled by Sir Cooper Rawson, Conservative M.P. for Brighton, in 1931, when he defeated his Labour Party opponent by 75,205 votes to 12,952, a majority of 62,253. The largest number of voters in any one constituency was the estimated 217,900 in Hendon (Middlesex) in 1941. The lowest majority on record was at Ilkeston in 1931 when the National Labour candidate, Mr. A. J. Flint, scraped home ahead of his Labour Party opponent, Mr. G. H. Oliver, by a majority of 2, the votes cast being 17,587 against 17,585. This result was almost matched at Peterborough in 1966 where the Conservative candidate defeated his Labour opponent by 3 votes. Dead heats were recorded in Bishop's Castle, Shropshire, in 1820 and in Ashton-under-Lyne in 1886.

Outside Great Britain, Zanzibar had the closest possible result in a General Election held in January 1961, when the Afro-Shirazi Party won by a single seat, the seat being gained by a single vote! India staged the largest election in the world in February 1967, when 152,724,611 votes were recorded.

(Further reading: Butler, *The electoral system in Britain since 1918*, 1963; Ross, *Elections and Electors*, 1955; Schofield, *Parliamentary elections*, 1959, and *Supplement*, 1964.)

ELECTORAL ADVISORY CONFERENCE

See SPEAKER'S CONFERENCE.

ELECTORAL COLLEGES

Electors usually choose their representatives in a legislature by actually voting for them, but there are indirect elections, held usually for an upper House, where the electors choose or appoint an intermediary body to choose the representatives. This body is known as an electoral college; e.g., the Council of States, the Indian upper House, is elected by such a body composed of the elected members of the legislatures of the States forming the Union. The President of the United States is elected by an electoral college the members of which are elected by the people.

ELECTORAL QUOTA

The Second Schedule to the House of Commons (Redistribution of Seats) Act, 1949, sets out rules for the redistribution of seats and provides that the electorate of any constituency shall be as near as practicable to the electoral quota. The electoral quota, which was redefined by the House of Commons (Redistribution of Seats) Act, 1958, is a number obtained by dividing the electorate of each part of the United Kingdom by the number of constituencies, and is to-day about 60,000. The Act of 1958 provides that the constituencies must be reviewed at intervals of not less than ten nor more than fifteen years.

ELECTORAL REGISTER

A list of persons qualified to vote at elections. In the United Kingdom it is the principal duty of the Registration Officer to prepare the register for each constituency for which he acts and to publish it not later than 15 February every year. The expense of compiling the register is shared between the Government and the local authority, whose Clerk is Registration Officer. All British subjects and citizens of the Republic of Ireland who qualify are entitled to vote as electors, but they must have their names on the register.

ELECTORAL TRUCE

Under an electoral truce the parties in a Coalition Government, such as the 1940–5 wartime coalition under Churchill's leadership, agree that when a seat falls vacant they will not put up a candidate against the person nominated by the party that held the seat before the vacancy. This means that a by-election would be uncontested, unless an independent or a member of a party not included in the coalition decided to contest the seat.

ELEVEN O'CLOCK RULE

See TEN O'CLOCK RULE.

ELIZABETH I (1533–1603) AND PARLIAMENT

Elizabeth I ascended the Throne of England on 17 November 1558 at a dark period in the country's history. The nation was bankrupt and threatened on all sides by enemies; poverty, pestilence, and famine stalked the land and the plight of the common people was desperate; and to add horror to an already grim situation England shuddered under the hideous religious persecution introduced by Elizabeth's predecessor and half-sister, Mary. England's prestige abroad was at its lowest level and at home the people were engulfed in a sink of misery, despair, and humiliation. The feeling in the country against the Church of Rome was one of frantic loathing, and the accession of Elizabeth was received by her stricken realm as nothing less than a deliverance. No greater tribute could be paid to the young woman who came to the throne at this dark hour than to point to the facts that within a year of her accession not only had a new hope dawned among the people but stability and security had begun to return to the land, and that at the end of her long and spectacular reign England was at the summit of her power and glory. Whatever may be justly spoken against Elizabeth (and she was not without serious faults) nothing can detract from her greatness as a Sovereign or the magnificence of her age.

Elizabeth was in no sense a constitutional monarch and throughout her reign she made full and free use of the Royal Prerogative (q.v.). In the forty-five years she ruled she summoned only ten Parliaments and she showed no more disposition than her predecessors to tolerate any boldness on the part of her faithful Commons. Parliament she regarded primarily as an instrument of taxation, a body to be called together as and when she found herself to be in need of money. Of the many glorious features which gave lustre to her reign the growth of constitutional freedom was most certainly not one. Nevertheless, these years were important ones in the history of Parliament. It is important to remember that the Commons had emerged as an independent and self-assertive body before Elizabeth came to the throne; that they had won certain well-defined and jealously guarded privileges; and that in addition to their taxing function their power to legislate in concert with the House of Lords had long been established and unchallenged. Elizabeth's Parliaments further consolidated the gains of the past and strengthened the parliamentary institution with the establishment of several important constitutional precedents. The enormous prestige and popularity enjoyed by Elizabeth undoubtedly exercised a restraining influence upon the Commons in their dealings with her, but there were also very definite manifestations in each of her Parliaments of the spirit which was later to overthrow the tyranny of absolute monarchy. From the widespread anti-Catholic feeling which had been engendered by the excesses of Mary's reign there had emerged the Puritan movement, violent in its hatred of papal doctrines and resolved upon nothing less than the total extirpation of the Roman Church in England. It was inevitable that this faction should be reflected in the Parliaments of Elizabeth and become the radical wing of the Protestant majority. From the ranks of the Puritans emerged the boldest spirits of the Elizabethan House of Commons, men who, whilst undeviating in their loyalty to and admiration for the Queen, nevertheless refused to be browbeaten in their disputes with the Crown, and indeed exhibited an amazing stubbornness even in the face of the royal displeasure. Elizabeth endeavoured to counteract the growing independence of the Commons in the manner of her immediate predecessors, by creating or restoring rotten boroughs for the purposes of parliamentary representation. The House of Commons thus included a very large number of Crown nominees, 62 members being added during the reign.

Elizabeth opened her first Parliament on 25 January 1559. The Abbot of Westminster sat among the peers on this occasion, the last on which any abbot appeared in Parliament. The Commons immediately set themselves to the task of re-establishing the Protestant faith. The authority of the Pope was repudiated, Mary's religious legislation was repealed, and the Church was restored upon a similar basis to that which existed prior to Mary's accession. An Act of Supremacy, appointing the Sovereign the head of the Church, and an Act of Uniformity, prescribing the use of the Protestant prayer book and requiring conformity with the restored faith, were carried through both Houses. Elizabeth had no cause for complaint at the financial provision the Commons made for her. Not only did they vote her lavish supplies exceeding all they had withheld from Mary, but the incomes from vacant bishoprics were made available to her, the properties of religious orders revived by Mary and now suppressed were restored to the Crown, and a further source of revenue was provided by the passing of a First Fruits Act and a Tonnage and Poundage Act. On 6 February the Speaker of the House of Commons with the Privy Council and thirty Members of the House of Commons sought an audience of the Queen and requested her to take a husband. The Queen's famous reply, delivered on the 10th, announced her intention to remain unmarried and ended with the words, 'This shall be for me sufficient, that a marble stone shall declare that a Queen, having reigned such a time, died a virgin.'

Four years elapsed before Elizabeth called her second Parliament, which she opened on 12 January 1563. The question of her marriage and the related matter of the succession had been causing great concern, particularly in the light of the activities of Mary, Queen of Scots, who was already being spoken of by her supporters as Queen of England. Elizabeth, however, refused to commit herself on the matter of the succession despite numerous attempts by Parliament to persuade her to do so. During this session an important penal statute against Catholics was carried in the face of some opposition, providing severe penalties for priests who refused to take the oath of supremacy. The obligation to take the oath was widely extended by the measure, and was imposed on all future Members of the House of Commons, thus excluding Roman Catholics from the lower House, but peers were exempted, 'the Queen's Majesty being otherwise sufficiently assured of their faith and loyalty'. Amongst other measures passed during this session was one to identify the office of Lord Chancellor with that of Lord Keeper of the Great Seal.

Having been prorogued on six successive occasions on account of the plague, Parliament did not meet after October 1563 until September 1566. The question of the Queen's marriage was again raised and Parliament managed to elicit from Elizabeth a promise that she would marry. Both Houses pressed for a more definite undertaking, however, and the Queen rebuked them for their importunity, informing them that she would marry where it should please her, with whom it should please her, and as soon as it should please her. She further observed that while she was not surprised at the Commons ('They had small experience and had acted like boys') the fact that the Lords had gone along with them filled her with wonder. The Queen forbade any further discussion of the subject, but Paul Wentworth, one of the bolder spirits of the Commons, inquired of the Speaker whether such an injunction was not against the liberties of Parliament. A long debate ensued which resulted in the Queen sending for the Speaker and commanding him to permit no further argument. But the Commons refused to be subdued and prepared a petition asserting their privileges, in consequence of which the Queen revoked her order. The royal concession was received by the Commons 'most joyfully, with most hearty thanks and prayers for the same'. This session Parliament also came into conflict with the Crown over ecclesiastical matters. A religious Bill was initiated in the Commons to which the Queen objected on the ground that it constituted an encroachment on her prerogative. When the Bill was referred to the Lords Elizabeth gave the order to proceed no further with it. The Commons retaliated by employing obstructive tactics in dealing with government legislation, and as neither Queen nor Commons would yield the session closed very unprofitably. On 2 January 1567 Elizabeth dissolved Parliament, highly incensed against her faithful Commons, to whom she delivered an angry rebuke. Never before had the Commons displayed such a resolute attitude in matters so directly concerning the Sovereign, and the session of 1566 is thus an important one in parliamentary history.

Over four years elapsed before Elizabeth called another Parliament, financial necessity compelling her to do so. The questions of her marriage and the succession were as far from being settled as ever. On 2 April 1571 she opened her third Parliament, and when the Commons met for business it was resolved that the Speaker should read prayers at the beginning of each day's session, a custom which has been continued to this day. The conspiratorial activities of the adherents to the

Roman Church, culminating in the Northern Rebellion, had been giving much cause for alarm, and matters were brought to a head in 1570 when the Pope issued the famous bull excommunicating Elizabeth and absolving her subjects from their allegiance to her. With zeal and determination the new Parliament devoted its energies to the legislation which the situation demanded. Many stringent measures were passed, including an Act providing the penalties of high treason for such offences as describing the Queen as a usurper or heretic, calling in question her title, or designating as her heir and successor any but the natural issue of her body, and another directed against papal interference providing a similar penalty for the publication of a papal bull and the penalties of praemunire for aiding and abetting the Roman Church in various other ways. At the same time the Thirty-nine Articles of Religion were enforced by statute.

The session of 1571 was of great importance for its debates on the constitution of the House of Commons and the qualifications of its members. The principle that a member is returned to Parliament not only to represent his own constituents but to serve the nation as a whole was asserted for the first time. The requirements which determined a man's fitness to sit in Parliament were discussed at length. One member opined that only a resident or inhabitant of a borough should be chosen to represent that borough in the House of Commons. Another urged that 'none should be of the House not of thirty years of age at least' and that 'for the choice of townsmen, there should be one of their own elected, or some gentleman near them, who had knowledge of the state of the country; and the second member should be a man learned and able to utter his mind and opinion'. Another member objected to the practice of the nomination of members on the part of noblemen who owned the boroughs for which they sat. This member, Mr. Bell, may well have been the first advocate of parliamentary reform, but his views do not appear to have been widely shared. Far from condemning the nomination system the majority regarded it as being very much in the local interests of the towns concerned, but exception was taken to any interference at elections in the interests of the government.

In this same session a Puritan member named Strickland was prohibited from attending Parliament for having introduced a Bill which proposed to alter the prayer book. The matter was raised in the House of Commons as an issue of privilege and was debated with great warmth and boldness. Sir Francis Knollys, speaking for the government, insisted that the Bill was 'against the prerogative of the Queen, which was not to be tolerated'. Christopher Yelverton replied that 'the precedent was perilous' and 'to say the Parliament had no right to determine of the Crown was high treason. Men are not there for themselves, but for their countries. It was fit for princes to have their prerogatives, but straitened within reasonable limits. The prince of herself could not make, neither, by the same reason, break them.' This was bold speaking indeed, and Knollys and his fellow Privy Councillors in the House began to realize that they were on the losing side of the argument. The debate was terminated on the motion of the Speaker, but it had achieved its purpose, for on the following day the Queen discreetly removed the prohibition on Strickland and he reappeared in the House to the great delight of his friends. As a result of the obligation upon members to take the oath of supremacy the House of Commons of 1571 was the first to contain no avowed Catholics.

Elizabeth's fourth Parliament was called the following year and was opened on 8 May 1572. It was unusual for one Parliament to follow so closely on the heels of another (although there had been annual Parliaments during the reign of Edward III, as the new Speaker pointed out in his speech after being elected) but the urgency of the situation which had been created by the conspiracies involving Mary, Queen of Scots, gave Elizabeth no alternative but to summon the two Houses to assemble once again. In January the Duke of Norfolk had been found guilty of high treason and with the greatest reluctance the Queen signed the warrant for his execution. But she shrank from taking this extreme step against the Scottish Queen, now in captivity in England. Her chief minister, Lord Burghley, had long been pressing her to assent to the initiation of proceedings against Mary, and backed by the insistence of both Lords and Commons the pressure upon Elizabeth became strong. A deputation from both Houses waited on her and she stated her wish that Parliament should not impeach her cousin for high treason but adopt some milder course. A Bill was carried to disqualify Mary from succeeding to the Throne of England, but even to this measure Elizabeth was reluctant to assent.

A number of prorogations took place before Parliament again assembled on 8 February 1576. A notable precedent was established at the beginning of this session enabling the eldest sons of peers to sit in the House of Commons. Lord Russell, the son of the newly created Earl of Bedford, was ordered to continue to sit in the lower House as the burgess for Bridport, notwithstanding the fact that he was the heir to the earldom. The most noteworthy incident of this session was a bold defence of liberty by Peter Wentworth, brother of the Paul Wentworth referred to previously. During the course of a speech of unprecedented outspokenness he observed that 'two things do very great hurt in this place, of the which I do mean to speak. The one is a rumour that runneth about the House, and this it is: "Take heed what you do. The Queen's Majesty liketh not of such a matter: whosoever preferreth it, she will be much offended with him." Or the contrary: "Her Majesty liketh of such a matter: whosoever speaketh against it, she will be much offended with him." The other is: sometimes a message is brought into the House, either of commanding or inhibiting, very injurious unto the freedom of speech and consultation. I would to God, Mr. Speaker, that these two were buried in Hell: I mean rumours and messages.' To the dismay of the House his speech developed into a direct attack upon the Queen. 'Certain it is, Mr. Speaker, that none is without fault: no, not our noble Queen. Since, then, Her Majesty hath committed great faults—yea, dangerous faults to herself and the state—love, even perfect love, void of dissimulation, will not suffer me to hide them to Her Majesty's peril, but to utter them to Her Majesty's safety. And these they are. It is a dangerous thing in a Prince unkindly to intreat and abuse his or her nobility and people, as Her Majesty did the last Parliament. And it is a dangerous thing in a Prince to oppose or bend herself against her nobility and people, yea against most loving and faithful nobility and people. And how could any Prince more unkindly intreat, abuse, and oppose herself against her nobility and people than Her Majesty did the last Parliament?' Wentworth was eventually forbidden to continue what was probably the most remarkable speech ever to have been heard in the House of Commons, and his audacity earned him a month's imprisonment in the Tower. He was liberated before the end of the session, and it was stated to the Commons on the Queen's behalf that 'she was absolutely persuaded that his speech proceeded of abundance of zeal towards her' and that she had 'not only forgiven but also forgotten the inconsiderateness of the same, and did accept him to be in as good grace and favour as ever she did before'. This gesture of royal magnanimity serves to illustrate that even in the days of absolute monarchy an English sovereign could tolerate, even appreciate, the spirit which moves a man to speak his mind.

Parliament was prorogued no less than twenty-six times before it assembled again for business on 16 January 1581. In the House of Commons Paul Wentworth moved that a fast should be observed, to which the House agreed by 115 votes to 100. The Queen was highly incensed at this, for not only had the House again usurped her authority in matters of religion, but she saw in the resolution a resumption of the tactics of the Puritan opposition which had been a source of vexation to her previously. Angrily she sent for the Speaker and commanded him to inform the House of her displeasure. The matter was smoothed over by the Commons' acceptance of a compromise motion agreeable to the Queen. The session of 1581 records the first conflict of opinion between the two Houses. A Bill for fortifying the northern borders which had been sent down by the Lords was returned by the Commons and a substitute Bill sent up in its stead. The Lords recorded their objection to this action on the part of the lower House, describing it as 'derogatory to the superiority of the place, and contrary to the ancient course of both Houses'. The objection was entered in the Journal, 'lest so evil an example may hereafter be used as a precedent', but the Lords accepted the Commons' Bill and the precedent they feared was established despite their lordships' solemn precaution. In this same session the House of Lords was first recognized as a Court of Appeal.

The House of Commons decisively asserted its right to punish its own members in the 1581 session. A number of knights, burgesses, and citizens were fined and deprived of their wages for absence without leave, but the most outstanding case of disciplinary action was that of Arthur Hall, the burgess for Grantham, who was expelled from the House, fined, and imprisoned for publishing a book 'not only reproaching some particular good Members of the House, but also very much slanderous and derogatory to its general authority, power and state, and prejudicial to the validity of its proceedings in making and establishing of laws'. Hall's case is cited by Hatsell (q.v.) as the leading precedent for the power of expulsion which the Commons have always retained. Elizabeth's fourth Parliament, the longest of her reign, was after further prorogations finally dissolved on 19 April 1583, having lasted eleven years yet having assembled for only three sessions totalling less than six months between them.

The fifth Parliament of the reign met on 23 November 1584, at a time of great national anxiety. The unceasing conspiracies of the papists had brought about a situation of the utmost gravity and the problem of the succession was still far from being determined. The Queen was now fifty-one and the question of her marriage had ceased to be an issue as no hopes of an heir could be based upon any union she might now contract. A Bill directed against the Jesuits was carried with little difficulty, the only fierce opposition to it in the House of Commons coming from Dr. William Parry, who was subsequently executed for conspiring against the Queen's life. The national danger had become so alarming that in 1585 the Commons debated the state of the nation, and the Lords deemed it necessary to bring in a Bill providing for the protection of the Queen's person. In this tense and foreboding atmosphere Elizabeth at last yielded to the pressure which had long been exerted upon her to proceed against Mary, Queen of Scots. On 29 October 1586 Elizabeth's sixth Parliament was opened by commission, having been summoned for the special purpose of attainting Mary Stuart. Both Houses were insistent upon her execution and a joint petition was presented to Elizabeth calling for the visitation of the supreme penalty upon her cousin. But the Queen was loth to agree to this extreme step and she asked Parliament if no alternative measure could be devised to secure the safety of the kingdom. Parliament replied that there was no other course, and when the Lord Chancellor and the Speaker sought audience of the Queen at Richmond they finally persuaded her of the necessity of the step she dreaded. Unanimously condemned by both Houses of Parliament, Mary, Queen of Scots, superbly courageous to the end, suffered death on the block on 8 February 1587. The Parliament of 1586, following a precedent of 1542 when Catherine Howard was attainted, sat not as a legislative assembly but as a judicial tribunal, a precedent which was again to be asserted by the Commons in 1649 when Charles I came to be tried and judged.

The execution of Mary, Queen of Scots, put paid to Elizabeth's enemies at home, but it drove the Spanish King into waging open war upon England. His aggressive action proved his own undoing. Parliament and the country rallied to their Sovereign with a patriotic fervour, liberal supplies were voted by the Commons for the defence of the realm, and the fate of the formidable Spanish Armada needs no re-telling.

In the session of 1587-8 the Commons again came into collision with the Queen over ecclesiastical matters. Puritan feeling had been progressively mounting in strength, and although various steps had been taken to curb its growth, including the establishment of the High Commission Court in 1583 for the trial of religious offences, they had failed to induce the uniformity intended. A member named Cope now brought forward a Bill to abolish the existing canon law and proposing a revised form of common prayer which was set out in a book which accompanied the Bill. The Speaker ruled against the introduction of the Bill on the ground that the Queen had on previous occasions commanded the Commons not to meddle in such matters. The Puritan members treated the ruling as an infringement of privilege and the issue was warmly debated, whereupon the Queen sent for the Speaker and commanded him to deliver up to her the offending Bill and book. This action led Peter Wentworth to formulate a number of questions relative to the liberties of the House which he presented to the Speaker with the demand that they be read. Instead, however, Wentworth, Cope, and others who had spoken in favour of the latter's motion were committed to the Tower, and although their release was demanded by the House they remained confined until the dissolution three weeks later.

The seventh Parliament of the reign, which sat from 4 February to 29 March 1589, was comparatively uneventful. The Royal Assent was received to all the Bills passed by both Houses, but the Queen intercepted two Commons measures, one which sought to check the abuses in the exchequer and the other dealing with purveyance, on the ground that such grievances were not matters for legislation and could be otherwise redressed.

Elizabeth's eighth Parliament met on 19 February 1593, and a stern warning was issued to the Commons at the very outset. They were instructed by the Lord Keeper to lose no time in idle speeches but to devote themselves entirely to necessary business. He recalled that in the past members had been wont to 'delight themselves in vain orations, full of verbosity and of vain ostentations, more than in speaking of things of substance'. On the 22nd the Commons presented their Speaker, Sir Edward Coke, at the Bar of the upper House, and in answer to his customary claim for the privilege of free speech the Lord Keeper made it clear that the privilege was merely the right to say 'Aye' or 'No', and 'not to speak every one what he listeth, or what cometh into his brain to utter'. The warning had little effect, for at the very first meeting of the Commons, the indomitable Peter Wentworth sought leave to introduce a Bill entailing the succession to the Crown. The Queen, infuriated, ordered the commitment of Wentworth and the three members supporting his petition. Wentworth remained in the Tower until his death in 1596, a sufferer in the cause of parliamentary freedom. A fifth member named Morrice was imprisoned shortly afterwards for introducing a Bill directed against the High Commission Court, and once again the Queen repeated her warning to the Commons not to meddle in ecclesiastical matters. The lower House appears to have thoroughly succumbed to royal intimidation this session as a motion for the release of the imprisoned members was rejected without a division. In their dealings with the Lords, however, the Commons exhibited a far stouter resolution. The upper House let it be known that it considered as inadequate the Supply which the Commons proposed to grant to Her Majesty, and suggested a joint conference of the two Houses on the matter. Francis Bacon, who first entered Parliament in 1593, rose in defence of the financial privilege of the lower House, pointing out that the right to grant a subsidy rested solely with the Commons. The House endorsed Bacon's view by 217 votes to 128, and although the conference was in actual fact held and the grant substantially increased, the Commons made it clear that no departure from principle was involved by emphasizing that 'these large and unusual grants, which are made to a most excellent Princess, on a most pressing and extraordinary occasion, may not at any time hereafter be drawn into a precedent'.

Towards the end of the session, when the attendance of members was sparse, a government Bill proposing to extend the penalties imposed upon recusants to Protestant nonconformists slipped through the House of Commons. This legislation and the generally repressive policy of the state towards dissenters drove the Puritans from mere opposition into outright hostility towards the Crown and the national Church, the full effects of which were destined to be felt most forcibly in the next century.

Elizabeth's ninth Parliament met on 24 October 1597 and sat until 9 February 1598. It devoted itself mainly to domestic legislation and was marked by an absence of the ecclesiastical disputes which had hitherto been prominent features of the Elizabethan Parliaments. The new Speaker, Serjeant Yelverton, introduced a touch of novelty into the customary speech excusing himself from taking office by elaborating ingeniously upon his multifarious disabilities, ranging from the financial to the physical. He subsequently went astray in a number of his rulings, insisting on one occasion that an adjournment of the Lords involved an adjournment of the Commons. Much time was wasted during this session on insignificant matters and there were frequent clashes between the two Houses on minor issues. One of the more important questions raised, and one which was to be revived in the following Parliament, was that of the abuses arising from monopolies. A petition praying for redress was presented to the Queen, who promised to afford a remedy, but she was loth to sacrifice the royal privilege of granting patents.

The tenth and last Parliament of Elizabeth's long reign met on 27 October 1601, and the Commons again addressed themselves to the grievances arising from monopolies, an issue which constituted the main business of the session. A debate occupying four days revealed the most flagrant abuses which for the most part pressed heavily on the poor. When the list of patents was read out one member was moved to exclaim, 'Is not bread among the number?' The Queen's ministers were left in little doubt of the popular feeling on the matter by the conclusion of the debate, but the problem was resolved by typically shrewd action on the part of Elizabeth herself, who issued a proclamation revoking all monopolies that should be found injurious by fair trial at law. Another heated debate in the Commons took place this session over a Bill for compelling attendance at church. On a division being taken 105 were shown to be in favour of the Bill and 106 against, upon which the minority claimed that the Speaker should have a vote additional to his casting vote. A scene of great uproar developed around the argument but the vote of the majority was held to be good and the Bill was lost.

Parliament was prorogued in December and the Queen died on 24 March 1603, before the Houses assembled again. Parliament played an important part during the reign of Elizabeth, and although she ruled largely through her Privy Council and periodically commanded the Commons not to meddle in matters of the state and the Church she did not remain unmoved by the voice of popular opinion as expressed in the lower House. Although they themselves knew it not, men like the Wentworths were the forerunners of the mighty movement which in a later age was to sweep away absolute monarchy and establish parliamentary government on a firm and durable basis.

(Further reading: Neale, *The Elizabethan House of Commons*, 1949; Neale, *Elizabeth I and her Parliaments*, 2 vols., 1953–7.)

ELSYNGE, HENRY (1598–1654)

Clerk of the House of Commons from 1632 to 1648 and a scholar of great learning. He was highly regarded in his own day as an authority on the law and history of Parliament, and it was said of him that for 'his abilities and prudence, more reverence was paid to his stool than to the Speaker's Chair'. Elsynge resigned his office in 1648 to avoid taking part in the proceedings against Charles I. In recognition of his loyalty the first Parliament after the Restoration granted the sum of £500 for the relief of his children.

Elsynge's father, who was also named Henry, was Clerk of the House of Lords and died before his son took office. He was 'a person of great abilities' and the author of a treatise first published in 1660 which went through several editions in the 17th century entitled 'The Ancient Method and Manner of holding Parliaments in England'. It was republished from the original manuscript by Tyrwhit in 1768. He also wrote 'The Method of Passing Bills in Parliament' (actually confined to the House of Lords) which appears in the Harleian Miscellany.

EMANCIPATION ACT

See ROMAN CATHOLICS IN PARLIAMENT.

EMERGENCY ADJOURNMENT MOTIONS

With the adoption of a revised Standing Order No. 9 in 1967 the phrase 'definite matter of urgent public importance' has become obsolete as a parliamentary term. However, the procedure for seeking an emergency debate on a matter requiring urgent consideration remains unchanged in principle. It is open to any member to rise after Questions on Monday, Tuesday, Wednesday or Thursday and seek leave to move the adjournment of the House for the purpose of discussing 'a specific and important matter that should have urgent consideration'. These words have replaced the phrase 'definite matter of urgent public importance' in the Standing Order for reasons which are explained below.

The acceptance of a motion under Standing Order No. 9 lies within the discretion of the Speaker who must indicate that he is prepared to entertain it before the question may be put to the House. If the Speaker is satisfied that the matter proposed to be discussed is of the kind envisaged by the Standing Order he will ask whether the motion has the leave of the House. If there is any dissent, he will call upon the members supporting the motion to rise and if as many as 40 members rise in their places it is assumed that the motion has leave. If less than 40, but more than 10, members rise, the question of whether leave is granted is put to the vote. When leave is given, the motion stands over until the commencement of public business on the following day (or on the following Monday if the motion is proposed on Thursday), although the Speaker may direct that the debate on it shall take place at 7 p.m. on the same day if he deems this to be justified by reason of urgency. The debate on such a motion is interrupted after it has continued for three hours.

A member proposing to take advantage of Standing Order No. 9 is required to give notice to the Speaker by noon of the same day or, if the urgency of the matter has not become apparent at that hour, as soon thereafter as is practicable. When leave to move the motion is sought the Speaker may defer giving his decision as to whether or not he will allow it until a named hour when he may interrupt the proceedings of the House for the purpose.

In stating whether or not he is satisfied that the matter is proper to be discussed, the Speaker is not permitted to give the reasons for his decision. However, in arriving at his decision he is required to consider the extent to which it concerns the administrative responsibilities of ministers of the Crown or could come within the scope of ministerial action, and to have regard to the probability of the matter being brought before the House in time by other means.

Standing Order No. 9 was revised in accordance with the recommendations of the Select Committee on Procedure, 1966–7. Under the previous rule the conditions under which emergency debates were granted had become so stringent as the result of accumulated precedents that the acceptance of the required motion by the Chair had become extremely rare. Reporting in 1966, the Committee pointed out that only 15 debates had been permitted in the previous twenty years as compared with 102 debates in the first twenty years of the century. It concluded that a relaxation of the restriction was desirable and that the Speaker's discretion in the allowance of Emergency Adjournment Motions should be widened. The abandonment of the phrase 'definite matter of urgent public importance' was recommended because each word had come to acquire a special significance in the light of rulings of successive Speakers and it had thus become a formidable obstacle to a member seeking to invoke the Standing Order. The words 'specific and important matter that should have urgent consideration' have no special significance of their own, and it was to ensure that they acquire none that the Committee proposed that the Speaker should be prohibited from stating the reasons for his decision in allowing or disallowing motions under the Standing Order. Explanations, as the Committee pointed out, tend to add to the force of precedents, thus diminishing the scope of the Standing Order. A number of prohibitions which applied under the previous Standing Order are no longer applicable. An emergency debate may now be granted even though a previously arranged debate on an adjournment motion has already been set down for that day. A matter calling for a legislative remedy is now an acceptable subject for debate, as is a matter which is not currently one of ministerial responsibility. The conduct of a person who, by the normal practice of the House, may only be criticized upon a substantive motion may now be discussed in the course of an emergency adjournment debate.

Restrictions which continue to apply include the requirement that the matter must be based on fact and not on hearsay; that it must be raised at the earliest opportunity and in the public interest require the immediate attention of the House; and that it raise a larger issue than a purely individual grievance.

Additional opportunities for raising urgent matters at short notice are available to the Opposition through the earmarking of 4 half-days out of the 29 Supply days for debates on such matters.

The Standing Orders of most of the other Parliaments of the Commonwealth make provision for an emergency adjournment procedure to enable matters of urgent public importance to be debated. In 1968 the Canadian House of Commons revised its own rule along lines similar to that of the new British rule. In the Australian Parliament such motions are regarded as something akin to emergency motions of censure against the Government, and the Opposition's right to invoke this procedure is interpreted with some latitude. The Indian House of the People provides for the discussion of such matters by a special procedure which requires no formal motion to be brought before the House. It is also open to a member, with the permission of the Speaker, to call the attention of a minister to a matter of urgent public importance by means of a brief statement which may not be debated.

EMPIRE PARLIAMENTARY ASSOCIATION

See COMMONWEALTH PARLIAMENTARY ASSOCIATION.

EMPLOYMENT AND PRODUCTIVITY, SECRETARY OF STATE FOR

A senior Cabinet appointment first established in April 1968, the Secretary of State for Employment and Productivity took over all the functions formerly exercised by the Minister of Labour (q.v.) and assumed in addition crucial economic responsibilities relating to prices and incomes policy. The Ministry of Labour was abolished in consequence of the establishment of this office, Mrs. Barbara Castle becoming its first incumbent.

In 1970, following a major reorganization of the machinery of central government, the responsibilities of this Minister in relation to government policy towards monopolies, mergers and restrictive trade practices were transferred to the Secretary of State for Trade and Industry. (*See* TRADE AND INDUSTRY, SECRETARY OF STATE FOR.)

The office of Secretary of State for Employment and Productivity was in consequence renamed Secretary of State for Employment.

ENABLING LEGISLATION

Acts of Parliament conferring powers, the exercise of which may be obligatory or discretionary, as distinguished from peremptory or prohibitory Acts. An early example of this type of legislation is an Act passed in 1540 (32 Hy.8, c.28) relating to leases.

ENGROSSING A BILL

The old method of engrossing Bills, i.e., transcribing them upon parchment, was continued until 1849. Until then the question 'That this Bill be engrossed' was put on the report stage, but after that Bills were printed. The omission of the formal question and division necessary to the old procedure saved a certain amount of time, although it was not used for Bills brought from the Lords, which were already engrossed.

ENTRENCHED CLAUSE

A section in a constitution which can only be repealed or altered by special process, and which normally deals with such matters as the liberties of the subject and the fundamental institutions of government. The constitutions of a number of the newer Commonwealth countries include entrenched clauses, and some also include 'specially entrenched' clauses, in respect of which the conditions governing their amendment are especially stringent. The process for amending entrenched and specially entrenched clauses varies with each constitution, and may involve a popular referendum, a fixed parliamentary majority of two-thirds or more, a system of delayed legislation, or a combination of two or more such factors.

The South Africa Act, subsequently superseded by South Africa's republican Constitution, included entrenched clauses relating to the equality of the two official languages and the voting rights of persons of mixed race in the Cape Province. The requirement for the repeal or amendment of these clauses was a two-thirds majority of both Houses of Parliament sitting together at the third reading of the Bill concerned.

ENVIRONMENT, SECRETARY OF STATE FOR THE

This Minister and his Department were created in 1970 as a result of a major reorganization of the machinery of central government. The new Department of the Environment has been formed from the unification of three other departments, the Ministry of Housing and Local Government, the Ministry of Public Building and Works and the Ministry of Transport. The Secretary of State for the Environment will be responsible, in the words of the White Paper on the Reorganization of Central Government (Cmnd 4506), 'for the whole range of

[250]

functions which affect people's living environment'. His responsibilities will include the planning of land, the construction industries, including the housing programme, the transport industries, pollution control, the preservation of natural amenities and the preservation of historic towns and monuments.

The Secretary of State is a Cabinet Minister with a salary of £8,500 a year, and he receives an additional £1,250 if he is a Member of the House of Commons. He is assisted by three non-Cabinet ministers: a Minister for Local Government and Development, a Minister for Housing and Construction and a Minister for Transport Industries.

ESTATES OF THE REALM

The Lords Spiritual, the Lords Temporal, and the Commons are the three estates of the realm which theoretically survive, notably in the enacting formula of an Act of Parliament, from the three broad classes of medieval society, the clergy, the barons, and the commons. For all practical purposes the clergy have ceased to be a seperate estate. They are represented in the House of Lords by the spiritual peers, and in the Commons by the popular representatives elected by clergy and laity alike. Actually, the 'Grades' or 'Estates' in the 14th-century Parliaments were many and not merely three in number—and they were not distinctions of birth. The judges were called an estate, and so were the clerical proctors; yet the one was composed of royal nominees and the other of representatives whose birth might be on any grade from base to noble. The description of Parliament as the 'Three Estates' arose in the 15th century out of a mistaken French analogy, and the phrase was never a true definition of an English Parliament. The whole conception of caste implied in the words was alien to English law and politics: every man's place in Parliament was determined by tenure and not by status, by writs of summons and not by class distinctions. So far from the English Parliament being a system of three estates, it was the difference between such systems and the English Parliament that enabled our system to survive and grow, while most systems of estates dwindled away and died.

ESTIMATES

The anticipated financial requirements of the public service for the forthcoming financial year. The Estimates now consist of two main divisions, the Civil Estimates and the Defence Estimates. The Civil Estimates consist of the following eleven classes: (1) Government and Finance; (2) Commonwealth and Foreign; (3) Home and Justice; (4) Communications, Trade and Industry; (5) Agriculture; (6) Local Government, Housing and Social Services; (7) Education and Science; (8) Museums, Galleries and the Arts; (9) Public Buildings and Common Governmental Services; (10) Other Public Departments;

(11) Miscellaneous. The Revenue Departments' Estimates, formerly printed separately, have been included with Class 1 since the publication of the Civil Estimates for 1962–3. Each class is divided into 'votes', a vote representing a public department and being a unit of appropriation. Some departments administer several votes, e.g., the Home Office is responsible, in addition to its own vote, for those in respect of Civil Defence, Police, Prisons, and Child Care. Each vote is divided into two parts. Part I, which is the operative part, simply specifies in the broadest terms the services for which the Estimate is required, and the total net amount of the Estimate which Parliament is being asked to approve. Part II is a breakdown of the vote under explanatory subheads, listing the various items of expenditure and receipts, if any, and showing comparable figures for the previous year. Explanatory notes and appendixes provide further information where appropriate. Prior to the reorganization of the Ministry of Defence in terms of the Defence (Transfer of Functions) Act, 1964, the Estimates of the Ministry, the Royal Navy, Army and Royal Air Force were published as separate divisions. All have now been incorporated as the Defence Estimates.

Substantial changes in the form of the Civil Estimates, designed to simplify and shorten them, were implemented in those for 1962–3. The form of the Estimates is controlled by the Crown, acting through the Treasury, but since it would be contrary to established usage to make any radical changes in their form without the consent of the House of Commons, the Treasury proposals were submitted to the Committee of Public Accounts and the Estimates Committee (qq.v.) prior to their adoption, certain modifications proposed by the latter Committee being also incorporated.

The Estimates are prepared by the various departments concerned. They must be passed by the Treasury and approved by the Cabinet, after which they are presented to the House of Commons. Printed on the cover of each volume of Estimates are the words, 'Presented by Command of Her Majesty', for these Estimates comprise the 'aids and supplies' which the Commons are being asked to grant to the Crown in order to meet the needs of the public service. Also printed on the covers are the words, 'Ordered by the House of Commons to be printed [followed by a date]', for the Estimates are published as House of Commons Papers (q.v.). The Estimates constitute the bulk of the financial business of the session. They were considered in the Committee of Supply prior to its abolition in December 1966. Under the new financial procedure they are now considered in the House with the Deputy Speaker in the Chair, and they must be approved by means of Supply resolutions passed in the House before legislation can be introduced to give them statutory effect.

The Estimates detail the anticipated expenses of each department and the specific purposes for which the money is required, such as salaries, stores and equipment, the maintenance of services, grants to various bodies and organizations, travelling expenses, etc. A large proportion of the money required goes to pay salaries and under Part II of each vote limited details concerning the staff of the department are given, showing the number of officers in each senior grade, the appropriate salary scale for the grade, and the total sums required for the payment of salaries. The equivalent estimate for the previous year is given in a parallel column against each item for the purpose of comparison. Most departments include in their Estimates sums in respect of 'appropriations-in-aid'. These represent receipts from sales and services, and they are deducted from the gross estimate, the approval of Parliament being required only for the remainder. Appropriations-in-aid cannot be reduced but if they exceed the total estimated expenditure the department concerned calculates its Estimates in such a manner as to provide for a net expenditure of (normally) £1,000 which the House votes as a 'token vote'. The purpose of the token vote is to maintain the principle of parliamentary control over expenditure. Any surplus appropriations-in-aid are paid into the Exchequer. Until the passing of the Public Accounts and Charges Act, 1891, all such receipts were paid direct into the Exchequer. By enabling the departments to make direct use of any moneys received both time and labour are saved through the avoidance of unnecessary transfers.

The Estimates provide for each financial year as a self-contained period. Surpluses may not be carried over from one financial year into another but must revert to the Exchequer. This system has been criticized on the ground that it encourages wastefulness. A very serious view is taken if a department overspends its estimate and therefore (assert the critics) a department may be tempted to over-estimate its requirements and indulge in needless expenditure at the end of the year in order to avoid a surplus. However, with the many effective checks on expenditure which are afforded by Treasury control, the auditing of public accounts, and the financial committees of the House of Commons (not to mention the high standard of integrity maintained by the public service generally), it is doubtful whether such practices could be carried to any great extent.

In addition to the main Estimates, which account for most of the time spent by the House of Commons considering Supply, there are four other forms of Estimates to be considered: Votes on Account, Supplementary Estimates, Supplementary Estimates on Account, and Excess Votes. A fifth type, Votes of Credit, is normally only utilized in time of war or other grave emergency. Under existing procedure twenty-nine days, known as Supply days, are allotted during each session to the consideration of all Supply. These days are normally utilized for general debates on subjects selected by the Opposition rather than for the consideration of the Estimates themselves. Although the practices relating to Supply days have changed, the principle underlying them remains the same. Parliament is exercising its right to discuss the policies behind the Government's proposed expenditures before voting the monies required to implement them. Under the former procedure, when twenty days were allotted to Supply, Supplementary Estimates and Excess Votes fell outside the allotted days, and there was no limit to the debate which could take place upon them. It will be convenient to consider Votes on Account, Supplementary Estimates, Excess Votes and Votes of Credit separately.

VOTES ON ACCOUNT. The main Estimates, which constitute the bulk of the financial business of the session, are seldom passed before July or August, well after the beginning of the financial year for which they provide. It is necessary, therefore, to provide the departments with funds to cover their immediate needs and to carry them over until the main Estimates are approved. Provisional Estimates are prepared and presented to the House of Commons in the normal manner and given special priority consideration. They must necessarily be approved before 31 March, and under the system of closure (q.v.), which is a feature of the existing procedure in Supply debates, this part of the financial business is expedited accordingly. The House approves these provisional Estimates by passing Votes on Account. Under former procedure, although the August closure operated in respect of the main Estimates, the passage of the Votes on Account was not assisted by the 'guillotine' (q.v.) which operates to-day. When this closure is applied the question is put without further debate on all Votes on Account which remain undiscussed, and also on any Supplementary Estimates and Excess Votes which have not been passed.

One result of the recent changes in financial procedure is that the procedure relating to Votes on Account is the same for the armed services as for the civil departments. The Defence Estimates are now divided by function rather than by service and their form is now similar to that of the Civil Estimates. The need for the special arrangements which formerly existed to meet the immediate financial needs of the armed services has thus been eliminated. Under the former practice, the armed services were permitted by means of the power of virement to meet a deficit on one vote from the surplus on another. It was customary to give an early passage to the vote concerned with the pay of service personnel, the most substantial item of expenditure, in place of a Vote on Account.

SUPPLEMENTARY ESTIMATES. It usually happens that some departments, having submitted their main Estimates, find that they have under-estimated their requirements and are compelled to ask

Parliament for more money. Estimates of the additional requirements, known as Supplementary Estimates, are prepared in a form similar to the main Estimates, details of the proposed expenditure being set out in the same way to inform the House of the purposes for which the extra money is required. It is important to emphasize that Supplementary Estimates are prepared and presented to Parliament well before the end of the financial year for which they provide, and in order to avoid a deficit being carried over into the next financial year (beginning 1 April) they must be passed by the House before 31 March. In the session of 1963–4, following a recommendation of the Estimates Committee, Supplementary Estimates on Account were presented for the first time and were available to the House at the very beginning of the session. The main object of this procedure was to improve parliamentary control over supplementary expenditure by having the departments provide provisional figures. In order to avoid any confusion regarding the Supplementary Estimates, it should be remembered that the parliamentary session overlaps two financial years, the latter months of one financial year corresponding with the first months of the session. Consequently, the consideration of the Supplementary Estimates is amongst the first financial business of the session and not the last. The main Estimates which they supplement will, of course, have been passed during the previous session. Under the new financial procedure introduced in December 1966 the Winter Supplementary Estimates must be disposed of not later than 6 February provided they shall have been presented not less than seven days previously.

Excess Votes. It sometimes happens at the end of a financial year that a department discovers it has exceeded its Estimates. By this time it is too late to present Supplementary Estimates and the department is faced with a deficit and the necessity of explaining it to the Committee of Public Accounts (q.v.). Excess expenditure is automatically deplored although in certain circumstances there may be a satisfactory explanation. Departments naturally take great care to avoid exceeding their Estimates, for an overdraft suggests incompetent accounting and reflects upon the efficiency of the department concerned. Consequently excesses seldom occur and when they do occur they usually involve only insignificant sums. However, when an Estimate is exceeded legal provision must be made for the excess, and Parliament effects this in the first instance by passing an Excess Vote. The mistake is thus pardoned, but a large excess would not be so readily excused and would be regarded with the utmost seriousness.

An Excess Vote is required in respect of the Civil Estimates when any single vote has been exceeded. Prior to the introduction of a Defence Vote on Account under the new financial procedure, the armed forces were empowered by the Appropriation Act to apply with the consent of the Treasury any surplus remaining from one vote to cover any deficit incurred on another, the power known as 'virement'. It is important to distinguish between Excess Votes and Supplementary Estimates. The former are designed to legalize excess expenditure *after* it has been incurred, while the latter seek the provision of increased funds *before* any overspending has taken place, this being a perfectly normal and regular procedure. Excess Votes, if any, form a part of the first financial business of the session and are passed to cover deficits incurred in the *previous* financial year.

VOTES OF CREDIT. Under conditions of national emergency and in particular during wartime it is usually either impossible or contrary to the national interest to draw up detailed Estimates of expenditure. In these circumstances Parliament is asked to pass a Vote of Credit, the effect of which is to place a large sum of money at the disposal of the public service for unspecified purposes. Votes of Credit were frequently passed during the two World Wars, e.g., in 1943, the House approved a Vote of Credit of one thousand million pounds for the prosecution of the war. Although sometimes rendered necessary by emergency conditions, Votes of Credit are obviously undesirable in principle.

The annual statutes which give legal effect to all the Estimates once they have been approved in the House are the Consolidated Fund and Appropriation Acts. The Appropriation Act (q.v.) is the main Act and is passed after the main Estimates have been agreed to. Statutory authority for Votes on Account, Supplementary Estimates, and Excess Votes is provided by the Consolidated Fund Act (q.v.), which is passed earlier in the session. If the financial business of the session is particularly heavy it may be necessary to pass more than one Consolidated Fund Act before the main Estimates are finally passed.

A thorough and detailed consideration of the Estimates is not feasible in the House itself, and Supply debates are concerned with matters of policy rather than financial detail. The Estimates are, therefore, referred to the Estimates Committee (q.v.) for more specific consideration.

See also PROCEDURE, FINANCIAL; SUPPLY.

ESTIMATES COMMITTEE

A Sessional Committee (q.v.) of the House of Commons, formerly appointed by order of the House, but now set up under a Standing Order passed in 1960. It consists of 33 members, 7 being a quorum, and its function is to consider the details of the Estimates. Its size was reduced from 43 following the setting up of various Specialist Committees (q.v.). Close scrutiny of the Estimates is not feasible in the

House, where debate tends to be wide and discursive and devoted rather to matters of policy than to the Estimates themselves. The Estimates Committee is debarred from considering policy, its order of reference being 'to examine such of the Estimates presented to this House as may seem fit to the committee and report how, if at all, the policy implied in those Estimates may be carried out more economically and, if the committee think fit, to consider the principal variations between the Estimates and those relating to the previous financial year and the form in which the Estimates are presented to the House'. The committee is empowered to send for persons, papers and records, to sit notwithstanding an adjournment of the House, to adjourn from place to place, to report from time to time, and to appoint sub-committees empowered to deal with any of the matters referred to the committee. The committee takes full advantage of its power to appoint sub-committees, and its investigations are largely conducted through its sub-committees, on whose reports the reports of the full committee are founded. The quorum of a sub-committee is 3. In 1960 the committee's membership was increased from 36 to 43 to permit of more sub-committees being appointed and additional reports being made, specifically on supplementary Estimates and the variations in Estimates between one year and another. However, with the appointment of new Specialist Committees, the Estimates Committee has been reduced in size and appoints fewer sub-committees. The committee's reports are considered in the House and may be debated on a Supply day (q.v.) at the request of the Opposition. (Following a statement by the Leader of the House in July 1960, three days were made available for debating the reports of the Estimates and Public Accounts Committees, two being Supply days and the third being provided in Government time.)

The Estimates Committee was first set up in 1912 on the motion of Lloyd George, when it numbered 15 members. Since then it has been regularly appointed each session except during the years 1915 to 1920 and 1939 to 1945, when its place was taken by a Select Committee on National Expenditure (see below). During the years it has functioned, and particularly prior to 1939, the committee has not been considered an unqualified success, although it has made a number of useful recommendations, the reclassification of the Estimates which took place in 1927 being one of the results of its work. The committee is unfortunately beset by many handicaps. Its order of reference imposes a difficulty at the outset, for financial policy, which the committee is precluded from considering, is inextricably bound up with the Estimates themselves. Also, owing to the very nature of its functions, the committee, if it is not extremely cautious, can expose itself to the charge of interfering in the internal administration of government departments. The main problem, however, lies in the actual examination of the Estimates. Although some scrutiny is attempted, it has been found that a detailed examination of such a prodigious volume of figures is equally impossible in a Select Committee as in the House or (prior to the introduction of the new financial procedure in December 1966) in Committee of Supply. The committee has only five months in which to complete its task, for the Estimates are presented to Parliament in February and must be passed by August. Unlike the Committee of Public Accounts (q.v.) the Estimates Committee has no expert advice on which to rely and nothing corresponding to an audit to guide it in selecting lines of inquiry. Since 1945, however, the committee has evolved a method of procedure more suitable than that of its pre-war predecessor. Following along the lines adopted by the wartime National Expenditure Committee it has concentrated upon the more practicable task of inquiring into selected ranges of current expenditure with a view to promoting economy and efficiency. The pursuit of its investigations through sub-committees has been an important factor in contributing to the comparative success of the committee's efforts in relation to those of its predecessor. In recent years as many as 7 sub-committees have been at work. Inspections and visits have become a normal part of sub-committee procedure, and with several sub-committees able to conduct simultaneous inquiries the amount of work accomplished has been considerably multiplied. However the number of sub-committees has been reduced to 4 with the appointment of an increasing number of Specialist Committees.

The unity of the committee as a whole is maintained by a co-ordinating sub-committee consisting of the Chairmen of all other sub-committees presided over by the Chairman of the full committee, its function being to decide on possible lines of inquiry. The pre-war Estimates Committee was also empowered to appoint sub-committees but very seldom did so.

In 1946 the Select Committee on Procedure recommended that the Estimates Committee and the Public Accounts Committee should be combined into a single Expenditure Committee, but this recommendation was not accepted. A warmer reception was given to the proposal of the 1968–9 Procedure Committee that the Estimates Committee be replaced by a Select Committee on Expenditure which would work through 8 functional sub-committees, each consisting of 9 members. The Government promised to examine the proposal and place a recommendation before the House. In October 1970, following a change in Government, a Green Paper was published entitled 'Select Committees of the House of Commons' (Cmnd 4507) which endorsed the Procedure Committee's recommendations in modified form. (*See also* EXPENDITURE, SELECT COMMITTEE ON; SPECIALIST COMMITTEES.)

During the two World Wars the Estimates Committee was replaced by a Select Committee on National Expenditure with terms of reference confining it to the consideration of war expenditure. The abnormal

[258]

conditions of war made scrutiny of the Estimates impracticable, for in the interests of security they were never published in full, and Parliament often voted money in the form of Votes of Credit, in which case the purposes for which the money was required were not specified. Thus the National Expenditure Committee was charged with a somewhat different task from that of the Estimates Committee. Its investigations were directed wherever money was being spent in large amounts, and particularly where it had reason to suspect waste, inefficiency, or maladministration. At the outset of the recent war the committee appealed to the public for any information which would lead to the discovery of bad practices in the expenditure of public money, and as a result of a very helpful response (the informants' names never being revealed) the committee's attention was drawn to a number of minor abuses and irregularities. Like the present Estimates Committee the National Expenditure Committee conducted its investigations to a very great extent through sub-committees which travelled all over the country, visiting such places as factories and aerodromes, subjected departmental activities to searching examination, and heard evidence from Government officials under conditions of strictest secrecy. The National Expenditure Committee was a diligent and enthusiastic body which effected many improvements during the war. There is no doubt that the overriding considerations of war provided both the incentive and the conditions which made for the committee's success.

(Further reading: Chubb, *The control of public expenditure*, 1952; Einzig, *The control of the purse*, 1959.)

EXAMINERS (OF PRIVATE BILLS)

When a Private Bill (q.v.) is promoted certain preliminaries are required by Standing Orders. To ascertain that these steps have been complied with two examiners are appointed, one from the staff of each House. Notice of the examination is given to promoters of Private Bills, who must appear, either in person or represented by parliamentary agents, otherwise the petition will be struck out. No Bill can proceed unless the examiners certify that Standing Orders have been complied with.

EXCEPTIONAL GRANTS

A term which, according to Erskine May, covers several different kinds of expenditure of an unusual character. They may be presented as Estimates (q.v.), in which case they receive legislative sanction in the annual Appropriation Act (q.v.), or they may be dealt with on a financial resolution (q.v.), in which case a special Act is required to legalize them.

The following charges may be cited as examples of exceptional grants:

A grant to cover a non-recurring expense in connexion with an imperial undertaking, such as the purchase of the Suez Canal shares;

A special grant for a novel purpose, such as the presentation of a Mace to a new Commonwealth legislature;

A grant for 'the maintenance of the dignity and well-being of the Crown', such as provision for the Civil List (q.v.) on the demise of the Crown;

A grant to provide for rewards to individuals for distinguished public service.

EXCESS VOTES

See ESTIMATES; PROCEDURE, FINANCIAL.

EXCHEQUER

See TREASURY.

EXCLUSION BILL

See ROMAN CATHOLICS IN PARLIAMENT.

EXCLUSIVE LIST

A list of subjects appended to a federal constitution in respect of which only the federal legislature has power to make laws.

EXECUTIVE COUNCIL

This body formulates policy in a colonial government and is also the authority on all disciplinary questions relating to the Overseas Service in the territory. It is composed of *ex-officio* members, who are usually the Chief Secretary, the Attorney-General, and the Financial Secretary, and official and sometimes unofficial members who are nominated by the Governor. Government measures are considered by the Executive Council before being submitted to the Legislative Council in the form of Bills. The Governor summons and presides over the Council, whose proceedings, like those of a Cabinet, are confidential, but it differs from a Cabinet in that it is only advisory, although the Governor is bound to consult it, and it has no collective responsibility. A colonial Governor is empowered to overrule his Executive Council, but if he does so he must give his reasons to the Secretary of State.

In a country with a federal constitution, a provincial or state Cabinet is sometimes more properly termed an Executive Council (e.g., in the Canadian Provinces), but in such cases the Premier is normally the President of the Executive Council and the principle of collective responsibility applies.

EXEMPTED BUSINESS

Business which is exempted from the operation of the House of Commons Standing Order which provides for the automatic interruption of business at 10 p.m., known as the Ten o'clock Rule (q.v.). (On Fridays the moment of the automatic interruption of business is at 4 p.m.)

The following is a complete list of Exempted Business as of 1969:

(1) Proceedings on a Bill brought in upon a Ways and Means Resolution or any Consolidated Fund Bill or Appropriation Bill. (*See* APPROPRIATION ACT; CONSOLIDATED FUND ACTS; *and* FINANCE ACT.)

(2) Proceedings on a motion authorizing expenditure in connexion with a Bill, but only for a period of three-quarters of an hour following the usual moment of the automatic interruption of business.

(3) Proceedings in pursuance of an Act of Parliament, including resolutions made under the Church of England Assembly (Powers) Act, 1919, the Statutory Orders (Special Procedure) Act, 1945, and the House of Commons Disqualification Act, 1957. Motions for the annulment of Statutory Instruments (q.v.) (commonly called 'prayers' in that they take the form of an Address to the Crown) are exempted for a limited time (i.e. until 11.30 p.m.). Such motions are normally made by private members and are in order only in cases where the authorizing statute expressly provides for such proceedings.

(4) Proceedings on motions made pursuant to certain Standing Orders, including proceedings following upon the 'naming' of a member; proceedings relating to the committal of Public Bills; proceedings on a resolution of the Business Committee (q.v.); proceedings relating to the reference of Scottish Bills to the Scottish Grand Committee and Scottish Standing Committee (q.v.); proceedings relating to the approval of certain contracts in terms of Standing Order No. 92; and proceedings relating to the withdrawal of strangers from the House.

Any business other than the above can be exempted on the affirmed motion of a Minister of the Crown.

EX-OFFICIO MEMBER

A member of a colonial legislature who holds his seat by virtue of an office under the Crown. He was formerly subject, like a Colonial Governor, to the direction of the Secretary of State for the Colonies. However, the dwindling size of the Colonial Empire led to the merging of this office in 1967 with that of Secretary of State for Commonwealth Affairs whose functions were in turn merged with those of the Secretary of State for Foreign Affairs in 1969. The *ex-officio* members consist of the *ex-officio* members of the Executive Council, who form the nucleus of the Legislative Council as well, and the holders of certain other prescribed offices.

EXPENDITURE

See APPROPRIATION ACT; CIVIL LIST; COMMITTEE OF PUBLIC ACCOUNTS; CONSOLIDATED FUND; CONSOLIDATED FUND ACTS; ESTIMATES; ESTI- MATES COMMITTEE; EXCEPTIONAL GRANTS; FINANCIAL RESOLUTION; PRIVILEGE, FINANCIAL; PROCEDURE, FINANCIAL; SUPPLY.

EXPENDITURE, SELECT COMMITTEE ON

This Committee, which at the time of writing (November 1970) has not been set up, was proposed by the Select Committee on Procedure 1968–9 as a substitute for the Estimates Committee (q.v.). This Com- mittee would work through eight functional sub-committees, each consisting of 9 members, which would examine the Estimates of expenditure and administrative efficiency in specified areas of govern- ment activity. The proposed sub-committees would each deal with the following areas: industry, technology, manpower and employment; power, transport and communications; trade and agriculture; education, science and the arts; housing, health and welfare; law, order and public safety; defence; external affairs.

The recommendation was warmly received and the Government promised to study it prior to making its own recommendation later. In October 1970, following a change of Government, a Green Paper was published entitled 'Select Committees of the House of Commons' (Cmnd 4507) which was debated in the House on 12 November 1970. This paper proposed the establishment of a dual system of Committees whereby the Select Committee on Nationalized Industries and certain Specialist Select Committees would be retained alongside an Expendi- ture Committee of about 45 members which would replace the Estimates Committee and have functions similar to those proposed by the Select Committee on Procedure. The Green Paper stated the view that such a system 'would provide for the increased scrutiny by Parliament of the longer-term projection of public expenditure which the Select Committee on Procedure saw to be desirable, while building on the foundations laid in the last Parliament by the Specialist Com- mittees'. The proposals were well received by the House and at the time of writing their implementation is awaited.

EXPIRING LAWS CONTINUANCE ACT

An Act passed in the British Parliament each session to provide for the continuance of temporary Acts. These are Acts which are valid for a limited period, such as those passed to meet some special emer- gency. Others may be of an experimental nature, and if they do not succeed in their object lapse automatically unless included in the Schedule to the annual Expiring Laws Continuance Act.

EXPLANATORY MEMORANDUM

A memorandum which explains the contents and object of a Bill in non-technical language. Such a memorandum is prepared when required and circulated with the Bill.

See also FINANCIAL MEMORANDUM.

EXPULSION FROM PARLIAMENT

The House of Commons has always retained the right of expulsion, the leading precedent being the case of Arthur Hall (q.v.) in 1581. Members have been expelled for offences committed against the House itself or for grave misdemeanours which do not of themselves, like treason and felony, automatically disqualify a person from membership. The most recent case of expulsion from the House of Commons was in December 1954, the expelled member having been convicted of a criminal offence and sentenced to a term of imprisonment. In October 1947, a member was expelled after the House of Commons had found him guilty of gross contempts of the House. Expulsion does not involve disqualification, and an expelled member is eligible to serve again in Parliament, including the same Parliament which expelled him, if re-elected, a principle which was established in 1782 as a result of the case of John Wilkes (q.v.). Erskine May points out that 'the purpose of expulsion is not so much disciplinary as remedial, not so much to punish Members as to rid the House of persons who are unfit for membership'.

The House of Lords has the right, although obsolete, to disqualify a peer from sitting in the House by its sentence, when the offender has been tried and found guilty on impeachment (q.v.). Such disqualification may be permanent or temporary and is removable only by pardon from the Crown.

F

FAGGOT VOTING

A device, dating back to the days of the early Stuarts, for extending the right to vote on the basis of a property qualification. Where the rooms of a tenement building were leased to a number of individuals, the right to exercise the franchise which the property conferred upon its owner or lessee could be split amongst the inhabitants of the building, thus creating a multiplicity of votes where there should have been only one. Another example was the possibility of buying property mortgaged to its full value for the purpose of obtaining a vote. Even the Reform Act (q.v.) of 1832 failed to abolish this practice, the last vestiges remaining until the passing of the Representation of the People Act of 1918.

FALKLAND ISLANDS LEGISLATIVE COUNCIL

The Constitution of the Falkland Islands incorporates a Legislative Council and an Executive Council. The former consists of 2 *ex-officio* members (Colonial Secretary and Colonial Treasurer), 4 elected members and 2 unofficial members nominated by the Governor. The latter consists of the 2 *ex-officio* members, the 2 nominated members and 2 of the elected members. The principle of universal adult suffrage for the election of the elected members was introduced in 1949.

FATHER OF THE HOUSE

The title given to the Member of the House of Commons who has served the longest without a break, even though he may have represented different constituencies. Thomas William Coke, afterwards Earl of Leicester, was referred to in his obituary in *The Times* as 'Father of the House', although his service between 1776 and 1831 was not uninterrupted. Christopher Talbot had more right to the title as he sat continuously from 1830 to 1890, but his record for long service was beaten by C. P. Villiers, who was Member for Wolverhampton from 1835 to 1898. Villiers became Father in 1895, following Gladstone, who had succeeded Talbot in 1890. Subsequent Fathers have been Sir John Mowbray, 1898, W. W. B. Hicks-Beach, 1899, Sir Michael Hicks-Beach, 1901, George Henry Finch, 1906, Sir Henry Campbell-Bannerman, 1907, Sir John Henry Kennaway, 1908, Thomas Burt,

1910, T. P. O'Connor, 1918, David Lloyd George, 1929, Earl Winterton (who afterwards went to the House of Lords as Baron Turnour), 1944, Sir Hugh O'Neill (afterwards Lord Rathcavan), 1951, the Rt. Hon. David Grenfell, 1952, Sir Winston Churchill, 1959, and Robert Turton, 1965.

It is reported that when Sir Winston Churchill became the Father of the House a member asked the Clerk what his duties were in that capacity. On being told that there were none the member remarked: 'That answer won't satisfy the Member for Woodford. If there are no duties then he will proceed to invent some!'

In the Canadian House of Commons the term 'Dean of the House' is employed in preference to 'Father of the House'.

FAWKES, GUY

See GUNPOWDER PLOT.

FEDERAL PARLIAMENTS

The formation of a federation is a recognition that certain governmental tasks cannot be performed adequately by the separate states and require handling on a broader basis. Therefore it is essential for a federal legislature to ensure that it can carry out the functions assigned to it and be able to act to meet the needs of the larger community. At the same time it must take account of the interests of the various sections of the new community and of the continuing responsibility of the member states for their fields of government. Although the needs and interests of the federation must normally prevail over those of individual states, the federation should exercise its powers so as not to impede unnecessarily the use by the member states of the powers they retain, although the constitution is the primary safeguard against improper extension of federal authority. The majority of federal Parliaments are bicameral, the upper House, in addition to its revisory rôle, being designed to reflect the interests of the constituent states, either as regions or as political entities. For the smaller states with limited representation in the lower House, representation in the upper House gives them greater influence in federal affairs than their populations alone would justify. Federalism is, in effect, a system of Government by compromise—in fact, Sir Ivor Jennings has written that 'nobody would have a federal constitution if he could possibly avoid it'. It recognizes regional autonomy and the desirability of protecting a regional minority from the power of a national majority where issues of local importance are concerned. It thus depends upon the division of power and the decentralization of administration and policy making. The Commonwealth has seen the birth, and more recently the death, of a number of Parliaments working under a federal or quasi-federal constitution. The first federal Parliament in the British Empire was that of Canada established in 1867 under the British North America Act. In 1901 the Federal Parliament of the Commonwealth of Australia came into being, and in 1949 India adopted its present federal constitution. Among the newer nations of the Commonwealth, Kenya is a federal state in all but name, comprising seven regions each with a Regional Assembly having certain decentralized powers. The latest federal experiment in the Commonwealth was the association of Aden with the scattered amirates and sheikdoms on the Arabian peninsula under British protection to form the Federation of South Arabia.

It would be impossible to claim that federalism in the Commonwealth has been an unqualified success. Two federations, those of Rhodesia and Nyasaland and the West Indies, were unable to survive. The Federation of Malaysia formed in 1963 was faced two years later with the secession of Singapore. Pakistan was a federation from 1947 to 1956 when its constitution was suspended and military government imposed. The new constitution introduced in 1962, while preserving certain federal characteristics, provided essentially for a unitary form of government. The Federation of Nigeria, which became independent in 1960, experienced a revolution in 1966 when it too was brought under military rule. In the same year the Prime Minister of Uganda announced that a unitary form of government would be introduced to replace the former constitution, which had incorporated certain federal characteristics resulting from a compromise agreed to at the time of Uganda's achievement of independence.

Even the Commonwealth's most stable federations have experienced difficulties. In 1933 the Commonwealth of Australia was faced with a strong secessionist bid from Western Australia, which was supported at the time by both the Government and the people of the State. In India the State of Nagaland, formerly a part of Assam, was created in response to pressure from the Naga people for independence, and dangerous frictions also underlay the separation on a linguistic basis of the former State of Bombay into the States of Maharashtra and Gujarat. Canada is currently experiencing a wave of French-Canadian nationalism which, in its most extreme form, is calling for the separation of Quebec from the rest of Canada. While outright secession is demanded by only a minority of the people of Quebec, most French-Canadians would probably favour a greater measure of autonomy for the Province.

There are many conditions to be fulfilled if a federal system of government is to succeed, and the disintegration of the Federation of Rhodesia and Nyasaland and the West Indies Federation was due in each case to entirely different reasons. The former Federation was born in 1953 during a period which could be described as the tail-end of the colonial era in Africa. It consisted of the self-governing Colony of Southern Rhodesia and the Protectorates of Northern Rhodesia and Nyasaland, brought together under a white federal government, but with the promise that racial partnership would be promoted. The African nationalists in the Protectorates regarded the Federation as nothing more than a device to perpetuate white supremacy in Central Africa, and mounted a militant campaign aimed at its destruction. The British Government eventually gave way to African nationalist pressure and, without the consent of the Federal Government, decided to permit the secession of the two Protectorates, which led to the dissolution of the Federation in 1963. Nyasaland and Northern Rhodesia became the independent states of Malawi and Zambia while Southern Rhodesia reverted to its status as a self-governing Colony and declared its independence unilaterally in 1965 after a prolonged dispute with the British Government.

Whereas there were clear economic advantages to be derived from the association of the Central African territories, the West Indies Federation held very little promise at its inception in 1956. The prospect of economic benefits was somewhat nebulous; there was no necessity to unite against a common danger; and the widely separated components of the Federation had enjoyed a long-established parochialism. The opposition to federation came mainly from Jamaica, where it was felt that the country was putting more into the Federation than it was receiving. This feeling was endorsed by a referendum held in 1961, and Jamaica seceded, to become an independent member of the Commonwealth in 1962.

Meanwhile, Trinidad and Tobago also asked for secession and the British Government decided in February 1962 to dissolve the Federation. The decision was taken, as in the case of the Federation of Rhodesia and Nyasaland, despite opposition from the Federal Government itself. Trinidad and Tobago, like Jamaica, became independent in the same year, and the question arose of maintaining a political association among the remaining smaller islands of Barbados, Antigua, Dominica, Grenada, Montserrat, St. Kitts/Nevis/Anguilla, St. Lucia and St. Vincent. The Regional Council of Ministers of these islands, being now aware of the high mortality rate among federations, included among their recommendations in October 1964 a proposal to the effect that no unit of the new Federation could secede without the consent of the other members. In February 1965 the Regional Council issued a draft scheme for federation, but Dominica, St. Lucia and St. Kitts disagreed with certain of the proposals, while Grenada preferred union with Trinidad and the ruling party of Barbados opted for unilateral independence rather than independence within a federation. When to these difficulties are added a lack of enthusiasm among the inhabitants of these islands for a further attempt at federation, there

[267]

would seem to be little chance of any new federal scheme reaching fruition.

A federal constitution makes provision for the division of powers between the federation and the states, and the subjects on which the federal and state Parliaments are empowered to legislate are usually to a large extent specified. Subjects falling within federal jurisdiction are normally embodied in an exclusive list, while matters on which the federation and the states exercise a concurrent jurisdiction are specified in a concurrent list. In the concurrent area federal law will normally prevail in the event of a conflict. Some federal constitutions, notably those of Canada and India, include a third list specifying the powers of the states, the undistributed residue of powers being vested in the central government. In certain other federal constitutions the powers of the states are not specified, it being understood that the jurisdiction of the states encompasses the unspecified residue. On the other hand, the tendency towards the strengthening of government at the centre, such as has taken place in Australia, suggests that where a constitution is flexible with regard to the distribution of residual powers, the jurisdiction of the federation is likely to expand more than that of the states. Some federal constitutions confer emergency powers on the central government whereby the federal authorities can take over the direct government of a state in the interests of public order and security. It is under such powers that the Government of India has assumed direct control of various States from time to time, and the Nigerian Government took over the government of the Western Region in 1962.

(Further reading: Wheare, *Federal government*, 1953.)

FEDERATION OF NIGERIA

See NIGERIAN PARLIAMENTS.

FEES OFFICE

Originally an office for the collection of fees on Private Bills, now only a small part of the work of the office, it is responsible under the Clerk (Administrator) for the preparation of the Estimates for the three departments of the House of Commons, the control of the expenditure of the grant voted, the payment of members and staff salaries and wages, and the operation of the free travel scheme for Members of Parliament.

FERRERS, GEORGE, CASE OF

The case which established for the Commons the privilege of immunity from arrest. In 1543 George Ferrers, a member, was arrested for debt while on his way to the House. The Commons sent their Serjeant-at-Arms (q.v.) with the Mace (q.v.) to demand the release of

Ferrers, but he was roughly turned away by the Sheriffs of London. The Commons thereupon summoned the Sheriffs, together with the person who had taken legal action against Ferrers, to appear at the Bar of the House. They were committed to prison, and King Henry VIII himself confirmed the action of the Commons in asserting their privilege.

FIJI PARLIAMENT

The State of Fiji became an independent member of the Commonwealth on 10 October 1970 under a Constitution which confirms Her Majesty the Queen as Head of State. The Constitution provides for a bicameral Parliament, comprising a Senate of 22 members and a House of Representatives of 52 members.

Of the 22 members of the Senate, 8 are nominated by the Council of Chiefs, 7 by the Prime Minister, 6 by the Leader of the Opposition and 1 by the Council of Rotuma which is a dependency of Fiji. Senators hold their seats for six years regardless of a dissolution of Parliament, 11 retiring every three years.

The 52 members of the House of Representatives are elected by an elaborate system of cross-voting which involves the use of four electoral rolls. There are three communal rolls, one for Fijians, one for Indians and a general communal roll for voters who are neither Fijians (nor other Pacific Islanders) nor Indians. In addition there is a national roll comprising the voters on all three communal rolls. The ethnic composition of the House of Representatives comprises 22 Fijians (12 elected by the Fijian communal roll voters and 10 by the national roll voters); 22 Indians (12 elected by the Indian communal roll voters and 10 by the national roll voters); and 8 members of other races (3 elected by the general communal roll voters and 5 by the national roll voters). Citizenship and a minimum age of twenty-one are the basic qualifications for the franchise, and the usual disqualifications apply. The life of the House of Representatives is five years unless dissolved earlier on the advice of the Prime Minister.

The Senate is not empowered to initiate legislation but may delay the passage of a Bill for a period of six months except in the case of a Money Bill or a Bill in respect of which the Governor-General, acting in accordance with the advice of the Prime Minister, has certified that its enactment is a matter of urgency. The Senate's most substantial power relates to the process of constitutional amendment. A Bill to amend the Constitution, unless it seeks to amend the entrenched clauses, requires the support of a two-thirds majority of the members of each House voting separately. A Bill to amend the entrenched clauses, which include those relating to fundamental rights, requires the support of not less than three-quarters of the members of each House. A constitutional amendment affecting Fijian lands or customs may be carried only if 6 out of the 8 Senators nominated by the Council of Chiefs are included in the majority supporting it.

The Constitution places no limit on the size of the Cabinet but specifies that the Attorney-General must be a member of Parliament. The official language of Parliament is English although the Constitution provides that a member may speak in Fijian or Hindustani. The Constitution also makes specific provision for an Ombudsman and for the office of Leader of the Opposition.

The history of legislative institutions in Fiji since 1937 reflects the orderly progress of this island colony to statehood and independence. Letters patent of 1937 provided for a Legislative Council in which Fijians, Indians and Europeans were represented, the Fijian members being nominated from a panel submitted by the Council of Chiefs. The Fijian Affairs Ordinance of 1944 conferred a wide measure of control on the Fijian people over government at the local level, and also established the Fijian Affairs Board which advised the Governor and could make regulations subject to the sanction of the Legislative Council.

In 1960 a Commission of Inquiry expressed the opinion that the Council of Chiefs had ceased to be fully representative of Fijian opinion and that the time had come for Fijians to elect their own representatives directly to the Legislative Council.

In 1963 the Legislative Council was expanded to consist of a Speaker, 19 official members (reduced in practice to 10) and 18 unofficial members (6 Fijians, 6 Indians and 6 Europeans). All the unofficial members were directly elected except for 2 Fijians who were elected by the Council of Chiefs. In 1964 the 'member' system (q.v.) was introduced and the Executive Council reconstituted to consist of 4 official and 6 unofficial members (2 of each race), 3 of whom were directly associated with the supervision of government departments.

A constitutional conference held in London in July–August 1965 made further recommendations for constitutional advance. The Legislative Council was further enlarged to consist of 36 elected members and not more than 4 officials nominated by the Governor. The 36 elected members comprised 14 Fijians, 12 Indians and 10 members of other races. A system of cross-voting, designed to encourage political integration among the races, was first established at this time and has been retained in the independence Constitution. Under the independence Constitution the Legislative Council became the first House of Representatives pending the holding of the first post-independence General Election in 1971.

FILIBUSTERING

The obstruction of business in a legislature by dilatory tactics, such as speaking merely to consume time. The use of the word in this sense is almost confined to the United States, where the late Senator Huey Long spoke for nearly sixteen hours in 1935. He introduced such irrelevancies as recipes for fried oysters and the life of Frederick the Great in a speech alleging an offence by the Executive in placing in high-salaried positions men whose names had not been submitted to the Senate for confirmation. Long's record was beaten in 1953 by Senator Wayne Morse who spoke for 22 hours and 26 minutes, but even this marathon speech is excelled by Senator Kilmer Corbin of the Texas State legislature who on one occasion harangued his fellow senators for $28\frac{1}{4}$ hours. Although Private Members' Bills are often 'talked out' in the House of Commons, the American type of filibustering would not be allowed under Standing Order No. 22, which says: 'Mr. Speaker or the chairman, after having called the attention of the House, or of the committee, to the conduct of a member, who persists in irrelevance, or tedious repetition either of his own arguments, or of the arguments used by other members in debate, may direct him to discontinue his speech.'

FINANCE ACT

The annual statute which gives legal force to the taxation proposals contained in the Budget (q.v.). It is based upon Ways and Means resolutions which must approve all Budget proposals before legislation can be introduced to give them the force of law. Until 1967 the necessary resolutions were required to be passed in the Committee of Ways and Means and subsequently approved by the House. Under the new financial procedure the Committee of Ways and Means has been abolished and Ways and Means resolutions are now considered in the House itself. Provision for the abolition of the Committee of Ways and Means was contained in the Finance (No. 2) Bill, 1967, legislative action being required because the Provisional Collection of Taxes Act, 1913 (consolidated and re-enacted in 1968), made specific reference to resolutions passed in the Committee of Ways and Means.

The scope of the Finance Act is not necessarily limited to the imposition and alteration of taxation, however, and it very often includes other provisions of a permanent nature relating to the collection of revenue. As a result it frequently happens that a Finance Bill does not conform to the definition of a Money Bill (q.v.) laid down in the Parliament Acts, 1911 and 1949 (q.v.). When it is desired to bring a Finance Bill within the scope of the statutory definition of a Money Bill it is usual to restrict its provisions to matters of taxation and to embody all other provisions in a separate Bill known as a Revenue Bill.

The debate on the second reading of a Finance Bill is always very wide in scope and the entire financial policy of the Government generally comes under review. It is a Bill, therefore, on which the Commons can expect to spend a considerable amount of time. The Finance Bill of 1909 and the Ways and Means resolutions on which it was based together occupied seventy sitting days, but this was a very exceptional case. Like Consolidated Fund Bills, the Finance Bill is Exempted Business (q.v.), and debate on its various stages is not subject to interruption under the automatic adjournment or Ten o'clock Rule (q.v.). It is not permissible to consider more than one stage of the Bill in any one day. In 1968 the Finance Bill for the first time received clause-by-clause consideration in a Standing Committee instead of in a Committee of the Whole House.

The Finance Act is an Act to raise revenue on behalf of the Crown and therefore contains a special enacting formula expressing the predominance of the Commons in matters of finance. It differs from that of the Appropriation Act (q.v.) and Consolidated Fund Acts (q.v.), which authorize expenditure, and runs as follows:

> Most Gracious Sovereign, We, Your Majesty's most dutiful and loyal subjects, the Commons of the United Kingdom in Parliament assembled, towards raising the necessary supplies to defray Your Majesty's public expenses, and making an addition to the public revenue, have freely and voluntarily resolved to give and grant unto Your Majesty the several duties hereinafter mentioned; and do therefore most humbly beseech Your Majesty that it may be enacted, and be it enacted by the Queen's most Excellent Majesty, by and with the advice and consent of the Lords Spiritual and Temporal, and Commons, in this present Parliament assembled, and by the authority of the same, as follows:—

The procedure which is observed when a Finance Bill receives the Royal Assent (q.v.) corresponds to that in respect of Consolidated Fund Bills (*see* APPROPRIATION ACT).

See also ACT OF PARLIAMENT.

FINANCIAL COMMITTEES

See COMMITTEE OF PUBLIC ACCOUNTS; COMMITTEE OF THE WHOLE HOUSE; ESTIMATES COMMITTEE; EXPENDITURE, SELECT COMMITTEE ON.

FINANCIAL MEMORANDUM

A memorandum which, on the recommendation of the Estimates Committee, is required to accompany all Bills involving expenditure. It explains the financial effect of such a Bill, together with an estimate of the amount of money involved.

See also EXPLANATORY MEMORANDUM.

FINANCIAL PRIVILEGE

See PRIVILEGE, FINANCIAL.

FINANCIAL PROCEDURE

See PROCEDURE, FINANCIAL.

FINANCIAL RESOLUTION

In addition to the ordinary annual expenditure as embodied in the Estimates and authorized by means of Supply resolutions, the House is sometimes called upon to consider new or extraordinary expenditure which is unrelated to the regular business of Supply. A Bill whose main purpose is to sanction such expenditure is founded upon a financial resolution passed in the House. In the case of a Bill containing expenditure clauses which are incidental to its main purpose, only those particular clauses, which are printed in italics, require preliminary authorization by means of a financial resolution. The committee stage of such Bills may not be taken until the financial resolution has been agreed to. The debate on the committee stage of such Bills is limited to three-quarters of an hour or 10.45 p.m., whichever is the later. Financial resolutions require the Queen's recommendation (q.v.), the means by which the initiative in financial matters is restricted to the Government. The Queen's Recommendation is signified in writing to the Clerk of the House and its signification is noted on the Order Paper. The procedure described above was first introduced in December 1966. It supersedes the earlier practice which required that a financial resolution first be passed in a Committee of the Whole House and subsequently endorsed by the House.

The forms of expenditure requiring a preliminary financial resolution of the type described above are exceptional grants (q.v., although these may be presented in the form of Estimates), expenditure in connexion with Bills other than Consolidated Fund Bills, and expenditure for special purposes such as the erection of a monument to a deceased statesman. The procedure adopted in the latter case is to agree to an Address to the Crown for action involving expenditure with the intimation that 'this House will make good the same'. The Queen's Recommendation is given in answer to the address. If a new item of expenditure is intended to become an annual charge, the Act which gives legislative effect to it is also deemed to authorize its subsequent inclusion in the Estimates.

FINANCIAL SECRETARY TO THE TREASURY

In the House of Commons the Financial Secretary holds the most important of the junior ministerial posts. He is, under the Chancellor of the Exchequer, the working political chief of the Treasury, and is responsible, under the Leader of the House, and in conjunction with the Parliamentary Secretary to the Treasury (the Chief Whip), for the arrangement of financial business. The Financial Secretary presents the Estimates for the Civil and Revenue Departments and the Vote on Account, answers questions addressed to the Chancellor of the Exchequer, and has many duties in connexion with the business of

Ways and Means. His Private Secretary is a member of the Treasury Establishment, and this arrangement enables him to preserve constant touch with the higher officials and to obtain from the permanent staff any information or help that he may require beyond what reaches him in the form of written minutes and memoranda. He is *ex-officio* a member of the Public Accounts Committee, but since 1922 has not usually attended their meetings because of the increased demands on his time and the fact that the Treasury is already represented on the committee by the Treasury Officers of Accounts at the meetings at which evidence is taken. In 1957 the office was equated to that of a Minister of State and the salary attached to the office is now £5,625, in addition to which the holder is entitled to £1,250 of his parliamentary salary.

FINANCIAL STATEMENT
See BUDGET.

FINES IN PARLIAMENT
See ATTENDANCE OF MEMBERS.

FIRST LORD OF THE ADMIRALTY
Formerly a minister of Cabinet rank with departmental responsibility for the Admiralty, this historic office was abolished, together with the Admiralty itself, with the coming into force of the Defence (Transfer of Functions) Act, 1964. It was superseded by the office of Minister of Defence for the Royal Navy, a minister below Cabinet rank who was subordinate to the Secretary of State for Defence, but this post was also dispensed with under a ministerial reorganization of January 1967 (*see* DEFENCE, SECRETARY OF STATE FOR).

The First Lord of the Admiralty was the President of the former Admiralty Board which was commissioned by letters patent to execute the duties of the Lord High Admiral of the United Kingdom, an office which was abolished in 1708 except for a brief period during the year 1827–8 when the Duke of Clarence was Lord High Admiral. The office of Lord High Admiral was first in commission from 1628 to 1636, and the office of First Lord of the Admiralty can be traced back to this period. Under an Order in Council of 1904 the Admiralty Board consisted of the First Lord (a civilian), 5 Sea Lords (who were Admirals), the Vice-Chief and the Deputy Chief of Naval Staff, the Permanent Secretary, and 2 junior ministers, the Parliamentary and Financial Secretary and the Civil Lord, who, like the First Lord, were Members of Parliament. Although the old Admiralty Board is no more, its name is perpetuated in one of the three Boards (namely the Admiralty Board, Army Board and Air Force Board) which now administer the three services under the Defence Council. The style 'Admiralty Board' was adopted in preference to that of 'Navy Board' as the result of a House of Lords amendment to the Defence (Transfer of Functions) Bill.

A chronological list of First Lords of the Admiralty appears as Appendix 8.

FIRST LORD OF THE TREASURY

This office is now invariably combined with that of Prime Minister (q.v.), whom it places at the head of the most important government department, the Treasury. His departmental duties are, however, apart from patronage, only nominal, as the working head of the Treasury is the Chancellor of the Exchequer. In the 18th and early 19th centuries, before the reform of the Civil Service and the parliamentary franchise, the fact that the First Lord of the Treasury exercised a very extensive patronage over official appointments meant that the Prime Minister, by combining the two offices, could control departmental appointments and was thereby assisted in obtaining a majority for his party in the House of Commons.

The last occasions when the two offices were held separately were during Lord Salisbury's administrations of 1891–2 and 1895–1902 in which A. J. Balfour served as First Lord of the Treasury.

FIRST READING

See BILL, PASSAGE OF.

FIRST SECRETARY OF STATE

A very senior Cabinet appointment created in July 1962 and first held by Mr. R. A. Butler who was at the same time designated Deputy Prime Minister (q.v.). There was some speculation at the time as to whether the naming of a Deputy Prime Minister was strictly constitutional on the ground that the Royal Prerogative respecting the choice of Prime Minister might thereby be infringed. The office of First Secretary of State and the designation of Deputy Prime Minister both lapsed when Sir Alec Douglas-Home became Prime Minister in October 1963, but the former was reinstated when Mr. Harold Wilson formed his Government in October 1964. Mr. George Brown became First Secretary of State and Minister for Economic Affairs with the implied status though not the designation of Deputy Prime Minister. It was stated at the time of Mr. Brown's appointment that he would act for the Prime Minister when the latter was out of the country.

No Minister was designated First Secretary of State when Mr. Edward Heath formed his Government in June 1970.

[275]

FLASH VOTING

A system by which votes in a legislature are recorded by means of an electric apparatus. A good example is provided by the West Bengal Assembly, where at each member's seat there is a small box containing three buttons, green for Aye, black for Abstain, and red for No. The votes given in these three categories and the total number of votes are shown on the indicator board on the wall opposite the Speaker's chair. On each side of this board are the lamp fields for members arranged in accordance with the seats. Each member has four lamps, red, green, and white (abstain), and another white lamp for recording his presence in the Chamber. If a secret ballot is required, the Speaker presses a different button to start the voting, and the votes are recorded, but instead of a member's light indicating *how* he voted, only a white light appears to show that he *has* voted.

The advantage of this system of recording divisions is of course the saving of time—in West Bengal it was found that while a regular division through the lobbies took fifteen minutes, voting by the new method took only about three minutes. In one day 37 divisions were called and the voting was completed in about ninety minutes.

The upper House of the Indian Parliament, the Rajya Sabha, also uses an automatic vote recorder.

FLOOR OF THE HOUSE

That part of a legislative chamber which is technically 'within the House', i.e., between the Bar of the House (q.v.) and the Speaker's Chair. Debate may not take place outside these limits and a member may only address the House from the Floor. Members are permitted to stand outside the prescribed area and listen to proceedings without participating.

See also CROSSING THE FLOOR.

FOOD, MINISTER OF

The Ministry of Food was formed in 1939 out of a Food (Defence Plans) Department set up in the Board of Trade in 1936. The Government decided in 1945 to make the Ministry a permanent Department of State, and this decision was implemented in 1946 by the Ministers of the Crown (Transfer of Functions) Act, but in 1954 the Ministry of Food was absorbed by the Ministry of Agriculture and Fisheries. The Minister was responsible for food supplies and their rationing when necessary, and he took over from the Minister of Health and the Minister of Agriculture various functions under the Food and Drugs Acts. A Minister of Food was appointed in 1917 and the department was abolished in 1921, the Ministers being Lord Devonport, Lord Rhondda, J. R. Clynes, G. H. Roberts, and C. A. McCurdy.

Ministers appointed during the second life of the Ministry from 1940 were Lord Woolton, Col. J. J. Llewellin (afterwards Lord Llewellin), Sir Benjamin Smith, John Strachey, Maurice Webb, Major Lloyd George, and Derick Heathcoat Amory.

FOREIGN AND COMMONWEALTH AFFAIRS, SECRETARY OF STATE FOR

This office was brought into being on 17 October 1968 as a result of the merging of the Foreign Office with the Commonwealth Office. The first step towards the merger was taken in 1965 with the setting up of the Diplomatic Service Administration Office which served the Commonwealth and Foreign Offices equally while being part of neither. A number of joint departments were set up in areas where the work of the two diplomatic departments overlapped. The unified department now covers the entire field of Britain's external relationships while preserving the special association with Commonwealth countries and making provision for dealing with the affairs of the remaining dependent territories. In accordance with these requirements a Commonwealth Co-ordination Department and a Dependent Territories Administration Division have been incorporated in the new Foreign and Commonwealth Office. Otherwise, the departments within the office are based upon rational, geographical groupings with the addition of functional diplomatic departments which are concerned with issues affecting more than one geographical department.

The Foreign Secretary first emerged as a minister in his own right in 1782 when the work of the two Secretaries of State (q.v.) was re-allocated, the Secretary for the Northern Department becoming the Secretary of State for Foreign Affairs. He has always been one of the most senior ministers in the Cabinet and following the merging of his office with that of Secretary of State for Commonwealth Affairs, he is now concerned with the formulation and conduct of the whole range of external policy and is responsible for the diplomatic service and British missions overseas. He maintains direct contact with the diplomatic representatives of foreign and Commonwealth states and he is also responsible for Great Britain's relationship with the United Nations. He is assisted by one Minister of State (q.v.) and three Parliamentary Under-Secretaries of State.

The Minister's salary is £8,500 per annum plus an additional £1,250 if he sits in the House of Commons. The last peer to hold office as Foreign Secretary was the Earl of Home who was appointed in 1960. A debate on the principle of appointing a peer to this vital office took place on 28 July 1960.

A chronological list of Foreign Secretaries appears as Appendix 17.

In other Commonwealth countries the parallel office to the Secretary of State for Foreign and Commonwealth Affairs is usually styled

'Minister for External Affairs'. In Canada this minister is known as the Secretary of State for External Affairs.

FOURTH CLERK-AT-THE-TABLE

See CLERK OF THE OVERSEAS OFFICE.

FRANCHISE

In the United Kingdom the franchise is enjoyed by all British subjects and citizens of the Republic of Ireland who have reached the age of eighteen (reduced from twenty-one in April 1969), the only other qualification required being one of residence. A person must be registered as an elector for the electoral district in which he or she resides in order to exercise the right to vote. Each elector has one vote, plural voting (i.e., the exercise of a business or a university vote in addition to a residential vote) having been abolished by the Representation of the People Act, 1948. A British or Irish adult is entitled to be registered as an elector if he or she is resident in any constituency upon a 'qualifying date'. The Act of 1948 substituted a 'qualifying date' for the 'qualifying period' which had applied previously, although an exception was made in the case of Northern Ireland. In order to prevent citizens of Eire from influencing an election by obtaining the franchise merely by establishing residence in Northern Ireland on a qualifying date, the qualifying period has been retained, and continuous residence for a period of three months is a condition of eligibility.

Apart from minors and aliens, persons falling into the following categories are also ineligible for the franchise:

Peers. Peers are prohibited by the Common Law of Parliament from voting at a parliamentary election although they appear to be under no statutory prohibition. However, a peer who disclaims his peerage under the Peerage Act, 1963, acquires the status of a commoner and becomes eligible for the franchise.

Persons of unsound mind. A certified lunatic is automatically disqualified, but other such persons may vote during lucid intervals.

Felons. A person sentenced for treason or felony to a term of imprisonment exceeding twelve months is disqualified until the sentence has been served or a free pardon granted.

Persons convicted of corrupt or illegal practices. A person convicted on indictment of corrupt or illegal practices in connexion with elections is ineligible to vote for five years from the date of conviction.

There are certain variations in the electoral systems of the other countries of the Commonwealth, some of which are noted below.

Canada. Canadian citizens and other British subjects of both sexes who have been ordinarily resident in Canada for twelve months preceding the election are entitled to vote. Certain persons are disqualified, including the Chief and Assistant Chief Electoral Officers, the Returning Officer in each district (who is, however, permitted a casting vote should the occasion arise), and every judge appointed by the Governor-General-in-Council. In 1960 the right to vote in federal elections was extended to all adult Indians. Previously Indians ordinarily resident on a reserve had been disqualified unless they had served in the armed forces or had waived their right to exemption from taxation. In October 1969 it was announced that legislation would be introduced to lower the voting age from twenty-one to eighteen. The voting age has already been reduced in most of the Canadian Provinces for the purpose of provincial elections.

Australia. All persons who have lived in Australia for six months continuously and who are natural born or naturalized subjects of the Queen are entitled to vote. Both enrolment and voting are compulsory except for the aboriginal natives of Australia who, nevertheless, were given the right to vote by an Act of 1962.

New Zealand. All Europeans other than aliens who have been resident in New Zealand for one year and in an electoral district for three months, and all Maoris who have resided in any of the four Maori electoral districts for three months, are entitled to the franchise. There are separate electoral rolls for both races, a person of mixed race having the right to decide whether to register as a European or a Maori. Registration, but not voting, is compulsory. New Zealand enjoys the distinction of being the first British country to confer the vote upon women. Women were enfranchised in 1893. In 1969 the voting age was reduced from twenty-one to twenty.

India. All Indian citizens are eligible to vote. Referring to universal adult suffrage in India in his book, *The Constitution of India,* G. N. Joshi writes: 'Its importance and significance can be easily appreciated when it is remembered that under the Constitution Act of 1935 hardly 14 per cent of the population was enfranchised, while under this Constitution more than 50 per cent of the population is enfranchised. When it is also remembered that 85 per cent of the population is illiterate, its significance is further emphasised. Reliance on the sound common sense of the masses is the basis of this great liberal step. It is a bold and hazardous experiment in a country where democracy is not yet firmly rooted in the soil.'

Ceylon. Since 1949 the franchise has been based on citizenship and residence, adults of both sexes being eligible. The property and literacy qualifications which were required before Ceylon gained independence no longer apply. An Act of 1959 reduced the voting age from twenty-one to eighteen.

The principle of 'one man, one vote' has in general been adopted in the other countries of the Commonwealth, except in the predominantly Moslem Northern Region of Nigeria where, prior to the imposition of

K [279]

military government, the vote was limited to adult males and in Rhodesia, where the franchise depends upon a complex system of educational and income qualifications and two separate voters' rolls. Malawi and Zambia formerly made provision for the special representation of European minorities. In Pakistan the right of the individual to vote was exercised through a system of 'basic democracies', institutions of local government which themselves elected the President, the National Assembly and the Provincial Assemblies, in the manner of electoral colleges. Certain Commonwealth countries have shown a constitutional instability which makes a discussion of their electoral systems somewhat difficult. In Cyprus, for example, the representative balance between the Greek and Turkish communities provided for in the Constitution has been negated by the secession of the Turks from the Legislature and the Government. The union between Tanganyika and Zanzibar to form the Republic of Tanzania does not appear to have involved the adoption of a common electoral system.

(For the history of the franchise *see* REPRESENTATION.)

FRANKING PRIVILEGES

In 1660 Members of Parliament were given the privilege of sending their letters post free by signing their names on the cover. When the postage on a letter was 10*d.* to 1*s.* 6*d.* this privilege was sometimes abused by members signing packets of covers for their friends, and by 1837 nearly seven and a half million letters so franked were sent out during the year, involving the Post Office in a loss of over one million pounds. Members did not confine their franking privilege to letters. Furniture, and even a pack of hounds, were held to be covered by it, while an Irish member franked his wife and family on a holiday from Galway to Dublin and back. At the end of the 18th century the daily allowance to members of both Houses was limited to ten letters sent by a member and fifteen received by him with postage to pay. Franking was abolished on the introduction of the penny post in 1840, but in these days a member has such a heavy volume of correspondence that there has been some agitation for the revival of the privilege. Members may send letters to government departments post free by marking them 'O.H.M.S.'

In the Parliaments of Ceylon and Malaysia postage is free on official correspondence, while in New Zealand members have free franking on all letters posted from Parliament Buildings during the session and £7 a month towards other postal services. Canadian Members of Parliament enjoy virtually unrestricted franking privileges during parliamentary sessions.

FREEDOM FROM ARREST

See PRIVILEGE.

FREEDOM OF ACCESS TO THE SOVEREIGN
See PRIVILEGE.

FREEDOM OF SPEECH
See PRIVILEGE.

FRONT BENCHES

In the House of Commons and other Commonwealth Parliaments where applicable, the Front Bench as far as the centre gangway on the Government side (to the right of the Speaker) is occupied by ministers and other members of the Government. This is sometimes referred to as the 'Treasury' Bench. On the other Front Bench sit the Leaders of the Opposition—the 'shadow cabinet'. The distance between the two Front Benches in the House of Commons is traditionally said to be two swords' lengths. The distance referred to is probably that between the two white lines behind which Front Bench Members sit. In Newfoundland and Prince Edward Island the Government side is to the left of the Speaker.

The Government Front Bench is reserved by custom, but only by custom, for members of the Government. On 23 November 1960 this privilege was invaded by Dame Irene Ward, who occupied a seat on the Government Front Bench in protest against the Government's inaction in improving the lot of certain categories of pensioners.

FUEL AND POWER, MINISTER OF
See POWER, MINISTER OF.

G

GAMBIA HOUSE OF REPRESENTATIVES

The Gambia (Constitution) Order in Council, 1954, which came into operation on 8 September 1954, marked a considerable advance in responsible government in the Gambia. It established a Legislative Council consisting of the Governor, a Speaker appointed by the Governor, 4 *ex-officio* members, 1 nominated official and 2 nominated unofficial members, 4 elected members to represent the Colony and 7 to represent the Protectorate, and 3 other elected members. The new legislature, which had a life of six years, was the first to have an elected, as distinct from an unofficial, majority. It had the usual legislative powers, subject to the Governor's reserve powers. The first session was opened on 14 December 1954. As a result of the Governor's recommendations, the Secretary of State for the Colonies approved further constitutional changes in September 1959. These changes provided for an increase in the membership of the Legislative Council (renamed the House of Representatives in 1960) to 34, including 7 elected members from the Colony and 20 from the Protectorate. Of the 20, 8 were elected by the Chiefs and 12 by universal adult suffrage which had previously been confined to the Colony area. The 5 official and 2 nominated unofficial members remained as before. The Executive Council consisted of 4 official and not fewer than 6 unofficial members, presided over by the Governor. Not more than 6 members of the Executive Council ranked as ministers, of whom not fewer than 3 had portfolios.

Following a constitutional conference held in July 1961, which recommended a wide measure of internal self-government, a new Constitution came into force after elections held in May 1962. It increased the House of Representatives to 39 members, presided over by an elected Speaker. Of these, 32 members were elected on the basis of universal adult suffrage and 4 were elected by Chiefs. Two further members, without votes, could be nominated by the Governor, and the Attorney-General was also a non-voting member. The Executive Council consisted of the Governor as President, a Premier, and not fewer than 8 ministers drawn from the House. The Governor remained responsible for internal security, external affairs, defence and the public service but otherwise acted in accordance with the advice of the Executive Council. Full internal self-government was introduced on

[282]

4 October 1963. The Premier became Prime Minister, the Executive Council became the Cabinet and certain aspects of external affairs and security were delegated to ministers.

The Gambia became a fully independent member of the Commonwealth on 18 February 1965, and a republican Constitution was adopted following a referendum held on 24 April 1970. An earlier referendum in 1965 had failed to produce the two-thirds majority necessary to effect a change in the Constitution. The republican Constitution makes provision for a President with executive responsibilities and his election is linked to that of the House of Representatives so that presidential and parliamentary elections can take place simultaneously.

GENERAL ASSEMBLY

The term which continues to apply to the single-chamber Parliament of New Zealand despite the abolition of the upper House in 1950. The chamber itself is known as the House of Representatives.

GENERAL ELECTIONS

See ELECTIONS.

GENTLEMAN USHER OF THE BLACK ROD

The Gentleman Usher of the Black Rod is an officer of the House of Lords whose parliamentary appointment dates from the reign of Henry VIII. By the constitution of that Sovereign he was to be chief of all the Ushers of the Kingdom and have care and custody of all the doors of the 'High Court called the Parliament'. Since that time he has been appointed from time to time by letters patent conferring upon him all the 'privileges, fees, etc., rights and liberties whatsoever now or heretofore belonging or appertaining to the Usher of the Black Rod as one of the Officers of the Garter'. The ancient decree establishing the office says it must be filled by 'a gentleman famous in arms and in blood'. Therefore it is traditionally bestowed on retired naval or military officers. The autobiography of Sir Brian Horrocks, *A Full Life*, published in 1960, reveals some interesting information concerning the origin of the appointment of Black Rod:

The appointment goes back to 1361 when Edward III founded the Order of the Garter. The first holder of this office was a certain William Whitehorse who received the not inconsiderable salary of twelve pence per day for life. He walked in front of the Sovereign carrying on his shoulder the Black Rod. . . . If anyone offended against the Order of the Garter it was the duty of the Gentleman Usher to tap him on the shoulder with the Black Rod, whereupon the offender was expelled and William Whitehorse received £5. . . .

Such is the continuity of things in this country that the Gentleman Usher of the Black Rod still walks in front of the Sovereign during the Garter ceremonies which are held annually at Windsor. (pp. 287-8.)

Attendance at the Garter ceremonies is Black Rod's only surviving Court function, and the only duty he is required to undertake in addition to his parliamentary responsibilities. The official dress of the Gentleman Usher of the Black Rod is a black cut-away tunic, knee-breeches, silk stockings, silver-buckled shoes, a sword, and a cocked hat carried under the left arm. He is so called because of the short ebony rod of office surmounted by a golden lion rampant which he carries in his right hand.

He or his deputy, the Yeoman Usher, is present whenever the House sits, and he controls the admission of strangers. If occasion were to arise he is the officer responsible for the commitment of parties guilty of breach of privilege or contempt. He also assists at the introduction of peers. Black Rod's salary (1970) is £4,390.

It is the Gentleman Usher of the Black Rod who, in accordance with ancient custom, is sent to desire the attendance of the Commons in the House of Lords at the Opening and Proroguing of Parliament. On every such occasion the ancient ceremony is repeated of barring the door of the Commons Chamber in his face until he has rapped three times with his ebony rod, in which a sovereign is embedded. The practice dates from the stormy period of English constitutional history when the Commons often dreaded interruption, particularly from a Royal Messenger, in which capacity Black Rod comes, and it is intended to demonstrate the right of the Commons to close their doors and deliberations against all comers if they so wish. When the door of the House of Commons is opened to admit him an Usher precedes him to the Bar and cries: 'Black Rod!' The Speaker rises to receive the message from the Sovereign but the members retain their seats. Black Rod slowly advances to the Table and during his progress bows three times to the Chair. On reaching the Table he says: 'The Lords Commissioners desire the immediate attendance of this honourable House in the House of Peers'. When the Sovereign is present in person in the House of Lords the message runs: 'The Queen commands this honourable House to attend Her Majesty immediately in the House of Peers.' Having delivered the message Black Rod retires backwards to the Bar, bowing as he goes, where he awaits the Speaker and escorts him, followed by the ministers and other members of the Commons, to the House of Lords.

Prior to the passage of the Royal Assent Act in 1967 a similar ceremony took place whenever the Royal Assent was signified to Bills. Upon Black Rod's arrival the Commons were obliged to suspend whatever business they happened to be engaged in while the Speaker led a procession of members to the Bar of the House of Lords to hear the Royal Assent signified to Bills by three Lords Commissioners. These interruptions caused considerable inconvenience to members as they frequently took place when important debates were in progress, and for the member holding the floor at the time the arrival of Black Rod was particularly galling.

On 13 April 1960 an unfortunate incident arose out of the observance of this ancient ceremony. Black Rod arrived at the House of Commons with his summons at a moment when an extremely heated debate was in progress on the Government's announcement of the abandonment of the Blue Streak missile. Members protested very strongly against the interruption, and Black Rod was unable to make his voice heard above the tumult. The Opposition, with the exception of their Leader and Chief Whip, remained in their places, as the procession made its way to the House of Lords, as an expression of their indignation. On the return of the other members, points of order were immediately raised as to the right of Black Rod to enter the Commons Chamber without the consent of the House, and the Speaker undertook to seek advice as to the constitutional position.

A further protest was registered on 5 August 1965 when Black Rod arrived to deliver his summons to the Commons some twenty minutes before Parliament was due to rise for the summer recess. A group of members not only remained in the Chamber but continued to debate the issue under discussion, notwithstanding the Speaker having left the chair, as a demonstration against what one of their number, Sir Geoffrey de Freitas, described as a 'ludicrous exercise'.

In December 1966 the Lord Privy Seal announced that arrangements were under consideration to remove the inconvenience which Black Rod's summons so frequently caused. The new procedure, which would involve legislation, would provide for the retention of the ceremony at prorogation and on at least one other occasion during the session. At other times the announcement of Royal Assent to Bills would be made without ceremony by the Lord Chancellor in the House of Lords and the Speaker in the House of Commons.

In 1967 this undertaking was given effect with the passage of the Royal Assent Act. On 10 May 1967 it received the Royal Assent in the traditional manner, and on that day Black Rod probably made his last historic journey between the Lords and the Commons, the first and last days of a session excepted.

GEORGE I (1660–1727) AND PARLIAMENT

King George I was proclaimed in his absence on 1 August 1714, the day of the death of Queen Anne. Whatever his personal failings may have been, George was in every respect a constitutional monarch who, unlike so many of his predecessors, observed the rights and liberties of the people and refrained throughout his reign from infringing the privileges of Parliament. His first action upon coming to the throne was to dismiss Bolingbroke, who had favoured a Stuart restoration, from the office of chief minister, and to appoint a new Whig administration headed by Townshend, Stanhope, and Walpole. He created an important precedent in government by forming his great officers of state into a Sovereign's council, a body which has developed into the Cabinet (q.v.) of the present day. Parliament readily voted £700,000 for the Civil List, thus continuing the income which the Crown had enjoyed during the previous reign, and on 31 January 1715 Parliament was dissolved, having continued the statutory six months beyond the death of the former Sovereign.

The political sympathies of the King were revealed early in his reign, and at the ensuing elections he threw all the influence he could command on to the side of the Whigs, who won a decisive victory. From these elections, the first of the reign of the first Hanoverian monarch, dated a long period of Whig ascendancy. The new Parliament met on 17 March and the King's speech was read by the Lord Chancellor, His Majesty being unable to speak English. The speech promised to uphold the Constitution and the established Church and criticized the Peace of Utrecht. The latter was roundly condemned in subsequent debates in both Houses of Parliament, and a committee was appointed by the government to investigate the activities of the previous ministry which had conducted the peace negotiations. As a result of the committee's findings, Oxford and Bolingbroke, the leaders of the previous administration, were impeached of high treason. The latter fled the country (although he was permitted to return some years later) but the proceedings against Oxford were subsequently dropped.

In anticipation of a Jacobite rising Parliament passed the Riot Act in the session of 1715. A rising was, in fact, attempted during that year but was easily suppressed and its leaders were executed. In view of the state of public agitation which prevailed, the government decided to introduce the Septennial Act, feeling their position too insecure to risk the elections required under the Triennial Act of 1694. Although it met with heated opposition, the Bill passed both Houses by large majorities. To enable the King to go abroad, Parliament in 1716 repealed without opposition one of the clauses of the Act of Settlement (q.v.). Ministerial changes also took place at this time as a result of Townshend having lost the King's favour. Stanhope was appointed chief minister and Townshend, Walpole, and Pulteney resigned in consequence.

In 1717 Convocation was prorogued by the Government as a result of violent disputes precipitated by the Low Church Bishop Hoadly of Bangor. Hoadly, the author of a famous tract against the non-jurors, was supported by both the King and his ministers but condemned by a majority in Convocation, which was not again summoned until 1852. In 1718 the Schism Act and the Occasional Conformity Act were both repealed. The most important measure of the 1719 session was the Peerage Bill, which was rejected by the Commons by a substantial majority. Its purpose was to deprive the King of his prerogative of unlimited creation of peers, and was designed to prevent the son of George I, in the event of his succeeding his father, from overthrowing the Whig administration by the creation of sufficient Tory peers. The King, who was antagonistic to his son, was only too ready to relinquish his prerogative and substantial inducements were offered to the Commons in order to secure the passage of the measure, but to no effect. The proposal was unquestionably unconstitutional, aimed as it was at establishing a permanent majority in the House of Lords for the Stanhope ministry, and if carried it would have turned the upper House into 'an almost unchangeable body, entirely beyond the control of King, or Minister or Commons' (Lecky). Amongst legislation passed during the session of 1719 was a Bill enabling the Parliament at Westminster to legislate for Ireland, a measure which was to remain in force until 1782.

In 1720 the nation was rocked by the collapse of the disastrous South Sea scheme, a catastrophe from which Walpole was able to snatch a personal triumph. The shock of the South Sea Bubble proved fatal to Stanhope, who died from a heart attack brought on whilst delivering a passionate reply in the House of Lords to the Duke of Wharton's attack upon himself and his administration. Aislabie, the Chancellor of the Exchequer, was expelled from the House of Commons and committed to the Tower for bribery and corruption in connexion with the South Sea scheme. Sunderland, although declared innocent of any corrupt activities, became so unpopular that he was compelled to resign. In the midst of the chaos Walpole took office as First Lord of the Treasury and Chancellor of the Exchequer, and through his great financial ability he restored the public credit. Thus in 1721 Britain's first Prime Minister, as he became in fact if not in name, began the phenomenal rise which was to place him for twenty-one years at the head of the administration. The King reposed such great confidence in Walpole that he withdrew from Cabinet meetings, where he was in any case severely handicapped through his inability to speak the English language, and left his chief minister to preside over the Sovereign's council. To preside over the Cabinet is to-day an automatic function of the Prime Minister.

Further Jacobite agitation occurred in 1722, and the House of Commons, incensed by the conspiratorial activities of the Pretender's supporters, exceeded the limits of parliamentary privilege by committing to prison the proprietor of a Jacobite newspaper for an alleged libel. There was no question of any breach of privilege or contempt

K*

of Parliament having been committed, and in arrogating to itself the right to punish a purely political offender the House of Commons gravely overstepped the bounds of its authority.

In 1725 the Lord Chancellor, the Earl of Macclesfield, was impeached on charges of corruption and judgment was given against him after a trial lasting some twenty days. During the same year difficulties arose in the realm of foreign affairs resulting from a treaty concluded between Austria and Spain. Hostilities were begun which dragged over the next two years, and shortly after peace was concluded the King died suddenly whilst returning to England from Hanover on 9 June 1727. George I's great virtue as a ruler was his moderation, but he failed to endear himself to the nation, to which he was very much an alien. He never troubled to learn the language and his frequent visits to Germany tended to make him unpopular in England. His German mistresses, together with the other foreigners he introduced into his Court, were notorious for their corruption and resented by the people. The King himself had no personal graces to help him win the popular affection. But it can be said that the national institutions were effectively safe-guarded under his rule, and the Constitution and the Church were never threatened as they had been so often in the past.

GEORGE II (1683–1760) AND PARLIAMENT

The second monarch of the Hanoverian dynasty succeeded to the British throne on the death of his father, 9 June 1727. He immediately named Sir Spencer Compton (afterwards Lord Wilmington) as his Prime Minister, but the influence of Walpole was such that Compton declined to form a Government. On the advice of Queen Caroline, the King agreed that Walpole should continue in office, and one of the chief minister's first acts of the new reign was to persuade Parliament to increase the Civil List by the substantial figure of £130,000 to the unprecedented sum of £830,000. Before being dissolved Parliament passed the first annual Bill of Indemnity for failure to observe the Test and Corporation Acts.

The first elections of the reign returned a great majority for the Government to the House of Commons, and Parliament was opened on 11 January 1728. Arthur Onslow (q.v.), the greatest and most famous occupant of the Chair of the House of Commons, was unani-mously elected Speaker. With its huge majority the Government had no difficulty in carrying its proposals, and although Pulteney, for the Opposition, strenuously attacked Walpole on various issues, Parlia-ment on the whole was remarkably docile.

The reporting of parliamentary debates became a major issue at this period. Parliament had always regarded the reporting of its proceedings as a flagrant breach of privilege, but the popular demand for informa-tion on the activities of the nation's legislators had induced certain publishers to issue surreptitious reports for public consumption. In 1728 the publisher Edward Cave was summoned to the Bar of the House of Commons, confined for several days, and rebuked for suffering reports of parliamentary proceedings to appear in the *Gloucester Journal*. The following year Cave's friend Robert Raikes was censured for the same offence. On this occasion the House of Commons unanimously resolved that the publication of its debates and proceedings was a breach of privilege and that offenders would be proceeded against with the utmost severity. The forbidden reports continued to be compiled, however, and appeared in the *Gentleman's Magazine*, started by Cave in 1731, and in the *London Magazine*, which was started shortly afterwards. The matter reached a climax in 1738 when an important debate took place in the House of Commons at the instigation of Speaker Onslow. The debate showed that, far from moderating its views on the subject, the attitude of the House had, if anything stiffened. Both Walpole and Pulteney roundly condemned the practice of reporting parliamentary debates, and amongst all the members, Sir William Wyndham, a leading Tory, was alone in supporting the right of the public to know more of what went on inside Parliament. The debate concluded with the unanimous resolution 'That it is a high indignity to, and a notorious breach of the privileges of, this House to print the debates or other proceedings of the House, as well during the recess as the sitting of Parliament, and that this House will proceed with the utmost severity against such offenders'. Far from being discontinued, however, the practice became even more widespread. (For further details *see* HANSARD *and* PRESS AND PARLIAMENT.)

In 1729 was concluded the Treaty of Seville, a defensive alliance between England, France, Spain, and subsequently Holland, in the negotiation of which William Stanhope was largely instrumental. Britain's difficulties with Spain were to a great extent adjusted by the treaty, but it greatly displeased the Austrian Emperor as it alienated both England and Spain from the Emperor and represented a diplomatic triumph for France. Gibraltar had proved a controversial issue in Anglo-Spanish relations, and the Government was known to have considered the cession of the territory in return for a satisfactory equivalent. Public opinion was strongly opposed to cession and parliamentary debates on the subject were frequent and heated. As the Treaty of Seville made no mention of Gibraltar, Spain was considered to have renounced her claims. In view of the treaty the Emperor realized the necessity of strengthening his own position, and in 1731 he concluded the second Treaty of Vienna with England, Spain, and Holland. Under it, England guaranteed the Pragmatic Sanction, which secured the hereditary succession of the states of Austria in the female line, thus enabling Maria Theresa to succeed her father, Charles VI.

In 1730 the final breach occurred between Walpole and Townshend.

They had frequently quarrelled, the former's jealousy of personal power causing him to resent bitterly any suggestion of rivalry. The friction between the two ministers was brought to a head by the Pension Bill, a measure which sought to disqualify the recipients of pensions from sitting in Parliament. The Government was opposed to the Bill, but it was strongly supported in the House of Commons where Walpole allowed it to pass, leaving Townshend to incur the unpopularity for its rejection by the Lords. This issue precipitated a violent quarrel between the two ministers which resulted in Townshend's resignation from the Government in the realization that the influence of his colleague was too powerful for him. Instead of joining forces with the Opposition Townshend retired altogether from public life. He was succeeded as Secretary of State by Stanhope, who had been created Lord Harrington. In the same year Carteret resigned the office of Lord-Lieutenant of Ireland to join the Opposition and become one of Walpole's chief opponents.

The year 1733 was notable for two of Walpole's most important financial schemes. The first was a proposal to apply money from the Sinking Fund, a fund which should properly have been reserved for the discharging of debts, to purposes of expenditure. The scheme was opposed by Pulteney and others, and the precedent set proved to be a bad one as it led eventually to the total absorption of the Sinking Fund. In consequence the country's debts were never diminished until the Sinking Fund was restored and reorganized by the younger Pitt. The proposal was carried mainly because Walpole threatened a land tax if it was rejected. The second of Walpole's measures was his famous excise scheme. It was eventually abandoned by its author in order to avert what would have amounted to a riot had it been pushed through. Although Walpole justified his scheme in a masterly speech in which he gave illustrations of the type of tax evasions which had lately been practised and which the scheme would have frustrated, excise duties were so thoroughly detested in the country that he failed to convince his opponents of the merits of the proposal.

The elections of 1734 returned Walpole's party to power but with a considerably reduced majority. The session of 1735 was a barren one from the point of view of legislation, but the 1736 session was notable for a number of measures, including a Gin Act, which sought to reduce drunkenness by the imposition of a prohibitive duty, the repeal of the inhuman Witchcraft Act, a measure for the better lighting of the streets of London which had suffered severely through lawlessness, and a Mortmain Act. A Bill for the relief of Quakers passed the Commons with the support of Walpole but was rejected in the Lords. It was at this period that Walpole lost the support of the Dissenters, who for a long time had looked to him for the removal of the legal disabilities under which they suffered. When asked point-blank when the time of the Dissenters' emancipation was to come, Walpole alienated himself from them with his one-word answer, 'Never!' To do him justice, Walpole in actual fact had considerable sympathy for the Dissenters, as was shown by his support for the Quakers' Bill. But in openly championing their cause he felt he would be embarking upon a hopeless struggle, and he was particularly anxious to avoid offending the Church.

The Porteous riots in Edinburgh in 1736 led to the introduction of a vindictive measure in 1737 providing for, amongst other punitive action, the abolition of the city's charter. So fierce was the opposition to the Bill, however, that when it was eventually passed it had been stripped of its worst features and merely disabled the Provost from holding any public office in the future. Walpole's famous Playhouse Bill, which was supported by the Opposition, was also introduced in 1737. It was strongly opposed by Lord Chesterfield, who delivered one of his most brilliant speeches in condemning it, predicting that it would prove to be the ruin of liberty. While there is no doubt that the scandal and indecency which were paraded on the stage had reached outrageous proportions, there is also little doubt that Walpole and his fellow members were strongly motivated by their own objections to being savagely lampooned. The Lord Chamberlain retained his powers under the Act until their abolition in 1968.

The opposition to Walpole's policies and to the minister personally had by now grown very strong. The Prince of Wales threw all the weight of his influence against the Prime Minister, and the Opposition was headed by a group of the Prince's closest associates, including Pulteney, Carteret, Chesterfield, Bubb Dodington, the Grenvilles, and the rising William Pitt, who were collectively known as the Leicester House Party. Early in 1737 the Prince came to an open rupture with his father in the matter of his income, which he demanded should be fixed by Parliament. In the House of Commons Pulteney moved that the King should be petitioned to settle an annual income of £100,000 upon the Prince. Walpole replied that he was authorized to offer only £50,000 together with the revenues of the Duchy of Cornwall. In the subsequent division Walpole secured a majority of only 30. A similar motion in the Lords by Carteret was rejected by a much larger majority. After failing to get his own way in the matter of his income the Prince of Wales proceeded to widen the breach between himself and his parents still further by removing his wife, Augusta of Saxe-Coburg, who was in the throes of childbirth, to the Palace of St. James's, which had been standing empty and unaired. The action was callous in the extreme, and the King never forgave his son. When Queen Caroline, shortly afterwards, was on her deathbed, the Prince implored to be allowed to see her but the King curtly refused the request and the Queen herself expressed no wish to see her son.

Walpole's policy of peace was particularly unpopular with the

Opposition, and when he concluded a convention with Spain strong voices were raised against him. The English and Spanish governments were entitled by treaty to search each other's ships, and many were the complaints lodged by British merchants against the alleged abuses of this right on the part of the Spaniards. The case of 'Jenkins's ear' (Jenkins was the master of a trading vessel who asserted that his ear had been torn off by Spaniards searching his ship) enflamed the public indignation, and much was made of the incident by the forces opposing Walpole. Nevertheless the convention was approved in both Houses, although by very small majorities. In the Commons the most vehement speech for the Opposition came from Pitt, who was rapidly coming to the fore as a leading opponent of Walpole. In the Lords an address was carried to the Crown complaining of Spanish atrocities. Feeling against Spain ran very high. The King himself favoured going to war, and even one of Walpole's own colleagues, the Duke of Newcastle, shared the King's view and secretly intrigued against the Prime Minister. It was thus in a most dangerous and difficult atmosphere that Walpole fought hard to maintain peace. As a result of the unpopular ministerial victory the Opposition took the extraordinary course of seceding from the House of Commons in a body. Wyndham, in taking his leave of the House, spoke so strongly that Pelham rose to move his committal to the Tower, but Walpole interposed and sought instead to hold his opponents up to ridicule, remarking that his only fear was that they would fail to be as good as their word and would return, as indeed they did. During the absence of the Opposition the Government carried all its measures without difficulty, but the mood of the country was such that Walpole realized that he must either declare war on Spain or be forced to resign. Against his own better judgment he yielded to the wishes of the King and the nation, and in 1739 England went to war with Spain. It was a disastrous war for England and proved to be a vindication of Walpole's foreign policy.

By this time Walpole's power was unquestionably on the decline. Government measures continued to be carried, but by steadily diminishing majorities, and there were many who sought to blame him for all the nation's misfortunes. His time had not yet come, however, and an attempt to overthrow him in 1741 proved unsuccessful. In this year a motion was introduced in the Commons for Walpole's dismissal on various grounds, including his conduct of the war. Fierce attacks were delivered against the Prime Minister by Pitt and Pulteney, and able speeches were made in his defence by Pelham and Fox. But it was his own powerful speech which was largely instrumental in saving the day for Walpole. The motion against him in the Commons was rejected by a large majority, and a similar motion by Carteret in the Lords was also lost. But although temporarily reprieved, Walpole's fall was not to be long delayed.

[292]

The elections of 1741 returned a Government majority of only 16 to the House of Commons. Parliament was opened on 1 December and Walpole's first defeat occurred when the Opposition secured the election of their candidate as Chairman of Ways and Means. There followed a succession of acrimonious debates on the election petitions, which at that time were regarded as purely party issues and were heard and decided in Committee of the Whole House. It was on the Chippenham election petition that Walpole was finally overthrown, but before this occurred he survived another powerful attack upon himself and his administration. In January 1742, Pulteney moved that certain papers relating to the war should be referred to a Secret Committee. The debate developed into a bitter battle during which it emerged that the real intention of the Opposition was to bring accusations against the Prime Minister. In a speech which was a masterpiece of invective Walpole lashed his opponents and ridiculed their charges. Yet he was able to muster a majority of only three.

Walpole's defeat on the Chippenham election petition is a typical illustration of how, in politics, great men can be brought down on trivial issues. In the final decision on the petition he was defeated by 16 votes and he immediately resigned all his offices. He was shortly afterwards created Earl of Orford with a pension of £4,000 a year, much to the resentment of his enemies. On tendering his resignation he advised the King to send for Pulteney, who declined office on account of a condition that no charges should be pressed against Walpole. Lord Wilmington was then invited to form a Government. His administration included Carteret, who swiftly became its virtual leader, Newcastle, Hardwicke, Pelham, and Grafton. Pulteney entered the Cabinet but without office, and his elevation to the Lords shortly afterwards lost him much of his influence. One of the first acts of the new administration was the prosecution of Walpole and a Secret Committee was appointed to inquire into Walpole's administration for the past twenty years. It failed to substantiate any major charges against the former Prime Minister although the committee itself was riddled with prejudice against him. He was spared the further triumph of his foes and in 1745, three years after his fall, he died. A great and shrewd statesman, Walpole served the best interests of his country for twenty critical years. To his discredit it has been said that he lowered the tone of public life and descended to corruption in order to gratify his lust for power, but it is for his ability and his services to the nation that he is best remembered.

In 1743 Parliament passed the Place Bill, which disqualified the holders of certain offices from sitting in Parliament. In the same session the Gin Act, which had never been successful, was repealed and a modified measure passed in its stead. Lord Wilmington died in July and Henry Pelham was appointed First Lord of the Treasury in his place. The following year Pelham headed the so-called Broad-bottom Administration which was formed after the resignation of Carteret, now Earl Granville, as Secretary of State. Granville regarded Pelham with extreme contempt and his obstructive tactics had caused the Government considerable embarrassment. He was popular with the King on account of his unqualified support of all measures in the Hanoverian interest, but he became increasingly unpopular with Parliament and the people as a result. The time came when the King was reluctantly compelled to choose between Granville and Pelham, and he was obliged to accept the former's resignation. The Broad-bottom Administration received the support of all parties and for some years the Opposition was reduced to insignificance. Two developments had taken place which united all factions, with the exception of the extreme Tories. The first was the war with France over the question of the Austrian succession into which Pelham had been compelled to lead the country, and the second was the renewed activities of the Jacobites. Heavy supplies were voted to meet the emergency and the Habeas Corpus Act was suspended for two months. In May 1745, the English sustained a defeat at the hands of the French at Fontenoy, and this reverse gave heart to the Jacobites and encouraged the famous rebellion in Scotland. On 25 July the Young Pretender landed in Scotland and was joined by Lochiel and other Highland chiefs. He defeated an English army at Prestonpans and then invaded England. He took Carlisle and advanced as far as Derby, after which he was compelled to retreat northwards. He reached Glasgow and was victorious at Falkirk, but he was finally overwhelmed and defeated at Culloden. Although the Pretender escaped, Culloden had sealed the fate of the Jacobite cause. The rising was followed by severe punitive measures against the Highlanders.

At the height of the rebellion a ministerial crisis occurred as a result of the King refusing to admit Pitt to office. Pelham resigned and Granville was called upon to form a Government. When he failed to do so the previous ministers were recalled and the King was forced to give way and accept Pitt.

In 1748 the Treaty of Aix-la-Chapelle brought the war to an end. The French King agreed to recognize Maria Theresa as Empress of Austria and to exclude the Pretender from France. The treaty was followed by some important legislation. Subsidies were voted on behalf of the Empress and the German princes, and the annual Mutiny Act was amended by the addition of a clause subjecting all half-pay officers and men at home to martial law. The latter measure provoked violent controversy, and the Government was forced to abandon a similar amendment to the Marine Mutiny Act, thus causing a glaring inconsistency between the two services. The session of 1749 was also notable for a financial scheme devised by Pelham for reducing the interest on the National Debt, and a Bill for the protection of ship-wrecked vessels which made the plunder of ships in distress a capital offence.

On 20 March 1751 the Prince of Wales died, and a Regency Act was passed appointing a council of regency, with the Princess of Wales as regent should the King die before the heir apparent should come of age. The chief measure of the 1751 session was the reform of the calendar according to a scheme drawn up by Lord Chesterfield and others. The new style of calendar was adopted under which the legal year would begin on 1 January instead of 25 March.

A curious incident occurred during the session of 1751 which did not redound to the credit of the House of Commons. A certain Alexander Murray was summoned to the Bar of the House to receive sentence for an alleged offence arising out of a disputed election. On being ordered to kneel down as the custom required, Murray steadfastly refused, protesting that he knelt only to God. The entry recorded in the Journal of the House of Commons relative to the episode reveals the deep displeasure of the House at Murray's behaviour:

Resolved, That it having been resolved by this House that the said Alexander Murray should receive, upon his Knees, at the Bar of this House, the said Sentence of this House against him; and he having, in a most insolent and audacious Manner, at the Bar of this House, absolutely refused to be upon his Knees, as required by the said Resolution, is guilty of a high and most dangerous Contempt of the Authority and Privilege of this House.

The House ordered that Murray should be committed a close prisoner to Newgate, should be denied the use of pen, ink, and paper, and that no person should be permitted to have access to him. Murray's case aroused much public sympathy for the victim and led to the suppression of the humiliating custom. In 1772 it was abolished by Standing Order.

Several important measures became law in the session of 1753. The Marriage Act framed by Lord Hardwicke had as its object the prevention of clandestine marriages. Although it put an end to a great deal of abuse it was gravely resented by the Dissenters as it provided that, with the exception of Jewish and Quaker marriages, no marriage should be valid unless solemnized according to certain formalities by an Anglican clergyman. The Jews' Naturalization Bill, a magnanimous measure, passed both Houses but was so vehemently opposed in the country that the Government was forced to repeal it the following year. A great event of the year was the founding of the British Museum, the funds for which were raised by means of lotteries under an Act of Parliament.

In 1754 the Government sustained a great loss through the death of Pelham. When the King heard the news he is said to have exclaimed,

'Now I shall have no more peace!' and the next few years of inefficient administration justified the prophesy. The Duke of Newcastle became the head of the Government and formed an administration largely drawn from the peerage. Pitt was later offered a seat in the Cabinet on the condition of his supporting the Government, but he declined and was dismissed from the office of Paymaster of the Forces. Shortly afterwards Fox became Secretary of State and leader of the House of Commons. When Parliament resumed in November 1755, one of the longest debates on record took place in the House of Commons on the subsidy treaties with Russia and Hesse. On this occasion the Member for Petersfield, William Gerard Hamilton, delivered the brilliant oration which earned for him the nickname of Single Speech Hamilton. A powerful speech against the Government was contributed by Pitt, who struck particularly at the coalition between Newcastle and Fox. The coalition was soon to be broken, however. In 1756 England entered into an alliance with Prussia and went to war with France over the rival ambitions of the two countries in India and North America. The Seven Years War began in Europe, and in the midst of these grave developments a ministerial crisis was precipitated at home. Fox broke with Newcastle, who was compelled to resign office, and Pitt's great opportunity had arrived. The Duke of Devonshire became Prime Minister and Pitt was appointed Secretary of State.

Various measures were passed in the session of 1757 to meet the emergency caused by the war, and in the same year the King took the ill-advised step of dismissing Pitt, against whom he had always entertained feelings of antagonism. His action was probably influenced by his displeasure at the attempts of Pitt to save Admiral Byng, who had recently been executed for his conduct in the face of the enemy which had resulted in the capture of Minorca by the French. The King was soon to realize his mistake and Pitt was not long out of office. For three months the country, although plunged into war, was without a Government while the Duke of Newcastle strove in vain to form a ministry. Eventually the King was compelled to accept Pitt, who was reinstated as Secretary of State in a Government nominally headed by Newcastle, and which included Granville, Legge, Holderness, Temple, and Grenville. Pitt's great rival Fox joined the Government in an inferior office and without a seat in the Cabinet. For all practical purposes Pitt was the head of the administration and he began to prosecute the wars in which England was engaged with great energy and earnestness. In 1757 the victories of Clive in India gave the country cause for rejoicing, and the conquest of Quebec by Wolfe in 1759 which established Canada as a British dominion was the culminating success of a year of brilliant British victories in all theatres of operation. The prestige and influence of Pitt were now at their height. He was held in the highest esteem by Parliament and the nation, and was referred to as 'the Great Commoner'.

At this period of national triumph and rejoicing the country lost its Sovereign. King George II died on 25 October 1760. His private failings were numerous, but as a monarch he behaved in a constitutional manner throughout his reign. In his relations with Parliament and his use of the Royal Prerogative history records little for which he can be reproached. Although lacking in regal qualities he knew how to discharge the duties of a constitutional ruler, and his reign, in the words of Lord Stanhope, 'left the dynasty secure, the constitution unimpaired, and the people prosperous'.

GEORGE III (1738–1820) AND PARLIAMENT

George III succeeded to the throne upon the death of his grand-father, George II, on 25 October 1760. His reign, which in length and eventfulness is second only to that of Queen Victoria, opened a new phase in the parliamentary history of the United Kingdom. George III came to the throne determined to regain for the Crown that power which it had lost since the Revolution of 1688, and which, under his two predecessors, had been completely surrendered to the politicians. The first two Georges had leaned heavily on the support of the great Whig families, and it was the influence of this faction that the young George III resolved to break. By disregarding the party system and choosing his ministers without considering their political connexions he believed he could attain his object. But in order to destroy the Whig oligarchy which for so long had been in the ascendancy he was com-pelled to throw in his lot with the Tories, thus removing himself from the position of constitutional monarch and becoming little more than a party leader, the slave of the very machine he was bent on breaking. George III believed in the unlimited exercise of the Royal Prerogative, and although he earnestly desired to use his power solely for the good of the state, his methods proved that despotic rule is the only alternative to party government. It was an inevitable consequence of King George's policy that the government should be placed in the hands of his personal friends and that he should attempt to exert a personal influence on Parliament which led to the wholesale dismissal of office holders who incurred his displeasure by failing to vote in accordance with his wishes. In the first ten years of the reign the struggle between the King and the politicians was so intense that no less than seven ministries were formed. The Crown and the ministry became two distinct and often opposite influences: the patronage of the former was no longer at the disposal of the latter; and the monarch assumed a rôle unfamiliar to contemporary generations.

George III's accession was heralded with popular acclamation. He was the first truly English Sovereign of the Hanoverian dynasty, and his issue of a proclamation against profaneness and immorality (one of his first acts as King) was received with general approval. It was well known that the King conducted his own life according to the moral principles he expressed. His speech on opening Parliament in November 1760, in which he stated that he gloried in the name of Briton and expressed his concern for the welfare of his people, made a highly favourable impression on both Houses. Supplies were voted amounting to £20 million and the Civil List was fixed at £800,000, the King surrendering the branches of the hereditary revenues. In March of the following year Speaker Onslow (q.v.) retired after thirty-three years' occupancy of the Chair of the House of Commons.

The young King was greatly under the influence of the Earl of Bute, whom he appointed to the Privy Council two days after his accession. The King was determined to get rid of the ministers he had inherited from the previous reign and to establish his favourite at the helm. In March 1761 Holderness was persuaded to resign as Secretary of State and Bute was appointed in his stead. Bute strongly advised the King to make peace with France, but realizing that such a step would meet with the strongest opposition from Pitt he conspired with the King to remove Pitt from the Cabinet. Pitt for his part was earnestly entreating his colleagues to declare war on Spain, which power was making preparations to join with France, but finding himself supported by only one other minister he felt himself compelled to resign, and he left the Government on 5 October.

The elections which took place in March and April of 1761 were the most corrupt which had ever been held, and the sale of boroughs on a widespread scale may be dated from these elections. Seats were openly sold to the highest bidder and one was even publicly advertised for sale. The new Parliament met on 3 November 1761 and Sir John Cust was elected Speaker. The Duke of Newcastle was still nominally Prime Minister, and although he had been persistently snubbed and cold-shouldered by the new King he had continued to cling to office. Finding that he was never consulted in matters of policy or patronage he was eventually constrained to resign in June 1762. The King immediately made Bute his Prime Minister, and other changes in the Government took place at the same time, George Grenville becoming Secretary of State and Francis Dashwood Chancellor of the Exchequer. Acting on Bute's suggestion and hoping to divide the Whigs, the King persuaded Henry Fox to take over the leadership of the House of Commons.

Peace was signed at Fontainebleau in November and the Treaty of Paris was formally concluded on 10 February 1763. Those who had opposed the peace soon found themselves the victims of Bute's vindictiveness. The Dukes of Newcastle and Grafton and the Marquis of Rockingham were deprived of their lord-lieutenancies, and the Duke of Devonshire, who resigned the office of Lord Chamberlain, was struck off the list of the Privy Council by the King's own hand. Even the most inferior officials were penalized by dismissal, and the King's policy assumed the appearance of a persecution of the Whigs. Bute had by this time become extremely unpopular in the country, and Dashwood's budget did little to improve the popularity of the administration. Additional wine duties and a tax on cider, a favourite drink of the poorer classes, were imposed, and it is interesting to record that the passage of the Cider Bill through the House of Lords was the occasion for the first division on a Money Bill to take place in the upper House. The conduct of the Government generally and Bute's oppressive tactics in particular aroused such popular hostility that on 7 April 1763 the Prime Minister suddenly resigned, and with him Dashwood and Fox. George Grenville became First Lord of the Treasury and Chancellor of the Exchequer and Lords Halifax and Egremont were made Secretaries of State, the three being collectively known as the Triumvirate. Bute, however, continued to wield a powerful influence behind the scenes.

Shortly after the formation of the Grenville Ministry there occurred the first of a number of incidents which secured a place in history for John Wilkes, the notorious libertine and possibly the strangest champion of liberty Britain has ever produced. Wilkes first entered Parliament in 1757 when he bought himself a seat at Aylesbury. In 1761 he started his paper, the *North Briton,* in which he fearlessly attacked authority and aroused much public antagonism towards Bute. On 23 April 1763 there appeared the famous issue, No. 45, in which the King's speech was fiercely assailed. Grenville had Wilkes arrested on a general warrant, a warrant on which no names were specified but which authorized the arrest of any persons suspected of or connected with the offence in question. He was examined by Halifax and Egremont and afterwards committed to the Tower, but moving for a writ of *habeas corpus* he was brought before Chief Justice Pratt, who ordered his release by reason of his privilege as a Member of Parliament. When Parliament met in November Wilkes complained of his imprisonment during the recess, but the House of Commons resolved that No. 45 constituted a 'false, scandalous and seditious libel' and that parliamentary privilege did not confer immunity upon the authors of such libels. The issue was brought to a head during Wilkes's absence from the House (he had been ordered to attend in his place but had been wounded in a duel), and after fierce debates he was expelled from the House by unanimous vote. Wilkes, undaunted, proceeded to bring an action for damages against the Government for illegal imprisonment, at the same time instigating similar proceedings on behalf of the forty-eight other persons arrested with him under the general warrant. All the plaintiffs obtained favourable verdicts. The court declared that general warrants were illegal and the Government paid out thousands of pounds in damages. Authority obtained its revenge on Wilkes shortly afterwards by prosecuting him for the publication of his 'Essay on Woman', an obscene parody of Pope's 'Essay on Man'. Anticipating that the judgment would go against him Wilkes absented himself from England during the trial, and he was found guilty and outlawed whilst abroad. For the time being Wilkes retired from the scene, but history had by no means finished with him, and his withdrawal from public activity was to be but temporary. Shortly after the trial a debate took place in the House of Commons on the subject of general warrants. It was a debate which should never have taken place, for in attempting to decide a question of law the House was openly usurping the function of the courts. In spite of the ruling by Chief Justice Pratt in Wilkes's case, a resolution endorsing his view that general warrants were illegal was defeated by the Government by a majority of 14.

In September 1763 important changes took place in the Government as a result of the death of Lord Egremont. Lord Sandwich was appointed Secretary of State and the Duke of Bedford was persuaded to accept office as President of the Council, the coalition thus formed becoming known as the Bedford–Grenville Ministry. In 1764 the disastrous policy was initiated which was eventually to cost Great Britain her American Colonies. Grenville decided that the colonists should be called upon to contribute something to the cost of the late war, and without consulting them in the matter he imposed duties on a number of articles of American trade. In the following session he introduced the Stamp Bill, which imposed more or less the same duties in America as those which were in force at home. The Bill passed through Parliament with little opposition, but there was a violent reaction on the part of the colonists, who took their stand on the principle of no taxation without representation. They were supported in their view by Pitt, whose warmth of feeling on the subject inspired him to one of the most powerful orations he ever delivered when the House met in January 1766. Whilst upholding the right of the English Parliament to legislate for the Colonies, he maintained that taxation without representation was illegal and called for the repeal of the Stamp Act. Influenced by the force of Pitt's arguments the Government did repeal the Stamp Act, and simultaneously brought in a Bill asserting the power of Parliament to make laws for the Colonies. A further Bill repealed or modified some of the duties imposed in 1764, and all three measures were carried after spirited debates.

Prior to these events the King suffered the first attack of the mental affliction which was ultimately to reduce him to insanity, and upon his recovery in 1765 it was deemed advisable to introduce a Regency Bill. The King desired that the power of appointing a regent should rest with him, but fearful of the influence of Bute, who was a favourite of the Dowager Princess of Wales, the Government persuaded the

King to consent to a clause limiting his choice to the Queen and the descendants of the late King, warning him that otherwise the Commons might exclude the Dowager Princess by name. When the Bill came before the Commons, far from behaving as Grenville had predicted they voted by an overwhelming majority to include the Princess's name, and such was the chagrin of the King that the incident led to the fall of the Bedford–Grenville Ministry. The King turned to Pitt, but the latter was not prepared to enter a Government which excluded Lord Temple, who in turn was loyal to Grenville, and the King had no alternative but to place the administration in the hands of the Marquis of Rockingham, the leader of the Whig aristocracy. Two of the new Government's first actions received popular approval, the repeal of the cider tax and the endorsement of a resolution declaring general warrants to be illegal, but it was so inherently weak that it fell in July 1766. Once again the King approached Pitt, who this time agreed to join a Government as Lord Privy Seal and accepted elevation to the peerage as the Earl of Chatham. The Duke of Grafton was the nominal Prime Minister but the real power lay in the hands of Chatham. The Government was a strong one and included Townshend as Chancellor of the Exchequer, Northington as Lord President, Camden as Lord Chancellor, and Conway and Shelburne as Secretaries of State. At the time of the formation of this ministry a critical situation developed due to the scarcity of corn, and to avert public disorder Chatham issued his famous Order in Council imposing an embargo on corn and detaining in port a number of ships which were laden with grain and ready to sail. In spite of the crisis Chatham did not put forward the meeting of Parliament, and when both Houses assembled in November he was vigorously attacked both for issuing the Order in Council and for his delay in calling Parliament together. The first action he defended on the ground of national necessity, and his lack of action in the second instance he justified by the need to avoid creating alarm. Shortly after these difficulties Chatham was stricken with a strange illness and was compelled to withdraw from public life. Grafton became Prime Minister in fact as well as in name, and the Government, deprived of the influence and wisdom of the first statesman of the age, reverted to the disastrous American policy which had been initiated by Grenville. A Bill for taxing American imports was introduced by Townshend, who died in September 1767 before its full effects became apparent, and another Bill was passed prohibiting the legislature of New York State from passing any legislation until the American Mutiny Act had been complied with, this measure having been overruled by the local legislators. Townshend was succeeded as Chancellor of the Exchequer by Lord North.

The first Parliament of George III was now drawing to its close, the final session being notable for a measure introduced by Sir George

Savile, a leading member of the Opposition, commonly known as the *Nullum Tempus* Act. Its purpose was to protect the property of a subject after sixty years' possession from any ancient claim on the part of the Crown, and so strongly was public opinion in favour of it that it passed without difficulty.

Parliament was dissolved on 11 March 1768, and the elections which followed were, if anything, more venal than those of 1761. Seats were bought and sold openly and shamelessly, a borough fetching a price between £4,000 and £5,000. So flagrant was the practice of bribery that in several instances the authorities were unable to overlook it and punitive action was taken against certain offenders. Amongst the members returned to the Parliament of 1768 were the irrepressible Wilkes and a newcomer of outstanding ability, John Dunning. Although proscribed as an outlaw Wilkes had returned to England, had offered himself and been rejected as a candidate for the City of London, and had stood for the county of Middlesex, which elected him by a large majority. In spite of his dubious character his exploits in the name of freedom had won him an overwhelming popularity with the masses, and the cry of 'Wilkes and liberty!' was frequently heard. His outlawry was reversed by the Court of King's Bench, but on the original charge against him he was sentenced to a fine and imprisonment. He petitioned the House of Commons against his imprisonment on the ground of his privilege as a member. He also wrote a scurrilous attack upon Lord Weymouth, one of the Secretaries of State, in the form of a letter, for which the House of Lords might with justification have proceeded against him, but instead the Commons impulsively decided to take action, and in consideration of his offences both past and present they resolved upon Wilkes's expulsion from the House. The unconstitutional nature of the expulsion was realized by a number of Wilkes's contemporaries including Edmund Burke and George Grenville, both of whom opposed the resolution. Wilkes had been called to account for all his offences save that against Lord Weymouth, in respect of which it would have been proper to prosecute him in the courts. Nevertheless the resolution for his expulsion was carried by a large majority. He was immediately re-elected for Middlesex, but on the day following his re-election the Commons resolved by 235 to 89: 'That Mr. Wilkes, having been in this session of Parliament expelled the House, was, and is, incapable of being elected a Member to serve in this present Parliament.' The election was declared void and a new writ issued. Wilkes was again re-elected and the process was repeated. A fourth time Wilkes was returned, and although he was this time opposed by three other candidates (one of whom polled no votes at all) his majority was overwhelming. The Commons again declared Wilkes's election to be null and void, and by 197 to 143 they declared the second candidate, Luttrell, who had polled 296 votes against Wilkes's 1,143, as the lawfully elected member. The electors of Middlesex petitioned the House against the return of Luttrell, but although they were supported in their arguments by Burke, Grenville, and Wedderburn, Luttrell's election was confirmed by a majority of 69.

By now the issue had become a *cause célèbre*, affecting not merely the merits or demerits of Wilkes's own claim as an individual, but the far wider principle of the right of the electors to return a candidate of their own choosing. Wilkes's personal popularity increased to such an extent that he became an alderman of the City of London and a subscription was raised to pay his debts. In 1770 Lord Chatham denounced the resolution of the Commons as denying to the subject his common right and depriving the electors of Middlesex of their free choice of a representative, and Lord Chancellor Camden described the proceedings as 'a direct attack upon the first principles of the Constitution'. In the Commons Dunning, Savile, and Dowdeswell espoused Wilkes's cause, and motions were introduced with the object of reversing the decision against him, but without success. The matter was again raised in the upper House when Lord Rockingham moved a resolution similar to one introduced by Dowdeswell in the Commons, but the Lords took the view that the Commons enjoyed a complete jurisdiction in the matter of elections and that interference on the part of the upper House would amount to a breach of the privilege of the lower. Rockingham's motion was lost, but forty-two peers, including Chatham, signed a protest against its rejection. Over the next four years the struggle continued to be waged in both Houses. The City of London petitioned the King for a dissolution of Parliament and the removal of his 'evil ministers', complaining that 'the majority of the House of Commons have deprived your people of their dearest rights'. The King denounced the petition as 'disrespectful to himself, injurious to Parliament, and irreconcilable with the principles of the Constitution', and a joint address of both Houses rebuked the City for its action. Chatham defended the petitioners and the right of petition, and having moved unsuccessfully for a dissolution, he introduced a Bill to reverse the judgment of the Commons which was defeated by a large majority. In 1771 Chatham again brought forward a motion to dissolve Parliament, and in the lower House Savile on three successive occasions, in 1772, 1773, and 1774, attempted to introduce a Bill safeguarding the rights of electors.

In 1774 Parliament was dissolved and Wilkes was once again returned for Middlesex. This time he was permitted to take his seat as his disqualification from membership lasted only for the duration of the previous Parliament. Determined to vindicate the rights of himself and his electors he moved in 1775 that the resolution against him be expunged from the Journal as 'subversive of the rights of the whole body of electors'. He secured 171 votes in support of his motion, which he renewed unsuccessfully in 1776, 1777, 1779, and 1781. At last in 1782 his efforts were crowned with success and his motion was carried by 115 votes to 47. All previous orders and resolutions relating to his election for Middlesex were expunged by order of the House, and a great constitutional battle had been won. Long before his final victory in this issue Wilkes scored a signal success, upholding another constitutional principle arising out of the reporting of parliamentary debates. Parliament had always regarded the reporting of its proceedings in the Press as a breach of privilege, and when in 1771 a number of printers were arrested by order of the House, Wilkes, who was at the time an alderman of the City of London, seized the opportunity of forcing the issue to a head. The struggle, which led amongst other incidents to the committal of the Lord Mayor of London to the Tower, brought little glory to Parliament, and its outcome amounted to a tacit acceptance by both Houses of the right of the people to know something of the activities of their legislators. (For fuller details of this matter *see under the heading* PRESS AND PARLIAMENT.)

To return to the year 1768: Chatham's ill-health compelled him to retire from the Government altogether, a factor which was to have a profound effect upon the course of history. In 1769 the Duke of Grafton proposed in Cabinet the total repeal of all import duties imposed upon America, but was defeated by one vote. Had Chatham's health been spared the result might have been different. Lord Chancellor Camden would also most probably have supported Grafton's proposal, but he had ceased to attend Cabinet councils on account of the Government's American policy and its actions in the matter of Wilkes's election, and in January 1770 he too withdrew from the administration. Later in the same year Grafton, unable any longer to carry on the work of government in the face of extreme difficulty, resigned office, and Lord North became the head of the Government in his stead. North's administration was a long and ignoble one, principally notable for its disastrous American policy. North himself was little more than the King's instrument, but in fairness to his memory his qualities of intellect, moral character, and good nature should not be overlooked. He had not long been in office before Chatham accused him of being under the domination of Bute and spoke of a power behind the throne greater than the throne itself. The ministry of Lord North, in which he himself held office as First Lord of the Treasury and Chancellor of the Exchequer, included Earl Gower as Lord President, the Earl of Halifax as Lord Privy Seal, and Lords Sandwich, Rochford, and Hillsborough as Secretaries of State. Later Sandwich became First Lord of the Admiralty and Grafton replaced Halifax as Privy Seal.

In 1770 Grenville carried his Bill for the trial of controverted elections, a measure which aimed at improving the methods by which the House decided such questions. Prior to the Grenville Act election petitions were decided in Committee of the Whole House and were regarded as purely political issues. Grenville's measure provided that the function should be taken over by a committee consisting of 13 members chosen by a somewhat complicated system of ballot and selection, and although it did little to remove election questions from the political arena it effected a practical improvement which was a step in the right direction. Grenville died shortly afterwards, thus removing one of the Government's leading opponents from the parliamentary scene.

In the same year Chatham raised the subject of parliamentary reform, predicting that if Parliament did not reform itself from within it would be reformed with a vengeance from without. Some years previously he had described the borough representation as the rotten part of our Constitution, and he now proposed a strengthening of the county representation as a first step towards reform. Sixty-two years were yet to elapse before the more flagrant abuses in the system of representation were corrected by the Reform Bill, but a great deal more was to be heard on the subject before the close of the reign of George III.

In 1772 the passing of the Royal Marriage Bill provided that no descendants of George II could contract a legal marriage without the consent of the reigning Sovereign until reaching the age of twenty-five. The Bill imposed the further conditions that no royal marriage could take place unless twelve months' notice of the intention to marry had been given to the Privy Council and the marriage had not been petitioned against by Parliament. Charles James Fox resigned his office as Junior Lord of the Admiralty to oppose the Bill. When it was carried he rejoined the Government as a Junior Lord of the Treasury in 1773, only to be removed at the instance of the King in 1774.

By 1774 matters in America had reached a crisis. It is true that in 1770 the Government had partially repealed the American import duties but the tax on tea had been retained. On 16 December 1773 the people of Boston seized the cargoes of three tea ships which lay in the harbour and pitched them into the water. The reaction of the home Government was to pass the Boston Port Bill, a punitive measure closing the port until such time as order should be restored and compensation paid for the destruction of the tea. Simultaneously another measure was passed withdrawing the constitution of Massachusetts, whose Assembly had called for a congress of the American Colonies and the removal of its governor. Both Acts severely antagonized the colonists, who held their proposed congress at Philadelphia and passed resolutions condemning the principle of taxation without representation, calling for the repeal of the recent measures against them, and suspending all trade with the mother country until their demands had been met. In the same year a General Election was held in Britain, which resulted in victory for the Government, who owed much of their support to the popular indignation which had swept through the country following the destruction of the tea cargoes. The City of London, however, petitioned on behalf of the colonists, and early in 1775 Chatham moved in the House of Lords that steps should be taken to improve the situation in America. Speaking with passionate eloquence he forecast that if the Government did not voluntarily retract from its position they would ultimately be compelled to do so, and the prestige of the Crown would suffer in consequence. His motion was supported by Camden and Shelburne but was lost by 68 votes to 16. Nevertheless he introduced a Bill for settling the troubles with America along the lines he had proposed, but this also was rejected by 61 to 32 votes. In the House of Commons Burke moved a series of resolutions directed towards the same end, but they were lost by 270 votes to 78.

Hostilities finally broke out in April 1775, when the battle of Lexington was fought, and on 4 July 1776 the thirteen Colonies met in congress and issued the Declaration of Independence. Soon after the outbreak of the war the Duke of Grafton resigned from the Government in protest against Lord North's American policy. Further harsh measures against America were passed by the Government and were so deplored by the Whig Opposition that in 1776 they ceased, for a time, their attendance in the House of Commons. In 1776 and again in 1777 Chatham repeated his attempts to bring about a cessation of hostilities, but his inspired oratory failed to move the majority of his fellow peers. A similar attempt in the Commons, moved in the form of an amendment to the address, was heavily defeated in spite of the efforts of Burke and Fox. By 1778 the Government began to appreciate the need for conciliation, and three measures were introduced repealing the tea duty, renouncing the claim of Parliament to tax the Colonies, and restoring the constitution of Massachusetts. But it was too late to attempt to turn back the clock. America was determined to secure her independence and was not prepared to compromise. Later in the year the Duke of Richmond moved in the upper House for the recognition of American independence, and it was during the course of this debate that Chatham collapsed in his last illness while addressing the Lords. One month later, on 11 May, the greatest statesman of the age passed away.

In this same session Savile, seconded by Dunning, brought in a Bill for the relief of Roman Catholics which both Houses passed unanimously. The Bill removed only the more oppressive disabilities, yet it was sufficient to stir a group of extremists, led by the fanatical Lord George Gordon, into provoking the serious disturbances known as the Gordon Riots. In the following session of 1779 a Bill for the relief of Dissenters, under which schoolmasters and ministers were no longer obliged to subscribe to the Thirty-nine Articles, also passed through both Houses.

In 1780 the subject of economic reform claimed the attention of Parliament. This contentious issue, involving as it did the much-resented power and influence of the Crown, had become one of great concern within the country, and Parliament found itself faced with strongly supported petitions emphasizing the necessity for reforms and complaining of the elaborate system of Crown patronage and the corrupt means by which it was maintained. In the Lords Shelburne moved for an inquiry into the public expenditure and in the course of the debate Lord Rockingham revealed the extent to which the Government was dominated by the influence of the Crown. The subsequent action of the King in dismissing two peers from their lord-lieutenancies for supporting Shelburne's motion went far towards substantiating Rockingham's assertion. Three days after the debate in the Lords, Burke placed before the House of Commons his famous scheme of economic reform, its main proposals being a reduction of offices, improvement of financial administration, diminution of the pension list, and the payment of all pensions at the Exchequer. The scheme was defeated by 233 votes to 190. Two months later, however, Dunning was successful in carrying his notable resolution against the power of the King, and by 233 votes to 215 the House of Commons affirmed 'That the influence of the Crown has increased, is increasing, and ought to be diminished'. A second resolution asserting the right of the House of Commons to correct the abuses in all branches of the public expenditure including the Civil List, and a third affirming the duty of the House in securing redress of the grievances complained of in the petitions, were carried without divisions. The Speaker, Sir Fletcher Norton, himself endorsed the truth of the resolutions. The King was highly incensed at these proceedings in the lower House, but the Commons had done no more than give voice to a rising tide of public opinion which was to mark the beginning of the decline of the political power of the Crown.

To revert to the matter of parliamentary reform: in 1776 John Wilkes proposed a scheme providing for the abolition of 'rotten' boroughs, the enfranchisement of the big industrial cities of the Midlands and the North, and the improvement of county representation, and embodying most of the other principles advocated by reformers before and after. His motion for leave to bring in a Bill giving effect to this scheme was negatived without a division. In 1780 the Duke of Richmond raised the issue in the Lords by introducing a Bill for establishing annual Parliaments, universal suffrage, and equal electoral districts. Richmond's attempt met with the same fate as Wilkes's, but in 1782 the cause was taken up by a man destined to match his father's greatness, the young William Pitt. Having drawn attention to the serious deficiencies in the system of representation he moved unsuccessfully for a committee of inquiry. In 1783 he moved resolutions directed against bribery and corruption at elections and proposing an increase in the representation of the counties and the capital. He managed to muster 149 votes in support of his resolutions against the majority of 293 which rejected them. Pitt's third and last effort in the cause of reform was made in 1785 shortly after he became Prime Minister, when he sought to introduce a Bill to amend the representation. It was rejected by 248 votes to 174 and he did not again revive the matter.

In 1782, following several determined moves to bring the American war to a close, Lord North resigned after twelve years at the head of a ruinous administration. When a resolution was carried branding as enemies to King and country all who should advocate a continuance of the war, North, realizing that the mood of the House was too strong for him to attempt resistance, announced that he was prepared to give effect to its views. Fox immediately denounced the principle of a minister remaining in office to implement a policy forced upon him by his opponents, and two motions expressing lack of confidence in the Government were introduced within a few days of each other and defeated only by very slender margins. Before another such attack could be launched Lord North had resigned. The King was now compelled, much against his will, to accept the Marquis of Rockingham as his Prime Minister. Rockingham stipulated as his conditions for taking office the concession of independence to America and the reform of the Civil List. His Government was a strong one, including Camden as Lord President, Cavendish as Chancellor of the Exchequer, Shelburne and Fox as Secretaries of State, and Burke and Dunning in lesser offices. The problem of the Civil List was first tackled, and legislation was introduced abolishing sinecure offices, reducing the pension list, and providing for the better control of expenditure. Measures were passed to correct certain electoral abuses, and the Government gave every indication of continuing as it had begun. Unfortunately, Rockingham died only three months after taking office and Shelburne became the head of the Government. Fox, Burke, and Cavendish all refused to serve under Shelburne and resigned their offices. Thomas Townshend took Fox's place as Secretary of State and William Pitt, at the age of twenty-three, became Chancellor of the Exchequer.

In 1783 the Treaty of Versailles was concluded between England, France, Spain, and the United States, under which Britain acknowledged the independence of America and ceded Pondicherry and other possessions in India back to France. The treaty was fiercely assailed by both Fox and Lord North, strange political bedfellows, who declared that it spelt disgrace and dishonour for Great Britain, and carried a vote of condemnation by 224 to 208. Shelburne thereupon resigned, and for thirty-seven days the country was without a Government. The King turned first to Pitt, who shrewdly declined to take office under circumstances which would have placed him at a distinct disadvantage, and in an endeavour to avoid the only alternative of a Fox–North coalition King George decided to bide his time in the hope that such an unusual political association might break down. Eventually the King was compelled to give way, and a coalition Government was formed under the Duke of Portland, with Lord North as Home Secretary, Fox as Foreign Secretary, and Cavendish as Chancellor of the Exchequer. The King's reactionary principles and his failure to appreciate the nature of his own constitutional position were never better revealed than in his conduct upon his new Government taking office. He informed Lord Temple that he would never repose his confidence in such a ministry and would seize the first opportunity which offered itself to get rid of them. He found, or made, his opportunity when Fox, whom he particularly detested, introduced his India Bill. The Bill passed the Commons, but the King instigated a campaign against it in the House of Lords, authorizing Lord Temple to state that whoever voted for the Bill was not only not His Majesty's friend but would be considered by him as an enemy. This unconstitutional behaviour drew indignant protests from the Commons and from a number of peers, including the Duke of Portland, but the Bill was nevertheless rejected by the upper House and the King dismissed the Government.

The King again applied to Pitt, who, judging that his moment had come, consented to form a ministry. On 23 December 1783 Pitt became, at twenty-four, Britain's youngest Prime Minister, at the head of a Government drawn from both parties with himself as First Lord of the Treasury and Chancellor of the Exchequer. He took office in the face of the most formidable opposition, led by Fox and North who for three months directed a bitter onslaught in the lower House against the Government with all the forces they could command. Yet this youthful statesman, whose acceptance of office had been received by his opponents with derision, by means of the most consummate political skill contrived to reduce the adverse majority against him to one, and to hold off a dissolution of Parliament until the time he accurately judged to be the most favourable to his party. Inspired by the unfailing ability and ingenuity of Fox, the Opposition attempted again and again to force the resignation of the Government by all the legitimate means at their disposal. Motions condemnatory of the Government were carried by clear, if not substantial, majorities. The Government's India Bill was thrown out; a motion for postponing the supplies was adopted; and the Mutiny Bill was held over. On 8 March 1784 a motion by Fox for a representation to the King on the state of the nation was carried by a single vote only, and on the 25th the King dissolved Parliament on his Prime Minister's advice. The elections which followed brought triumph for Pitt and bore testimony to the wisdom of his judgment. The Opposition were crushingly defeated, some 160 supporters of the Fox–North coalition losing their seats. The dissolution of 1784 has a significant importance in that it established the precedent of the ultimate appeal to the country in the event of a Government losing the confidence of the House of Commons. Unfortunately, the result of the election temporarily arrested the decline in the influence of the Crown for which Dunning's motion had pressed and which Rockingham's short administration had begun to bring about. The election was no less a victory for the King than it was for Pitt, and the former was only too ready to seize his opportunity to augment his personal power.

The new Parliament met in May and embarked upon a very full programme of legislation which included the reintroduction of the previously rejected India Bill, this time passed by a majority of 271 to 60. In one matter, however, Pitt failed to secure the approbation of the House in spite of his overwhelming party majority. At the General Election Fox had been returned for Westminster after a close and exciting contest, but the High Bailiff withheld the return in order to carry out a scrutiny of the votes. Such a scrutiny entailed an investigation into the qualifications of each individual voter, half the cost being defrayed by the Government and the other half by the candidate. The length of time it would take to conduct an inquiry of this sort was obviously so great as to have the effect of permanently excluding the elected candidate from Parliament, not to mention the likelihood of its bringing financial ruin upon him. The House of Commons sought to relieve Fox from his unenviable position by expediting the proceedings, but Pitt showed himself callously disinclined to come to the assistance of his rival. Fox, as it happened, had also been returned for Kirkwall and was therefore able to take his seat as the representative of this other constituency. The House made its views known by passing a vote of censure upon Pitt and also a Bill to prevent a recurrence of such a case.

The session of 1786 was notable for Pitt's reorganization of the Sinking Fund and the impeachment of Warren Hastings. The trial of Hastings before the House of Lords on twenty charges arising out of his activities during his governor-generalship of India began on 13 February 1788, in Westminster Hall. The principal managers of the impeachment included Fox, Burke, Sheridan, and Grey (afterwards Earl Grey of the Reform Bill). Much impressive eloquence, accompanied by suitable dramatic effect, was heard from these masters of oratory during the first days of the trial, which was to drag on for seven years. When Parliament was dissolved in 1790 Hastings and his friends hoped that the proceedings would be automatically dropped, but the House of Commons resolved otherwise and thus finally established the precedent that the proceedings upon an impeachment are not terminated by the prorogation or dissolution of Parliament.

Judgment was not pronounced until 23 April 1795, when Hastings was acquitted.

A number of attempts were made between 1787 and 1790 to relieve Dissenters by the repeal of the Test and Corporation Acts, but none succeeded. A motion by Fox in 1790 was opposed by Pitt and defeated by 294 votes to 105, after which the matter was not revived for many years.

The session of 1788 was notable for the vigorous efforts of Wilberforce and other reformers to suppress the slave trade. Wilberforce, who had the sympathy and support of Pitt, Fox, and Burke in his noble but thankless task, profoundly stirred the conscience of the Commons and the country in his campaign against the odious traffic, yet effective support for his aim was slow to accumulate. In 1791 a motion for abolition was lost in the Commons by 163 to 88, both Pitt and Fox voting in the minority. In 1792, however, the abolitionists were successful in carrying a Bill through the lower House only to see it meet with obstruction in the Lords. It was not until 1804 that Wilberforce managed to bring in another anti-slavery Bill, which was again passed by the Commons but rejected by the Lords. The following year, however, the Government took action of its own accord and introduced a modified form of prohibition, but it was not until 1807 that slavery was totally abolished by the General Abolition Act.

In 1789 the need for a Regency Bill again arose in view of a recurrence of the King's mental illness. Fox asserted the claims of the Prince of Wales to the appointment of Regent, but Pitt, knowing that one of the Prince's first actions upon assuming the power of sovereignty would have been to make Fox his Prime Minister, insisted that the Prince had no more right than any other subject except by decision of Parliament. The matter swiftly became a political issue, but the King's sudden recovery left the matter in abeyance.

Parliament was dissolved in 1790 and the elections brought another victory for Pitt, Fox having lost much popularity over his declaration of sympathy with the French Revolution. When Parliament met in 1791 the most important measure which came before the Houses was the Canada Bill. This enlightened piece of legislation, in providing for the administration of the territory, recognized for the first time the principle of independent representation within the Colonies. During the debates on the Bill Fox and Burke came to violent disagreement which led to a final rupture between the two friends, and during the short time he remained in Parliament Burke became a supporter of the Government. Two further notable measures of this session were Fox's Libel Bill, which passed the Commons without a division and became law during the following session, and a Catholic Relief Bill which considerably eased the disabilities pressing upon adherents of the Roman Church.

L   [311]

The last decade of the 18th century saw widespread activity in the cause of parliamentary reform. Whilst much of this activity was properly conducted and supported at a high level, a number of extreme movements arose and encouraged violence and disorder. These tumults, together with a threatening international situation which in 1793 led to war with France, drove the Government into introducing a series of measures for the suppression of popular liberties, to the dismay of the Opposition. The first serious disturbance occurred on 14 July 1791, the anniversary of the storming of the Bastille. Towards the end of 1792 the Government alleged that continued seditious practices had brought about such an enflamed and dangerous situation that it had become necessary to call out the militia. Fox and Sheridan condemned the Government's action, denying that such a situation existed, and when war was declared Fox moved a condemnatory resolution which was heavily defeated. In the upper House Lord Grenville introduced the Alien Bill which gave the Government control over foreigners and the power to remove them from the kingdom. It passed through both Houses and was followed shortly afterwards by a measure prohibiting any form of trade or correspondence with the French. In 1794, following a succession of vindictive prosecutions for treason and sedition, the Habeas Corpus Act was suspended. The following year a Treasonable Practices Act and a Seditious Meetings Act, two measures which drastically curtailed the rights and liberties of the subject, were passed in the face of furious opposition from Fox, Sheridan, and the minority supporting them. Such was the strength of the Government in both Houses that these unpopular measures were carried by over-whelming majorities. But the mood of the country, which had been reflected in the hostile demonstrations which had taken place when the King had opened Parliament in 1795, was very different. In 1797 Fox vainly moved for the repeal of the Treasonable Practices and the Seditious Meetings Acts, observing in the course of a powerful speech that 'liberty is order; liberty is strength'. Shortly afterwards the King struck Fox's name from the list of Privy Councillors with his own hand. Various measures restricting the activities of the Press became law during this decade, and a Bill passed in 1799 for the suppression of certain political organizations completed the Government's security programme.

In the meantime the moderate reformers had continued to advocate their cause. In 1792 an association calling itself the Society of the Friends of the People had been formed to promote parliamentary reform. One of the leaders of the movement was Grey, who in 1793 moved a resolution in the Commons calling for correction of the abuses in the electoral system. The society sought to achieve its objects by constitutional methods and entirely repudiated other contemporary organizations of a more virulent nature. Its activities were hampered by the Treasonable Practices Act which practically banned political discussion, but in 1797 Grey moved for leave to bring in a Bill largely similar to the great measure he was to carry successfully thirty-five years later. He was ably supported by Fox and Erskine, another leader of the society who distinguished himself in a remarkable speech, but the feeling of the House in the light of the current conditions caused the motion to be rejected by 256 to 91.

Important changes took place in the Government in 1794, the Duke of Portland and Lord Grenville becoming Home Secretary and Foreign Secretary respectively. Windham was made Secretary-at-War, and an additional office of Secretary *for* War was created to which Dundas was appointed. In 1795 Huskisson joined the Government as Under-Secretary for War, the young and promising George Canning was appointed Under-Secretary for Foreign Affairs in 1796, and Castlereagh became Secretary for Ireland in 1798.

In order to meet the heavy commitments imposed upon the country by the war, Pitt embarked upon a revolutionary financial policy in 1798 and 1799, and the latter year first saw the introduction of the income tax.

The outstanding legislative development of the year 1800 was the union of the two kingdoms of Great Britain and Ireland, an accomplishment which reflected no credit on either Pitt or Castlereagh, brought about as it was by means of the most scandalous system of bribery and intimidation. In fairness to Pitt it must be conceded that he earnestly believed that union offered the only solution to the turbulent problem of Ireland, and knowing that such a scheme had no hope of voluntary acceptance by the Irish themselves he was prepared to resort to highly distasteful methods in order to push it through, no doubt pacifying his conscience with the thought that the end justified the means. His proposals on the matter were carried by the British House of Commons by 149 votes to 24 and by the Lords without a division. They were eventually passed by both Houses of the Irish Parliament (q.v.) and legislation was prepared to embody the Articles of Union. The Bill received the Royal Assent in England on 2 July and in Ireland on 1 August. The Act came into operation on 1 January 1801 and the first Parliament of the United Kingdom of Great Britain and Ireland met on 22 January. As in the case of Scotland, the Irish Parliament ceased to exist with the coming into force of the Union, and although a substantial change in the constitution of the English Parliament was involved there was no prior dissolution. Ireland was represented in the House of Lords by 4 bishops sitting in annual rotation and 28 temporal peers elected for life by the Irish peerage, and in the House of Commons by 100 members. When Parliament met all members were required to take the oath afresh and a Speaker was elected as at the beginning of a new Parliament, the former Speaker, Addington, being re-elected.

Having effected the Irish Union Pitt resolved to follow it up by introducing measures for Catholic relief as a means of propitiating the Irish. The King, however, was staunchly opposed to such a proposal and Pitt found himself at serious variance with his Sovereign. Neither was prepared to give way on the issue and in February Pitt, who had the full backing of his Cabinet colleagues, resigned office after seventeen years of power. Addington succeeded Pitt as Prime Minister and formed a Government which was probably weaker and more ill-equipped to govern than any of its many predecessors. Addington, who had been an excellent Speaker, was no administrator, and although nominally Prime Minister he looked for guidance to Pitt, who did not formally hand over the seals of office until 14 March, some weeks after his resignation. The main event of the Addington administration was the negotiation of the Treaty of Amiens on 25 March 1802, which called a temporary halt to the war which had been dragging on since 1793. Pitt supported the peace without attempting to praise it, realizing that it offered the country no more than a much-needed respite. It is interesting to note that under the terms of the treaty the King of England renounced his ancient but meaningless title of King of France. Hardly more than a year elapsed before it became clear from the activities of Napoleon Bonaparte that England would soon be at war again. Pitt, who was fully aware of the Government's incompetence to deal with a situation calling for courageous and decisive action, went into opposition with Fox and Grenville. Addington, unable to withstand the powerful forces ranged against him, resigned and was created Viscount Sidmouth. One important measure passed during the Addington administration was the Act disqualifying clergymen from sitting in the House of Commons. It was passed in consequence of the return of Horne Tooke, the zealous campaigner in the cause of parliamentary reform who was prosecuted and acquitted on a charge of high treason in 1794, for the 'pocket' borough of Old Sarum.

Once again Pitt found himself at the head of affairs, but at a time when the country stood in vital need of a strong and determined Government the Prime Minister's attempt to form such a team was frustrated by opposition from the King. Pitt wished to include Fox and Grenville, but the King's hatred of Fox was so intense that he refused to have him in the Cabinet. Grenville declined to serve in a Government from which Fox was excluded, and Pitt was thus compelled to entrust high offices to second-rate men, many of whom had served under Addington. The formation of the new Government was completed in May 1804, with Pitt, the one tower of strength, holding his previous offices of First Lord of the Treasury and Chancellor of the Exchequer. He set himself to the task of prosecuting the war with characteristic vigour and resourcefulness, but he was an ailing man and his burdens pressed heavily upon him. In the session of 1805 he was sorely grieved when his great friend Henry Dundas, Viscount Melville, was impeached on charges of misappropriation during his term of office as Treasurer of the Navy. The motion for the impeachment was carried on the casting vote of the Speaker, Charles Abbot, the numbers in the division being equal. Pitt staunchly defended his friend's innocence but unfortunately did not live long enough to see him acquitted by the Lords. Melville's case is the last instance of an impeachment in the British Parliament.

Parliament was prorogued in July and the following October the country was able to celebrate Nelson's great victory at Trafalgar. The following December the allies suffered a terrible reverse at Austerlitz, and some weeks later, on 23 January 1806, Pitt died while travelling to London for the Opening of Parliament. The son of an equally great statesman, William Pitt the Younger possessed a natural genius for leadership which won him the confidence of the King, Parliament, and the country. Although unpopular at various times in his career all looked to him in times of stress and danger. He was every inch a man of Parliament, the natural progeny of the House of Commons, who could exert an influence over that unique institution which few statesmen have ever equalled. He brought great assets to the nation with his wise commercial treaties and his outstanding financial ability. It is one of the ironies of fate that a man possessed of such talents for promoting prosperity in peace should have gone down to posterity as one of our greatest political leaders in war. His brilliant career was cut off at the early age of forty-seven and at a time of national disaster which, it is said, went far towards hastening his end. His outstanding services to his country redeem his memory from those deeds, such as the means he employed to effect the Irish Union, which fail to reflect credit upon him.

Upon the death of Pitt, the King sent for Grenville, who insisted that any Government he should form must include Fox. The King assented to this condition, and the Ministry of 'All the Talents' was formed with Grenville as First Lord of the Treasury, Fox, Foreign Secretary, Erskine, Lord Chancellor, Grey, First Lord of the Admiralty, Sidmouth, Lord Privy Seal, Lord Henry Petty, Chancellor of the Exchequer, Lord Spencer, Home Secretary, and Windham, War and Colonial Secretary (the War and Colonial Departments having been united under one minister in 1801, a fusion which was to continue until 1854). The Lord Chief Justice, Ellenborough, was also appointed to the Cabinet, a highly unconstitutional proceeding though not without precedent. The House of Commons protested strongly against the appointment, contrary as it was to the principle of the separation of the judiciary from the executive.

Fox set himself the goal of restoring a real and lasting peace to Europe, but on 13 September 1806, before he could make any notable advances in his foreign policy, the great Whig leader died, surviving his rival Pitt by less than eight months. Grey, now Lord Howick, became Foreign Secretary, and shortly afterwards all hopes of peace were shattered when Napoleon issued his Berlin Decrees against Britain.

In 1807 the Grenville administration fell, like Pitt's Government before it, as a result of its stand on the issue of Catholic emancipation. The Army and Navy Service Bill proposed to relieve Catholics and Dissenters serving in the forces from their disabilities, but the King was adamantly opposed to such a measure and insisted that the Bill be withdrawn. The Government, however, refused to give an undertaking that the matter would not be revived, and was dismissed by the King. The one outstanding achievement of the Grenville ministry was the final abolition of the slave trade.

A new Government was formed under the Duke of Portland, with Spencer Perceval as Chancellor of the Exchequer, Canning, Foreign Secretary, Castlereagh, War and Colonial Secretary, Hawkesbury (later Lord Liverpool), Home Secretary, Eldon, Lord Chancellor, and Huskisson, Secretary to the Treasury. It immediately came under fire in both Houses for condoning by implication, in its acceptance of office, the unconstitutional dismissal of the previous ministry. A resolution in the Commons, 'That it is contrary to the first duties of the confidential servants of the Crown to restrain themselves by any pledge, expressed or implied, from offering to the King any advice which the course of circumstances may render necessary for the welfare and security of the empire', was lost by 258 to the large minority of 226. Perceval insisted that the King had acted without advice in his dismissal of the Grenville Government, but no modern constitutional authority would attempt to deny the responsibility of any Government which consented to take office in such circumstances, as the Sovereign cannot constitutionally act without advice.

Parliament had been dissolved in October 1806, during the period of Grenville's administration, and the new Parliament was therefore still in its first session. Nevertheless, the Government decided to go to the country again, thinking it prudent, in view of the King's hostility to Catholic emancipation, to take advantage of the anti-Catholic feeling prevalent in the country, and Parliament was dissolved on 27 April 1807. The elections provided the result the Government had hoped for, a large Tory majority being returned to the Commons. When the new Parliament met in June resolutions condemning the dissolution were heavily defeated in both Houses. In 1809 the weakness of the Duke of Portland brought about his resignation from the head of the Government and he was succeeded by Perceval. Lord Wellesley became Foreign Secretary, and two rising young statesmen were appointed to the Government, the twenty-four-year-old Lord Palmerston as Secretary-at-War and Robert Peel, at twenty-two, Under-

Secretary for the Colonies. In the session of 1810 the Government faced censure from the Opposition over the disastrous Walcheren expedition, an incident which had led to a serious breach and a duel between Castlereagh and Canning and the subsequent resignation of both ministers. In the same session the two leading political issues of the day, Catholic emancipation and parliamentary reform, were again raised. Motions in favour of both were decisively rejected in the Commons. A question of privilege arose which involved the Member for Westminster, Sir Francis Burdett, in conflict with the House of Commons over its commitment of a publisher for issuing an objectionable political placard. Burdett denounced the action of the House and was voted guilty of a breach of privilege and ordered for commitment to the Tower. He was arrested and imprisoned, having secured himself in his house for three days, and on his release at prorogation he brought actions against the Speaker and the Serjeant-at-Arms. The authority of the House was upheld in the Court of King's Bench and subsequently on appeal by the Exchequer Chamber and the House of Lords, but popular sympathy was on the side of the victim.

In the latter half of 1810 the King's insanity became permanent and a Regency Bill was passed, receiving the Royal Assent by commission on 5 February 1811. The Prince of Wales became Regent and, to the general surprise, made no change in the Government. A year later the Prince assumed the full powers of sovereignty, the original term for which the regency had been fixed having expired. The ten years of the regency were remarkable for great military victories abroad, including the final subjugation of Napoleon at Waterloo in 1815, and, at home, for bad government, civil violence, and agitation in the two notable causes of Catholic emancipation and parliamentary reform. In 1812 Grenville and Grey declined an offer to join Perceval's Government on account of their support for the Catholic emancipation movement. It was in this year that the movement, led by the noble-spirited Irishman, Henry Grattan, began to gain strength. Canning and Lord Wellesley, who resigned from the Government and was replaced as Foreign Secretary by Castlereagh, both espoused the cause. A motion by Canning in the lower House proposing that the laws imposing disabilities upon Catholics should be considered was carried by the unexpectedly high majority of 129, whilst a similar motion by Wellesley in the Lords was lost by only one vote. Supporters of Catholic emancipation came forward from the ranks of the Government itself, and in 1813 Castlereagh supported a motion by Grattan which was carried by a majority of 40. Grattan followed up his success by moving a far more definite resolution which was carried by an even greater majority. Thus encouraged, he introduced a Bill based upon his resolution which passed its second reading by 245 votes to 203, only to meet with obstruction and resultant abandonment in the committee

[317]

stage. Up to the time of Grattan's death in 1820 a number of further attempts were made in Parliament to relieve Roman Catholics, but all failed. Motions favouring parliamentary reform which were brought forward during this period came nowhere near the success which at first seemed to smile upon the cause of Catholic emancipation.

On 11 May 1812 Spencer Perceval was assassinated in the lobby of the House of Commons, and he was succeeded as Prime Minister by Lord Liverpool, whose administration continued for nearly fifteen years beyond the death of the ailing monarch. His Government as first constituted included Castlereagh as Foreign Secretary, Sidmouth, Home Secretary, Eldon, Lord Chancellor, Vansittart, Chancellor of the Exchequer, Palmerston, Secretary-at-War, and Peel, Secretary for Ireland. Liverpool's administration was to a regrettably large extent inefficient, repressive, and reactionary, producing extreme suffering for the poorer classes due to high food prices, unemployment, and trade restrictions, of which the most notorious example was the Corn Law of 1815. The domestic unrest to which Liverpool's policies gave rise was met with legislation of the utmost severity, including the suspension of the Habeas Corpus Act and the suppression or control of political clubs, debating societies, and public meetings. In 1817 Lord Sidmouth, who, as Home Secretary, was responsible for implementing the Government's stern domestic policy, issued a circular to all lord-lieutenants of counties authorizing magistrates to proceed against the authors and vendors of offensive publications under the Hawkers' and Pedlars' Act. The legality of the 'Sidmouth Circular' became a matter for discussion in both Houses, Lord Grey in the upper House and Samuel Romilly in the lower pointing out that the power thus given to the magistrates had not been conferred by statute or in any recognized constitutional manner.

On 10 June 1818 the Prince Regent dissolved Parliament without warning, a proceeding without precedent since Charles II dismissed the Oxford Parliament (q.v.) in 1681. The Prince had in actual fact acted to oblige his ministers. The King's death was expected at any time, and in the event of the demise of the Crown taking place prior to the day appointed for a new Parliament to assemble, the dissolved Parliament would have been recalled. The elections did not deprive the Government of its majority although they added strength to the Opposition, and the new Parliament met in January 1819. In August of that year the popular feeling was outraged by the 'Peterloo Massacre', an incident which served to emphasize the inimical relationship which existed between the Government and the people. The clash took place when the military charged a crowd gathered for a political meeting in St. Peter's Field, Manchester, and inflicted many casualties, including several killed. Indignant demands for an inquiry were made throughout the country, and motions calling for investigation into the affair were introduced in both Houses of Parliament. But far from heeding moderate counsels, the Government's reaction was to pass the repressive measures known as the 'Six Acts', which provided, amongst other things, for the taxing of newspapers, restraint upon popular gatherings, and more effective means of preventing libellous and seditious writings.

Parliament adjourned on 29 December 1819, and before it could reassemble the long and eventful reign of George III had reached its end. The King died on 29 January 1820, at a time of domestic turmoil and distress, having reigned for sixty years. His age had been a great one in all fields of endeavour and achievement, and is noteworthy for the number of its outstanding statesmen alone. It is one of the anomalies of fate that in a span of years which produced so many individuals of the first eminence there should have reigned a King whose limitations prevented that period of British history from reaching the summit of glory.

GEORGE IV (1762–1830) AND PARLIAMENT

George IV assumed the title of King upon the death of George III on 29 January 1820, having exercised the full power of sovereignty as Regent for the previous ten years during his father's insanity. No man could have been more ill-suited to the rôle of monarch than this selfish, spineless, dissolute dandy. Disloyal to his family, false to his friends, and indifferent to the welfare of his people, it is scarcely possible to point to a redeeming feature in his character. Perhaps the best that can be said of him is that England has been ruled by men more infamous, and that his occupancy of the throne brought with it a decided diminution in the personal power of the Crown. When he died it is doubtful whether the prestige of the monarchy had ever been at a lower ebb. Such reforms as were achieved during his reign, far from owing anything to his influence, were rather accomplished in spite of him; in fact the extent to which liberal policies prevailed at this period can be attributed in no small measure to the lack of royal influence. Nevertheless, the power of the Crown, which had increased so appreciably during the previous reign and had led to the passing of Dunning's famous resolution by the House of Commons in 1780, was still regarded with sufficient concern by the middle of 1822 as to bring forth a motion from Brougham calling for its reduction. The motion was negatived by 216 votes to 101 in spite of the mover's insistence that the power of the Crown had increased since Dunning's day.

On the accession of the new King the House of Commons fixed the Civil List at £845,727, but he received in addition a number of revenues, including substantial incomes from Scotland and Ireland, which considerably extended his financial resources. George IV had not been long on the throne before the Cato Street conspiracy was uncovered, a plot which had for its objects the assassination of Sidmouth,

Castlereagh, and other members of the Government and the incitement of a popular revolution. The betrayal of the conspiracy by one of its adherents led to expressions of grave concern in Parliament over the employment of spies and informers by the Government.

The main constitutional issues of the reign of George IV were the cruel and unjust proceedings which the King instituted against his wife, Caroline of Brunswick; the mounting pressure and eventual cession of the Roman Catholic claims for emancipation; and the popular agitation in favour of parliamentary reform. George had repudiated his consort many years before he became King, and upon his accession he refused to recognize her right to the title of Queen and denied her the courtesies due to that exalted rank. Caroline, who had been living abroad since 1814, returned to England when her husband became King and laid claim to her title. The King resolved upon divorce, and pressed the Government to formulate charges of infidelity against her, based upon evidence which the Cabinet knew to be far from conclusive. In spite of the fact that Caroline had been entirely cleared when similar allegations had been made against her in 1807, the Government succumbed, albeit reluctantly, to the insistence of the King, and to the perpetual shame of Lord Liverpool and his colleagues a Bill was introduced providing for the Queen's degradation and the dissolution of her marriage. Canning, who with Brougham had championed the cause of the wronged Queen, resigned from the Government in disgust at this proceeding. The Whigs and Radicals, backed by the country generally, rallied to Caroline's support, and when the third reading of the Bill was taken in the House of Lords the majority in its favour was only nine. Realizing that it would be hopeless to attempt to carry the Bill through the Commons the Government abandoned it and the nation rejoiced. The unhappy Caroline died shortly after her honour had been vindicated, but not before her despicable husband had inflicted one final humiliation upon her by disallowing her attendance at his coronation, a lavish and extravagant ceremony which provoked nothing but resentment in a people many of whom were starving.

At the beginning of 1822 Lord Sidmouth retired from office and was succeeded as Home Secretary by Robert Peel. Shortly afterwards Lord Londonderry, formerly Castlereagh, committed suicide, and Canning became Foreign Secretary in his place. Further important ministerial changes at this period included the appointment of Robinson, later Lord Goderich, as Chancellor of the Exchequer, and Huskisson as President of the Board of Trade. The progressive commercial policy of the latter minister did much to further the cause of free trade and bring about the eventual repeal of the Corn Laws.

During the course of the next few years the issue of Roman Catholic emancipation was one which frequently demanded the attention of the two Houses. The House of Commons, where a small majority generally voted in favour of granting some measure of relief to Catholics, showed itself more liberal in its attitude than the House of Lords, where, until 1829, a reactionary hard core of peers, outstanding amongst whom were the Duke of York and Lord Eldon, invariably contrived to influence the voting against such reforms. The King, of course, was emphatic in his opposition to any such proposal. In 1821 Plunket, upon whose shoulders the mantle of Grattan had fallen, had moved successfully in the lower House for a committee to consider the question of the Roman Catholic oaths. A Bill which he brought in subsequently, based upon the committee's resolutions, passed its third reading in the Commons by 19 votes but was thrown out by the Lords by a majority of 39. In 1822 Canning, who had throughout been an unfailing supporter of the Catholic claims, endeavoured to secure the removal of the disability upon Catholic peers to sit and vote in the upper House. His motion was opposed by Peel, his colleague in the Cabinet, but accepted by the House by the narrow majority of 5. A Bill incorporating Canning's proposal was carried in the Commons only to be rejected by their lordships. Further attempts in the cause of Catholic emancipation, including Burdett's Relief Bill of 1825, were similarly frustrated, and in the same year that Burdett introduced his Bill a measure for suppressing Daniel O'Connell's Catholic Association for three years was passed by Parliament. In 1827 the hopes of the Catholics rose when Lord Liverpool retired and Canning became Prime Minister (to the great reluctance of the King, it need hardly be added). Wellington, Peel, and Eldon refused to serve under Canning, who formed a ministry including Lord Lyndhurst as Lord Chancellor, Lord Dudley, Foreign Secretary, Sturges Bourne, Home Secretary, Palmerston, Secretary-at-War, and Goderich, Colonial Secretary. Canning himself took the offices of First Lord of the Treasury and Chancellor of the Exchequer, but only four months after taking office this great statesman, whose chief claim to fame rests upon his enlightened and constructive foreign policy, died. Lord Goderich became Prime Minister on Canning's death, but being unable to reconcile the internal dissensions within his ministry he resigned after five months and was succeeded by the Duke of Wellington. Wellington formed a Government drawn from both parties, but after a few months its Liberal members, including Palmerston, Dudley, Huskisson, and Lamb (afterwards Lord Melbourne), withdrew from it, and the Prime Minister reconstituted the ministry entirely from the Tories. It is one of those historical paradoxes that a Government formed from the party opposing Catholic relief should have been the one which was ultimately to implement that reform. In 1828 the Home Secretary, Peel, announced his conversion to the cause of Catholic emancipation, and Wellington, Lyndhurst, and other members of the Government agreed that the time had come to consider the granting of the Catholic claims. The urgent insistence of Peel induced a softening in the hitherto unyielding attitude of the King, who was persuaded to recommend the matter for the consideration of Parliament when opening Parliament on 5 February 1829. Peel, in order to test the views of his constituents, resigned his seat for Oxford University and contested it afresh. He was defeated by 146 votes, but he stood and was returned for the borough of Westminster shortly afterwards. Upon learning that the Government's proposed Relief Bill provided for the alteration of the oath of supremacy the King changed his mind and informed his ministers that he would withhold his consent to the measure, whereupon Wellington, Peel, and Lyndhurst resigned. They immediately resumed office when the vacillating monarch informed them he would yield to their wishes, and on 5 March Peel introduced the Catholic Relief Bill in the House of Commons. It passed the lower House with the resounding majority of 320 to 142, and the upper House agreed to it by 213 to 109, a large voting strength for the House of Lords which, in the reign of George IV, numbered only 372 members. Most of the spiritual peers opposed the measure, together with a group of diehard lay lords including, of course, Lord Eldon and Lord Sidmouth. The Relief Act was followed by a measure raising the qualifications for the franchise in Ireland, its purpose being to disfranchise the small freeholders whose votes, it was feared, would otherwise have been influenced by the priests. The Duke of Norfolk and other Catholic peers took their seats in the House of Lords, and Daniel O'Connell, who had been elected for County Clare, attempted to take his seat in the Commons, but was prevented from doing so as the Relief Act had not been made retrospective. He was forced to wait until a new writ was issued and the electors of Clare again returned him.

Another great liberal measure of this period, passed about a year prior to the Catholic Relief Act, was the Bill inspired by Lord John Russell for the repeal of the Test and Corporation Acts, two statutes which had long pressed heavily upon Dissenters. It is strange to note that Canning, who had fought so hard for Catholic emancipation, never gave his support to the cause of the Protestant Nonconformists. Russell's Bill passed both Houses, but a clause inserted during the committee stage in the upper House had the effect of disqualifying Jews from sitting in Parliament by introducing into the oath of allegiance the words, 'on the true faith of a Christian'.

Efforts in the interest of parliamentary reform were numerous during the reign of George IV, but although it was a cause backed by strong and influential support it failed to make any practical advance. Lord John Russell was a conspicuous campaigner in the movement for reform, and motions for the disfranchisement of corrupt boroughs, the enfranchisement of the large industrial towns, and the prevention of bribery at elections were unsuccessfully introduced by him at various times throughout the ten years George IV reigned. In 1827 Huskisson and other Liberals resigned from the Government on account of its opposition to even the most moderate reforms. In 1830 a motion by Daniel O'Connell in favour of triennial Parliaments, the introduction of the ballot, and universal suffrage was defeated by 319 votes to 13, and a resolution by Russell moderately proposing the extension of the basis of representation was rejected by 213 to 117. When one recalls that the great Reform Bill was destined to pass through both Houses a mere two years later it is obvious to what extent these majorities represented the forces of reaction. Nevertheless, a more liberal age had already dawned in spite of the character of the Government, as evidenced by the spirit of religious toleration which made possible the enactment of the measures referred to above. Other reforms effected during the period included a relaxation of restrictions upon the Press and a more humanitarian administration of the criminal law. The matter of law reform received attention during this period, and in 1828 Brougham delivered his celebrated speech of six hours, the longest in parliamentary history, advocating many improvements which have since been incorporated into the legal system. In 1830 a generous Budget brought considerable relief to the common people.

George IV died on 26 June 1830, and the accession of his successor heralded a new phase in the history of the institution of Parliament.

GERRYMANDER

To divide a country into electoral districts in such a way as to give a political advantage to the party in power. The word perpetuates the memory of Governor Gerry of Massachusetts, who resorted to this stratagem in 1812, and is formed by coupling his name with the latter half of the word 'salamander'. The story runs that while a group of politicians were studying an electoral map one of them, commenting on the unusual shape of one of the constituencies, remarked, 'It looks like a salamander,' whereupon another rejoined, 'You mean a gerrymander!'

Sir Ivor Jennings has given a simplified example of how much depends on the way in which boundaries are drawn. In a town entitled to elect four members, it is assumed that one-quarter of the electors belong to the working class, live in the centre of the town, and normally vote Labour, while the rest belong to the middle-class, live in the suburbs, and normally vote Conservative. If the town is divided diagonally into four quarters, each including part of the centre as well as part of the suburbs, it will return four Conservative members. If the centre forms one constituency and the suburbs are divided into three constituencies, the town will return one Labour member and three Conservatives.

'GETTING THE SPEAKER OUT OF THE CHAIR'

The ancient right of the Commons to debate grievances before considering Supply had traditionally found expression in the practice of debating the motion 'That Mr. Speaker do now leave the Chair' before the House resolved itself into Committee of Supply. It was a practice which often led to repetitive debate, since the matters discussed on the motion frequently anticipated those which were dealt with in Committee of Supply itself. In the 1880s, therefore, the right to debate the motion for 'getting the Speaker out of the Chair' was restricted to the three occasions when the main Civil, Army, and Navy estimates first came up for consideration. This procedure remained largely unchanged, save for the introduction of a fourth opportunity provided by the Air Estimates, until 1947, when, as a part of a general reform of Supply procedure, the moving of such motions ceased to be obligatory. Nevertheless, the practice of debating a motion to 'get the Speaker out of the Chair' on the first occasion of going into Committee of Supply on each of the four main branches of the Estimates was continued until 1956, and a ballot for notices of motion on going into Committee of Supply on the Civil Estimates was continued until 1960.

With the introduction of the new financial procedure in December 1966, the Committee of Supply has been abolished and Supply debates take place in the House itself with the Deputy Speaker presiding. The practice of debating the motion 'That the Speaker do now leave the Chair' is therefore now obsolete. When the House goes into committee on a Bill the Speaker leaves the Chair automatically without any question being put. Prior to the abolition of the Committee of Supply it was customary for the Speaker to leave the Chair without putting any question whenever an Order of the Day was read for the House to go into committee. However, a debate did sometimes take place when the Committee of Supply stood as the first Order and a Minister of the Crown moved 'That Mr. Speaker do now leave the Chair'. The effect of this procedure was to confine the initiative in launching such a debate to the Government. In former years the motion to 'get the Speaker out of the Chair' provided an opportunity for a discursive debate, but during the years immediately preceding the introduction of the new financial procedure it was largely used for debating a particular aspect of government policy, an amendment to the main question being moved for the purpose of confining debate to the matter it was intended to discuss. Such debates were, for all practical purposes, substitutes for debates in Committee of Supply, and the reports of the Public Accounts and Estimates Committees were frequently considered by means of this procedure. The practice of discussing matters of Supply on an amendment to the motion 'That

Mr. Speaker do now leave the Chair' was first established on 12 February 1948.

With regard to the Estimates of the armed services, it has been customary since May 1957 for a general debate to take place in each case on Vote A.

GHANA PARLIAMENT

Ghana became an independent country in the Commonwealth on 6 March 1957 and a Republic on 1 July 1960 following the adoption of a republican Constitution by Parliament and a plebiscite. The President of the Republic combined the functions of head of state and head of the Government. Dr. Kwame Nkrumah, who had been elected the first President of Ghana, was deposed by a military *coup d'état* in February 1966 after attempting to consolidate his power under an oppressive personal system of government.

Following a period of military rule a constituent assembly of 150 members was indirectly elected in 1969 and approved a new Constitution which was promulgated in August of that year. The first General Election under the new Constitution took place on 29 August 1969.

The Constitution places great emphasis on the need to protect democratic government and provides for elaborate safeguards against authoritarian practices and the abuse of freedom. It refers to the previous experience of 'a régime of tyranny', and affirms that no person shall be detained for more than twenty-four hours without being brought to trial and that no child shall be denied education or medical treatment because of a religious or philosophical belief.

The Constitution provides for a President, who would act as a constitutional head of state, a National Assembly, and a Cabinet headed by a Prime Minister. The President is elected by an electoral college consisting of Parliament and the regional assemblies. He appoints as Prime Minister the leader of the majority party in the National Assembly and on his advice appoints and determines the salaries of the Chief Justice, the Attorney-General, the Governor of the Bank of Ghana and an Ombudsman. He may exercise a delaying power of not more than two weeks over Bills passed by the National Assembly and he has certain supervisory functions over the activities of professional bodies. In discharging his functions as President he is assisted by a Council of State which includes the Chief Justice, the Prime Minister, the Speaker of the National Assembly, the Leader of the Opposition, the Attorney-General and the Commander-in-Chief of the Armed Forces.

The National Assembly consists of 140 members elected by universal adult suffrage for individual constituencies. The Prime Minister and his Cabinet are appointed from the membership of the National Assembly and are collectively responsible to Parliament, being constitutionally obliged to resign in the event of a vote of no confidence being carried against the Government. An unusual feature of the Constitution is that it provides for parliamentary procedure in some detail. It specifies that all Bills must be examined in Committee. It also provides that members who absent themselves from 15 consecutive sittings without the leave of the Speaker or who change their party shall automatically lose their seats, and that members who defame their colleagues without apologizing within seven days shall be subject to penalty.

The declaration of a state of emergency requires the approval of both the President and the National Assembly. An amendment of the Constitution requires a two-thirds majority vote of the National Assembly and in some cases an amendment could come into force only after six or twelve months.

When the Constitution came into force the powers of the President were being exercised by a Commission of three, the constituent assembly having resolved that this Commission should carry out the functions of President for three years or until the National Assembly decided otherwise.

Legislative institutions in Ghana, formerly the Gold Coast Colony and Protectorate, date back to the last century, African representation having been introduced as far back as 1888. It was not until 1946, however, that legislative jurisdiction over the Colony and Protectorate came to be centralized with the establishment of a new Legislative Council with jurisdiction over Ashanti as well as the Colony, a jurisdiction which in 1951 was extended also to the Northern Territories. This Legislative Council was the first legislature in British Africa to include a majority of African members and in 1949 it became the first to be presided over by an African Speaker.

In 1951 a new Constitution came into force providing for an enlarged legislature, the Legislative Assembly, with an elected Speaker and 75 elected members out of a total of 84. The Executive Council included a majority of African ministers drawn from the Legislative Assembly. In 1954 the Gold Coast was brought to the threshold of independence under a Constitution providing for a wholly elected Legislative Assembly of 104 members and a Cabinet system of government. The Constitution under which Ghana achieved independence provided for a number of Regional Assemblies to which substantial local powers were transferred but these Assemblies were dissolved by the Nkrumah Government in 1959. Regional Assemblies have been restored to Ghana under the new Constitution.

GIBRALTAR HOUSE OF ASSEMBLY

A Legislative Council was first established in Gibraltar in 1950 and was formally inaugurated by the Duke of Edinburgh on 23 November of that year. It originally consisted of the Governor as President, 3 *ex-officio* members (Colonial Secretary, Financial Secretary and Attorney-General), 2 members appointed by the Governor, and 5 members (subsequently increased to 7) elected by proportional representation (q.v.) on the principle of the single transferable vote. In 1958 a Speaker was appointed and the 'member system' (q.v.) was introduced, whereby elected members of the Legislative Council were associated with the administration of government departments.

Under the Gibraltar (Constitution) Order in Council, 1964, Gibraltar was granted a wide measure of internal self-government, which was further enhanced following constitutional talks which took place in July 1968. The Legislature is now known as the Gibraltar House of Assembly. It replaces the former Legislative Council and City Council. It consists of 15 elected members elected by universal suffrage and 2 *ex-officio* members, the Attorney-General and the Financial Secretary. The life of the Assembly will be four years. The Chief Minister, known prior to 1964 as the Chief Member, is also the Leader of the House and has been responsible for the management of government business since 1964. Elected members with departmental responsibilities have been designated ministers and carry full responsibility for their departments.

The Gibraltar Council and the Council of Ministers, established in 1964, remain under the new Constitution. The former consists of the Governor, the Deputy Fortress Commander, the Deputy Governor, the Attorney-General, the Financial Secretary, the Chief Minister and 4 other ministers appointed by the Governor after consultation with the Chief Minister. The Governor acts in consultation with the Gibraltar Council in relation to matters for which he is exclusively responsible, namely external affairs, defence and internal security. He may act contrary to its advice, but if he does so he is required to make a report to the Secretary of State. The Council of Ministers consists of the Chief Minister and not more than 8 other ministers appointed by the Governor after consultation with the Chief Minister. The Council of Ministers is responsible for matters of domestic concern and in such areas its decisions normally take effect, although the Governor has the right to require that decisions falling within the scope of matters for which he is executively responsible should be referred to the Gibraltar Council.

Following the integration of the City Council with the Legislature, the Mayor is now elected from the House of Assembly by the elected members of the Assembly.

The Constitution also provides for a code of human rights, the establishment of an Appeal Court intermediate between the Gibraltar Supreme Court and the Judicial Committee of the Privy Council, and the integration of the Gibraltar Government Service and the employees of the City Council into a single public service.

[327]

GILBERT AND ELLICE ISLANDS LEGISLATURE

A new Constitution came into force for the Gilbert and Ellice Islands at the end of 1967 which provided for a directly elected House of Representatives for the first time. The House of Representatives replaces the former Advisory Council and is presided over by the Resident Commissioner. It consists of 7 official members (the Assistant Resident Commissioner, the Attorney-General and 5 other members nominated by the Resident Commissioner) and 23 unofficial members elected by universal adult suffrage. The elected members represent 18 electoral districts, 5 of which return 2 members and the remaining 13 one apiece. Elections normally take place every two years.

The former Executive Council is replaced by a Governing Council consisting of the Resident Commissioner as President and 10 members, half of whom are officials and the other half elected members. The official members of the Governing Council are the Assistant Resident Commissioner, the Attorney-General and 3 of the nominated members; the unofficial representation comprises the Chief Elected Member, who is elected to that office by his 23 elected colleagues and 4 other elected members chosen by the 23 from among themselves. The Governing Council advises the Resident Commissioner and consents to legislation. The House of Representatives has no legislative authority of its own but considers any legislation which is submitted to it.

The new Constitution for the Islands exemplifies a new pattern of constitutional development in the smaller territories still administered by the United Kingdom. While combining executive and legislative functions in a single body, it recognizes the importance of direct participation in government by the elected representatives of the people, both through an advisory House of Representatives and through a direct sharing of responsibility in the Governing Council. Since the participation of civil servants in constitutional development is also indispensable they are permitted to stand as candidates for the House of Representatives.

GOLD COAST PARLIAMENT

See GHANA PARLIAMENT.

GOOD PARLIAMENT

The Parliament that assembled in 1376 in the reign of Edward III has been called by this name because of its measures against the corruption of the Court and government. Several of the ministers were impeached, and the King's mistress, Alice Perrers, was particularly singled out for censure by the Commons. Their growing activity in this Parliament received much encouragement from the Black Prince, but after his death John of Gaunt's Parliament undid the good work of its predecessor and imprisoned the Speaker, Sir Peter de la Mare.

GOVERNMENT
See PARLIAMENTARY GOVERNMENT.

GOVERNMENT BUSINESS
The responsibilities of government in the latter half of the 20th century have become so extensive that government business consumes by far the greater part of parliamentary time. The establishment of the Cabinet system made the Government the leaders of the majority in the House of Commons, but owing to the tenacity with which the House clung to the principle of the equality of members, any priority for Bills, motions, etc. introduced by the Government was not formally secured until the first half of the 19th century. During the 18th century the old practice of the Speaker arranging business gradually ceased, and a new distinction was made between Order Days, when business set down by order of the House was taken, and Notice Days for new business. Although by 1852 the Government had appropriated three of the Order Days a week, the whole of this time was not available because members in those days could avail themselves of technicalities of procedure for obstructing and interrupting Government business. After the passing of the 1832 Reform Bill, the procedure of the House began to be defined and regularized by means of Standing Orders (q.v.), and in 1902 the Government finally secured its hold upon the greater part of the time of the House.
See also BUSINESS OF THE HOUSE; PRIVATE MEMBERS' TIME.

GOVERNMENT DRAFTSMEN
See DRAFTSMEN.

GOVERNOR
The Governor and Commander-in-Chief of a Colony is appointed by the Crown, formerly on the advice of the Secretary of State for the Colonies. The rapidly diminishing extent of the colonial empire led to the abolition of that office in 1967, and the few colonial Governors remaining are to-day appointed on the advice of the Secretary of State for Foreign and Commonwealth Affairs. The office is created by letters patent, and as the agent of the Crown the Governor carries on executive government in its name. His duties and authority are defined in Royal Instructions and by a Commission, but generally he is empowered to appoint members of the Legislative and Executive Councils, to issue election writs for the legislature and to summon and dissolve it, and to assent or refuse assent to Bills, or to reserve them for the Crown's assent. Where a Legislative Council consists entirely of nominated members he may initiate taxation and appropriation measures and usually other Bills. In addition to these powers, Governors

have authority conferred on them by various statutes in respect of customs, defence works, naturalization of aliens, and many other matters.

Governors of the Australian States, appointed by the Crown, and Lieutenant-Governors of the Canadian Provinces, appointed on the advice of the Canadian Government by the Governor-General, are not agents of the Crown as are the colonial Governors, but are the Crown's representatives. In both cases they are as much the representatives of the Queen for all purposes of state or provincial government as the Governors-General are for the federal governments.

GOVERNOR-GENERAL

The Report of the Inter-Imperial Relations Committee, which was adopted by the Imperial Conference of 1926, stated that it was an essential consequence of the equality of status existing among the members of the British Commonwealth 'that the Governor-General of a Dominion is the representative of the Crown, holding in all essential respects the same position in relation to the administration of public affairs in the Dominion as is held by H.M. the King in Great Britain', and, like the Sovereign, he opens, prorogues, and dissolves Parliament, and assents to Bills. He exercises the prerogative of pardon and the seldom-used power to refuse a dissolution of Parliament. The report also made it clear that a Governor-General is not the representative or agent of H.M. Government in Great Britain or of any department of that Government. The Imperial Conference of 1930 further declared that the consequence of the Governor-General being the representative of the Sovereign only was that 'the constitutional practice that His Majesty acts on the advice of responsible ministers applies also in this instance'. It follows that the appointment of a Governor-General becomes a matter of local concern, and that the ministers whose advice is taken are those of the country concerned. In the modern Commonwealth the office of Governor-General has application only in those countries which acknowledge the Queen as Head of State and, in most of them, the convention has become established that the appointment should be held by a local citizen. Australia was the first country to set the precedent with the appointment of Sir Isaac Isaacs in 1931.

GRAND COMMITTEES

At the beginning of the 17th century the Standing Committees on religion, grievances, courts of justice, and trade were given the name of 'Grand' Committees. They were in form Committees of the Whole House, but unlike these, which have always had to ask leave to sit again, they were given power in 1626 to adjourn themselves. After the Restoration they began to take the committee stage of Bills, and soon became indistinguishable from Committees of the Whole House, although the formality of setting them up at the beginning of the session was continued until 1832.

Since December 1957 the Scottish Standing Committee in its plenary form has been officially known as the Scottish Grand Committee. A Welsh Grand Committee was set up in 1960.

GRAND REMONSTRANCE

A great documentary protest prepared and passed by the House of Commons in 1641 which purported to place before the King 'a faithful and lively representation of the state of the kingdom'. It contained 206 clauses describing the state of the nation, reciting the King's misdemeanours and the grievances of the Commons, stating the reforms which had already been effected by Parliament and the obstructions thereto, and finally demanding further remedial measures, including the enforcement of laws against Roman Catholics, improvements in the administration of justice, and the appointment of ministers in whom Parliament could confide. The remonstrance was provoked by the duplicity of Charles I in his dealings with Parliament, but the Royalist party in the Commons, whilst accepting the declaratory clauses, fiercely opposed those proposing further reforms. When a vote was taken on 23 November after a long and stormy debate, the figures of 159 in favour and 148 against revealed a large minority in sympathy with the King. Cromwell is recorded as having said, 'If the remonstrance had been rejected I would have sold all I had the next morning and never have seen England any more; and I know there are many other honest men of this same resolution.' The debate proved to be the first trial of strength between the two parties which eventually waged the Civil War.

The Grand Remonstrance was really intended to justify Parliament in the eyes of the people, and on the same day that it was passed a second vote was taken on a motion that it should be printed and was lost by 124 votes to 101. But the popular side refused to accept the decision as final, and a second debate was held on 15 December which resulted in a reversal of the decision by 135 votes to 83. It is recorded that tumult broke out in the House but order was restored by the strong, calm influence of John Hampden. The remonstrance thus became a direct appeal to the nation, and throughout its considerable length lay the implication that the Roman Church was conspiring against and was responsible for all the evils besetting the nation. As a result of its publication, the King, fearing for the Queen whose intrigues on behalf of the Catholic faith were no secret, was induced to make his celebrated attempt to arrest the five leaders of the party responsible for its authorship.

See also CHARLES I AND PARLIAMENT.

GREAT CHARTER
See MAGNA CARTA.

GREAT OFFICERS OF THE REALM
'An Acte for the placing of the Lordes in Parliamt', which was put on the Statute Book by Henry VIII in 1539, states who are to be considered the twelve Great Officers of the Realm and lists them in order of precedence. The offices of Ecclesiastical Viceregent, Lord Treasurer, Lord Admiral, and King's Secretary no longer exist and there are now only eight, namely, the Lord Chancellor (q.v.), the Lord President of the Council (q.v.), the Lord Privy Seal (q.v.), the Lord Great Chamberlain (q.v.), the Lord High Constable, the Earl Marshal, the Lord Steward of the Household, and the Lord Chamberlain. Of these eight, three are often for convenience, though without any known recorded authority, colloquially described as 'Great Officers of State'. These are the Lord Great Chamberlain, the Lord High Constable, and the Earl Marshal. The Lord Steward and the Master of the Horse, who has always been considered a 'Great Officer of the Household', might also be described as 'Great Officers of State'. The Lord Chancellor, the Lord Privy Seal, and the Lord President of the Council are active politicians, and receive their appointments from the party in power.

GREAT SEAL
The office of Lord Keeper of the Great Seal (q.v.) is now combined with that of the Lord Chancellor (q.v.). Although with Sir Nicholas Bacon in the reign of Elizabeth I the two posts of Keeper and Chancellor were united, it was not until the time of George III that the modern system of conferring the Great Seal and the title of Lord Chancellor simultaneously became customary. The documents to which the Great Seal is affixed are proclamations, writs, letters patent, and the documents which give power to sign and ratify treaties. Authority for affixing the Great Seal is given by a Royal Warrant under the Queen's Sign Manual and countersigned by the minister responsible for tendering the advice to which the document is to give effect. The duties in connexion with the use of the seal are now performed by the officers of the Keeper in the Crown Office, but he is responsible for its safe custody. Whenever a new Great Seal is adopted, at the beginning of a new reign, or a change of the royal arms, or when the old seal is worn out, it becomes the property of the Lord Chancellor. On the accession of William IV a dispute arose between Lord Lyndhurst and Lord Brougham as to who should possess the old seal. The former had been Chancellor when the order was made for the engraving of the new seal; the latter had occupied the Woolsack (q.v.) when the new seal

was finished and ordered to be put into use. The King decided that the seal should be divided between the two Chancellors, and when the same difficulty arose in 1878 Queen Victoria followed the precedent set in 1831 by the Solomon-like wisdom of King William.

In early times, the King used occasionally to deliver to the Chancellor several seals of different materials—perhaps one of gold and one of silver—with the same impression, although, with the exception of the rival Great Seals used by the King and the Parliament during the Civil War, there has not been for many centuries more than one Great Seal in existence at the same time. The Close Rolls abound with curious details of the careful manner in which the Great Seal was kept in its 'white leathern bag and silken purse' under the private seal of the Chancellor. There was a rule that it should not be taken out of the realm, but this was broken by Cardinal Wolsey, who took it to Calais with him in 1521. This supposed violation of duty formed one of the articles of his impeachment. On two occasions in its history the Great Seal has been abstracted—by James II, who dropped it into the Thames—and by burglars in 1784 from the house of Lord Chancellor Thurlow.

Queen Elizabeth II approved a new Great Seal of the Realm at a meeting of the Privy Council in August 1953. It was designed by Gilbert Ledward, R.A., and engraved in silver at the Royal Mint. The impression has a diameter of 6 inches, and as it is suspended from a document it has to have an obverse and a reverse impressed by the seal, which weighs 135 ounces, and by a counterseal weighing 3 ounces less. The practice, dating from the time of William the Conqueror, of depicting the Sovereign on horseback on the obverse and enthroned and robed on the reverse has been adhered to for the new seal.

The Imperial Conference of 1930 discussed the use of the Great Seal in connexion with the conduct of foreign relations by Commonwealth countries, and changes were later introduced in the form of the warrant for the release of the Great Seal to indicate that the Sovereign was acting on the advice of his ministers in the country concerned. South Africa had its own Great Seal instituted by the Royal Executive Functions and Seals Act of 1934, many years before she became a Republic, and Canada passed the Seals Act in 1939 authorizing the Great Seal of Canada (i.e., the Governor-General's seal) to be used instead of the Great Seal of the Realm.

GRENADA LEGISLATURE

One of the four islands of the Windward Islands group, Grenada's Constitution in 1951 provided for a Legislative Council consisting of the Administrator as President, 2 *ex-officio* members, 3 nominated members and 8 elected members, and an Executive Council comprising the Administrator, 2 *ex-officio* members, and 1 of the nominated and

4 of the elected members of the Legislative Council. In 1956 an additional elected member was appointed to the Executive Council, which became the principal instrument of policy with a majority of elected members, 3 of whom were appointed ministers.

In 1959 further constitutional changes became effective in Grenada. The Legislative Council was reconstituted to consist of 1 official, 2 nominated unofficial and 10 elected members, presided over by an elected Speaker. On 1 January 1960 the Leader of the Government became the Chief Minister and the Executive Council was reconstituted to comprise 5 unofficial members (including the Chief Minister and 3 other Ministers) and one official member (the Law Officer). The offices of the Governors of the Leeward Islands and the Windward Islands were abolished and their powers transferred to the Administrators of the various islands comprising these groups.

In 1962 the short-lived West Indies Federation, of which Grenada had been a member, was dissolved, and when negotiations for an alternative form of federation for the smaller West Indian Colonies failed to produce agreement, new constitutional proposals were published in 1965 (Cmnd. 2865) whereby six British territories of the Eastern Caribbean could, if they wished, enter into an associate status with Great Britain. Grenada decided to take advantage of these arrangements, and a new Constitution for the island was agreed at a conference held in April and May 1966 (Cmnd. 3021).

Under the West Indies Act, 1967, Grenada has shed her colonial status and has entered into an associate status with Great Britain. The new Constitution provides for full internal self-government, control of external affairs and defence being reserved to Great Britain, who will consult closely with the Government of Grenada in the discharge of these responsibilities.

The Legislature of Grenada consists of the Queen, represented by the Governor, a Senate and a House of Representatives. The Senate consists of 9 members appointed by the Governor, of whom 5 are appointed on the advice of the Premier, 2 on the advice of the Leader of the Opposition, and 2 on the advice of the Premier after he has consulted with such organizations or interests as he considers should be represented. The House of Representatives consists of 10 elected members. Both Houses elect a President and Speaker respectively from among their own membership.

A Money Bill which has been passed by the House of Representatives may be presented to the Governor for assent one month after it has been sent to the Senate if the Senate has failed to pass it within that time without amendment. Any other Bill may be presented for assent if it has been passed by the House of Representatives in two successive sessions and rejected by the Senate on both occasions. If the Bill concerned is a Bill to amend a basic clause of the Constitution it may be submitted to a referendum of the electorate after it has been rejected by the Senate for the second time.

The Constitution includes a number of basic clauses which relate to such matters as fundamental rights and freedoms, the Legislature, the franchise and elections, and the judicial system. A Bill seeking to alter the Constitution requires the approval at its third reading of not less than two-thirds of the total membership of the House of Representatives, and if it seeks to alter a basic clause it must in addition be submitted to the electorate at a referendum and approved by a majority of not less than two-thirds of the valid votes cast. No referendum would be required in respect of a Bill seeking the termination of the association between Great Britain and Grenada for the purpose of enabling the latter to enter into a federation, union or other association with an independent Commonwealth country in the Caribbean.

GREY, ANCHITELL (d. 1702)

The compiler of Grey's Debates, a contemporary record of the debates of the House of Commons from 1667 to 1694. Originally compiled for his own convenience, these debates were published in ten volumes in 1769. Grey was himself a Member of Parliament, and his work was the first continuous record of contemporary debates to be published. Grey's Debates are one of the main sources from which Cobbett and Wright compiled the Parliamentary History (q.v.).

GUERNSEY, STATES OF

See CHANNEL ISLANDS LEGISLATURES.

GUILLOTINE

A development of the closure (q.v.) which is applied to the various stages of Bills and is also known as the 'closure by compartments'. It can only be called into operation if a motion for the purpose has been agreed to by the House. Unlike a closure motion which has to be passed when a question is actually before the House, an allocation of time or 'guillotine' motion is passed in advance of the debate it is proposed to limit.

A 'guillotine' motion is designed to expedite the passage of a Bill, and seeks to do so by means of a time-table allotting a certain number of days proportionately to each stage and, in respect of the committee and report stages, stipulating the number of clauses which must be considered on each day or portion of a day. At the end of the allotted time the question under consideration must be put, followed by any further questions necessary to conclude the business which has been assigned to that day or period, opportunity for any further discussion being now lost. 'Guillotine' motions usually contain other provisions such as the prohibition of dilatory motions and the postponement of other business.

The 'guillotine' is unpopular on all sides of the House. It renders opposition ineffective and severely impairs the value of debate. Its only virtue is that of saving time, although a certain amount of time is always lost in the discussion of the motion itself. A Government is usually reluctant to propose its use, and will only do so as a matter of urgency. For instance, a Government might seek to call the 'guillotine' into operation if it is being unduly harassed by delaying tactics, or if fierce and prolonged debate is anticipated on a measure which threatens to disrupt the programme for the session.

On the recommendation of the Select Committee on Procedure of 1946 the 'guillotine' can be applied to proceedings in Standing Committees, although every motion proposing its application must be passed in the House itself.

GUNPOWDER PLOT

The name given to the conspiracy to blow up the Houses of Parliament which was engineered by a group of Catholics in 1605. The explosion was planned to take place on 5 November at the time when the King was due to open Parliament, but the plot was discovered the night before. According to the most popular account of the discovery, Guy Fawkes was caught red-handed in the act of setting the fuse which was to ignite the thirty-six barrels of gunpowder which had been deposited in the vault immediately beneath the Chamber of the House of Lords. The Journal of the House of Commons records: 'This last night the Upper House of Parliament was searched by Sir Tho. Knevett; and one Johnson (the name assumed by Fawkes), servant to Sir Thomas Percy, was there apprehended; who had placed thirty-six barrels of gunpowder in the vault under the House, with a purpose to blow King, and the whole company, when they should there assemble.'

The history of the conspiracy is surrounded by much confusion and opinions conflict over the question of its origins. It is generally accepted that the plot was provoked by the repressive measures to which, since the beginning of Elizabeth's reign, Catholics in England had been subjected. It has been alleged, however, that it was initiated by an *agent-provocateur* at the instigation of Salisbury, the Secretary of State, with the object of incriminating Catholics generally as a prelude to a fierce persecution designed to suppress Catholicism entirely. Whether this be true or false, there is no doubt that the government had some prior knowledge of the plot and deliberately falsified much of the evidence after the arrest of the conspirators.

The plot is supposed to have been conceived by Robert Catesby and confided by him to Thomas Winter and John Wright in a house in Lambeth. The conspiracy was later joined by Winter's brother

Robert, Wright's brother Christopher, Thomas Percy, John Grant, Ambrose Rookwood, Robert Keyes, Sir Everard Digby, Francis Tresham, Catesby's servant Thomas Bates, and Guy Fawkes, who has become the most famous of the persons concerned although his rôle was a relatively minor one. On 25 March, after some attempts at underground excavation, the ground-level vault immediately beneath the Lords' Chamber, which had previously been leased to a coal merchant, was hired by Percy, and here were concealed the barrels of gunpowder under a heap of firewood.

On 26 October an anonymous letter was delivered to Lord Monteagle, a Catholic peer and brother-in-law of Tresham, warning him not to attend the Opening of Parliament if he valued his life. The authorship of the letter has never been established. Certain evidence tends to throw suspicion on Tresham although other facts suggest otherwise. There is little doubt, however, that the warning came as no surprise to Monteagle who is believed to have had full knowledge of the plot. Monteagle had himself taken part in Catholic conspiracies in the past, but had been restored to favour with the Crown on declaring his support for James I on his accession. The part played by Monteagle in the affair under consideration is open to speculation, but his action upon receiving the letter was to reveal it to Salisbury and other ministers. On 4 November the vault beneath the House of Lords was searched, the gunpowder was discovered, and Guy Fawkes was arrested. Catesby and the others fled into the country, but all were eventually hunted down and either killed or arrested. Eight of the conspirators lived to stand trial — the two Winters, Digby, Rookwood, Keyes, Grant, Bates and Fawkes. They were executed on 30 and 31 January 1606, with all the dreadful accompaniments which in those days formed a part of the punishment for treason. Tresham died in the Tower before he could be tried.

Three Jesuit priests were also involved in the plot, but the extent of their implication was probably limited to the fact that it had been revealed to them in confession. One of them, Garnet, was arrested and executed, but the other two, Tesimond (alias Greenway) and Gerard, managed to escape.

It is doubtful whether the true history of the Gunpowder Plot will ever be known. As generally told it rests upon two accounts—the confessions taken from Thomas Winter and Guy Fawkes after their arrest. Those of the latter were extracted under torture and Winter's confession was probably forged; in any case, all their statements were certainly tampered with and there is no doubt that the evidence was consistently falsified to make it accord with the version which the government of the day wished the world to believe.

An interesting custom which still survives as a result of the Gunpowder Plot is the traditional searching of the cellars by the Yeomen of the Guard which takes place before the opening of each session of Parliament.

A useful book on the subject is Hugh Ross Williamson's *The Gunpowder Plot*, published in 1951.

GURNEY, JOSEPH (1744–1815)
See SHORTHAND WRITER TO THE HOUSE.

GURNEY, WILLIAM BRODIE (1777–1855)
See SHORTHAND WRITER TO THE HOUSE.

GUYANA PARLIAMENT

The State of Guyana, formerly the Colony of British Guiana, became independent on 26 May 1966 following a somewhat chequered constitutional history. Its Parliament is unicameral, consisting of the President and a National Assembly of 53 members elected by proportional representation. The life of the National Assembly is five years unless it is sooner dissolved. One minister has a special responsibility for Amerindian affairs, and the Prime Minister is entitled to include in his Cabinet not more than 4 ministers who are not members of the National Assembly. As non-elected ministers they are entitled to speak but not to vote in the National Assembly. The Constitution also provides for the appointment of an ombudsman, and requires the Prime Minister to consult with the Leader of the Opposition with regard to certain high judicial, public service, and police appointments.

An important step towards representative government in British Guiana was taken with the introduction in 1953 of a Constitution providing for a House of Assembly of 3 *ex-officio* and 24 elected members and an upper House, called the State Council, of 9 members appointed by the Governor. The first General Election under this Constitution was held on 27 April 1953, but as a result of a constitutional crisis precipitated by the People's Progressive Party, which obtained 18 of the 24 seats in the Assembly, the Constitution was suspended by the British Government on 9 October 'to prevent Communist subversion'. British Guiana temporarily reverted to Crown Colony government from 22 December with an Executive Council and a Legislative Council appointed by the Governor. An independent commission reported (Cmd. 9274) in November 1954 that 'so long as the People's Progressive Party retains its present leadership and policies there is no way in which responsible government can be restored without the certainty that the country will again be subjected to constitutional crisis'.

On 25 April 1956 the Colonial Secretary announced in the House of Commons that the time had come when some progress could safely be made in re-introducing democratic institutions in British Guiana, and it was finally proposed that the Legislative Council should have 28 members (excluding the Speaker), at least 14 of whom would be elected, not more than 11 nominated, and 3 *ex officio*. The Executive Council was to consist of the 3 *ex officio*, 2 nominated, and 5 elected members of the Legislative Council. These proposals were incorporated in the British Guiana (Constitution) (Temporary Provisions) (Amendment) Order in Council made on 19 December 1956, which also gave the Governor the power to suspend an elected member and left the way open for reversion to a wholly nominated Council if events necessitated it. The first elections under this amended Constitution were held in August 1957.

The British Guiana Constitutional Conference held in London in March 1960 (Cmnd. 998) recommended that a new Constitution conferring full internal self-government should be introduced. The Conference proposed that the legislature should be bicameral. The Legislative Assembly, or lower House, should consist of not less than 32 and not more than 35 members, all elected, and the Senate should comprise 13 members nominated by the Governor. There would be an Executive Council of 10 ministers, including 3 senators, presided over by the Premier. A General Election was held under this Constitution in August 1961 and 35 members were elected to the Legislative Assembly.

Further conferences were held in 1962 and 1963, but no decisions were reached as the leaders of the three political parties represented at the conferences were unable to agree on the system of voting at elections and whether or not fresh elections should be held before independence. In view of the continuing disagreement between the political leaders they requested the British Government to settle all outstanding constitutional issues and undertook to abide by the decisions made. As a result the British Government introduced the British Guiana (Constitution) Order, 1964, which provided for a House of Assembly of 53 members in a unicameral Parliament and an electoral system based on proportional representation. A General Election was held under this Constitution in December 1964 and, after a further conference held in London in 1965, it was announced that British Guiana would become independent on 26 May 1966 with the option of becoming a Republic after 1 January 1969. On 23 February 1970 Guyana became the world's first 'co-operative' Republic in terms of a new philosophy which, in the words of the Prime Minister, Mr. Forbes Burnham, was designed as the first real attempt to improve the lot of the small man. The function of implementing this basic policy is vested in a Co-operative Department which controls and promotes the formation of co-operative societies throughout the country. The Guyana National Co-operative Bank has been established to help finance co-operative ventures.

H

HAKEWILL, WILLIAM (1574–1655)

The author of a treatise on parliamentary procedure, originally published in 1641 under the title, 'The Manner how Statutes are enacted in Parliament by passing of Bills'. According to the *Dictionary of National Biography*, the work had remained in manuscript for many years, and numerous copies had found their way abroad, one of which was anonymously published as 'The Manner of holding Parliaments in England' (not to be confused with the work of similar title by Hakewill's contemporary, Elsynge (q.v.)).

Hakewill was at various times a Member of Parliament and represented several Cornish constituencies. The *D.N.B.* records that when examining the parliamentary writs in the Tower of London, he discovered that the three Buckinghamshire boroughs, Amersham, Marlow, and Wendover, had formerly returned members to Parliament but had allowed the privilege to lapse. At his suggestion they claimed their rights, and from 1625 they were recognized. Hakewill was returned as Member for Amersham in 1628, but in 1629 he retired permanently from parliamentary life.

HALL, ARTHUR, CASE OF

The leading precedent on which the House of Commons bases its right of expulsion. Arthur Hall was expelled from the House in 1581 for having published an offensive book in which he questioned the authority of the House and slandered individual members.

See also ELIZABETH I AND PARLIAMENT; EXPULSION FROM PARLIAMENT.

HANSARD

The official verbatim report of parliamentary debates, which takes its name from the Hansard family whose firm originally published the report. Hansard constitutes a complete and accurate record of every word which is spoken in Parliament, and each House issues its own separate report. In addition to speeches delivered in the course of debate the report includes the answers to questions (q.v.), both oral and written, and it records divisions (q.v.) in full. Hansard is issued in daily and weekly parts and also in bound volumes which are issued periodically during a session. The number of volumes which are filled by the debates of a complete session varies, but twelve may be taken as an average for the Commons and six for the Lords. A sessional index is published as a separate volume to either series. The debates of Standing Committees (q.v.) of the House of Commons are published in separate parts and volumes.

Hansard is published by Her Majesty's Stationery Office. It is issued free of charge to Members of Parliament and may be purchased by the public. The daily Hansard is available and on sale on the day following the sitting whose proceedings it reports. The schedule of prices and subscriptions, which varies from time to time, is published on the inside cover of each issue of the daily parts.

Parliamentary debates are recorded by highly skilled shorthand writers who are members of the staff of Parliament. The Hansard staff of the Commons consists of an Editor of Debates, an Assistant Editor, and twenty-one reporters, two of whom act as sub-editors; that of the Lords consists of an Editor, Assistant Editor, and eight reporters. The following description of the House of Commons reporting organization could apply equally well, with insignificant variations, to the similar but smaller organization of the House of Lords.

Hansard reporters occupy places in the Press (or Reporters') Gallery, a special trench which runs along the front of the gallery being reserved for them. They perform their reporting duties on a rota system, taking turns of ten minutes at a time. A second reporter sits beside the duty reporter and takes a check note with him (a wise arrangement which helps to resolve any doubts which might occur in the transcript), whilst a third reporter awaits his turn to take over. On the completion of the duty reporter's turn the check reporter, who has been watching the clock, whispers 'Right' to his colleague and settles down to his own turn. The retiring reporter completes the sentence he is in the process of recording and departs to transcribe his 'take'. The reporter standing by slips into the seat beside the new duty reporter and takes over as check reporter, and at about the same time another reporter enters the gallery to take his place in the rotation. The job of a Hansard reporter is an arduous one and punctuality is one of his essential virtues. In his fraternity to be late for a turn of duty is the unpardonable sin, so intense and gruelling is the nature of his work.

Having completed a turn of duty a Hansard reporter immediately proceeds to transcribe his 'take'. He first dictates to a typist from his notes and then revises the transcript while the proceedings he has just recorded are fresh in his mind. Revision is limited to the correction of grammar, spelling, and punctuation, ensuring that the correct parliamentary forms are observed, striking out superfluous repetition, and making any amendments necessary in the interests of clarity, common sense, and good English. No material alterations may be made, nor any amendments which would in any way tend to change the sense of what has been spoken. The transcript must remain an accurate, and as far as possible an exact, report of what has been said. A certain amount of revision is bound to be necessary, however. For instance, the tangled sentence and confusion of ideas which are such common features of extempore speaking, particularly when subject to interruption, must be sorted out if they are to make sense when committed to paper; the split infinitive and other solecisms which frequently occur in speech must be corrected; the mixed metaphor and other varieties of *lapsus linguæ*, those dreaded pitfalls in public speaking, must not be perpetuated in print; and the Member who refers to 'the Honourable and gallant Member' when he should have said 'the Right Honourable and learned Member' must have his error corrected in the transcript. The speeches of the poor speaker must be made to read as intelligibly as those of the master orator. A Hansard reporter requires more than a very high shorthand speed; a knowledge of parliamentary procedure, an excellent command of the English language, and plenty of sound common sense are highly important qualifications.

When a reporter has completed his transcript he takes it to the office of the Assistant Editor, after which he is free until his next turn of duty. The Assistant Editor and the two sub-editors are responsible for the preparation of the day's transcripts for publication. They read and assemble the transcripts and if necessary revise them further. They, of course, have the advantage of being able to follow the continuity of the speeches individually and the debate as a whole. Sometimes, although not officially, the editors consult with members themselves for the sake of ensuring accuracy. A member has no right to alter his speech in any way, and it rests with the Editor as to whether or not a member's correction shall be admitted. Unless he can prove he has been misreported, a member may not change the sense of anything he has been recorded as saying; neither is he permitted to make any insertion as an afterthought, nor strike out a passage which he regrets having uttered. Hansard is an enduring historical record and nothing is allowed which would impair its accuracy. The record is not coloured in any way. Descriptive comments such as 'prolonged applause' or 'ironical cheers' (which frequently appear in press reports) are totally banned. A simple comment such as 'laughter' is admissible if referred to by a member in the course of a speech. Hansard is a plain, ungarnished record. No pride of place is given to any speech, and the immortal perorations of Sir Winston Churchill appear upon equal terms with the less inspired utterances of the humblest of back-benchers. Throughout the afternoon and evening of the normal parliamentary day Hansard transcripts flow continuously into the office of the Assistant Editor, and batches of corrected copy are taken by a messenger to the printing works of Her Majesty's Stationery Office at half-hourly intervals. On the following morning the daily part is printed and ready for distribution. In the event of an all-night or exceptionally late sitting a certain amount of copy must inevitably be held over, and the decision as to where the cut shall be made rests with the Assistant Editor.

Parliament reposes great confidence in the accuracy of Hansard, and on various occasions members, including the Speaker, have paid tribute to the Hansard reporters. It has often been asked why recording machines have not replaced shorthand writers for this work in view of the fact that a verbatim record is required. The answer to this is simply that no machine can edit the speeches it records. If Hansard reporting was merely a matter of taking down every word exactly as spoken, regardless of grammatical errors, cumbersome phraseology, and unfinished sentences, then a recording machine might profitably be used in preference to a human agency. As it is, a mechanically recorded report would require scrupulous editing which would need to be undertaken by a staff of editors not having the advantage of having heard the original speeches. Furthermore, the possibility of a mechanical breakdown would always be present. Nevertheless, a number of legislative chambers in the Commonwealth employ a mechanical means of recording debates. In some cases, as in the House of Lords, tape-recorders are used only as an aid to the short-hand writers. They were also used for this purpose in the now defunct Federal Assembly of Rhodesia and Nyasaland. But in most Commonwealth Parliaments debates are reported in the same manner as at Westminster, and the term 'Hansard' is in general use throughout the Commonwealth.

Although Hansard is the official report of parliamentary *debates* it is not the official record of Parliament's *proceedings* and cannot be accepted as such in a court of law (see Speaker's Rulings of 16 and 17 February 1949: Hansard, vol. 461, cols. 1146-7 and 1347-50).

HISTORY OF HANSARD. The history of Hansard is inextricably bound up with the struggle between Parliament and the Press over the reporting of parliamentary debates in the newspapers. For many years Parliament regarded any report of its proceedings as a breach of privilege (*see* PRIVILEGE, BREACH OF) and technically still regards it as such to-day. In opposing the Press, however, Parliament also found itself in conflict with public opinion and was forced to relax its attitude. But whilst resigning itself to the fact that newspaper reports could not be suppressed, Parliament continued to forbid the actual taking of notes in the Public Gallery. This ban is still in operation to-day, although the Press are no longer affected by it now that they have their own gallery. Before special provision was made for them, newspaper reporters were severely hampered by this ban on taking notes; they were forced to rely upon their memories and as a result the reports of debates which appeared in the Press were usually garbled and inaccurate

M

versions. By the beginning of the 19th century Parliament had come to regard the Press with more tolerance. Reporters were taking notes quite openly and without fear of ejection, and soon the back row of the Public Gallery was exclusively reserved for them. After the fire of 1834 the Press began to come into their own. In 1835 the first Press Gallery was opened in the temporary House of Commons chamber, and when Sir Charles Barry's new Parliament building was opened in 1852 both chambers included a gallery for the exclusive use of reporters. Parliament had at long last recognized the claims of the Press. In the House of Lords the Reporters' Gallery faces the Throne and in the House of Commons it is above the Speaker's Chair. The Commons chamber designed by Barry was destroyed in 1941, but the Press Gallery is similarly situated in the new chamber which was opened in 1950.

In 1803 William Cobbett began to include a regular report of parliamentary debates in his *Political Register*. There was, of course, no attempt at verbatim reporting at this time, but the innovation was a great step forward as Cobbett brought a high spirit of integrity and fair-mindedness to his task which kept his report free from any partisan bias. After eight years he sold his interest to a printer named Thomas Curson Hansard, who was the son of Luke Hansard, the printer to the House of Commons. In its early years Hansard was compiled from newspaper reports and appeared at monthly intervals. It competed against a number of rival concerns including *The Mirror of Parliament* which at one time employed Charles Dickens. In 1855, however, the Hansard concern was threatened with bankruptcy from which it was rescued by a sales guarantee of one hundred sets on the part of the Treasury. In 1878 a Select Committee was appointed to consider the entire question of parliamentary reporting, and as a result of its recommendations Hansard received a partial subsidy from the Stationery Office on condition that the quality of the report was improved. Towards the fulfilment of this condition the first Hansard reporter was appointed and charged with the duty of attending the debates himself and supplementing the material drawn from newspaper reports. The standard of the report continued to be inadequate, and ten years later another Select Committee recommended a wider measure of Government control. It urged that the work should be carried out upon a contract basis, the contractor to employ a staff of reporters who could maintain between them a constant attendance in the gallery. As a result of this recommendation the concern passed from the control of the Hansard family. They were unable to satisfy the conditions required and in 1890 they sold their interest to a company called the Hansard Publishing Union, which itself soon became bankrupt. Thenceforward the contract was held by a series of different firms which all failed to make a success of it. The report was issued in volumes at intervals of roughly a month. Speeches were not fully reported, verbatim notes were only taken on special occasions, and the standard of accuracy was not high. At last, in 1907, a Select Committee recommended that the reporting of debates should be entirely taken over by the Government. This recommendation was accepted, and in 1908 the appointment of an Editor of Debates and ten reporters to the staff of the House of Commons was announced. Their joint task was to be the compilation of a complete and accurate verbatim record of the debates of the House, and in 1909, in conformity with this requirement, appeared the first Official Report of the debates of the House of Commons. The House of Lords did not at first follow the example of the Commons. Prior to 1909, a summary of the Lords' debates had been included in the same volume with the Commons' debates. Since that year the debates of the upper House have been separately published, and in 1920 they too were taken over by the Stationery Office.

Since 1909 Hansard has never looked back, and the very name is now officially recognized. In 1892 the word 'Hansard' was dropped and the report became known as the 'Authorized Edition' of parliamentary debates. In 1909 it became the 'Official Report', and has remained so ever since, but in 1943 the word 'Hansard' was restored and now appears in brackets upon each title page.

See also PARLIAMENTARY DEBATES; PARLIAMENTARY HISTORY; PRESS AND PARLIAMENT.

HANSARD, LUKE (1752–1828)

The printer of the Journal of the House of Commons (q.v.) from 1774 until his death. His biography was written by J. C. Trewin and E. M. King under the title *Printer to the House*, and published in 1952.

HANSARD SOCIETY FOR PARLIAMENTARY GOVERNMENT

Founded on 2 August 1944, the Hansard Society for Parliamentary Government is a supra-national, non-profit-making, unofficial educational body dedicated to promoting the cause of the institution of parliamentary government in all its democratic forms. The name *Hansard* is derived from the circumstance that the Society in its present form evolved from a small body called the *Friends of Hansard* founded by Sir Stephen King-Hall (afterwards Lord King-Hall) in 1940. From these small and struggling beginnings the Society has acquired a secure and honoured international status. It is the only body in the world undertaking this work. The government of the Society is vested in an international council elected annually by the members, who are either individuals or corporate members (firms, schools, Trade Unions and other associates). From 1944 until his death in 1966 Lord King-Hall was Chairman of the Council and Honorary Director of the Society.

The Society publishes a quarterly journal entitled *Parliamentary*

Affairs, the first issue of which appeared in the winter of 1947. It contains articles by distinguished contributors on every aspect of parliamentary institutions throughout the world. The Society also publishes books and pamphlets on parliamentary subjects. It has recently established American and African sections and a research department. The American section is at present promoting knowledge in British schools of the American system of government, and the African section is engaged on educational work in the service of West Africans. In 1957 the Ford Foundation made it a grant of £5,000 per annum for five years. The expanding activities of the Society include the organization of lectures, exhibitions and other educational work, particularly in schools. The work of the Society is financed by subscriptions from its two categories of membership (approximately 800 individuals and 500 corporate members) and donations. It is not liable for tax.

Institutions and individuals desirous of knowing more about the work of the Society, the privileges of membership, etc., should apply to The Secretary, The Hansard Society for Parliamentary Government, 162 Buckingham Palace Road, London, S.W.1.

HANSARD, THOMAS CURSON (1776–1833)

Eldest son of Luke Hansard, he began to print the Parliamentary Debates (q.v.) for Cobbett's *Political Register* in 1803. In 1812 he bought the interest from Cobbett and it remained with the Hansard family until it was resold in 1890.

HATSELL, JOHN (1743–1820)

Clerk of the House of Commons from 1768 until his death in 1820 and a leading authority on parliamentary practice. Redlich describes Hatsell and Sir Thomas Erskine May (q.v.) as 'the two distinguished writers on whose systematic works our whole acquaintance with the historic and current law of Parliament is based'. Hatsell's greatest and most valuable work was his prodigious collection of precedents which was first published in four volumes in 1781 under the title *Precedents of Proceedings in the House of Commons, under separate titles; with observations*. The best edition of this work is the fourth, published in 1818 with additions by Speaker Abbot. Hatsell was also the author of *A Collection of Cases of Privilege of Parliament, from the earliest records to 1628*, published in 1776.

Although Hatsell retired from the practical exercise of his duties in 1797 and appointed a deputy, John Ley, to carry on in his place, he remained titular Clerk of the House until his death. He continued to draw the emoluments attached to the office, sharing them with Ley, and remained in occupation of the Clerk's official residence. (*See* Williams, O. C., *The Clerical Organization of the House of Commons, 1661-1850*, Oxford University Press, 1954.)

HAXEY, THOMAS, CASE OF

The earliest recorded instance of the Commons asserting their right to liberty in conducting their proceedings was in 1397 when the Lords, at the instigation of Richard II, convicted Thomas Haxey of treason for his work in connexion with a Bill to which the King took exception. In the first Parliament of the following reign the Commons petitioned for a reversal of the judgment on the ground that it was 'against right and the course which had been usual in Parliament in violation of the customs of the Commons'. The petition was allowed and an important principle of privilege was thus recognized. Although this case is often regarded as having led to the first affirmation of the Commons' privilege of freedom of speech this assumption is not strictly correct since Haxey himself was not a member. The first specific claim for freedom of speech, also successful, was not made until 1455 when a member, Sir Thomas Yonge, complained of having been imprisoned for words he had spoken in the House, 'notwithstanding that by the old liberty and freedom of the Commons of this land had, enjoyed and prescribed, from the time that no mind is, all such persons as for the time being assembled in any Parliament for the same Commons, ought to have their freedom to speak and say in the House of their assembly, as to them is thought convenient or reasonable, without any manner of challenge, charge or punition'.

See also PRIVILEGE.

HEALING PARLIAMENT

The Convention Parliament (q.v.) which met on 25 April 1660 and restored Charles II to the throne a few days later. This action, it was hoped, would 'heal' all remaining wounds and differences existing in the nation.

HEALTH, MINISTER OF

This office became obsolete in 1969 with the merging of the Ministry of Health and the Ministry of Social Security under a Secretary of State for Social Services (*see* SOCIAL SERVICES, SECRETARY OF STATE FOR). The Ministry of Health had originally been created in 1919 and the Minister's responsibilities covered all matters affecting the health of the country including research, the publication of statistics and national health insurance. The Minister also took over the supervision of the local authorities from the Local Government Board (created in 1871), but in 1951 these matters, with the exception of public health, were taken over by the Minister of Local Government and Planning, who has now become the Minister of Housing and Local Government. Under the National Health Service Act of 1946, the Minister of Health had the duty of providing a comprehensive health service for England

and Wales designed to secure improvement in the physical and mental health of the people and the prevention, diagnosis, and treatment of illness.

A chronological list of Ministers of Health is included as Appendix 18.

HENRY I (1068–1135)

Youngest son of William I, crowned King of England 5 August 1100. He succeeded his brother, William II, and issued a charter of liberties on his accession.

HENRY II (1133–1189)

The first Plantagenet King, son of Matilda, only daughter of Henry I, and Geoffrey Plantagenet. He was crowned King of England on 19 December 1154. His first act upon his accession was to issue a charter of liberties. He initiated many great reforms in government and established the rule of law.

See also PARLIAMENT.

HENRY III (1207–1272)

Eldest son of John, succeeded his father while still a minor and was crowned on 28 October 1216. He was confirmed in his title on 17 May 1220, when a second coronation took place. His reign is an important one in the early development of Parliament (q.v.). It was in the age of Henry III that the term 'Parliament' first came to be regularly used and that the national assembly of the realm began to develop representative characteristics (*see* SIMON DE MONTFORT'S PARLIAMENT).

HENRY IV (1367–1413)

Son of John of Gaunt, was acclaimed King by Parliament on 30 September 1399, the day of the deposition of Richard II. The first King of the House of Lancaster, Henry re-established the monarchy upon a constitutional basis and adhered to the principle of government through Parliament (q.v.).

HENRY V (1387–1422)

Eldest son of Henry IV by his first wife, succeeded his father on 20 March 1413. Although in his short reign he distinguished himself as a warrior rather than as an administrator, he was a just and constitutional ruler who maintained good relations between the Crown and Parliament (q.v.).

HENRY VI (1421–1471)

The only son of Henry V and Catherine of France, succeeded his father on 31 August 1422, whilst still an infant. On 18 November 1423 he attended the Opening of Parliament (q.v.) at Westminster in his mother's arms. The reign of this weak and ill-fated monarch was torn by strife, and the history of Parliament has never been more turbulent than at this period, its powers falling into the hands of the factions engaged in the Wars of the Roses. Henry VI came to a violent end on 21 May 1471, at the hands of his Yorkist adversaries.

HENRY VII (1457–1509)

Son of Edmund Tudor, Earl of Richmond, and grandson of Catherine, widow of Henry V, defeated Richard III at Bosworth in 1485, and although his title was questionable, he was crowned King of England on 30 October of that year. He greatly strengthened the monarchy and left it secure for his successor.

HENRY VIII (1491–1547)

Second son of Henry VII, succeeded his father on 22 April 1509. During his reign the power of the Crown reached its height, and although he ruled theoretically through Parliament (q.v.) the legislature became, in reality, nothing more than the instrument of the King's will. The two major developments in the parliamentary history of the reign were the emergence of the House of Commons as the stronger of the two Houses and the total destruction of the parliamentary influence of the Church.

HIGH COURT OF PARLIAMENT

This expression now refers to the legislature, but it is a reminder that the British Parliament was, and still is, a court—the highest court in the land. In those distant ancestors of Parliament, the Witenagemot and the *Curia Regis* (qq.v.), the judicial, executive, and legislative powers were fused, and although the function of some early Parliaments, such as the Model Parliament (q.v.) of Edward I, was primarily judicial, at the end of the 14th century both Houses passed resolutions that the judicial power of Parliament was not vested in the House of Commons. The jurisdiction of the House of Lords, after its separation from the *Curia* in the reign of Edward III, extended to trial of peers by peers for treason or felony (*see* PEERS), appeals from the common law courts, and (after 1376) impeachment (q.v.). All that remains to the House of Lords is its appellate jurisdiction (*see* HOUSE OF LORDS) and judicial functions with regard to claims to ancient peerages. It also shares with the Commons certain judicial functions with regard to privilege and in connexion with Private Bills (q.v.), where the procedure assumes a quasi-judicial character when counsel and witnesses are heard on behalf of contending parties.

[349]

A Committee of Inquiry may be set up by either House, and under the Tribunals of Inquiry (Evidence) Act of 1921 has all the powers of the High Court as regards examination of witnesses and production of documents. Tribunals were so appointed in 1936 to inquire into a leakage of information about the forthcoming Budget and in 1948 (the Lynskey Tribunal, Cmd. 7616) to investigate allegations of bribery and corruption in Government circles.

South Africa in 1952 passed a High Court of Parliament Act which laid down that any past or future judgment of the Appellate Division declaring any Act of Parliament invalid was to be subject to review by the High Court of Parliament, 'which shall be a court of law'. It was to consist of every Member of Parliament with a president appointed by the Governor-General. The object in creating this High Court was to reverse a decision by the Appellate Division that an Act putting coloured voters on a separate roll was invalid, but on application by coloured voters to the Cape Provincial Division the High Court of Parliament Act was declared null and void, and on appeal by the Government to the Appellate Division this judgment was confirmed.

(The standard work on this subject is *The High Court of Parliament and its Supremacy*, by C. H. McIlwain, Yale Univ. Press, 1934.)

HISTORY OF PARLIAMENT TRUST

In May 1928 Josiah Wedgwood (later Lord Wedgwood) began to organize a petition to the Prime Minister for the compilation of a parliamentary history, and within a few months had collected the signatures of 200 Members of Parliament. In March 1929 a departmental committee was appointed to consider the whole question, and their interim report published in 1932 strongly advocated that the work of compiling a full record of Parliament, including biographies of members and a reconstruction of procedure, should be set on foot. Wedgwood subsequently set to work to raise the necessary funds by private subscription, and in 1934 the Government agreed to put up one-half of the estimated cost (£30,000) if subscriptions were sufficient to cover the remainder. The first two volumes were published in 1936 and 1938, and in 1940 the History of Parliament Trust was founded. Lord Wedgwood died in 1943, but the Second World War had already brought the scheme to an end, and its assets and historical collections were put in the care of trustees. In 1951 the Chancellor of the Exchequer announced that the Government would give financial support to a revised and improved scheme by means of annual grants-in-aid. Trustees were drawn from both Houses, and an Editorial Board was invited to direct the preparation of the History. A basic feature of the new History, which will be divided into sections of roughly forty years, will be its concise biographies of Members of the House of

Commons. Each section will be published as soon as it is ready, and the new volumes will replace those issued under Wedgwood's supervision. Work on the new History began officially in 1953, and the first three volumes, covering the period 1754–1790, were published in 1964.

HOME DEPARTMENT, SECRETARY OF STATE FOR THE

The office of Secretary of State for the Home Department originated in 1782, when the work of the two Secretaries of State (q.v.) then existing was divided into Home Affairs and Foreign Affairs. The Secretary of State for Home Affairs was also responsible for Ireland and the Colonies until they were taken over by additional secretaries. The Home Secretary is the medium of communication between the Church of England and the Queen, the British Government and Northern Ireland, the Isle of Man, and the Channel Islands, and he collaborates with the Secretary of State for Scotland on certain matters affecting that country. He is responsible for the administration of justice, apart from matters dealt with by the Lord Chancellor (q.v.), which includes the appointment of the Director of Public Prosecutions, the exercise of the Royal Prerogative of mercy, direct control of the Metropolitan Police and indirect supervision of the local forces, and the prisons and probation of offenders. Among the large variety of affairs also within the province of the Home Secretary are the naturalization and supervision of aliens, the preparation of registers for parliamentary and local elections, the Fire Service, Civil Defence, and miscellaneous duties imposed by the two Children Acts of 1933 and 1948 and the Shops Acts.

This Minister is invariably in the Cabinet and his salary is £8,500 per annum. He is entitled to a further £1,250 if he sits in the House of Commons. A chronological list of Home Secretaries appears as Appendix 19.

The Home Secretary's counterpart in other Commonwealth countries is variously styled. In Australia he is the Minister for the Interior, as also in Ghana, Cyprus and Sierra Leone. New Zealand, Nigeria, Uganda and Rhodesia employ the term Minister of Internal Affairs, and Minister of Home Affairs is the style in use in India, Pakistan, Ceylon, Malaysia, Tanzania, Jamaica, Trinidad and Tobago, Kenya, Malawi, Zambia, and Northern Ireland. In Canada there is no such minister, the subjects which normally come under the jurisdiction of a Home Department being distributed among various other ministries.

HOME SECURITY, MINISTER OF

Created in 1939, this office was first held by Sir John Anderson (afterwards Viscount Waverley) concurrently with that of Home Secretary (q.v.). Herbert Morrison, who was appointed Home

Secretary in 1940, was also appointed Minister of Home Security, which office he held until 1945, when the latter ministry was abolished. The Minister was responsible for civil defence and air-raid precautions, which have now been taken over by the Home Secretary.

HONG KONG LEGISLATIVE COUNCIL

Great Britain took formal possession of Hong Kong in 1841, and the Legislative Council, established under the Royal Charter which made the island a separate Colony, first met in 1844. Until 1858 the Council met *in camera*. Unofficial members first made their appearance in 1850, and the present composition of the Council, enlarged from July 1964, includes 13 nominated unofficials, 9 of whom are Chinese and 1 Indian. Twelve official members and the Governor as President complete the Council. The Executive Council now comprises the Governor, 5 *ex-officio* and 6 unofficial members, including 3 Chinese and 1 Portuguese, and 1 nominated official member. A notable variation from House of Commons procedure is that on the first reading of a Bill the mover explains its object and the reasons for introducing it. The Legislative Council occupies an annexe to the Secretariat Wing of the new government offices, which is equipped with two radio booths for broadcasting debates and commentaries. The Chamber is fan-shaped and provides accommodation for the Press and about eighty seats for the public.

HOUSE OF ASSEMBLY

The name given to the lower Houses of the Parliaments of the Bahamas, Barbados, Bermuda, South Australia, and Tasmania. It is also applied to the unicameral legislatures of Newfoundland, Nova Scotia, Papua and New Guinea, Dominica, St. Lucia and St. Kitts/Nevis/Anguilla, and Gibraltar.

HOUSE OF COMMONS

The lower House of the British Parliament, consisting of 630 members, including the Speaker (q.v.), elected by popular franchise and each representing a specific constituency of the United Kingdom. England returns 511 members, Scotland 71, Wales 36, and Northern Ireland 12. The numerical strength of the House has been altered from time to time by various Acts of Parliament. In 1900 there were 670 members, and in 1918 the number was increased to 707. In 1922, after the establishment of the Irish Free State, the number was reduced to 615, at which figure it remained until 1935 when it was increased to 640. The effect of the Representation of the People Act, 1948, was to reduce the membership to 625 with effect from 1950, and also to abolish the 12 university seats, the 12 double-member constituencies, and the business vote. In 1955 5 extra seats were allocated to England, bringing the total to its present figure of 630, Scotland, Wales, and Northern Ireland remaining unaffected by the increase.

The House of Commons is the lower House in name and tradition only. In reality it is the more powerful of the two Houses of Parliament. The Government depends for its existence upon the support of a majority of the Commons and is answerable to the House for all its actions. It must at all times be prepared to justify itself in the House, where it can expect to be subjected to constant criticism of its policy and administration. Members of the Opposition enjoy exactly the same rights and privileges as members who support the Government, and when in the House the Prime Minister himself has no privileges beyond those of any other member. All major legislation is initiated in the House of Commons, and no law can be enacted unless it is passed by a majority of the members present. The House of Commons also has exclusive control over the nation's finances, and no Supply can be granted nor taxation levied without the Commons' approval.

Just as the Government is responsible to the House of Commons, so are the Commons responsible to the country. The Commons have been representative in character from the earliest times, even though universal adult suffrage is a very recent institution. The principle of appealing to the country for the ultimate decision as to who is to govern, and the official nature of the Opposition's functions, are essential to the modern parliamentary system, which provides the means whereby a change of government can be effected without causing disruption to the life and economy of the country. It is a system which was developed through centuries of conflict between the Crown and the Commons before it became finally established in its present form.

HISTORY OF THE HOUSE OF COMMONS. The Commons made their first appearance in Parliament during the 13th century, when the practice arose of summoning the knights and burgesses of the shires and towns in addition to the bishops, earls, and barons. The precedent was created as a result of the King's ever-increasing financial needs. Before the Great Charter, King John had been forced to rely more and more upon extraordinary revenues for the prosecution of his wars and the indulgence of his other extravagances, and had raised the money principally by means of scutages, a form of regular taxation. The Great Charter, which resulted from the action taken by the barons to check the abuses of this monarch, forbade the King to levy scutages 'except by common counsel of our kingdom'. In drawing up the Charter the barons had not calculated on the Commons having any voice in the counsels of the kingdom, but as the royal requirements increased the King was forced to seek aids from the shires and boroughs as well as from the nobility. Under the feudal system of local government the shires and boroughs were self-contained communities or 'communes'—hence, Commons—which had achieved a considerable measure of self-government including the right to assess their own taxes. In 1254, as a result of the Lords' reluctance to take the responsibility for raising the supplies demanded by the King, two knights from each county were summoned to the Parliament, and in 1265 there also came two citizens from each city and two burgesses from each borough.

In the reign of Edward I, Parliaments began to assume a more representative character, although the purpose of summoning the Commons remained solely a financial one. The King had need only of their money, not their counsel. The Parliament of 1295, known as the Model Parliament (q.v.), was the most fully representative that had ever been called, and included the lower clergy for the first time. The 14th century saw the emergence of the Commons as a separate body, sitting and deliberating independently of the Lords. They now began to assert themselves, for the dependence of the Crown upon the Commons for the grant of aids and supplies gave them a strong bargaining power. In 1348 they demanded redress of their grievances before they would grant Supply, a practice which they claimed as a right and were to adopt on many subsequent occasions. The influence of the Commons upon legislation also becomes apparent in this century. Thanks to that very effective weapon, the power to withhold Supply, the King was compelled to make concessions to the Commons. Thus the measures they proposed to remedy the nation's grievances came to be accepted, and they gradually became the initiators of legislation instead of mere petitioners.

Successive monarchs endeavoured to circumvent Parliament by employing various extra-parliamentary devices to raise the revenues they required. These took the form of various taxes, compulsory gifts, or loans, and, in the reign of James I, the sale of titles. It was natural that these tactics should provoke protests from the Commons, and there began the long struggle to establish the principle that no taxation should be levied without the consent of Parliament. It was finally conceded at the Restoration when parliamentary control of taxation was accepted by the King and has never since been challenged. By this time the supremacy of the Commons over the Lords in matters of finance had also been established. As far back as 1395 grants were made 'by the Commons with the advice and assent of the Lords', and by the end of the 17th century even the right of the Lords to amend Money Bills had fallen into abeyance. It was not until the Parliament Act of 1911, however, that the Lords were finally deprived of their right to reject financial legislation.

Having gained control over taxation it was a logical development that the Commons should also establish control over expenditure. This, the final financial victory, was accomplished during the reign of George III, whose repeated extravagances made such deep inroads into the Civil List revenues that the Commons raised their voices in protest. In 1777 they refused to pay one of the royal debts until accounts had been presented. Their control of expenditure was confirmed in 1782 when the King agreed, under pressure from Lord Rockingham, to certain reforms, including that of the Civil List.

The modern parliamentary system, whereby the Government depends upon the support of a majority in the Commons in order to govern effectively, began to evolve after the Revolution of 1688. The right of the Sovereign to choose his ministers had never been challenged and although after the revolution the King had regard for the feelings of Parliament in selecting them, they were not controlled by, nor responsible to, either House. A ministry did not automatically resign, as is the custom to-day, if an election returned a hostile majority to the House of Commons. Both William III and Anne, however, found themselves compelled to adjust the composition of their ministries according to the political complexion of Parliament, as parliamentary support for the administration proved to be necessary to effective government. The year 1712 marked an important development in the establishment of the supremacy of the Commons over the Lords, when a predominantly Tory lower House came into conflict with the Whig majority in the Lords, who threatened to reject the Peace of Utrecht. The deadlock was broken by the creation of a sufficient number of Tory peers to ensure its acceptance by the upper House. As the head of the government it was customary for the Sovereign himself to preside over the ministry, but when George I withdrew from an active part in government a new presiding officer had to be found. In assuming this position, Sir Robert Walpole became the first, although unofficial, Prime Minister (q.v.). He had been appointed First Lord of the Treasury (an office which has come to be associated with that of Prime Minister), and unlike previous chief ministers he had not accepted elevation to the peerage but had chosen instead to remain a Member of the House of Commons. He thus became answerable in the Commons for the conduct of the administration as a whole. For twenty-one years he commanded a majority in the Commons, but when in January and February of 1742 he suffered two defeats at their hands, he resigned office, and thus established, if only fundamentally, the principle that the Government is responsible to the House of Commons and reliant on its support. In 1782 the principle was carried a considerable stage further when Lord North's entire ministry resigned because of insufficient support in the Commons for the Government's policy. After the passing of the Reform Bill, which effectively destroyed all means of predetermining the result of an election, the power of the Commons to decide the political complexion of the Government was finally confirmed.

The House of Commons has always been a representative assembly, and there is evidence of the responsibility of the member to his constituency as early as 1339, when the Commons declared themselves unable to grant an aid without first consulting those they represented. Indications of the modern relationship between the member and his constituents become apparent after the Restoration, but nearly three centuries were to elapse before the right to vote was won for every adult citizen. (For the history of the franchise *see under the heading* REPRESENTATION.)

ADMINISTRATION OF THE HOUSE OF COMMONS. The House of Commons is under the overall administrative authority of the Speaker, and since April 1965 he has shared with the Lord Chancellor the control of the greater part of the accommodation in the Palace of Westminster (q.v.). Control over the building was formerly vested in the Lord Great Chamberlain (q.v.), but those parts of the Palace of Westminster occupied by or on behalf of the House of Commons now fall within the exclusive jurisdiction of the Speaker.

For administrative purposes the staff of the House are organized into the following five departments: the Department of the Clerk of the House, the Department of the Speaker, the Department of the Library, the Administration Department and the Department of the Serjeant-at-Arms.

The Department of the Clerk of the House was reorganized in 1967 and is responsible for the conduct of the business of the House. It includes the Clerk Assistant and the Second Clerk Assistant and Clerk of Committees, who are the two permanent officers next in seniority to the Clerk himself, and the following six offices:

(1) Committee Office, under the Second Clerk Assistant and Clerk of Committees, which is responsible for the staffing of Standing Committees and Select Committees.

(2) Public Bill Office, under the Clerk of Public Bills, which is responsible for procedure on Public Bills and the financial procedure of the House.

(3) Journal Office, under the Clerk of the Journals, which is responsible for compiling the Journal of the House of Commons, the Votes and Proceedings, and for relevant research.

(4) Table Office, under a Principal Clerk, which is responsible for receiving questions to ministers and ensuring that they comply with the conditions relating to questions, and for the preparation of the Notice Paper and Order Book.

(5) Private Bill Office, under the Clerk of Private Bills (who is also Examiner of Private Bill Petitions), which is responsible for the conduct of private legislation and the staffing of Private Bill Committees.

(6) The Overseas Office, headed by a Principal Clerk, which is responsible for relations of the House of Commons with Commonwealth and Foreign Parliaments, participation in international parliamentary activities, parliamentary seminars, bilateral parliamentary exchanges, etc.

The Department of the Speaker includes the Speaker's Counsel, Chaplain and Trainbearer and the following four offices:

(1) Speaker's Office, under the Speaker's Secretary, who deals with his official correspondence and assists him with his social and official relations with members.

(2) Office of the Official Report, under the Editor of the Official Report of Debates, which is responsible for the daily production of Hansard.

(3) Vote Office, under the Deliverer of Votes, which is responsible for the issue of all parliamentary papers to members.

(4) Sale Office, under a Chief Office Clerk, which is responsible for the sale of papers and other material purchased by members.

The Library, previously included in the Department of the Speaker, became a separate department in 1967.

The Administration Department is headed by the Clerk Administrator (Services), who is answerable to the Clerk of the House, and includes the Fees Office, which is responsible for the control of House of Commons expenditures, and the Establishment Section.

The Department of the Serjeant-at-Arms is responsible for the upkeep and maintenance of the premises, the admission of strangers, and the maintenance of order within the precincts of the House. The housekeeping duties of the Serjeant-at-Arms derive from the House of Commons (Offices) Act, 1812, and include the allocation of accommodation, the organization of members' amenities, and cleaning. The doorkeepers, storekeepers, attendants, office keepers, watchmen, cleaners, and police assigned to duty in the House of Commons all come under the supervision of the Serjeant's department. The Admission Order Office and the issue of passes to the galleries are likewise under the control of this department.

The staff of the House of Commons totals approximately 320 people, at all levels. Their pay and conditions are settled by the House of Commons Offices Commission (q.v.), and most salary and wage scales are to-day linked to those of corresponding grades in the Civil Service.

Since December 1965 the administrative organization of the House of Commons has been under the central co-ordination of the House of Commons (Services) Committee (q.v.), a sessional committee appointed to advise the Speaker on the control of accommodation and services.

MEETING-PLACES OF THE HOUSE OF COMMONS. The earliest recorded meeting-place of the House of Commons is the Painted Chamber of the House of Lords where the knights, citizens, and burgesses assembled in 1341. In 1352 the Commons met in the Chapter House of Westminster Abbey, and in 1368 in the Little Hall or White Hall which later became the Court of Requests. The Chapter House was used again in 1384 and probably on a number of other occasions during the 14th century, but no reference to it appears in the existing records after 1395. During the next twenty years the Refectory of the Abbey was used as their debating chamber. No further record appears until 1547 when the Commons acquired their permanent meeting-place, St. Stephen's Chapel. It was granted to them by Edward VI and it remained their Chamber for nearly three hundred years until its destruction by fire in 1834. After the fire the Commons moved into the Court of Requests, which was vacated by the Lords who moved into the Painted Chamber. Here they remained until the new Commons Chamber, built by Sir Charles Barry, was ready for occupation in 1852. This was the Chamber which was destroyed by a German bomb on the night of 10 May 1941, when the Commons were forced to move again. They moved temporarily into Church House in Great Smith Street and, shortly afterwards, for the second time in their history, they took over the Chamber of the House of Lords for their deliberations, the Lords moving into the King's Robing Room. In December 1943, a Select Committee was appointed to consider the rebuilding of the Commons' Chamber, and recommended that its design should be in the style of the old one. The new Chamber was designed by Sir Giles Gilbert Scott and was officially opened on 26 October 1950.

THE NEW CHAMBER. The style of the new Chamber is a form of Gothic which retains characteristics similar to those of the one designer by Barry. It stands upon the original foundations of the formed Chamber and has the identical floor dimensions, 68 feet by $45\frac{1}{2}$ feet. Above the level of the galleries the dimensions are larger, 103 feet by 48 feet, thus providing additional seating capacity for visitors. It is 46 feet in height and has a shaped ceiling composed of a large number of glass panels which admit most of the light which illuminates the Chamber, but which are so coloured as to give them the appearance of oak in daylight. There is seating capacity for 437 members; thus, whenever an important debate draws a large majority of the members into the Chamber the latecomers are forced to stand.

A number of modern refinements have been incorporated into the design. Heating and ventilation are controlled by means of air conditioning plants which adjust the temperature and humidity to the desired degree. The Chamber is lit by 150 glass daylight panels, each with a fluorescent tube mounted in front of a reflector. In addition there is a system of indirect floodlighting to illumine the ceiling and subsidiary lights have been placed under the galleries. The lighting system can be regulated to provide the required degree of illumination. The Chamber is provided with microphones and miniature loudspeakers set into the backs of the seats.

Much of the furniture of the Chamber consists of gifts from the countries of the Commonwealth and Empire. The Speaker's Chair was presented by the Commonwealth of Australia, the entrance doors are the gifts of India and Pakistan, and the Table of the House came from Canada. The Union of South Africa (now the Republic of South Africa) presented the three Clerks' chairs, the Serjeant-at-Arms' chair came from Ceylon, and the two despatch boxes from New Zealand. A complete list of the gifts appears as Appendix 3.

HOUSE OF COMMONS, CANADA

See CANADIAN PARLIAMENT.

HOUSE OF COMMONS OFFICES COMMISSION

The body responsible for the salaries and conditions of service of the officers and staff of the House of Commons, originally established under the House of Commons Offices Act, 1812. It consists of the Speaker as Chairman and, provided they are Members of the House of Commons, the Secretaries of State, the Chancellor of the Exchequer, the Attorney-General and the Solicitor-General. The original membership included the Master of the Rolls, an office which now disqualifies its holder from membership of the House of Commons. The Act authorizes the Speaker and two other members to exercise the powers of the full Commission.

HOUSE OF COMMONS PAPERS

A series of papers, numbered from 1 onwards throughout the session, which bear on their covers the words 'ordered by the House of Commons to be printed'. They include reports and returns which have to be presented to the House in pursuance of some special provision in an Act; reports from Government officials produced in compliance with a direct order of the House, including the detailed financial statistics accompanying the Estimates, and returns from the Treasury, Post Office, and Revenue departments. Reports of Select Committees and Minutes of Standing Committees also appear as House of Commons Papers. These papers are listed as presented in Votes and Proceedings and the Journal, and are available to members on demand at the Vote Office. House of Lords Papers include Bills and are numbered in parentheses in one sequence.

HOUSE OF COMMONS (SERVICES) COMMITTEE

A Sessional Select Committee of 16 members first appointed on 7 December 1965 to control the accommodation and services in that part of the Palace of Westminster (q.v.) occupied by or on behalf of the House of Commons. The appointment of this committee followed from the arrangements, agreed by Her Majesty the Queen in the previous April, for the control of the precincts of the Palace of Westminster.

The committee is empowered to send for persons, papers and records, to sit notwithstanding an adjournment of the House, to report from time to time, and to appoint sub-committees. Each sub-committee must consist of 2 members of the full committee and not more than 5 other members nominated by the House on the recommendation of the committee. The quorum of the committee is 5, and of each sub-committee, 3. The following sub-committees have been appointed:

(1) The Catering Sub-Committee, which takes over the functions of the former Kitchen Committee (q.v.).

(2) The Administrative Sub-Committee, which is concerned with the administrative problems of the Department of the Clerk of the House and the Department of the Speaker (excluding the Library), the arrangements for the reporting and publishing of debates and the form and distribution of the Notice Papers of the House.

(3) The Library Sub-Committee, which replaces the informal library committee formerly appointed to advise the Speaker.

(4) The Accommodation and Housekeeping Sub-Committee, which is concerned with the improvement of accommodation, the facilities for members and staff and the security of the premises.

(5) The New Building Sub-Committee, which is concerned with the allocation of new accommodation as it becomes available and further plans for expansion.

(6) The Broadcasting Sub-Committee, which is concerned with the question of the broadcasting and televising of the proceedings of the House of Commons, a matter which has also occupied the attention of other Select Committees.

The committee has also taken over the functions of the former Select Committee on Publications and Debates Reports (q.v.),which now fall within the sphere of the Administrative Sub-Committee.

The Chairman of the committee answers questions in the House, both oral and written, on matters falling within the committee's jurisdiction and he may, should he think fit, delegate the answering of a question to the Chairman of the appropriate sub-committee.

HOUSE OF KEYS
See MANX PARLIAMENT.

HOUSE OF LORDS

The upper House of the British Parliament—the oldest and largest second Chamber in the world, still largely composed of hereditary peers. At the end of 1970 there were over 1,000 persons with a claim to membership of the House of Lords, although only a minority of them are politically active and regularly exercise their right to sit and vote. The total complement of hereditary peers and other Lords of Parliament at that time comprised 4 royal princes, 2 archbishops, 25 dukes, 30 marquesses, 162 earls and countesses, 109 viscounts, 24 bishops, and 720 barons and baronesses, in that order of precedence. These figures include the very small number of hereditary peers who, being minors, do not yet qualify for membership of the House. The archbishops and bishops are described as the Lords Spiritual (q.v.), the remainder being collectively known as the Lords Temporal (q.v.).

All hereditary peers who have attained the age of twenty-one and are not otherwise disqualified as aliens, bankrupts, lunatics, or by reason of serving a sentence following a conviction for treason or felony, are entitled to a writ of summons to attend Parliament with the right to sit and vote in the House of Lords. The membership of the House also includes a number of life peers (q.v.) whose rank is that of a baron, but since the essence of a peerage is its hereditary character, they, together with the Lords Spiritual, might more properly be described as Lords of Parliament. Life peers fall into two categories, judicial and non-judicial. The former category consists of the Lords of Appeal in Ordinary (q.v.) and the retired Lords of Appeal in Ordinary, appointed under the Appellate Jurisdiction Acts, 1876–1947, to assist in the hearing and determination of appeals when the House sits in its judicial capacity. They are not debarred from sitting and voting when the House sits in its legislative capacity. The majority of the life peers are non-judicial and are appointed under the Life Peerages Act, 1958. At the end of 1970, 181 life peers had been appointed under this Act since it first came into force.

The Life Peerages Act, 1958, also removed the general disqualification to which women had formerly been subject in respect of membership of the House of Lords. The Act permits the conferring of life peerages on women, but it did not not remove the disqualification upon hereditary peeresses from sitting and voting in the House in their own right. This disability was ultimately removed, however, by the Peerage Act, 1963, and a woman holding an hereditary peerage in her own right is now qualified for membership of the House of Lords on the same conditions as a man in similar circumstances. Thus, men and women are now on an equal footing with regard to admission to the upper House as well as to the lower House of Parliament.

Until the passing of the Peerage Act, 1963, the peers of Scotland were represented in the House of Lords by 16 of their number, elected by themselves at every General Election. Scottish peers are now in exactly the same position as the peers of England, Great Britain and the United Kingdom, all now being entitled to admission to the upper House. Irish peers, who were also at one time represented in the House of Lords, have not been placed on a similar footing, but they are not disqualified by reason of their peerages from sitting in the House of Commons or voting at General Elections. (*See* REPRESENTATIVE PEERS).

The most important effect of the Peerage Act, 1963, is the provision which it makes for an hereditary peer to disclaim his peerage, thus abandoning all the rights and privileges of peerage and assuming the rights and status of a commoner. (*See* PEERAGE, DISCLAIMER OF.)

In 1969 a Bill to reform the House of Lords was abandoned because its opponents prevented it from making progress at the committee stage. Its provisions are dealt with under the heading HOUSE OF LORDS REFORM.

The early House of Lords was small and, before the Reformation, when the abbots and priors were summoned, spiritual peers were in the majority—in 1301 in addition to the 2 archbishops and 18 bishops there were 80 abbots and priors who were entitled to sit in the House, while in those times the temporal peers rarely exceeded 50. This number was increased under the Stuarts, but it was not until the 18th century that the lavish creation of peers began, and between 1880 and 1920 433 new lords were added to the Roll. Of the existing peerages only a very small proportion are really ancient. These early peerages were created by writ of summons to Parliament, but from the end of the 14th century the practice grew up of creating a peerage by the more formal method of granting letters patent. This system superseded the earlier one under which the right to attend Parliament as a peer depended on a writ of summons having been issued to an ancestor, though whether this was how the hereditary factor originated in the peerage has been disputed. A list of the Lords Temporal is prepared by the Garter King of Arms, and a copy of this Roll of the Lords inscribed on parchment is laid by him on the Table of the House at the beginning of every session of Parliament. This Roll was first laid in 1621, and a similar Roll, including the Lords Spiritual, has been laid upon the Table by the Clerk of the Parliaments and ordered to be printed by H.M. Stationery Office since 1827.

The House of Lords is the lineal descendant of the Great Council or King's Council of the Norman and Plantagenet Kings, with which the Saxon Witenagemot (q.v.) was deemed to be incorporated. The

Lords became separated from the Commons in Parliament in the reign of Edward III, and the upper House became a definite body, although it was not called the House of Lords until the 16th century. The removal of the abbots and priors during the reign of Henry VIII ended for ever the ecclesiastical majority in the House of Lords, and the increase in the number of temporal peers went on rapidly during the reign of the earlier Stuarts. A week after the execution of Charles I the monarchy and the House of Lords were abolished by unanimous vote of the Commons, in spite of their previous declarations that they intended to respect the rights of the peers. The House of Lords was restored in the Convention Parliament of 1660 by no special Act or resolution—it reassembled with no greater formality than was customary after an adjournment. The bishops, who had been excluded by an Act of the Long Parliament, were still absent, but were readmitted by an Act passed by the next Parliament in 1661. After the Restoration the two Houses were on a more or less equal footing, but throughout the 18th and early 19th centuries the composition of the House of Commons was to a large extent controlled by peers who, as the patrons of parliamentary boroughs, were able to nominate their own candidates at elections. This state of affairs was remedied by the Reform Act of 1832, but although the House of Commons came into its own, the powers of the House of Lords remained formidable. Deadlock between the two Houses became a frequent occurrence and Liberal Governments found themselves unable to implement their legislative programmes on account of the obstruction of the Lords. It was a situation which could not continue, and the crisis came in 1909 when the Lords rejected the Finance Bill. Two years later the first of the Parliament Acts (q.v.) deprived the House of Lords of most of its effective power. The House of Lords is a typical example of the British aptitude for adapting ancient institutions to modern requirements. Originally the more powerful of the two Houses, it is to-day a second Chamber very much subordinate to the popular House, but owing to its considerable prestige it can still influence the course of legislation and the affairs of the nation.

The most important difference between the work of the two Houses of Parliament is the strict limitation of powers for dealing with finance which is imposed on the House of Lords. Henry IV in 1407 assented to the principle that money grants were to be initiated by the Commons, but it was not until after the Restoration by the resolutions of 1671 and 1678 that they asserted their exclusive right to control taxation. These resolutions were emphasized in 1860, at the time of the dispute between the two Houses over the repeal of the paper duty, when the House of Commons passed a famous resolution to the effect that the Lords ought not to impose or amend any legislation which imposed a charge on the people, or interfere in the administration or application of money raised by such a charge. The rejection of the Finance Bill by the Lords in 1909 resulted in the Parliament Act, 1911, which drastically curtailed the powers of the upper House. Its effect was to remove from the House of Lords all power but that of a limited delay. The Act, as amended by the Parliament Act, 1949, provides that any Bill passed by the House of Commons but rejected by the House of Lords can become law after one year, or in the case of a Money Bill (q.v.) after one month. (*See also* PRIVILEGE, FINANCIAL.)

Until the 19th century the procedure of both Houses of Parliament was very similar, but since then the changes in the procedure of the Commons have been very much more drastic owing to the effect of the Reform Acts, the necessity of counteracting obstruction of business, and the increasing pressure of Government business. The rules of debate and the methods of maintaining order are very different in both Houses, and this arises from the difference between the Speaker of the House of Commons and the Lord Chancellor, who, although he is called the Speaker of the House of Lords, is appointed like a minister from the ranks of the party in power and can support it by taking part in debates. This he does by moving away from the Woolsack (q.v.), which is said not to be within the confines of the House, to show that he is speaking as a peer and not as Speaker. Also, unlike the Speaker of the House of Commons, he votes in divisions, has no casting vote and is not responsible for maintaining order. He does not call on speakers who rise to address the House nor are speeches addressed to him. When the House is in committee the Lord Chairman presides. A quorum consists of 3 lords, but a division on any stage of a Bill cannot take place unless 30 are present. Order in the Lords is maintained by the House itself, speeches are addressed to the House, and members rise to speak without being called on. If more than one insists on speaking, the House would call for the speaker they wished to hear next. If the House thinks that a speaker has gone on for too long, it may move 'that the noble lord be no longer heard', but this procedure has only been resorted to five times in the last hundred years. The processes of passing Bills are the same in both Houses, but in the Lords a peer can introduce a Bill without obtaining the leave of the House and move its first reading, although a Bill not introduced by the Government has a very slender chance of reaching the Statute Book. A debate may also take place on a question addressed to H.M. Government, unless it is 'starred', when it is for information only, although there is no motion before the House. The more important debates take place on resolutions or on 'motions for papers'. These papers are usually non-existent, but such a motion is the formula adopted when it is desired to debate a subject without proposing any specific resolution upon it. There is no time fixed by Standing Order for the adjournment of the House of Lords; business arranged for the day is continued until it is finished, but the House seldom sits after dinner in the evening. The Standing Orders have recently been revised and brought into line with modern conditions, but the ceremonial proceedings which take place in the House are governed by tradition rather than by Standing Order. The House of Lords' Chamber, being technically the 'Parliament Chamber', is the scene of the sittings of Parliament in which the Sovereign participates, either in person or by Commission, at the opening and proroguing of a session, the approving of a Speaker of the House of Commons, and the giving of the Royal Assent (q.v.) to Bills which have been passed by both Houses. On these occasions the original layout of the full Parliament of Plantagenet times is reproduced; the Sovereign on the Throne (or represented by robed Commissioners seated in front of the Throne), the Lords ranged down either side of the Chamber, and the Commons, headed by their Speaker, at the Bar. Nowadays the Sovereign appears in person only at the opening of a parliamentary session and on this occasion the Peers, Temporal and Spiritual, wear their robes and the judges take their seats on Woolsacks in the centre of the Chamber. In the early days, as soon as the legislative programme outlined by the Royal Speech on this occasion had been dealt with, business was concluded. When the right to discuss other matters had been established the custom arose in both Houses of giving a first reading to a formal Bill before considering the Speech from the Throne. In the House of Commons the measure given its first reading is the Outlawries Bill (q.v.) and in the House of Lords the Select Vestries Bill (q.v.), and of course neither is proceeded with any further. The introduction of a new peer is also attended with some ceremony, which dates back many centuries. After receiving on bended knee his patent and writ from the Lord Chancellor, the new peer with his two supporters in their robes proceeds to the Table of the House where his patent and writ are read and where he takes the oath of allegiance. He is then conducted to the bench of his precedence, where he thrice raises his hat and bows to the Lord Chancellor. (*See also* PEERS.)

The House of Lords shares most of its functions with the House of Commons, but its judicial functions as the highest Court of Appeal are peculiar to itself. Maitland has established that Parliament at the end of the 13th century was regarded as the highest court of royal justice. Further research has confirmed the essentially judicial character of the earliest Parliaments, and that even under Edward III, although Parliaments devoted a considerable part of their time to political and economic business, the dispensation of justice remained their chief function. The control of the House of Lords by way of appeal over the action of the English Courts of Common Law may be traced back to the time when it was the King's Great Council. The control was afterwards extended to the courts of chancery or equity in England, and to the courts of Scotland and Ireland, but it has never been extended to the ecclesiastical courts or to the courts in other countries or colonies of the British Commonwealth, whose appeals are heard by the Judicial Committee of the Privy Council. Appeals are, however, heard from decisions of the Northern Ireland Judiciary via the Court of Appeal in Belfast, for although Northern Ireland has her own Parliament, in certain matters the authority of the British Parliament prevails. The judicial functions of the House of Lords have varied considerably through the centuries, both in their activity and the manner in which they have been exercised. The Commons left the judicial proceedings of Parliament to the Lords when they broke away early in the 14th century, as the Lords were at that time the older and more important body, but during the 15th and 16th centuries they did very little judicial work. In 1677 the Lords were conceded the right to hear appeals in equity from the Court of Chancery, and thus the House gathered within its appellate jurisdiction the last court to evade the direct supervision of Parliament. The Lords were able to summon the Common Law judges to assist them, but when the Union with Scotland and Ireland resulted in their appeals having to be heard, coupled with an ever-increasing population and new laws, the House found more and more difficulty in finding judicial time and judicial personnel. The judges were fully occupied in their own courts, and when Lords with no legal qualifications were excluded from voting on judicial questions the Lord Chancellor remained to hear appeals 'with two mute, untrained Lords in the background to represent the collective wisdom of the court', as Erskine May puts it. An attempt was made to create a judicial life peer in 1856 to alleviate the situation, but it needed the threat of an Act passed in 1873 which transferred the appellate jurisdiction of the Lords to a Supreme Court before this came about. The operation of this Act was suspended until 1876, when the Appellate Jurisdiction Act was passed, upon which the modern judicial powers and practice of the House are built. This Act restored its appellate jurisdiction and provided for its exercise by salaried 'Lords of Appeal in Ordinary'. These Lords of Appeal (who now number 9) were to hold their peerages only during their term of office, but an Act of 1887 allowed them to retain their peerages for life. The 1876 Act provides that no appeal can be heard unless at least 3 qualified legal personages are present, but as the Act does not disqualify any member of the House of Lords from taking part in the proceedings the judgment is still technically the judgment of that House. Actually, of course, its judicial functions are performed by the Lords of Appeal, or Law Lords as they are usually called, and any of the other qualified peers who can be invited to attend if a sufficient number of Law Lords are not available. The fusion of the parliamentary and judicial character of the House of Lords is epitomized in the Lord Chancellor, who is Speaker of the House and also Head of the Justiciary. In 1947, owing to the noise of rebuilding operations near the Lords' Chamber, appeals were heard by an Appellate Committee in a distant committee room, and this practice has been continued even though peace has been restored in the Palace of Westminster. It was found an advantage to be able to arrange judicial business without reference to the sittings of the House of Lords; appeals were formerly heard in the mornings in the Lords' Chamber, and the House sat in the afternoons. The Appellate Committee only hears argument and reports to the House, to which alone judgment is reserved.

Besides its function as the highest Court of Appeal, the House of Lords has had original jurisdiction of three kinds—in impeachment, trial of peers, and peerage claims. Of these, impeachment of offenders by the Commons and their trial by the Lords is obsolete (the last was brought against Lord Melville in 1806), the individual privilege of trial by fellow peers on charges of treason or felony was abolished by the Criminal Justice Act of 1948, and for all practical purposes only the third jurisdiction remains. These peerage claims are referred to the House of Lords by the Crown and are dealt with by the Lords' Committee for Privileges before whom counsel may be heard. With the loss of the privilege of trial by their peers, the privileges of the House of Lords and its members are now very similar to those of the House of Commons. The Lords, as the hereditary counsellors of the Sovereign, have the now rather archaic privilege of individual access to the Sovereign, while the Commons only have the collective right of access through their Speaker.

The House of Lords does not, in practice, exercise freely either the right to reject a Bill sent from the Commons if it is not in accordance with their own views, or the right to make substantial alterations. What they claim, according to a leading member of their House, is the right and duty 'to arrest the progress of such measures whenever we believe that they have been insufficiently considered and that they are not in accord with the deliberate judgment of the country'. The effective core of the House of Lords to-day—about one-tenth of its membership —consists of men of high attainments and notable achievement, not necessarily in party politics, whose knowledge of public affairs is extensive, whose public services are distinguished, and whose intellectual attainments are often outstanding. It is not surprising, therefore, that the House of Lords debates are often on a very high level and frequently surpass in wisdom and disinterestedness the speeches made in the House of Commons. Until 1957 Members of the House of Lords were unpaid, but in that year they became entitled to a tax-free expense allowance of up to 3 guineas a day. This allowance was increased to £4 16s. 6d. in 1964 and to £6 10s. in 1969.

For administrative purposes the House of Lords is divided into departments under the jurisdiction of the Lord Chancellor, the Lord

Chairman of Committees, the Clerk of the Parliaments, the Gentleman Usher of the Black Rod, the Librarian, and the Lord Great Chamberlain.

MEETING-PLACES OF THE LORDS. The Lords met in the White Chamber of the old Palace of Westminster until 1801, when the Union with Ireland introduced extra members to the House of Lords, and it moved to more commodious quarters in the White or Lesser Hall. The white or ancient Parliament Chamber had disappeared altogether by 1823, and some twenty years later the Royal Gallery (q.v.) was built on its site. After the fire of 1834 the Lords occupied the Painted Chamber, which had been re-roofed, until they were able to take possession of their present Chamber in 1847. From 1941 until 1950 the Chamber of the House of Lords was taken over by the Commons, their own Chamber having been destroyed by a German bomb. During this period the Lords met in the King's (now the Queen's) Robing Room, returning to their own renovated Chamber on 29 May 1951.

In the Queen's Speech opening Parliament on 31 October 1967 legislation was foreshadowed to reform the House of Lords by reducing its delaying powers and abolishing its hereditary basis.

HOUSE OF LORDS OFFICES COMMITTEE

A Sessional Committee (q.v.) of the House of Lords which is concerned with all matters relating to the staff, accommodation, finance and other domestic affairs of the House. Its membership is large (about 50) and includes the Lord Chancellor and Lord Chairman of Committees. The Lord President of the Council and the Lord Privy Seal are also members if they happen to be peers. The Committee appoints three sub-committees to deal respectively with the House of Lords Chamber, the Library and the Refreshment Department.

HOUSE OF LORDS REFORM

The question of reforming the House of Lords has long been a subject of controversy, and the fundamental overhaul of its structure which many people would like to see has not as yet been achieved. An attempt to do so in 1969 was abandoned after the Bill in question had been successfully obstructed by its opponents at the committee stage. The Bill was based upon a White Paper published in November 1968 (Cmnd. 3799), the key proposals of which were as follows:

(1) The reformed House of Lords should be a two-tier structure comprising voting peers, with a right to speak and to vote, and non-voting peers, with a right to participate in debate, ask questions, move motions and serve on committees but not to vote in the House or in any committee considering legislation.

(2) An hereditary peerage should no longer carry the right to a seat in the House of Lords but existing peers by succession would have the right to sit

as non-voting members for their lifetime. Some peers by succession would be created life peers and thus become qualified as voting peers.

(3) The voting House would initially consist of about 230 peers which would include a 'cross-bench' of peers having no party allegiance. The Government would have a small majority over the Opposition parties but not a majority of the voting House as a whole when the 'cross-bench' peers were included. Voting peers would be paid and would be required to attend at least one third of the sittings of the House and would be subject to an age of retirement.

(4) The reformed House would continue to include law lords and bishops, although the number of bishops sitting in the House would be gradually reduced from 26 to 16. A suitable number of peers able to speak with authority on the problems of Scotland, Wales, Northern Ireland and the regions of England would also be included.

(5) All peers should be qualified to vote in parliamentary elections and those who renounce their membership of the House of Lords should be eligible to sit in the House of Commons.

(6) The power of the House to delay a non-financial public Bill would be reduced from one year to six months. It would also be deprived of its power to veto subordinate legislation.

Such reforms as have been implemented in recent years have been of a piecemeal nature and have left the hereditary system on which the composition of the upper House is still largely based to a great extent untouched. Nevertheless, the changes which have been made since 1958 are in their way quite radical, although they are not such as to satisfy those who wish to see the hereditary system or the House of Lords as a whole abolished altogether.

The Life Peerages Act, 1958, and the Peerage Act, 1963, introduced certain reforms which had long been advocated. The former provided for the creation of life peers (q.v.) other than judicial life peers, and by making women eligible for such life peerages it also removed the general disqualification from membership of the House of Lords to which women had formerly been subject. The first appointments under the Act were made on 23 July 1958 and consisted of 10 male and 4 female life peers. The Peerage Act made provision for hereditary peers to disclaim their peerages under certain conditions and thus become eligible for election to the House of Commons and to vote at General Elections (see PEERAGE, DISCLAIMER OF). It also abolished the system whereby the peers of Scotland, and formerly the peers of Ireland, were represented in the House of Lords on an elective basis (see REPRESENTATIVE PEERS). It placed Scottish peers on the same footing as the peers of England, Great Britain and the United Kingdom, and in the case of Irish peers, while not admitting them to membership of the House of Lords, it guaranteed them the political rights of commoners unrestricted by virtue of their peerages. Finally, it extended to women holding hereditary peerages in their own right the same entitlement to membership of the House of Lords as men who are similarly qualified.

The Life Peerages Act was opposed when in its Bill form by the Labour Party on the grounds that it left the House of Lords an overwhelmingly hereditary body and that its powers remained intact. The Peerage Act, however, was passed with the co-operation of all parties since, in the light of the Wedgwood Benn case, the removal of the disqualification from service in the House of Commons, which succession to the peerage automatically entailed, was generally regarded as a matter of urgent necessity. Nevertheless, the Act did not fully meet the objections expressed by the Labour Party during the passage of the Life Peerages Bill. The Peerage Act was based on the report of a Joint Committee which had been appointed 'to consider whether any, and if so what, changes should be made in the rights of Peers of England, Scotland, Ireland, Great Britain or of the United Kingdom, and of Peeresses in their own right, to sit in either House of Parliament, or to vote at Parliamentary elections, and whether, and if so under what conditions, a Peer should be enabled to surrender a peerage permanently or for his lifetime or for any less period having regard to the effects and consequences thereof'. Reporting in December 1962, the Committee indicated that they had 'interpreted their order of reference as excluding the curtailment of any existing rights save in so far as such curtailment may be the appropriate consequence of the surrender of a peerage'. The hereditary system has thus been modified only to the extent that a person succeeding to a peerage can on certain conditions disclaim it, while the powers of the House of Lords itself continue untouched. It is true, of course, that in the light of the Parliament Acts, 1911 and 1949 (q.v.), these powers are severely limited in relation to those of the House of Commons.

The Parliament Acts, although they diminished the power of the House of Lords, did not provide for any of the reforms advocated during the last hundred years. The preamble of the 1911 Act certainly declared that 'it is intended to substitute for the House of Lords as it at present exists a Second Chamber constituted on a popular instead of hereditary basis', but nothing on these lines has yet been attempted. After the passing of the Reform Bill in 1832 a second chamber predominantly hereditary in its composition seemed even more a survival of feudalism and unduly representative of landed wealth, and indeed the Lords themselves passed a resolution in 1910 to the effect that 'the possession of a peerage should no longer in itself give the right to sit and vote in the House of Lords'. The fact that the average daily attendance in the House of Lords is only about 10 per cent of the total number of peers also aroused criticism, and it is not surprising that numerous proposals for reform were forthcoming. The earliest suggestion, appearing during the second half of the 19th century, was for the creation of life peers as a means of improving the quality of the debates in the upper House. Another proposal was that the peers should elect the second Chamber from among themselves as the Scottish Representative Peers were elected, and this was advocated by Lord Rosebery in 1888. A Select Committee of the House of Lords under Lord Rosebery's chairmanship repeated this proposal in 1908, recommending that 200 Lords of Parliament should be elected by the hereditary peers. Three years later a similar proposal was made in a Bill introduced by Lord Lansdowne. Lord Rosebery also suggested the election of a number of members to the upper House by outside bodies, and Lord Lansdowne the election of 120 members by Members of the House of Commons sitting for the larger constituencies. In 1917 a conference was appointed under the chairmanship of Lord Bryce to investigate and report on the question of reform in the Lords and the powers a reformed House would exercise. The majority recommended that one section of the proposed upper House should consist of about 250 members elected by members of the House of Commons grouped in territorial areas (roughly Lansdowne's suggestion) and a second section of about 80 members chosen by a joint Standing Committee of both Houses, appointed at the beginning of each Parliament, from among the peers and bishops. It was proposed that members of both sections should hold their seats for twelve years, and the powers of this House were to remain substantially the same as the present House of Lords. A group of Conservatives under the chairmanship of Sir Cuthbert Headlam published in 1946 'Some Proposals for Constitutional Reform' in which they made recommendations for House of Lords Reform which were substantially the same as those made by an all-party conference on the subject which met in 1948. The Report of this Conference (Cmd. 7380) contains the following proposals:

(1) The Second Chamber should be complementary to, and not a rival to, the Lower House, and, with this end in view, the reform of the House of Lords should be based on a modification of its existing constitution as opposed to the establishment of a Second Chamber of a completely new type based on some system of election.

(2) The revised constitution of the House of Lords should be such as to secure as far as practicable that a permanent majority is not assured for any one political party.

(3) The present right to attend and vote based solely on heredity should not by itself constitute a qualification for admission to a reformed Second Chamber.

(4) Members of the Second Chamber should be styled 'Lords of Parliament' and would be appointed on grounds of personal distinction or public service. They might be drawn either from hereditary Peers, or from commoners who would be created life Peers.

[371]

(5) Women should be capable of being appointed Lords of Parliament in like manner as men.

(6) Provision should be made for the inclusion in the Second Chamber of certain descendants of the Sovereign, certain Lords Spiritual and the Law Lords.

(7) In order that persons without private means should not be excluded, some remuneration would be payable to members of the Second Chamber.

(8) Peers, who were not Lords of Parliament, should be entitled to stand for election to the House of Commons, and also to vote at elections in the same manner as other citizens.

(9) Some provision should be made for the disqualification of a member of the Second Chamber who neglects, or becomes no longer able or fitted to perform his duties as such.

There was general agreement on these recommendations at the time, and they have now to a great extent been implemented. But it was found impossible to reach agreement with regard to the powers which should be vested in any reformed upper House, and this remains a subject on which conflict of opinion continues. The Labour Party manifesto of 1935 called for the abolition of the House of Lords, a course still regarded in radical circles as the logical and desirable solution.

At the end of 1952 Lord Simon introduced a Bill authorizing the Crown to appoint 10 life peers a year who would sit and vote in the House of Lords, but it was opposed by the Government on the grounds that more general reforms were being planned. Sir Winston Churchill in 1953 invited the Labour and the Liberal parties to take part in further conversations, but the Leader of the Labour Party replied: 'In view of the fact that the previous discussions in 1948 revealed a fundamental cleavage of opinion between the Labour and Conservative parties on what is the proper part to be played by the House of Lords as a second chamber under the Constitution, we have come to the conclusion that no useful purpose would be served by our entering into such a discussion'. On 9 March 1955 Viscount Samuel, who had long been an advocate of reform, inaugurated a two-day debate in the House of Lords based on the proposals of the 1948 Conference. He pointed out the reasons for the waning influence of the House of Lords, and suggested what must be done to restore its prestige and to prevent it 'dying of inanition before our eyes'. The Leader of the Opposition stated that the Labour Party would not be willing to enter into a preliminary conference to reach an agreed solution to the problem, but the Marquess of Salisbury, then Leader of the House, promised that the Government would appoint a committee and proceed on its own with plans for a reconstituted House of Lords.

In the debate already referred to, Viscount Samuel mentioned the difficulty of maintaining a link between the self-governing territories of the Commonwealth and Westminster, and pointed out that a new

House of Lords might well contain considerably more representatives from these countries than there are at present.

HOUSE OF REPRESENTATIVES

The name given to the legislative chambers of New Zealand, Cyprus, Sierra Leone, Malta, the Gambia and St. Vincent, and to the lower Houses of the Parliaments of Australia, Ceylon, Malaysia, Nigeria, Jamaica, Trinidad and Tobago, Kenya, Antigua and Grenada.

HOUSE OF THE PEOPLE

The lower House in the Indian Parliament (q.v.).

HOUSES OF PARLIAMENT

See BIG BEN; CENTRAL HALL; CHURCHILL ARCH; CLOCK TOWER; COURT OF REQUESTS; COURTYARDS; CRYPT CHAPEL; HOUSE OF COMMONS; HOUSE OF LORDS; MOSES ROOM; NEW PALACE YARD; OLD PALACE YARD; PAINTED CHAMBER; PALACE OF WESTMINSTER; PARLIAMENT; PRINCE'S CHAMBER; QUEEN'S ROBING ROOM; ROYAL GALLERY; ST. STEPHEN'S HALL; VICTORIA TOWER; WESTMINSTER HALL.

HOUSING AND LOCAL GOVERNMENT, MINISTER OF

This Minister's Department, together with those of the Minister of Transport (q.v.) and the Minister of Public Building and Works (q.v.), were absorbed by the new Department of the Environment established in consequence of a major reorganization of the machinery of central government in 1970. The new Department is headed by a Minister styled the Secretary of State for the Environment.

The office of Minister of Housing and Local Government was descended from that of Minister of Town and Country Planning (1943) and Minister of Local Government and Planning (1951) and was created by the Conservative Government which came to power at the end of 1951 to mark the change of emphasis in its policy. The Minister was responsible for housing and new towns and the planning and control of the use of land, general oversight of the work of local authorities and also financial responsibility towards them.

The importance of the office of Minister of Housing and Local Government was downgraded in October 1969 with the appointment of a Secretary of State for Local Government and Regional Planning with overall responsibility for the Ministry of Housing and Local Government and the Ministry of Transport. Both these Departments have now ceased to exist with the establishment of the Department of the Environment. The Secretary of State for Scotland continues to discharge the functions which in England and Wales were exercised formerly by the Minister of Housing and Local Government and now by the Secretary of State for the Environment.

The first Minister of Town and Country Planning was W. S. Morrison (elected Speaker of the House of Commons, 1951). He held office until the formation of the 1945 Labour Government when Lewis Silkin (afterwards Lord Silkin) was appointed to the office. He was succeeded by Hugh Dalton, who became the Minister of Local Government and Planning. In 1951 Harold Macmillan became the first Minister of Housing and Local Government.

HUSTINGS

Before the passing of the Ballot Act in 1872, candidates for Parliament were nominated on a platform known as the 'hustings', from which they addressed the electors. This word afterwards came into use to describe the whole proceedings at a parliamentary election.

HYBRID BILL

A Hybrid Bill is a Public Bill to which the Standing Orders relative to Private Business are applicable. In other words, it is a Bill which although general in its application affects certain private or local interests. For instance, a Bill to acquire property for the Post Office might affect some privately owned land, and would thus be a Hybrid Bill. Such Bills are subject to a special procedure during their passage through Parliament. Broadly speaking, it is correct to say that they are treated like Private Bills (q.v.) after the second reading.

After the first reading, all Bills are examined in the Public Bill Office with a view to ascertaining whether they affect private interests. Any Bill which is found to affect private interests is referred to the examiners (q.v.), and until they have reported the Bill may not be set down for second reading.

After second reading a Hybrid Bill is committed to a Select Committee nominated, as a general rule, partly by the House and partly by the Committee of Selection (q.v.). An order is made by the House that any petitions against the Bill shall be referred to the committee, but if none are received by a stipulated date the order committing the Bill to the Select Committee shall be discharged and the Bill committed to a Committee of the Whole House (q.v.) or a Standing Committee (q.v.). Unless the order expressly provides that petitions against the Bill may be deposited in the Public Bill Office they must be presented to the House as public petitions (for description of procedure *see* PETITIONS). The proceedings in a Select Committee on a Hybrid Bill were formerly similar to those in a committee on a Private Bill, but a modified procedure, which may be varied at the discretion of the committee, was recently adopted. Fees are charged to opponents of a Hybrid Bill as if it were a Private Bill.

I

ILBERT, SIR COURTENAY PEREGRINE (1841–1924)

Clerk of the House of Commons from 1902 to 1921, Ilbert began his career as a parliamentary draftsman and assistant to Sir Henry (afterwards Baron) Thring, the first Parliamentary Counsel to the Treasury (q.v.). A brilliant legal scholar, Ilbert was in a large measure responsible for the drafting of the Statute Law Revision Act, 1881, and the Civil Procedure Act, 1883. After spending four years in India he returned to England to become Assistant Parliamentary Counsel to the Treasury, and in 1899 he succeeded his chief as Parliamentary Counsel, retaining this appointment until he became Clerk of the House.

Ilbert's publications include *The Government of India* (1898), *Legislative Methods and Forms* (1901), *Parliament* (1911, revised by Sir Cecil Carr, 1953), and *The Mechanics of Law-making* (1914).

IMPEACHMENT

A trial before the Lords on the accusation of the Commons for 'high crimes and misdemeanours'. According to Maitland, there have not been seventy during the whole course of English history, and a full quarter of all of them belong to the years 1640–2. During the Oxford Parliament in 1681 the impeachment of Fitzharris was rejected by the Lords, and the Commons passed a resolution 'That it is the undoubted right of the Commons to impeach before the Lords any Peer or commoner for treason or any other crime or misdemeanour, and that the refusal of the Lords to proceed in Parliament upon such impeachment is a denial of justice and a violation of the constitution of Parliament'. The Commons also decided that any civil law court which should dare to deal with the case of Fitzharris should be answerable to them for its action. The earliest recorded impeachment was that of Lord Latimer in 1376 and the last was in 1806, when Lord Melville (Dundas) was charged by the Commons, but acquitted, of misappropriating official funds. As Jennings remarks in his *Parliament*, impeachment in the 17th and early 18th centuries was a means for 'liquidating' opponents, and the procedure may now be regarded as obsolete. The ballot boxes are now available for political opponents and the criminal courts for criminals. A full description of the procedure of impeachment is given by Hatsell in vol. 4 of his *Precedents*.

N

The Select Committee on Parliamentary Privilege which reported in December 1967 recommended that the right of impeachment should be formally abandoned by means of legislative action.

INDEPENDENT LABOUR PARTY

A non-Marxian organization formed under the inspiration of Keir Hardie at Bradford in 1893 with the object of uniting local labour parties into one national organization. Its leaders, including MacDonald, Snowden, Clynes, and Margaret Bondfield, who in the 1929–31 Labour Government became the first woman Cabinet Minister, were more concerned with social reform than with dogmatic Socialism, and were much influenced by the doctrines of the Fabian Society and its brilliant supporters Bernard Shaw and Sidney Webb. After seven years' struggle, the I.L.P. persuaded some trade unions to join the Socialists in setting up the Labour Representation Committee, which became the Labour Party (q.v.). The I.L.P. continued as a separate body within the federal structure of the Labour Party, but owing to its anti-war attitude it was practically a separate group from 1914–18. After the War, the I.L.P. suffered internal dissension over its future policy and its function in the Labour movement, now that the Labour Party had adopted a broadly Socialist programme, and by its new constitution (1918) had become a mass-party based on individual as well as on affiliated membership. In spite of this, the number of I.L.P. candidates returned to the House of Commons rose from 32 in 1922 to 46 in 1923. Meanwhile, the party continued to press for a much more radical advance to Socialism than many of the trade unionists in the Labour Party were ready to accept. The I.L.P. leaders, who carried more intellectual equipment than most of the trade unionists, had been the driving force in the Labour Party, but MacDonald and Snowden were now turning away from the I.L.P. to the Labour Party itself to further their ideas. This was particularly noticeable after the general strike of 1926 and the Labour Party Conference of 1927, where an I.L.P. proposal for family allowances had been condemned by Mac-Donald. Subsequently the I.L.P. refused to nominate him even as a delegate to the conference, and henceforward his membership of the party was purely nominal. Snowden resigned from it in 1928. At the I.L.P. Conference in 1928, James Maxton, who had become its leader, defined the party's mission to be 'a Socialist party within the Labour Party', but it was becoming increasingly obvious that it could not much longer retain that position. In the 1929 election 37 I.L.P. members gained seats in the House, and at their conference in 1931 the Labour Government was severely criticized for its luke-warm attitude to the cause of Socialism. In the General Election of the same year the result of increasing enmity between the two parties was the withdrawal of Labour Party endorsement from I.L.P. candidates, and although the I.L.P. was still formally affiliated to the Labour Party it really stood as an independent party. In the general collapse of the Labour Party the I.L.P. only retained 5 seats after this election. At a special conference in 1932 the I.L.P. decided to break its affiliation with the Labour Party by 241 votes to 142 and revert to the independence it enjoyed from 1893 to 1900. In doing so it lost many of its members, and after the 1935 election its parliamentary representation had dwindled to 4, all representing Glasgow constituencies. Only 3 of these were re-turned at the 1945 election, and when Maxton died in 1946, regretted by all parties, the I.L.P. applied for re-affiliation to the Labour Party. The application was rejected, and in 1947 the 3 I.L.P. members in Parliament decided to conform and to receive the Labour Party whip. The I.L.P., although it has continued its activities outside Parliament, has not been represented in the House of Commons since that time. However, the result of the 1970 General Election produced one member bearing the label 'Independent Labour'. He was Mr. S. O. Davies, who had represented Merthyr Tydfil since 1934 as the official Labour member. In 1970 his constituency association declined to renominate him on account of his age (83) but Mr. Davies responded by campaigning independently and, as it turned out, successfully.

INDEPENDENT MEMBER

A Member of Parliament is described as Independent if he acknow-ledges no allegiance to any political party, whether he has obtained his seat without the aid of any party organization or whether he leaves his party to become independent after he has been elected. 'Independent' at one time meant independent of the King or the Court supporters, and during the 18th century, of the Government. It was not until the second half of the 19th century, when political parties were more distinct and better organized, that independence was related to party. Men like Savile, Wilberforce, Cobden, and Bright were independents by nature although known as Whigs, Tories, or Radicals, and the fact that in those days there was more independence within a party made it unnecessary for a member to describe himself as Independent. Party discipline was tightened up, but it was not until 1915 that Pemberton Billing was elected as the first avowed Independent. The university seats before their abolition provided some of the best-known Independents of the modern variety, and the late Miss Eleanor Rathbone, associated with family allowances and the champion-ship of refugees, and Sir Alan Herbert, who owes much of his parlia-mentary fame to his Matrimonial Causes Bill, were typical examples.

The Independent member had certain advantages and some dis-advantages over the member tied to a party. He was able to vote as he pleased and was only governed by his conscience as to the regularity of his attendance at the House. He was free of party committees and social engagements. He could also take up causes that a party member could not, and his chances of being called to speak in debates, owing to the care taken not to disregard minorities in the House, were better than those of the back-bencher party member. On the other hand, he had none of the resources of a great political organization behind him, and except perhaps in wartime could not expect to become a minister. Also, although free from the obligation to attend party meetings, his absence from these discussions left him rather isolated and out of the swim of parliamentary life.

Sir Harold Nicolson has described five types of Independent: the true Independent, who fights his own battle entirely on his own resources; the fortuitously Independent, elected during a period of party truce; the academic Independent returned for a university seat; the temperamental Independent, 'who belongs to a party but cannot stay put'; and the forlorn Independent, survivor of a dead party.

Mainly due to the abolition of the university franchise, there have been few Independent members in the Parliaments elected since 1950 and their absence has been a matter for regret on both sides of the House.

INDEPENDENT MOTION

See SUBSTANTIVE MOTION.

INDIA AND BURMA, SECRETARY OF STATE FOR

The first Charter of the East India Company was granted by Queen Elizabeth I in 1600, and the more direct interposition of the British Parliament in Indian affairs was marked by the establishment of the Board of Control in 1784, which was made responsible for the supervision by the Government of the operations of the Company. The office of Secretary of State for India was created by the Government of India Act of 1858, whereby the powers and functions of the East India Company were transferred to the Crown, and Queen Victoria assumed the title of Empress of India in 1877. The India Office arose from the amalgamation of the Company's headquarters in London with the office of the Board of Control, whose President became the Secretary of State, and the personnel of the new government department was at the outset formed by uniting the clerks of the two old establishments. Henceforth, of course, the India Office was one of the departments of the Home Civil Service. But it differed from the other departments in one very important aspect—its cost was defrayed entirely from the revenues of India, and not from the United Kingdom, until, at the end of the 19th century, the Report of the Welby Commission on Indian Finance led to a contribution from the Treasury towards certain heads of Indian expenditure. By the Government of India Act of 1919 the salary of the Secretary of State for India was for the first time put upon the Parliamentary Estimates. A second important distinction between the Secretary of State for India and the other Secretaries of State lay in the fact that for most purposes the supreme authority under the Crown and Parliament for the control of Indian affairs was the Secretary of State in Council of India, and not a sole minister, although the Secretary of State possessed considerable powers apart from his Council. The Council ceased to exist from 1 April 1937, when some of its functions passed to a body of Advisers. The increasing measure of autonomy given to India by the Acts of 1919 and 1935 culminated in the Indian Independence Act of 1947, which set up two 'independent Dominions' to be known as India and Pakistan. The office of Secretary of State was therefore abolished in that year. The Government of Burma Act, 1935, created the office of Secretary of State for Burma, which was held by the Secretary of State for India. This office also lapsed in 1947 on the passing of the Burma Independence Act.

A chronological list of Secretaries of State for India appears as Appendix 21.

INDIAN PARLIAMENT

Although India became a Republic in 1947 it decided to continue as a member of the British Commonwealth of Nations with the Queen as a symbol of their free association.

The main objects of passing the Government of India Bill of 1935—the longest Bill in British parliamentary history—were the establishment of an Indian Federation and the grant of self-government to the Provinces of British India. Owing to the advent of war in 1939, only the second of these was carried into effect, and the Central Government remained as constituted under the Government of India Act of 1919. In 1946 a Constituent Assembly met which was elected by the Legislative Assemblies of the then existing Provinces, and included representatives of the Indian States on the basis of one member for every million inhabitants. Subsequently the British Government announced its intention to hand over power to popular representatives of India not later than June 1948, but finding no arrangement that was acceptable to both Hindus and Moslems, it decided to partition the country, and India and Pakistan came into existence on 15 August 1947 by virtue of the India Independence Act of that year. The members of the Constituent Assembly became members of two separate Assemblies, one for each new Dominion, and both had full powers to frame their own Constitutions.

The Constituent Assembly of India adopted their new Constitution on 26 November 1949. It is a Federal Constitution providing for a Union of States (17 States and 10 Union Territories) and comprises 395 articles and 9 schedules. The seventh schedule lists subjects within the legislative jurisdiction of the Union and of the States legislatures, and subjects over which both have concurrent jurisdiction. The Constitution came into force on 26 January 1950 and established a President and a bicameral legislature—the House of the People (Lok Sabha) and the Council of States (Rajya Sabha). The former is the lower House, and consists of not more than 500 directly elected members to represent the 17 States and not more than 25 members to represent the Union Territories chosen in such manner as Parliament may by law provide. In addition the President may nominate 2 members to represent the Anglo-Indian community if in his opinion it is not adequately represented. Following the General Election of 1967 the elected membership of the House of the People is 521, including the representatives of Jammu and Kashmir, who were formerly appointed by the President on the recommendation of the State Legislature. The President is elected by the elected members of the House of the People and the State Legislative Assemblies.

The Council of States consists of not more than 250 members, of whom 12 are nominated by the President and the rest elected. The representatives of the States are elected by the elected members of the Legislative Assembly of each State by means of proportional representation. The representatives of the Union Territories are chosen in such manner as Parliament may by law provide. The nominated members are selected from among people who have distinguished themselves in the arts, sciences, and social services. The strength of the Council of States as of 1967 was 238. The Council is a permanent body not liable to dissolution, but a third of the members retire every second year. The Vice-President of India is the *ex-officio* Chairman of the Council, and a Deputy Chairman is elected to preside in the absence of the Vice-President. They may speak and take part in the proceedings as does the Speaker of the House of Lords. Both Houses have a Secretariat, the Secretary being Clerk of the House in each case.

While Indian parliamentary procedure owes a great deal to British practice, it has, in certain of its aspects, evolved independently of external influences. The procedure of the House of the People has to a great extent been moulded by successive Speakers, the powers of the Indian Speaker being wider than those of any other Speaker in the Commonwealth. He may vary the hours of sitting, determine the order of seating, impose time limits on speeches and debates, and order any words which he deems to be offensive to be expunged from the record of proceedings. In consultation with the Leader of the House he determines the order of business which can only be varied with his consent. He is in supreme control of all parliamentary committees, some of which he appoints himself, and all committee chairmen are appointed by him. He himself is Chairman of the Rules Committee, which considers matters of procedure and the conduct of business, and such is the Speaker's influence that the committee's proposals are invariably agreed to. Like the British Speaker, the Indian Speaker also decides the admissibility of questions, resolutions and amendments, and he is empowered to accept or reject a dilatory motion, a closure motion, and an emergency adjournment motion, and to select amendments. The Speaker may address the House at any time to assist it in the course of its deliberations. From time to time he amplifies or elucidates the rules and practice of the House, and the Standing Orders empower him to determine the practice to be followed in cases for which the rules do not provide.

Although the Speaker retains his political affiliations while in office, and has been known to express himself publicly on matters of broad national concern, he maintains his aloofness from political activity sufficiently to ensure that his impartiality is never called in question. This precaution is of particular importance in a Parliament where, prior to the General Election of 1967, the Government commanded a large and disciplined majority and where the organization of the opposition forces was minimal. The Indian Speaker wears no wig nor any distinctive robes of office.

Indian parliamentary procedure makes no provision for the Committee of the Whole House (q.v.). Bills are referred for their committee stage to *ad hoc* Select Committees, and the following sessional committees are provided for in the Standing Orders: Business Advisory Committee; Committee on Private Members' Bills and Resolutions; Committee on Petitions; Committee on Public Accounts; Committee on Estimates; Committee of Privileges; Committee on Subordinate Legislation; Committee on Government Assurances; Committee on Absence of Members from the Sittings of the House; and the Rules Committee. Some of these committees have their counterparts in other Commonwealth Parliaments, but the Committee on Government Assurances was an Indian innovation, its functions being to scrutinize the undertakings given from time to time by Ministers of the Government and to report on the extent to which they have been implemented.

As in the House of Commons, the House of the People makes provision for a motion to adjourn the House for the purpose of discussing a definite matter of urgent public importance, but provision is also made for the raising of such matters other than by the adoption of the emergency procedure. With the permission of the Speaker and the support of at least two other members, a member may initiate a short discussion on a matter of urgent public importance on a date fixed by the Speaker in consultation with the Leader of the House. A further Standing Order provides the opportunity for a member, with the permission of the Speaker, to make a brief statement after Questions in which he may draw the attention of a minister to a matter of urgent

[381]

public importance, no debate being allowed. Provision is also made for half-hour discussions arising from the answers to questions, a procedure comparable to the daily half-hour debate on the adjournment motion which takes place at Westminster. These half-hour discussions, together with the discussions on matters of urgent public importance, underline an interesting variation from British procedure in that debate may take place although there is no formal motion before the House.

In order to raise a question of privilege a member requires the consent of the Speaker and, in the event of objection being raised, the leave of the House signified by at least 25 members. A motion of no confidence in a minister is admissible only if the leave of the House is signified by no less than 50 members. Divisions may be recorded electronically or by the members going into the lobbies, the decision as to which method shall be used resting with the Speaker.

In common with the other Commonwealth Parliaments, the financial initiative is reserved to the lower House and Money Bills are introduced only in the House of the People. The Constitution provides for the holding of joint sessions of both Houses when disagreement arises between them over legislation.

The executive power of the Indian Union is vested in the President, but like a constitutional monarch he follows the advice of his ministers tendered to him through the Prime Minister. The President is aided and advised by a Council of Ministers which includes all members of the Cabinet, Ministers of State and Deputy Ministers, the federal character of the Government being reflected in the composition of the Council which includes as far as possible representatives from every State. The Cabinet is a separate entity which includes all ministers in charge of departments. It exercises all the power that its British counterpart does—and more. When the House is not sitting it can make laws, suspend fundamental liberties by declaring a state of emergency, and alter the boundaries of States—but all these powers are ultimately subject to the approval of Parliament.

Parliament House in New Delhi was formally opened in 1927 by Lord Halifax when he was Viceroy. It is an impressive circular building one-third of a mile in circumference, with a continuous open verandah on the first floor fringed with 144 columns. There is a Central Hall whose dome is 98 feet high, and radiating from this centre are the Chambers of the two Houses and the old Princes Chamber, which is now occupied by the Parliamentary Library. Both the legislative Chambers are of horse-shoe design and a seat is allotted to each member. The House of the People can accommodate 530 and the Council of States 250.

Following the General Election of 1967 the representation of the States and Union Territories in the Indian Parliament is made up as follows:

	Council of States	House of the People
Andhra Pradesh . . .	18	41
Assam	7	14
Bihar	22	53
Gujarat	11	24
Hariana	5	9
Jammu and Kashmir . .	4	6
Kerala	9	19
Madhya Pradesh . . .	16	37
Madras	18	39
Maharashtra	19	45
Mysore	12	27
Nagaland	1	1
Orissa	10	20
Punjab	6	13
Rajasthan	10	23
Uttar Pradesh . . .	34	85
West Bengal	16	40
Andaman and Nicobar Islands	–	1
Chandigarh	–	1
Dadra and Nagar Haveli .	–	1
Delhi	3	7
Goa, Daman and Diu . .	–	2
Himachal Pradesh . . .	2	6
Laccadive	–	1
Manipur	1	2
Pondicherry	1	1
Tripura	1	2
North-East Frontier Tract .	–	1

(Further reading: Lal, *The Indian Parliament*, 1956; More, *Practice and procedure of the Indian Parliament*, 1960; Morris-Jones, *Parliament in India*, 1957).

INDIANS IN PARLIAMENT

Dadabhai Naoraji was the first Indian member of the Imperial Parliament. Elected in 1892 for Central Finsbury as a Liberal by the narrow majority of 3 votes, he served until the General Election of 1895. In that year Sir Mancherjee M. Bhownagree was returned as Conservative member for North-East Bethnal Green, a seat he held until 1906. S. Saklatvala was a Communist member for North Battersea from 1922 until 1923. All these members were Parsees. The House of Lords includes an Indian peer, Lord Sinha, the holder of a barony created in 1919. The Indian Parliament apart, other Commonwealth legislatures in which Indian members sit or have sat include those of Malaysia, Singapore, Kenya, Tanzania, Uganda, Malawi and Mauritius.

INDIAN STATE PARLIAMENTS

Prior to 1 November 1956 the Indian Union consisted of 27 States, divided into three categories, and the territory of the Andaman and Nicobar Islands. Most of the States had their own legislatures, some of them bicameral. From the above date the Indian States were reorganized, their boundaries redrawn, and the whole country divided into 14 states and 6 centrally administered territories, subsequently increased to 17 and 10 respectively. The 17 States are Andhra Pradesh, Assam, Bihar, Gujarat, Hariana, Jammu and Kashmir, Kerala, Madhya Pradesh, Madras, Maharashtra, Mysore, Nagaland, Orissa, Punjab, Rajasthan, Uttar Pradesh, and West Bengal. In September 1956 a Delimitation Commission was appointed to determine the Parliamentary and State Assembly constituencies into which each new State should be divided, the number of seats to be allotted to each, and the number of seats in the House of the People and the State Assemblies to be reserved for scheduled castes and tribes. The first elections for the State Parliaments after the reorganization were held simultaneously with the General Election for the Indian Parliament in March 1957.

In Assam, Gujarat, Hariana, Kerala, Nagaland, Orissa, and Rajasthan, Parliament consists of a Governor and a single chamber, the Legislative Assembly (Vidhan Sabha). In the other States, Parliament consists of a Governor and two Houses, the Legislative Council (Vidhan Parishad) being the upper chamber and the Legislative Assembly the lower. The Legislative Assemblies are all popularly elected, although in some States the Governor is empowered to appoint additional members to represent the Anglo-Indian community if he considers it is inadequately represented. A State Legislative Assembly must consist of not more than 500 and (except in the case of Nagaland) not less than 60 members chosen by direct election from territorial constituencies in the State. The normal duration of an Assembly is five years unless it is previously dissolved.

The composition of the State Legislative Councils is governed by the Legislative Councils Act, 1957. The strength of a Legislative Council must be not greater than one-third of the total number of members in the Legislative Assembly and in no case less than 40. Approximately one-third of the members of each Council are elected by the members of the Legislative Assembly, one-third by local authorities, one-twelfth by registered teachers who teach at secondary school level and above, one-twelfth by registered graduates of more than three years' standing, and the remainder are nominated by the Governor of the State from among those who have distinguished themselves in the arts, sciences, and social services. The Legislative

Councils are permanent bodies, one-third of their members retiring every second year.

The State Parliaments are empowered to make laws on any subject appearing in the State and Concurrent Lists which form a part of the seventh schedule to the Indian Constitution, Union legislation prevailing in the event of a conflict. A State Governor may reserve certain State legislation for the consideration of the President of India. No provision is made for joint sittings to take place between the two Houses of a State Parliament, but if the Legislative Assembly gives a second passage to a Bill which has been rejected by the Legislative Council it automatically becomes law after one month, irrespective of the action of the Legislative Council. A Legislative Council has no powers in respect of financial legislation except to recommend changes, provided the recommendations are made within fourteen days of the Bill being sent up from the Legislative Assembly.

The States of Gujarat and Maharashtra were created in 1960 from the former single State of Bombay. The Naga-Tuensang area of Assam was accorded separate statehood in 1962 under the name of Nagaland. The State of Hariana was created in the latter part of 1966 from the division of the State of Punjab into two States. Hariana's legislature consisted of 54 members in the first instance and was increased to 81 with effect from the 1967 General Election.

The Indian State Parliaments were composed as follows after the elections of 1967:

Andhra Pradesh
   Legislative Council: 90 members; Legislative Assembly: 287 members.

Assam
   Legislative Assembly: 126 members.

Bihar
   Legislative Council: 96 members; Legislative Assembly: 318 members.

Gujarat
   Legislative Assembly: 168 members.

Hariana
   Legislative Assembly: 81 members.

Jammu and Kashmir
   Legislative Council: 36 members; Legislative Assembly: 75 members.

(In the event of the Pakistan-occupied areas of the State being returned to the Indian Union the strength of the Legislative Assembly will be increased by 25.)

Kerala
Legislative Assembly: 133 members.

Madhya Pradesh
Legislative Council: 90 members; Legislative Assembly: 296 members.

Maharashtra
Legislative Council: 78 members; Legislative Assembly: 270 members.

Mysore
Legislative Council: 63 members; Legislative Assembly: 216 members.

Nagaland
State Assembly: 52 members, including 12 nominated for the Tuensang district.

Orissa
Legislative Assembly: 140 members.

Punjab
Legislative Council: 34 members; Legislative Assembly: 104 members.

Rajasthan
Legislative Assembly: 184 members.

Tamil Nadu (formerly *Madras*)
Legislative Council: 63 members; Legislative Assembly: 234 members.

Uttar Pradesh
Legislative Council: 108 members; Legislative Assembly: 425 members.

West Bengal
Legislative Council: 75 members; Legislative Assembly: 280 members.

INFORMATION, MINISTER OF

This Minister's department was created in 1939 soon after the beginning of the war to disseminate information and for 'the enlightenment of the people here and overseas', to quote the Lord Privy Seal, who represented the first Minister (Lord Macmillan) in the

Commons. At the end of 1945 it was decided to abolish the Ministry and form a new unit with similar functions to be called the Central Office of Information.

Lord Macmillan was succeeded in office by Sir John (afterwards Lord) Reith, Alfred Duff Cooper (afterwards Lord Norwich), Brendan Bracken (afterwards Lord Bracken), Geoffrey Lloyd, and E. J. Williams. In 1946 the Postmaster-General was appointed by the Labour Government to take over the department pending its abolition.

INGROSSING A BILL

See ENGROSSING A BILL.

INITIATIVE

See REFERENDUM.

INSTRUCTIONS TO A COMMITTEE

There are two types of instruction which may be given a committee by the House—permissive and mandatory. The permissive instruction gives the committee power to do something which it could not otherwise do, the mandatory instruction *directs* it to do something which it would not otherwise do. While both types of instruction can be given to Select Committees and Private Bill Committees, and with the concurrence of both Houses to Joint Committees, only the permissive form can be given to a Committee of the Whole House, and then only to a committee on a Bill, and to Standing Committees. A member must give notice that he intends to move an instruction to a committee, and amendments thereto also require notice. Instructions are frequently proposed which are unnecessary, as a committee to which Bills are committed already has power under the Standing Orders to make such amendments as they think fit, 'provided they be relevant to the subject matter of the Bill'. Instructions are, however, always needed by a committee which seeks to divide a Bill into two or more Bills, to consolidate two Bills into one Bill, to give priority to part of a Bill with power to report such part separately to the House, and to extend the operation of a Bill geographically to a part of the country not included in its original form.

INTER-PARLIAMENTARY UNION

The object of the I.P.U., according to the first article of its statutes, is 'to promote personal contacts between members of all Parliaments, constituted into National Groups, and to unite them in common action to secure and maintain the full participation of their respective States in the firm establishment and development of democratic institutions and the advancement of the work of international peace and co-operation'. Sir William Randal Cremer, a British M.P., and a French Deputy, Monsieur Frédéric Passy, held a preliminary meeting in Paris in 1888, and the next year the first I.P.U. Conference was held in London. Annual conferences have been held since, except during the war years, usually in one of the world's capital cities, the inviting country providing all the facilities for the conference. The current practice is to hold two conferences each year, a preliminary one in the Spring and the main one in the Autumn. The proceedings include a general debate on the Secretary-General's Report on World Affairs, and debates on various resolutions and reports prepared during the previous year by the study committees of the Union. The conference in effect constitutes an informal international Parliament, at which M.P.s of all countries and parties can meet and freely discuss the problems of the day. Apart from the conferences, there are frequent interchanges of visits of Members of Parliament from each National Group providing a valuable education for the M.P.s and an insight into the problems of their respective countries.

The central direction of the affairs of the I.P.U. is carried out by the Inter-Parliamentary Council, on which each Parliamentary Group is represented by two delegates. There is an Inter-Parliamentary Bureau at Geneva under the direction of the Secretary-General which is supervised by an executive committee of eleven members including the President. The President of the Union is *ex-officio* the President of the Inter-Parliamentary Council and of the Executive Committee. Members of the Executive Committee are elected for an initial term of three years, an average of three members retiring on a rotational basis each year.

In 1970 the Inter-Parliamentary Union consisted of member groups from sixty-six countries. The official organ of the Union is the *Inter-Parliamentary Bulletin* published in Geneva four times a year in both English and French. Related to the Inter-Parliamentary Union is the Association of Secretaries-General of Parliaments, membership of which is open to Clerks at the Table and certain other parliamentary officers.

The British Group of the I.P.U. numbers about 500 Peers and Members of the House of Commons, and the Lord Chancellor and the Speaker are its Honorary Presidents. The other officers of the group are the President, Vice-Presidents, Chairman, Vice-Chairmen, Hon. Treasurers, Hon. Secretaries, and an Administrative Secretary.

INTRODUCTION OF A MEMBER

A Member of Parliament returned at a by-election is usually introduced to the Speaker and the House immediately after Question Time is over—that is, before the Orders of the Day and Notices of Motion have been entered on. He remains below the Bar until the Speaker says:

'Members desiring to take their seats will please come to the Table.' In compliance with a Resolution of 1688 he must be 'introduced' or accompanied by two Members of the House, who walk with him to the Table where the oath is administered by the Clerk. He then signs the Test Roll and shakes hands with the Speaker in the same way as do members after taking the oath in a new Parliament.

IRISH NATIONALIST PARTY

After the Rebellion of 1798 in Ireland, the subsequent union of that country with Great Britain in 1800 was accompanied by much discontent among the Irish, and the struggle was carried on in the British Parliament by the members elected to represent Ireland in the House of Commons. Apart from their nationalist feelings, the Irish were determined to secure Catholic emancipation, the abolition of tithes collected by the Established Church of Ireland (Protestant) and ultimately its disestablishment. The leader of the Irish Party in the Commons, O'Connell, quickly achieved the emancipation of the Catholics, although the Reform Bill of 1832 rather counteracted its effect by raising the property qualification for Irish voters, but his caution and reluctance to face a violent solution to the other problems led to his downfall. The Whig and Tory landowners were still able to control many constituencies, and Ireland had to wait forty years for the disestablishment of the Church of Ireland. Repeal of the Union was unthinkable to the English, and without the restoration of the Irish Parliament (q.v.) the other reforms could not be obtained. Until the 1870's the Irish Party was not strong enough to make itself felt, but in 1870 the Home Government Association of Ireland was formed and 1872 saw the passing of the Ballot Act. This Act instituted the secret ballot, and the comparative absence of corruption in the 1874 election resulted in 59 Home Rulers being returned to Westminster. Under Isaac Butt and Parnell the Irish Party was well organized and became a thorn in the Government's flesh. From 1877 Parnell and the other Irish members missed no opportunity of obstructing Government business in the House, and their activities resulted in a tightening-up of the rules of debate, culminating in Mr. Gladstone's procedural reforms in 1882. These followed the incident in 1881 during the discussions on the Protection of Person and Property (Ireland) Bill, when the Irish Nationalists prolonged a debate for forty-one hours which Speaker Brand (q.v.) concluded on his own authority.

The General Election of 1885 resulted in an alliance between the Parnellites and the Gladstonian Liberals, and Mr. Gladstone tried to solve the Irish problem by the introduction of a modified Home Rule Bill in 1886, which was rejected by the Commons. Parnell died in 1891, having lost his leadership of the Irish Party as the result of appearing as the co-respondent in a divorce case. Gladstone became Prime Minister again in 1892, and in 1893 he submitted his second Home Rule Bill to Parliament. It passed the Commons by a majority of 34, but a week later was rejected in the House of Lords by a majority of 419 to 41. Following this setback and a split in the Nationalist Party caused by the Parnell controversy, politics ceased for a time to interest the Irish. The formation of the United Irish League in 1898, whose object was the compulsory expropriation of all landlords, effected a reconciliation between the Parnellites and the anti-Parnellites, and the reconstruction of the party under John Redmond. The Irish Councils Bill introduced by the Liberal Government in 1907 conferred extensive powers of self-government on Ireland, and although it was accepted by Redmond as a step in the right direction, it was withdrawn on its being rejected by a National Convention which met at Dublin. The General Election of 1910 placed the balance of power in Redmond's hands, and his price for supporting the Liberals in legislation to limit the power of the House of Lords (*see* PARLIAMENT ACTS, 1911 & 1949) was Home Rule. The third Home Rule Bill (Government of Ireland Bill) was introduced in 1912, passed by the Commons in January 1913, and rejected again by the Lords. The Bill, similar to that of 1893, gave only limited self-government to Ireland, but to the Nationalist Party, who had borne the brunt of the long-continued struggle, it seemed a satisfactory compromise. However, to Sinn Fein, the more extreme isolationist party in Ireland which came forward in 1902, it appeared totally inadequate. In Ulster (Northern Ireland) where loyalty to the United Kingdom was strong, agitation was started to resist the Bill at all costs. This attitude, the Bill having been rejected a second time by the Lords, influenced the Government to announce the introduction of an Amending Bill whereby any county might vote to be excluded from the operations of the Home Rule Bill for a period of six years. This compromise was acceptable to Redmond, but was rejected by the Ulster leader, Sir Edward Carson. In 1914 the Home Rule Bill passed the Commons for a third time, and under the Parliament Act of 1911 nothing but the Royal Assent was needed for it to become law. Soon after the outbreak of war in August 1914, the Government announced its intention of placing Home Rule on the Statute Book, accompanied by a Suspensory Act to prevent it becoming immediately operative, but it was not carried out. After the suppression of the rebellion in 1916 Lloyd George declared he was willing to grant Home Rule immediately to any part of Ireland which demanded it, and in March 1917 he announced the appointment of a Convention to frame a constitution for Ireland within the Empire. This was produced, but nothing was done as the Government's condition of conscription for Ireland was not acceptable to Sinn Fein or the Catholic clergy. For some years before the General Election of 1918 the Nationalist Party had been losing touch with many of the movements which attracted the younger nationalists, and they underestimated the importance of Sinn Fein. These and other factors were responsible for the collapse of the Irish Nationalist Party at this election, where they returned 7 members and Sinn Fein 73. A new Home Rule Bill was introduced in 1920 giving two separate Parliaments to Ulster and the rest of Ireland, but it was resisted by Sinn Fein, which wanted an undivided Ireland with complete control over its own affairs. The Ulster Parliament was opened in 1921, but the discontent of the rest of Ireland resulted in the Anglo-Irish treaty of 1921, which made Southern Ireland a Free State with the political status of Canada, and gave liberty to Ulster to retain her independence. The Irish Free State acquired a new constitution in 1937 under which the name of Eire was restored. In 1948 the country seceded from the British Commonwealth and became an independent republic.

IRISH PARLIAMENT

The origin of the Irish Parliament can be traced back to a meeting of the Great Council in 1297 at Kilkenny, to which two knights from each county and liberty were summoned, but it was not until 1310 that the system of representative government was fully established and Ireland obtained a Parliament of her own. However, as the English settlers who followed the invasion of Ireland by the Normans in 1169 were the wealthiest and most influential in the country, it was inevitable that they alone would be consulted on matters of taxation. Following the invasion of the Scots and the decline of the Colony, the Parliament became even more of a close corporation from which the Irish were rigorously excluded. This exclusion from Parliament and the refusal to the Irish of the privilege of living by the English law lasted practically until the reign of James I, when all classes of the population were taken under his protection and accredited with equal rights. In an attempt to restore the economic value of the Colony Edward III sent his son Lionel, Duke of Clarence, to Ireland where he held the famous Parliament of Kilkenny in 1366. Here was passed the Statute of Kilkenny, which was directed towards preventing the relations between the colonists and natives which, in Edward's opinion, were undermining the national character of the Colony and weakening the authority of the Crown, and also to reform the administration of justice and abuses such as the private wars which were sapping the strength of the Colony. In spite of these efforts the degeneration of the Colony continued, and by Henry VII's time English authority over Ireland had reached its lowest point. Sir Edward Poynings was sent over as Lord Deputy and restored order, and in 1494 the Parliament passed the Poynings' Act which provided that no Parliament should be held in Ireland without the sanction of the King and Council, who should also be able to disallow statutes passed by the Irish Parliament. These provisions practically annulled the legislative independence of the English Colony in Ireland, and as they remained in force for nearly three hundred years proved to be one powerful means of maintaining the subordination of the island. A Parliament held at Dublin in May 1536 imposed the Reformation on Ireland, and Henry VIII was declared supreme head of the Church in Ireland. No serious objections were taken to these measures in the Irish House of Commons, but in the upper House, where the Lords Spiritual possessed a majority, the Supremacy Bill encountered fierce opposition.

In the Parliament of 1542 Ireland was raised to the dignity of a Kingdom, and instead of the old title of Lord of Ireland Henry was now created by statute King of Ireland. When Elizabeth I came to the throne she sent the Earl of Sussex to Ireland as Lord Deputy. He called a Parliament in 1560 which re-established the Protestant faith, but as its statutes were disregarded another Parliament was summoned in 1569 which revealed a strong party opposed to the Crown. Queen Elizabeth had done much to alienate the sympathies of the Anglo-Irish gentry of the Pale (the native Irish were outside the Pale). Complaints were made of the irregular return of members, and the judges declared that those returned for towns not incorporated, and the magistrates who returned themselves, were incapable of sitting in Parliament; but they decided in favour of non-resident Englishmen who had been returned for places they had never seen, which still left a majority who supported the Crown.

After Ireland had been without a Parliament for twenty-seven years, James I summoned one in 1613, having taken measures to secure a docile Protestant majority, and the Catholics seceded for a time from Parliament. With regard to the parliamentary representation of Ireland in the 17th century, in 17 out of 32 counties there was no town that returned burgesses before the reign of James I, and the whole number in the rest was not more than 30. James created some 40 boroughs, and the number of the Commons in 1613 was 232. The extensions of the franchise were not made in the popular interest, and in the 18th century at least two-thirds of the members were slavishly returned by the tenants of the aristocracy. The Irish House of Lords in 1634 numbered 122. The rapacity and perfidy of Charles I and his Viceroy, Lord Strafford, combined with the decision of the English House of Commons that no toleration was to be given to the Catholic religion in Ireland, were the causes of the terrible Rebellion of 1641. After the Cromwellian Settlement of Ireland in 1652 Cromwell's son Henry governed Ireland for nearly four years. The first Irish Parliament to be held for twenty years met in 1661 and passed the Bill of Settlement, which was strongly opposed by the Catholics. They found favour, however, with James II, and the Parliament which met in

1689 consisted almost entirely of Catholics. It declared its own legislative independence by repealing Poynings' law and passed the first Act establishing religious equality. Matters looked promising for the Catholics until the Revolution under William of Orange changed the aspect of affairs and Protestantism triumphed during the reigns of William III and Anne, when statutes of unparalleled severity were passed against the Catholics. They were banished from the Irish Parliament by an English Act of 1691 which imposed the oath of supremacy upon its members, and in 1727 they were forbidden to vote at parliamentary elections. The struggle for parliamentary independence received a set-back in 1696 when all the Acts of James's Irish Parliament were nullified, but in 1719 Parliament again made an effort to assert its supremacy without success. When George III came to the throne the Irish Parliament was at a low ebb. Only one-sixth of the population—the Protestants—formed the electorate, patrons of boroughs by acting together could command a majority in the House, and self-interest and corruption were all but universal. However, there was a reforming party which secured the passage of a Septennial Bill, which was to ensure the election of a new Parliament every seven years, but the English Parliament insisted on eight years, and the first octennial Parliament was dissolved in 1776. As a result of the great national Volunteer movement in Ireland, Grattan was at last able to secure legislative independence for the Irish Parliament in 1782, but his efforts to secure reforms were unsuccessful. An exclusively Protestant House of Commons in Ireland, largely nominated by landed proprietors, was not a likely body to reform itself. Although the franchise and other civil liberties were accorded to the Catholics in 1792–3, there was bitter enmity between them and the Protestant Orangemen, and party strife culminated in the Rebellion of 1798. When the Rebellion had been crushed, Pitt felt that the only hope for Ireland lay 'in the mild and impartial rule of British statesmen and a united Parliament'. His resolution to that effect was carried in the British House of Commons by 149 votes to 24, and in the Lords without a division. The plan for Union was rejected in the Irish Parliament by a narrow margin, so a system of unblushing bribery was resorted to, and over £1¼ million was expended in indemnifying the borough and county interest, the patrons of boroughs receiving £7,500 for each seat in the Parliament that was to be dissolved. The Articles of Union were ultimately carried through both Irish Houses, and brought before the British Parliament on 2 April 1800. The Act of Union received the Royal Assent on 2 July in England and in Ireland on 1 August, and as it was to come into operation on 1 January 1801, on that date the incorporate union of Great Britain and Ireland became an accomplished fact. Under the Act of Union Ireland was to be represented in the Imperial Parliament by 4 bishops, sitting in annual rotation, 28 temporal peers elected for life by the Irish peerage, and by 100 members of the House of Commons. Irish peers not chosen for a seat in the House of Lords were eligible for election to seats in the House of Commons. The 4 bishops were withdrawn after 1 January 1871 on the disestablishment of the Irish Church by the Irish Church Act, 1869, and since Ireland became an independent Free State in 1922 there has been no election of representative peers for Ireland. The last survivor, the Earl of Kilmorey, died in 1961.

PARLIAMENTS HELD IN IRELAND

1559 Jan.	12	to	1559 Feb.	1	1703 Sept.	21	to 1713 May	6
1568 Jan.	17	„	1571 April	25	1713 Nov.	25	„ 1714 Aug.	1
1585 April	26	„	1586 May	14	1715 Nov.	12	„ 1727 June	11
1613 May	18	„	1615 Oct.	24	1727 Nov.	28	„ 1760 Oct.	25
1634 July	14	„	1635 April	18	1761 Oct.	22	„ 1768 May	28
1639 March	16	„	1648 Jan.	30	1769 Oct.	17	„ 1776 April	5
1661 May	8	„	1666 Aug.	8	1776 June	18	„ 1783 July	25
1689 May	7	„	1689 July	20	1783 Oct.	14	„ 1790 April	8
1692 Oct.	5	„	1693 June	26	1790 May	20	„ 1797 July	11
1695 Aug.	27	„	1699 June	14	1798 Jan.	9	„ 1800 Dec.	31

See also NORTHERN IRELAND PARLIAMENT.

ISLE OF MAN

See MANX PARLIAMENT.

J

JAMAICAN PARLIAMENT

From its discovery by Columbus in 1494 Jamaica remained in the possession of Spain until it was taken by the English in 1655. For the first few years it was governed by court martial, then in 1661 a Council was elected to advise the Governor, and subsequently a House of Assembly. In 1728 full legislative power was ceded to the Colony in return for an annual subsidy to support the civil government. As a result of riots and disturbances in 1865 the island surrendered its Constitution and agreed that a new one should be made by Order in Council. A single-chamber legislature was thereafter established, partly elected and partly nominated, which lasted until a new Constitution was granted in 1944. This provided for a Privy Council to advise the Governor, an Executive Council to be 'the principal instrument of policy', a Legislative Council (the upper House), and a House of Representatives. The Privy Council performed the functions of an Executive Council, the Executive Council occupying the position of a Cabinet. The Privy Council has been retained to advise the Governor-General on the exercise of the Royal Prerogative and to be responsible for disciplinary matters relating to the Civil Service. The 1944 Constitution could not properly be called even semi-responsible, as the elected members of the Executive Council were in a minority, but it was changed by an amendment in 1953 which altered the composition of the Council so that it should contain a majority of elected members. It comprised the Governor, the Chief Minister, 7 other ministers, the Colonial and Financial Secretaries, and 2 members nominated by the Governor from the Legislative Council. The upper House, or Legislative Council, consisted of 3 *ex-officio* members, not more than 2 official members and not less than 10 unofficial members appointed by the Governor. The lower House, or House of Representatives, had 32 members elected on an adult franchise. In November, 1957, however, Jamaica achieved virtual self-government when the Executive Council was replaced by a Cabinet of Ministers consisting of 9 members of the House of Representatives and 3 from the Legislative Council, the 3 officials who sat on the former Executive Council being dropped.

Further constitutional reforms came into effect with the General Election of July 1959. The Cabinet then consisted of a Premier and not less than 11 other ministers, 2 or 3 being members of the Legislative

Council and the remainder being members of the House of Representatives. The size of the House of Representatives was increased to 45 members elected by universal adult suffrage. The Legislative Council comprised 18 members appointed by the Governor, and an additional 2 or 3 members appointed on the advice of the Premier who were available as Ministers without Portfolio. The reserved powers of the Governor were removed, with the result that Jamaica attained complete internal self-government.

In 1958 Jamaica became a member of the former West Indies Federation, but seceded following a referendum held in September 1961 at which 53·8 per cent of the electorate voted in favour of leaving the Federation. Jamaica then expressed her desire for independence within the Commonwealth, and a conference was held in London in February 1962 at which it was agreed that a new Constitution providing for independence should come into force on the following 6 August.

The new Constitution provides for a Governor-General, a Privy Council of 6 members appointed by the Governor-General after consultation with the Prime Minister, and a bicameral Parliament consisting of a Senate and a House of Representatives. The Senate consists of 21 members appointed by the Governor-General, 13 on the advice of the Prime Minister and 8 on the advice of the Leader of the Opposition. The size of the House of Representatives remains at 45 but provision has been made for a possible increase of up to 60 members on the recommendation of a Standing Committee of the House of Representatives which will be responsible for reviewing constituencies and their boundaries. The life of a Parliament is five years unless sooner dissolved. The Cabinet consists of a Prime Minister and not less than 11 other ministers, of whom not less than 2 and not more than 3 must be Ministers without Portfolio appointed from the Senate. The Attorney-General may or may not be a member of either House. Parliamentary Secretaries may be appointed from either House provided the number appointed from the Senate does not exceed 3.

The Constitution incorporates provisions for the safeguarding of fundamental freedoms and a special procedure for constitutional amendment. There are ordinarily entrenched and specially entrenched provisions. The former may be amended by Parliament alone provided at least two-thirds of the membership of each House vote in favour of the amending Bill, and provided at least three months elapse between the introduction of the Bill and the commencement of the debate upon it and between the conclusion of the debate and the passing of the Bill by the House of Representatives. A specially entrenched provision is subject to the same procedure but requires in addition the approval of the electorate voting at a referendum. Should the Senate fail to approve by a two-thirds majority any Bill for the amendment of an ordinarily entrenched or a specially entrenched provision, the matter may nevertheless be submitted to a referendum, in which case a three-fifths and a two-thirds majority of the votes cast are respectively required before the Bill in question may be presented for the assent of the Governor-General.

Jamaica's Parliament Building, known as Headquarters House, was built at the end of the 18th century for a wealthy landowner's residence. It was later taken over by the officer commanding the forces in Jamaica, and after the great earthquake of 1907 became the Chamber of the then Legislative Council. It has remained the Chamber of the Legislature ever since, but there are plans afoot to erect a Parliament Building to mark the tercentenary of Jamaica's association with Great Britain, which occurred in 1965.

JAMES I (1566–1625) AND PARLIAMENT

James VI of Scotland became also James I of England on 24 March 1603. He had not long been on the throne before he made quite clear his views on government, views which are amply set forth in his treatise, 'The True Law of Free Monarchies'. This work asserts the principle of absolute sovereignty and exalts the King above the law. It claims that a monarch is ordained by God to rule over his people, that the state therefore owes him absolute obedience, and that to rebel against him under any circumstances is wickedness. No such doctrine could ever be acceptable to a nation such as the English, and it was inevitable that the King's dogmatic adherence to it should precipitate the great constitutional struggle between Parliament and the Crown which was destined to lead his son and successor to the block. In spite of his assertion of the Divine Right of Kings, James was not a man of evil intentions. But he was intolerant of opposition and, although of high academic attainment, short-sighted to the point of stupidity. Furthermore, he lacked the immense personal prestige which had enabled his imperious predecessor, Elizabeth, to avert the impending conflict.

James's first Parliament met on 19 March 1604, two months after the famous Hampton Court conference which, although it failed in its main object of reconciling the Puritan clergy to the Anglican Church, produced one enduring result in the authorized translation of the English Bible. The Commons were sympathetic to the Puritan cause and the circumstances were thus not very favourable to a harmonious relationship between the King and the lower House. They entered upon their first disagreement almost immediately. The Commons claimed exclusive jurisdiction in the issuing of writs for elections, but those for the recent elections which had returned the Parliament then sitting had been issued under a Royal Proclamation in violation of this privilege. Contrary to one of the provisions of the proclamation an outlaw, Sir Francis Goodwin, had been returned for the county of Buckinghamshire. The election had been declared void and a second candidate, Sir John Fortescue, chosen in place of Goodwin. The Commons, however, declared that Goodwin had been lawfully elected and should be allowed to take his seat. The matter was eventually settled by compromise when the King proposed that neither candidate should be returned and a new writ should be issued. The claim of the Commons was never again challenged, and as a conciliatory gesture they passed a Bill disqualifying outlaws for the future.

In accordance with past precedents the Commons passed a Bill granting the King tonnage and poundage for life, but later in the session they showed such reluctance in granting a subsidy that James was moved to write to them declining any further supply. This disobliging tendency on the part of the Commons was no doubt a reflection of their dissatisfaction at the King's manner of dealing with them during this session, as a request for a subsidy was by no means unreasonable at the beginning of a new reign. The proceedings of the lower House prior to this incident had greatly displeased the King. The Commons had attempted to persuade him to abandon his right of purveyance and his feudal rights in exchange for a revenue which he considered to be inadequate. They had shown no enthusiasm for a complete and immediate union between England and Scotland, a scheme on which the King had set his heart. His proposal that he should be styled King of Great Britain was later perforce abandoned upon the Commons declaring that they were not competent to legislate for Great Britain. When they insisted on debating church matters in defiance of his wishes James decided that the time had come to administer a formal rebuke and on 30 May he came down to Parliament for the purpose. The Commons' reaction was to appoint a committee to prepare a vindication of their proceedings. The resulting document, entitled 'A Form of Apology and Satisfaction to be delivered to His Majesty', was a firm assertion of their rights and liberties and a total refutation of James's doctrine of Divine Right. The Commons claimed that their privileges were their right and inheritance no less than their lands and goods; that to withhold from them their privileges was to wrong the state as a whole; that the formal request to enjoy their privileges at the beginning of a Parliament was only an act of manners and did not weaken the right; that their House was a court of record; that there was no higher court in the land than the High Court of Parliament; and that they were the sole proper judge of the election of members to their House. They declared that their privileges had been more dangerously impugned than at any time previously, their freedom of speech threatened, and their House made contemptible in the eyes of the world. They reminded the King that in all the matters he complained of they had proceeded according to their constitutional rights, and continued significantly: 'What cause we, your poor Commons, have to watch over our privileges, is manifest in itself to all men. The prerogatives of princes may easily, and do daily, grow. The privileges of the subject are, for the most part, at an everlasting stand. They may be by good providence and care preserved; but being once lost, are not recovered but with much disquiet.' This document, although read in the House, was never presented to the King, but the Commons were satisfied in having placed their contentions on record.

In considering the grievances of the subject, the Commons discussed the matter of the trading monopolies which seriously restricted the activities of merchants who did not belong to the privileged companies such as the Merchant Adventurers, the Levant Company, and the Muscovy Company. They passed a Bill to free foreign trade, but it was rejected by the Lords. Amongst the other matters which occupied the Commons during this session was a question regarding their own constitution which resulted in the disqualification of mayors from sitting in the House, and a matter of privilege affecting a member, Sir Thomas Shirley, who had been committed to prison for debt. The release of the member was effected, and the resulting statute passed by Parliament to protect those having the custody of such persons and to empower a creditor to proceed with an action against a debtor no longer sheltered by privilege has been described as the first legislative recognition of privilege.

Only on one matter did the Commons find themselves in agreement with the King. The rising tide of popery was causing the King to regret his former tolerance towards Catholics and he indicated his wish for new laws to restrict their activities. The intolerance and indeed the hatred which were felt for the Roman Church in the 17th century may not easily be comprehended in this more enlightened age; but her power was formidable and dangerous to those she regarded as heretics. She made no secret of her determination to destroy heresy by force, neither did she shrink from extreme ruthlessness. In oppressing innocent Catholics at home many a righteous Englishman believed he was doing his duty in protecting his country and his religion. It was not surprising, therefore, that in the House of Lords a peer was committed to prison for observing, 'We have been misled to forsake the religion of our fathers, and to follow some light persons.' One of Parliament's last deeds of the session was to pass an Act confirming the cruel penal statutes which had been passed against Catholics during Elizabeth's reign. Shortly afterwards, on 7 July, the King prorogued Parliament, again scolding the Commons for their refractory behaviour.

The second session of James's first Parliament began on that celebrated date, 5 November 1605. The enforcement of the laws against recusants had provoked a group of Catholics to hatch the notorious Gunpowder Plot (q.v.) which was discovered and foiled at the eleventh hour. The conspirators were either killed or captured and subsequently executed. The revelation of the plot naturally heightened the intensity of the feeling against Catholics, although the vast majority of the English Catholics were in no way associated with it. Nevertheless, Parliament in a spirit of revenge set about imposing even further grievous burdens upon recusants during this session. In opening the session the King affirmed his view that Parliament was the Sovereign's great council and not a place 'for every rash and hare-brained fellow to propose new laws of his own invention' or for a member to make a show of his eloquence. The Commons were not unduly offended at this admonition and agreed to vote liberal subsidies in order to relieve the King's financial stresses. No doubt their sense of common deliverance from the machinations of the gunpowder conspirators had induced a more complaisant mood where the King was concerned. But they were not as yielding as the King could have wished, as the subsidy Bill was accompanied by a list of grievances and also by another attempt to restrict the King's right of purveyance. Parliament was prorogued on 26 May and assembled again for its third session on 18 November.

The third session was mainly devoted to a consideration of the King's project for a complete union of the two countries over which he ruled. Although he was ably supported in the House of Commons by Sir Francis Bacon, the lower House continued to show a marked lack of enthusiasm for the scheme; neither were any signs of support forthcoming from the Scottish Parliament. The only concession which the Commons were prepared to make was to repeal the statutes under which Scots were regarded as enemies and aliens provided the Scottish Parliament would reciprocate in favour of the English. James also secured a legal decision in his favour ruling that the *post-nati* (i.e., Scots born since his accession to the English throne) were entitled to the rights and privileges of English subjects.

Displeased at the attitude of the Commons, James prorogued Parliament on 4 July 1607, and determined to defer another session as long as possible. In the two and a half years which elapsed before Parliament assembled for its fourth session on 9 February 1610 much had occurred to occasion popular discontent. Religious differences had become aggravated, particularly by the attitude of the Anglican clergy in supporting the King's claim to absolute power. The ecclesiastical courts, which enjoyed the King's favour, had been in continual conflict with the Courts of Common Law. James had maintained the odious Tudor practice of proclaiming new offences and penalties without regard for the existing law. The most pressing grievance, however, was the levying of impositions upon merchandise without parliamentary consent. These exactions were in violation of a statute of Edward I, many times reaffirmed, providing that no charges could be levied upon the people without the consent of Parliament. Despite these illegal duties the King was sorely in need of Supply, but the Commons were bent on securing redress of their grievances. They proceeded to discuss the impositions, and the King sent a message imperiously forbidding them to encroach upon his prerogative. But the Commons were not to be bullied into submission, and being in great need of money James suffered them to continue with their consideration of the matter. There followed a great debate in which Bacon spoke on behalf of the Crown, but for all his ability he was overshadowed by the opposition speakers. The Commons fully realized that to acknowledge the right of the King to impose duties according to his will would be to surrender their own control over all taxation. They therefore agreed to draw up a petition for the removal of the impositions. At this stage the King proposed a compromise to the effect that duties already imposed should be retained but that no new ones should be levied. A Bill was drawn up embodying this proposal but it was rejected by the Lords, and the entire matter remained in dispute.

Early in the session the Commons scored a victory by securing the suppression of a law dictionary entitled *The Interpreter* which had been written by one Dr. Cowell. This work gave unqualified support to the doctrine of Divine Right, asserting that the King had full legislative power independently of the two Houses of Parliament, and its publication had given great offence to the Commons. Even James was forced to admit that Cowell had gone too far and he agreed to the suppression of the book.

When Salisbury, the Lord Treasurer, made known the King's financial requirements, the Commons revived their proposal that James should surrender his feudal rights in exchange for a fixed annual income of £100,000. This was not acceptable to the King and he demanded a considerably higher compensation which the Commons rejected. The matter was reopened after the debate on the impositions had taken place, and negotiations ensued which resulted in a settlement known as the Great Contract. The parties agreed that the King should receive an income of £200,000 in return for a number of concessions, including the abolition of purveyance and military tenures. Parliament was prorogued on 23 July, but when it reassembled on 16 October both sides had had second thoughts. The Commons were unwilling to conclude the bargain until their grievances were redressed, and the King had decided that the terms of the settlement were not sufficiently favourable to him. The negotiations proved abortive and, despairing of a subsidy, James dissolved his first Parliament on 9 February 1611. He parted on very harsh terms with the Commons, to whom he delivered a bitter rebuke.

With the death of Salisbury in 1612 James lost his ablest counsellor, and for the remainder of his reign he was influenced by his own rash judgment or by some capricious favourite. One such intimate was Robert Carr, who was later created Earl of Somerset and was the first Scot to take his seat in the House of Lords. With his connivance, the King resorted to various devices for raising money, including the sale of baronetcies, but he was unable to close the gap between his income and his expenditure, and by 1614 he was driven to the necessity of calling a new Parliament. The problem facing the King was how to win the favour of the Commons without being forced into making concessions distasteful to him. The only answer was to attempt to influence the elections, and efforts were made by a group of courtiers who became known as the 'undertakers' to secure the return of candidates amenable to the royal will. The attempt failed, and James's second Parliament, which met on 5 April 1614, proved as unyielding as the last. The Commons immediately brought up the matter of impositions and called for a conference with the Lords. The Lords rejected the proposal, thus provoking a dispute between the two Houses which was further aggravated by some remarks uttered by Bishop Neile to which the Commons took exception. Frayed tempers led the Commons into prolonged and futile discussions which kept them from their normal business. This was most trying to the King whose needs had become urgent, but he could do nothing with them. In a fit of rage he sent for them and tore all their Bills before their faces, and on 7 June he dissolved Parliament. No Parliament before or since has ever proved so unfruitful. It granted no Supply and passed not a single Bill, and has in consequence become known to history as the Addled Parliament (q.v.).

For seven years no further Parliament was summoned. During that time the King resorted to illegal methods of raising money, including the exaction of benevolences, the letting out of monopolies, and the sale of peerages. Popular feeling was further antagonized by the proceedings of the Court of Star Chamber, and the unjust execution of Sir Walter Raleigh did not tend to enhance the reputation of the King. These years also witnessed the fall of the Earl of Somerset and the rise of another favourite, George Villiers, afterwards Earl of Buckingham, the dismissal of Chief Justice Coke, and the promotion of Bacon to the Lord Chancellorship.

The third Parliament of the reign met on 30 January 1621. In opening the first session James endeavoured to create a conciliatory atmosphere and even took upon himself some of the blame for former disagreements. He ascribed his misunderstandings with his first Parliament to his lack of familiarity with the customs of the kingdom, and the failure of his second to 'a strange kind of beasts called undertakers'. He pledged himself to the protection of the Church and reminded the Commons that he had received no grant of Supply for ten years. But the Commons were as resolute as ever over their grievances. The opposition leaders of the former Parliament had again been returned, together with Coke, who since his loss of office had espoused the popular cause, and John Pym, who was destined to win great fame in the following reign. The Commons began, as they had begun the previous Parliament, by taking communion in a body in order to exclude any Catholics who might have been elected, and they urged the enforcement of the penal laws against recusants. Coke moved for a Committee of the Whole House to consider grievances, which began by discussing past violations of the privilege of freedom of speech. The King reminded the Commons of his requirements, and in token of their goodwill they voted two subsidies, but they quickly returned to their grievances and concentrated particularly on the monopolies and the gross abuses associated with them. Much scandalous corruption was exposed and a number of impeachments resulted from the investigations of the Commons, notably that of Sir Giles Mompesson who had been granted a patent empowering him to issue licences to innkeepers. The Commons performed a great public service in bringing to book a bunch of scoundrels and relieving many an honest tradesman from oppressive hardship. The next victim of the Commons' reforming zeal was, however, far removed from the breed of Mompesson. A committee which had been appointed to investigate judicial corruption disclosed some grave malpractices in the courts of justice. Charges were laid before the House of Lords, and there followed the most famous impeachment of the reign, that of Lord Chancellor Bacon. Bacon was a great and wise man whose career was unfortunately not free from discreditable episodes. If he had not been wilfully corrupt he had certainly been recklessly indiscreet in his acceptance of gifts. He offered no defence in the face of the evidence submitted against him and was adjudged guilty. Although his sentence of a fine and imprisonment was not enforced he was ruined and retired a broken man. It neither excuses Bacon's conduct, nor does it detract from the high credit due to the Commons, to regret the downfall of one of the most eminent men of the age.

There was one case during this session which redounded to the credit of neither House. A Roman Catholic barrister named Floyd was alleged to have used certain words to which the Commons took exception and he was ordered to the Bar of the House to answer for his offence. He was found guilty and sentenced to stand three times in the pillory and to pay a fine of £1,000. The King questioned the jurisdiction of the Commons in the matter and referred the case to the House of Lords. With inexcusable savagery the Peers increased the severity of the sentence by raising the fine to £5,000 and adding perpetual imprisonment and a public flogging to the penalties. In this affair the King emerged very favourably. He at once remitted the flogging and at the end of the session he also remitted the fine and caused Floyd to be released.

The Commons were still immersed in their grievances when the King, growing impatient, ordered Parliament to adjourn on 4 June. When it reassembled on 20 November a fresh issue arose between the King and the Commons in the shape of foreign policy. In Europe the Thirty Years War had broken out. Predominantly a religious struggle between the Catholic and Protestant rulers of Central Europe, the starting-point of the conflict had been the claim of Frederick, the Elector Palatine, to the throne of Bohemia. In the course of events the Palatinate itself was invaded and lost to Frederick. Whilst sympathizing with the Protestant cause on the Continent, the Commons were not unduly concerned over so remote an issue as the loss of the Palatinate. Their hatred was directed against Spain as the arch-enemy of non-Catholic Christendom. The King, for his part, was anxious to avoid war with Spain, for not only did he fancy himself as the international mediator but he was keen to promote a Spanish marriage for his son Charles. The King's policy was totally repugnant to the Commons, who drew up a petition urging the enforcement of the laws against popery and pressing for a war with Spain and the abandonment of the negotiations for a Spanish match. On hearing of the petition James wrote an angry letter to the Speaker commanding him 'to make known our name unto the House, that none therein shall presume henceforth to meddle with anything concerning our Government or deep matters of state'. The Commons at once devoted themselves to the matter of privilege, setting aside all other business. In answer to a second petition the King asserted that they enjoyed their privileges only by grace of the Sovereign. Unable to allow this claim to pass unchallenged, the Commons, on 18 December 1621, entered the following famous Protestation in their journals:

The Commons now assembled in Parliament, being justly occasioned thereunto, concerning sundry liberties, franchises, privileges and jurisdictions of Parliament, amongst others nor herein mentioned, do make this protestation following:

That the liberties, franchises, privileges and jurisdictions of Parliament are the ancient and undoubted birthright and inheritance of the subjects of England; and that the arduous and urgent affairs concerning the King, State and defence of the realm, and of the Church of England, and the maintenance and making of laws, and redress of mischiefs and grievances, which daily happen within this realm, are proper subjects and matter of counsel and debate in Parliament; and that in the handling and proceeding of those businesses every member of the House of Parliament hath, and of right ought to have, freedom of speech to propound, treat, reason and bring to conclusion the same; that the Commons in Parliament have like liberty and freedom to treat of those matters in such order as in their judgments shall seem fittest; and that every such member of the said House hath like freedom from all impeachment, imprisonment, and molestation (other than by censure of the House itself) for, or concerning, any bill, speaking, reasoning, or declaring of any matter or matters touching the Parliament or Parliament business; and that if any of the said members be complained of, and questioned for anything said or done in Parliament, the same is to be showed to the King by the advice and assent of all the Commons assembled in Parliament before the King give credence to any private information.

The King was furious and, sending for the journals, he tore out the Protestation with his own hand. On 8 February 1622 he dissolved Parliament. The Spanish marriage did not take place and Charles eventually married Henrietta Maria of France.

James's fourth and last Parliament met on 12 February 1624. Again the popular leaders were returned together with two others destined to fame, John Selden and Sir John Eliot. In his opening speech the King declared that it was his wish to maintain the liberties of the Commons, but he went on to enjoin them, 'Let not any stir you up to law questions, debates, quirks, tricks and jerks, but continue yourselves in that honest modesty, whereby you may have my prayers to God for you, and procure the love of me, and a happy end to this Parliament.' The Commons, strongly Protestant as ever, were united in their hatred of Spain and their eagerness to enforce the laws against recusants, whilst the King was anxious to avoid war with Spain but keen to recover the Palatinate on behalf of his son-in-law, Frederick. The Commons were persuaded into voting subsidies amounting to £300,000, but they specified the purposes for which the grant was made, namely, to take measures in readiness for a war with Spain. They also insisted that the money should be paid over to treasurers appointed by Parliament. This Parliament is notable for the passing of the greatest statute of the reign, that abolishing the monopolies. The second outstanding incident was the impeachment of the Earl of Middlesex, the Lord Treasurer, for corrupt activities, a proceeding largely engineered by his bitter enemy, Buckingham. In spite of Buckingham's personal motives it transpired that the Earl had committed some unpardonable misdemeanours and he was found guilty.

The King soon became irritated by the insistence of the Commons on their attitude towards Spain and the Catholics at home, and on 29 May he prorogued Parliament. It was prorogued on three subsequent occasions but never summoned again, for on 27 March 1625 James died.

During the reign of this monarch the popular cause made considerable advances. The Commons successfully reasserted their rights of freedom of speech, appropriating supplies, determining contested elections, and impeachment; they secured the statutory abolition of monopolies; and in the impeachments of Bacon and Middlesex can be detected the first signs of the principle, now unquestioned, of ministerial responsibility to Parliament.

As a monarch James I, in spite of many deficiencies, had redeeming qualities. In some respects his views were more advanced than those of the popular party, notably on the matters of religious toleration and the union of the two kingdoms. But his convictions were incompatible with those of a freedom-loving people and, inherited as they were by his successor, could only bring disaster to the dynasty.

JAMES II (1633-1701) AND PARLIAMENT

James II came to the throne on 6 February 1685. Although he was an acknowledged Catholic his accession provoked no immediate unrest; in fact, the attitude throughout the country seemed to favour giving the new reign an opportunity to succeed. The new King was supported by moderate opinion, and those who opposed him kept their views to themselves. To begin with he adopted an inoffensive policy, promising that the established Church would be protected and that the prerogative would not be abused. He announced, however, that his brother had died in the Catholic faith; shortly afterwards he attended a public celebration of Mass and at his coronation the Anglican ritual was curtailed.

In spite of his promises James was a typical Stuart. He was no believer in free Parliaments, and his only motive in deciding to call one was to legalize the question of the Crown revenues which he had been collecting without parliamentary sanction. He made quite certain, however, that the elections would produce a result favourable to himself by manipulating the charters of towns in order to give his supporters control of the franchise. The charters of the City of London had been confiscated by Charles II in consequence of that monarch's displeasure with the capital, and they had been restored in much mutilated form with the object of making the corporation the mere instrument of the King's will. The elections thus returned an overwhelming Tory majority to the House of Commons.

James's one and only Parliament met on 19 May 1685. In his speech opening Parliament, the King made quite clear his real views on the matter of Parliament and the prerogative, and it contained a veiled threat to the effect that if the Commons failed to vote him the supplies he wanted they could expect him to follow in his father's footsteps and govern without Parliaments. The Commons agreed to the grants required without demur. The Lords, for their part, repealed a resolution which had provided that proceedings begun on an impeachment by the Commons should not be annulled by a dissolution, and Danby and others were released in consequence. But there was one matter, that of religion, on which the King could not command the subservience of Parliament. The first sign of dissension appeared when the

Commons recommended that the penal laws should be put into operation against all dissenters from the Church of England. The King could not have complied with this request without including his fellow Catholics amongst the victims, and by threats of his personal displeasure he induced the Commons to amend their resolution to one expressing confidence in His Majesty's undertaking to protect the established Church.

Parliament remained loyal to the King when the Monmouth Rebellion broke out in June and passed a Bill of Attainder against the Duke together with an extraordinary vote of Supply and a Bill for the protection of the King's person. On 2 July Parliament was prorogued and four days later Monmouth's Rebellion was effectively suppressed at Sedgemoor. A similar rising in Scotland, led by the Earl of Argyll, had been dealt with even more easily and its leader executed. Monmouth soon followed Argyll to the scaffold, and the notorious Bloody Assizes ensued to which James gave his fullest approval, Jeffreys being shortly afterwards promoted to the Lord Chancellorship.

The King's true regard for parliamentary government and the law was soon evidenced when Parliament reassembled on 9 November. In opening the session he announced his intention of raising a standing army, referring to the recent rebellion in justification of his decision. He also made it clear that he intended to defy the Test Act, a measure passed during the previous reign under which Catholics were disqualified from holding commissions in the army. At the same time he failed to repeat his assurances with regard to the established Church. He could not have resolved on a course more hateful to the country at large. The question of military authority had long been a point at issue between the Crown and Parliament, for the personal power of a sovereign with a standing army under his direct control could well become irresistible, thus rendering Parliament ineffectual. In violating the Test Act the King not only demonstrated his disregard for the law but gave a practical indication of his religious policy. The Commons agreed to a grant of Supply for which the King asked, but they made it clear that they would tolerate neither a standing army nor the violation of the Test Act. Strenuous opposition was expressed to the King's support and encouragement of popery, and an address was prepared and presented to James reminding him of the law and desiring him to dismiss his Catholic officers. The King's reaction to the address was so restrained that the majority of the Commons were mollified. They even committed one of their number, Coke, to the Tower for 'his indecent and undutiful reflecting on the King and this House' in remarking, 'I hope we are all Englishmen, and are not to be frighted out of our duty by a few high words.' The Lords, however, were not so readily satisfied by the King's reply. The Bishop of London, Henry Compton, in a speech of great force and conviction warned the House

o   [407]

of the implications which a violation of the Test Act would involve. 'If it were acquiesced in,' he declared, 'all the higher posts would very soon be filled with Catholics, and the whole administration would assume a Catholic character.' With these words he hit upon the King's very objective, which was ultimately nothing less than the re-establishment of the Roman Catholic religion in the country.

It was the attitude of the Lords which precipitated a dissolution. The King saw the danger to his plans in the steps which the Lords might propose to take, particularly if they appealed to the judges and obtained a legal decision against his actions. Although both Houses were prepared to indemnify his Catholic officers against the penalties they had incurred by accepting commissions, James was not prepared to abandon his designs and preferred to forgo his grant of Supply. He prorogued Parliament on 20 November before the Lords could resume their debate, and prorogued it six times in all before he finally dissolved it on 4 July 1687.

The developments which led up to the Revolution of 1688 and the abdication of the King may be briefly summarized. By now James had alienated many of his former supporters and the country was left in no doubt as to his intentions. He proceeded to govern without Parliament, like his father before him, and he conferred high offices on Roman Catholics. To further the Catholic ascendancy he revived the Court of High Commission as a result of whose action popery was introduced into the universities, the fellows of Magdalen College, Oxford, being expelled through his personal intervention. On 4 April 1687, the King issued his first Declaration of Indulgence in favour of all Dissenters, thus hoping to win Nonconformist support against the Anglican Church. His second Declaration of Indulgence followed on 27 April 1688, and was ordered to be read in all churches on two successive Sundays. This provoked the famous petition of the seven bishops protesting against the illegal use of the dispensing power in matters connected with the Church. The bishops were committed to the Tower and sent for trial on a charge of libel, but popular pressure proved stronger than that of the court and the jury returned a verdict of not guilty. The King now faced the first serious reverse of his reign, and the birth of a son to the Queen at this time probably strengthened the resolve of the people to get rid of the Stuart dynasty once and for all. On the same day as that on which the bishops were acquitted seven of the most prominent men in the country representative of all sections of Protestant opinion invited the Prince of Orange to England. William had close ties with England as a grandson of Charles I and through his marriage with Mary, the King's daughter. There were those who during the previous reign had entertained hopes of securing the succession in William's favour, and in the light of recent developments many eyes were now turned towards him. This trend was further accelerated by a fear existing in the country that the aggressive alliance which had been concluded between Charles II and the King of France had been renewed by James. Conscious of the rapidly growing feeling against him James realized the need for concessions. He agreed to the abolition of the High Commission, the restoration to Magdalen College of its previous constitution, and to the City of London and other boroughs their confiscated charters. He even consented to the permanent exclusion of Catholics from the House of Commons. But he shrank from calling a new Parliament, knowing full well that elections would not turn in his favour.

James's relations with William of Orange had deteriorated, the former's suspected alliance with France being a strong contributory factor, and the King's failure to summon a Parliament heightened the agitation at home. On 10 October William issued a declaration setting forth the grievances of the British people and demanding the calling of a Parliament. James, in a desperate effort to rally the country to his side in the face of a threatened Dutch invasion, made further concessions to popular feeling, but William issued a second declaration refuting the value of any concessions which failed to guarantee the security of religion and the end of arbitrary government. On 5 November William landed with his forces at Torbay. Strangely enough he was not received with the enthusiasm he had expected. The country had fallen into a state of apathy, no doubt temporarily lulled by the King's recent concessions. Had James at this time acted with shrewdness and determination, had he at once called a Parliament and dismissed all Catholics from office, he could probably have rallied the nation to his side and taken advantage of the Briton's natural repugnance to a foreign invader. But James was not a man of this calibre, neither was he in harmony with the feelings of his people. His concessions had been made in no spirit of understanding or generosity but merely as a matter of expediency, and now that he was faced with a situation demanding firm action he could only vacillate and waver. After some days of inactivity, the leading men in the nation began to join William. The revolution was a relatively peaceful one and little blood was shed. James's courage failed him and he decided on flight, eventually making his escape to France on 22 December. With the abdication of this misguided monarch, Stuart tyranny and misgovernment perished for ever.

JERSEY, STATES OF
See CHANNEL ISLANDS LEGISLATURES.

JEWEL TOWER
Tucked away behind the buildings in Old Palace Yard, facing the House of Lords, the Jewel Tower is a comparatively unknown part

of the Palace of Westminster. Yet it is historically one of the most interesting as it was probably built in the reign of Richard II. It was used by Edward III as a repository for the State jewels, and the name then given to the tower has been perpetuated to the present day. It was then used as a depository for the parliamentary records until the building of the Victoria Tower. After the fire of 1834, the Jewel Tower formed part of the Speaker's residence, and in 1866 part of the Weights and Measures Office.

JEWS IN PARLIAMENT

The first Jew to be elected a Member of the House of Commons was Baron Lionel de Rothschild. He was returned for the City of London in 1847, but as he could not take the oath which then contained the words 'on the true faith of a Christian' he was not allowed to take his seat. He waited for two years hoping that the Jewish Disabilities Bill would be passed to enable him to take the oath in the manner of his people, but although it passed its third reading in the Commons it was thrown out by the Lords. He thereupon resigned his seat, but was re-elected for the same constituency. Still the Commons refused to allow him to take his seat in the House, and for seven years he occupied a seat below the Bar without the right to vote. In 1851 Sir David Salomons, elected member for Greenwich, took his seat and voted in the House, for which offence he was fined £500. At last, after much opposition from the Lords, a Bill was passed in 1858 giving each House power to provide by resolution for the admission of Jews. Baron de Rothschild was the first to take advantage of the change—eleven years after his first election.

The most famous parliamentarian of Jewish birth was of course Benjamin Disraeli, who although a baptised Jew lost no opportunity of referring to his race with pride. The first Jewish Member of the House of Lords was the son of the first Jewish Member of the House of Commons. He was raised to the peerage as Lord Rothschild in 1885. There are at present (1970) 28 Jewish peers, including 16 life peers, and 40 Jewish Members of the House of Commons.

JOHN (1167?–1216)

Sixth and youngest son of Henry II, succeeded his brother Richard I and was crowned on 27 May 1199. His reign was an inglorious one, notable, however, for Magna Carta (q.v.), the last great constitutional development before the coming of Parliament (q.v.).

JOHNSON, DR. SAMUEL (1709–1784)

Amongst Dr. Johnson's lesser-known works are his reports of parliamentary debates which were published in the *Gentleman's Magazine* from July 1741 to March 1744. Johnson was never in the gallery himself and he did not report the actual speeches made in Parliament. He re-wrote them in his own unmistakable and rather ponderous style, and it is said that some of his reports bore little relation to the real debates. A strong Tory himself, he took no pains to conceal his bias, and on one occasion he is reported as having remarked, 'I took good care that the Whig dogs should not have the best of it.'

In Johnson's day the reporting of parliamentary proceedings was punishable as a breach of privilege, and the *Gentleman's Magazine* took certain precautions to avoid any possible consequences. Fictitious names were used for members (very often rather obvious anagrams of the real names were employed), and the debates purported to be those of the 'Senate of Lilliput'. Publication was often delayed until some time after the session, and the last report by Johnson was of a debate on 22 February 1743.

Johnson's *Parliamentary Debates* were published with his collected works in two separate volumes in 1787. They are one of the sources used by Cobbett and Wright in the compilation of the Parliamentary History (q.v.).

JOINT COMMITTEES

Joint Committees composed of an equal number of members of both Houses are appointed from time to time at the instance of one House or the other. They generally consider some matter which has aroused interest in both Houses, and the general concern over the question of India resulted in the appointment of the Joint Committee on Indian Constitutional Reform in 1933. A Joint Committee which is set up every session deals with the committee stage of Consolidation Bills, thus saving the detailed committee work in both Houses. The powers given to a Joint Committee are those which may be given to a Select Committee, and the procedure adopted is that of the committees of the House of Lords. For example, the Chairman of a Joint Committee votes like the other members and has no casting vote as in the House of Commons committees. If the votes are equal the question is decided in the negative. An interesting feature of a Joint Committee is that there is no common quorum—the Commons members must have a quorum (which has been given them by their House) and the Lords must have theirs (3 members) as if it were a meeting of two separate committees.

The report of a Joint Committee is presented to both Houses—by the Chairman to the House to which he belongs, and by a member selected by the committee to the other House. If the Joint Committee has been considering a Bill the report is made to the House which originated it. Since 1935 it has been the practice, when both Houses order the report of a Joint Committee to be printed, to publish the report as a joint House of Lords and House of Commons paper.

JOINT SESSION

The meeting together of both Houses of a bicameral legislature for the purpose of settling a disagreement between them (e.g., this is allowed by Section 57 of the Australian Constitution) or where it is necessary that a majority of both Houses sitting together should be obtained before changes can be made to the Constitution or certain types of legislation passed. There is no provision for joint sessions of the House of Commons and the House of Lords, but they can be held in the Parliaments of Australia and India. The latter Parliament's first joint session was held on 6 May 1961 in connexion with the Dowry Prohibition Bill.

JOURNAL OF CONSTITUTIONAL AND PARLIAMENTARY ACTIVITIES

Issued quarterly in New Delhi by the Institute of Constitutional and Parliamentary Studies, this journal publishes articles on legislative institutions in India and abroad and is intended as 'a vehicle of advanced and specialist study of comparative constitutional laws and parliamentary procedures'. It was first published in 1967, superseding the Journal of Parliamentary Information, the first number of which appeared in April 1955.

JOURNAL OFFICE

One of the offices in the House of Commons in the department of the Clerk of the House. Its principal duty is the compilation of the daily Votes and Proceedings (q.v.) and the Journal of the House of Commons (q.v.), and it also arranges for the tabling of papers presented to the House. This office also deals with petitions and the activities of the Committee on Public Petitions. A similar office exists in the House of Lords.

JOURNAL OF THE HOUSE OF COMMONS

The official permanent record of the proceedings of the House of Commons, not to be confused with Hansard (q.v.) which is a verbatim report of the debates. The Journal, which is prepared in the Journal Office from the Votes and Proceedings and the minute books of the Clerks-at-the-Table, is published annually and usually records the proceedings of one session. It is compiled in the form of a continuous narrative, except for proceedings in Committee of the Whole House which are recorded in the language of the Votes and Proceedings; according to Erskine May, this is possibly because until 1829 proceedings in committee were not noticed in the Journal.

The Journal of the House of Commons was begun in 1547 by John Seymour, the Clerk of the House. Except for a break during the reign of Elizabeth I from 1584 to 1601 the compilation of the Journal has been continuous since that year. Seymour appears to have undertaken the task voluntarily as there is no record of its forming part of his official duties. His journal began as a simple record of the readings of Bills, and although he expanded it over the years from three pages to eleven pages per session it was always in the form of notes. Fulke Onslow, Clerk of the House from 1567 to 1602, continued Seymour's work on a larger scale. His journal provided a reasonably detailed account of each day's proceedings, including annotations of members' speeches. In 1628, however, as a result of the King expressing a desire to see a speech entered in the Journal, the House resolved that 'the entry of the clerk of particular men's speeches was without warrant at all times'.

It is not known when the Journal became the official record of the proceedings of the House. According to Mackenzie (*The English Parliament*), the first evidence of this appears in February 1623/4, when the House resolved to appoint a committee to 'survey the clerk's Book of Entries every Saturday in the afternoon'. The earliest reference to its use as an authoritative source of precedent comes from June 1580/1, when a precedent was sought for the procedure to be followed upon a vacancy in the Speakership.

The Journal of the House of Commons was first ordered to be printed following a report of a Select Committee in 1742. An index to the Journals from 1547 to the death of Queen Anne was compiled under the supervision of Sir Thomas Erskine May (q.v.) Until 1866 the days and months of the year were given in Latin, but to-day the English form is used. The Journal of the House of Lords retains the Latin form, however. As the official record of the proceedings of the House the Journal is accepted as evidence in a court of law.

Both Houses of the Canadian Parliament also maintain a Journal of their proceedings.

JOURNAL OF THE HOUSE OF LORDS

The official record of the proceedings of the House of Lords, not to be confused with the official verbatim report of debates known as Hansard (q.v.). The Journal is compiled from the Minutes and Proceedings and is a far more detailed record. It records the names of peers attending each sitting and the name of a member who moves the second reading of any Bill. Proceedings in Committee of the Whole House are entered in detail and Select Committee reports included in full. The letters patent and writ of summons of a newly created peer are entered verbatim upon his introduction into the House, and a peer succeeding by descent may, if he wishes, lay upon the Table of the House the letters patent by which the title he inherits was granted in order that they may be entered in the Journal.

As a complete record the Journal of the House of Lords dates from the year 1509, but surviving fragments of earlier journals prove that a record was being compiled early in the 15th century. In the opinion of Mackenzie (*The English Parliament*), the Lords Journals were probably originated by John Fawkes, Clerk of the Parliaments from 1447 to 1470/1. The Journal did not become an official record until 1620/1 when the Lords appointed a committee 'to view and examine the entries of the Journal Book'.

Like the Journal of the House of Commons, the Lords Journal is published annually. The Lords appoint a committee every session 'to peruse and perfect the Journals of this and former sessions of Parliament', but no meetings of this committee have taken place for a long time.

JOURNAL OF THE SOCIETY OF CLERKS-AT-THE-TABLE IN COMMONWEALTH PARLIAMENTS

See SOCIETY OF CLERKS-AT-THE-TABLE IN COMMONWEALTH PARLIAMENTS.

JOURNALS, COMMITTEE FOR THE

See COMMITTEE FOR THE JOURNALS.

JUDICIAL COMMITTEE OF THE PRIVY COUNCIL

See PRIVY COUNCIL.

JUDICIAL OFFICE

One of the offices of the House of Lords which deals with its appellate jurisdiction. It supervises the preparation and arrangements for the hearing of appeals, as well as the taxation of judicial costs.

K

KANGAROO
See SELECTION OF AMENDMENTS.

KENYA PARLIAMENT
Kenya was administered by the Foreign Office from 1895 to 1905 when control was transferred to the Colonial Office. The East African Order in Council of 1906 replaced the Commissioner by a Governor and provided for Executive and Legislative Councils, to which latter body was transferred the power of making ordinances, hitherto vested in the Commissioner. Its first session was held in August 1907 and it consisted of 6 official and 2 (subsequently increased to 4) nominated unofficial European members. An ordinance of 1919 provided for the election of 11 European members and the official membership was increased at the same time to preserve the Government majority. An ordinance of 1924 provided for the election of 5 Indians and 1 Arab, and in 1927 the Legislative Council was enlarged on the basis of the recommendations of the Devonshire Commission of 1923. It then consisted of 20 official members (11 *ex-officio* and 9 nominated of whom one represented Arab interests) and 18 unofficial members comprising 11 elected Europeans, 5 elected Asians, 1 elected Arab, and 1 nominated member to represent African interests. In 1938 a second unofficial member to represent African interests was appointed. In 1944 the first African took his seat in the Legislative Council, and a second was appointed in 1946. In June 1948 the Legislative Council assembled for the first time with a majority of unofficial members. In the same year a Speaker was appointed, and the Council consisted, in addition to the Governor and Speaker, of 16 official and 22 unofficial members, the latter comprising 11 elected Europeans, 5 elected Asians, 4 nominated Africans, 1 elected and 1 nominated Arab. In 1952 further legislation increased the size of the Council to 54. The number of officials was increased to 26 (8 *ex-officio* and 18 nominated) and the 28 unofficial members comprised 14 Europeans, 6 Africans, 6 Asians, and 2 Arabs. In 1956 legislation was passed providing for the election of 8 African members for which purpose the Colony was divided into 8 electoral districts. The first election of African members took place in 1957. A system of multiple voting was introduced for these elections whereby male and female Africans over twenty-one could exercise from one to three votes according to their educational and other qualifications.

o*

[415]

The franchise for Europeans and Asians was one of universal adult suffrage within their own communities, and for Arabs universal adult male suffrage subject to a simple literacy test.

Following proposals made by the Colonial Secretary in November 1957 (Cmnd. 309) further changes were introduced into the composition of the Legislative Council. Six additional seats were provided for elected African members and provision was made for 12 special members designed to represent the people on a non-communal basis. Provision was also made for the Governor to appoint as many nominated members as would ensure an adequate Government majority and, in 1960, the size of the Legislative Council, excluding the Speaker, stood at 91, including an elected membership of 18 Africans, 18 Europeans, 9 Asians and 3 Arabs.

In 1954 a Council of Ministers was set up as the principal instrument of government, exercising collective responsibility for policy decisions. It comprised the Governor and Deputy Governor, 6 *ex-officio* members, 2 nominated members, and 6 unofficial members of whom 3 were Europeans, 2 Asians, and 1 an African. In 1958 the Council of Ministers was enlarged by the addition of 2 unofficial members, a European and an African. Provision was also made for not less than 3 and not more than 6 Assistant Ministers of whom 2 should be Africans, 1 an Asian, and 1 an Arab. The Executive Council, which had continued to exercise certain functions when the Council of Ministers was first created, was abolished. The 1958 Constitution also provided for a Council of State with powers of delay and revision to protect any one community against legislation which discriminated disadvantageously. It consisted of a Chairman and 10 members, none of them members of the Legislative Council, nominated by the Governor and included representatives of all races.

A constitutional conference held in London in 1960 led to further constitutional reforms, the Legislative Council being reconstituted to include 65 elected members of whom 53 were elected on a common voters' roll. The representation of minority communities was safeguarded by the reservation of 10 seats for Europeans, 8 for Asians and 2 for Arabs, and a system of primary elections was introduced for these seats whereby any candidate securing 25 per cent of the total votes cast by his own racial community at the primary election became eligible as a candidate at the main election, when all races voted together on a common roll. Twelve of the elected members were designated National Members and were elected by the other 53 elected members sitting as an electoral college on the basis of proportional representation. Elections under this Constitution were held in February 1961, and represented an important step towards the establishment of universal adult suffrage. The Council of Ministers comprised 4 official and 8 elected members, but in 1962 its size was increased to 16, including only 2 official ministers responsible respectively for Legal Affairs and Defence.

Following a conference held in 1962, Kenya attained self-government on 26 May 1963 and full independence on the following 12 December. The new Constitution introduced a quasi-federal system with a strong central government based on a central legislature designated the National Assembly and consisting, at the outset, of a Senate and a House of Representatives. As originally constituted, the Senate consisted of 41 members elected by universal adult suffrage and was equipped with a delaying power restricted to one month in the case of money bills and one year or two sessions in the case of other legislation. The House of Representatives consisted of 117 members elected by universal adult suffrage and 12 specially elected members elected by the House sitting as an electoral college. However, the National Assembly is now unicameral, legislation amalgamating the Senate and the House of Representatives into a single chamber having been passed in December 1966. In December 1969, 158 constituencies were contested by candidates of the governing party at primary elections, which have been retained under Kenya's electoral system even though racial representation has been abolished. Since the governing party, KANU, was the only party contesting the election the successful candidates were returned unopposed at the General Election which took place later in the same month.

Kenya consists of Nairobi (the capital) and seven Regions, namely Coastal, Central, Eastern, Rift Valley, Western, Nyanza and North-East. Each Region has an elected Regional Assembly consisting of one member from each District of the Region and one specially elected member for each 8 constituency members elected in the same way as the 12 specially elected members of the House of Representatives. Each Regional Assembly is empowered to make laws in respect of matters specified in the Constitution as being under exclusive regional jurisdiction or concurrent jurisdiction, and to exercise the executive authority of the Region through committees. All residual powers are vested in the central legislature, which is also competent, subject to affirmative resolutions passed by 65 per cent of the membership of the National Assembly, to assume the legislative or executive authority of a Regional Assembly in certain circumstances. The Central Government may delegate any of its functions to a Regional Assembly, but a Regional Assembly may not delegate its executive functions to the Central Government. The boundaries of the Regions are specified in the Constitution, but they may be amended by the decision of a two-thirds majority of each of the Regional Assemblies concerned and a simple majority of the National Assembly.

The Constitution incorporates a Bill of Rights, provides for a central and seven regional Public Service Commissions, the majority

[417]

of whose members must be independent of political influence, and sets up an Electoral Commission, principally composed of regional representatives, which is required to review the number and boundaries of constituencies at least every eight years.

Kenya became a Republic on 12 December 1964, the first anniversary of independence, the President being also the head of the executive. On 10 November 1964 Kenya temporarily became a one-party state, when the party in Opposition in the National Assembly dissolved itself and merged with the Government party. However, following a rupture between the President, Mr. Jomo Kenyatta, and the Vice-President, Mr. Oginga Odinga, a new parliamentary opposition emerged in April 1966. This development led to the passing of a law requiring any member of the National Assembly who resigns from the party for which he originally stood as a candidate to vacate his seat and submit himself for re-election.

KHAKI ELECTION

In September 1900 the Conservative Government dissolved Parliament and appealed to the country on the ground that it was necessary to bring to an issue the question of fighting the war in South Africa to a finish. The General Election in October, which was the work of Chamberlain, became known as the 'Khaki Election' because it was felt that the dissolution of Parliament was an attempt to capitalize the emotions of military victory in terms of votes for the Government. The Conservatives were returned to power with a majority of 134. The 'Coupon Election' (q.v.) of 1918 is also sometimes known as the 'Khaki Election'.

KING'S COUNCIL

See CURIA REGIS.

KING'S ROBING ROOM

See QUEEN'S ROBING ROOM.

KITCHEN COMMITTEE

Until it was superseded by the House of Commons (Services) Committee (q.v.) in December 1965, the catering arrangements of the House of Commons were under the control of a Sessional Committee colloquially known as the Kitchen Committee. Its full title was the Select Committee on Kitchen and Refreshment Rooms (House of Commons), and it was unique among committees of the House in that its powers were not confined merely to making recommendations. It had full control over the management of the catering facilities of the House, the appointment of staff, and the spending of money within the scope of its responsibilities. Its powers and functions have now been taken over by the Catering Sub-Committee of the House of Commons (Services) Committee.

The Kitchen Committee consisted of 13 members, and its quorum was 4. It was empowered to send for persons, papers and records (although it rarely summoned witnesses), to sit notwithstanding any adjournment of the House, and to delegate any of its powers to sub-committees. It normally met once a month and reported to the House once a year when it submitted a statement of accounts and balance sheet for the previous year. The Chairman of the Kitchen Committee answered questions in the House when called upon to do so, although complaints were normally dealt with privately. The Committee appointed three sub-committees to deal respectively with buying, staff and wine. The Manager of the Refreshment Department was appointed by the Committee, attended meetings by invitation, and worked closely with the Chairman in running the department. All these responsibilities now fall within the province of the House of Commons (Services) Committee.

The catering arrangements of the House of Commons date from 1848 when a Select Committee was appointed following the destruction of Bellamy's Kitchen (q.v.) in the fire of 1834 'to inquire into the proposed arrangements of the Kitchen and Eating and Accommodation Rooms for Members and Officers of the House of Commons in the new Palace of Westminster'.

The Committee recommended that a Sessional Committee be appointed to control the catering arrangements. The actual work of catering was initially left to a contractor who received a grant from public funds and supplied refreshments at fixed rates. Eventually the Committee assumed these duties itself and since 1884 the Refreshment Department has been run by a Manager answerable to the Kitchen Committee, and latterly to the House of Commons (Services) Committee, in the manner of a club.

The Refreshment Department is not self-supporting and is subsidized to the extent of about £12,000 a year. In 1906 Speaker Lowther decided that while the catering arrangements were the exclusive responsibility of the Kitchen Committee he must reserve to himself the decisions as to which persons are permitted to make use of the rooms within the precincts of the House of Commons.

L

LABOUR, MINISTER OF

The office of Minister of Labour was superseded by that of Secretary of State for Employment and Productivity in April 1968. (*See* EMPLOYMENT AND PRODUCTIVITY, SECRETARY OF STATE FOR.) A new department of Employment and Productivity with enlarged responsibilities was created to take the place of the Ministry of Labour and Mrs. Barbara Castle was appointed its first Secretary of State. This Minister inherited all the duties previously exercised by the Minister of Labour and was also given overall responsibility for prices and incomes policy which was previously vested in the Department of Economic Affairs.

The first Minister of Labour was appointed in 1917 under the authority of the Ministries and Secretaries Act of 1916. Until 1939 he was Minister of Labour only, but in that year he was also appointed Minister of National Service by an Order-in-Council. His reconstituted department took over the administration of the Factories Acts from the Home Office, the apportionment of manpower between the armed services and industry and the administration of the National Service Act. His title reverted to Minister of Labour with the abolition of National Service in 1959.

The main responsibilities inherited by the Secretary of State for Employment and Productivity from the Minister of Labour were control of the employment exchanges and appointment offices, the settlement of industrial disputes, the publication of labour statistics and information and the consideration of international labour questions. Statutory duties include those relating to the Employment and Training Acts, 1948 and 1950, the Disabled Persons (Employment) Acts, 1944 and 1958, the Wages Councils Act, 1945 and other Wages Acts, and the Factories Acts.

A chronological list of Ministers of Labour appears as Appendix 22.

LABOUR PARTY

The Labour Party was formed at a conference of trade unionists and Socialists held in February 1900. It was then known as the Labour Representation Committee, and it was not until 1906 that its title was changed to The Labour Party. Its immediate forerunner was the Independent Labour Party (q.v.) of Keir Hardie, who worked to persuade the trade unions to support the party instead of the Liberals. In the General Election which returned the Liberals to power in 1906 the

Labour Party gained 29 seats with 50 candidates, and a new factor in politics had appeared. In spite of some successes, however, the prestige of the party declined, partly due to defective leadership and partly because many Socialists and industrial workers would not accept the limitations imposed on the party's actions by its constitution and by the demands of parliamentary democracy. The party also had a set-back in a judgment given by the Law Lords that a trade union was acting illegally in raising a compulsory levy on its members for political purposes, and if the payment of M.P.s had not been introduced in 1911 many trade union men would have had to resign from Parliament. The Trade Unions Act of 1913 permitted the unions to raise money from their members for political purposes subject to certain conditions. At the beginning of the First World War the Labour Party was not making much headway, but most Labour M.P.s supported the Government's war policy and the coalition subsequently formed. The Independent Labour Party and five of its members in the House, including Keir Hardie, MacDonald, and Snowden, were anti-war. Ramsay MacDonald resigned from the leadership of the Parliamentary Labour Party, a position he had held since Keir Hardie's retirement from that post in 1911, and no longer took a leading part in debates. Arthur Henderson was responsible for proposals to amend the constitution of the party in order to admit individual members and to set up electoral machinery in the constituencies. Early in 1918 a conference was held at which it was agreed to continue the existing system of direct affiliation by trade unions and other national organizations, but to establish in addition constituency parties in each parliamentary area. It is the constituency party which appoints the agent, confirms the selection of individuals to fight local government elections, nominates the parliamentary candidate, and designates the delegates to the Annual Conference, the supreme authority in the party. In the 'Coupon Election' (q.v.) in 1918 at the end of the war the anti-war Labour leaders were heavily defeated, but in the 1922 election which followed the break-up of the coalition the Labour Party gained 142 seats, and under the leadership of Ramsay MacDonald became for the first time His Majesty's official Opposition. Another General Election followed a year later at which the Labour Party gained 191 seats and with Liberal consent formed a Government under the leadership of MacDonald. After eleven months it was thrown out by the Conservatives and Liberals, but not before it had passed legislation improving the conditions of the unemployed, the old-age pensioners and the war-disabled and launched a housing project. The following election, the third in two years, was notable for the use made of the Zinoviev letter (q.v.) by the party's opponents, and the Bolshevik bogey assisted the Conservatives to return to power with Baldwin as Prime Minister. The Labour Party lost 40 seats but increased its poll by over a million votes. This second Baldwin administration was notable from the party point of view for the issue of *Labour and the Nation*, a detailed re-statement of Labour policy, and for the General Strike of 1926. The failure of this strike did not have an unfavourable effect on the party's fortunes in the General Election of 1929, and the second Labour Government was returned with 287 seats. This Government was soon faced with the effects of a world economic depression, and in 1931 a split occurred in the party, Ramsay MacDonald, Snowden, and J. H. Thomas joining the Liberals and Conservatives to form a National Administration, while the rest of the Labour ministers and most of the Labour members formed an Opposition under Arthur Henderson. An election followed at which the number of Labour members was reduced to 52. After the defeat of Henderson in 1931, Lansbury led the party until his extreme pacifism conflicted with its policy, and under Attlee's leadership the party trebled its membership after the 1935 election. Following the outbreak of war in 1939, the Labour Party resisted a coalition under Chamberlain, but in 1940 accepted it under Churchill's leadership; and Attlee, Bevin, Morrison, Greenwood, and Dalton joined the Government. The 1945 General Election swept Labour into its first overwhelming victory, with a clear majority over all other parties of 146. During its five years of office the party carried out the nationalization of the coal mines, electricity and gas supply, civil aviation, railways, and the Bank of England, and retained the war controls over private business as well. All but a very few schools came under Government control and in some respects the National Insurance and Health Schemes instituted went beyond the recommendations of the Beveridge Report. In 1950 the Labour Party celebrated its jubilee—in fifty years its paying membership had grown from under 376,000 to over 5,000,000, and its income from less than £300 a year to nearly £200,000. The General Election of 1950 gave the Labour Party an unworkable majority of 6 in the House of Commons, and a year later another election was held. The party had been weakened by the death of Ernest Bevin and the resignation of Sir Stafford Cripps, and in April 1951 Aneurin Bevan resigned from the Government as a result of his disagreement with the Budget and the rearmament programme. The 1951 election resulted in a Conservative Government with a majority of 17, although the Conservatives actually received 231,000 fewer votes than the Labour Party. Labour also lost the 1955 election by 58 seats, but their poll on this occasion was nearly one million below that of the Conservatives. They subsequently gained a number of seats in by-elections during the life of this Parliament, but in spite of this they failed to win the 1959 election, securing only 258 seats against the Conservatives' 365. The party was to suffer two further serious blows while still in Opposition. In July 1960 it lost a tower of strength with the death of Aneurin Bevan, whose brilliance and powerful personality had established him as probably the most significant individual force in the entire Labour movement. Early in 1963 Hugh Gaitskell, who had led the party since Attlee's retirement in December 1955, also died prematurely, thus leaving the party in a pre-election year very short of leaders with previous experience of Cabinet office.

Mr. Harold Wilson was elected leader of the Labour Party in February 1963 at a time when the popularity of the Conservative Government was sinking. In October 1964 he led the party to a very narrow victory, thus restoring it to power after thirteen years in Opposition. Yet even in victory Labour's run of bad luck seemed to continue. One of the party's most experienced members, Mr. Patrick Gordon-Walker, lost his seat at the General Election, notwithstanding which Mr. Wilson appointed him Foreign Secretary with the intention of bringing him back into the House of Commons by means of a by-election. A supposedly safe Labour seat was found for Mr. Gordon-Walker at Leyton, but to the surprise of all concerned he was again defeated, and therefore felt himself compelled to resign from the Government. Mr. Wilson's Government was thus left to function in the House of Commons with the wafer-thin majority of 4, its task further exacerbated by a serious economic situation. Nevertheless, in spite of the grave difficulties confronting it, the Labour Government succeeded in winning a wide measure of public confidence, Mr. Wilson achieving considerable personal popularity as Prime Minister. A further General Election in March 1966 confirmed the party in office with the resounding majority of 97, probably the most significant General Election result since 1945.

Such are the fortunes of political life, however, that Mr. Wilson's Government, grappling with serious economic difficulties which culminated in the devaluation of the pound in 1967, rapidly lost favour with the electorate. Continued by-election losses and a serious defeat in the Greater London Council elections of 1967 dragged the fortunes of the party down to an unprecedentedly low level. Nevertheless, by 1970, the economic situation in the country having become more stable, the public opinion polls began to indicate that the Labour Party was recovering its popularity. An election was called in June of that year which Labour was confidently tipped to win, but contrary to most expectations the Conservatives were returned to power with an overall majority of 30.

It has already been mentioned that the Annual Conference is the supreme authority in the Labour Party. It is responsible for policy, and receives reports on the activities of the preceding year from the National Executive Committee and the Parliamentary Party. The National Executive is directly elected by the conference itself, and stands in a closer relationship to it than the Parliamentary Labour

Party, whose members are elected by their constituents. They attend Conference therefore only in an *ex-officio* capacity, and although they take part in discussion are not allowed to vote unless they are also there as delegates from an affiliated organization. The Leader of the Party is always an *ex-officio* member both of Conference and of the National Executive Committee, but he is actually elected by the Parliamentary Party.

LADIES' GALLERY

The attitude of the House of Commons to the presence of women in the Chamber has varied from total exclusion to allowing them to occupy seats by the side of members on the sacred floor of the House. In the 17th century, although officially barred from the Chamber, their occasional presence was treated with some leniency, but towards the end of the 18th century they were allowed to sit anywhere in the Chamber. In the year 1778, however, during an important debate on the state of the nation, a member, noticing that the ladies were occupying seats to the exclusion of his male friends, drew attention to the presence of strangers, and an order was given to clear the galleries. There was an immediate and evidently unlady-like uproar, and it was two hours before the last of the fair sex was ejected. Afterwards, so rigorous was the ban against women that Mrs. Sheridan had to wear male attire in order to hear her husband's speeches. This state of affairs lasted for more than half a century, but eventually, as a great concession, ladies were admitted to a room above the Chamber where they were allowed to peer through an iron grating above the chandelier which lighted the old House.

After the fire of 1834, a Select Committee recommended 'that a portion of the Strangers' Gallery, not exceeding a quarter of the whole, and capable of containing 24 ladies, be set apart for their accommodation, divided by a partition from the rest of the gallery, and screened in front by an open trellis work, and that the Gallery so proposed be called the Ladies' Gallery'. This referred to the temporary Chamber in the old Court of Requests, but when the new Houses of Parliament were built a similar recommendation was carried—not without considerable opposition. In 1888 some women applauded a speech, and this resulted in the Ladies' Gallery being closed to the public until 1909. The 'trellis work' was removed in 1918, and in this year of their political emancipation women were permitted, if they preferred, to sit with the opposite sex in the Strangers' Gallery. The new Chamber of the House of Commons has no Ladies' Gallery, as such, but the Speaker's Gallery is customarily reserved for women. The Canadian House of Commons has a Ladies' Gallery, but men are admitted to it provided they are accompanied by a lady.

LAND AND NATURAL RESOURCES, MINISTER OF

An appointment created in October 1964 and abolished in February 1967, and held throughout this period by Mr. Frederick Willey as a Minister of Cabinet rank but without a seat in the Cabinet itself. This office was a somewhat controversial one from the outset, since its responsibilities included the setting up of a Land Commission, as foreshadowed in the Labour Party's 1964 Manifesto, for the public acquisition of building land. Other matters under the jurisdiction of this Minister included the Nature Conservancy, National Parks, forestry, mineral rights, geological survey, and certain other functions relating to land use. When the task of co-ordinating matters relating to land and natural resources under a single department was completed, this Minister's functions were absorbed by the Minister of Housing and Local Government (q.v.).

LAW LORDS

See LORDS OF APPEAL.

LAW OFFICERS OF THE CROWN

The King could not appear in his own Courts in person to plead his cause where his own interests were concerned, so from very early times he used the services of an attorney, or agent, to appear on his behalf. The list of Attorneys-General begins early in the reign of Edward I and the Solicitor-General appears first in Edward IV's reign. The Solicitor-General is a subordinate of the Attorney-General, and frequently gives a joint opinion with him on legal matters at the request of a government department. It is essential in practice that both should be in Parliament, although that opinion was by no means always held by the House of Commons, which for the first three centuries of its existence was always anxious to exclude the holders of great offices under the Crown. Indeed, in 1614 the House, jealous of the influence of the Court, appointed a committee to search for precedents for the Attorney-General being a member of the House—a hit at Sir Francis Bacon, who was both. The committee failed to find anything illegal in the position, and the House allowed Sir Francis to remain a member but recommended that 'never any Attorney-General shall serve for the future'. This rather illogical ruling remained in force until Francis North became Attorney-General in 1673, and after the Revolution it was the general practice for the Attorney-General to be a member of the House of Commons.

The law officers are not only the legal advisers and representatives of the Sovereign: they are at the service of the state where offences against the good order of the community are not left to a private prosecution, but are dealt with by the Government of the day in the person of the Director of Public Prosecutions, who is instructed by the Attorney-General. The latter would normally prosecute in criminal cases involving serious constitutional considerations, and in murder cases there is a tradition that he should always prosecute in a case of murder by poisoning. The law officers may also intervene to vindicate the rights of the public at the instance of private persons. The Government may call for their advice, and so may each department of government; they are expected to defend in the House of Commons the legality of ministerial action if it is called in question, and no appeal can be taken to the House of Lords without the authority of the Attorney-General. The law officers are not necessarily, or until recent years usually, Privy Councillors, but they receive a writ of attendance, together with the judges, to the House of Lords at the commencement of every Parliament. The Crown, or it is more true to say the Government, has its legal advisers for Scotland and for Northern Ireland: the Lord Advocate and Solicitor-General for Scotland, the Attorney-General for Northern Ireland. The Lord Advocate and the Irish law officer are Privy Councillors. The Solicitor-General for Scotland is not always in Parliament.

The law officers of the Crown play a various part. They are the legal advisers of the Crown, the Ministry, and the departments of government. They are members of the Ministry, but are seldom included in the Cabinet. Sir Rufus Isaacs was the first Attorney-General to be appointed to the Cabinet by Mr. Asquith in 1912, but no Solicitor-General has ever enjoyed Cabinet rank. The law officers are members of the House of Commons and come and go with the change of party majorities. They are responsible to Parliament for the advice given to the Crown and its servants; they are the chiefs of the legal profession in their respective countries, and in England and Northern Ireland represent the Bar when the Bar takes collective action. Both the law officers are now precluded from private practice during tenure of office.

The Law Officers Act, 1944, provides that functions which are required to be discharged by the Attorney-General may be discharged by the Solicitor-General if (1) the office of Attorney-General is vacant, or (2) the Attorney-General cannot act owing to absence or illness, or (3) the Attorney-General authorizes the Solicitor-General to act in a particular matter (e.g., where the former has a personal interest).

The Attorney-General's salary is £13,000, the Solicitor-General's £9,000, and the Lord Advocate's £8,000. They also draw £1,250 as M.P.s.

In most other Commonwealth countries the law officers are Civil

Servants, but in Australia and New Zealand the Attorney-General, and in Canada the Solicitor-General, are ministers.

(Further reading: Edwards, *Law Officers of the Crown*, 1964.)

LEADER OF THE HOUSE

According to Gladstone, the Leader of the House 'suggests, and in a great degree fixes, the course of all principal matters of business, supervises and keeps in harmony the actions of his colleagues, takes the initiative in matters of ceremonial procedure, and advises the House in every difficulty as it arises'. The details of the arrangement of Government business are settled, subject to his control, by the Chief Whip, and the Leader of the House announces the business for the following week every Thursday after Questions. Herbert Morrison, who spoke with authority as a former Leader of the House, says that the Leader should be Chairman of the Cabinet Committee on Legislation and of the committee dealing with the future legislative programme. He should also be conscious of five responsibilities: to the Government, to the Government's own supporters on the back benches, to the Opposition, to the House as a whole, and to the individual minister in charge. He should, within reason, be accessible to both sides of the House. His relations with the Government Whips should be close, cordial, and co-operative, and he must be ready to listen to them even though he is not always bound to agree with their view. He should keep in mind the duty of the Government to promote all reasonable facilities for the House to debate matters about which it is genuinely concerned, and must regard himself not only as a member of the Government but as one of the principal guardians of the rights of the House of Commons as a whole.

The title of Leader of the House as a technical term does not appear to have been thoroughly established until the middle of the 19th century. As late as 1840, Lord John Russell, who was the chief Minister of the Crown in the House of Commons when the Prime Minister (Lord Melbourne) was in the House of Lords, is referred to in a debate as 'the noble Lord who has to conduct, on the part of the Crown, the business of the country in this House'. In those days, when it was not uncommon for the Prime Minister to be in the House of Lords, a leading minister had to take his place in the Commons. Thus, whether the term was used or not, Lord Althorp was Leader of the House under Lord Melbourne until his succession to a peerage in 1834, and so were Castlereagh and Canning before him. If the Prime Minister is Leader of the House, as he usually was until 1942, unless he was a peer, he appointed a minister to act as Deputy Leader. Mr. Attlee as Lord Privy Seal acted in that capacity until Mr. Eden was appointed Leader in 1942. The Leader of the House of Lords performs a similar function to his opposite number in the Commons, and like him is a member of the Cabinet Legislation Committee.

LEADER OF THE OPPOSITION

The Member of the House of Commons who is for the time being the Leader in that House of the party in opposition to the Government having the greatest numerical strength. Her Majesty's Opposition is Her Majesty's alternative Government, and the Leader of the Opposition is probably Her Majesty's alternative Prime Minister. The British Constitution assumes that at any moment if the Government resigns, or is defeated on a major issue, a new one can be formed from the Opposition. The Leader of the Opposition holds an office which arose, like that of the Leader of the House, out of practice but has no official functions either according to legislation or to the rules of the House. Actually his duties, which have been described as 'multifarious', include the arranging of the business programme in consultation with the Leader of the House and the Whips. According to the Ministers of the Crown Act of 1937, if any doubt arises as to which party in opposition has the greatest strength, or as to who is the Leader in the House of such a party, the question shall be decided by the Speaker.

In the British House of Commons the Leader of the Opposition receives a salary of £4,500, charged directly on the Consolidated Fund (q.v.) and he is entitled to an additional £1,250 as a Member of Parliament.

Canada was the first Commonwealth country to pay its Leader of the Opposition, when a sessional allowance was granted him in 1905. Since 1920, a salary has been provided for the Leader of the Opposition in the Australian House of Representatives, the practice having already been adopted by all six states before that date. In Canada and Australia a salary or allowance is also paid to the Leader of any minority party with a minimum specified strength—10 members in Australia, 12 in Canada. New Zealand first paid its Leader of the Opposition in 1951, while in Canada and Australia there is also a salary payable to the Leader of the Opposition in the Senate. The salaries of Leaders of the Opposition in other Commonwealth Parliaments appear in Appendix 2 (Members' Salaries).

LEEWARD ISLANDS GENERAL LEGISLATIVE COUNCIL

The Leeward Islands Federation, established by an Act of 1871, included Antigua and Barbuda, St. Kitts–Nevis and Anguilla, Montserrat, and the British Virgin Islands (qq.v.). The Leeward Islands Act, which received the Royal Assent on 15 March 1956, abolished the federation, and with it the General Legislative Council, and provided that each of the four Presidencies should become a separate Colony.

LEGISLATION BY REFERENCE

The alteration of a law by means of references in an amending Act to previous legislation. This practice obviates the necessity of repealing an old statute and replacing it with a new one incorporating the required amendments. In spite of the extreme complexity which this method of legislation tends to introduce into the wording of a statute, it is advantageous from the point of view of time-saving and printing economy.

LEGISLATIVE ASSEMBLY

The name given to the Indian and Malaysian state legislatures and most of the Canadian provincial and the Australian state legislatures (where the Parliament is bicameral it is applied to the lower House). Since 1923 the Rhodesian legislature has been termed the Legislative Assembly, although following Rhodesia's unilateral declaration of independence in 1965 the Prime Minister announced that it would henceforth be re-designated Parliament, a term regarded as being more commensurate with the sovereign status assumed by that country.

LEGISLATIVE CHAMBER

See CHAMBER.

LEGISLATIVE COUNCIL

The name usually given to the colonial legislatures of the British Commonwealth. It is also applied to the upper Houses of some bicameral legislatures, including those of the Indian and Australian States.

LEGISLATIVE DRAFTING

See DRAFTSMEN.

LEGISLATURE

The body of persons in a country or state invested with power to make, alter, and repeal laws. It may consist of one or two Chambers, with similar or differing powers, and in the monarchies of the British Commonwealth the legislature is incomplete without the Sovereign (q.v.) whose assent is constitutionally required before any measure can become law. In the United Kingdom there are two legislative Chambers, the House of Commons (q.v.) and the House of Lords (q.v.); in Canada, the House of Commons and the Senate; in India, the House of the People and the Council of States. Australia, Ceylon, Malaysia, Jamaica and Trinidad and Tobago each have Parliaments which include a Senate and a House of Representatives. New Zealand's unicameral Parliament is known as the General Assembly and its single Chamber is the House of Representatives. Cyprus, Malta, Sierra Leone and the Gambia also have single-chamber Parliaments with a House of Representatives, while the term National Assembly is employed in Ghana, Tanzania, Kenya, Uganda, Malawi, Zambia, Guyana and Botswana. Barbados has a Senate and a House of Assembly. Nigeria had a Senate and a House of Representatives and Lesotho a Senate and a National Assembly prior to the *coups d'état* in these states.

The term Legislative Council has been applied to a colonial legislature and to the upper House of a provincial or state legislature. The popularly elected House of a provincial or state legislature is usually termed a Legislative Assembly. In a federal state the term legislature is sometimes applied to the provincial or state legislative bodies to distinguish them from the central Parliament.

See also BICAMERAL LEGISLATURE; UNICAMERAL LEGISLATURE.

LENTHALL, WILLIAM (1591–1662)

Speaker of the House of Commons from 1640 to 1655 (with the exception of two short breaks in 1647 and 1653) and from 1659 to 1660. Lenthall's fame rests upon his term of office during the Long Parliament (q.v.), and in particular upon his behaviour on the occasion of the attempted arrest of the five members by the King. This incident is dealt with in full under the heading CHARLES I AND PARLIAMENT.

Some historians have written in great praise of Lenthall whilst others have found little good to say about him. There is evidence that he was regarded unfavourably by a number of contemporary critics, but, as Dasent so aptly expresses it, 'In the case of an office like the Speaker's there can be no posthumous fame without contemporary appreciation.' The truth probably lies somewhere between the two extremes. Lenthall was neither an outstanding character nor a great Speaker, but on one occasion at least he rose to the heights of greatness both as man and Speaker, and declared for the first and for all time where a Speaker's first duty lay. Lenthall's words on this historic occasion are well-known and are repeated elsewhere in this work, but it is not inappropriate that they should appear under this heading also. On 4 January 1642 Charles I came without warning to the House of Commons to make his famous attempt to arrest five members on a charge of treason. When he turned to the Speaker to demand where they were, Lenthall fell upon his knees and delivered his memorable reply:

'May it please Your Majesty, I have neither eyes to see, nor tongue to speak in this place, but as the House is pleased to direct me, whose servant I am here; and I humbly beg Your Majesty's pardon that I cannot give any other answer than this to what Your Majesty is pleased to demand of me.'

Lenthall presided over the House when the ordinance for bringing the King to trial was introduced, although he personally is believed to have opposed the measure. He continued as Speaker after the King's execution, but years later on his deathbed admitted quite frankly that he was motivated by fear of the consequences had he declined to continue in office. During the first years of the Commonwealth the Speaker was accorded precedence as the first man in the realm, but in practice his power was strictly limited. On two occasions, however, he used his casting vote to save prominent royalists from the scaffold. On 20 April 1653 Cromwell forcibly dismissed the Long Parliament. Lenthall was ejected from the Chair, and did not become a member of the ensuing Barebones Parliament (q.v.). He was, however, summoned to the first Parliament held after Cromwell became Protector, and again elected Speaker.

Lenthall became Speaker for the last time on 7 May 1659, when he presided over the restored Long Parliament, or Rump Parliament (q.v.). He supported Monk and the Restoration, and stood as a candidate for the Convention Parliament (q.v.) but was not elected. He was pardoned by the King for his part during the Commonwealth, but he was incapacitated by the House of Lords from holding any office of trust. He died on 3 September 1662, and in a dying confession he expressed penitence for his share in the trial and execution of King Charles I.

LESOTHO PARLIAMENT

On 30 January 1970, parliamentary government was suspended in Lesotho by the Prime Minister following a General Election in which the Opposition gained the majority of seats. A state of emergency was declared, Opposition leaders were arrested, and the King, who was accused by the Prime Minister of actively supporting the Opposition, was placed under restriction. What follows therefore applies to the situation as it existed prior to the suspension of the Constitution.

Lesotho, formerly Basutoland, became independent on 4 October 1966. The Constitution provides for the establishment of Motlotlehi (the Paramount Chief) as Head of State, and a Parliament consisting of Motlotlehi, a Senate and a National Assembly. The Senate consists of the 22 principal chiefs or their nominees and 11 other persons nominated by Motlotlehi acting in his absolute discretion. Motlotlehi's nominations are for the duration of a Parliament and are not revocable. The National Assembly consists of 60 members elected by universal adult suffrage and representing single-member constituencies.

The Senate is not empowered to initiate legislation but may refer

Bills back to the National Assembly with amendments. Any Bill passed by the National Assembly may be submitted for the assent of Motlotlehi should the Senate have failed to pass it within 90 days (30 days in the case of a Money Bill) or passed it only with amendments unacceptable to the lower House. The Senate is not empowered to delay the Appropriation Bill.

The life of a Parliament is five years unless earlier dissolved. The power to prorogue and dissolve Parliament rests with Motlotlehi who normally acts on ministerial advice, but who in certain circumstances may be guided by his own discretion. He may refuse a dissolution if he believes it contrary to the national interest and is satisfied that the Government can be carried on without a dissolution. He may dissolve Parliament if the National Assembly passes a resolution of no confidence in the Government (proposing at the same time the name of an alternative Prime Minister) and if the Prime Minister fails to resign or advise a dissolution himself within three days. He may also dissolve Parliament if the Prime Minister's office is vacant and he finds himself unable to nominate a Prime Minister who could command the support of a majority in the National Assembly.

The Cabinet consists of the Prime Minister and not less than 7 other ministers appointed by Motlotlehi on the Prime Minister's advice. The Constitution also provides for the appointment of Assistant Ministers. Motlotlehi acts in accordance with ministerial advice except where the Constitution specifically provides that he may act on his own discretion. He exercises an absolute discretion in the appointment of 11 members of the Senate, the approval of appointments to his personal staff and the National Planning Board, and in carrying out certain functions relating to disciplinary proceedings against chiefs. In certain other cases the Constitution specifies the scope of his discretion. In the exercise of his discretionary powers he is advised by a Privy Council consisting of the Prime Minister and two persons nominated by himself, one on the advice of the Prime Minister.

The Constitution entrenches the institution of Chieftainship and establishes the College of Chiefs, which consists of the 22 principal chiefs with the power to co-opt up to 3 other persons. Its function is to determine matters of Basuto law and custom including those relating to the succession to the office of Motlotlehi. The Constitution also provides for the protection of fundamental human rights and freedoms, and consists of specially entrenched provisions, entrenched provisions and ordinary provisions. The specially entrenched provisions include those concerning the nature of the State of Lesotho, the office of Motlotlehi, Motlotlehi's Privy Council, the protection of human rights and freedoms, the Chiefs and the College of Chiefs, land, and the principal sections relating to the judicature. These provisions may be amended by means of the normal legislative process, subject to the proviso that any such legislation must subsequently be approved at a referendum in which all registered voters shall be eligible to participate. Entrenched provisions, which include those concerning the franchise; the holding of elections; the duration, prorogation, and dissolution of Parliament; and the composition, powers, and procedure of both Houses, may be amended either by the procedure specified for the amendment of specially entrenched Provisions or by an Act of Parliament passed by a two-thirds majority of each House voting separately. Ordinary provisions may be amended by means of the ordinary legislative process.

Basutoland first achieved a measure of internal self-government in 1959 with the establishment of a National Council of 80 members, half of whom were elected. The Council acted as a consultative body in matters reserved to the High Commissioner, which included external affairs, defence, internal security, customs and excise, postal services, broadcasting and the public service. A new Constitution, envisaging the achievement of independence within a short period following its adoption, came into operation with the holding of a General Election on 1 May 1965. This Constitution established a Parliament whose composition has remained unchanged with the emergence of Lesotho as an independent state, except that the Paramount Chief, formerly the Queen's representative, is now himself established as the Head of State.

LIBERAL NATIONAL PARTY
See NATIONAL LIBERAL PARTY.

LIBERAL PARTY
After Stuart days Members of Parliament tended to collect into small influence groups. But apart from their individual opinions on various problems most were either Whig or Tory. In those days, broadly speaking, the Tory sympathized with the old rule of Privilege and the Crown, and the Whig was the democrat. 'Whig' is probably a shorter form of whiggamore, and the whiggamores were a body of insurgents from the west of Scotland who marched on Edinburgh in 1648. The supporters of the Presbyterian cause in Scotland were called the real whigs, and the name was applied derisively to those Members of Parliament who wished to exclude James, Duke of York, from the throne in 1679. The Whigs were in power for the greater part of the 18th century and although the Liberals were the immediate heirs of the Whigs, they were not identified with them to as great an extent as the Conservatives were with the Tories. At the beginning of the 19th century the reforming ideas of the Spanish *liberales* and the French *libéraux* were detested by the Tories, and they applied the term 'Liberals' to the advanced section of the Whigs, who accepted it at its

face value and became the Liberal Party. The agitation preceding the Reform Bill of 1832 consolidated the position of the Liberals, and although some Members of Parliament continued to use the name of Whig for twenty years after this, 1832 may fairly be regarded as the year of the birth of the Liberal Party.

Under Lord Palmerston (1846–66) the Liberals were a powerful and influential party and acted as a brake on many schemes for political reform. They were supported by the growing commercial and business interest of the times and stood for a minimum of Government interference in business and for the rights of the individual.

After Lord Palmerston, Mr. Gladstone dominated the party and they in turn dominated the political scene. As a party they became more closely knit and better organized and until 1874 they suffered no eclipse. From then until 1906 they remained a powerful and influential party and were generally supposed to be supported by a vast middle-class urban vote and by the large business interests.

Although 1906 was the year of a great Liberal electoral victory, it also marked the beginning of the shrinking of the party, due to the significant arrival of the Labour Party in Parliament some thirty strong. In parenthesis, this perhaps explains the decline of the party for it failed in the years before the First World War to attract the newly enfranchised working classes. They tended to go either into the Conservative fold (since a great deal of Conservative legislation in the second half of the 19th century was beneficial to the working man) or to rally under Labour's flag. The party still, however, attracted great leaders; Asquith, Lloyd George, Churchill, Ramsay MacDonald, and many others were to follow, and much important legislation was to be carried out, in particular the Old Age Pensions Act and the foundations of the later Welfare State.

The party was in power in 1914 when war broke out and in 1916 was split when Lloyd George formed a coalition with the Conservatives. But in the 1918 election the party proper dropped to 34. In 1923 the coalition broke up and the Liberal Party recovered a little with 158 members, but later in 1928 they dropped to 59, to 21 in 1935, to 12 in 1945, and 6 in 1951. In the 1955 election the party retained 6 seats but lost 1 as the result of a by-election in 1957. In 1958 a minor sensation was caused when the Liberal candidate won the Torrington seat at a by-election from the Conservatives. Hopes arose in Liberal circles that this victory presaged a revival in the party's fortunes. These hopes were to some extent dashed by the result of the 1959 election at which, in spite of polling over one and a half million votes, the party failed to increase its representation in the House of Commons. Although one new seat was gained (North Devon) this advantage was cancelled out by the loss of Torrington. However, a further boost to Liberal morale came in 1962 when the former Conservative stronghold of Orpington was gained at a by-election. In the General Election of 1964 the Liberal Party increased its strength to 9, Orpington being retained, and a further by-election success at the expense of the Conservatives subsequently brought the strength of the Liberal team to 10. In the General Election of 1966 the Liberals lost 2 seats but gained 4, thus increasing their parliamentary strength to 12, further increased to 13 by a subsequent gain at a by-election. Only 6 Liberal candidates were successful in retaining their seats at the General Election of 1970, however, thus demonstrating that occasional modest successes cannot be said to presage a Liberal revival. The overall voting pattern in the country continues to suggest that the Conservative and Labour Parties are the only significant contenders for power. Both the Conservative and the Labour Parties have played their part in the decimation of the Liberal Party. After the First World War the Liberals lost some of their leaders to the Conservatives and those who remained, conscious of their party's radical tradition, tended to support the growing Labour opposition. This policy led paradoxically to the displacement of the Liberal Party by the Labour Party which emerged as the new opponent of the Conservatives and the new popular party with the electorate. It is noteworthy that the Liberal Party to-day remains a radical group, in some respects more so than the Labour Party, although it tends to draw its electoral support from voters who would probably prefer the Conservatives to Labour in the absence of a Liberal candidate.

LIBRARIES OF PARLIAMENT
See PARLIAMENTARY LIBRARIES.

LIFE PEERS
The hereditary basis of the summons to Parliament of the lay lords became established in the course of centuries, and the possibility of breaking away from the hereditary principle seems not to have been seriously considered until the Wensleydale case in 1856, although a few life peerages were created between the reigns of Richard II and Henry VI, and several women received life peerages between the reigns of Charles II and George II. When, to strengthen the judicial side of the House of Lords, Sir James Parke, a distinguished judge, was created Baron Wensleydale 'for the term of his natural life', four hundred years had elapsed since the creation of a male life peer. A new patent was made out, however, conferring a hereditary barony on Lord Wensleydale, because the Committee for Privileges of the House of Lords decided that he was not entitled to sit and vote in Parliament on the terms of his original creation.

In 1870 it was proposed to confer life peerages on men distinguished in any form of public service and, although nothing came of the proposal at the time, it figured in most of the subsequent plans which were put forward for the reform of the House of Lords. The principle of granting life peerages was accepted six years later with the passing of the Appellate Jurisdiction Act, 1876, under which the first four Lords of Appeal in Ordinary (q.v.) were appointed with the rank of baron. Their number was increased by statute to 6 in 1913, to 7 in 1929, and to 9 in 1947, with the proviso that unless their number falls below 7 the vacancies will not be filled unless the Lord Chancellor, with the concurrence of the Treasury, is satisfied that it is necessary to fill them. At the present time (1970) they are at full strength, and there are in addition a number of retired Lords of Appeal in Ordinary who retain their membership of the House of Lords as life peers.

Until 1958 life peerages were exclusively judicial in nature, and indeed no provision existed for the appointment of life peers other than Lords of Appeal in Ordinary. The creation of non-judicial life peers was made possible with the passing of the Life Peerages Act, 1958, which also removed the general disqualification under which women had been debarred from membership of the House of Lords. On 23 July 1958 the first 14 life peers were appointed under this Act, 4 of them being women. By 1970 their numbers had been increased to 181, including 23 women. During the years 1965 to 1970 no new hereditary peerages were created.

All life peers hold the rank of baron, but their titles do not descend to their heirs. They are entitled to a writ of summons for life, but they hold office subject to good behaviour and are removable on an address of both Houses of Parliament.

See also LORDS OF APPEAL.

LIMITATION OF DEBATE

See CLOSURE; GUILLOTINE; SUPPLY DAYS.

LITTLE PARLIAMENT

See BAREBONES PARLIAMENT.

LOBBY CORRESPONDENT

Lobby (or political) correspondents are a special class of parliamentary journalists who provide the background to happenings in Parliament for their papers. They are allowed direct contact with members in the Members' Lobby, and are thus enabled to present a clear picture of political trends and the political scene generally with some authority. There are only about fifty who are allowed the exclusive right of entry to the Lobby in the House of Commons, but some of their names are very well known to the public and they wield a great deal of influence in the political arena.

Lobby correspondents derive their privilege from a precedent set in 1884 when one gentleman of the Press was given official permission 'to enter and remain in the Members' Lobby of the House of Commons'. To-day they are a highly respected group of journalists united by an *esprit de corps* and a code of honour which ensures that their sources of information are never revealed. While they often work individually, they also meet together under their own Chairman and invite ministers and other members to address them and submit to their questioning as a body.

Lord Hill of Luton who, having been responsible for the co-ordination of official information services from 1957 to 1961, is a particularly authoritative commentator on the Parliamentary Lobby, points out that ' "non-attributability" lies at the heart of the whole system, and the Lobby would deal brusquely with any member who ignored it'. (*Both Sides of the Hill*, 1964.)

(Further reading: Tunstall, *The Westminster lobby correspondents*, 1970.)

LOBBYING

The practice of frequenting the lobby of a legislature for the purpose of influencing members' votes on some proposed legislation.

See also PRESSURE GROUPS.

LOCAL ACTS

See PRIVATE ACTS.

LOCAL BILLS

See PRIVATE BILLS.

LOCAL GOVERNMENT AND PLANNING, MINISTER OF

The Minister of Town and Country Planning became the Minister of Local Government and Planning early in 1951, but his title was again changed, when the Conservative Government came in at the end of the year, to Minister of Housing and Local Government (q.v.).

LOCAL GOVERNMENT AND REGIONAL PLANNING, SECRETARY OF STATE FOR

Temporarily established in October 1969, this Minister assumed overall control of the Ministry of Housing and Local Government and the Ministry of Transport although both departments retained their own separate Ministers of non-Cabinet status. The Secretary of State's responsibilities covered all those vested in the two departments including the Regional Economic Board and Councils, and matters concerned with environmental pollution. The first holder of this office, Mr. Anthony Crosland, was also given personal charge of the negotiations on local government reform arising out of the proposals of the Redcliffe–Maud Commission.

[437]

LOCUS STANDI

The right of a petitioner to be heard in opposition to a Private Bill, Hybrid Bill, Provisional Order Bill or Special Procedure Order (qq.v.). This is not a right enjoyed by the petitioner automatically. It depends on whether his personal property or interests stand to be adversely affected by the passage into law of the measure concerned, and if its promoters can succeed in establishing that he will not be directly affected in such a manner as would entitle him to be heard on his petition, he is said to have no *locus standi*. Questions of *locus standi* in relation to Bills are determined in the House of Commons by the Court of Referees and in the House of Lords by the committee dealing with the Bill. They are determined by the Lord Chairman and the Chairman of Ways and Means in relation to Special Procedure Orders.

LONGEST PARLIAMENTS

The longest parliaments in England have been the Parliament of 1572–83 (*see* ELIZABETH I AND PARLIAMENT); the Long Parliament (q.v.), 1640–53; the Cavalier Parliament (q.v.), 1661–79; and the two World War Parliaments, which lasted from 1911–18 and 1935–45 respectively.

LONG PARLIAMENT

The fifth and last Parliament to be summoned by Charles I. It met on 3 November 1640, and in 1642 it took up arms against the King. It is possibly the most historic assembly ever to have sat at Westminster, and it was said of it that many thought it would never have a beginning, and afterwards that it would never have an end. During its long life, which extended over twenty years, it underwent many changes. In 1648 it was purged of those members who were too favourable to the King; in 1649 it abolished both the monarchy and the House of Lords; it was expelled by Cromwell in 1653; recalled and expelled again in 1659; restored for the last time, with its excluded members later recalled, at the end of that year; and finally dissolved on 16 March 1660. It commenced its long existence as a formidable and enthusiastic assembly, bent upon drastic reform, the champion of the liberties of the people against the tyranny of the King. It sank eventually into corruption, ignominy, and discredit, having subverted the Constitution it had set out to uphold, and having lost many of its greatest members through death or exclusion.

When the Long Parliament was first summoned the House of Lords consisted of 150 peers and the House of Commons of 504 members, more than half of whom had sat in the previous Short Parliament (q.v.), which had been summoned earlier in the same year. Cromwell, Pym, Hampden, Holles, Haselrig, Strode, Fiennes, Selden, Waller, Hyde,

St. John, Whitelocke, and the two Vanes were amongst the original members. William Lenthall (q.v.) was elected Speaker. The Commons immediately set about the removal of their grievances and introduced various legislation, including a Triennial Bill and measures to check the royal power of dissolution, to abolish the Star Chamber and other special courts with arbitrary jurisdiction, and to prohibit taxation without the consent of Parliament. Simultaneously they impeached Strafford, the minister who had been entrusted by the King with the administration of Ireland, and Pym conducted the indictment at the Bar of the House of Lords. Later they proceeded against Strafford by way of a Bill of Attainder. The King found himself in circumstances which compelled him to accept the measures insisted on by the Commons, including Strafford's Attainder Bill, and he reluctantly signed his minister's death-warrant. The impeachment of Archbishop Laud shortly followed that of Strafford, but he was not proceeded against until 1644. Writing of the Long Parliament, Hallam stated that 'it usurped from the first, legislative, executive, and judicial functions'.

The party system can trace its origin to the stormy sessions of the Long Parliament, and the issue which first split the Members of the House of Commons into factions was the vital one of church reform. Measures such as the 'Root and Branch' Bill, which proposed the abolition of episcopacy, were furiously debated, and led to the formation of a constitutional Royalist party in opposition to the Puritans. Once parties had arisen over religious issues, political differences were not slow in developing. The vote on the Grand Remonstrance (q.v.) revealed a large minority of the Commons in favour of the King, but he alienated many of his supporters by his ill-advised and unconstitutional attempt to arrest five of the leading opposition members on charges of treason shortly afterwards. The Civil War was not long in following this incident and every member was forced to choose his side.

After the parliamentary victory, dissension arose between the Presbyterians, who were in the majority in the House of Commons, and the army leaders who dominated the faction known as the Independents. Their differences were both religious and political. In the first place, the Presbyterians sought to impose their system of religion upon the whole country, whilst the Independents favoured toleration for Dissenters; secondly, the Independents were the republican party, whilst the Presbyterians favoured an agreement with the King. The army eventually won the upper hand, and the Presbyterians were excluded from the House of Commons as a result of Pride's Purge (q.v.). The depleted Commons then proceeded to bring the King to trial.

After the King's execution, the remnant of the House of Commons wielded complete sovereignty and they proceeded to abolish the

P

monarchy and the House of Lords in February 1649. A Council of State was elected to govern, but Parliament had by no means solved all its difficulties. The country was torn with internal dissension and had become a prey to faction. Many who had deplored the abuses of Charles I's personal government had never become anti-Royalist in principle and they found themselves bitterly opposed to the new system; others with episcopalian sympathies withheld their support on religious grounds. Parliament was thus unpopular with a large section of the community, and the general feeling throughout the country was that these members who had sat for so long should depart and make way for new blood. Parliament, for its part, feared for the entire Puritan cause if the composition of a new Parliament were to be left to the free decision of the country, and therefore decided to prolong its own life. A scheme was introduced permitting sitting members to retain their seats and empowering them to exclude any new members elected to fill vacant seats if they considered them unfit. The scheme met with emphatic opposition from Cromwell and the army who maintained that Parliament was merely attempting to perpetuate its own power. It had by this time degenerated into a corrupt and contemptible assembly, and its scandalous activities at length drove Cromwell, under pressure from the army, to take a drastic decision. On 20 April 1653, his resolve hastened by Parliament's defiance of his objections to its scheme, he proceeded with a body of soldiers to the House of Commons, where, in an impassioned speech, he bitterly reproached the members both collectively and individually for their deeds and for the lives they led, and finally dismissed them, calling in his soldiers to effect the expulsion.

But history had not heard the last of the Long Parliament. Six years later, on 23 April 1659, its remnant, which became known as the Rump Parliament (q.v.), was recalled by the army leaders. Richard Cromwell, who succeeded his father as Protector, had dissolved his one and only Parliament under pressure from the army, and at General Lambert's instigation it was decided to restore the Long Parliament, for it was held that it had never been legally dissolved. Headed by Speaker Lenthall, 42 members returned to Westminster where they were subsequently joined by others. Richard Cromwell resigned his protectorship, and the restored Parliament reiterated its intention to maintain a republican form of government but without a single person at its head. It was resolved that there should be no House of Lords and a new Council of State was appointed. But the old quarrel between Parliament and the army quickly revived. The army demanded that it should be independent of parliamentary control, but Parliament insisted that supreme military authority should be vested in itself. The latter passed a number of measures aimed at strengthening its position and reducing the power of the army, whereupon the army decided, not for the first time, to assert its authority by force. On 13 October the Long Parliament was forcibly expelled for the second time in its history. On 26 December, the army's administration having fallen into complete chaos, it was restored for the last time. It was at this time that General Monk came into prominence upon the parliamentary scene. He realized the necessity for drastic changes if the nation's welfare was to be preserved, and supported by the citizens of London he demanded that the present Parliament should dissolve itself and that new and long overdue elections should be held for a new one. Monk was enthusiastically acclaimed for his action; yet decayed and moribund though it was, the pathetic shadow of the once great Long Parliament, the restored Rump endeavoured to cling to its precarious power. Realizing the full implication of Monk's demand, it played for time. But Monk was a man of action, and a week or so later, the writs for fresh elections not having been issued within the period he had stipulated, he circumvented the Parliament by inviting those members who had been excluded since Pride's Purge to return and take their seats. They soon found themselves in the majority, most of the republicans having abandoned the House. The way was now clear for the restoration of the monarchy, and many of the restored members spoke openly in favour thereof. A Bill was passed providing for dissolution and on 16 March 1660 the Long Parliament finally ceased to exist.

The Long Parliament spanned twenty momentous years of British history. There were no regrets at its passing although it had achieved great reforms during its early years; but for all its grave shortcomings and misdeeds the Long Parliament established beyond question, albeit unconsciously, the imperishable nature of England's ancient Constitution and the impossibility of conducting the nation's government upon any other basis.

See also CHARLES I AND PARLIAMENT; CHARLES II AND PARLIAMENT; COMMONWEALTH, 1658–1660; CROMWELL AND PARLIAMENT.

LONG PARLIAMENT OF THE RESTORATION
See CAVALIER PARLIAMENT.

LORD ADVOCATE
See LAW OFFICERS OF THE CROWN.

LORD CHAIRMAN OF COMMITTEES
See CHAIRMAN OF COMMITTEES, HOUSE OF LORDS.

LORD CHANCELLOR
The office of Lord High Chancellor of Great Britain and Keeper of the Great Seal is the most historic and dignified under the Crown.

In the course of its nine centuries of existence it has attracted to itself a mass of tradition which is closely interwoven with the constitutional development of the country. The Lord Chancellor, or the Lord Keeper, as he was earlier called, has always been a splendid figure, wielding on occasions a power little inferior to that of the Crown itself. He is the highest civil subject in the land, and if he is a peer takes precedence, after the Royal Family, of all Her Majesty's subjects excepting the Archbishop of Canterbury. To slay him is accounted high treason. Though the office is now held by a lawyer of great distinction, the Lord Chancellor was originally an ecclesiastic, of which Thomas à Becket and Cardinal Wolsey were famous examples. The last prelate to fill the office was John Williams, Archbishop of York from 1621 to 1625, although there had been lay Chancellors before this date, notably Sir Thomas More. With the coming of the Reformation the law finally took the place of the Church in supplying Lord Chancellors.

The Lord Chancellor is appointed by the party in power and shares in the responsibilities of the Government of the day as a member of the Cabinet. He is not necessarily a peer, although ennoblement invariably follows his appointment, but he must not be a Roman Catholic, as he is historically the Keeper of the King's conscience and must therefore belong to the established Church. As well as presiding over the debates of the House of Lords, the Lord Chancellor is President of the highest Court of Appeal in the land and of the Chancery Division of the High Court of Justice and a Privy Councillor. As head of the justiciary he appoints all Justices of the Peace, recommends to the Sovereign the judges for the Court of Appeal, and appoints certain church livings in the gift of the Crown. As Speaker of the House of Lords the Chancellor has an unimportant part to play, his duties being confined to formal proceedings and putting the question at the termination of a debate, whether the 'contents' or the 'not-contents' have it. He does not decide points of order, the House taking upon itself that duty, but unlike the Speaker of the House of Commons he has the privilege of intervening in a debate. When he exercises this right he steps aside from the Woolsack (q.v.) and thus severs himself temporarily from his office and takes his place in the House as a peer. He is not as Speaker addressed in debate, the peer speaking beginning his address with 'My Lords'. He takes part in divisions and votes first but he has no additional casting vote. The Lord Chancellor is the formal medium of communication between the Queen and Parliament, and in her absence from the Opening of Parliament it is his duty to read the Speech from the Throne, and all other messages from the Sovereign to Parliament. If Parliament is being opened by commission he informs the House of Lords, and the Commons after they have been summoned, and gives the Queen's approval to the election of their Speaker. It is also his duty to report the Royal Assent (q.v.) to Bills.

The salary of the Lord Chancellor as Speaker of the House of Lords is £4,000, and he receives £10,500 as President of the Supreme Court and of the Chancery Division.

See also GREAT SEAL; LORD KEEPER OF THE GREAT SEAL.

LORD GREAT CHAMBERLAIN

One of the Great Officers of State, this is an hereditary office, and the co-heirs in whom it is at present invested are the Marquess of Cholmondeley, the Earl of Ancaster and the descendants of the late Charles Robert, Marquess of Lincolnshire. The Lord Great Chamberlain was the nominal chief authority in the Palace of Westminster (the Houses of Parliament) which is still a royal palace but, on 23 March 1965, the Prime Minister announced in the House that from the following 26 April the Speakers of the House of Commons and House of Lords would assume control over their respective parts of the Palace. The control of Westminster Hall and the Crypt Chapel would be vested jointly in the two Speakers and the Lord Great Chamberlain. The latter, in view of his responsibilities in connexion with the Opening of Parliament (q.v.), has not relinquished control over the Royal Gallery and the Queen's Robing Room, which play an important part in the ceremony.

The Lord Great Chamberlain also has duties at the introduction of new peers into the House of Lords and at the homage of bishops after their consecration. His office should not be confused with that of the Lord Chamberlain, who is appointed by the Government as chief officer of the Royal Household and whose best-known function was the licensing of plays for public performance.

LORD HIGH STEWARD

When members of the House of Lords still retained the right to be tried by their peers for treason or felony (abolished by the Criminal Justice Act of 1948) a Lord High Steward was appointed to regulate the proceedings of a Lord High Steward's Court. He acted as a chairman rather than as a judge, since the peers were the judges and the Lord High Steward had a vote with the rest as a peer. However, if the trial took place during a recess, he was the sole judge of matters of law. If Parliament was sitting, the trial was properly before the High Court of Parliament.

LORD KEEPER OF THE GREAT SEAL

In early times the Lord Chancellor (q.v.) was usually entrusted with the personal custody of the Great Seal (q.v.) and was called the Lord Keeper. Later on between the death of one Chancellor and the appointment of another the Great Seal, instead of remaining with the Sovereign, was entrusted to a temporary Keeper. This lead to the practice of

[443]

occasionally appointing a person to hold the Great Seal with the title of 'Keeper', who held it permanently in his own right and discharged all the duties belonging to it. Queen Elizabeth I appointed Sir Nicholas Bacon to this office, but objections were made to the legality of some of his acts, and to obviate these a statute was passed declaring that 'the Lord Keeper of the Great Seal shall have the same place, pre-eminence and jurisdiction as the Lord Chancellor of England'. Since then, of course, there has never been a Chancellor and a Keeper concurrently. During the 17th and 18th centuries there were various instances of the Great Seal being delivered to a 'Lord Keeper' who was sometimes raised to the dignity of 'Lord Chancellor', but since the beginning of the reign of George III the title of 'Lord Chancellor' has always been conferred in the first instance with the Great Seal. The last Lord Keeper was Sir Robert Henley, afterwards Lord Northington, who died in 1772.

LORD PRESIDENT OF THE COUNCIL

One of the Great Officers of State, the Lord President is in charge of the Privy Council office, for whose work he is responsible, and at the infrequent formal meetings of the Council he presents the business to the Queen and her Councillors. However, his departmental duties are slight, and he is usually entrusted by the Prime Minister, like the other holders of non-departmental offices, with some special task. For example, after the Ministry of Information was abolished the Lord President was appointed to co-ordinate the information services and was Chairman of a Cabinet Committee on the subject, while Lord Woolton, when he was Lord President, was entrusted with co-ordinating the policy of the Ministries of Agriculture and Food. The Lord President is frequently a member of the House of Lords, and before the last war his political influence was not very great. He first emerged as a powerful senior Minister in the Churchill War Government of 1940–5.

Under the Labour Government which took office in 1945 the Lord President of the Council became responsible for the general oversight of scientific research and civil scientific policy, and among the bodies for which he was answerable to Parliament were the Department of Scientific and Industrial Research, the Medical Research Council, the Agricultural Research Council, the Nature Conservancy and the Atomic Energy Authority. In 1959 a Minister for Science was designated, an office which was coupled in the first instance with that of Lord Privy Seal and subsequently (in 1960) with that of Lord President of the Council, Mr. Quintin Hogg (then Lord Hailsham) being the Minister to hold these appointments jointly. In 1963 the office of Secretary of State for Education and Science was established, and

Mr. Hogg was appointed to it while remaining Lord President of the Council.

When the Labour Party returned to office in October 1964 the functions of Lord President of the Council and Secretary of State for Education and Science were separated under a general reorganization of ministerial responsibilities. The latter minister became responsible for scientific research and civil scientific policy and became answerable for the work of such bodies as the Medical Research Council, Agricultural Research Council and Science Research Council. The Nature Conservancy became the responsibility of the Minister of Lands and Natural Resources (whose functions were afterwards absorbed by the Minister of Housing and Local Government) and the Department of Scientific and Industrial Research and the Atomic Energy Authority were placed under the jurisdiction of the newly created office of Minister of Technology (q.v.).

The Lord President of the Council was thus released for other Cabinet duties, and since Mr. Harold Wilson formed his government in October 1964 the office has been coupled with that of Leader of the House (q.v.).

The salary of the Lord President of the Council is £8,500 per annum, and when he sits in the House of Commons he is entitled to a further £1,250. A chronological list of the holders of this office appears as Appendix 23.

LORD PRIVY SEAL

The early Kings of England used their private seal when the Great Seal (q.v.) was not available, or was considered too cumbrous for everyday use, and in the reign of King John it was being affixed to letters patent. There is no doubt that in the 13th century the private seal was regarded as the particular instrument of the Royal Prerogative. Edward I used it to seal acts (and even charters) which bore no relation to the ordinary work of the Household, in spite of complaints from barons and commons. From 1275 there was a Keeper of the Privy Seal who became in 1311 a Minister of State on the same footing as the Chancellor and the Treasurer, though of somewhat lower dignity. In the 15th century the office of Keeper of the Privy Seal became detached from the Household, and the use of the Privy Seal became specially connected with financial business as a warrant for payment from the Exchequer, and for the affixing of the Great Seal to letters patent.

The use of the Privy Seal was abolished by a statute of 1884, but long before this the office of Lord Privy Seal had ceased to involve any personal action by its holder. However, the Lord Privy Seal, who may be a member of either House, can be a very useful auxiliary minister, able to give his attention to any matter of urgency which may arise.

In 1932 Anthony Eden was appointed to the office and deputed to deal with League of Nations business, while Lord Waverley (then Sir John Anderson) was Lord Privy Seal in 1938–9 with the job of instituting more effective air-raid precautions. When the Labour Government was in office in 1951 the Lord Privy Seal was responsible for co-ordinating the policy of the Home Information Services, and was made answerable to Parliament on questions of major broadcasting policy. In 1959 Lord Hailsham was appointed to the office with duties synonymous to those of a Minister for Science, and later in the same year this office was officially created, Lord Hailsham being designated Lord Privy Seal and Minister for Science. (*See also* LORD PRESIDENT OF THE COUNCIL.) Mr. Edward Heath succeeded Lord Hailsham as Lord Privy Seal in 1960 and was given the special function of acting as the Government's spokesman in the House of Commons on foreign affairs, a peer (Lord Home) having been appointed Foreign Secretary (q.v.).

The Lord Privy Seal is appointed by letters patent and the delivery of the Privy Seal, and his salary when a member of the Cabinet is £8,500. When he sits in the House of Commons he is entitled to a further £1,250. A chronological list of the holders of this office appears as Appendix 24.

LORDS AMENDMENTS, CONSIDERATION OF
See BILL, PASSAGE OF.

LORDS COMMISSIONERS
Before the opening of a new Parliament the Queen issues, by the advice of the Privy Council, a Commission conferring on the Lord Chancellor and other Lords of the Privy Council, or any three or more of them, full powers in her name (1) 'to begin and hold' the Parliament which she has ordered to be holden, (2) to 'open and declare the causes of holding the same', (3) to 'proceed upon' the arduous and urgent affairs mentioned in the writ, and (4) 'if necessary to continue, adjourn and prorogue the said Parliament'. A week before the Speech from the Throne, the Lord Chancellor and usually 4 Lords Commissioners summon the Members of the House of Commons and their Clerk and Serjeant-at-Arms to the House of Lords, where the Lord Chancellor informs them that it is Her Majesty's pleasure that they 'retire to the place where you are to sit, and there proceed to the choice of some proper person to be your speaker'. The next day the Lords Commissioners sit again to receive the new Speaker, who announces his election and is assured by the Lord Chancellor that the Queen approves him as Speaker. Prior to the passage of the Royal Assent Act in May 1967 it was the custom for some hundred years for the Sovereign to appoint Lords Commissioners as for the Opening of Parliament to

give the Royal Assent (q.v.) to Bills, except that usually only 3 Commissioners sat instead of 5. Lady Horsburgh was the first woman to act as a Commissioner in May 1961. The Royal Assent Act, while making other arrangements for the signification of the Royal Assent to Bills, continues to permit the signification of the Royal Assent in the historic manner, that is by the Queen in person or by Royal Commission. However, the Royal Assent has not been signified by the Sovereign in person since 1854, and it is anticipated that the practice of pronouncing the Royal Assent by Royal Commission will be observed in future only on the last day of a session.

LORDS, HOUSE OF

See HOUSE OF LORDS.

LORDS OF APPEAL

The Law Lords, as they are often called, are persons with great legal knowledge and experience who sit in the highest Court in the United Kingdom—the House of Lords. They consist of the Lord Chancellor, ex-Lord Chancellors, peers who are, or who have been, members of the Judicial Committee of the Privy Council or judges of the superior Courts, and the Lords of Appeal in Ordinary (including those retired). These latter are appointed by the Crown under the Appellate Jurisdiction Act, 1876, and they become life peers (q.v.), having the same rights and privileges as hereditary peers. Parliamentary rules of order are still observed when the House of Lords is sitting in its judicial capacity, and the Lords of Appeal address their speech or opinion to the other Lords and not to the litigants or their counsel. Their function is not to give a judgment, but to clarify the law and to give a considered opinion regarding an appeal. The speeches of the Law Lords may contain varying opinions and conclusions, and as the proceedings are taking place in Parliament the usual method of determining the will of the House is employed—the Lord on the Woolsack 'putting the question' in the ancient form. The first 4 Lords of Appeal in Ordinary were appointed in 1876. Their number was increased to 6 in 1913, to 7 in 1929, and to 9 in 1947. In terms of their creation as life peers retired Lords of Appeal in Ordinary are entitled to continue to sit and vote in the upper House. When the House of Lords sits in its capacity as a Court of Appeal only the active judicial peers normally take part in the proceedings. In theory, however, the entire House is deemed to be present, and any other peers are at liberty to attend should they so desire. Under the Appellate Jurisdiction Act provision is made for the Lords of Appeal to hear and determine appeals notwithstanding a prorogation or dissolution of Parliament.

LORDS OF APPEAL IN ORDINARY

Those Lords of Appeal (q.v.) who are appointed under the Appellate Jurisdiction Act, 1876, and who are normally life peers (q.v.).

LORDS OF THE ARTICLES

See SCOTTISH PARLIAMENT.

LORDS OF THE TREASURY

The Commissioners who since 1714 have exercised the functions of the office of Treasurer. They consist of the First Lord of the Treasury (q.v.), who nowadays is invariably the Prime Minister (q.v.), the Chancellor of the Exchequer (q.v.), and 5 junior lords who are Government Whips (q.v.) in the House of Commons.

See also TREASURY.

LORDS SPIRITUAL

It is sometimes not realized that the 2 archbishops and the 24 bishops of the Church of England who sit in the House of Lords are as much Members of Parliament as those members elected to sit in the House of Commons. There are now many more Temporal Lords in Parliament than Spiritual, but before the suppression of the monasteries by Henry VIII in 1539, when the abbots and priors sat with the bishops, the Lords Spiritual actually exceeded the Lords Temporal in number. This was in spite of the fact that during the 14th century an increasing number obtained exemption from attendance—in 1295 Edward I sent writs of summons to 70 abbots and priors, but after Edward II's reign the number fell to 27, which was less than one-tenth of the total number of abbots in the country. In the early period of parliamentary history these church dignitaries were supposed to sit, like the temporal lords, by virtue of tenure, but many were summoned from time to time who had not this qualification. This practice helped to provide the King with the ablest counsellors, for the ecclesiastics were the sole repositories of learning, and from their ranks the greatest officers of state were often selected. They were the possessors of enormous wealth, at least part of which was spent in the public service. In days when the proudest baron saw no cause for shame in the confession of his inability to read and write, the assistance of clerics in Council was essential. To all this must be added the fact that the bishops, abbots, and priors exercised an unbounded influence over the lower orders of society. It is not surprising, therefore, that their services were in great demand, and that, prior to the Reformation, they should have out-numbered the lay peers in the House of Lords. Even when the abbots and priors had been removed, the bishops alone formed about one-third of the House. But while the temporal lords have been multiplied since that period about fourteen-fold, the English archbishops and bishops sitting in Parliament have only been increased from 21 to 26—to whom were added, for a time, the 4 Irish bishops. The ecclesiastical element in our legislature has thus become relatively inconsiderable and subordinate. Instead of being a third of the House of Lords it now forms a thirty-third part of it. But however small their numbers, the presence of the bishops in Parliament has often provoked opposition. Repudiated by every sect of Dissenters and ejected from Parliament by the Puritans, they have had to contend against many popular opinions and prejudices. In 1834, the Commons refused leave to bring in a Bill 'for relieving the bishops of their legislative and judicial duties in the House of Peers', by a majority of two to one, and in 1826 they refused to affirm by an even greater majority 'that the attendance of the bishops in Parliament is prejudicial to the cause of religion'. After the following year, when they denied with equal emphasis the proposition that the sitting of the bishops in Parliament 'tends to alienate the affections of the people from the Church', there have been no adverse motions in Parliament in relation to the legislative functions of the bishops. In 1847, on the creation of the bishopric of Manchester, it was enacted that the number of bishops sitting in Parliament should not be increased in consequence, and a similar provision has been made in the case of bishoprics which have been created subsequently.

Although the importance of the bishops in the political arena has now become negligible, their influence was strong until comparatively recently. Few bishops can now attend debates regularly and keep up with their diocesan duties, but in 1733 Walpole's Whig Government was twice saved from defeat by the almost solid vote of the bishops. A hundred years later the bishops were supporting the Conservatives, principally because the Nonconformists, considered a threat to the established Church, were Liberals. The bishops are now entirely free from party allegiance, and their appointments are not made with any political considerations. The last bishop to hold ministerial office was the Bishop of Bristol, who was Lord Privy Seal in 1711. The clergy of the Church of England are disqualified from membership of the House of Commons, so that an important function of the bishops in the House of Lords is to advise on and explain Church Assembly Measures (q.v.) which have to receive the assent of Parliament.

To-day the Spiritual Lords in Parliament consist of the 2 Archbishops of Canterbury and York, the Bishops of London, Durham, and Winchester, and the 21 next in seniority irrespective of their sees.

The Bishop of Sodor and Man is not eligible for a seat in the House of Lords as he has his own legislative position in the House of Keys of the Isle of Man.

[449]

LORDS TEMPORAL

The secular members of the House of Lords as opposed to the bishops or Lords Spiritual (q.v.). During the reigns of Richard II and Henry IV some changes were introduced in the mode of describing the assent of the Lords to an Act of Parliament. In earlier reigns the assent was usually said to be that of the prelates, dukes, earls, barons, and other magnates. In the 3rd year of Richard II they were described collectively as 'the Lords', in the 4th year as the 'Prelates and Lords', and in the 9th year the old form reappears. In the 13th year a new form was used, 'the Prelates and Lords Temporal', but in the 21st year and in the 1st and 2nd years of Henry IV the dukes, earls, etc., are again specified. In the latter year the words the 'Lords Spiritual and Temporal' are used also as being synonymous. In the 4th year of the reign of Henry IV the 'Lords Spiritual and Temporal' are mentioned for the first time in the commencing words of a statute, and although there are some exceptions, this was ever afterwards the usual form.

LOWER CHAMBER

See BICAMERAL LEGISLATURE.

M

MACE

The Mace figures in the ceremonial of both Houses of Parliament. It is the symbol of the royal authority and, in consequence, of the authority of Parliament. In the House of Commons it further symbolizes the authority of the Speaker, for, as Lord Campion has stated, 'the authority of the Speaker and of the House are indivisible'. The Mace is also the warrant for the Serjeant-at-Arms (q.v.) to execute his authority when acting under the direction of the Speaker, as, for instance, when he is called upon to effect an arrest. Many precedents exist for this practice, and the following extract from the Journal of the House of Commons for 27 February 1575 may be cited as an example:

After sundry Reasons, Arguments, and Disputations, it is Resolved, That Edward Smalleye, Servant unto Arthure Halle Esquire, shall be brought hither Tomorrow, by the Serjeant; and so set at Liberty, by Warrant of the Mace; and not by Writ.

A certain mystical quality surrounds the Mace, due no doubt to the remoteness of its origin and the ancient traditions with which it is associated. Lord Campion has written that 'there is in the halo surrounding the Mace something also of the prerogative'. A correspondence concerning the significance of the Mace, in which Lord Campion participated, and to which those desirous of pursuing this aspect of the matter should refer, took place in *The Times* during February 1954.

The Mace is an essential part of the regalia of Parliament. Without it the House of Commons is not constituted and no proceedings may take place. When the Speaker is in the Chair, that is, when the House is sitting as a House, the Mace lies on the Table of the House, resting in the upper brackets, the orb and cross surmounting it pointing towards the Government of the day. When the Speaker leaves the Chair, that is, when the House sits as a Committee of the Whole House (q.v.), the Mace is removed into the lower brackets beneath the Table. In attending and leaving the Chamber the Speaker is preceded by the Mace, which is borne by the Serjeant-at-Arms on the right shoulder. To sum this up in the words of Hatsell, 'When the Mace lies upon the Table the House is a House; when under, it is a Committee; when out

[451]

of the House, no business can be done; when from the Table and upon the Serjeant's shoulder, the Speaker alone manages.'

A curious incident, in the course of which these words were quoted, took place in the House of Commons on 6 December 1961 when, during a debate in committee which had generated considerable heat, the Chairman of Ways and Means was forced to assume the Chair as Deputy Speaker and suspend the sitting for half an hour. In the confusion the position of the Mace was overlooked, and it remained in the lower brackets when the Chairman took the Chair as Deputy Speaker. Points of order were raised when the sitting was resumed and, doubts having arisen as to the validity of the suspension, the House adjourned pending a ruling from the Speaker. On the following day the Speaker ruled that while an act of the House, such as a vote, would probably be invalidated if the Mace were in the wrong position, an act of the Chair in isolation, such as the suspension of a sitting for reasons of grave disorder, would not be so invalidated. This ruling is of particular interest since it does not seem to be entirely consistent with the conception of the Mace as the symbol of the Speaker's authority.

The importance with which the Mace is regarded can be well illus-trated from several historical incidents. On an occasion in 1626, for instance, the House was in a state of uproar and the Serjeant-at-Arms attempted to close the sitting by removing the Mace. A member seized it from him, replaced it on the Table, and locked the door of the House. On another occasion King Charles I attempted to suspend the pro-ceedings of Parliament by sending for the Mace. It need hardly be added that the Commons refused to relinquish it. In the middle of the last century it once happened that the House was forced to postpone its sitting because the official who held the key of the Mace cupboard was missing. On 17 July 1930 a Member named Beckett attempted to carry away the Mace as a protest against the naming of another Member by the Speaker. Needless to say he was himself named for 'grossly dis-orderly conduct'. Various other occasions are recorded of members wrestling with each other for possession of the Mace, some holding it down on the Table to prevent others from removing it. But perhaps the most famous occasion on which the indispensable nature of the Mace was demonstrated was on 20 April 1653, when Cromwell dismissed the Long Parliament (q.v.). Having called in his soldiers to clear the House and having had the Speaker forcibly ejected from the Chair, he ordered one of his men to remove the Mace, which he contemptuously referred to as 'this bauble'. This incident had the opposite effect to that which Cromwell intended, for instead of reducing the Mace to an object of contemptible insignificance it established even more firmly the tradition that the House could not sit without it.

The Mace is an indispensable feature of a number of parliamentary ceremonies, notably the election of a new Speaker. The election cannot take place unless the Mace is present, but in the absence of a Speaker until a new one is elected or the former re-elected, it reposes in the brackets below the Table whilst the Clerk of the House officiates. As soon as a Speaker has been elected and has taken the Chair, the Serjeant-at-Arms places the Mace in the brackets upon the Table. After his election the Speaker has still to seek the royal approval of his appointment, and during the procession to the House of Lords the Serjeant-at-Arms carries the Mace with the head resting in the crook of his left arm. On the return journey to the Commons, the royal approval having been signified, the Mace is borne shoulder-high. (*See also* SPEAKER, sub-heading *Election of Speaker*.) On this occasion the Mace is left at the door of the House of Lords in the charge of an attendant. Only on certain rare occasions may the Speaker enter the House of Lords preceded by the Mace, namely, in the event of an impeachment and in seeking the arraignment of and, if convicted, the judgment against the person impeached. This precedent was established by Speaker Richard Onslow on 23 March 1709, as the following extract from the Commons Journal illustrates:

When Mr. Speaker came to the Door of the House of Lords, to demand Judgment against Doctor Henry Sacheverell, entering in with the Mace, the Deputy Gentleman Usher of the Black Rod put his Rod across the Door, to stop Mr. Speaker, and his Mace, from going in; upon which Mr. Speaker bid him acquaint the Lords, that he insisted upon it as his Right, to go to the Bar with the Mace; And the Door being shut, after some short time the Black Rod returned, and opened the Door; and Mr. Speaker went, with the Mace on his right Hand, towards the Bar; where the Black Rod attempting to interpose between Mr. Speaker and the Serjeant with the Mace, Mr. Speaker said, 'My Lords, If you do not immediately order your Black Rod to go away, I will immediately return to the House of Commons.' Upon which, the Black Rod was directed by the Lords to go from thence; which he accordingly did; and Mr. Speaker, with the Mace, went up to the Bar.

Whenever the Speaker and other Members of the House of Commons proceed anywhere as a House, as for instance when they adjourn to the Bar of the House of Lords to hear the Royal Assent (q.v.) signified to Bills, they are preceded by the Serjeant-at-Arms bearing the Mace. If the Sovereign is present in person upon any formal occasion outside the House of Lords, as when King George VI attended Westminster Hall for the opening of the new Commons Chamber in 1950, the Mace is covered with a cloth, the symbol being unnecessary in the presence of the actual authority. If both Houses attend a state function together the House of Commons Mace is covered in the presence of the House of Lords Mace, signifying that the royal authority in Parliament is transmitted through the medium of the upper House. In the presence of the Sovereign herself both Maces would be covered. When a person or persons are brought to the Bar of the House of Commons as offenders, as witnesses, or as petitioners, they are attended at the Bar by the Serjeant-at-Arms with the Mace.

The present House of Commons Mace dates from 1660, and the following description of it is taken from Sir Bryan Fell's *Houses of Parliament* (1944):

> The Mace is silver-gilt and measures 4 ft. 10½ in. in length. The shaft consists of one short and two long sections, which are chased throughout with longitudinal branches from which spring roses and thistle flowers. The head is divided into four panels containing respectively a crowned rose, a thistle, a harp, and a fleur-de-lis. The whole is surmounted by a Royal Crown with the orb and cross. On the cap are the Royal Arms with the garter supported by crowned lion and unicorn, with the motto *Dieu et mon droit* and the initials C. R. The Mace is not hall-marked and bears no inscription, date or maker's mark.

The Mace used by the House of Commons prior to 1649 was destroyed or otherwise disposed of by Cromwell with the rest of the regalia of monarchy. In the same year a new Mace, shorn of the orb and cross and all other regal ornamentation, was made for the House by one, Thomas Maundy. This was the 'bauble' which Cromwell ordered to be removed four years later. On the restoration of the monarchy in 1660 the House of Commons ordered that another Mace should be made with the symbols of monarchy restored. Most authorities agree, however, that no new Mace was manufactured, but that the head of the existing Mace was replaced or remodelled to incorporate the Royal Crown and badges and the initials 'C.R.', and the orb and cross restored. If this is so, the present House of Commons Mace is that very same 'bauble' of Cromwell's suitably adapted at the Restoration. Others assert that the House is using a Mace which was entirely new in 1660, and a number of claims have been made regarding the possession of the Mace which was in use during the Commonwealth.

The House of Lords has two Maces, the earlier dating from the reign of Charles II and the later from the reign of William III. The reason for the two Maces arises from the fact that the Lord Chancellor is also Speaker of the House of Lords and therefore has two distinctly separate spheres of authority. To quote from Sir Bryan Fell's book again, the older Mace 'is of silver-gilt, 5 ft. 1 in. in length and bears no hall-mark. Round the head, in four panels, are a rose and portcullis, a fleur-de-lis, a thistle and a harp, severally crowned and with the initials C II R. The other Mace . . . was made by Francis Gathorne, a silversmith of London. It is also of silver-gilt, 5 ft. 1¾ in. in length and is made up of pieces of more than one Mace, the foot-knop being of different work from the rest of the Mace. The head bears the initials G.R. but the G. replaces an earlier W. On the cap of the crown are the Royal Arms.'

Like the Speaker of the House of Commons, the Lord Chancellor is preceded by the Mace when attending and leaving the Chamber and on other ceremonial occasions such as the opening of the Law Courts. When the House is sitting the Mace reposes upon the Woolsack (q.v.) behind the Lord Chancellor, unless the Sovereign is present in person (e.g. when she attends the State Opening of Parliament). Unlike the House of Commons practice the position of the Mace remains unchanged when the House goes into committee. Between a dissolution and the summoning of a new Parliament the Maces of both Houses are kept at St. James's Palace in the Lord Great Chamberlain's office.

The Maces of other Commonwealth Parliaments follow a design which is fundamentally similar to those at Westminster, although they vary in size and decorative detail, the ornamentation usually having a local significance. It has become customary for the House of Commons to present a Mace or some other article of parliamentary furniture to other Commonwealth Parliaments to mark significant occasions, such as the attainment of national independence or the opening of new parliamentary buildings. The House of Representatives of Australia, of Ceylon and of Sierra Leone are among the Commonwealth Legislative Chambers to which a Mace has been presented. No two parliamentary Maces in the Commonwealth are alike, except that the Mace in use by the House of Assembly of South Africa, when that country was a member of the Commonwealth, was a replica of the House of Commons Mace and formerly belonged to the House of Assembly of the old Cape Colony.

Some Maces, such as those of Ceylon and Fiji, are designed in the likeness of a traditional war club. Kenya's Mace is unusual in that it is made of gold and ivory. Wooden Maces are in use in British Honduras and Montserrat, and the Malaysian Mace has sealed within its base small samples of the country's principal products (rubber, rice, tin, etc.). Among the oldest Maces in the Commonwealth are those belonging to the legislatures of the British West Indies (*see* Sir Harry Luke's *Caribbean Circuit*, 1950, Chapter 12: 'The Maces of the British West Indies'). Some legislative Chambers of the Commonwealth do not use a Mace at all. Among these are the Australian Legislative Assemblies of New South Wales and Queensland and, until recently, the Canadian Legislative Assembly of Prince Edward Island. For many years the legend persisted that Prince Edward Island's Mace was removed by an enemy raiding party in the war of 1812 and that tradition forbade its replacement. This theory was belied by recent research and, in January 1966, a Mace was presented to the legislature of Prince Edward Island by the Canadian Federal and Provincial Branches of the Commonwealth Parliamentary Association.

In 1965 the Canadian House of Commons came to the assistance

[455]

of the Bahamas House of Assembly with the loan of a Mace. The Bahamas Mace had been thrown out of a window and broken in two during an acrimonious debate, and had not been repaired in time for the forthcoming meeting of the House on 1 July. When the Canadian Speaker became aware of the dilemma he authorized the loan to the Bahamas of a wooden replica of the Canadian Mace which had been destroyed in the fire of 1916, a museum-piece which was normally displayed in a glass case in his office.

Some interesting variations of procedure concerning the Mace are observed in Jersey. The Mace of Jersey is the Bailiff's Mace and it is never covered even in the presence of the Sovereign. It always stands erect unless the office of Bailiff is vacant in which case it lies recumbent pending the appointment of a successor. It is carried on the left shoulder instead of the right as is usual in other Parliaments. This variation probably has no special significance, but it has been suggested that the tradition derives from the fact that the islanders have long been accustomed to military training, a gun being carried on the left shoulder.

The mace was originally a weapon of offence and was designed to be capable of breaking through the strongest armour. The Serjeants-at-Arms of the King's Bodyguard, established in France by Philip II and in England by Richard I, were equipped with maces for the protection of the King's person, and as the duties of these officers included the apprehension of malefactors and the summoning of persons to the royal presence, the mace came to be regarded as the symbol and warrant of the King's authority. In this manner it developed its ceremonial significance, and early in the 13th century these maces were being ornamented with jewels and precious metals. During this century civic maces began to be carried before Mayors at civic ceremonies, but the bearing of an ornamented mace was considered an infringement of the privileges of the Royal Serjeants-at-Arms, for in 1344 the House of Commons drew the King's attention to the fact by means of a petition stating that 'the King's Serjeants are alone worthy to bear maces enriched with costly insignia'. It was not long, however, before civic authorities were granted the right to carry ornamented maces, and by the 16th century they were in general use. The earliest ceremonial maces retained the aggressive shape and style of the military mace, the head or flanged end being borne uppermost whilst the Royal Arms appeared on a small button, known as a 'knop', at the base of the shaft. Gradually the blades and spikes of the war mace gave way to more ornamental appurtenances, and the end bearing the Royal Arms acquired a greater importance. This resulted in a reversal of the position in which the Mace was carried, the base thus becoming the head, and by the reign of James I mace heads were being richly decorated with heraldic devices.

It is not known when a Mace was first carried before the Speaker of the House of Commons, but the use of a Mace in Parliament probably dates from before the separation of the two Houses. It is probable that when the King first appointed a Serjeant-at-Arms to attend upon the Speaker a Mace went with him as the symbol of the authority delegated to the Speaker.

MAD PARLIAMENT

The Parliament summoned on 11 June 1258 at Oxford was so called by supporters of Henry III, but in reality its proceedings were very businesslike. It appointed a commission of 24 who drew up a plan of reform called the Provisions of Oxford (q.v.).

MAGNA CARTA

Sealed by King John at Runnymede on 15 June 1215, under pressure from the barons, the constitutional importance of Magna Carta lies not in its specific provisions but in its establishment of the principle that the King cannot override the law. As one would expect of the product of a feudal age, the Charter was in fact a statement of feudal law and custom, and it did not hold for those who drafted it the constitutional significance it acquired in later generations. It became the venerated symbol of popular liberty and was many times invoked during the following four centuries. Its provisions have given rise to many divergences of opinion, and principles have been read into it as implicit which are not specifically stated, e.g., parliamentary consent to taxation and trial by jury. The rights of the individual with regard to property and justice are, however, plainly set down.

Magna Carta had no direct bearing on the evolution of Parliament which was to assume its recognizable form later in the century. But it is the supreme example in the early Middle Ages of successful organized resistance to tyrannical rule, thus foreshadowing the constitutional developments of the future, and it was the first great milestone in the struggle for liberty which Parliament was to wage so indefatigably many years later.

The 750th anniversary of the signing of Magna Carta was commemorated by a special service of thanksgiving held in St. Paul's Cathedral on 10 June 1965.

(Further reading: MacKechnie, *Magna Carta*, 1914; Thompson, *Magna Carta*, 1950.)

MAIDEN SPEECH

A member's first speech in the House. By courtesy it is not subject to interruptions, and a member wishing to make his maiden speech is given precedence over other members who rise at the same time. He generally craves the indulgence of the House, and it is the custom for the following speaker to congratulate him. According to Sir Alan

Herbert, the advice given by old hands in the House of Commons is not to be in too great a hurry to make your maiden speech. He himself did not take this friendly warning to heart, and, as he says, 'roared into action' on the second day of the new Parliament and produced what Sir Winston Churchill described as 'a brazen hussy of a speech'. William Cobbett was equally precipitate, and having listened to his first debate he rose and said: 'Mr. Speaker, it appears to me that since I have been sitting here I have heard a great deal of vain and unprofitable conversation.' The self-confidence of a man who became an earl and Lord Chancellor was evident in the person of William Cowper who on the first day of taking his seat in the Parliament of 1695 addressed the House no less than three times—and was applauded on each occasion! Some members have risen to make their maiden speech and have had to sit down again without saying a word. Joseph Addison, the essayist, nearly came into this category, but at least his failure caused a great deal of amusement. He rose, and having said: 'Mr. Speaker, I conceive,' paused, as if frightened by the sound of his own voice. He again commenced: 'I conceive, Mr. Speaker,' when he stopped, until encouraged by cries of 'Hear! Hear!' when he tried once more with 'Sir, I conceive. . . .' Power of further utterance was denied, so he sat down amidst the scarcely suppressed laughter of the House, which was quite irrepressible when a member remarked to the Speaker: 'Sir, the honourable gentleman has just conceived three times and brought forth nothing.' Mr. Gladstone waited several months before he caught the Speaker's eye. His caution did not do him a lot of good, however, as he was reported in the Press to have made a few remarks which were not audible in the Gallery!

MALAWI PARLIAMENT

Malawi, formerly the Nyasaland Protectorate, became a fully independent member of the Commonwealth on 6 July 1964, and a Republic on 6 July 1966. Parliament consists of the President and a National Assembly of 55 members, 50 of whom are elected by universal adult suffrage, the other 5 being nominated to represent interests not otherwise represented. Malawi is a one-party State.

Malawi's Constitution is substantially similar to that under which the country became self-governing on 1 February 1963. The adjustments consequent upon independence included the redesignation of the Legislative Assembly as the National Assembly, its enlargement from 28 to 53 members, the replacement of the Financial Secretary in the Cabinet by an elected Minister of Finance, and the relinquishment by the British Government of responsibility for external affairs and defence. The Constitution embodies a Bill of Rights.

In 1907 the British Central Africa Protectorate was renamed the Nyasaland Protectorate and its first Legislative Council was established.

It met for the first time on 7 May 1908 and consisted of the Governor as President, the Deputy Governor, the Treasurer, the Attorney-General, and 3 appointed unofficial members, all Europeans. The first Legislative Council had a life of five years, but subsequently unofficial members were appointed for a period of three years only until 1955 when the duration of a Council was fixed at four years. In 1932 the Legislative Council was enlarged to comprise 4 official and 4 unofficial members presided over by the Governor. The unofficial members were nominated by the Governor without regard to any specific considerations of representation and were selected as persons most likely to be of assistance to him in the discharge of his duties. By this time, however, two concessions to the representative principle had become apparent. The Chamber of Agriculture and Commerce had been accorded the right to put forward 2 nominees in order of preference for any unofficial vacancy arising on the Council, the final selection resting with the Governor, and it had also become the practice to appoint one unofficial member from one of the Missionary Societies, thus giving a form of indirect representation to the African people. During the Second World War the Legislative Council was increased in size and reconstituted on a representative basis to consist of the Governor, 6 officials, and 6 nominated unofficial members of whom 4 were nominated from a list submitted by the Nyasaland Convention of Associations, one by the Northern Provinces Association, and one selected by the Governor from one of the Missionary Societies to represent African interests.

In 1949 the Constitution was revised to provide for group representation. The Legislative Council was enlarged by the addition of 6 members comprising 2 Africans appointed by the Governor on the recommendation of the African Protectorate Council, 1 Asian selected from a list put forward by the Indian Chamber of Commerce, and 3 officials to preserve the parity between official and unofficial members. In 1953 a further African member was appointed together with an additional official to maintain equality, and at this time the Legislative Council thus consisted of the Governor as President, 10 officials (including the 3 *ex-officio* members of the Executive Council), 6 unofficial European members, 3 unofficial African members, and 1 unofficial Asian member.

In 1953 Nyasaland became a member of the ill-fated Federation of Rhodesia and Nyasaland while still remaining a Protectorate. Radical constitutional reforms were announced for Nyasaland in June 1955. They provided for the direct election of the non-African unofficial members and the country was divided into 6 constituencies for the purpose. Europeans and Asians voted together in each constituency for candidates who could themselves be either European or Asian. The number of African members was increased to 5 and they were elected by the African Provincial Councils. Elections were held in March 1956 after which the Legislative Council consisted of the Governor as President, 4 ex-officio members (Chief Secretary, Attorney-General, Financial Secretary, and Secretary for African Affairs), 7 other officials, 6 elected non-African members, and 5 African members elected by the African Provincial Councils. In February 1958 a Speaker was appointed to preside over the Legislative Council in place of the Governor. In July 1959 the Council acquired a Mace and an African Serjeant-at-Arms was appointed.

In 1959 a state of emergency was declared following unrest which resulted from African opposition to Nyasaland's membership of the Federation. Interim changes were made in the composition of the Legislative Council, including an increase in the number of officials to 14 and an increase in the number of African members to 7, thus giving the Africans a majority over the unofficial non-African members for the first time.

Further constitutional changes were agreed to in 1960 and implemented in 1961. The Legislative Council was reconstituted to comprise a Speaker and 33 members, of whom 28 were elected, thus providing Nyasaland's legislature with its first unofficial majority. The Chief Secretary, Attorney-General and Financial Secretary continued to sit ex-officio together with two other nominated official members. The provision of two electoral rolls with differential qualifying requirements ensured that 20 of the elected members would be Africans and 8 would be non-Africans. The Executive Council consisted of the Governor, the 3 ex-officio and 2 nominated official members, and 5 elected members, of whom 3 were required to be elected by the lower-roll voters and 2 by those on the higher roll.

A further conference held in 1962 led to the establishment of self-government in 1963. On 1 February the Executive Council became a Cabinet consisting of 9 elected ministers including a Prime Minister and an ex-officio Minister of Finance (the Financial Secretary). On 9 May the Cabinet ceased to be advisory to the Governor except in respect of financial matters, the public service and public order. The official members withdrew from the Legislature (renamed the Legislative Assembly) with the exception of the Financial Secretary while he remained a member of the Cabinet. The Federation of Rhodesia and Nyasaland was finally dissolved on 31 December 1963, and Nyasaland's transition to independence was completed the following year.

MALAYSIA FEDERAL PARLIAMENT

The Federation of Malaysia consists of the 11 States of the Malay Peninsula and the States of Sarawak and Sabah (formerly North Borneo). In 1948 the Malayan Federation was formed in succession to the Malayan Union from the States of Johore, Kedah, Kelantan, Negri Sembilan, Pahang, Perak, Perlis, Selangor and Trengganu and the British Settlements of Penang and Malacca, with Kuala Lumpur as the federal capital. The Federation became an independent member of the Commonwealth in August 1957 and, on 16 September 1963, it was enlarged under the name of Malaysia to include the State of Singapore and the Borneo territories of Sarawak and Sabah. A third Borneo territory, Brunei, decided to remain outside the Federation, and in 1966 Singapore seceded from the association.

The Supreme Head of the Federation is the Yang di-Pertuan Agong, and he is elected for a period of five years by the Rulers of the States from among themselves. He appoints the Prime Minister, summons, prorogues and dissolves Parliament, and acts according to the advice of the Cabinet.

The Federal Parliament consists of the Supreme Head of the Federation and two chambers, the Senate (Dewan Negara) and the House of Representatives (Dewan Ra'ayat). The Senate consists of 48 members, 2 elected by the Legislative Assemblies of each Malay State, 2 elected by the legislature of Sarawak, 2 elected by the legislature of Sabah, and 22 nominated by the Federal Government from among people who have rendered outstanding public service or have otherwise distinguished themselves. The President of the Senate (Yang di-Pertua Dewan Negara) is elected by the Senators from among themselves. The Senate is not subject to dissolution and Senators hold office for six years, one-half of them retiring every three years. A Senator must be at least thirty years of age. Bills passed by the lower House may be delayed by the Senate for thirteen months or, in the case of a Money Bill, for twenty-one days, after which they may be submitted to the Supreme Head of the Federation for his assent whether or not they have been passed by the Senate. The House of Representatives may not, however, overrule the Senate on a Bill for the amendment of the Constitution. The House of Representatives consists of 144 members, reduced from 159 following the secession of Singapore from the Federation. The 11 Malay States are represented by 104 members, Sarawak by 24 and Sabah by 16. The members for Sarawak and Sabah were in the first instance elected by their state legislatures but it is anticipated that all the members of the House of Representatives will be directly elected at future General Elections. The Speaker (Yang di-Pertua Dewan Ra'ayat) is elected by the members from among themselves. The qualifying age for a member of the lower House is twenty-one years.

The matters over which the state legislatures exercise control include Moslem law, land, agriculture and forestry, local government, and water supply, and concurrently with the Federal Parliament social welfare, town and country planning and public health. Federal powers

[461]

in relation to immigration and education are subject to certain reservations in order to accommodate the Borneo territories. Although the Federation is a Moslem country there is no state religion in Sarawak and Sabah, and where federal law provides for the granting of financial aid to Moslem institutions proportionate amounts are granted to the Borneo States for the purposes of social welfare.

Each State has a unicameral legislature consisting of the Ruler of the State and a Legislative Assembly, known in the Malay States as Dewan Negeri. The legislatures of Sarawak and Sabah are dealt with under their own headings. Those of the Malay States are composed as follows:

Johore, 32; Kedah, 24; Kelantan, 30; Malacca, 20; Negri Sembilan, 24; Pahang, 24; Penang, 24; Perak, 40; Perlis, 12; Selangor, 28; Trengganu, 24.

MALTA PARLIAMENT

Malta became an independent member of the Commonwealth, acknowledging the Queen as Head of State, on 21 September 1964. Parliament consists of a Governor-General and a House of Representatives of 50 members, elected on the principle of proportional representation by means of the single transferable vote, from 10 electoral divisions. The Constitution makes provision for the protection of the Roman Catholic religion and the fundamental rights and freedoms of the individual, and specifies Maltese and English as the official languages of Malta.

Very soon after the annexation of Malta to the British Crown in 1814 a demand for self-government is recorded, and in 1849 the Council of Government, established in 1835, was reconstituted with 10 official members and 8 elected unofficial members. In 1887 the official members were reduced to 6 and the elected members increased to 14, but in 1903 a new Constitution was introduced which reverted to the Crown Colony type, and the official members were increased to 10 while the unofficials were reduced to 8. A new Constitution was granted in 1921 by which control of the island was divided between the legislature (a Senate and Legislative Assembly) and a Nominated Council presided over by the Governor, who, after consultation with the Council, was empowered to make ordinances in respect of 'reserved matters'. These included defence, coinage and currency, immigration, and everything connected with the naval, military, and air forces in Malta. The Constitution also established an Executive Council composed of ministers, and a Privy Council consisting of the Executive Council and the Nominated Council for the consideration of matters not within the exclusive responsibility of the Executive Council. After this Constitution had been twice suspended in 1930 and 1933, during which time the Governor had legislative and executive authority, new letters patent provided in 1936 for a Constitution which included an Executive

Council composed of 5 *ex-officio* members and not less than 3 members appointed by the Governor. In 1939 Malta was granted yet another Constitution (known as the 'MacDonald Constitution' after the Colonial Secretary at the time) which provided for an Executive Council of 5 *ex-officio* members appointed and presided over by the Governor and a Council of Government of 8 official, 10 elected, and 2 unofficial members nominated by the Governor. Responsible government was restored to Malta by the 1947 Constitution, which remained in force until its suspension in 1959 and was essentially the same as that of 1921, except that it did not include a Senate.

The Legislative Assembly had 40 members elected from 8 electoral divisions on the proportional representation system. Sittings were held in the historic Tapestry Chamber in what was once the Palace of the Knights of St. John of Jerusalem, Valletta, and is now the Governor-General's Palace.

In February 1956 Malta decided by a referendum on integration with the United Kingdom, but after prolonged negotiations failed to produce agreement on the economic aspects of this step the Prime Minister, Mr. Mintoff, and his Cabinet resigned in April 1958. The resignations were accepted by the Governor, who thereupon declared a state of emergency and assumed direct responsibility for the administration of the island.

In April 1959 the 1947 Constitution was revoked, and an interim Constitution was introduced providing for an Executive Council composed of 3 official members and 4 members nominated by the Governor. The Governor was empowered to enact ordinances, but he acted, with certain exceptions, in consultation with the Executive Council. Plans for the early restoration of representative government to Malta were announced in the House of Commons on 27 July 1960, and a new Constitution was promulgated in October 1961. It provided for a Legislative Assembly of 50 members and designated the island the State of Malta. In July 1963 a conference was held in London to discuss independence for Malta, but it proved impossible to reach agreement on the form of the future Constitution. The Prime Minister of Malta, Dr. Borg Olivier, therefore decided to submit the Constitution proposed by his Government to the Legislative Assembly and to a referendum. It was approved by the Assembly on 1 April 1964 and by a majority of the electorate early in May, after which further negotiations ensued. The Constitution finally agreed upon (Cmnd. 2406) is very similar to that drafted by the Maltese Government.

MANITOBA LEGISLATIVE ASSEMBLY

The Act of the Canadian Parliament of 1870 creating the Province of Manitoba made provision for the appointment of a Lieutenant-Governor and the establishment of a bicameral legislature—a Legislative Council appointed by the Lieutenant-Governor in Council and an elected Legislative Assembly. The first Parliament met on 15 March 1871, but in 1876 the Legislative Council was abolished, and since then the legislature has been unicameral. There are 57 members directly elected for five years by single-member constituencies, the previous electoral system which was based on proportional representation having been abolished in 1955. The Electoral Divisions Act, 1957, created 36 rural and 21 urban seats. The Province is represented by 6 members in the Canadian Senate and 13 in the House of Commons at Ottawa. Manitoba's magnificent Legislative Building, formally opened in 1920, is of classic design, with a central tower and dome rising to a height of 180 feet above the main roof level.

In 1963 the Manitoba Legislative Assembly elected a woman Speaker, Mrs. Thelma Forbes. Mrs. Forbes thus became the second woman in the Commonwealth to hold office as Speaker, the first being Mrs. Nancy Hodges who was elected Speaker of the British Columbia Legislative Assembly in 1950.

MANNER OF HOLDING PARLIAMENTS IN ENGLAND

See ELSYNGE, HENRY; HAKEWILL, WILLIAM; MODUS TENENDI PARLIAMENTUM.

MANX PARLIAMENT

The Parliament of the Isle of Man, the Tynwald Court, is of Norse origin and one of the oldest legislatures in the world, having originated with the Viking invasions of the 10th century. The accepted derivation of the island's name is the Norse word for 'chosen', and 'Tynwald' is derived from the words *Thing Vollr* meaning 'Parliament Field'. The sovereignty of the isle was for many centuries vested in grantees of the Crown who were called 'Lords of Man and the Isles', but the sovereignty was purchased by George III in 1765 for £70,000. The island still enjoys a semi-autonomous Constitution, the supreme legislative authority being vested in the Crown, the Lieutenant-Governor, the Legislative Council, and the House of Keys, which together form the Tynwald Court. The Lieutenant-Governor is appointed by the Crown on the advice of the Home Secretary, who is the intermediary between the Manx and the British Parliaments. The Legislative Council consists of the Lieutenant-Governor, the First Deemster (or judge), the Bishop of Sodor and Man, the Attorney-General, 2 members appointed by the Lieutenant-Governor, and 5 members elected by the House of Keys. The latter is the lower House, and was formerly chosen by the Lords of Man, but since 1866 the 24 members have been elected by ballot. They receive a salary of £150 a year for expenses. All men and women over twenty-one have a vote, and the Isle of Man led the world by granting the franchise to unmarried women and widows in 1881, some years before the cry of 'votes for women' was heard in England. The island is administered in accordance with its own laws by the Tynwald Court and it is not bound by Acts of the British Parliament unless specially mentioned in them. An Executive Council to assist the Governor in framing legislation, particularly financial, was set up in 1946, and consists of 5 members of the House of Keys and 2 of the Legislative Council. In 1967 the Speaker of the House of Keys was included in the Executive Council, and his appointment aroused some controversy. There is little trace of party politics in the Tynwald and there are no party Whips since most of the members are independent.

In 1869 the seat of Government was transferred from Castletown to Douglas and housed in its present building. The Keys debate in their own chamber, but they sit with the Council in the Tynwald Chamber for a Tynwald Court. In this room there is a 'Floor' occupied by the Keys under their Speaker, and a 'Gallery' for the members of the Council, presided over by the Governor. The Speaker's seat in this Chamber is directly below that of the Governor, who presides over the Court, in the gallery above. In the Tynwald the Speaker of the House of Keys, whose title dates from the end of the 18th century, may speak as an ordinary member of the Court as well as represent to the Council the views of the Keys. In case of disagreement between the two Houses, any member of the Keys may move 'that the Keys retire to their own Chamber'. The Tynwald Court sits to transact executive business and to sign Bills, which before they become law require the signatures of the Governor, 2 members of the Council, and 13 members of the Keys. Bills are then sent to the Queen for the Royal Assent, and then must be promulgated in English and Manx from Tynwald Hill at the annual open-air ceremony on 5 July. The constituencies in the Isle of Man are the six 'sheadings', or local sub-divisions, and the four municipalities of Douglas, Castletown, Peel, and Ramsey. The electorate numbers about 40,000.

MARQUESS

This title has the next place of honour to that of a duke. Blackstone says that the office of a marquess (German *Markgrave*) was formerly to guard the frontier and limits of the kingdom, which were called marches, but it is doubtful if these soldier lords were the original marquesses of the English peerage. The first English marquessate was conferred by Richard II upon Robert de Vere, who was created Marquess of Dublin in 1385. The creations were not very numerous, however, and it would appear that the new honour was not greatly coveted by the old nobility. When John de Beaufort was deprived of his marquessate by Henry VI the Commons petitioned the King to restore it to him. The marquess opposed the petition, saying that 'it was a new dignity altogether unknown to his ancestors, and that, therefore, he neither craved it, nor in any wise would he accept it'. In spite of this the title from 1475 was constantly in existence in the peerage until the reign of Edward VI; thenceforward it became a regular and common grade of nobility. A marquess is created by letters patent under the Great Seal, and takes the style of 'Most Honourable'. He is officially addressed by the Crown as 'Our right trusty and entirely beloved Cousin'. The mantle of a marquess is the same as a baron's, but has three rows and a half of ermine on the cape. The coronet is a circle of silver gilt, surmounted by four gold strawberry leaves and four silver balls, alternately, the latter a little raised on points above the rim. There are at present (1970) 30 Marquesses.

MARY I (1516–1558)

Daughter of Henry VIII and Catherine of Aragon and half-sister to Edward VI, succeeded to the throne after an unsuccessful attempt on the part of the Duke of Northumberland to cause her to be disinherited in favour of his daughter-in-law, Lady Jane Dudley. Edward VI died on 6 July 1553, and on the 10th the Privy Council proclaimed Lady Jane Queen. Mary then proceeded to Framlingham Castle in Norfolk and was herself proclaimed Queen at Norwich on the 13th. Supporters soon began to rally to her cause and on the 19th she was proclaimed in London. Her coronation took place on 1 October. Mary I was the first Queen Regnant in England's history, and in 1554 a Royal Marriage Act removing the difficulties which stood in the way of the accession of a female Sovereign was passed by Parliament (q.v.).

MARY II (1662-1694)

See WILLIAM III AND PARLIAMENT.

MATERIALS, MINISTER OF

The Ministry of Materials Act, 1951, created a department to deal with the problems of obtaining raw materials and supervising their distribution in view of the rearmament programme. The Ministry took over certain functions of the Ministry of Supply and the Board of Trade, and Richard Stokes was appointed its first head while retaining his office of Lord Privy Seal (q.v.). In the Conservative Government which came into office later in 1951 Lord Swinton was appointed Chancellor of the Duchy of Lancaster (q.v.) and Minister of Materials. He was succeeded as Minister of Materials by Sir James (afterwards Lord) Salter and subsequently by Lord Woolton, who combined the office with that of Chancellor of the Duchy of Lancaster. Lord Woolton remained the Minister until his ministry was dissolved and its remaining functions transferred to the Board of Trade in July 1954.

MAURITIUS LEGISLATIVE ASSEMBLY

Mauritius became independent on 12 March 1968 under a Constitution based on an agreement which had been reached at a Conference held in London in September 1965. At this Conference it had been decided that Mauritius would become independent after a period of six months' internal self-government, if the Legislative Assembly resolved by a simple majority to ask for independence.

Under the Constitution, Parliament consists of the Queen represented by a Governor-General and a Legislative Assembly. The Assembly consists of 62 members representing as many constituencies and 8 additional members appointed from among party members who have stood as candidates for election but have not been returned. These 8 additional seats are designed to ensure a fair and adequate representation of each community. The Cabinet consists of the Prime Minister and not more than 14 ministers.

The Constitution provides for an Electoral Boundaries Commission which reviews the boundaries of constituencies every ten years or after the holding of a census, and an Electoral Supervisory Commission which is responsible, *inter alia*, for making recommendations to the Governor-General for the appointment of the 8 additional members.

The Constitution also provides for fundamental rights and freedoms, citizenship, the public service and the judicature. Mauritius is the first Commonwealth country to provide for the establishment of the office of Ombudsman within its basic constitutional document. The power to prescribe the procedure to be observed in the performance of the functions of the office is reserved to Parliament.

The Constitution also provides for its own amendment, a special procedure being prescribed for the amendment of entrenched and non-entrenched provisions. The entrenched provisions, which include those relating to Parliament, the electoral system, the judicial system, fundamental rights and freedoms and the constitutional amendment procedure, may be amended only with the support of not less than three-quarters of the total membership of the Legislative Assembly. A Bill to amend any other provision requires the approval of a two-thirds majority.

The first Legislative Council of Mauritius with a majority of elected members was established in 1947 and consisted of the Governor as President, 3 *ex-officio*, 12 nominated and 19 elected members. In 1951 the Government first appointed 'liaison officers' from among the unofficial members whose duty it was to keep in touch with government departments and thus obtain a fuller knowledge of policy which would help them to take a share in forming it. This was the prelude to the introduction of the ministerial system in 1956. In the same year a Speaker was appointed to preside over the Legislative Council in place of the Governor. In 1958 universal adult suffrage was introduced and the number of elected members of the Legislative Council increased to 40. In 1964 the second stage of a two-stage plan conferring internal self-government came into operation, the Legislative Council becoming the Legislative Assembly, the Executive Council being replaced by a Council of Ministers and the Chief Minister becoming the Premier. In the following year the Conference took place which led to the emergence of Mauritius as a fully independent State.

MAY, SIR THOMAS ERSKINE (1st BARON FARNBOROUGH) (1815–1886)

Clerk of the House of Commons from 1871 to 1886, and author of the standard work on parliamentary practice, *Treatise on the Law, Privileges, Proceedings and Usage of Parliament*. The first edition was published in 1844, and the latest edition, the 17th, was edited by the present Clerk of the House, Sir Barnett Cocks. The work is used in all Commonwealth Parliaments and is the acknowledged text-book on the subject.

Prior to becoming Clerk of the House, Erskine May was assistant librarian of the House of Commons in 1831 and examiner of petitions for Private Bills and taxing-master for both Houses of Parliament from 1847 to 1856. From 1866 to 1884 he was president of the Statute Law Revision Committee. Erskine May became a barrister of the Middle Temple in 1838, was made a Knight Commander of the Bath in 1866, a Privy Councillor in 1885, and created Baron Farnborough in 1886. His other works include a *Constitutional History of England*, first published in 1861, and he also compiled an index to the Journals of the House of Commons from 1547 to the death of Queen Anne.

MEASURES

See CHURCH ASSEMBLY MEASURES.

MEMBER OF PARLIAMENT

A member of a legislature may be elected, nominated, or sit by hereditary right as in the House of Lords. Edmund Burke, in his well-known address to the electors of Bristol in 1774, declared that a Member of the House of Commons was not just the delegate of his constituents, but that when he was elected he became a representative of the whole nation, and must vote in agreement with what he or his party considered to be the best interests of the country as a whole. This does not mean that a member must neglect his constituents' personal difficulties or their local affairs, indeed a large proportion of time not spent in the Chamber is devoted to them, but in regard to the nation's affairs he is, as Burke told his electors, 'not a Member of Bristol, but he is a Member of Parliament'. In the early days of parliamentary history, when the functions of the Commons were mainly to present petitions for the redress of grievances and to grant taxes, members were definitely sent to Parliament as delegates from local authorities. They received wages from their constituents and were required to live in their constituencies. Andrew Marvell, the poet, was the last person known to have been paid such a regular wage as a Member of Parliament. He was returned as Member for Hull from 1660 to 1678 by the Mayor and Aldermen, and wrote regularly to them asking for instructions and sending news of happenings in Parliament. Burke's speech put instructions from a constituency out of favour, and after the 1832 Reform Act came into operation, larger and more popular constituencies rendered precise instructions impracticable. The Redistribution Act of 1885 strengthened the view that a member represents the whole country, which is divided into electoral districts merely for the convenience of election. Most members enter Parliament as supporters of one of the major political parties, and the electors know that in national affairs their member will act in accordance with his party's policy. If he changes his party he is not compelled to resign his seat, but he may decide to resign and offer himself for re-election in order to find out whether his action meets with the approval of the majority of his constituents. An M.P. will deal with local matters concerning his constituency by writing to the minister concerned or addressing a question to him in the House, or he may raise a local question on an adjournment debate. The only occasion on which a member is expected to dwell on the progress of his own constituency and the sterling qualities of its inhabitants (it is important to remember that he represents the minority who did not vote for him as well as the majority who did) is if he is chosen to move or second the debate on the address (q.v.).

Apart from national and local representation, an M.P. may also represent some particular interest or section of the community, such as the textile industry or the coal miners. Members obviously draw on their own experience in considering proposed legislation, and it is only natural that they should see that the interests of the professional, industrial, or economic group to which they belong are taken into account.

The life of a Member of Parliament is one of very strenuous activity. The late Lord Snell wrote in his *Daily Life in Parliament*, 'As a result of seven years' experience, I am convinced that the average M.P. works at greater pressure and for longer hours than nine-tenths of those who elected him, and that if the factory worker, miner, or engineer had the same strain put upon him, he would down tools within a month and demand better conditions of work.' As well as listening to debates in the House—and waiting for a chance to 'get in' himself—he may have to serve on Standing or Select Committees, attend party and other meetings, and meet constituents and conduct parties of them round the parliamentary buildings. He is faced with a formidable pile of letters every day, mostly from constituents needing help or advice, and there is no free secretarial service provided. His week-ends are occupied with meetings and social engagements in his constituency, where he is expected to open fêtes and flower-shows and attend the functions of local organizations and charities, to which he is also expected to subscribe. Parliamentary duties and obligations can make considerable financial demands upon a member, but it was not until 1911 that British M.P.s were paid a salary by the state. It started at £400 a year, but was increased to £600 in 1937 and to £1,000 in 1946 with a £2 a day sessional allowance added in 1954. In 1957 this allowance was abolished and an annual allowance of £750 substituted in its place. This represented a financial improvement of nearly £500 a year. In 1964 salaries were again increased and consolidated at £3,250. In December 1969 an additional allowance of £500 was awarded, subject to the presentation of accounts, for secretarial assistance. Members also enjoy free rail, sea, or air travel between their constituencies and homes and Westminster. (Salaries of Members of other Commonwealth Parliaments will be found in Appendix 2.) A member may also receive financial assistance from bodies outside Parliament, such as trade unions. Whether these payments involved a breach of privilege was discussed by the House of Commons Committee of Privileges in 1947, and they reported that they did not, provided that a member's complete independence was not fettered by his undertaking to press some particular point of view on behalf of an outside interest, whether for reward or not. The Report was agreed to by the House on 15 July 1947, when it was emphasized that the duty of a member was to his constituents and the country as a whole, rather than to any particular section thereof.

(Further reading: Richards, *Honourable Members*, 2nd ed., 1964).

See also ABSENCE, LEAVE OF; DISQUALIFICATION FROM MEMBERSHIP; INDEPENDENT MEMBER; INTRODUCTION OF A MEMBER; PAYMENT OF MEMBERS; PRIVILEGE.

MEMBERS' SALARIES

See PAYMENT OF MEMBERS; APPENDIX 2 for Members' Salaries in the Parliaments of the Commonwealth.

'MEMBER' SYSTEM

A system whereby unofficial members of a colonial legislature are associated with Government departments. They are expected to take a particular interest in the department to which they are appointed, but unlike a minister they are not responsible for its activities. The 'member' system is an early stage in the evolution of the cabinet system in colonial government.

MEMORIAL

A form of petition usually associated with a Private Bill (q.v.). Any person may send in a memorial to the examiners of a Private Bill, complaining that Standing Orders have not been complied with by the promoters of the Bill. Such a person is entitled to appear at the examination in person or be represented by a parliamentary agent (q.v.) and produce witnesses. Memorials are, however, becoming increasingly rare, and proceedings before the examiners usually consist of the handing in of affidavits by the promoters' agents, and personal evidence as to other facts by those responsible for the preparation of Bills and notices.

MERCILESS PARLIAMENT

The Parliament summoned in the 11th year of Richard II's reign, and which met on 3 February 1388, was so called because of the bitter reprisals it took against members of the Court party, who had supported the King in his attempt to regain control of the government. A number of them were condemned to death on such flimsy charges that the sentences amounted to judicial murder. 'The Parliament that wrought wonders' was the title bestowed on it by those who approved of its activities.

MESSAGE

See CROWN AND PARLIAMENT.

MINISTERIAL STATEMENT

Statements by ministers regarding the Government's domestic or foreign policy and announcements on public business arrangements or legislative proposals are usually elicited by arrangement in reply to a Private Notice Question. But the older practice under which these explanations were volunteered in the House of Commons by the minister concerned is often followed. Notice of such statements has to be given to the Speaker, but the leave of the House is not required, and they are made before the commencement of Public Business.

A ministerial statement may not be debated, since no motion is

Q   [471]

before the House when such a statement is made, but members are permitted to question a minister on a statement he has just made provided the questions are kept within reasonable limits. The degree of latitude allowed in such questions rests with the discretion of the Speaker, but it is his function to ensure that no debate develops.

MINISTER OF STATE

The designation 'Minister of State' is usually, but not invariably, applied to a minister below Cabinet rank but senior to a Parliamentary Secretary. Such ministers are normally appointed to departments where the ministerial load is particularly heavy, and in respect of certain departments it is now usual for more than one Minister of State to be appointed. The Cabinet Ministers in charge of such departments retain their overall control and are responsible to Parliament for any action their subordinate colleagues may take.

There is, however, no shortage of precedents for the appointment of a Minister of State with Cabinet rank. In 1941 Sir Winston Churchill brought Lord Beaverbrook into his War Cabinet as Minister of State, and later the same year Mr. Oliver Lyttelton joined the War Cabinet as Minister of State, Resident Middle East. As recently as 1964 Sir Edward Boyle was appointed Minister of State for Education and Science while retaining his seat in the Cabinet, thus enjoying equality of status with the Secretary of State for Education and Science, an office held by Mr. Quintin Hogg concurrently with that of Lord President of the Council.

The practice of appointing Ministers of State to departments in an intermediate capacity was instituted during the Second World War when Mr. Richard Law was appointed Minister of State at the Foreign Office. The practice was continued by subsequent Governments with the result that Ministers of State have been appointed at one time or another to most of the principal Departments of State. In recent years a new category of Minister has arisen which has come to be termed Senior Minister of State. Among the Ministers who may fall into this category is the Chief Secretary to the Treasury, an office first given statutory authority by the Ministers of the Crown Act, 1964. The two Ministers of Defence subordinate to the Secretary of State for Defence, who were included in Mr. Harold Wilson's Government prior to its defeat in 1970, also fell into this category. Senior Ministers of State receive salaries only marginally lower than that of a full Cabinet Minister. The Chief Secretary to the Treasury is, in fact, sometimes a member of the Cabinet himself.

The House of Commons Disqualification Act, 1957, as amended by the Ministers of the Crown Act, 1964, defines a Minister of State as 'a member of Her Majesty's Government in the United Kingdom, who neither has charge of any public department nor holds any other of the offices specified in the Second Schedule to this Act or any office in respect of which a salary is payable out of moneys provided by Parliament under section 2 of the Ministerial Salaries Act, 1946'. The Act of 1964 makes provision for the appointment of up to 19 Ministers of State, and leaves the determination of salary to the discretion of the Prime Minister within the limit of a Cabinet Minister's salary. An office therefore need not carry the designation 'Minister of State' in order to conform to the statutory definition, and provision remains for the appointment of a Minister of State to full Cabinet status.

The Government formed by Mr. Edward Heath in June 1970 included 2 Ministers of State at the Home Office, 2 at the Ministry of Technology and 1 at each of the following Ministries: the Foreign and Commonwealth Office, the Treasury, the Ministry of Defence, the Department of Health and Social Security, the Ministry of Housing and Local Government, the Scottish Office, the Welsh Office and the Board of Trade.

The salary of a Senior Minister of State is £7,625 a year, that of a Minister of State £5,625. A Minister of State with Cabinet rank would, of course, receive a Cabinet Minister's salary of £8,500. All such ministers receive an additional taxable allowance of £1,250 if they are Members of the House of Commons.

MINISTER OF THE CROWN

The holder of one of the chief political offices of Her Majesty's Government in the United Kingdom or of her governments overseas. The majority of ministers are in charge of specified departments of state, although a few, notably the Prime Minister (q.v.), unless he also takes upon himself the responsibility for a specific department, have no, or very slight, departmental duties. Ministers falling into this category, who include the Lord President of the Council (q.v.), the Lord Privy Seal (q.v.), the Chancellor of the Duchy of Lancaster (q.v.), and the Paymaster-General (q.v.), are therefore available for special duties or able to devote their time exclusively to the business of the Cabinet (q.v.). Occasionally, and more particularly outside the United Kngdom, two or more offices may be combined in one individual. In other Commonwealth countries it is a general practice to give more than one portfolio to certain ministers.

Ministers are chosen by the Prime Minister and appointed by the Crown on his advice. They may or may not be members of the Cabinet, the selection of Cabinet Ministers also resting with the Prime Minister. They are by established usage Members of Parliament, although exceptions were made in the cases of Gladstone (1845-6), Smuts (1917-18), and Sir A. Griffith-Boscawen (1922-3), who were at those times Cabinet Ministers without a seat in either House. Whether inside or outside the Cabinet, every departmental minister is fully responsible for the work of his department and of any sub-departments falling within his jurisdiction. Although he may (and, of course, is compelled to) delegate authority to his Parliamentary Secretary (q.v.) and his permanent officials, he remains responsible for all decisions taken by them. The minister's task is to relate the policy of his department to that of the Government and to serve as the link between his department and Parliament. He receives guidance on the affairs of his department from his expert advisers, the permanent officials, but it is a weak minister who will rely on his experts to such an extent as to be led by them. The function of a minister is not to follow a lead but to give one. His task is therefore to assess the advice of his experts and to use his own judgment in taking decisions, if necessary in the face of conflicting views. Whilst it is no light matter to disregard the advice of permanent officials, based as it is bound to be on long experience and deep consideration of the problems in hand, a minister is under no obligation to his subordinates to accept their advice or to refrain from seeking the views of persons outside his own department. The most valuable attribute with which a minister can hope to be endowed is an ability to grasp essentials and to arrive at sound judgments. The majority of daily administrative decisions are obviously taken within the department itself, so that the minister must rely upon the permanent officials bringing to his attention any matters involving policy or of sufficient importance to warrant a ministerial decision.

When one appreciates the true function of a minister it becomes apparent that an expert knowledge of the affairs of the department he controls is not an essential qualification. A country could no doubt be governed with considerable efficiency by its Civil Service alone, but without a political chief at the head of each department there could be no co-ordination of policy, no contact with public opinion, no independent minds to resolve disputes within and between departments and to foresee consequences which are unavoidably beyond the vision of the relatively narrow departmental sphere. To borrow the words of Sir William Harcourt, 'The value of political heads of departments is to tell the permanent officials what the public will not stand.' It is only fair, however, to add Sir Ivor Jennings's observation 'that there are occasions when the permanent officials have to tell the politicians what the public will not stand'.

Parliamentary experience ranks high in importance as a ministerial qualification, although it is not always possible to take this into account when appointing ministers. Nevertheless, a minister who has served previously as a Parliamentary Secretary or Parliamentary Private Secretary (qq.v.) has a valuable training behind him. Varied experience also has its advantages and the ministerial reshuffles which periodically take place are not without their merits from this point of view. There is therefore little justification in the criticism which is commonly levelled at the ministerial system on the ground that a political head of a department seldom stays in any one office long enough to become intimately acquainted with the affairs of that department. At the same time, only through a long period of tenure of a single office can any minister hope to leave his personal impression upon a government department.

Under the Ministerial Salaries and Members' Pensions Act, 1965, the great majority of Ministers of Cabinet rank receive salaries of £8,500 a year. (The salary of a Cabinet Minister, other than the Prime Minister and Lord Chancellor, had previously been £5,000 in terms of the Ministers of the Crown Act, 1937.) Provision is made for the salaries of the Lord President of the Council, the Lord Privy Seal, the Chancellor of the Duchy of Lancaster and the Paymaster General to be determined by the Prime Minister within the limit of £8,500 when those ministers are not appointed to the Cabinet. All ministers receive an additional taxable allowance of £1,250 if they are Members of the House of Commons. A minister who sits in the House of Lords is not, however, entitled to the peers' attendance allowance of up to £4 14s. 6d. a day. Since 1906 no minister has been permitted to hold a directorship. There is also a general ban on the writing of political articles by ministers for the Press.

At one time a Member of the House of Commons appointed to ministerial office was obliged, under the Succession to the Crown Act, 1707, to submit himself for re-election, but this requirement was first modified and then abolished by the Re-election of Ministers Act, 1919, and a subsequent amending Act in 1926.

No minister is debarred from sitting in either House of Parliament by reason of the office he holds. In theory, the Lord Chancellor could be a Member of the House of Commons, but in practice he is always a peer, and when the appointment is made from the Commons the member concerned is invariably elevated to the peerage at the same time. Similarly there is no statutory prohibition on the Prime Minister sitting in the House of Lords, as many Prime Ministers have done in the past, but modern convention requires the Prime Minister and the majority of his colleagues to be Members of the House of Commons.

There has long been a statutory limitation on the number of ministers who may sit in the House of Commons, and the Ministers of the Crown Act, 1937, and the House of Commons Disqualification Act, 1957, were both designed to ensure that a minimal representation of the Government in the House of Lords would be guaranteed. The position is now governed, however, by the Ministers of the Crown Act, 1964, which places an overall limit of 91 (formerly 70) on the number of ministers (senior and junior) who may sit in the House of Commons, and abolishes the former limit of 27 on the number of senior ministers who may sit in that House. It also provides for the appointment of up to 9 Secretaries of State (q.v.), up to 19 Ministers of State (q.v.), and up to 36 Parliamentary Secretaries (q.v.) plus not more than 2 Treasury Secretaries. For all practical purposes the Act removes any obligation upon a Prime Minister to include any peers in his Government, with the possible exception of the Lord Chancellor whose office is omitted from the relevant schedule of the Act.

Under the law as it stood prior to the passing of the Act of 1964 the limits could be exceeded provided the additional ministers were unpaid and not listed in the second schedule of the Act of 1957. Mr. Harold Wilson did in fact exceed those limits when he formed his Government in 1964, and certain of his ministers were obliged to serve without a ministerial salary pending the amendment of the law.

See also MINISTER OF STATE; SECRETARIES OF STATE.

MINISTERS' SALARIES
See APPENDIX 2.

MINISTER WITHOUT PORTFOLIO

A Minister without a department, who is usually appointed by the Prime Minister to do some special work which the ministers with departments are not in a position to undertake. For example Mr. Anthony Eden (afterwards Lord Avon) was appointed a Minister Without Portfolio in 1935 to take charge of League of Nations affairs, while in 1967 Mr. Patrick Gordon Walker was given this office with the special responsibility of co-ordinating the social services. A Minister Without Portfolio ranks as a Minister of State (q.v.) unless he is a member of the Cabinet (q.v.).

MINISTRY

Usually the word 'ministry' is applied to a government department for which a Minister is responsible to Parliament, but it can also mean the Government of the day as a whole. It is not used in this sense now as much as it was in the 19th century, when writers referred to Governments led by particular Prime Ministers as the Aberdeen Ministry or the second Derby Ministry, etc.

MIRROR OF PARLIAMENT, THE

A record of parliamentary debates, started in 1828 by John Henry Barrow, which during its lifetime was a keen rival to Hansard (q.v.). For a time it employed Charles Dickens as one of its reporters. *The Mirror of Parliament* ceased publication in 1841 owing to financial difficulty.

MODEL CLAUSES COMMITTEE

This committee was appointed in 1948 to revise and redraft model clauses for use in private legislation. It is presided over by the Speaker's Counsel (q.v.) and consists of the Counsel to the Lord Chairman together with representatives of parliamentary agents (q.v.) and government departments. A volume of model clauses has been issued, which is revised by the committee at each session of Parliament, and this is of great assistance to the promoters of Private Bills (q.v.).

MODEL PARLIAMENT

The Parliament summoned on 13 November 1295 by Edward I, and afterwards so called because it settled the general type of Parliament for the future. It is generally regarded as the first fully representative assembly, particularly notable for the fact that 2 knights from each shire, 2 citizens from each city, and 2 burgesses from each borough (all elected) were summoned, together with representatives of the lower clergy, to sit with the bishops, earls, and barons in the council of the realm. The King called this Parliament because he was in need of money and, as its composition indicates, he enlisted the aid of all classes of society instead of turning only to the nobles for assistance.

The details of the constitution of the Model Parliament are as follows: the 2 archbishops and all the bishops, 67 abbots, 8 earls, 41 barons, the Masters of the Temple and of Sempringham, the prior of the Hospital of St. John of Jerusalem, the prior and archdeacons of the dioceses of Canterbury and York, 1 proctor from the chapter of each cathedral, 2 proctors from the parochial clergy of each diocese, and the representatives of the shires, cities, and boroughs referred to above.

The Model Parliament was not the first Parliament to which the Commons had been summoned. Simon de Montfort's Parliament (q.v.) of 1265 had included knights, citizens and burgesses although it cannot be regarded as a truly representative assembly. The first time the Commons were included in a genuinely national council was in 1275 when 'four knights more discreet in the law and also six or four citizens, burgesses or other honest men from each of the cities' were summoned to a Parliament by King Edward I 'to discuss together with the magnates the affairs of our kingdom'. There is evidence that the Commons were present in several other Parliaments during the reign, but it was not until the Model Parliament set the pattern for future Parliaments that they came to be summoned as a matter of course.

MODUS TENENDI PARLIAMENTUM

A document of the 14th century, this is the earliest existing account of the constitution of Parliament in the Middle Ages. It is not generally regarded as a reliable authority. Sir Courtenay Ilbert described it as 'too fanciful to be trustworthy', and William Stubbs acknowledged that it is frequently misleading, although he added, 'it may be accepted as a theoretical view for which the writer was anxious to find a warrant in immemorial antiquity'. A. F. Pollard did not, however, share the prevailing view regarding its unreliability (see *The Evolution of Parliament*, 2nd ed., p. 68). He agreed that it does not give a valid account of the method of holding Parliaments in Anglo-Saxon times, but believed it to be of some value as a contemporary record. He pointed out that it seemed to be regarded as authoritative in the 15th century, as a revised version was sent over to Ireland in 1418 as a guide to the holding of Parliaments in Dublin.

Its composition has been assigned to the early years of the reign of Edward III, mainly because it makes no mention of dukes, marquesses, and viscounts, but only earls and barons. At least three extant manuscripts date from the 14th century. An edition was published in 1846 by Sir Thomas Duffus Hardy, and excerpts (in the original Latin) are included in the 9th edition of Stubbs's *Select Charters*.

MONEY BILLS

As distinct from the statutory definition which is given below, a Money Bill is taken to mean a Public Bill whose main object is to authorize expenditure or to impose taxation. The Standing Orders relating to financial business in the House of Commons require that any such Bill be founded on a resolution of the House. Prior to the introduction of the new financial procedure in December 1966 preliminary authorization was given by a resolution passed in a Committee of the Whole House and subsequently endorsed by the House. Except in the case of a Bill which is required to be brought in on a Ways and Means resolution, a Money Bill may be presented or brought in on an Order of the House by a Minister of the Crown and the charge shall not require to be authorized by a resolution of the House until the Bill has passed its second reading.

A Money Bill is defined in the Parliament Act, 1911, as 'A Public Bill which in the opinion of the Speaker of the House of Commons contains only provisions dealing with all or any of the following subjects, namely, the imposition, repeal, remission, alteration, or regulation of taxation; the imposition for the payment of debt or other financial purposes of charges on the Consolidated Fund, or on money provided by Parliament, or the variation or repeal of any such charges; supply; the appropriation, receipt, custody, issue or audit of accounts of public money; the raising or guarantee of any loan or the repayment thereof; or subordinate matters incidental to those subjects or any of them'. In this definition the expressions 'taxation', 'public money', and 'loan' respectively do not include any taxation, money, or loan raised by local authorities or bodies for local purposes. Money Bills, as defined in the Act, must be endorsed as such by the Speaker before they are sent to the House of Lords. The Lords are not entitled to initiate or amend a Money Bill, and although they may constitutionally reject such a Bill *in toto* the effect of so doing would be inoperative as the Act provides that a Money Bill may receive the Royal Assent notwithstanding the consent of the Lords having been withheld. Under the Act, a Bill containing provisions other than those defined is not a Money Bill unless they are subordinate matters incidental to the financial provisions.

At a first glance the shades of difference between the statutory definition of a Money Bill and the meaning of the term as generally understood will probably not be apparent. To a very great extent their meanings overlap, but one important difference lies in the fact that the former stipulates that the *sole* object of the Bill must be financial, whereas with the latter usage it is understood that the *main* object is financial, although a Bill whose *sole* object is financial could equally well be embraced by the second meaning as by the first. On the other hand, financial Bills which do not impose charges on the people, and which would not require the authorization of a financial resolution, have been certified as Money Bills as required by the Act, although they would not normally be referred to as such. The differences may seem slight but they are very important in practice, because a Bill which has not been endorsed as a Money Bill in terms of the Parliament Act can be delayed for a year if the House of Lords withholds its consent, whereas a certified Money Bill can only be held up for a month. Thus the annual Finance Bill (q.v.) which embodies the year's financial proposals is frequently not a Money Bill as defined by the Act because it often contains provisions other than those stated in the Act. It will be realized that the responsibility of the Speaker in deciding whether or not to endorse a Bill as a Money Bill is a very great one. He consults (to quote the Act) 'if practicable, two members to be appointed from the Chairmen's Panel at the beginning of each Session by the Committee of Selection'.

A Bill containing a clause or clauses imposing a charge which is incidental to the main proposals is not a Money Bill and does not require to be founded on a financial resolution. The financial clause or clauses, however, require authorization before they can be considered by the committee on the Bill. Such clauses are printed in the Bill in italics. If similar provisions are contained in Bills which are sent down from the Lords they are omitted when the Bill is before the upper House to avoid any infringement of the financial privileges of the Commons. When the Bill comes before the Commons the relevant clauses are inserted, underlined, and enclosed in square brackets, and are thus initiated in the lower instead of the upper House.

Q*

MONEY RESOLUTION

See FINANCIAL RESOLUTION.

MONK RESOLUTIONS

The resolutions by which parliamentary approval was given to the passing of a virement (q.v.) in the votes of the armed services, so called because they were first moved in 1879 by a member named Charles James Monk. These resolutions were rendered obsolete with the substitution of a Defence Vote on Account under a new procedure adopted in 1969.

See also ESTIMATES; PROCEDURE, FINANCIAL.

MONTSERRAT LEGISLATIVE COUNCIL

Now a separate Colony, Montserrat belonged to the Leeward Islands Federation until its abolition in 1956. The Legislative Council consisted of the Commissioner as President, 2 *ex-officio*, 2 nominated, and 5 elected members. The Executive Council included, besides the Commissioner, 2 *ex-officio* members, 2 of the Legislative Council's elected members, and 1 of the nominated members.

In June 1959 constitutional changes for Montserrat were agreed upon by the Leeward and Windward Islands Constitutional Conference. The Legislative Council now consists of 2 official members (the Attorney-General and Financial Secretary), 1 nominated unofficial member, and 7 elected members, and is presided over by the Administrator. Other constitutional changes became effective on 1 January 1960. The Leader of the Government became the Chief Minister and the Executive Council, where the 'member' system (q.v.) had been in operation, was reconstituted to comprise 4 unofficial members (including the Chief Minister and 2 other ministers) and 2 official members. The powers of the Governors of the Leeward Islands and the Windward Islands (whose posts are abolished) were transferred to the Administrators of the various islands comprising these groups. Montserrat was a member of the now defunct West Indies Federation.

MORE, SIR THOMAS (1478–1535)

Speaker of the House of Commons for four months during the year 1523 and Lord Chancellor of England from 1529 to 1532.

More was elected Speaker on the recommendation of Wolsey in April 1523, and his short tenure of office was distinguished by a conscientious regard for his duties as guardian of the privileges of the House of Commons. He was the first Speaker to crave the King's indulgence for any words which might be spoken by individual members during the course of debate. In his speech following his election as Speaker he besought the King 'to give to all your Commons here assembled your most gracious licence and pardon freely, without doubt of your dreadful displeasure, every man to discharge his conscience, and boldly in everything incident among, declare his advice, and whatsoever happeneth any man to say, it may like your noble Majesty of your inestimable goodness to take all in good part, interpreting every man's words, how uncunningly soever they may be couched, to proceed yet of a good zeal towards the profit of your Realm and honour of your Royal person. . . .' A few days after his appointment as Speaker, More was called upon to defend the rights of the Commons. The Lord Chancellor, Wolsey, made what Dasent describes as a wholly unconstitutional irruption into the Chamber to demand a grant of £800,000 (in those days an enormous sum) for the prosecution of the war with France. Appalled at the amount, the Commons decided to ask the King to accept a lesser sum, but Wolsey remained implacable and repeated his demand. The House remaining silent, Wolsey called upon the Speaker to make answer on their behalf. Falling upon his knees More reminded the Lord Chancellor, respectfully but firmly, that for the House to deliver an answer without an opportunity for unhindered debate 'was neither expedient nor agreeable with the ancient liberty of the House', and as for himself, 'except every one of them could put into his one head all their several wits, he alone in so weighty a matter was unmeet to make his Grace answer'. On receiving this rebuke, Wolsey departed.

On the fall of Wolsey, More became Lord Chancellor, the first layman to hold that high office. The events which led up to the resignation in 1532 and the subsequent fall of this remarkable man are beyond the scope of this work. The measure of More's greatness may however, be assessed by the indelible impression he left during his brief appearance in the ever-moving pageant of Parliament.

MOSES ROOM

A room situated to the west of the Peers' Lobby in the House of Lords, so called from the large fresco by J. R. Herbert, R.A., showing Moses bringing down the Tablets from Mount Sinai.

MOTHER OF PARLIAMENTS

A term often applied to the British Parliament as the progenitor of all other Parliaments. The expression was originally applied to the English nation by John Bright in 1865.

MOTIONS

Proposals made in order to elicit a decision of the House. There are two classes of motions, independent or substantive motions (q.v.)

and dependent or subsidiary motions (q.v.), and a motion once proposed can only be withdrawn by leave of the House. The motion is the form in which debate on any subject must originate, and when a motion has been moved and seconded the Speaker *proposes* the question, in the same terms as the motion, as the subject of debate. The decision of the House is made known by the Speaker *putting* the question at the conclusion of the debate.

A motion must be moved by the member in whose name it stands except in the case of a minister who may move a motion on behalf of another minister. Formerly all motions in the House of Commons required to be seconded with the exceptions of motions to carry into effect an order of the House, motions moved by a Privy Councillor or a minister, motions for unopposed returns (q.v.), and motions moved in Committee of the Whole House (q.v.). As the result of a recent procedural amendment, no motion or amendment now requires to be seconded before the question thereon is put from the Chair, except on ceremonial occasions, such as the occasion of moving an address in reply to the Queen's Speech opening a new session of Parliament.

See also ANCILLARY MOTION; DILATORY MOTION.

MOTIONS FOR PAPERS

Questions or motions of which notice is given in the order paper of the House of Lords may be, and frequently are, the occasion of general debate. If a peer wishes to reserve to himself the right to reply to the debate, he adds at the end of his question the words 'and to move for papers', since, under Standing Order No. 28 of the House of Lords, the mover of any motion has a right of reply. The 'papers' are, of course, mythical and merely provide a *modus operandi*.

Such motions are not normally pressed to a division, and the Committee of the House of Lords on Procedure of the House, reporting in May 1966, recommended that this practice should not be changed. The committee pointed out that the purpose of such a debate is to give the House an opportunity to express its opinion through the speeches made by its members rather than on division. Such motions are regarded as neutral motions, and according to the view expressed by the committee, to press a motion for papers to a division without due notice would be unfair to the House. On the other hand, the committee considered that a peer genuinely seeking documentary information should specify in his motion the kind of papers which he requires and ask the House for positive action in the form of a resolution.

In the Canadian House of Commons a motion for the production of papers is a procedural device frequently used by Private Members desiring access to documents which would not otherwise be tabled. Such a motion is debatable if so desired by the member proposing it

[482]

or by a Minister of the Crown, in which case debate is limited to the desirability or otherwise of tabling the papers concerned.

MULTIPLE VOTE

See PLURAL VOTING.

MUNITIONS, MINISTER OF

Lloyd George was appointed Minister of Munitions in 1915, and was followed by E. S. Montague, Dr. C. Addison (afterwards Lord Addison), and Winston Churchill. The functions of the Minister of Munitions were adopted by the Minister of Supply (q.v.) in the last war, when Canada, Australia, and New Zealand all had ministers responsible for the production of munitions of war.

MURDER IN PARLIAMENT

Disregarding the many unrecorded acts of violence which no doubt took place within parliamentary precincts during the turbulent years of the Middle Ages, the only murder known to have been committed in recent times was on 11 May 1812, when the Prime Minister, Spencer Perceval, was assassinated by a man named Bellingham, who fired a pistol at him as he was entering the Lobby of the House of Commons. The spot where the assassin stood is now covered by the statue of Burke.

In September 1958 the Deputy Speaker of the East Pakistan Legislative Assembly died as a result of injuries received when assaulted in the Chamber by some Members of the Opposition. On 1 September 1965 the Speaker of the Aden State Legislative Council was shot dead by terrorists, although this outrage was committed outside the precincts of the legislature.

Perhaps the most sensational case of a murder within parliamentary precincts was the assassination on 6 September 1966 of the late Prime Minister of South Africa, Dr. H. F. Verwoerd, who was stabbed to death as he sat on the Government front bench in the House of Assembly by a man employed as a parliamentary messenger.

MUTINY BILL

See ARMY ACT.

N

'NAMING' A MEMBER

If a Member of the House of Commons defies the authority of the Chair by refusing to withdraw offensive language or in some other way abuses the rules of the House, he can be directed by the Speaker or Chairman to leave the Chamber for the remainder of the day's sitting. If the member refuses and is persistent in his disregard of the Chair, the Speaker refers the matter to the House by rising and saying, 'I must name the Hon. Member for . . ., Mr. . . ., for disregarding the authority of the Chair.' The Leader of the House then moves that the Member be suspended from the service of the House, and the motion must be put to the question 'without amendment, adjournment or debate'.

If the member is named in Committee of the Whole House by the Chairman, the latter immediately suspends the proceedings and reports the circumstances to the House when the Speaker has resumed the Chair. From this point matters proceed as described above.

If the House agrees to the suspension, the Speaker again directs the member to withdraw and, if he still persists in refusing to do so, even when summoned under the Speaker's orders by the Serjeant-at-Arms, force is resorted to. If this is necessary, the Speaker calls the attention of the House to the fact, and in such a case the suspension of the member is for the remainder of the session. The normal period of suspension is now fixed at five sitting days for the first offence and twenty for the second, the uncompleted portion of the sitting during which the offence was committed counting as one day. The first offence is taken to mean the first during that session.

A member who is suspended is not exempt from serving on a Private Bill Committee but, apart from this exception, suspension from the service of the House of Commons means exclusion from the precincts of the Palace of Westminster.

A similar procedure is adopted in other Commonwealth Parliaments for the punishment of offenders.

A member guilty of a breach of privilege or contempt may be suspended without being named, but in such a case the motion for his suspension would be subject to debate. The practice of 'naming' a member was first introduced by Speaker Lenthall (q.v.) in 1641.

The procedure which follows upon the 'naming' of a member clearly asserts the ultimate authority of the House in matters of discipline. It also places a clear obligation upon the House to take certain action after a member has been 'named', and a serious reflection on the Chair would be involved should the House decline to carry the motion for suspension. Until this procedure was codified by Standing Order there was some doubt as to the consequences which should follow the 'naming' of a member, since the function of the Speaker was merely to draw the attention of the House to the member's misconduct. When the question was put to Speaker Arthur Onslow he is said to have replied, 'The Lord in Heaven only knows!'

NATIONAL DEMOCRATIC PARTY

An offshoot of the Labour Party, including a number of prominent trade union leaders, which was formed in 1918 to support the continuation of the Lloyd George Coalition Government. In the 1918 General Election (the 'Coupon' Election) 10 of its 28 candidates were elected. One of these reverted to the Labour Party, and the brief history of the N.D.P. ended with the defeat of the other 9 by Labour candidates in the General Election of 1922. Thus passed away the predecessor of the National Labour Party (q.v.) of 1931, which was to perish hardly less ingloriously in its turn.

NATIONAL EXPENDITURE COMMITTEE

See ESTIMATES COMMITTEE.

NATIONAL INSURANCE, MINISTER OF

See SOCIAL SECURITY, MINISTER OF.

NATIONALIZED INDUSTRIES, SELECT COMMITTEE ON

See SELECT COMMITTEE ON NATIONALIZED INDUSTRIES.

NATIONAL LABOUR PARTY

The party that followed Ramsay MacDonald when he accepted the leadership of a National Government of all parties formed in 1931 as a result of the economic crisis. The Labour Party regarded his action as a betrayal, and only 15 of them became members of the National Labour Party. Three of MacDonald's former Cabinet colleagues, Snowden, Sankey, and J. H. Thomas, agreed to join the National Government. In the General Election which followed in October 1931 only 13 (out of 20) National Labour Party candidates were returned to Parliament among the 554 who supported the National Government. The National Labour Party was really a party of leaders with no followers, and after the 1935 election only 8 of its members were left in Parliament, with Thomas as the sole survivor of the Labour Cabinet seceders of 1931. MacDonald was defeated but was returned as M.P. for the Scottish Universities in 1936 and died the following year. Thomas resigned in 1936 following a leakage of Budget information, and after that the National Labour Party quietly faded away.

NATIONAL LIBERAL PARTY

The Liberals had always strongly advocated Free Trade, but the economic crisis of the 1930's raised doubts among some of them as to whether this doctrine could always be strictly adhered to. These Liberals decided to support the MacDonald National Government and the 10 per cent *ad valorem* general tariff, and in four days a new party was organized and staffed under the leadership of Sir John Simon (afterwards Viscount Simon). The party called itself 'Liberal National' to distinguish it from the National Liberal Federation, but its supporters were often referred to as 'Simonites' or 'Simonite Liberals'. In the 1931 General Election the Liberal Nationals secured 35 seats, and in 1935 32 seats in Parliament. In 1936 the National Liberal Federation, which was the Liberal federation of constituency associations, was dissolved and its place was taken by the Liberal Party Organization. This removed the Simonites' objection to the name 'National Liberal', and after the Second World War the Liberal National Party became the National Liberal Party. Also in 1936 the party held its first representative conference, and although its leaders insisted that they were remaining true to Liberal principles while supporting the National Government, their protestations could not undo the effect of a prophetic remark made by Mr. Baldwin just before the conference, that the Liberal Nationals would inevitably be drawn into the Tory Party in course of time. The 1945 election saw 13 National Liberal candidates returned, and in 1946 the party approached the Liberals with a view to reuniting with them. The Liberals insisted that reunion could only be acceptable on the understanding that the combination would be opposed to both Labour and Conservatives, and as the National Liberal Party could not agree to this stipulation they entered into an agreement with the Conservatives in 1947 for a closer relationship. This was known as the Woolton–Teviot Agreement, from the names of the Chairmen of the respective party organizations. By this agreement combined constituency associations were formed, and after the 1950 election the National Liberals and other Conservative supporters, i.e., the Conservative and National Liberals, Conservative and Liberals, National Liberal and Conservatives, and Liberal and Conservatives, formed a National Liberal Unionist Group in the House of Commons, with its own Chairman and Whip. At the 1951 election 20 Liberal Unionists were returned to Parliament, 22 in the 1955 General Election, and 19 in the 1959 General Election. Thereafter a tendency developed among the National Liberals to merge themselves more completely with the Conservatives. In the 1964–6 Parliament the number of Conservative supporters using the National Liberal label had dropped to 6. Of the

Conservative members elected in March 1966 two sat as National Liberal and Conservative and one as Conservative National. None of the Conservatives elected at the General Election of 1970 carried anything other than a straight Conservative label.

NATIONAL SERVICE, MINISTER OF

Neville Chamberlain was appointed Director-General (he was not then a Member of Parliament) of the Ministry of National Service when Lloyd George became Prime Minister in 1917. Later Sir Auckland Geddes was appointed Minister, which office he held until the Ministry was abolished in 1919. Until the appointment of a Minister, Arthur Henderson, a Minister Without Portfolio, represented the Ministry in the House of Commons. From 1939 to 1959 national service was the concern of the Minister of Labour under the title of Minister of Labour and National Service.

NAURU LEGISLATURE

The island of Nauru, formerly administered under a trusteeship agreement with the United Nations by Great Britain, Australia and New Zealand (Australia being the administering power), became an independent Republic on 31 January 1968. The Constitution, which is unusual in a number of respects, provides for a President and a Legislature, the President being both head of State and head of the Executive. The President is himself a member of the Legislature and is elected by its members for a maximum period of three years. He appoints 4 or 5 members of the Legislature who with himself constitute the Cabinet which is collectively responsible to the Legislature.

The Legislature consists of 18 members representing 8 constituencies, a quorum being 9, and has a statutory life of not more than three years. The head of state is not, as is generally found under the British parliamentary system, considered to be one of the component parts of the Legislature. The legislative functions usually performed by a head of state are performed by the Speaker, although the concurrence of the President is required in the case of proroguing and dissolving Parliament. The Speaker exercises only a casting vote in the House, as is usual in Commonwealth Parliaments.

Should the Legislature pass a vote of non-confidence in the Cabinet, an election for the President must take place immediately, and if not completed within seven days, the Legislature is automatically dissolved.

The Constitution in addition to making provision for the President, the Executive, the Legislature and the Judicature contains a number of special features. It makes elaborate provisions for the Public Service, provides that only persons native to Nauru (with certain exceptions) may qualify for citizenship, and protects the revenues derived from

[487]

the phosphate deposits which form the mainstay of the island's economy. The Constitution also incorporates a Bill of Rights based on the pattern which has become standard among the recently independent countries of the Commonwealth. The Constitution may be amended by a two-thirds majority of the Legislature, although a referendum is also required where certain provisions of the Constitution are concerned. An interval of 90 days must occur between the introduction and the passing of a Bill to amend the Constitution.

Nauru has been granted special membership of the Commonwealth which confers all the normal privileges of membership except representation at meetings of Commonwealth governments.

NEW BRUNSWICK LEGISLATIVE ASSEMBLY

The government of New Brunswick is vested in a Lieutenant-Governor assisted by an Executive Council and a Legislative Assembly of 58 members (increased from 52 in 1967) elected for 22 constituencies returning 1, 2, 3, 4 and 5 members. Election is by popular vote and the life of a Legislature is five years unless sooner dissolved. Until 1892 the legislature was bicameral. The Province, which is one of the original members of the Canadian Confederation, sends 10 members to the Canadian Senate and 10 to the House of Commons.

NEWFOUNDLAND HOUSE OF ASSEMBLY

Sir Humphrey Gilbert took possession of Newfoundland in 1583 in the name of Queen Elizabeth I, and it became in 1610 the first territory to be colonized by the English. The first representative Assembly met in 1833, and in 1855 responsible government was granted with a bicameral legislature and Dominion status in 1917. In 1933 Newfoundland requested the U.K. Government to appoint a Royal Commission to investigate the financial situation, which recommended that until the island became self-supporting again the existing Constitution should be suspended and a Commission of Government established. In 1934 6 Commissioners were appointed, 3 from Newfoundland and 3 from the U.K., under the chairmanship of the Governor, and parliamentary government was suspended. The U.K. Government announced in 1945 that a National Convention would study and discuss the financial and economic situation of the island and make recommendations as to its future government. Forty-five members were elected to the Convention in 1946, and in 1948 it proposed that a referendum should be held to decide between confederation with Canada, the continuation of the Commission for five years, and responsible government as it existed in 1933. It became necessary to hold two referenda, as in the first held in June 1948 no one form of government received a clear majority of votes. The Commission received the fewest votes, however, and when a second referendum was held in July on the other two alternatives, the decision was for confederation. This accordingly took place on 31 March 1949, and Newfoundland became the tenth Province of Canada. The upper House was dropped when the legislature was revived and the Government now consists of the Lieutenant-Governor, an Executive Council of the Premier and 10 ministers, and the House of Assembly, whose membership now stands at 42. There are 41 constituencies, 1 of which returns 2 members. The Coast of Labrador became part of Newfoundland an an additional constituency after confederation. Procedure is based on that of the House of Commons of Westminster, but a reform of the rules is currently under consideration. Speaking at a Speakers' Conference in Ottawa in September 1966, Newfoundland's Speaker said that some of the proposed revisions were based on recent changes which have been implemented in the Australian Parliament (q.v.). An unusual feature of the House of Assembly is that the Government sits on the left of the Speaker. Newfoundland now has universal adult suffrage, the Terms of Union with Canada having extended the suffrage to women at the age of twenty-one (previously twenty-five).

Newfoundland sends 7 members to the Canadian House of Commons and 6 Senators to the Senate.

The House of Assembly chamber is now housed in an administrative building newly constructed in the capital, St. John's.

NEW MEMBER, INTRODUCTION OF

See INTRODUCTION OF A MEMBER.

NEW PALACE YARD

After Westminster Hall (q.v.) was completed in 1098 under William Rufus the open space outside its main entrance was called New Palace Yard to distinguish it from Old Palace Yard (q.v.). During the nine hundred years of its history New Palace Yard has been the scene of many strange and tragic events. Many famous historical figures have passed through it to face trial in Westminster Hall, and many an offender, including Perkin Warbeck and Titus Oates, has been exposed in the pillory which was once a feature of the Yard.

NEW PARTY

Founded by Sir Oswald Mosley in 1931 to put forward a solution to the economic crisis which the Government had not been able to accept. It was joined by 5 other Members of the House of Commons, but at the General Election later in the year all its 24 candidates were defeated. The party was already defunct when its founder went over to Fascism in 1933.

Recent attempts by Sir Oswald Mosley to re-enter active political life since 1959, as a Union Movement candidate advocating a restrictive policy towards coloured immigration, have been consistently frustrated by the electorate.

NEW SOUTH WALES PARLIAMENT

New South Wales became a British possession in 1770, and from 1788 until 1824 was administered by a Governor. The latter year saw the appointment of a Council of not more than 7 or less than 5 members to advise the Governor. In 1828 the Council was increased to 15 members—though still nominated by the Crown—and the Governor still retained the exclusive right to initiate legislation, although petitions could be presented to him praying for the enactment of laws. After the cessation of transportation of convicts in 1842, a Legislative Council of 36 members, with 24 elected by the colonists, was constituted and first met in 1843. The Governor ceased to preside over the Council, which elected its own Speaker, subject to the Governor's approval. In 1851 New South Wales lost part of its territory to form a new State —Victoria—and as some recompense was granted responsible government with a nominated Legislative Council and an elected Legislative Assembly. In this connexion it is interesting to note that New Zealand and all the Australian States, with the exception of Western Australia, were once part of the Colony of New South Wales. The new Parliament first met in 1856 and the secret ballot was introduced two years later. Universal suffrage was achieved when women were given the vote in 1902, and compulsory voting was introduced in 1930. In 1934 the Council was reconstituted and became an elective House, the electors being the members of the Council and Assembly. Membership is now for twelve years, 15 of the 60 members being elected every three years by a system of proportional representation. Before this change the President of the Council was appointed by the Governor, but he is now elected by the Council itself. The question of abolishing the Council has been under consideration in New South Wales, and legislation providing for a referendum on the matter was declared constitutionally valid by the State Supreme Court in September 1960. The referendum was held in April 1961, and the Government's campaign for abolition was defeated by a majority of 286,681 out of 1,941,084 votes recorded, voting being compulsory. The Legislative Assembly was enlarged in 1949 from 90 to 94 members, who are elected for the three-year term of each Parliament. Under an Act passed in 1950, no Bill extending the life of a Parliament beyond three years may be presented to the Governor for assent unless the Bill has been approved by a referendum of the people. There are a number of variations in the procedure of the New South Wales Parliament from that of the United Kingdom, such as the Speaker being elected in a new Parliament *after* the swearing-in of the members. Practice in regard to motions varies considerably, and the procedure on Private Bills, which have become almost un-known in New South Wales, is entirely different from that of the House of Commons. For a comparative study of these points refer to Walcott, *Report on practice etc. of the House of Commons* (Government Printer, Sydney, 1948).

Parliament House in Sydney was originally part of the old General Hospital buildings. It was appropriated in 1829 for the second session of the Legislative Council. This building, with additions and alterations, has housed the legislature ever since. The last extensive rebuilding was put in hand between 1934 and 1936, when the Council Chamber was also re-lined and air-conditioned and extra rooms were provided for members.

NEW ZEALAND PARLIAMENT

In 1852, twelve years after New Zealand had been formally annexed to the British Empire, the United Kingdom Parliament passed the New Zealand Constitution Act, which provided for a General Assembly consisting of the Governor, a Legislative Council, and a House of Representatives. The first meeting of Parliament was in May 1854, but the shadow of the Colonial Office was still upon it, and there was a strong demand from Members of the lower House for the removal of the old-time officials from office so that the administration would be entirely in the hands of the ministers responsible to Parliament. The United Kingdom agreed to this in 1855, and responsible government was introduced a year later. An Act amending the Constitution Act was passed in 1857 giving the Assembly power to amend, alter, suspend, or repeal, with certain exceptions, any of the provisions of the 1852 Act. The Constitution also provided for Provincial Councils, but they were abolished in 1876. The Statute of Westminster (q.v.) was adopted by New Zealand in 1947.

The General Assembly now comprises the Governor-General, representing the Queen, and the House of Representatives. The Legislative Council, or upper House, was abolished in 1950 because the Government came to the decision that it performed no useful function. The way was left open for its restoration, however, at such time as this should become desirable. Parliaments in New Zealand were first elected for five years, but since 1881 the term has normally been for three years, following the passing of the Triennial Parliaments Act in 1879. The New Zealand Constitution provided for not more than 42 nor less than 24 members to be elected to the House of Representatives, and the first popular Chamber, elected in 1853, had 37. With the growth of the country the number of members has progressively increased, and there are now 84, increased from 80 in 1969, including 4 Maori members. A quorum is 20, including the Speaker. As there are over 40 Departments of State most Cabinet ministers carry more than one portfolio. In the execution of the authority vested in him, the Governor-General must be guided by the advice of the Executive Council (Cabinet), but if he does not agree with it he may act in opposition to their opinion. In this case he must report the matter to the Queen and give his reasons for so acting. However, in the political circumstances of the 1970's this power must be regarded as largely theoretical.

Since the abolition of plural voting in 1889 and the introduction of women's suffrage in 1893 all adults have been eligible to vote. The minimum voting age was reduced from twenty-one to twenty in 1969. All registered electors, subject to the usual disqualifications, are eligible for adoption as parliamentary candidates, women becoming qualified in 1919 under the Women's Parliamentary Rights Act.

There was no developed party organization in New Zealand until the 1880's. The Liberal Party emerged in 1890 and introduced laws for the improvement of labour conditions, land reform, the franchise for women, and old-age pensions. The Reform Party which formed a Government in 1912 adopted a conservative policy and stood mainly for the farming interests, but it was defeated by a combination of the United Party and the Labour Party in 1928. The United Party remained in power until the withdrawal of Labour support in 1930, when it formed a Coalition Government with the Reform Party, and in 1935 the Labour Party took office. The Labour Party was defeated in 1949 by the National Party, which was also returned in the two subsequent General Elections. In 1957 the Labour Party was once more returned to power, but was defeated in 1960, 1963, 1966 and 1969.

The procedure of the New Zealand Parliament is based upon that of the House of Commons and, like that of the House of Commons, has recently been revised in certain respects. The following points are of particular interest:

Financial Procedure. In 1968 financial procedure was radically revised, the new procedure closely resembling that which was adopted by the Australian House of Representatives in 1963. The Committees of Supply and Ways and Means and other financial committees of the Whole House have been abolished, together with the requirement that all financial legislation must be founded on resolutions adopted in a Committee of the Whole House. Under the new procedure the main Estimates are conveyed to the House by a Message which recommends an appropriation of revenue. The minister then presents the Appropriation Bill with a motion for introduction and, its title being read by the Clerk, forthwith moves the second reading. The Budget statement is delivered on the second reading of the Bill which provides the occasion for the ensuing wide-ranging debate on public affairs. The Estimates are subsequently debated in Committee of the Whole House on the schedules of the Appropriation Bill, consideration of the clauses being postponed until after all the items in the schedules have been dealt with. An Imprest Supply Bill (i.e., a Bill providing for the grant of interim Supply) is introduced in the same manner and the Standing Orders provide for the moving of an amendment relating to public affairs to the motion for second reading. Supplementary Estimates are introduced in the same manner as the main Estimates and are considered on the schedules of the Bill giving them legislative effect. The motion for second reading of a Bill giving effect to the Supplementary Estimates is now regarded as formal and the House proceeds without debate to the committee stage of the Bill. Provision is made for an enlarged debate to take place on the third reading of such a Bill, the aim being to provide a vehicle for a general debate at the end of a session. Resolutions relating to the Customs and Excise Duty and Sales Tax are introduced without notice and may be debated in the House, each member being restricted to four five-minute speeches. When agreed to, these resolutions stand referred to the Committee on the Bill giving them statutory effect.

Questions. The procedure for questioning ministers is similar to that observed in the British House of Commons, although certain variations may be noted. Notice is required of all questions except in circumstances of urgency, and they are placed on the order paper in the order in which they are received. A member desiring to ask a question without notice on the ground of urgency in the public interest must furnish a copy to the Speaker and the minister concerned, and if the Speaker is prepared to allow it he states its nature to the House, after other oral questions have been disposed of, and the member is permitted to put the question to the minister. Oral questions are distinguished by an asterisk and thirty minutes are allotted to them on Tuesdays, Wednesdays, Thursdays and Fridays. A question which is not reached is placed on the order paper for the next sitting day and is given priority over the questions already set down for that day. Supplementary questions may be asked at the discretion of the Speaker. Provision exists for the transfer to a supplementary order paper of all questions, written and oral, together with their answers should this be requested by a member, and for these to be debated on alternate Wednesdays for one hour.

Time Limits on Speeches. Unless otherwise provided, there is a general time limit of twenty minutes on speeches. An exception is made during financial debates where thirty minutes are allowed. Speeches on Private Members' motions, Emergency Adjournment motions and reports of Select Committees are limited to ten minutes. Speeches on the motion to elect a Speaker are limited to five minutes. Extended periods are allowed to the member in charge of a Bill and the leading speakers in a major debate, and no restriction is applied to the Minister of Finance when he presents his Budget statement.

Select Committees. Bills on certain questions—such as Labour, Agriculture, Local Government, Health, or Maori Affairs—are referred to Select Committees after a pro-forma second reading. Select Committees consist of from 5 to 10 members, selected according to party affiliations. Usually there are 6 from the Government and 4 from the Opposition. Proceedings in Select Committees follow those of a Committee of the Whole House and all Select Committees have power to call for persons, papers, and records; they may also suggest amendments to Bills. The Standing Orders Committee of 1968 recommended that consideration should be given to the establishment of committees specializing in certain subject areas comparable to those appointed in the House of Commons.

Order Papers. The House of Representatives has no Votes and Proceedings but only an order paper which lists Orders of the Day, Notices of Motion, and Questions and papers for consideration. Questions (other than urgent questions) are printed on the following day's order paper. They are transferred each Saturday to a supplementary order paper which is reprinted with the ministerial replies, and circulated on the following Wednesday afternoon for discussion in the House.

Radio Broadcasting. Sound broadcasting of the debates of the House of Representatives was introduced in 1936. Commencing with the session of 1937 continuous broadcasting of the proceedings was instituted. The broadcasts normally cease at 10.30 p.m. but may be extended if the House sits longer.

The present Parliament House, occupying an imposing 5-acre site, comprises three distinct buildings, an old wooden structure completed for the use of the Governor in 1871, the Library wing, erected over fifty years ago, and the main building, which has not been quite completed since work on it was interrupted in 1922. The first of these buildings was partly reconstructed in 1944 and 1952, and new dining-rooms and bars for Bellamy's (q.v.) were erected. An unusual law requires that after the meeting of a new Parliament, the Clerk of the House must conduct a poll on the question as to whether liquor shall be sold and consumed within the precincts of Parliament House. There is usually a large majority in favour of this. The library wing houses the General Assembly Library of about 300,000 volumes. The Library receives two copies of every New Zealand publication under the Copyright Act. The main building contains the Chamber of the House, the former Legislative Council Chamber, ministerial suites, committee rooms, and accommodation for members.

NIGERIAN PARLIAMENT

In February 1966 parliamentary government in Nigeria was suspended following a military *coup d'état* and steps were taken towards the establishment of a unitary form of government. A second *coup* later in the same year overthrew the first revolutionary government and restoration of a federal system was decreed. In May 1967 the Eastern Region announced its decision to secede from the Federation and the ill-fated Republic of Biafra was founded. The Federal Government immediately denounced the move and declared its intention to divide the country into twelve separate regions. A civil war then broke out which came to an end with the collapse of Biafra in January 1970. From the present vantage point there is no means of predicting if and when parliamentary government will be restored in Nigeria. What follows, therefore, is of historical interest only.

On 1 October 1954, while still a Colony, Nigeria became a Federal State, and on 1 October 1960 the Federation of Nigeria became an independent member of the Commonwealth. On 1 October 1963 a republican constitution came into force, and the Governor-General Dr. Nnamdi Azikiwe, who had been the first African to hold this office, became the country's first President. At the outset of its existence as a federation Nigeria had consisted of three Regions, the Northern Region, the Eastern Region and the Western Region. Following a referendum in August 1963 a fourth Region was created, the Mid-Western Region, comprising the provinces of Benin and Delta which had formerly formed a part of the Western Region.

Nigeria's Federal Constitution provided for a federal Parliament and a regional legislature for each Region, all of which were bicameral. The Federal Parliament consisted of a Senate of 44 members and a House of Representatives of 312 members, the latter elected by universal adult suffrage except in the Northern Region where the franchise was limited to males. Each regional legislature consisted of an elected House of Assembly and a nominated House of Chiefs.

A small nominated Legislative Council was established in 1861 in the old Colony of Lagos, which became part of the Colony and Protectorate of Southern Nigeria in 1906, Northern and Southern Nigeria being amalgamated in 1914. This Legislative Council, whose jurisdiction did not extend to the Protectorate, remained in existence until 1922. In that year a new Legislative Council was set up for the Colony and the southern part of the Protectorate which, though it had an official and non-African majority, included the first elected Africans in any legislature of British tropical Africa. This Council, which remained almost unchanged until 1946, had a maximum membership of 46, of whom 27, including the Governor, were officials and 19 unofficials. Of the unofficials 4 were elected Africans, the rest being nominated Europeans and Africans. The Executive Council in the period 1922–46 consisted mainly of officials, but 3 African and 2 European unofficials were added in 1943. As a result of the proposals of the then Governor, afterwards Lord Milverton (Cmd. 6599), a new Constitution was granted to Nigeria in 1946. The principal features were the introduction of Regional Councils for the Northern, Eastern, and Western groups of provinces, and a Legislative Council (16 official and 28 unofficial members) whose competence covered the whole of the territory. In 1951 there were more constitutional changes. The regional legislatures were enlarged and given increased powers; the Executive Council was transformed into a Council of Ministers, as the principal instrument of policy, with 6 *ex-officio* members and 12 ministers (4 from each region); and the Legislative Council became a much enlarged House of Representatives with a majority of elected members.

With the introduction of a new Constitution on 1 October 1954, Nigeria became a Federation with a single-chamber legislature sited in Lagos, the capital and federal territory. The Federal House of Representatives comprised a Speaker appointed from outside the legislature, 3 *ex-officio* members, up to 6 special members appointed by the Governor-General, and 184 elected members comprising 92 for the Northern Region, 42 each for the Western and Eastern Regions, 6 for the Southern Cameroons, and 2 for Lagos. The Council of Ministers comprised the 3 *ex-officio* members and 10 ministers, 3 from each Region and 1 from the Southern Cameroons.

The main effect of the 1954 Constitution was to give greater autonomy to the Regions and to carry them a considerable way towards internal self-government. The greater responsibilities of the regional legislatures was recognized by the appointment of a Governor for each Region in place of the former Lieutenant-Governor, and by replacing the office of Governor of the Federation by that of Governor-General. The Eastern and Western Regions became fully autonomous in 1957 and the Northern Region in 1959.

A constitutional conference held in 1957 and 1958 initiated further constitutional changes which paved the way for Nigeria's attainment of independence in 1960. The Federal Constitution provided for the division of legislative powers between the Federation and the Regions and a charter of fundamental rights which could be amended only by a two-thirds majority of both Houses of the Federal Parliament sitting separately and affirmative resolutions of both Houses of at least two of the regional Parliaments.

The administration of the former trusteeship territory of the Cameroons became separated from that of Nigeria when the latter achieved independence. Shortly afterwards separate plebiscites were held in the Northern and Southern Cameroons which resulted in the former voting in favour of union with Nigeria and the latter opting for union with the Republic of Cameroon. The Northern Cameroons became merged with the Northern Region of Nigeria on 1 June 1961 and was renamed Sardauna Province.

(Further reading for the colonial period: Wheare, *The Nigerian Legislative Council*, 1950.)

NINETEEN PROPOSITIONS, THE

The final terms which Parliament despatched to Charles I on 2 June 1642, before the outbreak of the Civil War. They amounted to a demand that henceforward Parliament and not the King should be the sovereign power of the nation. The main demands were that church government and the liturgy should be reformed in accordance with the wishes of Parliament and the laws against Catholics be enforced; that all appointments to the Privy Council and high offices of state should require the approval of Parliament; that the King should resign the control of the army to Parliament; that judges should hold office during good behaviour; that no new peer should sit or vote in Parliament without the consent of both Houses; and that parliamentary approval be required for those persons appointed to educate the King's children, and for any subsequent marriage of his children.

The King rejected the propositions, describing them as the sort of conditions which are made with a prisoner.

See also CHARLES I AND PARLIAMENT.

NINETEEN TWENTY-TWO COMMITTEE

The Conservative Members' Committee in the House of Commons consisting of the entire back-bench membership of the Conservative Party. The 1922 Committee takes its name from the famous meeting of Conservative members at the Carlton Club in October 1922 which led to the ending of the coalition and the downfall of Austen Chamberlain as Conservative leader in the House of Commons. Prior to 1922 there was no effective back-bench organization of Conservative members in the House of Commons, and the first initiative in this direction was taken when a back-bench committee was formed by a group of new members who were returned in the election immediately following the fall of the coalition. To begin with the committee concentrated on providing guidance for new members, but shortly after its inception all Conservative back-benchers were admitted to membership, and it became the forum of Conservative opinion in the House of Commons and thus to some extent a counterpart of the Parliamentary Labour Party.

To-day the 1922 Committee is a significant force in Conservative Party counsels. The Chairman is a senior back-bencher who enjoys direct access to the party leader and keeps him informed of back-bench opinion. The committee also elects 2 vice-chairmen, 2 secretaries, a treasurer and 12 other members who with the Chairman constitute an Executive Committee which meets regularly before each weekly meeting of the full Committee. Four members of the Executive Committee sit on the Executive Committee of the National Union of

Conservative and Unionist Associations, all Conservative M.P.s being members of its Central Council.

The 1922 Committee is essentially a committee for the discussion of forthcoming business. When the Conservative Party is in office, ministers, even junior ministers, do not attend meetings of the committee except by invitation. The Whips attend but have no voting rights. When the party is in opposition the entire parliamentary membership is entitled to attend, but the leader by custom attends only by special arrangement.

See also CONSERVATIVE PARLIAMENTARY PARTY; CONSERVATIVE PARTY.

NO CONFIDENCE, VOTE OF
See VOTE OF CONFIDENCE.

'NODDING THROUGH'

The House of Commons has an established system of absent voting in divisions which is called 'nodding through', and is intended to relieve the strain upon members who are sick. The member is required to be in the precincts of the Palace of Westminster when the division is called, and a Whip of his own party visits him to be told how he wants his vote recorded. The Whips accept without question the word of their opposite numbers that members 'nodded through' are in the precincts at the time. This arrangement is particularly valuable when the Government has a very small majority, as it enables sick members to be brought to the House by ambulance or car, and their possibly vital votes recorded without their having to leave the vehicle.

NOMINATED MEMBER
See OFFICIAL MEMBER; UNOFFICIAL MEMBER.

NORTH BORNEO
See SABAH.

NORTHERN IRELAND PARLIAMENT

As an attempt to provide some measure of self-government for Ireland, the Government of Ireland Act of 1920 kept the whole country within the framework of the United Kingdom but set up two subordinate governments to deal with purely local affairs, one in Belfast for Northern Ireland (Ulster) and the other in Dublin for Southern Ireland. There was to be a council of representatives from both to discuss and settle matters of common interest, but the Act was ignored by Southern Ireland, which preferred complete separation and a republic. However, elections were held in Northern Ireland in 1921, and the first Parliament was opened by King George V on 22 June in its temporary home, the Presbyterian Assembly's College in Belfast. Although the Governor summons, prorogues, and dissolves Parliament and assents to Bills as in distant countries of the British Commonwealth, Northern Ireland by its Constitution is an integral part of the United Kingdom of Great Britain and Northern Ireland and elects 12 members to the United Kingdom Parliament. The taxation of the province is on the same basis as that in other parts of the United Kingdom and, with the exception of a few local duties, its revenue goes into the United Kingdom exchequer. Also many Acts passed at Westminster apply to Northern Ireland in the same way as to other parts of the United Kingdom, but there is a considerable range of local affairs which have been passed over to the care of the Northern Ireland Government. These are indicated by departments represented by ministers—Finance, Home Affairs, Social Services, Education, Agriculture, Commerce, and Health and Development.

Parliament has two Houses—the House of Commons with 52 members and a Senate with 26 members. Members of the House of Commons are elected for five years by universal adult franchise (women were enfranchised in 1928) from single-member constituencies. Twenty-four members of the Senate are elected by the House of Commons by proportional representation for eight years, and half the seats fall vacant at the end of every fourth year. The other two senators hold their seats by virtue of their office—the Lord Mayor of Belfast and the Mayor of Londonderry.

A number of important electoral reforms took effect prior to the General Election of February 1969. A permanent Boundary Commission was established to review constituency boundaries which, despite significant shifts in population, had not been changed in over thirty years. The 4 university seats, representing Queen's University, Belfast, were abolished and 4 new seats were created in their place which enabled the representation of populous areas to be more evenly distributed. The business franchise, which allowed an additional vote to the owner of business premises, was also abolished.

Parliamentary procedure is very similar to that of the Westminster House of Commons, but as a result of the very much smaller membership of the Northern Ireland Parliament there is one important difference. A minister can introduce Bills, answer questions, or make statements in both Houses, although he will be a member of one only—most ministers are members of the House of Commons. A minister without any departmental duties who is a member of the Senate is sometimes appointed to represent the Cabinet in the Senate and to act as Leader of the House.

[499]

Parliament House stands on a hillside in a 300-acre estate at Stormont five miles south-east of Belfast, the capital of the province. The building, where Parliament first met in 1932, was presented by the Imperial Government, and is one of the most beautiful and impressive legislatures in the Commonwealth. It is designed in the Greek Classical tradition, and the sculpture around the building is particularly fine. There are four main floors, and the whole structure is 365 feet by 164 feet and 70 feet high, rising to a height of 92 feet at the centre of the main façade. The decorative character of the ceilings and the lighting effects of the Great Hall (100 feet by 48 feet) and the two Chambers are outstanding features of the building.

(Further reading: Mansergh, *The government of Northern Ireland*, 1936.)

NORTHERN RHODESIA

See ZAMBIA PARLIAMENT.

NORTHERN TERRITORY LEGISLATIVE COUNCIL

Transferred by South Australia to the Commonwealth of Australia in 1911, the Northern Territory was governed by an Administrator from 1931 until the Council was inaugurated in 1948. It consists of the Administrator as President, 6 official and 11 elected members. An Act of 1968 amended the composition of the Legislative Council by abolishing the seats of 3 nominated unofficial members and substituting elected members in their place. All ordinances require the assent of the Administrator, and whether assented to or disallowed must be laid before the Commonwealth Parliament. Both the Governor-General and the Administrator may refer ordinances back to the Legislative Council for reconsideration or with suggested amendments. Money votes may be proposed only by the Administrator, or by his permission or direction. The Governor-General may withhold assent from part of an ordinance, the advantage of this procedure being that an unacceptable provision may be disallowed without necessitating a veto on the ordinance as a whole.

The Administrator's Council, which is concerned with the executive government of the Territory, consists of the Administrator, 2 official, 2 elected and 2 nominated unofficial members.

In 1955 the Council occupied a new and permanent Chamber and offices in Darwin, erected on the site of a post office building which was destroyed by Japanese bombers in 1942. The Northern Territory elects one member to the Federal House of Representatives. Since 1968 he has enjoyed full voting rights, whereas previously, although he was permitted to participate in all debates, he had no vote in the House except on matters directly affecting his own constituency.

NORTHSTEAD, MANOR OF

See CHILTERN HUNDREDS.

NORTH-WEST TERRITORIES COUNCIL

The North-West Territories of Canada comprise those parts of the country east of the Yukon and north of the 60th parallel with the exception of the northern part of the Province of Quebec and a small portion of Newfoundland. The Territories, which consist of the districts of Mackenzie, Keewatin and Franklin, do not as yet have provincial status and their administration is directly controlled by the Canadian Government. Under the North-West Territories Act the government is vested in a Commissioner and a Territorial Council with certain legislative powers. The Commissioner is appointed by the Canadian Government and receives his instructions from the Governor-General-in-Council, and specifically from the Minister of Indian Affairs and Northern Development. The Territorial Council consists of 12 members, of whom 5 are appointed by the Governor-General-in-Council (including the Deputy Commissioner) and 7 are elected. 4 of the elected members represent the 4 constituencies which comprise the district of Mackenzie, and 3 (who were added in 1966) are elected by the voters, mainly Eskimoes, of the districts of Keewatin and Franklin. In 1965 an Eskimo was appointed to the Council for the first time. The Commissioner and the Council carry out their legislative functions in much the same manner as the Lieutenant-Governor and the Legislature of a Province.

The North-West Territories are represented in the Canadian House of Commons by 1 member.

NOTICE OF MOTION

A member intending to introduce a motion is normally required to give notice to the House of his intention.

See also MOTIONS.

NOTICE PAPER

That part of the Vote (q.v.) which includes questions (q.v.) put down for future days, Notices of Motions (q.v.), notices of amendments to Bills, and notices of committees which are to meet that day.

NOVA SCOTIA LEGISLATIVE ASSEMBLY

After the confederation of the Canadian Provinces in 1867, Nova Scotia continued with its bicameral legislature, the upper House, the Legislative Council, having 21 nominated members. This was abolished in 1926 after having been in existence for 170 years. The government of the Province is now vested in a Lieutenant-Governor, an Executive Council under the presidency of the Premier, and a Legislative Assembly of 46 members, increased from 43 in 1967. There are 43 constituencies, 3 of them returning 2 members each, and the term of a legislature is five years unless sooner dissolved. Nova Scotia sends 10 members to the Canadian Senate and 11 to the House of Commons.

(Further reading: Beck, *The Government of Nova Scotia*, 1958.)

O

OATHS

Every member elected to a seat in the House of Commons must, before taking his seat, take the oath of allegiance or make the affirmation required by law. At one time Members of Parliament had to take three oaths—the oaths of supremacy, of allegiance, and of abjuration. By an Act of 1679 the oaths of supremacy and allegiance, formerly taken before the Lord High Steward, were required to be taken by the Lords and Commons at the Tables of their respective Houses. The oath of supremacy was a repudiation of the spiritual or ecclesiastical authority of any foreign prince, person, or prelate, and of the doctrine that princes deposed or excommunicated by the Pope might be murdered by their subjects. The oath of allegiance was a declaration of fidelity to the Sovereign, and the oath of abjuration introduced in 1702 was a repudiation of the right and title of descendants of James II to the throne. To these was added a declaration against transubstantiation, which with the oath of supremacy effectively barred Roman Catholics from Parliament, while the oath of abjuration, which concluded with the words 'on the true faith of a Christian', could not be taken by a Jew. The Roman Catholic Relief Act of 1829 provided an oath acceptable to members of that church and also abolished the declaration against transubstantiation, while Jews were enabled to sit in the House after the passing of an Act in 1858 permitting the omission of the words 'on the true faith of a Christian' in individual cases. In the same year a single form of oath was prescribed instead of the former three, and by the Parliamentary Oaths Act of 1866 the words which caused the difficulty were omitted from the statutory form required.

By Acts passed in 1678, 1701, and 1714 severe penalties were inflicted on members of either House who sat or voted without taking the oath, and by the 1866 Act the offence incurs a penalty of £500. In the Commons, however, it is necessary to move a new writ immediately the omission is discovered, as the member's seat is vacated. The Chiltern Hundreds (q.v.) may be accepted before the oath is taken, and a member is entitled to all his other privileges (but not to his salary).

At the opening of a new Parliament the Speaker is the first to take the oath after his election and return from the House of Lords. He is followed by the members, but the oath must be taken or affirmation made with a full quorum of members in the House. The Promissory

R

Oaths Act, 1868, substituted for various earlier forms the oath which is now in the following form: 'I . . . do swear that I will be faithful and bear true allegiance to Her Majesty Queen Elizabeth, her heirs and successors, according to law. So help me God.'

On the accession of a new Sovereign members of both Houses again take the oath, although on the authority of Sir D. Somervell the obligation ceased to be statutory in the 18th century and has since been continued by custom of Parliament. Ministers on appointment take the oath of allegiance and the official oath. The form of the latter is: 'I . . . do swear that I will well and truly serve Her Majesty Queen Elizabeth in the office of. . . .'

See also AFFIRMATION; BRADLAUGH, CHARLES.

OFFICE OF PROFIT UNDER THE CROWN

In the time of James I the House of Commons insisted that an office the duties of which entailed prolonged absence from the House was inconsistent with a seat therein, and various Bills were introduced after the Restoration to exclude executive officers in order to diminish the influence of the Crown over Parliament. By the end of the 18th century the principle was also established that the control or influence of the executive government over the House by means of an undue proportion of office-holders being members should be limited. Commissioners of Stamps and Excise were excluded from membership of the House by statutes of 1694 and 1699, but the principle of the exclusion of what subsequently became the Civil Service was established by the Succession to the Crown Act of 1707. Apart from the statutory limitation on the number of ministers that can be appointed, the Re-election of Ministers Acts of 1919 and 1926 removed the necessity for a member appointed to a 'political' office to seek re-election. The acceptance of an 'office of profit', such as the stewardship of the Chiltern Hundreds (q.v.), enables a member to resign his seat, which according to a settled principle of parliamentary law he could not otherwise do. Even where an office has no salary or profits attached, acceptance of it could vacate a seat. A recent example of this was the disqualification of the member elected in a Mid-Ulster by-election in August 1955, but such members are indemnified by a special Act from the heavy fines incurred by sitting and voting illegally. The House of Commons Disqualification (Temporary Provisions) Act, 1941, allowed the appointment of a member to an 'office of profit' if the Prime Minister certified that it was necessary to the war effort. The debates on this Bill brought into prominence the fact that, to quote Sir Winston Churchill, 'the whole of this question of offices and places of profit is in a state of great legal complexity and obscurity'. The result was the appointment of a Select Committee (the Herbert Committee) which recommended legislation to reform and consolidate the law on this subject. Fifteen years later the House of Commons Disqualification Bill was introduced and closely followed the recommendations of the Select Committee. The consolidation of the existing law involved the repeal or partial repeal of 118 Acts, and the schedules to the Bill help to clarify the position by actually listing the offices disqualifying for membership and those which do not. The Bill was passed by the House of Commons without a division, and received the Royal Assent in 1957.

See also DISQUALIFICATION FROM MEMBERSHIP OF PARLIAMENT.

OFFICIAL MEMBER

A member of a colonial legislature (q.v.) who is nominated by the Governor from the public service of the Colony. Official members, together with *ex-officio* members, should be distinguished from the representative or unofficial members of a colonial legislature.

OFFICIAL REPORT OF DEBATES

See HANSARD; PARLIAMENTARY DEBATES.

OLD PALACE YARD

Surrounded by houses in medieval times, in one of which lived Geoffrey Chaucer, Old Palace Yard is now the space on the west side of the Palace of Westminster (q.v.) where the equestrian statue of Richard I by Marochetti is situated. A bomb which fell here during the Second World War blew out the south window of Westminster Hall (q.v.) and bent, but did not break, King Richard's sword.

Sir Walter Raleigh and Guy Fawkes were amongst the unfortunate victims executed in Old Palace Yard, so called to distinguish it from New Palace Yard (q.v.).

OLD PARLIAMENTARY HISTORY

A compilation published as the Parliamentary or Constitutional History of England to the Restoration, in twenty-four volumes, including index, 1751–62. It was the work of a number of hands but was published without the name of any editor. The bulk of the work relates to the Commonwealth and Restoration periods, and it is a valuable work of reference, albeit a defective one. It was one of the sources used by Cobbett and Wright in compiling the Parliamentary History (q.v.).

OMBUDSMAN

See PARLIAMENTARY COMMISSIONER FOR ADMINISTRATION.

'ONE MAN, ONE VOTE'

This phrase, adopted as a slogan by the advocates of parliamentary reform (q.v.), was coined by Major Cartwright, a famous Radical Member of the House of Commons in the first quarter of the 19th century.

ONSLOW, ARTHUR (1691–1768)

Speaker of the House of Commons from 1728 to 1761 and a member from 1720. It is probably no exaggeration to describe Onslow as the greatest Speaker ever to preside over the House of Commons. Certainly he set the high standards and traditions which have come to be associated with the office and, in the words of Dasent, 'was the first in the long catalogue to realize the supreme importance of the independence and impartiality of the Chair'. Most of Onslow's predecessors had held, in addition to the speakership, lucrative offices under the Government which had always been regarded as the special perquisites of the occupant of the Chair. By resigning the office of Treasurer of the Navy and contenting himself with the income derived from fees on Private Bills, Onslow raised the speakership above politics, on which high level (with the exception of lapses on the part of his immediate successors) it has remained ever since. Onslow may be regarded as the first of the modern Speakers.

Onslow was a zealous guardian of the privileges of the House of Commons and, to quote Horace Walpole, 'against encroachments of the House of Lords he was an inflexible champion'. Many testimonies exist to his integrity and ability, the dignity and authority with which he sustained his office, and the high regard in which he was held by his contemporaries. He introduced many improvements in the clerical organization of the House of Commons, and it was due to his influence that the House, in 1742, ordered its Journals to be printed.

Onslow retired from the Chair and from the House on 18 March 1761, and took his leave of Parliament with a simple and moving speech in which he expressed what his life's work had meant to him. This speech and the Commons' high tribute to him can be found in the House of Commons Journal (vol. 28, p. 1108). He was the third of the Onslow family to occupy the Chair of the House of Commons, and he held and still holds to-day the record for length of service as Speaker.

ONTARIO LEGISLATIVE ASSEMBLY

The powers and rights of this single-chamber legislature are defined in the British North America Act of 1867. Ontario before Confederation was known as Upper Canada, and afterwards, with the other three original Provinces, ceded certain authority to the Federal Parliament. The Government consists of the Lieutenant-Governor, the Executive Council or Cabinet, and the Legislative Assembly, which has 117 members (increased from 98 in 1963 and from 108 in 1967), who are elected for a term of five years on an adult-suffrage basis. Unlike some unicameral Parliaments which send their Bills to the Governor or Governor-General for the Royal Assent, the Lieutenant-Governor of Ontario signifies it personally in the Legislative Chamber. He has the right either to withhold assent or to reserve the Bill in order to submit it to the Governor-General of Canada for his consideration. In the rare event of his taking either of these actions, his decision is announced to the Legislative Assembly by the Clerk, who also explains the reasons for the Governor's action.

In 1969 a number of important procedural changes were recommended to the Legislature by the Select Committee on Rules and Procedures. Principal among them were the following:

(1) The abolition of a notice requirement for questions and the imposition of a time limit on the question period of one hour on Mondays, Tuesdays and Thursdays and one half-hour on Wednesdays and Fridays.

(2) The revision of the emergency adjournment procedure so as to require a member to give written notice to the Speaker and to permit him to present his case for an emergency debate in a speech of not more than five minutes' duration.

(3) The revision of the committee stage of the legislative process so as to require notice of amendments in Committee of the Whole House, to provide that only those sections of a Bill to which amendments have been proposed shall be called, and to permit the House to proceed directly from second to third reading in cases where no amendments have been proposed.

(4) The revision of Supply procedure so as to limit the amount of time which may be spent considering Estimates in Committee of Supply and to provide for the reference of some departments to one or more Standing Committees on Estimates.

(5) A simplified method of holding divisions in Committee of the Whole House.

(6) The limitation of Private Members' time to twenty hours in a session, to fall between 5 p.m. and 6 p.m. on Mondays as early as possible in the session.

(7) The introduction of a new method of initiating the Debate on the Address, whereby the Premier will move the motion for the Address and deliver a speech in which he will review the affairs of the Province.

A distinctive feature of the Ontario House is the Eton-collared page-boys who are employed as messengers.

Ontario sends 24 Senators to the Canadian Senate and 88 members to the House of Commons.

The main Parliament Building is in the Romanesque style and was completed in 1892. It contains the Legislative Chamber, which was formally opened in 1893, and covers 4 acres of ground. A new east block was completed in 1927 to relieve congestion in the main building.

OPENING OF PARLIAMENT

Early Parliaments were opened in the Painted Chamber (q.v.) until 1536, when the modern practice of opening in the House of Lords seems to have begun. The British Parliament is opened by the Sovereign, who proceeds from Buckingham Palace in the State Coach, escorted by the Household Cavalry, down the Mall and along Whitehall, through lines of troops, to the House of Lords. Here the Queen is met by the Great Officers of State and escorted to the Robing Room, where a procession is formed which passes through the Royal Gallery (q.v.) and the Prince's Chamber (q.v.) to the House of Lords. At the head of the procession are the four pursuivants, Rouge Croix, Bluemantle, Rouge Dragon, and Portcullis, wearing their tabards embroidered with the Royal Arms, followed by heralds and officers of the Court in full dress. The Comptroller and Treasurer of the Household carry white wands, the Private Secretary and the Keeper of the Privy Purse follow in their uniforms; after them come the Lord High Chancellor carrying his Purse which contains the Royal Speech, the Lord President of the Council, and two peers, one holding aloft the Sword of State, the other the red velvet Cap of Maintenance trimmed with ermine. Preceded by the Lord Great Chamberlain and the Earl Marshal walking backwards, the Queen, in her ermine and velvet robe and wearing the Imperial Crown, enters the House of Lords. As she does so the lights are turned up and the entire assembly rises to its feet. It is a brilliant gathering—peeresses in gowns of every hue, wearing tiaras, peers in their scarlet robes, archbishops, bishops, and judges in their ceremonial robes, and the Diplomatic Corps displaying a galaxy of uniforms and sparkling orders. When the Queen has taken her seat on the Throne she says: 'My Lords, pray be seated.' The Speaker and Members of the House of Commons having been summoned by Black Rod, the Lord Chancellor hands the Queen a copy of the Royal Speech (which is, these days, an outline of the legislative programme for the session and is prepared by the Government of the day), which she reads to the assembled Lords and Commons. The Speaker and the Members of the House of Commons then return to their own Chamber, the Queen drives back through cheering crowds to Buckingham Palace, and the glorious pageant disperses.

In the House of Commons the business of the session, after certain formal motions have been agreed to, then begins by the Speaker informing the House of the reasons for their summons by reading the Royal Speech, of which, 'for greater accuracy', he has obtained a copy. But before this happens, the Clerk of the House has risen and given out the title of a Bill—the Outlawries Bill (q.v.). The reading of this Bill affirms the right of the Commons to discuss any business they please, irrespective of what may be in the Royal Speech. The House then proceeds to the debate on the address (q.v.).

An interesting custom which still survives is the searching of the cellars by the Yeomen of the Guard prior to the opening ceremony, a practice which was instituted as a result of the Gunpowder Plot (q.v.).

On 28 October 1958 the ceremony of the Opening of Parliament at Westminster was broadcast for the first time over both the sound and television services of the B.B.C. At the Opening of Parliament on 21 April 1966 television cameras were allowed into the House of Commons Chamber for the first time. (*See also* BROADCASTING IN PARLIAMENT.)

OPPOSED AND UNOPPOSED BUSINESS

Business is said to be opposed if even one member objects to its transaction. In the House of Commons no opposed business may be considered after 10 p.m. on Mondays to Thursdays, and 4 p.m. on Fridays, unless it is Exempted Business (q.v.). Opposed Private Business may not be taken at the special time allotted to Private Business.

See BUSINESS OF THE HOUSE.

OPPOSITION, THE

The importance of the Opposition in the system of parliamentary government has long received practical recognition in the procedure of the Parliaments of the British Commonwealth. Both the name and the fact of 'Her Majesty's Opposition' date from the early days of the 19th century, and the expression has been constantly in use ever since. 'His Majesty's Opposition' was a phrase first used by John Cam Hobhouse (afterwards Lord Broughton) in 1826. The Opposition is the party in the House for the time being in the minority, organized as a unit and officially recognized, which has had experience of office and is prepared to form a Government, with its leader as Prime Minister, when the existing ministry has lost the confidence of the country. The Leader of the Opposition (q.v.) and his 'Shadow Cabinet' (q.v.) sit on the Front Bench on the Speaker's left hand, with their supporters behind them, as from the beginning of the 18th century the front bench on the right of the Speaker came to be reserved for members of the Cabinet and their ministerial colleagues. Under modern conditions it has fallen to the Opposition to discharge what was regarded before the institution of Cabinet Government as the primary function of the House as a whole—the control by criticism of the Government. Its leader is paid a salary charged directly on the Consolidated Fund, which means that he is beyond the reach of the majority vote without formal legislation. It is organized like the Government party and it has its own rights over the time of the House, as apart from being consulted as to the length of time required for discussion on the different stages of Government Bills, the Opposition has by a convention of about fifty years' standing the right to choose the subjects to be debated on the days allotted to Supply and the Bills by which it is finally authorized. The amount of time which is controlled by the Opposition in this and other ways is very substantial. Regarded as a parliamentary institution, it may be claimed for the Opposition that no better system has yet been devised for ensuring that the indispensable function of criticism shall be effectively co-ordinated and exercised in a constructive and responsible spirit. There is a well-known saying of Lord Randolph Churchill's to the effect that the function of the Opposition is to oppose, but its real function is more subtle. It is to act as the responsible outlet for criticism, as the incorruptible searcher after scandals needing exposure, the organized expression of legitimate grievances, and to act as a partly formed, trained, responsible team prepared to take over the reins of Government. To quote Professor Keith, 'The Opposition seeks power to effect the changes it desires, but it does not seek power by means which deny democracy. There are standards of fair dealing which are normally respected, and which, if any party should violate, it endeavours to prove in reality still intact. It follows, therefore, that there must be co-operation, above all in arranging the business of the House. It is not the right of the Government to stifle criticism; it must, therefore, put down for discussion such financial items as the Opposition wish to discuss. It must find time for the discussion of a vote of censure. On the other hand, it expects reasonable aid from the Opposition in dealing with non-contentious business and in arranging the use of Parliamentary time. . . . Co-operation is also sought when issues approach such a crisis that inaction would be dangerous to the public welfare.' It would seem to be established usage now that in moments of supreme national crisis the members of both parties unite in a national coalition, and it also seems established that when the crisis is over the parties should separate into the normal conflicting teams composed of Her Majesty's Government and Her Majesty's Opposition.

ORDER BOOK

In the House of Commons this serves as a programme, as far as has been notified, of the future business of the session. It includes questions, motions, and orders set down for particular days and Notices of Motion for which no day has been fixed. The daily printing of this paper was begun in 1856.

ORDER IN THE HOUSE

See DEBATE, RULES OF; DISORDER IN THE HOUSE; 'NAMING' A MEMBER;
UNPARLIAMENTARY EXPRESSIONS.

ORDER PAPER

The agenda for a day's sitting of the House.
See also VOTE, THE.

ORDERS AND RESOLUTIONS

Both orders and resolutions result from the acceptance of a motion
by the House. An order of the House is an instruction relating to its
domestic affairs, such as a direction to certain members or officers of
the House that a specific action be taken, or a command that a certain
person or persons should appear at the Bar of the House. A resolution
is an expression of the opinion of the House or of its intention to
take a certain course of action. Legislation is sometimes based (invariably in the case of financial legislation) on preliminary resolutions.

On ceremonial occasions, as when an address of condolence or
congratulation is presented to the Sovereign, orders and resolutions
are sometimes declared by the Speaker to have been passed *nemine
contradicente*. The House of Lords on these occasions uses the form
nemine dissentiente. The forms of procedure by which the House
varies its previously expressed opinion are discharge in the case of an
order, repeal in the case of a Standing Order (vacation in the Lords),
recession in the case of a resolution, and an order that proceedings be
null and void. The latter form is adopted when there has been some
irregularity or inadvertence in procedure whereby there is no order
that can be discharged or resolution which can be rescinded, or when
the previous position cannot be restored merely by discharging an
order or rescinding a resolution.

See also FINANCIAL RESOLUTION.

ORDERS IN COUNCIL

An Order in Council is technically a decree of the Sovereign issued
with the advice of her Privy Council. The power to legislate by
Order in Council exists in common law, although in this context it is
now limited to the making of laws for newly conquered or ceded
territories. It is a survival of the days when the right to make laws was
a prerogative of the Crown. It is thus older than Parliament, but it
continues to exist only at the will of Parliament. The existence of a
power to legislate without the immediate control of Parliament

(exercisable by Proclamation and Letters Patent as well as by Order in Council) has, however, been of great importance in the comparatively recent past—as, for example, when the Crown, on the advice of Gladstone's Government, abolished the purchase of Army commissions in 1870, a measure which would never have secured the agreement of the House of Lords had it been introduced in the form of a Bill.

Orders in Council are to-day classed as subordinate legislation and are published with the Statutory Instruments (q.v.). In these days they are usually made in terms of an enabling Act, and are used for a variety of purposes. It has, for example, become customary to issue a new constitution for a colonial or newly independent territory by means of an Order in Council in terms of an enabling Act.

Another method of granting a constitution to an overseas territory is by Letters Patent in terms of the Royal Prerogative, a means which was employed in respect of Southern Rhodesia in 1923 and Malta in 1947. The Order in Council has largely superseded Letters Patent for this purpose, possibly because the latter tends to circumvent Parliament as a means of legislating. Orders in Council made in terms of an Act of Parliament are normally open to objection in either House of Parliament during a specified period, whereas Letters Patent issued by the Crown would be subject to debate only on a substantive motion.

See PRIVY COUNCIL; STATUTORY INSTRUMENTS.

ORDERS OF THE DAY

The ordinary Public Business of the House consists of Orders of the Day and Notices of Motion. The distinction is now in substance one between the stages of Bills or other matters which the House has ordered to be considered on a particular day and new matters brought before the House in the form of motions. Technically it is a distinction between business partly considered and new business, as a motion, when the debate upon it is adjourned, becomes an Order of the Day, and a Bill may still be introduced on a motion. When the Orders of the Day are reached after Questions, the Speaker directs the Clerk to read them without any question being put, and they are thereupon disposed of following the order in which they stand on the Notice Paper (q.v.).

OUTLAWRIES BILL

An obsolete Bill which is given its first reading at the beginning of every session of the House of Commons before the debate on the address (q.v.) but is never proceeded with. The long title of the Bill is 'A Bill for the more effectual preventing clandestine outlawries', but its original purpose remains rather obscure. The first reading of the Outlawries Bill is yet another symbol of the ancient rights and privileges of the Commons, and serves to show that they are not compelled to give priority to the Sovereign's business. The ceremony dates from before 1603.

In 1946 a member attempted to initiate a debate upon the Bill but was ruled out of order by the Speaker. The member, C. S. Taylor, raised a point of order and referred to an occasion in 1749 when Sheridan raised a debate on the first reading of the Bill. On a further point of order, another member, W. J. Brown, supported Mr. Taylor and requested the Speaker to reconsider his ruling 'in the light of precedent, and in the light of the tradition of this House', submitting 'that the purpose of the Outlawries Bill is to insist upon the right of the House to discuss some item or other of its own business before going on to consider the King's Speech'. The Speaker, however, adhered to his original ruling. (*See* Hansard, vol. 430, cols. 3-4.)

See also SELECT VESTRIES BILL.

OVERSEAS DEVELOPMENT, MINISTER OF

Originally created in October 1964 as an office of Cabinet rank, this Minister's department absorbed the former Department of Technical Co-operation which had been set up in 1961. Mrs. Barbara Castle was appointed the first Minister of Overseas Development, having charge of the provision of technical assistance to Commonwealth and foreign countries, including Britain's contributions to United Nations Agencies.

Following a major reorganization of central government implemented in 1970, this Minister's department was brought under the jurisdiction of the Foreign and Commonwealth Office while retaining a separate administrative identity. The Minister of Overseas Development now discharges his functions by delegation from the Secretary of State for Foreign and Commonwealth Affairs and no longer has Cabinet status. The White Paper on the Reorganization of Central Government (Cmnd. 4506) stated the Government's view that ultimate ministerial responsibility for overseas aid should rest with the Secretary of State for Foreign and Commonwealth Affairs, while recognizing that the management of overseas aid was a function distinct from the general conduct of foreign affairs.

OXFORD PARLIAMENT

The fifth and last Parliament of Charles II which met at Oxford on 21 March 1681. The King appointed Oxford as the meeting-place of this Parliament in order to demonstrate his displeasure with the City of London, hoping also for a greater measure of success with his legislators by removing them from the place where his wishes had been consistently opposed. Sixteen peers drew up a petition of protest against the move, praying that Parliament might be allowed to sit, as usual, at Westminster. The King remained adamant, in spite of the fact that the elections had returned a majority to the House of Commons no more likely to prove amenable to his will than the members of the previous Parliament, and he repaired in great state to Oxford on 14 March. The gallery at the Public Schools was adapted for the Lords and the Convocation House accommodated the Commons.

Oxford had also provided the location for some of the earlier Parliaments in our history, but the term 'Oxford Parliament' is generally taken to refer to the last Parliament of Charles II.

P

PAINTED CHAMBER, PALACE OF WESTMINSTER

This was situated in the old Palace of Westminster and was so called because of the medieval paintings on the walls which were revealed when the tapestries were removed in 1800. It was previously known as St. Edward's Chamber, as Edward the Confessor is traditionally supposed to have died there. In the 14th century it was used for the Opening of Parliament and as a meeting-place for the Commons until they moved to the Abbey Chapter House at the end of the century. The Painted Chamber was largely consumed by the fire of 1834, but by means of certain adaptations, including the addition of a new roof, it was converted into a temporary Chamber for the House of Lords.

PAIRING

A system which enables a member who wishes to absent himself to agree with another member from the opposite side of the House to absent himself at the same time, thus neutralizing their votes in any division which might take place during their absence. Members make use of the pairing system not only on specific questions or for one day's sitting alone, but for periods of weeks and months at a time. Consequently two members might have a more or less permanent arrangement to pair. The system is said to have had its origin in the time of Cromwell.

According to Erskine May, although the practice has never been condemned there can be no parliamentary recognition of it, and pairing arrangements are made privately or through the party Whips. The system is not restricted to the lower House, and it is one which is observed in other Commonwealth Parliaments. In the Canadian House of Commons it is customary for a paired member to announce after a division with whom he was paired and to state the manner in which he would have voted had he not been paired.

PAKISTAN PARLIAMENT

A Constituent Assembly for Pakistan, which also functioned as the federal legislature, was set up under the scheme embodied in the Cabinet Mission Plan (Cmd. 6821) dated May 1946 and the Statement on Indian Policy (Cmd. 7136) of June 1947, on the basis of one seat for every million of population. The Dominion of Pakistan came into being on 15 August 1947, and the first meeting of the Assembly was held in Karachi on 23 February 1948. At first there were 69 members, later increased to 79. At the General Election held in June 1955 for Pakistan's second Parliament 80 members were elected, half of whom represented East Bengal and a further 21 the Punjab. At the end of 1954 the Provinces and Princely States in West Pakistan were integrated into a single administrative unit, thus making the country a federation of two Provinces—West Pakistan and East Pakistan, each with its own provincial assembly.

On 2 March 1956 the Governor-General gave his assent to a new Constitution Bill, which provided for a single-chamber legislature (the National Assembly) of 300 members, divided equally between East and West Pakistan, who were elected for five years on the basis of universal adult suffrage. For the first ten years 10 additional seats were to be specially reserved for women, who were to represent five territorial women's constituencies in each of the two Provinces. For a Bill passed by the Assembly to become law it required the President's assent, but if this was withheld it was returned to the Assembly, and if it was again passed, by a majority of two-thirds of the members present and voting, the President was obliged to assent to it.

Pakistan followed India in becoming a Republic. On 23 March 1956 she officially declared herself a sovereign and independent Islamic Republic, with a President as the head of the state, but continuing as a full member of the British Commonwealth and acknowledging the Queen as the head and symbol of this free association of independent nations.

On 7 October 1958 the President issued a proclamation abrogating the Constitution described above, dissolving the National and Provincial Assemblies, dismissing all ministers from office, and proclaiming martial law. This action was taken because the President was convinced that the political parties were responsible for the 'chaotic internal situation'. The riotous scenes in the East Pakistan Assembly during which the Deputy Speaker was fatally injured were one of the reasons for this grave decision.

The first step towards a return to constitutional government was taken in October 1959 with the introduction of a system of 'basic democracies'. This consisted of a five-tier series of Councils. Those at the first tier were responsible for the agricultural, industrial, and community development of each town and village. Those at the second tier were responsible for co-ordinating the activities of the first-tier Councils in their respective areas, while the third tier consisted of District Councils with responsibilities relating to education, health and the general development of the district. Divisional Councils formed the fourth tier while the fifth tier consisted of two Provincial Development Advisory Councils, one for East Pakistan and one for West Pakistan, which co-ordinated the activities of all the subordinate authorities in the Province, formulated development plans, and advised the Central Government on matters pertaining to all the Local Councils. Direct elections took place only at the first-tier level, the Councils at this level being responsible for matters most closely affecting the daily lives of the people. The Councils at the other levels were composed of *ex-officio* members, appointed members and the chairmen of Councils at lower levels.

This system operated until 1962 when a new presidential Constitution was introduced providing for a President having executive authority, a National Assembly of 150 members (75 from each Province) elected by the elected members of the Basic Democracies, and two Provincial Assemblies each having 155 members. Six seats were reserved for women in the National Assembly and 5 in each Provincial Assembly. In 1967 the Provincial Assemblies were increased in size to 218 members, of which 8 seats were reserved for women and 10 were reserved for distinguished persons who had held high office or acquired high academic or professional distinction. Under an Act passed in 1964 an Electoral College of some 80,000 members elected by universal adult suffrage was established to elect the President, the National Assembly and the two Provincial Assemblies. This Electoral College also formed the membership of the Basic Democracies responsible for local government.

In March 1969 martial law was again proclaimed in Pakistan following the resignation of President Ayub Khan and the succession to the presidency of General Yahya Khan, Commander-in-Chief of the Army. In the following July the new President announced the appointment of a Chief Electoral Commissioner to prepare for General Elections within 12 to 18 months and in a broadcast on 28 November 1969 he outlined his plans for the restoration of the parliamentary system and a federal form of government. He announced that General Elections would be held on 5 October 1970 on the basis of 'one man—one vote' for a National Assembly which would have the task of formulating a new Constitution. If the task were not completed within 120 days the National Assembly would be dissolved and a new one elected. He also announced that provincial autonomy would be strengthened and that the one-unit system for West Pakistan would be abolished and its former Provinces restored.

PALACE OF WESTMINSTER (HOUSES OF PARLIAMENT)

Built on the site of the ancient Royal Palace, the Palace of Westminster was the chief residence of the Kings of England from Edward the Confessor to Henry VIII. It ceased to be a royal residence after St. James's Palace was built in 1532, but to this day it remains a Royal

Palace. There is evidence that Parliaments were held at Westminster from quite early times. As soon as a royal residence was established there, it was necessarily the meeting-place of the King's Council; but the King maintained several other palaces, and it was only when Westminster became the usual residence of the Sovereign that it became the habitual meeting-place of Parliament.

After the great fire of 1834, which destroyed all the Palace with the exception of Westminster Hall (q.v.), the Crypt, and the Cloisters, the designs of Mr. (afterwards Sir) Charles Barry were accepted for the present building. Construction commenced in 1837, and ten years later the House of Lords was ready for occupation. In 1850 the House of Commons had a trial sitting, and 1852 saw the official opening of the new Palace by Queen Victoria. In 1857 it was completed except for the Victoria Tower (q.v.). It is built of magnesium limestone (from Anston in Yorkshire) which has not stood up to the corrosive effects of the London atmosphere, and extensive replacement and repair were commenced in 1928, held up during the war, and completed in 1953. The east or River Thames front is 872 feet long, including the Terrace, which is 678 feet long and 33 feet wide. The south front from the Victoria Tower to the river is 323 feet in length, and overlooks the Victoria Tower Gardens, while the north side from the Clock Tower (q.v.) to the river is 232 feet long, and overlooks Speaker's Green. This portion of the building is occupied by the official residences of the Speaker and the Serjeant-at-Arms. The Palace covers 8 acres and contains 11 open courtyards, 1,100 rooms, 100 staircases, and 2 miles of corridors. The buildings were damaged by air raids on twelve different occasions between 11 September 1940 and 10 May 1941, and the Commons Chamber, Members' Lobby, most of the Cloisters, and the north side of the Peers' Court were destroyed. The new Commons Chamber was formally opened on 26 October 1950. (*See* HOUSE OF COMMONS, sub-heading *New Chamber*.)

Until April 1965 the entire precincts of the Palace of Westminster were under the control of the Lord Great Chamberlain (q.v.). Under the new arrangement the Lord Chancellor and the Speaker of the House of Commons have assumed control of those parts of the building which are occupied by the House of Lords and the House of Commons respectively. The Speaker is assisted by the House of Commons (Services) Committee (q.v.) and the Lord Chancellor by an administrative committee of the House of Lords. The Lord Chancellor and the Speaker of the House of Commons share with the Lord Great Chamberlain the control of Westminster Hall and the Crypt Chapel. The Lord Great Chamberlain remains in control of the Royal Gallery and the Queen's Robing Room and he retains his functions in the Palace of Westminster on royal occasions, such as the Opening of Parliament (q.v.).

PALGRAVE, SIR REGINALD FRANCIS DOUCE (1829–1904)

Clerk of the House of Commons from 1886 to 1900 and a leading authority on parliamentary procedure. The successor in office to Sir Thomas Erskine May (q.v.), Palgrave did much to ensure the continuity of Erskine May's outstanding work. Together with Alfred Bonham Carter he edited the much enlarged 10th edition (1893) of May's *Parliamentary Practice*, and he was responsible for the 8th, 9th, 10th, and 11th editions of the *Rules, Orders, and Forms of Procedure of the House of Commons*. Palgrave's other publications include *The House of Commons, Illustrations of its History and Practice* (1869, revised edition 1878) and *The Chairman's Handbook, Suggestions and Rules for the Conduct of Chairmen of Public and other Meetings based upon the Procedure and the Practice of Parliament*, first published in 1877 and many times reprinted.

PAPUA AND NEW GUINEA HOUSE OF ASSEMBLY

Papua has been controlled by the Federal Government of Australia since 1901 while New Guinea was first administered by Australia under a League of Nations mandate of 1921, and subsequently under a United Nations trusteeship agreement of 1947. The Papua Act, 1905, under which the political transfer of Papua was completed, also provided for the establishment of a Legislative Council. After the resumption of civil government, which was suspended during the Japanese invasion (1942–5), the two territories, while retaining their own status and identity, were formed into an administrative union with its headquarters at Port Moresby. From 1945 to 1951 power to make ordinances was vested in the Governor-General of Australia, but a new Legislative Council was inaugurated in 1951 under the Papua and New Guinea Act, 1949, of Australia. The Legislative Council consisted of the Administrator as President, 16 official members and 12 non-official members who included 3 elected and 3 native members. The Act also provided for an Executive Council of 9 officials appointed by the Governor-General of Australia.

Following a resolution of the United Nations Trusteeship Council in June 1960 recommending that the rate of political progress should be accelerated in these territories, the Australian Minister of Territories stated that his Government's proposals for political advancement and reform included an increase in the non-official membership of the Legislative Council, and the direct representation of the large section of the indigenous population who were covered by local government councils and were familiar with the process of choosing members to represent them.

In 1960 legislation was enacted in the Australian Parliament increasing the size of the Legislative Council to 37. The Administrator continued to preside, and the other members comprised 14 officials, 12 elected members and 10 appointed unofficial members, one half of the elected members and one half of the appointed unofficial members being natives of Papua and New Guinea. An Administrator's Council consisting of 3 official and 3 unofficial members, at least 2 of whom were elected, replaced the former Executive Council.

The Australian Minister for Territories said at the time that although separate electoral rolls for natives and Europeans had been established it was the intention of the Government to introduce a common electoral roll as a second stage in the constitutional development of Papua and New Guinea. This policy was implemented by legislation in 1963 and, in 1964, the Legislative Council was replaced by a House of Assembly of 64 members of whom 54 were elected. In 1966 the membership was increased to 94. Sixty-nine members are elected by universal adult suffrage and a preferential voting system; the 10 seats previously reserved for non-indigenous residents have been abolished in favour of 15 regional seats which are open to candidates possessing a minimum educational qualification; and the number of official members has been retained at 10.

The former Administrator's Council has been replaced by the Administrator's Executive Council and a limited form of ministerial government has been introduced. The Council consists of the Administrator, 3 official members, 7 ministerial members selected from the elected members of the House, and one elected member nominated by the Administrator.

There are no organized political parties in Papua and New Guinea and, in view of the political immaturity of the indigenous people, the Australian Government launched an instruction programme prior to the 1964 Election under which leading Papuans and New Guineans were given the opportunity to receive education in the theory and practice of parliamentary government.

PARLIAMENT

The word 'parliament' originally meant a talk, and was derived from the French *parler* (to speak or parley) and the Latin *parliamentum*. In the latter form it was applied to the after-dinner conversations held by monks in their cloisters, talk which the monastic statutes of the 13th century condemn as unedifying. The term was also used to describe conferences such as that held between Louis XI of France and Pope Innocent IV in 1245 and the diplomatic parley between Alexander II of Scotland and Richard, Earl of Cornwall, in 1244. Matthew Paris of St. Albans was the first to apply the word 'parliament' to a great council of prelates, earls, and barons in 1239 and again in 1246. From this time on it was used increasingly, though not exclusively, for such an assembly, but the term did not necessarily connote the presence of the Commons. The word having at first signified the talk itself was by degrees transferred to the body of persons who assembled for discussion, and from the reign of Edward I it came to be regularly used in reference to a national assembly.

The British Parliament, often called the Mother of Parliaments, consists of the Sovereign, the House of Lords, and the House of Commons. Together they exercise the legislative functions of government. The entire executive authority resides in the Sovereign, but under the conventional law of the Constitution she acts only upon the advice of her ministers who sit in the two Houses of Parliament. The ministers in turn are responsible to Parliament and through the House of Commons to the electorate. The Crown is restrained by statute from ruling without a Parliament. The power of Parliament is transcendent and its Acts bind every subject, even the Sovereign when specifically mentioned, and no authority other than Parliament can create, amend, or abrogate a statute. The two Houses also exercise a judicial authority as the High Court of Parliament (q.v.) and the House of Lords has been recognized since the reign of Elizabeth I as a Court of Appeal.

The history of the British Parliament may be divided into four main periods: the medieval, the period of evolution, during which Parliament assumed the fundamental form familiar to us to-day, the Model Parliament of 1295 setting the pattern for future Parliaments; the period from 1485 to 1688, when Parliament emerged as an independent body under the Tudors, rose to power under the Stuarts, and finally entered into a triumphant conflict with the Crown; the period between 1688 and 1832 when Parliament became established in its modern rôle and in its constitutional relationship to the Crown; and the modern period from 1832 when the Reform Act reconstituted the House of Commons on a more truly representative basis. The parliamentary history of each reign from that of Elizabeth I to that of Victoria is dealt with under the headings of the Sovereigns concerned (e.g., CHARLES I AND PARLIAMENT). The remainder of this article is devoted to an outline of the earlier history of Parliament.

The origin of Parliament can be traced to the Witenagemot (q.v.) of the Anglo-Saxon Kings, an assembly of the wise men of the realm. It had no definite Constitution, it was not elected, and although it was deemed to be a representative body it contained no element of popular representation as we know it. Nevertheless it was a supreme legislative, administrative, and judicial assembly, it could elect and depose a monarch, and no ancient British King attempted to legislate or impose taxes without its advice and approval. It is thus of great importance to a study of the origins of Parliament. The Norman Conquest brought with it many constitutional changes, notably the introduction of the feudal system, but English laws and customs, and in particular the local political organization of the shires, remained unaltered. The structure of the county court or shiremoot bore a close resemblance to the composition of the national assemblies which were to follow; in fact, Parliament became, in the words of Bishop Stubbs, 'the concentration of all the constituents of the shiremoots in a central assembly'. The sheriff of the county who had always presided at the shiremoot continued to do so after the Conquest, but he became a royal appointee and the local government of the shires thus became directly dependent on the King. The feudalization of land tenure created a supreme landlord in the person of the King himself. All land was held directly or indirectly from the King, the great landowners being the King's tenants-in-chief, their vassals in turn holding land directly under them. All landholders, however small, owed direct allegiance to the King as well as to their immediate overlords. The Norman system of government was a completely despotic one, but most historians agree that it made for national unity and strength. The councils and assemblies which supplanted the Witenagemot were neither legislative nor representative bodies, although they were presumably convened to offer advice to the King when he sought it. The Great Council probably consisted of the King's tenants-in-chief, and other bodies more numerous were called together as the occasion demanded. The supreme council of state which emerged under the Normans was the *Curia Regis* (q.v.), a body which has been the subject of conflicting statements, and which seems to have been derived partly from the Witenagemot and partly from the Norman feudal court. It consisted of the greatest men of the realm and included the great officers of state—justiciar, chancellor, treasurer, etc.—who eventually formed an inner or privy council (q.v.). The various functions of government had not as yet been differentiated and the *Curia Regis* sat in a judicial, legislative, executive, and financial capacity alike. The Anglo-Saxon Chronicle records that the Conqueror attended its sessions: 'Three times every year he wore his crown, as often as he was in England; at Easter he wore it at Winchester, at Whitsuntide at Westminster, and at Christmas at Gloucester, and then there were with him all the powerful men over all England, archbishops and bishops, abbots and earls, thegns and knights.'

The reign of Henry II was of great constitutional importance. This monarch, as just as he was able, initiated the rule of law, and his sagacious reforms provided a foundation for the English Constitution. Although a despot like his predecessors Henry exercised his power for the benefit of the people as he conceived it. He enlarged the *Curia Regis* and called it at frequent intervals, reserving for his own hearing the causes in which it failed to do justice. There was thus formed a court of appeal consisting of the King and council, 'the body,' writes Stubbs, 'from which at later dates the judicial functions of the Privy Council and the equitable jurisdiction of the Chancellor emerged. It is this council which, in conjunction with the elements of Parliament, summoned to meet, but not under the proper parliamentary style, constitutes the *Magnum Concilium* of the next century, from the mixture of whose powers the House of Lords received its judicial character as a court of appeal, and the Privy Council derived its legislative character, which it attempted to carry out in the form of ordinances.' Henry II gave form and permanence to the jury system, and in 1188 when he imposed the famous Saladin tithe for the expenses of a crusade the liability of individuals to be taxed was assessed in each district by a body of local jurors. The Saladin tithe was the first tax to be imposed on personal property and in the method employed for its assessment (implying, as it did, a connexion between taxation and representation) can be detected the first glimmer of the principle of parliamentary control over taxation. The reign of John was, of course, notable for Magna Carta (q.v.), the last great constitutional milestone before the coming of Parliament, which confirmed the supremacy of the law and the principle of consent to taxation.

The growth of representation owes much to that great constitutional reformer, Simon de Montfort, who has been referred to as the creator of the House of Commons, and the reign of Henry III may be said to have heralded the age of Parliament. Throughout his reign Henry was in conflict with the barons and a national assembly called in 1242 was the first to issue a written protest and to have its proceedings formally recorded. From 1246 Parliaments, as they were now coming to be called, were held frequently, until in 1254 two knights from each shire were summoned in addition to the prelates, earls, and barons to attend a Parliament held on 26 April. On 11 June 1258 the so-called Mad Parliament (q.v.) drew up the Provisions of Oxford (q.v.), a determined assault upon regal tyranny, calling for observance of the charters of liberties, the regular summoning of Parliaments, and reserving to Parliament the right of appointing the justiciar, chancellor, and treasurer. It is to the famous Parliament of 1265, called at the instance of Simon de Montfort, that the origin of popular representation can be traced. Although it marked a great step forward in the representative system, representatives of the cities and boroughs being summoned to Parliament for the first time, it was not a constitutional assembly in the modern sense as all the known opponents of de Montfort were excluded. The clergy were well represented (although the Archbishop of Canterbury was a notable absentee), but only 5 earls and 18 barons attended. Its most important feature, however, was the representation of the shires, cities, and boroughs, 2 knights, 2 citizens, and 2 burgesses being summoned from each respectively as well as delegates from the Cinque Ports. Simon de Montfort was killed at the Battle of Evesham later in the same year, and although his death was followed by an immediate recovery of power on the part of the King, his introduction of the principles of constitutional government to a land long oppressed by feudalism set in motion a process which the tyranny of succeeding ages failed to stem. Even in this early stage of our constitutional history there were very definite signs that certain of the principles which were eventually to lead to parliamentary sovereignty were beginning to be recognized. It is significant, for instance, that although Henry III never himself conceded the principle of consent to taxation the barons frequently refused him the aids he demanded and the King never claimed the right of general taxation; and it is like stumbling across an anachronism to discover a 13th-century judge observing that 'the King can do nothing on earth, being a minister of God, but what he can do by law; and law is not any mere will of the prince, but that which is established by the advice of the counsellors, the King giving his authority, and deliberation being had upon it'.

Of supreme importance in parliamentary history was the reign of Edward I, the great legislator. Under him the institutions of our government advanced with a rapidity hitherto unmatched. Edward's first Parliament, to which knights, citizens and burgesses were summoned, met in 1275 and enacted the first Statute of Westminster (q.v.), a just and enlightened measure safeguarding the rights and liberties of the subject. In 1285 was passed the second Statute of Westminster, an important landmark in the history of English law. But the climax in the constitutional history of the reign was reached in 1295 with the summoning of the celebrated Model Parliament (q.v.). It met on 13 November and was called because the King stood in urgent need of money. This Parliament became the model for all future Parliaments. It is generally regarded as the first truly representative assembly of the three estates of medieval society, the clergy, the barons, and the commons. It consisted of the 2 archbishops and all the bishops, the greater abbots, 8 earls, and 41 barons, all of whom received a separate summons; the head of each cathedral chapter, the archdeacons, 1 proctor from the chapter of each cathedral and 2 proctors from the parochial clergy of each diocese, all summoned through their archbishops and bishops; and 2 knights from each shire, 2 citizens from each city, and 2 burgesses from each borough elected by the county court in terms of a writ directed to the sheriff of each county. The national assembly was thus no longer a feudal court in which the qualification for membership was solely one of land tenure, and the Commons had arrived in Parliament to stay. The *Rotuli Parliamentorum* (*see* ROLLS OF PARLIAMENT) which began in 1278 first refer to the Commons in 1304. The King surrendered to the Model Parliament his power of arbitrary taxation and, although subsequently infringed, the parliamentary control of taxation became an accepted constitutional principle from that date. It is interesting to note at this stage the reluctance of the lower clergy to sit in Parliament with the laity, and in the 14th century they ceased to attend altogether. The Commons also showed very little eagerness to be represented in Parliament at the outset, little realizing (as little, indeed, as the King who summoned them) the potential power which was being placed in their hands. In 1382, nearly a century later, a statute was passed compelling the attendance of all who had been summoned, from dukes and archbishops to citizens and burgesses.

The political power of Parliament developed rapidly under the later Plantagenets. At a Parliament called by Edward II on 27 April 1309, the Commons presented to the King a prepared list of grievances which they insisted should be redressed before they would make any grant of Supply. This condition, repeated in subsequent Parliaments, was fully established as a recognized principle before the 14th century had run half its course. In 1322 an important resolution of the three estates affirmed that legislation affecting the entire community should be approved by the representatives of all classes, legislative authority being vested in the King with the assent of the prelates, lords, and Commons assembled in Parliament. In 1327 Parliament recalled a power of the ancient Witenagemot by resolving on the deposition of Edward II in favour of his son. The Parliament was constitutionally summoned, the Great Seal having been obtained from the King, who was being held a prisoner, and the writs of summons issued under it. A deputation delivered Parliament's resolutions to the King, who surrendered the crown and sceptre in token of his resignation. The ensuing reign of Edward III was one of great constitutional development and marked a significant milestone in the history of Parliament in the separation of the two Houses. Since their first appearance in the national assemblies of the realm the knights of the shires, as landowners, had associated themselves with the barons. The greater landowners were distinguished from the lesser by the separate summons which they were entitled to receive, and the title of baron, which originally meant merely a man, came to be confined to the former class. The knights of the shires gradually drew apart from the barons and in the first Parliament of Edward III they threw in their lot with the representatives of the cities and towns. The union thus formed was strengthened by the withdrawal of the lower clergy, and from this time forward the Commons consisted of the knights, citizens, and burgesses sitting together. In the Parliament of 1332 the earls and barons, the prelates, and the Commons each deliberated separately, but the final division of Lords (including prelates) and Commons into two Houses dates from 1341. The necessities of Edward III greatly strengthened the position of Parliament and throughout the reign the two Houses were summoned annually and sometimes even more frequently. The calling of frequent Parliaments continued as a regular practice until the end of the reign of Henry VI.

The most important Parliament of Edward III was held in 1376, towards the end of the reign, and is usually referred to as the Good Parliament (q.v.). The work of this Parliament was a measure of the extent to which the parliamentary institution had advanced as a power in the realm. It set itself with great determination to the correction of abuses and the overthrow of corrupt ministers. From this Parliament comes the first recorded instance of an impeachment (q.v.) by the Commons before the Lords. The activities of the reformers were strongly supported by the Black Prince, a fact which undoubtedly gave a great advantage and incentive to the Good Parliament, but he unfortunately died while the work of reform was at its height and most of it was reversed the following year. The Commons of the Parliament of 1376 elected Sir Peter de la Mare as their spokesman, and although he was not technically the first Speaker (q.v.) he virtually acted as such. The first Speaker to be so styled, Sir Thomas Hungerford, was elected by the Commons in the Parliament of the following year, the last Parliament of Edward III.

Richard II, the son of the Black Prince, was eleven years of age when he came to the throne and during his minority Parliament played a great part in the actual government of the country, although the machinations of John of Gaunt made for neither a sound administration nor harmonious relations between Lords and Commons. The Commons successfully asserted their right to examine the public accounts and appropriate the supplies, a right which they allowed to fall into disuse after the reign of Henry IV but which was revived in the reign of Charles I and finally established as a constitutional principle in 1666. To meet an imminent threat of invasion Parliament sought to raise money by means of a poll tax, but when it failed to yield an adequate revenue the Commons, dissatisfied with the handling of the nation's finances, petitioned for the removal of the chief officers of state and the appointment of new ministers by Parliament. The King conceded the petition and after the new appointments had been made the Commons, when Parliament assembled in 1380, agreed to a Lords proposal that another poll tax should be imposed. It was this tax which precipitated the Peasants' Revolt of 1381, an insurrection which united the Lords and the Commons in a resolve to effect many necessary reforms and incidentally led to a decline in the power of John of Gaunt. From 1389 the King took over the government of the country personally and for some years he ruled constitutionally. Towards the end of his reign, however, he became a despot and thereby encompassed his own downfall. A subservient Parliament meeting at Shrewsbury in 1398 confirmed Richard as an absolute monarch, delegating its authority to a committee of 18 persons who were little more than creatures of the King. Seemingly secure in his power, Richard banished Thomas Mowbray, Duke of Norfolk, and Henry Bolingbroke, Duke of Hereford, in consequence of their mutual antagonism, and on the death of John of Gaunt, the latter's father, he seized upon the estates which should rightfully have been inherited by Bolingbroke. Returning to England to avenge the King's treachery Bolingbroke found an army of 60,000 ready to follow him, and thus encouraged he was emboldened to lay claim to the crown itself. The King on returning from a visit to Ireland found himself abandoned and with no alternative but to yield to Bolingbroke. Richard executed a formal deed of resignation which was accepted by a Parliament summoned to meet on 30 September 1399. In the course of a century Parliament had thus deposed two monarchs, a significant testimony to the power and influence which had accrued to Parliament since the reign of Edward I. The deposition of Richard II foreshadowed the mighty battle between Royal Prerogative and parliamentary sovereignty which was destined to be fought to a finish during the reigns of the Stuarts. The end of the 14th century and of the Plantagenet period coincided with the end of a distinct phase of parliamentary history. To this period can be traced the origin of the ceremonies connected with the Opening of Parliament (q.v.) and the Royal Assent (q.v.) to Bills, together with many salient features of parliamentary procedure such as the stages of a Bill (see BILL, PASSAGE OF).

Henry Bolingbroke was crowned Henry IV on 13 October 1399, fully acknowledging that the Crown was his by the will of Parliament and the nation. The first Sovereign of the House of Lancaster, his claim to the throne rested solely upon popular consent and he realized that his position depended upon the avoidance of any serious conflict between himself and the power which had made him. He thus reigned as a constitutional King and established the principle of governing through Parliament, the latter exercising an effective control over the executive. Parliament, and in particular the Commons, had never before been so strong as at this period, and over two hundred years were to elapse after the death of Henry IV before that strength was regained.

Reverting to matters of finance, the three estates had originally taxed themselves independently, but before the end of the 14th century Lords and Commons were making grants jointly. As the main burden of taxation fell upon the Commons it was agreed that they should be accorded precedence in financial matters, and a formula to that effect was adopted and first used in 1395. In 1407 the Commons objected to interference on the part of the King and the Lords in the granting of aids and supplies; they claimed that the right of initiating grants should rest solely with themselves, that no grant should be reported to the King until both Houses had agreed to it, and that the report should then be made by the Speaker of the House of Commons. The King accepted the claim of the lower House and an important constitutional principle was thus established. To this day the procedure relating to a Money Bill (q.v.) incorporates the traditional formalities begun in 1407. Having passed through both Houses, a Money Bill, unlike all other Bills, is returned to the House of Commons, and on the day it receives the Royal Assent it is carried up to the Bar of the House of Lords by the Clerk of the House of Commons, handed by the latter to the Speaker, who personally delivers it to the Clerk of the Parliaments, the officer responsible for pronouncing the words signifying Her Majesty's concurrence. (*See also* PRIVILEGE, FINANCIAL.) However, some modification of this procedure no doubt became necessary with the passage of the Royal Assent Act, 1967, which provides that the Royal Assent to Bills may now be announced by the Lord Chancellor and the Speaker of the House of Commons in their respective Houses.

In 1414, when Henry V had been on the throne one year, the Commons won another important concession for which they had been repeatedly pressing. In a famous petition, notable as the first in which the English language was employed, the Commons prayed that 'from this time forward there never be no law made and engrossed as statute and law, neither by addition nor diminution, by no manner of term or terms, the which would change the sentence and the intent asked'. The King in his reply undertook that 'from henceforth nothing be enacted to the petition of the Commons contrary to their asking, whereby they should be bound without their assent'. From this precedent the practice developed of sending up to the King ready-drafted statutes instead of petitions (q.v.). Throughout the 14th century the Commons had been petitioners rather than legislators, and although their concurrence to legislation had been required along with that of the Lords they had always played only a subordinate part in legislative proceedings. With the development of the new practice, which became fully established by the end of the reign of Henry VI, the Commons acquired a new and improved status. They drafted their own Bills, to which the King could either assent or dissent but which he could not amend, and the elevation of the Commons to the status of a legislative body was acknowledged in a new formula which placed the two Houses on an equal footing. Statutes were now enacted by the advice and consent of the Lords and Commons, and before the middle of the 15th century the significant words 'and by the authority of the same' were added to the formula. Thus, before the end of the Middle Ages, Parliament had become the legislative authority which we know to-day, although a very strong power was still reserved to the Sovereign in his right, frequently exercised for many years to come, to withhold his assent to measures which had been agreed to by both Houses. To this period may be traced the growth of both Public and Private Bills (qq.v.).

During the Wars of the Roses Parliament became the instrument of the warring factions, and the overthrow of the House of Lancaster brought with it a temporary eclipse of the great Lancastrian constitutional principle of government through free Parliaments. In the reigns of Edward IV, Edward V, and Richard III constitutional progress was at a standstill, but in 1485 the advent of the Tudor dynasty heralded a new parliamentary era. Under the Tudors Parliament was restored to the position of sovereignty in which it had been confirmed by Henry IV, but the Tudors also established a strong and authoritarian monarchy, and although they governed through Parliament they saw to it that Parliament was always an instrument of the royal will, with the result that the power of Parliament was the power of the Sovereign. The Houses were only summoned when it suited the monarch's convenience to call them together, and the Tudor period is therefore one of infrequent Parliaments, although some of them lasted much longer than had previously been known. Henry VII summoned only seven Parliaments in the twenty-four years of his reign, and of these the first was by far the most important. Henry's claim to the throne was a very disputable one, and he permitted very little time to elapse after his coronation on 30 October 1485 before calling a Parliament to confirm him in his royal title. The Parliament which met on 7 November was only too ready to comply with the new King's wishes and the Crown was settled upon him and his descendants. Henry nevertheless felt insecure in his new dignity, and although his marriage with Elizabeth of York united the red and white rose factions and diminished the threat of her House asserting its hereditary right, he yet sought further means of strengthening his possession of the Crown. The policy he followed was a wise one, one which recognized that the surest path to security lay in maintaining the King's popularity with the people. He took the precaution, however, of manipulating the constitutions of municipal corporations in order to bring them under his personal domination and thus destroy the independence of the boroughs. In many boroughs a system of close election was introduced for the purpose of returning burgesses to Parliament, thus ensuring the election of a large number of Crown nominees to the lower House of the legislature, which in turn was more readily subjected to the royal will. Henry VII left a stable throne to his successor and some have even gone so far as to designate him the refounder of the English monarchy.

Henry VIII succeeded his father on 21 April 1509, and began an eventful reign during which he augmented the power of the Crown to a degree which had never before been surpassed. Although he accepted and applied the principle that a King should rule through Parliament, so completely did he subordinate his Parliaments to his own will and authority that there has never been a reign before or since in which Parliament so consistently and unprotestingly carried out the bidding of the monarch. As we have already seen, the powers which Parliament had gathered unto itself over the centuries were by no means insignificant, and there existed a number of clearly recognized limitations upon the Royal Prerogative, but so great was the fear and respect with which Henry VIII was regarded that these powers were allowed to lie dormant while he occupied the throne. Yet in spite of the slavish obedience of Henry's Parliaments to their Sovereign the House of Commons was transformed during the reign (in the words of Froude) 'into the first power in the State under the Crown'. The most important Parliament of the reign was the Reformation Parliament (q.v.), in which the Commons wrested the initiative from the Lords and emerged for the first time as the more powerful of the two Houses. This Parliament gave effect to the great religious revolution upon which the King was determined, destroyed the parliamentary influence of the Church, curbed the power of the nobles, and ruthlessly crushed all the opponents of the new policy. Never before had such great and terrible things been attempted as were accomplished by the Parliaments of Henry VIII at the direct instance of the King. So pliable were these Parliaments that during the course of the reign one or another of them released the King from his obligation to pay his debts, allowed him to exact forced loans, declared him Supreme Head of the Church and denied the jurisdiction of the Pope, altered the succession in obedience to the royal command, condemned by Act of Attainder Anne Boleyn, Catherine Howard, Thomas Cromwell, the Duke of Norfolk, the Earl of Surrey, and others of whom the King desired to be rid, and altered the laws of treason to accord with his requirements. Henry VIII was a cruel monarch with many evil deeds to his discredit, yet he enjoyed the confidence of his subjects to such an extent that he could safely invest his House of Commons with a power never before wielded by the popular representatives and remain secure in the knowledge that his own supremacy and control would not be challenged.

Under the youthful Edward VI, who succeeded to the throne on 28 January 1547, the work of the Reformation was advanced, and the two Parliaments of the reign showed a strong and healthy independence. One of the greatest enactments of the period was the treason law which re-adopted the standards laid down in the famous statute of Edward III. The latter had long been accepted as providing a reasonable definition of the limits of the crime of treason, but these limits were greatly extended by Henry VIII. In amending the treason law Parliament proceeded with a Bill of its own in preference to one proposed by the government, an unmistakable indication of the fact that at this period the framing of statutes was recognized as falling within the exclusive jurisdiction of Parliament. The accession of Mary I in 1553 reversed the religious trend of the two previous reigns and the nation returned temporarily to the fold of the Roman Church. But although Mary's Parliaments did not resist the re-establishment of the Roman Catholic faith in England, they did not prove entirely tractable in other matters. Her first Parliament protested strongly against her proposed marriage with Philip of Spain, and the Speaker of the House of Commons received a wrathful rebuke from the Queen when he boldly urged her to marry an Englishman. The Commons also made it clear that they were opposed to the penalization of nonconformists. Mary's second Parliament, meeting in 1554, settled a controversial constitutional point when they passed a Royal Marriage Bill which declared that the Royal Prerogative could be exercised with equal validity by a male or a female Sovereign. Later in the same year the third Parliament of the reign, the Reconciliation Parliament (q.v.), provided the world with the humiliating spectacle of an abject surrender to the Church of Rome. But as the heresy statutes began to be enforced and the fires of persecution commenced to blaze Parliament showed itself less inclined to be obliging. In 1555 Mary's fourth Parliament refused her a subsidy, and a Bill providing for the surrender of first fruits to the Pope was so bitterly opposed in the Commons that it only passed by a vote of 193 to 126. So intractable did this Parliament become that Mary dissolved it and sent several of its members to the Tower. Mary's fifth and last Parliament was not summoned until 1558, the year of her death. The reign of this unhappy and bigoted Sovereign was one of the blackest in English history, but it was followed by one destined to rank amongst the most glorious.

Before leaving the early history of Parliament reference should be made to its place of meeting and to the numerical composition of the two Houses. Although the Plantagenet Parliaments were often summoned to various provincial towns (York, Lincoln, Oxford, Gloucester, Marlborough, Shrewsbury, and Northampton amongst them), Westminster had always been the most usual meeting-place. As far back as the reign of Edward the Confessor Westminster was recognized as the home of the national assembly, but for the convenience of the monarch it was customary for Parliament to assemble wherever the King happened to be residing. As Westminster became the usual royal residence so it became the permanent and exclusive home of Parliament.

Until the reign of Henry VIII the spiritual peers were the more numerous body in the House of Lords. The temporal peers were originally few in number and seldom exceeded 50 in the 15th century. When the abbots and priors were expelled from the upper House by the

Reformation Parliament the spiritual peers lost and never regained their preponderance of numbers. The Commons were always a more numerous body than the Lords. Some 275 Commons attended the Parliaments of Edward I and in the reign of Henry VI the average number was 300. Henry VIII added 27 members for Wales and 4 for the county palatinate of Chester. Mary I granted or restored the privilege of parliamentary representation to 14 boroughs which between them returned 25 members. In her first Parliament the lower House consisted of 430 members.

See also DURATION OF PARLIAMENT; HOUSE OF COMMONS; HOUSE OF LORDS; PRIVILEGE; REPRESENTATION.

PARLIAMENT ACTS, 1911 and 1949

The main purpose of these Acts is to restrict the powers of the House of Lords. Together they provide that a Money Bill (q.v.) which has passed the House of Commons may be presented for the Royal Assent (q.v.) after one month even though the consent of the Lords has been withheld, and that the delaying power of the Lords in respect of other Public Bills shall be limited to one year, after which time they may receive the Royal Assent notwithstanding the Lords' consent being withheld. A special enacting formula is provided for Bills presented for the Royal Assent which the Lords have refused to pass, running as follows:

Be it enacted by the Queen's most Excellent Majesty, by and with the advice and consent of the Commons in this present Parliament assembled, in accordance with the provisions of the Parliament Acts, 1911 and 1949, and by authority of the same, as follows:

The 1911 Act defines a Money Bill and requires that all Money Bills be endorsed as such by the Speaker before they are sent to the Lords. It also provides that 'nothing in this Act shall diminish or qualify the existing rights and privileges of the House of Commons'. A further provision is the substitution of five years as the maximum period for the duration of a Parliament in place of the seven years provided by the Septennial Act, 1715. The 1911 Act conceded a delaying power of two years to the Lords which was reduced to one year by the 1949 Act.

The following extract from the preamble to the 1911 Act is of particular interest:

And whereas it is intended to substitute for the House of Lords as it at present exists a Second Chamber constituted on a popular instead of hereditary basis, but such substitution cannot be immediately brought into operation:

It is hardly necessary to point out that this intention has not been fulfilled, but its expression in an Act of Parliament might be regarded as evidence of the strong feeling which existed against the House of Lords at the time on account of their rejection of the 1909 Budget. It was, of course, this action which brought about the Parliament Act, 1911.

PARLIAMENTARIAN, THE

A publication of the Commonwealth Parliamentary Association (q.v.), formerly entitled the *Journal of the Parliaments of the Commonwealth*, and first published in 1920 as the *Journal of the Parliaments of the Empire*. It consists of summarized extracts from the debates of Commonwealth legislatures and articles on parliamentary subjects, and its distribution is limited to members of the association.

PARLIAMENTARY AFFAIRS

The quarterly journal of the Hansard Society for Parliamentary Government (q.v.).

PARLIAMENTARY AGENT

The person acting for the promoters of a Private Bill (q.v.) or the petitioners opposing such a Bill is known as a parliamentary agent. His is a specialized profession, and his function is to undertake all the work involved in promoting or opposing a Private Bill and to look after the interests of his client.

A register of parliamentary agents is kept in the Private Bill Offices of the House of Commons and the House of Lords, and no person may style himself a parliamentary agent unless he is so registered. Parliamentary agents are very often solicitors, and before they are eligible for registration they must fulfil certain conditions, amongst which they must satisfy the Speaker and the Lord Chairman that they have practical knowledge of the Standing Orders and procedure of the House of Commons regulating Private Business. Any applicant for registration who is not a solicitor must produce a 'certificate of his respectability from a Member of Parliament, a Justice of the Peace, a Barrister, or a Solicitor'. No Member of Parliament or Officer of the House may practise as a parliamentary agent. The register is open to public inspection.

In 1949, the Speaker drew the attention of the House to the fact that certain persons were representing themselves as parliamentary agents without possessing the necessary qualifications. He referred to the rules on the subject, and stated that any person contravening them was liable to be dealt with by the House for a contempt. The rules relating to parliamentary agents are set out in full in Erskine May's *Parliamentary Practice* (17th ed., pp. 913-16).

PARLIAMENTARY AND SCIENTIFIC COMMITTEE

The origins of this committee go back to 1933 when a group of Members of Parliament, officers of the British Science Guild, the Association of Scientific Workers and a few scientific and professional institutions came together under the title of the Parliamentary Science Committee. This was reorganized in 1939 as the Parliamentary and Scientific Committee, which is now composed of about 200 members of all parties from both Houses of the British Parliament, and representatives from about 30 scientific, technical and professional institutions.

The aims of the Committee are:

(1) To provide Members of Parliament with authoritative scientific information from time to time in connexion with debates.

(2) To bring to the notice of Members of Parliament and government departments the results of scientific research and technical development which bear upon questions of current public interest.

(3) To arrange for suitable action through parliamentary channels whenever necessary to ensure that proper regard is had for the scientific point of view.

(4) To examine all legislation likely to affect the above and take such action as may be suitable.

(5) To watch the financing of scientific and technological research, education and development.

(6) To provide its members and other approved subscribers with a regular summary of scientific matters dealt with in Parliament.

The committee meets once a month in a committee room of the House of Commons, the Chairman usually being selected from the party in power and the Deputy Chairman from the Opposition.

See articles by S. A. Walkland in *Parliamentary Affairs*, vol. XVII, 1964, nos. 3 and 4.

PARLIAMENTARY BAR

The parliamentary bar consists of the barristers who represent the parties concerned in promoting and opposing Private Bills (q.v.).

PARLIAMENTARY COMMISSIONER FOR ADMINISTRATION

An Act establishing the office of Parliamentary Commissioner for Administration received the Royal Assent on 22 March 1967. The office was inspired by the example of the Scandinavian Ombudsman, and the legislation was based upon proposals which had been published by the Government in October 1965 (*see* Cmnd. 2767). Sir Edmund Compton was appointed the first Parliamentary Commissioner, having been nominated in anticipation of the Bill becoming law. The salary attaching to the office is £14,000 a year, increased from £9,800 by resolution of the House of Commons in 1970.

The function of the Parliamentary Commissioner is to investigate the complaints and grievances of private citizens (and to a lesser extent of corporate bodies) arising out of administrative action on the part of the departments of central government. The Act recognizes, however, that Parliament is the traditional forum wherein the grievances of the citizen are ventilated, and it was drafted in such a way as to avoid any erosion of the functions of Members of Parliament. It does not, therefore provide any machinery inconsistent with the historic framework of the British Constitution. Accordingly, the Parliamentary Commissioner is empowered to undertake an investigation only on the initiative of a Member of Parliament. He does not cut across the channel of communication between member and constituent, and a complainant will, as in the past, continue to make his representations to a member (although not necessarily to the member for his own constituency).

The Parliamentary Commissioner is an independent officer appointed by the Crown. His salary and pension is directly charged to the Consolidated Fund, and therefore not subject to annual review by Parliament, and he is secure from dismissal except by parliamentary motion. He is required to report to Parliament each year and otherwise as the occasion requires. He is empowered to take evidence, on oath if necessary, and to compel the production of departmental documents other than those of the Cabinet and its committees. He is concerned only with faults in the administration and does not have the right to criticize policy. He has a discretionary power in deciding whether or not to pursue a complaint. Where he finds a complaint is justified he may invite the department concerned to put the matter right. Should the department fail to respond it is open to him to make an *ad hoc* report to Parliament.

Certain matters are excluded from his jurisdiction. He is not, for example, empowered to investigate complaints involving national security, relations with other countries, or the administration of colonial territories. It is not within his competence to investigate the actions of departments in relation to personnel or orders and discipline in the armed forces. The consideration of official appointments, the exercise of the prerogative of mercy, and the conferring of honours by the Sovereign are also excluded from his sphere of operations, and he does not normally investigate matters falling within the competence of the courts.

The House of Commons appoints a Select Committee of 11 members to consider the reports made by the Parliamentary Commissioner and to report to the House from time to time.

New Zealand was the first Commonwealth country to appoint a Parliamentary Commissioner, the term 'Ombudsman' being adopted in acknowledgment of the Scandinavian origin of the institution. New Zealand's first Ombudsman was installed in his duties on 1 October 1962. Guyana, Mauritius, Ghana and Fiji are also among the Commonwealth countries which have adopted the principle of the Ombudsman, the office being provided for in the Constitutions of all four countries. Mauritius was the first Commonwealth country to make provision for an Ombudsman in its basic constitutional document. In April 1967 the Canadian Province of Alberta appointed an Ombudsman, the first such appointment to be made in Canada.

PARLIAMENTARY COUNSEL TO THE TREASURY

The officer responsible for the drafting of Bills. The office was established in 1869 and its first occupant was Henry Thring (afterwards Lord Thring). The Parliamentary Counsel is an established Civil Servant and is provided with an assistant, known as Second Parliamentary Counsel, and a staff of draftsmen (q.v.). His salary is £14,000 per annum.

PARLIAMENTARY DEBATES

Together with the Parliamentary History (q.v.) the Parliamentary Debates form a great legislative history of Great Britain and the United Kingdom from the Norman Conquest to the present day. They commenced in the year 1803, when William Cobbett began to include a report of parliamentary debates in his *Political Register*. From 1812 to 1890 they were published by the Hansard (q.v.) family and thus acquired the famous name by which they have become generally known.

The Parliamentary Debates consist of five series, as follows:

First Series: 41 volumes covering the 2nd to the 6th Parliaments of the United Kingdom (1803–20);

Second Series: 25 volumes covering the 7th and 8th Parliaments of the United Kingdom (1820–30);

Third Series: 356 volumes covering the 9th to the 24th Parliaments of the United Kingdom (1830–91);

Fourth Series: 199 volumes covering the 24th to the 28th Parliaments of the United Kingdom (1892–1908);

Fifth Series: The current series which commenced in 1909. In that year the publication of the Parliamentary Debates was taken over by the Government and became known as the Official Report. Since 1909, also, the Lords and Commons Debates have been published separately. By the end of 1970, 808 volumes of Commons Debates and 313 volumes of Lords Debates had been published in this series. Volume 800 of the Commons Debates was reached in April–May 1970.

The first continuous record of contemporary debates, from 1667 to

1694, was compiled by Anchitell Grey (q.v.), and published as Grey's Debates. For many years, however, Parliament regarded the publication of its proceedings as a breach of privilege, and twice during the 18th century (in 1738 and 1762) declared it as such. By the beginning of the 19th century Parliament had relaxed its attitude and even went so far as to reserve a part of the Public Gallery for the Press. Nevertheless, the reporting of parliamentary debates in the Press is still technically a breach of privilege, although neither House would to-day take exception to any fair and honest accounts of its proceedings.

Other compilers of parliamentary debates prior to Cobbett include Richard Chandler, Ebenezer Timberland, John Almon, John Debrett, Dr. Johnson, and William Woodfall (qq.v.). The Journals of Sir Simonds D'Ewes (q.v.) constitute a record, although not a contemporary one, of the proceedings of the Elizabethan Parliaments. His manuscript diary is the best authority for the debates of the early years of the Long Parliament (q.v.). Various other collections and diaries, including those of Rushworth, Somers, Hardwicke, and Burton, provide valuable records of the Parliaments of James I, Charles I, and the Commonwealth, and a number of manuscript records, including Sir Ralph Verney's *Notes of Proceedings in the Long Parliament*, have been published by the Camden Society. In 1956 the Library of the House of Commons compiled a bibliography of the Parliamentary Debates of Great Britain which was published by H.M. Stationery Office. In 1959 the University of London published a thesis entitled 'Sources for Debates in the House of Commons, 1768-1774,' by Peter D. G. Thomas.

See also HANSARD.

PARLIAMENTARY DRAFTSMEN

See DRAFTSMEN.

PARLIAMENTARY GOVERNMENT

The British Commonwealth Parliaments provide examples of the true parliamentary type of executive government—a Cabinet chosen from the political party commanding a majority in the legislature and responsible to that legislature for its actions. Parliamentary government is responsible government (q.v.), as opposed to presidential government, where the head of the executive, the President, is not responsible to the legislature. Under the Cabinet system, the Government carries on the general administration of the country, with the help of Parliament, which help is expressed in a permanent and general control of governmental acts, destined to guarantee that the directing ideas which inspire the Government's policy correspond with the opinions predominating in Parliament, and that control is made effective by the political responsibility of the Government before Parliament.

PARLIAMENTARY HISTORY

A compilation of thirty-six volumes, begun by William Cobbett in 1806 and completed by J. Wright, which constitutes a legislative history of Great Britain and the United Kingdom from the Norman Conquest to the year 1803. It is the forerunner of the Parliamentary Debates (q.v.) which consist mainly of Hansard (q.v.).

The chief sources from which the Parliamentary History was compiled are the Old Parliamentary or Constitutional History of England, 24 volumes, which goes down to the Restoration; the Journal of Sir Simonds D'Ewes; the collections of Rushworth, Somers, and Hardwicke; the Debates of the Commons in 1620 and 1621; Chandler and Timberland's Debates, 22 volumes; Grey's Debates of the Commons from 1667 to 1694, 10 volumes; Almon's Debates, 24 volumes; Debrett's Debates, 63 volumes; and Dr. Johnson's Debates in Parliament.

Although not free from errors of detail, the Parliamentary History is a valuable work of reference.

PARLIAMENTARY LABOUR PARTY

In 1906 the Labour Party (q.v.) secured 29 seats in the House of Commons, and this group organized itself into the Parliamentary Labour Party. The Chairman and Leader of the party is recognized as the Leader of the Labour Party not only in Parliament but also in the country, and he, the Deputy Chairman and Deputy Leader, and the Chief Whip are elected by the P.L.P. at the beginning of each parliamentary session when the party is in opposition. The Leader and Deputy Leader are *ex-officio* members of the National Executive Committee of the Labour Party, with which the P.L.P. may confer on the work or programme of the party. The work of the P.L.P. is directed by a Parliamentary Committee which consists of the Chairman and Deputy Chairman (i.e., Leader and Deputy Leader), the Chief Whip, the Chairman of the Labour Group in the House of Lords, the Chief Whip of the Labour peers, 12 elected representatives of the Labour members of the House of Commons and 1 peer elected to represent the Labour peers. These members form the Shadow Cabinet (q.v.), and occupy the Opposition Front Benches when the party is in Opposition, whether they are ex-ministers or not. Labour peers are members of the Parliamentary Party, and are free to attend its meetings, though they do not vote on matters of special concern to the Commons. A full-time Secretary and a small permanent secretariat are in charge of the party's business, and a set of Standing Orders (suspended from 1946 to 1952) regulates the conduct of members. These state that membership of the P.L.P. involves the acceptance of the decisions of the Party Meeting and the right of the party to withdraw the Whip (q.v.) on account of things said or done by members of the party in the House. Since 1944 the P.L.P. has established Subject and Area Groups with their own chairmen and vice-chairmen. The Subject Groups meet to discuss matters within their terms of reference, e.g., education, foreign affairs, or nationalized industries, and the Area Groups questions affecting their regions.

The practices described above are dispensed with when the Labour Party is in power as they are incompatible with the operation of the Cabinet system as it is understood in Great Britain. The right of a Prime Minister to select his colleagues, a fundamental British constitutional principle, would be usurped if the party were to elect a Cabinet in the same way as it elects its Parliamentary Committee when in Opposition. The Labour Party when in office has therefore always conformed to the traditional constitutional practice.

PARLIAMENTARY LIBRARIES

Even the smallest legislature in the Commonwealth has a collection of books for the use of its members, the Speaker, and the parliamentary staff, and the older and larger Parliaments have magnificent libraries —in Australia the Federal Parliamentary Library has even developed into a National Library which has now become a separate institution. In every country the making of new laws continues relentlessly, and as more matters are subjected to legislation, so the coverage of the parliamentary library must increase and its book stock expand. To-day there are few subjects which might not conceivably claim the attention of Parliament, since the responsibilities of government extend into almost every area of national activity. There are, perhaps, certain subjects which do not call for extensive coverage, for example in the range of the fine arts, religious doctrines, and esoteric philosophy, or in highly technical fields, but even in these areas the library should be able to provide the minimal information normally available in the general reference collection of encyclopædias, dictionaries, year-books and glossaries. Apart from the usual reference and information services provided for Members of Parliament, parliamentary libraries issue bulletins, lists of recent accessions, reading lists and statistical material on subjects of topical interest—in fact they make readily available any material which will help a member to compose a speech, a motion, or a question, or to answer a query from a constituent.

A recent development in certain parliamentary libraries of the Commonwealth, notably those of Great Britain, Canada and Australia, is the provision of a research service with the function of providing members with information in depth. This type of service was pioneered in the United States, the Congressional Research Service of the Library of Congress being the prototype. The modern Member of Parliament is invariably under great pressure, and in order to perform his duties effectively he needs to be informed on a very wide range of subjects. To undertake all the study necessary without research assistance would be a virtual impossibility, and the establishment of a research service in a parliamentary library is a recognition of this fact of parliamentary life. The successful operation of a research service depends upon a highly qualified staff which will normally include lawyers, economists, scientists and other subject specialists. Their function is to prepare projects at the request of members, and to analyse, interpret, and prepare in a usable and assimilable form the material available on the subject concerned.

In addition to performing these very vital functions, the parliamentary library is the natural repository of its country's parliamentary records and publications, including those papers and reports which by statute have to be laid before Parliament. The importance attached to the library of Parliament is shown by the rapid development in recent years of the House of Commons Library, which, as the result of a Report by a Select Committee in 1946, has increased its staff about fourfold since that date. Parliamentary libraries are not 'special libraries' as understood by librarians, but they must obviously possess special collections on parliamentary subjects and constitutional law and history and the laws of their own and other Commonwealth countries. They are also particularly interested in social and economic questions and in forming a general collection of books of national or local interest.

PARLIAMENTARY PAPERS

See BLUE BOOK; COMMAND PAPERS; HOUSE OF COMMONS PAPERS; STATUTORY INSTRUMENTS; WHITE PAPER.

PARLIAMENTARY PRIVATE SECRETARIES

A minister appoints a Parliamentary Private Secretary (not to be confused with a Parliamentary Secretary) from among the Members of Parliament. He is often one of the younger back-benchers who shows promise of becoming a useful member of the party in office, and who thus acquires valuable experience of ministerial duties. He is able to advise the minister on the state of parliamentary opinion and the general feeling of the House regarding matters which concern his department. He is a valuable channel of information and contact with back-benchers, additional to the Whips (q.v.) and the Parliamentary Secretaries (q.v.), and if he is unable to satisfy them he can arrange interviews with the minister. The Parliamentary Private Secretary is unpaid, i.e., he receives only his salary as a Member of Parliament. The Select Committee on Offices or Places of Profit under the Crown recommended in 1941 the establishment of a convention that there should not be more than one Parliamentary Private Secretary for each department, but that recommendation has not been strictly implemented. A Parliamentary Private Secretary must be a member of the same house as the minister he serves.

A Parliamentary Private Secretary, who has no officially recognized status, has never had clearly defined duties, and in practice they can range from those of a relatively humble ministerial assistant to those of an unofficial junior minister. The action of Mr. Harold Wilson in dismissing 7 Parliamentary Private Secretaries in May 1967 for failing to support his Government's policy in relation to the European Common Market would suggest that they are expected to consider themselves bound by the principle of collective responsibility. It also indicates that while the appointment of a Parliamentary Private Secretary is the prerogative of the Minister concerned, the Prime Minister reserves the right of dismissal.

PARLIAMENTARY REFORM

The movement for parliamentary reform developed as a serious political force in the middle of the 18th century. It received an impetus from the Earl of Chatham, whose enormous prestige gave great weight to any views expressed by him. In 1766 he described the borough representation as 'the rotten part of our Constitution' and declared that 'if it does not drop it must be amputated'. In 1770 he suggested that a third member should be added to each county 'in order to counterbalance the weight of the corrupt and venal boroughs' which were under the control of wealthy and powerful patrons. Chatham predicted that if Parliament did not reform itself from within it would be reformed with a vengeance from without. In 1776 the cause was taken up independently by John Wilkes (q.v.) and John Cartwright. Wilkes brought forward a scheme in Parliament to disfranchise the 'rotten' boroughs, enfranchise the populous towns of the Midlands and the North, and improve the county representation, and on 21 March he unsuccessfully moved for leave to introduce a Bill incorporating these principles. In the same year Cartwright founded the Society of the Supporters of the Bill of Rights, the first organized radical movement and the progenitor of many other radical institutions. In 1780 the Duke of Richmond introduced a Bill in the House of Lords providing for universal suffrage, equal electoral districts, and annual Parliaments, proposals so sweeping and revolutionary that it is hardly necessary to add that their lordships rejected the Bill without a division. Two years later the younger Pitt took up the issue when he moved for a committee of inquiry on the state of the representation, pointing out amongst other anomalies that the Nabob of Arcot, as patron of several boroughs, had seven or eight nominees sitting in the House. His motion was rejected, as were his further resolutions, introduced in the following year, directed against bribery and corruption at elections and proposing an increase in the county representation and that of the capital. The short-lived Rockingham ministry of 1782 eliminated two serious electoral abuses by disqualifying government contractors from membership of the House of Commons and disfranchising revenue officers. There were many boroughs where revenue officers had controlled the voting, as, for example, in Bossinney where the electorate was reduced to a single voter after they were rendered ineligible. In excluding government contractors from the House the Government struck at a particularly odious form of bribery whereby persons had secured contracts in exchange for their votes in Parliament.

Pitt's last effort in the cause of parliamentary reform was made in 1785, shortly after he became Prime Minister. He sought leave to introduce a Bill which proposed to disfranchise 36 'rotten' boroughs and to distribute the 72 members which they returned among the counties and the capital, the enfranchisement of copyholders in the counties, and the redistribution of a number of other seats in order to give representation to the more populous towns. The one distasteful feature of the Bill was the provision it made for the compensation of the proprietors of disfranchised boroughs, a grave sacrifice of principle. The Bill was thrown out nevertheless, and Pitt did not again champion the popular cause. In 1790 a member named Flood moved for the amendment of the representation by the addition of 100 county members, and Pitt, whilst expressing his sympathy for the proposal, withheld his support from it.

In 1792 the Society of the Friends of the People was formed, an association which had for its object the promotion of parliamentary reform. The society numbered among its leaders Grey and Erskine, the exponents in Parliament of the new and growing radicalism. In 1793 the Friends of the People claimed to have proved that 200 Members of the House of Commons were returned by towns with less than 100 electors and that 357 members were returned by 154 patrons. Armed with these facts Grey introduced a motion for reform accompanied by a petition exposing the disgraceful state of the representation. The time was far from opportune for a reformer, however. The excesses of the French Revolution had caused widespread alarm among the property-owning classes in Britain and there was a definite tendency to identify an advocate of reform with an apostle of violence. Furthermore, the parliamentary Opposition had disintegrated following the rupture between Burke and Fox, and Grey's motion was decisively rejected. In 1797 Grey attempted to bring in a Bill based upon his resolution of four years earlier. It proposed to increase the county representation, to extend the franchise, and to introduce a uniform electoral qualification; in fact it anticipated the great measure which Grey was destined to carry thirty-five years later, but on this occasion it was rejected by a large majority. A number of other political associations came into being during this period including the London Corresponding Society, the Society for Constitutional Information, the Revolution Society, and the Societies of United Englishmen, Scotsmen, and Irishmen. Some were unquestionably extreme in their policies and were totally repudiated by the Society of the Friends of the People. All such organizations were suppressed under the repressive programme of legislation embarked on by Pitt's Government during the final decade of the 18th century in consequence of its fear of public disorder.

For a number of years activity in the interest of reform suffered a decline and no noticeable progress was made until Lord John Russell emerged as its advocate in 1820, from which date the Whigs, under the leadership of Grey, became definitely pledged to the cause. In the intervening years the doughty and ardent campaigner, Sir Francis Burdett, who had been returned to Parliament in 1807, conducted an unequal struggle on behalf of parliamentary reform. In 1818 he proposed the introduction of universal male suffrage, equal electoral districts, voting by ballot, and annual Parliaments, but he could not muster a single supporter for his resolutions in the Division Lobby. A further motion by Burdett in the following year, proposing merely to consider the question of reform, was rejected by a substantial majority.

During the reign of George IV the reform movement gathered strength, but as a substantial majority in both Houses of Parliament remained opposed to any change no practical advance was achieved beyond the disfranchisement of the notoriously corrupt borough of Grampound and the assignment of its two members to the county of York. The Bill for this purpose was twice carried through the House of Commons by Lord John Russell in 1820 and 1821 and had originally proposed that the two vacant seats be allocated to the unrepresented town of Leeds, but the amendment substituting the county had been accepted in the upper House. A motion by Lambton, afterwards Lord Durham, proposing to abolish the borough representation and to substitute a system based on a division of the counties and to extend the franchise to every householder, was rejected by the House of Commons in 1821. In 1822 Russell introduced a resolution calling for consideration of the state of the representation which was defeated by a majority of 105. The same resolution repeated in 1823 and 1826 was negatived by even heavier majorities. Attempts by Russell and others to strike at bribery, to disfranchise corrupt boroughs, and to enfranchise the densely populated towns all met with a similar fate. In the sessions of 1829 and 1830 the Marquis of Blandford and Daniel O'Connell distinguished themselves by their reforming zeal. A motion by the former condemning the practice of patronage was supported by a most disheartening minority, and O'Connell fared even worse with his motion in favour of the ballot, universal suffrage, and triennial Parliaments, for which he could muster only 13 votes against 319. A motion by Russell in 1830 calling for an extension of the basis of

s*

the representation was lost by 213 to 117, Sir Robert Peel remarking during the course of the debate that he considered the voice of the people to be already sufficiently heard in the House of Commons.

Yet in spite of the formidable opposition of the reactionary majority in Parliament the feeling throughout the country was intensely in favour of reform. In 1830 the fulfilment of the reformers' object was far closer than they themselves can have realized. Shortly after the accession of William IV, the Prime Minister, the Duke of Wellington, sealed the fate of his Tory Government when he unwisely declared that 'the legislature and the system of representation possessed the full and entire confidence of the country'. On the same day Brougham gave notice that he intended to raise the question of the representation, and a few days later the Government was defeated on a motion for a committee of inquiry into the Civil List. The Government resigned and Earl Grey formed a Whig administration pledged to secure the reform of the House of Commons. Considerable difficulty remained to be overcome, however, before the celebrated Reform Bill passed both Houses in 1832.

See also REPRESENTATION; WILLIAM IV AND PARLIAMENT.

PARLIAMENTARY REGISTER

See ALMON, JOHN.

PARLIAMENTARY SALARIES

See APPENDIX 2.

PARLIAMENTARY SECRETARIES

All Ministers of the Crown (q.v.) who control a major department have one or two Parliamentary Secretaries to assist them. If the Minister is a Secretary of State (q.v.) his Parliamentary Secretary is designated an Under-Secretary of State. As well as helping their ministers in their parliamentary work and deputizing for them in the House, they are accessible to members who seek information or wish to make representations or complaints, and many such matters are dealt with on the Parliamentary Secretaries' own responsibility. They are selected by the Prime Minister, in consultation with the minister concerned, and as they are not appointed by the Sovereign they are not Ministers *of the Crown* but junior ministers. If the minister is a peer it is usual for his Parliamentary Secretary to be a Member of the House of Commons, and not infrequently a minister in the House of Commons has a Parliamentary Secretary in the House of Lords, possibly in addition to another in his own Chamber. As Junior Ministers the Parliamentary Secretaries must accept the doctrine of collective responsibility, and a Parliamentary Secretary to the Ministry of Food was required to resign after making a public statement on agriculture which conflicted with Government policy. Herbert Morrison's

Government and Parliament contains a 'Parliamentary Secretaries' Charter' which suggests that Parliamentary Secretaries should be allowed to play a bigger part in the administration of their respective ministries. A Parliamentary Secretary's salary is £3,750 a year plus £1,250 if he is a member of the House of Commons. The senior Parliamentary Secretary is the Chief Government Whip who is automatically the Parliamentary Secretary to the Treasury and receives a salary of £5,625, plus an additional £1,250 as a Member of the House of Commons. Under the Ministers of the Crown Act, 1964, the number of Parliamentary Secretaries is limited to 36.

The office of Parliamentary Secretary is familiar to most Commonwealth countries, although in New Zealand the designation Parliamentary Under-Secretary is employed while India, Ceylon and Rhodesia use the term Deputy Minister. Until 1959 the Canadian counterpart was Parliamentary Assistant, but the designation was changed to Parliamentary Secretary and legislation was enacted providing for a maximum of 16 such appointments. In Canada a Parliamentary Secretary does not have the status of a junior minister and his duties approximate more closely to those of a Parliamentary Private Secretary (q.v.) in the British Parliament. It is also of interest to note that in Canada the term Deputy Minister is used to describe the permanent head of a Government Department.

PARLIAMENTARY UNDER-SECRETARIES OF STATE

See PARLIAMENTARY SECRETARIES.

PARLIAMENT, DISSOLUTION OF

See DISSOLUTION OF PARLIAMENT.

PARLIAMENT, DURATION OF

See DURATION OF PARLIAMENT.

PARLIAMENT OF BATS

The name given to the Parliament of 1426, when members came armed with bats and clubs in consequence of a ban upon the carrying of more deadly weapons. Also known as the Club Parliament.

PARLIAMENT OF WHITE BANDS

A Parliament held at Westminster on 15 July 1321, which was attended by a discontented faction wearing 'odd party-coloured habits yellow and green, with a white band across their breasts'.

PARTY SYSTEM

The position to-day whereby political parties organize themselves in order to further their own plans and ideas of government is accepted by democratic countries without much question. Not only does a party hold itself in readiness to take over the reins of government but it continually strives to influence the policy of the party in power. The origins of the party system lie far in the past, and even before a representative Parliament had arrived there was a party which strove to influence the party in power, i.e., the King. The King and his counsellors were in effect the party permanently in power, and the prominent nobles who became the chosen counsellors were in effect the Government. Since the characters of kings varied, it followed that at certain times the opposing factions were more active and perceptible when a weak king was on the throne, and naturally on the succession of a minor the rivalry between various groups was accentuated. The first recognizable political parties were produced by the Civil War, and the Cavaliers and the Roundheads became the Tories and the Whigs respectively. These party names were first used in 1679.

Under Charles II the Tory party supported the King, and for a while the combination was successful. But the question of the succession of a Roman Catholic King broke the ranks of the Tories, and although the names Whig and Tory persisted, it cannot be said that a consistent policy was a characteristic of either party. By the 18th century parliamentary power and influence had increased, but still the name Whig or Tory labelling a member gave no certain idea of his sympathies or of his likely course of action. It was popular to suggest that political factions were venal self-seeking conspirators, and that few Members of Parliament had a sense of duty to the people they were supposed to represent and the country whose destinies they were helping to guide. The original Tory party suffered eclipse in 1714, and for most of the 18th century the country was ruled by Whig Governments.

The beginning of the 19th century brought signs of change. Parties were apt to be called after their leaders, and the Canningites and Pittites were more definite in their policies and ideas. The Reform Act of 1832 which extended the franchise is the first great landmark in the history of the British party system, and it is with that Act that parties in the modern sense of the term, with recognizable principles and more stable policies, began.

The number of parties forming a Government varies from the single party, popular in totalitarian states, to the multi-party system of France. For all practical purposes Great Britain has always had a two-party system, whether it was Whigs and Tories, Liberals and Conservatives, or Conservatives and Labour. The rise of the latter party at the beginning of this century might have produced a three-party system, but the two-party system triumphed in the end with the elimination of the Liberals or their absorption by the Conservatives. In Australia three parties are represented in Parliament, two of them being in coalition. A two-party system operates in New Zealand, although in the General Election held in November 1966 a member of the Social Credit Party was returned, the first time in twenty-three years that a third party has gained representation in the New Zealand House of Representatives. Five parties were represented in the Canadian House of Commons, after three elections prior to 1968 had failed to give any single party an overall majority. Nevertheless, only two of these parties, the Liberals and Progressive Conservatives, have in the past been serious contenders for power, the minor parties being dependent for their support on concentrations of local strength. As M. Duverger points out in his *Political Parties*, the natural movement of societies tends towards the two-party system. It seems to correspond to the nature of things, i.e., political choice usually takes the form of a choice between two alternatives. There is no doubt also that parliamentary government works best under this system. Its stability is assured because when either party falls from power, the opposing party accedes to it. The leaders of the party out of office are the prospective leaders of the alternative Government, and the Opposition (q.v.) itself is a part of the machinery of government. Although the multi-party system may be able to reflect from the electorate more shades of opinion, no party can expect to have an absolute majority of its own, and has to rely on the support of other parties to form a Government. There are several alternative Governments which may take the place of one which is defeated—the certainty of the two-party system disappears and, as experienced in France prior to 1958, Governments tend to be less stable and shorter-lived.

However, as MacIver says in *The Modern State*, in any event the advantages and disadvantages of the two and multi-party systems are relative to the intelligence and culture of the community. The essential thing is that government should rest on as broad a basis of opinion as possible, maintaining, in spite of its party character, the unity of a whole people.

(Further reading: Bulmer-Thomas, *The growth of the British party system*, 2 v., 1965; Hansard Society, *The British party system*, 1952; McKenzie, *British political parties*, 1963).

PATRONAGE SECRETARY

See WHIPS.

PAYMASTER GENERAL

In Great Britain the public revenue is paid into the Bank of England to the credit of the Exchequer, and an order under the Royal Sign Manual countersigned by two Lords of the Treasury directs the Treasury Commissioners to transfer sums granted by the Consolidated Fund Acts (q.v.) or the Appropriation Act (q.v.) to the credit of the various government departments. The Treasury Commissioners also send an authority to the Comptroller and Auditor General (q.v.) who directs the Bank to transfer the money to the account of the Paymaster General, who then pays it over to the appropriate departments. After 1835 the offices of Paymaster General of the Forces and Treasurer of the Navy were combined in the office of Paymaster General. The Paymaster General's appointment is a political one, and as his powers are delegated to the permanent staff of the Pay Office and his Treasury duties are insignificant, he is entrusted by the Prime Minister with some special function. For instance, in the Conservative Government formed in 1951 Lord Cherwell became Paymaster General with the exceptional status of Cabinet membership. He was put in charge of atomic energy development and directed the Prime Minister's Statistical Section. When Mrs. Judith Hart was appointed to the office in 1968 it was stated that her special responsibilities would include matters involving youth, greater public participation in government, and decentralization and devolution of powers to Scotland and Wales.

The salary of the Paymaster General is variable within the maximum of £8,500 a year, the salary to which he is entitled when a Member of the Cabinet. In the Government of Mr. Harold Wilson the office was equated with that of a Senior Minister of State, the salary being £7,625. When a Member of the House of Commons the incumbent is entitled to an additional £1,250.

As the late Lord Morrison has written: 'The fact that the position of Paymaster General can range between a full Cabinet Minister and a minor office illustrates how usefully adaptable the ministerial structure can be.'

A chronological list of the holders of this office appears as Appendix 25.

PAYMENT OF MEMBERS

As far back as the 13th century the representatives of the shires, cities, and boroughs were remunerated for their attendance at Parliament, knights receiving four shillings a day and citizens and burgesses two shillings a day for the duration of the Parliament. These payments were the legal responsibility of the constituencies, and although Members of Parliament are now paid from national funds the liability upon the constituencies has never been legally removed. Andrew Marvell was reputedly the last person to receive a parliamentary salary paid by the constituency of Hull until his death in 1678, but as late as 1681 Thomas King presented a petition stating that he had not been paid his wages by the borough of Harwich. Although, generally speaking, the payment of members by their constituents had ceased by the end of the 17th century, it is stated in Lyson's *Cornwall* that the practice in that county continued into the 18th century. Samuel Pepys in his Diary entry for 30 March 1668 remarks, 'At dinner . . . all concluded that the bane of the Parliament hath been the leaving off the old custom of the places allowing wages to those that served them in Parliament, by which they chose men that understood their business and would attend it, and they could expect an account from, which now they cannot.' The question was raised again in 1780, when a committee appointed by the electors of Westminster with Fox as chairman, recommended the payment of members and their report was adopted by the influential Society for Constitutional Information whose president was the Duke of Richmond. Lord Blandford's Reform Bill of 1830 and the People's Charter of 1839 also proposed that Members of Parliament should be paid. Motions or Bills supporting such a proposal were brought before the House of Commons in 1870, 1888, 1892, 1893, and 1895, but membership of Parliament remained an unpaid occupation until 1912, when, by a resolution passed the previous year in the face of substantial opposition, Members of the House of Commons became entitled to draw a salary of £400 a year. In 1937 this salary was increased to £600, remaining at this figure until 1946 when the House of Commons voted that the salaries of its members should be raised to £1,000. A Select Committee reporting in 1954 recommended a further increase of £500, a recommendation which was endorsed by a majority of the House of Commons, but the Government declined to implement it. However, in order to relieve the financial difficulties suffered by some members, the Government agreed to the introduction of a sessional allowance of £2 a day for each day the House sat, Fridays excepted. In July 1957 the Prime Minister announced in the House of Commons a proposal to pay members an annual allowance of £750 instead of the £2 a day sessional allowance which had amounted to about £280 a year. The total salary was thus consolidated at £1,750 all of which was taxable. It was announced at the same time that peers, who had previously drawn neither salaries nor allowances, would in future be paid a tax-free expense allowance of up to three guineas for each day's attendance, but ministers sitting in the House of Lords would not be entitled to this allowance in addition to their salaries. Further increases in parliamentary salaries came into effect in 1964, the salary of a member of the House of Commons being increased to £3,250 and a peer's allowance to £4 14s. 6d. a day. Increases were also given to all ministers, both senior and junior, the Leader of the Opposition, the Speaker, the Chairman of Ways and Means and Deputy Chairman, the Lord Chairman and the Comptroller and Auditor General. The payment of a salary to the Opposition Chief Whip was an innovation introduced at the same time. Previously he had drawn a salary as a Member of Parliament, but was unpaid in his capacity as a Whip. In December 1969 members were awarded an additional allowance, subject to the

[549]

presentation of accounts, of £500 for secretarial assistance and an increased motor-car allowance, and the peer's allowance was increased to a maximum of £6·50 a day.

The payment of members was established in Canada, Australia, and New Zealand many years before it was re-adopted in Great Britain. Members were receiving payment in Canada even before the British North America Act brought the Canadian Confederation into being, and an Act of 1867 continued the practice for the federal Parliament of Canada. In New Zealand the Members of both Houses were paid from their first session in 1854.

Canadian Members of Parliament enjoy the distinction of being paid the highest parliamentary salaries in the Commonwealth. Their sessional indemnity amounts to $26,000, $8,000 of which is tax free, in addition to which they are entitled to a variety of perquisites. The legislators of Ceylon are probably the least well paid. They receive no salary but only an allowance which, for an ordinary member, amounts to about £636 a year.

See also Appendix 2 for Members' Salaries in other Commonwealth countries.

(Further reading: Taylor, *Payment of Members*, 1870.)

PEACE TOWER, OTTAWA

The dominating feature of Canada's Parliament Building, this campanile is 300 feet high and contains a carillon of 53 bells ranging from 10 pounds to 10 tons. The four dials of its clock are 15 ft. 9 in. in diameter, the hour hands 5½ feet long, the minute hands 9 feet, and its chime is the same as Big Ben's in the clock tower of the British Houses of Parliament. Like this tower it also shows a light when Parliament is sitting. The cornerstone of the Peace Tower, which is a memorial to the Canadians who died in the 1914–18 War, was laid to commemorate the 60th anniversary of the Dominion Confederation by the Prince of Wales (now Duke of Windsor) in 1919, the original tower having been destroyed by fire in 1916. The inscription on the stone, 'This stone was laid by Edward Prince of Wales, Sept. 1st, in this year of victory. FINIS CORONAT OPVS', gives the 'year of victory' if all the letters representing Roman numerals are added together.

PEERAGE, DISCLAIMER OF

The right to disclaim an hereditary peerage under certain conditions was established by the Peerage Act, 1963. Prior to its passing the renunciation of a peerage was contrary to settled law, although it was not a matter for which any statutory provision existed. Since a peerage automatically disqualified its holder from membership of the House of Commons and from voting at General Elections, the fact that no means existed whereby a peerage could be relinquished was clearly inconsistent with the realities of modern political life. Public attention was focused upon this problem by the case of Mr. Anthony Wedgwood Benn, whose campaign to rid himself of an unwanted peerage led to the appointment of a Joint Committee on House of Lords Reform in April 1962. In the following December the Joint Committee, having been re-appointed in the 1962-3 session, produced the report on which the Peerage Act was largely based.

The Act provides that a person holding or succeeding to an hereditary peerage in the peerage of England, Scotland, Great Britain or the United Kingdom may, under certain conditions and subject to certain time limits, disclaim that peerage by delivering to the Lord Chancellor an instrument of disclaimer, the form of which is set out in Schedule 1 of the Act. A peerage must be disclaimed within the following time limits:

(1) In the case of a person succeeding to a peerage after the commencement of the Act, within twelve months of the day on which he succeeds, or, if he succeeds before reaching the age of twenty-one, within twelve months of his twenty-first birthday.

(2) In the case of a Member of the House of Commons, within one month of the date of his succession.

(3) In the case of a successful candidate at a General Election held in pursuance of a writ issued before his succession, within one month of the declaration of the result.

(4) In the case of a person who succeeded to a peerage before the commencement of the Act, whether or not he had applied for a writ of summons to attend the House of Lords, within twelve months of the commencement of the Act or, if he is under twenty-one, within twelve months of his twenty-first birthday. This provision gave the opportunity to peers who were already in active membership of the House of Lords to enter or return to the wider political arena of the hustings and the House of Commons.

The Act provides for extensions of the time limits where justified by illness and other circumstances.

Life peers (q.v.), persons who accept hereditary peerages after the commencement of the Act, and hereditary peers who succeed after the commencement of the Act and apply for a writ of summons to attend the House of Lords are ineligible to disclaim their peerages.

The effect of a disclaimer is irrevocable for the lifetime of the individual concerned although it does not extinguish the peerage. The peerage remains dormant until the death of the disclaiming peer, at which time the heir becomes entitled to succeed unless he too chooses to disclaim. A disclaiming peer renounces all rights, titles and privileges of peerage in respect of himself and his wife, and assumes with his wife the rights and status of a commoner. He becomes ineligible for any other hereditary peerage, although the Act does not disqualify him from the acceptance of a life peerage.

The remaining provisions of the Act relate to Scottish and Irish peerages and hereditary peeresses. (*See* HOUSE OF LORDS; HOUSE OF LORDS REFORM; PEERS; REPRESENTATIVE PEERS; WOMEN IN PARLIAMENT.)

As the result of an amendment carried in the House of Lords although previously rejected in the House of Commons, the Peerage Act came into force immediately on the signification of the Royal Assent. The first peer to disclaim his peerage was Viscount Stansgate, better known as Mr. Anthony Wedgwood Benn, for whom the passage of the Act represented the successful culmination of an eight-year campaign. He was present in the gallery of the House of Lords at the moment when the Peerage Act passed into law on 31 July 1963, and was ready to deliver his instrument of disclaimer as soon as the words of the Royal Assent had been pronounced. He was followed ten minutes later by Lord Altrincham who became once again plain Mr. John Grigg. In the following October Sir Alec Douglas-Home renounced the earldom of Home and five other peerages following his appointment as Prime Minister, and one month later Mr. Quintin Hogg relinquished the viscounty and barony of Hailsham. By the end of 1966 four further peers had disclaimed their peerages—Lord Southampton (Charles Fitzroy), Lord Monkswell (William Collier), Lord Beaverbrook (Maxwell Aitken) and the Earl of Sandwich (Victor Montagu). Lord Fraser of Allander (Sir Hugh Fraser) disclaimed in 1967, and Lord Lambton disclaimed the earldom of Durham in 1970.

Although the renunciation of a peerage, prior to the passage of the Peerage Act, 1963, had been regarded as contrary to settled law, the fact remains that surrenders of peerages had taken place in the past, even as late as in the reign of Charles I. They were normally relinquished either to the Crown in exchange for a higher rank or a grant of money or land, or to another person subject to subsequent confirmation by the Crown. The *Complete Peerage*, in an appendix to volume 3, lists 17 cases of surrendered peerages in England between 1232 and 1640, but on 1 February 1640/41 the House of Lords resolved very definitely that there was no means whereby any peer could 'alien or transfer his honour, drown or extinguish it'. Their lordships also agreed that there was no form either of surrender, grant, fine, or any other conveyance to the King by which the descent of a peerage could be stopped. There were also frequent cases of surrendered peerages in Scotland, but the *Complete Peerage* points out that, after the Act of Union came into force in 1707, the Kingdom of England and the Kingdom of Scotland ceased to have any legal existence as separate entities, and therefore the power of the Crown to add to or to abrogate the limitations of dignities in either kingdom was completely lost.

Modern interest in the question arose entirely because of the disqualification from the service of the House of Commons which a peerage imposed on its holder. Several attempts to remove this disqualification had been made prior to the Wedgwood Benn case by persons who had fallen victim to it. In 1895, in the case of Viscount Wolmer, a Select Committee of the House of Commons found that disqualification arose from the fact of succession and not from the receipt of a writ of summons. Lord Ponsonby was equally unsuccessful in 1936 when he tried to persuade the House of Lords that peers should be allowed to stand for election to the House of Commons and to vote at General Elections, but that they should vacate their seats in the Lords if elected. In 1950 Viscount Hailsham made no headway when he requested legislation which would have enabled him to retain his seat in the House of Commons. It was Mr. Wedgwood Benn who brought the issue to a head by pursuing his objective with a tenacity that could not be ignored. There can be no doubt that his determined efforts to avoid the disqualification incurred by succession to a peerage, and the public controversy aroused by them, were in large measure responsible for the re-examination of the question of House of Lords reform and the consequent passage of the Peerage Act.

Mr. Wedgwood Benn commenced his campaign before the death of his father, the first Viscount Stansgate. In 1955 he sought permission for the introduction of a Personal Bill in the House of Lords which would have enabled him to renounce the peerage, but it was refused on the ground that the subject was properly one for a Public Bill. Accordingly his father moved the second reading of the Wedgwood Benn (Renunciation) Bill in the Lords on 26 April 1955, but it was defeated by 52 votes to 24. On 17 November 1960 the first Viscount Stansgate died, and on the 29th Mr. Wedgwood Benn, being a Member of the House of Commons at the time of h's father's death, petitioned the House against his disqualification as a member. The petition, which was referred to the Committee of Privileges, held *inter alia* that the disqualification of peers from sitting and voting in the House of Commons had never been laid down by statute nor judicially determined; that the petitioner had executed an instrument of renunciation of his viscounty; that the House of Commons Disqualification Act, 1957, conferred a statutory right on Members of the House of Commons to refuse to accept places which would disqualify them from sitting in the House of Commons; and that no member succeeding to a peerage could lose his right to sit in the House of Commons until he had received a writ of summons to the House of Lords.

The Committee of Privileges, by a majority, rejected Mr. Wedgwood Benn's contentions. They held that the fact of succession to a peerage was in itself a disqualification from membership of the

House of Commons and that no peer could surrender or renounce his peerage. They also recommended against the introduction of a Bill enabling Mr. Wedgwood Benn to remain a Member of the House of Commons. The report of the Committee of Privileges was considered in the House of Commons on 13 April 1961 and accepted after a division. Mr. Wedgwood Benn's seat was thereupon declared vacant, but he was re-adopted as a candidate by the Labour Party and returned at the subsequent by-election with an impressive majority. On 8 May 1961 he was prevented from entering the Commons Chamber by order of the Speaker, and the House, after a division, carried a Government-sponsored resolution confirming the Speaker's ruling.

Following the by-election result, Mr. Wedgwood Benn's defeated opponent, Mr. Malcolm St. Clair, petitioned the Court of Queen's Bench challenging the validity of Mr. Wedgwood Benn's election. On 28 July the Election Court ruled that the election of Mr. Wedgwood Benn was invalid, and three days later Mr. St. Clair took his seat in the House of Commons as the lawfully elected member for Mr. Wedgwood Benn's former constituency. As soon as the Peerage Act became law, however, Mr. St. Clair resigned his seat in accordance with a pledge which he had given by applying for the stewardship of the Manor of Northstead, and a further by-election was held, uncontested by the Conservative and Liberal Parties, at which Mr. Wedgwood Benn was again decisively returned.

Throughout his long and complex campaign Mr. Wedgwood Benn conducted and argued his own case. Probably the most telling point he advanced, notwithstanding the skill with which he presented his legal arguments before the Committee of Privileges and the Election Court, was his submission that in view of the constitutional changes which the House of Lords had undergone, elevation to the peerage no longer involved a call to higher service. Instead ' . . . it now involves nothing more than imposing a lifetime disqualification on service in the Commons which is now the highest service in the State'.

PEERS

The grades in the British peerage are, in ascending order, baron, viscount, earl, marquess, and duke (see under these headings). The word *pares*, from which the word peers is derived, came into use during the 14th century, and merely meant equals. It was a very early principle of law that a man should be tried by his equals, and thus a man's *pares* came to mean those who, standing on the same level as himself, were competent to be his judges. In spite of a long struggle for their own courts of law, the barons only succeeded in establishing that lords should be tried by lords for the crimes of treason and felony. It was this privilege which helped to define a class of *pares*, who in feudal times were tenants-in-chief of the Crown and the peers of one another. This ancient right of trial was finally surrendered by the peers themselves, who were responsible for inserting the words 'privilege of peerage in relation to criminal proceedings is hereby abolished' in the Criminal Justice Act of 1948. Lord de Clifford was the last to be tried, for manslaughter, by his peers in 1935. Peers and peeresses, however, enjoy other privileges attached to their rank, such as exemption from serving on juries, and peers who sit in the House of Lords also possess privileges as Members of Parliament. Under the Peerage Act, 1963, peeresses are now automatically entitled to sit in the House of Lords. The Lords enjoy rights and exercise functions in five distinct characters: (1) They possess titles of honour which give them rank and precedence; (2) They are, individually, hereditary counsellors of the Crown; (3) They are, collectively, together with the Lords Spiritual, when not assembled in Parliament, the permanent council of the Crown; (4) They are, collectively, together with the Lords Spiritual, when assembled in Parliament, a court of judicature; (5) They are, conjointly with the Lords Spiritual and the Commons, in Parliament assembled, the legislative assembly of the Kingdom, by whose advice, consent, and authority, with the sanction of the Crown, laws are made. Magna Carta ordained that the archbishops, bishops, earls, and greater barons should be summoned to the Council by writ, and although the development of the hereditary principle in connexion with the peerage is rather obscure, a peer once summoned might continue to receive the writ to attend further meetings of the Council, although this did not necessarily follow, and on his death it could be transferred to his heir. The creation of peers by writ of summons has for a long time been discontinued in favour of creation by letters patent, except in the case of the eldest sons of dukes, marquesses, and earls, on attaining their majority, in respect of their fathers' baronies. This, however, does not involve the creation of a new barony.

When a new peer is introduced in the House of Lords he is sponsored by two peers of the same rank as himself. During the ceremony it is customary for the new peer and his sponsors to rise three times, each time raising their hats to the Lord Chancellor. The origin of this custom is obscure, but according to Lord Halifax (*Fulness of Days*, 1957) two possible explanations have been advanced for it. The first suggests that it was intended as a salutation to the three Persons of the Blessed Trinity; the second that it originated as a courtesy acknowledgment of the three earliest orders of the peerage.

The peerage consists of five classes or creations—those of England, Scotland, Ireland, Great Britain and the United Kingdom. The right to create new peers is a Royal Prerogative, in practice now exercisable only in respect of the United Kingdom. No Scottish peerages have been created since the Act of Union with Scotland came into force in 1707. The Act of Union with Ireland in 1800 provided that the number of Irish peerages should be kept to 100, but no new Irish peerages have been created since 1898 when an Irish barony was conferred on Lord Curzon.

The system whereby Scottish and, formerly, Irish peers were represented in the House of Lords by a proportion of their total number was abolished by the Peerage Act, 1963 (*see* REPRESENTATIVE PEERS). To-day all peers of England, Scotland, Great Britain and the United Kingdom are entitled to sit and vote in the House of Lords unless they disclaim their peerages in the manner prescribed by the Peerage Act, 1963 (*see* PEERAGE, DISCLAIMER OF). Irish peers are not similarly qualified, although they are entitled to vote and offer themselves as candidates at General Elections, rights formerly enjoyed only by non-representative Irish peers and denied even to non-representative Scottish peers. Perhaps the most famous Irish peer ever to sit in the House of Commons was Viscount Palmerston. An Irish peer may claim membership of the House of Lords by virtue of a peerage held in one of the other classes, even if it is of inferior rank to his Irish peerage. For example, Earl Winterton, an Irish peer who sat for many years as a Member of the House of Commons, took his seat in the House of Lords on becoming a baron of the United Kingdom. Prior to the passing of the Peerage Act, 1963, Scottish peers other than representative peers were also debarred from membership of the House of Lords unless they were qualified by virtue of a peerage of England, Great Britain or the United Kingdom.

It is interesting to note that in May 1966 12 Irish peers presented a claim to the House of Lords Committee for Privileges that their right to be represented in the House of Lords was 'transcendental and fundamental'. They claimed they were entitled to sit not as representatives of the Irish Republic or Northern Ireland, but as peers of Ireland, and that no enactment could erase that privilege.

Under the Appellate Jurisdiction Acts, 1876–1947, nine Judges of Appeal may be appointed to the House of Lords as life peers (q.v.) with the rank of baron, their function being to assist in the hearing and determination of appeals when the House sits in its judicial capacity. Since the passing of the Life Peerages Act, 1958, non-judicial life peers may also be appointed. This Act in conjunction with the Peerage Act, 1963, also places women on the same footing as men with regard to membership of the House of Lords. Previously subject to a general disqualification, women became eligible for life peerages under the former Act, while the latter extended to women holding hereditary peerages in their own right the same entitlement to membership of the House of Lords as men in similar circumstances.

The 2 archbishops and 24 bishops who sit in the House of Lords do so not as peers but as Lords Spiritual (q.v.) of Parliament.

A peer is entitled to an expense allowance of £6.50, increased in 1969 from £4 14s. 6d., for each day he attends the House of Lords.

See also HOUSE OF LORDS; LIFE PEERS; LORDS SPIRITUAL; LORDS TEMPORAL; REPRESENTATIVE PEERS.

PENSIONARY PARLIAMENT
See CAVALIER PARLIAMENT.

PENSIONS AND NATIONAL INSURANCE, MINISTER OF
See SOCIAL SECURITY, MINISTER OF.

PENSIONS, MINISTER OF
See SOCIAL SECURITY, MINISTER OF.

PENSIONS OF MEMBERS OF PARLIAMENT
United Kingdom. The only Member of the House of Commons entitled to a pension as a right is the Prime Minister who is paid £4,000 a year on his retirement. A retiring Speaker is normally granted a pension of £4,000 by resolution of the House, an Act authorizing payment being passed on his especial behalf.

A pension scheme for ex-Members of Parliament and their widows and orphans was first introduced in 1939 with the passing of the House of Commons Members' Fund Act. The present scheme came into operation with the passing of the Ministerial Salaries and Members' Pensions Act in 1965. All members (other than those who have been or may become Prime Minister, Speaker of the House of Commons or Lord Chancellor), who cease to be members after 16 October 1964, may qualify for a pension. They pay £150 a year into the Members' Contributory Pension Fund and the Exchequer contributes annually an amount equal to the total amount paid into the fund by members. The Exchequer also makes an additional annual contribution (the initial deficiency contribution) which in the first instance amounted to £132,000. This payment is to continue for not more than twenty-five years from the commencement of the Act. An ex-member becomes entitled to a pension on reaching the age of sixty-five (later if his membership continues beyond that age) provided he has served for at least ten years. The pension is payable at the rate of £60 a year for the first fifteen years of service and thereafter at the rate of £24 a year, subject to a maximum period of service of forty-five years. Widows of members are entitled to one half of the pension received by the deceased member, and widowers may receive the same reduced pension in certain circumstances. The Pension Fund is administered by managing trustees, who must be Members of the House of Commons, and the Public Trustee acting as a custodian trustee. Ex-members whose service terminated prior to 16 October 1964 may receive grants from a separate fund in cases of need.

Canada. A former Prime Minister who has held the office for at least four years is entitled to an annual allowance equal to two-thirds of the salary payable to the Prime Minister commencing on the day he ceases to hold office or reaches the age of seventy, whichever is the later. The allowance is not payable during any period that he is a senator or Member of the House of Commons. Widows of former Prime Ministers qualify in certain circumstances for an allowance of one-third of that paid to the deceased husband.

The payment of pensions to members of both Houses is governed by the Members of Parliament Retiring Allowances Act, 1952, as amended in 1953, 1955, 1963, 1965 and 1970. With effect from 1970 the rate of contribution is $7\frac{1}{2}$ per cent for a member of the House of Commons and 6 per cent for a senator. In addition they are required to contribute a further $\frac{1}{2}$ per cent to a Supplementary Retirement Benefits Account. The Prime Minister, other Ministers and Parliamentary Secretaries are also required to contribute to this account. A member wishing to secure a higher pension for himself on retirement may elect to increase his contributions in respect of previous sessions of Parliament. A member qualifies for an allowance if he retires following a minimum of six years' service. The amount of the retirement allowance is calculated according to a formula based upon length of service and the amount of contributions which have been paid. The effect of the amending legislation passed in 1970 was to raise the maximum pension from $9,000 to a possible $13,500. A member's widow becomes entitled to an allowance equal to three-fifths of the allowance which would have been payable to her deceased husband.

Australia. The Parliamentary Retiring Allowances Trust was established in 1948 to administer a pension fund for ex-members. A member contributes $11\frac{1}{2}$ per cent of his parliamentary allowance to the fund and the Government contributes 70 per cent of the amount of each pension paid. An ex-member who has reached the age of forty and who has served for at least three Parliaments (or eight years if he retires voluntarily) is entitled to a pension equal to 30 per cent of his parliamentary allowance, increasing by 4 per cent for each additional year to a maximum of 50 per cent at the age of forty-five and over. A member's widow is entitled to a pension equal to five-twelfths of the parliamentary allowance payable to the member at the time of his death.

Under the Parliamentary Retiring Allowances Act, 1964, a Ministerial Retiring Allowances Fund was established which permits the payment of an additional pension to former ministers and others. A minister and the Leader of the Opposition in the House of Representatives contribute $37 a month to the fund, the Leader of the Opposition in the Senate and the Deputy Leader of the Opposition in the lower House pay $18·50, and the Deputy Leader of the Opposition in the Senate pays $9·25, In return they are entitled to an additional pension related to their length of service, amounting to $18 a week for the first eight years of service rising to a maximum of $42 a week after fourteen years' service or more. The widow of a deceased office-holder has the option of receiving a pension calculated at the rate of five-sixths of the pension received by her deceased husband, or a refund of his contributions. Prime Ministers are entitled to an additional pension varying from $4,000 a year after two years in office to $6,000 after six years, and their widows half these amounts.

New Zealand. Prime Ministers who have served for not less than two years receive a pension at the rate of £200 a year for each full year in office subject to a maximum of £1,000.

A contributory pension scheme for Members of Parliament was first introduced by the Superannuation Act, 1947. Under the Act as amended members are required to contribute 10 per cent of their basic salary (i.e., $465 a year) to a superannuation fund. To qualify for a pension an ex-member must have reached the age of fifty and served for a minimum of nine years. He then becomes entitled to a pension calculated at the rate of one thirty-second of a member's basic salary for each year of service subject to a maximum of two-thirds of that salary. A member's widow is entitled to one half of the pension received by her deceased husband or to a refund of his contributions.

Other Commonwealth Countries. Most of the remaining Commonwealth countries provide for no pension schemes for their Members of Parliament, an exception being Malta which introduced a scheme in 1966.

In Kenya provision is made for pensions or *ex gratia* payments to be paid to ex-members of the National Assembly in cases of need, while Uganda provides for the payment of gratuities to the Prime Minister, the Speaker, and ministers at all levels including Parliamentary Secretaries.

In Nigeria a former Prime Minister is entitled to a pension of £1,500 a year, while Ghana's National Assembly Act of 1961 makes provision for the payment of gratuities to members and ministers. However, in both these countries parliamentary government was upset in 1966 by military *coups*, although it has been restored in Ghana.

'PEOPLE'S BUDGET'

Introduced by Lloyd George in a $4\frac{1}{2}$-hour speech in the House of Commons in 1909 with the object of raising the extra funds needed for old-age pensions and other intended reforms. It introduced super-tax, but it was the proposals for land taxes that aroused the most controversy. The Conservative opposition to the passage of the ensuing Finance Bill through the House was intense and fierce and seventy parliamentary days were needed, during which there were 554 divisions, before the Bill passed its third reading. It was rejected by the House of Lords by 350 votes to 75, and an immediate dissolution of Parliament followed, as no Government could continue without the passing of the Budget. Although the 'People's Budget' was abortive, it resulted in a curtailment of the power of the House of Lords by means of the first of the Parliament Acts (q.v.) passed in 1911.

PERSONAL ACTS

See PRIVATE ACTS.

PERSONAL BILLS

See PRIVATE BILLS.

PERSONAL BILLS COMMITTEE

A Sessional Committee (q.v.) of the House of Lords, consisting of the Lord Chairman of Committees and 4 other Lords, 3 forming a quorum, whose function is to consider petitions for Personal Bills. A Personal Bill is a Private Bill (q.v.) concerned with personal matters, such as names and estates, and is always introduced in the House of Lords. Such a Bill, like any Private Bill, must be based on a petition, which in turn must be deposited by the promoters, together with a copy of the Bill, in the Committee and Private Bill Office of the House of Lords. Such a petition automatically stands referred to the Personal Bills Committee which reports to the House as to whether its purpose is a proper subject for a Personal Bill and whether the provisions of the Bill are properly framed to achieve that purpose.

PERSONAL EXPLANATION

A statement made by a member before the commencement of Public Business, permission having previously been obtained from the Speaker, explaining his conduct in regard to a particular question or occasion, replying to an accusation made by another member, or correcting an alleged misrepresentation. No debate should follow, and general arguments or too distinct a reference to previous debates are out of order. The Speaker of the House of Commons himself made a personal statement on 11 December 1947, when he apologized for having treated a member unfairly.

When a member makes a personal statement the House assumes that he does so with complete integrity. As Mr. Harold Wilson put it, in the course of the debate on the Profumo case on 17 June 1963, 'this House allows freedom of personal statement without question or debate on the premise that what is said is said in good faith'. The resolution passed by the House three days later left no doubt that the abuse of this right constitutes a grave contempt of Parliament.

PETITION OF RIGHT

A declaratory statute asserting the rights and liberties of the subject which was passed by both Houses of Parliament in 1628. Commencing with a recital of past statutes which had secured these rights and liberties, and of recent violations of those laws, the Petition besought the King 'that no man hereafter be compelled to make or yield any gift, loan, benevolence, tax, or such-like charge without common consent by Act of Parliament; that none be called to answer or take such oath, or to give attendance, or be confined or otherwise molested or disquieted concerning the same or for refusal thereof; that no free-man in any such manner as is before mentioned be imprisoned or detained; that Your Majesty would be pleased to remove the said soldiers and marines, and that your people may not be so burthened in time to come; that the aforesaid commissions for proceeding by martial law may be revoked and annulled; and that hereafter no commissions of the like nature may issue forth to any person or persons whatever, to be executed as aforesaid, lest by colour of them any of Your Majesty's subjects be destroyed or put to death contrary to the laws and franchises of the land.'

The Petition of Right has been regarded by many historians as the greatest constitutional milestone since Magna Carta. In prohibiting arbitrary imprisonment and unparliamentary taxation it was directed against the two most consistent abuses of the prerogative, but a deeper significance underlay the prohibition of martial law in peacetime and the billeting of soldiers. The contemporary soldier was more often than not a brutal ruffian drawn from the criminal classes, and the compulsory billeting of such persons upon the ordinary citizen was a terrible infliction. Martial law not only empowered the King to form a peacetime army completely subject to his will but enabled him forcibly to recruit the outcasts of society into his armed forces. The restriction thus aimed at removing an intolerable burden from the people.

The King at first returned a characteristically vague and evasive reply to the Petition, but under the pressure of popular opinion he gave his assent in the customary form, *Soit droit fait comme est desiré*, on 7 June 1628.

See also CHARLES I AND PARLIAMENT.

PETITIONS

The right of petitioning the Crown and Parliament for redress of grievances is acknowledged as a fundamental principle of the Constitution. In considering the history of the petition it should be realized that law originated as unwritten custom and as such could not be changed. The petition was the innovation of Edward I and provided a method of seeking redress from the King by virtue of his prerogative power where none could be sought through the ordinary course of law. The prerogative power being above the law thus established precedents. The grants of favours and rights to individuals and communities were in the nature of private laws, while the grant of a petition on behalf of the realm as a whole would make a public law.

From the reign of Edward I, the Commons appointed a Committee of Grievances at the commencement of each Parliament, and the King, or the Lord Chancellor on his behalf, nominated Receivers of Petitions together with auditors called Triers. The function of the Receivers was to examine petitions to make sure they complied with certain forms and were properly addressed, while the duty of the Triers was to 'try out whether the remedies sought for were reasonable and fit to be propounded'. In 1740 a motion to discontinue the appointment of Receivers and Triers was introduced into the House of Lords but was defeated. Although they had long ceased to serve any purpose these officials continued to be appointed at the commencement of every Parliament until 1886.

During the reign of Edward I the volume of petitions greatly increased, and by 1280 they had become too numerous for the King and his council to deal with. Consequently they were divided into five groups, and it was provided that 'all petitions which concern the seal shall come first to the Chancellor; and those which touch the exchequer to the exchequer; and those which concern the justices and the law of the land to the justices; and those which concern the Jews to the justices of the Jews; so that the King and his council may, without the load of other business, attend to the great business of the realm, and of other foreign countries'. The fifth group, which was dealt with by the King himself, contained only those petitions 'which are so great or so much of grace that they are to come before the King'. Petitions of the more general kind resulted in decisions which in effect created laws or statutes.

As the Commons developed as an independent body, so petitions came to be presented by them affecting matters of national interest. The first petition recorded as being presented by the Commons was that of 1327, consisting of forty-one articles and dealing with various matters. This might well be regarded as the first Public Bill (q.v.) although to-day each individual matter would be embodied in a separate Bill. Thus petitions concerning the nation as a whole came to be separated from those of a purely personal or local nature.

The modern form of petitions was evolved in the 17th century. In these days they usually deal with public grievances and seldom seek redress of private injustices. The rights of petitioners and the power of the House to deal with petitions were laid down by two resolutions of the Commons in 1669:

That it is the inherent right of every commoner in England to prepare and present petitions to the House of Commons in the case of grievance, and the House of Commons to receive the same.

That it is an undoubted right and privilege of the Commons to judge and determine, touching the nature and matter of such petitions, how far they are fit and unfit to be received.

Petitions are no longer addressed directly to the Crown, but to one of the two Houses of Parliament, and petitioners are required to observe a prescribed form in drawing up their petitions. Petitions to the House of Lords should be superscribed, 'To the right honourable the Lords Spiritual and Temporal in Parliament assembled', and to the House of Commons, 'To the honourable the Commons of the United Kingdom of Great Britain and Northern Ireland in Parliament assembled.' A general designation of the parties to the petition should follow, and if there be one petitioner only, his name after this manner: 'The humble petition of (name or other designation) sheweth.' The substance of the petition follows, concluding with the 'prayer' which expresses the object of the petition. To the whole petition are generally added the words, 'And your petitioners, as in duty bound, will ever pray, &c.', to which are added the signatures of the petitioners.

A petition should be hand-written on parchment or paper, and will not be received if printed or typewritten. Many other conditions need to be observed: for instance, a petition must be free from interlineations or erasures; it must have no letters, affidavits, or other documents attached to it; it must be in the English language, or accompanied by a translation which the member who presents it states to be correct; it must bear original signatures or marks, except in the case of incapacity or illness when it is permissible for another person to sign on behalf of the petitioner; and each sheet must be headed by the prayer, which may be reproduced in print or by other mechanical process on every sheet after the first. A petition must be respectfully worded and free from language offensive to the Sovereign, to Parliament, the courts of justice, or other constituted authority.

Foreigners who are resident in the country are entitled to present a petition as well as British subjects. The petition of a corporation may be presented under the common seal of the corporation. The Corporation of the City of London enjoys the privilege of presenting petitions directly at the Bar of the House through its sheriffs. The last occasion on which this privilege was exercised was in 1948 when the corporation petitioned against the abolition of the separate constituency of the City of London. The City of Dublin formerly enjoyed a similar privilege, exercised on its behalf by the Lord Mayor. Petitions from all other persons or bodies are presented to Parliament by a member of the

House to which they are addressed (except in the case of a petition on a Private Bill), but a member cannot be compelled to present one. A member who has not taken the oath or made affirmation may not present a petition, and neither, according to established usage, may the Speaker of the House of Commons do so. The manner of presentation differs in the two Houses. In the House of Lords a peer may comment upon a petition at the time of presentation and a debate may ensue. In the House of Commons discussion of public petitions was abolished in 1842. A member presenting a petition is permitted to make a brief statement upon its source and content, but no debate is allowed unless the petition affects the privileges of the House or complains of a personal grievance requiring immediate remedy. All other petitions are referred to the Committee on Public Petitions for consideration. According to Lord Campion (*Parliament: a Survey*, p. 145n.), 'public petitions, though still presented, are intended merely as demonstrations, since no parliamentary action is now possible on them.' The original purpose of the public petition, to voice the grievances of those classes which were denied parliamentary representation, fell away with the extension of the franchise. The parliamentary question (q.v.) has largely superseded the petition as a means of airing grievances.

A Member of the House of Commons who wishes to present a petition should rise for the purpose before Question Time or, should he prefer to do so, deposit it in the petition bag which is kept behind the Speaker's Chair.

Petitions promoting or opposing Private Bills (q.v.) are subject to a different procedure and are not presented in the manner described above. They are deposited in the Private Bill Office of the House of Lords or the House of Commons either by a Member of Parliament, the petitioner himself, or his agent.

PLURAL VOTING

The objection to an elector possessing more than one vote was voiced by the Radicals in the first quarter of the 19th century with their cry of 'one man, one vote'. Plural voting rested chiefly on the property qualification in counties, and the 'faggot votes' (q.v.) which resulted from this first became a serious political issue when they were denounced by the Liberals prior to the passing of the Franchise Act of 1884. Bills abolishing plural voting were passed by the House of Commons in 1906, in 1912, and in 1913, but were defeated by the House of Lords. The right to exercise more than one vote at a parliamentary election was finally abolished by the Representation of the People Act, 1948. Previously an elector might qualify for a residential, a business, and a university vote, but if he was entitled to a business vote *and* a university vote he could use only one of these. Thus it was not possible for anyone to exercise more than two votes. A form of plural voting advocated by J. S. Mill is known as the multiple or 'weighted' vote. Under this system an elector may have several votes, the number depending on his educational qualifications and his position in society. It was adopted for the direct election of African members to the Kenya Legislative Council, following a report on electoral procedure (the Coutts Report) published in 1955, but ceased to operate when the 1960 constitutional proposals were implemented.

'POCKET' BOROUGH

See 'ROTTEN' BOROUGH.

POINT OF ORDER

Any Member of Parliament can and should bring to the Speaker's immediate notice any instance of what he considers a breach of order or a transgression of any written or unwritten law of the House which the Chair has not perceived, and he may also ask for the guidance and assistance of the Chair regarding any obscurities in procedure. A member is entitled, in such cases only, to interrupt a debate by rising and saying, 'On a point of order, Mr. Speaker', and then to lay the point in question concisely before him, although there is often some doubt among members as to what exactly constitutes a point of order, and the reply is quite frequently, 'That is not a point of order.' As Speaker Morrison said in the House of Commons on 26 March 1952, when members raise points of order the Speaker or Chairman have no idea what they are going to say until they deliver themselves. He went on to say that in too many cases the point raised is not a point of order at all but an attempt either to score a debating point or to delay the proceedings of the House. To raise a point of order during a division (q.v.) a member must be seated and covered.

POLICE IN PARLIAMENT

The important duties performed by the police in the Parliaments of the Commonwealth are obvious to the most casual visitor, and they have become an indispensable adjunct to the parliamentary system of government. As well as maintaining order and preventing the intrusion of unauthorized persons, they have their part to play in the ceremonial of Parliament—and sometimes, as at Ottawa, where the Royal Canadian Mounted Police are on duty, a very colourful part. A sessional order of the British House of Commons directs that the police shall keep the streets leading to the Houses of Parliament free and open, and that no obstruction shall be permitted to hinder the passage thereto of the Lords or Members of the Commons. The police accordingly give every facility to members and officers of the two Houses to cross the street and approach the Houses of Parliament without interruption, and when necessary hold up the traffic for this purpose.

The police maintain order in the lobbies and corridors of the House of Commons, and the only occasion on which they were called into the Chamber for this purpose was in 1901. Twelve Irish Nationalists had been suspended but refused to leave the Chamber, and Speaker Gully eventually sent for a body of police to remove them. Nine of the Irishmen, fiercely resisting to the last, were borne on the shoulders of constables out of the Chamber amidst a tremendous uproar. During the session the House of Commons has an inspector, a sergeant, and 28 constables on duty under the control of the Serjeant-at-Arms, the cost being borne by the House of Commons. The Metropolitan Police have performed duty at the Houses of Parliament since the constitution of the Force in 1829. Four policemen are assigned to permanent duty in the Palace of Westminster, while the remainder are stationed there during sessions only.

POLITICAL REGISTER

See COBBETT, WILLIAM; HANSARD; PARLIAMENTARY DEBATES.

POSTAL VOTE

See ELECTIONS.

POSTS AND TELECOMMUNICATIONS, MINISTER OF

Legislation for the reorganization of the Post Office as a public corporation, based upon a White Paper published on 21 November 1967 (Cmnd. 3233), came into operation on 1 October 1969. The office of Minister of Posts and Telecommunications was established simultaneously, that of Postmaster-General being abolished.

The Minister has overall responsibility for the Corporation although he is not accountable to Parliament for its day-to-day operations. He appoints the Chairman and members of the Corporation and the members of the Users National Council and of the separate Users Councils for Scotland, Wales and Northern Ireland. He is empowered to give directions of a general nature to the Corporation when these appear to be in the national interest, including directions to remedy any defects brought to light by the Users Councils. He also assumed the functions of the Postmaster-General in respect of broadcasting, including responsibility for broadcasting policy. The Minister, although not normally in the Cabinet, enjoys Cabinet rank and is assisted by a parliamentary secretary.

Prior to the passing of the Post Office Act in 1657 the head of the Post Office had been known by various titles—Master of the Posts, Comptroller-General of the Posts, Messengers, and Couriers, and Postmaster of England. With the passing of the Act the title of Postmaster-General came into regular use. Between 1691 and 1823 the office was held jointly by two appointees, and in 1710 it became statutory. Not until 1866 was the Postmaster-General allowed to sit in the House of Commons although his office had been regarded as a political one since 1837. The Postmaster-General was appointed by Letters Patent and exercised the royal monopoly of carrying letters for reward, and subsequently the monopoly of the telegraph and telephone services also.

His responsibility for broadcasting was established under the Wireless Telegraphy Act of 1904 and, like his successor, he was answerable to Parliament in a limited degree for the British Broadcasting Corporation whose governors are appointed by the Crown on the advice of the Prime Minister. The Minister of Posts and Telecommunications has inherited from his predecessor the power to forbid the transmission of any matter and, in an emergency, to take over control of transmissions entirely. He also retains his predecessor's function in relation to the Independent Television Authority in terms of the Independent Television Act, 1954.

The Post Office, which employed the largest staff of any government department, was formerly subordinate to the Treasury but in 1933 it became a separate department with a wider control over its considerable revenue.

A list of the holders of the office of Postmaster-General since 1823 appears as Appendix 27.

POWER, MINISTER OF

In October 1969 this office was merged with that of the Minister of Technology, which was in turn merged with that of the President of the Board of Trade in 1970 to form a new Department of Trade and Industry under a Minister styled the Secretary of State for Trade and Industry and President of the Board of Trade.

A Minister of Fuel and Power was first appointed in 1942 under the Ministers of the Crown (Emergency Appointments) Act, 1939, and put on a permanent basis by the Ministry of Fuel and Power Act, 1945. This Minister was responsible for the administration of the Acts dealing with the industries concerned with the supply of electricity, gas, coal and oil. The functions of the Board of Trade in relation to gas and electricity were taken over by the Ministry, and it absorbed the Board of Trade's Mines and Petroleum Department. In January 1957 the Ministry was renamed the Ministry of Power, when it also took over iron and steel from the Board of Trade, and was given in addition the responsibility for extending the use of atomic energy as a source of industrial power.

'PRAYER'

A motion to annul a Statutory Instrument (q.v.). Such motions count as Exempted Business (q.v.) and are taken at the end of the day's

T

sitting. They must be moved during the forty days after the order is laid on the Table, at the expiration of which it automatically becomes law. The form of these motions provides the reason for their name— 'That an humble Address be presented to Her Majesty praying that the —— Regulations . . . be annulled.'

PRAYERS IN PARLIAMENT

In the early days of parliamentary history the work of the session was preceded by mass, usually in the Chapel of St. Stephen. Later, when the two Houses separated, the custom was kept up, the practice in Tudor times being for the House of Lords to attend service in the Abbey and for the Commons to resort to St. Margaret's Church. This church has been adopted by the House of Commons ever since as its parish church, and is used for its thanksgiving and memorial services. Occasionally, as happened in 1426, the presence of legislators in a body at church was taken advantage of by ecclesiastics to read them a lesson on the errors of their public ways. In that year the Archbishop of Canterbury took his opportunity and delivered an impassioned harangue against the statute which disqualified foreigners from holding any ecclesiastical dignity in the country. With a full appreciation of the value of this law, Parliament elected to keep it on the Statute Book, where it remains to this day. In the reign of Elizabeth I we find the first mention, in D'Ewes's Journal, of devotions in the Legislative Chamber itself. He records that the Litany was said by the Clerk kneeling, and answered by the whole House on its knees. In 1571 the Speaker, Christopher Wray, suggested that he should add a prayer himself 'such as he should think fittest for the time', but perhaps they were too long-winded as the Clerk is again recorded as reading them nine years later. Either the Clerk or the Speaker read the daily prayers in the House until 1643, when the Journal of the House of Commons records 'that one of the ministers of the assembly shall be appointed to pray with the House every morning'. A further stage was reached in 1650, when the House resolved: 'The Governor of the College of Westminster do take care that some fit and able person or persons do attend *de die in diem* to pray in Parliament, and that they give their attendance accordingly.' The first regular Speaker's Chaplain was appointed in 1659, and since that time the Chaplain has used the following prayer at the commencement of each day's business: 'Almighty God, by whom alone Kings reign and Princes decree justice, and from whom alone cometh all counsel, wisdom and understanding; we Thine unworthy servants here gathered together in Thy name do most humbly beseech Thee to send down Thy heavenly wisdom from above, to direct and guide us in all our consultations: And grant that, we having Thy fear always before our eyes, and laying aside all private interests, prejudices and partial affections, the result of all our counsels may be to the glory of Thy blessed Name, the maintenance of true Religion and justice, the safety, honour and happiness of the Queen, the publick wealth, peace and tranquillity of the Realm, and the uniting and knitting together of the hearts of all persons and estates within the same, in true Christian Love and Charity one towards another.' The Speaker does not take the Chair, the Clerks remain outside the Chamber, and strangers are excluded from the Public Galleries until prayers are finished.

In the House of Lords prayers were formerly read by the Lord Keeper of the Great Seal, then by ministers called in from outside, and afterwards by the youngest bishop. Now the practice is for a selected bishop to officiate according to arrangement.

Prayers precede the day's sitting in other Commonwealth Parliaments with the exception of Ceylon, where there is too great a diversity of religious belief amongst the members.

(If further reading is required an article on this subject by Philip Laundy was published in the issue of *Parliamentary Affairs* for Autumn 1958.)

PREAMBLE

That part of a Bill which sets out the reasons for and intended effects of the proposed legislation. It is not an essential feature of a Public Bill (q.v.) and is not often incorporated except where constitutional matters are involved, e.g., the Government of India Act of 1919, or the Statute of Westminster, 1931. It is the last part of the Bill to be considered, as amendments to the Bill may necessitate an alteration to the preamble. Unlike the practice in regard to those Public Bills in which it appears, the preamble which is always part of a Private Bill (q.v.) is first considered, and if it is opposed the petitioners against the Bill are heard and the question is put to the Committee on Opposed Bills 'That the preamble is proved', which is resolved either in the affirmative or in the negative.

PRECEDENCE

The order in which persons should be placed on ceremonial occasions by virtue of their rank received statutory recognition by an Act of 1539. Although this Act was concerned directly only with the Great Officers of State, it has since been considered the chief authority for the marshalling of dignities, and confirmed regulations made since the first 'order of all Estates of Nobles and Gentry of England' was framed in 1339. Important decrees of precedence were made in 1612 and 1616, and James I himself decided that the newly created order of baronets should follow barons' and viscounts' younger sons. Precedence must come from father or husband, and cannot be derived from a female, unless in the case of a peeress in her own right. In the United Kingdom the Prime Minister, by a Royal Warrant of 2 December 1905, takes precedence, after the Royal Family, the archbishops, and the Lord Chancellor, of all peers and commoners. The Prime Minister is followed by the Lord President of the Council, and then the Speaker of the House of Commons, whose precedence was established by an Order in Council of 30 May 1919.

PRECEDENT

A previous decision by the Chair, or a well-established procedure or usage which serves as an authority or guide when a similar point or circumstance arises in Parliament. A large part of parliamentary procedure rests upon precedents which form for Parliament the source of its customary law. This is ascertained and made available to the Speaker or Chairman for deciding questions of procedure by reference to a similar case in the Journals of the House or to the rulings given by past Speakers. A well-known collection of parliamentary precedents is that compiled by John Hatsell (q.v.), Clerk of the House of Commons at the end of the 18th century.

See also SPEAKERS' RULINGS.

PREFERENTIAL VOTE

See ALTERNATIVE VOTE.

PREROGATIVE

See ROYAL PREROGATIVE.

PRESIDENT OF THE BOARD OF TRADE

In 1970 this office ceased to have an independent existence following a major reorganization of the machinery of central government. One result of this reorganization was the merger of the Ministry of Technology and the Board of Trade to form a new Department of Trade and Industry headed by a Minister with the title of Secretary of State for Trade and Industry and President of the Board of Trade.

Together with the Ministries of Agriculture and Education, the Board of Trade differs from other Government departments in that it developed from a committee of the Privy Council. When Britain's overseas trade began to grow the Privy Council was responsible for its protection, but during the 17th century it was evident that the Council was unable to cope with all the work that was involved. It therefore delegated these functions to committees and 'Commissioners for Trade', and in 1696 a Committee of Privy Councillors and Members of Parliament was created and called the Board of Trade and Plantations (i.e., Colonies). This Board was abolished by an Act of 1782, but it was reconstituted by William Pitt in 1786 under the title of 'the Committee of the Privy Council for Trade and Foreign Plantations' with Lord Hawkesbury as its first President. The Order in Council of 23 August 1786 which constituted the committee provided for no quorum, thus enabling the President to act alone on its behalf. To quote from Hugh Dalton's *The Fateful Years* (p. 387, footnote):

The last recorded meeting was held on December 23rd 1850, but for the previous thirty years only the President and Vice-President had attended. The practice of weekly, and often twice weekly, meetings of the Board continued with steadily flagging attendance from 1786 to 1850, but the minute books do not record a full attendance at any of these many meetings.

In addition to the President the Board, as now constituted, comprises the Archbishop of Canterbury, First Lord of the Treasury, First Lord of the Admiralty (now a defunct office), the Principal Secretaries of State, Chancellor of the Exchequer, Speaker of the House of Commons, and (if they are Privy Councillors) the Chancellor of the Duchy of Lancaster, Paymaster-General, Treasurer of the Navy (now a defunct office), and the Master of the Mint. The Vice-President was replaced in 1867 by a Parliamentary Secretary.

The new Secretary of State is answerable to Parliament for the matters dealt with by the Board, which besides the promotion of export trade is responsible for export credits, trade statistics, patents, designs and trade marks, and the registration of companies. The functions of the Ministries of Labour, Transport, and Power (formerly Fuel and Power) which became fully detached departments with widened responsibilities, were at one time exercised by the Board of Trade. It was also concerned with the registration of ships and the administration of the Merchant Shipping Acts until these matters were transferred in 1939 to what became the Ministry of Transport. When the Ministry of Materials was dissolved in July 1954 its remaining functions were transferred to the Board of Trade.

The new Secretary of State is a Cabinet Minister with a salary of £8,500. If he sits in the House of Commons he is entitled to a further £1,250. The President of the Board of Trade was also invariably a Cabinet Minister.

A chronological list of Presidents of the Board of Trade appears as Appendix 30.

PRESS AND PARLIAMENT

The cordial and co-operative relationship which to-day exists between Parliament and the Press represents the achievement of centuries of struggle between the champions of liberty and the forces of intolerance. The reporting of parliamentary proceedings was for many years regarded as a flagrant breach of parliamentary privilege, and (an interesting survival from a less enlightened era) is still technically so to-day. The freedom which the Press enjoys to-day was not lightly won, and it was in comparatively recent times that unfettered journalism was accepted as a healthy and essential feature of a democratic society.

A thirst for news has ever been a British characteristic, but it was not until the abolition of the Star Chamber in 1641 that journalism was able to enjoy a temporary and very much restricted freedom. The rapidly strengthening power and influence of Parliament had stirred the political consciousness of the nation, and a demand became apparent amongst the literate populace for news of Parliament's activities. Various news books came into being which reported parliamentary proceedings as their main feature. Some reports, such as those appearing under the title of 'Diurnal Occurrences of Parliament' which were started in 1641 and continued until the Restoration, were recognized officially, but those which offended Parliament were suppressed and their authors and printers punished. So seriously did the Commons regard unlicensed reporting that Sir E. Dering was expelled from the House and imprisoned for printing a collection of his own speeches. There was considerable journalistic activity between 1641 and 1660 in spite of the dangers involved, and in spite of the re-imposition of censorship in 1643 which spurred Milton into writing the *Areopagitica*. It was in this essay that Milton gave expression to the advanced thought 'that freedom of speech and freedom of action are not evils to be tolerated, but blessings essential to the life and progress of any nation'. (C. E. Vaughan's preface to the Everyman edition of Milton's *Areopagitica*.) 'Give me the liberty to know, to utter, and to argue freely, according to conscience, above all other liberties', wrote Milton, but many were to suffer before authority recognized the right of the individual to enjoy this liberty.

Shortly after the Restoration the activities of the Press were severely curtailed. On 25 June 1660, the House of Commons resolved 'that no person whatsoever do presume at his peril to print any votes of proceedings of this House without the special leave and order of this House'. In 1662 the Licensing Act was passed limiting the number of master printers to twenty, and for over thirty years the Press was virtually suppressed. Surreptitious publications continued to appear, however, and in 1694 a printer named Dyer was brought to the Bar of the House of Commons and reprimanded for reporting parliamentary proceedings. At the same time the Commons passed a resolution warning writers of newsletters against the commission of Dyer's offence. When the Licensing Act was allowed to lapse in 1695 there was a great revival of journalistic activity, but Parliament remained as firm as ever in its insistence that its debates and proceedings should receive no attention from the Press. But the popular demand for parliamentary information was as strong as ever. In the closing years of Queen Anne's reign summaries of debates, compiled from memory, began to appear in Boyer's *Political State of Great Britain*. In the following reign similar reports started to appear in the *Historical Register*. Ever jealous of its privileges, an alert Parliament took great pains to bring offending journalists to book. In 1704, John Tutchin, editor of the *Observator*, expressed political views which displeased Parliament, and the House of Commons passed a resolution declaring that the offending issues of Tutchin's paper contained 'matter scandalous and malicious, reflecting on the proceedings of the House, tending to the promotion of sedition in the kingdom', and ordered Tutchin, together with the printer and the publisher, into custody. Even its own members were not immune from punitive action, and in 1714 Richard Steele was expelled from the House of Commons for editing a seditious newspaper.

In 1712 Parliament attempted to muzzle the Press by imposing a tax on newspapers. A paper printed on a half-sheet was liable for a stamp tax of a halfpenny; if printed on a whole sheet the tax was a penny. Editors were swift to find a loophole in the law, and began to publish six-page newspapers, printed on one sheet and a half, thereby escaping the tax. This loophole was closed in 1725 when all newspapers, regardless of their size, became liable for the tax and had to bear a red stamp. Taxation did not have the effect which Parliament desired, and as the sales of newspapers increased so their number grew. The tax was doubled in 1757, and taxation of the Press in one form or another continued for nearly a hundred years after this date.

In 1721 the House of Commons exceeded its jurisdiction by assuming the right to punish a journalist for a purely political offence, no breach of parliamentary privilege being involved. A newspaper of Jacobite sympathies called *Mist's Journal* had advocated the restoration of the Pretender, and the matter was brought before the Commons who resolved 'that the said paper is a false, malicious, scandalous, infamous, and traitorous libel, tending to alienate the affections of His Majesty's subjects, and to excite the people to sedition and rebellion, with an intention to subvert the present happy establishment and to introduce popery and arbitrary power'. The proprietor, Nathaniel Mist, was committed to Newgate, and was later compelled to fly the country. Even after his departure his paper continued to be published under the name of *Fog's Journal*.

It was in 1731 that the enterprising publisher, Edward Cave (q.v.), launched the *Gentleman's Magazine* and published parliamentary reports on a larger scale than ever before. Cave had already been in trouble with Parliament, and in 1727 he had been committed to prison by the House of Commons for supplying information on the proceedings of Parliament to his friend Robert Raikes for publication in the

Gloucester Journal. In 1729 Raikes himself had been summoned to the Bar of the House for censure, and on this occasion the Commons unanimously resolved 'that it is an indignity to, and a breach of the privilege of, this House for any person to presume to give in written or printed newspapers any account or minutes of the debates or other proceedings of this House, or of any committee thereof', and 'that upon discovery of the authors, printers, or publishers, this House will proceed against the offenders with the utmost severity'. Cave, nothing daunted, achieved astonishing success with his reports in the *Gentleman's Magazine*, which was followed shortly afterwards by the rival *London Magazine*. On the reports contained in these two periodicals, the Parliamentary History (q.v.) for the period is chiefly based. It is interesting to note that although Parliament as a body took strong exception to the reporting of its debates, Cave received considerable assistance in the supply of material and the correcting of proofs from members themselves. He is even said to have forwarded proofs to the Speaker of the House of Commons for correction. He was thus able to ensure the accuracy of his reports and authentic parliamentary reporting may be said to have started with Cave's reports.

The issue of parliamentary reporting came to a head in April 1738, when an important debate took place in the House of Commons as a result of Cave having published a speech before it had been delivered. Much eloquence was expended on the subject, most of the members who spoke vigorously condemning the practice in the strongest terms. 'If we do not put a speedy stop to this practice,' declared Winnington, 'you will have every word that is spoken here by gentlemen misrepresented by fellows who thrust themselves into our gallery. You will have the speeches of this House every day printed, even during your session, and we shall be looked upon as the most contemptible assembly on the face of the earth.' Sir William Wyndham was alone in upholding the right of the public 'to know somewhat more of the proceedings of the House than what appears from the votes'. The debate ended in the unanimous resolution 'That it is a high indignity to, and a notorious breach of the privileges of this House to print the debates or other proceedings of the House, as well during the recess as the sitting of Parliament, and that this House will proceed with the utmost severity against such offenders'.

This debate and its resultant resolution marked a setback for parliamentary journalism. The matter had been brought before the House by Speaker Onslow with a view to ascertaining the final opinion of the House upon it. The House had stated its resolution unanimously and in most definite terms, and to disregard it might well have involved greater hazards than before as Parliament could be expected to increase its vigilance over the activities of the Press. Also, members themselves deemed it advisable to cease to be as co-operative as in the past. Cave was not the man to admit defeat, however, and he continued to publish reports in which the locale and the names of the speakers were disguised and which were constructed from brief notes smuggled out of the Public Gallery by persons specially placed there for the purpose. The first man to construct these reports was a writer named William Guthrie and he was followed in 1740 by the young Samuel Johnson (q.v.). The reports appeared in such forms as 'Debates in the Senate of Great Lilliput' and 'Debates of the Political Club'. The names of the speakers were disguised in such a way that they could be easily recognized, usually in the form of anagrams of the real names. In 1747 Cave and Astle (the editor of the *London Magazine*) were summoned before the House of Lords for publishing an account of Lord Lovat's trial in their two journals. They were compelled to make abject apology but were spared further punishment. After this incident Cave ceased his reports until 1752, after which he does not appear to have been molested.

The eventual removal of the ban on parliamentary reporting was largely due to the activities of the notorious but colourful John Wilkes (q.v.). In 1762 Wilkes commenced his paper, the *North Briton,* and from the very first issue he fearlessly asserted the right of the individual to criticize authority. He wrote scathing political articles, making no effort to conceal the names of those he assailed (a precaution which other writers usually observed), until the weight of official displeasure descended on him with the publication of the famous 'No. 45', in which he fiercely attacked the King's Speech on proroguing Parliament. (For further details of Wilkes's brushes with authority at this stage and subsequently *see* GEORGE III AND PARLIAMENT.) Having fled the country and been proclaimed an outlaw, Wilkes returned to England in 1768 and was elected to Parliament as the member for Middlesex. His long struggle with Parliament over the right of the Middlesex electors to return him as their member is dealt with under the heading referred to above, but it was at the outset of this constitutional battle that the incident arose which resulted in the tacit removal of the ban on parliamentary reporting. In 1771 two printers, Thompson of the *Gazetteer and New Daily Advertiser* and Wheble of the *Middlesex Journal,* were summoned to the Bar of the House of Commons for 'misrepresenting the speeches and reflecting on several members of this House'. When neither of them attended as directed they were ordered to be taken into custody. Wheble was arrested in circumstances suggestive of collusion and appeared before Wilkes, now an alderman of the City of London, who had encouraged the printers in their defiance of the House. Wilkes discharged the prisoner and bound him over to prosecute the person who had arrested him. Thompson was arrested on the same day and appeared before another alderman named Oliver, who discharged him on the ground that no accusation had been made against him. The following day a third printer named Miller of the *London Evening Post*, another journal which had offended the House of Commons, was arrested by a House of Commons messenger on a warrant signed by the Speaker. Miller called for a constable who took both men before the Lord Mayor, Wilkes, and Oliver. They dismissed the charge against Miller and committed the messenger for trial for assault. The Commons, on learning of these events, fumed with indignation and ordered the Lord Mayor and Oliver, who were members, to attend in their places, and Wilkes to appear at the Bar. Wilkes replied that he was the lawfully elected Member for Middlesex and would attend only as a member. After he had disobeyed three summonses the Commons discreetly allowed the matter to drop, but the Lord Mayor and Oliver, having attended in their places and expressed their defiance, were both committed to the Tower. They were released a few weeks later on the prorogation of Parliament, and the popular demonstration in favour of the aldermen alarmed the Commons to such an extent that they made no further attempt to suppress the reporting of parliamentary debates and proceedings. From this time the freedom of the Press may be said to have been secured. There were subsequent occasions on which Governments took steps to fetter the activities of the Press, but the profession of journalism was never without its champions in the House of Commons. In the session of 1810, for instance, Sheridan was inspired to utter the following noble sentiments: 'Give me but the liberty of the Press, and I will give the minister a venal House of Peers, I will give him a corrupt and servile House of Commons, I will give him the full swing of the patronage of office, I will give him the whole host of ministerial influences, I will give him all the power that place can confer upon him to purchase submission and overawe resistance; and yet, armed with the liberty of the Press, I will go forth to meet him undismayed; I will attack the mighty fabric he has reared with that mightier engine; I will shake down from its height corruption, and lay it beneath the ruins of the abuses it was meant to shelter.' In 1803 the House of Commons recognized the right of the Press by reserving special seats in the Public Gallery for the use of reporters, and in 1835 the first gallery exclusively for the use of the Press was opened. (*See also* HANSARD.)

To-day Parliament and the Press have a healthy respect for each other, but newspapers are bound to report parliamentary proceedings accurately and to observe and respect the legitimate privileges of Parliament and its members. There have been occasions in recent years when Parliament has proceeded against persons who have transgressed in this respect, and examples may be cited from two Commonwealth countries, the United Kingdom and Australia. In the first case, an article published in the *World's Press News* in 1947 by the then Member for Gravesend reflected upon the conduct of some of the author's fellow members, and the matter was referred to the Committee of Privileges, the usual procedure in such cases. After considering the committee's report, the House of Commons found the author of the article and the editor of the *World's Press News* guilty of a gross contempt of the House. The former was expelled from the House and the latter was summoned to the Bar and reprimanded by the Speaker. Further facts which were established as a result of this case led to another member being reprimanded for supplying confidential information to a newspaper in return for payment, and the editor and political correspondent of the newspaper concerned apologizing at the Bar of the House for refusing to reveal the name of their informant when questioned by the Committee of Privileges. Another case arose in 1957 when the editor of the *Sunday Express* was called to the Bar of the House of Commons (24 January) to answer for a contempt resulting from a leading article which appeared on 16 December 1956 on the subject of petrol rationing.

A serious case arose in Australia in 1955 when the proprietor of a suburban newspaper in New South Wales, the *Bankstown Observer*, published defamatory allegations against a member of the lower House of the Federal Parliament. The complaints of the member concerned were investigated by the Committee of Privileges, which reported that the proprietor of the newspaper and the writer of the offending articles were guilty of a serious breach of privilege. The House of Representatives unanimously agreed with the findings of the committee and voted, on a division, to commit both offenders to prison for three months.

Following upon the disclosures brought to light by the *World's Press News* case in 1947, the House of Commons adopted a resolution some weeks later 'That, if in any case hereafter a Member shall have been found guilty by this House of corruptly accepting payment for the disclosure and publication of confidential information about matters to be proceeded with in Parliament, any person responsible for offering such payment shall incur the grave displeasure of this House; and this House will take such action as it may, in the circumstances, think fit'. A similar motion had been introduced previously, but its wording had occasioned doubts in the minds of some members that it might be taken to imply a general criticism of the Press. The revised motion was opposed on the grounds that the action it empowered the House to take was too vague, that it constituted an extension of privilege, and that it implied the existence of widespread corruption. The debate which took place (on 10 December 1947) gave a clear indication of Parliament's anxiety to safeguard the legitimate rights of a free Press whilst taking the necessary steps to protect itself from the activities of unscrupulous journalists who form a very small minority in an honourable profession. It is a very different outlook from that which flourished in the days of Edward Cave and John Wilkes.

PRESS GALLERY

Every Commonwealth Parliament provides a gallery for the exclusive use of the Press. In the House of Commons it is situated above the Speaker's Chair, and in a number of other Parliaments it is similarly placed. In the House of Lords the Press Gallery faces the Throne. Admission to the Press Gallery is reserved to accredited representatives of newspapers, news agencies, or the B.B.C. They are admitted on production of a press card which is issued by the Serjeant-at-Arms.

The first Press Gallery was opened in the House of Lords in 1831 and in the House of Commons in 1835, in a temporary chamber which was being used following the great fire of 1834 which destroyed the Parliament building. When the new Houses of Parliament were opened in 1852 both Chambers included a Press Gallery. Previously, parliamentary correspondents were forced to join other members of the public in the Strangers' Gallery, although by the beginning of the 19th century a special row had come to be reserved for them. During the previous century reporters had been severely handicapped by the ban on taking notes, for in those days Parliament regarded any report of its proceedings as a breach of privilege. This is technically still the case (*see* PRIVILEGE, BREACH OF), and to this day the taking of notes is forbidden in all the public galleries other than the Press Gallery.

Special places in the Press Gallery are also reserved for Hansard (q.v.) reporters.

PRESSURE GROUPS

When industrial, commercial, professional, or other sections of the community, represented by societies, trade unions, or professional associations, try to influence Parliament to promote, withdraw, or repeal legislation, they are commonly known as 'pressure groups'. The methods by which a Government may be persuaded to take a certain course of action in respect of any matter involving the interests of a special group vary from an interview with a minister to a national campaign sponsored by the interests concerned. This facet of the British political system is thoroughly examined in the following books: Stewart (J. D.), *British Pressure Groups*, 1958; Finer (S. E.), *Anonymous Empire*, 1958; Eckstein (H.), *Pressure Group Politics*, 1960.

'PREVIOUS QUESTION'

A motion which is moved for the purpose of preventing the House coming to a decision on a subject of debate. It now makes a very infrequent appearance in the House of Commons (it was last moved in 1943) but 150 years ago the motion played quite a large part in procedure. It is moved in the words, 'That the question be not now put'; the mover, however, merely says, 'I move the previous question.' If the motion is carried, the question which was before the House when the 'previous question' was moved disappears. If the motion is negatived, the question which was previously before the House must be put immediately, and the result is the same as if the closure (q.v.) had been carried. The mover must be a member who has not spoken in the debate on which the 'previous question' is moved.

In the House of Lords the 'previous question' is proposed from the Chair in the words, 'Whether the said original question be now put', which form entails the mover voting *against* the motion. The 'previous question' was last moved in the House of Lords in 1950. Prior to 1888 the procedure relating to the 'previous question' was the same in the House of Commons as in the House of Lords.

The 'previous question' is so called because the question whether the question before the House should be put at all is, in the logical order of business, previous in its nature.

PRIDE'S PURGE

The forcible exclusion of the Presbyterian Members of the House of Commons which was carried into effect on 6 December 1648. The army leaders were determined that Charles I should be brought to trial, but realized that they could not secure the concurrence of the House of Commons unless the majority which favoured continued negotiation with the King was excluded. With the connivance of the Independents in the Commons, three regiments surrounded the House, and as each member arrived, Colonel Pride, one of the commanders, checked his name from a list. Those to whom the army objected were denied admission, and many who resisted were imprisoned, including D'Ewes, Prynne, Fiennes, Strode, and Waller. The purge was an unconstitutional and wholly indefensible act of violence. It achieved its object, however, and it was a greatly reduced and violently anti-Royalist House of Commons which resolved to bring the King to trial and finally condemned him.

See also CHARLES I AND PARLIAMENT.

PRIMARY ELECTIONS

A primary election is a preliminary public election conducted at public expense whose purpose is the selection of candidates for nomination at a subsequent main election. Primary elections are held in the United States of America where there are a very large number of offices to be filled by election, and there is consequently a need to reduce the number of candidates to manageable proportions.

Primary elections were unknown in the British Commonwealth until 1961 when they were introduced in Kenya. Kenya's Constitution at the time provided for an African majority in the Legislative Council and the representation of minorities by the reservation of 10 seats for Europeans, 8 for Asians, and 2 for Arabs. Prior to a General Election, the candidates for these seats contested a primary election in which the voting was restricted to the racial communities whom the candidates were intended to represent. Any candidate for these seats who secured at least 25 per cent of the total votes cast at the primary elections went forward to the main election at which all the candidates were elected by all the races voting together on a common roll. Thus a candidate who won a primary election was by no means certain of success at the main election.

Although racial representation was abolished when Kenya became independent, primary elections were retained for the purpose of selecting those candidates of the governing party who would go forward as candidates at a General Election. In December 1969 over 600 government party candidates presented themselves at primary elections in 158 constituencies. Those nominated were returned unopposed at the ensuing General Election since no other party was contesting the election.

PRIME MINISTER

The Prime Minister, besides being the leader of the Government, is also the leader of one of the main political parties. On the one hand he is the trustee of the principles of his supporters, and on the other he is responsible to the Crown for the administration of public affairs. Lord Esher said, 'He is the supreme co-ordinating authority, and as the architect and constructor of the Cabinet it is his function to hold it together. On his death or retirement it is automatically dissolved, though it may be re-formed under another chief.' As well as choosing the members of the Cabinet, the Prime Minister can secure the removal of ministers in order to maintain Cabinet harmony. Keith, in his *British Cabinet System*, says that the polite description of the Prime Minister as *primus inter pares* (first among equals) which satisfied Lord Morley is inadequate to describe his real position if by temperament he is willing to assert to the full the position which he can assert if he so desires. His power grows, not diminishes, and this is inevitable when the sources whence it is derived are borne in mind. The root of the matter lies in the fact that since the Reform Act of 1832, the Prime Minister has become the choice of the electorate, and General Elections have frequently been fought on personalities rather than on principles. The reason for this lies in the fact that democracies find it easier and wiser to form judgments on men rather than on doctrines, and they feel, after a man has been before them in high office, that they can trust him or not to further the kind of views which will appeal to them. Mr. Harold Macmillan's dismissal of one-third of his Cabinet, including the Chancellor of the Exchequer, the Lord

Chancellor and the Minister of Defence, in July 1962 lent emphasis to the view that the Prime Minister is an all-powerful figure who dominates the Government. There can be no doubt that his right to select and dismiss his colleagues, to ask for a dissolution of Parliament, and to dispense patronage amount to a formidable total of power. Yet one should not lose sight of the fact that a Prime Minister is dependent on the support of his colleagues, his party and ultimately the country. An important article by G. W. Jones on the subject of the Prime Minister's power, which challenges the widely held view regarding the extent of his dominance, was published in *Parliamentary Affairs*, vol. XVIII, no. 2, 1965.

The Prime Minister is now invariably a member of the House of Commons, although 18 of the 47 Prime Ministers we have had so far have sat in the House of Lords during their term of office, the last being Lord Salisbury. In 1721 Sir Robert Walpole was installed at the head of the administration as First Lord of the Treasury and Chancellor of the Exchequer, and this is usually regarded as the first occasion on which there was a real Prime Minister. Lord Melbourne said that Walpole's powerful position was the result of the very great confidence which both George I and George II reposed in him, and from the difficulty which they had in transacting business from their imperfect knowledge of English. The title of Prime Minister was not a popular one at first—it was even used in a derogatory sense. Lord North would never allow himself to be called *Prime* Minister because he said it was an office unknown to the Constitution, and this was so until 1905, when by Royal Warrant the holder of the office was given precedence next after the Archbishop of York. Since Walpole's time the position of the head of the Government has generally been united with that of the First Lord of the Treasury. From the days of Queen Elizabeth I the first minister was nearly always the Treasurer. There have been some Prime Ministers who did not combine these two offices, such as Lord Chatham, who was also Lord Privy Seal, and Lord Salisbury, who was successively Foreign Secretary and Lord Privy Seal on two occasions whilst leading an administration. The Lord Treasurer or First Lord of the Treasury originally concerned himself with the fiscal duties of his office, and he was often Chancellor of the Exchequer also when he sat in the Commons. The two offices have not been held together for over a hundred years, except in the case of Mr. Gladstone during portions of his first two Governments and by Stanley Baldwin in 1923. In 1924 Ramsay Macdonald coupled the office with that of Foreign Secretary, a decision for which he was strongly criticized. It would clearly be difficult in modern conditions for a Prime Minister to hold any other office with substantial duties, although since the establishment of a Civil Service Department (with which was integrated the Civil Service Commission) in 1968 the Prime

Minister has also taken on the responsibility of Minister for the Civil Service. The Ministers of the Crown Act of 1937 recognized the special position of the Prime Minister by giving him a salary of £10,000 a year as Prime Minister and First Lord of the Treasury. In 1964 this salary was increased to £14,000, in addition to which he draws £1,250 as a Member of the House of Commons. From 1940 to 1945 Sir Winston Churchill was also Minister of Defence, and though this second office carried with it no statutory duties and no department, it served to symbolize a very active direction of the military side of the war effort.

The Prime Minister accepts his place from the Sovereign not by the delivery of a staff or a seal nor by a declaration in Council, as do other high officers of state, but by kissing hands like an ambassador. He receives no letters patent, his appointment being merely noted in the Court Circular, although his commission as First Lord of the Treasury is gazetted. The Prime Minister as such possesses no distinctive uniform, and like other Cabinet Ministers he wears on state occasions the ordinary full-dress of a Privy Councillor. Apart from his salary, a rate- and tax-free house is assigned to him at 10 Downing Street. Downing Street was called after Sir George Downing, a Secretary of State in the time of Charles II, and the house was originally offered to Sir Robert Walpole by George II as a private residence. Walpole refused it as such, but accepted it as an official residence for himself and his successors in the Treasury. While he is in office the Prime Minister also has the use of Chequers in the Chiltern Hills, a country house and estate, with sufficient capital to maintain them, which were settled by Lord Lee of Fareham in perpetuity on the Prime Minister for the time being.

The record length of service for any Prime Minister in the Commonwealth was recently held by the late Mackenzie King of Canada with 7,829 days in office, although not in one unbroken period. Britain's first Prime Minister, Walpole, came very near to equalling this with an unbroken period of 7,620 days. Early in 1955, however, Mackenzie King's record was broken by Sir Godfrey Huggins (now Lord Malvern), as Prime Minister of Southern Rhodesia and later as Prime Minister of the Federation of Rhodesia and Nyasaland. When he retired in October 1956 his service in that high office amounted to 8,419 days. The record for the unbroken tenure of the premiership at the head of one government is held by Sir Thomas Playford, Premier of New South Wales, who broke Walpole's record on 14 September 1959.

History was made in Ceylon in 1960 when Mrs. Bandaranaike became the world's first woman Prime Minister. In 1966 India followed Ceylon's example when Mrs. Indira Gandhi became Prime Minister of her country.

As Lord Mersey remarks in his book on the Prime Ministers of

Britain, there is one final position which a Prime Minister, if he rises rightly to his high trust, can always command—the first place after his Sovereign in the estimation of his fellow-countrymen.

Chronological lists of the Prime Ministers of Commonwealth countries appear as Appendix 7.

(Further reading: Benemy, *The elected monarch*, 1965; Carter, *The office of Prime Minister*, 1956.)

PRINCE EDWARD ISLAND LEGISLATIVE ASSEMBLY

The first legislature was established in this Canadian Province in 1773, and responsible government was achieved in 1851. The Legislative Council (the upper House) was made elective in 1862, but after the island had joined the Confederation in 1873 a political system consisting of a Lieutenant-Governor, Cabinet, and a bicameral legislature, in addition to 6 members and 4 Senators in the Federal Parliament, suggested over-government for so small a Province. In 1874 a resolution was introduced into the Assembly which sought to abolish the Council and reduce the Assembly by one-third, but in spite of similar attempts in 1879 and 1880 the required reform was not accepted by the Government. The Legislative Council's reply to the two latter Bills was the suggestion that both branches of the legislature should be reduced by a half and that the remaining members should combine to form one House. In spite of steady opposition from the Government, this was finally achieved in 1893, half the members of the Assembly being elected on the old Council property vote and the remainder by universal male and female suffrage.

The Government of Prince Edward Island now consists of a Lieutenant-Governor, appointed by the Federal Government, an Executive Council or Cabinet, and a Legislative Assembly of 32 members (increased from 30 in 1966) representing 16 electoral districts. Each district returns a Councillor and an Assemblyman elected by all the voters of the Province. Prior to the election of 1966 the former was elected by property-holders only, the latter by property-holders and non-property holders. Another innovation introduced in 1966 was the use of an official voters' list to replace the unofficial system of voters' registration which had been in operation previously.

Since 1784 the Executive Council has consisted of 9 members, including the Premier who is also its President, the Cabinet thus occupying an unusually dominant position both in the legislature and in the caucus. In the Chamber, contrary to the usual practice in Commonwealth legislatures, the Government sits to the left of the Speaker. Until recently the Legislative Assembly was denied the main adjunct to parliamentary ceremonial—the Mace. According to local legend, this was removed by an enemy raiding party during the war of 1812 and it was long held that tradition forbade its replacement.

[583]

However, in February 1966 a Mace was presented to the Legislative Assembly as a joint gift from the Canadian branches of the Commonwealth Parliamentary Association, federal and provincial.

Prince Edward Island is now represented in the Canadian Parliament by 4 members of the House of Commons and 4 Senators.

(Further reading: MacKinnon, *The Government of Prince Edward Island*, 1951.)

PRINCE'S CHAMBER, HOUSE OF LORDS

An ante-chamber to the House of Lords which is situated behind the Throne. It is richly decorated with bas-reliefs in bronze by William Theed, depicting historic events of the Tudor period, panel portraits of Kings and Queens, and a frieze carved with the arms of the Sovereigns of England. The dominating feature of the chamber is a massive statue of Queen Victoria seated on the Throne, carved in marble by J. Gibson, R.A. The figures of Justice and Mercy formerly on either side of the Queen were removed following a recommendation of the Select Committee on House of Lords Offices which was adopted by the House in December 1955.

The Prince's Chamber is so called to commemorate the apartment of that name which adjoined the House of Lords in the ancient Palace of Westminster.

PRIVATE ACTS

Acts with a local or personal application only, such as one extending the powers of a local authority or regulating a private estate. Private Acts are divided into three classes:

Local and Personal Acts. Until 1798 such Acts were printed with the other statutes of the year, but since that year they have been distinguished from Public Acts and printed in a separate series. Since 1868 certain statutes previously included among the Public General Acts (q.v.) have been transferred to the category of the Local and Personal Acts. They are Acts which, though passed as Public Bills, are local in their character, and Acts for the confirmation of provisional orders (*see* PROVISIONAL ORDER BILL). During the past century much private legislation has been dealt with in the form of Provisional Order Bills and latterly under the Statutory Orders (Special Procedure) Act, 1945.

Private Acts Printed. From 1798 to 1815 the Private Acts, not declared public, were not printed by the King's Printers, and could only be given in evidence by obtaining authenticated copies from the statute rolls in the Parliament Office. Since 1815 the greater part of such Private Acts have been printed by the King's Printers, and have contained a clause declaring that a copy so printed 'shall be admitted as evidence thereof by all judges, justices, and others'. Since 1851 this evidence clause has been retained, with the addition of an enactment that the 'Act shall not be deemed a Public Act'. These Acts are now mainly Estate Acts.

Private Acts not Printed. This last class of Private Acts is rapidly falling in numbers. They are of a strictly personal nature and many types, such as Naturalization and Divorce Acts, have completely disappeared.

PRIVATE BILL OFFICE

An office in the department of the Clerk of the House (q.v.) which supplies the clerks for Private Bill Committees and assists in the conduct of Private Bill legislation in all its stages. One of the clerks from this office acts as secretary to the Chairman of Ways and Means (q.v.). There is a similar office in the House of Lords with which is incorporated their Committee Office.

PRIVATE BILLS

Bills which confer particular powers or benefits on any person or body of persons, including individuals, local authorities, statutory companies, and private corporations. They should not be confused with Private Members' Bills (q.v.). The essential difference in procedure between a Public Bill (q.v.) and a Private Bill is that, whereas the former is either presented direct to the House or introduced on a motion by a Member of Parliament, the latter is solicited by the parties who are interested in promoting it and is founded on a petition (q.v.). It sometimes occurs that a Public Bill affects private interests, and such a Bill is regarded as a Hybrid Bill (q.v.) and is treated like a Private Bill after second reading.

The majority of Private Bills are local in character, but some, which are not now common, deal with personal matters such as estates, names, naturalization, and divorce. Naturalization Bills are uncommon because of general legislation which has conferred certain powers on the Home Secretary, and the need for Divorce Bills has been removed by judicial methods of divorce and other factors. When the need for such a Bill does arise it is always introduced in the House of Lords and is known in that House as a Personal Bill. A Personal Bills Committee is set up by the House of Lords at the beginning of every session to consider any petitions for Personal Bills which may be presented. If this committee recommends that a Personal Bill be proceeded with, the subsequent procedure is substantially the same as that on any other Private Bill.

The originators of Private Bills are mainly local authorities and other statutory bodies, and the measures proposed usually concern the regulation of public utilities. The necessity for private legislation has been greatly reduced by the growth of administrative powers, including the power of making Provisional Orders (*see* PROVISIONAL ORDER BILL) and Special Procedure Orders (q.v.).

A special procedure is prescribed for Private Bills, and separate sets of Standing Orders exist in both Houses for the regulation of Private Business. Private Bills originate from petitions which are deposited by the promoters in the Private Bill Office. With rare exceptions, the opportunity arises once a year only, 27 November being the final date for the deposit of the petition and Bill, and 30 January the last day for the presentation of petitions against the Bill.

It is assumed that the Bill will seek powers and privileges to which others will object, and notices of intention to promote the Bill must be given by newspaper advertisement and gazette notices. Individual notices must be given to owners, lessees, and occupiers of land and houses affected by the proposals. Once deposited, the petition and Bill are open to inspection, and printed copies must be made available for the use of members and officers of Parliament and government departments. To ascertain that all the conditions required by Standing Orders have been complied with, two examiners are appointed, one by each House, who begin to examine all petitions on 18 December. They sit separately, each considering a certain number of petitions each day. Any petition which, in the opinion of an examiner, has not complied with Standing Orders is referred to the Standing Orders Committee, which considers the matter further and reports its recommendations to the House.

After the examiners have reported, the Chairman of Ways and Means and the Lord Chairman of Committees together decide in which House the respective Bills shall be introduced. Once a Bill is laid upon the Table of the appropriate House it is deemed to have been read a first time. Petitions objecting to a Bill are considered in the House of Commons by the Court of Referees in the event of the promoters of the Bill questioning the *locus standi* (q.v.) of the petitioners. The Court consists of the Chairman of Ways and Means, the Deputy Chairman, the Speaker's Counsel, and not less than 7 members of the House. Three members form a quorum, and the decisions of the Court constitute legal decisions against which there is no appeal.

A Private Bill goes through the same stages as a Public Bill (*see* BILL, PASSAGE OF), and the procedure is similar in both Houses. Most Private Bills go through without opposition from members of the House, but if objection is voiced time has to be found for debate. Normally the second reading is taken as unopposed Private Business before Questions. Quite apart from any opposition from the House itself, a Private Bill is deemed to be opposed if a petition has been presented against it in which the petitioner or petitioners have prayed to be heard, or if the Chairman of Ways and Means reports to the House that in his opinion it should be treated as opposed. After second reading, every Private Bill is referred to the Committee of Selection (q.v.) whose task is to allocate each measure to an appropriate committee for its committee stage. All unopposed Bills are referred to the Committee on Unopposed Bills, which consists of the Chairman of Ways and Means, the Deputy Chairman, and 3 other members, and is assisted by the Speaker's Counsel. In the House of Lords, the function of this committee is fulfilled by the Lord Chairman of Committees. Opposed Bills are referred either individually or in groups to committees consisting of a Chairman and 3 members 'not locally or otherwise interested therein'. These committees sit in a semi-judicial capacity and hear the case for and against the Bills argued by counsel representing the promoters and those petitioning against them. The function of all Private Bill Committees is to determine whether it is in the public interest that a Private Bill should be passed, and if so in what form.

If a Private Bill is amended in committee it is ordered to lie on the Table of the House so that the amendments may be moved in the House. Usually the report stage is a pure formality, as are the third reading and the passage through the other House. In neither the Lords nor the Commons may amendments be moved unless they have been submitted to the Chairman of Ways and Means or the Lord Chairman of Committees, as the case may be.

The progress of a Private Bill is dependent upon the payment of fees by the promoters, and the actual work involved in promoting such a measure or in taking proceedings to oppose it is carried out by a parliamentary agent (q.v.).

In 1930 a Select Committee of the House of Commons under the chairmanship of Sir Herbert Dunnico made a number of recommendations which had the effect of simplifying Private Bill procedure and keeping down the costs of private legislation. In 1955 a Joint Committee of both Houses was appointed with similar terms of reference to those of the Dunnico Committee, namely, 'to consider what alterations, if any, are desirable in the practice and the Standing Orders of the two Houses relating to private legislation, having special regard to the desirability of lessening the expense at present incurred.' The Joint Committee reported in May 1955, and amongst other changes recommended an enlargement of the panel for the consideration of unopposed Bills; the standardization of the Standing Orders and procedure on Private Bills in both Houses; the introduction of a uniform and considerably reduced scale of fees for both Houses; and provision for reviewing the scales of charges of parliamentary agents.

The volume of private legislation was at its height towards the middle of the 19th century on account of the prodigious development in railway construction at that time. In 1846 alone 1,130 Private Bills became law.

(Further reading: F. Clifford, *History of Private Bill Legislation*,

2 vols., 1885–7; T. L. Landers, *Private Bills in Parliament,* 1919; and O. C. Williams, *The historical development of Private Bill Procedure and Standing Orders in the House of Commons,* 2 vols., H.M.S.O., 1948–9.)

PRIVATE MEMBER

A Member of the House of Commons who is neither an office-holder in the Government nor an Opposition leader; also known as a 'back-bencher'.

PRIVATE MEMBERS' BILLS

Public Bills which are introduced by private members instead of by the Government, not to be confused with Private Bills (q.v.). The time allotted to Private Members' Bills during a session is ten days, Friday being the day on which such measures are considered. Of those Private Members' Bills which reach the Statute Book the majority are balloted Bills, although other methods of introducing Bills are available to private members. At the beginning of each session a ballot is held to determine the precedence which is to be given to private members who wish to introduce Bills, and all members desiring to take part enter their names on the ballot sheet. The draw takes place in a committee room in the presence of the Chairman of Ways and Means. Under present procedure the ballot for Private Members' Bills takes place on the second Thursday on which the House shall sit during the session, and members who are successful present their Bills on the fifth Wednesday. A member who is successful in the ballot but who has no Bill of his own to introduce may promote a Bill on behalf of another member. Alternatively, if he is a Government supporter he may, by arrangement with the Government Whips, promote a Bill which the Government desires to introduce but cannot fit into its generally overcrowded programme. Similarly, an Opposition member may introduce a Bill on behalf of his party. Private Members' Bills pass through the same stages as all other Public Bills (*see* BILL, PASSAGE OF), but for the committee stage they are referred to a Standing Committee which gives precedence to Private Members' Bills.

Private Members' Bills are subject to many hazards and only comparatively few ever reach the Statute Book. If a Bill does reach a second reading the member promoting it is fortunate if he gets it through in the limited time allotted to it, and many Private Members' Bills are either defeated or talked out. A member promoting a Bill naturally endeavours to win as much support for his proposed measure as possible, but he is also likely to encounter opposition. There have, however, been some notable Private Members' Bills which have survived to become Acts of Parliament, Sir Alan Herbert's Matrimonial

Causes Bill, 1937, being a famous example. A more recent example of a Private Member's Bill which attracted much public attention was the Murder (Abolition of Death Penalty) Bill which became law at the end of 1965. It was introduced by Mr. Sydney Silverman and sponsored by members from all parties. The Government allowed time for the consideration of the Bill, and at one stage morning sittings were introduced in order to expedite its passage through the House of Commons.

In spite of the formidable obstacles which confront the private member in his attempts to initiate legislation, his right to do so is a very healthy feature of our parliamentary system, and many a worthy cause has benefited as a result. A private member may not promote a Bill whose principal object is financial. A balloted Bill (but not one introduced under the 'ten minutes rule') may contain money clauses and be given a second reading in anticipation of the Government sponsoring a money resolution to cover them. If this is not forthcoming the money clauses are struck out at the committee stage.

Private Members' Bills may also be introduced under the 'ten minutes rule' (q.v.), but this procedure is usually adopted only for the purpose of attracting some publicity to a proposed measure as its chances of a successful passage are very remote.

In the House of Lords a Bill may be introduced by any peer with the leave of the House.

One of the most famous Bills to be sponsored by a private member and passed into law in a Commonwealth country other than the United Kingdom was the Electoral (Compulsory Voting) Bill introduced in Australia in 1924. It established the compulsory voting requirement which is a notable feature of that country's electoral system.

(Further reading: Bromhead, *Private Members' Bills*, 1956.)

PRIVATE MEMBERS' TIME

In addition to Question Time and the daily half-hour Adjournment Motion, a certain amount of time is devoted each session to private members' business, which consists of Bills and motions. Under the present arrangement, the first 20 Fridays of the session are given over to private members' business, Bills and motions being considered on alternate Fridays. There are also four other days during the session on which private members' business takes precedence until 7 p.m. Bills may be considered on days reserved for motions although the latter take priority. The precedence which is to be given to private members wishing to introduce Bills or motions is determined by ballot. The ballot for Private Members' Bills (q.v.) is usually held in a committee room and conducted by the Chairman of Ways and Means, but in the case of private members' motions the ballot takes place in the House with the Speaker in the Chair, and is held after Question Time on such days during the session as the House appoints for the purpose. A recent Select Committee on Procedure recommended that these two ballots should be combined.

The complaint is often heard that private members' time is being constantly whittled down. The complaint is undoubtedly justified (during the War all private members' time was absorbed), but the pressure of Government business has become so heavy in recent years that other business must necessarily be curtailed. The claims of the Opposition are also ever-increasing, with the result that the Government is hard pressed to complete its legislative programme. Even private members' time is sometimes made to serve the ends of Government and Opposition, as a private member with no business of his own may introduce a Bill or motion on behalf of his party. The member who specializes in worthy causes may well reflect sadly upon his lost opportunities when he recalls that in 1832 the Government took precedence on two days a week only.

PRIVATE NOTICE QUESTIONS
See QUESTIONS.

PRIVILEGE

Erskine May defines parliamentary privilege as 'the sum of the peculiar rights enjoyed by each House collectively as a constituent part of the High Court of Parliament, and by members of each House individually, without which they could not discharge their functions, and which exceed those possessed by other bodies or individuals. Thus privilege, though part of the law of the land, is to a certain extent an exemption from the ordinary law'. The privileges of the Commons as distinct from the Lords have been defined as 'the sum of the fundamental rights of the House and of its individual members as against the prerogatives of the Crown, the authority of the ordinary courts of law and the special rights of the House of Lords'. The Lords, originally the more powerful of the two Houses, have always enjoyed special privileges as peers distinct from those which they enjoy, together with the Commons, as Members of Parliament. Thus privilege falls into three categories which respectively apply to Members of Parliament individually, to each House collectively, and to both Houses jointly. (*See also* PEERS.)

Parliamentary privilege is both extensive and indefinite, and its growth and development form a subject which is discussed at great length in all constitutional histories. Important accounts can be found in Erskine May (Chaps. 3-10) and Sir William Anson's *Law and Custom of the Constitution* (Chap. 4). The history of parliamentary privilege is to a great extent the story of the fierce and prolonged struggle of the

Commons to win the rights and freedoms which they enjoy to-day. At the commencement of every Parliament it is the custom for the Speaker 'in the name, and on behalf of the Commons, to lay claim by humble petition to their ancient and undoubted rights and privileges', and in particular he specifies freedom from arrest and all molestations, liberty of speech in all their debates, and the right of access to the Sovereign. He concludes by praying that 'all their proceedings may receive from Her Majesty the most favourable construction'. To this petition the Lord Chancellor replies that 'Her Majesty most readily confirms all the rights and privileges which have ever been granted to or conferred upon the Commons by Her Majesty or any of her royal predecessors'. This has become a traditional ceremony at the Opening of Parliament.

The earliest recorded instance of the Commons claiming their right to certain liberties occurred in 1397 when the Lords convicted one Thomas Haxey, of treason for introducing a Bill of reforms to which the King objected. The judgment was later reversed on the petition of the Commons, who claimed that it was 'against right and the course which had been usual in Parliament in violation of the customs of the Commons'. In the Parliament of 1401 the Speaker, upon his election, besought the King to disregard unofficial reports of the proceedings in the Commons, and in the reign of Henry IV it became the custom for the Speaker to claim for himself the right to inform the King of the mind of the Commons and to request that the most favourable construction be put upon their utterances. In 1523 the Commons asserted their right to freedom of debate, when they rejected Wolsey's demand for the sum of £800,000 (in those days an enormous sum of money) for the prosecution of the war with France, before they had had an opportunity to discuss the matter amongst themselves. In 1536 came the demand for the right of access to the Crown, and in 1541 freedom of speech was specifically claimed for the first time. In 1554 appears the first record of the petition which has now become a part of the ceremony of the Opening of Parliament. In the Journal of the House of Commons for 12 November of that year, it is recorded that 'Mr. Speaker made an excellent Oration, comparing a Body Politick to a Body Natural; and in the End made Three Petitions, viz. For free Speech in the House, Privilege from Arrest and Troubles for the Common House, and their Servants, and to have Access to the King and Queen, for the Cases of the House'. The claiming of these privileges became a regular practice at the Opening of a new Parliament, and from here on they may be considered separately.

FREEDOM OF SPEECH. In the reign of Elizabeth I the granting of this privilege had become an established precedent, but in reality it was a concession of a very doubtful nature. The Queen made it clear on various occcasions that she did not intend the privilege to be taken too literally. In 1621 James I went much further than Elizabeth when, in a letter to the Speaker, he commanded him 'to make known our name unto the House, that none therein shall presume henceforth to meddle with anything concerning our Government or deep matters of State'. The Commons' reply was the famous Protestation which the King himself tore from the Journal. It read:

That the liberties, franchises, privileges and jurisdictions of Parliament are the ancient and undoubted birthright and inheritance of the subjects of England: And that the arduous and urgent affairs concerning the King, State and defence of the realm, and of the Church of England, and the maintenance and making of laws, and redress of mischiefs and grievances, which daily happen within this realm, are proper subjects and matter of counsel and debate in Parliament: and that in the handling and proceeding of those businesses every member of the House of Parliament hath, and of right ought to have, freedom of speech to propound, treat, reason and bring to conclusion the same. . . .

The climax of the struggle for freedom of speech was reached during the reign of Charles I when the long constitutional conflict between the Crown and Parliament came to a head. On 4 January 1641 (1642 according to our present calendar), the King, attended by an armed escort, entered the Commons Chamber and attempted to arrest five members on a charge of treason resulting from their proceedings in the House. He took the Speaker's Chair and called upon the five members by name, but the House maintained an angry silence. He then turned to the Speaker and demanded that the members be pointed out to him, upon which the Speaker, Lenthall (q.v.), fell on his knees and delivered his famous reply: 'May it please Your Majesty, I have neither eyes to see, nor tongue to speak in this place, but as the House is pleased to direct me, whose servant I am here. . . .'

The entry in the Journal for the following day shows clearly and in no uncertain terms the view which the House took of the King's unwarranted intrusion. After prayers it was ordered 'that the door be locked and the key brought up; and the outward doors cleared of all persons but servants to Members of the House; and that no Member do offer to go out without leave; and also that some Members do send forth their servants, to see what numbers of people are repairing towards Westminster; and to bring notice to this House'. A committee of ten members was then appointed and ordered to retire immediately 'to consider of some way for vindicating the Privileges of Parliament; and for providing for the safety of both Kingdoms; and present it to the House with all speed'. The Journal then continues:

Whereas His Majesty, in his Royal Person, Yesterday being the Fourth Day of January, 1641, did come to the House of Commons, attended with a great Multitude of Men, armed in a warlike Manner with Halberds, Swords, and Pistols; who came up to the very Door of this House, and placed themselves there, and in other Places and Passages near to the House, to the great Terror and Disturbance of the Members thereof then sitting, and, according to their Duty, in a peaceable and orderly Manner, treating of the great Affairs of both the Kingdoms of England and Ireland; and His Majesty having placed himself in the Speaker's Chair, did demand the Persons of divers Members of That House to be delivered unto him: It is this Day declared by the House of Commons, that the same is a high Breach of the Rights and Privilege of Parliament, and inconsistent with the Liberties and Freedom thereof. . . .

The privileges of Parliament were never effectively challenged after the Restoration, and freedom of speech was finally confirmed after the Revolution of 1688 by the Bill of Rights (q.v.) which declared: 'That the freedom of speech, and debates on proceedings in Parliament, ought not to be impeached or questioned in any court or place out of Parliament.'

The importance of the privilege to-day lies in the immunity it confers upon Members of Parliament from the law of slander. All members are, however, subject to the discipline of the House itself and it is their bounden duty not to abuse the privilege. The protection extends to the publication of any papers printed by order of the House, and a newspaper editor who publishes fair and honest reports of what has been said in the House is also protected. A Member of Parliament is not protected by privilege from the consequences of any words he utters outside the House, or of publishing on his own initiative any speeches he has made inside the House.

FREEDOM FROM ARREST. This privilege has ceased to be of any great importance as it does not confer immunity from arrest on any criminal charge; the Commons themselves had always excluded 'treason, felony and breach of the peace' from their claim for this privilege. Until comparatively recent times, however, it was a very necessary protection in view of the frequent use made of imprisonment in cases of debt and other civil actions. A member is immune from arrest for the duration of a session and for forty days before and after, this period having its origin in the ancient protection which the King extended to persons travelling to and from his court. By ancient custom a peer enjoys immunity at all times, his person being 'for ever sacred and inviolable'.

Although this privilege had been claimed by the Commons as far back as the 15th century it was not conceded as a right until 1543, when George Ferrers, a member who had been arrested for debt, was released by the Serjeant without any writ or warrant, 'only by show of his Mace, which was his warrant'.

FREEDOM OF ACCESS TO THE SOVEREIGN. This right is exercised by the Commons as a body through the Speaker and is not accorded to individual members. Members may, of course, attend the Speaker, and the privilege was once an important one as it meant that the Sovereign could not refuse to receive an address which came from the House as a whole. However, in these days, its significance is largely of a ceremonial nature.

In addition to the privileges which are specifically claimed there are others which have always been asserted and enforced by the Commons. These include the right to provide for their own constitution, to regulate their own proceedings, and to punish those guilty of breaches of privilege (*see* PRIVILEGE, BREACH OF). The right to regulate their own proceedings includes the right to initiate any business and to consider all matters in any order they choose (*see* OUTLAWRIES BILL).

Some privileges are based solely on custom and precedent while others have been confirmed by statute. In the 19th century the limits of privilege were defined and agreed to by Parliament, the Crown, and the courts, and it was further agreed that no new privilege can be created.

In 1967 a Select Committee was appointed to consider the whole question of parliamentary privilege and it reported in December of that year. The Report, which made far-reaching recommendations, some of them requiring legislative action, was debated in the House on 4 July 1969. Its principal recommendations concern complaints of contempt and the penal jurisdiction of the House and they are considered in the ensuing entry. The committee also proposed that the immunity of members and officers of the House from jury service should be retained and the immunity of members and officers of the House from attendance as witnesses should be retained in limited form.

(Further reading : Lord Kilmuir, *The Law of Parliamentary Privilege*, 1959).

See also PRIVILEGE, FINANCIAL.

PRIVILEGE, BREACH OF

Both Houses of Parliament claim the right to punish offences which violate their privileges, whether committed by a member or an outsider, and whether directed against an individual or against the House collectively. Certain other offences against the authority and dignity of Parliament, whilst not breaches of specific privileges, are also punishable and are more correctly called contempts (q.v.). Giving evidence before the Committee of Privileges on 1 March 1965 the Clerk of the House explained that 'the term "breach of privilege" means really a breach of a known, established privilege of which the two great privileges are freedom of speech and freedom from arrest in civil cases or freedom from molestation. . . . If the offence is more vague or less easily distinguished then it is called generally a contempt'. It has become the custom, however, to refer to all such offences as breaches of privilege.

The acts which constitute breaches of privilege are many, and are dealt with exhaustively in Erskine May (Chap. 8). Anson summarizes them as disrespect to any member of the House, as such, by a person not being a member; disrespect to the House collectively, whether committed by a member or any other; disobedience to orders of the House, or interference with its procedure, with its officers in the execution of their duty, or with witnesses in respect of evidence given before the House or a Committee of the House. Disrespect to a member includes attempts to threaten or intimidate him, any libel concerning his conduct in the House, and the offering of a bribe. Disrespect to the House collectively is described by Lord Campion as 'the original and fundamental form of breach of privilege', and includes libels on the House at large, upon the Speaker, and upon Select Committees. Amongst those breaches of privilege which may be classed as disobedience to the orders of the House, mention should be made of the publication of debates, which was formerly an offence and was frequently punished as such. Even to-day their publication is permitted only on sufferance, and it still remains within the power of the House to treat such action as breach of privilege. The publication of false or misrepresented reports of debates is still censured as though the very publication constitutes the offence. Abuse of the right of petition, premature publication of evidence given before a committee, and proceeding against a member or officer of either House in the courts for his conduct in obedience to the orders of Parliament, are further instances of breach of privilege.

The power to punish breaches of privilege is essential to the authority of any legislative assembly and is enjoyed by all the Parliaments of the Commonwealth. In the case of the House of Lords and the House of Commons it has been held that their power to inflict punishment for breaches of privilege is inherent in the two Houses as a High Court of Parliament. The power of commitment, described by Erskine May as the keystone of parliamentary privilege, has always been held by the House of Lords and was claimed by the Commons in the 16th century. It is the most serious penalty which either House can inflict upon its members or upon outside offenders. The Commons cannot order imprisonment for a period beyond the duration of the session, but the Lords are not so restricted. The Lords are also empowered to impose fines, but there seems to exist some doubt as to whether the Commons also possess this power, although it is one which they have exercised in the past. The last occasion on which the House of Commons imposed a fine was in 1666. An offender who is punished by imprisonment is confined in the Clock Tower if he is a member, otherwise he is committed to one of Her Majesty's prisons.

Offences which are not sufficiently grave to warrant imprisonment are punished by admonition or reprimand, the latter being the more serious punishment of the two. The punishment is administered by the Lord Chancellor in the House of Lords and by the Speaker in the House of Commons. If the offender is a member he stands uncovered in his place; if a non-member he is summoned to the Bar of the House to receive his punishment, attended in the Lords by Black Rod and in the Commons by the Serjeant-at-Arms bearing the Mace. It was formerly the practice to make offenders kneel at the Bar when hearing the judgment of the House.

Members of Parliament who commit offences are liable to two further penalties: suspension from the service of the House and expulsion.

At the beginning of every session the House of Commons appoints a Committee of Privileges (q.v.) and the House of Lords appoints a similar committee designated the Committee for Privileges (q.v.).

In the House of Commons it is open to any member to raise a complaint of privilege on the floor of the House provided he does so at the earliest opportunity and, if the Speaker rules that a *prima facie* case has been established, the matter takes precedence over all other business. It is not the Speaker's function to decide whether or not the matter complained of constitutes a breach of privilege or contempt, but only to determine whether or not the complaint meets the conditions which justify its taking precedence over all other business. A matter of privilege may also be raised by way of a motion, of which notice is required, in which case it takes its place in the normal order of business, and it is open to a member to proceed in this way should the Speaker rule that his complaint does not constitute a *prima facie* case. Regardless of the method employed the final decision respecting matters of privilege rests with the House itself.

The proceedings which follow upon a complaint of privilege may vary according to whether the complaint is directed against a member or a non-member and whether or not it is founded upon a document. Most complaints, if they are dealt with at all, are referred to the Committee of Privileges and the House usually takes no action until the committee has reported. When a complaint is raised in the House and the Speaker rules that a *prima facie* case has been made out, it is customary for a motion to be made at once referring the matter to the Committee of Privileges. Little, if any, debate normally takes place at this stage. The member raising the matter states the grounds of his complaint and, if it is directed against a fellow-member, the latter usually makes a statement in explanation or exculpation, after which he withdraws from the House. If the ensuing motion is debated he remains outside the Chamber for the duration of the debate.

Certain recent cases have tended to demonstrate that the border-line between a breach of privilege or contempt of Parliament and legitimate political comment can be somewhat thin. In the session of 1963–4, for example, a complaint was raised against Mr. Quintin Hogg concerning a public speech he made in the course of which he alleged that the then Government's 'elbows had been jarred in almost every part of the world by individual Labour members' partisanship of subversive activities'. The matter was referred to the Committee of Privileges which acknowledged that in certain circumstances reflections upon members, whether they were identified or not, can amount to reflections upon the House itself, but that it was by no means clear whether such an interpretation would be valid 'otherwise than in respect of their conduct within the precincts of Parliament or in the transaction of the service or business of the House'. The Committee found that the words complained of did not constitute a contempt and recommended that no further action should be taken. The Committee's report included the following important observations:

Your Committee recognise that it is the duty of the House to deal with such reflections upon Members as tend, or may tend, to undermine public respect for and confidence in the House itself as an institution. But they think that when the effect of particular imputations is under consideration, regard must be had to the importance of preserving freedom of speech in matters of political controversy and also, in cases of ambiguity, to the intention of the speaker. It seems to them particularly important that the law of parliamentary privilege should not, except in the clearest case, be invoked so as to inhibit or discourage the formation and free expression of opinion outside the House by Members equally with other citizens in relation to the conduct of the affairs of the nation.

It has long been accepted that neither House of Parliament has any power to create new privileges. Your Committee believe that it would be contrary to the interest of the House and of the public to widen the interpretation of its privileges especially in matters affecting freedom of speech. Your Committee and the House are not concerned with setting standards for political controversy or for the propriety, accuracy or taste of speeches made on public platforms outside Parliament. They are concerned only with the protection of the reputation, the character and the good name of the House itself. It is in that respect only and for that limited purpose that they are concerned with imputations against the conduct of individual Members. (H.C. 247, 1963–4.)

This report did not seem to deter members from raising similar complaints during the first session of the new Parliament which was elected in October 1964. Six complaints were made all told, three of which failed to satisfy the Speaker with regard to the requirements of establishing a *prima facie* case. The other three were referred to the Committee of Privileges. The first, to take them in chronological order, arose from a complaint concerning a speech by a Labour member in which he was alleged to have said that some Conservative M.P.s were 'half-drunk and disgusting to look at' during certain debates in the House. Reporting on 8 March 1965, the Committee found that the member had been guilty of a gross contempt of the House and a breach of its privileges, but in the light of a written apology made by the member concerned recommended that no further action be taken. (H.C. 129, 1964–5.) The second case arose from a threatening letter sent to certain members of Parliament by a racial extremist, and the Committee, while finding that the letter constituted a breach of privilege, chose to treat it with the contempt it deserved and recommended in their report of 27 May 1965 that no action be taken. (H.C. 228, 1964–5.)

The third case arose from words which had been used in a public speech by the Chancellor of the Exchequer, Mr. James Callaghan, and had the effect of bringing to a head the entire issue of the latitude which a politician may allow himself in the course of his public speaking. Mr. Callaghan, in referring to the prolonged debates on the Finance Bill, had been reported as saying that he did not think of certain Conservative members as members for particular constituencies. 'I look at them and say Investment Trusts, Capital speculators or that is the fellow who is the Stock Exchange man who makes profit on Gilt Edge. I have almost forgotten their constituencies, but I shall never forget their interests. I wonder sometimes whom they represent? The constituents or their own or friends' particular interests?'

After this case was referred to the Committee of Privileges a number of Labour members let it be known that they intended to repeat Mr. Callaghan's words in public while the matter was still before the Committee. This was indeed a throwing-down of the gauntlet, for had the Conservatives responded by raising further complaints in the House a farcical situation could have arisen and the dignity of the House been gravely threatened. Fortunately common sense prevailed.

Reporting on 12 July 1965 the Committee quoted from the report of its predecessor in relation to the Quintin Hogg case (*see* second paragraph of the extract from H.C. 247, 1963–4 quoted above) and, having invited Mr. Callaghan to explain his words, found that there had been no contempt of the House (H.C. 269, 1964–5).

In the course of a memorandum submitted to the Committee of Privileges during the consideration of the Callaghan case, the Clerk of the House pointed out that 'under the law of privilege offences against the House are not civil but quasi-criminal in character. . . . Libels on the House or on its members relating to their service in the House are therefore not comparable with libel in civil actions, and certainly justification has never been accepted by the Committee of Privileges as a defence; it does not appear, therefore, that it could be pleaded.'

In 1967 a Select Committee was appointed to examine the whole question of parliamentary privilege in the light of a widespread feeling, reflected in press comments and debates in the House as well as in the Reports of the Committee of Privileges, that such an examination was necessary. Reporting in December of that year, it made important recommendations largely concerning complaints of contempt and the penal jurisdiction of the House. The Report was debated in the House on 4 July 1969, and it is noticeable that the Reports of the Committee of Privileges in the past two years have been in keeping with the spirit of the recommendations. The Committee recommended, *inter alia*, that:

(1) the House should retain its penal jurisdiction but that it should be exercised as sparingly as possible;

(2) where a member has a remedy in the courts he should not be permitted to invoke the penal jurisdiction of the House;

(3) in deciding whether or not a contempt has been committed, the House should take into account the truth of the allegations made and whether or not the person making them was motivated by considerations of public interest;

(4) complaints of a trivial character should be dismissed without benefit of investigation;

(5) in appropriate cases legal aid should be made available to persons appearing before the Committee of Privileges;

(6) the reporting of the proceedings of the House or its Committees from which the public are not excluded, and the advance publication of unrestricted information relating to divisions, questions or notices of motion, should not constitute contempts and

(7) a member who speaks upon a specific topic in which he has a financial interest should disclose such interest.

The Committee also recommended that the expression 'parliamentary privilege' should be abolished, that the House should speak of its 'rights and immunities' rather than 'rights and privileges' and of 'contempt' rather than 'breach of privilege' and that the Committee of Privileges should be renamed the Select Committee of House of Commons Rights. The Committee also indicated that the implementation of some of its recommendations would require legislation.

PRIVILEGE, FINANCIAL

The nation's finances are controlled exclusively by the House of Commons, whose rights in this respect may well be regarded as the most important collective privilege of that House. The House of Lords can neither initiate nor amend Bills sanctioning taxation or expenditure or Bills dealing with local rates. Although they are still constitutionally entitled to reject such Bills altogether, such action would be devoid of practical effect to-day since the Parliament Act, 1911, provides that a Money Bill (q.v.) can receive the Royal Assent (q.v.) even though it has not been assented to by the Lords.

In respect of private legislation and certain minor charges upon the people, the Commons have permanently relaxed their privileges, and they have been known to waive them under other circumstances whilst creating no precedent. (For full details see Erskine May, Chap. 28.) The Commons would not be prepared to consider any Bill sent down from the Lords which infringed their financial privileges in any way, although the Lords would not deliberately offend the Commons in this manner; in fact, so completely do they recognize the financial privileges of the lower House that they do not go into committee on the annual Finance and Consolidated Fund Bills. Any interference with these Bills on the part of the Lords would, of course, be regarded as an intolerable breach of privilege by the Commons, for they are the modern counterparts of the ancient 'Bill of aids and supplies' which, to quote Erskine May, 'are felt by them (the Commons) to embody privilege in its most essential form.'

From the earliest times the Commons have claimed the right to grant or withhold aids and supplies, but being a legislative enactment a grant also required the advice and consent of the Lords. The procedure remained unchanged until the 17th century when two famous resolutions denied to the Lords the right of interference. In 1671 it was resolved 'that in all aids given to the King by the Commons, the rate or tax ought not to be altered by the Lords'. The second resolution of 1678 also asserted the right of the Commons to decide the purposes to which their grants should be put; it was resolved 'that all aids and supplies, and aids to His Majesty in Parliament, are the sole gift of the Commons; and all Bills for the granting of any such aids and supplies ought to begin with the Commons; and that it is the undoubted and sole right of the Commons to direct, limit, and appoint in such Bills the ends, purposes, considerations, conditions, limitations and qualifications of such grants, which ought not to be changed or altered by the House of Lords.' On these two resolutions the present practice is based. Two important incidents were to occur, however, before the exclusive right of the Commons in financial matters was finally established and accepted. In 1860 the Lords rejected the Paper Duties Repeal Bill. In reply the Commons reasserted their claims, and the proposal contained in the rejected measure was reintroduced in a Finance Bill which embodied all the financial proposals for the year, a practice which has been adopted ever since. In 1909 the Lords took more drastic action still, and rejected the Finance Bill for that year (i.e., the Budget). The crisis caused thereby resulted in the passing of the Parliament Act, 1911, which abolished the necessity for the Lords' assent to a Money Bill, thus robbing the upper House of all power to impede the progress of financial legislation.

Throughout the Commonwealth the principle is generally accepted that the upper House is not entitled to interfere with financial measures.

However, in 1957, the dormant rights of the Canadian Senate were reasserted in an academic way in the Report of the Special Committee on the Rights of the Senate in Matters of Financial Legislation.

See also PARLIAMENT ACTS, 1911 and 1949.

PRIVILEGE OF PEERAGE

See PEERS.

PRIVILEGES, COMMITTEE FOR

See COMMITTEE FOR PRIVILEGES.

PRIVILEGES, COMMITTEE OF

See COMMITTEE OF PRIVILEGES.

PRIVY COUNCIL

Originally the executive organ of government, the administrative powers of the Privy Council declined in the 18th century with the growth of the Cabinet (q.v.), and from the accession of George I its functions have been purely formal. 'The Lords and others of Her Majesty's most Honourable Privy Council' to-day number about 340. They are appointed by letters patent and consist of persons who hold or who have held high political, legal, or ecclesiastical office in Great Britain and other countries of the Commonwealth and Empire, peers and persons distinguished in their professions. All Cabinet Ministers are included by convention, the two archbishops by prescription, and others (e.g., the Speaker of the House of Commons, the Lord Chief Justice, and leading statesmen from Commonwealth countries overseas) by custom. A Privy Councillor, who must be a British subject, is required to take the special Privy Councillor's oath in addition to the oath of allegiance. He is liable to dismissal from the Council by the Sovereign, but such drastic action is rarely taken, the last such occasion being in 1921. In June 1963 Mr. John Profumo was removed from the Privy Council, at his own request, although no direct precedent existed for the procedure adopted. Until 1707 a Privy Councillor remained in office for the duration of the Sovereign's life. The Succession to the Crown Act of that year extended the period of office for six months following the Sovereign's death, and since the Demise of the Crown Act, 1901, it has been customary for the new Sovereign to renew the appointment.

The main function of the Privy Council to-day is to give formal effect to Proclamations and Orders in Council, which are issued by the Crown under prerogative or statutory powers. Such instruments are enacted 'by and with the advice of Her Majesty's Privy Council', but in actual fact the Crown acts on the advice of the Government in the exercise of the prerogative, and where statutory provision exists the power has, of course, been authorized by Parliament through an Act of Parliament. Proclamations are issued for such matters as proroguing, dissolving, and summoning Parliament and declaring war or peace. Orders in Council may be legislative, executive, or judicial in effect. They are generally issued under powers conferred by statute, and may provide for anything from a colonial Constitution to the setting up of a government department. A Privy Council is called for certain ceremonial occasions, such as the acceptance of office by a newly appointed minister, as well as for the purposes described above.

When a meeting of the Council takes place, only those Privy Councillors who are summoned attend, the quorum being 3. The usual number summoned is 4, being the ministers concerned with the matter which is to be dealt with. The Queen presides, and the meeting is attended by the Clerk to the Council who authenticates Her Majesty's assent to a measure with his own signature. He also records the names of the Councillors present, who are responsible for the business transacted. Unless the Sovereign or a royal deputy is present at a meeting of Privy Councillors, that meeting cannot be said to constitute a Council but only a committee. There are a number of Standing Committees of the Privy Council, including the important Judicial Committee. Committees are also set up for specific purposes such as the consideration of a petition for the grant of a Royal Charter. Some committees exercise advisory functions on matters relating to the Channel Islands, the universities, and the conferring of honours; others exist to direct various fields of research. The Judicial Committee was constituted by statute in 1833 'for the better administration of justice in His Majesty's Privy Council'. It has inherited what survives of the ancient judicial powers of the Privy Council, and has appellate jurisdiction from the Courts of the Channel Islands, the Isle of Man, and the Colonies (originally called 'foreign plantations'), the Ecclesiastical Courts, the Admiralty Court, and the Prize Court.

The Privy Council, in common with the other institutions of central government excepting the House of Commons, is descended from the ancient *Curia Regis* (q.v.), and became a distinct body by the end of the 14th century. At first it was a heterogeneous assembly, including among its members the Great Officers of State, officials of the royal household, judges, lawyers, barons of the Exchequer, and a varying number of the nobility both lay and ecclesiastical. Most of the work of government was performed by the officials and the King's favourites, but the insistence of the barons upon a stronger measure of power for themselves led to a series of struggles for domination until the end of the reign of Edward III. With the accession of Richard II, due to the King's minority and the closer parliamentary control over its composition, the Privy Council became a more defined body. By the end of the reign of Henry V it had acquired a very different character from that of the earlier councils, and during the reign of Henry VI, due again to the close parliamentary control which resulted from the King's minority, its composition became very strictly defined. It usually consisted of the Chancellor, the Lord Treasurer, the Keeper of the Privy Seal, the Chamberlain, the Steward of the Household, the 2 archbishops, and from 10 to 15 other members. Others distinguished in law and other branches of knowledge were also occasionally summoned. During Henry VI's minority this Council governed the country. But the civil strife which rent the country during this unfortunate reign eventually brought about the disintegration of the Council, which was not revived until the advent of the Tudors, when Henry VII reformed it as an instrument of the Crown. In the reign of Henry VIII a distinction was drawn between Privy Councillors and 'ordinary councillors'. The latter were men of inferior rank who were chosen for their learning and ability but were not accorded the full status of a Privy Councillor. This distinction probably bears some relation to the separation, which becomes apparent at this time, of the executive and the judicial functions of the Council. To quote Professor Baldwin, 'Henceforth the monarchy was generally successful in maintaining two co-ordinate boards working simultaneously. The one following the King was commonly known as the "council at court", while the other continued to be called "the King's Council in the Star Chamber" ' (i.e., the Court of Star Chamber). The former body continued to be known as the Privy Council. The Court of Star Chamber and other special courts which were created during this period, including the Court of High Commission and the Court of Requests, evolved from the King's Council in its judicial capacity. With the accession of the Stuarts there arose the great constitutional conflict between the Crown and Parliament and these courts of arbitrary jurisdiction were singled out for attack as being associated with the much abused Royal Prerogative. In 1641 the Long Parliament abolished both the Court of Star Chamber and the Court of High Commission by statute. The Civil War swept away the administrative system as it had hitherto existed with all the other accoutrements of royalty, but the Privy Council, although it fell into abeyance, was never legally abolished. It was revived as a functioning body at the Restoration when its members were drawn from the Commons as well as from the peerage and clergy. Henceforward the numerical strength of the Council steadily increased, a process which was accompanied by a corresponding decline in its powers. The emergence of the Cabinet system at length eclipsed the Privy Council as an executive organ, although there was an attempt in the Act of Settlement (q.v.) of 1701 to restore the Council to its lost position. But the Cabinet maintained its pre-eminence and had completely usurped the functions of the Privy

Council by the time the first Hanoverian monarch ascended the Throne of England.

A Privy Councillor is entitled to the prefix 'The Right Honourable' and to use the initials 'P.C.' after his name. In Parliament it has long been the custom to accord priority to Privy Councillors wishing to speak in a debate, although it lies within the Speaker's discretion as to whether or not they are called (see Speaker's ruling of 5 March 1953: Commons Hansard, vol. 512, col. 567). In 1959 a select committee recommended the aboliton of this custom, but no formal action has been taken in this regard (see ruling of 14 November 1962: Commons Hansard, vol. 667, col. 432). A Privy Councillor's motion has never required a seconder. To-day Privy Councillors are no longer privileged in this respect, as a recent amendment to the procedure of the House of Commons has abolished the necessity for the seconding of any motion except on ceremonial occasions.

A full Privy Council is summoned on only two occasions these days —to sign the Proclamation of the accession of a new Sovereign, and on the occasion of a Sovereign announcing an intention to marry.

THE PRIVY COUNCIL FOR CANADA. Canada is the only full member of the Commonwealth other than the United Kingdom with a comparable Privy Council. It consists of about 120 members, most of whom are present and former Ministers of the Crown. They are sworn members of the Privy Council by the Governor-General on the advice of the Prime Minister and retain their membership for life. The Privy Council of Canada does not meet as a functioning body and its constitutional responsibilities are discharged by the ministers constituting the Cabinet of the day. However, whenever the Cabinet meets for the purpose of tendering formal advice to the Governor-General it resolves itself into a Committee of the Privy Council. A Committee of the Privy Council, composed of members of the Cabinet of the day, also meets regularly to consider Orders in Council which are subsequently recommended to the Governor-General for his approval. The Cabinet thus never formally substitutes itself for the Privy Council when discharging the constitutional responsibilities of the latter. From 1921 to 1957 the office of President of the Privy Council was held by the Prime Minister, but since April 1957 it has become a regular Cabinet portfolio held by another minister, although it carries no statutory responsibilities. Members of the Privy Council for Canada are not entitled to the prefix 'The Right Honourable' unless they are also members of the United Kingdom Privy Council.

(Further reading: Fitzroy, *History of the Privy Council*, 1928.)

PRIVY SEAL, LORD

See LORD PRIVY SEAL.

PROCEDURE

Lord Campion, a former Clerk of the House of Commons, has pointed out that parliamentary procedure is a combination of two elements, the traditional and the democratic. The latter is a growth of the last century and is embodied in the Standing Orders (q.v.), while the former is the 'practice of the House'—the body of rules and precedents which grew up during the early and middle periods of Parliament. It is this 'ancient practice' and not the Standing Orders which remains the essential basis of procedure.

The greater part of the rules which govern debate and regulate behaviour in the House were well established by the beginning of the 17th century, but they tended more to protect minorities and the individual member than to facilitate the business of the House. The Standing Orders introduced from 1832 onwards were really amendments to the established practice and not a separate code. Their effect was to prevent the obstruction of business, and gradually to introduce more efficient methods of forcing the ever-increasing volume of business through the House. Methods which were employed by small groups to bring the business of the majority to a standstill included the discussion of petitions (abolished by Standing Order in 1842), the moving of dilatory motions (q.v.), and talking at length on non-contentious subjects to delay progress on more obnoxious items.

In the 1880's, under the pressure of Irish Nationalist obstruction, the House drastically revised its rules. Numerous devices were introduced for the limitation of debate, and the powers of the Speaker were greatly augmented. It is interesting to note that the Standing Orders devised at this time, arising as they did from the necessity to counter obstruction, have become the basic machinery of procedure without which the House would never dispose of the heavy volume of business which is always before it. Among the rules dating from this period are those relating to the closure and 'guillotine' (qq.v.), dilatory motions, the unnecessary claiming of divisions, the adjournment of the House for the purpose of holding emergency debates on matters of sudden urgency, the Speaker's leaving the Chair without putting the question when a committee stage of Supply stands as an Order of the Day (no longer applicable since December 1696), and the disciplinary powers of the Chair in checking disorderly conduct and persistent irrelevance or tedious repetition. The system of 'allotted days' (*see* SUPPLY DAYS) was introduced in 1896 on the initiative of Balfour and cut down the time taken for the consideration of financial business. In 1907 the extension of the use of Standing Committees (q.v.) accelerated the passage of legislation by enabling the committee stages of more than one Bill to be considered simultaneously.

In brief, therefore, parliamentary procedure consists of three elements—traditional practice, the Standing Orders, and the parliamentary case-law. The traditional practice has evolved as Parliament itself has evolved, while the Standing Orders have modified the older procedures and introduced new ones according to the changing requirements of the day. Parallel with these two planks of procedure—the ancient and the modern—is the case-law—the precedents embodied in the accumulated rulings of successive Speakers and Chairmen in interpretation of both traditional practice and Standing Orders.

Various officers of both Houses have rendered invaluable services to Parliament by codifying its practice and procedure. The first authoritative manual was produced by Henry Elsynge, Clerk of the Parliaments and father of the Henry Elsynge who was Clerk of the House of Commons during the early years of the Long Parliament. The Clerk of the House of Commons during the Cromwellian era, Henry Scobell, provided in his *Memorials* the main authority for 17th-century procedure. John Hatsell's *Precedents* form the standard authority on 18th-century procedure, whilst Sir Thomas Erskine May's famous *Treatise on the Law, Privileges, Proceedings and Usage of Parliament* has been the standard work on the subject since the first edition appeared in 1844. Lord Campion, in addition to editing the 14th and 15th editions of Erskine May, has made a number of valuable contributions to the literature of the subject, including his *Introduction to the Procedure of the House of Commons*.

As the result of the report of the Select Committee on Procedure which was presented to the House of Commons in 1946, far-reaching changes were made in the procedure of the lower House. To quote from Lord Campion's preface to the 15th edition of Erskine May, 'Partly in the light of wartime experience, the procedure relating to the sittings of Parliament, Questions, motions for the adjournment of the House, the business of Supply, the reception of notices, the machinery of the guillotine, and the constitution and functions of standing committees, was overhauled and adapted to present conditions. Other changes were made on the initiative of the Government with the familiar purpose of expediting business and cutting down the stages of bills and financial resolutions.' The House of Commons is in the habit of reviewing its procedure periodically, and since 1964 Select Committees have been appointed for the purpose in every session. The matters considered by these committees have included financial procedure, Question Time, the reference of Bills to Second Reading Committees for consideration in principle, the holding of morning sittings, the appointment of specialist committees, methods of voting, the procedure relating to matters of urgency, and numerous matters of detail. Many important reforms have resulted from the work of these committees, among the most recent being the inauguration of a new annual debate based upon an economic forecast prepared by the

Government and the establishment of a Select Committee on Expenditure to take the place of the Estimates Committee (q.v. and *see also* EXPENDITURE, SELECT COMMITTEE ON and PROCEDURE, FINANCIAL). In spite of these far-reaching developments procedure committees are usually less radical than some of those who give evidence before them, while the House has normally shown itself to be even more cautious than its committees and selective in the acceptance of the various recommendations they put forward. So far the House has never appointed a Select Committee on Procedure by sessional order but, since the subject of procedure is a hardy perennial, one can assume that it will be a matter for continuing investigation. Members and those who advise them are more conscious than ever before of the need to promote the effectiveness of Parliament and to effect procedural reforms which are compatible with modern conditions. Various books have been written in recent years, by academics and practitioners alike, proposing solutions which merit consideration, and bodies such as the Study of Parliament Group (q.v.) have given a considerable stimulus to the promotion of parliamentary studies. In an article in *The Times* on 17 November 1966, Lord Redmayne, a former Conservative Chief Whip, even recommended the provision of two Chambers in which separate debates could take place simultaneously. More detailed accounts of the machinery of procedure will be found under separate and more specific headings.

The procedure of the House of Lords differs in many respects from that of the House of Commons, although until the 19th century it was much the same so far as the freedom and elasticity afforded by the 'ancient practice' was concerned. The most striking difference is to be found in the rules of debate and the maintenance of order, and this arises from the difference in the position of the Speaker (q.v.) and that of the Lord Chancellor (q.v.). Legislative procedure is much the same in both Houses. Bills are required to pass through the same stages, but certain differences have developed. In the Lords a peer can introduce a Bill without obtaining the leave of the House and move its first reading. The deliberative functions of the Lords are carried out by debates arising out of resolutions, motions, or questions. Debates may take place on a question addressed to the Government although there is no motion before the House, but the more important debates take place on resolutions or on 'motions for papers' (q.v.), a formula which is adopted when it is desired to debate a subject without proposing any specific resolution on it. The mover then has the right of reply at the conclusion of the debate as there is a motion before the House. Recent innovations include the institution of 'starred questions' asked for the purpose of obtaining specific information. An interesting simplification of procedure has been introduced in the form of the question by which amendments are put. Under the former procedure, where the amendment was for the omission of certain words from a clause, the rather confusing question was put, 'that the words proposed to be left out stand part of the clause'. Now in all amendments the simpler question is put, 'that this amendment be agreed to', each amendment being treated as self-contained.

Procedure in the other Parliaments of the Commonwealth is based on that of the House of Commons with variations which depend on the size of the legislature and other local conditions. Further information will be found under the appropriate country headings.

PROCEDURE, FINANCIAL

The financial procedure of the House of Commons was radically revised in 1966 and 1967. The most radical innovation is the abolition of the requirement that all financial measures must be founded on resolutions passed in a Committee of the Whole House. Formerly this requirement was fundamental to all financial procedure, and was a practice deeply rooted in parliamentary history. It was abolished on the recommendation of the Select Committee on Procedure, Session 1965–6, on the ground that it had become meaningless and unnecessary. As a result the Committee of Supply, in which the principal annual debates relating to public expenditure formerly took place, was abolished in December 1966. Abolished at the same time was the requirement that any public expenditure other than Supply be initially authorized by a financial resolution passed in a Committee of the Whole House. The Committee of Ways and Means, which was concerned mainly with the Budget (q.v.) resolutions, was abolished in 1967. Legislative action was required to effect the abolition of this committee because the Provisional Collection of Taxes Act, 1913 (consolidated in 1968), which sanctions the provisional collection of taxes on the authorization of financial resolutions, was so drafted as to relate specifically to the resolutions of the Committee of Ways and Means. The Committee of Ways and Means had two functions: to authorize taxation and to approve the issue from the Consolidated Fund (q.v.) of the sums formerly voted by the Committee of Supply for the needs of the public service. The latter function, which was purely formal, fell away with the abolition of the Committee of Supply.

An important stage in the conduct of financial business has thus been eliminated. The business of Supply and Ways and Means is now taken in the House itself, the annual Budget statement being now delivered by the Chancellor of the Exchequer in the House instead of in Committee of the Whole House. The Chairman of Ways and Means, who presides over all Committees of the Whole House and thus formerly presided over the Committee of Supply and the Committee of Ways and Means, now presides over the House in his capacity as Deputy

Speaker whenever the House considers the Estimates or the business of Ways and Means. One result of the new procedure is that all the subterfuges formerly employed to permit the discussion of Supply on an allotted day are no longer necessary. Previously, devices were frequently resorted to to enable a selected subject to be debated, such as the moving into and out of Committee of Supply when there were no Estimates to be debated; the reporting of progress when none had been made; the elaboration of schedules of token votes, none of which was discussed in detail; and the choice of votes which would be unlikely to attract debate, all of which were designed to permit the business of Supply to be taken formally and the day's business conducted on some other motion. Under the new procedure Supply debates may take place on motions introduced by the Opposition or motions for the adjournment of the House, and specific subjects are no longer allocated to Supply days.

For the sake of clarity it may be convenient to tabulate the basic features of financial procedure. Any variations between the old and the new procedure which have not been dealt with in the foregoing preamble will be indicated in the course of the following account.

(1) The House of Commons has exclusive control over financial business and all financial legislation is initiated in that House (*see* PRIVILEGE, FINANCIAL). The House of Lords is not empowered to amend a Money Bill (q.v.) and since the passing of the Parliament Act, 1911, the rejection of such a Bill by the upper House would have no effect.

(2) The granting of public money and the imposition of taxation are strictly the functions of Parliament, but they can only be proposed on the Queen's Recommendation (q.v.). The effect of the Queen's Recommendation, which is of course made on the advice of her ministers, is to restrict the initiation of financial proposals to Her Majesty's Government.

(3) The great financial Bills of the year are founded on resolutions of the House. The Consolidated Fund and Consolidated Fund (Appropriation) Bills, which provide for expenditure, are based on Supply resolutions; Finance Bills, which authorize taxation, are based on Ways and Means resolutions. The two main financial statutes of the year are the Finance Act (q.v.) which incorporates the Budget proposals and the Appropriation Act (q.v.) which gives statutory authority to the Estimates (q.v.). Prior to the Appropriation Act there are always at least two Consolidated Fund Acts, which between them give statutory effect to the Supplementary Estimates for the current financial year and the Votes on Account which provide the departments of government and the armed services with the funds they need pending the final endorsement of the main Estimates.

(4) Under the new procedure twenty-nine whole days, which must fall before 5 August, are allotted to the consideration of Supply. Three

additional days were added to compensate for the withdrawal of the right to debate the third reading stage of Consolidated Fund and Consolidated Fund (Appropriation) Bills. For the purposes of the Standing Order relating to the allotted days the business of Supply is defined to include the Estimates in all their forms (excluding war expenditure), substantive motions, motions for the adjournment of the House, and proceedings on the reports of the Committee of Public Accounts and Estimates Committees.

(5) Under the new procedure Supply debates may take place in the House on motions introduced by the Opposition and on motions for the adjournment of the House. The choice of subjects for discussion on Supply days is the prerogative of the Opposition, and the new procedure has been designed to clarify the real objective of Supply debates: the provision of opportunities to the Opposition to examine government activities of their own choice. The new procedure does not, however, infringe the basic right of the House of Commons to grant or deny the financial requirements of the executive.

Until recently the ancient right of the Commons to discuss their grievances before granting Supply nominally survived in the limited retention of the procedure which enabled a debate to be held on the motion 'That Mr. Speaker do now leave the Chair'. Until 1956 such a motion was debated on each of the four occasions when the House first went into Committee of Supply on the four main branches of the Estimates. These debates were very discursive and provided opportunities for raising various matters not directly concerned with Supply. In recent years the motion for 'Getting the Speaker out of the Chair' (q.v.) was used more restrictively, Supply debates being very wide in scope in themselves. With the abolition of the Committee of Supply the device of debating a motion 'That Mr. Speaker do now leave the Chair' has fallen away completely. The new procedure recognizes that the right to debate grievances before granting Supply to the Crown is of diminished significance in the circumstances of the 20th century. Of greater moment is the right of the Opposition to decide which areas of government policy should form the subjects of Supply debates. The closest modern equivalent to the 'grievances before Supply' procedure is the debate which takes place three times in the session on the second reading of the three Consolidated Fund Bills. These debates are recognized as back benchers' occasions, during which they are accorded priority and entitled to raise any matter within the Government's responsibility.

(6) Parliament budgets for each financial year quite separately, and any surpluses must be paid back into the Exchequer at the end of the year and not carried over into the next. The parliamentary session, however, overlaps the financial year, which begins on 1 April. Consequently, one session is concerned with both the current and the

forthcoming financial year, and, if there are any Excess Votes to be considered, with the previous financial year as well.

(7) The main features of the financial system are the Consolidated Fund, described by Campion as 'the reservoir into which all revenue flows and from which all expenditure issues'; the Estimates, which are detailed statements, prepared by the various departments of government, of the sums of money which are estimated to be required for the forthcoming year and the purposes for which they are required; the Supplementary Estimates (*see* ESTIMATES) which are prepared by those departments which find they have underestimated in the main Estimates and which must be submitted to Parliament *before* the end of the financial year; Votes on Account (*see* ESTIMATES), or provisional Estimates which are designed to meet the immediate needs of the public service and to cover the period from the beginning of the financial year until such time as the main Estimates are finally passed; and Excess Votes (*see* ESTIMATES) which must be passed in the event of departments overspending to legalize the deficit from the previous financial year. Votes of Credit (*see* ESTIMATES) are a feature of wartime financial procedure, and are sums of money voted for unspecified purposes.

(8) The Standing Orders provide for the appointment each session of two important financial committees (not of the Whole House) which deliberate regularly and report to the House from time to time. The Committee of Public Accounts (q.v.) is appointed to examine the Appropriation Accounts of past financial years and the reports thereon of the Comptroller and Auditor General (q.v.), and to draw the attention of the House to any extravagances and anomalies. The Estimates Committee (q.v.) has the function of examining the Estimates in detail, but within the framework of Government policy, detailed scrutiny being impractical in the House.

If the facts enumerated above are borne in mind, the course of the financial procedure for a session may be outlined as follows:

During the course of her speech opening Parliament (the Opening of Parliament usually takes place in the late autumn) the Queen informs the Commons that 'The Estimates for the Public Service will be laid before you'. This constitutes the Queen's Recommendation in respect of the programme of expenditure set out in the Estimates. The first financial business of the session is the consideration of the Supplementary Estimates for the current financial year and the Votes on Account for the forthcoming financial year. The practice of submitting Winter Supplementary Estimates on account was established in the 1963–4 session, thus enabling the House to learn at an early stage of all major prospective increases in the Estimates. This has resulted in the passage of a regular Consolidated Fund Bill early in the year, and under the new procedure the Supplementary Estimates are subject to a closure on the sixth allotted Supply day, being a day not later than 6 February, provided they shall have been presented to the House not less than seven clear days previously. This is the first of three Supply guillotines (under the former procedure there were only two). The Votes on Account must be passed before the beginning of the new financial year in order to supply the various departments of government with sufficient funds to carry them through until the passage of the main Estimates later in the year. Under a procedure adopted in 1969 the Civil Vote on Account is presented well before Christmas and passed before the first guillotine comes into operation. The Defence Vote on Account, which takes the place of a former procedure whereby certain selected Defence Votes were passed to meet the immediate needs of the armed services, must be disposed of before the second guillotine comes into operation. The second closure comes into operation on the tenth allotted Supply day, being a day before 25 March, and applies to Votes on Account, Excess Votes, if any, and any outstanding Supplementary Estimates. The way is then open for the introduction of the Consolidated Fund (No. 2) Bill, which empowers the Government to spend the sums of money voted by the House.

With the passage of the first two Consolidated Fund Bills the immediate needs of the public service are provided for, and the House can proceed in more leisurely manner to discuss the main financial business of the year. As noted above, the right of initiating Supply debates is reserved to the Opposition, and they take place on Opposition motions and on motions for the adjournment of the House. Consideration of the main Estimates continues until the twenty-nine allotted Supply days have run their course and the third and final closure comes into operation on 5 August.

On the three occasions when the guillotine falls the question is put on all the outstanding motions to which the particular closure applies, but although no further debate is permitted, it is open to members to vote against all or any of the proposals being decided. Under the new procedure, however, members intending to vote against any of the proposals being decided on guillotine days are required to give notice of their intention on the previous day, thus permitting the unopposed Estimates to be put in a single question, the purpose being to save the time of the House. On guillotine days the closure now comes into operation at 10 p.m. instead of 9.30 p.m. as previously.

One of the traditionally recognized methods of expressing dissatisfaction with a specific service is to move a reduction in the Estimate concerned. This practice has no financial significance and merely enables a complaint to be registered and discussed. To move an increase in the vote would be out of order, and the only alternative, therefore, is to move for a reduction, although the intention of the member concerned could well be to call attention to the inadequacy of the provision which has been made. The new procedure has necessitated a change in the method of moving such amendments. Now that the Estimates are debated in the House, a standard method of moving amendments to Estimates has been introduced, and is one which does not preclude further debate on the Estimate concerned when the amendment has been disposed of. The standard form of amendment is now 'That (the Estimate concerned) be reduced by £5', and it is put by the Chair in the form of a main question.

Following the passage of the main Estimates, the Consolidated Fund (Appropriation) Bill is brought in to give legislative effect to the Supply resolutions adopted by the House. This differs from other Consolidated Fund Bills in that it details the purposes for which the money is to be used (to a certain extent it reproduces the Estimates themselves), and on receiving the Royal Assent (q.v.) it becomes known as the Appropriation Act (q.v.).

Proceedings on the Consolidated Fund and Consolidated Fund (Appropriation) Bills do not fall within the twenty-nine allotted Supply days, and they thus provide further opportunity for debating the business of Supply. Under the new procedure the third reading stage of such Bills is not debatable, but the second reading stage is now given over exclusively to private members. Backbenchers thus have a specific opportunity to raise any grievance they may have against the administration before final approval is given to the grant of Supply.

During the months when the business of Supply is under consideration, the House has also to consider ways and means of raising more money to replenish the Consolidated Fund. The basis of these debates is that item of parliamentary business which arouses more discussion outside Parliament than any other, namely, the Budget. Since Budget procedure was only recently reformed, both the traditional and the new procedure will be outlined for purposes of comparison. Under the traditional procedure the Budget was introduced by the Chancellor of the Exchequer in the Committee of Ways and Means, since it was the function of that committee to consider and approve all taxation proposals. The days following the Budget statement were, as now, usually devoted to a general debate of very wide scope. On the conclusion of the Financial Statement (or Budget speech) it was the practice for the Chairman of Ways and Means to put the question on all the Budget resolutions except the last one, which served as the peg for the entire debate. The adoption of the other resolutions permitted the provisional collection of taxes in terms of the Provisional Collection of Taxes Act, 1913. When the Budget debate was concluded the resolutions were reported to the House with the Speaker in the Chair.

Under the new procedure, the Committee of Ways and Means has been abolished and all proceedings relating to the Budget now take place in the House itself. As in the case of Supply, an entire stage has been eliminated from Budget procedure. As soon as the Chancellor has delivered his speech, the House immediately passes a provisional resolution designed to enable the Provisional Collection of Taxes Act, as amended and consolidated in 1968, to take effect. The Budget debate then takes place on the first Budget resolution instead of the last, thus enabling considered decisions to be taken on all the resolutions at the end of the debate.

Following the passage of the Budget resolutions, they are incorporated into the annual Finance Bill which has yet to be passed before the proposals can become law. The second reading of this Bill provides yet another opportunity for wide and discursive debate, and the entire financial policy of the Government generally comes under review. Eventually the Finance Bill passes through all its stages to become an Act of Parliament. The rejection of the Finance Bill, which in these days is a very unlikely event, would, of course, constitute a major defeat for the Government involving its resignation.

On 23 July 1969 the Select Committee on Procedure presented an important report to the House on the scrutiny of public expenditure and administration which led to a further change in the financial procedure of the House. For some years concern had been expressed at the weakening of Parliament's control over public expenditure and the ever-increasing growth of executive power resulting from the heavy responsibilities of modern government. The Select Committee concluded that Parliament could retrieve some measure of influence only if it were given the opportunity of considering forward surveys, which would of course depend upon Government willingness to reveal its plans of future expenditures and priorities. In its evidence to the Committee the Government announced its intention to publish an annual White Paper on projected public expenditure over five years. The Committee therefore recommended that an annual debate should take place on this White Paper, and expressed the view that it should come to occupy as important a place in the programme of parliamentary business as the Budget debate. The first such debate took place in January 1970.

The Committee also recommended the appointment of a new Select Committee on Expenditure (q.v.) to replace the Estimates Committee (q.v.) It would work through eight functional sub-committees, each of which would examine the Estimates of expenditure and administrative efficiency in a specified area of Government responsibility. This recommendation was well supported and the Government promised to examine it.

To ensure that the funds made available to the civil departments and the three armed services are utilized in the manner specified by the Appropriation Act, an annual audit of the accounts of all departments is carried out by the Comptroller and Auditor General, who reports his findings to the House. The report of the Comptroller and Auditor

General, together with the Appropriation Accounts themselves, are considered by the Committee of Public Accounts. The committee subjects the report and the accounts to the most rigid scrutiny and examines witnesses from the departments themselves. The committee reports to the House which considers its reports, along with those of the Estimates Committee, on Supply days.

There remains one feature of the financial process over which Parliament's control is limited and that is the matter of borrowing. Borrowing is authorized in the Appropriation and Consolidated Fund Acts, a necessary provision since the incoming revenue does not replenish the Consolidated Fund fast enough to meet the frequent demands upon its reserves. The only limit which is specified to these loans is that they must not exceed the total sum appropriated by the Act. Furthermore, certain payments, known as Consolidated Fund Services, are paid directly from the Consolidated Fund under permanent legislation and do not require regular parliamentary approval; these include payments of interest on the National Debt which, owing to enormous emergency loans due to the War and other factors and the fluctuating rate of interest, which has at times been very high, imposes a heavy liability upon the nation. In these matters Parliament is forced to allow considerable freedom of action to the executive, for under present-day conditions it would not be feasible to restrict its financial activities too severely.

It is interesting to note that in 1963 the Australian House of Representatives also eliminated the Committees of Supply and Ways and Means, and the major financial debates of the year now take place on the legislation itself. The Budget speech is made, and the Budget debate ensues on the second reading of the main Appropriation Bill, and the details of the Estimates, which are contained in a schedule to the Bill, are considered in Committee of the Whole House at the committee stage. Similar practices were adopted in New Zealand in 1967, and in 1968 Canadian financial procedure was revised along comparable although not exactly similar lines.

PROCEDURE OF THE HOUSE, SELECT COMMITTEE ON
See SELECT COMMITTEE ON PROCEDURE OF THE HOUSE.

PRODUCTION, MINISTER OF
Lord Beaverbrook was appointed the first Minister in 1942, with responsibility for war production in accordance with the policy of the Minister of Defence and the War Cabinet. It included the allocation of available resources of productive capacity and raw materials (including arrangements for their import), the settlement of priorities of production where necessary, and the supervision and guidance of

the various departments and branches of departments concerned. Lord Beaverbrook was very shortly succeeded by Oliver Lyttelton (afterwards Lord Chandos), who remained in office until the forming of the Caretaker Government in May 1945, when he combined it with that of President of the Board of Trade. The office was abolished when the Labour Government was returned later in the same year. When the Ministry of Defence was created in 1946 a Ministerial Production Committee was appointed.

PROPORTIONAL REPRESENTATION

A method of representation which is designed to secure the election of candidates in proportion to the numerical strength of each section of political opinion, thus accurately reflecting the political feeling of the country in Parliament. The system was advocated by John Stuart Mill, who maintained that no form of representation was truly democratic unless all minorities were represented in accordance with the measure of support they could command. Proportional representation has never been introduced into the United Kingdom (except in respect of some of the late university constituencies), but the Proportional Representation Society since its foundation in 1884 has been pressing for its introduction, and the matter has at various times been discussed.

Any system of proportional representation which is to fulfil the aims of Mill and the Proportional Representation Society depends on large constituencies returning several members, and the system most widely advocated is that of the single transferable vote. It operates in Malta, Guyana, the Australian State of Tasmania and in Eire, and was also used, before their abolition, in those university constituencies which returned more than one member. The elector has one vote only, but as with the alternative vote, he may indicate his choice of candidates in the order of his preference. All candidates who poll the necessary minimum quota of votes are declared elected; for instance, in a constituency returning three members the quota would be one-quarter of the votes cast plus one, for three other candidates could not each have more; similarly, in a four-member constituency the quota would be one-fifth of the votes plus one and in a five-member constituency one more than a sixth, and so on. The surplus votes cast for the candidate or candidates at the top of the poll go to swell the totals of the other candidates according to the preferences indicated on the ballot papers. Candidates at the bottom of the poll are eliminated and their votes are distributed amongst the other candidates according to the preferences indicated, the process of elimination continuing until the number of candidates remaining in the poll is reduced to the number of vacancies.

The advantage of this method over the present system may be demonstrated by means of a simple example. Let us assume that the imaginary county borough of Barchester is divided into ten divisions for the purposes of parliamentary representation and that the total electorate is 500,000, comprising 250,000 Conservative voters, 200,000 Labour voters, and 50,000 Liberal voters. Under the present system the Conservative candidates could quite conceivably win all 10 Barchester seats, in some cases by very slender majorities; on the other hand, they might possibly win less than half the seats through their votes being concentrated into heavy majorities in those areas where they command most of their support. The Liberal candidates would stand little chance of winning any seats. Proportional representation would obviate these possibilities. Barchester would become a single constituency returning 10 members, and by the use of the single transferable vote the successful candidates would reflect the political feeling of Barchester; in other words, the constituency would return 5 Conservative members, 4 Labour members, and 1 Liberal member. This example is, of course, simple in the extreme, but it serves to illustrate the system's basic claim to consideration.

A further form of proportional representation is the list system which is used in several European countries. Its characteristic feature is the presentation of lists of candidates by the various party organizations. Under this system the vote has a twofold significance: in the first place, it is a vote for a party, and is used for determining the number of seats to be allotted to each party; in the second place, it is a vote for a particular candidate or selection of candidates from a party list. The detailed operation of the list system varies widely, and a full description is beyond the scope of this work.

The main advantages which have been claimed for proportional representation are as follows:

It would ensure fair and accurate representation of the people. Under the present system any but the stronger minorities are virtually disfranchised, the result of an election is influenced by the drawing of constituency boundaries, and it is not unusual for a minority of voters to return a majority of representatives or a small majority of voters to return an overwhelming majority of representatives.

It would widen the choice of the electors, and where a particular candidate was unacceptable, would provide an alternative choice without detriment to the interests of the political party concerned.

It would strengthen the House of Commons by ensuring the election of the ablest men of all parties and reducing the influence of party organizations in the House.

It would ensure that no votes were wasted at an election, as surplus votes and votes for unsuccessful candidates would be redistributed.

The main arguments which have been used against the system are:

It would reduce the personal contact between the member and his constituency.

It would be prejudicial to stable government in that it would tend to do away with the broad-based political party and encourage the rise of splinter parties and the formation into separate groups of each varying shade of opinion. The tendency of the present system to return a party with a majority disproportionate to the size of its poll is in the interests of stable government and is therefore an asset rather than a disadvantage.

It would improve the chances of the isolated crank or fanatic entering Parliament.

Its advantages would be limited to General Elections as the system could not be applied to by-elections.

It is altogether too complex a system, and is liable to confuse the voter and impose an undue burden on the Returning Officer.

(Further reading: Humphreys, *Proportional representation*, 1911; Lakeman, *How Democracies Vote*, 1970.)

See also ALTERNATIVE VOTE.

PROROGATION

A session of Parliament is terminated by prorogation, Parliament being prorogued by exercise of the Royal Prerogative (q.v.). The prorogation is effected at the close of a session by an announcement made in the House of Lords by commissioners appointed by the Sovereign for that purpose. The prorogation is to a specified date which may either be postponed or advanced by Royal Proclamation issued with the advice of the Privy Council. Parliament can be prorogued by the Sovereign in person, but since 1854 it has always been prorogued by commissioners. Under this procedure a message is sent from the Lords Commissioners to the House of Commons requesting their attendance. The same message may request attendance to hear the Royal Assent given to the last Bills of the session as well as to hear announcement of prorogation. After the Royal Assent has been given, and before the prorogation is announced, the Lord Chancellor reads to both Houses a Speech from the Throne, reviewing the proceedings of the session. The Speaker, followed by the Members of the House of Commons who have attended him at the Bar of the House of Lords, then returns to the Commons Chamber without the Mace preceding him. He takes his seat in the Chair usually occupied by the Clerk of the House and again reads the Speech from the Throne. He then shakes hands with all the members present, but this little ceremony has been omitted in recent years when Parliament is to reassemble after only a short interval.

The effect of a prorogation is at once to suspend all business until

Parliament is summoned again. Not only are the sittings ended, but all proceedings pending at the time, except impeachments by the Commons and appeals before the House of Lords, are brought to a close. Every Bill which has not secured a passage through all its stages is required to be reintroduced at the new session if it is to receive further consideration. Similarly, all committees cease to exist and must be newly appointed if they are to continue their work in the new session.

PROTEST BOOK

Members of the House of Lords possess the privilege, when they dissent from any measure which the House accepts, of recording their reasons in the Protest Book kept by the Clerk. The 'protest' is enternd in the Journal of the House, together with the names of all the peers who concur in it. This privilege is restricted to those who were present and voted on the question to which they desire to express their dissent. When the Reform Bill was finally passed by the Lords in 1832, 105 of the opposition peers took advantage of the Protest Book to express their objections to the Bill. The right of protest is not frequently made use of in these days, the last occasion on which it was exercised being in 1954.

PROVISIONAL ORDER BILL

A Bill to confirm a provisional order issued by a Minister of the Crown under the authority of an Act of Parliament. Provisional order procedure originated with the Public Health Act of 1848 and was introduced as a simplified means of legislating upon matters which would otherwise require the promotion of a Private Bill (q.v.). Its advantages are a saving of parliamentary time and a reduction of the expenses normally incurred in private legislation, but it has been largely superseded, except in Scotland, by an even quicker procedure introduced by the Statutory Orders (Special Procedure) Act, 1945 (*see* SPECIAL PROCEDURE ORDER). The procedure for issuing provisional orders varies and in each case reference must be made to the provisions of the relevant statute. As with a Private Bill a provisional order, which is usually made at the instance of a local authority or other body, must be given adequate publicity and interested parties notified, the responsibility for protecting the interests affected resting with the minister concerned instead of with Parliament. The fact that a power to issue provisional orders exists does not prohibit the promotion of a Private Bill. Once a provisional order has been made the Bill to confirm it may be introduced in either House of Parliament. It is introduced as a Public Bill but the subsequent proceedings on it are similar to those on a Private Bill.

In the case of Scotland a general power is conferred on the Secretary of State for Scotland under the Private Legislation Procedure (Scotland)

Act, 1936, to issue a provisional order in regard to any interest in Scotland which could be a matter for private legislation.

PROVISIONS OF OXFORD

The new Constitution which was drawn up by a commission of 24 members appointed from the so-called Mad Parliament (q.v.) summoned to meet at Oxford in 1258. It established a standing council of 15, with whose advice and consent Henry III was henceforth to exercise all his authority. Thrice in the year another committee of 12 was to treat with the 15 on the common affairs of the realm, and another 24 members of this Parliament were appointed to make grants of money to the Crown. All aliens were to be expelled from office, and new ministers and other officials were appointed under stringent conditions. The original 24 were authorized to draw up schemes for the reform of the Royal Household.

PROXY VOTE

See ELECTIONS.

PUBLIC ACCOUNTS COMMITTEE

See COMMITTEE OF PUBLIC ACCOUNTS.

PUBLIC BILL

A Bill which relates to matters of public policy and usually has a general application over the entire nation, as distinct from a Private Bill (q.v.). In common with the Private Bill, the Public Bill developed from the petition (q.v.). As the Commons came to present their petitions on behalf of the nation as a whole, so their influence upon early legislation increased. The endorsement of the Commons, consisting of the words, *Soit baille aux seigneurs* (a formula which is still inscribed on every Commons Bill before it is sent to the Lords), gave their demands the authority naturally due to a petition which had received the general approval. Nevertheless, the medieval House of Commons was still only a body of petitioners and not legislators. True, they held a decisive weapon in their power to refuse Supply until their grievances had been remedied, and when in 1348 they stipulated that redress of grievances should precede grant of Supply, the pressure thus brought to bear upon the Crown produced concessions more readily. But throughout the 14th century the Commons were constantly complaining that laws made at their request did not correspond to the petitions on which they were based. In 1414 they prayed the King 'that there never be no law made and engrossed as statute and law neither by additions nor discriminations by no manner of term or terms which should change the sentence and the intent asked'. In reply the King conceded that in the future 'nothing be enacted to the petition of the

Commons contrary to their asking, whereby they should be bound without their assent'. This led to an important change in the framing of statutes. It became the custom to send to the King not a petition but a statute in draft which could be accepted or rejected but not amended. The Bill thus replaced the petition, and by the end of the reign of Henry VI the practice had become firmly established. The growing importance of the Commons in the framing of legislation was recognized in the reign of Henry VII when the enacting formula of an Act of Parliament (q.v.), which is still in use to-day, was first introduced. (*For matters relating to procedure see* BILL, PASSAGE OF.)

PUBLIC BILL OFFICE

An office in the House of Commons in the department of the Clerk of the House. It is responsible for all matters relating to Public Bills and for communications with the House of Lords regarding them. It is also responsible for financial procedure and prepares financial resolutions for use in relation to the business of Supply and the consequential Consolidated Fund Bill. This office arranges ballots for Private Members' Bills and Notices of Motion. A similar office exists in the House of Lords.

PUBLIC BUILDING AND WORKS, MINISTER OF

In 1970 this Minister's department was absorbed by the new Department of the Environment in consequence of a major reorganization of the machinery of central government. The new department is headed by a Minister styled the Secretary of State for the Environment.

The Department of the Commissioners of Works and Public Buildings was created by an Act of 1851 to take over the royal palaces and parks and public buildings from the former Commissioner of Woods, Forests, and Land Revenues. It was controlled by a First Commissioner, the Secretaries of State, and the President of the Board of Trade. The department was known as the Office of Works until 1942, when under the Ministry of Works and Planning Act it acquired a Minister in place of the First Commissioner and took over most of the town and country planning functions of the Ministry of Health. Planning, however, was soon afterwards assigned to a new Minister of Town and Country Planning by an Act of 1943, and the Minister of Works and Planning became the Minister of Works. The responsibilities of this minister increased substantially during the War, when he controlled the construction of aircraft and munitions factories and planned post-war building under the direction of the Minister of Reconstruction. In 1951 his department assumed responsibility for the Festival of Britain.

In July 1962 the Minister of Works was re-designated the Minister of Public Building and Works and given extended responsibilities.

He was responsible, as before, for the upkeep of royal palaces and parks, diplomatic and consular offices, and the preservation of ancient monuments, regarding which his department published a useful series of guide-books. In addition he was responsible for the efficiency of the building industry in general and for the licensing of civil building. The scope of his work was subsequently broadened to include the problems of the industry as a whole and the promotion of building productivity, and in particular to ensure (in co-operation with the Minister of Housing and Local Government, whose department has also now been absorbed by the new Department of the Environment) that a proper balance was maintained between residential and non-residential building including Government construction.

The Minister of Public Building and Works, although not normally a member of the Cabinet, was a minister of Cabinet rank.

A chronological list of First Commissioners and subsequent Ministers appears as Appendix 33.

PUBLIC GALLERY

See STRANGERS.

PUBLIC GENERAL ACTS

The statutes of general application which are published in annual volumes by H.M. Stationery Office with the Church Assembly Measures (q.v.) as the Public General Acts and Measures. They are Acts of Parliament (q.v.) which originated as Public Bills (q.v.), and they comprise the bulk of the nation's legislation as finally agreed to by Parliament and assented to by the Sovereign. They do not include Private Acts (q.v.), which originate as Private Bills (q.v.). Until 1798, all Acts, public and private, were published together, but in that year the Public General Acts were distinguished from Local and Personal Acts which have since been published separately.

Owing to the great and ever-expanding bulk of legislation, it becomes necessary from time to time to consolidate the statute law— a mighty task which is carried out under the supervision of the Statute Law Committee appointed by the Lord Chancellor. These consolidations are known as the Statutes Revised. The latest edition, which is the third, brings the law up to date to the end of 1948. Repealed Acts and Private Acts are excluded. It consists of 32 volumes and is supplemented by the annual volumes of Public General Acts and Measures.

(Further reading: Hughes, *The British Statute Book*, 1957.)

PUBLIC PETITIONS, COMMITTEE ON

See COMMITTEE ON PUBLIC PETITIONS.

Q

QUEBEC NATIONAL ASSEMBLY

Prior to 31 December 1968, Quebec was the only Canadian Province with a bicameral Legislature, the Upper House being the Legislative Council and the Lower House the Legislative Assembly. On that date the Legislative Council was abolished and the Quebec Legislature was restyled the National Assembly. When the new session of the National Assembly was opened on 25 February 1969, certain other concessions to republican sentiment were in evidence. The Lieutenant-Governor's speech from the Throne was redesignated the 'inaugural speech' and the Speaker and Clerk of the House were restyled the President and Secretary respectively. At the opening of the 1970 session the role of the Lieutenant-Governor was significantly reduced. His speech was drastically abbreviated, the motion for an address in reply was eliminated and the main speech of the day was made by the Premier.

Constitutionally, however, Quebec remains a province of the Canadian confederation, the Lieutenant-Governor being appointed by the Governor-General-in-Council, that is by the Government of Canada. He performs the usual constitutional functions of summoning, proroguing and dissolving the Legislature, appointing the Premier and assenting to Bills duly passed by the National Assembly. The Premier of the Province is the President of the Executive Council, however, and in all matters relating to the Government of Quebec, the Lieutenant-Governor acts on the advice of his ministers.

The Legislative Council, like the Senate of Canada, was a survival of the early colonial upper Chamber, its prototype being the House of Lords. It consisted of 24 members appointed for life by the Government of the day, although provision had been made for the compulsory retirement of all Legislative Councillors appointed after 1 July 1963 on reaching the age of seventy-five. The Legislative Councillors were appointed to represent constituencies which corresponded exactly with the 24 ridings into which Quebec was divided when it was the Colony of Lower Canada.

The National Assembly consists of 108 members (increased from 95 in 1966) elected by popular vote. It is elected for five years unless sooner dissolved. Women were enfranchised in Quebec in 1940 and the voting age was lowered to eighteen with effect from 1966. The President of the National Assembly is elected by the members from among themselves in the normal manner of a popular Chamber.

The procedure of the National Assembly has also come under review for the purpose of modernizing and streamlining the conduct of parliamentary business. Although constitutional changes have been implemented in certain areas, the procedure of the National Assembly remains fundamentally based on the practices familiar to the British parliamentary system. Recent procedural changes have included a restructuring of the Standing Committees and the reference of Estimates and most Bills to them for consideration in detail; the abolition of appeals from the Speaker's rulings; and the introduction of time limits and other devices designed to expedite the business of the House.

The Province of Quebec is represented in the Canadian House of Commons by 74 members and in the Senate by 24 senators who represent the same historic electoral divisions as the former Legislative Councillors.

QUEEN'S CONSENT

Not to be confused with the Royal Assent (q.v.) to Bills, the Queen's Consent has to be given by a Privy Councillor to Bills (and occasionally amendments) affecting local and personal interests which concern the Royal Prerogative, the hereditary revenue or personal property or interests of the Crown or the Duchy of Cornwall. If there is a Prince of Wales who is of age, his consent is signified in matters affecting the Duchy. The Queen's Consent is usually given on the third reading of such Bills in order that account may be taken of any amendments made before Consent to the whole Bill is given. If the matters affecting the royal interests form the main or a very important part of a Bill, the Communication from the Queen is signified on the second reading. If the Queen's Consent is not obtained for a Bill which requires it, the proceedings on such a Bill are rendered null and void. The constitutional right of the Sovereign to give or withhold the Royal Assent to a Bill is in no way vitiated by her having consented to its being considered.

QUEENSLAND PARLIAMENT

Formerly a part of New South Wales, Queensland became a separate Colony with responsible government in 1859. It is the only State in Australia with a unicameral legislature, but its Parliament possessed a Legislative Council as well as a Legislative Assembly from 1860 to 1922. From 1950 to 1960 there were 75 members of the Legislative Assembly, 24 from Brisbane, 28 from the southern area outside Brisbane, 13 from North Queensland, and 10 from Western Queensland, but since the 1960 General Election there have been 78 members elected from three electoral zones. Elections are held every three years, and since 1915 voting has been compulsory by all adults who have had three months' residence in the State, six months in Australia, and one month in the electoral district. Women were given the vote in 1905, and first exercised it in the 1907 election. The system of preferential voting was in force until 1942, but after that the candidate who obtained the highest number of votes in the electoral district was elected. The Governor is President of the Executive Council of Ministers, of whom there are 11. The Premier is also Chief Secretary and Vice-President of the Executive Council. The Standing Orders of the Legislative Assembly are based on those of the House of Commons, and when made require the approval of the Governor. A Serjeant-at-Arms (who is also the Clerk Assistant) is employed, but a Mace is not used. The Legislative Assembly did not acquire the powers, privileges, and immunities of the Commons, but only such powers as were necessary to the existence of such a body and the proper exercise of the functions it is intended to execute.

The first meeting of the Queensland Parliament in 1860 was held in the old Military and Convict Barracks, but these somewhat unsuitable premises were only occupied until 1868, when Parliament was summoned to meet in its present fine building. This was completed when the western wing was occupied in 1891.

In August 1957 Queensland elected its first non-Labour government in twenty-five years.

QUEEN'S RECOMMENDATION

The consideration of all financial business is the function of the House of Commons alone, but the originating of such business is reserved to the Crown. Thus, no expenditure or taxation may be proposed without the Queen's Recommendation, the practical effect of which is to reserve the initiative in financial matters to Her Majesty's Government. The Queen's Recommendation to a financial proposal is signified in writing to the Clerk of the House and the fact of its signification is indicated by means of a note on the Order Paper. Prior to the introduction of the new financial procedure in December 1966 a Minister of the Crown (q.v.) was required to signify the Queen's Recommendation in person. The Government is as much bound by the terms of the resolution, however, as a private member, and no new or increased charge may be proposed in the form of an amendment. Recommendation of the annual Estimates (q.v.) is given in the Speech from the Throne at the beginning of a session.

The historical significance of this procedure and the constitutional theory underlying it are effectively summarized by Erskine May (17th ed., page 705) as follows:

The Sovereign, being the executive power, is charged with the management of all the revenue of the State, and with all payments for the public service. The Crown, therefore, acting with the advice of its responsible ministers, makes known to the Commons the pecuniary necessities of the government; the Commons, in return, grant such aids or supplies as are required to satisfy these demands; and they provide by taxes, and by the appropriation of other sources of the public income, the ways and means to meet the supplies which they have granted. Thus the Crown demands money, the Commons grant it, and the Lords assent to the grant: but the Commons do not vote money unless it be required by the Crown; nor do they impose or augment taxes, unless such taxation be necessary for the public service, as declared by the Crown through its constitutional advisers.

The financial relations between the Crown and Parliament defined in the preceding paragraph took shape during the period while the King still governed through ministers responsible to himself, and the House of Commons only exercised a negative control through its power to withhold supplies. These constitutional relations have been maintained in essential continuity, despite the establishment of Cabinet government dependent upon the support of the House of Commons.

See also FINANCIAL RESOLUTION; PROCEDURE, FINANCIAL.

QUEEN'S ROBING ROOM

From 1941 to 1950 the King's Robing Room, as it then was, was adapted for use as the Chamber of the House of Lords, the peers having given up their own Chamber to the House of Commons after the bombing of the latter in May 1941. It is interesting to record that according to the general opinion the standard of debate in the upper House was improved during this period by the more intimate atmosphere of a smaller Chamber.

The Robing Room is 54 feet long, 37 feet wide, and 25 feet high. It contains a chair of state beneath an impressive canopy of carved oak depicting the rose of England, the thistle of Scotland, the shamrock of Ireland, and Queen Victoria's monogram. The room is decorated with eighteen carved panels by H. Armstead portraying incidents from the Arthurian legends and five fresco paintings by W. Dyce, R.A., also illustrating the legends.

In April 1965 when the Lord Chancellor and the Speaker of the House of Commons assumed control of those parts of the Palace of Westminster occupied by their respective Houses, the Lord Great Chamberlain (q.v.), who previously controlled the entire precincts of the Palace, retained control of the Queen's Robing Room and the Royal Gallery (q.v.). These rooms are used on royal occasions such as the Opening of Parliament (q.v.), the arrangements for which are the responsibility of the Lord Great Chamberlain.

QUEEN'S SPEECH

See DEBATE ON THE ADDRESS; OPENING OF PARLIAMENT; PROROGATION.

QUESTION

When a motion has been moved and seconded in the House of Commons, the Chair proposes the question, in the same terms as the motion (with certain recognized exceptions), as the subject of debate. In the House of Lords the question is proposed in the form, 'That the motion be agreed to'. The question is put from the Chair at the conclusion of the debate in order to elicit the decision of the House, and every matter dealt with must be resolved in this manner. No speech is permissible except to a question—or to move or second a motion which becomes a question—and every speech must be confined to the terms of the question.

QUESTIONS TO MINISTERS

The practice whereby a Member of Parliament can put a question to a minister on a matter concerning his department is universal throughout the British Commonwealth. The late Sir Herbert Williams, who asked about four thousand questions during his parliamentary career, described questions in the House as 'perhaps one of the most powerful implements of democracy in our country'. Questions to ministers cover the whole administration of the country, and range from foreign relations to the individual victim of bureaucracy, so that it is quite apparent how important they are in enabling the private member to investigate any Government or departmental activity which does not satisfy him. Nothing could more weaken the control of Parliament over the executive than the abolition or curtailment of the right of a Member of Parliament to ask a question in the House, and so important has this method of ventilating grievances become that it has been responsible for a corresponding decline in public petitions. The first formal question to a minister was put in 1721 in the House of Lords and questions first appeared on the order paper in 1835. At first a member could ask any number of questions, but it was later fixed at 8 in 1909, 4 in 1919, 3 in 1920, and finally in 1960 at 2 oral questions in any one day—there is no limit to questions requiring a written answer. To ask his question a member rises when called by name in his turn by the Speaker, and merely says, 'Number . . ., Sir.'

In the British House of Commons Question Time begins not later than 2.45 and finishes not later than 3.30. Two days' notice must be given to allow time for the answer to be prepared by the minister and department concerned and, by a resolution of 27 October 1965, not more than twenty-one days' notice may be given in order to prevent congestion of the Notice Paper. Questions requiring an oral answer are marked with an asterisk on the order paper—otherwise answers, and also answers to questions which are not reached in time, are printed in Hansard. As it is not possible for all questions to be answered in the House, their order is so arranged as to give every minister his turn at answering questions orally on certain days each week. The Prime Minister answers questions orally on specified days only. Since 18 July 1961 the Prime Minister has agreed to answer questions from 3.15 p.m. on Tuesdays and Thursdays, while on Mondays and Wednesdays Question Number 45 and subsequent questions, if reached, are by custom addressed to him. Under this arrangement the House can be sure that the Prime Minister will answer questions for a quarter of an hour on at least two days a week. Question Number 45 is frequently not reached, and under the former procedure there was no guarantee that the Prime Minister would answer questions on a specified day. All questions have to be passed and perhaps edited by the Table Office in the House of Commons, and there are a considerable number of rules governing what is and what is not admissible —Erskine May lists twenty-nine types of question which are not allowed, including questions affecting the Royal Family, questions based on hearsay, and questions which seek a legal opinion. The object of a question is to extract information or press for action, not to seek an expression of opinion from a minister, but it is proper to put a question about the legislative or administrative intentions of his department. Members must not repeat rumours or newspaper gossip in their questions, which must be founded on facts for whose accuracy the member himself takes entire responsibility. One of the most important rules is that questions can only be addressed to a minister who is responsible for the matter of the question and whose department is directly involved. A Minister is not bound to answer a question, but unless there are obvious reasons for not doing so, such as national security, a refusal to answer would create a most unfavourable impression in the House. Difficulties arose in Great Britain over the lack of a minister responsible for the nationalized industries to whom questions could be put. In December 1951 the House of Commons appointed a Select Committee 'to consider the methods by which the House is informed of the affairs of the Nationalized Industries'. In their Report the committee explained that they concentrated on questions to ministers because 'the Parliamentary Question was the most immediate and convenient way open to Members to obtain information about public matters'. The problem was subsequently solved by the appointment on a sessional basis of a Select Committee on Nationalized Industries (q.v.).

A member asking a question, or any other member, is allowed to ask supplementary questions arising out of the answer received, and a member of the Opposition often puts down a question which looks innocent enough, but which gives opportunity for effective scoring against the Government through supplementary questions. However, a minister's department provides him with the ammunition to counter all the obvious 'sups' which may be asked, although it is impossible to prepare for every contingency.

Questions which have not appeared on the order paper, if they are of an urgent character relating to matters of public importance or the arrangement of business, may be taken at the end of Questions if they have been submitted to the Speaker and accepted as satisfying the above conditions. Such questions are known as Private Notice Questions, and the minister concerned must be informed before they can be put. Under a recent change in the rules relating to questions, the rule against anticipation does not apply to a Private Notice Question when there is no reasonable prospect of a question already tabled receiving an early oral answer.

In the House of Lords questions for oral and written answers are addressed to Her Majesty's Government, and debates may take place on them although there is no motion before the House. A postwar innovation is the institution of 'starred' questions, which are those asked in order to obtain specific information. No speech may be made in asking these and no debate may take place upon them, although supplementary questions may be asked. Starred questions are limited to four per member per day, although Question Time itself is of no fixed duration. The practice of the House of Lords in the questioning of ministers permits considerably more latitude than that of the House of Commons. However, the Committee of the House of Lords on Procedure of the House, reporting in May 1966, recommended that the attention of the House be drawn to three categories of questions which are regarded as 'not in accordance with the traditions of the House'. These categories are:

(1) Questions casting reflections on the Sovereign and Royal Family;
(2) Questions relating to matters which are *sub judice*;
(3) Questions which are phrased offensively.

The Canadian procedure with regard to questioning ministers is somewhat unorthodox by British standards. In the Canadian House of Commons two kinds of question are admissible: the written question, which appears on the order paper and of which notice is given; the oral question, which is asked daily at the commencement of business and of which no notice is required. Until recently, only the written question was recognized by the Standing Orders, the asking of oral questions having developed as a customary procedure and being in theory restricted to matters of urgency. If a written question is starred it is answered orally in the House but, as the Government is under little pressure to answer them, some of them remain on the order paper for months, and ministers answer them as and when they see fit. The political impact lies in the daily oral question period when ministers are subjected to a barrage of questions on the burning issues of the day. The fact that no notice is required of these questions makes it very difficult for the Speaker to regulate them. They frequently infringe the basic rules of questioning ministers, in that they are based on hearsay or raise matters which do not fall within ministerial responsibility. While the Chair is empowered to rule a question out of order, or to rule that it be transferred to the order paper, it is not always easy to enforce the rules, particularly since many bad practices have become accepted through long-standing custom.

(Further reading: Chester and Bowring, *Questions in Parliament*, 1962; Howarth, *Questions in the House*, 1956.)

QUORUM

In the House of Commons 40 members, including the Speaker, form a quorum. In the House of Lords only 3 peers are needed to form a quorum, although if a division is called upon any stage of a Bill the question is declared not decided unless 30 Lords are present to vote.

In the House of Commons it is the duty of the Speaker to ascertain whether or not a quorum is present before he takes the Chair, after which the House becomes responsible. Under former practice, if, after prayers, the Speaker found there was not a quorum present, he refrained from taking the Chair and waited either until a quorum assembled or until four o'clock when he again counted the House. To-day he takes the Chair and will only count the House if his attention is drawn to the fact that a quorum is not present. If a quorum is not present at four o'clock (1 p.m. on Fridays) he adjourns the House until the next sitting day without putting the question.

If, at any time after he has taken the Chair, the Speaker's attention is drawn to the fact that fewer than 40 members are present, or notice is taken that there are fewer than 40 members voting in a division, he will direct strangers to withdraw and members are summoned as if for a division. After the expiration of two minutes the Speaker proceeds to count the House, the outer door being kept open meanwhile. If a quorum is not present he will suspend proceedings either until four o'clock or until the required 40 members are assembled. If the House is counted out after four o'clock the Speaker will immediately adjourn the House.

In Committee of the Whole House the Chairman follows the same course if his attention is drawn to the fact that a quorum is not present. When he has ascertained that less than 40 members are assembled he leaves the Chair and the Speaker returns and counts the House. If a quorum has meanwhile been made and the Speaker counts the requisite 40 members the House again goes into committee.

There are certain times and occasions, specified in Standing Order No. 30, when a count may not take place. The House may not be counted out between 7.30 and 8.30 p.m. (1.15 and 2.15 p.m. on Fridays), in order to permit members to dine, nor after 10 p.m. However, if a division is called during such periods and 40 members are not present to vote, the business must stand over until the next sitting. No count may take place during proceedings on any Consolidated Fund Bill or Appropriation Bill or during proceedings in the course of which Mr. Speaker is directed to put forthwith any question. There are also certain established conventions regarding counts and quorums. For instance, it is recognized that once the presence of a quorum has been established by a count or division a reasonable period must elapse before another count is called. A 'reasonable period' has been regarded as one hour. A member who has called a count is entitled to absent himself while it takes place.

If a member wishes to call the Speaker's attention to the fact that a quorum is not present he does so in the following words: 'Mr. Speaker, I beg to take notice that there are not 40 members present.' Division bells are then rung throughout the building, and the policemen in the corridors call 'Count!' Members are given four minutes in which to assemble.

The quorum of 40 members is a usage which dates from 1640 and is subject to alteration by resolution of the House. In that year Speaker Lenthall had occasion to complain of the difficulty of constituting a House, remarking on 'the conduct of Members so unworthy to sit in Parliament that could so run forth for their dinners, or to the play-houses and bowling alleys, leaving business of great weight'. On 5 January it was therefore resolved, 'That Mr. Speaker is not to go to his Chair till there be at least forty in the House'. An explanation of why forty was chosen for a quorum, which was advanced at the time, was that it coincided with the number of counties into which England was divided at that period. It was not until 1729 that the House was 'counted out' in consequence of the absence of a quorum.

In other Commonwealth Parliaments the quorum varies according, usually, to the size of the legislature. The Canadian House of Commons, the New Zealand House of Representatives, and the Ceylon House of Representatives all require 20 members to form a quorum. The Australian House of Representatives, however, requires one-third of its members for a quorum, and the Standing Orders of this House provide (presumably to facilitate the making of so large a quorum) that at the commencement of the day's business no member may leave the Chamber until a quorum has been made. Malaysia's House of Representatives requires a quarter of its membership to form a quorum.

R

RADICALS

A term once applied to Members of Parliament who pressed for thorough or radical social reforms, particularly parliamentary and electoral. They formed an extremist section of the Whigs or Liberals, and although they came together to further causes which they supported, such as the Reform Bill and extension of the franchise, they never formed a separate political party. The first use of the word 'radical' in a political sense is attributed to Charles James Fox, who expressed his desire in 1797 for 'radical reform'. However, the birth of Radicalism actually took place thirty years earlier, during the struggle against the increasing domination of Parliament by George III. By 1776 the whole question of the 'rotten' boroughs (q.v.) had been investigated, and it was then that John Wilkes made his contribution to the history of parliamentary reform with his motion in the House of Commons, 'That leave be given to bring in a Bill for a just and equal representation of the people in Parliament'. It was Tom Paine in the two parts of his *Rights of Man* published in 1791 and 1792 who provided the inspiration for working-class Radicalism for the next fifty years. Many Radicals were not quite so revolutionary in their ideas as Paine, and rather favoured Bentham's utilitarian principles. They were all opposed to privilege and patronage in or out of Parliament. Many ultra-Radicals were Dissenters with a strong aversion to ceremonial and the pomp and circumstance which surrounds a monarchy, and after 1832 30 to 50 Radicals were always found to support a motion to reduce the Civil List (q.v.). In the first Parliament to be elected after the passing of the Reform Bill, which the Radicals helped to force through, there were nearly 200 members who might have been described as Radicals, but there were probably not more than 50 who would have voted against the Whigs on any vital issue. Apart from preoccupation with suffrage questions, the Radicals campaigned for the repeal of the Corn Laws and several church reforms. Dissenters were freed from compulsory church rates in 1868 after a struggle which lasted over thirty years, and the abolition of Anglican tests at the universities was achieved in 1871. Other reforms which had been demanded by Radicals for decades were the substitution of the magistrates in the administration of the counties by elected county councils (County Councils Act of 1888), and the more democratic organization of the smaller local government bodies as carried out in the Local Government Act of 1894. A new statement of Radical policy was embodied in the 'Newcastle Programme' of 1891, but it was overshadowed by the Home Rule dispute and nullified by the return of the Conservatives to power in 1895. The Liberal triumph at the General Election of 1906 was also a victory for the Radicals, and there followed in 1907 the first recognition for the purposes of income tax of the difference between earned and unearned income, in 1908 the Old Age Pension Act, in 1909–10 the great struggle over the 'People's Budget', regarded as the first step in a new Radical campaign against the landowners, and in 1911 the Parliament Act which reduced the power of the House of Lords. After the First World War, Radical politicians and voters were absorbed by the Labour Party, and the result of Lloyd George's failure to recapture working-class confidence was the disappearance of the Radicals from the British political scene. Most of the reforms they had struggled for had been obtained, and the names of their great men, such as Hume, Grote, Cobden, Bright, and Joseph Chamberlain, will always have an honoured place in the political history of England.

READING CLERK

A Clerk in the House of Lords who sits at the Table of the House with the Clerk of the Parliaments (q.v.) and the Clerk Assistant. He records attendances of peers, reads aloud the letters patent and writs of summons of newly created peers when they are introduced, and administers the oath. He also reads the commissions for Royal Assent to Bills, prorogation (qq.v.), etc.

READINGS OF BILLS

The stages through which a Bill passes in both Houses of Parliament include a first, second, and third reading. After the first reading Bills are printed and are available to members for study prior to the debate which takes place on the second reading. Before printing was invented Bills were actually read out in full by the Clerk as the only means of informing members of their contents, and this practice extended well into the 18th century, when the distribution of printed copies rendered the reading unnecessary.

See also BILL, PASSAGE OF.

REASONED AMENDMENT

A method of opposing a Bill on second or third reading is to move a reasoned amendment, in which objections to the Bill or reasons for opposing its progress are clearly stated. Unlike the amendment, 'that the Bill be read upon this day six (or three) months', the effect of a reasoned amendment, if carried, is not necessarily one of outright rejection as the Bill can be brought up again on a subsequent occasion.

Nevertheless, a Bill in respect of which a reasoned amendment had been carried on the second or third reading is unlikely to make any further progress. Since 1967 it is now possible to have a second division on the main question after the defeat of a reasoned amendment in recognition of the fact that the opponents of the Bill might not necessarily agree with the terms of the amendment.

The categories into which a reasoned amendment may fall are listed by May as follows:

(1) It may be declaratory of some principle adverse to, or differing from, the principles, policy or provisions of the Bill;

(2) It may express opinions as to any circumstances connected with the introduction or prosecution of the Bill, or otherwise opposed to its progress;

(3) It may seek further information in relation to the Bill by committees, commissioners, the production of papers or other evidence.

As an example of a reasoned amendment we may instance that which was moved by Sir Winston Churchill on the third reading of the Representation of the People Bill, 1948. To the question, 'That the Bill be now read the Third time', Sir Winston moved the omission of the words after 'that' and the substitution of the following: 'this House, while recognizing the necessity for an equitable scheme of redistribution, declines to give a Third Reading to a Bill which repudiates agreed recommendations of Mr. Speaker's Conference, 1944, and disregards for the purpose of Party advantage the findings of the Boundary Commission, thereby bringing discredit on Ministers of the Crown and lowering the traditional standards of our public life.' (Hansard, vol. 452, col. 1377.)

RECALL
See REFERENDUM.

RECEIVERS OF PETITIONS
See PETITIONS.

RECESS
The period between a prorogation (q.v.) of Parliament and the opening of a new session, as distinct from the period between a dissolution (q.v.) and the calling of a new Parliament. The term is popularly applied to a period between an adjournment and the resumption of a session, e.g., the parliamentary vacations. Usually the recesses of the House of Lords and House of Commons coincide, but in 1947 the Lords met while the Commons were still in recess, or more correctly had adjourned for the summer vacation.

RECOMMITTAL OF BILL

See BILL, RECOMMITTAL OF.

RECONCILIATION PARLIAMENT

The third Parliament of the reign of Mary I which met on 12 November 1554 to deal with the question of reuniting England to the Church of Rome. Both Houses made supplication to the Pope beseeching his pardon for their past defection, and out of 360 members in the House of Commons only 2 raised any objection to these proceedings. Later, however, 33 members seceded from the lower House when they realized the full implications of the new policy, an action for which they were duly prosecuted. This Parliament reversed the attainder against Cardinal Pole and in the presence of the Queen both Lords and Commons humbly received absolution from this prelate. The Reconciliation Parliament completely swept away all the ecclesiastical legislation passed during the reign of Henry VIII.

RECONSTRUCTION, MINISTER OF

Lord Woolton was appointed Minister of Reconstruction in 1943 to assume general direction of the efforts of the government departments in preparing schemes for reconstruction after the War—the switching over of industry from war to peace, and the provision of adequate supplies of food and houses. The Ministry was abolished in 1945 when Lord Woolton became Lord President of the Council. During the First World War the 1st Viscount Addison was appointed Minister of Reconstruction in 1917.

RECORDS OFFICE, HOUSE OF LORDS

See VICTORIA TOWER.

REDISTRIBUTION OF SEATS

See CONSTITUENCY.

'RED LETTER' ELECTION

See ZINOVIEV LETTER.

RED PARLIAMENT

A Scottish Parliament which met at Perth in 1606, so called because by order of King James VI the nobles appeared in scarlet robes. This Parliament gave the King particular satisfaction as it declared by one of its enactments that his prerogative extended 'over all estates, persons, and causes whatsoever'.

REFERENDUM

The machinery of the referendum has been used in a number of Commonwealth countries—but not in the United Kingdom—to obtain for the Government a direct decision from the electorate on a specific subject involving legislation, and parliamentary voters are entitled to express their opinion by voting for or against the Government's proposition. The referendum has been used in Canada and New Zealand on the question of prohibition, and in Australia to introduce amendments to the Constitution. A referendum was also held in Southern Rhodesia in 1953 which decided that the Colony would form a federation with Northern Rhodesia and Nyasaland and in 1960 South Africa decided by referendum that she would become a republic. It is argued that the use of the referendum makes the sovereignty of the people a reality, and that the responsibility of making a decision compels them to think carefully of the laws that govern them, but actual experience in some countries has shown that the referendum does not create interest in legislation and the percentage of voters who participate is usually small unless the issue to be decided is of far-reaching importance.

Allied to the referendum is the initiative, a system whereby a certain fixed number of voters are entitled to command a legislature to introduce a particular law. One type of initiative, the formulative, allows voters to draft a Bill and compel the legislature to consider it. The Canadian Provinces of Alberta and British Columbia make provision for the use of the initiative by means of Direct Legislation Acts. Alberta's Liquor Act of 1916 was enacted under the provisions of its Direct Legislation Act, but British Columbia's Direct Legislation Act has never been formally proclaimed although it remains on the statute book as potential law.

A type of referendum known as the recall is a device intended to give an electorate a direct control over its representative by voting for his resignation. It has never been used in the British Commonwealth.

REFORM

See HOUSE OF LORDS REFORM; PARLIAMENTARY REFORM; REFORM ACT; REPRESENTATION; WILLIAM IV AND PARLIAMENT.

REFORM ACT

The term generally applied to the Representation of the People Act, 1832, the first of a series of statutes which substantially amended the state of the parliamentary representation in the United Kingdom. It provided for a drastic redistribution of seats including the abolition of 56 'rotten' boroughs (q.v.), the enfranchisement of populous towns previously unrepresented, an increase in county representation, the extension of the franchise, and the reduction of election expenses. The measure was carried by Earl Grey's Whig Government after two previous Bills had been rejected by the House of Lords. It radically altered the constitution of the House of Commons although it effected no change in the number of seats.

Strangely enough, this great liberal measure, which swept away so many electoral abuses, was the first specifically to exclude women from voting. Prior to 1832 the ban on female suffrage had been not statutory but customary, but the Reform Act specifically confined the vote to male persons in all those new boroughs which were created in place of the 'rotten' boroughs.

See also REPRESENTATION; WILLIAM IV AND PARLIAMENT.

REFORMATION PARLIAMENT

The fifth Parliament of Henry VIII and the first of the Reformation. It sat from November 1529 until April 1536, during which time it enacted a volume of statutes to give legal effect to the religious revolution which had been brought about by the King. The Commons seized the legislative initiative and the Lords found themselves compelled to endorse all the measures sent up to them by the lower House, according as they did with the will of the King and of the country at large. In this Parliament the Commons emerged for the first time as the more powerful of the two Houses, and the dissolution of 1536 left the influence of the Lords severely curtailed. In excluding the abbots from the upper House the Reformation Parliament put an end to the dominant influence which the Church had wielded over the legislature. This Parliament has also been termed, by those who disliked its proceedings, the Black Parliament.

REMONSTRANCE

A form of petition (q.v.) making a declaration of grievances. To be received by either House it had to be respectfully worded and include the proper form of 'prayer', in which the particular object of the petitioner is expressed. However, the use of the word 'remonstrance' was not favoured by Parliament, and a document headed as a remonstrance, although complying with the other requirements, was refused in 1843.

See also GRAND REMONSTRANCE.

REPORTERS' GALLERY

See PRESS GALLERY.

REPORT STAGE
See BILL, PASSAGE OF.

REPRESENTATION

Parliament has been a representative assembly from the earliest times. When the King's Council of the early Middle Ages deliberated, the whole nation was deemed to be present, and when the Commons arrived in Parliament during the 13th century the principle of representation became more than theoretical. The first representatives of the common people were the 2 knights from each shire who were summoned to the Parliament of 1254, and who were the forerunners of our modern county members. In 1265 they were joined by 2 citizens from each city and 2 burgesses from each borough, and thereafter the Commons began to develop as a separate representative body. The Commons have always been elected by the communities, or constituencies, they represent, although the manner of election, distribution of seats, and qualifications for the franchise bear little similarity to-day to the system which operated for four centuries before the passing of the Reform Bill in 1832.

The history of the county franchise is fairly straightforward. The sheriffs of the counties were directed by their writs to cause an election to be held of 2 knights to represent each shire. The knights were elected by the county courts, which were the centres of local administration in feudal England, from amongst their own members. The sheriff, who was in charge of the proceedings, probably determined the manner of election. An Act of 1430, which regulated the county franchise until the Reform Act of 1832, imposed a property qualification on voters, requiring a man to be the owner of freehold land or tenement to the value of 40 shillings a year in order to be eligible for the franchise. Leaseholders and copyholders were excluded. Originally, 37 counties were represented by 74 knights, the counties palatinate of Chester and Durham being excluded. The Welsh counties, Monmouthshire, and Chester were enfranchised by Henry VIII, raising the county membership to 90. The Scottish and Irish counties were included in 1707 and 1800 respectively, and on the eve of the Reform Bill there were 114 county constituencies represented by 188 members.

The history of the borough franchise is far more complex. Cities and boroughs were not specified in the sheriff's writ; they were assumed to be known, and it is probable that the places to be so treated were chosen at the discretion of the sheriff. In the 13th and 14th centuries, parliamentary representation was considered a doubtful privilege, and it is likely that towns preferring to remain unrepresented made arrangements with the sheriff accordingly. Later the outlook changed, and there are signs early in the 15th century that the towns were beginning to recognize the advantages of representation. The 16th century saw a rapid increase in the number of boroughs. Many were created by Royal Charter under the Tudor monarchs, whilst others were revived or restored to borough status.

The practice of creating boroughs of insignificant voting strength in order to secure the election of members who could be relied upon to support the policies of the Crown appears to have arisen during the reign of Edward VI. Elizabeth I frequently resorted to this means in her attempts to gain control over parliamentary representation, and her reign produced a profusion of 'pocket' or 'rotten' boroughs as these constituencies came to be called. By the end of her reign there were 374 borough members in the House of Commons as compared with 90 county members. The selection and distribution of parliamentary boroughs were quite arbitrary. The south of England was more heavily represented than the north, and there were dense clusters of boroughs in certain areas. The county of Cornwall was a particularly flagrant example, 18 members being returned for the Liskeard area alone. Even in Elizabeth's reign it was recognized that borough representation was too high, but apart from a few minor attempts to correct them, the abuses in the electoral system remained unchecked until the Reform Act of 1832.

The borough franchise before 1832 was unregulated, inconsistent, and confused, and depended entirely on local custom. The boroughs could be roughly divided into two classes, the 'open' and the 'close'. In the open boroughs the franchise was fairly wide. In the so-called 'scot and lot' boroughs, for instance, anybody liable to pay 'scot' (local dues) or to bear 'lot' (local duties) was entitled to the vote, and broadly speaking this included all rate-payers. In the 'potwalloper' boroughs the franchise was enjoyed by all heads of families. (A 'potwalloper' can roughly be taken to mean a breadwinner, or one not dependent upon any other person for his food.) At the other end of the scale were the 'burgage' boroughs, where the right to vote depended on showing title to a property by the form of tenure known as burgage tenure. Sometimes residence was also a condition, but in other cases, it was neither necessary nor possible. The notorious 'rotten' borough of Old Sarum, where two members were returned by seven voters, consisted of fields which could not even provide a barn to shelter the Returning Officer. Burgages were easily bought and sold as the occasion arose, and where a residence qualification existed a broken-down hovel often sufficed as the qualifying property. Different again were the nomination boroughs, the closest of them all, where the member owed his seat to a patron whose interests he was expected to look after. They consisted of two groups, the 'corporation' boroughs and the 'freemen' boroughs. In the former the franchise was restricted by charter to those, usually self-elected and often non-resident, who belonged to

x* [639]

the governing body of the borough. In the latter it was enjoyed only by those who held the freedom of the borough, a privilege which could be acquired by birth, marriage, gift, purchase, and other means. In all nomination boroughs the electorate was an easily controlled body which existed to endorse the choice of the patron. Candidates wishing to be independent of any control could buy their seats. They could be bought and sold quite openly and were even advertised in the Press. The sale of a seat merely amounted to bribery of the patron on the part of the candidate, and of the electors by the patron. The Government itself participated in these transactions, and Treasury boroughs were reserved for those whose election the Government was desirous of securing. In 1830 the average price for a seat in Parliament appears to have been £6,000. The fact that keen reformers and men of high scruples such as Ricardo, Romilly, Burdett, and Hume bought their seats serves to indicate that this was the only method of entering Parliament which was open to the man who wished to maintain his independence.

In 1793 the Society of the Friends of the People estimated that 51 boroughs with a combined total of less than 1,500 electors were returning 100 members to the Commons. Constituencies of 50 and fewer voters were returning 2 members apiece, whilst growing cities such as Manchester, Birmingham, Leeds, and Sheffield were unrepresented. In some districts twin boroughs existed which had been created originally for the sole purpose of doubling their parliamentary representation, but which were united for all other purposes. Such were Weymouth and Melcombe Regis and East and West Looe. The Cornish fishing village of Bossinney, once a borough, could produce but one elector after an Act of 1782 had disfranchised revenue officers, most of whom had held their appointments as favours in return for their votes. Other 'rotten' boroughs such as Gatton and Old Sarum are, of course, well known. In 1827 John Wilson Croker estimated that no less than 276 members were returned by patrons. At the end of the 18th century the voters' roll in England was estimated to include only 2 per cent of the population, and the proportion in Scotland was two voters per thousand head of population.

Such was the state of the electoral system before the passing of the Reform Bill, a system which had been defended by eminent men such as Edmund Burke. Prior to 1832 both Chatham and the younger Pitt had attempted to introduce reforms, and one scheme proposed by the Duke of Richmond in 1780 had even advocated universal adult suffrage. It was not until 1830, however, when a Whig administration was returned pledged to the ideal of reform, that the problem was tackled with the seriousness it required.

The Reform Bill of 1832, which was passed after two previous Bills had been rejected by the Lords, was a milestone in British history, although its immediate effects were not as far-reaching as its supporters had hoped or as its opponents had feared. It did not of itself put an end to all abuse and corruption, but it was a substantial step forward. It set in motion the machinery of reform and paved the way for further progress. It was the inevitable effect of a tide which was sweeping away the old traditions of government, for the unrepresented masses had been by no means voiceless.

The Bill had four main purposes: to redistribute seats, to increase county representation, to extend the franchise, and to reduce election expenses. Before its passing, the House of Commons consisted of 658 seats, made up of 188 county, 465 borough, and 5 university seats. The Reform Bill, and the similar Bills which were passed for Scotland and Ireland in the same year, left the total number of seats unaltered but they were drastically redistributed. Fifty-six 'rotten' boroughs were abolished altogether and 30 were deprived of one member. Of the 143 seats thus obtained, 65 went to the counties, 65 to towns previously unrepresented, and 13 to Scotland and Ireland. The total effect of the redistribution was to reduce the number of members for England from 489 to 471, and to give 29 seats to Wales, 53 to Scotland, and 105 to Ireland, whereas before the numbers had been 24, 45, and 100 respectively. Thus the reformed House of Commons consisted of 253 county, 399 borough, and 6 university members.

The Bill retained the 40-shilling freehold franchise in the counties and enfranchised four new classes: the possessors of the £10 copyhold, the £10 long leaseholders, the £50 short leaseholders, and the occupiers paying a minimum rent of £50 per annum. In the boroughs a uniform franchise was introduced, the vote being given to all householders paying an annual rent of £10. The effect of these provisions was to enfranchise the middle classes. The Bill also introduced the system of registration of voters, and the strength of the electorate which registered for the first time in 1832 was 813,000. It was estimated that this figure represented an increase in the electorate of some 300,000, although allowance was not made for plural voters.

Once the Reform Act, 1832, a much-needed and long overdue measure, had come to the Statute Book, other measures were not long in following. A Bill to abolish the nomination of members by their patrons was passed soon after in 1835. The Representation of the People Act, 1867, was the next important step forward. In the counties it reduced the £10 qualification for copyholders and leaseholders to £5, and enfranchised occupiers of premises with a £12 rateable value. Its effects were far more significant in the boroughs, where the franchise was conferred on all householders and on lodgers paying an annual rent of £10. The vote was thus conferred upon the urban working man, and it is estimated that the strength of the electorate was raised to two millions as a result.

In 1872 the Ballot Act introduced the system of voting by secret ballot. The measure met with serious opposition and was only passed eventually as an experimental law subject to annual renewal. For fifty-five years it was renewed annually by the Expiring Laws Continuance Act of each year before it became established as a permanent measure in 1918. The Ballot Act also removed the distinction between knights, citizens, and burgesses, and classed them all as members.

The next stage in the advance towards universal adult suffrage came with the Representation of the People Act, 1884, and the Redistribution of Seats Act, 1885. By bringing in the householders and lodgers in the counties, and introducing a standard £10 occupation qualification for both boroughs and counties, the former Act established a uniform franchise throughout the country. Just as the Act of 1867 had enfranchised the urban working man, so the Act of 1884 did the same for his rural counterpart. The Act of 1885 raised the number of seats from 658 to 670 and redistributed them more evenly according to the size of the population. As far as possible the country was divided into equal electoral districts each returning a single member. Twenty-seven constituencies, including the City of London and the universities of Oxford, Cambridge, and Dublin, continued to return 2 members. Boroughs with less than 15,000 inhabitants were merged with the county.

The Representation of the People Act, 1918, altered the electoral system fundamentally, and was the most notable advance since the Reform Act. The sweeping changes introduced by the Act included the enfranchisement of women who had reached the age of 30, provided they were local government electors or the wives of local government electors, and the substitution of a simple franchise for the old form, residence or the occupation of business premises for a period of six months being the sole qualification. In addition to his residential vote, a qualified elector was allowed to exercise either a university vote or a business vote. The Act also made provision for absent voters, enabling them to vote by post or proxy. It modified the system of registration, provided that Returning Officers' expenses (subject to a fixed maximum) be paid out of the Exchequer, and introduced the condition which requires each candidate to deposit £150 with the Returning Officer on nomination day. As a result of the Act the electorate was increased by about 8 millions and the number of seats was raised to 707. The House of Commons remained at this strength until 1922 when the withdrawal of the Southern Irish members reduced the number to 615. It was raised to 640 by the interim revision which preceded the General Election of 1945.

The final disqualifications upon women were removed by the Representation of the People (Equal Franchise) Act, 1928. The Act enfranchised all women upon their reaching the age of 21 on the same conditions as those which applied to men. Thus universal adult suffrage was finally attained, and after the passing of this Act the electorate stood at over 28 millions.

The Representation of the People Act, 1948, abolished the university seats, the business vote, and the twelve remaining double-member constituencies. The Cities of London and Westminster, which previously returned 2 members each, were merged into one constituency. The Act thus put an end to plural voting and established 625 constituencies each returning one member, residence being the sole qualification required by the voter provided he or she is a British subject or citizen of the Republic of Ireland of full age. Prior to the General Election of 1955 the number of constituencies was increased to 630 and it remained unaltered for the General Elections of 1959, 1964, 1966 and 1970.

In 1969 the voting age was reduced from 21 to 18, and to-day the strength of the electorate stands at some 40 millions. Of the 630 members they return to the House of Commons, 335 represent borough constituencies and 295 county constituencies. There are 511 constituencies in England (289 borough, 222 county), 36 in Wales (10 borough, 26 county), 71 in Scotland (32 borough, 39 county), and 12 in Northern Ireland (4 borough, 8 county). The 5 seats added in 1955 all went to England, which previously had 291 borough and 215 county constituencies.

The law relating to elections was consolidated by the Representation of the People Act, 1949.

See also ALTERNATIVE VOTE; ELECTIONS; FRANCHISE; HOUSE OF COMMONS; PARLIAMENTARY REFORM; PROPORTIONAL REPRESENTATION; UNIVERSITY REPRESENTATION.

REPRESENTATIVE PEERS

The system whereby the peers of Scotland, and formerly the peers of Ireland, were represented in the House of Lords on an elective basis was abolished by the Peerage Act, 1963. To-day all Scottish peers are eligible to sit and vote in the House of Lords. The Act did not extend the same right to Irish peers, but it abolished all limitations on their eligibility to vote and stand as candidates at General Elections.

For over 250 years, following the coming into force of the Act of Union with Scotland in 1707, the Scottish peers were represented in the House of Lords by 16 of their own number elected by themselves. They sat for the duration of a Parliament and were re-elected at each General Election. No provision was made for Spiritual Lords, the established Church of Scotland being Presbyterian. Scottish peers who were not elected as representative peers did not enjoy the political rights of commoners and were not eligible for membership of the House of Commons. Under the Peerage Act, 1963, Scottish peers are on the same footing as the peers of England, Great Britain and the United Kingdom. They remain ineligible to vote at General Elections and to become Members of the House of Commons, but they have the right, in common with other hereditary peers, to disclaim their peerages under the conditions specified in the Act, in which case they forfeit the rights, titles and privileges of peerage and assume the rights and status of commoners (*see* PEERAGE, DISCLAIMER OF).

The Irish peerage was represented in the House of Lords from 1800, the date of the union with Ireland, but the provisions of the Act of Union respecting the House of Lords differed from those of the Act of Union with Scotland. 28 Irish representative peers were to be elected for life, and the rest were eligible to vote at General Elections and to be elected to the House of Commons for seats other than Irish seats. The total number of Irish peerages was to be limited to 100. Four Irish Spiritual lords were admitted to the House of Lords, but they lost their seats when the Church of Ireland was disestablished in 1869.

No election of Irish representative peers had taken place since the constituting of the Irish Free State in 1922. From this date the offices of Lord Chancellor of Ireland and Clerk of the Crown and Hanaper were abolished together with the machinery for filling vacancies among the Irish representative peers (the last time an election had actually taken place was in 1919). There was no surviving Irish representative peer when the Peerage Act was passed in 1963, the last of them, the fourth Earl of Kilmorey, having died in 1961.

In May 1966, 12 Irish peers presented a claim to the House of Lords' Committee for Privileges that their right to be represented in the House of Lords was 'transcendental and fundamental'. They claimed they were entitled to sit not as representatives of the Irish Republic or Northern Ireland but as peers of Ireland, and that no enactment could erase that privilege. Not unexpectedly their claim was denied.

(Further reading: Fergusson, *The Sixteen Peers of Scotland*, 1960.)

REPRIMAND AND ADMONITION

An offender against the privileges of the House of Commons or the House of Lords may be subjected to a reprimand by the Speaker of either House in any case not sufficiently serious to warrant imprisonment. Members receive a reprimand standing in their place, while non-members are brought to the Bar of the House attended by the Serjeant-at-Arms. This punishment was last inflicted in 1968. An admonition is a milder form of reprimand, and was last administered in 1930.

See also PRIVILEGE, BREACH OF.

RESERVATION OF SPEECH

The mover of an Order of the Day in the House of Commons may, if he wishes, reserve his speech until later in the debate. It is customary for this intention to be indicated by the member raising his hat whilst seated. The same right is accorded to the seconder of a substantive motion in legislatures where motions require seconders.

RESERVED POWERS

The Governor of a Colony has power to reserve certain Bills submitted to him by the legislature by withholding his assent until Her Majesty, through her Secretary of State for the Colonies, has considered the principles involved. This is a prerogative power of the Crown which is usually embodied in the Colony's Constitution, and its exercise by the Governor may be either obligatory by reason of the subject matter, or discretionary. A colonial Governor has also in most Colonies a positive control of legislation, having reserved powers to enact Bills over the heads of the unofficial majority in the interests of public order, public faith, or other essentials of good government. Apart from those reserved powers delegated to a Governor, the Crown has power to legislate by Order in Council and to disallow ordinances already passed. There have been constitutions (e.g., the 1923 Constitution of Southern Rhodesia) under which the Governor is required to reserve certain specified legislation, but otherwise he acts invariably on the advice of the locally constituted government. As a result of the recommendations of the Imperial Conferences of 1926 and 1930, embodied in the Statute of Westminster (q.v.), neither the Crown nor the Governor-General retains reserved powers in respect of those countries which are full members of the Commonwealth.

RESIGNATION OF SEAT

See CHILTERN HUNDREDS.

RESOLUTION, FINANCIAL

See FINANCIAL RESOLUTION.

RESOLUTIONS

See ORDERS AND RESOLUTIONS.

RESPONSIBLE GOVERNMENT

Responsible government is a term which has been used in a variety of senses. In the days of the former British Empire it was used to denote a form of colonial self-government which provided for a wide measure of internal autonomy while reserving certain powers, notably in respect of external affairs, to the mother country. This form of government was first introduced in the Canadian colonies in 1848 and was widely extended subsequently.

In the modern sense of the term, responsible government is open to at least three interpretations. In the first place, it is used to denote a system of government which is responsive to public opinion. In this sense it can be used to distinguish between a democratic form of government, which recognizes an obligation to consult public opinion, and a totalitarian régime, in which the rights of the individual are subordinated to the monolithic state.

In another sense the term is used to denote concepts of public duty and moral responsibility. There are few who would deny that the prime duty of a government is to govern in the national interest, and that when the national interest is in conflict with public opinion, the former must take precedence. The late L. S. Amery has written: 'A British government is not merely responsible to those who have appointed it or keep it in office in the sense in which an agent is responsible to his principal. It is an independent body which on taking office assumes the responsibility of leading and directing Parliament and the nation in accordance with its own judgment and convictions.'

In the third place, the term responsible government is used to signify the accountability of the government and individual ministers to an elected assembly, a usage which is current in any country with a parliamentary system of government. The Cabinet is collectively responsible to Parliament for government policies and individual ministers are personally responsible for the work of their departments. The elected assembly is thus, in principle, the truly sovereign institution in the system of government.

In a democratic state each of the three concepts of responsible government described above has validity, although it is clear that the objectives implied in each case are not always compatible. For example, public opinion is not always consistent with what is prudent or practical, and a government which was guided solely by public opinion would soon find itself pursuing contradictory policies. The best that any government can hope to do is to strike a healthy balance between conflicting objectives, and in this process the representative system is a vital factor. It is impossible to consider the concept of responsible government in any of its aspects without considering the representative system also. As Professor A. H. Birch has written:

'It is largely through this system [the representative system] that public demands are expressed, modified and presented to the government. The political parties absorb a wide variety of opinions on controversial issues and merge them, with varying degrees of success, into a limited number of alternative policies. Political leaders use party conferences and election meetings to increase public understanding of their programmes. Periodic elections ensure that some weight is given to the opinions of inarticulate and unorganized citizens, as well as to those of people who know how to make their views felt. A representative system thus provides a way of bridging the gulf between the policies a government would follow if it responded to the varying day-to-day expressions of public opinion and those it must follow if its policies are to be coherent and mutually consistent. . . .' (A. H. Birch, *Representative and responsible government*, 1964.)

RESTITUTION BILLS

Bills for the restoration of honours and land, restitution in blood, and the reversing of attainders. Such Bills are always initiated in the House of Lords and are presented to that House by command of the Sovereign. They pass through the ordinary stages of Public Bills (q.v.) and are sent to the House of Commons where they are committed to a Select Committee (q.v.) after second reading. The Royal Assent (q.v.) is signified in the words, *Soit fait comme il est desiré.*

Such Bills are very infrequent and since 1848 there have been only seven: Maxwell's Restitution Bill, 1848; Drummond's (Duke de Melfort's) Restitution Bill, 1853; Lord Lovat's Restitution Bill, 1854; Carnegie's Restitution Bill, 1855; Bruce's Restitution Bill, 1869; Earldom of Mar Restitution Bill, 1885; and Alexander's Restitution Bill, 1916.

RHODESIAN PARLIAMENT

Until 1964, when the territory previously known as Northern Rhodesia adopted the name of Zambia upon becoming independent, the country known to-day as Rhodesia was called Southern Rhodesia to distinguish it from its northern neighbour.

The present *de facto* Constitution of Rhodesia, the legality of which is not recognized outside the country, was brought into force following a referendum held in June 1969. It provides for a Republican form of government, a bicameral Parliament consisting of a Senate and House of Assembly and an electoral system based upon two separate voters' rolls, one for Europeans and one for Africans. The Senate consists of 23 members, comprising 10 elected Europeans, 10 African Chiefs elected by the Council of Chiefs, and 3 persons of any race appointed by the President. The House of Assembly consists of 66 members, of whom 50 are Europeans and 16 are Africans. One half of the African members are elected by African voters voting in 8 constituencies and the other half are elected by tribal electoral colleges of Chiefs and other office-holders in tribal trust lands. The franchise is dependent upon income and educational qualifications in the case of both European and African voters. The Constitution provides for increases in African representation in the House of Assembly through a process related directly to increases in the proportion of personal income tax contributed by the African population, with the proviso that African representation may never exceed parity with European representation.

The Constitution also provides for a Declaration of Rights and protects a new land tenure system whereby all land in Rhodesia is divided into areas reserved for Europeans and areas reserved for Africans. The main power of the Senate is one of delay, particularly in reference to Bills which the Legal Committee of the Senate considers to be inconsistent with the Declaration of Rights. However, it is also provided that no court will have the right to inquire into or pronounce upon the validity of any law upon the ground that it is inconsistent with the Declaration of Rights.

Until 1923 both Southern and Northern Rhodesia were administered by the British South Africa Company in terms of a Royal Charter granted in 1889. The powers conferred upon the Company included the right to make laws, to maintain a police force and to administer justice. The Southern Rhodesia Order-in-Council, 1898, provided the Colony with its first semblance of representative government. Executive power was vested in one or more Administrators appointed by the Company, the previous Administrator's Council becoming an Executive Council divested of primary legislative powers. The power to make laws was conceded to a Legislative Council including elected members, the Company surrendering its former power to make ordinances in London. Ordinances passed by the Legislative Council required the assent of the High Commissioner who was also empowered to legislate concurrently by proclamation. (From 1910 the office of High Commissioner was combined with that of Governor-General of the Union of South Africa, and he retained certain functions in respect of the constitutional machinery of Southern Rhodesia until 1937.) Further imperial control over the Company's administration was provided by a British Resident Commissioner, who was *ex-officio* a member of both the Legislative and Executive Councils, and the power of the Secretary of State for the Colonies to disallow any legislation within a year of its enactment.

The first Legislative Council consisted of the Administrators of Mashonaland and Matabeleland (in 1901 the two appointments were merged into the single office of Administrator of Southern Rhodesia), the British Resident Commissioner, 5 members nominated by the British South Africa Company with the approval of the Secretary of State for the Colonies, and 4 members elected by the registered voters of the Colony. The number of elected members on the Legislative Council increased with the growth of the European population. By 1907 the elected members were in the majority on the Council and by 1923 their number had reached 13. In the previous year a referendum was held to decide whether Southern Rhodesia should be granted internal self-government or become a Province of the then Union of South Africa. The electorate decided in favour of the former proposition and in 1923 a Constitution was issued by letters patent conferring responsible government on Southern Rhodesia. In addition to the usual powers which were in those days reserved to the Crown in respect of its self-governing colonies, the Southern Rhodesian Constitution contained reservations relating to native affairs, all legislation which was racially discriminatory being subject to the approval of the Imperial Government.

The 1923 Constitution provided for a fully elected Legislative Assembly of 30 members, the first session of which was opened by the Governor of the Colony on 30 May 1924. Its size remained unchanged until December 1962 when the first election was held under the new Constitution of 1961. In the meantime much was to happen which would affect the constitutional future of Southern Rhodesia.

In 1953 Southern Rhodesia entered into a Federation with its two northern neighbours, Northern Rhodesia and Nyasaland, and surrendered a wide range of powers to a Federal Parliament and Federal Government. The Federation was ill-fated and short-lived, being dissolved ten years later as the result of African nationalist pressure in the northern territories. At the time the Federation was formed, following a referendum in Southern Rhodesia and with the blessing of the British Government, the rapid pace of political emancipation in Africa had not been foreseen. In 1953 Africa was still largely a colonial continent. Southern Rhodesia, although self-governing, was controlled by its European minority while Northern Rhodesia and Nyasaland were Protectorates of the British Crown. The pattern of the Federal Government approximated to that of Southern Rhodesia and was thus inconsistent with the African political ambitions which emerged in the ensuing decade. In 1963 nearly all the former African Colonies of the European powers had either become independent or were on the verge of becoming so. In this context the Federation of Rhodesia and Nyasaland had become an anachronism.

Before the dissolution of the Federation, a new Constitution was granted to Southern Rhodesia, having been approved by the electorate at a referendum in 1961. The new Constitution removed most of the reservations embodied in the previous Constitution but fell short of conceding the Colony full independence. It provided for a Legislative Assembly of 65 members and incorporated a highly complex franchise system which, while not approaching universal adult suffrage, guaranteed wider voting opportunities than before to the African people. Provision was made for two voters' rolls, the franchise being based upon various combinations of educational and income qualifications. The qualifications required for registration on the lower roll were considerably less than those required for registration on the upper roll, and while neither roll was restricted to any one race the great majority of the more highly qualified voters were Europeans. All African chiefs and headmen, however, were automatically qualified for registration on the upper roll. 50 of the 65 members of the Legislative Assembly were elected by the voters on the upper roll, the remaining 15 by the voters on the lower roll. The electoral law also provided for a system of cross-voting between the two rolls, but the preferential vote which was introduced for the first time in 1958 was subsequently abolished.

The Constitution also enshrined a Declaration of Rights and provided for a Constitutional Council with certain advisory and delaying functions designed to prevent the passage of legislation which discriminated unfairly between the races or contravened the Declaration of Rights.

The first election to be held under the new Constitution took place in December 1962, 14 of the 65 members elected being Africans, the first ever to sit in the Southern Rhodesian Parliament. Nevertheless, the nature of the result was not such as to offer any hope for the continuance of the Federation of Rhodesia and Nyasaland which was dissolved exactly one year later. Nyasaland and Northern Rhodesia shortly afterwards became the independent states of Malawi and Zambia, while Southern Rhodesia reverted to its previous status as a self-governing Colony. Thereafter a prolonged dispute began between Rhodesian and successive British Governments, the former claiming Rhodesia's right to full independence, the latter declining to concede it while the control of the government remained indefinitely in the hands of a white minority. The dispute reached a climax on 11 November 1965 when the Prime Minister of Rhodesia, Mr. Ian Smith, declared the independence of his country unilaterally. His action was condemned by most of the countries of the world, but although his régime is unrecognized outside Rhodesia it remains at the present time (1970) the *de facto* government of the country.

The Parliament building was erected during the period 1897 to 1899, and it was originally designed as an hotel. The Chamber is well-proportioned and lofty, and the Speaker's Chair was used by the administrators in the early days of the British South Africa Company's history. The building houses a fine collection of portraits of past Administrators, Governors, Prime Ministers, and Speakers, and unusual features are the two lamp standards at the foot of the main staircase made from elephant tusks of exceptional size—one weighing 75 and the other 73 lb.

RICHARD I (1157–1199)

Third son of Henry II, crowned King of England on 3 September 1189.

RICHARD II (1367–1400)

Younger son of the Black Prince and grandson of Edward III, succeeded to the throne of England upon his grandfather's death on 21 June 1377. He was deposed by Parliament (q.v.) in 1399 in favour of Henry of Lancaster, son of John of Gaunt, the second monarch to be thus deprived of his crown since the Conquest. Richard's formal resignation was accepted by Parliament on 30 September, he himself dying shortly afterwards in mysterious circumstances.

RICHARD III (1452–1485)

Younger brother of Edward IV, assumed the Crown on 26 June 1483, a Parliament having been persuaded to declare the illegitimacy of Edward V and his younger brother, the sons of Edward IV. He was defeated at Bosworth by Henry Tudor on 22 August 1485, and was himself slain on the battlefield.

RIDING

Normally defined as an administrative division of a county, this term is sometimes used overseas, notably in Canada, to denote an electoral district or constituency (q.v.).

ROLLS OF PARLIAMENT

The most ancient parliamentary records in existence. They were commenced in 1278 and continued until 1503, and it is probable that the principal duty of the Clerk of the Parliaments (q.v.) during those years was to keep the records up to date. The Rolls consist mainly of petitions (q.v.), some of a private but most of them of a public character, and the answers to them. Reports of the actual proceedings of Parliament are included to a lesser extent, but many of the entries are obscure or incomplete and important events are all too often treated with an exasperating brevity. The opening proceedings, including the Chancellor's speech declaring the cause of summons and the appointment of receivers and triers of petitions, are usually dealt with in some detail. In spite of their shortcomings, however, the Rolls are of considerable value to the historian. They are written partly in Norman French, partly in Latin, and partly in medieval English. In the 18th century (1767–77) they were printed in six folio volumes under the title *Rotuli Parliamentorum*. An index, which provides an excellent guide to the information contained in these ancient chronicles, was published in 1832 by order of the House of Lords.

ROMAN CATHOLICS IN PARLIAMENT

Roman Catholics had been subject to various penal laws since 1559 and in 1678, following the revelation of the so-called Popish Plot, a Bill was passed which had the effect of excluding them from sitting in either House of Parliament. In 1680 a Bill to exclude the King's brother, the Duke of York (afterwards James II), from the succession on the ground of his Catholic faith was passed by the House of Commons but rejected by the House of Lords by 63 to 30, 14 bishops voting in the majority. James inherited the Crown, but his reign was short-lived, and after the Revolution of 1688 Catholics continued to be excluded from Parliament, not expressly as Roman Catholics but by reason of a passage in the oath of supremacy denying the spiritual and ecclesiastical jurisdiction of the Pope, and a declaration against transubstantiation administered to members before they were permitted to take their seats. The Act of Settlement (q.v.) of 1701 disqualified non-members of the Church of England from succeeding to the throne. Various disabilities of the Catholics were removed by Acts of 1778 and 1791, and in 1793 Irish Catholics were admitted to the franchise. However, it was not until the Irish leader Daniel O'Connell was elected for Clare in 1828 that the question of political emancipation came to a head. The prospect of a rebellion of the Irish Catholics and the security risks of tying up five-sixths of the infantry force of the United Kingdom in Ireland convinced the Government that they would have to yield at last. Peel decided to support the Prime Minister, the Duke of Wellington, and even to conduct through the Commons a measure which he had hitherto consistently opposed. The objections of George IV, a bitter anti-Catholic, were overcome, and the Emancipation Bill was introduced in the House of Commons by Peel on 5 March 1829. It passed that House by 320 votes to 142, and the Lords by 217 to 112, and received the Royal Assent on 13 April. The Act removed the most serious disabilities and amongst other things it admitted Catholics to the franchise and made it lawful for any Roman Catholic who was a peer or was returned as a Member of the House of Commons to sit and vote in either House respectively. The first Roman Catholic peers to take their seats were the Duke of Norfolk and Lords Dormer and Clifford on 28 April 1829. On 4 May the Earl of Surrey, eldest son of the Duke of Norfolk, took his seat in the Commons for the borough of Horsham, of which his father was the owner—the first Catholic member under the new Act. Daniel O'Connell had hoped to be the first, but as he had been elected in 1828 the Speaker ruled that the Emancipation Act was not retrospective and he would be obliged to take the old oaths of allegiance, abjuration, and supremacy. This of course he refused to do, and the House decreed his election to be null and void. However, he was immediately re-elected and finally took his seat on 4 February 1830.

An Act of 1926 removed most of the disabilities left by the 1829 Act. Those which remain are exclusion from the succession to the throne, exclusion from the offices of Regent, Lord Chancellor, and Keeper of the Great Seal, and exclusion from various ecclesiastical appointments. Roman Catholic priests, in common with the Anglican clergy, may not sit in the House of Commons. There are at present

(1970) 61 Catholic peers and 28 Catholic members of the House of Commons.

See also GEORGE IV AND PARLIAMENT.

'ROTTEN' BOROUGH

The term applied to those parliamentary constituencies, of which there were a large number before the passing of the Reform Bill of 1832, which were entirely at the disposal of patrons, the patron in many instances being the Crown. The term owes its origin to Chatham's description of the borough representation as 'the rotten part of the constitution'. Bribery and corruption at elections flourished openly and shamelessly throughout the 18th and the early part of the 19th centuries. Parliamentary seats were bought and sold without any attempt at concealment of the fact; in some cases they were publicly advertised for sale. In addition to wealthy patrons the purchasers included candidates themselves who wished to be independent and were possessed of the necessary means. The majority of the boroughs were controlled, however, and their representatives were merely the nominees of powerful interests who expected their orders to be obeyed.

Of the more notorious 'rotten' boroughs, Old Sarum, which could not provide a shelter for the Returning Officer and where 7 voters returned two members; Dunwich, which was half under water and whose 14 voters also returned two members; Gatton with its population of 135; and Bossinney, a Cornish fishing village which, after the disfranchisement of revenue officers in 1782, boasted one voter, may be cited as typical examples. The term 'pocket' borough is also used in reference to such constituencies, no doubt in recognition of the fact that the member was 'in the pocket' of the patron.

See also REPRESENTATION.

ROTULI PARLIAMENTORUM

See ROLLS OF PARLIAMENT.

ROYAL ASSENT

When a Bill has been finally agreed to by both Houses of Parliament it requires the Royal Assent before it becomes an Act of Parliament (q.v.). The Bill becomes an Act and has the force of law immediately the Royal Assent has been signified, unless a specific date has been provided in the Act itself for the commencement of its operation.

Under the Royal Assent Act, 1967, the Royal Assent to Bills may be signified by the Queen in person or by Lords Commissioners (q.v.), or it may be announced by the Lord Chancellor and the Speaker of the House of Commons in their respective Houses. The latter method will henceforth constitute the usual practice, although the historic ceremony described below will probably be retained at least on the occasion of the prorogation of a session.

The traditional method of signifiying the Royal Assent is an ancient and interesting ceremony, although the last occasion on which it was given by the Sovereign in person was on 12 August 1854. It is generally given by commission, three or more Lords Commissioners representing the Sovereign. Attired in robes and three-cornered hats and seated on a form between the Throne and the Woolsack in the House of Lords, they command the Gentleman Usher of the Black Rod (q.v.) to inform the Commons that their attendance is desired in the House of Peers to hear the commission read. When the message has been delivered, the Commons immediately suspend their business and headed by the Speaker they proceed to the Bar of the House of Lords. The commission is then read at length by the Reading Clerk (q.v.). The title of each Bill is read by the Clerk of the Crown and the Royal Assent is signified by the Clerk of the Parliaments in Norman French and is so entered in the Journal of the House of Lords. In the case of public and local Acts the Royal Assent is pronounced in the words, *La Reyne le veult*, and for personal Acts the formula is *Soit fait comme il est desiré*. Bills for granting aids and supplies to the Crown, that is, Bills involving finance, are carried by the Clerk of the House of Commons, handed to the Clerk of the Parliaments by the Speaker, and receive the Royal Assent before all other Bills, the formula being, *La Reyne remercie ses bons sujets, accepte leur benevolence, et ainsi le veult*. This variation in procedure is another symbol of the Commons' declared right in matters of finance. If the Royal Assent were to be denied, the words used would be, *La Reyne s'avisera*, but the last occasion on which this power was exercised was in 1707 by Queen Anne. To quote Erskine May, 'The necessity of refusing the Royal Assent is removed by the strict observance of the constitutional principle, that the Crown has no will but that of its Ministers, who only continue to serve in that capacity so long as they retain the confidence of Parliament.' When the Commons have returned to their own Chamber, the Speaker reports that the Royal Assent has been given to certain Acts and this is recorded in the Votes and Proceedings and the Journal of the House of Commons.

Bills awaiting the Royal Assent are kept in the custody of the Clerk of the Parliaments, except Bills for granting aids and supplies to the Crown, which are returned to the Commons after their passage through the Lords. When the necessity arises, the Lord Chancellor receives notice that a commission is required, and the Clerk of the Parliaments then prepares two sets of the titles of all the Bills, one set being for the Clerk of the Crown to insert in the commission and the other for the Sovereign's inspection before signing. Bills for granting aids and supplies to the Crown are placed first, followed by other Public Bills, and finally Private Bills.

Prior to the end of the 17th century the Royal Assent to Bills was normally signified by the Sovereign in person. The first occasion on which it was pronounced by a Royal Commission was in 1541 when in order to spare the feelings of Henry VIII the Royal Assent to the Bill of Attainder against Katherine Howard was signified on his behalf by a Commission of Peers. The Act which sanctioned this practice remained on the statute book until its repeal in 1967 although it was not until the accession of the Hanoverian monarchs that Royal Assents came to be signified by commission as a regular practice.

The passage of the Royal Assent Act was designed to end the inconvenience which so often resulted when the business of the House of Commons was interrupted by the arrival of Black Rod. In recent years members had frequently complained about these interruptions, and in December 1966 it was announced that legislation would be introduced to enable the procedure relating to the signification of the Royal Assent to be changed. The Royal Assent Act itself received the Royal Assent in the traditional manner on 10 May 1967. In future it is probable that Black Rod will make his historic journey between the Lords and the Commons only on the first and last days of a session.

Under certain circumstances a Bill can become an Act upon the Royal Assent being given even though it has not been consented to by the Houses of Lords. Under the Parliament Acts, 1911 and 1949 (q.v.), a Money Bill (q.v.) which, having been passed by the House of Commons and referred to the House of Lords at least one month before the end of the session, is not passed by the Lords without amendment within one month after it has been sent up, may be presented for the Royal Assent; and any other Public Bill may be similarly presented if it has been passed by the House of Commons in two successive sessions and, having been referred to the upper House at least one month before the end of the session, has been rejected by the Lords on both occasions, provided that one year has elapsed between the second reading in the first session and the passing of the Bill for the second time.

The ceremony of the Royal Assent to Bills, as performed in the Mother of Parliaments, is necessarily unique in view of the unique character of the upper House, but a similar procedure is followed in some other Commonwealth Parliaments. In Parliaments consisting of only one Chamber no ceremony is possible, but some of the Commonwealth's bicameral Parliaments observe the tradition. The Canadian ceremony seems to be that which most closely resembles the original.

In Commonwealth Parliaments overseas, except in those countries where the Queen of Britain is not recognized as Sovereign, the Royal Assent is signified by the Governor-General or the Governor, as the case may be, on behalf of the Crown. In certain circumstances a Bill is reserved for the signification of the Royal Assent by the Sovereign; for example, in New Zealand, the Shipping and Seamen Amendment Bill, 1946, was so reserved because it had extra-territorial effect.

ROYAL GALLERY, HOUSE OF LORDS

Built on the site of the ancient White Chamber, the Royal Gallery is 110 feet long, 45 feet wide, and 45 feet high. It is appropriately so called because the Sovereign passes through it on the way to the Houses of Lords Chamber at the opening of Parliament. On the walls are two paintings in the water-glass process by Daniel Maclise, R.A., which he finished in 1865. They represent the meeting of Wellington and Blücher after the Battle of Waterloo and the death of Nelson on board the *Victory*. There are also portraits of Queen Victoria and the Prince Consort, Edward VII and Queen Alexandra, George V and Queen Mary, and statues of earlier Kings and Queens.

The gallery was used for the trials of Earl Russell and Lord de Clifford by their peers in 1901 and 1935, and it has been the scene of dinners during Imperial Conferences. The gallery has also been used for the presentation of addresses of congratulation to the Sovereign after both World Wars, receptions to foreign potentates and ministers, and the business sessions of the 1961 Commonwealth Parliamentary Conference. History was made on 9 February 1967 when the Russian Premier, Mr. Kosygin, addressed both Houses of Parliament in the Royal Gallery.

The Royal Gallery is one part of the Palace of Westminster which has remained under the control of the Lord Great Chamberlain following the arrangements made in April 1965 whereby the Lord Chancellor and Speaker of the House of Commons assumed control of those parts of the building occupied by their respective Houses.

ROYAL INSTRUCTIONS

These are issued to Governors-General and Governors on their appointment, and, like the letters patent constituting their office, contain directions as to their duties and the exercise of the prerogative of pardon. Instructions for the Governor of a Colony also set out the composition of his Executive Council.

ROYAL PREROGATIVE

Blackstone defines the Royal Prerogative as 'that special pre-eminence, which the King hath, over and above all other persons, and out of the ordinary course of the common law, in right of his regal dignity'. He goes on to say that the term can only be applied to those rights and capacities which the King enjoys alone, in contradistinction to others, and not to those which he enjoys in common with any of his subjects. 'Out of the ordinary course of the common law' does not mean that the Sovereign is above the law, as the Courts have authority to determine whether or not an alleged prerogative exists. The expression Royal Prerogative is now used to refer to the Crown's discretionary authority, that is, to what the Queen or her servants can do without the authority of an Act of Parliament. The prerogative may be limited by statute.

Hood Phillips divides the prerogative into two main classes—personal and political. The personal ones include the supposition that the Sovereign can do no wrong (and is therefore immune from all actions, civil or criminal), never dies, is not bound by statutes unless named therein, and is never an infant. The political prerogatives are divided into domestic and foreign, the domestic including executive (appointment of ministers, creation of peers, and the summoning, proroguing, and dissolution of Parliament), judicial (includes the prerogative of pardon), legislative (providing courts and legislatures for British countries overseas), and ecclesiastical prerogatives. The foreign prerogatives include the right to make war and peace, to make treaties, and to receive and send ambassadors and other diplomatic representatives from and to foreign states. The political prerogative's practical use is that it provides a convenient mechanism for certain important governmental activities already referred to—the summoning of Parliament, ratification of treaties, and appointments to office. These are effected by Orders in Council, orders, commissions, or warrants under the Sign Manual, and proclamations, writs, or letters patent under the Great Seal. Ministers of the Crown are now responsible for the exercise of the Royal Prerogative, and this responsibility is secured by the requirement that a seal should be used of which the minister has the custody, or that the counter-signature of a minister should be affixed to the document concerned. There is hardly anything official which the Sovereign can do without the intervention of written forms, and little for which a minister is not responsible. As Sir Winston Churchill once remarked, 'The prerogatives of the Crown have become the privileges of the people.' However, most constitutional authorities agree that the prerogative, even to-day, embraces an indefinable reserve of power which can come into operation under abnormal circumstances. For example, should a Prime Minister resign without tendering advice as to the appointment of a successor, the prerogative regarding the appointment of a Prime Minister would assume a semblance of reality. This situation arose as recently as 1957 when Sir Anthony Eden resigned as Prime Minister.

The Royal Prerogative extends to other Commonwealth countries unless otherwise prescribed by United Kingdom or local enactment. It is delegated to colonial Governors in regard to public government and the right of pardon, and more extensively to Governors-General.

RULES OF DEBATE

See DEBATE, RULES OF.

RUMP PARLIAMENT

The term which is sometimes applied to the extension of the Long Parliament (q.v.) which continued to sit after the House of Commons had been depleted by Pride's Purge (q.v.) and which was expelled by Cromwell on 20 April 1653; and, more commonly, to that remnant of the Long Parliament which was recalled in 1659, consisting at first of 42 members, and gradually increasing until it numbered 91. Later in the same year the restored Rump was expelled by the army for the second time, only to be recalled again, even further depleted in numbers, at the end of 1659. Early in 1660, the excluded members were invited to return by General Monk, and finding themselves in the majority they paved the way for the restoration of the monarchy and passed a Bill finally dissolving the Rump Parliament (and with it the Long Parliament) on 16 March 1660.

See also COMMONWEALTH, 1658-1660; CROMWELL AND PARLIAMENT.

RUNNING PARLIAMENT

The name given to the Scottish Parliament of 1556 because it met at intervals. There were several other 'Running Parliaments' in Scottish history, but the term is more particularly applied to that of 1556.

RUSHWORTH, JOHN (1612?–1690)

Clerk Assistant to the House of Commons during the Long Parliament (q.v.). Rushworth was appointed on 25 April 1640 at the request of the Clerk of the House, Henry Elsynge (q.v.), and it is due to him that we have a verbatim record of the famous incident of 4 January 1642, when King Charles I came to the House of Commons to demand the surrender of the five members. Rushworth, who wrote a system of shorthand, recorded the King's speech and the memorable reply of Speaker Lenthall (q.v.), although he was not authorized to do so. On his appointment he was prohibited from taking notes except by order of the House, only the Clerk being entitled to record the proceedings. On this occasion, however, Elsynge decided to discontinue the record, and the entry in the House of Commons Journal stops abruptly, as follows: 'His Majesty came into the House; and took Mr. Speaker's Chair. "Gentlemen, I am sorry to have this Occasion to come unto you. . . ."' Fortunately for posterity, Rushworth decided to ignore the prohibition imposed upon himself. He was observed by the King whilst taking notes, and the same evening the King sent for him and demanded a copy of the report of his speech. Rushworth attempted to excuse himself by reminding the King that to disclose words spoken in Parliament constituted a breach of privilege; 'to which,' reports Rushworth, 'His Majesty smartly replied, "I do not ask you to tell me what was said by any Member of the House, but what I said myself." ' Rushworth then transcribed his notes, and the King had the speech printed.

This does not appear to be the only occasion upon which Rushworth violated the conditions of his appointment, for his great compilation, *Historical Collections*, upon which his fame rests, contains copious notes of the proceedings and some of the speeches made during the Long Parliament. Rushworth has, in fact, been called the 'Father of Parliamentary Reporting'.

In 1657 Rushworth entered Parliament as the Member for Berwick, and was re-elected for the same constituency to the Convention Parliament of 1660. He was singularly fortunate in that he was in favour and held a number of appointments during the period of the Commonwealth, yet managed to secure the favour of the King after the Restoration. He died, however, in poverty and debt in the King's Bench prison at Southwark, where he spent the last six years of his life.

S

SABAH LEGISLATURE

Until July 1946 North Borneo was a Protected State with a Legislative Council constituted under the Royal Charter granted to the British North Borneo Company in 1881. This Council enacted legislation but exercised no financial control, this being reserved to the Court of Directors of the company in London. When the territory (including the island of Labuan) became a Colony in 1946, an Advisory Council was established to assist the Governor which was superseded by the Executive and Legislative Councils in 1950.

In 1963, North Borneo became the independent State of Sabah when it joined the Malaysian Federation. The legislature now consists of the Head of State (the Yang di-Pertua Negara) appointed by the Federal Supreme Head and the Legislative Assembly. The latter has a Speaker appointed by the Head of State from outside the legislature, 32 elected and not more than 6 nominated members. The Cabinet consists of a Chief Minister and not more than 8 or less than 4 other members appointed by the Head of State on the advice of the Chief Minister.

ST. CHRISTOPHER

See ST. KITTS/NEVIS/ANGUILLA LEGISLATURE.

ST. EDWARD'S CHAMBER

See PAINTED CHAMBER, PALACE OF WESTMINSTER.

ST. KITTS/NEVIS/ANGUILLA LEGISLATURE

The islands of St. Kitts, Nevis and Anguilla formed a part of the Leeward Islands Federation until its abolition in 1956. From 1952 to 1960 the Legislative Council of this territory consisted of the Administrator as President, 2 *ex-officio*, 3 nominated and 8 elected members. In 1960 it was reconstructed to comprise 1 official member (the Law Officer), 2 nominated unofficial members and 10 elected members, presided over by an elected Speaker. In the same year the Leader of the Government became the Chief Minister and the Executive Council was reconstituted to comprise 5 unofficial members (including the Chief Minister and 3 other ministers) and the Law Officer. The posts of the Governors of the Leeward Islands and the Windward Islands were abolished and their powers transferred to the Administrators of the various islands comprising these groups.

Following the dissolution of the West Indies Federation, of which the territory formed a part, in 1962, attempts to reach agreement with regard to the formation of a new Federation of the smaller British islands in the Caribbean failed to meet with success. It therefore became necessary to consider alternative constitutional arrangements for those West Indian islands which lacked the economic viability necessary to support independence. In 1965 the British Government published a white paper (Cmnd. 2865) setting out a scheme under which these colonies could enter into an associate status with Great Britain if they wished, and St. Kitts/Nevis/Anguilla decided to take advantage of this opportunity.

At a conference held in May 1966 (Cmnd. 3031), a new Constitution was agreed upon for St. Kitts/Nevis/Anguilla. Under the West Indies Act, 1967, the territory sheds its colonial status and enters into an association with Great Britain. It now enjoys full internal self-government, Great Britain retaining responsibility for external affairs and defence, which will be discharged in close consultation with the territorial government. The British Parliament will not legislate for the territory except at its request or with its consent.

The Legislature consists of the Queen, represented by a Governor, and the House of Assembly. The House will consist of a Speaker, elected members and nominated members. The elected members will represent single-member constituencies of which there will be at least 7 in St. Kitts, at least 2 in Nevis and at least 1 in Anguilla. 2 nominated members will be appointed on the advice of the Premier and 1 on the advice of the Leader of the Opposition or by the Governor acting in his discretion if there is no Leader of the Opposition. The Attorney-General may also be nominated to the House of Assembly, and if he is a Civil Servant he will sit *ex-officio*. A nominated member may vote in the House except on a motion of no confidence in the Government or on Bills for the amendment of the Constitution. The Speaker may be elected from among the elected members of the House or from outside the House, and if he is not an elected member he becomes a member of the House by virtue of his office.

The Constitution includes a number of basic clauses relating to fundamental rights and freedoms, the structure, powers and composition of the Legislature, the franchise and elections, the judicial system, and other basic institutions of government. The Constitution may be amended by a two-thirds majority of the House of Assembly, and if the proposed amendment affects the basic clauses the Bill embodying them must also be approved by a two-thirds majority of the valid votes cast at a referendum. In addition, a Bill which seeks to amend the Constitution in such a way as to affect local government in Nevis and Anguilla must be approved by the electors of the island concerned voting in a referendum, a two-thirds majority being required.

The association between Great Britain and St. Kitts/Nevis/Anguilla may be terminated by either side, and if terminated by the latter for the purpose of entering into a federation, union or other association with an independent Commonwealth country in the Caribbean, the necessary constitutional Bill will not be subject to a referendum.

In 1967 an attempt was made by the island of Anguilla to sever its association with St. Kitts and Nevis and the British Government subsequently appointed a Commission to investigate the island's grievances and determine its future. Reporting in 1970 the Commission recommended that Anguilla should remain in its present constitutional association with the other two islands.

ST. LUCIA LEGISLATURE

The St. Lucia (Legislative Council) Order in Council, 1951, made provision for universal adult suffrage and reconstituted the Legislative Council to comprise the Administrator as President, 2 *ex-officio*, 3 nominated and 8 elected members. The Executive Council (which was presided over by the Governor of the Windward Islands if he was in St. Lucia) consisted of the Administrator, who normally presided, the 2 *ex-officio* members, 1 nominated member and 3 of the elected members, increased to 4 in 1956 when the Executive Council became the principal instrument of policy, 3 of the elected members being appointed ministers. Further constitutional changes were agreed in June 1959 when the Legislative Council was reconstructed to comprise 1 official member (the Law Officer), 2 nominated unofficial members and 10 elected members, presided over by an elected Speaker. From 1 January 1960 the Leader of the Government became the Chief Minister and the Executive Council was reconstituted to comprise 5 unofficial members (including the Chief Minister and 3 other ministers) and the Law Officer. The posts of the Governors of the Leeward Islands and the Windward Islands were abolished and their powers transferred to the Administrators of the various islands comprising these groups.

In 1962 the West Indies Federation, to which St. Lucia belonged, was dissolved, and attempts to negotiate an alternative federation of the smaller British islands in the Caribbean proved unsuccessful. It therefore became necessary to make other constitutional arrangements for the future of these Colonies. Accordingly, the British Government in 1965 published a white paper (Cmnd. 2865) embodying a scheme whereby they could if they wished enter into an associate status with Great Britain. St. Lucia decided to take advantage of this opportunity, and a new Constitution was agreed at a conference which took place in April and May 1966.

Under the West Indies Act, 1967, St. Lucia sheds its colonial status and enters into an association with Great Britain. It now enjoys full internal self-government, the British Government retaining its responsibilities in relation to external affairs and defence, which will nevertheless be discharged in close consultation with the St. Lucia Government. The British Parliament will not legislate for St. Lucia except at its request or with its consent.

The Legislature consists of the Queen, represented by a Governor, and a House of Assembly. Provision is also made for a Senate which may be established by the decision of a majority of the House of Assembly. The House of Assembly consists of 10 elected members, the Attorney-General and, pending the constitution of a Senate, 3 nominated members. Two of the nominated members are appointed on the advice of the Premier, and 1 by the Governor after consultation with the Premier and such other persons as he may in his discretion wish to consult. The nominated members may not vote on a motion of no confidence in the Government or on constitutional questions. The Speaker may be elected from among the membership or from outside the House. If a non-member is elected Speaker he will become a member by virtue of his office.

The Constitution includes a number of basic clauses relating to such matters as fundamental rights and freedoms, the Legislature, the franchise and elections, the judicial system and citizenship. A Bill to amend the Constitution requires a majority at its third reading of not less than two-thirds of the elected members of the House of Assembly, and if it seeks to alter a basic clause it must in addition be approved at a referendum by a two-thirds majority of the valid votes cast. No referendum is required in respect of a Bill which seeks to terminate the association between Great Britain and St. Lucia for the purpose of enabling St. Lucia to enter into a federation, union or other association with an independent Commonwealth country in the Caribbean.

ST. MARGARET'S CHURCH

Referring to St. Margaret's the Journal of the House of Commons has an entry in 1735 which reads, 'It is as it were a National Church for the use of the House of Commons', and it is in this church that the Commons assemble on occasions of national mourning or rejoicing. The connexion between the House and St. Margaret's began in 1621, when members attended for the first time in their official capacity because, the majority being staunch Puritans, they objected to the continued use of wafer-bread at Communion which the then Dean of Westminster favoured in the Abbey. Prior to that date, the Commons had either, like the House of Lords, attended Westminster Abbey, whose Chapter House had until the death of Henry VIII been the scene of its deliberations, or had accompanied its many legal members to the Temple. The building of a gallery in 1644 in the north aisle of the church provides the first instance of the definite allocation of seats to the House, a custom which has continued to the present time. In 1642 both Houses of Parliament, the Assembly of Divines, and the Scottish Commissioners gathered in St. Margaret's to take the 'Solemn League and Covenant', to swear they would 'extirpate popery, prelacy, superstition, schism and profaneness'. Although no remuneration in the way of pew rents has ever been paid by the House in spite of the large amount of accommodation afforded to it over three centuries, it contributed about £28,000 between 1799 and 1876 towards the upkeep and restoration of the church. Further links between St. Margaret's and the Commons include the ringing of the church bells when a new Speaker is admitted to office and the calling of the banns of members married in the Crypt Chapel (q.v.) and the registering of baptisms therein by the church of the House of Commons.

The House of Lords attended St. Margaret's with the Commons in 1918 for a special service on the anniversary of the declaration of the First World War, but after the Second World War they held their thanksgiving services in Westminster Abbey where they have attended divine service from the earliest times.

ST. STEPHEN'S HALL, PALACE OF WESTMINSTER

The present hall stands on the site of St. Stephen's Chapel which was built by King Stephen about 1141. The chapel was partially destroyed by fire in 1298 and rebuilt by Edward III in the Gothic style, being completed in 1364. It was suppressed with other free chapels in 1547 and handed over by Edward VI to the Commons for permanent use as their Chamber. The Commons occupied it until the Palace of Westminster was destroyed by fire in 1834.

St. Stephen's was the stage of many of the greatest dramas in parliamentary history. The struggle for constitutional government was fought there by Eliot, Pym, and Hampden, and it heard the historic orations of Pitt and Fox and the long debates on the Reform Bill.

St. Stephen's Hall is 95 feet long and 30 feet wide, and is adorned with panels illustrating historical scenes by famous artists and statues of Burke, Chatham, Clarendon, Falkland, Fox, Grattan, Hampden, Mansfield, the younger Pitt, Selden, and Walpole.

The stained-glass windows show coats of arms of many of the cities and boroughs represented in the House of Commons. 1960 saw the completion of two years' work of restoration on the Hall by artists, architects, stone-masons, and Ministry of Works officials.

ST. VINCENT LEGISLATURE

In 1763 King George III granted St. Vincent a Constitution by which the first organized government was set up with a Council and an Assembly of representatives of the people. In 1786 the Assembly consisted of 19 elected members, but with the abolition of slavery in the Colony in 1838 the planters' interest in self-government slowly waned, and frequently there were not sufficient members present in the Assembly to carry on the business of the House. In 1867 the House of Assembly and the Legislative Council, created in 1856, were replaced by a single Legislative Assembly with 12 members, 3 *ex-officio*, 3 nominated by the Crown, and 6 elected by the people. There then followed a long period of administration by the Colonial Office, which began with the meeting of a Legislative Council in 1878 with no elected members. During the First World War a movement was started for a return to representative government, and following the Report by a Commission sent to the Colony by the British Government, a new Constitution was granted in 1924. This provided for a Council of 3 official members, 1 nominated and 3 elected members with the Administrator as President. In 1936 the nominated members were increased to 3 and the elected members to 5, and in 1951 a new Constitution increased the elected members to 8 and provided for universal adult suffrage.

The Executive Council at that time consisted of 2 *ex-officio* members (in addition to the Governor of the Windward Islands who presided when he was in St. Vincent), 1 nominated member and 3 elected members of the Legislative Council. In March 1956 the Executive Council became the principal instrument of policy, and its elected membership was increased to 4, 3 being appointed ministers. Further constitutional changes were agreed in June 1959, and the Legislative Council was reconstituted to comprise 1 official member, 2 nominated unofficial members and 9 elected members, presided over by an elected Speaker. From 1 January 1960 the Leader of the Government became the Chief Minister and the Executive Council was reconstituted to consist of 5 unofficial members (including the Chief Minister and 3 other ministers) and 1 official member (the Law Officer). The posts of the Governors of the Leeward Islands and the Windward Islands were abolished and their powers transferred to the Administrators of the various islands comprising these groups.

In 1962, the West Indies Federation, to which St. Vincent belonged, was dissolved, and attempts to negotiate an alternative federation of the smaller West Indian Colonies proved unsuccessful. It therefore became necessary to make other constitutional arrangements for the future of these islands, none of which enjoyed the advantage of economic viability. In 1965 the British Government published a white paper (Cmnd. 2865) embodying a scheme whereby they could if they wished enter into an associate status with Great Britain, at the same time enjoying internal self-government, and a new constitution for St. Vincent was agreed to at a Conference which took place in London in April and May 1966.

Although St. Vincent became eligible for associate statehood under the West Indies Act, 1967, it was not until 27 October 1969 that the island finally shed its colonial status and entered into an association with Great Britain. The island is internally self-governing, Great Britain retaining responsibility for external affairs and defence, but acting in these areas only in close consultation with the Government of St. Vincent. The British Parliament does not legislate for St. Vincent except at its request or with its consent.

The Legislature consists of the Queen, represented by a Governor, and a House of Assembly. The House of Assembly consists of a Speaker, 9 elected members (to be increased to 13 with effect from the first General Election following statehood) and, until the Legislature provides otherwise, 3 nominated members, 2 of whom are appointed on the advice of the Premier and one on the advice of the Leader of the Opposition. The Attorney-General, if not otherwise a member of the House, sits as an *ex-officio* member. The Speaker may be elected from among the members or from suitably qualified persons outside the House.

The Constitution includes a number of basic clauses relating to such matters as fundamental rights and freedoms, the office of Governor, the Legislature, the franchise and elections, the judicial system, and other basic institutions of government. A Bill to amend the Constitution requires the approval of a two-thirds majority of the elected members of the House of Assembly at both the final vote and the vote before the final vote. If the Bill seeks to amend a basic clause it must in addition be submitted to the electorate by way of a referendum and approved by not less than two-thirds of the valid votes cast. A Bill seeking to terminate the association between Great Britain and St. Vincent for the purpose of enabling the island to enter into a federation, union or other association with an independent Commonwealth country in the Caribbean will not be subject to a referendum.

In 1948 the then Administrator, Sir Ronald Garvey, was instrumental in obtaining a Mace for the Legislative Council, and it was first used in December of that year.

SALARIES OF MEMBERS

See APPENDIX 2; PAYMENT OF MEMBERS.

SARAWAK LEGISLATURE

On 1 April 1957 a new Constitution came into force for Sarawak, which provided for a legislature with an elected unofficial majority and an executive in which half the members were elected. The Council Negri, which has financial as well as legislative jurisdiction, consisted of 45 members, of whom 24 were elected unofficials, 14 *ex-officio*, 4 nominated by the Governor, and 3 standing members, who as members of the Council prior to the cession of Sarawak to Great Britain in 1946 were granted life membership as long as they remained members of the Sarawak Civil Service. The Supreme (or Executive) Council consisted of 3 *ex-officio* members, 2 nominated by the Governor from the Council Negri, and 5 elected by the unofficial members of the Council Negri from among the elected, nominated, or standing members of that Council. In 1962 a Speaker was appointed by the Governor to the Council Negri, the 14 *ex-officio* members reduced to 3, the 24 elected members retained, and the 4 nominated members increased to not less than 4 or more than 15. In 1963, the elected members were increased to 36 and the nominated members reduced to not more than 3.

The ministerial system was introduced in 1963 with the appointment of a Chief Minister who now presides over the Supreme Council. In the same year Sarawak became a member of the Federation of Malaysia, retaining a considerable measure of local autonomy. The Legislature consists of the Governor and the Council Negri, which retains its former composition. The Supreme Council consists of the Chief Minister, Deputy Chief Minister, 6 other elected ministers, and the 3 *ex-officio* members of the Council Negri (State Secretary, State Attorney-General and State Financial Secretary).

Elections in Sarawak are indirect, members of the Council being chosen by electoral colleges formed from the district councils and the divisional advisory councils.

SASKATCHEWAN LEGISLATIVE ASSEMBLY

The Canadian Province of Saskatchewan was created, together with the neighbouring Province of Alberta, in 1905. The Government consists of the Lieutenant-Governor (appointed by the Federal Government), the Executive Council (presided over by the Premier of the Province) and a Legislative Assembly of 60 members. The statutory life of a legislature is five years. Women were enfranchised in 1916 and the voting age was recently reduced from twenty-one to eighteen.

The procedure of the Legislative Assembly is based on British parliamentary practice and was recently subjected to a far-reaching review by a Special Committee of the House which reported in December 1969. Among the recommendations made by this Committee the following are of particular interest:

(1) It is proposed that the procedure for initiating emergency debates should no longer hinge upon an adjournment motion. A person desiring to raise a matter of urgent public importance would instead ask leave to move 'that this Assembly do grant "Priority of Debate" (stating the subject) as a matter of urgency'. Two hours' notice of such a motion would be required but the Speaker would have the right to waive notice.

(2) The Committee of Supply and the Committee of Ways and Means should be combined and re-designated 'The Committee of Finance'. The Committee contended that the terms 'Supply' and' Ways and Means' had become archaic and that a more modern terminology was desirable. The Budget would be introduced in the Committee of Finance and the Budget debate, which would not exceed five sitting days, would take place on the motion 'That this Assembly do now resolve itself into a Committee of Finance'.

(3) The second and third readings of the Appropriation Bill should be combined in a single motion and the debate thereon should not exceed two days.

(4) The duration of the debate on the Speech from the Throne should be reduced from seven days to six.

(5) The motion requesting leave to introduce a Bill prior to first reading should be dispensed with.

(6) A Select Standing Committee to be known as the 'Non-Controversial Bills' Committee should be established with a view to expediting the passage of Bills which provoke no opposition. An interesting feature of this proposed committee is that it would have a majority of Opposition members. Bills would be referred to it only with the unanimous consent of the House.

(7) A Standing Committee of the Legislature on Members' Services should be established.

(8) The Lieutenant-Governor's recommendation with respect to Money Bills should be noted on the Order Paper and it should not be necessary for a Minister to deliver it orally in the House.

In view of the difficulties experienced in the House of Commons with regard to ministerial responsibility for the nationalized industries, it is interesting to record that the Saskatchewan Legislative Assembly has devised a unique procedure to ensure legislative scrutiny of the operations of Crown corporations, such as those charged with the administration of power, transport, telephones, etc. The managing board of each corporation is headed by a minister designated as the 'responsible' minister, and scrutiny of the annual reports and financial statements of the corporations is effected through a Select Standing Committee, whose functions are similar to those of the British Public Accounts Committee. Its meetings are attended by the 'responsible' minister and the general manager and accounting officer of the corporation under examination, and answers to questions put by members may only be refused on grounds of 'public interest'.

The Saskatchewan legislature was the first in the world to produce its Hansard from dictaphone recordings. Arrangements for recordings were made before the last war, but had to be abandoned until an experimental sixteen-microphone installation was tried out in 1947. The following year the installation became permanent with thirty microphones, one for each two members, in the Chamber and an additional system in the main Committee Room. Typescript copies of each day's proceedings are available on the morning of the next day.

The Legislative Assembly of Saskatchewan introduced the sound broadcasting of its proceedings in 1946, the first Canadian legislature to do so. Coverage is mainly confined to the debate on the Speech from the Throne and the Budget debate, and the broadcasts take place on about twenty days of the session from 2.45 p.m. to 4 p.m. The broadcasts are repeated later in the evening from other stations in the Province. The Select Standing Committee on Radio Broadcasting of Selected Proceedings allocates the broadcasting time between the parties during the session and the Whips arrange for the distribution of the time among individual members.

The Legislative Building, opened in 1912, is cruciform in shape and 542 feet long by 275 feet at its greatest width, with a central dome 188 feet high. It has 265 rooms and grounds of 167 acres, reputedly the largest of any government in the world. The Library, of some fifty thousand volumes, contains the 'Confederation Table' at which the 'Fathers of Canadian Federation' sat in 1867. Saskatchewan returns 13 members to the Canadian House of Commons and 6 senators to the Senate.

SCIENCE, MINISTER FOR

See EDUCATION AND SCIENCE, SECRETARY OF STATE FOR; LORD PRESIDENT OF THE COUNCIL.

SCOBELL, HENRY (d. 1660)

Appointed Clerk of the House of Commons in 1648 on the resignation of Elsynge (q.v.), Scobell is regarded as the authority on parliamentary procedure during the Commonwealth. His *Memorials of Method and Manner of Proceedings of Parliament in passing Bills* is an important treatise on 17th-century practice. During the year of his appointment an Act was passed conferring the appointment on him for life. In 1658 he also claimed to be Clerk of the other House which Cromwell substituted for the Lords. In 1659 he fell from favour and was summoned to the Bar of the House of Commons to account for an entry he had made in the Journal for 20 April 1653. This was the day on which Cromwell had dismissed the Long Parliament, and Scobell had written, 'This Day his Excellency the Lord General dissolved this Parliament.' The entry was declared a forgery, having been made without the consent of the House, and was ordered to be expunged from the Journal. The House also ordered that a Bill be brought in to repeal the Act under which Scobell had been appointed Clerk for life.

Scobell's *Memorials* were first published in 1656, and reissued in 1658, 1670, and 1692. His other works include *Remembrances of some Methods, Orders and Proceedings of House of Lords*, 1657, and *Power of Lords and Commons in Parliament in Points of Judicature*, 1680.

SCOTLAND, SECRETARY OF STATE FOR

Before 1885 Scottish affairs were in the province of the Home Secretary (q.v.) and various other departments, but in that year a Secretary for Scotland with a Scottish office was created by statute. Under the Secretaries of State Act of 1926 he became a Secretary of State, and the Conservative Government in 1951 appointed a Minister of State, Scottish Office, to act as deputy to the Secretary of State, with his headquarters normally in Scotland. The Secretary of State is the Keeper of the Great Seal of Scotland, which the Act of Union requires to be used for Scottish matters. He exercises in Scotland most of the powers of a Secretary of State, and is one of the Commissioners of Crown Lands (q.v.). His administrative departments are the Department of Agriculture for Scotland, the Scottish Education Department, the Department of Health for Scotland, and the Scottish Home Department. The salary of the Secretary of State for Scotland is £8,500, that of the Minister of State £7,625, and the three Under-Secretaries of State each receive £3,750. They are all entitled to a further £1,250 if they sit in the House of Commons.

In this century the Secretary of State for Scotland has always been a member of the Cabinet (q.v.) except when a War Cabinet has been in existence.

A chronological list of Scottish Secretaries appears as Appendix 28.

SCOTTISH BILLS

Under a House of Commons Standing Order originally introduced in 1948 Bills dealing with Scotland exclusively are submitted to the Scottish Grand Committee before second reading for consideration of the principles of these Bills. The committee cannot reject a Bill, but reports its deliberations to the House. After the second reading, unless objection is taken, the Bill is returned to the Scottish Standing Committee for its committee stage on the motion of a minister, and is deemed to have received its second reading. A debate on second reading must take place in the House if six or more members give notice of an amendment.

SCOTTISH GRAND COMMITTEE AND SCOTTISH STANDING COMMITTEES

Standing Order No. 61 makes provision for two Scottish Standing Committees which differ from other Standing Committees in certain important respects. When considering certain business a Scottish Standing Committee is known as the Scottish Grand Committee and consists of all the members who sit for Scottish constituencies together with from 10 to 15 other members appointed by the Committee of Selection (q.v.) with a view to their qualifications and the preservation of relative party strengths. It considers Bills and other business relating exclusively to Scotland, the certification of such Bills being the responsibility of the Speaker.

The Scottish Grand Committee may consider Scottish Bills in relation to their principle, when debate follows the lines of a second reading debate in the House. When the order for the second reading of a Scottish Bill is read in the House it is open to a Minister of the Crown to move that it be referred to the Scottish Grand Committee, the motion being decided without amendment or debate. If not less than ten members signify their objection to the motion by rising in their places the Speaker must declare that the Noes have it.

The Scottish Grand Committee may also consider the Scottish Estimates on not more than six days in any session. The selection of Estimates for discussion by the Committee is arranged by the Government at the request of the Opposition, and it is open to a Minister of the Crown to move that such Estimates be referred to the Scottish Grand Committee, the motion being decided without amendment or debate. The Committee, having considered such Estimates, makes a report to the House. Provision is also made for the reference of other matters relating exclusively to Scotland to the Scottish Grand Committee and, provided no objection is registered by not less than ten members, such matters may be considered by the Committee on not more than two days in a session.

A Bill certified by the Speaker as relating exclusively to Scotland is automatically referred to one of two Scottish Standing Committees for its committee stage. The first consists of 30 members representing Scottish constituencies and not more than 20 additional members. The second Committee consists of not less than 16 or more than 50 members of whom not less than 16 must represent Scottish constituencies. The members of both Scottish Standing Committees are nominated by the Committee of Selection in respect of each Bill. Their membership is, therefore, subject to change, but in nominating members, regard is had to their individual qualifications and the composition of the House. A second Scottish Standing Committee was first appointed in the 1962–3 session specifically to consider Private Members' Bills relating exclusively to Scotland.

Y*   [671]

When a Scottish Bill has been considered in relation to its principle and so reported to the House by the Scottish Grand Committee, it is open to a minister, when the order for second reading is subsequently read in the House, to move that it be committed to a Scottish Standing Committee, provided no notice of an amendment to the second reading has been given by 6 or more members. The report stage of a Scottish Bill may also be referred to the Scottish Grand Committee or a Standing Committee on the motion of a Minister of the Crown, provided no objection is registered by 20 or more members.

The power to consider Scottish Bills in relation to their principle was first given to the Scottish Standing Committee in 1948, and such a Committee in its plenary form has been known as the Scottish Grand Committee since December 1957. The functions of the Scottish Grand Committee and the two Scottish Standing Committees are set out in detail in Standing Orders 61–4.

SCOTTISH NATIONAL PARTY

The Scottish National Party came into being in 1934 as a result of the merger of two other nationalist movements, the National Party of Scotland and the Scottish Party. The party made little progress at the polls until April 1945 when it recorded its first electoral success at a by-election in Motherwell. In taking his seat as his party's first representative in the House of Commons, Mr. R. D. McIntyre caused a minor storm by declining to accept sponsors. The Speaker pointed out that it was the uniform practice of the House that a member coming into the House for the first time following a by-election should be introduced by two other members. A motion to dispense with the practice to enable Mr. McIntyre to take his seat was rejected following a debate, but on the following day he allowed himself to be introduced by two independent members. Mr. McIntyre lost his seat at the General Election later in the same year when it was won by the Labour Party.

Although it continued to be active outside Parliament, the Scottish National Party made very little further impact upon the voters until 1967. In March of that year the party polled very well at a by-election in the Glasgow constituency of Pollok and in the following November went on to win Hamilton from the Labour Party at another by-election, Mrs. Winifred Ewing becoming the second member of the party to take her seat in the House of Commons. In 1968 the party polled extremely well in the Scottish municipal elections, but thereafter it began to show a decline. At the General Election of 1970 Mrs. Ewing lost Hamilton and the Labour Party regained the seat. However, the Scottish National Party registered an unexpected gain in the Western Isles, where Mr. D. J. Stewart defeated Mr. Malcolm Macmillan, who had held the seat for the Labour Party since 1935.

SCOTTISH PARLIAMENT

The first mention in Scottish history of a King acting with the concurrence of a National Council is in 1120, but such Councils were not called a 'Parliament' until 1215 when King Alexander II 'tenuit Parliamentum' in Edinburgh. The real founder of the Scottish Parliament was King Robert the Bruce, who at the Parliament of Cambuskenneth in 1326 summoned the burgesses as well as 'other free tenants of the Kingdom'. It is in this Parliament that we meet with the first development in Scotland of what are now considered the fundamental principles of a representative constitution—a claim of right, redress of grievances, a grant of supplies, and a strict limitation of the grant to its proper purposes. Although the burgesses were summoned to this Parliament they did not become an essential part of all parliaments until the middle of the 15th century. They then formed one of the three 'Estates' of the realm. The other two were the Lords Spiritual and the barons—the word 'Estates' was frequently used for Parliament. By the beginning of the 15th century the smaller barons had almost ceased to attend Parliament, and although James I passed an Act in 1427 freeing them from attendance and replacing them with representatives from each shire it remained inoperative until after the Reformation. James I also attempted to create the office of Speaker at the same time, but this attempt was equally unsuccessful, and the Lord Chancellor continued to preside over the single-chamber legislature. The officers of state had seats in the Scottish Parliament by virtue of their offices, and the judges of the Court of Session sat round a table in the centre of the hall between the barons and the commons. If the King was not present the Royal Assent to Bills or 'articles' was given by touching them with the royal sceptre. The Parliament of Scotland was apt to be the tool either of a strong King or of the greater barons during the reign of a weak King, and its ineffectiveness before the Reformation was not helped by the absence of the shire representatives, whose combination with burgess members was the strength of the English House of Commons. Another weakening factor was the delegation of the work of Parliament to a committee. In 1367 certain persons were elected by the three Estates to hold the Parliament, and the rest were allowed to go home 'because of the harvest'. The Committee of the Lords of the Articles, as it was called, had the effect of reducing the burgess element in Parliament, and in the later centuries the Crown employed it to obtain complete control. During the 16th century it was the custom for the Estates to meet in full only on the first and last day of its session—on the first to appoint the Lords of the Articles and on the last to endorse what they had done. The 1427 Act was ratified in 1585 when 'two wise men' were to be elected from each shire, but the restriction of the electors to those with forty-shilling freeholds considerably limited the right of voting, and up to the Reform Act of 1832 the number of electors for Scottish counties varied from ten to about two hundred. The Parliament's unrepresentative character prevented its development after the Restoration. Also in those years in the General Assembly of the Church the country possessed a more really representative body than the Parliament ever was, so that when Parliament was not taking its orders from the King it was following the lead of the Assembly. The Parliament which met in 1560 and abolished the Roman Catholic faith was one of the few which the burgesses and the smaller barons attended freely and where they voted in accordance with their own feelings. James VI, after his accession to the Throne of England, acquired complete control over the appointment of the Lords of the Articles, and thus over Parliament, and his methods were followed by Charles I, who of all the Stuarts was the least considerate of Scotland. The Parliament of 1639 left the old Tolbooth and met in their new Parliament House, which became one of the most admired buildings in Edinburgh. In that year the Earl of Argyle carried a vote at a sitting of the Lords of the Articles that henceforth each Estate should choose its own representatives in that body. During the Commonwealth there was only one Imperial Parliament, in which Scotland was represented by twenty members from the counties and ten from the boroughs. The Scottish Parliament met again after the Restoration in 1661 and passed Acts which abolished all the laws made after the year 1633 and re-established the ancient government of the church by archbishops and bishops, who were thus restored to Parliament, from which they had been banished by the Glasgow Assembly of 1638. Between 1660 and 1689 the Scottish Parliament was once more only the instrument for official sanction, but in the latter year a Convention of the Estates was held which deposed James VII, and affirmed that William and Mary were now King and Queen of Scotland and that the Scottish Church was Presbyterian. When the acceptance of William and Mary converted the Convention into a Parliament it achieved a great triumph by abolishing the Lords of the Articles, and henceforward, until the Treaty of Union with England took effect, there was parliamentary independence in Scotland as far as purely internal affairs were concerned. The last Scottish Parliament, the memorable Union Parliament, met in 1703 and it was distinguished by the first appearance in Scotland of parliamentary parties. The Act ratifying and approving the Treaty of Union with England was carried in this Parliament by 110 to 69 votes on 16 January 1707, but it continued to sit until the treaty was accepted by England, and decided that the representative peers (q.v.) as well as the commoners for Scotland should be chosen to sit in the Parliament of Great Britain from their own members. Queen Anne gave the Royal Assent to the Act of Union passed by the English Parliament in person in the House of Lords on 6 March 1707, and from 1 May the two Kingdoms were united.

(Further reading: Rait, *The Scottish Parliament before the Union*, 1901.)

PARLIAMENTS AND CONVENTIONS OF THE ESTATES OF SCOTLAND

27-37	David II	1357-67	19-20	Charles I	1643-4
29-30	James I	1434-5	20-22	,, ,,	1644-7
3-22	James II	1439-58	23	Charles I ⎫	1648-51
3-26	James III	1462-87	3	Charles II ⎭	
1-22	James IV	1488-1509	12-15	,, ,,	1661-3
1-28	James V	1513-40	17	,, ,,	1665
1-26	Mary	1542-67	18	,, ,,	1667
1-43	James VI	1567-1609	21-26	,, ,,	1669-74
46	,, ,,	1612	30	,, ,,	1678
50	,, ,,	1617	33	,, ,,	1681
50	,, ,,	1617	1 & 2	James VII	1685-6
54	,, ,,	1621	1	William & Mary	1689
54 & 55	,, ,,	1621	1-5	William & Mary ⎫	
1	Charles I	1625	7-13	William ⎬	1689-1702
4-9	,, ,,	1628-33	1	Anne ⎭	
15-17	,, ,,	1639-41	2-6	,,	1703-7

SCOTT, SIR GILES GILBERT (1880–1960)

The architect who designed the present House of Commons Chamber which was opened in October 1950.

SECOND BALLOT

See ALTERNATIVE VOTE.

SECOND CHAMBERS

See BICAMERAL LEGISLATURE.

SECOND CLERK ASSISTANT

See CLERKS ASSISTANT.

SECOND READING COMMITTEE

The second reading of a Bill is the stage at which it is considered in principle, and only the House can decide the question as to whether or not a Bill should be given a second reading.

The debate on second reading normally takes place on the Floor of the House, but there are precedents whereby a Bill may be considered in principle by a Standing Committee (q.v.), the right to decide the question for second reading being nevertheless reserved to the House. The Scottish Grand Committee (q.v.) has long been empowered to consider in principle all Bills relating to Scotland, provided no objection is registered by 10 or more members. On 27 October 1965 this practice was extended in the House of Commons by an order of the House having effect in the first instance for the 1965–6 session. It was continued in the new Parliament which began in 1966. Provision was made for the reference of Government Bills to a Second Reading Committee on the motion of a Minister of the Crown of which ten days' notice is required. The question must be decided without amendment or debate and is negatived if not less than 20 members object. A Second Reading Committee is a Standing Committee consisting of not less than 16 or more than 80 members nominated by the Committee of Selection (q.v.) in respect of each Bill, regard being had to their qualifications and the composition of the House.

The function of a Second Reading Committee is to consider a Bill in principle and to recommend to the House whether or not the Bill should be proceeded with, the question for the second reading of such a Bill being decided in the House without amendment or debate. The purpose of the procedure is to expedite the passage of non-controversial legislation and to provide an opportunity for the passage of desirable legislation which, in the normal course of events, would be crowded out of the parliamentary timetable.

SECRETARIES OF STATE

Her Majesty's Principal Secretaries of State are heads of important government departments for whose administration they are responsible to Parliament, and constitutionally they also function as channels of communication between the Crown and its subjects. They are appointed by the delivery to them of three seals engraved with the royal arms, and the recall of these seals terminates the office. Constitutionally any one of them can exercise the functions of any of the others.

We first hear of the King's Secretary in the reign of Henry III, and until after the time of Henry VIII he belonged to the Royal Household. Even in the 15th century the King's business began to require more than one Secretary and in 1433 a second Secretary had become necessary for the transaction of royal affairs in France. The reign of Henry VIII marks an important advance in the position of the Principal Secretary. His use of the King's Signet is confirmed by statute, he ranks next to the greater household officers, and he has a seat in Parliament and the Council. If he is a baron, he sits above all other barons, and if a bishop above all other bishops. In 1539 the two Principal Secretaries were both members of the Commons, but one was always to sit in the upper House and one in the lower, interchanging weeks, unless the King was present in the House of Lords, in which case both were to be there. The growing importance of the office is indicated not only by the precedence given to the holders but by the quality of the men who held it. Thomas Cromwell was for a short time Secretary to Henry VIII, and Sir William Cecil was Secretary to Elizabeth I from her accession until he was made Lord Treasurer in 1571. During the greater part of this reign there was only one Secretary, who by now was no longer attached to the Household, but at the close of it Sir Robert Cecil shared the duties with another, he being called 'Our Principal Secretary of Estate', and the other 'one of Our Secretaries of Estate' or 'Second Secretary'. The Secretary was expected to possess a general knowledge of relations with other countries, including the affairs of Wales and Ireland, and to take charge of the royal correspondence with foreign princes. After the Restoration he also had to prepare business for the inner Council, of which by then he was a member, and attend meetings of the larger body, the Privy Council (q.v.). From the beginning of the 17th century until 1794 there were two Secretaries of State, except in 1616, from 1707 to 1746, when there was usually a third Secretary for Scottish business, and from 1768 to 1782, when there was a third Secretary for colonial business. From the Revolution until 1782, except during the temporary existence of the Scottish and Colonial Secretaries, one Secretary was in charge of the Northern Department and the other of the Southern Department. The Northern Department included the northern powers of Europe within its jurisdiction, while the Southern as well as our dealings with the Latin countries, Switzerland, and Turkey, embraced Irish and colonial business and the work of the Home office. These two Secretaries down to 1782 were described as 'His Majesty's Principal Secretaries of State for Foreign Affairs', but after 1782 the Southern Department became the Home Office, retaining Irish and Colonial business, the Northern Department became the Foreign Office, and the Colonial Secretaryship, which had been in existence for fourteen years, was abolished.

About this time it was realized that the numerous authorities responsible for military affairs needed a guiding hand in time of war, and in 1794 a third Secretary of State was appointed, for War. In 1801 the new Secretary took over the Colonial Office as well, and during the peaceful times following the fall of Napoleon his War duties became rather neglected—so much so that when the Crimean War came along the chaotic state of this department necessitated the appointment of a Principal Secretary of State for War, and the Secretary of State for War and the Colonies was relieved of his responsibility for the army. Other Secretaries of State appointed by Queen Victoria included one for India, who held and discharged the powers and duties vested in the East India Company when the Crown took over its territories in 1858. This office lapsed when India became independent in 1947.

The development of air warfare led to the appointment of a

Secretary of State for Air in 1917, and in 1925 the Colonial Secretary assumed the new Secretaryship of State for Dominion Affairs. A separate Secretary of State for Dominion Affairs was appointed in 1930 and, in 1947, this minister's title was altered to Secretary of State for Commonwealth Relations. The offices of Secretary of State for Commonwealth Relations and for the Colonies were again combined under one minister in July 1962, only to be separated again when Mr. Harold Wilson formed his Government in October 1964. However, the Colonial Secretary's office was finally abolished in 1966 and his functions were absorbed by the newly styled Secretary of State for Commonwealth Affairs. In 1926 the Secretary for Scotland was raised to the status of a Secretary of State. In 1951 Lord Leathers was appointed Secretary of State for the Co-ordination of Transport, Fuel and Power, but the creation of 'overlords', as such appointments were popularly called, aroused much criticism, and the office was not continued after the resignation of Lord Leathers in September 1953.

In July 1962, Mr. R. A. Butler was appointed First Secretary of State with the status of Deputy Prime Minister in Mr. Harold Macmillan's Government. This appointment lapsed when Sir Alec Douglas-Home became Prime Minister in October 1963, but was reinstated when Mr. Harold Wilson formed his Government exactly one year later. In October 1964, Mr. George Brown became the second minister to hold this office, and was simultaneously appointed Secretary of State for Economic Affairs. In 1963 Mr. Edward Heath was appointed Secretary of State for Industry, Trade and Regional Development, while concurrently holding office as President of the Board of Trade. In 1964 the office of Secretary of State for Defence was created with the passing of the Defence (Transfer of Functions) Act. The same Act also abolished the offices of Secretary of State for War and Secretary of State for Air (not to mention that of First Lord of the Admiralty which was one of the most historic of ministerial offices).

In 1964 Mr. Quintin Hogg was designated Secretary of State for Education and Science while holding office as Lord President of the Council. It is noteworthy that Sir Edward Boyle was simultaneously appointed Minister of State for Education and Science while retaining cabinet rank. The Labour Government formed in October of the same year continued the appointment of Secretary of State for Education and Science, and also included for the first time a Secretary of State for Wales. Among the first legislation introduced by this Government was a Machinery of Government Bill which was passed into law as the Ministers of the Crown Act, 1964. This Act provides, *inter alia*, for the appointment of up to 9 Secretaries of State, no portfolios being specified.

In 1968 the Foreign Office and the Commonwealth Office were

merged under a single minister who is now designated Secretary of State for Foreign and Commonwealth Affairs. The same year saw the appointment of a Secretary of State for Employment and Productivity and a Secretary of State for Social Services. In 1969 a Secretary of State for Local Government and Regional Planning was appointed. Two new Secretaryships of State were created in 1970 in consequence of a major reorganization of the machinery of central government. The Ministry of Technology and the Board of Trade were merged to form a department headed by a minister styled the Secretary of State for Trade and Industry and President of the Board of Trade. A Secretary of State for the Environment was also appointed to head a department formed from the unification of the Ministry of Housing and Local Government, the Ministry of Transport and the Ministry of Public Building and Works. A wide measure of latitude will no doubt continue to exist with regard to the portfolios allocated to those ministers who are designated Secretaries of State, the use which is made of this particular ministerial office lying mainly within the discretion of the Prime Minister of the day.

The salary of a Secretary of State is £8,500 a year, with an additional £1,250 if he is a Member of the House of Commons. A Secretary of State normally has at least one Minister of State (q.v.) and one or more Parliamentary Under-Secretaries of State to assist him. The salary of a Minister of State is £7,625 or £5,625 depending on seniority, and that of a Parliamentary Under-Secretary of State £3,750, plus the additional allowance of £1,250 if they are Members of the House of Commons.

The only other country of the Commonwealth where the office of Secretary of State exists is Canada where the Cabinet includes a Secretary of State for External Affairs and a minister styled simply Secretary of State whose functions relate largely to cultural affairs.

SECRET BALLOT

First introduced in parliamentary elections by South Australia in 1856.

See BALLOT ACT, 1872; ELECTIONS.

SECRET SESSION

Should either House of Parliament desire to conduct certain proceedings in private it can adopt a resolution to go into secret session. So far secret sessions have been held only in war-time, and in these days it is inconceivable that Parliament would ever debate in secret except in the interests of national security. A motion to go into secret session requires the support of a majority of the House, and it is first necessary to 'take notice that strangers are present'. The mover (probably the Leader of the House if the motion is on behalf of the

Government) rises and says, 'Mr. Speaker, I spy strangers.' The Speaker immediately puts the question, 'that strangers do withdraw', no debate being allowed. If the motion is agreed to the Public and Press Galleries are immediately cleared. The Hansard reporters also depart as debates in secret session are not recorded. After all strangers have withdrawn the motion is made that the remainder of the day's sitting or certain proceedings should be held in secret. If the House is opposed to a secret session the procedure would not reach this stage as the majority would vote against the motion to exclude strangers. The custom of 'spying strangers' is a survival from the days when Parliament imposed a ban on the reporting of its proceedings and the presence of outsiders. At one time it was sufficient for a single member to 'spy strangers' in order to oblige the Speaker to order the clearing of the galleries (*see also* STRANGERS).

During a secret session barriers are erected at the end of corridors leading to the Members' Lobby and access is denied by the police to all save members and certain officers of the House, namely the Clerks-at-the-Table and (in the House of Commons) the Serjeant-at-Arms and the Deputy and Assistant Serjeants-at-Arms and (in the House of Lords) the Gentleman Usher of the Black Rod and Yeoman Usher of the Black Rod. Members of the House of Lords are permitted to attend secret sessions in the House of Commons, and *vice versa*. It constitutes a contempt to reveal any proceedings which have taken place during a secret session while they are still held to be secret.

The considerations leading to a subject being debated in secret session were described by the Lord Privy Seal (Sir Stafford Cripps) in the House of Commons on 9 July 1942. On 19 December 1945 it was resolved that no proceedings held in secret session during the previous Parliament should be any longer secret.

SELECT COMMITTEE ON HOUSE OF COMMONS (SERVICES)

See HOUSE OF COMMONS (SERVICES) COMMITTEE.

SELECT COMMITTEE ON NATIONAL EXPENDITURE

See SELECT COMMITTEE ON ESTIMATES.

SELECT COMMITTEE ON NATIONALIZED INDUSTRIES

One of the most recently constituted of the Sessional Committees (q.v.) of the House of Commons, this Committee has risen rapidly in importance since it was first appointed in 1955 following the recommendation of an earlier Select Committee. It consists of 14 members, 5 being the quorum, and owes its origin to back-bench pressure. There had long been concern in all parts of the House at the lack of parliamentary control over the nationalized industries in the absence of any specific ministerial responsibility for them. In 1951 a Select Committee was appointed to consider improvements in the methods whereby Parliament could be informed of the affairs of the nationalized industries, but in its first report it recommended against the questioning of ministers on the subject. It reported again in 1953, having in the meantime been re-appointed, this time recommending the appointment of a Sessional Committee as the solution to the problem. The recommendation was accepted, although certain of the committee's proposals were turned down, with the result that the Select Committee on Nationalized Industries is not appointed in terms of a Standing Order, it is not empowered to appoint sub-committees, and it has no technical expert to guide its lines of inquiry.

The main task of the committee is to inquire into the financial state of the nationalized industries and to investigate their current, as distinct from their general, policies. It has the usual power to send for persons, papers and records, and is assisted by liaison officers from the Treasury and other Government departments where necessary. Since it is not possible to direct questions to ministers on the nationalized industries this committee provides the House with its only means of keeping a check on the activities of these great spending concerns.

SELECT COMMITTEE ON PROCEDURE OF THE HOUSE

A Sessional Committee (q.v.) of the House of Lords with terms of reference which are largely self-explanatory. It includes the Lord Chancellor and the Lord Chairman of Committees.

It is noteworthy that there is no such Sessional Committee in the House of Commons, although the Commons have frequently appointed Select Committees on Procedure on an *ad hoc* basis. It seems that the Lords have chosen to keep their procedure under continuing review through a Sessional Committee, whereas the Commons prefer to appoint a committee as and when their rules and practice, or certain aspects thereof, appear due for a revision.

SELECT COMMITTEE ON PUBLICATIONS AND DEBATES REPORTS

Formerly a Sessional Committee of the House of Commons consisting of 11 members, the functions of this committee have now been taken over by the House of Commons (Services) Committee (q.v.). It had previously been appointed to assist the Speaker by considering the arrangements for the reporting and publishing of debates and the form of the Votes and Proceedings, Order Paper, Notice Paper, etc. It also inquired into the expenditure of printing and stationery for the House of Commons generally.

In the 1964–5 session this committee, interpreting its terms of reference rather widely, decided to consider the question of televising parliamentary proceedings, and took evidence from the B.B.C. and the Independent Television Authority on the matter. Its special report on the subject was referred to the House of Commons (Services) Committee when the latter was first appointed.

SELECT COMMITTEE ON STATUTORY INSTRUMENTS

A Sessional Committee (q.v.) of the House of Commons consisting of 11 members, the quorum being 3, which has been appointed regularly since the session of 1943–4 with the duty of scrutinizing statutory instruments (q.v.). It is assisted by the Speaker's Counsel (q.v.), and is empowered to require the submission of memoranda or the attendance of witnesses from Government departments to explain the purport and content of any statutory instruments, including those which may be before Parliament in draft form.

The Committee performs a strictly 'watchdog' function. It is excluded by its terms of reference from considering the merits of or the policy behind delegated legislation. It is concerned solely with the manner in which the executive uses its powers and with drawing the attention of Parliament to any tendency on the part of the executive to exceed them. Instruments which impose a charge on public revenues, which confer immunity from challenge in the courts, which have an unauthorized retrospective effect, which reveal an 'unusual or unexpected' use of a statutory power, or which otherwise exceed the authority delegated by the parent statute, are examples of the cases on which the committee would be expected to report. It is also authorized to report any case of delay in presentation or publication, and to make special reports from time to time on general tendencies in delegated legislation. One of the latter led to the passing of the Statutory Instruments Act, 1946.

SELECT COMMITTEES

Both Houses of Parliament appoint Select Committees to perform duties for which the House itself is unsuited. Detailed investigation, the hearing and sifting of evidence, and the discussion of matters on which little public or political interest centres are tasks more efficiently undertaken by a small committee than by a numerous assembly. In recent years the Royal Commission and the departmental committee have tended to move into the province of the Select Committee, but there remain many areas of investigation in which only Select Committees can perform, and they are fundamental to the committee system of both Houses. When Select Committees from both Houses sit together on the same investigation they are known as a Joint Committee (q.v.).

Members of a Select Committee are 'selected' by the House which appoints it, although until 1819 they were sometimes chosen by ballot.

To-day they are normally appointed on the motion of a Government Whip, the relative party strengths being preserved in the composition of the committee, and the Whips of each party having first ascertained which of their members would be willing and best qualified to serve. (In certain cases the Committee of Selection (q.v.) participates in the nomination of a Select Committee.) The names of the members of a Select Committee are normally proposed *en bloc* immediately after the motion appointing the committee has been agreed to. A member, having been appointed to a committee, cannot resign from it, although it is open to the House to entertain a motion that he be discharged from it.

In the House of Commons, Standing Order No. 69 provides that a Select Committee may not, except with the leave of the House, consist of more than 15 members, and with the notable exception of the Estimates Committee (q.v.), this rule is generally applied. The House of Lords specifies no limits with regard to the size of its Select Committees. The membership of a Select Committee may subsequently be altered or enlarged by resolution of the House. Its quorum is fixed at the time of its appointment. When a Select Committee comprises 7 members or less the quorum is normally fixed at 3, and at 5 when it consists of 8 or more. In the case of an exceptionally large committee the quorum may be 7 or even as high as 9. If no quorum is specified the committee cannot function unless all the members are present.

A Select Committee is confined by its terms of reference, and is empowered only to make recommendations. Except in the case of the House of Commons (Services) Committee (q.v.) and the Kitchen Committee (q.v.) which it superseded, Parliament has never followed the practice common in other spheres of government of delegating executive authority to committees, although the prestige of certain parliamentary committees (e.g., the Committee of Privileges and the Public Accounts Committee [qq.v.]) is such that their recommendations tend to be accepted without debate or question. The fact remains that either House can debate, accept, reject or even ignore the recommendations of one of its committees. A committee is completely responsible to the House which appoints it. The House defines its terms of reference and only the House can alter them.

Select Committees are appointed for a specific purpose and are given the powers they require in order to conduct the inquiry assigned to them. They are normally authorized to 'send for persons, papers and records'—that is, to summon witnesses and to call for certain documents. Powers sometimes but not regularly conferred on Select Committees include the power to appoint sub-committees, to appoint persons from outside to serve on such sub-committees, to confer with persons outside their own body, and to sit outside the precincts of the House.

The matters with which Select Committees are concerned are many and various, but the committees themselves may be divided into three broad categories:

(1) Sessional Committees (q.v.), regularly appointed by order of the House or under a Standing Order.

(2) Select Committees appointed to consider a Bill.

(3) Select Committees appointed *ad hoc* to conduct a particular inquiry.

The Sessional Committees of the House of Commons are the Committee of Privileges; Select Committee on Statutory Instruments; Committee on Public Petitions; Select Committee on Nationalized Industries; and House of Commons (Services) Committee (all appointed by order of the House); Committee of Public Accounts; Estimates Committee; Committee of Selection; Standing Orders Committee; and Business Committee (all appointed under Standing Orders). All these committees are dealt with under their own headings. In 1968, following the establishment of the office of Parliamentary Commissioner for Administration (q.v.), a Select Committee was appointed to consider the reports of the Parliamentary Commissioner, and it can be expected that this committee will also be appointed every session. Sessional Committees of the House of Lords are the Committee of Selection; Standing Orders Committee; Special Orders Committee; and Personal Bills Committee (all appointed by Standing Order); Committee for Privileges; Select Committee on Procedure of the House; House of Lords Offices Committee; and Committee for the Journals (qq.v.).

At the time of writing (1970) the select committee system of the House of Commons is undergoing review in the light of certain proposals by the Select Committee on Procedure, 1968–9, a Green Paper published by the Government (Cmnd. 4507) and a debate in the House on 12 November 1970. It is anticipated that a Select Committee on Expenditure will replace the Estimates Committee (*see* EXPENDITURE, SELECT COMMITTEE ON) and that the system of specialist committees (q.v.) first instituted in December 1966 will be continued.

When a Select Committee is appointed to consider a Bill, the Bill itself is the order of reference. The House sometimes refers a Bill after second reading to a Select Committee instead of to a Standing Committee (q.v.), in which case it undergoes a preliminary committee stage and is subsequently re-committed to a Committee of the Whole House. A Bill is normally referred to a Select Committee when the House deems it desirable that evidence should be heard in relation to it, in which case the Committee will be empowered to send for persons, papers and records. Once the evidence, if any, is concluded, the Committee considers the Bill in accordance with the procedure which operates in a Committee of the Whole House or a Standing Committee, except that the Chairman is not empowered to select amendments or to entertain a closure motion. A Select Committee can consider a money clause if it has previously been sanctioned by a financial resolution. When a Select Committee has completed its consideration of a Bill it reports the Bill to the House, with or without amendment. Should it wish to express its views on the matters dealt with by the Bill it may make a special report which is submitted to the House together with the Bill itself. If, after hearing evidence, a Select Committee comes to the conclusion that the Bill should not be allowed to pass, it normally makes a special report to this effect, at the same time reporting the Bill without amendment.

A Select Committee elects its own Chairman and controls the times of its own sittings, except that it cannot without the leave of the House sit on a day which falls after the House has adjourned. The procedure in a Select Committee is basically similar to that of the House, although it tends to be less formal. For example, the Chairman may participate in the discussion, although he does not vote unless the numbers in a division are equal; members may speak more than once to the same question, and they refer to each other by name; motions have never required seconders (in recent years this requirement has been abolished in the House itself) and there is no provision for the limitation of debate. On the whole, Select Committees pursue their activities in an atmosphere of cordiality and impartiality, and neither the discussions nor the voting follow partisan lines as a rule. The public may be admitted to a sitting when evidence is being taken, but they may be ordered to withdraw at any time and are invariably excluded when the committee deliberates. Members of the House who are not members of the committee are entitled to attend meetings in an observer capacity unless the House has ordered that the committee shall be a committee of secrecy (no such committee has been appointed since 1857), but they normally withdraw out of courtesy when the committee deliberates.

Having completed its investigation a Select Committee proceeds to the consideration of its report. A draft report is usually prepared by the Chairman with the assistance of the clerk to the Committee and circulated among the members. The draft report is considered paragraph by paragraph; each paragraph is open to amendment and new paragraphs may also be proposed. It is open to any member of the committee to submit an alternative draft report which, if desired by the committee, may also be considered in detail. No provision exists for the presentation of minority reports by dissenting members of Select Committees, although all draft reports submitted are published with the minutes. Once a Select Committee has agreed on its report it becomes the report of the committee as a whole. Members who object to parts or the whole of the agreed report are able to place their dissent on record by dividing the committee, all divisions being recorded in the minutes. They could in addition express their disagreement on the Floor of the House itself in the event of the report being debated in the House. Once a report has been agreed and submitted to the House a Select Committee has reached the limit of its powers, and, unless it is empowered to report from time to time, its work is deemed to be at an end. The report of a Select Committee cannot be amended by the House, but it may be referred back to the committee, a course of action which has the automatic effect of reconstituting the committee.

The Select Committee system is a part of the machinery of all Commonwealth Parliaments, although certain variations in terminology are to be found. In Canada, for example, a Sessional Select Committee is known as a Standing Committee, a term which has a different significance at Westminster, and an *ad hoc* Select Committee is termed a Special Committee. Such differences are, however, purely superficial.

SELECTION, COMMITTEE OF

See COMMITTEE OF SELECTION.

SELECTION OF AMENDMENTS

Any member is entitled to put forward amendments at any stage of a debate on a Bill or motion, and the Speaker and, in Committee of the Whole House, the Chairman of Ways and Means or Deputy Chairman are empowered to decide which amendments should be selected for consideration. The power cannot be exercised in the House by the Deputy Speaker unless the Speaker's absence has been formally announced. The purpose of conferring this power upon the Chair is to ensure that the limited time available is used to the best advantage, and it lies within the discretion of the Chair to decide which amendments represent the leading sections of opinion. Although not compelled to give any reasons for passing over certain amendments, the occupant of the Chair might decide to announce a reason in respect of a particular amendment, or he might invite the mover of an amendment to explain its objects before taking a decision. In exercising his discretion his main concern is to interpret the wishes of the House.

The power of selecting amendments was first introduced in limited form in 1909 and its exercise required a special decision of the House. A Standing Order of 1919 established it as a permanent power of the Chair. In 1934 it was extended to the Chairmen of Standing Committees.

Because it involves 'jumping' over certain amendments on the order paper, the process of selecting amendments is known as the 'kangaroo'. It is usual to give notice of an amendment so that it appears on the order paper for the following day; an amendment of which notice has not been given is very unlikely to be selected.

SELECT VESTRIES BILL

A Bill with no legislative significance, the first reading of which is taken in the House of Lords before the debate on the address in reply to the Queen's Speech. It asserts the right of the Lords to conduct their business in any order they choose and corresponds to the Outlawries Bill (q.v.) in the House of Commons.

SENATE

The term frequently applied to the upper House of a legislature. In the British Commonwealth it is the name given to the upper House of the Parliaments of Canada, Australia, Ceylon, Malaysia, Nigeria, Jamaica, Trinidad and Tobago, Fiji, Antigua and Grenada. The word means literally an assembly of old men or elders, and is therefore applied to a council with the highest deliberative and legislative functions. The Roman Senate was the supreme council of State, and the British Parliament is sometimes alluded to rhetorically as the Senate.

SEPTENNIAL ACT, 1715

See DURATION OF PARLIAMENT.

SERJEANT-AT-ARMS

In the House of Commons the Serjeant-at-Arms attends the Speaker (q.v.) in a ceremonial capacity. He also has his own department and controls a large staff, including a Deputy Serjeant and Assistant Serjeant, his counterpart in the House of Lords being the Gentleman Usher of the Black Rod (q.v.). Until 1970 there was also a Serjeant-at-Arms in the House of Lords. He was an officer in the department of the Lord Chancellor who attended the Lord Chancellor with the Mace (q.v.) and, according to Erskine May, was an officer of the Lord Chancellor rather than of the House of Lords. In 1970 the office was abolished and its functions combined with those of the Gentleman Usher of the Black Rod.

The duties of the Serjeant-at-Arms in the House of Commons are in many respects traditional, but he is also housekeeper of the House under the House of Commons (Offices) Act, 1812, and therefore performs administrative as well as ceremonial duties. He is appointed by the Crown under a warrant from the Lord Chamberlain and by patent under the Great Seal (q.v.) 'to attend upon Her Majesty's person when there is no Parliament; and at the time of every Parliament, to attend upon the Speaker of the House of Commons'. Once appointed, he becomes the servant of the House and may be dismissed by the House in the event of a breach of conduct. His full style is 'Serjeant-at-Arms in Ordinary to Her Majesty', and the appointment is usually held by a retired officer of Her Majesty's forces.

[687]

The Serjeant-at-Arms is the custodian of the Mace, which features prominently in the performance of his ceremonial duties. Bearing the Mace upon his right shoulder he precedes the Speaker when the latter enters and leaves the Chamber at the beginning and the end of a day's sitting; he does likewise when the Speaker attends the Bar of the House of Lords and when the House of Commons proceeds anywhere as a House. The only occasion on which the Mace is not borne shoulder-high is during the ceremony attendant upon the election of a new Speaker (q.v., sub-heading *Election of Speaker*). When a person appears at the Bar of the House as a petitioner, witness, offender, or in any other capacity, he is attended at the Bar by the Serjeant-at-Arms bearing the Mace. When the Gentleman Usher of the Black Rod arrives as a messenger from the House of Lords he is introduced into the Chamber by the Serjeant-at-Arms.

The Serjeant-at-Arms is responsible for the maintenance of law and order throughout the precincts of the House of Commons. He is empowered to take into custody or order the withdrawal of strangers who are guilty of misconduct or who have been irregularly admitted and, if ordered to do so by the Speaker, to take disciplinary action against members themselves should the occasion arise. Under the direction of the Speaker he executes the orders of the House including the commitment of persons ordered into custody. He controls the admission of strangers to all galleries and other parts of the building, and the police on duty in the lobbies and passages are under his supervision. As housekeeper of the House he is responsible for the upkeep and maintenance of the building, and the doorkeepers, office keepers, attendants, cleaners, and watchmen come under his jurisdiction.

The Serjeant-at-Arms wears a traditional uniform consisting of a cocked hat, black cut-away coat, lace ruffles at the throat, white lace cuffs, knee-breeches, black silk stockings, and silver-buckled shoes. The rapier and scabbard girt to his side are the symbol of his power and authority. Whilst the House is sitting he occupies a chair at the Bar of the House, raised above the level of the floor and facing the Speaker. He is relieved from time to time by the Deputy Serjeant-at-Arms, who wears the same uniform. On occasions of official mourning the normal dress is varied by means of a black sword with black mountings, black knee and shoe buckles and black gloves.

It was probably during the reign of Richard II that a Serjeant-at-Arms was first appointed by the King to attend the Speaker of the House of Commons. Serjeants-at-Arms were originally members of a King's Bodyguard which was established in France by Philip II and introduced into England probably by Richard I. In executing the orders of the King they were the representatives of the royal authority, the Maces they carried were their warrants, and their ceremonial functions evolved as the necessity for protecting the King's person diminished. In addition to the Serjeant-at-Arms specially assigned to Parliament there are 8 Royal Serjeants whose duties are purely ceremonial. Similarly, the 2 Serjeants-at-Arms formerly assigned to Parliament for the protection of the Lord Chancellor and the Speaker respectively acquired ceremonial functions in place of their duties as bodyguards. During the course of the centuries the Speaker's election by the Commons has ceased to be influenced by the Crown, the Lord Chancellor has become the nominee of the Government of the day, but the office of Serjeant-at-Arms has remained a royal appointment.

The present (1970) salary of the Serjeant-at-Arms in the House of Commons is £6,000 per annum and he has an official residence in the Palace of Westminster.

SESSION

The period beginning with the day Parliament is opened and ending with the day it is prorogued, or in the case of the final session of a Parliament, dissolved. During the session a House may adjourn itself of its own motion to such date as it pleases, and whereas a prorogation terminates a session, an adjournment is an interruption in the course of one and the same session. A list of the usual parliamentary session months throughout the Commonwealth is given at the beginning of each volume of *The Table*, the Journal of the Society of Clerks-at-the-Table (q.v.).

A session opens with the Speech from the Throne, usually delivered by the Sovereign herself, and in her territories overseas by the Governor-General or Governor, as the case may be. A Speech from the Throne is also delivered by the Lord Chancellor in the House of Lords when Parliament is prorogued.

SESSIONAL COMMITTEES

Select Committees (q.v.) which are automatically appointed at the beginning of each session, either by Standing Order or by order of the House. They are committees which have a continuing function, as distinct from *ad hoc* committees appointed to undertake a specific investigation.

In the House of Commons the following Sessional Committees are appointed under Standing Orders: Committee of Public Accounts, Estimates Committee, Committee of Selection, Standing Orders Committee and Business Committee (qq.v.). The following are appointed by order of the House: Committee of Privileges, Committee on Public Petitions, Select Committee on Statutory Instruments, Select Committee on Nationalized Industries, House of Commons (Services) Committee (qq.v.), and the Committee which is appointed to consider the reports of the Parliamentary Commissioner for Administration (q.v.).

However, at the time of writing (1970) the select committee system of the House is under review and a number of important changes are anticipated, notably the replacement of the Estimates Committee by a Select Committee on Expenditure (*see* EXPENDITURE, SELECT COMMITTEE ON).

In the House of Lords the following Sessional Committees are appointed under Standing Orders: Committee of Selection, Standing Orders Committee, Special Orders Committee and Personal Bills Committee (qq.v.). Those appointed by order of the House are: the Committee for Privileges, Select Committee on Procedure of the House, House of Lords Offices Committee and Committee for the Journals (qq.v.).

A Joint Committee of both Houses on Consolidation Bills (q.v.) is also appointed sessionally.

In other Commonwealth Parliaments a sessionally appointed Select Committee is normally called a Standing Committee, a term which has a different significance at Westminster.

SESSIONAL ORDERS

Regulations made by the House of Commons which are renewed at the beginning of each session. They deal with double election returns, exclusion of peers from voting, bribery at elections, tampering with witnesses, false evidence in any case before the House or any committee thereof, directions to the police, the printing of Votes and Proceedings and the Journal, and the appointment of certain sessional committees (q.v.). The order first mentioned appeared at the end of the 17th century, and by the end of the 18th there were considerably more than there are to-day. They included additional orders prohibiting strangers in the House or gallery, regulations for the delivery of letters to members and for the adjournment of committees as soon as a sitting of the House commenced, and orders prohibiting gambling by members' footmen and their presence in the Lobby of the House.

SEYCHELLES LEGISLATIVE ASSEMBLY

The Seychelles (Legislative Council) Order in Council, dated 11 March 1948, introduced elected members for the first time. The Council then consisted of the Governor as President, 6 official members, 4 elected members, and 2 nominated unofficial members.

In 1967 a new Constitution was introduced providing for a single Governing Council consisting of the Governor as President, 3 official members, up to 4 nominated members and 8 elected members. This Constitution embodied a system of government by committee, there being 3 committees of the Governing Council under the chairmanship of elected members and a fourth, the Finance Committee, under the chairmanship of the Financial Secretary. Each committee had responsibility for groups of government departments, although the Governor retained his full reserve powers.

Under a new Constitution introduced in 1970 a Legislative Assembly and a Council of Ministers have been established. The Legislative Assembly consists of a Speaker, 3 *ex-officio* members (Deputy Governor, Attorney-General and Financial Secretary) and 15 elected members directly elected in 8 constituencies. The Council of Ministers consists of a Chief Minister and up to 4 other ministers selected from the elected members of the Legislative Assembly and the 3 *ex-officio* members, presided over by the Governor. Members of the Council of Ministers have charge of portfolios covering the full range of government business except for those subjects which remain within the direct responsibility of the Government, namely external affairs, defence, internal security, the public service and the government broadcasting service and newspaper.

An unusual feature of the Constitution is that it makes provision for a public accounts committee of the Legislative Assembly and for an advisory committee to assist the Governor in the discharge of his responsibilities for the government publicity media.

SEYMOUR, JOHN

A Clerk of the House of Commons who first began the Journal of the House (q.v.) in 1547 in the form of a diary of events in the Commons. This first volume was known as 'Seymour', and covered the years 1547–66.

SHADOW CABINET

A group of the leaders of the Opposition party who cover the various portfolios of the Government and lead for the Opposition in any debate concerning their special area of responsibility. Each member contributes expert knowledge, often gained by official experience, to the task of directing criticism of Government policy from the point of view of a party which is bidding for the support of the nation. Members of the Shadow Cabinet can normally expect senior ministerial office in the event of their party being returned to power.

When the Conservative Party is in Opposition their leader personally selects the members of the Shadow Cabinet (which is known technically as the Consultative Committee), just as a Prime Minister would choose his Cabinet. When the Labour Party is in Opposition the Shadow Cabinet (or Parliamentary Committee) is elected annually by the Parliamentary Labour Party, except for the leader, deputy leader and Chief Whip who are *ex-officio* members.

(Further reading: Turner, *The Shadow Cabinet in British Politics*, 1969).

SHIPPING, MINISTER OF

A Controller of Shipping was appointed in 1917 who later in the same year became Minister of Shipping. At the beginning of the War in 1939 Sir John Gilmour was appointed to this office, and he was followed by R. H. Cross and R. S. Hudson (afterwards Lord Hudson). In 1941 F. J. Leathers (afterwards Lord Leathers) was appointed Minister of Shipping and Transport.

See also TRANSPORT, MINISTER OF.

SHORTEST PARLIAMENT

The shortest Parliament ever held was that which met on 30 September 1399 and deposed Richard II. It sat only for one day, and although Parliament assembled six days later with the same members, Henry IV decreed that this assembly constituted a new Parliament.

SHORTHAND WRITER TO THE HOUSE

The shorthand reporting of evidence taken before select committees was first introduced in 1802 when William Brodie Gurney and his father Joseph Gurney were assigned to take notes of evidence before select committees of both Houses of Parliament. In 1813 W. B. Gurney was formally appointed shorthand writer to the Houses of Parliament with the responsibility for providing shorthand writers for all committees engaged in hearing evidence. He was paid two guineas a day for attendance and one shilling a folio for the transcript of his notes. Joseph Gurney was the first of the famous shorthand-writing family to undertake parliamentary work, his first assignment being in the House of Lords in 1783. The firm of Gurneys still supplies the shorthand writers for select committees, the Hansard reporters being engaged solely in recording debates.

SHORT PARLIAMENT

The first of the two Parliaments summoned by Charles I in 1640, the second being the Long Parliament (q.v.). The King demanded an immediate grant of supplies for the purpose of raising an army to send against Scotland, but the Commons insisted that the nation's grievances should receive priority over the King's needs. The Short Parliament was disposed to be as drastic in its demands as the Long Parliament, in fact, eventually was, and it was prepared to insist on the abandonment of the war with Scotland. It was dissolved after it had sat for three weeks.

It was during the Short Parliament that Pym emerged as the leader of the group opposed to the King. In a famous speech which was received with great enthusiasm in the House he enumerated the grievances of Parliament and the nation. Details of the elections to the Short Parliament are almost completely lacking.

See also CHARLES I AND PARLIAMENT.

SIERRA LEONE PARLIAMENT

Sierra Leone became an independent member of the Commonwealth on 27 April 1961. Parliament consists of the Queen, represented by a Governor-General, and a House of Representatives which, with effect from the General Election held in May 1962, has consisted of 74 members, 62 elected by universal adult suffrage for single-member constituencies and 12 Paramount Chiefs elected by tribal authorities. The Cabinet formed on 29 April 1964 consisted of the Prime Minister and 14 other ministers, five fewer than the previous Cabinet. The Constitution provides for the protection of fundamental rights and freedoms, this provision being entrenched along with other basic provisions, notably those relating to the duration of Parliament and the frequency of its sessions, the holding of elections, the office of Paramount Chief, and most of those relating to finance, the judiciary and the public service. An entrenched provision may be amended only by a bill which has twice been passed by a two-thirds majority of all the members of the House of Representatives, a dissolution of Parliament having taken place between the two occasions. Other provisions may be amended by a Bill passed by a two-thirds majority on a single occasion. However, following an inconclusive election result in April 1967, the government of the country was taken over by the military, and parliamentary government was suspended but restored in April 1968.

The Colony of Sierra Leone was first governed by the Sierra Leone Company at the end of the 18th century, but the members of the Legislative Council were all nominated by the Governor until 1924. Election by ballot was first introduced in that year, when 2 members were elected for the urban district and 1 for the rural area. Sierra Leone included a Protectorate, as well as a Colony, which was first represented in 1924 by 3 of its Paramount Chiefs (nominated by the Governor) among the 7 unofficial members. There were also 11 official members with the Governor as President. The first major change in the legislature was in 1951, when the membership of the Council was increased to 31, of whom 7 were elected directly from the Colony and 14 were elected to represent the Protectorate. In 1953 the 6 official members of the Executive Council received the title of minister for the departments for which they were responsible. New constitutional advances were approved by the British Government in October 1956, and these provided for a House of Representatives composed of 14 members elected from the Colony and 24 from the Protectorate, 12 paramount chiefs, 1 member elected from the Bo urban area, 2 nominated unofficials to represent special interests (with power to speak but not to vote), and 4 *ex-officio* members. A Speaker was elected by a two-thirds majority vote of the members from either inside or outside the House, and the Deputy Speaker from among the members by a simple majority. The Governor retained the right to convene and address the House, although he ceased to preside over the legislature. A further step towards eventual self-government was taken in 1958. From 14 August of that year the Chief Minister became the Premier and the Executive Council was reconstituted and its authority enhanced. The *ex-officio* members were removed from both the House of Representatives and the Executive Council, although the Governor continued to preside over the latter. In June 1960 the Executive Council was replaced by a Cabinet consisting of a Prime Minister and not less than 7 other ministers, all drawn from the elected membership of the House of Representatives. The Prime Minister presided over the Cabinet, on whose advice the Governor normally acted.

Following the recommendations of the Electoral Reform Commission, which reported in 1954, the franchise in Sierra Leone was gradually extended over the following eight years. The first stage of reform took effect in 1957 with the introduction of a modest property qualification in the Colony and a qualification based on the payment of taxes in the Protectorate. Universal adult suffrage was introduced for the election of 1962. With the achievement of independence in 1961 the existing House of Representatives, with the exception of the 2 nominated members, continued in being for an interim period prior to the election.

SIMON DE MONTFORT'S PARLIAMENT

Simon de Montfort has often been referred to as the creator of the House of Commons, due to the fact that it was at his instance that the representatives of the cities and boroughs were first summoned to the national assembly. This was in 1265 when 2 knights from each shire, 2 citizens from each city, and 2 burgesses from each borough were summoned to a Parliament which, whilst it included most of the bishops, was attended by only 5 earls and 18 barons. Two knights from each shire had previously been called to a Parliament in 1254. Although the origin of popular representation can be traced to the Parliament of 1265 it was a very partisan assembly whose delegates were selected from the known supporters of Simon de Montfort, and it cannot therefore, like the Model Parliament (q.v.), be considered to have been truly representative.

The 700th anniversary of this Parliament was celebrated by the presentation of addresses to the Queen in Westminster Hall by the

Lords and Commons on 22 June 1965 and by the issue of commemorative postage stamps.

SINGAPORE PARLIAMENT

A Legislative Council was constituted by the Singapore Colony Orders in Council, 1946 to 1953, made under the Straits Settlements (Repeal) Act of 1946 and the British Settlements Acts of 1887 and 1945 passed by the United Kingdom Parliament. These Orders in Council and the Royal Instructions issued in 1946, as subsequently amended, provided for a Governor, an Executive Council, with the Governor as Chairman, 4 *ex-officio* members, 2 nominated official, 4 nominated unofficial, and 2 elected members, and a Legislative Council consisting of 4 *ex-officio* members, 5 nominated official, 4 nominated unofficial, and 12 elected members. As the result of the appointment by the Governor of a Constitutional Commission (the Rendel Commission) in 1953, a revised constitution introducing a ministerial system and a Legislative Assembly with a Speaker and a majority of elected members was brought into force in April 1955. In the following July the newly elected Legislative Assembly adopted a resolution requesting that a new Constitution providing for self-government should be granted immediately. A conference was accordingly held in London in April 1956, but reached a deadlock on the question of responsibility for internal security, defence, and external affairs. A further conference was held in March–April 1957, which resulted in agreement that Singapore should receive internal self-government, shed its colonial status, and become known as the State of Singapore. A General Election marking the inauguration of the new Constitution was held on 30 May 1959 at which voting was compulsory. The office of Governor was abolished and replaced by a Malayan-born Head of State known as the Yang di-Pertuan Negara. The Legislative Assembly was reconstituted as a fully elected body of 51 members representing single-member constituencies. The Chief Minister became the Prime Minister presiding over a Cabinet directly responsible to the Assembly.

In September 1962 Singapore voted by means of a referendum to become a member of the Federation of Malaysia, but with a larger measure of local autonomy than the other states of the Federation. The Federation was formed in September 1963 from the States of the Malayan Federation, Sabah (formerly North Borneo), Sarawak, and Singapore. In August 1965, however, Singapore seceded from the Federation, but agreed to enter into a treaty of external defence and mutual assistance with Malaysia, and also to co-operate in economic affairs. The British Government announced its recognition of Singapore as an independent state on 10 August 1965.

On 22 December 1965 the Legislative Assembly passed legislation formalizing the constitutional and legal changes consequent upon secession. Singapore is now a Republic within the Commonwealth, the first President being the former Yang di-Pertuan Negara. The Legislative Assembly has been renamed Parliament, and now consists of 58 members representing single-member constituencies. The Speaker may be chosen from the membership of Parliament or from outside the House, but if a non-member he may not exercise a casting vote. He is removable only through a dissolution of Parliament.

The official languages of Singapore are Malay, Chinese, Tamil and English. All adult citizens are enfranchised without distinction of race or sex.

SINGLE TRANSFERABLE VOTE
See PROPORTIONAL REPRESENTATION.

SITTINGS OF THE HOUSE OF COMMONS

Under Standing Order No. 1 the House of Commons sits on Mondays, Tuesdays, Wednesdays, and Thursdays at 2.30 p.m. and on Fridays at 11 a.m. Business is automatically interrupted at 10 p.m. and on Fridays at 4 p.m., unless it is Exempted Business (q.v.) or the House agrees to suspend the automatic adjournment rule on the motion of a Minister of the Crown. The House may vary the times of its sittings by resolution and normally does so when circumstances, such as the intervention of public holidays, render a variation convenient or desirable. An unprecedented variation was announced in the House on 11 March 1965 after the Murder (Abolition of Death Penalty) Bill was discharged from a Standing Committee and ordered to be taken on the Floor of the House. It was decided that the Bill should be taken in Committee of the Whole House at the same time as it would normally have been taken in the Standing Committee, i.e., from 10.30 a.m. to 1 p.m. The Committee sat every Wednesday morning from 24 March to 26 May, when the Bill was reported.

On 1 February 1967, morning sittings on Mondays and Wednesdays were instituted on a regular basis but were abolished during the same year because of the difficulties which were encountered in securing the attendance of members. A system of 'suspended sittings' has been adopted in their place. Under this procedure it is open to a minister at any time after 10 p.m. to move that the sitting be suspended to enable the business under discussion to be completed at a more reasonable hour the following morning. The motion is not subject to amendment or debate. The experiment with morning sittings was designed to find time for the consideration of non-controversial business and it was provided that no division or count of the House could take place during these sittings. While morning sittings lasted, the debate on the adjournment motion on Mondays and Wednesdays took place between

12.30 p.m. and 1 p.m. instead of at the end of the day. (*See* ADJOURN-MENT OF THE HOUSE.)

Occasionally a temporary suspension of business takes place, there being various reasons which may require a pause in the proceedings. Such a suspension always takes place on the first day of a session after the Commons return to their own Chamber from the House of Lords, where the Queen traditionally reads the Speech from the Throne opening the new Parliament. The sitting may be suspended if attention is drawn to the absence of a quorum (q.v.) before 4 p.m. (or 1 p.m. on a Friday), or if the House becomes grossly disorderly. Further occasions on which a sitting may be suspended are referred to in Erskine May (17th ed., p. 324).

The longest continuous sitting so far is $41\frac{1}{2}$ hours, and this took place from 31 January to 2 February 1881 when the House was debating the Protection of Persons and Property (Ireland) Bill, known as the Coercion Bill. The obstruction of the Irish members on this occasion led to the introduction of the closure (q.v.). The next two longest sittings were $34\frac{1}{4}$ hours (22-4 July 1936) and $31\frac{3}{4}$ hours (11-12 June 1951). The record for a committee was set up by the Scottish Standing Committee which sat for nearly 26 hours on 21-2 May 1957.

The shortest sitting of the House of Commons on record took place on Friday, 25 November 1910, when the House sat for precisely nine minutes. The last item of business on the previous day, Thursday, had been a motion that the House at its rising should adjourn until the Monday following, a motion which in the normal course of events would have found automatic acceptance. However, before this final item of business could be disposed of, a member called the Speaker's attention to the lack of a quorum. The House was counted out, most of the members having already departed for their homes or constituencies, with the result that no further business could be transacted and the House had no option but to meet again on the following day. As Parliament was on the eve of its dissolution there were no effective orders of the day and consequently little with which to detain members when the House met for its brief Friday sitting.

SNAP DIVISION

An unexpected division which is sometimes engineered by the Opposition in the hope that Government supporters will be unprepared and in insufficient numbers to avoid a defeat.

SOCIAL SERVICES, SECRETARY OF STATE FOR

This office was instituted on 1 November 1968 when the Ministry of Health and the Ministry of Social Security were merged as the

Department of Health and Social Security. Its establishment was designed to permit the co-ordination of the whole range of social services and to facilitate the implementation of policies which had previously cut across departmental boundaries. Mr. Richard Crossman was appointed the first Secretary of State to head the new department, and he was at that time assisted by two Ministers of State and two joint Under-Secretaries of State.

The Ministry of Social Security, which was superseded by the new department, was established on 3 August 1966 and brought together the Ministry of Pensions and National Insurance and the National Assistance Board, thus eliminating the distinction which had previously existed between benefits related to contributions and non-contributory benefits. At that time the Minister of Pensions and National Insurance became the Minister of Social Security, Miss Margaret Herbison becoming in the process the first holder of this office.

The office of Minister of Pensions and National Insurance had been created in 1953 when the Ministry of Pensions and the Ministry of National Insurance were combined under one Minister. The first Minister was Osbert Peake (now Viscount Ingleby).

The Ministry of Pensions had been created in 1916 to take over the duties of the Admiralty, the Army Council and the Commissioners of Chelsea Hospital in relation to war pensions, and the minister's duties were increased by the creation of the R.A.F. and the outbreak of the Second World War. The Ministry of National Insurance arose as the result of the implementation of the comprehensive scheme of social insurance largely based on the Beveridge Report, and was established in 1944. This department took over much of the work relating to insurance which had formerly been administered by the Ministries of Labour and Health and the Home and Scottish Offices. The minister became responsible for the administration of unemployment insurance, although the actual payment of benefits was made at the local offices of the Ministry of Labour. There were 5 Ministers of National Insurance during the period that this office existed independently. Sir William Jowitt (afterwards Earl Jowitt) was the first and he was succeeded by Leslie Hore Belisha, James Griffiths, Dr. Edith Summerskill and Osbert Peake. When the last-named became Minister of the combined departments of Pensions and National Insurance, his responsibilities extended to both service and civil pensions.

A chronological list of the holders of the office of Minister of Pensions and its successors appears as Appendix 26.

SOCIETY OF CLERKS-AT-THE-TABLE IN COMMONWEALTH PARLIAMENTS

Founded in 1932 by Owen Clough, C.M.G., Clerk of the South African Senate from 1910 to 1929, this society was formed to facilitate a general interchange of views and information between the Clerks of the Parliaments throughout the Commonwealth on procedure and precedent in the legislatures which they serve. The society publishes an annual journal, of which Mr. Clough was the editor from its inception in 1932 until 1952, when he became Honorary Life President of the Society. In his editorial in the first issue, Mr. Clough wrote:

This is perhaps the first instance of the members of the same profession within the British Empire organizing themselves into a Society for their mutual interest and benefit. Notwithstanding the many textbooks on the subjects of parliamentary procedure and constitutional law in its relation to the Legislature, there is much knowledge required of the 'Clerk of the House' which is only obtainable either from one's own practical experience or from that of others long engaged in the same occupation.

The British House of Commons of today, with its highly developed procedure, its large membership and its great pressure of business, all working under the enviable elasticity of what is, practically, an unwritten Constitution, does not always afford helpful precedents in parliamentary practice suitable to the simpler needs of the smaller and younger Legislature overseas. Even the Parliaments of the Dominions, often by reason of particular provisions in their Constitutions not in force in the United Kingdom, are building up their own precedents, or are being guided by those of other Dominion Parliaments where similar provisions exist. Therefore, although the wealth of precedents and age-long experience in parliamentary practice afforded by the Mother of Parliaments, so readily accessible in textbooks, etc., will continue to be invaluable to the overseas Clerk, the want has long been felt of some means by which he may also have a general knowledge of the working of other overseas Parliaments.

The Journal, now known as *The Table*, receives contributions from Officers of Parliament throughout the Commonwealth, and it includes a number of regular features incorporating information received in answer to the annual questionnaire which the society circulates amongst Commonwealth legislatures. They cover such matters as Speakers' rulings, applications of privilege, constitutional amendments, amendments to Standing Orders, and expressions which have been ruled as unparliamentary.

SOLICITOR-GENERAL

See LAW OFFICERS OF THE CROWN.

SOUTH AUSTRALIAN PARLIAMENT

From its founding in 1836 South Australia was administered by the Governor and other officials and 7 Resident Commissioners, who were responsible for the sale of Crown land. The Commissioners' authority was abolished in 1838, and in 1843 a nominated Legislative Council was established under British Acts of 1842. In 1851 a Council of 24 members was created, two-thirds of whom were elected, and in

1857 responsible government was granted with a Legislative Council (upper House) and a House of Assembly. Since 1915 there have been 20 members in the Council elected by five 4-member districts—2 metropolitan and 3 country. South Australia was the first Australian State to extend the franchise to women in 1894, and in 1902, after federation, the number of members elected to the Assembly was reduced from 54 to 42. In 1938 single electorates were introduced, and each of 39 districts now has one member. Members of the Council are elected for six years, half the members retiring every three years, and members of the Assembly for three years, the normal life of a Parliament since 1938. A system of preferential voting is in operation, and voting for the House of Assembly has been compulsory since 1942. South Australia has the distinction of being the first to introduce the secret ballot in 1856.

The following are the main divergences from House of Commons procedure:

(1) The main Estimates for any financial year are presented during the currency of that financial year, and not before the commencement of the year to which they relate. Supply Acts are put through to provide finance to carry on until the Appropriation Act is passed. They have the same effect as the Votes on Account of the House of Commons.

(2) All Public Bills (unless transmitted by the Governor by message, or sent from the Council) are initiated either by motion for leave to bring in the Bill, or by a motion for a committee of not less than 2 members to prepare and bring it in, or by an Order of the House.

(3) Amendments may not be made on the report stage of a Bill.

(4) The Legislative Council has equal power with the Assembly except in relation to Money Bills, which can only originate in the lower House.

(5) If one House insists on its disagreement with alterations made to its Bills by the other, a Conference between them may be arranged. Five members (who are called Managers in this rôle) from each House meet, and after some formalities are 'at liberty to confer freely by word of mouth'. The Conference has proved to be a valuable method of reaching a satisfactory compromise on matters in dispute between the two Houses, and as a last resort has been the means of saving a number of Bills which might otherwise have been lost.

(6) All answers to questions, which may be asked without notice, are given orally in the House.

(7) There is no adjournment debate, and no fixed time for the adjournment of either House.

(8) Owing to the comparatively small number of members, there is no provision for the guillotine, and the closure has not been resorted to in recent years.

In 1966 the House of Assembly adopted a number of important

procedural changes. Principal among them was the elimination of the archaic requirement that every Money Bill be founded on a resolution of a Committee of the Whole House. This change in financial procedure reflected a principle previously implemented in the Australian and British Parliaments and subsequently adopted in the Canadian and New Zealand Parliaments. Another new rule requires the Printing Committee to draw the attention of the House every year to any papers which have not been presented to the House in compliance with statute. Other changes include the recognition of the precedence of government business by Standing Order, the granting of the right of reply to the mover of the third reading of a Bill, and the modernizing of the forms of the closure and the previous question.

The first portion of South Australia's fine Parliament House in Adelaide was completed in 1889, and the second wing, housing the Legislative Council and the Library, was opened in 1939. It has some 175 rooms, and provides, as well as the normal facilities, the rather unusual luxury of a desk and an individual telephone for each member.

(Further reading: Combe, *The Parliament of South Australia*, 1960.)

SOVEREIGN

The Parliaments of the British Commonwealth (excluding those of the Republics within the Commonwealth) are composed of the Sovereign, or the Sovereign represented by a Governor-General (q.v.), and the upper and lower Houses of the legislature, or the single chamber if the Parliament is unicameral as is the case in New Zealand, which several powers collectively form the legislature. The Anglo-Saxon Kings were elected by the Witenagemot (q.v.), and although the doctrine of hereditary succession was introduced by the Normans, the principle of election and consent continued until the reign of Edward IV, when the new theory arose that the King never dies, thus ensuring that henceforward the throne was never vacant. Originally the Sovereign personally exercised all the functions of government, but through the centuries most of the powers attached to the throne have been lost to its occupant. 'The Queen reigns but she does not rule', although, according to Bagehot, three rights remain to her with regard to the government of the country—the right to be consulted, the right to encourage, and the right to warn. The Sovereign's powers as the supreme executive authority in the state are almost entirely delegated to her ministers. Her main constitutional functions are to appoint as Prime Minister the leader of the majority party in the House of Commons, to grant on the advice of the Prime Minister a dissolution of Parliament (and in very special circumstances to refuse or to insist on a dissolution), to summon, open, and prorogue Parliament, to approve the House of Commons' choice of a Speaker, to assent to Bills, and to create peers. With respect to this last power, there have been occasions when a Prime Minister, wishing to secure the passage through the House of Lords of a measure supported by the House of Commons, has applied to the Sovereign for the creation of a sufficient number of peers to achieve his purpose, a notable instance being that of Earl Grey and the Reform Bill (*see* WILLIAM IV AND PARLIAMENT). Should such an occasion arise the right is reserved to the Sovereign to refuse to create the necessary peers should she consider that the House of Commons lacks the full support of the country on the issue in question. In actual practice the powers of the House of Lords have been so curtailed that it is doubtful whether such a contingency could arise to-day. The only occasion on which the Sovereign is present in Parliament is at the opening ceremony, when she reads the Speech from the Throne, prepared by the Cabinet and approved by her, outlining the Government's legislative programme for the session. Her other parliamentary functions, such as the assent to Bills, are performed by her representatives, the Lords Commissioners (q.v.).

The privilege of access to the Sovereign is enjoyed by the House of Commons through their Speaker, but the House of Lords is not only entitled as a body to free access to the throne, but each peer, as one of the Sovereign's hereditary counsellors, is entitled to a personal audience. The relationship between the Sovereign and Parliament is best stated, as Herbert Morrison (afterwards Lord Morrison) has pointed out, in the recital of every Act of Parliament: 'Be it enacted by the Queen's most Excellent Majesty, by and with the advice and consent of the Lords Spiritual and Temporal, and Commons, in this present Parliament assembled, and by the authority of the same, as follows:—'. Whilst the enactment is by the Queen, it is made effective not only by and with the advice of both Houses of Parliament but by and with their consent, and the authority for the statute is clearly stated to be that of Parliament. The assertion of parliamentary responsibility could not be more clear, yet it is put in the best possible way from the point of view of the dignity of the Sovereign by the commencing words. Moreover, before a Bill can become an Act it requires the Royal Assent (q.v.) even though the power to withhold this has been dormant since the reign of Queen Anne.

Gladstone said that there was a vital distinction between the Sovereign and the Crown, which is often overlooked because the law and the conventions do not distinguish between the rights, powers, and prerogatives of the Sovereign as a person and those of the Crown. The latter is a legal idea, and the distinction has been made clearer since the passing of the Crown Proceedings Act in 1947, which enables the Crown, but not the Sovereign, to be sued in a court of law. The Sovereign is the oldest and what has proved to be the most essential part of the Constitution, and is now firmly established as the head of the British Commonwealth of Nations and its symbol of unity.

[702]

Until 1953 legislation regarding the title of the Sovereign was undertaken only by the Parliament of the United Kingdom with the assent of the Dominions, in accordance with the Statute of Westminster (q.v.). At the end of 1952 it was agreed among the full members of the Commonwealth that each Commonwealth country should be free to pass its own legislation on the subject. Speaking on the Royal Titles Bill in the House of Commons on 3 March 1953, the then Home Secretary said:

'The Commonwealth . . . has moved beyond the Statute of Westminster; and today, rather than that legislation on the title of the Sovereign should be undertaken only by the United Kingdom Parliament with the assent of the Dominions as recited in the Statute of Westminster, it is more appropriate that each Commonwealth country concerned should take the action appropriate to its own constitutional requirements.

'The Prime Ministers and the heads of delegations agreed that the appropriate action in the established constitutional relationship would be for each member country to use for its own purpose a form of title which would suit its own particular circumstances, but that all should retain a common element. They agreed that the common element in the title of the Queen should include a reference to Her Majesty's other realms and territories and her title as head of the Commonwealth. The titles in the other Commonwealth countries are matters on which it will be for those countries to take the appropriate constitutional action. In this country the normal procedure is for Parliament to authorize the Sovereign to issue a Royal proclamation setting out the Royal titles, and that is what this Bill does in Clause 1.' (Hansard, vol. 512, col. 194.)

In the United Kingdom the Queen's title reads:

Elizabeth II, by the Grace of God, Queen of the United Kingdom of Great Britain and Northern Ireland and of her other realms and territories, Queen, Head of the Commonwealth, Defender of the Faith.

In Canada her title reads:

Elizabeth II, by the Grace of God, of the United Kingdom, Canada and her other realms and territories, Queen, Head of the Commonwealth, Defender of the Faith.

In Australia and New Zealand a similar style has been adopted.

The Queen's title in those countries where she is not regarded as Head of State is:

Elizabeth II, Queen of the United Kingdom and of her other realms and territories, Head of the Commonwealth.

See also CROWN AND PARLIAMENT; ROYAL PREROGATIVE.

SPEAKER

The Speakership is an ancient and honourable office and an essential feature of the parliamentary system. The Speaker is the presiding

z*

officer of the House of Commons and his authority is recognized and respected on all sides of the House. (The Speaker of the House of Lords is the Lord Chancellor (q.v.).) The only occasion on which he, or the Deputy Speaker (q.v.), leaves the Chair while the House is sitting is when the House goes into committee and the Chairman of Ways and Means (q.v.) presides over its deliberations. The function of the Speaker is to regulate debate and enforce the observance of the rules which govern its conduct. He calls upon members who wish to speak and uses his own discretion in selecting them. He is also the representative of the House of Commons in its external relations with the Crown, the House of Lords, and other authorities and persons outside Parliament. The quality most essential to a Speaker is strict impartiality, and in the House of Commons (although not in all the Parliaments of the Commonwealth) a member who accepts the office retires permanently from the political arena. One of his most important duties is to protect the rights of minorities and to ensure that their voices are heard. All members look to him for guidance in matters of procedure, and he decides points of order and gives rulings when required. These rulings constitute precedents by which subsequent Speakers are guided. A Speaker's ruling may not be questioned, and the conduct of the Speaker may only be debated upon a substantive motion (q.v.). So great is the prestige attaching to the office that an affront to the Speaker is an affront to the House as a whole. Much has been written of the personal qualities required for the Speakership, but perhaps they are best summarized in a newspaper article quoted by Viscount Ullswater, who himself occupied the Chair of the House of Commons as Speaker Lowther: 'The office of Speaker does not demand rare qualities. It demands common qualities in a rare degree.'

The Speaker is the guardian of the privileges of the House and it is through him that the Commons claim and enjoy their right of access to the Sovereign. As the servant of the House he executes all its orders, such as the punishment of those found guilty of breach of privilege (q.v.). His authority is derived partly from custom and precedent and partly from the Standing Orders (q.v.) of the House, which clearly indicate certain duties, such as the punishment of unruly behaviour and the checking of irrelevance in debate.

The Speaker does not vote in the House except in the event of the numbers in a division being equal, in which case he is expected, if possible, to vote in such a manner as to leave the matter open for further consideration. He takes no part in debates, although according to certain precedents it is permissible for him to do so when the House is in committee. No Speaker has exercised the right since 1870, however, and for all practical purposes it may be regarded as obsolete.

The Speaker is possessed of wide discretionary powers, and in addition to interpreting the law of Parliament he is called upon to decide such matters as whether or not a *prima facie* case has been established when a breach of privilege is complained of, or whether a motion to adjourn the House 'for the purpose of discussing a specific and important matter that should have urgent consideration' conforms to the provisions of the appropriate Standing Order. He also has a number of duties imposed on him by statute: for instance, under the Parliament Act, 1911 (q.v.), he is responsible for deciding which Bills are Money Bills (q.v.) and he must certify them before they are sent to the Lords.

Until 1919 the Speaker of the House of Commons ranked as the first commoner in the land. Under an Order in Council of 30 May 1919, he takes precedence immediately after the Lord President of the Council (q.v.). He is provided with a residence within the Palace of Westminster and is the only subject who holds levees which are attended in Court dress.

On entering and leaving the Chamber the Speaker is attended by a traditional ceremonial procession in which he is always preceded by the Serjeant-at-Arms (q.v.) bearing the Mace (q.v.) upon his shoulder. While the Speaker is in the Chair the Mace lies upon the Table of the House. During the performance of his office the Speaker wears a full-bottomed wig and Court dress under a black silk gown. A gold-embroidered ceremonial gown is kept for special occasions such as the Opening of Parliament (q.v.).

Attempts have been made in the past to establish a convention which would ensure an unopposed return to a Speaker seeking re-election at a General Election, but recent trends have indicated a marked tendency to discount this custom. Since the Reform Act the Speaker has been opposed in his constituency on seven occasions—in 1885, 1895, 1935, 1945, 1950, 1955 and 1964. In 1951 and 1959 the Speaker did not seek re-election, while in 1950 and 1955 his opponent was without official party backing. In 1964, however, Sir Harry Hylton-Foster was opposed by official candidates of the Labour and Liberal Parties, indicating a change in the attitudes of those parties to the question. The fact that at the time Conservative Speakers had been in continuous occupation of the Chair since 1928 may well have had a bearing on the matter. However, following Sir Harry's untimely death in 1965, a Labour Speaker, Dr. Horace King, was elected to the Chair unanimously, and at the elections of 1966 and 1970 he was not opposed in his constituency by either a Conservative or a Liberal candidate, although his seat was contested by Independents. The election of Dr. King, the first Labour Speaker to succeed to the office, was something of a milestone in the history of the Speakership.

It is an established principle that any Speaker who takes part in a General Election does not participate in political campaigning. The Speaker must be a Member of Parliament (although there are certain

Commonwealth Parliaments which do not apply this rule), but it has been suggested that the Speaker's constituency is denied proper representation because of the restraint imposed upon his parliamentary activities by virtue of his office. Remedies which have been put forward, and which were considered by a Select Committee which sat in 1938, are that the Speaker's should be a two-membered constituency or that some fictitious constituency should be created which he should always represent. It seems unlikely, however, that any change will be made to the position which obtains at present.

ELECTION OF SPEAKER. The Speaker is elected by the Members of the House of Commons from amongst themselves. He is elected at the beginning of every new Parliament, but it is customary to re-elect the Speaker of the former Parliament should he be returned to the House. The office is therefore normally held until retirement or death. When electing a new Speaker it is usual and desirable for the Government and the Opposition to agree upon a candidate and elect him to the Chair unanimously. He is normally proposed by a Government back-bencher and seconded by an Opposition back-bencher. Sometimes, however, as in 1895 and more recently in 1951, there is a contested election when the parties fail to agree upon a candidate. When the election of a Speaker takes place, the Clerk of the House (q.v.) acts as presiding officer and indicates the proposer by pointing to him. The proposer then moves that his candidate 'do take the Chair of this House as Speaker', and after he has spoken the Clerk indicates the seconder in the same manner. The custom of pointing to instead of calling upon the proposer and seconder signifies that the House has no voice while it is without a Speaker. If the election is contested a similar motion is made and seconded on behalf of the rival candidate, and a debate ensues which usually ends in a division. It is the custom under these circumstances for each candidate to vote in favour of his rival.

Although the election of the Speaker was not contested in 1959, a dispute arose between the Conservative and Labour Parties over the manner of the nomination of the candidate. The Conservative majority had indicated that they would have been prepared to support an Opposition nominee, but when the member who would have been acceptable to them declined to allow his name to go forward, the Conservatives proposed a candidate from their own ranks. The Leader of the Opposition, Mr. Gaitskell, expressed his party's resentment at the fact that the Conservatives had refused to consider an alternative candidate from the Labour benches, and claimed 'that on this occasion there was a peculiarly strong case for such a man to have been chosen from the Opposition benches'. (Hansard, vol. 612, col. 7).

When the Speaker elect has been chosen, he expresses his sense of the honour it is proposed to confer upon him and submits himself to the will of the House. It was formerly the custom for the chosen member to protest his unworthiness for the office, sometimes at great length. He even went further and, until the custom was broken by Speaker Onslow (q.v.) in 1728, the Speaker elect would offer physical resistance to his proposer and seconder when they came to conduct him to the Chair with the result that he was actually dragged to it. This custom had its origin in the genuine reluctance with which Speakers of former times often accepted office. So many came to grief through offending the King in the course of duty that the Speakership became a most unpopular appointment. To-day a Speaker elect contents himself with a token show of reluctance more akin to modesty.

When he has been conducted to the Chair, the Speaker elect, standing on the upper step of the dais, once again expresses his thanks and appreciation to the House, after which he takes his seat. The Mace, which has meanwhile been resting in the brackets beneath the Table, is now laid upon the Table, and the Speaker elect is congratulated by leading members on all sides of the House. When he leaves the House after it adjourns he is not preceded by the Mace because his appointment requires the Royal Approbation before it is confirmed. The following day the Speaker elect takes the Chair and awaits the arrival of the Gentleman Usher of the Black Rod (q.v.) to summon him to the House of Lords. Attended by Members of the Commons and preceded by the Serjeant-at-Arms bearing the Mace in the crook of his arm, he proceeds to the Bar of the House of Lords where he acquaints the Lords Commissioners (q.v.): 'That in obedience to Her Majesty's command, Her Majesty's most faithful Commons have, in the exercise of their undoubted right and privileges, proceeded to the election of a Speaker', and submits himself with all humility, as the Speaker elect, to Her Majesty's gracious approbation. The Royal Approbation is confirmed by the Lord Chancellor (q.v.); the only instance of its being refused was in the case of Sir Edward Seymour in 1678. The Speaker then claims on behalf of the Commons 'all their ancient and undoubted rights and privileges', which being confirmed he retires, together with the members who attended him and the Serjeant-at-Arms who this time bears the Mace upon his shoulder. During the proceedings described above the Speaker elect wears a small bob-wig. On his return to the Commons he retires for a brief period to change into the full-bottomed wig which he will normally wear.

HISTORY OF THE SPEAKERSHIP. The roll of Speakers, from Sir Thomas Hungerford, who was appointed Speaker in 1377 and was the first to be so designated, is almost unbroken. Earlier presiding officers were variously styled 'parlour', 'prolocutor', and 'procurator', and Dasent's catalogue of Speakers gives Peter de Montfort, who apparently presided over the Mad Parliament (q.v.) at Oxford in 1258, as the earliest on record. Sir Peter de la Mare, who immediately preceded Hungerford, was Speaker in all but name, and in an interesting article in *Parliamentary Affairs* (vol. XVIII, no. 1, 1964/5) Mr. Enoch Powell presses the claims of Henry de Keighley to recognition as an early Speaker for the rôle he played in the Parliament of 1301. The principal function of the Speaker in those early days was to act as the mouthpiece of the Commons and to communicate their resolutions to the King. It was often an unenviable task, and at least nine Speakers are known to have died a violent death, four of them during the turbulent period of the Wars of the Roses. On the other hand, the Speaker frequently turned out to be a King's man, and in the Tudor period he is described by Stubbs as being 'the manager of business on the part of the Crown and probably the nominee either of the King himself or the Chancellor'. He frequently held high office in addition to the Speakership. It has been suggested that the practice of the Speaker vacating the Chair when the House goes into committee owes its origin to the mistrust once felt by the Commons for their presiding officer, but there is little evidence to support this theory. The Speaker was entitled to participate in committee proceedings himself, so that the fact of his vacating the Chair would not of itself have prevented him from carrying tales to the King. However, the Speaker had no control over debate when the House was in committee, so that the Commons enjoyed greater freedom of debate and were less vulnerable to manipulations of procedure when the Speaker was out of the Chair.

The reign of Charles I saw the climax to the struggle between Crown and Commons and the establishment of the principle that the Speaker's first duty is to the House. In the early years of that reign the Speaker was still the King's minion, as evidenced by Speaker Finch's rebuke to an angry House: 'I am not less the King's servant for being yours.' But when in 1642 the King came to the House attended by an armed escort and demanded of Speaker Lenthall (q.v.) the surrender of five members on a charge of treason, Lenthall's famous reply left no doubt as to where the Speaker's first duty lay. Falling on his knees he said: 'May it please Your Majesty, I have neither eyes to see, nor tongue to speak in this place, but as the House is pleased to direct me, whose servant I am here, and I humbly beg Your Majesty's pardon that I cannot give any other answer than this to what Your Majesty is pleased to demand of me.'

Attempts on the part of the Crown to interfere with the appointment to the Speakership did not entirely cease subsequent to this historic occasion, but they never met with any marked success. For instance, when Charles II refused to confirm the election of Sir Edward Seymour he failed to secure the election of his own candidate and was forced to compromise with the Commons on a third choice. The Commons had won the struggle and no Speaker was ever again to be a mere creature of the Crown.

The Speaker continued to have strong associations with the Government until the election of Speaker Onslow in 1728. He resigned the office of Treasurer of the Navy, which had come to be regarded as a perquisite of the Speakership, and contented himself with the proceeds of fees from Private Bills. To this great Speaker, whose term of office continued until 1761, is due the credit for setting the high standards which are to-day associated with the office. Although Onslow's level was not at first maintained by his successors, it is to him that we can trace the development of the Speakership in its modern form.

The principle of the continuity of the Speaker's office and its final removal from the arena of partisanship was established in 1841 when the Liberal Speaker Shaw-Lefevre was re-elected by a House controlled by a Conservative majority. Six years previously a Whig majority had refused to re-elect the Conservative Speaker Manners-Sutton, and in 1841 there were a number of Conservatives who were inclined to take retaliatory action. They were restrained from doing so by Sir Robert Peel, who gave five important reasons in favour of Shaw-Lefevre's re-election:

First, I do not think it for the public advantage that the election for the Chair should necessarily be made the object of a party.

Secondly, I do not think it would be just towards a Speaker who has shown himself well qualified for his office, and has in my opinion acted fairly and impartially, to reject him.

Thirdly, I think the late Speaker, if he be re-elected with the general goodwill of the House, will have greater authority and power to preserve order than a Speaker elected after a party contest.

Fourthly, I do not think we have any person to propose who would appear to advantage as Speaker, all things considered, when compared with Lefevre.

Fifthly, it is not a very high or satisfactory ground to allege for opposing Shaw-Lefevre that the Whigs and Radicals opposed Lord Canterbury [Manners-Sutton]. We said it was unjust and unpolitic to oppose Lord Canterbury, and it seems to me more becoming to a great party to act upon its own principle, and even apply it against itself, than to say to its opponents —'Though our principle was the right one, yet by way of retaliation we will adopt yours.'

In recent years successive Speakers have upheld and increased the prestige attaching to the Chair of the House of Commons and have successfully resisted all assaults upon its dignity. Perhaps the most notable instance in this connexion was the action taken by Speaker Brand (q.v.) in 1881 in applying the closure (q.v.) on his own responsibility as the only effective means of opposing the deliberately obstructive tactics of the Irish Nationalists. Brand's own words are worth quoting here: 'The usual rules have proved powerless to ensure

[709]

orderly and effective debate. . . . The dignity, the credit, and the authority of this House are seriously threatened, and it is necessary that they should be vindicated.' Brand's action was firmly endorsed, and shortly afterwards the discretionary powers of the Speaker were greatly extended.

It is no exaggeration to describe the development of the Speakership as a great and truly British achievement. It is a tribute to the fair-mindedness and democratic spirit of the nation that the office is held in such high regard. To-day the Speaker is the House of Commons' man in the strictest sense. Once elected, he forgets party affiliations and is immune to external influences in any form. His salary equates with that of a Cabinet Minister. In 1834 it was fixed by statute at £5,000 per annum, at which figure it remained until 1957 when, in common with all other Members of the House of Commons, his emoluments were increased by £750. In 1964, as a part of a general revision of parliamentary salaries and allowances, the Speaker's salary was increased to £8,500 plus a parliamentary allowance of £1,250. On retirement he is normally honoured with a viscounty and voted a pension of £4,000, an arbitrary figure which has not varied since 1832. In 1964 it was proposed that the Speaker's pension be fixed at £6,000, but the Government preferred that it should be decided by the House, as in the past, at the time of a Speaker's retirement.

A chronological list of Speakers appears as Appendix 5.

THE SPEAKERSHIP IN OTHER COMMONWEALTH PARLIAMENTS. The tradition of the Speakership has been inherited by Parliaments through-out the Commonwealth, but usually with certain modifications. Whilst in the Chair the functions of a Speaker overseas correspond with those of the Speaker of the House of Commons, and similar ceremonial attends his entering and leaving the Chamber. The dissociation of the Speaker from party politics, however, has not been achieved throughout the Commonwealth in so complete a manner as has been found possible in Great Britain. It is common for the Speaker to enter the political field when he is not occupying the Chair, and the continuity of office which has become an established principle of the Speakership of the House of Commons irrespective of any change of government, is not a feature of the appointment in many other Parliaments. In Ceylon, Australia, and New Zealand, for instance, the Speakership is regarded as a privilege of the party in power, and the occupant of the Chair usually changes with the Government. The Speaker is generally opposed in his constituency during a General Election, and fights for his seat like any other candidate. In some Parliaments, when the House goes into committee the Speaker does not necessarily refrain from taking part in debates and voting in divisions. It is possible that in these relatively small Parliaments which are accustomed to precarious majorities the

Speaker's vote in committee is regarded as too important to sacrifice. Although the subject of much criticism, this system does not necessarily reflect upon the impartiality of the Chair. It is still possible for an active politician to discharge the duties of Speaker with fairness, although it is unlikely that he can acquire the same position of detachment and prestige which characterizes the Speaker of the House of Commons and which is such a desirable attribute of the office.

In Canada an important precedent was established in June 1968 with the re-election of the Speaker in his constituency as an Independent with the support of the two major parties. He was subsequently re-elected to the Chair unanimously on a motion of the Prime Minister, seconded by the Leader of the Opposition. The principle of the independence of the Speakership having been established in Canada, it remains to promote the continuity of the office, the successful accomplishment of which will depend on further agreements between the political parties. In the past it had been the custom, although not an invariable one, for the Speaker to change with each Parliament, an English-speaking Speaker alternating with a French-speaking Speaker. Prior to 1968 the Speakership had sometimes been regarded as a stepping-stone to higher office and had tended to remain dependent to some extent on party patronage. Until recently the Speaker was also at a disadvantage because all his rulings were subject to appeal from the Floor of the House, and there are recent instances of a Speaker's ruling being overturned by a vote in the House. This rule was invariably used for political purposes, without regard for precedent or good procedure, and was an ever-present threat to the Speaker's authority. The very fact of invoking the rule could be damaging, for at worst it could reverse the Speaker's considered judgment, while at best it called upon a party majority to sustain it. The ill effects of this rule were emphasized during the notorious pipeline debate of 1956, when the Speaker was dragged into the thick of a most heated political conflict to find himself fighting a procedural battle on behalf of the Government against a hostile Opposition. Twenty-five rulings from the Chair were challenged during eighteen days of acrimonious debate which culminated in the only motion of censure against a Speaker ever known in the Canadian House of Commons. The rule permitting appeals from Speaker's rulings was abolished provisionally in 1965 and on a permanent basis in 1968.

In Australia the Speakership has long been regarded as a political appointment, and while some Australian Speakers have striven to discharge their duties with impartiality, others have been openly partisan. Provision exists in the Australian House of Representatives for challenging a Speaker's ruling and, as with the Canadian experience, there is no evidence to suggest that the existence of such a rule is anything other than inimical to the promotion of good procedure. It is significant that in neighbouring New Zealand, where there is no such rule, relations between the Chair and the Opposition have been consistently good.

The Indian Speakership, originally patterned on the British model, has developed in accordance with local requirements along more individualistic lines. Indian parliamentary procedure varies in many respects quite radically from that of Westminster, and the influence of the Speaker has been the most important single factor in its evolution since independence. Indian parliamentarians repose great confidence in their Speaker, to whom wide discretionary powers are entrusted in relation to procedural matters. Mr. Speaker Dhillon was the first Indian Speaker to resign from membership of his party on being elected to the Chair in August 1969.

The constitution of Uganda provides that the Speaker may be chosen either from among the members of the National Assembly or from outside Parliament. The same provision has long existed in Rhodesia under both the Constitutions of 1923 and 1961. This principle can usefully be adopted in a small legislature where the appointment of a Speaker from the sitting membership can make a big and even a vital difference to the voting strength. The Standing Orders of the Rhodesian Parliament which were revised some time before the Unilateral Declaration of Independence provide that the Speaker has neither an original nor a casting vote.

In the newer states of the Commonwealth the Speakership, while superficially modelled on that of Westminster, is not invariably in accord with the British concept of the office. Although the parliamentary system operates in most Commonwealth countries in one form or another, concepts of politics and government in many of these countries differ radically from those of the West, and it has therefore been found necessary to adapt the institutions which have been inherited from Britain to the requirements of local political reality. As far as the Speakership is concerned, it would be difficult to form any general conclusions as to likely evolutionary trends in the newer states of the Commonwealth, particularly those of Africa. An interesting provision exists in the Constitution of Singapore whereby a Speaker cannot be removed from office save through a dissolution of Parliament.

The costume of the Speaker of the House of Commons is usually worn by the Speakers of the older Commonwealth Parliaments, with local variations. The Speaker of the Canadian House of Commons wears neither wig nor knee-breeches, but he wears a tricorne hat when in procession. Wig and gown are normally worn by the Australian Speaker, although they are dispensed with when the Labour Party is in power in deference to the party's distaste for such special insignia of office. The Indian Speaker wears no special costume, although this example has not invariably been followed by the other Commonwealth states of Asia and Africa, where a wig or gown or both usually feature in the costume of the Speaker. The costume of the Rhodesian Speaker most exactly resembles that of his counterpart at Westminster.

The Legislative Assembly of British Columbia created an interesting precedent in 1950 by appointing the Commonwealth's first woman Speaker, Mrs. Nancy Hodges, an example which was followed by the legislature of Manitoba in 1963 with the appointment of Mrs. Thelma Forbes.

During the comparatively recent years when most of Britain's former Colonies had yet to attain independence, it was frequently the custom for the colonial Governor to preside over the legislature, and the appointment of a Speaker came to be regarded as a symbol of a Colony's constitutional progress.

(Further reading: Dasent, *Speakers of the House of Commons*, 1911; Laundy, *The Office of Speaker*, 1964; MacDonagh, *Speaker of the House*, 1914.)

SPEAKER, HOUSE OF LORDS

The Lord Chancellor (q.v.) acts as Speaker of the House of Lords, and in this capacity he receives a salary of £4,000. He does not exert the same authority and disciplinary powers in the regulation of debate as the Speaker of the House of Commons.

SPEAKER'S CHAIR

An essential and imposing article of furniture in the House of Commons and many other legislative chambers. It stands upon a dais and is so situated as to afford its occupant a commanding view of the entire Chamber. The present Speaker's Chair in the House of Commons was the gift of the Australian Federal Parliament. It is a magnificent specimen of the art of the woodcarver, and as one would expect of such a chair, is fully in keeping with the dignity and authority of the office of Speaker.

It has become customary for the House of Commons to present an article of parliamentary furniture to other Commonwealth Parliaments to mark a significant event such as the attainment of national independence. A Speaker's Chair was the gift selected when Ghana and Tanganyika became independent, and also when the Federation of Malaysia was formed.

SPEAKER'S CHAPLAIN

The first regular chaplain to the House of Commons was appointed in 1659. In the time of William III the custom was adopted of providing for the chaplain at the termination of his office by obtaining for him from the Crown an appointment to a benefice, but it was abandoned in 1835 owing to the opposition of Hume. Since then the chaplain has been nominated by the Speaker, and he receives a nominal salary. He takes part in the Speaker's daily procession into the House and conducts prayers before the commencement of each sitting. There is an old parliamentary joke to the effect that the chaplain looks at the assembled Members of Parliament and prays for the country.

See also PRAYERS IN PARLIAMENT.

SPEAKER'S CHOP

The term applied to an unofficial adjournment of the House which was instituted in the 19th century to enable the Speaker to have his dinner. Nowadays the Speaker can be relieved by a deputy at any time without the specific leave of the House and there has ceased to be any necessity for such an institution.

According to Sir Henry Lucy, a member who was mentally deranged once went behind the Chair and 'tried to eat the Speaker's chop' !

The 'Speaker's chop' was reinstituted for a short period in 1924 as the result of a difficult constitutional situation which arose after the General Election of December 1923. Although the Conservative Party had been defeated in the election by the combined strength of the Liberal and Labour parties, it still remained the largest single group represented in the House of Commons. The Prime Minister, Stanley Baldwin, therefore decided to remain in office until such time as his Government sustained a defeat in the House of Commons. When Parliament met Baldwin proposed the re-election of the Chairman of Ways and Means and Deputy Chairman, but the leader of the Labour Party, Ramsay Macdonald, warned him that under the circumstances the appointments would not be allowed to pass without a division. The matter was therefore left in abeyance, and there being no Deputy Speaker to relieve the Speaker, the House reverted temporarily to the practice of allowing a break in the proceedings to afford the Speaker an opportunity to partake of refreshment.

SPEAKER'S CONFERENCES

The term 'Speaker's Conference' is normally used to denote a conference of Members of Parliament meeting under the chairmanship of the Speaker of the House of Commons to consider questions of electoral reform. The first such conference was held in 1916 and its recommendations were subsequently embodied in the Representation of the People Act, 1918, which implemented the most sweeping electoral reforms since 1832. They included the partial enfranchisement of women, the introduction of a simple franchise based on residence or the occupation of business premises, the modification of the registration system, the redistribution of seats on an equitable basis, and the introduction of the condition which requires a parliamentary candidate to deposit £150 with the returning officer.

In 1929 Lord Ullswater who, as Speaker Lowther had presided over the 1916 conference, was called out of retirement to preside over another conference which considered proportional representation (q.v.) and the alternative vote (q.v.), but after fifteen sittings it was unable to agree on any recommendations.

The third Speaker's Conference on electoral reform was convened in 1944, receiving its stimulus, like the first, from the circumstances arising out of a World War. It considered the redistribution of seats, the reform of the franchise (both parliamentary and local government), election expenses and methods of election. This conference overwhelmingly rejected the introduction of proportional representation and the alternative vote, but made certain recommendations regarding redistribution which were eventually embodied in the House of Commons (Redistribution of Seats) Act, 1949, which established the four permanent Boundary Commissions for England, Scotland, Wales and Northern Ireland. Its recommendations respecting the retention of the business and university franchises and the preservation of the City of London as a two-member constituency were not destined to find acceptance, and the Representation of the People Act, 1948, established a single franchise based on residence, all constituencies returning a single member.

On 12 May 1965 the Speaker announced the terms of reference of a further conference on electoral reform, which included the reform of the franchise in particular relation to the minimum voting age and registration procedure generally, methods of election including preferential voting, and the conduct of elections with particular reference to such matters as absent voting, polling hours, election expenses, undue influences and the use of broadcasting. It was open to Members of Parliament, party organizations and other bodies to submit representations to the conference on matters falling within its terms of reference. The appointment of an Electoral Advisory Conference, consisting of representatives of Government Departments, registration officers and the representatives of political parties, to consider detailed questions of election procedure was announced at the same time. One of the recommendations to emerge from this conference on electoral reform was the reduction of the voting age to twenty, but the Representation of the People Act passed in 1969 went further and reduced it to eighteen.

In 1919–20 a conference was held under the chairmanship of the Speaker on a matter other than electoral reform, namely, the devolution of powers to subordinate legislatures within Great Britain. Although it published a report, the conference failed to reach satisfactory conclusions, and the matter was not further proceeded with.

In June 1965 a Conference of Commonwealth Speakers was held in London, and similar conferences (this time including the presiding officers of upper Chambers) were held in Ottawa in September 1966 and September 1969. Regular conferences are also held among the federal and state or provincial Speakers in Canada, Australia, India and Malaysia, and among the Speakers, Presiding Officers and Clerks of the Commonwealth countries of the Caribbean.

SPEAKER'S COUNSEL

First appointed in 1838 as the result of a recommendation made by the Select Committee on Private Business in the session of 1837/8. He advises the Chairman of Ways and Means on Private Bill legislation, and is a member of the Court of Referees (q.v.). He acts as legal adviser to the Statutory Instruments Committee, and has the general duty of advising the Speaker on any point of law not concerned with procedure. He also acts as Chairman of the Model Clauses Committee (q.v.) and is available to members seeking advice on statutory instruments (q.v.) and other legal matters connected with the government of the country. The present salary of the Speaker's Counsel (1970) is £6,000 a year.

In the House of Lords the Lord Chairman of Committees also has the assistance of a counsel who performs a function similar to that of the Speaker's Counsel, and who also acts as adviser to the Special Orders Committee.

SPEAKER'S PROCESSION

It is the custom in Commonwealth Parliaments for some ceremony to be observed in the passage of the Speaker from his office or apartments to the Chair at the commencement of a sitting. The formal procession in the House of Commons is led by a Badge Messenger followed by the Serjeant-at-Arms with the Mace, the Speaker, his train-bearer, and finally his chaplain and secretary. In other Parliaments the Clerks often take the place of the chaplain and secretary in the procession.

During the last war, when the Commons' Chamber was destroyed and they were using the Lords' Chamber, the Speaker's procession had to take a longer route through the Central Hall. This was very popular and enabled many visitors to see the procession, and now that the Chamber of the House of Commons has been rebuilt the longer route has been retained instead of returning to the shorter pre-war route, which only crossed the Members' Lobby.

No account of the origin of the Speaker's procession would seem to be extant. However, in view of the parliamentary custom of commencing each day's proceedings with a prayer, the procession may originally have been associated with some more elaborate form of worship. Alternatively, it may owe its origin to the necessity which existed in more turbulent times for protecting the Speaker's person, and the inclusion in the procession of the Serjeant-at-Arms with the Mace would seem to strengthen this possibility.

SPEAKERS' RULINGS

Lord Campion has described Speakers' rulings as the third main basis of procedure (q.v.), the other two being the 'practice of the House' and the Standing Orders (q.v.). He points out that some Standing Orders give the Chair discretionary powers and others lay down mandatory rules which it is the duty of the Chair, as of other members, to follow. However, cases arise which contain some element of doubt or some feature which was not foreseen or provided for by the Standing Order in question. When in such cases disagreement arises among members as to the application of the Standing Order, it becomes the duty of the Speaker or Chairman to explain the interpretation he puts upon it—in other words to 'give a ruling from the Chair'. All rulings are preserved for future reference as precedents, and during the last hundred years have been printed for official use. The more important rulings are incorporated into successive editions of Erskine May's *Parliamentary Practice*.

SPEAKERS' SALARIES

See APPENDIX 2.

SPEAKER'S STATE COACH

The oldest of the three great ceremonial coaches, the others being the Royal State Coach and the Lord Mayor's Coach, used by the Speaker of the House of Commons on special state occasions such as the coronation of a new Sovereign. It was built in 1698, weighs $2\frac{3}{4}$ tons, and is lavishly ornamented. Not every Speaker has the opportunity of using the coach, but the coats of arms of those who have used it are inscribed upon it.

When in use it is drawn by brewers' dray-horses, a custom which originated from the relationship between a former Speaker and the brewing firm of Whitbreads. The coachman is a drayman and the footmen are stablemen from Whitbread's brewery.

SPECIALIST COMMITTEES

Until recently the appointment of select committees (q.v.) to investigate special subject areas was not a normal practice in the House of Commons, mainly because the consideration of questions of policy had not been regarded in the past as a suitable function of a select committee. However, committees such as the Estimates Committee and the Select Committee on Nationalized Industries (qq.v.) have experienced ever-increasing difficulty in separating the consideration of policy from the consideration of efficient management in respect of the departments and undertakings which come under their scrutiny. In December 1965 a concession to subject specialization was made when the Estimates Committee reorganized its sub-committees upon this basis.

The House itself first gave its endorsement to the principle of specialist committees in December 1966 when two new select committees were appointed on an experimental basis: a Select Committee to consider the activities in England and Wales of the Ministry of Agriculture, Fisheries and Food and a Select Committee to consider Science and Technology. The Leader of the House, Mr. Richard Crossman, in moving for the appointment of these committees, acknowledged that the time had come when back-bench members should be given a share in the investigation of government policies. He agreed that the distinction between administration and policy is often very blurred, and that this blurring had enabled the Select Committee on Nationalized Industries to do its most valuable work.

The Agriculture Committee was later discontinued, but other specialist committees appointed subsequently included one on Scottish Affairs, one on Education and Science and one on Race Relations and Immigration. When a new Parliament was opened in 1970 the future of the specialist committees remained in doubt. However, a Green Paper published in October 1970 entitled 'Select Committees of the House of Commons' (Cmnd. 4507) proposed that certain specialist committees should continue to be appointed and that they should operate alongside a new Select Committee on Expenditure (*see* EXPENDITURE, SELECT COMMITTEE ON). The Green Paper was debated on 12 November 1970 and its proposals received the qualified endorsement of the House.

In the Canadian House of Commons the appointment of specialist committees has long been an established practice. At the present time (1970) there are a number of standing committees, appointed sessionally under a standing order, each having terms of reference corresponding with the jurisdiction of one or more government departments. The subjects covered by these committees include the entire range of government responsibilities, and since 1968, in addition to dealing with *ad hoc* investigations, Bills and departmental Estimates have been automatically referred to them. These committees are empowered to consider matters of policy, and ministers regularly appear before them, very often making important policy statements.

SPECIAL ORDER

A term in use in the House of Lords denoting a statutory instrument (q.v.) which requires affirmative resolutions of both Houses to give it the force of law. Erskine May describes special orders, as originally introduced in 1919, as 'a minor variant upon the provisional order system', the difference between a special order and a provisional order being that the former required affirmative resolutions and the latter a confirming Bill (*see* PROVISIONAL ORDER BILL). To-day this definition does not exactly fit the term as it is understood in the House of Lords. In 1924 the upper House set up a Special Orders Committee whose function was, and is, to examine all rules and orders requiring affirmative resolutions of both Houses and to report to the House on any questions of principle, policy, and precedent which such rules and orders might raise. These statutory instruments have become known in the House of Lords as special orders, and the affirmative resolutions required to give them the sanction of the upper House may not be moved until the Special Orders Committee has reported on them.

SPECIAL PROCEDURE ORDER

A statutory order issued by a minister in terms of the Statutory Orders (Special Procedure) Act, 1945. Special procedure orders are made in connexion with matters which would otherwise require private legislation, and they have largely superseded (except in Scotland) the provisional order system which was itself originally introduced as a means of reducing the volume of Private Bills (q.v., *and see also* PROVISIONAL ORDER BILL). The Statutory Orders (Special Procedure) Act, 1945, provides a simplified machinery for conferring powers upon local authorities and other bodies. Under the provisional order procedure an Act of Parliament is required to confirm each order issued, but the special procedure order has dispensed with this necessity and parliamentary confirmation is not normally required to give such an order the force of law. Copies of all special procedure orders must, however, be laid before both Houses, and any order can be annulled by resolution of either House. As with provisional orders, special procedure orders must be given all necessary publicity, and parties whose interests are affected by an order must be notified and are entitled to petition against it. A petition may be one of general objection or it may merely pray for amendment. Petitions of the latter class, once they have been certified by the Lord Chairman and the Chairman of Ways and Means as 'proper to be received', are referred for consideration to a Joint Committee consisting of 3 members from each House, unless a motion for annulling the order concerned has previously been carried. A petition of general objection is normally considered in the House itself, but it may be referred to a Joint Committee if either House considers that it requires more detailed scrutiny. A resolution to annul a special procedure order may be moved notwithstanding that no petition has been presented against it.

[719]

SPEECHES IN PARLIAMENT

Until the time of the elder Pitt speeches in the House of Commons were not notable for their length. His orations, however, made the 2- or 3-hour speech popular with parliamentarians, and by 1831 Lord Brougham brought the trend to a climax with a 6-hour speech on law reform. Chancellors of the Exchequer have more excuse than others for making long speeches, and Gladstone when occupying that office in 1853 achieved 5 hours, while Lloyd George did nearly as well with 4 hours 51 minutes when introducing his Budget in 1909. The longest speech in recent years on the part of a House of Commons back-bencher was made by Mr. M. K. Macmillan on 15–16 March 1961 when he spoke for 157 minutes.

Speeches must always be addressed to the Chair, and in Commonwealth Parliaments are made from the member's place—in many foreign Parliaments members leave their seats and speak from a rostrum. The reading of written speeches has never been recognized in the British Parliament, although it has been allowed in Australia since 1963. Members may use notes and read extracts from documents, while ministers sometimes read statements when they are of an abstruse nature, but generally speaking the language used by a member must be delivered in the form of an unwritten composition. The purpose of this rule is primarily to maintain the cut and thrust of debate, which depends on successive speakers moulding their speeches to some extent upon the arguments of earlier speeches. The House of Lords has shown more tolerance to the reading of speeches than the lower House, although they recommended in 1641 'that reading of formal Speeches and Answers out of Papers in this House is no Parliamentary way'. Nearly three hundred years later their Lordships had to take notice of the question again, and in 1936 approved a resolution: 'That in the opinion of this House the growing practice of reading speeches is to be deprecated as alien to the custom of the House and injurious to the traditional conduct of its debates.' Their Lordships also approved a motion by Lord Egremont on 13 July 1965 that speeches in the House should be shorter, although the mover did not press for any definite time-limits.

Most of the Parliaments of the Commonwealth impose time-limits on speeches, the United Kingdom Parliament being the notable exception. These limitations vary according to the nature of the business under discussion—e.g., in Australia 45 minutes are allowed to the mover of the second reading of a Bill and other members may speak for 30 minutes on these occasions, while on a motion for allotment of time when urgent business is to be discussed a member is only allowed 5 minutes. Speech-timing clocks with a single hand are operated by the Deputy Clerk, who moves the hands on the clocks on each side of the

[720]

Chamber to indicate the number of minutes allowed for a particular speech. As the time is used up, the hands return in an anti-clockwise direction to the zero or twelve o'clock position. A warning light appears on the clock faces when there is one minute to go. In the Indian House of the People the Speaker may prescribe a time-limit for speeches after taking the sense of the House. The Queensland Legislative Assembly imposed no time-limit on speeches until a member took advantage of the fact to speak for eleven hours. A system of light signals for timing speeches is described under RHODESIAN PARLIAMENT.

SPEECH FROM THE THRONE
See DEBATE ON THE ADDRESS.

'SPYING STRANGERS'
See SECRET SESSION; STRANGERS.

STAGES OF BILLS
See BILL, PASSAGE OF.

STANDING COMMITTEES

The committee stages of Bills other than Money Bills are normally considered in Standing Committees, which are miniature Committees of the Whole House in which relative party strengths are preserved and the same procedure and rules of debate observed. The debates of Standing Committees are recorded verbatim and the public are admitted to their sittings except in the rare event of a Standing Committee ordering otherwise.

Until 1882 the committee stages of all Bills were taken in Committee of the Whole House. Standing Committees originated under the pressure of Irish obstruction, and were brought into being on the simple calculation that two committees could deal with twice as much work as one. Originally only 2 Standing Committees were appointed. In 1907 their number was increased to 4 and in 1919 to 6. They are now appointed under Standing Order No. 59 and since 1947 no limit has been placed on their number. In practice, owing to the limitations imposed by the availability of staff and accommodation, 9 are the maximum number which have ever sat simultaneously.

Under Standing Order No. 40 (1) all Bills other than Money Bills are automatically referred to Standing Committees after second reading unless the House orders otherwise. If a Bill is referred to a Committee of the Whole House, as is usual in the case of Bills which are highly controversial or of great national importance, the necessary motion is normally made immediately after second reading. The appointment of members to Standing Committees is made by the Committee of Selection (q.v.), and with the exceptions of the committees specifically concerned with Scotland and Wales, each Standing Committee consists of not less than 16 nor more than 50 members appointed specifically for the consideration of each Bill allocated to it. In appointing members to Standing Committees the Committee of Selection is required to have regard to the composition of the House and the qualifications of members in relation to the Bill under consideration. The average size of a Standing Committee is 45 members and its quorum is 17 or one-third of its membership excluding the Chairman, whichever is the less. The Law Officers of the Crown are permitted to attend and speak in any Standing Committee, but may only vote or move amendments or motions in committees of which they are themselves members.

Excepting the Scottish Grand and Standing Committees and the Welsh Grand Committee (qq.v.), there is little to distinguish one Standing Committee from another. A Standing Committee has no permanence or individuality and is not, strictly speaking, a Standing Committee at all. Its composition changes with each Bill that comes before it; it is distinguished only by a letter of the alphabet; and it does not receive one type of Bill more than another. It is, however, provided that there shall be one Standing Committee in which Government business shall not have precedence, and Private Members' Bills are normally allocated to this committee. The distribution of Bills among the Standing Committees is a responsibility of the Speaker. The Scottish Standing Committee receives all Scottish Bills, and the Standing Orders also provide that for the consideration of all Bills relating exclusively to Wales and Monmouthshire the Standing Committee shall be so constituted as to comprise all members sitting for constituencies in Wales and Monmouthshire.

The Chairmen of Standing Committees are appointed by the Speaker from the Chairmen's Panel (q.v.). They exercise the same powers as the Chairman of Ways and Means in a Committee of the Whole House, including the power to select amendments and to accept or reject a closure motion. For the closure to be carried in a Standing Committee the minimum number of members required to vote with the majority corresponds to the quorum of the Committee. An allocation of time order may be made in relation to Standing Committee proceedings, but a motion proposing its application must be passed by the House itself. The same rules of decorum apply in a Standing Committee as in the House or a Committee of the Whole House. Members address the Chair standing, and may not refer to other members by name, or smoke. All members of the House have the right of access as spectators to the sittings of Standing Committees of which they are not members.

Standing Committees are entitled to meet on any day of the week from Monday to Friday inclusive, but normally meet during the mornings of Tuesday, Wednesday and Thursday. A record sitting of nearly 26 hours was set up by the Scottish Standing Committee on 21–2 May 1957.

In 1966 the Committee of the House of Lords on Procedure of the House considered the desirability of the adoption of a Standing Committee system by the House of Lords. The committee recommended against the proposal, however, mainly because it felt that it would be impossible to obtain a realistic political balance in a body which would, by its very nature, require to be a smaller replica of the House itself.

In other Commonwealth Parliaments the term 'standing committee' generally refers to Select Committees which are appointed every session, and which would be known at Westminster as Sessional Committees. Standing Committees of the precise Westminster pattern are unknown elsewhere. The practice of taking the committee stages of Bills in Committee of the Whole House is normally followed in those Commonwealth Parliaments whose legislative Chambers are much smaller numerically than the House of Commons.

STANDING ORDERS

The printed rules which regulate procedure, debate, and the conduct of members in a legislature. According to Lord Campion, the Standing Orders of the House of Commons in their process of development may be divided roughly into two groups: (1) those adopted between 1832 and 1878, the purpose of which was to give the Government rights over the order of business and the distribution of the time of the House commensurate with the increased importance of the Cabinet in the parliamentary system, and (2) those passed since 1878, which reflect the impatience of democratic governments in the face of obstacles to the achievement of a vast annual output of legislation. Before 1832 the procedure of the House of Commons formed an unwritten code based on precedent and developed by various interpretations and Speakers' rulings (q.v.). In the 18th century the financial rules were defined, and prior to their amendment in December 1966 they were the oldest of the modern Standing Orders. After 1832 precedent and improvisation were no longer adequate to provide for the increasing pressure of business, and the House began for the first time in its history deliberately to create and reform its procedure. The recommendations of numerous Select Committees appointed to examine different aspects of procedure during the 19th century became Standing Orders, where they were approved by the House, and by the end of the century those relative to Public Business had grown to nearly a hundred. There are also Standing Orders for the regulation of Private Business, and these affect every stage of a Private Bill (q.v.) prior to and after presentation. Standing Orders can be suspended by order of the House for various purposes.

The Standing Orders of the House of Lords were superimposed on the old unwritten practice of Parliament—for instance, the order forbidding a peer from making more than one speech on any motion was made a Standing Order in 1626, and was alluded to even then as the 'ancient order of the House'. A revision of the Standing Orders was made in 1888, but no radical revision had been made for nearly two hundred years until 1954, when as the result of the appointment of a Select Committee many obsolete orders were excised and some new ones added. The committee recommended that those orders which were of great historical interest but which were not now applicable should be preserved in an Appendix to the revised Standing Orders. A Companion to the Standing Orders was published in 1955.

STANDING ORDERS COMMITTEE

HOUSE OF COMMONS. The Standing Orders Committee is appointed by Standing Order each session, and consists of the Chairman of Ways and Means (who, when present, is *ex-officio* Chairman of the Committee), the Deputy Chairman, and 8 members appointed by the Committee of Selection (q.v.) at the commencement of every session. Three form the quorum, and the committee has the assistance of the Speaker's Counsel. The function of the committee is to determine whether, and to what extent, and under what conditions, compliance with Standing or Sessional Orders may be dispensed with in the case of Private or Hybrid Bills, and to perform certain other duties in relation to such Bills. They report their decisions to the House.

HOUSE OF LORDS. A similar committee is appointed at the beginning of each session in the House of Lords, consisting of the Lord Chairman of Committees (who is always Chairman of the committee), and such other Lords as are named by the House. Three peers, including the Chairman, form a quorum on opposed cases, while it is the practice on unopposed cases that one member can act alone.

Other Commonwealth Parliaments which are concerned with private legislation also appoint Standing Orders Committees.

STATUTE

A statute was originally a decree of the Sovereign. The word 'statutum' (it is decided) from which it is derived suggests the exercise of a prerogative power. To-day a statute is a law or enactment of a legislative authority, such as an Act of Parliament (q.v.).

See also CITATION OF STATUTES.

[724]

STATUTES OF WESTMINSTER

The first Statute of Westminster was passed in 1275. It laid down among other things that elections should be free and undisturbed and that girls should not be married until they were seven years old, but it seems unlikely that the elections mentioned were parliamentary. There were two more Statutes of Westminster in 1285 and 1290 dealing with such subjects as the appointment of justices of assize and the alienation of land, but *the* Statute of Westminster is the one passed in 1931 which put the status of equality of the self-governing Dominions with the United Kingdom on a statutory basis. As early as 1921, at the first Imperial Conference held after the First World War, Lloyd George said, 'They (the Dominions) have achieved full national status. They now stand beside the United Kingdom as equal partners in the dignities and the responsibilities of the British Commonwealth.' This principle received formal expression in the historical definition agreed to at the Imperial Conference at Ottawa in 1926. Describing the position and mutual relations of the group of self-governing communities composing Great Britain and the Dominions, it said, 'They are autonomous Communities within the British Empire equal in status, in no way subordinate one to another in any aspect of their domestic and external affairs, though united by a common allegiance to the Crown and freely associated as Members of the British Commonwealth of Nations.' The result of discussions at that Conference was the appointment of the Inter-Imperial Relations Committee under Lord Balfour, and its report showed that there still remained certain forms and machinery forming part of the old system of centralized control which had become obsolete. Ministers in the United Kingdom could exercise control over Dominion legislation by advising the King to disallow an Act; after it had been passed by one of the legislatures and assented to by the King's representative, the Governor-General, it could be nullified by an order from England. There was also the method of reservation, by which the Governor-General could be directed not to assent to a Bill which had been passed by the local legislature, and a Bill so reserved could not come into operation until the King's Assent had been given to it on the advice of his ministers in the United Kingdom. Another limitation of powers was a general provision embodied in the Colonial Laws Validity Act (q.v.) of 1865, the effect of which was that the Dominion law, if repugnant to a provision of a United Kingdom Act extending to the Dominion, was void to the extent to which it was repugnant—in other words, there was an overriding power in Acts of the United Kingdom. Lastly, there was a limitation to the power of Dominion Parliaments to give extra-territorial effect to their legislation. The legal problems involved in the consideration of these matters were too intricate to be dealt with by the 1926 Conference, and a special

Conference on the Operation of Dominion Legislation met in 1929, whose Report was approved and adopted by the Imperial Conference of 1930. Its recommendations were designed both to carry into full effect the principle of equality of status and to indicate methods for maintaining and strengthening the practical system of free co-operation. The 1930 Conference set out in its Report the clauses which would be required in a United Kingdom statute to remove the limitations already mentioned, and settled the procedure by which the Dominion Parliaments (Canada, Australia, New Zealand, South Africa, the Irish Free State, and Newfoundland) were to be asked to approve and request the passage of legislation by the United Kingdom Parliament. This was agreed to by the Governments concerned, and the Statute of Westminster received the Royal Assent on 11 December 1931. It is important to note that although this statute abolished the remnants of imperial legislative power, it left the Sovereign intact as the constitutional centre of the Commonwealth. Its preamble expressly states that the British Commonwealth is united by a common allegiance to the Crown, and that any alteration in the law touching the succession to the throne or the Royal Style and Titles shall require the assent of all the Parliaments of the Dominions as well as that of the United Kingdom Parliament.

To-day, however, the Commonwealth has moved beyond the Statute of Westminster. For example, it was not envisaged in 1931 that the Commonwealth would one day include republics among its members, and that these states, while recognizing the Queen as the Head of the Commonwealth, would appoint or elect their Heads of State from among their own nationals. It was in recognition of the altered structure of the Commonwealth that it was agreed in 1952 that each Commonwealth country should legislate separately, and in a manner appropriate to its own constitutional requirements, for the Royal Style and Titles.

See also SOVEREIGN.

STATUTES REVISED

See PUBLIC GENERAL ACTS.

STATUTORY INSTRUMENTS

Rules and regulations made by ministers and government departments under the authority of a statute. An Act of Parliament conferring this power always contains a section of which the following is a typical example: 'Any power conferred by this Act on the Minister to make regulations shall be exercisable by statutory instrument which shall be subject to annulment in pursuance of a resolution of either House of Parliament.'

Some Acts also give power to a statutory instrument to appoint the day on which they shall come into force; others provide for the amendment of their own schedules by statutory instrument.

Statutory instruments are classified, like statutes, as either general or local and personal. In peace-time the local instruments far outnumber the general, but in war-time the general predominate as a result of emergency legislation which gives the Government wide powers to make regulations. An example is provided by the Goods and Services (Price Control) Act, 1941, under which hundreds of regulations were made. About half the statutory instruments made are required to be laid before Parliament, and some automatically become law by an affirmative resolution of the House, generally where a major issue is concerned. In other cases a statutory instrument can be annulled if a member succeeds in moving a 'prayer' (q.v.) against it during the forty days after it has been laid, when it is vulnerable to such action. Statutory instruments cannot be amended by Parliament, although this was advocated in the Preservation of the Rights of the Subject Bill, which reached a second reading in the House of Lords in 1947.

Statutory instruments laid before Parliament are referred to a Select Committee which was established in 1944 and is appointed each session. The duties of the committee are to scrutinize statutory instruments for those which impose a charge on public revenues or make unusual or unexpected use of the powers conferred by the Act, and to those containing ambiguities or which are not clearly expressed. The committee reports to the House such orders as seem to call for special attention, but it cannot report detailed opinions on them.

Rules, orders, and regulations made under an Act of Parliament were previously known as statutory rules and orders, and were first published in annual volumes in 1890. The Statutory Instruments Act, 1946, which was brought into force on 1 January 1948, gave the more comprehensive name of statutory instruments to all this subordinate legislation. Statutory instruments which are required to be laid before Parliament are 'laid on the Table' of both Houses for the specified period, and in the House of Lords they are examined by the Special Orders Committee. Statutory instruments dealing with finance are laid before the House of Commons only.

An edition of Statutory Rules and Orders and Statutory Instruments revised to 31 December 1948 has appeared in 25 volumes, and supplementary volumes are issued annually.

See also DELEGATED LEGISLATION.

STATUTORY INSTRUMENTS, SELECT COMMITTEE ON

See SELECT COMMITTEE ON STATUTORY INSTRUMENTS.

STEPHEN (1097?–1154)

Son of the fourth daughter of William I and the Count of Blois, whose claim to the English Crown was preferred to that of Matilda, daughter of Henry I. Crowned in December 1135.

STRANGERS

Any person within the precincts of the Palace of Westminster who is neither a peer, nor a Member of the House of Commons, nor an officer of either House, is officially regarded as a stranger. The term is used in the cry, 'Hats off, strangers', which heralds the approach of the Speaker in procession, and the Public Galleries are more correctly called 'Strangers' Galleries'. The term is also used in the wording of a motion to clear the galleries, which has become the customary preliminary procedure when the House wishes to go into secret session. It is the custom for a member introducing such a motion to look up at the galleries and pronounce the words, 'I spy strangers!', whereupon the Speaker puts the question, 'That strangers do withdraw.' At one time it was sufficient for a single member to 'spy strangers' to require the instant clearing of the galleries, but as the result of a distasteful incident which occurred on 27 April 1875, when no less a person than the Prince of Wales was compelled to withdraw from the House of Commons gallery because one member drew attention to the presence of strangers, a resolution was adopted requiring a majority vote of the House before strangers could be excluded. No debate is permitted on the motion, 'That strangers do withdraw', and no amendment to the motion may be moved.

These days any member of the public wishing to listen to a parliamentary debate can do so provided there is room for him in the gallery, but Parliament has not always been so hospitable in its attitude towards strangers. One of the original duties of the Serjeant-at-Arms was the 'taking into custody of such strangers who presume to come into the House of Commons'. Instances are recorded of strangers, having wandered either deliberately or involuntarily into the precincts of Parliament, receiving extremely rough handling, for great importance was attached to preserving the secrecy of debate. However, Parliament came to view strangers with greater tolerance, and in the late 18th and early 19th centuries the doorkeepers and messengers were able to supplement their incomes substantially by receiving gratuities from strangers in return for admitting them to the galleries.

Select Committees (q.v.) have the right to admit strangers to their sittings when witnesses are being examined, and it is of interest to note that this right was specifically included in the terms of reference of the two specialist committees on agriculture and on science and technology which were appointed in December 1966.

[728]

The official use of the word 'stranger' is yet another symbol of the ancient privileges of Parliament, implying as it does the distinction between a member and a non-member and the fact that an outsider is permitted within the confines of the Palace of Westminster on tolerance only and not by right.

STUDY OF PARLIAMENT GROUP

A private group of university teachers and officers of both Houses of Parliament which was formed to further serious study of the working of Parliament. It has been meeting since 1964, under the chairmanship of Sir Edward Fellowes, a former Clerk of the House of Commons.

SUB JUDICE RULE

It is a general principle of parliamentary procedure that a matter awaiting a judicial decision should not be referred to in debate nor form the subject of a motion or a question to a minister, including a supplementary question. The purpose of the rule is to avoid any proceeding which might be prejudicial to a case awaiting or undergoing trial. The rule does not apply to Bills on the ground that legislation is action designed to alter the circumstances on which a court must reach a decision, and the right of Parliament to legislate as and when it pleases must not be limited.

The *sub judice* rule is based on precedents dating back to 1844, when the Chair first ruled on the subject, and it was codified for the first time in a resolution of the House of Commons passed on 23 July 1963. Subject to the discretion of the Chair, the rule bans references to all cases, criminal and civil, awaiting or under adjudication in all courts at all levels, including courts martial; and to all cases which have been referred by the House to a judicial body, such as a Tribunal of Inquiry, for investigation and report. The ban ceases to apply once a decision has been rendered or a report has been presented. The interpretation of the rule lies with the Chair, which is guided by the available precedents, the possibility of prejudicial effect, and (since 1963) the resolution of the House.

SUBSIDIARY LEGISLATION

Legislation imposed by the executive by means of statutory instruments (q.v.), orders, or regulations made by authority of an Act of Parliament, as opposed to principal legislation which is imposed by statute.

See also DELEGATED LEGISLATION.

SUBSIDIARY MOTION

This type of motion is dependent upon, or related to, other motions, or it may follow upon some proceeding in the House. Amendments and dilatory and ancillary motions are all subsidiary motions, and are dealt with under their respective headings. The mover of a subsidiary motion has no right of reply.

SUBSTANTIVE MOTION

A motion which is not incidental to any other business of the House, but is a self-contained proposal submitted for its consideration, and drafted in such a way as to be capable of expressing its decision. A substantive motion usually requires notice, whereas a subsidiary motion (q.v.) does not. The actions of certain high personages can only be discussed on a substantive motion: they are the Sovereign, the Heir to the Throne, the Governors-General of the Dominions, the Lord Chancellor, the Speaker, the Chairman of Ways and Means, Members of the Lords and Commons, and Judges of the Superior Courts of the United Kingdom. The mover of a substantive motion has the right of reply.

SUFFRAGE

The right or privilege of voting, or the exercise of that right. Universal adult suffrage is the system whereby every national has a vote on reaching adult age, now usually eighteen. In the early years of the 19th century the idea of universal suffrage, without any income, property, sex, or literacy qualification, was repugnant to all but the more advanced thinkers. Even much later in the century many people, including J. S. Mill in his *Representative Government*, found it difficult to reconcile such a wide application of the suffrage with illiteracy. However, this obstacle was removed in Britain with the spread of universal and compulsory education, and now in countries such as those in Asia and Africa, which have a large proportion of illiterates, literacy is not considered to be an essential qualification for obtaining a vote. It is now recognized that adult suffrage is the only method which secures the fair representation of all elements of the population and absolute equality of political rights to every adult citizen.

See also ELECTIONS; FRANCHISE; REPRESENTATION.

SUFFRAGETTES

The term applied to female agitators for votes for women. John Stuart Mill was among the first to bring this question into prominence, and as well as pleading for political equality for women in his writings, constantly advocated it in the House of Commons. Lord Brougham was responsible for the passing of an Act in 1849 which declared that 'words importing the masculine gender shall be deemed to include females, unless the contrary is expressly provided', but the 1832 Reform Act had introduced the term 'male person', and that was to stand for nearly a century. In 1870 Jacob Bright introduced a Women's Suffrage Bill, but he received no support from his more famous brother John, and still less from Mr. Gladstone, who for once was in complete agreement with Queen Victoria in her dislike of the idea of women's emancipation—whether political or otherwise. From 1870 onwards, frequent attempts were made in Parliament to enfranchise women, and at least seven Bills got as far as a second reading before the vote was obtained. Outside Parliament, agitation began with the formation of Women's Suffrage Societies in 1867, and before the First World War three hundred of these societies were affiliated to the National Union of Women's Suffrage Societies. By 1905, the question was a live political issue which received more support from Labour than from the two older parties. The Women's Social and Political Union, founded in 1903 by Mrs. Pankhurst, introduced the militant 'suffragette' as opposed to the constitutional suffragist represented by the Women's Suffrage Societies. The latter were entirely opposed to the new methods of demonstrations, monster processions, destruction of public and private property, and in fact any action, whether legal or illegal, which would induce the Government of the day to accede to their demands. A Parliamentary Franchise (Women) Bill passed its second reading in 1910, and a Women's Enfranchisement Bill in 1911 reached the same stage, but they were Private Members' Bills and the Government, faced with a constitutional crisis regarding the House of Lords, could give them no facilities. These Bills were known as Conciliation Bills because they proposed, as a first step, to give the vote only to women who were householders. As a result of this disappointment the suffragettes increased their activities, and many women were imprisoned. In 1913 one of them threw herself in front of the King's horse while the Derby was being run and was killed. The disturbances caused by the suffragettes undoubtedly diminished public sympathy for their cause, and further Bills introduced in Parliament in 1912, 1913, and 1914 were still unsuccessful. At the outbreak of the First World War the suffragettes called off the struggle and devoted themselves to war-work. In 1917 a Speaker's Conference (q.v.) reported unanimously in favour of some measure of suffrage for women, and in 1918 the goal was reached with the passing of the Representation of the People Act— the fourth 'Reform Act'. Under this Act the minimum age for women voters was thirty, but by the passing of the Representation of the People (Equal Franchise) Act in 1928 women achieved absolute equality with men as regards both parliamentary and local government elections.

(Further reading: Fulford, *Votes for women*, 1957; Pankhurst, *Unshackled*, 1959.)

SUPERSEDING MOTION

Dilatory motions and the 'previous question' (qq.v.) come under this class because if carried they supersede the original question, and must be disposed of before the debate on the original question can be resumed.

SUPPLEMENTARY ESTIMATES

See ESTIMATES; PROCEDURE, FINANCIAL.

SUPPLEMENTARY QUESTIONS

See QUESTIONS.

SUPPLY

The grants of money which are voted annually by Parliament for the maintenance of the Civil Service and the armed forces. The requirements of the various public departments are drawn up in the form of Estimates (q.v.) which are presented to Parliament for consideration. The right of considering and approving grants of Supply and of initiating financial legislation is reserved to the House of Commons (q.v., *and see also* PRIVILEGE, FINANCIAL). Supply resolutions, which are founded on the Estimates, are debated in the House with the Deputy Speaker in the Chair, and the Consolidated Fund and Consolidated Fund (Appropriation) Bills which give legislative effect to the Estimates are based on these resolutions. Prior to December 1966 the Estimates were debated in a Committee of the Whole House known as the Committee of Supply. Under the new financial procedure the traditional requirement that financial legislation must be based upon resolutions made in a Committee of the Whole House has been abolished, with the result that the Committee of Supply no longer exists. The consideration of Supply constitutes the bulk of the session's financial business, and twenty-nine days (increased from twenty-six in December 1966), known as Supply days, are specifically allotted each session to this purpose. (*See also* PROCEDURE, FINANCIAL.)

The expenses of government are those of the Crown, and originally this was a literal as well as a technical fact. The King, like his nobles and gentry, was a great landed proprietor with his own incomes out of which he was expected to find the wherewithal to govern. That which we know as the Treasury (q.v.) once consisted of the King's own personal resources. As the expenses of government increased the Treasury became insufficient to meet them and the King was compelled to seek assistance from Parliament. It was due to the King's ever-increasing financial needs, and to no other reason, that the Commons were originally summoned to attend Parliament. As the King came to rely more and more upon the Commons for money, it was only natural that they should make use of the weapon which their Sovereign's necessity placed in their hands, and it became customary to demand redress of their grievances before they would consent to grant Supply. (Incidentally, the early meaning of the word 'supply' was 'to make up a deficiency'.)

Prior to December 1966 this ancient right of the Commons nominally survived in the use which was made of the motion for 'getting the Speaker out of the Chair' (q.v.) on certain occasions when the House resolved itself into Committee of Supply. Until 1956 it was the custom for such motions to be debated on the four occasions when the House first went into Committee of Supply on each of the main branches of the Estimates. These occasions were the recognized opportunities for members to raise any matters covered by the Estimates, the scope of debate being very wide indeed. Even before the introduction of the new financial procedure this opportunity had become curtailed. A limited use was made of the motion for 'getting the Speaker out of the Chair', but as the debates in Committee of Supply were themselves very broad in scope the use of the motion as a means of providing opportunities for debate had to a great extent fallen away.

The Committee of Supply was eliminated from Australian parliamentary procedure in 1963, and as a result the principle of 'grievances before Supply' has received new emphasis in the Australian House of Representatives. A general debate now takes place on the question 'that grievances be noted' and a day set down for such a debate is known as 'Grievance Day'.

Although the preliminary consideration of financial resolutions in a Committee of the Whole House has been abolished, the former procedure retains its historic interest. The Committee of the Whole House developed its two distinct functions as Committee of Supply and Committee of Ways and Means in 1641. The main function of the Committee of Supply became the approval of expenditure, that of the Committee of Ways and Means the authorization of taxation. Originally the distinction was not so clear as all grants were raised by directly assigning the proceeds from certain taxes to specific purposes. Both committees therefore performed a similar function, although it would seem that the Committee of Supply was concerned with regular taxes which yielded a more or less constant revenue, whilst the Committee of Ways and Means was set up to devise new methods of raising money. During the course of the 18th century the authorizing of expenditure became clearly distinguished from the imposition of taxation, the former becoming the special function of the Committee of Supply. The procedure on Bills for granting aids and supplies was evolved in the first half of the 17th century and remained fundamentally the same until December 1966. Supplies were initially voted in the form of resolutions in Committee of the Whole House and the authorizing Bill was drafted in accordance with these resolutions. The essential characteristic of such a Bill was that it granted money to the Sovereign by the authority of Parliament and predominantly of the Commons, and this is still made apparent to-day in the preamble of a Bill of aids and supplies (*see* APPROPRIATION ACT *and* FINANCE ACT).

Although the Commons controlled the provision of money it was not until the 18th century that they gained full control over public expenditure. Before the Restoration no regular provision was made for the ordinary expenses of government and the King relied upon his hereditary revenues and other non-parliamentary incomes, together with such aids and supplies as Parliament could be persuaded to grant. After the Restoration the practice arose of granting the Sovereign a regular income to cover the ordinary expenses of government, whilst extraordinary expenditure was met by special grants which were voted annually. Both Charles II and James II received an annual allowance of £1,200,000, voted by Parliament 'for the constant yearly support of His Majesty'. No other purpose was specified for the money and it was left to the King to dispose of it as he thought fit. The annual Supply grants which were voted to meet extraordinary expenditure were, however, assigned to particular purposes. The principle of appropriation dates back to the 14th century, but it was after the Restoration that it came to be applied in earnest. Thus, in the latter half of the 17th century provisos came to be included in Supply Bills specifying the purposes for which the money was being made available and stipulating that it should be used 'to no other purpose whatsoever'. During the reign of William III the annual income which Parliament granted to the Sovereign came to be known as the Civil List (q.v.), and as the sum of money granted was invariably insufficient the Sovereign was compelled to ask the Commons from time to time for 'grants-in-aid of the Civil List'. It therefore became necessary to relieve the burden upon the royal income, which meant that further public expenses had to be met from annual Supply grants. At the same time the need to maintain a standing army and navy necessitated a recurring expenditure hitherto unknown, and the expenses of the two armed services took their places alongside the Civil List as major branches of regular expenditure. Before long the civil expenses met from Supply grants exceeded the Civil List itself and yet a new branch of expenditure came to be created known as the Miscellaneous Supply Services. Thus towards the end of the 18th century three of the great divisions of expenditure we know to-day had taken form and the 'extraordinary' expenses which Supply grants had originally been designed to meet had assumed their permanent character.

Until the reign of George III the Commons made no attempt to direct the expenditure of the Civil List revenues; indeed, proposals to do so were more than once turned down as being contrary to tradition and derogatory to the Crown. It was not until 1777 that the Commons, disturbed by the King's repeated extravagances, demanded that accounts be presented before agreeing to meet his huge debts. In 1782 Lord Rockingham stipulated the reform of the Civil List as one of the conditions of his forming a Government, and parliamentary control over ordinary civil expenditure thus became established. To-day the expenses of government are no longer charged upon the Civil List, which has become the Sovereign's personal income.

Parliament thus controls all expenditure. Under modern procedure the expenses of government fall into two divisions: those charged directly upon the Consolidated Fund (q.v.), the great financial pool of the nation which was inaugurated by Pitt in 1786, and those which are voted annually. The former include the Civil List, payments of interest on the National Debt, and the salaries of certain high officials. These charges are fixed by statute and are not subject to annual review. The expenses which are considered annually are those of the Civil Service and the armed forces. The Sovereign, therefore, no longer supports the government, but the government supports the Sovereign; the hereditary revenues of the Crown have become state revenues, and the machinery of government is paid for with Supply grants. Once voted, grants of Supply are also charged upon the Consolidated Fund. Under former practice they were met from the proceeds of certain taxes specifically assigned to the purpose, but to-day all revenue is paid into the Consolidated Fund and all expenditure issues from it.

SUPPLY, COMMITTEE OF

See COMMITTEE OF THE WHOLE HOUSE; ESTIMATES; PROCEDURE, FINANCIAL; SUPPLY.

SUPPLY DAYS

Under the new financial procedure introduced in December 1966, twenty-nine days are allotted each session by Standing Order to the business of Supply (q.v.) Supply debates are not necessarily confined to these twenty-nine allotted days but they represent the minimum amount of time which must be devoted to Supply during a session. With the abolition of the Committee of Supply all Supply days are now held in the House, the Deputy Speaker presiding when the Estimates (q.v.) are under discussion. It is customary for the Opposition to select the subject for discussion on these occasions, but it is no longer necessary to assign specific subjects to Supply days. The business of Supply includes debates on substantive motions tabled by the Opposition and adjournment debates, as well as the proceedings on all forms of Estimates, save those relating to war expenditure, and the consideration of reports from the Committee of Public Accounts and the Estimates Committee. Prior to December 1966 there were twenty-six Supply days. The three additional days were added to compensate for the withdrawal of the right to debate the third reading stage of Consolidated Fund Bills (q.v.). Four half-days are earmarked out of the twenty-nine Supply days to enable the Opposition to raise urgent matters for debate at short notice.

The provisions of the Standing Order are such as to define an allotted day as a day on which the whole of the time for public business up to 10 p.m. is devoted to the business of Supply, two Fridays counting as one day. The Standing Order also provides for a system of closure whereby all twenty-nine Supply days are required to fall before 5 August.

See also PROCEDURE, FINANCIAL.

SUPPLY, MINISTER OF

The Ministry of Supply Act, 1939, created this Ministry and gave the Minister general powers to buy, manufacture, and sell articles for the public service. His responsibilities were greatly increased when the war began, as besides being the supply department of the War Office, his Ministry controlled many branches of war production affecting all the Government departments. It was responsible for the supply of aircraft and munitions, including atomic weapons and guided missiles, and of raw materials in general. The wartime Ministry of Aircraft Production was absorbed by the Ministry of Supply in 1946.

The Ministry of Supply was wound up after the 1959 General Election, its functions being assumed mainly by the newly created Ministry of Aviation and the War Office.

A chronological list of Ministers of Supply appears as Appendix 29.

SUSPENSION OF A MEMBER

See 'NAMING' A MEMBER.

SUSPENSION OF SITTING

See SITTINGS OF THE HOUSE OF COMMONS.

SWAZILAND PARLIAMENT

A parliamentary system of government was first introduced in Swaziland by an Order in Council of 1963 (S.I.2094), and the new Constitution came into operation with elections held in June 1964. Executive power was vested in Her Majesty's Commissioner for Swaziland, formerly the Resident Commissioner, who was appointed by the Crown in the manner of colonial Governors and was directly responsible to the Secretary of State for the government of the territory.

The Legislative Council consisted of a Speaker appointed by Her Majesty's Commissioner, 4 official members (including the Chief Secretary, Attorney-General, and Secretary for Finance and Development), 24 elected members, and up to 3 members nominated by Her Majesty's Commissioner. 8 of the elected members were Swazis who were elected by traditional methods; 8 were Europeans, of whom 4 were elected by the voters on a European roll and 4 by the voters on a national roll; and 8 were members of any race elected by voters on a national roll. The national roll franchise was based virtually on universal adult suffrage. Eurafricans had the option of registering on the European roll or the national roll, and they were also eligible for election by Swazi traditional methods provided they could fulfil the requisite conditions. The Commissioner's power to nominate members was used only to secure the representation of interests not otherwise adequately represented, or to provide for the conduct of the government under abnormal circumstances.

In April 1967 a new Constitution came into effect providing for internal self-government for Swaziland as a protected state. The Constitution recognizes the Ngwenyama (Paramount Chief) as King of Swaziland and Head of State, and provided for the continuance of British protection until the attainment of full independence which took place in September 1968. During the interim period the Commisioner retained ertain responsibilities in relation to external affairs, defence, internal security, finance and the public service, which he exercised with a consultative council consisting of representatives of the British and Swaziland Governments.

The new Swaziland Parliament consists of two Chambers, a Senate and a House of Assembly. The former consists of 6 members elected by the House of Assembly and 6 appointed by the King. The latter consists of a Speaker, 24 members elected by adult suffrage in 8 three-member constituencies, 6 members appointed by the King, and a non-voting Attorney-General. The former Executive Council, which was presided over by the Commissioner, is replaced by a Cabinet consisting of a Prime Minister, a Deputy Prime Minister, and up to 6 other Ministers.

The rights and immunities of the Ngwenyama are protected under the Constitution and the title to the Swazi Nation Land and the national mineral rights are vested in him. However, agreement had not been reached, at the time of the Constitution coming into force, as to the method of consultation whereby the King would exercise his right to grant mineral concessions.

T

TABLE OFFICE

In the House of Commons this office assists the Clerks-at-the-Table in the preparation of the Notice Paper and the Order Book, but its principal work is dealing with Notices of Questions addressed to ministers from members, and the office is staffed outside sitting hours and on Saturdays for the purpose of receiving them. It also prepares the regular schedule showing the daily order in which ministers attached to the various departments will answer questions. This office has part of its accommodation adjoining the Chamber, where it is convenient for members to find out whether their questions are in order and to obtain advice on motions and amendments or other matters regarding procedure.

TABLE OF THE HOUSE

An essential part of the furniture of the House of Commons and other Commonwealth legislative chambers. The Table is situated in front of the Speaker's Chair between the two front benches, so close that front-bench members are often seen with their feet resting on the Table. The Clerk of the House (q.v.) and his colleagues on duty in the Chamber sit at the Table with their backs to the Speaker (hence the term 'Clerks-at-the-Table'). The Mace (q.v.), always present when the House is in session, reposes in brackets on top of the Table when the Speaker is in the Chair, and is transferred to lower brackets when the Chairman of Ways and Means (q.v.) presides. Both sets of brackets are situated at the end of the Table opposite to that at which the Clerks sit. The Table of the House also accommodates the two Despatch Boxes (q.v.). When the House is in committee the Chairman also sits at the Table, occupying the chair of the Clerk of the House next to the Clerk Assistant (q.v.). Papers and reports presented to the House are said to be 'laid upon the Table', and in some legislatures, but not in the House of Commons, these documents are literally placed upon the Table where they lie for a specified period.

In the 18th century a Table was reputedly designed for the House of Commons by Wren. This Table was one of the few objects which escaped destruction in the fire of 1834 and is now preserved in the Lower Waiting Hall.

TABLE, THE

See SOCIETY OF CLERKS-AT-THE-TABLE IN COMMONWEALTH PARLIAMENTS.

TANGANYIKA

See TANZANIA PARLIAMENT.

TANZANIA PARLIAMENT

Tanganyika (formerly German East Africa) was administered by the United Kingdom under a League of Nations Mandate after the First World War, and subsequently under a trusteeship agreement approved by the General Assembly of the United Nations in 1946. The special status of Tanganyika was recognized in United Kingdom legislation and Orders in Council, where it was referred to as the Trust Territory of Tanganyika. The first Legislative Council met in 1926, since when it followed the usual pattern of development in colonial legislatures. Prior to April 1955 the Legislative Council consisted of the Governor as President, 15 officials, and 14 nominated unofficial members of whom 7 were Europeans, 4 Africans, and 3 Asians. The Tanganyika (Legislative Council) (Amendment) Order in Council, 1955, enlarged the Legislative Council considerably, following the recommendations of a Constitutional Committee composed of all races which had been appointed by the Governor in 1949 and reported in 1951. From the session commencing in April 1955 the Legislative Council consisted of a Speaker and 61 members comprising 17 officials, 14 unofficial members who accepted the Government whip, and 30 representative members (10 African, 10 Asian, and 10 European) who were nominated by the Governor after consultation with bodies representing the various communities and interests in the Territory. The Government was thus assured of a majority of 31 to 30. In May 1958 the Legislative Council passed a Bill providing for a qualitative franchise and the election on a common voters' roll of 3 members (1 African, 1 Asian, and 1 European) from each of 10 constituencies, thus substituting direct election for nomination in respect of the 30 representative members. Elections for five constituencies were held in September 1958 and for the remaining five in February 1959. Following the report of a committee headed by Sir Richard Ramage it was announced that the membership of the Legislative Council would be increased to provide for 71 representative members, and that further elections would be held in 1960 on a much wider franchise. The new franchise, which was based on residence and literacy or income qualifications, increased the number of voters from some 60,000 to about 1½ million. Asians were allotted 11 seats and Europeans 10, while the remaining 50 seats were available to candidates of all races, thus ensuring an African majority in the legislature.

[739]

In April 1957 the ministerial system was introduced and the official members of the Executive Council were re-designated ministers. Six assistant ministers were appointed in the following month from the unofficial members of the Legislative Council. In July 1959 a Council of Ministers (which later replaced the Executive Council) was set up in which unofficial members, including Africans, were appointed to full ministerial office for the first time. Of the 12 ministers comprising the Council 5 were unofficial members (3 Africans, 1 Asian, and 1 European). After the 1960 Election the Council of Ministers was re-formed on the basis of an unofficial majority. It was headed by an elected Chief Minister and included only 2 officials who held office as Attorney-General and Minister of Information. Of the 12 ministers, 7 were Africans (including the Chief Minister), 4 were Europeans (including the 2 officials), and 1 was an Asian.

Tanganyika achieved internal self-government on 1 May 1961, the Legislative Council being replaced by a National Assembly of 71 elected members, the Council of Ministers being replaced by a Prime Minister and Cabinet. On 9 December 1961 Tanganyika became fully independent, and exactly one year later became a Republic within the Commonwealth following an election for a President with executive powers. The election of the President was linked with the election every five years of the National Assembly. The former was thus unable to dissolve the latter without bringing his own term of office to an end. The President may withhold his assent to a Bill passed by the National Assembly, but if it is thereafter again passed by the Assembly with a two-thirds majority he is required to give his assent to the measure within twenty-one days.

On 27 April 1964 Tanganyika joined with Zanzibar to become the United Republic of Tanganyika and Zanzibar, subsequently re-designated the United Republic of Tanzania on the following 29 October. Pending the adoption of a new Constitution by a constituent assembly the new Republic is governed under the Constitution of Tanganyika, suitably modified to allow Zanzibar a measure of local autonomy. The President presides over a Cabinet which includes two Vice-Presidents, the first of whom is also the President of Zanzibar. In spite of the union Zanzibar appears to be continuing to pursue her own independent policies both internally and externally.

The appointment of a commission to formulate a new Constitution for the Republic was postponed pending the report of a presidential commission on the establishment of a one-party State. This report was published on 7 April 1965, and its recommendations included the proposal that the size of the National Assembly should be increased by the addition of nominated 'national members' who would not be concerned with constituency or local interests. It also proposed that the election of the President should no longer be tied to the election of the National Assembly.

On 5 July 1965, following a debate in the National Assembly, a provisional Constitution was adopted which provided that Tanzania should be a one-party State and that the Constitution of the ruling party, the Tanganyika African National Union, should be incorporated into the Constitution of the State.

The National Assembly now consists (1970) of up to 204 members, comprising 107 elected members representing Tanganyika, 15 members elected by the National Assembly to represent national institutions, 20 regional commissioners who sit *ex officio*, up to 32 members of the Revolutionary Council of Zanzibar, and up to 30 members appointed by the President. The members representing Zanzibar are all nominated, but voters in both Tanganyika and Zanzibar participated in the presidential election of 1965.

TASMANIAN PARLIAMENT

Second oldest of the Australian settlements, Tasmania, or Van Diemen's Land as it was first called, celebrated the 150th anniversary of its foundation in 1953. It started as a dependency of New South Wales, but in 1825 it obtained its independence, and Executive and Legislative Councils were appointed to advise the Lieutenant-Governor. As early as 1826 there was agitation for some form of representative government, and successive years saw petition after petition addressed to the Imperial Government for reform on these lines. In the 1840's there was much indignation over the attempt to make the Colony pay for the maintenance of thousands of convicts sent there from England. The continuance of transportation became the burning question of the day, and it was realized that until it was abolished attempts to achieve self-government were doomed to failure. The Australasian Anti-Transportation League was founded in 1851—the first major move to bring the Australian Colonies together on matters of common interest —and its efforts were crowned with success in 1853. In the meantime, this achievement was foreshadowed by the passing by the British Government in 1850 of an Act for the Better Government of the Australian Colonies, which gave Tasmania a Legislative Council of 24 members, 16 to be elected and 8 nominated by the Crown. With the passing in 1853 of transportation, the Legislative Council submitted a new draft Constitution to the Imperial Government, which received the Royal Assent in 1855. By this Constitution Tasmania was the first of the Australian Colonies to be granted responsible government and a fully-elected bicameral legislature—the Legislative Council and the House of Assembly—and the name of the Colony was changed from Van Diemen's Land to Tasmania as from 1 January 1856. The first Parliament was opened on 2 December of the same year.

[741]

Since 1947 the Legislative Council has consisted of 19 members. The House of Assembly consists of 35 members (increased in 1959 from 30, which figure had remained unchanged since 1906), elected under a system of proportional representation. Members of the Legislative Council are elected by owners of freeholds of £10 annual value and occupiers of any property of £30. They sit for six years, 3 retiring annually over five years and 4 every sixth year. There is no power to dissolve the Legislative Council. Members of the House of Assembly are elected for five years by adults who have lived in the State for at least six months. By the Constitution Act (No. 2) of 1954 the life of a House of Assembly may be reduced to three years if equal numbers of the two political parties (Labour and Liberal) are elected. When this happens, the party obtaining the lowest aggregate number of votes may nominate one of its members for election as the Speaker. If they do not, the 'majority' party can elect a Speaker from among its own members, and in this case the member chosen must resign his seat and a by-election follows. Voting has been compulsory since 1928 for both Houses, women obtaining the vote in 1903 and eligibility for election to either House in 1921.

In 1967 the procedure of the House of Assembly was radically revised following a comprehensive review of the Standing Orders. The most important change was the revision of financial procedure in accordance with the principles adopted by the Australian House of Representatives in 1963 (*see* AUSTRALIAN PARLIAMENT). Other changes included the abolition of the procedure relating to Private Bills and the substitution of two categories of Bills, namely Public Bills and Semi-Public Bills, for the previous three; and an alteration in the procedure relating to a motion of dissent against a Speaker's ruling, whereby such a motion must now be decided before the debate on the question which gave rise to the ruling is allowed to proceed.

The building which has constituted the Houses of Parliament for more than a hundred years is one of the finest of its type remaining in Australia. It was first used by the nominee Legislative Council in 1840, and the Assembly met where the Parliamentary Lounge is now located from 1856 until 1940, when the present modern House of Assembly was occupied. In 1970 the Tasmanian Cabinet comprised 9 ministers, both the Premier and Deputy Premier holding portfolios in addition to their other responsibilities. The Tasmanian Parliament publishes no Hansard, but newspaper reports of its debates are reprinted weekly.

(Further reading: Green, ed., *A Century of Responsible Government 1856-1956*, 1958.)

TAXATION

See BUDGET; FINANCE ACT; PRIVILEGE, FINANCIAL; PROCEDURE, FINANCIAL; WAYS AND MEANS.

TECHNOLOGY, MINISTER OF

This Minister's department was merged with the Board of Trade to form a new Department of Trade and Industry as a result of a major reorganization of the machinery of central government which took place in 1970. The new department is headed by a Minister styled the Secretary of State for Trade and Industry and President of the Board of Trade.

The appointment of Minister of Technology was first created in October 1964, Mr. Frank Cousins becoming the first holder of the office. In 1967 this Minister absorbed the functions of the former Minister of Aviation and in October 1969 his department was enlarged and he assumed the functions of the Minister of Power with responsibilities for industry in both the private and public sectors. Prior to the absorption of his functions by the Secretary of State the responsibilities of the Minister of Technology included the nationalized industries and the production that flows from them; aviation; engineering; shipbuilding; electronics and nuclear industries; various technological and research activities; functions relating to the distribution of industry and investment grants and loans which were taken over from the Board of Trade; and control of the industrial reorganization corporation which had been taken over from the defunct Department of Economic Affairs. All these responsibilities together with those of the President of the Board of Trade (q.v.) are now vested in the new Secretary of State.

TELEVISION IN PARLIAMENT

See BROADCASTING IN PARLIAMENT.

TELLERS

See DIVISIONS.

TEN MINUTES' RULE

The term applied to the Standing Order of the House of Commons which provides that Notices of Motions for leave to introduce Bills and for the nomination of Select Committees may be set down for consideration at the commencement of Public Business on Tuesdays and Wednesdays and, if given by a minister, on Mondays and Thursdays also. The mover is permitted to make a brief explanatory statement if he thinks fit. Only one member is permitted to speak in opposition, after which the Speaker puts the question without further debate. Such speeches, as the term implies, are supposed to be limited to ten minutes. Ten Minutes' Rule Bills are limited to one on any one day, and a week's notice must be given of their introduction.

Private Members wishing to introduce Bills frequently adopt this procedure as a means of securing early publicity for their proposed measures.

On 27 October 1965 the House resolved that for the duration of the 1965–6 session motions made under the Ten Minutes' Rule would be taken at the conclusion instead of at the commencement of public business. The House divided upon the proposal, which was carried by 128 to 118. Those opposing it drew attention to the difficulty in maintaining a quorum in the House at a late hour, and to the fact that the publicity value afforded by the Ten Minutes' Rule depended upon the business concerned being dealt with in the early afternoon. Supporters of the change emphasized that a private member's motion stood a better chance of being passed at a late hour when attendance would be sparse than during the day. The change was not continued, however, and in the ensuing session motions made under the Ten Minutes' Rule were restored to their original position at the commencement of public business.

TEN O'CLOCK RULE

The term which is applied to the Standing Order of the House of Commons which provides for the automatic interruption of business at 10 p.m. (Standing Order No. 1 (Sittings of the House), paragraph 2). It reads:

At ten of the clock on Mondays, Tuesdays, Wednesdays, and Thursdays, the proceedings on any business then under consideration shall, save as otherwise provided in paragraph (1) of Standing Order No. 2 (Exempted Business), be interrupted; and, if the House be in committee, the chairman shall leave the chair, and report progress and ask leave to sit again; and if a motion has been made for the adjournment of the House, or of the debate, or in committee that the chairman do report progress, or do leave the chair, every such motion shall lapse.

When business is interrupted by the Speaker under the rule, a day is named for the resumption of the interrupted business by the member in charge of it, and the remaining Orders of the Day (q.v.) are called out by the Clerk of the House. Those which are unopposed are dealt with immediately (provided no member wishes to speak upon them); the others are postponed to a later day. The last half-hour of the day from 10 to 10.30 p.m. is then devoted to a debate on the motion, 'That this House do now adjourn', a motion which provides private members with the opportunity of raising any matters to which they particularly wish to draw attention (*see* ADJOURNMENT OF THE HOUSE). During the experiment with morning sittings on Mondays and Wednesdays in 1967 the half-hour debate on the adjournment motion was transferred to the period 12.30 p.m. to 1 p.m., prior to the luncheon adjournment, on these days, thus enabling the House to terminate its sittings punctually at 10 p.m. on Mondays and Wednesdays.

[744]

In practice, the House very often continues with the business under discussion after 10 p.m. in spite of the rule. In the first place a Minister of the Crown may move the suspension of the rule at 10 p.m. in order to continue the debate, the motion being decided without amendment or debate. (This practice replaces the former procedure whereby a Minister was required to move the suspension of the rule at the commencement of the day's Public Business, and if he wished the suspension to apply beyond that particular day's sitting the motion was subject to both amendment and debate.) Secondly, certain business is automatically exempted from the rule (*see* EXEMPTED BUSINESS).

Prior to 1888 there was no automatic adjournment and the prolonging of a sitting was always considered a legitimate political weapon. It was abused to such an extent by the Irish Nationalist members, who on one famous occasion kept the House sitting continuously for $41\frac{1}{2}$ hours (31 January to 2 February 1881), that it became necessary to introduce some form of restriction. A Twelve o'clock Rule was introduced in 1888 which was altered in 1906 to an Eleven o'clock Rule. The present Ten o'clock Rule replaced the Eleven o'clock Rule in 1946. In each case the adjournment took place half an hour after the moment for the interruption of business.

TEST ROLL
When a Member of the House of Commons has taken the oath or made affirmation, he subscribes his name at the Table of the House on the Test Roll, a roll of parchment folded in the shape of a book.

THIRD READING
See BILL, PASSAGE OF.

THREE ESTATES
See ESTATES OF THE REALM.

TIMBERLAND, EBENEZER
See CHANDLER, RICHARD.

TOKEN VOTE
See ESTIMATES.

TONGA LEGISLATIVE ASSEMBLY
Tonga became a fully independent member of the Commonwealth on 4 June 1970. Previously it had enjoyed a unique status in the British Commonwealth as an independent kingdom under the protection of the British Crown. Its Constitution has hardly changed since it was granted by its King, George Tupou I, in 1875. Under a new treaty of friendship

signed in 1958 and ratified in 1959 Tonga remained a state under British protection but with increased local autonomy. In 1965 a direct medium of communication between Great Britain and Tonga was established in the British Commissioner and Consul in Tonga, an officer who was previously responsible to the Governor of Fiji. The Legislative Assembly consists of 7 nobles elected by their peers, 7 representatives elected by the people every three years, 7 Ministers of the Crown who are *ex-officio*, and a Speaker appointed by the King from among the 7 nobles. The right to vote was given to women in 1960.

TORY PARTY

See CONSERVATIVE PARTY; PARTY SYSTEM.

TOWN AND COUNTRY PLANNING, MINISTER OF

A Ministry of Town and Country Planning was established by an Act of 1943, the first Minister being William Shepherd Morrison. Early in 1951 the Minister's title was changed to Minister of Local Government and Planning, and when the Conservative Government was returned later in the year he became Minister of Housing and Local Government (q.v.).

A chronological list of these Ministers appears as Appendix 20.

TRADE AND INDUSTRY, SECRETARY OF STATE FOR

The office of Secretary of State for Trade and Industry, with which is also combined the historic office of President of the Board of Trade (q.v.), was created in 1970 as a result of a major reorganization of the machinery of central government. This Minister's department has taken over the functions of the Board of Trade and the Ministry of Technology (except for certain responsibilities which have been temporarily vested in a Minister of Aviation Supply (q.v.)). It has also taken over from the Department of Employment and Productivity responsibility for government policy towards monopolies, mergers and restrictive trade practices.

The responsibilities of the new Secretary of State, in the words of the White Paper on the Re-organization of Central Government (Cmnd. 4506), are 'concerned primarily with the strategic issues of policy and priority which determine the operations of his Department as a whole'. The objective of the department is 'to assist British industry and commerce to improve their economic and technological strength and competitiveness'. It is also responsible for the Government's relations with the great majority of industries in both the private sector and the public sector and to provide services in relation to export promotion, industrial research and advice to industry.

The Secretary of State is a Cabinet Minister with a salary of £8,500 a year, plus an additional £1,250 if he is a member of the House of

Commons. He is assisted by two non-Cabinet Ministers each of whom is responsible for a particular range of functions.

TRANSPORT, MINISTER OF

In 1970 this Minister's department was absorbed by the new Department of the Environment created in consequence of a major reorganization of the machinery of central government. A Department of Transport was first created by the Ministry of Transport Act, 1919 to take over certain functions relating to shipping exercised by the Board of Trade and generally to improve the means of and facilities for land and sea transport. The Bill was introduced as the Ministry of Ways and Communications Bill, which rather cumbrous title was afterwards changed to the Ministry of Transport. The Minister was answerable in the House for matters relating to railways, canals, roads, bridges, ferries, and docks and harbours and the issuing of regulations concerning licences and compulsory insurance under the Road Traffic Acts. In October 1969 he and his department were subordinated to the overall control of the Secretary of State for Local Government and Regional Planning. The new Secretary of State for the Environment has assumed even wider responsibilities.

In 1941 F. J. Leathers (afterwards Lord Leathers) was appointed Minister of Shipping and Transport. His title was soon afterwards changed to Minister of War Transport, which office he held until the advent of the Labour Government in 1945. Alfred Barnes was then appointed Minister of War Transport, reverting to the title of Minister of Transport on the dissolution of the Ministry of War Transport in March 1946. In 1951 the Departments of Transport and Civil Aviation were merged in a single Ministry until 1959 when responsibility for civil aviation was removed from the Minister of Transport.

A chronological list of Ministers of Transport appears as Appendix 31.

TREASURER OF THE NAVY

See PAYMASTER-GENERAL.

TREASURY

The Treasury is an offshoot of the Exchequer, which was constituted by Henry I at the beginning of the 12th century. The Exchequer was the *Curia Regis* or King's Court sitting for revenue purposes. The method of accounting gave rise to the name 'Exchequer', as the Treasurer and the barons sat round a table with a chequered cloth divided into columns of squares for pounds, shillings, and pence and multiples thereof—an adaptation of the abacus method of reckoning. The Exchequer consisted of two offices, the Upper and the Lower.

The Upper Exchequer, which audited and managed the King's accounts, developed into the Court of Exchequer which took over the judicial business (not only revenue cases), while the Lower Exchequer, from which the Treasury emerged, was concerned with the receipt of the royal revenue. The office of Treasurer dates from Norman times, while the Chancellor of the Exchequer (q.v.), who now has general control of the Treasury, was appointed in the reign of Henry II partly to take charge of the Seal of the Exchequer and partly to be a check on the Treasurer. Actually he had certain judicial duties in connexion with the Upper Exchequer, and his more strictly financial functions belonged to the post of Under Treasurer, which is now combined with that of Chancellor of the Exchequer. The office of Treasurer has been in commission since 1714—in other words his duties were taken over by a Board, the Lords Commissioners of H.M. Treasury, consisting of the First Lord of the Treasury (the Prime Minister), the Chancellor of the Exchequer, and 5 Junior Lords who, together with the Parliamentary Secretary, are Government Whips in the House of Commons. Apart from the Parliamentary Secretary, who is Chief Government Whip with a salary of £5,625 a year, the Commissioners have 3 other secretaries, a Chief Secretary and a Financial Secretary, who are ministers, and a Permanent Secretary who is head of the Civil Service. In the early part of the 18th century the Treasury Board met frequently, with the Sovereign in the chair. After the surrender of the royal revenues by George III in exchange for the Civil List (q.v.), the King ceased to attend. By the beginning of the 19th century meetings became more formal and less frequent as the business became too much for the Board as such, and meetings were discontinued altogether in 1856, although the Junior Lords still have certain formal functions, such as signing Treasury Warrants.

The functions of the Treasury have been summarized as follows: '(a) Subject to Parliament it is responsible for the imposition and regulation of taxation and the collection of revenue, for which purpose it has the assistance of the Revenue Departments (i.e., departments controlled by the Board of Inland Revenue, which collects taxes, the Board of Customs and Excise, which collects indirect taxes, and the Commissioners of Crown Lands (q.v.)); (b) It controls public expenditure through the preparation or supervision of the Estimates (q.v.) for Parliament; (c) It arranges for the provision of the funds required from day to day to meet the necessities of the public service, for which purpose it is entrusted with extensive borrowing powers; (d) It initiates and carries out measures affecting the public debt, currency, and banking; and (e) It prescribes the manner in which the public accounts should be kept.'

Other subordinate departments of the Treasury, in addition to the Revenue Departments, are H.M. Stationery Office, the Civil Service

Commissioners, the Treasury Solicitor's Office, and that of the Parliamentary Counsel. The senior official of the Treasury Solicitor's Office is H.M. Procurator-General and Treasury Solicitor, who in his latter capacity acts as solicitor in litigation to government departments which do not have their own solicitor's department. The Parliamentary Counsel (q.v.) are barristers who draft Government Bills.

(Further reading: Baxter, *The development of the Treasury, 1660-1702*, 1957.)

TREASURY BENCH

See FRONT BENCHES.

TRIERS OF PETITIONS

See PETITIONS.

TRINIDAD AND TOBAGO PARLIAMENT

From 1797, when the Spanish rulers of the island capitulated to the British, Trinidad was administered by a Governor. From 1801 to 1803 he had the assistance of a Council of Advice, and from 1803 to 1831 he was advised by a body described as His Majesty's Council. The legislature of Trinidad and Tobago (joined to Trinidad in 1889) was first established in 1831 as a Council of Government 'having full authority to make new, and repeal old, laws in furtherance of order and good government'. The same form of legislature continued with slight changes until 1924, when a small number of elected members were introduced, but *ex-officio* and nominated members were in the majority. In 1941 the elected membership of the Legislative Council was made equal to the *ex-officio* and nominated membership, but the Governor had a casting vote. In 1946 the franchise was amended and voting was carried on for the first time on the basis of adult suffrage. In 1950 a new Constitution was introduced, and the Council consisted of 3 *ex-officio*, 5 nominated, and 18 elected members, the Governor being replaced by a Speaker. Another advance was made in 1956 as the result of the appointment of a Constitutional Reform Committee by the Governor in January 1955 which reported in February 1956. It recommended the creation of a Chief Minister elected by the Legislative Council as Leader of the Government, the replacement of the Financial Secretary by an elected Finance Minister, and an increase in the elected members of both Executive and Legislative Councils. The Speaker was also to be elected instead of nominated. In 1959 the Chief Minister became the Premier and the Executive Council was replaced by a Cabinet. The Legislative Council then had 2 *ex-officio* members, 5 nominated unofficials, and 24 elected members. The Cabinet consisted of the Premier as Chairman, 2 *ex-officio* members and 8 elected by the Legislative Council from among its own elected members.

In 1958 Trinidad and Tobago became a member of the short-lived West Indies Federation, and achieved internal self-government in 1961 prior to the dissolution of the Federation. The self-governing Constitution provided for a bicameral legislature with a Senate of 21 members appointed by the Governor and a House of Representatives of 30 members elected by universal adult suffrage. Following the secession of Jamaica from the Federation in 1961, Trinidad and Tobago also decided to withdraw, and a conference held in London in 1962 led to the framing of a new Constitution and the attainment of independence on 31 August of that year.

The Constitution provides for a Governor-General and the retention of the bicameral legislature which had been established under the self-governing Constitution. The size of the Senate was increased to 24 members and comprises 13 appointed on the advice of the Prime Minister, 4 on the advice of the Leader of the Opposition, and 7 on the advice of the Prime Minister after consultation with certain religious, economic and social bodies. The size of the House of Representatives remains at 30 members, but provision has been made to permit this number to be varied. The Speaker may be elected either from among the members or from outside the House. The Cabinet may include not more than 2 Senators, or not more than 3 if the Attorney-General is a Senator.

The Constitution includes provisions for the safeguarding of fundamental freedoms and incorporates a special amendment procedure. There are ordinarily entrenched and specially entrenched provisions, the former relating to such matters as human rights and fundamental freedoms, the prorogation of Parliament, the Public and Police Service Commissions, and the Auditor-General; the latter relating to the office of Governor-General, the establishment and composition of both Houses of Parliament, the Elections Commission and the Boundaries Commission, the judicature, and the amendment of the Constitution. The amendment of an ordinarily entrenched provision requires the agreement of at least two-thirds of the membership of each House, while the amendment of a specially entrenched provision requires the approval of at least three-quarters of the members of the House of Representatives and two-thirds of the members of the Senate.

The seat of the legislature is Port-of-Spain, and Parliament is housed in the administration building commonly known as the 'Red House'.

TURKS AND CAICOS ISLANDS LEGISLATIVE ASSEMBLY

Power to constitute a separate government for the Turks and Caicos Islands (previously administered as a dependency of Jamaica) was bestowed on the Queen by the Cayman Islands and Turks and

Caicos Islands Act of 1958. An Executive Council and a Legislative Assembly with 9 elected members was established under a Constitution proclaimed in July 1959 but, as Jamaica still retained power to apply her laws to the islands, they received a new Constitution in 1962, when Jamaica became independent. This provided for an Administrator, an Executive Council with 2 *ex-officio* members, one nominated from the nominated members of the Legislative Assembly and 2 elected by all members of the Assembly from among the elected members.

The Assembly has 2 or 3 *ex-officio*, and 2 or 3 nominated and 9 elected members and is presided over by the Administrator, or in his absence by a Deputy President elected by the Assembly and submitted to the Administrator for the Queen's Consent. He has power to enforce the passing of legislation if he considers it expedient.

In June 1963 a working party met at Nassau to consider a merger of the Administrations of the Turks and Caicos Islands and the Bahamas. The party's report indicated, however, that the practical problems involved made it impossible to recommend a merger at that time.

TWELVE O'CLOCK RULE

See TEN O'CLOCK RULE.

TYNWALD

See MANX PARLIAMENT.

U

UGANDA PARLIAMENT

Uganda became an independent country in the Commonwealth on 9 October 1962 under a Constitution which took account of the special position of the kingdom of Buganda and other monarchic districts. The original independence Constitution provided for a federal relationship between Buganda and the rest of Uganda and permitted certain rights in respect of local administration and legislation to other kingdoms and special districts within the country. Provision was made for a unicameral National Assembly consisting of a Speaker and 92 members, Buganda being represented in the National Assembly by 21 members indirectly elected by Buganda's own Parliament, the Lukiko, sitting as an electoral college. The Lukiko of Buganda consisted of 100 members of whom 68 were directly elected, 6 were nominees of the Kabaka (the King of Buganda), 20 were chiefs who sat *ex-officio*, and 6 were ministers elected by the Lukiko.

On 1 October 1963, the office of Governor-General was abolished and the Queen was replaced as head of state by a President, the Kabaka of Buganda becoming the first President of Uganda. On 24 February 1966, however, following the arrest of 5 Cabinet ministers, the Prime Minister, Dr. Milton Obote, announced the suspension of the Constitution and assumed all the powers of government. On 15 April a new interim Constitution was adopted by the National Assembly and Dr. Obote was himself sworn in as President. In February 1967 the Uganda High Court ruled that the new Constitution was lawful and on 8 September of the same year the Bill for a new permanent Constitution was unanimously adopted by the Uganda Parliament sitting as a Constituent Assembly.

Under the new Constitution Uganda is a unitary State, the four hereditary kingdoms of Buganda, Ankole, Bunyoro and Toro having been abolished. The President of Uganda is the head of both State and Government and his office is an elective one. The election of the President is linked to the election of the National Assembly. Each candidate at a General Election must declare which presidential candidate he supports, and the presidential candidate who is supported by the party gaining a majority of the seats in the National Assembly is normally declared President. The qualifications for a presidential candidate are that he be a citizen of Uganda, at least thirty-five years of age and qualified to be a member of the National Assembly. The

President summons the Assembly and has the power to prorogue and dissolve it at any time. He presides over the Cabinet, which is responsible to Parliament, and he appoints the Vice-President, ministers and deputy ministers from among the members of the National Assembly. The President's term of office is normally five years unless he is removed by vote of the National Assembly.

The Parliament of Uganda consists of the President and the National Assembly, the latter comprising 82 members elected in single-member constituencies by universal adult suffrage. The Constitution provides that the party having the greatest number of elected members in the National Assembly shall itself elect such further number of specially elected members as are required to give it a majority of not more than 10 over all non-government members combined. The duration of Parliament is five years unless sooner dissolved. A General Election must be held within sixty days of a dissolution and a new National Assembly must convene within thirty days after the holding of the election.

The Constitution, like its predecessor, provides for the protection of fundamental human rights and also for the process of constitutional amendment. The Constitution may be amended by ordinary Act of Parliament except for certain entrenched provisions which require not less than a two-thirds majority of the total membership of the National Assembly at both the second and third readings of the amending Bill.

Uganda's first Legislative Council was set up in 1921 and comprised 6 appointed European members. An Asian member was appointed in 1926 and in 1945 3 African members were appointed to the Council for the first time. In 1950 the membership of the Legislative Council comprised 16 official and 8 African, 4 Asian and 4 European unofficial members, all appointed. Various constitutional changes took place in the years preceding the achievement of independence, the main obstacle to constitutional progress being the question of Buganda's association with the central government. In 1955 the size of the Legislative Council was increased to 60, of which the African membership totalled 30, and in 1957 a Speaker was appointed for the first time. In 1958 the first direct elections took place for representative members on a qualitative franchise, and in 1961 elections were held for 82 elected members under a franchise which conferred the right to vote on about 80 per cent of the adult population. On 1 March 1962 Uganda became internally self-governing and thus arrived at the threshold of independence.

UNICAMERAL LEGISLATURE

A legislature consisting of one chamber only. It is not considered by most authorities as satisfactory in its operation as a Parliament which has an upper and a lower House (*see* BICAMERAL LEGISLATURE). However, there are many supporters of unicameralism, particularly in

Canada and the United States, who contend that a single chamber affords a simpler, more direct, and more expeditious method of legislation; also that it centralizes authority and fixes responsibility, and is therefore more responsive to public opinion. Single-chamber legislatures in the British Commonwealth include those of New Zealand, Ghana, Cyprus, Sierra Leone, Tanzania, Uganda, Malta, Malawi, Zambia, the Gambia, Guyana, Singapore, Botswana, Rhodesia, Western Samoa, the Australian State of Queensland, all the Canadian Provinces, the Indian States of Assam, Gujarat, Hariana, Kerala, Nagaland, Orissa and Rajasthan, and all the States of Malaysia.

UNIONIST PARTY

Formed in 1886 to support the maintenance of the parliamentary union between Great Britain and Ireland, and consequently to oppose Home Rule. It was actually a coalition of Conservatives and Liberal Unionists, whose principles and policy eventually became identified with the Conservative Party (q.v.). The name Unionist survives in the official title of this party—the Conservative and Unionist Party, and Conservative members of the House of Commons are still described as Unionists in Vacher's *Parliamentary Companion* (q.v.). Conservative supporters in Northern Ireland continue to call themselves Ulster Unionists.

UNIVERSITY REPRESENTATION

The representation of universities in the House of Commons came to an end with the Parliament of 1945–50. The university constituencies were abolished by implication by the Representation of the People Act, 1948, Section 1 of which states that there shall, for the purpose of parliamentary elections, be the county and borough constituencies, each returning a single member, and no other constituencies. Thus for the first time in nearly 350 years the House of Commons which was constituted after the General Election of 1950 included no members to represent the special interests of universities. In the Northern Ireland Parliament, 4 members represented Queen's University, Belfast until these seats were abolished prior to the General Election of February 1969.

Prior to their abolition there were seven university constituencies returning 12 members between them. Oxford and Cambridge, the ancient universities and the first to be represented in Parliament, each returned 2 members; London University, the University of Wales, and Queen's University, Belfast, each returned 1 member; the Universities of Durham, Manchester, Birmingham, Liverpool, Leeds, Sheffield, Bristol, and Reading were combined to form one constituency returning 2 members; and the Scottish universities, Edinburgh, St. Andrews, Glasgow, and Aberdeen, were combined to form a constituency returning 3 members. The electors who returned the university members were graduates of the universities concerned who had kept their names upon the universities' registers. A university voters' qualification entitled an elector to a university vote in addition to his residential vote. Many university voters had no residential vote, however, for the university electorate was scattered all over the world. At the 1945 election the total university electorate was 217,655, made up as follows: Oxford, 28,921; Cambridge, 42,012; London, 23,948; Combined English, 42,312; Scottish, 63,581; Wales, 11,847; Queen's, Belfast, 5,134.

University representation had always been a unique feature of the British parliamentary system and had for some years been a controversial issue, staunchly defended by some, roundly condemned by others. The main argument against this form of representation has always been that it confers a privilege upon a special class and is contrary to the democratic principle of 'one man, one vote'. Advocates of its retention have advanced various reasons in its justification: it affords representation of the professional classes who are otherwise under-represented in the Commons; the tendency of the universities to elect representatives who are free of party associations serves to introduce a healthy independent element into a House dominated by the major political parties; the vast responsibilities entrusted to universities require that they send representatives to Westminster, not only to safeguard their interests but to answer for their activities also; and most of the defenders of university representation agree that the fact of its being an ancient and harmless tradition which distinguishes the British Parliament from all other national assemblies is a sufficient reason for its retention. Two compromise suggestions which have been put forward in the past but never adopted are, firstly, that universities should be represented in the House of Lords, and, secondly, that an elector qualified as a university voter should be permitted to choose whether he will cast a university vote or a residential vote at an election. Sir Alan Herbert has argued against the former suggestion on the ground that there are many university issues, such as those involving finance, which could not be debated in the Lords. The alternative suggestion would seem to provide a hopeful compromise should the question ever be reopened, which seems unlikely.

Lawyers from the Universities of Oxford and Cambridge had been summoned to attend Parliament as early as the reign of Edward I, but university representation is usually regarded as having originated in 1603. In that year James I granted letters patent to both universities for the return of 2 burgesses to Parliament. Oxford and Cambridge were the only universities represented until 1800, when by the Act of Union with Ireland the University of Dublin was granted 1 seat in the House of Commons, and thus became the first university to be enfranchised by statute. The Reform Act, 1832, increased Dublin's representation to 2. The Representation of the People Act, 1867, recognized the claims of London University and granted it representation by 1 member. The Scottish Universities, whose claims had been overlooked at the time of the Reform Bill, were enfranchised in 1868. They were granted 2 seats, 1 for Edinburgh and St. Andrews and 1 for Glasgow and Aberdeen, bringing the total number of university members in the House of Commons to 9. At this time opposition to the principle of university representation began to be voiced. When London University was enfranchised, John Bright proclaimed his disagreement with the principle, although he did not oppose the enfranchisement of London specifically. In 1885 the Liberal member, James Bryce, moved the abolition of the university constituencies and cited various arguments in support of his views: representation was against the interests of the univerisites themselves as it introduced the turmoil of politics into what should be an atmosphere of academic calm; university members were elected not by the teaching bodies but by graduates scattered all over the country who lacked a proper understanding of university matters; the privilege of voting was obtained by the payment of fees, thus restricting the franchise to wealthier graduates. However, Bryce's proposal was defeated by a majority of 181. In 1912 a Liberal Government proposed the abolition of the university seats but nothing came of the attempt, the Bill containing the proposal being lost for entirely different reasons.

In 1918, in spite of the feeling which had existed against it, university representation was extended. It had long been held by the Liberals that the university seats were a preserve of the Conservatives, and to remove the grounds for this allegation it was decided to enfranchise the modern universities. Compromise having been reached by both parties at the Speaker's Conference on Electoral Reform in 1916, the Representation of the People Act, 1918, completely overhauled the system of university representation and made provision for several new seats. Oxford, Cambridge, and London retained their representation, and the other English universities (with the exception of Reading which was added in 1928 by a special Act) were formed into a single constituency returning 2 members. The Scottish Universities became a single constituency returning 3 members, and the University of Wales was given 1 seat. Graduation, together with a registration fee not exceeding £1, became the electoral qualification, and women graduates over the age of thirty were given the university vote. (The same Act conferred the general franchise upon women of the same age.) Proportional representation (q.v.) in the form of the single transferable vote was introduced in constituencies returning more than one member. By-elections excepted, a graduate of more than one university could only vote in one university constituency. Under the Redistribution of Seats (Ireland) Act, 1918, the National University of Ireland

and Queen's University, Belfast, were each granted representation by 1 member. The former never returned a member to Westminster, however, and Dublin University ceased to be represented in 1922 when the Irish Free State was established.

Abolition was again proposed by a Labour Government in the Representation of the People Bill, 1931, and again on a Labour motion in 1935. The matter was not discussed again until 1944, when another Speaker's Conference reported in favour of retaining the university seats, with the proviso that every graduate should be automatically registered without the payment of a fee. In this year also the Liberal Party withdrew its traditional opposition to the principle, declaring that university education was no longer the exclusive privilege of the wealthy and that the number of university voters had substantially increased. The party suggested that the university voter, instead of having a second vote, should choose which vote he would exercise. In spite of these developments, the Labour Government which took office in 1945 again proposed abolition in the Representation of the People Bill, 1948, and with its large majority in the Commons the Government won the day. Mr. (as he then was) Winston Churchill moved a reasoned amendment on the third reading of the Bill, and during the course of his speech he gave a pledge to restore the university seats should his party be returned to power. His amendment was defeated by 338 votes to 193. Although the Conservative Party was in office from 1951 to 1964, no move was made to restore these constituencies, probably due to its reluctance to revive such a controversial issue. Abolition was not opposed by the Conservative peers in the House of Lords, for, as the Marquess of Salisbury explained, it would have been improper for the Lords to attempt to interfere with the constitution of the other House. The Representation of the People Act, 1948, received the Royal Assent on 30 July of that year, and an institution which had survived for three and a half centuries ceased to exist, except in Northern Ireland. However, a form of university representation has been introduced in the Indian State Parliaments (q.v.), where one-twelfth of the total membership of each Legislative Council (upper House) is elected by graduates of the State of three years' standing.

The members representing the university constituencies at the time of their abolition were Sir Alan Herbert and Sir Arthur Salter (Oxford), Kenneth Pickthorn and Wilson Harris (Cambridge), Sir Ernest Graham-Little (London), Sir John Anderson, Sir John Graham Kerr, and Walter Elliot (Scottish Universities), Henry Strauss and Kenneth Lindsay (Combined English Universities), William Gruffydd (Wales), and Douglas Savory (Queen's, Belfast).

During the 350 years of their existence, the university constituencies returned many eminent men as their representatives, among them

Prime Ministers and Speakers of the House of Commons. Oxford has included Sir Robert Peel and Gladstone among its burgesses, and Sir Francis Bacon, Sir Isaac Newton, William Pitt the younger, and Lord Palmerston all sat for Cambridge. Dublin University has been represented by Lord Carson and the Scottish Universities by Lord Tweedsmuir.

The record of the university members in Parliament was an excellent one. At least two measures of great social importance resulted from the influence of university members; the Matrimonial Causes Act, 1937, was introduced and piloted through the House as a Private Members' Bill by Sir Alan Herbert, and the Family Allowances Act, 1945, was largely the achievement of Miss Eleanor Rathbone, who represented the Combined English Universities from 1929 until her death in 1946. The case of Ramsay MacDonald is bound to sound a note of irony, however. Speaking in 1931 of university representation he said: 'If you want materialism at its very worst masquerading under the most sacred guise, you find it in the university for generations. . . . Our view is that, if there be any special institution requiring representation here, it is certainly not the universities.' At the General Election of 1935 MacDonald lost his seat, but he was returned at a by-election during the following year as a Member for the Scottish Universities.

(Further reading: Humberstone, *University representation*, 1951; Rex, *University representation in England, 1604–90*, 1954.)

UNLEARNED PARLIAMENT

Lord Chancellor Beaufort, in framing the writ of summons to the Parliament of 1426, illegally inserted a prohibition that any man of law should be elected. This Parliament was afterwards branded as the Unlearned Parliament or *Parliamentum indoctum*, probably by the legal profession.

UNOFFICIAL MEMBER

A member of a colonial legislature who may be elected or nominated by the Governor and who holds no Colonial Office appointment. There are usually more elected unofficials than nominated, but in most cases the Governor has the right to appoint provisional members in place of those temporarily absent, and extraordinary members when the advice of particular persons is required regarding a subject under discussion in the Legislative Council. Unofficial members are usually included in a Colony's Executive Council.

UNOPPOSED BUSINESS

See OPPOSED AND UNOPPOSED BUSINESS.

UNOPPOSED MOTION

A substantive motion, which with the unanimous consent of the House is moved without notice, is known in some Commonwealth Parliaments as an unopposed motion. It is so-called because one dissenting voice is enough to block its introduction. The waiving of notice in respect of a motion which normally requires notice constitutes the suspension of a normal procedural requirement and therefore depends on the concurrence of all members present.

Such motions may be debated, but normally their use is confined to matters of a formal character, such as an expression of condolence, the adjournment of the House over a holiday, the leave of absence of a member, or the composition of a committee; or to matters concerning the convenience of the House, such as the rearrangement of business or the prolongation of a sitting. In the Canadian House of Commons the procedure of seeking the unanimous consent of the House to a course of action not envisaged by the rules is frequently resorted to.

If a private member desires to bring forward a matter of public concern without notice he must avail himself of the procedure by which he can propose the adjournment of the House for the purpose of holding an emergency debate.

UNOPPOSED RETURN

A motion may be moved in the House, notice having been given, for an unopposed return, i.e., for a paper compiled by a government department for the information of members. Such a motion requires the assent of the minister concerned, and unless this has been signified to the Speaker he will pass over the motion.

UNOPPOSED RETURNS (ELECTIONS)

Should only one candidate be nominated to stand for election to Parliament in any constituency, he is automatically declared elected without a contest. There is sometimes a small number of unopposed returns in a General Election. In the United Kingdom General Election of 1955, however, not a single candidate was returned unopposed, the first such occasion since 1832. Every seat was again contested in 1959, 1964, 1966 and 1970.

UNPARLIAMENTARY EXPRESSIONS

Expressions which may be ruled out of order in Parliament cover a wide range, and the Speaker or Chairman is often required to make a quick decision as to whether he can allow the Government to be accused of 'arrant political jobbery' or a member to be described as a 'pig'. What is allowed during one period of parliamentary history is not necessarily allowed at another. When Lord Shaftesbury took his seat as Lord Chancellor in 1672 the Duke of York called him a rascal and a villain. (The Chancellor replied that he was obliged to His Royal Highness for not calling him a coward and a papist as well.) On the other hand, Lord Melbourne said he remembered a Speaker ruling out of order a reference to a member as 'a member of the opposition'. In these days, any epithet which reflects upon the character of a member of either House is considered disorderly. The imputation that a minister or member is not telling the truth is never allowed; certainly 'terminological inexactitude' has been passed over, but not such circumlocutions as 'a complete distortion of the facts'. Apart from this ban on alluding to other members as liars or hypocrites, there is some disagreement throughout the Commonwealth as to what constitutes an unparliamentary expression. Obviously there are too many possibilities for any exact rules to be laid down, and the amount of latitude allowed in offensive language depends entirely on the Chair and the good taste of members. Some Speakers have rather high standards, and a Rhodesian Speaker objected strongly when a member described a road in his constituency as having more curves than a certain popular film star! Usually, as in this case, a member will withdraw an unparliamentary expression when directed to do so by the Speaker, but if he refuses to do so he can be suspended for the remainder of the sitting or named to the House for disregarding the authority of the Chair.

In some Parliaments it is out of order for one member to accuse another of 'wasting the time of the House'. Although not particularly offensive, the remark is construed as a reflection upon the Chair, it being the sole responsibility of the Chair to decide such matters.

Many an anecdote can be related involving the use of an unparliamentary expression. One of the most famous concerns the occasion when Disraeli was called to order for declaring that half the Cabinet were asses. 'Mr. Speaker, I withdraw,' he apologized, 'half the Cabinet are not asses!'

An interesting list of words and phrases allowed and disallowed in the Parliaments of the Commonwealth is given in each annual issue of *The Table*, the Journal of the Society of Clerks-at-the-Table in Commonwealth Parliaments.

UNPRINTED PAPERS

Reports, accounts, and other papers of institutions, corporations, and government departments which, although presented to Parliament under a statutory obligation, are not printed by either House as parliamentary papers, but may be, and often are, printed by the bodies concerned.

UNREPORTED PARLIAMENT

The Parliament of 1768–74, so called because of the rigid enforcement of the rule excluding strangers. The House of Lords first applied the rule, excluding even Members of the House of Commons, who immediately retaliated by excluding the peers from their Chamber. This, of course, involved the exclusion of the public. A record of the proceedings of this Parliament does exist, however, in the reports compiled by the Member for Lostwithiel, Sir Henry Cavendish (q.v.).

UPPER CHAMBER

See BICAMERAL LEGISLATURE.

'USUAL CHANNELS'

The Government and Opposition Whips constitute the 'usual channels', through which agreements are made with regard to the arrangement of business and other matters. Should the Opposition request facilities for debating a question additional to the programme, the Government Chief Whip would be likely to ask in return for the Opposition's co-operation in expediting the passage of certain other items of business in order that the necessary time may be found.

Negotiations through the 'usual channels' are of an informal nature, but are of great importance as a means of securing agreement between the parties as to a fair and equitable allocation of parliamentary time. As Sir Ivor Jennings pointed out in his *Parliament*, 'If either [side] pressed its rights to the uttermost, the parliamentary system would come to an end.'

The 'usual channels' are formalized to the extent that a Treasury Officer assists in the negotiations between the Whips in the capacity of an honest broker.

V

VACHER'S *PARLIAMENTARY COMPANION*

A pocket-sized work of reference which is issued quarterly and provides up-to-date lists of members of both Houses of Parliament. Founded in 1831, it contains much useful information, including members' addresses, ranks and titles of peers, constituencies represented by Members of the House of Commons, the composition of the Royal Household, Privy Council, and Cabinet, and lists of diplomatic representatives and the principal officers of both Houses of Parliament and government departments. The annual subscription is £1.50 and individual copies can be purchased for 45p.

VETO BILL

A Bill to curtail the powers of the House of Lords. Two such Bills were passed by the House of Commons in 1911 and 1949 and became the Parliament Acts, 1911 and 1949 (q.v.).

VICEROY

After the Indian Mutiny the administration of India was transferred in 1858 from the East India Company to the Crown, and the Governor-General received the new title of Viceroy. The first to bear this was Lord Canning and the last before India received her independence in 1947 was Earl Mountbatten.

VICTORIA (1819–1901) AND PARLIAMENT

The young Princess Victoria succeeded to the throne on 20 June 1837 and began the longest reign in the history of the British monarchy. The immediate effect of her accession was to separate the Crowns of England and Hanover, succession in the female line being prohibited in Hanover under the Salic Law. The Hanoverian Crown was inherited by the Duke of Cumberland, younger brother of the late King William IV and uncle to Victoria.

The memorable reign of Queen Victoria was of the highest constitutional importance for it realized the modern conception of a constitutional monarchy. Through her strict observance of constitutional forms and conventions Victoria established that relationship between the Crown and its ministers which is to-day recognized as proper and compatible with a democratic form of government. At her accession Victoria inherited a number of active prerogatives, but by the time her long reign reached its close almost all vestiges of personal authority had passed from the hands of the Sovereign. This was due to a combination of factors—her own meticulous regard for her constitutional position, the growth of radical institutions and the ascendancy of democratic ideals, and the reduction in the personal participation of the Queen in the affairs of government which was the inevitable result of her voluntary seclusion after the death of the Prince Consort and her frequent informal visits overseas. Although a woman of decided views and prejudices she never permitted them to influence her conduct as the Queen. She openly criticized policies she disliked, but never actively opposed ministers of whom she disapproved nor withheld from them the confidence which was their constitutional right. She recognized the supremacy of the popular will when it conflicted with her own inclinations, and although she made no secret of her political predilections she invariably submitted to the predominant feeling. She was, however, by no means disposed to regard the rôle of Sovereign as that of a mere figurehead. To the end of her reign she regarded the prerogative of dissolving Parliament as a personal one, her means of appealing to the country in the event of a failure to resolve a dispute with her ministers. She insisted on her right to be consulted and to express her views on policy and to the last she maintained that no ministerial decision could properly be taken without her prior knowledge. The field of foreign affairs was one within which she regarded the Sovereign as having a particular right to exert her influence, and this view led to serious difficulties between the Queen and one of her most masterful ministers, Lord Palmerston. She reacted strongly when Parliament dissolved the personal control of the Crown over the army, sincerely believing that her ministers had destroyed a prerogative which should have been regarded as inalienable. She spared no effort in studying and attempting to master the details of government and her influence was on many an occasion exerted to the advantage of the nation and the Empire. Possessed of no outstanding intellectual attainment, she had strength of will and character, she was conscientious in her devotion to duty, and often shrewd in her judgment. Whatever her personal limitations she also possessed truly regal qualities, and however much of an autocrat she may have appeared in her private life she was inspired as a ruler by the finest democratic principles. In her husband she had a counsellor on whom she implicitly relied, but after his death she relied increasingly upon her ministers.

On her accession she continued Lord Melbourne (who was her political tutor and closest counsellor during the earliest years of her reign) in office, and at the General Election which followed the dissolution of Parliament in July 1837 the Liberals maintained an adequate, if not commanding, majority over the Conservatives of 348 to 310. On 20 November the Queen opened her first Parliament. The Civil List was fixed at £385,000 and was never altered during the reign.

In 1839 Victoria came face to face with her first ministerial crisis, and she handled the situation with a rather clumsy obduracy which she was never to repeat. Upon his majority falling to five in a crucial division, Melbourne rightly felt that he had lost the confidence of Parliament and tendered his resignation, advising the Queen to send for Sir Robert Peel. Peel agreed to form a Government on condition that the Queen's ladies, who had been drawn from the leading Whig families, were replaced by ladies with Tory associations. The Queen completely failed to appreciate Peel's motives in stipulating such a condition, and Melbourne's fatherly counsel does not seem to have been in evidence on this occasion. Upon her indignant refusal to comply with what she regarded as an insolent request, Peel declined to take office, and at the Queen's persuasion Melbourne returned to the prime ministership and continued to lead the Government for another two years. The Queen subsequently confessed quite frankly to the error of which she had been guilty, and the practice of choosing the ladies of the household from one political party shortly afterwards ceased.

Victoria's marriage to Prince Albert on 10 February 1840 heralded a new phase of her life, one of unblemished domestic happiness but many public anxieties also. The Prince was a devoted husband and a wise counsellor, but he failed to inspire affection and confidence in the country. Throughout his life he was subjected to ill-informed criticism and attack. Even before his marriage to the Queen she was distressed by an undignified parliamentary wrangle which took place over the proposed status and income of the Prince. Parliament rejected a proposal to accord him precedence next the Queen and above the other members of the Royal Family and carried a reduction in his proposed annuity from £50,000 to £30,000. This so incensed Lord John Russell that he declared somewhat rashly that the action of the House was intended as a mark of disrespect to the Queen. The Prince's influence over the Queen was far from the malevolent one which many people supposed and the welfare of his adopted land was his first concern in his capacity as the Queen's adviser. On 11 September 1846 he was admitted to the Privy Council and he subsequently summarized his functions as 'the husband of the Queen, the tutor of the royal children, the private secretary of the Sovereign and her permanent minister', an accurate description of himself, albeit a dangerous one from the point of view of the constitutional considerations involved.

In June 1841 Melbourne's Government was defeated by 36 votes on a proposal to reduce the sugar duty and a vote of confidence was carried against him by one vote. On 29 June Parliament was dissolved and the ensuing elections returned a large Conservative majority to the House of Commons. The Queen absented herself from the opening of the new Parliament on 19 August, thus indicating her disapproval of the composition of the new House of Commons, and her speech was read by the Lord Chancellor. On 28 August Melbourne, unable to hold on any longer in the face of a hostile majority, resigned office, and on his advice she invited Sir Robert Peel to form a Government. Both the Queen and her new Prime Minister behaved with extreme tact and the change of government was smoothly effected. Melbourne, whose retirement from office deeply distressed her at first, continued as her personal friend, but she very correctly relied upon her new Prime Minister for all political advice. In fact, to quote Peel himself, he found in the Queen 'a scrupulous and most punctual discharge of every public duty, and an exact understanding of the relation of a constitutional Sovereign to her advisers'.

In 1845 another ministerial crisis occurred. Great misery and distress threatened the working classes as a result of the failure of the potato crop in Ireland and the harvest in Britain, and Peel resolved, in spite of the attitude of his own party, on the repeal of the corn laws as the only remedy to a desperate situation. Although seriously disturbed at the prospect of such a measure the Queen unhesitatingly supported Peel in his resolve. Peel decided that it would be correct to allow the party which had advocated repeal in the past to carry the necessary legislation through Parliament, and he accordingly resigned to enable Lord John Russell to form a Liberal Government. But Russell's attempt proved abortive and Peel returned to office, and it was thus a Conservative Government which passed the Bill for repeal. On the day it became law, however, Peel was defeated on the Irish Coercion Bill, and a new Government was formed by Lord John Russell in July 1846. A rather stupid objection was raised by the protectionists because Prince Albert was present in the House of Commons' gallery to hear Peel explain his repeal proposals. They chose to regard his presence as implying partiality on the part of the Crown and the Prince treated the protest so seriously that he never again attended a debate in the House of Commons.

The return of a Liberal Government had been dreaded by the Queen as it also meant the return of Lord Palmerston to the Foreign Office. No Liberal administration would have considered the exclusion of Palmerston, who would have refused any office other than that of Foreign Secretary, and he had already crossed swords with the Queen during his previous tenure of that office. Her fears proved more than justified. Palmerston was a strong and independent minister, resentful of control, and reluctant to recognize any check upon his power outside Parliament. His encouragement of revolutionary movements in Europe was not at all to the Queen's liking, and she was greatly incensed by his continual disregard of her constitutional right to be consulted before committing the country to a particular course of action.

The Liberals were secured in office at the General Election of 1847, the new Parliament being composed of 325 Liberals, 226 protectionists, and 105 free traders or Peelites. The prorogation ceremony of 5 September 1848 took place for the first time in the Peers' Chamber of the new Houses of Parliament which had been rebuilt following the fire of 1834.

The breach between the Queen and Palmerston grew ever wider as Russell's ministry wore on and in 1851 it reached a crisis which resulted in Palmerston's dismissal. His persistent failure to comply with her demands provoked the Queen into drawing up the famous memorandum to Lord John Russell in 1850 in which she required '(1) that the Foreign Secretary will distinctly state what he proposes in a given case, in order that the Queen may know as distinctly to what she has given her royal sanction; (2) having once given her sanction to a measure, that it be not arbitrarily altered or modified by the minister; such an act she must consider as failure in sincerity towards the Crown, and justly to be visited by the exercise of her constitutional right of dismissing that minister.' On being informed of the Queen's displeasure Palmerston blandly expressed his regret and undertook to amend his ways, remained in office, and cheerfully carried on as before. But his action in the following year of committing the country to recognition of Louis Napoleon's *coup d'état* without consulting the Queen or his colleagues was too much for Lord John Russell who, in his exasperation, resolved the problem for the Queen by advising her to dismiss her Foreign Secretary. Palmerston, however, was immensely popular outside the Court and his influence was considerable. Within two months of his own dismissal he had encompassed the defeat of his former colleagues, who resigned on 20 February 1852, on the rejection of the Militia Bill. Lord Derby formed a Conservative Government with Disraeli as Chancellor of the Exchequer, but the General Election of the same year left the Conservatives in a minority and Derby's Government resigned when Disraeli's Budget was rejected. In December a Coalition Government was formed under Lord Aberdeen and Palmerston was back in office, this time as Home Secretary. The way to supreme power was now fully paved for Palmerston. In 1854, largely owing to his predominating influence, the Crimean War broke out, in spite of Lord Aberdeen's attempts to avert it. In January of the following year, as a result of his lukewarm and vacillating conduct of the war, Aberdeen was forced to resign, and the Queen was faced with the distasteful necessity of appointing Palmerston in his stead. The measure of her reluctance to appoint him may be gauged from the fact that she negotiated with both Derby and Russell before resigning herself to the inevitable, but it is to her great credit that having made the appointment she reposed the utmost confidence in her new Prime Minister. Peace was concluded on 30 March 1856, and the Queen acknowledged Palmerston as the architect of the victory by conferring the Garter upon him.

In 1858 Palmerston was defeated over his French Alliance policy and Lord Derby returned to office. On 2 August, following upon the Indian Mutiny, the administration of India was transferred from the East India Company to the Crown. The proclamation to the Indian people which was drawn up for the occasion is worthy to stand by itself as a tribute to the memory of Queen Victoria, for it is to her benign influence that its language, couched in terms of warm humanity and friendship, is due. The part she played in its composition did much to conciliate Indian feeling. Lord Derby's Government was defeated in April 1859 on its Reform Bill and Parliament was dissolved. The General Election result left the Conservatives in a minority of 43 and much against her will the Queen was compelled to recall Palmerston. The Queen's relations with this administration proved exceptionally difficult, the foreign policy pursued by Palmerston and Lord John Russell (the Foreign Secretary) meeting with her strongest disapproval. In 1861 there arose the affair of the *Trent*, an incident which might have precipitated war between England and America had it not been for the Prince Consort's intervention. America was at that time engaged in its disastrous civil war, and the Palmerston administration made no secret of its sympathies with the southern cause. When a federal warship fired on an English steamer, the *Trent*, which was known to be carrying two southern envoys, Palmerston drafted a strongly worded despatch to Washington which, had it been sent, would probably have involved England in war with America. The Prince Consort counselled moderation and re-drafted the despatch with the result that a crisis was averted. This was the last time that the Prince exerted his influence on behalf of the Government for on 14 December 1861 he died, leaving his widow desolate and inconsolable and on the threshold of an altogether fresh era of her life.

For five years following her husband's death the Queen declined to open Parliament in person and she never again read the Speech from the Throne herself. Her refusal to participate in ceremonial functions often caused her governments grave concern, particularly as a republican movement was developing within radical circles, and her action in withdrawing herself completely from public life lent force to their arguments in favour of the republican form of government. It was not generally appreciated that her bereavement in no way impaired her sense of duty. She did not once neglect affairs of state during her seclusion and she applied herself to the business of government with the same conscientious industry which had always characterized her.

In 1865 Parliament was dissolved and the Liberals slightly increased their majority at the General Election, but before the meeting of the new Parliament Palmerston died. In her tributes to this great statesman the Queen, with characteristic generosity, forgot the rancour of the past and sincerely mourned his passing. She charged Russell, who had become an earl in 1861, with the task of forming the new Government, and in response to his special request she consented to open Parliament on 10 February 1866. She insisted, however, on divesting the ceremony of its traditional colour and her speech was read on her behalf by the Lord Chancellor. On the six subsequent occasions when she opened Parliament the traditional procedure was never restored. In June of the same year Russell's Government was defeated on its Reform Bill, and to the chagrin of the Queen, who took the view that it was the Government's duty to remain in office because of the difficult foreign situation, Russell insisted on resignation. In July Lord Derby formed a new Government with Disraeli once again Chancellor of the Exchequer. The Queen was very anxious to see a settlement of the franchise problem which had overthrown Russell's Government, and in 1867 Disraeli successfully piloted another Reform Bill through Parliament. The Queen held liberal views on the subject of reform. She believed it to be in the interests of the monarchy, Parliament, and the Government to widen the basis of the electorate and was therefore favourably disposed to an extension of the franchise. Although conservative by inclination she was by no means reactionary when judged by the political standards of her time.

In 1868 Derby resigned office owing to ill health and Disraeli became the new Prime Minister. No other minister of the reign ever succeeded in winning the Queen's favour and confidence to the same extent as Disraeli. His tact, wit, charm of manner, and his punctilious observance of constitutional form combined to arouse in the Queen a regard for him which endured until his death. But his first term as her chief minister was not destined to last long. His parliamentary backing was precarious and shortly after accepting office he was defeated on the issue of the disestablishment of the Irish Church, brought forward by Gladstone, by the substantial majority of 65. The idea of disestablishment was personally repugnant to the Queen but she recognized that it was a matter for Parliament to decide. There were three courses open to her in the circumstances. She could accept Disraeli's resignation and thus be compelled to confer office on Gladstone, a course which did not appeal to her as it would inevitably associate the Crown with the cause of disestablishment before the people had an opportunity to pronounce a verdict upon it. She could dissolve Parliament, a course which did not recommend itself because it would force a General Election before the provisions of the 1867 Reform Act could be put into operation. Finally, she could keep Disraeli's Government in office for another six months and rely upon the Opposition not to force a dissolution within that period. Disraeli left it to the Queen to decide which of the three alternatives she would select, and on her own responsibility she chose the final one. The Prime Minister, who explained to the House of Commons the substance of his negotiations with the Queen, was assailed by the Opposition on the ground that he had failed to act in the proper capacity of a constitutional adviser by offering the Queen a choice of courses of action instead of definite advice. In spite of the objections the incident disposed of the illusion that the Sovereign was a mere figurehead and, if anything, added to the Queen's prestige. She very soon demonstrated her recognition of the limits upon her personal power when she assented to a petition from a strong majority of the Commons on the question of Irish Church patronage.

Disraeli was crushingly defeated in the General Election of 1868, the Liberals winning a majority of 128. He set a precedent by tendering his resignation to the Queen before the meeting of the new Parliament, and Gladstone began his first term of office as her Prime Minister. His Government embarked upon a lengthy programme of legislative reforms, of a nature largely distasteful to the Queen, but which she very correctly never resisted. Although Gladstone's policies were diametrically opposed to her own opinions she never permitted her personal views to obstruct the machinery of government. In fact, on the controversial Irish Church Bill it was actually her mediation which carried it through the House of Lords in the face of a threatened conflict between the two Houses. In 1870 the Government began to reorganize the administration of the army in a manner particularly offensive to the Queen. She had always claimed that the direct control of the army by the Crown through the Commander-in-Chief was an inalienable prerogative of the Crown, but one of the new proposals was to subordinate the office of Commander-in-Chief to that of the Secretary-of-State for War, thus bringing the army under direct ministerial control. In June she signed an Order-in-Council giving effect to this proposal. When the Bill embodying the army reforms reached the House of Lords it was thrown out, and the Queen was again faced with a situation she dreaded, a conflict between Lords and Commons. The Government thereupon proposed to the Queen an ingenious device for circumventing the upper House. The practice of purchasing commissions, which the Bill had been designed to abolish, had been established by Royal Warrant and not by statute, and it was proposed to the Queen that she could legally accomplish the Government's objective by the employment of the prerogative on ministerial advice. The usual legislative process, which required the agreement of both Houses, could thus be avoided. Although the Queen regarded this procedure as a sordid subterfuge she felt obliged to comply with it, in spite of her fear of alienating the peers from their attachment to the monarchy.

Republican sentiment was at this time gaining currency in the country and the formation of a republic in France had encouraged the feeling. The main plank used by the republicans in their attack upon the monarchy was the expense of maintaining a royal establishment, and rumours concerning the supposedly fabulous wealth of the Queen became widespread. The allegations were taken up in the House of Commons, and in March 1872 Sir Charles Dilke moved for an inquiry into the royal expenditure. The debate sparked off a disorderly scene in the House, but it was the republicans who were embarrassed in the outcome. Dilke and his seconder mishandled their case by an avowal of their republican convictions and the motion was overwhelmingly defeated, only two other members supporting them in the Division Lobby.

In March 1873 Gladstone was defeated on his Irish University Bill and he immediately resigned. Disraeli, however, declined to form a Government then and there, preferring to wait for the Conservative victory at the polls which he confidently expected. Gladstone was reluctantly compelled to return temporarily to office, complaining that Disraeli's refusal to accept responsibility was unconstitutional in that he had engineered the Government's defeat. The General Election of 1874 resulted in an overwhelming Conservative victory and to the Queen's delight she was enabled to recall Disraeli. Disraeli's policies were in accord with the Queen's own views and there followed a period of the most cordial relations between the Sovereign and her ministers. In actual fact Disraeli was no more influenced by the Queen than any of his predecessors. His personal popularity with her merely enabled him to reconcile her to a distasteful course far more success-fully than a less favoured minister. To quote his own remark: 'Glad-stone treats the Queen like a public department; I treat her like a woman.'

In the session of 1875 the House of Commons altered its procedure relating to the exclusion of strangers (q.v.). Previously, the objection of only one member was required to oblige the Speaker to order the galleries to be cleared, but under the revised rule a vote of the majority of the House became necessary.

In 1876 the Queen was highly gratified when Disraeli was instru-mental in having the title of Empress of India conferred on her. In 1877 Disraeli accepted a peerage and continued to lead the Government from the House of Lords as the Earl of Beaconsfield. During the latter years of this decade the Government became involved in a series of crises in Europe and elsewhere, and Disraeli's policies were vehemently attacked by Gladstone and his followers. The Queen backed her Government with an undeviating faith, but with public opinion Disraeli had lost a great deal of ground. Parliament was dissolved on 24 March 1880, and at the General Election Disraeli was decisively rejected by the country by a majority of 166. Much against her will the Queen invited Gladstone to form his second Government, and while observing a strict constitutional correctness, as always, in her dealings with her ministers, she found herself invariably displeased with their major policies. One of the members elected to the Parliament of 1880 was Charles Bradlaugh (q.v.) who, as an atheist, claimed his right to affirm his allegiance to the Crown instead of taking the oath as was customary. The stand which he took upon his principles involved him in a long struggle with the House of Commons during which he was thrice re-elected for Northampton but was not permitted to take his seat until 1886.

The session of 1881 was notable for the drastic procedural reforms which were adopted by the House of Commons in the face of the unrelenting obstruction of business carried on by the Irish Nationalist members under the leadership of Parnell. The foremost innovation was the closure (q.v.), first introduced on the initiative of Speaker Brand (q.v.), but many of the other rules which have since become integral features of modern procedure date from this period. In the latter half of 1882 the unusual step was taken of calling a special session of Parliament for the exclusive purpose of reforming the rules on a permanent basis.

As Gladstone's second administration continued the Queen grew ever more disquieted with its policies. She took great exception to further army reforms which it effected, deplored the Transvaal peace negotiations which it insisted on pressing to a conclusion, and held it directly responsible for the death of General Gordon at Khartoum, a tragedy resulting from what she regarded as a disastrous Egyptian policy. One measure which did command her support, however, was the Reform Bill of 1884, which proposed the extension of the franchise to the working classes. The Bill was rejected by the House of Lords, and when the Government announced its intention of reintroducing the Bill in the House of Commons a serious conflict between the two Houses appeared imminent. Not for the first time the Queen brought her influence to bear upon the upper House and the passage of the Bill was facilitated, although by way of compromise it was coupled with a second Bill providing for the redistribution of constituencies.

Gladstone's Government, which had forfeited a great deal of respect owing to its Egyptian policy, was defeated on its 1885 Budget, and Lord Salisbury, who had succeeded Disraeli as leader of the Conservative Party on the latter's death in 1881, was invited in the June to form a Government. Salisbury's first ministry was very short-lived. The General Election of November returned only 250 Conservatives against 334 Liberals and 86 Irish Nationalists. Five days after the opening of the new Parliament on 21 January 1886—the last Parliament which the Queen opened in person—Salisbury's Government was defeated and Gladstone returned to power. The burning controversy of the session which followed was the issue of Irish home rule. Gladstone had been newly converted to this policy, which, needless to say, was vigorously opposed by the Queen. A violent and angry session ended in the rejection of Gladstone's Home Rule Bill and the resignation of his Government. Parliament was dissolved and a second General Election was held within nine months, resulting in a heavy defeat for the home rulers. Lord Salisbury returned to office with a stable majority and harmonious relations between the Queen and her Government were restored.

On 20 June 1886 Queen Victoria began the fiftieth year of her reign and the year which followed witnessed her golden jubilee celebrations. They were attended by many representatives from India and the Colonies and it was this glittering occasion which firmly established the Queen in her great rôle as Mother of the Empire and the symbol of imperial unity. The growth of imperial sentiment brought about a corresponding decline in republican feeling and the Queen's reappearance at public functions encouraged the mounting enthusiasm. There were still active, however, certain elements which were hostile to the Crown, and in 1889 the Queen encountered fierce opposition when she requested Parliament to make financial provision for her grandchildren. The Government proposed the appointment of a committee to examine the Queen's request, but an amendment by Bradlaugh to refer the entire matter of Crown revenues to the committee was supported by 125 votes and defeated by only 63. It was Gladstone's intervention in the debate which secured a satisfactory settlement of the question and probably spared the Queen a particularly unpleasant form of embarrassment.

The General Election of 1892 resulted in victory for the home rulers, who secured a majority of 355 to 315. Gladstone returned to lead his fourth and final ministry at the age of 84. But although his Home Rule Bill was carried by the Commons it was, much to the Queen's relief, decisively rejected by the Lords, and the issue did not again arise to vex her during the remainder of her reign. On 2 March 1894 Gladstone, aged and ailing, finally retired. At his death four years later the Queen paid tribute to his character and intellect but refrained from any other expressions of admiration. On her own initiative she requested the Earl of Rosebery to succeed Gladstone, but his administration lasted only a short time. A coalition of Conservatives and Liberal Unionists under Lord Salisbury was returned in strength at the General Election of 1895 and this administration remained in office until the Queen's death.

On 23 September 1896 the Queen arrived at the day on which she had reigned longer than any other English Sovereign, and in 1897 her diamond jubilee celebrations re-kindled the patriotic fervour which her golden jubilee had inspired ten years before. An imperial theme was again chosen for the occasion and representatives from all corners of the Empire participated in the splendid public ceremonies. At a special reception all the colonial Prime Ministers were sworn members of the Privy Council. Altogether two weeks were devoted to the celebration of this great imperial occasion. Thus emphasized, the Queen's personification of the ideal of imperial family unity emerged as the outstanding characteristic of a momentous reign. She lived to see the formation of the Australian federation which was inaugurated at Sydney on 1 January 1901, and when she died she was the head of the greatest Empire the world had ever seen. In spite of a change in the concept of imperial unity, the ideal has proved to be one of the enduring achievements of the reign.

The General Election of 1900 returned the Unionists to power and Victoria's 15th and last Parliament was opened in December of that year. On 22 January 1901 the Queen died. Her son, the Prince of Wales, was proclaimed King Edward VII two days afterwards. With the passing of Victoria there passed also an era of history. She was mourned not only by a nation but by an Empire, an Empire which has since become a Commonwealth of Nations, many of which have inherited the parliamentary institutions of the mother country.

VICTORIA PARLIAMENT

The Australian State of Victoria achieved responsible government in 1856 and the first Parliament was opened on 21 November of that year.

There are two Houses in the Parliament of Victoria, the Legislative Assembly with 66 members and the Legislative Council with 34 members. Members of both Houses are elected on an adult franchise, women having received the vote in 1908. Compulsory voting (q.v.) was instituted for the Legislative Assembly in 1926 and for the Legislative Council in 1935. Members of the lower House, the Legislative Assembly, are elected for the duration of Parliament, which is limited to three years. Members of the Legislative Council hold their seats for six years, but 1 of the 2 members for each of the 17 provinces retires every third year. An unusual feature of the Legislative Assembly is that it has no fixed hour of sitting, the hours for one day being decided at the close of the previous day. Bills passed by Parliament are submitted by ministers for the Governor's assent in the form of Executive Council Minutes.

Parliament House in Melbourne was planned on a very lavish scale. Building began in 1856, and the colonnade and steps which are the outstanding feature of the west façade were not completed until 1892. The magnificent library of 120,000 volumes was opened in 1860. The Commonwealth Parliament occupied Victoria's Parliament House from 1901 to 1927, when it moved to Canberra. During this period the Victorian Parliament met in the Western Annexe of the Exhibition Building.

VICTORIA TOWER, PALACE OF WESTMINSTER

Built in 1860, the main structure is 337 feet high, 360 feet to the tops of the turrets, 391 feet to the top of the flagstaff, and 75 feet square. Original copies of Acts of Parliament, the Rolls of Parliament, and the ballot papers used in the constituencies of England and Wales are kept here in the Record office. The ballot papers are only kept for one year after every General Election.

Since the 14th century the Clerk of the Parliaments has been responsible for the records of Parliament, and since the 16th century they have been preserved in the House of Lords. The Royal Commission on Historical Documents started to calendar the records in 1867, but in 1896 the House of Lords took over their publication. Among those which may now be consulted in the Record Office are the Judicial Records from 1601, the House of Lords Journal from 1510, Committee Proceedings from 1621, documents laid on the Table, and Reports and Command Papers from 1531.

The Union Jack is flown from the Tower from sunrise to sunset when Parliament is sitting, and on special occasions such as royal birthdays, and the Royal Standard when the Sovereign arrives to open Parliament in person. In 1917 the 'Stars and Stripes' was flown side by side with the Union Jack to celebrate the entry of the United States into the War.

(Further reading: Bond, *The Records of Parliament*, 1964.)

VIREMENT

This is a French word meaning a transfer, and is used to describe the method whereby funds appropriated to a certain purpose detailed in the Estimates (q.v.) may be transferred and applied to another object. Prior to the revision of financial procedure the Department of Defence was permitted to make use of the virement procedure with the consent of the Treasury because of the unpredictable nature of armed services' expenditure, but this need has now fallen away. Departments may transfer funds within, but not between, votes.

VIRGIN ISLANDS

See BRITISH VIRGIN ISLANDS LEGISLATIVE COUNCIL.

VISCOUNT

The grade above a baron in the British peerage. A viscount or *vice-comes* was originally a sheriff of a county, and the title was not a noble one until Henry VI created John, Baron Beaumont, Viscount Beaumont by letters patent dated 12 February 1440. The honour was at first, as in this instance, conferred as an advancement to barons, but afterwards was frequently created with the barony; in modern times it is often conferred without the barony. The style of a viscount is 'Right Honourable', and he is officially addressed by the Sovereign as 'Our right trusty and well-beloved Cousin'. The mantle of a viscount is the same as a baron's, except that two rows and a half of ermine are worn on the cape. The coronet of a viscount is a circle of silver gilt, surmounted by sixteen silver balls. There are at present (1970) 109 viscounts.

VOTE, THE

In the House of Commons the 'Vote' is a collection of papers, consisting of a number of different serial issues, which are issued to members daily when the House is sitting. They are arranged in the following order: Votes and Proceedings, Private Business, Notice Paper of Public Business (the agenda for the day, including Questions, Orders of the Day, and Notices of Motion), Supplement to the Votes (amendments to Public Bills to be taken in Committee of the Whole House and in Standing Committees), Minutes of Proceedings on the previous day of Standing Committees, and finally Division Lists.

VOTE (DIVISIONS)

See DIVISIONS.

VOTE (ESTIMATES)

See ESTIMATES.

VOTE (FRANCHISE)

See ELECTIONS; FRANCHISE; REPRESENTATION.

VOTE OF CENSURE

If the Opposition wishes to put down a motion censuring the Government's policy in some direction the Government has to find time for its discussion. Such a motion is usually moved by the Leader of the Opposition. A whole day's sitting or more is occupied with the 'full-dress' debate which follows and nowadays if the motion is carried the fall of the Government invariably results.

[775]

A motion expressing no confidence in the Government is also spoken of as a vote of censure—e.g., Sir John Wardlaw-Milne's motion in July 1942, in which he used the words 'That this House . . . has no confidence in the central direction of the war'.

VOTE OF CONFIDENCE

A Prime Minister has the right to ask for a Vote of Confidence from the House in difficult times and the crises of war. Sir Winston Churchill described the procedure as 'thoroughly normal, constitutional and democratic' when he asked for such a vote in January 1942. On that occasion it was moved by Mr. Attlee with the words 'That this House has confidence in His Majesty's Government and will aid it to the utmost in the vigorous prosecution of the War'. After a three-day debate the House divided, and the motion was carried by 464 votes to 1. Mr. Maxton voted against it, and two other members of the I.L.P. acted as tellers for the 'noes'.

A motion expressing no confidence in the Government is dealt with under VOTE OF CENSURE.

VOTE OFFICE

The office in the House of Commons which is responsible for the provision and distribution of parliamentary papers; nearly a million of these are handled each session. The office is headed by a Principal Clerk who controls a staff consisting of an Assistant Clerk, Chief Office Clerk, and 6 Office Clerks, and part-time porters are appointed for the delivery of papers to addresses in the London area.

There is a similar office in the House of Lords called the Printed Paper Office.

VOTES AND PROCEEDINGS

The title given to a paper issued daily in the form of minutes which records what was done in the House on the previous day, but not what was said. The term 'votes' is used in the sense of decisions of the House. In the House of Commons it is published on the authority of a Sessional Order passed regularly on the first day of the session since 1680, and is prepared by the Journal Office from the minute books of the Clerks-at-the-Table. Prior to 1817 the Votes were as copious as the Journals, but since then, on the recommendation of a committee appointed in that year, the paper has been issued in a more abbreviated form. Questions are not recorded as they involve no decision of the House, but some votes are recorded which are not now actually taken—e.g., orders upon the presentation of public petitions—because such orders have the same force as those which the House is asked to decide. Also listed at the beginning of Votes and Proceedings are the documents presented that day to the House, such as Command Papers, Unprinted Papers, and House of Commons Papers (qq.v.).

See also VOTE, THE.

VOTES (DECISIONS OF THE HOUSE)
See VOTES AND PROCEEDINGS.

VOTES OF CREDIT
See ESTIMATES; PROCEDURE, FINANCIAL.

VOTES ON ACCOUNT
See ESTIMATES; PROCEDURE, FINANCIAL.

W

WALES, SECRETARY OF STATE FOR

A Secretary of State for Wales was first appointed to the Cabinet in October 1964, Mr. James Griffiths becoming the first holder of this office. The appointment, together with the establishment of a Welsh Office, was an implementation of a pledge made by the Labour Party before coming to power, and was designed to promote a more unified administrative structure in Wales. The Welsh Office is located in Cardiff, and the minister also retains a small office in London.

The Secretary of State for Wales took over from the Minister of Housing and Local Government and the Minister of Transport executive responsibility for housing, new towns, town and country planning, the organization of local government, and roads (including trunk roads) in Wales. He is involved in the matter of regional planning, and the Chairman of the Planning Board for Wales is appointed from the Welsh Office. He has local oversight of certain national policies, notably in respect of agriculture, education, health, transport, trade and labour, for which other ministers are centrally responsible. In other matters affecting Wales which do not involve the jurisdiction of other departments he has full responsibility.

The Secretary of State replaced the former Minister for Welsh Affairs, an office without a department which was created in 1951. This minister had no executive powers in relation to Wales, neither did he answer to Parliament for any services for which other ministers were departmentally responsible. His function was to keep himself informed with regard to Welsh Affairs, and to represent Welsh interests and aspirations in the Cabinet. From 1951 to 1957 the office was combined with that of Home Secretary, and from 1957 to 1964 with that of Minister of Housing and Local Government. During the latter period a Minister of State for Welsh Affairs was also appointed.

With the advent of a Labour Government in 1964 a Minister of State and a Parliamentary Under-Secretary were appointed to assist the Secretary of State at the Welsh Office. The salary of the Secretary of State for Wales is £8,500 a year plus an additional £1,250 if he is a Member of the House of Commons. The salaries of the Minister of State and the Parliamentary Under-Secretary are £5,625 and £3,750 respectively, plus the £1,250 allowance if they are Members of the House of Commons.

[778]

WAR, SECRETARY OF STATE FOR

Formerly a Minister of Cabinet rank and the political head of the War Office, the office of Secretary of State for War was abolished, together with the War Office itself, with the coming into force of the Defence (Transfer of Functions) Act, 1964. It was immediately superseded by the office of Minister of Defence for the Army, a minister below Cabinet rank and subordinate to the Secretary of State for Defence, but this office has also since been abolished (*see* DEFENCE, SECRETARY OF STATE FOR).

A Secretary-at-War had been appointed in England as early as 1642, but the office of Secretary of State for War was not created until 1794, and was first held by Henry Dundas, Viscount Melville. Between 1801 and 1854 colonial affairs were under this minister's jurisdiction, and during that period the office was styled Secretary of State for War and the Colonies. In 1854 the office of Secretary-at-War was combined with that of Secretary of State for War, and in 1863 the former office was abolished. Until 1904, when an administrative reorganization took place, the Secretary of State for War shared responsibility for the Army with the Commander-in-Chief and various other authorities. In that year the office of Commander-in-Chief was abolished, and the Secretary of State for War assumed full responsibility for the Army, acting with the advice of the Army Council which was constituted by letters patent and of which he was President. Since 1964 the organization of defence has been centralized in a single department, the Ministry of Defence, and the administration of the Army is now vested in the Army Board, a body subordinate to the Defence Council. A chronological list of the holders of the office appears in Appendix 32.

WAR TRANSPORT, MINISTER OF

See TRANSPORT, MINISTER OF.

WAYS AND MEANS

The provision of revenue to meet national expenditure. The nation's revenue is raised by methods known collectively as 'charges upon the people', taxation being the principal means. Prior to 1967 all such matters were required to originate in Committee of Ways and Means. They were, as now, initiated in the form of resolutions moved by a Minister of the Crown, and were required to be adopted both in Committee of Ways and Means and on report in the House before legislation could be introduced to give them statutory authority. Under the new financial procedure the Committee of Ways and Means has been abolished and Ways and Means resolutions are introduced and adopted only in the House. The abolition of the Committee of Ways and Means required legislative action because the Provisional Collection

[779]

of Taxes Act, 1913 (re-enacted in 1968), made specific reference to resolutions passed in the Committee of Ways and Means. The necessary legislative provision was included in the Finance (No. 2) Bill, 1967. All 'charges upon the people' which require to be initiated by Ways and Means resolutions are general charges imposed for general purposes, and the term embraces the following matters: all taxation, including the imposition of a new tax, the continuation of an expiring tax, an increase in the rate of an existing tax, and an extension of the incidence of a tax so as to include persons not already payers; the repeal or reduction of existing alleviations of taxation, such as an exemption; the delegation of taxing powers within the United Kingdom; the grant of borrowing powers to the Crown; and the payment into the Exchequer of receipts which do not arise from taxation.

With the exception of the Budget (q.v.) all Ways and Means resolutions are considered separately and the rule of relevance applies to all debate and amendments. No amendment may seek to increase the charge authorized by the resolution. The most important part of the business of Ways and Means is the consideration of the annual financial statement or Budget, and on this occasion a special procedure is observed which may best be explained by the following quotation from Erskine May:

> The resolutions which form the usual basis of the Chancellor's statement are the resolutions for the continuance, during the financial year, of the income tax, and the imposition of any new duties or alteration of permanent duties necessary for the purpose of adjusting the revenue to the expenditure of the year. . . . Their purpose is to provide the balance of revenue which, when added to the revenue derived from permanent taxes, will suffice to cover the estimated expenditure of the year. Hence the committee must be at liberty to consider the resolutions, proposed by the Chancellor of the Exchequer, as forming together with existing taxation a complete scheme of revenue to be debated as a whole; and must also be at liberty to consider expenditure in its relation to the burden of providing the necessary revenue. A general debate, which is on the broadest lines, is accordingly permitted, comprising all these resolutions and any financial resolutions necessary to the Budget . . .

With the abolition of the Committee of Ways and Means the Budget statement is now delivered in the House. As soon as the Chancellor sits down, the House proceeds to pass a resolution of a provisional nature which enables the Provisional Collection of Taxes Act to take effect. This resolution replaces the previous series of questions on all the Budget motions save the last. The Budget debate now proceeds on the first of the Budget resolutions instead of the last, thus enabling considered decisions to be reached on all the resolutions at the end of the debate. As with the old procedure, the new procedure provides no opportunity for debating individual Budget resolutions and subsequently no opportunity of moving amendments to them. The only resolution which is debated is the first (in place of the last as previously), this being accepted as the peg for a wide and discursive debate lasting several days, the normal rule of relevance being suspended for the purpose. The Budget proposals are eventually given statutory authority by the Finance Act (q.v.) which is introduced as a Bill once all the resolutions have been agreed to. A resolution which provides for the increase or renewal of an existing tax usually includes a declaration to give it statutory effect under the Provisional Collection of Taxes Act, 1968. In such a case the resolution comes into force without legislative sanction as soon as it is agreed to or upon a date specified in the resolution itself. Under the new statutory provisions it ceases to have effect if it is not agreed to in the House within the next ten days, if the Finance Bill has not passed its second reading within the next twenty-five days, or if the Finance Bill has not received the Royal Assent (q.v.) by 5 August. It would also cease to have effect in the event of a dissolution or prorogation of Parliament. The provisions of the Provisional Collection of Taxes Act, 1968, cannot apply to a new tax which was not in force during the previous financial year.

Although the Committee of Ways and Means and the Committee of Supply have been abolished they were for many years of fundamental importance to the financial procedure of the House of Commons and therefore retain their historic interest. The Committee of Ways and Means had two separate functions: in its taxing capacity it considered ways and means of replenishing the Exchequer, and in its spending capacity it authorized the issue from the Consolidated Fund (q.v.) of the sums of money voted in Committee of Supply for the purposes of expenditure. Like the Committee of Supply, the Committee of Ways and Means acquired its separate identity in 1641. It originated for the purpose of devising new methods of raising money, and an early mention of such a committee appears in the Journal of the House of Commons (q.v.) for 1 December 1641, in the following terms: 'The House resolved itself into a Committee to consider of some way of raising Monies.' At this time the Committee of Supply had also a taxing function, for in the absence of a common pool of revenue the basis of all expenditure was the assigning of specific taxes to particular purposes (see SUPPLY). Early in the 18th century the first step towards pooling the nation's revenues was taken with the establishment of the Aggregate Fund, and during the course of that century the authorization of expenditure became clearly distinguished from the imposition of taxation, the former becoming the particular function of the Committee of Supply and the latter that of the Committee of Ways and Means. On the creation in 1786 of the Consolidated Fund, which eventually became the great financial pool of the nation, the Committee of Ways and Means became responsible for authorizing the issue of the sums of money required to meet the grants voted in Committee of Supply, and thus acquired its spending function.

See also PROCEDURE, FINANCIAL.

WAYS AND MEANS, CHAIRMAN OF

See CHAIRMAN OF WAYS AND MEANS.

WAYS AND MEANS, COMMITTEE OF

See BUDGET; COMMITTEE OF THE WHOLE HOUSE; PROCEDURE, FINANCIAL; WAYS AND MEANS.

WEDGWOOD BENN CASE

See PEERAGE, DISCLAIMER OF.

WEIGHTED VOTE

See PLURAL VOTING.

WELSH GRAND COMMITTEE

A Standing Committee consisting of all the members of the House of Commons representing constituencies in Wales and Monmouthshire together with not more than 15 other members nominated by the Committee of Selection. The Welsh Grand Committee was first appointed by sessional order in the 1959–60 session and was established by Standing Order in 1969. The Welsh Grand Committee considers such matters, relating exclusively to Wales and Monmouthshire, as are referred to it by the House. A motion to refer a matter to the Welsh Grand Committee may be initiated only by a Minister of the Crown at the commencement of public business and is not subject to amendment or debate. The committee's powers are limited to considering the matters referred to it and reporting that they have been considered. Standing Order No. 60, which deals with the nomination of members to Standing Committees (q.v.), provides that for the consideration of all Public Bills relating exclusively to Wales and Monmouthshire the committee shall be so constituted as to comprise all members sitting for constituencies in Wales and Monmouthshire.

WESTERN AUSTRALIAN PARLIAMENT

A bicameral State Parliament consisting of a Legislative Council and a Legislative Assembly. The former consists of 30 members, 2 representing each of 15 electoral provinces for a six-year term, one half of the members retiring every three years. The latter consists of 50 members, each representing a single electoral district for the duration of a Parliament, which is normally three years. Only the Legislative

Assembly is subject to dissolution. The franchise is based on universal adult suffrage. Elections to the Legislative Council were formerly based on a property franchise, but the qualifications required of candidates and electors are to-day identical in respect of both Houses. The preferential system of voting is used in the State (*see* ALTERNATIVE VOTE), and voting is compulsory for all registered voters. Registration is also compulsory for all qualified persons except aboriginal natives, who are nevertheless entitled to enrol as voters if they so wish.

The original Legislative Council nominated by the Governor first sat in 1832, and partially representative government was instituted in 1870. After many difficulties and considerable opposition in the United Kingdom had been overcome, the Colony was granted a Constitution in 1890 and achieved responsible government. At first the Legislative Council was nominated by the Governor, but it was provided that as soon as the population figure reached 60,000 it should be elective. This did not take long, and by 1893 both Houses of Western Australia's Parliament were fully elected. Procedure is based on that of the House of Commons, but, as in some other Commonwealth Parliaments, Bills are considered in Committee of the Whole House and not by Standing Committees.

Western Australia's Parliament Buildings were opened in 1904. Like most upper Houses, the furnishings of the Legislative Council Chamber are in red, following the House of Lords tradition, but the Legislative Assembly has adopted blue instead of the more usual green.

WESTERN SAMOA LEGISLATIVE ASSEMBLY

Western Samoa was a Trust Territory which was administered by New Zealand from 1919. In 1921 New Zealand made provision for a civil administration which included a Legislative Council partly composed of unofficial members. In 1946 New Zealand undertook to adopt a policy in relation to Western Samoa which would eventually lead to self-government for that territory. Legislation enacted by New Zealand in 1956 and 1957 made provision for elected members of the Western Samoan legislature to assume responsibility for government departments. A system of ministerial government was thus introduced with the Executive Council functioning as a Council of Ministers, but at the end of 1959 this was replaced by a Cabinet in which the functions of the *ex-officio* members were assumed by Samoan ministers. The New Zealand High Commissioner, who presided over the Executive Council, also withdrew when the Cabinet was formed.

A Samoan constitutional convention was held in 1954 and its proposals were largely accepted by the New Zealand Government and came into operation with the elections held in November 1957. They provided for a Legislative Assembly of 48 members comprising 41 elected Samoans, 5 elected Europeans, and 2 official members (the previous strength of the legislature was 26). Provision was also made for the abolition of the Fono of Faipule, an advisory body of 41 members which had been established in 1905 and was continued under New Zealand administration.

Full independence followed a plebiscite held in May 1961, and was declared on 1 January 1962. Western Samoa thus became the first sovereign independent Polynesian State, and the Commonwealth Prime Ministers agreed that it would be treated as a Commonwealth country pending a decision on whether it would finally become a member. It became a full member of the Commonwealth on 28 August 1970. On 1 August 1962 Western Samoa signed a treaty of friendship with New Zealand under which the latter country acts, at the request of Western Samoa, as the official channel of communication between Western Samoa and other countries. The New Zealand High Commissioner is the only diplomatic representative accredited to the Government of Western Samoa.

Under the Constitution, Parliament consists of the Head of State ('O le Ao o le Malō') and the Legislative Assembly. The latter consists of 45 members, of whom 43 are elected for territorial constituencies by an electorate consisting of matais or chiefs. Two members are elected by universal suffrage. The Head of State appoints the Prime Minister and, on the Prime Minister's advice, the other eight ministers who comprise the Cabinet. In matters relating to the executive government he acts on the advice of the Cabinet. The present Head of State holds office under the Constitution for life, but future Heads of State will be elected by the Legislative Assembly for a five-year term.

WESTMINSTER HALL

The only remaining portion of the ancient Palace of Westminster (q.v.). The original hall was completed in 1099 and it is recorded that William Rufus held his first court there.

Westminster Hall is 238 feet long, 67½ feet broad, and 90 feet high. The famous hammer-beam roof was built by Richard II in 1394. It has suffered the ravages of the death-watch beetle and very extensive restorations were concluded in 1922. The beautiful roof was severely damaged by incendiary bombs in May 1941, and again in 1944, and the repairs were not completed until 1950. The oak for this restoration came from Lord Courthope's Wadhurst estate which, it is believed, supplied the original timber in the reign of Richard II.

Beginning as the Great Hall of the Royal Palace, Westminster Hall has been used for many purposes. Simon de Montfort's Parliament and the Model Parliament both met there, and from the middle of the 13th century until 1882 the Courts of Law were held in or adjoining it. It was a popular meeting-place and shopping market from the time of Edward III until the beginning of the 19th century. It has been the scene of many famous state trials, including those of Sir William Wallace (1305), the Duke of Buckingham (1520), the Earl of Essex (1601), the Gunpowder Plot conspirators (1606), Charles I (1649), and Warren Hastings, whose trial lasted from 1788 to 1795. It has seen many Coronation feasts (George IV held the last one) and state ceremonies, and in modern times it has been used for the lying-in-state of Kings and statesmen. Gladstone was the first statesman to be so honoured in 1898. In 1965 Sir Winston Churchill was similarly honoured. Westminster Hall has also been used for the celebration of special parliamentary occasions. For example, ceremonies were held there in 1950 to mark the opening of the new House of Commons Chamber and in 1965 in recognition of the seventh centenary of Simon de Montfort's Parliament.

The Hall has indeed witnessed many of the dramas and tragedies of British history, and some of these are recalled to the visitor by means of brass plaques set into the pavement on the spot where they took place, or as near as could be discovered.

Along with the rest of the precincts of the Palace of Westminster, Westminster Hall was under the authority of the Lord Great Chamberlain until April 1965. Since then its control has been vested jointly in the Lord Great Chamberlain, the Lord Chancellor and the Speaker of the House of Commons.

H. St. G. Saunders' *Westminster Hall* (published 1951) is recommended should further information be required.

WHARNCLIFFE ORDERS

Under what are known as the 'Wharncliffe' Standing Orders, certain Private Bills (q.v.) conferring particular powers upon companies have to be referred to the examiners in both the House of Commons and the House of Lords for proof that they have been duly approved of by the proprietors or members of the companies concerned. These orders (Standing Orders relating to Private Business Nos. 62–7) are named after Lord Wharncliffe, who was largely responsible for the original making of an order of this nature by the House of Lords.

WHIG PARTY

See LIBERAL PARTY; PARTY SYSTEM.

WHIP (DOCUMENTARY)

The Government and Opposition Chief Whips send out a document each week to their members which is known as the whip. It details the business for each day of the following week and may indicate who the chief speakers will be. Each item of business is underlined according to its importance—the present practice is to underline it once if no division is expected, twice if the business is fairly important and a division may take place, and a three-line whip means an important debate and a division which every member is expected to attend unless prevented by illness. The receipt of the weekly whip by a member is a recognition that he or she is a member of the party which issues it, so if it is withdrawn and no longer sent to a member it means that he is expelled or liable to expulsion from the party.

Mr. Quintin Hogg is on record as saying that a three-line whip is a summons to attend rather than a summons to vote. However, having regard to the nature of modern political life, it is doubtful that this interpretation would be widely accepted. Mr. Harold Wilson's recent rebuke to certain dissidents in the Labour Party, to the effect that a dog may be allowed one bite but if he continued to bite his licence might be revoked, reinforces the view that the main purpose of a three-line whip is to enforce party discipline in the division lobbies.

According to Porritt (*The Unreformed House of Commons*) whips were in vogue as long ago as 1621, when notices underlined six times were sent to the King's friends. Until fairly recently a whip was only issued when critical divisions on great party issues were expected, and the number of underlinings considered necessary has varied. Five-line whips formerly denoted the highest point of urgency, and one of these was sent out to Conservative members on the occasion of the second reading of Gladstone's first Home Rule Bill in 1886. After that four lines were considered sufficient to ensure a member's presence, and then Sir Wilfred Lawson explained pithily that a one-line whip meant 'you ought to attend'; a two-line whip 'you should attend'; a three-line whip 'you must attend'; and a four-line whip 'stay away at your peril'.

WHIPS

The word 'whip' (an abbreviation of 'whipper-in') in its parliamentary sense was borrowed in the 18th century from the fox-hunting vocabulary, where a whipper-in kept the hounds from straying from the pack. The Government and Opposition Whips have a similar task in regard to Members of Parliament—to round them up to support their party in divisions and to see that they are present on all other necessary occasions. But this is by no means their only function—the efficient and smooth running of the parliamentary machine depends largely on the Whips. Certain duties are common to Whips (who are all Members of Parliament) of all parties, such as supplying their members with information on forthcoming business (*see* WHIP (DOCUMENTARY)), securing their attendance, arranging pairing (q.v.), and supplying lists of members to serve on Standing and Select Committees. The most important duties devolve, however, on the Government Chief Whip, whose official title is Parliamentary Secretary to the Treasury. Disraeli said his office required 'consummate knowledge of human nature, the most amiable flexibility, and complete self-control'. He is sometimes referred to as the Patronage Secretary, which title comes from the days when the Chief Whip exercised a material influence on numerous Government appointments. His main work is the organization of Government business in consultation with the Opposition Chief Whip. The Government Chief Whip has a small staff of Civil Servants headed by the Private Secretary, and the Opposition Chief Whip discharges equally responsible duties for his own side. The latter was granted a special salary for the first time in 1964. The two Chief Whips together form the 'usual channels', a term often used in the House when referring to the arrangement of business or to the possibility of time being found for the discussion of some particular question. Both sides of the House have to ensure the presence of at least one Whip in the Chamber, and the Government Whips have the responsibility of seeing that Government business is not impeded by any procedural failure on the Treasury Bench. They are supplied with notes on the business of the day and indications when this or that must be moved and by whom. The Government Chief Whip also customarily moves the closure (q.v.). As well as its Chief Whip, each party has a Deputy Chief Whip and a varying number of junior Whips. Those on the Government side hold various offices and designations such as Lords Commissioners of the Treasury and political officers of Her Majesty's Household. A Government Whip in the House of Lords is known as a Lord-In-Waiting, and if the office is held by a woman in that Chamber she is known as a Baroness-In-Waiting. A woman Whip, Mrs. Harriet Slater, was appointed for the first time when Mr. Harold Wilson's Government came to power in 1964. All these Government Whips are paid out of public funds, but there are also Assistant Whips appointed who are unpaid. In order principally to prevent any possible breach of the friendly relations which exist between them, the Chief Whips do not usually take part in debates in the House.

WHITE BOOK

The list of members elected to the House of Commons which is brought to the Chamber and delivered to the Clerk Assistant by the Clerk of the Crown on the first day of a new Parliament.

WHITE PAPER

A colloquial term for a government report, statement of policy, or similar document, which is not of sufficient thickness to require the stout blue covers which would transform it into a Blue Book (q.v.).

'WHO GOES HOME?'

This cry is echoed by the policemen on duty through the lobbies and corridors of the House of Commons when it has concluded its sitting and is about to close its doors. The cry had its origin in the far-off time when a member, wending his way homeward alone at night, was liable to be attacked and robbed, and therefore the doorkeepers of the House made arrangements for parties living in the same district to go home together for mutual protection. 'Who goes home?' is not called when Parliament is prorogued—perhaps members were accustomed to having their coaches waiting to take them to their constituencies or country houses at the end of a session.

WILKES, JOHN (1727–1797)

Journalist, politician, and wit, Member of Parliament for Aylesbury and subsequently for Middlesex, whose importance in parliamentary history rests chiefly upon his achievements in vindicating the right of electors to return the candidate of their choice to the House of Commons and in securing for the Press the freedom to publish the debates and proceedings of Parliament without fear of penalization. In his later years he was also active in the cause of parliamentary reform (q.v.).

His journalistic activities incurred for him the odium of the Government, and on the publication of the famous 'No. 45' of his periodical, the *North Briton* (1763), in which he fiercely attacked the King's speech, he was prosecuted, discharged on the ground of his privilege as a Member of Parliament, but expelled from the House of Commons and subsequently outlawed. Returning to England in 1768 he was elected to Parliament for the county of Middlesex but was declared by the House of Commons to be ineligible to take his seat on the ground of his previous expulsion. He was three times re-elected for Middlesex, but on each occasion the election was declared invalid. He was returned again in 1774 at the beginning of a new Parliament and was permitted to take his seat, his disqualification applying only for the duration of the previous Parliament. After many attempts he was eventually successful in persuading the House to agree that all previous resolutions against him should be expunged from the Journals (1782). He remained a Member of Parliament until 1790.

For further details *see also* GEORGE III AND PARLIAMENT; PRESS AND PARLIAMENT.

WILLIAM I (1027?–1087)

King of England by conquest; crowned 25 December 1066.

WILLIAM II (1057?–1100)

Third son of William I, crowned King of England 26 September 1087.

[788]

WILLIAM III (1650–1702) AND PARLIAMENT

The parliamentary system as we know it to-day may be said to have begun with the reign of William III and the acceptance of the Declaration of Right. The revolution of 1688 and the abdication of James II put an end to the struggle for supremacy between Crown and Parliament which had commenced with the reign of the first James, and Parliament had emerged the victors. The reign of William III may be regarded as a great landmark in parliamentary history for it finally established Parliament as the supreme authority in the land and saw the emergence of the Commons as the ruling influence. It is notable also for the development of the strength of party influences, the appointment of the first parliamentary ministry, and the institution of the Cabinet system. It must not be supposed that relations between William and his Parliaments were invariably cordial or totally free from dissension. The King and the Commons offended each other on a number of occasions, and the former withheld his assent from more than one Bill which had been passed by both Houses. But William was a wise and just monarch. He respected Parliament and, unlike his Stuart predecessors, recognized the force of public opinion even though it might conflict with his own.

After the flight of James II the Prince of Orange was requested to take over the administration pending the summoning of the Convention. The Convention met on 22 January 1689, and consisted of two Houses. It was not formally opened by William, who had as yet not been proclaimed Sovereign and therefore had no constitutional status. The fact of the Throne being vacant created a perplexing constitutional position, for although there was no Sovereign in actual practice, theoretically the monarchy was continuous. The situation was debated at great length by both Houses of the Convention and various views and proposals were put forward. Eventually the following resolution, which went far towards reconciling the conflicting opinions on the matter, was passed by the lower House:

That King James II, having endeavoured to subvert the constitution of the kingdom by breaking the original contract between King and people, and, by the advice of Jesuits and other wicked persons, having violated the fundamental laws, and having withdrawn himself out of the kingdom, has abdicated the government, and that the throne is thereby become vacant.

Subsequently, the Lords also agreed with the view expressed by the Commons.

On the question of the succession there were three schools of thought. There were those who felt that the Prince of Orange should rule alone as King; others were in favour of offering the Crown to the Princess of Orange independently of her husband; whilst a third body of opinion advocated a joint government by William and Mary with the former

[789]

as actual ruler. The second proposal was unacceptable to both the Prince and Princess, and the third was at length agreed to as forming a favourable compromise. Meanwhile the Commons were engaged in preparing the celebrated Declaration of Right. This historic document, later confirmed by the legislation known as the Bill of Rights (q.v.), reasserted the laws, liberties, and religion of England, and resolved that William and Mary be declared King and Queen. William and Mary accepted the Crown under the conditions expressed in the Declaration of Right, undertaking to summon frequent Parliaments whose counsels should be regarded as supremely important. On 20 February 1689, the Convention declared itself a Parliament. In Scotland another Convention declared the deposition of James II and passed its own Claim of Rights, and on 11 May William and Mary were offered the Scottish Crown.

The first ministry of William and Mary was drawn from all parties, but it was not long before dissension broke out between the Whigs and the Tories. The King was anxious to arrive at a settlement of the revenue but the Whigs in the Commons were not disposed to be generous. The experiences of past reigns had made them chary of conferring upon the Sovereign a fixed income for life which might render him financially independent of Parliament. William considered himself entitled to the income of his predecessor, a fixed £1,200,000 per annum which had been agreed upon during the reign of Charles II. The Commons agreed to grant this sum to the King but voted it in the first instance for one year only. Unable to arrive at a mutually satisfactory arrangement, William, on the advice of his ministers, prorogued Parliament on 27 January 1690, and dissolved it ten days later. The Convention Parliament established the monarchy upon a secure constitutional foundation, but its subsequent proceedings greatly perturbed the King and caused wide antagonism.

A Tory majority was returned to the second Parliament of William and Mary which met on 20 March 1690. In his opening speech William asked for an immediate settlement of the revenue and for an Act of Indemnity in favour of all those who had been concerned in the proceedings of the previous reign. Both of these wishes were carried out. The Commons agreed to four revenue resolutions without a division, the effect of which was to grant to William and Mary the hereditary revenues and those parts of the customs and excise duties which had been received by James II; but in order to prevent the King from enjoying permanent financial independence the excise was voted for four years only. The Act of Grace, described by Macaulay as 'one of his (William's) noblest and purest titles to renown', was passed following the financial concessions. During its first session this Parliament also declared the acts of the Convention Parliament to be lawful.

When the King opened the second session of his second Parliament on 2 October 1690, he spoke urgently of the need to prosecute war against France. England, he said, was gravely threatened by that nation and additional funds were vitally necessary for war preparations. The King was strongly supported by the country and in recognition of the popular feeling the Commons voted a generous war grant of nearly £4½ million, but were forced to impose additional taxes in order to raise it. During the third session, which opened on 22 October 1691, further substantial grants were voted for the maintenance of the army and navy, both of which were greatly strengthened in manpower with the consent of the Commons. The lower House, however, reserved the right to examine, and if necessary to limit, the annual defence estimates, and also claimed control over the expenditure of public money. At this time the Lords and the Commons fell out over the appointment of a commission of inquiry into the public accounts. The upper House demanded a voice in the appointment of the commission, but the Commons regarded this as an infringement of their financial privilege, and circumvented the Lords by providing for the appointment in a special clause of a Money Bill which the peers did not venture to reject. The session ended on an inharmonious note with the King for the first time withholding his assent to a Bill which had been passed by both Houses. On 24 February 1692, he prorogued Parliament and announced that he was travelling abroad.

The conflict between the Whigs and the Tories continued undiminished, and when Parliament reopened on 4 November 1692 the Whigs complained bitterly of the mismanagement of the war and relentlessly attacked the chief ministers of the government. They also sponsored the Place Bill which, if passed, would have excluded all office-holders from Parliament. This measure, although passed by the Commons, was rejected by the Lords by only two votes. The most important business of this session concerned the Triennial Bill, which aimed to provide for a fresh Parliament every three years. This measure provoked violent argument but was eventually passed by both Houses. The King, however, refused his assent, much to the surprise of Parliament and the country. Although completely within his constitutional rights, William's action was ill-advised. Unlike the previous measure he had rejected (a Bill affecting the judiciary and the payment of judges' salaries), the Triennial Bill was one of profound importance to Parliament and the community, and in exercising his veto he caused widespread ill-feeling. On 14 March 1693, William closed the session. Shortly afterwards significant ministerial changes took place. The Whigs had greatly strengthened their position, having taken the initiative in a matter of major constitutional importance, and certain leading Whigs were appointed to high offices in the government, although the Tories remained in the majority.

The fifth session of the second Parliament of William and Mary opened on 7 November 1693. The Commons began the session by attacking the Admiralty for its mismanagement of the fleet. The Place Bill was reintroduced and this time passed both Houses but the King would not assent to it. Although angered by his refusal, the Commons continued to behave generously in voting supplies for the prosecution of the war. £5 million was granted for the maintenance of the army and navy together with an increase in manpower for the former. During this session the question of the revenue came in for further attention, and it was at this time that the principle was approved of providing a fixed income to meet the Sovereign's personal expenses, while defence expenditure was separated and placed under the direct control of the Commons. The pressing requirements of the war were responsible for two great innovations in 1694—the National Debt and the Bank of England. Both arose from the necessity of relieving the government of its financial difficulties. Parliament was prorogued on 25 April 1694, and the sixth session commenced on 12 November. Tonnage and poundage were granted to the King for a further period of five years, but to emphasize the fact that the grant lay within their benevolence the Commons allowed one day to elapse between the expiry of the old period and the renewal of the grant. The Triennial Bill was reintroduced and quickly passed through all its stages in both Houses, and this time the King gave the measure his assent, the prevalent rumour being that the renewal of the tonnage and poundage grant was conditional upon its acceptance. The Triennial Act was received with acclamation. It did not, of course, affect the right of the Sovereign to dissolve Parliament at any time before it had run its three-year course, should he think fit.

On 28 December 1694 the Queen died and William continued to reign alone. The effect of Mary's death was to strengthen the Whigs still further and to drive the Tories into opposition to the government. Many Tories had had misgivings over the conduct of the nation's affairs on the part of the administration, but had felt themselves muzzled owing to their connexions at Court, but with the death of the Queen these had largely fallen away. Tory ex-ministers began strongly to attack the government's policies, whilst the Whigs saw in these new developments an opportunity for breaking the power of the Tories and ousting them from the administration altogether. On 3 May 1695 Parliament was prorogued and on 11 October it was dissolved, the King having been advised to take advantage of the favourable circumstances to hold new elections.

William's third Parliament met on 22 November 1695. A number of leading Tories were defeated at the elections and a House of Commons largely favourable to the government was returned. Parliament promised wholehearted support for the war and voted a grant for the maintenance of the armed forces even greater than that which had been voted by the last Parliament. There was, however, a great obstacle in the way of raising this money. The coinage of the realm had become so depreciated through clipping and filing that it bore no relation to its original value. What good coin there was in circulation was generally hoarded, and it was decided that the only solution to the financial crisis which threatened was to recoin the money. Both the King and Parliament agreed that the loss involved should be borne by the state to avoid inflicting insupportable hardship upon the people. Nevertheless, new taxes were inevitable in order to meet the loss, and it was resolved to levy a window tax on all dwellings except cottages.

In spite of the pro-government majority in the House of Commons, the King received several checks from Parliament during this session. In the face of strong opposition he was compelled to recall a gift of Crown land, to abandon his support of the Darien Scheme, and to agree to the establishment of a Board of Trade. His policy on domestic issues at this time was to give way to Parliament in order to retain the support of the Commons for the prosecution of the war with France, his most cherished project. In this he demonstrated his wisdom, for the Commons did not deviate in their support of his foreign policy and agreed to some drastic measures in the face of the critical situation which had developed. Both Houses of Parliament, in testimony of their loyalty, drew up declarations which finally dispelled any doubts which might still have existed regarding William's constitutional right to the Crown, and a patriotic association was formed which was backed in the country by an overwhelming majority of the ordinary people. The national unity on the war issue, however, did little to abate the political conflict between the Whigs and the Tories. In 1696 a bitter financial quarrel was fought out between the two parties when the Tories, hoping to destroy the Bank of England, formed a company to establish a National Land Bank. Although it was encouraged by the King (whose need of money would have led him to encourage any promising project), the scheme was a failure and its collapse strengthened the Bank of England immeasurably. The latter resolved to lend the King a large sum of money which he had been striving desperately to raise and for which he was permanently grateful. This transaction brought the bank into alliance with the Whigs, whose powerful influence was the finest guarantee of its future security.

The second session of William's third Parliament, which opened on 20 October 1696, was mainly occupied with the proceedings against the Jacobite, Sir John Fenwick, who was executed after a Bill of Attainder had been passed against him. When the third session commenced on 3 December 1697, the country was at peace. The Treaty of Ryswick, concluded on 10 September, put an end to the eight-year conflict and won the recognition of all Europe for William as the King of England.

The Treasury, however, was by this time empty, having been drained of all its resources for the purposes of the war. The King in his opening speech spoke urgently of his need for Supply and of the necessity for maintaining the army in order to secure the peace. In spite of his plea the Commons voted by a majority of only three votes to take Supply as the first order of business, and much to William's chagrin they resolved that the army should be disbanded. On the question of a standing army in peace-time there was no party cleavage. The Commons were traditionally opposed to a standing army on principle, for the power of a Sovereign with an armed force under his direct control was enormously strengthened. Thus, in this matter the King was unable to rely upon his supporters in the Commons carrying the day for him. Nevertheless, the Commons were generous in relieving William of his financial difficulty and voted £700,000 for the Civil List. Later in the session the Whigs and the Tories joined issue with each other over the monopoly of the East India Company. A new company, the General East India Company, had been established with the support of the Whigs, and had for some years been disputing with the older company over the matter of trading rights. The Tories supported the interests of the original company and proposed that its privileges should be secured; but the Commons eventually agreed to the Whig counter-proposal setting up a new company altogether with exclusive trading rights. The old company was permitted an interest in the new one and, in fact, became its largest subscriber. The King gave the new venture his support and waived his prerogative to permit the passage of the necessary legislation. On 5 July 1698 Parliament was prorogued and two days later dissolved.

The elections were no triumph for either the government or the opposition. Both the Tories and the Whig supporters of the government suffered at the polls, and there was a large influx of new members, uncommitted to either party, who held the balance in the Commons. On 6 December 1698 William opened his fourth Parliament. In his speech he emphasized the importance of maintaining the armed forces and replenishing the exchequer. But this Parliament relished the idea of a standing army no better than the last, and deferred the discussion of Supply until this matter should have been considered. With popular feeling overwhelmingly ranged against them the government was powerless and the King with great reluctance assented to a Bill providing for the disbandment of the army. When they came to consider Supply the Commons were considerably less generous than their predecessors in the previous Parliament, and the King, greatly dissatisfied, closed the session on 4 May 1699. Various ministerial changes took place before the commencement of the second session of this Parliament on 16 November. Again the King in his opening speech dwelt upon the necessity for securing the nation against threats from without and supplying the needs of the Treasury. But the Commons were not disposed to be obliging, and instead of complying with the King's wishes they raised various difficulties and levelled attacks against certain ministers and judges. The most serious issue arose out of the disposal of the forfeited estates of Ireland. The King claimed that the right of disposal lay with himself, but the Commons insisted that they should be applied to the public interest, and resolved that a Bill should be brought in to that effect. Bitter feeling was engendered by this dispute; the parties flung out recriminations, and the majority in the Commons found themselves alienated from both the King and his ministers. In the House of Lords the Bill was adopted with a number of amendments, but the Commons would accept no compromise and threatened to withhold Supply unless the Bill was passed in its original form. Eventually the Lords yielded and carried the Bill as it stood by five votes. This was a major triumph for the Commons and a disaster for those Whigs who had opposed the measure, for its passing spelt their downfall. On 11 April 1700 the King came to the Houses of Parliament, gave his formal assent to a number of Bills, and without a word to the assembled Lords and Commons he ordered the prorogation of Parliament. On 19 December it was dissolved.

The ensuing elections returned a Tory majority to the House of Commons. At this time the situation in Europe was giving the King cause for grave concern, as the actions of Louis XIV in the matter of the Spanish succession were providing grim warning of the designs of France. When opening Parliament on 6 February 1701, he dwelt on the necessity for securing the Protestant religion and the peace of Europe. He also drew attention to the matter of the English succession which had been complicated by the death of the young son of the Princess Anne. In order to secure the Protestant succession a settlement was required which would forestall the claims of the son of James II. The House did not share the King's foresight in regard to the threat to the peace of Europe, although a resolution was passed pledging them to take any measures necessary for the safety of the kingdom. But they realized the urgency of the need for settling the succession. A committee was appointed to examine the question and on the basis of their resolutions a Bill was brought in which was quickly passed into law as the Act of Settlement (q.v.). It ignored all hereditary claims for the sake of securing the Protestant succession, and it provided among other things for the disqualification of any future potential successor not in communion with the Church of England.

Foreign affairs next occupied the attention of the Commons and the King and certain of his ministers were attacked for having concluded the second Partition Treaty of 1700, a treaty which had been designed to settle the Spanish succession and had been violated by Louis XIV. The Commons maintained that the treaty was inimical to the interests of the nation and proceeded to impeach the Whig ministers whom they held to be responsible, and requested the King to dismiss them permanently from his councils. Fortunately for the Whigs they were stronger in the Lords than in the Commons, and with the support of the bishops they carried an address to the King beseeching His Majesty to take no action against the accused ministers until they had stood trial before the upper House. By this time the attitude of the Commons was losing them the support of the country. William was a popular and trusted monarch, and his treatment at the hands of his fifth Parliament was arousing indignation among the people. Eventually, the voice of public opinion was heard in the famous Kentish Petition, signed by a large number of freeholders and justices of the peace, declaring the deep devotion in which the King was held by his subjects, and imploring the Commons 'to have regard to the voice of the people, that our religion and safety may be effectually provided for, that your loyal addresses may be turned into bills of supply, and that his most sacred Majesty (whose propitious and unblemished reign over us we pray God long to continue) may be enabled powerfully to assist his allies before it is too late'. This petition infuriated the Commons, who immediately took action against its initiators. But in so doing they alienated themselves from the popular feeling still further. Owing to much wrangling of a technical nature, the impeachments were dropped, and the proceedings which had led up to them proved very damaging to the Tory cause. Reacting at last to the national feeling, and perceiving rather belatedly the threat of which the King had given them warning, they fell in with the general view. At this juncture the King deemed it advisable to close an unsatisfactory session, and he prorogued Parliament until 7 August. On 16 September James II died in France, and the action of Louis XIV in recognizing his son as King of England made war inevitable. In the circumstances William decided on a dissolution of Parliament, the Tories in the Privy Council opposing the recommendation. It was a wise decision as his fifth Parliament had completely lost the confidence of the country.

The elections returned a substantial majority in favour of the King although there was little difference in the strength of each party, as represented in the House of Commons. William opened his sixth and last Parliament on 30 December 1701, and delivered his last and most memorable speech to the assembled Houses. He exhorted all members to unity in the face of the common danger and besought them to waste no time in taking the measures necessary to secure the safety of the land. He denounced the French King and the Pretender, and concluded with the warning, 'If you do in good earnest desire to see England hold the balance of Europe, and to be indeed at the head of the Protestant interest, it will appear by your right improving the present opportunity.' Both Houses returned an enthusiastic response to the King's exhortation and promised all the support necessary to achieve the common purpose. Bills to provide men for the armed forces were speedily passed, followed by a Bill attainting the Pretender. Yet other issues soon aroused party struggles. A Bill to make compulsory the taking of an oath of abjuration was fiercely resisted by the Tories and narrowly passed by both Houses. The question of reopening the trial of the Whig ministers impeached during the last Parliament was raised, the proposal being defeated in the House of Commons by only fourteen votes. The Commons by their vote established the principle that an accused person is entitled to a speedy trial, and this in turn led to the broader issue of the rights of the subject in relation to the privileges of Parliament. Many voices in the country, including that of Defoe, were claiming the subordination of Parliament to the will of the people. The Whigs supported this view and claimed that the representatives of the people were answerable to those who had elected them, and that the people, if dissatisfied with the conduct of affairs by Parliament, possessed the undoubted right of petitioning the Sovereign for a dissolution. The Tories claimed for Parliament the right to override any other interests. While this party strife was in progress the King suffered a serious riding accident from the effects of which he died on 8 March 1702. Thus the solution of the mighty issues to which he had devoted himself, including the war and the proposal for a union with Scotland, were to remain for his successor.

The reign of William III was notable for many great advances and achievements. The relationship between Sovereign and Parliament had been stabilized upon the foundation of the Bill of Rights. The annual Mutiny Act, first passed in 1689, had limited the power of the Crown by establishing parliamentary control over the army. Personal liberty had been further secured with the granting of freedom to the Press by the repeal of the Licensing Act of 1662 and the amendment of the law of treason. The recoining of the money, the establishment of the Bank of England, and the revision of the financial system were innovations of the highest importance in fiscal history. In religion, the Toleration Act had, in the words of Macaulay, 'removed a vast mass of evil without shocking a vast mass of prejudice'. And although the age of parliamentary reform and the universal franchise had yet to dawn, the accession of William and Mary to the Throne of England had heralded a new and enlightened era of popular liberty.

WILLIAM IV (1765–1837) AND PARLIAMENT

The third son of George III, William IV succeeded his brother George IV on the latter's death on 26 June 1830. Although his reign was a short one it is memorable in the annals of parliamentary history for the achievement of those major reforms in the representative system for which progressive thinkers had been battling for so many years. William IV, although he was in no way remarkable, was possessed of constitutional integrity as a Sovereign, and of the qualities of unselfishness and geniality as a man. At the elections which followed shortly after his accession the advocates of reform were returned to the House of Commons considerably increased in numbers. The Duke of Wellington and his Tory ministry were continued in office, but when Parliament opened on 2 November the Duke, during the debate on the address, made the rash statement which was to bring down his Government. Voicing the Government's opposition to parliamentary reform he said that 'the country possessed a legislature which answered all the good purposes of legislation' and that 'the legislature and the system of representation possessed the full and entire confidence of the country'. An assertion more contrary to the popular feeling could hardly have been made. On the same day Brougham gave notice that he intended to raise the subject of the representation, and a few days later the Government was defeated on a motion for a committee of inquiry into the Civil List (q.v.). Wellington and his colleagues resigned and the Whig leader, Earl Grey, was commissioned to form a Government. Grey's ministry was drawn entirely from the Whigs and their allies, and the new Prime Minister stipulated that reform should be a Cabinet question. The King was not easily convinced of the sagacity of a reform policy, but he was eventually persuaded to accept Grey's condition, and having done so it is to his credit that he did not waver in the support he gave to the Liberal Government. The new ministry was rich in talent, including Brougham as Lord Chancellor, Melbourne Home Secretary, Palmerston Foreign Secretary, Durham Lord Privy Seal, Lansdowne Lord President of the Council, Althorp Chancellor of the Exchequer, Goderich War and Colonial Secretary, and Lord John Russell Paymaster-General. The latter minister was delegated the Government's chief spokesman on the reform issue, his office being merely a sinecure.

The first Reform Bill was introduced in the House of Commons by Russell on 1 March 1831. It proposed the disfranchisement of 60 'rotten' boroughs, the removal of one member from each of 47 others, and a redistribution of seats which would have reduced the House of Commons from 658 to 596 members. It provided also for a uniform £10 household franchise in the boroughs and the abolition of the exclusive privileges of corporations. It was in a tense and excited House that Lord John Russell read out the names of the condemned boroughs whilst the outraged Tories opposite scoffed at the idea of their disfranchisement. For seven nights the House debated the introduction of the Bill, and on 21 March the second reading was agreed to by one vote in the fullest House which had ever assembled for a debate, the figures being 302 to 301. The Bill was committed on 18

April, and an amendment proposing that the number of members for England and Wales ought not to be diminished was carried against the Government by 299 to 291. On 21 April the Government announced its decision to proceed no further with the Bill, and on the following day it was defeated by 22 votes on a motion to adjourn. Lord Grey applied to the King for a dissolution, but the Parliament was barely six months old and the King did not immediately accede to Grey's request. This action on the part of the Prime Minister gave rise to scenes of unprecedented unruliness in both Houses of Parliament. In the Lords, on the afternoon of the 22nd, Lord Wharncliffe moved an address to the Crown against a dissolution, and Lord Mansfield, against a background of confusion, attacked the Government for 'conspiring against the safety of the State and making the Sovereign the instrument of his own destruction'. The proceedings were interrupted by the arrival of the King himself, who had decided to grant a dissolution. A scene of uproar was simultaneously being enacted in the House of Commons when Black Rod arrived to summon the lower House to attend His Majesty in the Lords. The King prorogued Parliament with a view to its immediate dissolution, having decided that it was his duty to stand by the defeated Government, and the dissolution was proclaimed on the following day.

At the elections the reform party was returned in very great strength. The second Reform Bill was introduced on 24 June 1831, and was followed by similar Bills for Scotland and Ireland. The second reading was taken on 4 July and after a debate lasting three nights it was agreed to by the substantial majority of 367 to 236. The dissentient minority adopted such obstructive tactics during the committee stage, however, that the Bill did not pass its third reading until 21 September when it received the approval of the House of Commons by 345 to 236. The country now waited tensely to see what would happen to the Bill in the House of Lords. The debate on the second reading carried on for five nights and Lord Grey in the most emphatic terms entreated the peers not to reject the measure. Nevertheless, when the division was taken the opponents of the Bill numbered 199 against 158 in its favour. Of the spiritual peers only one, the Bishop of Norwich, supported it. This action of the prelates incited the popular feeling against the Church and so exasperated was the country by the peers' rejection of the Bill at a time when Parliament was inundated with petitions calling for reform that there was grave cause for alarm at the insurrectionary trend of the popular reaction. The Government remained in office after the rejection of the Bill and the House of Commons passed a vote of confidence in Lord Grey and his colleagues by 329 to 198.

Lord John Russell introduced the third Reform Bill on 12 December 1831, and the second reading was agreed to in the Commons by 324

2C* [799]

to 162. The proceedings on the Bill in committee were protracted from the middle of January to the middle of March 1832, and the third reading was carried on 19 March by 355 to 239. A number of peers who had voted against the previous Bill had been much chastened by the events which had followed their action, and when the third Bill was referred to the House of Lords the second reading was passed by 184 to 175, the Archbishop of York and several bishops this time voting in its favour. In committee, however, Lord Lyndhurst moved that the disfranchising clauses of the Bill be held over until the enfranchising clauses had been considered. Grey, in opposing the amendment, let it be known that if the House accepted it the Government would regard the Bill itself as having been defeated, but the motion was nevertheless carried against the Government by 151 to 116. Grey now resorted to an extreme course. He requested the King to create a sufficient number of peers from amongst the advocates of reform to ensure the success of the Bill in the upper House, and upon the King's refusal to take this unprecedented step Grey and his colleagues resigned. Straight away the House of Commons passed a vote of confidence in the outgoing Government by 288 to 208, together with an address beseeching His Majesty 'to call to his councils such persons only as will carry into effect, unimpaired in all its essential provisions, the Bill for reforming the representation of the people which has recently passed this House'. The King turned first to the former Prime Minister, the Duke of Wellington, who failed to form a Government. He then recalled Lord Grey to office, who repeated his proposal regarding the creation of new peers. Reluctantly the King consented to create the additional peers should it become necessary, but he communicated his resolve to the opposition in the House of Lords and appealed to them to allow the Bill to pass. The threat and the appeal proved effective. The third Reform Bill was suffered to pass the House of Lords, and on 4 June 1832 the third reading was agreed to in the upper House by 106 to 22, most of the opposition peers having absented themselves. Similar Bills for Scotland and Ireland were also passed, and a great measure thus finally reached the Statute Book, due to no small extent to the personal influence of the Sovereign. The details of the changes made by the Act in the representative system will be found under the heading REPRESENTATION.

The first General Election to be held after the passing of the Reform Act gave an overwhelming victory to the Liberal Party which had carried it. The composition of the first reformed House of Commons was 486 Liberals and 172 Conservatives. The new Parliament was opened by commission on 29 January 1833, and Lord Grey continued in office as Prime Minister until 9 July 1834. His eventual resignation was brought about by his conduct of Irish affairs, which were a matter of grave concern throughout the reign of William IV. The collection of tithes in Ireland had been rendered virtually impossible by the violence and lawlessness which rent that turbulent country, and the Government was forced to pass measures for the relief of impoverished clergy. Simultaneously, a Coercion Act was passed providing for special powers to deal with unrest in Ireland. A further measure provided for sweeping church reforms in Ireland, but a clause dealing with the appropriation of surplus church revenues was abandoned as involving a controversial principle. The ministry itself was seriously disunited on the Irish question, and when in 1834 Grey proposed to renew the Coercion Act he lost the support of his closest colleague, Lord Althorp, and felt himself constrained to resign. Amongst other notable reforms for which Grey's administration is memorable are the abolition of colonial slavery, the protection of women and children working in industry under the Factory Act of 1833, the substantial improvement of the Poor Laws, and the repeal of the East India Company's trading monopoly.

Lord Melbourne succeeded Earl Grey as Prime Minister and Lord Althorp rejoined the Government as Chancellor of the Exchequer. Shortly afterwards the latter was elevated to the House of Lords as Earl Spencer, having succeeded to the title upon the death of his father and as Melbourne's Government had depended upon him to lead the House of Commons, the Prime Minister intimated to the King that a change of ministry might not be inadvisable. Acting on Melbourne's suggestion the King dismissed the Government and sent for the Duke of Wellington, who recommended that Sir Robert Peel should be entrusted with the formation of a new Government. Peel being abroad at the time, the Duke took over the reins of government pending his arrival, actually holding all the secretaryships of state personally during this period. Peel formed his administration in December, himself taking office as First Lord of the Treasury and Chancellor of the Exchequer, with Lyndhurst as Lord Chancellor, Wellington Foreign Secretary, Goulburn Home Secretary, and Lord Aberdeen War and Colonial Secretary. It was in this administration that William Ewart Gladstone was first called to office as Junior Lord of the Treasury, subsequently transferring to the Colonial Office as Under-Secretary of State. This great Liberal statesman originally entered Parliament in 1832 as a Tory.

Parliament was dissolved in December 1834, and the Conservatives improved their position at the General Election, although the Liberals retained a large majority in the House of Commons, securing 380 seats against the Conservatives' 273. Prior to the dissolution, a major catastrophe occurred when the Houses of Parliament were destroyed by fire on 16 October. Both the Lords' and Commons' Chambers were totally destroyed, but Westminster Hall was fortunately spared. A number of valuable documents were lost, but the greater part of the books and papers in the libraries escaped the ravages of the fire.

The new Parliament met in February 1835, and Peel's Government was defeated on the election of the Speaker and also on the address, when an amendment was carried attacking the dissolution of the previous Parliament. A Government measure for the commutation of tithes met with failure when the question of appropriation was raised by the Liberals. Lord John Russell moved resolutions urging that the surplus revenues of the Church of Ireland should be used for promoting the moral and religious welfare of the people and affirming that no measure on the subject of tithes which failed to embody this principle would prove acceptable. Both resolutions were carried in committee and Peel's Government resigned in consequence. Lord Melbourne returned to office as Prime Minister and formed a Government including Lord John Russell as Home Secretary, Palmerston Foreign Secretary, and Spring Rice Chancellor of the Exchequer. Government and Opposition having changed places, the battle over the Irish tithes continued as fiercely as ever. A Bill brought in by the new Government incorporating the controversial appropriation clauses passed its second reading in the House of Commons and the House of Lords, but during the committee stage in the upper House all the appropriation clauses were deleted and the Bill was abandoned. It was reintroduced the following year, 1836, when it met with a similar fate and provoked Lord John Russell to complain of the action of the House of Lords in interfering with a Money Bill. The Bill was revived again in 1837 but dropped owing to the dissolution which followed the King's death.

In 1835 Melbourne's Government took up the matter of municipal reform, a logical consequence of parliamentary reform, and Russell's Municipal Corporations Bill established many salutary innovations in the local government system. In 1836 two Acts were passed in favour of Dissenters, the one legalizing the solemnization of marriages in Nonconformist churches and the other providing for a civil record of births, marriages, and deaths. In the same year, following the appointment of several commissions of inquiry into the affairs of the Church of England, the Ecclesiastical Commissioners were appointed, and various church reforms recommended by them affecting episcopal dioceses and incomes were approved by Parliament.

William IV died on 20 June 1837. The seven years of his reign brought reforms so radical and sweeping that it is doubtful whether they could have been effected in any other country without the compulsion of a popular revolution. Much of the credit for the peaceful transition must go to Earl Grey, under whose Government the constitution of the House of Commons was first recast in the form familiar to us to-day.

(Further reading: Butler, *The passing of the great Reform Bill*, 1914.)

WITENAGEMOT

The council of the Anglo-Saxon Kings, known also as the Witan. It was a body of no specifically defined composition, yet it could wield great power, and the ancient English Kings were elected by it. It was called by the King when he wished, and if he was a strong King it was constituted as he desired. The Witan was a small, aristocratic assembly composed of the wise and noble men of the realm, and the bishops were its most permanent and at times its most powerful element. It was nevertheless a supreme legislative, governmental, and judicial assembly, and as such it may be said to have been an ancestor of Parliament. However, as Maitland points out, the whole business of a central government was as yet very small. Existing laws were few, new laws were made very infrequently, and taxation was practically unknown until the first tribute was raised in 991 to buy off the Danes. The rents of public lands and the profits of the Courts provided sufficient revenue to run such central government as existed. The Witan also acted as a court of justice, but until justice had failed suitors in the local courts, recourse to it was not encouraged.

WOMEN IN PARLIAMENT

Except during ancient times, women were ineligible to sit in the English Parliament until 1918. Some of the Anglo-Saxon Witenagemots (q.v.) were known to have included abbesses, but the participation of women in the councils of the realm must have ceased at a very early date as their presence is not recorded at any medieval Parliaments.

The election of women to the British Parliament was made possible by the passing of the Parliament (Qualification of Women) Act in 1918, and the first woman to be elected was the Countess Markiewicz (1868–1927) for a Dublin constituency in the same year. An Irishwoman who married a Pole, she was an uncompromising Republican, and like the other Sinn Feiners elected at the same time, did not take her seat in the House of Commons. The first woman to do so was Viscountess Astor, who sat for the Sutton Division of Plymouth from 1919 to 1945. The first woman to sit in a Commonwealth legislature overseas was Mrs. Ethel Tawse Jollie who was elected to the Legislative Council of Southern Rhodesia (now Rhodesia) in 1920. In 1924 she became a member of that Colony's first fully elected Parliament, the Legislative Assembly, which was established under the self-governing Constitution granted in the previous year.

The first woman to be appointed a Cabinet Minister was Miss Margaret Bondfield who held office as Minister of Labour from 1929–31. Other women to hold senior ministerial rank have included Miss Ellen Wilkinson (Education, 1945–7), Dr. Edith Summerskill (National Insurance, 1951), and Miss Florence Horsbrugh (Education, 1951–5.)

More recent appointments have included Mrs. Barbara Castle who was appointed Minister of Overseas Development in 1964, Minister of Transport in 1965 and Secretary of State for Employment and Productivity in 1968. Miss Margaret Herbison was appointed Minister of Pensions and National Insurance in 1964 and Minister of Social Security in 1966. Mrs. Judith Hart was appointed Minister of Social Security in 1967, Paymaster General in 1968 and Minister of Overseas Development in 1969. Mrs. Castle, Miss Herbison and Mrs. Hart all served in Mr. Harold Wilson's Labour Government. When the Government of Mr. Edward Heath took office in June 1970 he appointed Mrs. Margaret Thatcher as Secretary of State for Education and Science. Numerous women have held office as Ministers of State and Parliamentary Secretaries, some of the more recent including Mrs. Shirley Williams, Miss Alice Bacon, Baroness Lee of Asheridge (formerly Miss Jennie Lee), Mrs. Eirene White, the Baroness Serota and the Baroness Tweedsmuir. In 1964 Mrs. Harriet Slater became the first woman to be appointed as a Government Whip. In Canada the first woman Minister, Mrs Ellen Fairclough, was appointed to the Conservative Government formed in 1957. In 1960 Ceylon became the first country in the world to have a woman Prime Minister, Mrs. S. Bandaranaike. She held office until 1965 and was elected to a second term in 1970. The world's second woman Prime Minister also emerged in a Commonwealth country, when Mrs. Indira Gandhi succeeded Lal Bahadur Shastri as Prime Minister of India on the latter's death in 1965. In 1966 the Australian Prime Minister, Mr. Harold Holt, appointed Senator Dame Annabelle Rankin as Minister of Housing, the first woman to administer a federal government department in Australia.

Women have also occupied the Chair, and British Columbia has the distinction of having elected in 1950 the first woman Speaker in the Commonwealth, Mrs. Nancy Hodges. In 1963 the Legislative Assembly of Manitoba followed suit and elected Mrs. Thelma Forbes as its Speaker. India's House of the People has had women on its panel of Chairmen, while Ceylon has the distinction of being the first Commonwealth country to appoint a woman to preside over the upper House of Parliament, Lady Molamure having been appointed Deputy President and Chairman of Committees of the Ceylon Senate in 1959. The first woman to preside over the Members of the House of Commons was Mrs. F. Paton when acting as Temporary Chairman in 1948. The first woman to be appointed to one of the permanent chairmanships of the House of Commons was Miss Harvie Anderson who became Deputy Chairman of Ways and Means in June 1970. On 16 February 1966 Lady Wootton of Abinger became the first woman to sit on the Woolsack when deputizing for the Lord Chairman in the House of Lords. Apart from women who have distinguished themselves as members of the Government, others have made useful contributions to the Statute Book. Miss Eleanor Rathbone was responsible for the introduction of family allowances, and Lady Tweedsmuir introduced a Bill in 1954 which became the Protection of Birds Act. Mrs. Mavis Tate, by agreeing to join the parliamentary delegation which visited Belsen just after the War, demonstrated that women members expect to share the more unpleasant parliamentary duties with the men. The contribution of women M.P.s to discussions in the Parliaments of the Commonwealth has been most valuable where their special interests are concerned—health, education, welfare, and all matters affecting the family and the care of children, adolescents, and the aged. At the General Election of 1970, 96 women stood as candidates, of whom 26 were elected, 15 being Conservatives, 10 Labour and 1 an Independent. 80 women stood as candidates at the 1966 General Election, of whom 26 were elected, 19 being Labour and 7 Conservatives. At the 1964 election 29 were elected out of 89 candidates, and in 1959 25 out of 79 candidates. The number of women members in the House of Commons has thus remained fairly constant for a number of years.

It was thought that the Sex Disqualification (Removal) Act of 1919 would give women peers (peeresses in their own right) the same right as male peers to sit in the House of Lords, but the Committee for Privileges of the House of Lords decided in 1922 in the case of Viscountess Rhondda that the Act conferred no right to receive a writ of summons to Parliament. Following some correspondence in *The Times*, motions were moved in the House of Lords in March 1946 to enable peeresses to sit and vote in the House and to make it possible for women to be made peers on the same terms as men. In view of the opinions expressed by their Lordships, one of these motions was not moved and the other was withdrawn. A public petition was organized in 1947 to secure the admission of peeresses to the upper House, but a motion in favour of this was carried in the Lords on 27 July 1949 which rendered the presentation of the petition unnecessary. However, the Government were only prepared to deal with the question as part of the general reform of the House of Lords, regarding it as a constitutional matter and not merely as the removal of a sex disqualification. The Life Peerages Act of 1958 enabled women at last to sit in the House of Lords. The first four women to be appointed under the Act on 23 July 1958 were Dame Katherine Elliot, the Dowager Marchioness of Reading, Baroness Ravensdale, and Mrs. Barbara Wootton. Since then a number of eminent women have been appointed life peeresses including Dame Florence Horsbrugh, Dr. Edith Summerskill, Mrs. Gaitskell (widow of the former Leader of the Labour Party), Lady Violet Bonham Carter, Lady Churchill, Mrs. Mary Stocks and Lady Hylton-Foster (widow of a former Speaker of the House of Commons). In May 1961 Baroness Horsbrugh became the first woman to act as one of the Lords Commissioners to signify the Royal Assent to Bills. She did not emulate the male peers by raising her hat at the appropriate moments but preferred to nod.

The Life Peerages Act did not extend to hereditary peeresses an automatic right to membership of the House of Lords, but this final disability was removed by the Peerage Act, 1963, with the result that all peeresses are now able to sit in the upper House on the same terms as men. (*See* HOUSE OF LORDS REFORM.)

WOODFALL, WILLIAM (1746–1803)

The first parliamentary reporter to publish reports of debates on the morning after they had taken place. He achieved contemporary fame through his remarkable memory, which enabled him to write an accurate report of a speech merely by listening to it and without taking notes. He commenced his reports of parliamentary debates in 1789.

WOOLSACK

A square couch which tradition says was placed in the House of Lords in the time of Edward III. When the House is sitting the Woolsack is the seat of the Lord Chancellor (q.v.). At first it was stuffed with wool clippings as a reminder of England's staple trade, but in course of time it came to be stuffed with hair. In 1938 it was re-stuffed with a blend of wool from the British Isles and Commonwealth countries given by the International Wool Secretariat.

The Woolsack is considered to be outside the precincts of the House, and the Lord Chancellor, when he wishes to address his fellow peers, must 'enter' the House by standing aside from the Woolsack.

WOOLTON–TEVIOT AGREEMENT

See NATIONAL LIBERAL PARTY.

WORKS, MINISTER OF

See PUBLIC BUILDING AND WORKS, MINISTER OF.

WRIT

A document issued by the Clerk of the Crown in Chancery, or the Governor in the case of Northern Ireland, directing the Returning Officer of a constituency to hold an election for a Member of Parliament. Before a General Election the Queen in Council orders the Lord Chancellor to issue the writs, but for a by-election the Clerk of the Crown issues the writ on a warrant from the Speaker. When the House is sitting it orders the Speaker to issue his warrant, but during a recess it is his statutory duty, if a member has died or has been elevated to the peerage, to issue his warrant on the receipt of a certificate under the hands of two members. At the beginning of each Parliament the Speaker is required to appoint not more than 7 and not less than 3 members to issue writs in case of his own death, the vacation of his seat, or his absence abroad. Motions for new writs in the House of Commons are taken immediately after Prayers, and although any debate is unusual it is limited to fifteen minutes. It was found necessary to fix this limit because during the war years Common Wealth frequently challenged the motion on the grounds that the electoral register was out of date, and on one occasion used up half the time allotted to Questions in discussing the matter. In actual fact, owing to the time taken up by prayers, the time allowed for such a debate is less than fifteen minutes because in terms of Standing Order 8 (2) it would have to be terminated at 2.45 p.m. It is now the practice when a new writ is opposed for the Speaker to adjourn the debate until after Questions.

WRIT OF SUMMONS

In the 13th century those who were summoned to the King's Council in Parliament were the holders of a barony, and it came to be held that a person who had received a summons and had taken his seat acquired not only a right to be summoned to future Parliaments but an hereditary right to be summoned which descended to his heirs. Thus baronies came to be created by a writ of summons to Parliament, but Richard II introduced the modern method by creating a barony by letters patent under the Great Seal. However, the Lords Spiritual and Temporal are still summoned to the opening of a new Parliament by an individual writ of summons, issued by the Clerk of the Crown on behalf of the Queen, which commands them to be personally present with the Queen in the City of Westminster on the appointed day, and there to treat and give their counsel upon 'certain arduous and urgent affairs' concerning the Queen, the State, and the defence of the United Kingdom and the Church.

Y

YEOMAN USHER OF THE BLACK ROD

The deputy to the Gentleman Usher of the Black Rod (q.v.). The office was combined with that of Serjeant-at-Arms in the House of Lords from 1962 to 1970 when the latter was abolished and its functions taken over by Black Rod himself.

YONGE, SIR THOMAS, CASE OF

See HAXEY, THOMAS, CASE OF

YUKON TERRITORIAL COUNCIL

The Yukon Territory comprises that part of Canada which lies north of the 60th parallel and west of the North-West Territories. It does not as yet have provincial status and its administration is under the direct control of the Canadian Government. The Yukon Act provides for the government of the Territory by a Commissioner and a Territorial Council with certain legislative powers. The Commissioner is appointed by the Governor-General-in-Council, from whom he receives his instructions, the minister to whom he is directly responsible being the Minister of Indian Affairs and Northern Development. The Territorial Council is wholly elected and consists of 7 members elected for a three-year term of office. The Yukon has its own territorial Civil Service which administers the Territory with the assistance and advice of the federal Department of Indian Affairs and Northern Development.

The Yukon is represented in the Canadian House of Commons by 1 member.

Z

ZAMBIA PARLIAMENT

The Republic of Zambia, formerly the Protectorate of Northern Rhodesia, became an independent member of the Commonwealth on 24 October 1964. The President, who is head of the Government as well as Head of State, is elected at the same time as elections take place for the National Assembly. A presidential candidate must be nominated by at least 1,000 registered voters, and each candidate for election to the National Assembly must declare in advance the presidential candidate he supports. The voter thus votes simultaneously for the parliamentary candidate of his choice and the presidential candidate supported by the parliamentary candidate.

The National Assembly, which is unicameral, consists of 105 elected members, increased from 75 in terms of a constitutional amendment adopted in December 1967. The minimum voting age was lowered from twenty-one to eighteen years at the same time. The President is empowered to nominate up to 5 additional members should he see fit to do so. The 10 seats formerly reserved for Europeans fell away with the dissolution of Zambia's first Parliament in November 1968. The President is not a member of the National Assembly but may address it at any time. The Speaker is elected by the National Assembly from among its own members or from persons outside the Assembly who are qualified for membership. In the latter case the Speaker automatically becomes a member of the Assembly when elected.

The life of a Parliament is five years unless sooner dissolved, or unless Parliament itself varies this period by reason of an emergency. The power to summon, prorogue and dissolve Parliament is vested in the President, and a Bill passed by the National Assembly requires the assent of the President. Should the President withhold his assent to a Bill it may be returned to the Assembly and presented again for the presidential assent if it is passed by a two-thirds majority within six months. In this event the President must either assent to the Bill within twenty-one days or dissolve Parliament.

The Cabinet consists of the President, the Vice-President, the Leader of the House in the National Assembly, and not more than 14 other ministers. The Vice-President and the other ministers are all appointed by the President from among the members of the National Assembly.

The Constitution incorporates a Bill of Rights and also provides for a House of Chiefs having advisory functions including the right to examine such legislation and debate such matters as are referred to it by the President. A Bill to amend the Constitution requires a two-thirds majority of the National Assembly at both its second and third readings. Following a referendum held in June 1969, the holding of a referendum is no longer necessary for the amendment of an entrenched clause of the Constitution. The entrenched clauses include those relating to the Bill of Rights, the Judiciary and the procedure for constitutional amendment.

Zambian law requires that any member of the National Assembly who changes his party is liable to expulsion from the Assembly.

An interesting ruling was given by the Speaker of the new National Assembly at its opening on 22 January 1969 to the effect that he could not accord recognition to the African National Congress, which had won 23 of the 105 seats at the General Election, as the official opposition, on the grounds that it could form 'neither a quorum to execute the business of the House nor a government'. Among the effects of this ruling was the denial to the leader of the Party of the salary and accommodation to which the leader of the Opposition would normally be entitled.

Under an agreement with Barotseland, that territory, while a part of Zambia, enjoys a special position within the Republic. The Zambian Government recognizes the authority of the Litunga of Barotseland. The Litunga and his council are empowered to make laws for Barotseland on specified matters and retain their powers in relation to land matters under customary law and practice, the Barotse native courts having an original jurisdiction in respect of such land matters.

A Legislative Council was first constituted in Northern Rhodesia in 1924 when the administration of the territory was taken over by the British Government from the British South Africa Company. At first all the members were nominated, but elected members were introduced in 1926. In 1948 there was an unofficial majority for the first time and the first African members were appointed to the Council. In the same year a Speaker was appointed and the Governor ceased to preside over the Council.

In 1953 Northern Rhodesia became a part of the ill-fated Federation of Rhodesia and Nyasaland, and during the ensuing decade the constitutional development of the protectorate was crucially influenced by its membership of the Federation. In 1959 and in 1961 constitutional reforms were implemented which were notable mainly for their complexity. The franchise and the constituency boundaries were so designed as to ensure certain proportions of European and African representation, the principal purpose of these exercises being to find a compromise which would satisfy African political aspirations and at the same time enable Northern Rhodesia to remain in a federal association with the white-governed Colony of Southern Rhodesia.

These attempts failed and the Federation was dissolved as the result of African nationalist pressure on 31 December 1963.

In January 1964 Northern Rhodesia became self-governing under a Constitution which provided for a Legislative Assembly of 75 members, 65 of whom were elected by Africans in main-roll constituencies and 10 by Europeans in reserved-roll constituencies. (Voters who were neither African nor European were allowed to register on the roll of their choice.) The Executive Council was replaced by a Cabinet consisting of a Prime Minister and not more than 13 other ministers. Northern Rhodesia achieved independence later in the year on the basis of this Constitution, adjusted to provide for a republican form of government.

ZANZIBAR NATIONAL ASSEMBLY

The control of the Zanzibar Protectorate was transferred from the Foreign Office to the Colonial Office on 1 July 1913, legal effect being given to the change of administration in the following year. The government was vested in a High Commissioner, who was also Governor of the British East Africa Protectorate, and a British Resident. In 1925 the High Commissionership was abolished and a Protectorate Council established with His Highness the Sultan as President. It was of an advisory and consultative nature, and ceased to exist in 1926, when Executive and Legislative Councils were constituted. The Sultan presided over the Executive Council and the British Resident over the Legislative Council, which consisted of 4 *ex-officio*, 5 official, and 8 unofficial members. The unofficials were appointed by the Sultan and comprised 3 Arabs, 2 Indians, 2 Africans, and 1 European. In October 1955 new constitutional proposals were announced and legislative effect was given to them in March 1956, when the Councils Decree was passed. The Decree, which came into force in the following September, provided for the establishment of a Privy Council, the reconstitution of the Executive Council, and the enlargement of the Legislative Council to 25 members. The Privy Council consisted of the British Resident, the Chief Secretary, the Attorney-General, and 3 other members, its function being to advise the Sultan when requested. The Executive Council, from which the Sultan withdrew, consisted of the British Resident, 3 other *ex-officio* members, 4 official members, and 3 unofficial members of the Legislative Council. The 3 unofficials were specially associated with the Departments of Education, Health, and Agriculture, and this reform represented a first step towards the eventual establishment of a ministerial system. The Legislative Council continued to be presided over by the British Resident and included 3 other *ex-officio* members, 9 official members, and 12 unofficial members. The first elections took place in July 1957 under the Legislative Council (Elections) Decree, 1957. Six of the unofficial members were elected to represent six constituencies by a common voters' roll restricted to male subjects of the Sultan and the remaining 6 unofficials were nominated by the Sultan on the advice of the British Resident. In May 1959 further constitutional changes were announced in the House of Commons. The number of constituencies was increased to 8 (5 in Zanzibar and 3 in the neighbouring island of Pemba), thus increasing the elected members in the Legislative Council from 6 to 8 and reducing the nominated unofficial members from 6 to 4. The number of representative members on the Executive Council was increased from 3 to 5. The franchise was extended to women in 1959.

A report by Sir Hilary Blood published in June 1960 recommended the institution of a ministerial system based on an unofficial majority under a Chief Minister, and the introduction of an elected majority in the Legislative Council. A new Constitution embodying these proposals came into effect with an election held in January 1961. The Legislative Council was reconstituted to consist of an appointed Speaker, 3 *ex-officio* members, up to 5 members appointed by the Sultan, and 22 elected members. The January election resulted in a stalemate, the two major parties each obtaining 11 seats, and a further election was held in June, the number of elected seats being increased to 23 in order to avoid another dead heat. The Executive Council was comprised of the British Resident as President, the 3 *ex-officio* members of the Legislative Council, and 5 elected ministers one of whom was designated Chief Minister.

In April 1962 a constitutional conference met in London to consider the question of internal self-government and independence for Zanzibar. The former was achieved on 24 June 1963, and in the following month a National Assembly, consisting of a Speaker and 31 elected members, was elected to replace the Legislative Council. Zanzibar became independent on 10 December 1963, the Sultan being Head of State.

On 12 January 1964 a revolutionary Government deposed the Sultan and declared a Republic, and on 23 February this Government was recognized by the United Kingdom. On 27 April Zanzibar became united with Tanganyika as a single sovereign state, the United Republic of Tanganyika and Zanzibar, which was re-designated the United Republic of Tanzania on 29 October. Zanzibar nevertheless continues to retain its own National Assembly and President (who is also the First Vice-President of Tanzania), and in spite of the union continues to pursue its own independent policies.

See also TANZANIA PARLIAMENT.

ZINOVIEV LETTER

A letter purporting to have been sent in 1924 by Zinoviev, Chairman of the Communist International, to the Communist Party of Great

Britain instructing them to prepare an armed revolution. Unfortunately for the Labour Party it was issued to the Press by the Foreign Office together with a note of protest addressed to the Soviet Ambassador by Ramsay MacDonald, who was then Prime Minister and Foreign Secretary. At the General Election (the 'Red Letter' election) which followed a few days after its publication, the letter, although its authenticity was denied by the British Communist Party and the Soviets, became the most important issue and contributed largely to the fact that the Labour Party was not returned to power.

LIST OF APPENDIXES

PARLIAMENTS OF ENGLAND

(Listed according to the regnal year and the date of the first session
of each Parliament)

15	John	1213	15	Edward II	1322
10	Henry III	1226	16	,,	1322
38	,,	1254	17	,,	1323–4
45	,,	1261	18	,,	1324
49	,,	1264–5	19	,,	1325
3	Edward I	1275	20	,,	1326–7
11	,,	1282–3	1	Edward III	1327
11	,,	1283	2	,,	1327–8
18	,,	1290	2	,,	1328
22	,,	1294	2	,,	1328
23	,,	1295	2 & 3	,,	1328–9
24	,,	1296	4	,,	1329–30
25	,,	1297	4	,,	1330
26	,,	1298	5	,,	1331
28	,,	1299–1300	5	,,	1331
28	,,	1300	6	,,	1331–2
29	,,	1300–1	6	,,	1332
30	,,	1302	6	,,	1332
33	,,	1304–5	8	,,	1333–4
34	,,	1306	8	,,	1334
35	,,	1306–7	9	,,	1335
1	Edward II	1307	10	,,	1335–6
1	,,	1307–8	10	,,	1336
2	,,	1309	10	,,	1336–7
5	,,	1311	11	,,	1336–7
5	,,	1311	11	,,	1337
5	,,	1311–12	12	,,	1337–8
6	,,	1312	12	,,	1338
6	,,	1312–13	12 & 13	,,	1338–9
7	,,	1313	13	,,	1339
7	,,	1313	13	,,	1339–40
7	,,	1314	14	,,	1340
8	,,	1314	14	,,	1340
8	,,	1314–15	15	,,	1341
9	,,	1315–16	16	,,	1342
9	,,	1316	17	,,	1343
10	,,	1316	18	,,	1344
11	,,	1318	20	,,	1346
12	,,	1318	21	,,	1347–8
12	,,	1319	22	,,	1348
14	,,	1320	22	,,	1348–9
15	,,	1321	25	,,	1350–1

25	Edward III	1351–2	
26	,,	1352	
27	,,	1353	
28	,,	1354	
29	,,	1355	
31	,,	1357	
32	,,	1357–8	
34	,,	1360	
34	,,	1360–1	
36	,,	1362	
37	,,	1363	
38	,,	1364–5	
40	,,	1366	
42	,,	1368	
43	,,	1369	
45	,,	1370–1	
45	,,	1371	
46	,,	1372	
47	,,	1373	
50	,,	1375–6	
51	,,	1376–7	
1	Richard II	1377	
2	,,	1378	
2	,,	1379	
3	,,	1379–80	
4	,,	1380	
5	,,	1381	
5	,,	1382	
6	,,	1382	
6	,,	1382–3	
7	,,	1383	
7	,,	1384	
8	,,	1384	
9	,,	1385	
10	,,	1386	
11	,,	1387–8	
12	,,	1388	
13	,,	1389–90	
14	,,	1390	
15	,,	1391	
16	,,	1392	
16	,,	1392–3	
17	,,	1393–4	
18	,,	1394–5	
20	,,	1396–7	
21	,,	1397–8	
23	,,	1399	
1	Henry IV	1399	
2	,,	1400–1	

3	Henry IV	1401–2	
3	,,	1402	
5	,,	1403	
6	,,	1404	
7	,,	1405–6	
9	,,	1407	
11	,,	1409–10	
13	,,	1411	
14	,,	1412–13	
1	Henry V	1413	
2	,,	1413–14	
2	,,	1414	
3	,,	1415	
3	,,	1415–16	
4	,,	1416	
5	,,	1417	
7	,,	1419	
8	,,	1420	
9	,,	1421	
9	,,	1421	
1	Henry VI	1422	
2	,,	1423	
3	,,	1425	
4	,,	1425–6	
6	,,	1427	
8	,,	1429	
9	,,	1430–1	
10	,,	1432	
11	,,	1433	
14	,,	1435	
15	,,	1436–7	
18	,,	1439	
20	,,	1441–2	
23	,,	1444–5	
25	,,	1446–7	
27	,,	1448–9	
28	,,	1449	
29	,,	1450	
31	,,	1452–30	
33	,,	1455	
38	,,	1459	
39	,,	1460	
1	Edward IV	1461	
3	,,	1462–3	
7	,,	1467	
9	,,	1469	
10	,,	1470	
12	,,	1472	
17	,,	1477–8	

22	Edward IV	1482–3	35	Elizabeth I	1592–3
1	Richard III	1483–4	39	,,	1597
1	Henry VII	1485	43	,,	1601
3	,,	1487	1	James I	1603–4
5	,,	1489	12	,,	1614
7	,,	1491	18	,,	1620–1
11	,,	1495	21	,,	1623–4
12	,,	1496–7	1	Charles I	1625
19	,,	1504	1	,,	1625–6
1	Henry VIII	1509–10	3	,,	1627–8
3	,,	1511–12	16	,,	1640
6	,,	1514–15	16	,, (Long	
14	,,	1523		Parliament)	1640
21	,,	1529	Interregnum		1653
28	,,	1536		,,	1654
31	,,	1539		,,	1656
33	,,	1541–2		,,	1658–9
37	,,	1545		,,	1659
1	Edward VI	1547	12	Charles II	1660
7	,,	1552–3	13	,, (The Pen-	
1	Mary	1553		sionary Parliament)	1661
1	,,	1554	31	Charles II	1678–9
1 & 2	Philip and Mary	1554	31	,,	1679
2 & 3	,,	1555	33	,,	1680–1
4 & 5	,,	1557–8	1	James II	1685
1	Elizabeth I	1558–9	Convention		1688–90
5	,,	1562–3	2	William and Mary	1689–90
13	,,	1571	7	William III	1695
14	,,	1572	10	,,	1698
27	,,	1584	12	,,	1700–1
28	,,	1586	13	,,	1701
30 & 31	,,	1588–9	1	Anne	1702

PARLIAMENTS OF GREAT BRITAIN

4	Anne	1705	21	George II	1747
7	,,	1708	27	,,	1754
9	,,	1710	1	George III	1761
12	,,	1713	8	,,	1768
1	George I	1714–15	15	,,	1774
8	,,	1722	21	,,	1780
1	George II	1727	24	,,	1784
8	,,	1734	30	,,	1790
15	,,	1741	36	,,	1796

PARLIAMENTS OF THE UNITED KINGDOM

41	George III	1801	56	,,		1892
42	,,	1802–3	59	,,		1895
47	,,	1806–7	64	,,		1900
48	,,	1807–8	6	Edward VII		1906
53	,,	1812–13	10	,,		1910
59	,,	1819	1	George V		
1	George IV	1820	1 & 2	,,		1911
7	,,	1826	9 & 10	,,		1919
1	William IV	1830–1	13 & 14	,,		1922–3
2	,,	1831	14 & 15	,,		1924
4	,,	1833	15 & 16	,,		1924–5
6	,,	1835	20 & 21	,,		1929–3
1	Victoria	1838	22 & 23	,,		1931–2
4	,,	1841	26	,,		1935–6
10	,,	1847	9 & 10	George VI		1945–6
15	,,	1852	14	,,		1950
20	,,	1857	15 & 16	,,		1951–2
22	,,	1859	1	Elizabeth II		
29	,,	1866	4	,,		1955
32	,,	1868–9	8	,,		1959
37	,,	1874	13	,,		1964
43	,,	1880	15	,,		1966
49	,,	1886	19	,,		1970
49	,,	1886				

SALARIES OF MINISTERS, SPEAKERS, AND MEMBERS

COMMONWEALTH OF AUSTRALIA

Ministers' Salaries

Salary	Prime Minister	$21,250
	Deputy Prime Minister	$12,500
	Treasurer	$12,250
	Senior Ministers	$10,500
	Junior Ministers	$ 7,500
Allowances: Expense	Prime Minister	$10,300
	Deputy Prime Minister	$ 4,600
	Treasurer	$ 4,600
	Senior Ministers	$ 4,600
	Junior Ministers	$ 4,000
Other Privileges	All Ministers receive in addition their salaries as M.P.s. Expense allowance tax-free.	

Salaries of Speaker and Other Presiding Officers

Salary	President and Speaker	$7,500
	Chairman of Committees	$3,125
Allowances: Expense	President and Speaker	$4,000
Other Privileges	Both Speaker and Chairman receive in addition their salaries as M.P.s. Expense Allowance tax-free.	

Members' Salaries

Salary	Members and Senators	$9,500
	Leader of the Opposition	$10,500
	Deputy Leader of the Opposition (Representatives)	$5,000
	Leader of Opposition in the Senate	$5,000
	Deputy Leader of Opposition in the Senate	$1,625
	Leader of Third Party (subject to existing conditions)	$2,500
	Leader of second non-Government party in the Senate	$1,000
Allowances: Expense	Members representing an urban constituency	$2,750
	Members representing a rural constituency	$3,350
	Senators	$2,650

	Leader of the Opposition (Representatives)	$4,600
	Leader of Opposition in the Senate	$1,500
	Deputy Leader of Opposition (Representatives)	$1,500
	Deputy Leader of Opposition in the Senate	$750
	Leader of Third Party (subject to existing conditions)	$750
	Leader of second non-Government party in the Senate	$500
	Government Whip (Representatives)	$1,500
	Other Whips	$1,250

BAHAMAS

Salaries of Speaker and Other Presiding Officers		
Salary	Speaker	$B1857.14
	Deputy Speaker	$B1485.71
Allowances: Housing	Speaker, percentage of basic salary	5%
	Deputy Speaker, percentage of basic salary	5%
Additional	Speaker, percentage of basic salary	17½%
	Deputy Speaker, percentage of basic salary	17½%
	Ministers and other members receive neither salaries nor allowances.	

BERMUDA

Salaries of Speaker and Other Presiding Officers		
Salary	Speaker	£450
Allowances: Entertainment	Speaker	£350
	Deputy Speaker	£150
Members' Salaries		
Salary	Members, fee for each sitting attended	24s.
	Committee members, fee for each meeting attended	16s.
	Three members of House of Assembly's Finance Committee share additional fee of £100	

BOTSWANA

Ministers', Speaker's, Other Presiding Officers' and Members' Salaries		
Salary	Ministers	£2,500
	Assistant Ministers	£1,250
	Speaker	£600
	Members	£500
Allowances: Subsistence	Speaker and Members, when attending Parliament, per day	£3
Constituency	Members, depending on size of constituency	£50–£100
Other Privileges	Speaker and Members receive transport allowances for approved journeys between Gaberones and their homes based on 6d. a mile when a private vehicle is used or the cost of a first-class return fare by road, rail or air.	

BRITISH HONDURAS

Ministers' Salaries		
Salary	Premier	$7,600
	Ministers	$6,900
Allowances: Expense	Premier	$2,100
	Ministers	$2,100

Salaries of Speaker and Other Presiding Officers		
Salary	Speaker	$3,750
	Deputy Speaker	$3,375
	President of Senate	$2,800
	Vice-President of Senate	$2,400
Allowances: Entertainment	Speaker	$1,000
	President of Senate	$600
Expense	Deputy Speaker	$1,200

Members' Salaries		
Salary	Members	$3,000
	Leader of Opposition	$3,000
	Senators	$2,000
Allowances: Expense	Members	$1,200
	Leader of Opposition	$1,200
Special Expense	Leader of Opposition	$900

CANADA

Ministers' Salaries

Salary		
	Prime Minister	$25,000
	Other Ministers	$15,000
	Parliamentary Secretaries	$4,000
	All Ministers receive in addition the same sessional indemnity and expense allowance as other Members, amounting to	$26,000
Allowance: Car	All Ministers, except for Parliamentary Secretaries	$2,000
	All emoluments taxable except car allowance.	

Salaries of Speaker and Other Presiding Officers

Salary		
	Speaker of the House of Commons	$9,000
	Deputy Speaker	$6,000
	Deputy Chairman of Committees	$2,000
	Speaker of the Senate	$9,000
Allowances: Residence	Speakers of the House of Commons and Senate	$3,000
Car	Deputy Speaker	$1,500
	Speakers of the House of Commons and Senate	$1,000
Other Privileges	All receive in addition their sessional indemnities and allowances as M.P.s. All allowances tax-free. Speaker of the House of Commons has the use of a country residence a few miles from Ottawa.	

Members' Salaries

Salary		
	Members	$18,000
	Senators	$18,000
	Leader of the Opposition (additional)	$15,000
Allowances: Expense	Members and Leader of the Opposition	$8,000
	Senators	$4,000
Car	Leader of the Opposition	$2,000
Other Privileges	Each Member has his own office and secretary provided. Travel privileges include free pass on the railways and paid air passages between Ottawa and constituency. Franking privileges are virtually unrestricted and telephone calls from Ottawa may be made without charge to anywhere in Canada. Allowances tax-free.	

CEYLON

Ministers' Salaries

Salary	Prime Minister and other Ministers of Cabinet rank	Rs.18,000
	Parliamentary Secretaries	Rs.12,000
Allowances: Entertainment	Prime Minister	Rs.18,000
	Other Ministers	Rs.6,000
Clerical	Parliamentary Secretaries	Rs.1,200
Car	All Ministers except Prime Minister	Rs.6,060
Domestic staff	All Ministers except Prime Minister	Rs.4,320
Other Privileges	Official residence and car provided for Prime Minister. Entertainment allowance tax-free and in the case of the Prime Minister rental value of residence tax-free.	

Salaries of Speaker and Other Presiding Officers

Salary	Speaker	Rs.18,000
	Deputy Speaker	Rs.12,000
	Deputy Chairman of Committees	Rs.12,000
	President of the Senate	Rs.18,000
	Deputy President	Rs.12,000
Allowances: Entertainment	Speaker	Rs.10,000
	President	Rs.6,000
Clerical	Deputy Speaker	Rs.1,200
	Deputy President	Rs.1,200
Car	President, for upkeep	Rs.4,080
Other Privileges	Official car for President. Speaker receives allowances for travelling, upkeep of car, and employment of domestic staff. Allowances tax-free.	

Members' Salaries

Salary	Members	Rs.7,200
	Senators	Rs.3,600
	Leader of the Opposition	Rs.18,000
Allowances: Clerical	Members and Senators	Rs.1,200
Travelling	Senators	Rs.300
Other Privileges	Members are entitled to free rail travel at all times and free air travel on parliamentary business. Members from remote constituencies are entitled to free rail transport for their cars or Rs.75 per month in lieu. Postage, telegrams and telephone calls are free when related to parliamentary business. Rent-free telephone. Clerical allowance and one half of travelling allowance tax-free.	

Cyprus

<table>
<tr><td>Ministers', Speaker's, Other Presiding Officers' and Members' Salaries</td><td></td><td></td></tr>
<tr><td>Salary</td><td>Ministers</td><td>£2,200</td></tr>
<tr><td></td><td>President (Speaker)</td><td>£2,200</td></tr>
<tr><td></td><td>Vice-President (Deputy Speaker)</td><td>£1,800</td></tr>
<tr><td></td><td>Members</td><td>£960</td></tr>
<tr><td>Allowances: Representation</td><td>Ministers</td><td>£600</td></tr>
<tr><td></td><td>President</td><td>£700</td></tr>
<tr><td></td><td>Vice-President</td><td>£540</td></tr>
<tr><td></td><td>Members</td><td>£540</td></tr>
</table>

Ghana

(Applicable prior to the suspension of parliamentary government in 1966)

<table>
<tr><td>Ministers' Salaries</td><td></td><td></td></tr>
<tr><td>Salary</td><td>Cabinet Ministers and other Ministers including Regional Commissioners</td><td>£G3,000</td></tr>
<tr><td></td><td>Parliamentary Secretary (Government Chief Whip)</td><td>£G1,650</td></tr>
<tr><td></td><td>Deputy Ministers</td><td>£G1,500</td></tr>
<tr><td>Allowances: Basic</td><td>Cabinet Ministers</td><td>£G1,500</td></tr>
<tr><td></td><td>Other Ministers including Regional Commissioners</td><td>£G750</td></tr>
<tr><td>Secretarial</td><td>Cabinet Ministers</td><td>£G1,320</td></tr>
<tr><td></td><td>Other Ministers including Regional Commissioners</td><td>£G600</td></tr>
<tr><td></td><td>Parliamentary Secretary</td><td>£G400</td></tr>
<tr><td>Chauffeur</td><td>Cabinet Ministers and other Ministers including Regional Commissioners</td><td>£G144</td></tr>
<tr><td></td><td>Deputy Ministers and Parliamentary Secretary</td><td>£G180</td></tr>
<tr><td>Car</td><td>Cabinet Ministers and other Ministers including Regional Commissioners (Plus 4d. per mile travel allowance outside Accra.)</td><td>£G17</td></tr>
<tr><td></td><td>Deputy Ministers and Parliamentary Secretary (Plus 4d. per mile travel allowance outside Accra.)</td><td>£G156–£G174</td></tr>
</table>

Salaries of Speaker and Other
Presiding Officers

Salary	Speaker	£G3,000
	Deputy Speaker	£G1,500
Allowances: Table	Speaker	£G600
Entertainment	Speaker	£G750
Chauffeur	Speaker	£G216
	Deputy Speaker	£G180
Car	Speaker—9*d*. per mile outside Accra, plus maintenance	£G173
	Deputy Speaker	£G138
Basic	Deputy Speaker	£G500

Members' Salaries

Salary	Members	£G1,200
Allowances: Basic expense	Members	£G300
Other Privileges	Free rail or air travel on parliamentary business and transport allowance of 4*d*. per mile when using own car on parliamentary business. Free telephone at place of residence in Accra and all local calls free.	

GIBRALTAR

Ministers' Salaries

Salary	Chief Minister	£850
	Deputy Chief Minister	£550
	Ministers	£480

Members' Salaries

Salary	Speaker and other Members	£250

GUYANA

(*Note*—$4.80=£1 sterling. All salaries are monthly)

Ministers' Salaries

Salary	Prime Minister	$840
	Ministers	$840
	Attorney-General	$1,400
	Parliamentary Secretaries	$480
Allowances: Entertainment	Prime Minister	$200
	Ministers	$100
	Attorney-General	$100
Living	Prime Minister—free fully furnished residence or in lieu thereof a house allowance of $480 per month.	

Professional	Attorney-General	$600
Household	Prime Minister—not exceeding $1,248 per month for expenses in excess of $100 per month actually incurred in the employment of domestic staff at and in the upkeep of the official residence.	
Commuted	Prime Minister	$120
Travelling	Ministers	$120
	Attorney-General	$120
	Parliamentary Secretaries	$120
Chauffeur	Prime Minister	$120
	Ministers	$120
	Attorney-General	$120
Subsistence	Prime Minister, Ministers, Attorney-General and Parliamentary Secretaries, $4.80 per day for the first 14 days and $3.60 per day thereafter subject to the conditions of payment from time to time applying to officers in the public service.	
Other Privileges	Prime Minister—free telephone service at residence. Free travelling on transport services operated by the Transport and Harbours Department.	

Salaries of Speaker and Other Presiding Officers

Salary	Speaker	$500
	Deputy Speaker	$350
Allowances: Entertainment	Speaker	$60
Commuted Travelling	Speaker	$65
Chauffeur	Speaker	$80
Telephone	Deputy Speaker	$12
Subsistence	Deputy Speaker—$4.80 per day for the first 14 days and $3.60 per day thereafter, subject to the conditions of payment from time to time applying to officers in the public service.	
Other Privileges	Speaker—free telephone service at residence. Free travelling on transport services operated by the Transport and Harbours Department.	
	Deputy Speaker—free travelling on transport services operated by the Transport and Harbours Department. Variable travelling allowance.	

[828]

Members' Salaries

Salary	Members	$250
	Leader of the Opposition	$500
Allowances: Telephone	Members	$12
	Leader of the Opposition	$12
Subsistence	Members (including Leader of the Opposition)—$4.80 per day or actual expenses subject to the conditions of payment from time to time applying to officers in the public service.	
Other Privileges	Members (including Leader of the Opposition)—free travelling on transport services operated by the Transport and Harbours Department. Variable travelling allowance.	

INDIA

Ministers' Salaries

Salary	Prime Minister and other Ministers of Cabinet rank, per month	Rs.2,250
	Deputy Ministers, per month	Rs.1,750
Allowances: Sumptuary	All Ministers of Cabinet rank except Prime Minister, per month	Rs.500
Other Privileges	All Ministers—furnished rent-free residences. Salary and allowance taxable.	

Salaries of Speaker and Other Presiding Officers

Salary	Speaker of the House of the People, per month	Rs.2,250
	Deputy Speaker, per month	Rs.2,000
	Chairman of the Council of States, per month	Rs.2,250
	Deputy Chairman, per month	Rs.2,000
Allowances: Sumptuary	Speaker and Chairman, per month	Rs.500
Other Privileges	Furnished rent-free residences. Salary and allowances taxable.	

Members' Salaries

Salary	Members, per month	Rs.400
Allowances: Expense	Members, while on parliamentary business, per day	Rs.21
Other Privileges	Travelling expenses for journeys undertaken on parliamentary business. Free first-class railway pass valid throughout India. Free local telephone calls up to a maximum of 1,800 in any one year. Rent-free telephone. Daily allowance tax-free.	

[829]

JAMAICA

Ministers' Salaries

Salary	Prime Minister	£6,000
	Deputy Prime Minister	£3,250
	Other Ministers	£3,000
	Parliamentary Secretaries	£2,500
	Ministers without Portfolio	£2,250
Allowances: Duty	Prime Minister	£3,000
Entertainment	Prime Minister	£2,000
	Deputy Prime Minister and other Ministers	£500
	Parliamentary Secretary	£300
	Ministers without Portfolio	£300
Office	Prime Minister	£1,500
	Deputy Prime Minister and other Ministers	£700
	Parliamentary Secretary	£600
Chauffeur	Deputy Prime Minister and other Ministers, per week	£10
Travel	Ministers without Portfolio	£400
	All Ministers on Cabinet business	£500
	Ministers residing outside the Corporate Area of Kingston and St. Andrew, commuted allowance	£1,300
Other Privileges	All Ministers—furnished official residences at economic rental.	

Salaries of Speaker and Other Presiding Officers

Salary	Speaker	£2,500
	Deputy Speaker	£1,900
Allowances: Entertainment	Speaker	£300
Office	Speaker	£600
	Deputy Speaker	£500
Chauffeur	Speaker, per week	£10

Members' Salaries

Salary	Members	£1,800
	Senators—no salary.	
Allowances: Constit. Travel	Members	£400–£500
Travel	Members—plus 5d. a mile when on parliamentary business	£180
	Members and Senators residing outside the Corporate Area of Kingston and St. Andrew, while on parliamentary business, per day	£5
	Senators residing outside Corporate Area receive 1s. per mile.	
Office	Members	£450

Kenya

Ministers' Salaries

Salary	Ministers	£3,550
	Assistant Ministers	£2,260
Allowances: Constituency	All Ministers	£120

Salaries of Speaker and Other Presiding Officers

Salary	Speaker of the House of Representatives	£1,750
	Speaker of the Senate	£1,750
	(Prior to abolition of Senate.)	

Members' Salaries

Salary	Members	£1,200
Allowances: Attendance	Members, per day	£4
Subsistence	Members, per day	£2
Constituency	Members	£120
Other Privileges	Free first-class rail or air travel between constituency and Nairobi. Free stationery. All allowances tax-free.	

Malawi

Ministers' Salaries

Salary	Ministers	£2,200
	Parliamentary Secretaries	£2,000
Allowances	Ministers	£500
Other Privileges	Ministers and Parliamentary Secretaries are entitled to a furnished official residence for which they pay rent. Each Ministry is provided with an official car and driver on which the Minister has first call. Ministers' allowance tax-free.	

Salaries of Speaker and Other Presiding Officers

Salary	Speaker	£2,000
	Deputy Speaker	£600
	(Deputy Speaker also receives salary and allowance of a Member.)	
Allowances: Duty	Speaker	£240
Entertainment	Speaker	£200

Other Privileges	Speaker is provided with official residence, official car and chauffeur. Allowances tax-free.	

Members' Salaries

Salary	Members	£600
Allowances: Constituency	Members	£240
Attendance	Members, per day	£3
Subsistence	Members, while on parliamentary business away from home, per day	£2
Other Privileges	Free travel between home and constituency. Unrestricted franking privileges. Allowances tax-free.	

FEDERATION OF MALAYSIA

Ministers' Salaries

Salary	Prime Minister	$48,000
	Deputy Prime Minister	$36,000
	Other Ministers	$36,000
	Assistant Ministers	$24,000
Allowances: Entertainment	Prime Minister	$24,000
	Deputy Prime Minister	$6,000
	Other Ministers	$3,000
	Assistant Ministers	$1,800
Chauffeur	All Ministers except Assistant Ministers	$1,800
Additional	Prime Minister as Leader of the House	$12,000
	Entertainment allowances tax-free.	

Salaries of Speaker and Other Presiding Officers

Salary	Speaker of the House of Representatives, per month	$2,250
	President of the Senate, per month	$2,000
Allowances: Entertainment	Speaker of the House of Representatives, per month	$500
	President of the Senate, per month	$350
Other Privileges	Official car, furnished residence and domestic staff provided at Government expense. Entertainment allowance is tax-free.	

Members' Salaries

Salary	Members, per month	$750
	Senators, per month	$500
Allowances: Subsistence	Members—while on parliamentary business, per day	$35

| Other Privileges | Free railway passes for each Member and his wife. Exemption from registration fee on one car. Limited free air travel on parliamentary business. Unrestricted franking privileges and free telephone calls. Rent-free telephone. Daily subsistence allowance is tax-free. | |

MALTA

Ministers' Salaries

Salary	Prime Minister	£2,970
	Cabinet Ministers	£2,160
Allowances: Entertainment	Prime Minister	£750
Other Privileges	All Ministers provided with chauffeur-driven cars.	

Salaries of Members and Other Presiding Officers

Salary	Speaker	£1,080
	Deputy Speaker	£810
Other Privileges	Speaker is provided with chauffeur-driven car.	

Members' Salaries

Salary	Members	£648
Allowances: Travel	For each Member resident in Gozo	£50
Other Privileges	Free secretarial service, free postage on internal mail, free telephone service at home.	

MAURITIUS

Ministers' Salaries

Salary	Premier	Rs.48,000
	Ministers	Rs.36,000
	Parliamentary Secretaries	Rs.24,000
Allowances: Chauffeur	Ministers	Rs.2,400

Salaries of Speaker and Other Presiding Officers

Salary	Speaker	Rs.36,000
	Deputy Speaker	Rs.18,000
	Deputy Chairman of Committees	Rs.14,000
Allowances: House	Speaker	Rs.2,400
Chauffeur	Speaker	Rs.2,400

Members' Salaries

| Salary | Members | Rs.10,000 |

New Zealand

In August 1970 a Royal Commission on Parliamentary Salaries and Allowances recommended increases in the salaries and allowances of Members of Parliament in New Zealand. At the time of going to press the report of the Royal Commission has yet to be considered. In this section, therefore, the revised salaries and allowances proposed by the Royal Commission are given in brackets after the figures which pertain at present.

Ministers' Salaries

Salary			
	Prime Minister	$12,400	($17,000)
	Deputy Prime Minister	$9,150	($12,500)
	Ministers	$8,600	($11,250)
	Ministers without portfolio	$7,000	($9,650)
	Parliamentary Under-Secretaries	$6,450	($8,450)
Allowances: Expense	Prime Minister	$3,500	($4,000)
	Deputy Prime Minister	$1,400	($1,625)
	Ministers	$1,300	($1,500)
	Ministers without portfolio	$1,100	($1,275)
	Parliamentary Under-Secretaries	$1,100	($1,275)

Other Privileges — All Ministers—up to $12 per day travel allowance, plus additional allowance of same sum when necessarily accompanied by wife. Allowances are tax-free.

Salaries of Speaker and Other Presiding Officers

Salary			
	Speaker	$7,350	($10,000)
	Chairman of Committees	$5,950	($7,750)
Allowances	Speaker, allowances of Member plus	$1,000	($1,250)
	Chairman, allowances of Member plus	$600	($700)

Other Privileges — Both are provided with unrestricted free use of official cars for local running in Wellington at any time for Speaker and in connection with official duties for Chairman. Speaker is entitled to additional free use of official cars when engaged elsewhere in New Zealand on official duties or within his

[834]

	electorate for wife and himself. Taxis may be used if no official car available. Unrestricted air travel between her home and Wellington for wife.		

Members' Salaries

Salary	Members	$4,650	($6,100)
	Leader of the Opposition	$7,350	($10,500)
	Deputy Leader of the Opposition	$5,200	($6,850)
Allowances: Electorate	Members and Deputy Leader of the Opposition, depending on nature of constituency.	$80–1,000	($90–1,150)
	(Additional payments are proposed for the four Maori members whose electorates jointly embrace the whole country)		
Sessional	Members and Deputy Leader of the Opposition,		
	per day	$2.25 per day	($3.00 per day)
	per night	$6.00	($8.00)

Special Salary Allowances for Government and Opposition Whips

	Chief	$400	
	Junior	$200	
Basic expense allowance		$1,000	($1,250)
Expense	Leader of the Opposition	$1,300	
Travel	Leader of the Opposition	$1,100	
Car	Leader of the Opposition	up to $1,000	
Additional	Deputy Leader of the Opposition	$500	
Other Privileges	Free air, rail, and road travel. Sessional franking privileges provided to Leader of the Opposition.		
	Wives or husbands of Members to be entitled to 12 free single trips by air between their constituencies and Wellington.		
	Member with spouse using air travel within electorate to attend official functions are entitled to free travel of up to $70 per annum.		

NIGERIA

(Applicable prior to the suspension of parliamentary government in 1966)

Ministers' Salaries

Salary	Prime Minister	£4,500
	Other Ministers	£2,700
	Junior Ministers	£1,800
	Chief Whip	£1,980
	Deputy Chief Whip	£1,800
	Other Whips	£1,260
Allowances: Entertainment	Prime Minister	£1,000
	Other Ministers	£400
Residential	Prime Minister, for maintenance of official residence	£500
	Other Ministers, for maintenance of official residences	£250
Chauffeur	Other Ministers	£150
Transport	Other Ministers, per month	£80

Salaries of Speaker and Other Presiding Officers

Salary	Speaker of the House of Representatives	£2,700
	President of the Senate	£2,700
	Deputy Speaker	£1,620
	Deputy President	£1,620
Allowances: Entertainment	Speaker and President	£400
Residential	Speaker and President, for maintenance of official residences	£250
Chauffeur	Speaker and President	£150
Transport	Speaker and President, per month	£80
	Deputy Speaker and Deputy President	£266

Members' Salaries

Salary	Members of the House of Representatives	£900
	Senators	£900
	Leader of the Opposition	£1,800
Allowances: Transport	Members, Senators and Leader of the Opposition	£266
Additional	Members, Senators and Leader of the Opposition, when attending committee meetings during recess, per day	£3 3s.
Other Privileges	Free air, rail, sea or road travel on parliamentary business for Member, his wife and 2 servants. Free accommodation when Parliament is sitting and	

during meetings of its committees. Correspondence post-free and telephone calls and telegrams free when addressed to the Clerk of the Parliaments.

PAKISTAN

Ministers' Salaries

Salary	Ministers, per month	Rs.3,000
Allowances: Sumptuary	All Ministers, per month	Rs.500
Equipment	All Ministers, on appointment	Rs.2,000
Other Privileges	All Ministers—furnished residences or Rs.1,250 per month in lieu thereof. Official car provided. Special travel facilities and allowances. Allowances are tax-free.	

Salaries of Speaker and Other Presiding Officers

Salary	Speaker, per month	Rs.500
Allowances: Equipment	Speaker, on appointment	Rs.2,000
	Speaker receives same allowances as a Member.	

Members' Salaries

Salary	Members, per month	Rs.500
Allowances: Expense	Members, while on parliamentary business, per day	Rs.50
Other Privileges	Travelling expenses for journeys on parliamentary business. Free local telephone calls up to a maximum of 1,800 a year. Rent-free telephone. Daily allowances tax-free.	

RHODESIA
(At the time of U.D.I.)

Ministers' Salaries

Salary	Prime Minister	£3,500
	Other Ministers	£3,250
Allowances	Prime Minister	£750
	Other Ministers	£750
	Allowances tax-free.	

Salaries of Speaker and Other Presiding Officers

Salary	Speaker	£1,750
	Deputy Speaker	£500

Allowances: Residential	Speaker	£400
Entertainment	Speaker	£250
Subsistence	Speaker, per sitting day	£3 3s.
Other Privileges	Speaker receives a Member's constituency allowance, if a Member. Deputy Speaker receives in addition the same salary and allowances as other Members. Allowances are tax-free.	

Members' Salaries

Salary	Members and Leader of the Opposition	£1,000
Allowances: Special	Members and Leader of the Opposition	£150
Constituency	Members and Leader of the Opposition	£50–£202
Subsistence	Members and Leader of the Opposition, per sitting day	£1 1s.
	If resident more than 25 miles from Salisbury, per sitting day	£3 3s.
	Allowances tax-free.	

SIERRA LEONE

Ministers' Salaries

Salary	Prime Minister	£4,000
	Other Ministers	£3,000
	Ministers without Portfolio	£2,500
Allowances: Entertainment	Prime Minister	£600
	Other Ministers	£240
	Ministers without Portfolio	£120
Staff	All Ministers, for personal assistants	£360
Other Privileges	Prime Minister has free furnished house and official chauffeur-driven car. Other Ministers have free house or £300 in lieu thereof.	

Salaries of Speaker and Other Presiding Officers

Salary	Speaker	£2,500
	Deputy Speaker	£1,250
Allowances: Entertainment	Speaker	£240
Other Privileges	Speaker has free official car and free house or £300 per annum in lieu thereof.	

Members' Salaries

| Salary | Members | £920 |
| | Leader of the Opposition | £1,500 |

Allowances: Constituency	Members	£300
Accommodation	Members on parliamentary business, per day	£2 10s.
Rent	Provincial Members who retain accommodation in Freetown	£120
Entertainment	Leader of the Opposition	£180
Other Privileges	All Members—free air and rail travel on parliamentary business. Transport allowance of 1s. 6d. a mile when Member uses his own car. Free local telephone calls and limited franking privileges.	

SINGAPORE

Ministers', Speaker's, Other Presiding Officers, and Members' Salaries

Salary	Prime Minister, per month	$3,500
	Other Ministers, per month	$2,500
	Ministers of State, per month	$2,000
	Parliamentary Secretaries, per month	$1,500
	Speaker, per month	$3,000
Allowances: Entertainment	Speaker, per month	$400
Special	Members, Ministers, Ministers of State and Parliamentary Secretaries, per month	$500
Other Privileges	Provision is made for entertainment expenses for Ministers, the amount varying from Ministry to Ministry.	

TANZANIA

Ministers' Salaries

Salary	Ministers	£1,800
	Parliamentary Secretaries	£1,500
Allowances: Entertainment	Ministers	£1,000
	Parliamentary Secretaries	£300
	Entertainment allowances tax-free.	

[839]

Salaries of Speaker and Other Presiding Officers

Salary	Speaker	£2,400
	Deputy Speaker	£700
Allowances: Entertainment	Speaker	£300
Additional	Deputy Speaker	£500
Other Privileges	Deputy Speaker receives the allowances of a Member. Allowances tax-free.	

Members' Salaries

Salary	Members	£700
Allowances: Constituency	All Members	£300
Subsistence	All Members, while on parliamentary business, per day	£3
	If Member lives in Dar-es-Salaam	£1 10s.
Postage	All Members	£25
Other Privileges	Free air or rail travel or mileage allowance when on parliamentary business. Local telephone calls free when made from the Parliament Building. Allowances tax-free.	

TRINIDAD AND TOBAGO

Ministers' Salaries

Salary	Prime Minister	$12,960
	Cabinet Ministers	$11,520
Allowances: Chauffeur	Cabinet Ministers	$1,440
Other Privileges	Prime Minister has official car and chauffeur.	

Salaries of Speaker and Other Presiding Officers

Salary	Speaker	$9,000
	Deputy Speaker	$6,960
Allowances: Travel	Deputy Speaker	$600

Members' Salaries

Salary	Members	$5,520
	Senators	$5,520
Allowances: Travel	Members and Senators (Trinidad)	$1,200
	(Tobago)	$1,500
Subsistence	Members and Senators residing off mainland of Trinidad while in Trinidad on parliamentary business, per day	$50

UGANDA

Ministers' Salaries

Salary	Prime Minister	£4,500
	Cabinet Ministers	£3,000
	Deputy Ministers	£2,625
	Parliamentary Secretaries	£2,200
Allowances: Special	Parliamentary Secretaries	£144

Salaries of Speaker and Other Presiding Officers

Salary	Speaker	£2,700
	Deputy Speaker	£1,200
Allowances: Entertainment	Speaker	£200
Special	Deputy Speaker	£600
Other Privileges	Both are provided with rent-free furnished houses. Speaker has official car and chauffeur.	

Members' Salaries

Salary	Members	£1,200
Allowances: Attendance	Members, while on parliamentary business, per day	£3
Subsistence	Members while away from home on parliamentary business	£3
	If Member resides close to Parliament House	£1 15s.
Other Privileges	Free first-class air, road or rail travel on parliamentary business. Free secretarial services while Parliament sitting. Free use of telephones in Parliament House. Free postage on correspondence connected with parliamentary business. Charges for telegrams on parliamentary matters refundable. Salary and allowances tax-free up to a maximum of £1,800.	

UNITED KINGDOM

Ministers' Salaries

Salary	Prime Minister	£14,000
	Cabinet Ministers and Ministers of Cabinet rank	£8,500
	Senior Ministers of non-Cabinet rank	£7,625

	Ministers of State, Parliamentary Secretary and Financial Secretary to the Treasury	£5,625
	Parliamentary Secretaries and other Junior Ministers	£3,750
Allowances	All Ministers other than peers receive an additional parliamentary salary of	£1,250
Other Privileges	Part of Prime Minister's salary is tax-free.	

Salaries of Speaker and Other Presiding Officers

Salary	Speaker	£8,500
	Chairman of Ways and Means	£4,875
	Deputy Chairman of Ways and Means	£3,750
Allowances	All receive an additional parliamentary salary of	£1,250
Other Privileges	Speaker has an official residence in the Palace of Westminster. Part of his salary is tax-free.	

Members' Salaries

Salary	Members	£3,250
	Leader of the Opposition	£4,500
Allowances	Leader of the Opposition receives an additional salary as an M.P. of	£1,250
	Secretarial	£500
Attendance	Members of the House of Lords, for each day's attendance, up to (Members of the House of Lords receive no salary.)	£6.50
Other Privileges	Travel vouchers provided for journeys between London, constituency and home. Franking privileges when writing to Government departments. Local telephone calls free when made from the Houses of Parliament.	

ZAMBIA

Ministers' Salaries

| Salary | Ministers | £2,550 |
| | Parliamentary Secretaries | £1,950 |

Allowances: Special	Ministers	£950
	Parliamentary Secretaries	£500
Housing	Ministers	£360
	Parliamentary Secretaries	£300
	All allowances tax-free.	

*Salaries of Speaker and Other
  Presiding Officers*

Salary	Speaker	£2,550
	Deputy Speaker	£1,950
Allowances: Special	Speaker	£500
	Deputy Speaker	£300
Housing	Speaker	£360
	Deputy Speaker	£360

Other Privileges   Speaker is entitled to the same travelling and subsistence allowances as Ministers when on official duty. All allowances tax-free.

Members' Salaries

Salary	Members	£1,200
	Leader of the Opposition, additional	£1,200
Allowances: Special	Members	£500
Constituency	Depending on size	£150–£300
Subsistence	Members	£240
	If Member resides within 25 miles of Lusaka	£72
Postal	Members	£50

Other Privileges   Additional subsistence and travelling allowances for approved purposes authorized by the Speaker. Free travel on parliamentary business. Allowances tax-free.

LIST OF COMMONWEALTH AND COLONIAL GIFTS TO THE NEW HOUSE OF COMMONS

ADEN	Members' writing-room table
AUSTRALIA	Speaker's Chair
BAHAMAS	Minister's writing-desk and chair
BARBADOS	Minister's writing-desk and chair
BASUTOLAND	Two silver-gilt ashtrays
BECHUANALAND	One silver-gilt ashtray
BERMUDA	Two triple silver-gilt inkstands
BRITISH GUIANA	Four triple silver-gilt inkstands
BRITISH HONDURAS	Minister's writing-desk and chair and royal coat of arms
CANADA	Table of the House
CEYLON	Serjeant-at-Arms's chair
CYPRUS	Members' writing-room table
DOMINICA	One silver-gilt inkstand
FALKLAND ISLANDS	One silver-gilt ashtray
FIJI	One silver-gilt inkstand
GAMBIA	Two silver-gilt ashtrays
GIBRALTAR	Two oak table-lamps with bronze shades
GOLD COAST	Minister's writing-desk and chair
GRENADA	One silver-gilt inkstand
GUERNSEY	Minister's writing-desk and chair
HONG KONG	One triple silver-gilt inkstand
INDIA	One doorway to new Chamber
ISLE OF MAN	One silver-gilt inkstand and two silver-gilt ashtrays for Prime Minister's Conference Room
JAMAICA	Bar of the House
JERSEY	Minister's writing-desk and chair
KENYA	Minister's writing-desk and chair
LEEWARD ISLANDS	Six oak table-lamps with bronze shades
MALAYA	Minister's writing-desk and chair
MALTA	Three silver-gilt ashtrays
MAURITIUS	Minister's writing-desk and chair
NEWFOUNDLAND	Six chairs for Prime Minister's Conference Room
NEW ZEALAND	Two despatch boxes
NIGERIA	Furniture for one Division Lobby
NORTH BORNEO	One table and five chairs for Interview Room
NORTHERN IRELAND	Three Chamber clocks
NORTHERN RHODESIA	Two pairs of brackets for the Mace
NYASALAND	One triple silver-gilt inkstand and one silver-gilt ashtray
PAKISTAN	One doorway to new Chamber
ST. HELENA	One Chairman's chair for Prime Minister's Conference Room

St. Lucia	One silver-gilt inkstand
St. Vincent	One silver-gilt ashtray
Seychelles	Minister's writing-desk and chair
Sierra Leone	Minister's writing-desk and chair
Singapore	One table and five chairs for Interview Room
South Africa	Three chairs for Table of the House
Southern Rhodesia	Two silver-gilt inkstands for Chamber
Swaziland	One silver-gilt ashtray
Tanganyika	One table and five chairs for Interview Room
Trinidad	Minister's writing-desk and chair
Uganda	Furniture for one Division Lobby
Zanzibar	One silver-gilt ashtray

LORD CHANCELLORS AND KEEPERS OF THE GREAT SEAL

1067	Maurice, Bishop of London	1268	John Chishull
1068	Herfast	1269	Richard Middleton
1070	Osbern, Bishop of Exeter	1272	John Kirkeby
1073	Osmund, Bishop of Salisbury	1272	Walter de Merton
1078	Maurice, Bishop of London	1273	Robert Burnell
1083	William de Beaufeau	1292	John Langton
1086	William Giffard	1302	William Greenfield
1090	Robert Bloet	1304	William Hamilton
1093	Waldric	1307	Ralph de Baldock
1094	William Giffard	1307	John Langton
1101	Roger, Bishop of Salisbury	1310	Walter Reynolds
1103	William Giffard	1314	John Sandall
1104	Waldric	1318	John Hotham
1107	Ranulf	1320	John Salmon
1124	Geoffrey Rufus	1323	Robert de Baldock
1135	Roger of Salisbury	1327	John Hotham
1139	Philip	1327	Henry de Clyff
1142	Theobald, Archbishop of Canterbury	1327	Henry de Burghersh
		1330	John Stratford
1154	Thomas à Becket	1334	Richard Bury
1173	Ralph de Warneville	1335	John Stratford
1182	Geoffrey Plantagenet	1337	Robert Stratford
1189	William de Longchamp	1338	Richard Bynterworth
1197	Eustace, Bishop of Ely	1340	Archbishop Stratford
1199	Hubert Walter	1340	Robert Stratford
1205	Walter de Grey	1340	William Kildesby
1213	Peter des Roches	1340	Sir Robert Bourchier
1214	Walter de Grey	1341	Sir Robert Parnyng
1214	Richard de Marisco	1343	Robert Sadyngton
1226	Ralph Neville	1345	John Ufford
1238	Simon de Cantilupe	1349	John Thoresby
1240	Richard, Abbot of Evesham	1356	William Edington
1242	Silvester of Eversden	1363	Simon Langham
1246	John Mansel	1367	William of Wykeham
1250	William de Kilkenny	1371	Sir Robert Thorpe
1255	Henry Wingham	1372	Sir Richard Scrope
1258	Walter de Merton	1372	Sir John Knyvett
1260	Nicholas of Ely	1377	Adam Houghton
1261	Walter de Merton	1378	Sir Richard Scrope
1263	Nicholas of Ely	1379	Simon of Sudbury
1265	Thomas de Cantilupe	1381	Richard, Earl Arundel
1265	Walter Gifford	1382	Robert Braybrook
1266	Godfrey Gifford	1383	Sir Michael de la Pole

1386	Thomas Arundel, Archbishop of Canterbury	1587	Sir Christopher Hatton
1389	William of Wykeham	1591	Lord Burghley
1391	Archbishop Arundel	1592	Sir John Puckering
1396	Edmund Stafford	1596	Sir Thomas Egerton
1399	Archbishop Arundel	1617	Sir Francis Bacon
1399	John Scarle	1621	John Williams
1401	Edmund Stafford	1625	Sir Thomas Coventry
1403	Henry Beaufort	1640	Sir John Finch
1405	Thomas Langley	1641	Sir Edward Littleton
1407	Archbishop Arundel	1645	Sir Richard Lane
1410	Earl of Dorset	1649–60	Great Seal in Commission
1412	Archbishop Arundel	1660	Sir Edward Hyde
1413	Henry Beaufort	1667	Sir Orlando Bridgeman
1417	Bishop Longley	1672	Earl of Shaftesbury
1422	Simon Ganstede	1672	Sir Heneage Finch
1424	Henry Beaufort	1682	Sir Francis North
1426	John Kemp	1685	Baron Jeffreys
1432	John Stafford	1689–93	Great Seal in Commission
1450	John Kemp	1693	Sir John Somers
1454	Earl of Salisbury	1700	Sir Nathan Wright
1455	Thomas Bourchier	1705	William Cowper
1456	William of Waynflete	1710	Sir Simon Harcourt
1460	Thomas Bourchier	1714	Baron Cowper (formerly William Cowper)
1460	George Neville	1718	Baron Macclesfield (formerly Sir Thomas Parker)
1467	Robert Stillington		
1470	George Neville	1725	Baron King
1471	Robert Stillington	1733	Baron Talbot of Hensol
1473	Earl of Essex	1737	Earl of Hardwicke
1473	Laurence Booth	1757	Sir Robert Henley (the last Lord Keeper)
1474	Thomas Rotherham		
1475	John Alcock (Chancellor from April to September in absence of Rotherham)	1766	Baron Camden
		1770	Charles Yorke, Lord Morden
		1771	Baron Apsley
1483	John Russell	1778	Baron Thurlow
1485	John Alcock	1793	Baron Loughborough
1486	John Morton	1801	Baron Eldon
1500	Henry Deane	1806	Baron Erskine
1502	William Wareham	1807	Baron Eldon
1525	Cardinal Wolsey	1827	Baron Lyndhurst
1529	Sir Thomas More	1830	Baron Brougham
1532	Sir Thomas Audley	1834	Baron Lyndhurst
1544	Lord Wriothesley	1836	Baron Cottenham
1547	Lord St. John	1841	Baron Lyndhurst
1551	Thomas Goodrich	1846	Baron Cottenham
1553	Stephen Gardiner	1850	Baron Truro
1556	Nicholas Heath	1852	Baron St. Leonards
1558	Sir Nicholas Bacon	1852	Baron Cranworth
1579	Sir Thomas Bromley	1858	Baron Chelmsford

1859	Baron Campbell	1916	Baron Finlay
1861	Baron Westbury	1919	Earl of Birkenhead
1865	Baron Cranworth	1922	Viscount Cave
1866	Baron Chelmsford	1924	Viscount Haldane
1868	Baron Cairns	1924	Viscount Cave
1868	Baron Hatherley	1928	Viscount Hailsham
1872	Baron Selborne	1929	Viscount Sankey
1874	Earl Cairns (formerly Baron Cairns)	1935	Viscount Hailsham
		1937	Viscount Maugham
1880	Earl of Selborne	1939	Viscount Caldecote
1885	Baron Halsbury	1940	Viscount Simon
1886	Baron Herschell	1945	Earl Jowitt
1886	Baron Halsbury	1951	Viscount Simonds
1892	Baron Herschell	1954	Viscount Kilmuir
1895	Earl of Halsbury	1962	Viscount Dilhorne
1905	Earl Loreburn	1964	Baron Gardiner
1912	Viscount Haldane	1970	Lord Hailsham of St. Marylebone
1915	Baron Buckmaster		

PRESIDING OFFICERS AND SPEAKERS OF THE HOUSE OF COMMONS

1258	Peter de Montfort
1327	William Trussell
1332 (March)	
	Henry Beaumont
1332 (Sept.)	
	Sir Geoffrey Le Scrope
1340	William Trussell
1343	William Trussell again
1347–8	William de Thorpe
1351–2	William de Shareshull
1376	Sir Peter de la Mare
1377 (Jan.–Mar.)	
	Sir Thomas Hungerford (the first to be designated Speaker)
1377 (Oct.–Nov.)	
	Sir Peter de la Mare
1378 (Oct.–Nov.)	
	Sir James Pickering
1380	Sir John Guildesborough
1381–2	Sir Richard Waldegrave
1383–90	Sir James Pickering (during these years the records are defective and this Speaker's service might not have been unbroken)
1394–8	Sir John Bussy
1399 (Oct.)	
	Sir John Cheyne or Cheney
1399 (Oct.–Nov.)	
	John Dorewood
1401 (Jan.–Mar.)	
	Sir Arnold Savage
1402 (Oct.–Nov.)	
	Sir Henry Redford
1404 (Jan.–Apr.)	
	Sir Arnold Savage
1404 (Oct.–Nov.)	
	Sir William Sturmy or Esturmy
1406	Sir John Tiptoft
1407–11	Thomas Chaucer

1412	Speaker unknown
1413 (May–June)	
	William Stourton
1413 (June)	
	John Dorewood
1414 (May)	
	Sir Walter Hungerford
1414	Thomas Chaucer
1415 (Nov.)	
	Richard Redman or Redmayne
1416 (Mar.–May)	
	Sir Walter Beauchamp
1416–19	Roger Flower
1420	Roger Hunt
1421	Thomas Chaucer
1421	Richard Baynard
1422 (Nov.–Dec.)	
	Roger Flower
1423–4	Sir John Russell
1425 (May–July)	
	Sir Thomas Walton or Wauton
1426 (Feb.–June)	
	Sir Richard Vernon
1427–8	Sir John Tyrrell
1429–30	William Alington
1431 (Jan.–Mar.)	
	Sir John Tyrrell
1432 (May–July)	
	Sir John Russell
1433 (July–Dec.)	
	Roger Hunt
1435 (Oct.–Dec.)	
	John Bowes
1437 (Jan.–Mar.)	
	Sir John Tyrrell
1437 (Mar.)	
	William Burley or Boreley
1439–42	William Tresham
1445 (Feb.–Apr.)	
	William Burley

1447 (Feb.–Mar.)
 William Tresham
1449 (Feb.–July)
 Sir John Say
1449 (Nov. 8th)
 Sir John Popham
1449–50 William Tresham
1450–1 Sir William Oldhall
1453–4 Thomas Thorpe
1454 (Feb.–Apr.)
 Sir Thomas Charlton
1455–6 Sir John Wenlock
1459 (Nov.–Dec.)
 Sir Thomas Tresham
1460 (Oct.)
 John Green
1461–2 Sir James Strangeways
1463–8 Sir John Say
1469–71 No particulars known
1472–8 William Alington
1483 (Jan.–Feb.)
 John Wood or Wode
1484 (Jan.–Feb.)
 William Catesby
1485–6 Sir Thomas Lovell
1487 Sir John Mordaunt
1489–90 Sir Thomas Fitzwilliam
1491–2 Sir Richard Empson
1495 Sir Robert Drury
1496 (Oct.)
 Sir Reginald Bray (not a Speaker in the true sense of the word as he presided over a Great Council rather than a Parliament)
1497 Sir Thomas Englefield or Inglefield
1504 Edmond Dudley
1510 (Jan.–Feb.)
 Sir Thomas Englefield
1512–13 Sir Robert Sheffield
1515 (Feb.–Dec.)
 Sir Thomas Nevill
1523 (Apr.–Aug.)
 Sir Thomas More
1529–33 Sir Thomas Audley
1533–6 Sir Humphrey Wingfield
1536 (June–July)
 Sir Richard Rich

1539–40 Sir Nicholas Hare
1542–4 Sir Thomas Moyle
1545–52 Sir John Baker
1553 (March)
 Sir James Dyer
1553 (Oct.–Dec.)
 Sir John Pollard
1554 (Apr.–May)
 Sir Robert Brooke
1554–5 Sir Clement Heigham
1555 (Oct.–Dec.)
 Sir John Pollard
1558 (Jan.–Nov.)
 Sir William Cordell
1559 (Jan.–May)
 Sir Thomas Gargrave
1563 (Jan.–Apr.)
 Thomas Williams
1566–7 Richard Onslow
1571 (Apr.–May)
 Sir Christopher Wray
1572–6 Sir Robert Bell
1581–3 Sir John Popham
1584–7 Sir John Puckering
1589 (Feb.–Mar.)
 Thomas Snagge
1593 (Feb.–Apr.)
 Sir Edward Coke
1597–8 Sir Christopher Yelverton
1601 (Oct.–Dec.)
 Sir John Croke
1604–11 Sir Edward Phelips
1614 (Apr.–June)
 Sir Randolph Crewe
1621–2 Sir Thomas Richardson
1624–5 Sir Thomas Crewe
1626 (Feb.–June)
 Sir Heneage Finch
1628–9 Sir John Finch
1640 (Apr.–May)
 Sir John Glanville
1640–7 William Lenthall
1647 (July–Aug.)
 Henry Pelham
1647–53 William Lenthall
1653 (July–Dec.)
 Rev. Francis Rous
1654–5 William Lenthall
1656–8 Sir Thomas Widdrington

1657   Bulstrode Whitelocke (appointed *pro tem.* during absence of Widdrington through indisposition)

1659 (Jan.–Mar.)
Chaloner Chute

1659 (March)
Sir Lislebone Long

1659 (Mar.–Apr.)
Thomas Bampfylde

1659–60   William Lenthall

1660 (Jan.)
William Say (appointed *pro tem.* during Lenthall's absence)

1660 (Apr.–Dec.)
Sir Harbottle Grimston

1661–71   Sir Edward Turnour

1673 (Feb.)
Sir Job Charlton

1673–8   Sir Edward Seymour

1678 (Apr.–May)
Sir Robert Sawyer

1678–9   Sir Edward Seymour

1679 (Mar.–July)
Sir William Gregory

1680–1   Sir William Williams

1685–7   Sir John Trevor

1689 (Jan.–Feb.)
Henry Powle

1690–5   Sir John Trevor

1695–8   Paul Foley

1698–1700
Sir Thomas Littleton

1701–5   Robert Harley

1705–8   John Smith

1708–10   Sir Richard Onslow

1710–13   William Bromley

1714–15   Sir Thomas Hanmer

1715–27   Sir Spencer Compton

1728–61   Arthur Onslow

1761–70   Sir John Cust

1770–80   Sir Fletcher Norton

1780–9   Charles Cornwall

1789 (Jan.–June)
William Wyndham Grenville

1789–1801
Henry Addington

1801–2   Sir J. Mitford

1802–17   C. Abbot

1817–34   C. Manners-Sutton

1835–9   J. Abercromby

1839–57   C. Shaw-Lefevre

1857–72   J. E. Denison

1872–84   H. B. W. Brand

1884–95   A. W. Peel

1895–1905
W. C. Gully

1905–21   J. W. Lowther

1921–8   J. H. Whitley

1928–43   E. A. FitzRoy

1943–51   D. Clifton-Brown

1951–9   W. S. Morrison

1959–65   Sir Harry Hylton-Foster

1965–71   Dr. Horace King

1971–   Selwyn Lloyd

CLERKS OF THE HOUSE OF COMMONS

1363	Robert de Melton	1678	William Goldesbrough the younger
1385	John de Scardeburgh		
1414	Thomas Haseley	1683	Paul Jodrell
1440	John Dale	1727	Edward Stables
1461	Thomas Bayen	1732	Nicholas Hardinge
1503 (?)	Thomas Hylton	1748	Jeremiah Dyson
1510	William Underhill	1762	Thomas Tyrwhitt
1515	Richard Urmeston or Ormeston	1768	John Hatsell
		1820	J. H. Ley
1548	John Seymour	1850	Sir D. Le Marchant
1567	Fulk Onslow	1871	Sir T. Erskine May
1603–11	Ralph Ewens	1886	Sir R. F. D. Palgrave
1613	John Wright	1900	A. J. S. Milman
1640	Henry Elsynge	1902	Sir C. P. Ilbert
1649	Henry Scobell (later Clerk of the Parliament)	1921	Sir T. L. Webster
		1930	Sir H. Dawkins
1658	John Smythe	1937	Sir G. Campion
1658	Thomas St Nicholas	1948	Sir F. Metcalfe
1660	William Jessop	1954	Sir E. Fellowes
1661	William Goldesbrough the elder	1961	Sir Barnett Cocks

PRIME MINISTERS OF THE COMMONWEALTH

PRIME MINISTERS OF GREAT BRITAIN

1721	Sir Robert Walpole	1858	Earl of Derby
1742	Earl of Wilmington	1859	Viscount Palmerston
1743	Henry Pelham	1865	Earl Russell (formerly Lord
1754	Duke of Newcastle		John Russell)
1756	Duke of Devonshire	1866	Earl of Derby
1757	Duke of Newcastle	1868	B. Disraeli
1762	Earl of Bute	1868	W. E. Gladstone
1763	George Grenville	1874	B. Disraeli
1765	Marquess of Rockingham	1880	W. E. Gladstone
1766	Earl of Chatham	1885	Marquess of Salisbury
1767	Duke of Grafton	1886	W. E. Gladstone
1770	Lord North	1886	Marquess of Salisbury
1782	Marquess of Rockingham	1892	W. E. Gladstone
1782	Earl of Shelburne	1894	Earl of Rosebery
1783	Duke of Portland	1895	Marquess of Salisbury
1783	William Pitt	1902	A. J. Balfour
1801	H. Addington	1905	Sir H. Campbell-Bannerman
1804	William Pitt	1908	H. H. Asquith
1806	Lord Grenville	1916	D. Lloyd George
1807	Duke of Portland	1922	A. Bonar Law
1809	S. Perceval	1923	Stanley Baldwin
1812	Earl of Liverpool	1924	J. Ramsay MacDonald
1827	G. Canning	1924 (Nov.)	Stanley Baldwin
1827	Viscount Goderich	1929	J. Ramsay MacDonald
1828	Duke of Wellington	1935	Stanley Baldwin
1830	Earl Grey	1937	Neville Chamberlain
1834	Viscount Melbourne	1940	Winston Churchill
1834	Sir Robert Peel	1945	C. R. Attlee
1835	Viscount Melbourne	1951	Sir Winston Churchill
1841	Sir Robert Peel	1955	Sir Anthony Eden
1846	Lord John Russell	1957	Harold Macmillan
1852	Earl of Derby	1963	Sir Alec Douglas-Home
1852	Earl of Aberdeen	1964	Harold Wilson
1855	Viscount Palmerston	1970	Edward Heath

PRIME MINISTERS OF AUSTRALIA

1901	Sir E. Barton	1908	A. Fisher
1903	A. Deakin	1909	A. Deakin
1904	J. C. Watson	1910	A. Fisher
1904	Sir G. Reid	1913	Sir J. Cook
1905	A. Deakin	1914	A. Fisher

1915	W. M. Hughes	1941	J. Curtin
1923	S. M. Bruce	1945	F. M. Forde
1929	J. H. Scullin	1945	J. B. Chifley
1932	J. A. Lyons	1949	R. G. Menzies
1939	E. C. G. Page	1966	Harold Holt
1939	R. G. Menzies	1968	John Gorton
1941	A. W. Fadden	1971	William McMahon

PRIME MINISTER OF BARBADOS

1964   Errol Barrow

PRIME MINISTER (AFTERWARDS PRESIDENT) OF BOTSWANA

1966   Sir Seretse Khama

PRIME MINISTERS OF CANADA

1867	Sir J. A. Macdonald	1921	W. L. MacKenzie King
1873	A. MacKenzie	1926	A. Meighen
1878	Sir J. A. Macdonald	1926	W. L. MacKenzie King
1891	Sir J. Abbott	1930	R. B. Bennett
1892	Sir J. Thompson	1935	W. L. MacKenzie King
1894	Sir M. Bowell	1948	L. S. St. Laurent
1896	Sir C. Tupper	1957	J. G. Diefenbaker
1896	Sir W. Laurier	1963	Lester Pearson
1911	Sir R. Borden	1968	Pierre Elliott Trudeau
1920	A. Meighen		

PRIME MINISTERS OF CEYLON

1948	Don S. Senanayake	1960	Dudley S. Senanayake
1952	Dudley S. Senanayake	1960	Mrs. S. Bandaranaike
1953	Sir J. Kotelawala	1965	Dudley S. Senanayake
1956	S. W. R. D. Bandaranaike	1970	Mrs. S. Bandaranaike
1959	W. Dahanayake		

PRESIDENT OF CYPRUS

1960   Archbishop Makarios

PRIME MINISTER AND (since 1970) PRESIDENT OF THE GAMBIA

1965   Dauda Jawara

PRIME MINISTERS OF GHANA

1957   Kwame Nkrumah

(In 1960 Dr. Nkrumah assumed the title of President but remained the head of the Government. In 1966 he was overthrown by a military *coup* led by General Joseph Arthur Ankrah. In 1969 parliamentary government was restored to

Ghana under a new Constitution providing for a President as constitutional head of state and a Prime Minister at the head of the Government.)

1969   Kofi Abrefa Busia

Prime Minister of Guyana
1966   Forbes Burnham

Prime Ministers of India
1947   Shri Jawaharlal Nehru
1964   Lal Bahadur Shastri

1966   Gulzarilal Nandi
          (Interim Prime Minister)
1966   Mrs Indira Gandhi

Prime Ministers of Jamaica
1962   Sir Alexander Bustamante
1967   Donald Sangster
1967   Hugh Shearer

Prime Minister and (since 1964) President of Kenya
1963   Jomo Kenyatta

Prime Minister of Lesotho
1966   Chief Leabua Jonathan

Prime Minister and (since 1966) President of Malawi
1964   Dr Hastings Kamuzu Banda

Prime Ministers of Malaya and (since 1963) Malaysia
1957   Tunku Abdul Rahman
1959   Dato Abdul Razak bin Dato Hussein
1960   Tunku Abdul Rahman
1970   Tun Abdul Razak

Prime Minister of Malta
1962   Dr George Borg Olivier

Prime Minister of Mauritius
1964   Sir Seewoosagur Ramgoolam

Prime Ministers of New Zealand
1856   H. Sewell
1856   W. Fox
1856   E. W. Stafford
1861   W. Fox

1862   A. Domett
1863   F. Whitaker
1864   F. A. Weld
1865   E. W. Stafford

1869	W. Fox	1891	J. Ballance
1872	E. W. Stafford	1893	R. J. Seddon
1872	G. M. Waterhouse	1906	W. Hall-Jones
1873	W. Fox	1906	Sir J. G. Ward
1873	J. Vogel	1912	T. Mackenzie
1875	D. Pollen	1912	W. F. Massey
1876	Sir J. Vogel	1925	Sir F. Bell
1876	H. A. Atkinson	1925	J. G. Coates
1877	Sir G. Grey	1928	Sir J. G. Ward
1879	J. Hall	1930	G. W. Forbes
1882	F. Whitaker	1935	M. J. Savage
1883	H. A. Atkinson	1940	P. Fraser
1884	R. Stout	1949	S. G. Holland
1884	H. A. Atkinson	1957	K. Holyoake
1884	Sir R. Stout	1957	Walter Nash
1887	Sir H. A. Atkinson	1960	K. Holyoake

PRIME MINISTER OF NIGERIA

1960   Alhaji Sir Abubakar Tafawa Balewa

(In January 1966 the Government of Sir Abubakar Tafawa Balewa was overthrown by a military *coup*, the Prime Minister himself being killed as a result of the uprising. A military government was established under the leadership of General Aguiyi-Ironsi, who was himself overthrown in July of the same year by a second *coup* which resulted in the control of the Government being taken over by Lieutenant-Colonel Y. Gowon.)

PRIME MINISTERS AND (since 1958) PRESIDENTS OF PAKISTAN

1947	Liaquat Ali Khan	1957	I. I. Chundrigar
1951	Khawaja Nazi Muddin	1957	Malik Firoz Khan Noon
1953	Mohammed Ali	1958	Mohammed Ayub Khan
1955	Chaudri Mohamad Ali	1959	Yahya Khan
1956	Huseyn Shaheed Suhrawardy		

PRIME MINISTERS OF SIERRA LEONE

1961	Sir Milton Margai	1968	Siaka Stevens
1964	Sir Albert Margai		

PRIME MINISTER OF SINGAPORE

1959   Lee Kuan Yew

PRIME MINISTERS OF RHODESIA

1923	Sir Charles Coghlan	1953	R. S. Garfield Todd
1927	H. U. Moffat	1958	Sir Edgar Whitehead
1933	G. Mitchell	1962	Winston Field
1933	Sir Godfrey Huggins	1964	Ian Smith

(In 1965 Mr. Ian Smith declared the independence of Rhodesia unilaterally and was dismissed from office by the Governor. He has nevertheless continued to head the *de facto* government of the country since that time.)

Prime Ministers of Tanganyika and President of Tanganyika and (since 1964) Tanzania

1961	Dr. Julius Nyerere	1962 Dr. Julius Nyerere
1962	Rashidi Mfaume Kawawa	

Premier and (since 1961) Prime Minister of Trinidad and Tobago

1959   Dr. Eric Williams

Prime Minister and (since 1966) President of Uganda

1962   Dr. Milton Obote

President of Zambia

1964   Dr. Kenneth David Kaunda

LORDS HIGH ADMIRAL, FIRST LORDS OF THE ADMIRALTY AND (FROM 1964 TO 1967) MINISTERS OF DEFENCE FOR THE ROYAL NAVY

When no High Admiral is mentioned the office is in commission and there is a First Lord. Prior to these lists, the office was in commission on two occasions only, and then the office now known as that of First Lord was filled by (1) Lord Weston, 1628–36 and (2) W. Juxton, Bishop of London, 1636–8. Between 1638 and 1660, the office was held either by a Lord High Admiral or a Parliamentary Committee.

1660	James, Duke of York (Lord High Adm.)	1748	Earl of Sandwich
1673	King Charles II	1751	Lord Anson
1673	Prince Rupert	1756	Earl Temple
1679	Sir Henry Capell	1757	Earl of Winchilsea & Nottingham
1680	D. Finch	1757	Lord Anson
1684	King Charles II (Lord High Adm.)	1762	Earl of Halifax
		1762	George Grenville
1685	King James II (Lord High Adm.)	1763	Earl of Sandwich
1689	A. Herbert	1763	Earl of Egmont
1690	Earl of Pembroke & Montgomery	1766	Sir Charles Saunders
		1766	Sir Edward Hawke
1692	Lord Cornwallis	1771	Earl of Sandwich
1693	Viscount Falkland	1782	Adm. Keppel
1694	Adm. E. Russell	1783	Viscount Howe
1699	Earl of Bridgwater	1783	Viscount Keppel
1701	Earl of Pembroke & Montgomery	1783	Viscount Howe
		1788	Earl of Chatham
1702	Earl of Pembroke & Montgomery (Lord High Adm.)	1794	Earl Spencer
		1801	Earl of St. Vincent
1702	Prince George of Denmark (Lord High Adm.)	1804	Viscount Melville
		1805	Lord Barham
1708	Earl of Pembroke & Montgomery (Lord High Adm.)	1806	C. Grey
		1806	T. Grenville
1709	Earl of Orford	1807	Lord Mulgrave
1710	Adm. Sir John Leake	1810	C. Yorke
1712	Earl of Strafford	1812	Viscount Melville
1714	Earl of Orford	1827	Duke of Clarence (Lord High Adm.)
1717	Earl of Berkeley		
1727	Viscount Torrington	1828	Viscount Melville
1733	Sir Charles Wager	1830	Sir J. R. G. Graham
1742	Earl of Winchilsea & Nottingham	1834	Lord Auckland
		1834	Earl de Grey
1744	Duke of Bedford	1835	Lord Auckland
		1835	Earl of Minto

1841	Earl of Haddington	1916	Sir E. Carson
1846	Earl of Ellenborough	1917	Sir E. C. Geddes
1846	Earl of Auckland	1919	W. H. Long
1849	Sir F. T. Baring	1921	Lord Lee of Fareham
1852	Duke of Northumberland	1922	L. S. Amery
1853	Sir J. R. G. Graham	1924	Viscount Chelmsford
1855	Sir C. Wood	1924	W. C. Bridgeman
1858	Sir J. S. Pakington	1929	A. V. Alexander
1859	Duke of Somerset	1931	Sir Austen Chamberlain
1866	Sir J. S. Pakington	1931	Sir B. M. E. Monsell
1867	H. T. L. Corry	1936	Sir S. Hoare
1868	H. C. E. Childers	1937	A. Duff Cooper
1871	G. J. Goschen	1938	Earl of Stanhope
1874	G. Ward Hunt	1939	Winston Churchill
1877	W. H. Smith	1940	A. V. Alexander
1880	Earl of Northbrook	1945	Brendan Bracken
1885	Lord George Hamilton	1945	A. V. Alexander
1886	Marquess of Ripon	1946	G. H. Hall
1886	Lord George Hamilton	1951	Lord Pakenham
1892	Earl Spencer	1951	J. P. L. Thomas (afterward
1895	G. J. Goschen		Viscount Cilcennin)
1900	Earl of Selborne	1956	Viscount Hailsham
1905	Earl Cawdor	1957	Earl of Selkirk
1905	Lord Tweedmouth	1959	Lord Carrington
1908	R. McKenna	1963	Earl Jellicoe
1911	Winston Churchill	1964	Christopher Mayhew
1915	A. J. Balfour	1966	J. P. W. Mallalieu

PRESIDENTS OF THE BOARD OF AGRICULTURE AND MINISTERS OF AGRICULTURE, FISHERIES AND (SINCE 1955) FOOD

1889	H. Chaplin
1892	H. Gardner
1895	W. Long
1900	R. W. Hanbury
1903	Earl of Onslow
1905	A. Fellowes
1905	Earl Carrington
1911	W. Runciman
1914	Lord Lucas
1915	Earl of Selborne
1916	Earl of Crawford
1916	R. Prothero
1919	Lord Lee of Fareham
1921	Sir A. G. Boscawen
1922	Sir R. Sanders
1924	N. Buxton
1924	E. F. L. Wood (afterwards Earl of Halifax)
1925	W. Guinness
1929	N. Buxton
1930	C. Addison
1931	Sir J. Gilmour
1932	Walter Elliot
1936	W. S. Morrison
1939	Sir R. Dorman-Smith
1940	R. S. Hudson
1945	T. Williams
1951	Sir T. Dugdale
1954	D. Heathcoat Amory
1958	John Hare
1960	Christopher Soames
1964	Fred Peart
1968	Cledwyn Hughes
1970	James Prior

SECRETARIES OF STATE FOR AIR AND
(from 1964 to 1967)
MINISTERS OF DEFENCE FOR THE ROYAL AIR FORCE

1917	Viscount Cowdray
1917	Lord Rothermere
1918	Lord Weir
1919	Winston Churchill
1921	Sir L. Worthington-Evans
1921	F. E. Guest
1922	Sir S. Hoare
1923	Lord Thomson
1924	Sir S. Hoare
1929	Lord Thomson
1930	Lord Amulree
1931	Marquess of Londonderry
1935	Viscount Swinton
1938	Sir K. Wood
1940	Sir S. Hoare
1940	Sir A. Sinclair
1945	Harold Macmillan
1945	Viscount Stansgate
1946	P. J. Noel-Baker
1947	A. Henderson
1951	Lord de L'Isle & Dudley
1956	Nigel Birch
1957	George Ward
1960	Julian Amery
1962	Hugh Fraser
1964	Lord Shackleton

SECRETARIES OF STATE FOR THE COLONIES

1768	Earl of Hillsborough	1783	Lord North
1772	Earl of Dartmouth	1783	Lord Sydney (formerly
1776	Lord George St. Germaine		Thomas Townshend)
1782	W. Ellis	1789	W. W. Grenville
1782	Earl of Shelburne	1791	H. Dundas
1782	Thomas Townshend	1794	Duke of Portland

From 1794 to 1854 see WAR AND COLONIES

1854	Sir G. Grey	1915	A. Bonar Law
1855	Sidney Herbert	1916	W. H. Long
1855	Lord John Russell	1919	Viscount Milner
1855	Sir W. Molesworth	1921	Winston Churchill
1855	H. Labouchere	1922	Duke of Devonshire
1858	Lord Stanley	1924	J. H. Thomas
1858	Sir E. Bulwer-Lytton	1924	L. S. Amery
1859	Duke of Newcastle	1929	Lord Passfield
1864	E. Cardwell	1931	J. H. Thomas
1866	Earl of Carnarvon	1931	Sir P. Cunliffe-Lister
1867	Duke of Buckingham &	1935	M. MacDonald
	Chandos	1935	J. H. Thomas
1868	Earl Granville	1936	W. Ormsby-Gore
1870	Earl of Kimberley	1938	M. MacDonald
1874	Earl of Carnarvon	1940	Lord Lloyd
1878	Sir M. E. Hicks-Beach	1941	Lord Moyne
1880	Earl of Kimberley	1942	Viscount Cranborne
1882	Earl of Derby (formerly Lord	1942	O. Stanley
	Stanley)	1945	G. H. Hall
1885	F. A. Stanley	1946	A. Creech Jones
1886	Earl Granville	1950	J. Griffiths
1886	E. Stanhope	1951	O. Lyttelton
1887	Sir H. T. Holland	1954	A. T. Lennox-Boyd
1892	Marquess of Ripon	1959	Iain MacLeod
1895	Joseph Chamberlain	1961	Reginald Maudling
1903	A. Lyttelton	1962	Duncan Sandys
1905	Earl of Elgin & Kincardine	1964	Anthony Greenwood
1908	Earl of Crewe	1966	Earl of Longford
1910	L. Harcourt	1966	Frederick Lee

SECRETARIES OF STATE FOR DOMINION AFFAIRS
AND (FROM 1947 TO 1966)
SECRETARIES OF STATE FOR COMMONWEALTH RELATIONS
AND (FROM 1966 TO 1968)
SECRETARIES OF STATE FOR COMMONWEALTH AFFAIRS

1925	L. S. Amery
1929	Lord Passfield
1930	J. H. Thomas
1935	M. MacDonald
1938	Lord Stanley
1938	M. MacDonald
1939	Sir T. Inskip
1939	Anthony Eden
1940	Viscount Caldecote
1940	Viscount Cranborne
1942	C. R. Attlee
1943	Viscount Cranborne
1945	Viscount Addison
1947	P. J. Noel-Baker
1950	P. Gordon-Walker
1951	Lord Ismay
1952	Marquess of Salisbury
1952	Viscount Swinton
1955	Earl of Home
1960	Duncan Sandys
1964	Arthur Bottomley
1966	Herbert Bowden
1967	George Thomson

MINISTERS OF DEFENCE AND (SINCE 1964) SECRETARIES OF STATE FOR DEFENCE

1936 Sir T. Inskip
1939 Lord Chatfield
1940 Winston Churchill
1945 C. R. Attlee
1946 A. V. Alexander
1950 E. Shinwell
1951 Winston Churchill
1952 Lord Alexander of Tunis
1954 Harold Macmillan
1955 Selwyn Lloyd
1956 Sir W. Monckton
1956 Antony Head
1957 Duncan Sandys
1959 Harold Watkinson
1962 Peter Thorneycroft
1964 Denis Healey
1970 Lord Carrington

CHANCELLORS OF THE DUCHY OF LANCASTER AND CHANCELLORS OF THE DUCHY AND COUNTY PALATINE

Chancellors of the Duchy of Lancaster

1399	William Burgoyne	1431	Walter Shiryngton
1402	John Wakering	1449	William Tresham
1405	Thomas Stanley	1449	John Say
1410	John Springthorpe	1471	Sir Richard Fowler
1413	John Wodehouse	1477	Sir John Say

Chancellors of the Duchy and County Palatine

1478	Thomas Thwaites	1558	Sir Edward Waldegrave
1483	Thomas Metcalfe	1559	Sir Ambrose Cave
1485	Sir Reginald Bray	1568	Sir Ralph Sadler
1504	Sir John Mordaunt	1587	Sir Francis Walsingham
1505	Sir Richard Empson	1590	Sir Thomas Heneage
1509	Sir Henry Marney	1595	In Commission
1523	Sir Richard Wingfield	1597	Sir Robert Cecil
1525	Sir Thomas More	1599	In Commission
1529	Sir William Fitzwilliam	1601	(24 September for ten days only) Sir John Fortescue
1542	Sir John Gage		
1547	Sir William Paget	1601	(8 October to 4 November) In Commission
1552	Sir John Gates		
1553	Sir Robert Rochester	1601	Sir John Fortescue

Chancellors of the Duchy of Lancaster

1603	Sir John Fortescue	1658	John Bradshaw
1607	Sir John Fortescue ⎫ jointly Sir Thomas Parry ⎭	1660	William Lenthall
		1660	Sir Gilbert Gerrard
1615	Sir Thomas Parry ⎫ jointly Sir John Daccombe ⎭	1660	Lord Seymour of Trowbridge
		1664	Sir Thomas Ingram
1616	Sir John Daccombe	1672	Sir Robert Carr
1618	Sir Humphrey May	1682	Sir Thomas Chichley
1629	Lord Newburgh	1687	Lord Belasye 'and other Commissioners for ye Treasury'
1644	Lord Grey of Wake ⎫ William Lenthall ⎭ Commissioners		
		1689	Lord Willoughby de Eresby
1648	Sir Gilbert Gerrard	1697	Earl of Stamford
1649	John Bradshaw	1702	Sir John Leveson Gower
1653	John Bradshaw ⎫ jointly Thomas Fell ⎭	1706	Earl of Derby
		1710	Lord Berkeley of Stratton
1655	Thomas Fell	1714	Earl of Aylesford

1716	Earl of Scarborough	1882	Earl of Kimberley
1717	Nicholas Lechmere	1882	J. G. Dodson
1727	Duke of Rutland	1884	G. O. Trevelyan
1735	Earl of Cholmondeley	1885	H. Chaplin
1743	Lord Edgcumbe	1886	E. Heneage
1758	Viscount Dupplin	1886	Sir U. J. Kay-Shuttleworth
1762	Lord Strange	1886	Duke of Rutland
1771	Earl of Clarendon	1892	J. Bryce
1782	Lord Ashburton	1894	Lord Tweedmouth
1783	Earl of Derby	1895	Viscount Cross
1783	Earl of Clarendon	1895	Lord James of Hereford
1787	Lord Hawkesbury	1902	Sir W. Walrond
1803	Lord Pelham	1905	Sir H. H. Fowler
1804	Lord Mulgrave	1908	Lord Fitzmaurice
1805	Earl of Buckinghamshire	1909	H. L. Samuel
1806	Earl of Derby	1910	Lord Gainford
1807	S. Perceval	1911	C. E. H. Hobhouse
1812	Earl of Buckinghamshire	1914	C. F. G. Masterman
1812	C. Bathurst	1915	E. S. Montague
1823	Lord Bexley	1915	Winston Churchill
1828	Earl of Aberdeen	1915	H. L. Samuel
1828	C. Arbuthnot	1916	E. S. Montague
1830	Lord Holland	1916	T. M. Wood
1830	Earl of Haddington	1917	Sir F. Cawley
1834	C. W. W. Wynn	1918	Lord Beaverbrook
1835	Lord Holland	1918	Lord Downham
1840	Earl of Clarendon	1919	Earl of Crawford & Balcarres
1841	Sir G. Grey	1921	Viscount Peel
1841	Lord Granville Somerset	1922	Sir W. Sutherland
1846	Lord Campbell	1922	Marquess of Salisbury
1850	Earl of Carlisle	1923	J. C. C. Davidson
1852	R. A. C. Nisbet-Hamilton	1924	J. C. Wedgwood
1852	E. Strutt	1924	Viscount Cecil of Chelwood
1854	Earl Granville	1927	Lord Cushenden
1855	Earl of Harrowby	1929	Sir O. E. Mosley
1855	M. T. Barnes	1930	C. R. Attlee
1858	Duke of Montrose	1931	Lord Ponsonby of Shulbrede
1859	Sir G. Grey	1931	Marquess of Lothian
1861	E. Cardwell	1931	J. C. C. Davidson
1864	Earl of Clarendon	1937	Earl Winterton
1866	G. J. Goschen	1939	W. S. Morrison
1866	Earl of Devon	1940	Lord Tryon
1867	J. Wilson-Patten	1940	Lord Hankey
1868	T. E. Taylor	1941	A. Duff Cooper
1868	Lord Dufferin	1943	Ernest Brown
1872	H. C. E. Childers	1945	Sir A. Salter
1873	John Bright	1945	J. B. Hynd
1874	T. E. Taylor	1947	Lord Pakenham
1880	John Bright	1948	Hugh Dalton

1950	Viscount Alexander of Hillsborough	1963	Viscount Blakenhorn
1951	Viscount Swinton	1964	Douglas Houghton
1952	Viscount Woolton	1966	George Thomson
1956	Earl of Selkirk	1967	Frederick Lee
1957	Charles Hill	1969	George Thomson
1961	Iain Macleod	1970	Anthony Barber
		1970	Geoffrey Rippon

PRESIDENTS OF THE BOARD OF EDUCATION, MINISTERS OF EDUCATION AND (SINCE 1964) SECRETARIES OF STATE FOR EDUCATION AND SCIENCE

1900	Duke of Devonshire
1902	Marquess of Londonderry
1905	A. Birrell
1907	R. McKenna
1908	W. Runciman
1911	J. A. Pease
1915	A. Henderson
1916	Marquess of Crewe
1916	H. A. L. Fisher
1922	E. F. L. Wood (afterwards Earl of Halifax)
1924	C. P. Trevelyan
1924	Lord Eustace Percy
1929	Sir C. P. Trevelyan
1931	H. B. Lees-Smith
1931	Sir D. Maclean
1932	Lord Irwin (afterwards Earl of Halifax)
1935	O. Stanley
1937	Earl Stanhope
1938	Earl de la Warr
1940	H. Ramsbotham
1941	R. A. Butler
1945	R. K. Law
1945	Ellen Wilkinson
1947	G. Tomlinson
1951	Florence Horsbrugh
1954	Sir David Eccles
1957	Lord Hailsham
1957	Geoffrey Lloyd
1959	Sir David Eccles
1962	Sir Edward Boyle
1964	Quintin Hogg
1964	Michael Stewart
1965	Anthony Crosland
1967	Patrick Gordon Walker
1968	Edward Short
1970	Margaret Thatcher

CHANCELLORS OF THE EXCHEQUER

1714	Sir Richard Onslow	1873	W. E. Gladstone
1715	Sir Robert Walpole	1874	Sir S. Northcote
1717	Lord Stanhope	1880	W. E. Gladstone
1718	John Aislabie	1882	H. C. E. Childers
1721	Sir Robert Walpole	1885	Sir M. E. Hicks-Beach
1742	Samuel Sandys	1886	Sir W. Harcourt
1743	Henry Pelham	1886	Lord Randolph Churchill
1754	Hon. Henry Bilson-Legge	1887	G. J. Goschen
1761	Viscount Barrington	1892	Sir W. Harcourt
1762	Sir Francis Dashwood	1895	Sir M. E. Hicks-Beach
1763	George Grenville	1902	C. T. Ritchie
1765	William Dowdeswell	1902	Austen Chamberlain
1766	Hon. Charles Townshend	1905	H. H. Asquith
1767	Lord North	1908	D. Lloyd George
1782	Lord John Cavendish	1915	R. McKenna
1782	William Pitt	1916	A. Bonar Law
1783	Lord John Cavendish	1919	Austen Chamberlain
1783	William Pitt	1921	Sir R. S. Horne
1801	H. Addington	1922	Stanley Baldwin
1804	William Pitt	1923	Neville Chamberlain
1806	Lord Henry Petty	1924	P. Snowden
1807	S. Perceval	1924	Winston Churchill
1812	N. Vansittart	1929	P. Snowden
1823	F. J. Robinson	1931	Neville Chamberlain
1827	G. Canning	1937	Sir J. Simon
1827	J. C. Herries	1940	Sir K. Wood
1828	H. Goulburn	1940	Sir J. Anderson
1830	Viscount Althorp	1945	Hugh Dalton
1834	Sir Robert Peel	1945	Sir Stafford Cripps
1835	T. Spring-Rice	1950	Hugh Gaitskell
1839	F. T. Baring	1951	R. A. Butler
1841	H. Goulburn	1956	Harold Macmillan
1846	C. Wood	1957	P. Thorneycroft
1852	B. Disraeli	1958	D. Heathcoat Amory
1852	W. E. Gladstone	1960	Selwyn Lloyd
1855	Sir G. C. Lewis	1962	Reginald Maudling
1858	B. Disraeli	1964	James Callaghan
1859	W. E. Gladstone	1967	Roy Jenkins
1866	B. Disraeli	1970	Iain Macleod
1868	G. W. Hunt	1970	Anthony Barber
1868	R. Lowe		

SECRETARIES OF STATE FOR FOREIGN AFFAIRS
AND (SINCE 1968) SECRETARIES OF STATE FOR FOREIGN AND COMMONWEALTH AFFAIRS

1782	Charles James Fox	1880	Earl Granville
1782	Lord Grantham	1885	Marquess of Salisbury
1783	Charles James Fox	1886	Earl of Rosebery
1783	Marquess of Carmarthen	1886	Earl of Iddesleigh
1791	Lord Grenville	1887	Marquess of Salisbury
1801	Lord Hawkesbury	1892	Earl of Rosebery
1804	Lord Harrowby	1894	Earl of Kimberley
1805	Lord Mulgrave	1895	Marquess of Salisbury
1806	Charles James Fox	1900	Marquess of Lansdowne
1806	Lord Howick	1905	Sir E. Grey
1807	G. Canning	1916	A. J. Balfour
1809	Earl Bathurst	1919	Lord Curzon
1809	Marquess Wellesley	1924	J. Ramsay MacDonald
1812	Viscount Castlereagh	1924	Austen Chamberlain
1822	G. Canning	1929	A. Henderson
1827	Earl of Dudley	1931	Lord Reading
1828	Earl of Aberdeen	1931	Sir J. Simon
1830	Viscount Palmerston	1935	Sir S. Hoare
1834	Duke of Wellington	1935	Anthony Eden
1835	Viscount Palmerston	1938	Lord Halifax
1841	Earl of Aberdeen	1940	Anthony Eden
1846	Viscount Palmerston	1945	Ernest Bevin
1851	Earl Granville	1951	Herbert Morrison
1852	Earl of Malmesbury	1951	Sir Anthony Eden
1852	Lord John Russell	1955	Harold Macmillan
1853	Earl of Clarendon	1955	Selwyn Lloyd
1858	Earl of Malmesbury	1960	Earl of Home
1859	Lord John Russell	1963	R. A. Butler
1865	Earl of Clarendon	1964	Patrick Gordon Walker
1866	Lord Stanley	1965	Michael Stewart
1868	Earl of Clarendon	1966	George Brown
1870	Earl Granville	1968	Michael Stewart
1874	Earl of Derby (formerly Lord Stanley)	1970	Sir Alec Douglas-Home
1878	Marquess of Salisbury		

MINISTERS OF HEALTH

1919	C. Addison
1921	Sir A. Mond
1922	Sir A. Griffith-Boscawen
1923	Neville Chamberlain
1924	J. Wheatley
1924	Neville Chamberlain
1929	A. Greenwood
1931	Neville Chamberlain
1931	Sir E. Hilton Young
1935	Sir K. Wood
1938	Walter Elliot
1940	M. MacDonald
1941	Ernest Brown
1943	H. U. Willink
1945	A. Bevan
1951	H. A. Marquand
1951	H. Crookshank
1952	Iain Macleod
1956	R. H. Turton
1957	D. Vosper
1957	D. Walker-Smith
1960	Enoch Powell
1963	Anthony Barber
1964	Kenneth Robinson

(In 1968 this office was superseded by that of Secretary of State for Social Services.)

SECRETARIES OF STATE FOR THE HOME DEPARTMENT

1782	Earl of Shelburne	1873	R. Lowe
1782	Thomas Townshend	1874	Sir R. A. Cross
1782	Lord North	1880	Sir W. V. Harcourt
1783	Lord Sydney (Thomas Townshend)	1885	Sir R. A. Cross
		1886	H. C. E. Childers
1789	William Wyndham Grenville	1886	H. Matthews
1791	Henry Dundas	1892	H. H. Asquith
1794	Duke of Portland	1895	Sir M. W. Ridley
1801	Lord Pelham	1900	C. T. Ritchie
1803	C. P. Yorke	1902	A. Akers-Douglas
1804	Lord Hawkesbury	1905	H. J. Gladstone
1806	Earl Spencer	1910	Winston Churchill
1807	Lord Hawkesbury	1911	R. McKenna
1809	R. Ryder	1915	Sir J. Simon
1812	Viscount Sidmouth	1916	H. L. Samuel
1822	Robert Peel	1916	Sir G. Cave
1827	W. S. Bourne	1919	E. Shortt
1827	Marquess of Lansdowne	1922	W. C. Bridgeman
1828	Robert Peel	1924	A. Henderson
1830	Viscount Melbourne	1924	Sir W. Joynson-Hicks
1834	Viscount Duncannon	1929	J. R. Clynes
1834	H. Goulburn	1931	Sir H. Samuel
1835	Lord John Russell	1932	Sir J. Gilmour
1839	Marquess of Normanby	1935	Sir J. Simon
1841	Sir J. R. Graham	1937	Sir S. Hoare
1846	Sir G. Grey	1939	Sir J. Anderson
1852	S. H. Walpole	1940	Herbert Morrison
1852	Viscount Palmerston	1945	Sir D. B. Somervell
1855	Sidney Herbert	1945	J. Chuter Ede
1855	Sir G. Grey	1951	Sir D. Maxwell Fyfe
1858	S. H. Walpole	1954	G. Lloyd George
1859	T. H. S. Sotheron-Estcourt	1957	R. A. Butler
1859	Sir G. C. Lewis	1962	Henry Brooke
1861	Sir G. Grey	1964	Sir Frank Soskice
1866	S. H. Walpole	1966	Roy Jenkins
1867	G. Hardy	1967	James Callaghan
1868	H. A. Bruce	1970	Reginald Maudling

MINISTERS OF TOWN AND COUNTRY PLANNING AND (FROM 1951 TO 1970) MINISTERS OF HOUSING AND LOCAL GOVERNMENT

1943	W. S. Morrison
1945	Lewis Silkin
1950	Hugh Dalton
	(For a brief period in 1951 this Minister was designated Minister of Local Government and Planning.)
1951	Harold Macmillan
1954	Duncan Sandys
1957	Henry Brooke
1961	Charles Hill
1962	Sir Keith Joseph
1964	Richard Crossman
1966	Anthony Greenwood
1969	Anthony Crosland
	(Mr. Crosland was appointed the first Secretary of State for Local Government and Regional Planning, Mr. Greenwood remaining Minister of Housing and Local Government.)
1970	Peter Walker

SECRETARIES OF STATE FOR INDIA

1858	E. H. S. Stanley
1859	Sir C. Wood
1866	Earl de Grey and Ripon
1866	Viscount Cranborne
1867	Sir S. Northcote
1868	Duke of Argyll
1874	Marquess of Salisbury (formerly Viscount Cranborne)
1878	Viscount Cranbrook
1880	Marquess of Hartington
1882	Earl of Kimberley
1885	Lord Randolph Churchill
1886	Earl of Kimberley
1886	Viscount Cross
1892	Earl of Kimberley
1894	Sir H. Fowler
1895	Lord George Hamilton
1903	St. J. Brodrick
1905	Viscount Morley of Blackburn
1910	Earl of Crewe
1915	Austen Chamberlain
1917	E. Montagu
1922	Viscount Peel
1924	Lord Olivier
1924	Earl of Birkenhead
1928	Viscount Peel
1929	W. Wedgwood Benn
1931	Sir S. Hoare
1935	Marquess of Zetland
1940	L. S. Amery
1945	Lord Pethick-Lawrence
1947	Earl of Listowel

MINISTERS OF LABOUR
AND (SINCE 1968) SECRETARIES OF STATE FOR EMPLOYMENT AND PRODUCTIVITY

1917	J. Hodge
1917	G. H. Roberts
1919	Sir R. S. Horne
1920	T. J. Macnamara
1922	Sir M. Barlow
1924	T. Shaw
1924	Sir A. Steel-Maitland
1929	Margaret Bondfield
1931	Sir H. Betterton
1934	O. Stanley
1935	Ernest Brown
1940	Ernest Bevin
1945	G. A. Isaacs
1951	A. Bevan
1951	A. Robens
1951	Sir W. Monckton
1956	Iain Macleod
1959	Edward Heath
1960	John Hare
1963	J. B. Godber
1964	R. J. Gunter
1968	Barbara Castle
1970	Robert Carr

LORDS PRESIDENT OF THE COUNCIL

1679	Earl of Shaftesbury	1805	Earl Camden (formerly Lord Camden)
1679	Earl of Radnor		
1684	Earl of Rochester	1806	Earl FitzWilliam
1685	Marquess of Halifax	1806	Viscount Sidmouth
1685	Earl of Sunderland	1807	Earl Camden
1689	Earl of Danby	1812	Viscount Sidmouth
1699	Earl of Pembroke & Montgomery	1812	Earl of Harrowby
		1827	Duke of Portland
1701	Duke of Somerset	1828	Earl Bathurst
1702	Earl of Pembroke & Montgomery	1830	Marquess of Lansdowne
		1834	Earl of Rosslyn
1708	Lord Somers	1835	Marquess of Lansdowne
1710	Earl of Rochester	1841	Lord Wharncliffe
1711	Duke of Buckinghamshire & Normanby	1846	Duke of Buccleuch
		1846	Marquess of Lansdowne
1714	Earl of Nottingham	1852	Earl of Lonsdale
1715	Earl of Dorset	1852	Earl Granville
1716	Duke of Devonshire	1854	Lord John Russell
1717	Earl of Sunderland	1855	Earl Granville
1719	Duke of Kingston	1858	Marquess of Salisbury
1720	Viscount Townshend	1859	Earl Granville
1721	Lord Carleton	1866	Duke of Buckingham & Chandos
1725	Duke of Devonshire		
1730	Lord Trevor	1867	Duke of Marlborough
1730	Earl of Wilmington	1868	Earl de Grey & Ripon
1742	Earl of Harrington	1873	H. A. Bruce
1745	Duke of Dorset	1874	Duke of Richmond
1751	Earl Granville	1880	Earl Spencer
1763	Duke of Bedford	1883	Lord Carlingford
1765	Earl of Winchilsea & Nottingham	1885	Viscount Cranbrook
		1886	Earl Spencer
1766	Earl of Northington	1886	Viscount Cranbrook
1767	Earl Gower	1892	Earl of Kimberley
1779	Earl Bathurst	1894	Earl of Rosebery
1782	Lord Camden	1895	Duke of Devonshire
1783	Viscount Stormont	1903	Marquess of Londonderry
1783	Earl Gower	1905	Earl of Crewe
1784	Lord Camden	1908	Lord Tweedmouth
1794	Earl FitzWilliam	1908	Viscount Wolverhampton
1794	Earl of Mansfield	1910	Earl Beauchamp
1796	Earl of Chatham	1910	Viscount Morley
1801	Duke of Portland	1914	Earl Beauchamp
1805	Viscount Sidmouth	1915	Marquess of Crewe

1916	Earl Curzon of Kedleston	1943	C. R. Attlee
1919	A. J. Balfour	1945	Lord Woolton
1922	Marquess of Salisbury	1945	Herbert Morrison
1924	Lord Parmoor of Frieth	1951	Viscount Addison
1924	Marquess Curzon of Kedleston	1951	Lord Woolton
1925	Earl of Balfour	1952	Marquess of Salisbury
1929	Lord Parmoor of Frieth	1957	Earl of Home
1931	Stanley Baldwin	1957	Viscount Hailsham
1935	J. Ramsay MacDonald	1959	Earl of Home
1937	Viscount Halifax	1960	Viscount Hailsham
1938	Viscount Hailsham	1960	Viscount Hailsham (Quintin
1938	Viscount Runciman of		Hogg)
	Doxford	1964	Herbert Bowden
1939	Earl Stanhope	1966	Richard Crossman
1940	Neville Chamberlain	1968	Fred Peart
1940	Sir J. Anderson	1970	William Whitelaw

KEEPERS OF THE PRIVY SEAL

1307	William Melton	1415	John Wakering
1312	Roger Northburgh	1416?	Henry Ware
1316	Thomas Charlton	1418	John Kemp
1320	Robert Baldock	1421	John Stafford
1323	Robert Wodehouse	1422	William Alnwick
1323	Robert Ayleston	1432	William Lyndwood
1324	William Airmyn	1443	Thomas Beckington
1325	Henry Cliff	1444	Adam Moleyns
1325?	William Harleston	1450	Thomas Kent
1326	Robert Wyvill 'acted as keeper of the privy seal used by Edward, Duke of Aquitaine, while governing the realm in his father's name'	1450	Andrew Hulse
		1452	Thomas Kent
		1452	Thomas Lisieux
		1456	Lawrence Booth
		1460	Robert Stillington
1327	Richard Airmyn	1467	Thomas Rotherham
1328	Adam Limber (Lymbergh)	1470	John Hales (Keeper during the brief restoration of Henry VI)
1330	Richard Bury		
1334	Robert Ayleston		
1334	Robert Tawton	1471	Thomas Rotherham
1335	William de la Zouche	1474	John Russell
1337	Richard Bentworth	1483	John Gunthorp
1338	William Kilsby	1485	Peter Courtenay
1342	John Offord	1487	Richard Fox (first to be designated Lord Privy Seal)
1344	Thomas Hatfield		
1345	John Thoresby	1516	Thomas Ruthall
1347	Simon Islip	1523	Lord Marny
1350	Michael Northburgh	1523	Cuthbert Tunstall
1354	Thomas Bramber	1530	Thomas Boleyn, Earl of Wiltshire & Ormond
1356	John Winwick		
1360	John Buckingham	1536	Thomas Cromwell
1363	William of Wykeham	1540	Earl of Southampton
1367	Peter Lacy	1542	John Russell
1371	Nicholas Carew	1555	Sir Robert Rochester
1377	John Fordham	1555	Lord Paget
1381	William Dighton	1571	Lord Burghley (styled Keeper —Nicholas Bacon is said to have acted as Keeper at the beginning of Elizabeth's reign)
1382	Walter Skirlaw		
1386	John Waltham		
1389	Edmund Stafford		
1396	Guy de Mone		
1397	Richard Clifford	1572	Lord Howard of Effingham
1401	Thomas Langley	1573	Sir Thomas Smith
1405	Nicholas Bubwith	1576	Francis Walsingham
1406	John Prophet	1590?	Lord Burghley

1598	Robert Cecil		Abraham Stanyan ⎫
1608	Earl of Northampton	1731	Robert Jackson ⎭
1614	Earl of Somerset		Commissioners
1616	Earl of Worcester	1731	Duke of Devonshire
1628	Sir John Coke	1733	Viscount Lonsdale
1628	Sir Robert Naunton	1735	Earl of Godolphin
1628	Earl of Manchester	1740	Lord Hervey of Ickworth
1643	Sir Edward Nicholas	1742	John Leveson Gower
1644	Earl of Bath	1743	Earl of Cholmondeley
1655–7	Nathaniel Fiennes, 'Commissioner of His Highnes Privy Seale', received the customary allowance from March 1655 until June 1657 during the Protectorate	1744	Earl Gower (formerly John Leveson Gower)
		1755	Duke of Marlborough
		1755	Granville Leveson Gower
		1757	Earl Temple
		1761	William Sharpe ⎫ Jeremiah Dyson ⎭
1661	John Robartes		Commissioners
1673	Earl of Anglesey	1761	Duke of Bedford
1682	Marquess of Halifax	1763	Duke of Marlborough
1685	Earl of Clarendon	1765	Duke of Newcastle-upon-Tyne and Duke of Newcastle-under-Lyne
1687	Lord Arundell of Wardour		
1689	Marquess of Halifax		
1690	William Cheyne or Cheney ⎫ Sir John Knatchbull ⎬ Sir William Pulteney ⎭	1766	Earl of Chatham (in February 1768 the office was put in Commission for a short time. Chatham took the oath again in March 1768)
	Commissioners		
1692	Earl of Pembroke		
1699	Viscount Lonsdale		
1700	Earl of Tankerville	1768	Earl of Bristol
1701	Edward Southwell ⎫ Christopher Musgrave ⎬ James Vernon ⎭	1770	Earl of Halifax
		1771	Earl of Suffolk & Berkshire
		1771	Duke of Grafton
	Commissioners	1775	Earl of Dartmouth
1702	Duke of Buckinghamshire & Normanby	1782	Duke of Grafton
		1783	Earl of Carlisle
1705	Duke of Newcastle-upon-Tyne	1783	Duke of Rutland
1711	John Robinson	1784	William Fraser ⎫ Evan Nepean ⎬ Stephen Cottrell ⎭
1713	Earl of Dartmouth		
1714	Marquess of Wharton		
1715	Edward Southwell ⎫ Christopher Musgrave ⎬ Andrew Charlton ⎭		Commissioners
		1784	Marquess of Stafford
		1794	Duke of Marlborough
	Commissioners	1794	Earl of Chatham
1715	Earl of Sunderland	1798	Earl of Westmorland
1716	Duke of Kingston	1806	Viscount Sidmouth
1719	Duke of Kent	1806	Lord Holland
1720	Duke of Kingston	1807	Earl of Westmorland
1726	Lord Trevor of Bromham	1827	Duke of Devonshire
1730	Earl of Wilmington	1827	Earl of Carlisle
		1828	Edward Law

1829	Earl of Rosslyn	1919	A. Bonar Law
1830	Earl of Durham	1921	Austen Chamberlain
1833	Earl of Ripon	1923	Viscount Cecil
1834	Earl of Carlisle	1924	J. R. Clynes
1834	Earl of Mulgrave	1924	Marquess of Salisbury
1834	Lord Wharncliffe	1929	J. H. Thomas
1835	Lord Duncannon	1930	V. Hartshorn
1840	Earl of Clarendon	1931	T. Johnston
1841	Duke of Buckingham	1931	Earl Peel
1842	Duke of Buccleuch	1931	Viscount Snowden
1846	Earl of Haddington	1932	Stanley Baldwin
1846	Earl of Minto	1934	Anthony Eden
1852	Marquess of Salisbury	1935	Marquess of Londonderry
1853	Duke of Argyll	1935	Viscount Halifax
1855	Earl of Harrowby	1937	Earl de la Warr
1858	Marquess of Clanricarde	1938	Sir J. Anderson
1858	Earl of Hardwicke	1939	Sir S. Hoare
1859	Duke of Argyll	1940	Sir K. Wood
1866	Earl of Malmesbury	1940	C. R. Attlee
1868	Earl of Kimberley	1942	Sir Stafford Cripps
1870	Viscount Halifax	1942	Viscount Cranborne
1874	Earl of Malmesbury	1943	Lord Beaverbrook
1876	Earl of Beaconsfield	1945	A. Greenwood
1878	Duke of Northumberland	1947	Lord Inman
1880	Duke of Argyll	1947	Viscount Addison
1881	Lord Carlingford	1951	R. R. Stokes
1885	Lord Rosebery	1951	Marquess of Salisbury
1885	Earl of Harrowby		(formerly Viscount
1886	W. E. Gladstone		Cranborne)
1886	Earl of Cadogan	1952	H. F. C. Crookshank
1892	W. E. Gladstone	1956	R. A. Butler
1894	Lord Tweedmouth	1959	Viscount Hailsham
1895	Viscount Cross	1960	Edward Heath
1900	Marquess of Salisbury	1963	Selwyn Lloyd
1902	A. J. Balfour	1964	Earl of Longford
1903	Marquess of Salisbury	1965	Sir Frank Soskice
1905	Marquess of Ripon	1966	Earl of Longford
1908	Marquess of Crewe	1968	Lord Shackleton
1911	Marquess of Lincolnshire	1968	Fred Peart
1912	Marquess of Crewe	1968	Lord Shackleton
1915	Earl Curzon	1970	Earl Jellicoe
1916	Earl of Crawford		

PAYMASTERS GENERAL OF THE FORCES, TREASURERS OF THE NAVY AND PAYMASTERS GENERAL

PAYMASTERS GENERAL OF THE FORCES

1660	Sir Stephen Fox	1782	Edmund Burke and Isaac
1679	Nicholas Johnson and Charles		Barré
	Fox	1783	Edmund Burke
1682	Charles Fox	1784	William Wyndham Grenville
1689	Earl of Ranelagh		and Lord Mulgrave
1703	John Howe and C. Fox	1789	Lord Mulgrave and the
1707	J. Brydges		Marquis of Graham
1713	Thomas Moore and	1791	D. Ryder and T. Steele
	E. Nicholas	1800	T. Steele and G. Canning
1714	Robert Walpole	1801	T. Steele and Lord
1715	Earl of Lincoln		Glenbervie
1720	Robert Walpole	1803	T. Steele and
1721	Lord Cornwallis		J. H. Addington
1722	Spencer Compton	1804	G. Rose and Lord Charles
1730	Henry Pelham		Somerset
1743	Sir Thomas Winnington	1806	Earl Temple and Lord John
1746	William Pitt (afterwards Earl		Townshend
	of Chatham)	1807	C. Long and Lord Charles
1755	Earl of Darlington and T. Hay		Somerset
1757	Henry Fox	1813	C. Long and F. J. Robinson
1765	Charles Townshend	1817	Sir C. Long
1766	Lord North and George	1826	W. V. Fitzgerald
	Cooke	1828	J. Calcraft
1767	George Cooke and Thomas	1830	Lord John Russell
	Townshend	1834	Sir E. Knatchbull
1768	Richard Rigby	1835	Sir H. Parnell

TREASURERS OF THE NAVY

1660	Sir George Carteret	1724	P. Byng
1667	Earl of Anglesey	1734	Arthur Onslow
1672	Sir T. Osborne	1742	T. Clutterbuck
1673	Sir Edward Seymour	1742	Sir Charles Wager
1681	Viscount Falkland	1743	Sir John Rushout
1689	Edward Russel	1744	G. Bubb Dodington
1699	Sir T. Littleton	1749	H. B. Legge
1710	Robert Walpole	1754	George Grenville
1711	Charles Caesar	1756	G. Bubb Dodington
1714	John Aislabie	1756	George Grenville
1718	Richard Hampden	1762	Viscount Barrington
1720	Sir G. Byng	1765	Viscount Howe

1770	Sir Gilbert Elliot	1806	R. B. Sheridan
1777	W. Ellis	1807	G. Rose
1782	Isaac Barré	1818	F. J. Robinson
1782	Henry Dundas	1823	W. Huskisson
1783	Charles Townshend	1827	C. Grant
1784	Henry Dundas	1828	W. Fitzgerald
1800	D. Ryder	1830	T. F. Lewis
1801	C. Bragge	1830	C. P. Thompson
1803	G. Tierney	1834	Viscount Lowther
1804	G. Canning	1835	Sir H. Parnell

PAYMASTERS GENERAL

1836	Sir H. Parnell	1912	Lord Strachie
1841	E. J. Stanley	1915	Lord Newton
1841	Sir E. Knatchbull	1916	A. Henderson
1845	W. B. Baring	1916	Sir J. Compton Rickett
1846	T. B. Macaulay	1919	Sir J. Tudor Walters
1848	Earl Granville	1923	Neville Chamberlain
1852	Lord Stanley	1923	Sir W. Joynson-Hicks
1852	Lord Colchester	1923	A. B. Boyd-Carpenter
1853	Lord Stanley	1924	H. Gosling
1855	E. Pleydell Bouverie	1925	Duke of Sutherland
1855	R. Lowe	1928	Earl of Onslow
1858	Earl of Donoughmore	1929	Lord Arnold
1859	Lord Lovaine	1931	Sir J. Tudor Walters
1859	J. Wilson	1931	Lord Rochester
1859	W. F. Cowper	1935	Lord Hutchison
1860	W. Hutt	1938	Earl of Munster
1865	G. J. Goschen	1939	Earl Winterton
1866	W. Monsell	1940	Viscount Cranborne
1866	S. Cave	1941	Lord Hankey
1868	Lord Dufferin & Clandeboye	1942	Sir W. Jowitt
1872	H. C. E. Childers	1942	Lord Cherwell
1873	W. P. Adam	1946	A. Greenwood
1874	S. Cave	1947	H. A. Marquand
1880	D. R. Plunket	1948	Viscount Addison
1880	Lord Wolverton	1949	Lord Macdonald
1885	Earl Beauchamp	1951	Lord Cherwell
1886	Lord Thurlow	1953	Earl of Selkirk
1886	Earl Beauchamp	1956	Sir W. Monckton
1887	Earl Brownlow	1957	R. Maudling
1890	Earl of Jersey	1959	Lord Mills
1891	Lord Windsor	1961	Henry Brooke
1892	C. Seale-Hayne	1962	John Boyd-Carpenter
1895	Earl of Hopetoun	1964	George Wigg
1899	Duke of Marlborough	1968	Lord Shackleton
1902	Sir S. Crossley	1968	Judith Hart
1906	R. K. Causton	1969	Harold Lever
1910	Lord Ashby St. Ledgers	1970	Viscount Eccles

MINISTERS OF PENSIONS AND (FROM 1953 TO 1966) NATIONAL INSURANCE AND (SINCE 1966) MINISTERS OF SOCIAL SECURITY AND (SINCE 1968) SECRETARIES OF STATE FOR SOCIAL SERVICES

1916	G. N. Barnes
1917	J. Hodge
1919	Sir L. Worthington-Evans
1920	J. I. Macpherson
1922	G. C. Tryon
1924	F. O. Roberts
1924	G. C. Tryon
1929	F. O. Roberts
1931	G. C. Tryon
1935	R. S. Hudson
1936	H. Ramsbotham
1939	Sir W. Womersley
1945	W. Paling
1947	J. B. Hynd
1947	G. Buchanan
1948	H. A. Marquand
1951	G. A. Isaacs
1951	D. Heathcoat Amory
1953	O. Peake
1955	J. A. Boyd-Carpenter
1962	Niall Macpherson
1963	Richard Wood
1964	Margaret Herbison
1967	Judith Hart
1968	Richard Crossman
1970	Sir Keith Joseph

POSTMASTERS-GENERAL AND (SINCE 1969) MINISTERS OF POSTS AND TELECOMMUNICATIONS

1823	Earl of Chichester	1903	Lord Stanley
1826	Lord Frederick Montague	1905	S. Buxton
1827	Duke of Manchester	1910	H. L. Samuel
1830	Duke of Richmond	1914	C. E. H. Hobhouse
1834	Marquess of Conyngham	1915	H. L. Samuel
1834	Lord Maryborough	1916	J. A. Pease
1835	Marquess of Conyngham	1916	A. H. Illingworth
1835	Earl of Lichfield	1921	F. G. Kellaway
1841	Lord Lowther	1922	Neville Chamberlain
1846	Earl of St. German's	1923	Sir W. Joynson-Hicks
1846	Marquess of Clanricarde	1923	Sir L. Worthington-Evans
1852	Earl of Hardwicke	1924	V. Hartshorn
1853	Viscount Canning	1924	Sir W. Mitchell-Thomson
1855	Duke of Argyll	1929	H. B. Lees-Smith
1858	Lord Colchester	1931	C. R. Attlee
1859	Earl of Elgin & Kincardine	1931	W. G. A. Ormsby-Gore
1860	Duke of Argyll	1931	Sir K. Wood
1860	Lord Stanley of Alderley	1935	G. C. Tryon
1866	Duke of Montrose	1940	W. S. Morrison
1868	Marquess of Hartington	1943	H. Crookshank
1871	W. Monsell	1945	Earl of Listowel
1873	L. Playfair	1947	W. Paling
1874	Lord John Manners	1950	Ness Edwards
1880	H. Fawcett	1951	Earl de la Warr
1884	G. J. Shaw-Lefevre	1955	Charles Hill
1885	Lord John Manners	1957	Ernest Marples
1886	Lord Wolverton	1959	J. R. Bevins
1886	H. C. Raikes	1964	Anthony Wedgwood Benn
1891	Sir J. Fergusson	1966	Edward Short
1892	A. Morley	1968	Roy Mason
1895	Duke of Norfolk	1968	John Stonehouse
1900	Marquess of Londonderry	1970	Christopher Chataway
1902	Austen Chamberlain		

SECRETARIES AND SECRETARIES OF STATE FOR SCOTLAND

SECRETARIES FOR SCOTLAND

1885	Duke of Richmond & Gordon	1905	Marquess of Linlithgow
		1905	J. Sinclair
1886	G. O. Trevelyan	1912	T. M. Wood
1886	Earl of Dalhousie	1916	H. J. Tennant
1886	A. J. Balfour	1916	R. Munro
1887	Marquess of Lothian	1922	Viscount Novar
1892	Sir G. O. Trevelyan	1924	W. Adamson
1895	Lord Balfour of Burleigh	1924	Sir J. Gilmour
1903	A. Graham Murray		

SECRETARIES OF STATE FOR SCOTLAND

1926	Sir J. Gilmour	1945	J. Westwood
1929	W. Adamson	1947	A. Woodburn
1931	Sir A. Sinclair	1950	H. McNeil
1932	Sir G. Collins	1951	James Stuart
1936	Walter Elliot	1957	John Maclay
1938	D. J. Colville	1962	Michael Noble
1940	E. Brown	1964	William Ross
1941	T. Johnston	1970	Gordon Campbell
1945	Earl of Rosebery		

APPENDIX 29

MINISTERS OF SUPPLY

1939	E. L. Burgin
1940	Herbert Morrison
1940	Sir A. Duncan
1941	Lord Beaverbrook
1942	Sir A. Duncan
1945	J. Wilmot
1947	G. R. Strauss
1951	D. Sandys
1954	Selwyn Lloyd
1955	R. Maudling
1957	Aubrey Jones

PRESIDENTS OF THE BOARD OF TRADE

1786	Lord Hawkesbury	1888	Sir M. E. Hicks-Beach
1804	Duke of Montrose	1892	A. J. Mundella
1806	Lord Auckland	1894	J. Bryce
1807	Earl Bathurst	1895	C. T. Ritchie
1809	Viscount Melville	1900	G. W. Balfour
1812	Earl Bathurst	1905	Marquess of Salisbury
1812	Earl of Clancarty	1905	D. Lloyd George
1818	F. J. Robinson	1908	Winston Churchill
1823	W. Huskisson	1910	S. C. Buxton
1827	C. Grant	1914	J. Burns
1828	W. Vesey Fitzgerald	1914	W. Runciman
1830	J. C. Herries	1916	Sir A. H. Stanley
1830	Lord Auckland	1919	Sir A. C. Geddes
1834	C. E. Poulett Thomson	1920	Sir R. S. Horne
1834	A. Baring	1921	Stanley Baldwin
1835	C. E. Poulett Thomson	1922	Sir P. Lloyd-Greame
1839	H. Labouchere	1924	Sidney Webb
1841	Earl of Ripon (formerly F. J. Robinson)	1924	Sir P. Cunliffe-Lister (formerly Sir P. Lloyd-Greame)
1843	W. E. Gladstone	1929	W. Graham
1845	Earl of Dalhousie	1931	Sir P. Cunliffe-Lister
1846	Earl Clarendon	1931	W. Runciman
1847	H. Labouchere	1937	Oliver Stanley
1852	J. W. Henley	1940	Sir A. R. Duncan
1852	E. Cardwell	1940	O. Lyttelton
1855	Lord Stanley of Alderley	1941	Sir A. R. Duncan
1858	J. W. Henley	1942	J. J. Llewellin
1859	Earl of Donoughmore	1942	Hugh Dalton
1859	T. M. Gibson	1945	O. Lyttelton
1866	Sir S. H. Northcote	1945	Sir Stafford Cripps
1867	Duke of Richmond	1947	Harold Wilson
1868	John Bright	1951	Sir H. Shawcross
1870	C. S. P. Fortescue	1951	P. Thorneycroft
1874	Sir C. B. Adderley	1957	Sir David Eccles
1878	Viscount Sandon	1959	Reginald Maudling
1880	Joseph Chamberlain	1961	F. J. Erroll
1885	Duke of Richmond & Gordon	1963	Edward Heath
		1964	Douglas Jay
1885	E. Stanhope	1967	Anthony Crosland
1886	A. J. Mundella	1969	Roy Mason
1886	Sir F. Stanley	1970	Michael Noble

MINISTERS OF TRANSPORT

1919	Sir E. Geddes
1921	Viscount Peel
1922	Earl of Crawford & Balcarres
1922	W. Ashley
1923	J. Moore-Brabazon
1924	H. Gosling
1924	W. Ashley
1929	H. Morrison
1931	P. J. Pybus
1933	O. Stanley
1934	L. Hore-Belisha
1937	E. L. Burgin
1939	D. E. Wallace
1940	Sir J. Reith
1940	J. Moore-Brabazon
1941	Lord Leathers
1945	A. Barnes
1951	J. S. Maclay
1952	A. T. Lennox-Boyd
1954	J. A. Boyd-Carpenter
1956	H. Watkinson
1959	Ernest Marples
1964	Tom Fraser
1966	Barbara Castle
1968	Richard Marsh
1969	Frederick Mulley
1970	John Peyton

SECRETARY OF STATE FOR WAR

1794   Henry Dundas

SECRETARIES OF STATE FOR WAR AND THE COLONIES

1801	Lord Hobart	1833	E. G. Stanley
1804	Earl Camden	1834	T. Spring-Rice
1805	Viscount Castlereagh	1834	Earl of Aberdeen
1806	W. Windham	1835	C. Grant
1807	Viscount Castlereagh	1839	Marquess of Normanby
1809	Earl of Liverpool	1839	Lord John Russell
1812	Earl Bathurst	1841	Lord Stanley
1827	Viscount Goderich	1845	W. E. Gladstone
1827	W. Huskisson	1846	Earl Grey
1828	Sir G. Murray	1852	Sir J. S. Pakington
1830	Viscount Goderich	1852	Duke of Newcastle

SECRETARIES OF STATE FOR WAR AND (FROM 1964 TO 1967) MINISTERS OF DEFENCE FOR THE ARMY

1854	Duke of Newcastle	1914	H. H. Asquith
1855	Lord Panmure	1914	Earl Kitchener of Khartoum
1858	J. Peel	1916	D. Lloyd George
1859	Sidney Herbert	1916	Earl of Derby
1861	Sir G. C. Lewis	1918	Viscount Milner
1863	Earl de Grey & Ripon	1919	Winston Churchill
1866	Marquess of Hartington	1921	Sir L. Worthington-Evans
1866	J. Peel	1922	Earl of Derby
1867	Sir J. S. Pakington	1924	S. Walsh
1868	E. Cardwell	1924	Sir L. Worthington-Evans
1874	Viscount Cranbrook	1929	T. Shaw
1878	F. A. Stanley	1931	Marquess of Crewe
1880	H. C. E. Childers	1931	Viscount Hailsham
1882	Marquess of Hartington	1935	Viscount Halifax
1885	W. H. Smith	1935	A. Duff Cooper
1886	H. Campbell-Bannerman	1937	L. Hore-Belisha
1886	W. H. Smith	1940	Oliver Stanley
1887	E. Stanhope	1940	Anthony Eden
1892	H. Campbell-Bannerman	1940	H. D. R. Margesson
1895	Marquess of Lansdowne	1942	Sir J. Grigg
1900	St. John Brodrick	1945	J. J. Lawson
1903	H. O. Arnold-Foster	1946	F. J. Bellenger
1905	R. B. Haldane	1947	E. Shinwell
1912	J. E. B. Seely	1950	J. Strachey

1951	Antony Head	1963	J. B. Godber
1956	John Hare	1963	James Ramsden
1958	Christopher Soames	1964	Frederick Mulley
1960	John Profumo	1966	G. W. Reynolds

FIRST COMMISSIONERS OF WORKS, MINISTERS OF WORKS AND (FROM 1962 TO 1970) MINISTERS OF PUBLIC BUILDING AND WORKS

1851	Lord Seymour	1922	Sir J. Baird
1852	Lord Charles Manners	1924	F. W. Jowett
1853	Sir W. Molesworth	1924	Viscount Peel
1855	Sir B. Hall	1928	Marquess of Londonderry
1858	Duke of Rutland (formerly Lord Charles Manners)	1929	G. Lansbury
		1931	Marquess of Londonderry
1859	H. Fitzroy	1931	W. Ormsby-Gore
1860	W. F. Cooper	1936	Earl Stanhope
1866	Duke of Rutland	1937	Sir P. Sassoon
1868	A. H. Layard	1939	H. Ramsbotham
1869	A. S. Ayrton	1940	Earl de la Warr
1873	W. P. Adam	1940	Lord Tryon
1874	Lord Henry Gordon-Lennox	1940	Lord Reith (first Minister)
1876	G. J. Noel	1942	Lord Portal
1880	W. P. Adam	1944	D. Sandys
1881	G. J. Shaw-Lefevre	1945	G. Tomlinson
1885	Earl of Rosebery	1947	C. W. Key
1885	D. R. Plunket	1950	R. R. Stokes
1886	Earl of Morley	1951	George Brown
1886	Earl of Elgin & Kincardine	1951	Sir David Eccles
1886	D. R. Plunket	1954	Nigel Birch
1892	G. J. Shaw-Lefevre	1955	P. Buchan-Hepburn
1894	H. J. Gladstone	1957	Hugh Molson
1895	A. Akers-Douglas	1959	Lord John Hope
1902	Lord Windsor	1962	Geoffrey Rippon
1905	L. Harcourt	1964	Charles Pannell
1910	Earl Beauchamp	1966	Reginald Prentice
1914	Lord Emmott	1967	Robert Mellish
1915	L. Harcourt	1969	John Silkin
1916	Sir A. Mond	1970	Julian Amery
1921	Earl of Crawford & Balcarres		

BIBLIOGRAPHY

POLITICAL BIOGRAPHY: COLLECTED

Abdullah (A.) & T. C. Pakenham, *Dreamers of Empire*, 1930.
Atlay (J. B.), *The Victorian Chancellors*, 2 v., 1906–8.
Biggs-Davison (J.), *Tory lives*, 1952.
Bigham (C. C.), *The chief ministers of England, 920–1720*, 1923.
           The Prime Ministers of Britain, 1721–1921, 1923.
Campbell (Lord), *Lives of the Chancellors*, 7 v., 1846–7.
Cecil (A.), *British Foreign Secretaries, 1807–1916*, 1927.
Courtney (W. L. & J. E.), *Pillars of Empire*, 1918.
Hambro (C. J.), *Newspaper lords in British politics*, 1958.
Hayes (J. F.), *The Nation Builders*, 1968 (Canada).
Heuston (R. F. V.), *Lives of the Lord Chancellors, 1885–1940*, 1964.
Hutchison (B.), *Mr. Prime Minister, 1867–1964*, 1964 (Canadian Prime Ministers).
Maddyn (D. O.), *Chiefs of parties*, 2 v., 1859.
Norwich (Lord), ed., *British Prime Ministers*, 1953.
Park (J. H.), *British Prime Ministers of the nineteenth century*, 1950.
Pike (E. R.), *Britain's Prime Ministers from Walpole to Wilson*, 1968.
Russell of Liverpool (Lord), *The royal conscience* (lives of Lord Chancellors), 1961.
Salter (Lord), *Personality in politics*, 1947.
Taylor (G. R. S.), *Modern English statesmen*, 1920.
Whibley (C.), *Political portraits*, 1917.
Whittle (J.), *Great Prime Ministers*, 1966.
Williams (F.), *A Pattern of Rulers*, 1965.

POLITICAL BIOGRAPHIES (INCLUDING LETTERS AND MEMOIRS)

ABERDEEN (Lord)
    Balfour (Lady F.), *Life*, 2 v., 1923.
ACTON (Lord)
    Himmelfarb (G.), *Lord A.*, 1952.
    Mathew (D.), *A.*, 1946.
ADDISON (Lord), *Politics from within, 1911–18*, 2 v., 1924.
           Four and a half years, 1914–19, 2 v., 1934.
    Minney (R. J.), *Visct. A., Leader of the House of Lords*, 1958.
AGG-GARDNER (Sir J.), *Some parliamentary recollections*, 1927.

ALBERT, PRINCE CONSORT
    Bolitho (H.), *A., Prince Consort*, 1964.
    Eyck (F.), *The Prince Consort*, 1959.
    Fulford (R.), *The Prince Consort*, 1949.
AMERY (L. S.), *My political life*, 3 v., 1953–5.
AMORY (D. Heathcoat)
    Allen (W. G.), *Reluctant politician*, 1958.
ASTOR (Lady)
    Collis (M.), *Nancy Astor*, 1960.
ATHOLL (Duchess of), *Working partnership*, 1958.
ATTLEE (Lord), *As it happened*, 1954.
    Jenkins (R.), *Mr. A.*, 1948.
    Williams (F.), *A Prime Minister remembers*, 1961.
AVON (Lord), *The Eden Memoirs*, 3 v., 1960–5.
    Bardens (D.), *Portrait of a statesman*, 1955.
    Broad (L.), *Sir A. E.: chronicles of a career*, 1955.
    Campbell-Johnson (A.), *Sir A. E.*, 1955.
    Churchill (R. S.), *Rise and fall of A. E.*, 1959.
    Rees-Mogg (W.), *Sir A. E.*, 1956.
AWOLOWO (Obafemi), *Awo* (autobiog.), 1960.
AZIKIWE (Nnamdi)
    Ikeotuonye (V. C.), *Zik of new Africa*, 1962.
BACON (Sir Francis)
    Bevan (B.), *The real F.B.*, 1960.
    Bowen (C. D.), *F.B., the temper of a man*, 1963.
BAGEHOT (Walter)
    Buchan (A.), *The spare chancellor*, 1959.
    St. John-Stevas (N.), *W. B., His life with selections from his political writings*, 1959.
BALDWIN (Lord)
    Baldwin (A. W.), *My father: the true story*, 1955.
    Green (J.), *Mr. B.*, 1933.
    Middlemas (K.), & J. Barnes, *Baldwin: A Biography*, 1969.
    Somervell (D. C.), *Stanley B.*, 1953.
    Steed (W.), *The real S.B.*, 1930.
    Young (G. M.), *B.*, 1952.
BALFOUR (Lord), *Chapters of autobiography*, 1930.
    Alderson (B.), *A. J. B.*, 1903.
    Balfour (Lady F.), *A memoir of Lord B.*, 1924.
    Churchill (Sir W. S.), 'A. J. B.' (in his *Great Contemporaries*, 1938).
    Dugdale (B. E. C.), *A. J. B.*, 2 v., 1936.
    Judd (D.), *B. and the British Empire*, 1968.
    Malcolm (Sir I.), *Lord B.*, 1930.
    Midleton (Earl of), 'Lord B.' (in *The post Victorians*, 1933).
    Raymond (E. T.), *Mr. B.*, 1920.
    Young (K.), *Arthur James Balfour*, 1963.
BEACONSFIELD (Lord)
    Baumann (A. A.), 'B. Disraeli' (in Massingham, *The great Victorians*, 1932).

Blake (R.), *Disraeli*, 1966.
Briggs (A.), 'B. D. and the leap in the dark' (in his *Victorian People*, 1954)
Faber (R.), *Beaconsfield and Bolingbroke*, 1961.
Froude (J. A.), *The Earl of B.*, 1917.
Jerman (B. R.), *The young Disraeli*, 1960.
Maurois (A.), *Disraeli;* trans. Miles, 1949.
Monypenny (W. F.) & G. E. Buckle, *Life*, 2 v., 1929.
O'Connor (T. P.), *Lord B.*, 1905.
Pearson (H.), *Dizzy*, 1952.
Somervell (D. C.), *Disraeli & Gladstone*, 1932.
Taylor (G. R. S.), 'B. D.' (in his *Mod. Eng. Statesmen*, 1920).

BEAVERBROOK (Lord)
    Driberg (T. E. N.), *B.*, 1956.
    Howard (P.), *B., a study of Max the unknown*, 1964.
    Middleton (E.), *B.*, 1934.
    Wood (A.), *The true history of Lord Beaverbrook*, 1965.
    Young (K.), *Churchill and B.*, 1966.

BELLO (Sir Ahmadu), *My life*, 1962.

BENNETT (R. B.)
    Beaverbrook (Lord), *Friends: 60 years of intimate personal relations with R. B. B.*, 1959.
    Watkins (E.), *A biography*, 1963

BENTINCK (Lord G.)
    Beaconsfield (Lord), *Lord G. B.*, 1852.

BEVAN (Aneurin)
    Brome (V.), *A. B.*, 1953.
    Foot (M.), *A. B., 1897–1945*, v.1, 1962.
    Krug (M. M.), *A. B.: cautious rebel*, 1961.

BEVERIDGE (Lord), *Power & influence*, 1953.

BEVIN (Ernest)
    Bullock (A.), *Life and times of E. B.*, v.1, 1960, v.2, 1967.
    Evans (T.), *B.*, 1946.
    Williams (F.), *E. B.*, 1952.

BIRKENHEAD (Lord)
    Birkenhead (2nd Earl of), *Earl of B.*, 2 v., 1933–5.
    F. E., 1959.
    Camp (W.), *The glittering prizes*, 1960.

BLUNDELL (Sir Michael), *So rough a wind*, 1964.

BOLINGBROKE (Lord)
    Faber (R.), *Beaconsfield and Bolingbroke*, 1961.
    Hart (J), *Viscount B.*, 1966.
    Hassall (A.), *Life of B.*, 1889.
    Jackman (S. W.), *Man of Mercury*, 1966.
    Mansfield (H. C.), *Statesmanship and party government: a study of Burke and Bolingbroke*, 1966.
    Sichel (L.), *B. & his times*, 1901.

BONAR LAW (A.)
    Blake (R.), *The unknown Prime Minister*, 1955.
    Hailsham (Lord), 'A. B. L.' (in *The post Victorians*, 1933).

Taylor (H. A.), *The strange case of A. B. L.*, 1932.
BONDFIELD (Margaret), *A life's work*, 1949.
BORDEN (Sir R. L.), *Memoirs*, 2 v., 1938.
BRABAZON (Lord), *The B. story*, 1956.
BRADDOCK (Mrs. E.) & J. Braddock, *The Braddocks*, 1963.
    Toole (M.), *Mrs. Bessie B., M.P.*, 1957.
BRADLAUGH (Charles)
    Arnstein (W. L.), *The Bradlaugh case*, 1966.
    Bonner (H. B.), *C. B.*, 2 v., 1898.
    C. B. Champion of liberty, centenary vol., 1933.
BRENTFORD (Lord)
    Taylor (H. A.), *Jix—Visct. B.*, 1933.
BRIGHT (John), *Diaries*, ed. R. A. J. Walling, 1930.
    Ausubel (H.), *J. B.: Victorian reformer*, 1966.
    Briggs (A.), 'J.B. and the creed of reform' (in his *Victorian People*, 1954).
    Hirst (M. E.), *J. B.*, 1945.
    O'Brien (R. B.), *J. B.*, 1910.
    Trevelyan (G. M.), *Life of J. B.*, 1913.
BROCKWAY (Lord), *Inside the left*, 1947.
                   Outside the right, 1963.
BROUGHAM (Lord)
    Aspinall (A.), *Lord B. & the Whig Party*, 1927.
    Hawes (F.), *Henry B.*, 1957.
    New (C. W.), *The life of Henry Brougham to 1830*, 1961.
BROUGHTON (Lord), *Recolls. of a long life*, 6 v., 1910–11.
BROWN (George)
    'Cassandra', pseud., *G. B.*, 1964.
BURKE (Edmund)
    Copeland (T. W.), *E. B.: Six essays*, 1950.
    Magnus (Sir P.), *E. B.*, 1939.
    Mahoney (T.H.D.), *E.B. and Ireland*, 1960.
    Mansfield (H. C.), *Statesmanship and party government; a study of Burke and Bolingbroke*, 1966.
    Reynolds (E. E.), *E. B.*, 1948.
    Taylor (G. R. S.), 'E. B.' (in his *Mod. Eng. Statesmen*, 1920).
BURNS (John)
    Grubb (A. P.), *Life story of J. B.*, 1908.
    Kent (W.), *J. B., Labour's lost leader*, 1950.
BUTLER (R. A.)
    Boyd (F.), *R. A. B.*, 1956.
    Harris (R.), *Politics without prejudice: a polit. apprec. of R. A. B.*, 1956.
CAMPBELL-BANNERMAN (Sir H.)
    Spender (J. A.), *Life*, 2 v., 1923.
CANNING (George)
    Bagot (J.), *G. C. & his friends*, 2 v., 1909.
    Marriott (Sir J. A. R.), *G. C. and his times*, 1907.
    Petrie (Sir C.), *G. C.*, 1946.
    Rolo (P. J. V.), *G. C.: three biographical studies*, 1965.

CARNARVON (Lord)
    Hardinge (Sir A. H.), *The 4th Earl of C.*, 3 v., 1925.
CARSON (Lord)
    Hyde (H. M.), *C.*, 1956.
    Marjoribanks (E.) & I. Colvin, *Life*, 2 v., 1932–4.
CASTLEREAGH (Lord)
    Hassall (A.), *Viscount C.*, 1908.
    Leigh (I.), *C.*, 1951.
    Marriott (Sir J. A. R.), *C.: political life*, 1936.
CAVE (Lord)
    Mallet (Sir C.), *Lord C.*, 1931.
CECIL (Lord), *A great experiment*, 1941.
CHAMBERLAIN, family of
    Elletson (D. H.), *The Chamberlains*, 1966.
    Petrie (Sir C.), *The C. tradition*, 1938.
CHAMBERLAIN (Sir Austen), *Down the years*, 1935.
                                     Politics from inside, 1936.
    Petrie (Sir C.), *Life & letters of Sir A. C.*, 2 v., 1940.
CHAMBERLAIN (Joseph), *A political memoir, 1880–92*, 1953.
    Churchill (Sir W. S.), 'J. C.' (in his *Great Contemporaries*, 1938).
    Creswicke (L.), *Life*, 4 v., 1904.
    Fraser (P.), *J. C. radicalism and empire, 1868–1914*, 1966.
    Garvin (J. L.) & J. Amery, *Life of J. C.*, 4 v., 1932–51.
    Jeyes (S. H.), *Mr. C., his life and public career*, 1903.
    Ware (Sir F.), 'J. C.' (in *The post Victorians*, 1933).
CHAMBERLAIN (Neville)
    Feiling (K.), *Life*, 1946.
    Keith-Shaw (D.), *Prime Minister N. C.*, 1934.
    McLeod (I.), *N. C.*, 1961.
    Walker-Smith (D. C.), *N. C.: man of peace*, 1939.
CHANDOS (Lord), *Memoirs*, 1962.
CHATHAM (Lord)
    Ashbourne (Lord), *Pitt*, 1898.
    Green (W. D.), *W. Pitt*, 1901.
    Harrison (F.), *C.*, 1925.
    Plumb (J. H.), *C.*, 1965.
    Robertson (Sir C. G.), *C. & the British Empire*, 1948.
    Rose (J. H.), *Life of Pitt*, 1934.
    Rosebery (Lord), *C.: his early life etc.*, 1910.
    Rosebery (Lord), *Pitt*, 1891.
    Sherrard (O. A.), *Lord C.*, 3 v., 1952–8.
    Williams (B.), *Life*, 2 v., 1966.
CHIFLEY (J. B.)
    Crisp (L. F.), *Ben Chifley*, 1960.
CHILSTON (1st Viscount)
    Chilston (3rd Viscount), *Chief whip; the political life of the 1st Viscount Chilston*, 1961.
CHURCHILL (Lord Randolph)
    Churchill (Sir W. S.), *Lord R. C.*, 1951.

James (K. R.), *Lord R. C.*, 1959.
Rosebery (Lord), *Lord R. C.*, 1906.
CHURCHILL (Sir Winston),   *Thoughts & adventures*, 1932.
                    My early life, 1940.
                    A self-portrait, 1954.
    Bardens (D.), *C. in Parliament*, 1967.
    Bibesco (Princess), *Sir W. C.*, 1957.
    Bonham-Carter (Lady V.), *Churchill as I knew him*, 1964.
    Broad (L.), *W. C., 1874–1955*, 1956.
            W. C.: the years of preparation, 1963.
    Churchill (R. S.), *W. C., Youth, 1874–1900*, v. 1., 1966; *Young Statesman*,
       1901–1914, v. 2, 1967.
    Cowles (V.), *W. C.: the era and the man*, 1953.
    Eade (C.), ed., *C.: by his contemporaries*, 1953.
    Eden (G.), *Portrait of C.*, n.d.
    Guedalla (P.), *Mr. C.: a portrait*, 1943.
    James (R. R.), *Churchill: a study in failure, 1900–1939*, 1970.
    Lockhart (J. G.), *W. C.*, 1951.
    Marchant (Sir J.), ed., *W. C.*, 1954.
    Marsh (J.), *The young W. C.*, 1955.
    Martin (H.), *Battle: life story of W. C.*, 1940.
    Moran (Lord), *W. C., The struggle for survival, 1940–65*, 1966.
    Morin (R.), *C.: Portrait of greatness*, 1965.
    Observer, The, *C., by his contemporaries*, 1965.
    Sencourt (R.), *W. C.*, 1941.
    Stewart (H. L.), *Sir W. C. as writer & speaker*, 1954.
    Thompson (R. W.), *The Yankee Marlborough*, 1963.
    Thomson (M.), *Life of W. C.*, 1945.
    Times, The, *The Churchill years: 1874–1965*, 1965.
    Young (K.), *C. and Beaverbrook*, 1966.
CLARENDON (Lord)
    Wormald (B. H. G.), *C.: politics etc., 1640–60*, 1951.
CLYNES (J. R.), *Memoirs*, 2 v., 1937.
COBBETT (William)
    Carlyle (E. I.), *W. C.*, 1904.
    Cole (G. D. H.), *Life*, 1947.
COBDEN (Richard)
    Hammond (J. L.), 'R. C.' (in Massingham, *The great Victorians*, 1932).
    Hobson (J. A.), *R. C.: the international man*, 1918.
    Morley, (J.), *Life*, 2 v., 1881.
COCHRANE (Lord)
    Lloyd (C.), *Lord C.: Seaman-Radical-Liberator*, 1947.
COGHLAN (Sir C.)
    Wallis (J. P. R.), *One man's hand: Sir C. C. & the liberation of Southern
       Rhodesia*, 1950.
COKE (Sir E.)
    Bowen (C. D.), *The lion and the throne*, 1957.
COURTNEY (Lord)
    Gooch (G. P.), *Life of Lord C.*, 1920.

CREWE (Lord)
    Pope-Hennessy (J.), *Lord C., 1858–1945*, 1955.
CRIPPS (Sir Stafford)
    Cooke (C.), *Life of S. C.*, 1957.
    Estorick (E.), *S. C.*, 1949.
    Strauss (P.), *C.—advocate & rebel*, 1943.
CROFT (Lord), *My life of strife*, 1949.
CROKER (J. W.), *Corresp. & diaries*, 3 v., 1885.
    Brightfield (M. F.), *J. W. C.*, 1951.
CROMER (Lord)
    Zetland (Lord), *Lord C.*, 1932.
CROOKS (W.)
    Haw (G.), *W. C.*, 1907.
CURZON (Lord)
    Churchill (Sir W. S.), 'C.' (in his *Great Contemporaries*, 1938).
    Mosley, (L.), C., *The end of an epoch*, 1960.
    Nicolson (H.), *C.: the last phase, 1919–25*, 1934.
    Ronaldshay (Lord), *Life*, 3 v., 1928.
DALTON (Hugh), *Call back yesterday: memoirs, 1887–1931*, 1953.
                The fateful years: memoirs, 1931–45, 1957.
                High tide and after: memoirs, 1945–60, 1962.
DEAKIN (Alfred)
    La Nauze (J. A.), *A. D.*, 2 v., 1965.
DERBY (14th Earl of)
    Jones (W. D.), *Lord D. and Victorian conservatism*, 1956.
DERBY (17th Earl of)
    Churchill (R. S.), *Lord D.*, 1959.
DEVONSHIRE (Duke of)
    Holland (B.), *The 8th Duke of D.*, 2 v., 1913.
    Whibley (C.), 'The 8th Duke of D.' (in his *Political Portraits*, 1917).
DIEFENBAKER (John G.)
    Newman (P. C.), *Renegade in Power*, 1963.
DILKE (Sir C. W.)
    Gwynn (S.) & G. M. Tuckwell, *Life*, 1918.
    Jenkins (R.), *Sir C. D.*, 1965.
DISRAELI, *see* BEACONSFIELD
DODINGTON (George)
    Carswell (J.), 'G. D.' (in his *The Old Cause*, 1954).
DOUGLAS-HOME (Sir Alec)
    Dickie (J.), *The uncommon commoner*, 1964.
    Hughes (E.), *Sir A. D.-H.*, 1964.
    Young (K.), *Sir A. D.-H.*, 1970.
DRIBERG (T.), *Best of both worlds*, 1953.
DUPLESSIS (Maurice)
    Roberts (L.), *The chief*, 1963.
DURHAM (Lord)
    Cooper (L.), *Radical Jack*, 1959.
    New (C. W.), *Life*, 1929.
    Reid (S.), *Life & Letters of Lord D.*, 2 v., 1906.

EDWARD VII (King)
    Lee (Sir S.), *King E. VII*, 2 v., 1925–7.
    Magnus (P.), *King E. VII*, 1964.
    Maurois (A.), *King E. and his times*, 1933.
EDWARD VIII (King)
    Windsor (Duke of), *A King's story*, 1951.
ELIOT (Sir John)
    Hulme (H.), *Life of Sir J. E.*, 1957.
ESHER (Lord), *Journals & letters*, 4 v., 1934–8.
EWART (William)
    Munford (W. A.), *W.E.*, 1960.
FOSTER (Sir George)
    Wallace (W. S.), *Memoirs of Sir G. F.*, 1933.
FOX (Charles James)
    Carswell (J.), 'C. J. F.' (in his *The Old Cause*, 1954).
    Drinkwater (J.), *C. J. F.*, 1928.
    Eyck (E.), *Pitt vs. Fox*, 1950.
    Hobhouse (C.), *F.*, 1947.
    Lander (W. S.), *C. J. F.*, 1907.
    Lascelles (E.), *Life*, 1936.
    Reid (L.), *C. J. F., a man for the people*, 1969.
    Trevelyan (G. O.), *Early hist. of C. J. F.*, 1880.
FRASER (Peter)
    Thorn (J.), *P. F.: New Zealand's war-time P.M.*, 1952.
GAITSKELL (Hugh)
    Rodgers (W. T.), ed., *H. G., 1906–63*, 1964.
GALLACHER (W.), *The rolling of the thunder*, 1947.
              The last memoirs, 1966.
GEORGE V (King)
    Nicolson (*H.*), *King G. V*, 1952.
GEORGE VI (King)
    Wheeler-Bennett (J. W.), *King G. VI*, 1958.
GLADSTONE (Lord)
    Mallet (Sir C.), *Herbert G.: a memoir*, 1932.
GLADSTONE (W. E.)
    Burdett (O.), *W. E. G.*, 1927.
    Eyck (E.), *G.*, 1938.
    Hammond (J. L.) & M. R. D. Foot, *G. & Liberalism*, 1952.
    Hirst (F. W.), *G. as financier and economist*, 1931.
    Hyde (F. E.), *Mr. G. at the Board of Trade*, 1934.
    McCarthy (J.), *Story of G.'s life*, 1898.
    Magnus (P.), *G.*, 1954.
    Morley (J.), *Life of G.*, 3 v., 1903.
    Ponsonby (Lord), 'W. E. G.' (in Massingham, *The great Victorians*, 1932).
    Russell (G. W. E.), *W. E. G.*, 1917.
    Somervell (D. C.), *Disraeli & G.*, 1932.
    Williams, (W. E.), *Rise of G. to the leadership of the Liberal Party*, 1934.
GLYNN (Patrick McMahon)
    O'Collins (G.), *P. M. G.: a founder of Australian federation*, 1965.

GODOLPHIN (1st Earl)
   Lever (Sir T.), *G.*, 1952.
GODWIN (William)
   Fleisher (D.), *W. G.: a study in Liberalism*, 1951.
GORTON (John)
   Trengrove (A.), *John Grey Gorton: an informal biography*, 1970.
GOSCHEN (Lord)
   Colson (P.), *Lord G. & his friends*, n.d.
   Elliot (A. R. D.), *Visct. G.*, 2 v., 1911.
GRAHAM (Sir J.)
   Erickson (A. B.), *The public career of Sir J. G.*, 1952.
   Parker (C. S.), *Life & letters of Sir J. G.*, 2 v., 1907.
   Whibley (C.), 'Sir J. G.' (in his *Political Portraits*, 1917).
GRAHAM (Willie)
   Graham (T. N.), *W. G.*, 1948.
GRANVILLE (Lord)
   Fitzmaurice (Lord), *The 2nd Earl G.*, 2 v., 1905.
GREVILLE (C. C. H.), *The G. Memoirs*, 3 series in 8 v., 1874–1887.
GREY (Earl)
   Trevelyan (G. M.), *Lord G. of the Reform Bill*, 1920.
GREY (Sir George)
   Rutherford (J.), *Sir G.G.*, 1961.
GREY (Visct.) of Fallodon, *Twenty-five years*, 2 v., 1926.
   Politicus, *G. of Fallodon*, 1935.
   Trevelyan (G. M.), *G. of Fallodon*, 1945.
GRIGG (Sir James), *Prejudice & judgment*, 1948.
HALDANE (Lord), *An autobiography*, 1929.
   Leslie (S.), 'Lord H.' (in *The post Victorians*, 1933).
   Maurice (Sir F.), *H.*, 2 v., 1937–9.
   Sommer (D.), *H. of Cloan*, 1960.
HALIFAX (Lord), *Fulness of days*, 1957.
   Campbell-Johnson (A.), *Visct. H.*, 1941.
   Birkenhead (Lord), *H.*, 1965.
HALSBURY (Lord)
   Fox (A. W.), *The Earl of H.*, 1929.
HAMILTON (Lord G. F.), *Parliamentary reminiscences (1868–1906)*, 2 v., 1916–22.
HANSARD (L. G.), *Diary, 1814–41*, 1962.
HARCOURT (Sir W.)
   Gardiner (A. G.), *Life of Sir W. H.*, 2 v., 1923.
HARDIE (Keir)
   Cockburn (J.), *The hungry heart*, 1956.
   Fyfe (H.), *K. H.*, 1935.
   Hughes (E.), *K. H.*, 1956.
   Maxton (J.), 'K. H.' (in *The post Victorians*, 1933).
HARDWICKE (Lord)
   Yorke (P. C.), *Life of Earl of H.*, 3 v., 1913.
HARRIS (Sir Percy), *40 years in and out of Parl.*, 1947.

HEATH (Edward)
 Hutchinson (G.), *E. H.; a personal and political biography*, 1970.
HEMINGFORD (Lord), *Back-bencher & Chairman*, 1946.
HENDERSON (Arthur)
 Hamilton (M. A.), *A. H.*, 1938.
 Jenkins (E. A.), *From foundry to Foreign Office*, 1933.
HERBERT (Sir Alan)
 Independent member, 1950.
 A. P. H.: His life and times, 1970.
HICKS-BEACH (Sir M.)
 Hicks-Beach (Lady V.), *Sir M. H.-B.*, 2 v., 1932.
HILL (Lord), *Both sides of the hill*, 1964.
HILL (Sir Rowland)
 Smyth (E. C.), *Sir R. H.; story of a great reform*, 1907.
HOLMAN (W. A.)
 Evatt (H. V.), *Australian Labour leader; story of W. A. H. & the Labour movement*, 1954.
HORE-BELISHA (Lord), *Private papers*, 1960.
HUGHES (W. M.)
 Whyte (W. F.), *W. M. H., his life and times*, 1957.
HUSKISSON (W.)
 Brady (A.), *W. H. & Liberal reform*, 1928.
 Fay (C. R.), *H. & his age*, 1951.
IKRAMULLAH (Begum Shaista S.), *From purdah to Parliament*, 1963.
ISAACS (George)
 Eastwood (G. G.), *G. I.*, 1952.
JINNAH (M. A.)
 Bolitho (H.), *J.: creator of Pakistan*, 1954.
JOHNSON (Donald), *A cassandra at Westminster*, 1967.
JOHNSTON (Thomas), *Memories*, 1952.
JONES (Thomas), *A diary with letters, 1931–50*, 1954.
JOWETT (Lord)
 Brockway (A. F.), *Socialism over 60 years; life of J. of Bradford*, 1946.
KAUNDA (Kenneth David), *Zambia shall be free: an autobiog.*, 1962.
KILMUIR (Lord), *Political adventure: the memoirs of the Earl of Kilmuir*, 1964.
KING (W. L. Mackenzie)
 Dawson (R. M.), *W. L. M. K.*, v. 1, 1958.
 Ferns (H. S.) & B. Ostry, *The age of M. K.: the rise of a leader*, 1955.
 Hardy (H. R.), *M. K. of Canada*, 1949.
 Hutchison (B.), *M. K.: the incredible Canadian*, 1953.
 Ludwig (E.), *M. K.*, 1944.
 McGregor (F. A.), *The fall and rise of Mackenzie King, 1911–19*, 1962.
 Neatby (H. B.), *W. L. M. K., 1924–32*, 1963.
KIRKWOOD (David), *My life of revolt*, 1935.
KOTELAWALA (Sir J.), *An Asian Prime Minister's story*, 1956.
LABOUCHERE (H.)
 Pearson (H.), '*Labby*', 1936.
 Thorold (A. L.), *Life*, 1913.

LANG (J. T.), *I remember*, 1956.
LANSBURY (George), *My Life*, 1928.
    Lansbury (E.), *G. L.*, n.d.
    Postgate (R.), *Life of G. L.*, 1951.
LANSDOWNE (Lord)
    Newton (Lord), *Lord L.*, 1929.
LAURIER (Sir Wilfrid)
    Schull (J.), *Laurier, the first Canadian*, 1965.
LEE (Jennie), *This great journey*, 1963.
LIVERPOOL (Lord)
    Brock (W. R.), *Lord L. and liberal toryism*, 1967.
    Petrie (Sir C.), *Lord L. & his times*, 1954.
LLEWELLIN (Lord)
    Thomas (G.), *Llewellin*, 1961.
LLOYD GEORGE (D.)
    Beaverbrook (Lord), *The decline and fall of Lloyd George*, 1963.
    George (W.), *My brother and I*, 1958.
    Jones (T.), *L. G.*, 1951.
    Lloyd George (R.), *L. G.*, 1960.
    Ludwig (E.), '*L. G.*' (in his *Leaders of Europe*, 1934).
    Mallet (Sir C.), *Mr. L. G.*, 1930.
    Owen (F.), *Tempestuous journey; life of L. G.*, 1954.
    Spender (H.), *The Prime Minister*, 1920.
    Sylvester (A. J.), *The real L. G.*, 1947.
LONG (Walter)
    Petrie (Sir C.), *W. L. & his times*, 1936.
LONGFORD (Lord), *Born to believe*, 1953.
                  Five lives, 1964.
LOWE (Robert)
    Briggs (A.), 'R. L. and the fear of democracy' (in his *Victorian People*, 1954.)
LYNDHURST (Lord)
    Martin (Sir T.), *Life of Lord L.*, 1884.
MACDONALD (J. Ramsay), *Wanderings & excursions*, 1932.
    Elton (Lord), *Life (1866–1919)*, 1939.
    Tiltman (H. H.), *J. R. M.*, 1929.
MACDONALD (Sir John A.)
    Creighton (D.), *J. A. M.*, 2 v., 1952.
McGOVERN (J.), *Neither fear nor favour* (autobiog.), 1960.
McKENNA (Reginald)
    McKenna (S.), *R. M. 1863–1943*, 1948.
MACMILLAN (Harold)
    Winds of change, 1914–39, 1966.
    The blast of war, 1939–1945, 1967.
    Tides of Fortune, 1945–1955, 1969.
    Hughes (E.), *M., portrait of a politician*, 1962.
MACMILLAN (Lord), *A man of law's tale*, 1952.
MALVERN (Lord)
    Gann (L. N.) & M. Gelfand, *Huggins of Rhodesia*, 1964.
MANN (Jean), *Woman in Parliament*, 1962.

MANNERS (Lord J.)
 Whibley (C.), *Life*, 2 v., 1925.
MARSH (Sir Edward)
 Hassall (C.), *E. M.*, 1959.
MAUGHAM (Lord), *At the end of the day*, 1954.
MAXTON (James)
 McAllister (G.), *J. M.*, 1953.
 McNair (J.), *J. M.: the beloved rebel*, 1955.
MEIGHEN (Arthur)
 Graham (R.), *A. M.*, 3 v., 1960–5.
MELBOURNE (Lord)
 Cecil (Lord D.), *Melbourne*, 1965.
 Dunckley (H.), *Lord M.*, 1890.
 Torrens (W. T. McC.), *Memoirs of Lord M.*, 1878.
MELCHETT (Lord)
 Bolitho (H.), *Alfred Mond, 1st Lord M.*, 1933.
MELVILLE (Lord)
 Matheson (C.), *Life of H. Dundas, 1st Visct. M.*, 1933.
MENON (Krishna)
 George (T. J. S.), *K. M.*, 1964.
MENZIES (Sir R.), *The measure of the years*, 1970.
MERSEY (Lord), *Journal & memories*, 1952.
MORLEY (Lord), *Recollections*, 2 v., 1917.
MORRIS (Sir Rhys Hopkin)
 Evans (T. J.), *Sir R. H. M.*, 1958.
MORRIS-JONES (Sir H.), *Doctor in the whips' room*, 1955.
MORRISON (Lord), *Herbert M., an autobiography*, 1960.
NATHAN (Lord)
 Hyde (H. M.), *Strong for service,*1968.
NEHRU (J.), *An autobiography*, 1949.
 Brecher (M.), *N.*, 1959.
 Crocker (W. S.), *N.; a contemporary's estimate*, 1966.
 Karaka (D. F.), *N.*, 1953.
 Moraes (F.), *J. N.*, 1956.
 Nanda (B. R.), *The Nehrus, Molital and Jawaharlal*, 1962.
 Seton (M.), *Panditji*, 1967.
 Sheean (V.), *N., the years of power*, 1960.
 Tyson (G.), *Nehru: the years of power*, 1966.
NEWTON (Lord), *Retrospection*, 1941.
NICOLSON (H.), *Diaries and Letters, 1930–1939*, 1966.
       1939–1945, 1967.
       1945–1962, 1968.
NKRUMAH (Kwame), *Ghana*, 1957.
 Phillips (J.), *K. N. and the future of Africa*, 1960.
 Timothy (B.), *K. N.: his rise to power*, 1955.
NORTHCLIFFE (Lord)
 Pound (R.) & G. Harmsworth, *N.*, 1959.
NORWICH (Lord), *Old men forget*, 1953.

O'CONNELL (D.)
    MacDonagh (M.), *Life*, 1903.
O'CONNOR (T. P.), *Memoirs of an old parliamentarian*, 2 v., 1929.
ONSLOW (Lord), *Sixty-three years* (autobiog.), 1944.
    Vulliamy (C. E.), *The O. family, 1528–1874*, 1953.
O'SULLIVAN (Edward William)
    Mansfield (B.), *Australian democrat: the career of E. W. O'S.*, 1965.
OWEN (Robert)
    Cole (G. D. H.), *Life of R. O.*, 1965.
    Podmore (F.), *Life of R. O.*, 1906.
OXFORD & ASQUITH (Earl of), *50 years of Parliament*, 2 v., 1926.
                                     Memories & reflections, 2 v., 1928.

    Alderson (J. P.), *Mr. Asquith*, 1905.
    Asquith (H.), *Moments of memory*, 1938.
    Churchill (Sir W. S.), 'H. H. Asquith' (in his *Great Contemporaries*, 1938).
    Jenkins (R.), *Asquith*, 1964.
    Mitchell (R.), 'Lord O. and A.' (in *The post Victorians*, 1937).
    Spender (J. A.) & C. Asquith, *Life of A.*, 2 v., 1932.
PALMERSTON (2nd Viscount)
    Connell (B.), *Portrait of a whig peer*, 1957.
PALMERSTON (3rd Viscount)
    Ashley (E.), *Life*, 2 v., 1876.
    Bell (H. C. F.), *Lord P.*, 2 v., 1936.
    Bulwer (Sir H. L.), *Life*, 3 v., 1870.
    Guedalla (P.), *P.*, 1950.
    Marx (K.), *Story of the life of Lord P.*, 1899.
    Nicolson (H.), 'Lord P.' (in Massingham, *The great Victorians*, 1932).
    Pemberton (W. B.), *Lord P.*, 1954.
    Southgate (D.), *The most English minister—policies and politics of Palmerston*, 1966.
PARMOOR (Lord), *A retrospect*, 1936.
PARNELL (C. S.)
    Churchill (Sir W. S.), 'C. S. P.' (in his *Great Contemporaries*, 1938).
    Ervine (St. J.), *P.*, 1928.
    Lyons (F. S. L.), *Fall of P.*, 1960.
    O'Brien (C. C.), *P. & his party*, 1957.
    O'Brien (R. B.), *Life of P.*, 1910.
    O'Shea (K.) (Mrs. Parnell), *C. S. P.*, 2 v., 1914.
PEARCE (Sir G. F.), *Carpenter to Cabinet*, 1951.
PEEL (Sir Robert), *Memoirs*, 2 v., 1857.
    Gash (N.), *Mr. Secretary P.: life of Sir R.P. to 1830*, 1961.
    Laski (H. J.), 'R. P.' (in Massingham, *The great Victorians*, 1932).
    Lever (Sir T.), *Life, etc., of Sir R. P.*, 1942.
    Parker (C. S.), *Sir R. P. from his private papers*, 3 v., 1891–9.
    Ramsay (A. A. W.), *Life*, 1928.
    Thursfield (J. R.), *P.*, 1928.
PERCY (Lord) of Newcastle, *Some memories*, 1958.
PETHICK-LAWRENCE (Lord), *Fate has been kind*, 1942.
    Brittain (V.), *P.-L.: a portrait*, 1963.

PITT, family of
  Lever (Sir T.), *The House of Pitt*, 1947.
  Taylor (G. R. S.), 'The Pitt family' (in his *Mod. Eng. Statesmen*, 1920).
PITT (William), the younger
  Ashbourne (Lord), *P.: chapters of his life etc.*, 1898.
  Eyck (E.), *Pitt vs. Fox*, 1950.
  Rose (J. H.), *Life*, 2 v., 1934.
  Rosebery (Lord), *P.*, 1891.
  Wilson (P. W.), *W. P., the younger*, n.d.
PITT (William), Earl of Chatham, *see* CHATHAM
PRAED (W. M.)
  Hudson (D.), *A poet in Parl.*, 1939.
PRITT (D. N.), *The autobiography of D. N. P.*, 3 v., 1965–7.
PYM (John)
  Brett (S. R.), *J. P.*, 1940.
  Wade (C. E.), *J. P.*, 1912.
RAHMAN (Tunku Abdul)
  Miller (H.), *Prince and premier*, 1959.
RATHBONE (Eleanor)
  Stocks (M. D.), *E. R.*, 1954.
REAKES (G. L.), *Man of the Mersey*, 1956.
REDMOND (John)
  Redmond-Howard (L. G.), *J. R., the man & the demand*, 1911.
REEVE (Henry)
  Laughton (J. K.), *Memoirs of the life etc. of H. R.*, 2 v., 1898.
REEVES (William Pember)
  Sinclair (K.), *W. P. R.; New Zealand Fabian*, 1965.
RIDDELL (Lord), *Intimate diary of the Peace Conference & after*, 1933.
                More pages from my diary, 1908–14, 1934.
ROBSON (Lord)
  Keeton (G. W.), *A Liberal Attorney-General*, 1946.
ROEBUCK (John Arthur)
  Briggs (A.), 'J. A. R. and the Crimean War' (in his *Victorian People*, 1954).
  Leader (R. E.), *Life etc. of J. A. R.*, 1897.
ROSEBERY (Lord)
  Churchill (Sir W. S.), 'The Earl of R.' (in his *Great Contemporaries*, 1938).
  Coates (T. F. G.), *Lord R.*, 2 v., 1900.
  Crewe (Lord), *Lord R.*, 2 v., 1931.
  James (R. R.), *R.*, 1963.
  Raymond (E. T.), *The Man of Promise: Lord R.*, 1923.
  Thruston (E. H.), *Statesman and sportsman*, 1928.
RUSSELL (Lord John)
  Walpole (S.), *Life of Lord J. R.*, 2 v., 1889.
ST. LAURENT (Louis)
  Thomson (D. C.), *Louis St. Laurent: Canadian*, 1967.
SALISBURY (Lord)
  Cecil (Lady G.), *Life of S.*, 4 v., 1921–32.
  Kennedy (A. L.), *S., 1830–1903*, 1953.

Massingham (H.), 'Lord S.' (in his *The great Victorians*, 1932).
Traill (H. D.), *The Marquess of S.*, 1892.
SAMUEL (Lord), *Memoirs*, 1945.
Bowle (J.), *Viscount S.*, 1957.
SASTRI (V. S. S.)
Rao (P.), *The Right Honourable V. S. S. S.: a political biography*, 1963.
SHAFTESBURY (Lord)
Blackburn (B.), *Noble lord*, 1949.
Bready (J. W.), *Lord S. & social-industrial progress*, 1926.
Hammond (J. L. & B.), *Lord S.*, 1939.
Hodder (E.), *Life etc. of Lord S.*, 3 v., 1886.
SHAKESPEARE (Sir G.), *Let candles be brought in*, 1949.
SHINWELL (E.), *Conflict without malice: an autobiog.*, 1955.
SIDMOUTH (Viscount)
Ziegler (P.), *Addington*, 1965.
SIMON (Lord), *Retrospect*, 1952.
Roberts (B.), *Sir J. S.*, 1938.
SMYTH (Sir J.), *The only enemy* (autobiog.), 1959.
SNELL (Lord), *Men, movements and myself*, 1936.
SNOWDEN (Lord), *An autobiography*, 2 v., 1934.
Andreades (A. M.), *S.: the man and his financial policy*, 1930.
Bechofer-Roberts (C. E.), *S.: an impartial portrait*, 1929.
Churchill (Sir W. S.), 'P. S.' (in his *Great Contemporaries*, 1938).
Cross (C.), *Philip Snowden*, 1966.
STRAFFORD (Lord)
Burghclere (Lady), *S.*, 2 v., 1931.
SUNDERLAND (Earl of)
Kenyon (J. P.), *Robert Spencer, Earl of S.*, 1641-1702, 1958.
SUTHERLAND (Duke of), *Looking back*, 1957.
SWINTON (Lord), *I Remember*, 1949.
TEMPLEWOOD (Lord), *The unbroken thread*, 1949.
Nine troubled years, 1954.

THOMAS (J. H.)
Blaxland (W. G.), *J. H. T.: a life for unity*, 1964.
THORNE (Will), *My life's battles*, 1925.
TILLET (Ben), *Memoirs and reflections*, 1931.
TOMLINSON (George)
Blackburn (F.), *G. T.*, 1950.
ULLSWATER (Lord), *A Speaker's commentaries*, 2 v., 1925.
VANSITTART (Lord), *The mist procession*, 1958.
VICTORIA (Queen), *Letters*, 9 v., 1907-32.
Hardie (F.), *The political influence of Queen V.*, 1935.
WALPOLE (Horace)
Gwynn (S.), *Life*, 1932.
Ketton-Cremer (R. W.), *H. W.: a biog.*, 1946.
Taylor (G. R. S.), 'The Walpoles' (in his *Mod. Eng. Statesmen*, 1920).
WALPOLE (Sir Robert)
Morley (J.), *W.*, 1893.
Plumb (J. H.), *Sir R. W.*, 2 v., 1956-60.

WAVERLEY (Lord)
    Wheeler-Bennett (J. W.), *John Anderson, Viscount W.*, 1962.
WEBB (Sidney & Beatrice)
    Webb (B.), *Our partnership*, 1948.
    Diaries, 1912-32, 2 v., 1952-6.
WEDGWOOD (Lord), *Memoirs of a fighting life*, 1940.
    Wedgwood (C. V.), *The last of the Radicals: J. W.*, 1951.
WELENSKY (Sir Roy), *Welensky's 4000 days*, 1964.
    Allighan (G.), *The Welensky story*, 1962.
    Taylor (D.), *The Rhodesian*, 1955.
WELLINGTON (Duke of), *Despatches, corresp. & memoranda (1819–32)*, 8 v.,
    1867–80.
    Aldington (R.), *W.*, 1946.
    Guedalla (P.), *The Duke*, 1946.
    Petrie (Sir C.), *W., a reassessment*, 1956.
WEST (Sir A.), *Private Diaries*, 1922.
WHARTON (Thomas)
    Carswell (J.), 'T. W.' (in his *The Old Cause*, 1954).
WHITBREAD (Samuel)
    Fulford (R.), *S. W., 1764-1815: a study in opposition*, 1967.
WILBERFORCE (W.)
    Warner (O.), *W. W. and his times*, 1962.
    Coupland (R.), *W. W.*, 1945.
WILKES (John)
    Bleackley (H.), *Life*, 1917.
    Chevenix-Trench (C.), *Portrait of a patriot*, 1962.
    Postgate (R.), *That devil Wilkes*, 1956.
    Quennell (P.), 'J. W.' (in his *Four portraits*, 1945).
    Rude (G.), *W. and liberty*, 1961.
    Sherrard (O. A.), *Life of J. W.*, 1930.
WILLIAM IV (King)
    Allen (W. G.) *King W. IV*, 1960.
WILLIAMS (Sir Herbert), *Politics—grave & gay*, 1949.
WILSON (Harold)
    Foot (P.), *The Politics of H. W.*, 1968.
    Kay (E.), *Pragmatic Premier*, 1967.
    Noel (G. E.), *H. W. and the new Britain: the making of a modern Prime
        Minister*, 1964.
    Smith (D. G.), *H. W.: a critical biography*, 1964.
    Smith (L. G. D.), *H. W.: the authentic portrait*, 1964.
WINTERTON (Earl), *Pre-War*, 1932.
                        Orders of the Day, 1953.
                        50 tumultuous years, 1955.
    Broderick (A. H.), *Near to greatness: life of 6th Earl W.*, 1965.
WOLVERHAMPTON (Lord)
    Fowler (E. H.), *Life*, 1912.
WOOLTON (Lord), *Memoirs*, 1959.
ZETLAND (Marquess of), *'Essayez': memoirs*, 1957.

PARLIAMENT: UNITED KINGDOM AND GENERAL

Abraham (L. A.) & S. C. Hawtrey, *A parliamentary dictionary*, 3rd ed., 1970.
Abshagen (K. H.), *King, Lords & gentlemen*, 1939.
Allen (A.), *The story of our Parliament*, 1963 (juvenile).
Allyn (E.), *Lords v. Commons (1830–1930)*, 1931.
Bailey (S. D.), *The Palace of Westminster*, 1949.
British parl. democracy, 1962.
Barker (A.) & Michael Rush, *The member of Parliament and his information*, 1970.
Barker (Sir E.), *Reflections on govt.*, 1942.
Essays on govt., 1951.
Barnes (R. J.), *Central government in Britain*, 2nd ed., 1969.
Bassett (R.), *The essentials of parliamentary democracy*, 2nd ed., 1964.
Bateman (C. D.), *Your parliament*, 1968.
Battley (J.), *A visit to the Houses of Parl.*, 1949.
Benstead (C. R.), *Mother of Parliaments*, 1948.
Brayley (E. W.) & J. Britton, *The hist. of the ancient Palace & later Houses of Parl.*, 1836.
Brierly (J. L.), ed., *Law & govt. in principle & practice*, 1948.
Brown (E. T.), *The sovereign people*, 1954 (Australia).
Brown (W. J.), *Everybody's guide to Parliament*, 1946.
Bryce (Lord), *Mod. democracies*, 2 v., 1962.
Butler (D. E.), *British political facts 1900–1968*, 3rd ed., 1969.
Campion (Lord) & others, *British govt. since 1918*, 1950.
Parliament: a survey, 1952.
Carter (G. M.) & J. H. Herz, *Government and politics in the 20th century*, 1961.
Clarke (J. J.), *Outlines of central govt.*, 1961.
Cocks (T. G. B.), *The Parl. at Westminster*, 1952 (juvenile).
Collins (D.), *Aspects of British politics, 1904–19*, 1965.
Commonwealth Year Book (annual Europa publication).
Cooper (I. M.), *Meeting places of Parl. in the Palace of Westminster*, 1938.
Corry (J. A.), *Democratic govt. & politics*, 1952 (Canadian Govt. Series).
Craig (R.), *Hist. of oratory in Parl., (1213–1913)*, 1913.
Craigton (Lord), *Insight into government*, 1965.
Crick (B.) & S. Jenkinson, *Parliament and the people*, 1966.
Curtis (M. R.), *Central govt.*, 1958.
Dickinson (G. L.), *Development of Parl. during the 19th cent.*, 1895.
Dodd (A. H.), *Growth of responsible government from James I to Victoria*, 1965.
Dod's *Parliamentary companion* (Annual).
Dunnico (Sir H.), *The mother of Parls.*, 1951.
Eaves (J.), *Emergency powers and the parl. watchdog*, 1958.
Eden (G.), *The Parliament book*, 1953.
Edwards (W.), *Crown, Parl. & people*, 1937.
Fell (Sir B. H.), *The Houses of Parliament*, 1961.
Finer (H.), *Theory etc. of mod. govt.*, 1954.
Foot (M.), *Parliament in danger*, 1959.
Gilmour (I.), *The Body Politic*, 1969.
Gordon (S.), *Our Parliament*, 6th ed., 1964.

Government and Opposition (quarterly, 1965–).
Gwyn (W. B.), *Democracy and the cost of politics*, 1962.
Hailsham (Lord), *The purpose of Parl.*, 1948.
Halsbury (Lord), *Laws of England*, 3rd ed., v. 28 (pp. 295–479), 1959.
Hansard Society, *Papers on Parliament*, 1949.
Hansard Society, *Parliamentary Affairs* (quarterly).
Hansard Society, *Parliamentary government in England*, 1949.
Hanson (A. H.), *Parliament and public ownership*, 1961.
Harrison (W.), *The govt. of Britain*, 1966.
Haskins (G. L.), *Growth of Eng. representative govt.*, 1948.
Hastings (M.), *Parliament House*, 1950.
Hawgood (J. A.), *The citizen & govt.*, 1947.
Hearn (W. E.), *The govt. of England*, 1886.
Hemingford (Lord), *What Parl. is & does*, 1948.
Herbert (Sir,A.), *The point of Parl.*, 1946.
Hollis (C.) *Can Parliament survive?*, 1949.
             Has Parliament a future?, 1960.
Ilbert (Sir C.) & Sir C. Carr, *Parliament*, 1956.
Illingworth (F.), *The British Parl.*, 1948.
Inter-Parliamentary Union, *Parliaments: a comparative study*, 2nd ed., 1966.
James (Sir A.), *How Parl. works*, 1944.
Jenkins (R.), *Mr. Balfour's poodle*, 1954. (Struggle between House of Lords
    and Asquith's Govt.)
Jennings (G. H.), *Anecdotal hist. of Parl.*, 1899.
Jennings (Sir W. I.), *Parliament*, 2nd ed., 1957.
Joad (C. E. M.), *Principles of parl. democracy*, 1949.
Johnson (N.), *Our government and its functions*, 1966.
          Parliament and administration, 1966.
Johnston (J.), *Westminster voices: studies in parl. speech*, 1928.
Journal of Commonwealth Political Studies (quarterly, 1962–).
Journal of Parliamentary Information (Indian—twice yearly).
Keeton (G. W.), *The passing of Parl.*, 1954.
Keith (A. B.), *The King, the const., the Empire & foreign affairs*, 1938.
Kilpin (R.), *Conflict betw. public & private rights in Parl.*, 1943.
King (H. M.), *Parl. & freedom*, 1962.
Laski (H. J.), *Parl. govt. in England*, 1938.
LeMay (G. H. L.), *British govt. 1914–53: sel. docs.*, 1955.
Low (S.), *The governance of England*, 1914.
Lowell (A. L.), *The govt. of England*, 2 v., 1912 (Amer.).
Lucy (Sir H. W.), *Lords & Commoners*, 1921.
Macdonagh (M.), *Book of Parl.*, 1897.
   Parl.: its romance, comedy & pathos, 1905.
   The pageant of Parl., 2 v., 1921.
McIlwain (C. H.), *The High Court of Parl.*, 1934.
Mackenzie (K. R.), *The English Parl.*, 1962.
   Parliament (juvenile), 1959.
Mackenzie (W. J. M.), & J. W. Grove, *Central administration in Britain*,
    1957.
Mackintosh (Sir A.), *Echoes of Big Ben*, 1945.

Marriott (Sir J. A. R.), *English polit. institutions*, 1939.
  How we are governed, 1934.
  Mechanism of the mod. State, 2 v., 1927.
Menhennet (D.) & J. Palmer, *Parliament in perspective*, 1967.
Merrett (J.), *How Parl. works* (juvenile), 1960.
Morrison (H.) & W. S. Abbott, *Parl.: what it is & how it works*, 1935.
Morrison (Lord), *Govt. & Parliament*, 3rd ed., 1964.
Muir (R.), *How Britain is governed*, 1940.
Munro (W. B.), *The governments of Europe*, 1947.
Nicholson (Max), *The System: the misgovernment of modern Britain*, 1967.
Nicolson (H.), *The independent member* (Hansard Soc. Pamph. No. 2), 1946.
Nicolson (N.), *People and Parl.*, 1958.
Ogg (F. A.), *English govt. & politics*, 1947 (Amer.).
Ogg (F. A.) & H. Zink, *Mod. foreign govts* (Part I), 1949 (Amer.).
Parliament. The eloquence of the British Senate; sel. speeches, 1625–1802, 1807.
Parliamentarian, The (quarterly).
Plaskitt (H.) & P. Jordan, *Govt. of Britain, Commonw. countries & dependencies*,
  9th ed., 1968.
Political Studies: Journal of the Political Studies Assoc. of the U. K. (quarterly).
Pollard (A. F.), *The evol. of Parl.*, 2nd ed., 1964.
Pope-Hennessy (J.) & H. Wild, *The Houses of Parl.*, 1953.
Prentice (D.), *Your book of Parliament*, 1967 (juvenile).
Punnett (R. N.), *British Government and politics*, 1968.
Rayner (R. M.), *British democracy*, 1946.
Rose (R.) ed., *Studies in British politics*, 2nd ed., 1969.
Saunders (H. St. G.), *Westminster Hall*, 1951.
Schwann (D.), *The spirit of Parliament*, 1908.
Smellie (K. B.), *100 years of English govt.*, 1950.
Somervell (D. C.), *British politics since 1900*, 1950.
Spearman (D.), *Democracy in England*, 1957.
Spender (J. A.), *The public life*, 2 v., 1925.
Stacey (F.), *The government of modern Britain*, 1968.
Statesman's year-book (annual)
Stewart (M.), *The British approach to politics*, 5th ed., 1966.
          Modern forms of govt., 1959.
Strong (C. F.), *Parl. & people, 1837 to present day*, 1942.
Sykes (A.) & I. Sproat, *The wit of Westminster*, 1967.
Thatcher (M.), *What's wrong with politics*, 1968.
Thomas (M. W.), *Citizens all: British democracy at work*, 1947.
  The English heritage: our law & central govt., 1944.
Todd (A.), *Parl. govt. in England*, 2 v., 1892.
Tunstall (J.), *The Westminster lobby correspondents*, 1970.
Vacher's *Parliamentary Companion* (quarterly).
Wheare (K. C.), *Legislatures*, 1963.
White (L. W.) & W. D. Hussey, *Govt. in Gt. Britain, the Empire & the Common-
  wealth*, 1965.
Wilson (C.) ed., *Parliaments, Peoples and Mass Media*, 1970.
Wilson (N.), *The British system of government*, 1963.
Wiseman (H. V.), *Parliament and the executive*, 1966.

Wright (A.) & P. Smith, *Parl. past & present*, 2 v., 1902.
Wymer (N. G.), *Behind the scenes in Parliament*, 1966.
Young (G. M.), *The govt. of Britain*, 1941.
Young (R.), *The British Parliament*, 1962.

CABINET

Aspinall (A.), *The Cabinet Council 1783–1835*, 1952.
Blauvelt (M. T.), *Development of Cabinet govt. in England*, 1902 (Amer.).
Daalder (H.), *Cabinet reform in Britain, 1914–63*, 1963.
Ehrman (J.), *Cabinet govt. & war, 1890–1940*, 1958.
Gordon Walker (P.), *The Cabinet*, 1970.
Jenks (E.), *Parliamentary England: evol. of Cabinet system*, 1903.
Jennings (Sir W. I.), *Cabinet govt.*, 3rd ed., 1959.
Keith (A. B.), *The British Cabinet system*, 1952.
Loewenstein (K.), *British Cabinet Government*, 1967.
Mackintosh (J. P.), *The British cabinet*, 1968.
Mosley (R. K.), *The story of the Cabinet office*, 1969.
Torrens (W. M.), *History of Cabinets*, 2 v., 1894.
Wangteh Yu, *The English Cabinet system*, 1939.
Waverley (Visct.), *The machinery of govt.*, 1946.
Wheare (K. C.), *The machinery of govt.*, 1945.
Wiseman (H. V.), *The cabinet in the Commonwealth*, 1958.

CHANNEL ISLANDS

Hooke (W. D.), *The C. I.*, 1953 (Chap. 3).
Le Quesne (C.), *Const. history of Jersey*, 1856.
Sheridan (L. A.), 'The C. I.' (in Keeton & Lloyd, *The U.K.: develop. of its laws etc.*, 1955).

CONSTITUTIONAL LAW AND HISTORY

Adams, (G. B.) *Const. hist. of England*, revised by R. L. Schuyler, 1963.
          The origin of the English constitution, 1912.
   & H. M. Stephens, eds., *Sel. docs. of English const. hist.*, 1921.
Alexander (L.), *Const. law in a nutshell*, 1955.
Amery (L. S.), *Thoughts on the constitution*, 1953.
Amos (Sir M.), *The English const.*, 1930.
Andrews (W. G.), *Constitutions and constitutionalism*, 1963.
Anson (Sir W. R.), *Law & custom of the constitution*, 2 v. in 3, 1922–35.
Aylmer (G. E.), *The struggle for the constitution, 1603–1689*, 2nd ed., 1968.
Bagehot (W.), *The English constitution;* with an introduction by R. H. S. Crossman, 1964.
Baldwin (J. F.), *The King's Council*, 1913.
Benemy (F. W. G.), *The elected monarch; the development of the power of the Prime Minister*, 1965.
Berkeley (H.), *The power of the Prime Minister*, 1968.
Birch (A. H.), *Representative and responsible government*, 1964.
Brasher (N. H.), *Studies in British government*, 1965.
Broad (L.), *The path to power: rise to premiership from Rosebery to Wilson*, 1965.
Brooke (J.), *The Prime Ministers' papers 1801–1902*, 1968.
Carter (B. E.), *The office of Prime Minister*, 1956.

2G*

Chrimes (S. B.), *English const. hist.*, 3rd ed., 1965.
Costin (W. C.) & J. S. Watson, *Law & working of the const.*, 2 v., 2nd ed., 1961–4.
Courtney (L.), *The working const. of the U.K.*, 1901.
Cracknell (D. G.), *Constitutional law and the English legal system*, 1963.
Dicey (A. V.), *Law of the const.*, 10th ed., with an introduction by E. C. S. Wade, 1961.
    & R. S. Rait, *Thoughts on the Union betw. Eng. & Scotland*, 1920.
Elton (G. R.), *The Tudor constitution*, 1960.
Emden (C. S.), *The people & the const.*, 1956.
    Principles of British const. law, 1925.
    Sel. speeches on the const., 2 v., 1939.
Fitzroy (Sir A.), *Hist. of the Privy Council*, 1928.
Gardiner (S. R.), *Const. docs. of the Puritan revol., 1625–60*, 1951.
Gneist (H. R. von), *Hist. of the Eng. const.*, 2 v., 1886.
Great Britain. Parliament, *Report of Comm. on Ministers' powers*, 1932 (Cmd. 4060).
Greaves (H. R. G.), *The British const.*, 1955.
Hallam (H.), *Const. hist. of Eng.: Henry VII to Geo. II*, 3 v., 1930–6.
Hallgarten (A.) & J. Cooke, *Constitutional law and the English legal system*, 2nd ed., 1968.
Harvey (J.) & L. Bather, *The British constitution*, 2nd ed., 1968.
Haynes (C.) ed., *The essentials of the British constitution*, 1965.
Heuston (R. F. V.) ed., *Essays in const. law*, 2nd ed., 1964.
Holt (J. C.), *Magna Carta*, 1965.
Howard (A.) & R. West, *The making of the Prime Minister*, 1965.
Iwi (E. F.), *Laws & flaws*, 1956.
Jennings (Sir W. I.), *The British const.*, 5th ed., 1966.
    The law & the const., 1959.
    The Queen's Govt., 1954.
Jolliffe (J. E. A.), *The const. hist. of medieval Eng. from the English Settlement to 1485*, 4th ed., 1962.
Keeton (G. W.) & D. Lloyd, *The U.K.: develop. of its laws & const.*, 2 v., 1955.
Keir (Sir D. L.), *Const. hist. of mod. Britain since 1485*, 9th ed., 1969.
    & F. H. Lawson, *Cases in const. law*, 1954.
Keith (A. B.), *Const. law:* 7th ed. of Ridges, *Const. law of Eng.*, 1946.
    Const. of England from Victoria to Geo. VI, 2 v., 1940.
Kemp (B.), *King and Commons, 1660–1832*, 1957.
King (A. S.), *The British Prime Minister: a reader*, 1969.
Laski (H. J.), *Reflections on the const: the House of Commons etc.*, 1951.
Lawson (F. H.) & D. J. Bentley, *Constitutional and administrative law*, 1961.
Lodge (E. C.) & G. A. Thornton, eds., *Eng. const. docs., 1307–1485*, 1935.
Lovell (C. R.), *English constitutional and legal history*, 1962 (Amer.).
Low (S. J. M.), *The governance of Eng.*, 1914.
Lyon (B. D.), *Constitutional and legal history of medieval England*, 1960 (Amer.).
McKechnie (W. S.), *Magna Carta*, 1905.
Maitland (F. W.), *Const. hist. of England*, 1961.
Marcham (F. G.), *Constitutional history of modern England*, 1960.
Marshall (G.) & G. C. Moodie, *Some problems of the const.*, 1961.

May (Sir T. Erskine), *Const. hist. of Eng. since the accession of George III*, 3 v., 1912.
Medley (D. J.), *Orig. illusts. of Eng. const. hist.*, 1926.
Mitchell (J. D. B.), *Constitutional law*, 1964.
Petit-Dutaillis (C.) & G. Lefebvre, *Studies etc.* suppl. to Stubbs' *Const. hist.*, 1930.
Phillips (O. Hood), *Constitutional and administrative law*, 3rd ed., 1962. (Previously published as *Constitutional laws of Great Britain and the Commonwealth.*)
　Leading cases in const. law, 2nd ed., 1957.
Pickthorn (Sir K.), *Some hist. principles of the const.*, 1925.
Prothero (Sir G. W.), ed., *Sel. statutes of Eliz. I & James I*, 1949.
Public Law (quarterly).
Richardson (H. G.) & G. O. Sayles, *The governance of medieval England from the Conquest to Magna Carta*, 1963.
Ridges (E. W.), *Const. law*, 8th ed. by G. A. Forrest, 1950.
Robertson (Sir C. G.), ed., *Sel. statutes, cases etc.*, 1949.
Schuyler (R. L.) & C. C. Weston, *British constitutional history since 1832*, 1957 (Amer.).
Sharma (I. D.), *Modern constitutions at work*, 1962.
Stannard (H.), *The two constitutions: Brit. & American*, 1949.
Strong (C. F.), *Modern political constitutions*, 1958.
Stubbs (W.), *Const. hist. of Eng.*, 3 v., 1891–8.
　ed., *Sel. charters & other illusts. of Eng. const. hist.*, 1921.
Tanner (J. R.), *Const. docs. of reign of James I*, 1952.
　Eng. const. conflicts of the 17th cent., 1960.
　Tudor const. docs., 1940.
Taswell-Langmead (T. P.), *Eng. const. hist.*, 11th ed. by T. F. T. Plucknett, 1960.
Thompson (F.), *Magna Carta*, 1950.
Tout (T. F.), *Chapters in the admin. hist. of medieval Eng.*, 6 v., 1920–33.
Twysden (Sir R.), *Certaine considerations upon the govt. of Eng.*, 1849 (Camden Soc.)
Wade (E. C. S.) & G. G. Phillips, *Const. law*, 7th ed., 1965.
Webb (S.) & B. Webb, *A const. for the socialist commonwealth of Gt. Brit.*, 1920.
Wheare (K. C.), *Government by committee*, 1955.
White (A. B.), *The making of the Eng. const.*, 1908.
Wilkinson (B.), *Studies in the const. hist. of the 13th & 14th cents.*, 1952.
　Const. hist. of England, 1216–1399, 3 v., 1948–52.
　Constitutional history of England in the 15th Century (1399–1485), 1964.
Williams (E. N.), *The 18th century constitution, 1688–1815*, 1961.
Willson (F. M. G.) & D. N. Chester, ed., *The organization of British Central Government, 1914–1964*, 2nd ed., 1968.
Wilson (G. P.), *Cases and materials on constitutional and administrative law*, 1966.
Yardley (D. C. M.), *Introd. to British const. law*, 2nd ed., 1964.

CROWN

Altrincham (Lord), *Is the monarchy perfect?*, 1958.
Bailey (A.), *The succession to the English throne*, 1879.
Barker (Sir E.), *Brit. constit. monarchy*, 1951.

Benemy (F. W. G.), *The Queen reigns: she does not rule*, 1963.
Black (P.), *The mystique of modern monarchy*, 1953.
Edwards (W.), *Crown, people & parl.*, *1760–1935*, 1937.
Farrer (J. A.), *The monarchy in politics*, 1917.
Figgis (J. N.), *Divine right of kings*, 1914.
Hardie (F.), *The political influence of the British monarchy*, *1868–1952*, 1970.
Hardinge (N.), *The path of kings*, 1952.
Laird (D.), *How the Queen reigns*, 1959.
Lapsley (G. T.), *Crown, community & Parl. in the later Middle Ages*, 1951.
Lockyer (R.), *The monarchy*, 1965.
Macdonagh (M.), *The English King*, 1929.
Martin (K.), *The crown and the establishment*, 1962.
Michie (A. A.), *The Crown & the people*, 1952.
Morrah (D.), *The work of the Queen*, 1958.
Namier (Sir L.), *Monarchy & the party system*, 1952.
Nicolson (Sir H.), *Monarchy*, 1962.
Petrie (Sir C.), *Monarchy in the 20th cent.*, 1952.
    The modern British monarchy, 1961.
Windsor (Duke of), *The Crown & the people*, *1902–53*, 1953.

DEBATES, PARLIAMENTARY PAPERS, ETC.

Almon (J.), *Parl. Register*, 1742–81.
Aspinall (A.), 'Reporting and publishing of the House of Commons debates, 1771–1834' (in *Essays presented to Sir Lewis Namier*, ed. R. Pares & A. J. P. Taylor), 1956.
Bond (M.), *The records of Parliament*, 1964.
Bowyer (R.), *Parl. diary*, *1606–07*, 1931 (Amer.).
Cavendish (Sir H.), *Debates*, *1768–74*, 2 v., 1841–2.
Chandler (R.), *Debates (H. of C.)* *1660–1742*, 14 v., 1742–4.
Cobbett (W.), *Parl. hist. to 1803*, 36 vols.
Debrett (J.), *Debates of both houses*, *1743–74 & 1780–1803*, 63 vols.
Dering (Sir E.), *Parl. diary*, *1670–73*, 1940 (Amer.).
D'Ewes (Sir S.), *Journals*, ed. Notestein, 1923.
Ford (P.) & G. Ford, *A breviate of parl. papers*, *1917–39*, 1951.
    A breviate of parl. papers, *1900–16*, 1957.
    Guide to parl. papers, 1956.
    Sel. list of parl. papers, *1833–99*, 1953.
Grey (A.), *Debates of the H. of C.*, *1667–94*, 10 v., 1763.
Hansard (J.) & L. Hansard, *Hansard's cat. of parl. papers*, *1696–1834*, 1953.
Hoover (B. B.), *S. Johnson's parl. reporting*, 1953.
House of Commons Library, *Bibliog. of parliamentary debates of Gt. Britain*, 1956.
Journal of the H. of Commons, 1547 to date.
Journal of the H. of Lords, 1509 to date.
King (Horace M.), *Before Hansard*, 1968.
King-Hall (Lord), & A. Dewar, *Hist. in Hansard*, *1803–1900*, 1952.
Law (W.), *Our Hansard*, 1950.
Milward (J.), *Diary*, 1938.
Old Parl. History, 24 v., 1751–62 (Commonwealth & Restoration).

Parliamentary Debates, 1803 to date.
Rolls of Parliament, 1278–1503, 6 v., 1767–77. Index, 1832.
Thomas (P. D. G.), *Sources for debates of H. of Commons, 1768-74*, 1960.
Timberland (E.), *Proceedings in the H. of Lords, 1660–1742*, 8 v., 1742–3.
Trewin (J. C.) & E. M. King, *Printer to the House: story of Hansard*, 1952.

DELEGATED LEGISLATION

Allen (Sir C. K.), *Law & orders*, 1956.
  Administrative jurisdiction, 1956.
Carr (Sir C.), *Delegated legislation*, 1921.
  Concerning administrative law, 1941.
Committee on Ministers' Powers, *Report*, 1932 (Cmd. 4060).
Hewart (Lord), *The new despotism*, 1929.
Hewitt (D. J.), *Control of delegated legislation*, 1953.
House of Commons, Report of the Select Committee on delegated legislation, 1953 (H. C. 310).
Keeton (G. W.), *The passing of Parl.*, 1952.
Kersell (J. E.), *Parl. supervision of delegated legislative power*, 1960.
Molson (H.), *Delegated legislation*, 1947 (Hansard Soc.).
Select Committee on Statutory Instruments. Reports.
Sieghart (M. A.), *Government by decree*, 1950 (Britain & France).
Willis (J.), *The parl. powers of English govt. depts.*, 1933 (Amer.).

FINANCE

Adarkar (B. P.), *Principles etc. of federal finance*, 1933.
Beer (S. H.), *Treasury control*, 1956.
Brittain (Sir H.), *British budgetary system*, 1959.
Buck (A. E.), *The Budget in governments of today*, 1934 (Amer.).
Chubb (B.), *The control of public expenditure*, 1952.
Dalton (H.), *Principles of public finance*, 1954.
Durell (A. J. V.), *Principles & practice of the system of control over parl. grants*, 1917.
Einzig (P.), *Control of the purse*, 1959.
Hawtrey (R. G.), *The Exchequer & the control of expenditure*, 1921.
Hicks (J. R.), *Problem of budgetary reform*, 1948.
Hicks (U. K.), *The finance of Brit. govt., 1920–36*, 1938.
  Public finance, 1955.
Higgs (H.), *Financial reform*, 1924.
Hills (J. W.) & Sir E. A. Fellowes, *The finance of govt.*, 1932.
House of Commons Select Committee on Estimates, Treasury control of expenditure, 1958.
Ilersic (A. R.), *Govt. finance & fiscal policy in post-war Brit.*, 1955.
Kennet (Lord), *The system of national finance*, 1936.
Lutz (H. L.), *Public finance*, 1936.
Mallet (Sir B.) & C. O. George, *British budgets*, 3 v., 1913–33.
Normanton (E.), *The accountability and audit of governments: a comparative study*, 1966.
Pigou (A. C.), *A study in public finance*, 1951.
Prest (A. R.), *Public finance in theory and practice*, 1960.

Reid (G.), *The politics of financial control: the role of the House of Commons*, 1966.
Shirras (G. F.), *Federal finance*, 1944.
Singh (B.), *Federal finance & under-developed economy*, 1952.
Tew (B.), *Wealth & income: econ. & financial systems of Australia & Gt. Brit.*, 1955.

HISTORY OF PARLIAMENT

Aiken (W. A.) & B. D. Henning, *Conflict in Stuart England*, 1960.
Aspinall (A.) & others, *Parliament through seven centuries: Reading and its M.P.s*, 1962.
Bisset (A.), *Short hist. of the Eng. Parl.*, 1883.
Cecil (A.), *Q. Victoria & her Prime Ministers*, 1953.
Chrimes (S. B.), *Introd. to the admin. hist. of medieval Eng.*, 1952.
Clayden (P. W.), *Eng. under the Coalition, 1885–92*, 1892.
Dodd (A. H.), *The growth of responsible govt. from James I to Victoria*, 1956.
Elton (G. R.), *The Tudor revol. in govt.*, 1953.
Foord (A. S.), *His Majesty's Opposition, 1714–1830*, 1964.
Gneist (H. R. von), *The Eng. Parl. in its transformations through 1,000 years*, 1886.
    Hist. of the Eng. Parl., 800–1887, 1889.
Jane (L. C.), *The coming of Parl. (1350–1660)*, 1905.
Kemp (B.), *King & Commons, 1660–1832*, 1957.
Lehmberg (Stanford E.), *The Reformation Parliament, 1529–1536*, 1970.
McElwee (W.), *England's precedence*, 1956.
Mackenzie (K. R.), *The Eng. Parl.*, 1962.
May (T.), *Hist. of the Parl. of Eng. which began Nov. 3, 1640*, 1854.
Moir (T. L.), *The Addled Parl.*, 1958.
Namier (Sir L. B.) & J. Brooke, *The House of Commons, 1754–90*, 3 v., 1964 (the History of Parliament).
Neale (J. E.), *Eliz. I & her Parliaments*, 2 v., 1953–7.
Oleson (T. J.), *The Witenagemot in the reign of Edward the Confessor*, 1955.
Pares (R.), *King George III and the politicians*, 1953.
Parliament, *Hist. of Parl.: Biographies of Members, 1439–1509*, 1936.
    Register, 1439–1509, 1938. (H.M.S.O.)
Pickthorn (Sir K.), *Early Tudor govt.: Hy. VII*, 1949.
    Early Tudor govt.: Hy. VIII, 1951.
Powell (J. E.), *Great parl. occasions*, 1960.
Richardson (H. G.) & G. O. Sayles, *Parliaments and Great Councils in medieval England*, 1961.
Roberts (C.), *The growth of responsible government in Stuart England*, 1966.
Skottowe (C.), *Short history of Parliament*, 1892.
Smellie (K. B.), *A 100 years of Eng. govt.*, 1950.
Smith (G. B.), *Hist. of the Eng. Parl.*, 2 v., 1894.
Smith (L. B.), *Tudor prelates & politics*, 1953 (Amer.).
Thomas (N. P.), *Hist. of Brit. politics from 1900*, 1956.
Thompson (F.), *A short hist. of Parl.*, 1953 (Amer.).
Verney (Sir R.), *The Long Parl.*, 1845 (Camden Soc.).
Winstanley (D. A.), *Lord Chatham & the Whig opposition*, 1912.
Wright (A.) & P. Smith, *Parliament past & present*, 1902.

HOUSE OF COMMONS

Baker (A.), *The House is sitting*, 1958.
Belloc (H.), *The House of Commons and monarchy*, 1920.
Boardman (H.), *The glory of Parl.*, 1960.
Bodkin (M. McD.), *Grattan's Parliament*, 1912.
Bossom (Lord), *Our House*, 1965.
Braithwaite (W. J.), *Lloyd George's ambulance wagon*, 1957.
Briers (P. M.), *The Speaker* (Hansard Soc. Pamph. No. 3), 1946.
Brown (W. J.), *Everybody's guide to Parl.*, 1946.
Brunton (D.) & D. H. Pennington, *Members of the Long Parl.*, 1954.
Cawthorne (G.), *Mr. Speaker, Sir*, 1952.
Coombes (D. L.), *The Member of Parliament and the administration; the case of the Select Committee on Nationalised Industries*, 1966.
Dasent (A. I.), *The Speakers of the H. of Commons*, 1911.
Denison (J. E.), *Diary (1857–72)*, 1900.
Edwards (J. G.), *The Commons in medieval English Parls.*, 1958.
Escott (T. H. S.), *Gentlemen of the H. of Commons*, 2 v., 1902.
Farquharson (R.), *The H. of Commons from within*, 1912.
Finer (S. E.) & others, *Backbench opinion in the House of Commons, 1955–59*, 1961.
Forster (J.), *Arrest of the 5 members by Charles I*, 1860.
Glass (H. A.), *The Barbone Parl.*, 1899.
Graham (H. J. C.), *Mother of Parliaments*, 1911.
Gray (H. L.), *Influence of the Commons on early legislation*, 1932 (Amer.).
Griffith-Boscawen (Sir A.), *14 years in Parl. (1892–1906)*, 1907.
Hanson (A. H.) & Crick (B.), *The Commons in transition*, 1970.
Herbert (Sir A.), *The Ayes have it: story of the Marriage Bill*, 1937.
House of Commons, *Reports of Sel. Comm. on Accommodation etc.*, 1953–4.
   Report of the Select Committee on the office of Speaker, 1852–3.
   Report from the Select Committee on the Palace of Westminster, 1964–5.
House of Commons Library, *The Mace in the House of Commons*, 1957.
   Official dress worn in the House of Commons, 1960.
   Ceremonial in the House of Commons, 1961.
Howarth (P.), *Questions in the House*, 1956.
James (R. R.), *An introduction to the House of Commons*, 1961.
Jeans (W.), *Parl. reminiscences*, 1912.
Johnson (D. M.), *A doctor in Parl.*, 1958.
Judd (G. P.), *Members of Parl., 1734–1832*, 1955 (Amer.).
Lambert (J. D.), *The H. of C. in debate* (Hansard Soc. Pamph. No. 8), 1950.
Laundy (P. A. C.), *The office of Speaker*, 1964.
Lindsay (M.), *The H. of Commons*, 1947. ('Brit. in Pictures'.)
Lucy (Sir H. W.), *The Balfourian Parl.*, 1906.
   Diary of the Home Rule Parl., 1892–95, 1896.
   Diary of the Salisbury Parl., 1892.
   Diary of two Parls.: Disraeli Parl., 1874–80; Gladstone Parl., 1880–85, 2 v., 1885.
   Diary of the Unionist Parl., 1895–1900, 1901.
   Memories of 8 Parls., 1908.

Men & manner in Parl., 1919.

Peeps at Parl., 1903.

Lummis (E.), *The Speaker's Chair*, 1900.

Macdonagh (M.), *Reporter's gallery*, 1920.

The Speaker of the House, 1914.

Manning (J. A.), *Lives of Speakers of the H. of C.*, 1850.

Marsden (P.), *Officers of the Commons, 1363–1966*, 1966.

Masterman (J. H. B.), *The H. of Commons*, 1908.

Members of Parliament. (*Eng., 1213–1874, Scotland, 1357–1707, Ireland, 1559–1800*), H.M.S.O., 1874–91.

Mitchell (W. M.), *The rise of the revolutionary party in the English H. of Commons, 1603–29*, 1957 (Amer.).

Mowbray (Sir J.), *70 years at Westminster*, 1900.

Neale (Sir J. E.), *The Elizabethan H. of Commons*, 1963.

Nicolson (H.), *The Independent M.P.* (Hansard Soc. Pamph. No. 2), 1946.

Notestein (W.), *The winning of the initiative by the H. of C.*, 1924.

O'Connor (T. P.), *Gladstone's H. of C.*, 1885.

Owen (J. D.), *The rise of the Pelhams*, 1957.

Palgrave (R. F. D.), *The H. of C.*, 1869.

Pasquet (D.), *Origins of the H. of Commons* (*to 1341*), trans., 1964.

Porritt (E.) & A. G. Porritt, *Unreformed H. of C.* (*to 1832*), 2 v., 1963 (American reprint).

Richards (P. G.), *Honourable members: a study of the British backbencher*, 2nd ed., 1964.

Roskell (J. S.), *The Commons in the Parl. of 1422*, 1954.

The Commons and their Speakers in English Parliaments, 1376–1523, 1965.

Temple (Sir R.), *The House of Commons*, 1899.

Thomas (J. A.), *The H. of C., 1832–1901*, 1939.

The H. of Commons, 1906–11, 1958.

Times House of Commons, 1966.

Townsend (W. C.), *Memoirs of the H. of Commons*, 2 v., 1844.

White (W.), *Inner life of the H. of C.*, 2 v., 1898.

Whitty (E. M.), *St. Stephen's in the fifties*, 1906.

Williams (Sir H.), *A question in Parl.* (Hansard Soc. Pamph. No. 5), 1946.

Williams (O. C.), *Clerical organiz. of the H. of C., 1661–1850*, 1954.

Willson (D. H.), *The privy councillors in the H. of C., 1604–29*, 1940 (Amer.).

Witcombe (D. T.), *Charles II and the Cavalier House of Commons, 1663–74*, 1966.

HOUSE OF LORDS AND SECOND CHAMBERS

Bailey (S. D.), ed., *The future of the H. of L.*, 1954 (Hansard Soc.).

Benn (A. W.), *The Privy Council as a second chamber*, 1957.

Bromhead (P. A.), *The H. of L. and contemporary politics*, 1958.

Fergusson (Sir G.), *The 16 peers of Scotland*, 1960.

H.M.S.O., *House of Lords Reform*, Cmnd. 3799, 1968.

Jenkins (R.), *Mr. Balfour's poodle*, 1954.

Jones (Harry), *Liberalism and the House of Lords*, 1912.

Lees-Smith (H. B.), *Second chambers in theory & practice*, 1923.

Macpherson (W. C.), *The baronage and the senate: the House of Lords*, 1893.
McKechnie (W. S.), *The reform of the House of Lords*, 1909.
Marriott (Sir J. A. R.), *Second chambers*, 1927.
Merrivale (Lord), *H. of L., record & prospects*, 1935.
Morgan (J. H.), *H. of L. & the constitution*, 1910.
Muir (R.), *Peers and bureaucrats*, 1910.
Pike (L. O.), *Const. hist. of the H. of L.*, 1905.
Pine (L. G.), *Story of the peerage*, 1956.
Powell (E.), *The House of Lords in the Middle Ages*, 1968.
Roberts (G. B.), *The functions of an Eng. second chamber*, 1926.
Round (J. H.), 'Origin of the H. of L.' (in his *Peerage & Pedigree*, vol. 1), 1910.
Spalding (T. A.), *The H. of L.*, 1894.
Stead (W. T.), *Peers or people?*, 1907.
Temperley (H. W. V.), *Senates & upper chambers*, 1910.
Turberville (A. S.), *The H. of L. in the age of reform, 1784–1837*, 1958.
Weston (C. C.), *English constitutional theory and the House of Lords, 1556–1832*, 1965.
Wilkinson (K.), *The personal story of the upper House*, 1905.
Wontner (A.), *The Lords: their hist. & power.*, 1910.

IRISH AND SCOTTISH PARLIAMENTS

Calvert (H.), *Constitutional law in Northern Ireland: A study in regional government*, 1968.
Hunt (W.), *The Irish Parl., 1775*, 1907.
Keeton (G. W.) & D. Lloyd, *The U.K.: develop. of its laws & const.*, 1955.
Mansergh (N.) *The govt. of N. Ireland*, 1936.
Rait (Sir R. S.), *The Scottish Parl. before the Union*, 1901.
   Parliaments of Scotland, 1924.
Shearman (H.), *How N. Ireland is governed*, 1951.
Sigerson (G.), *The last independent Parliament of Ireland*, 1918.
Smith (G. B.), *Hist. of the Eng. Parl.*, 1894: Book 10, Scotland; Book 12, Ireland.

PARLIAMENTARY PROCEDURE

Blackmore (E. G.), *Speakers' decisions: Peel, Denison & Brand*, 4 v., 1887–1900.
Bourke (R.), *Decisions of C. Shaw Lefevre, Speaker, 1839–57*, 1857.
Bromhead (P. A.), *Private members' bills in the Brit. Parl.*, 1956.
Campion (Lord), *Introd. to procedure of the H. of Commons*, 3rd ed., 1958.
Chester (D. N.) & N. Bowring, *Questions in Parliament*, 1961.
Denison (J. E.), *Notes from my Journal when Speaker*, 1900.
Elsynge (H.), *The ancient method etc. of holding Parls.*: ed. Tyrwhitt, 1768.
Fell (Sir B.), *Parl. proc. as a link of Empire*, 1937.
Hakewill (W.), *The manner how statutes are enacted in Parl.*, 1641.
Hanson (A. H.) & H. V. Wiseman, *Parliament at work: a casebook of parliamentary procedure*, 1962.
Hatsell (J.), *Precedents*, 4 v., 1818.
H.M.S.O. *Select Committees of the House of Commons* (Cmnd. 4507), 1970.
House of Commons, *Decisions from the Chair*, 1936.
   Manual of procedure in the public business, 1959.
   Report from the Select Committee on Members' Interests (Declaration), 1969.

Report from the Select Committee on Parliamentary Privilege, 1967.
Reports from the Sel. Comm. on Procedure, as published.
Standing Orders, current edition.
House of Lords, *Standing Orders relating to the public business,* 1965 (as amended).
   Companion to the Standing Orders of the H. of L. on public business, 1955.
Hughes (C.), *The British statute book,* 1957.
Kilmuir (Lord), *The law of parl. privilege,* 1959.
May (Sir T. Erskine), *The law, privileges, proceedings & usage of Parl.,* 17th ed.
   1964.
Palgrave (Sir R. F. D.), *The chairman's handbook,* 1933.
Redlich (J.), *Proc. of the H. of Commons,* 3 v., 1908.
Russell (Sir A.), *Legislative drafting & forms,* 1938.
Table, The (the annual journal of the Soc. of Clerks-at-the-Table).
Taylor (E.), *The H. of Commons at work,* 7th ed., 1967.
Tregear (A. A.), *H. of Commons: rep. on procedure,* 1953. (Publ. by Australian
   Parl., Canberra.)
Walkland (S. A.), *The legislative process in Great Britain,* 1968.

POLITICAL PARTIES AND PRESSURE GROUPS

Attlee (Lord), *The Labour party in perspective,* 1949.
Bailey (S. D.), *The Brit. party system,* 1952 (Hansard Soc.).
Bassett (R.), *1931: political crisis,* 1958.
Bealey (F.) & H. Pelling, *Labour and politics, 1900–06,* 1958.
Beer (S. H.), *Modern British politics: a study of parties and pressure groups,* 2nd
   ed., 1969.
Belloc (H.) & G. K. Chesterton, *The party system,* 1911.
Beloff (M.), *The party system,* 1958.
Birch (N.), *The Conservative party,* 1949.
Blondel (J.), *Voters, parties and leaders,* 1966.
Bonham-Carter (V.), *In a Liberal tradition,* 1960.
Bow Group, *The Conservative opportunity,* 1965.
Brand (C. F.), *The British Labour Party: a short history,* 1965 (Amer.).
Bullock (A. L. C.) & M. Shock, eds., *The Liberal tradition from Fox to Keynes,*
   1956.
Bulmer-Thomas (I.), *The party system in Gt. Brit.,* 1953.
   The growth of the British party system, 2 v., 1965.
Butler (Sir G. G.), *The Tory tradition,* 1957.
Cecil (Lord H.), *Conservatism,* n.d.
Churchill (R.), *The fight for the Tory Party leadership,* 1964.
Cole (G. D. H.), *British working-class politics, 1832–1914,* 1950.
   Hist. of the Labour party from 1914, 1948.
Crosland (C. A. R.), *The Conservative enemy: a programme of radical reform for
   the 1960s,* 1962.
Cruikshank (R. J.), *The Liberal party,* 1948.
Dowse (R. E.), *Left in the centre: the Independent Labour Party, 1893–1940,*
   1966.
Duverger (M.), *Political parties,* 2nd ed., 1964.
Eckstein (H.), *Pressure group politics,* 1960.
Elliot (W.), *Toryism and the 20th century,* 1927.

Feiling (K. G.), *Hist. of the Tory party, 1640–1714*, 1924.
  The second Tory party, 1714–1832, 1951.
Finer (S. E.), *Anonymous empire*, 2nd ed., 1966.
Fulford (R.), *The Liberal case*, 1959.
Grimond (J. O.), *Liberal future*, 1959.
  The Liberal challenge, 1963.
Hall (W. G.), *The Labour party*, 1949.
Harris (W.), *Hist. of the Radical party in Parl.*, 1885.
Hoffman (J. D.), *The Conservative Party in opposition, 1945–51*, 1964.
Hogg (Q.), *The Conservative case*, 1959.
Hollis (C.), *The rise and fall of the ex-socialist government*, 1947.
Hunt (N. C.), *Two early political associations*, 1961.
Hunter (L.), *Road to Brighton Pier* (Labour Party), 1959.
Jackson (R. J.), *Rebels and whips*, 1968.
Jenkins (R.), *The Labour case*, 1959.
Jennings (Sir W. I.), *Party politics*, 3 v., 1960–2.
Jones (J. R.), *The first Whigs*, 1961.
Kebbel (T. E.), *Hist. of Toryism*, 1886.
Kent (C. B. R.), *Early hist. of the Tories, 1660–1702*, 1908.
Kirk (R.), *The conservative mind*, 1954.
Lyman (R. W.), *The first Labour govt., 1924*, 1957.
Lyons (F. S. L.), *The Irish Parl. party, 1890–1910*, 1951.
McCallum (R. B.), *The Liberal Party from Earl Grey to Asquith*, 1963.
Maccoby (S)., *Eng. Radicalism, 1762–1914*, 6v., 1935–61.
  ed., *The English radical tradition, 1763–1914*, 1966.
McDowell (R. B.), *British conservatism 1832–1914*, 1959.
McElwee (W.), *England's precedence*, 1956.
Macfarlane (L. J.), *The British Communist Party: its origin and development until 1929*, 1966.
McHenry (D. E.), *The Labour party in transition, 1931–38*, 1938.
McKenzie (R. T.), *Brit. polit. parties*, 2nd ed., 1963.
Magee (B.), *The new radicalism*, 1962.
Mathiot (A.), *The British political system*, 1958.
Michels (R.), *Political parties*, 1960.
Middlemas (R. K.), *The Clydesiders: a left-wing struggle for parliamentary power*, 1965.
Miliband (R.), *Parliamentary socialism*, 1961.
Morton (A. L.) & G. Tate, *The British Labour movement, 1770–1920*, 1956.
Namier (Sir L. B.), *The structure of politics at the accession of George III*, 1957.
  'Monarchy and the party system' (in his *Crossroads of power*, 1962).
Neumann (S.), ed., *Modern political parties*, 1956 (Amer.).
O'Brien (C. C.), *Parnell & his party, 1880–90*, 1957.
O'Donnell (F. H.), *Hist. of the Irish Parl. party*, 2 v., 1910.
Ostrogorski (M.), *Democracy and the organisation of political parties*, 2 v., 1902.
Pelling (H.), *Origins of the Labour party, 1880–1900*, 1965.
  America & the British left, 1956.
  The British Communist party, 1958.
  The challenge of socialism, 1954.
  A short history of the Labour Party, 2nd ed., 1965.

Poirier (P. P.), *The advent of the Labour party*, 1958.
Potter (A.), *Organized groups in British national politics*, 1961.
Rasmussen (J. S.), *The Liberal Party: a study of retrenchment and revival*, 1965.
Reid (J. H. S.), *Origins of the British Labour party, 1880–1900*, 1955 (Amer.).
Rodgers (W.) & B. Donoughue, *The people into Parliament; an illustrated history of the Labour Party*, 1966.
Shinwell (E.), *The Labour story*, 1963.
Smith (G.), *The rise of the Labour Party in Great Britain*, 1969.
Stewart (J. D.), *British pressure groups*, 1958.
Thayer (G.), *The British political fringe*, 1965.
Tracey (H.), ed., *The British Labour Party*, 3 v., 1948.
Turner (D. R.), *The Shadow Cabinet in British Politics*, 1969.
Vincent (J.), *The formation of the Liberal Party, 1857–68*, 1966.
Walcott (R.), *English politics in the early 18th century*, 1956.
Watkins (A.), *The Liberal dilemma*, 1966.
Watson (G.), ed., *Radical alternative: studies in Liberalism*, 1962.
White (R. J.), *The conservative tradition*, 1950.
Williams (F.), *Fifty years' march: rise of the Labour party*, 1949.
Wilson (T.), *The downfall of the Liberal Party, 1914–35*, 1966.
Woods (M.), *History of the Tory party*, 1924.

PRIVATE BILLS

Clifford (F.), *Hist. of private bill legislation*, 2 v., 1885–7.
Dodd (C.) & H. W. W. Wilberforce, *Private bill procedure*, 1898.
Great Britain: Parliament. Joint Comm. on Private Bill Procedure. *Report, etc.*, 1955.
Landers (T. L.), *Private bills in Parl.*, 1919.
Report of Joint Committee on promotion of private bills, 1959.
Williams (O. C.), *Hist. develop. of private bill procedure*, 2 v., 1948–9.

REFORM

Bagehot (W.), *Essays on parl. reform*, 1883.
Butler (J. R. M.), *Passing of the great Reform Bill*, 1964.
Christie (I. R.), *Wilkes, Wyvill and reform*, 1962.
Cowling (M.), *1867, Disraeli, Gladstone and Revolution: The passing of the Second Reform Bill*, 1967.
Crick (B.), *Reform of the Commons*, 1959.
    The reform of Parliament, 2nd ed., 1968.
Grey (Earl), *Parl. govt. considered with reference to a reform of Parl.*, 1858.
Hansard Society, *Parl. Reform*, 2nd. rev. ed. 1967.
Headlam (Sir C.) & others, *Some proposals for const. reform*, 1946.
Hill (A.) & A. Wichelow, *What's wrong with Parliament?*, 1964.
Hughes (E.), *Parliament and mumbo-jumbo*, 1966.
Jennings (Sir W. I.), *Parl. must be reformed*, 1941.
    Parl. reform, 1934.
Maehl (W. H.) ed., *The Reform Bill of 1832*, 1967.
Neave (A.), *Control by committee: the reform of the committee system of the House of Commons*, 1968.
Pollard (R. S. W.), *How to reform Parl.*, 1944.

Smith (F. B.), *The making of the Second Reform Bill*, 1966.
Study of Parliament Group, *Reforming the Commons*, v. XXXI, no. 491 of *Planning*, October 1965 (the journal of P.E.P.).
Veitch (G. S.), *The genesis of parl. reform*, 1965.

REPRESENTATION

Alexander (A.) & A. Watkins, *The making of the Prime Minister, 1970*, 1970.
Alford (R. R.), *Party and society; voting behaviour in the Anglo-American democracies*, 1964.
Benney (M.), A. P. Gray & R. H. Pear, *How people vote*, 1956.
Booth (A. H.), *British hustings, 1924–50*, 1956.
Butler (D. E.), *The Brit. Gen. Election of 1951*, 1952.
   The Brit. Gen. Election of 1955, 1955.
   The electoral system in Brit. since 1918, 1963.
   Political change in Britain: forces shaping electoral choice, 1969.
   & R. Rose, *The Brit. Gen. Election of 1959*, 1960.
   & A. King, *The British General Election of 1964*, 1965.
      The British General Election of 1966, 1966.
Chrimes (S. B.), *The General Election in Glasgow*, 1950.
Committee on Electoral Machinery, *Report*, 1942 (Cmd. 6408).
Cook (H. K.), *The free & independent: trials etc. of the parl. election*, 1949.
Daniels (S. R.), *The case for electoral reform*, 1938.
Davies (I. R. M.), *Trial by ballot*, 1950.
Deakin (N.), ed., *Colour and the British electorate 1964*, 1965.
Eyles (W. E.), *Parl. & local govt. elections*, 1936.
Fulford (R.), *Votes for women*, 1957.
Gash (N.), *Politics in the age of Peel: parl. represent., 1830–50*, 1953.
   Reaction and reconstruction in English politics, 1832–52, 1965.
Gibbons (P. A.), *Ideas of polit. represent. in Parl. (1660–1832)*, 1914.
Grego (J.), *Hist. of parl. elections & electioneering*, 1892.
Gwyn (W. B.), *Democracy and the cost of politics in Britain*, 1962.
Hanham (H. J.), *Elections and party management* (politics in the time of Disraeli and Gladstone), 1959.
Hogan (J.), *Election & representation*, 1945.
Holt (R. T.) & J. E. Turner, *Political parties in action: the battle of Barons Court*, 1968.
House of Commons, *Report of the Select Committee on Parliamentary Elections (Mr. Speaker's Seat)*, 1938–9.
Humberstone (T. L.), *University represent.*, 1951.
Humphreys (J. H.), *Proportional represent.*, 1911.
Institute of Electoral Research, *Parliaments and electoral systems; a world handbook*, 1962.
Knight (C.), *Handbook for presiding officers*, 1959.
Lakeman (E.) & J. D. Lambert, *How democracies vote*, 1970.
Leonard (R. L.), *Elections in Britain*, 1968.
McCallum (R. B.) & A. Readman, *The Brit. Gen. Election of 1945*, 1947.
MacKay (R. W. G.), *Coupon or free? Elect. reform & represent. govt.*, 1944.
Mackenzie (W. J. M.), *Free elections*, 1958.

McKisack (M.), *The parl. represent. of the Eng. boroughs during the Middle Ages*, 1962.
Mill (J. S.), *Representative govt.* (Everyman ed., 1947).
Milne (R. S.) & H. C. Mackenzie, *Straight fight; voting behaviour in Bristol, 1951*, 1954 (Hansard Soc.).
Marginal seat, 1955, 1958.
Mitchell (B. R.) & K. Boehm, *British parliamentary election results, 1950–64*, 1966.
Nicholas (H. G.), *The Brit. Gen. Election of 1950*, 1951.
To the hustings, 1956. (Extracts from English fiction.)
O'Leary (C.), *Elimination of corrupt practices in British elections, 1868–1911*, 1962.
Pankhurst (C.), *Unshackled*, 1959.
Parker (F. R.), *Powers, etc. of an election agent and a returning officer*, 6th ed., 1959.
Paterson (P.), *The selectorate: the case for primary elections in Britain*, 1967.
Rex (M. B.), *University represent. in Eng., 1604–90*, 1954.
Rose (R.), *Politics in England*, 1965.
Ross (J. F. S.), *Elections & electors*, 1955.
Parl. representation, 1948.
Schofield (A. N.), *Parl. elections*, 3rd ed., 1959.
Seymour (C.), *Elect. reform in Eng. & Wales, 1832–85*, 1915.
Smith (T. E.), *Elections in developing countries*, 1960.
Trenaman (J.) & D. McQuail, *Television and the political image*, 1961.
Williams (J. F.), *Proportional representation and British politics*, 1914.
Wilson (C.), *Parliaments, peoples and mass media*, 1970.

COMMONWEALTH PARLIAMENTS

CONSTITUTIONAL AND GENERAL

Bailey (S. D.), ed., *Parl. govt. in the Commonw.*, 1951 (Hansard Soc.).
Parl. govt. in Southern Asia, 1953 (Hansard Soc.).
Bowie (R. R.) & C. J. Friedrich, *Studies in federalism*, 1954.
Brady (A.), *Democracy in the Dominions*, 1959.
Burns (Sir A.), *Parliament as an export*, 1966.
Dawson (R. M.), *The develop. of dominion status*, 1937.
Egerton (H. E.), *Federations & unions within the Brit. Empire*, 1911.
Evatt (H. V.), *The King & his Dominion Governors*, 2nd ed., 1967.
De Smith (S. A.), *The new Commonwealth and its constitutions*, 1964.
Fawcett (J. E. S.), *The British Commonwealth in international law*, 1963.
Forsey (E. A.), *The royal power of dissolution of Parl.*, 1943.
Grey (I.) & L. Marriott, *Payments and privileges of Commonwealth parliamentarians*, 1965.
Halsbury (Lord), *Laws of England*, 3rd ed., v. 5 (pp. 427–714), 1953.
Hansard Society, *What are the problems of parl. govt. in West Africa?*, 1958.
Harvey (H. J.), *Consultation & co-operation in the Commonw.*, 1952.
Hodgkin (T.), *African political parties*, 1961.
Jeffries (Sir C.), *Transfer of power*, 1960.

Jenks (E.), *The govt. of the Brit. Empire*, 1918.
Jennings (Sir W. I.), *The approach to self-government*, 1958.
  The Commonw. in Asia, 1951.
  Const. laws of the Commonw., v. 1, 'The Monarchies', 1958.
  & C. M. Young, *Const. laws of the Commonw.*, 1952.
Keith (A. B.), *Const. law of the Brit. Dominions*, 1933.
  The Dominions as sovereign states, 1938.
  Dominion autonomy in practice, 1929.
  The govts. of the Brit. Empire, 1935.
  Imperial unity & the Dominions, 1916.
  The King & the imperial crown, 1936.
  The King, the const., the Empire & foreign affairs, 1938.
  Letters on imperial relations etc., 1916–35, 1935.
  Responsible govt. in the Dominions, 2 v., 1928.
  The sovereignty of the Brit. Dominions, 1929.
  ed., *Speeches & docs. on the Brit. Dominions, 1918–31*, 1932.
Latham (R. T. E.), *The law & the Commonw.*, 1949.
Leys (C.) & P. Robson, *Federation in East Africa: opportunities and problems*,
  1965.
Livingstone (W. S.), *Federalism in the Commonwealth*, 1963.
MacMahon (A. W.), *Federalism mature & emergent*, 1955 (Amer.).
Macmillan (W. M.), *The road to self-rule*, 1959.
Madden (F.), *Imperial constitutional docs.*, 1953.
Maitland (P.), *Task for giants*, 1957.
Marshall (G.), *Parl. sovereignty and the Commonw.*, 1957.
Milburn (J. F.), *Governments of the Commonwealth*, 1965.
Poley (A. P.), *The federal systems of the U.S. & Brit. Empire*, 1913.
Roberts-Wray (Sir K.), *Commonwealth and colonial law*, 1966.
Sawer (G.), ed., *Federalism*, 1952.
Schlosberg (H. J.), *The King's republics*, 1929.
Schuyler (R. L.), *Parliament and the British Empire*, 1963.
Simmons (J.), *From Empire to Commonw.*, 1949.
Todd (A.), *Parl. govt. in the Brit. colonies*, 1894.
Watts (R. L.), *New federations: experiments in the Commonwealth*, 1966.
Wheare (K. C.), *Federal govt.*, 4th ed., 1963.
  The Statute of Westminster, 1953.
  The const. structure of the Commonw., 1960.
Wight (M.), *The develop. of the Legis. Council, 1606–1945*, 1946.
Wiseman (H. V.), *The Cabinet in the Commonw.*, 1958.
  Britain and the Commonwealth, 1965.

AUSTRALIA

Australia. *Report of the Royal Commission on the Constitution*, 1929.
Australian Inst. of Political Science, *Federalism in Australia*, 1949.
Australian Parliament, *Report from the Joint Select Committee on Constitutional
  Review*, 1959.
Birch (A. H.), *Federalism, finance etc., in Canada, Australia & the U.S.*, 1955.
Bland (F. A.), *Planning the modern state*, 1945.
  ed., *Govt. in Australia*, 1944.

Brennan (T. C.), *Interpreting the constitution*, 1935.

Brett (P.), *Cases and materials in constitutional and administrative law*, 1962.

Campbell (E.), *Parliamentary privilege in Australia*, 1966.

Campbell (W. J.), *Australian state public finance*, 1954.

Canaway (A. P.), *The failure of federalism in Australia*, 1930.

Clark (C. I.), *The Parl. of Tasmania*, 1947.

Combe (G. D.), *Responsible govt. in South Australia*, 1957.
The Parl. of South Australia, 1960.

Cowen (Z.), *Federal jurisdiction in Australia*, 1959.

Crisp (L. F.), *The Australian Federal Labour party, 1901–51*, 1955.
Australian national government, 1965.

Davies (A. F.), *Australian democracy*, 1958.

Davis (S. R.), ed., *The government of the Australian States*, 1960.
& others, *The Australian party system*, 1954.

Deakin (A.), *The federal story*, 1944.
The crisis in Victorian politics, 1879–81, 1957.

Denning (W.), *Inside Parl.*, 1946.

Drummond (D. H.), *Australia's changing constitution*, 1943.

Else-Mitchell (R.), ed., *Essays on the Australian const.*, 1961.

Encel (S.), *Cabinet government in Australia*, 1962.

Garran (R. R.), *The coming Commonw.*, 1897.

Green (F. C.), ed., *A century of responsible government, 1856–1956* (Tasmania), 1958.

Greenwood (G.), *Future of Australian federalism*, 1946.

Jupp (J.), *Australian party politics*, 1964.
Australian Labour and the world, 1965.

Kennedy (W.), *The Parl. of Victoria*, 1951.

Kerr (D.), *Law of the Australian const.*, 1925.

Knowles (Sir G. S.), *The Commonw. of Australia Constitution Act*, 1936.
The Australian Const., 1937.

Latham (Sir J. G.), *Australia & the Brit. Commonw.*, 1929.

Lane (P. H.), *Some principles and sources of Australian constitutional law*, 1964.

Loveday (P.), *Parliament, factions and parties: the first 30 years of responsible government in New South Wales, 1856–1889*, 1966.

Lumb (R. D.), *The constitutions of the Australian states*, 1963.

McMahon (W.), *The Australian political party system*, 1954.

McMullin (Sir A.), *Introduction to the Australian Federal Parliament*, 1959.

Maughan (D.) & others, *Const. revision in Australia*, 1944.

Melbourne (A. C. V.), *Early const. develop. in Aust., 1788–1856*, 1964.

Melbourne University, Dept. of Political Science: *The government of Victoria*, 1958.

Menzies (Sir R.), *Central power in the Australian Commonwealth*, 1967.

Miller (J. D. B.), *Australian govt. & politics*, 1959.

Nicholas (H. S.), *The Australian const.*, 1952.

Odgers (J. R.), *Australian Senate practice*, 1959.

Overacker (L.), *The Australian party system*, 1952.

Paton (G. W.), *The Commonw. of Australia; develop. of its laws & const.*, 1952.

Pearl (C.), *Wild men of Sydney*, 1958.

Portus (G. V.), ed., *Studies in the Aust. const.*, 1933.
Quick (Sir J.), *Legislative powers of the Commonw. & states of Aust.*, 1919.
& R. R. Garran, *The annotated const. of the Aust. Commonw.*, 1901.
Ratchford (B. U.), *Public expenditure in Australia*, 1959 (Amer.).
Rawson (D. W.), *Australia votes; the 1958 Federal election*, 1961.
Labour in vain? a survey of the Australian Labour Party, 1967.
Reeves (W. P.), *State experiments in Aust. & N. Zealand*, 2 v., 1923.
Rydon (J.) & R. N. Spann, *New South Wales politics, 1901–10*, 1962.
Sawer (G.), *Cases on the const. of the Commonw. of Aust.*, 1964.
Australian federal politics and the law, 2 vols., *1901–29*, 1956, *1929–49*, 1963.
& others, *Federalism in Aust.*, 1949.
Spann (R. N.), *Public administration in Australia*, 1959.
Sweetman (E.), *Aust. const. development*, 1925.
Tew (B.), *Wealth & income: econ. & financial systems of Aust. etc.*, 1955.
Townsley (W. A.), *The struggle for self-government in Tasmania*, 1951.
Warner (K. O.), *Introd. to some problems of Australian federalism*, 1933 (Amer.).
West (K.), *Power in the Liberal Party: a study in Australian Politics*, 1966.
Whyte (W. F.), *The Aust. Parl. handbk.*, 1952.
Wood (F. L. W.), *Const. development of Australia*, 1933.
Wynes (W. A.), *Legisl., executive & judicial powers in Aust.*, 1962.

CANADA

Aitchison (J. H.), *The political process in Canada*, 1963.
Beauchesne (A.), *Rules & forms of the House of Commons of Canada*, 1958; supplement, 1961.
Canada's parl. Building, n.d.
Beck (J. M.), *The Government of Nova Scotia*, 1957.
Pendulum of power: Canada's federal elections, 1968.
Birch (A. H.), *Federalism, finance etc. in Canada etc.*, 1955.
Borden (Sir R. L.), *Canadian const. studies*, 1922.
Bourinot (Sir J.), *Const. hist. of Canada to 1901*, 1901.
Parl. procedure and practice in the Dominion of Canada, 4th ed., 1916.
British North America Acts, 1867–1965.
Buck (A. E.), *Financing Canadian govt.*, 1949 (Amer.).
Cameron (E. R.), *The Canadian const.*, 2 v., 1915–30.
Canada: Department of Secretary of State, *Organization of the government of Canada*, 1966.
Canada. Dominion Provincial and Interprov. Conferences, 1951.
Cheffins (R. I.), *The constitutional process in Canada*, 1969.
Clokie (H. McD.), *Canadian govt. & politics*, 1944.
Corry (J. A.) & J. E. Hodgetts, *Democratic govt. & politics*, 1959.
Coupland (Sir R.), *The Durham Report*, 1946.
Dawson (R. M.), *Democratic govt. in Canada*, 1949.
ed., *Const. issues in Canada, 1900–31*, 1933.
The govt. of Canada, 4th ed., 1963, ed. N. Ward.
Dawson (W. F.), *Procedure in the Canadian House of Commons*, 1962.
Donnelly (M. S.), *The government of Manitoba*, 1963.
Durham (Lord), *Rep. on the affairs of Brit. N. America*, 3 v., 1912.
Egerton (H. E.) & W. L. Grant, *Canadian const. development*, 1907.

Eggleston (W.), *The road to nationhood*, 1946.
Gerin-Lajoie (P.), *Const. amendment in Canada*, 1950.
Hambleton (G.), *The Parl. of Canada*, 1961.
Houston (W.), *Docs. illustrative of the Canadian const.*, 1891.
Irving (J.), *The Social Credit movement in Alberta*, 1959.
Kennedy (W. P. M.), *Const. of Canada, 1534–1937*, 1938.
  Docs. of the Canadian const., 1759–1915, 1918.
  Statutes, treaties & docs. of the Canadian const., 1913–29, 1930.
Kunz (F. A.), *The modern senate of Canada, 1925–63*, 1965.
Langstone (R. W.), *Responsible govt. in Canada*, 1931.
Laskin (B.), *Canadian constitutional law*, 3rd ed., 1966.
Lewis (A. C.), *Parl. procedure in Ontario*, 1940.
Lingard (C. C.), *Territorial govt. in Canada*, 1946.
Lower (A. R. M.), & others, *Evolving Canadian federalism*, 1958.
Lyon (J. N.) & R. G. Atkey, ed., *Canadian constitutional law in a modern perspective*, 1970.
MacKay (R. A.), *The unreformed Senate of Canada*, 1926.
MacKinnon (F.), *The government of Prince Edward Island*, 1951.
Martin (C.), *The foundations of Canadian nationhood*, 1955.
Meisel (J.), *The Canadian general election of 1957*, 1962.
Munro (J. E. C.), *The const. of Canada*, 1889.
Neuendorff (G.), *Studies in the evol. of dominion status: Governor-Generalship of Canada etc.*, 1942.
Ollivier (M.), *Problems of Canadian Sovereignty*, 1945.
Olmsted (R. A.), *Decisions of the Judicial Comm. of the Privy Council etc.*, 3 v., 1954.
Pickersgill (J. W.), *The Liberal Party*, 1962.
Pierson (C. G.), *Canada & the Privy Council*, 1960.
Regenstreif (P.), *The Diefenbaker interlude*, 1965.
Riddell (W. R.), *The const. of Canada etc.*, 1917.
Ross (Sir G.), *The Senate of Canada*, 1914.
Rowell-Sirois Report (Royal Comm. on Dominion–Provincial Relations), Ottawa, 1940.
Saywell (J. T.), *The office of Lieutenant-Governor*, 1957.
Schindeler (F. F.), *Responsible Government in Ontario*, 1969.
Shortt (A.) & A. G. Doughty, *Docs. relating to the const. hist. of Canada, 1758–91*, 2 v., 1935.
Thorburn (H. G.), *Politics in New Brunswick*, 1961.
Varcoe (F. P.), *Distrib. of legislative power in Canada*, 1954.
Ward (N.), *The Canadian H. of Commons: representation*, 2nd ed., 1963.
  The public purse; a study in Canadian democracy, 1962.
Williams (J. R.), *The Conservative party of Canada*, 1956.

CEYLON

Ceylon, *Rep. of the Special Commission on the Const.* (the Donoughmore Report, Cmd. 3131).
Ceylon, *Rep. of Commission on Const. Reform* (the Soulbury Report, Cmd. 6677).
Collins (Sir C.), *Public admin. in Ceylon*, 1951.

Jennings (Sir W. I.), *The const. of Ceylon*, 1953.
  & H. W. Tambiah, *Ceylon: develop. of its laws & const.*, 1966.
Namasivayam (S.), *The legislatures of Ceylon, 1928–48*, 1951.
Weerawardana (I. D. S.), *Ceylon General Election, 1956*, 1960 (Colombo).

GHANA

Apter (D.), *The Gold Coast in transition*, 1955.
Bennion (F. A. R.), *The constitutional law of Ghana*, 1962.
Elias (T. O.), *Ghana and Sierra Leone: the development of their laws and constitutions*, 1962.
Kimble (D.), *Political history of Ghana, 1850–1928*, 1963.
Rubin (L.) & P. Murray, *The constitution and government of Ghana*, 2nd ed., 1964.
Wight (M.), *The Gold Coast Legislative Council*, 1947.

HONG KONG

Endacott (G. B.), *Government and people in Hong Kong, 1841–1962: a constitutional history*, 1964.

INDIA

Aggarwala (O. P.), *Cases on the constitution of India*, 6 v., 1963.
Alexandrowicz (C. H.), *Const. developments in India*, 1957.
Auston (G.), *The Indian Constitution*, 1966.
Banerjee (A. C.), *Constituent Assembly of India*, Calcutta, 1947.
  Indian constitutional documents, 1757–1947, 4 v., 1961.
Basu (D. D.), *Commentary on the constitution of India*, 5 v., 1961–5.
  Shorter constitution of India, 1964.
Bhambhri (C. P.), *Parliamentary control over finance in India*, 1959.
  Parliamentary control over state enterprise, 1960.
Brecher (M.), *Political leadership in India*, 1968.
Coupland (Sir R.), *Rep. on the const. problem in India*, 3 parts, 1942–3.
  India: a restatement, 1945.
Desikachar (S.), *Centralised legislation: a history of the legislative system of British India from 1834–61*, 1963.
Eddy (J. P.) & F. H. Lawton, *India's new const.*, 1935.
Gledhill (A.), *The republic of India: develop. of its laws & const.*, 1964.
Gupta (M. G.), ed., *Aspects of the Indian Constitution*, 1956.
Gwyer (Sir M.) & A. Appadorai, *Speeches and documents on the Indian const., 1921–47*, 2 v., 1957.
India, Joint Comm. on Indian const. reform, 3 v., 1934.
Jain (M. P.), *Indian constitutional law*, 1962.
Jennings (Sir W. I.), *Some characteristics of the Indian const.*, 1953.
Joshi (G. N.), *The const. of India*, 1961.
Kaul (M. N.) & S. L. Shakdher, *Practice and Procedure of Parliament*, 1968.
Keith (A. B.), *A const. hist. of India, 1600–1935*, 1935.
Lal (A. B.), *The Indian Parl.*, 1956.
Menon (V. P.), *The integration of the Indian States*, 1956.
  The transfer of power in India, 1957.
More (S. S.), *Practice and procedure of the Indian Parliament*, 1960.

Morris-Jones (W. H.), *Parl. in India*, 1957.
  The government and politics of India, 2nd ed., 1967.
Mukherjea (A. R.), *Parliamentary procedure in India*, 2nd ed., 1967.
Palande (M. R.), *Introd. to Indian admin.*, 1951.
Pylee (M. V.), *Const. govt. in India*, 2nd ed., 1966.
  India's constitution, 1962.
Rau (B. N.), *India's constitution in the making*, 1961.
Santhanam (K.), *The constitution of India*, New Delhi, 1951.
Sastri (L. S.), *The const. of India*, 1950.
Schuster (Sir G.) & G. Wint, *India & democracy*, 1941.
Sen-Varma (S. P.), *Law of elections*, 1963.
Sharma (B. M.), *The Republic of India: constitution and government*, 1967.
Sharma (R.), *A const. hist. of India, 1765–1954*, 1955.
Shukla (V. N.), *Commentaries on the const. of India*, 1956.
Tope (T. K.), *The constitution of India*, 1963.
Varadarajan (M. K.), *The Indian states & the federation*, 1939.
Venkateswaran (R. J.), *Cabinet government in India*, 1967.
Weiner (M.), *Party politics in India*, 1957 (Amer.).

MALAYSIA
Sheridan (L. A.), ed., *Malaya and Singapore, the Borneo territories; the development of their laws and constitutions*, 1961.

NEW ZEALAND
Beaglehole (J. C.), *N.Z. & the Statute of Westminster*, 1944.
Chapman (R. M.) & others, *New Zealand politics in action: the 1960 General Election*, 1962.
Hight (J.) & H. D. Bamford, *The const. hist. of N.Z.*, 1914.
Lipson (L.), *The politics of equality: N.Z.'s adventures in democracy*, 1948.
McLintock (A. H.), *Crown colony government in New Zealand*, 1958.
Milne (R. S.), *Political parties in New Zealand*, 1966.
Mitchell (A.), *Government by party*, 1966.
Polaschek (R. J.), *Government and administration in New Zealand*, 1958.
Reeves (W. P.), *State experiments in Australia & N.Z.*, 2 v., 1923.
Robson (J. L.), *New Zealand: develop. of its laws & const.*, 2nd ed., 1967.
Scholefield (G. H.), *N.Z. parliamentary record, 1840–1949*, 1950.
Scott (K. J.), *The New Zealand constitution*, 1962.
Simpson (F. A.), *Parl. in N.Z.*, 1947.
Webb (L. C.), *Govt. in N.Z.*, 1940.

NIGERIA
Awa (E. O.), *Federal government in Nigeria*, 1964 (Amer.).
Ezera (K.), *Constitutional developments in Nigeria*, 2nd ed., 1964.
Mackintosh (J. P.), *Nigerian government and politics*, 1966.
Nwabueze (B. O.), *Constitutional law of the Nigerian Republic*, 1964.
Odumosu (O. I.), *The Nigerian constitution: history and development*, 1963.
Post (K. W. J.), *The Nigerian federal election of 1959*, 1963.
Tamuno (T. N.), *Nigeria and elective representation, 1923–47*, 1966.
Wheare (J.), *The Nigerian Legislative Council*, 1950.

PAKISTAN

Ahmad (M.), *Government and politics in Pakistan*, 1963.
Callard (K.), *Pakistan, a political study*, 1957.
Choudhury (G. W.), *Democracy in Pakistan*, 1963.
Coupland (Sir R.), *Rep. on the const. problem in India*, 3 parts, 1942–3.
Feldman (H.), *A const. for Pakistan*, 1955.
Gledhill (A.), *Pakistan, development of its laws and constitution*, 1957.
Jennings (Sir W. I.), *Const. problems in Pakistan*, 1957.
Newman (K. J.), *Essays on the constitution of Pakistan*, 1956.
Shankat Mahmud, *Commentary on the new constitution*, 1963.
Symonds (R.), *The making of Pakistan*, 1950.
Von Vorys (K.), *Political developments in Pakistan*, 1965 (Amer.).
Wilcox (W. A. O.), *Pakistan; the consolidation of a nation*, 1963.

RHODESIA

Leys (C.), *European politics in Southern Rhodesia*, 1959.
Palley (C.), *The constitutional history and law of Southern Rhodesia, 1888–1965, with special reference to imperial control*, 1966.

SIERRA LEONE

Elias (T. O.), *Ghana and Sierra Leone: the development of their laws and constitutions*, 1962.

TANZANIA

Cole (J. S. R.) & W. N. Denison, *Tanzania: the development of its laws and constitution*, 1964.

UGANDA

Low (D. A.), *Political parties in Uganda, 1949–62*, 1962.
Morris (H. F.) & J. S. Read, *Uganda: the development of its laws and constitutions*, 1966.

WEST INDIES

Ayearst (M.), *The British West Indies: the search for self-government*, 1960.
Craig (H.), *The Legislative Council of Trinidad and Tobago*, 1952.
Murray (D. J.), *The West Indies and the development of colonial government, 1801–34*, 1965.